Gwen Merkley

The Blackwell Dictionary

of

Judaica

Also by Dan Cohn-Sherbok

A Dictionary of Judaism and Christianity

Holocaust Theology

Issues in Contemporary Judaism

Jewish Petitionary Prayer: a Theological Exploration

On Earth as it is in Heaven: Jews, Christians and Liberation Theology

Rabbinic Perspectives on the New Testament

The Crucified Jew: Twenty Centuries of Christian Anti-Semitism

The Jewish Heritage

The Jews of Canterbury

As editor:

A Traditional Quest: Essays in Honour of Louis Jacobs

Contemporary Jewish Theology

Exploring Reality

Islam in a World of Diverse Faiths

Religion in Public Life

The Canterbury Papers: Essays on Religion and Society

The Salman Rushdie Controversy in Interreligious Perspective

The Sayings of Moses

Tradition and Unity: Sermons Published in Honour of Robert Runcie

Using the Bible Today: Contemporary Interpretations of Scripture

World Religions and Human Liberation

The Blackwell Dictionary
of
Judaica

Dan Cohn-Sherbok

BLACKWELL
Reference

First published 1992

Blackwell Publishers
108 Cowley Road
Oxford OX4 1JF

British Library Cataloguing in Publication Data

Cohn-Sherbok, Dan
The Blackwell dictionary of Judaica.
I. Title
296

ISBN 0-631-16615-7
ISBN 0-631-18728-6 (pbk)

Typeset in 10/12 pt Baskerville
by Butler & Tanner Ltd
Printed in Great Britain by T.J. Press (Padstow) Ltd, Padstow, Cornwall

For My Mother

Advisers

Contents

Contents

Preface

For more than fifteen years I have taught courses in Jewish studies to students at the University of Kent in Canterbury, England. During this time I have frequently directed students to such multi-volume encyclopedias of Judaism as the *Jewish Encyclopedia* and the *Encyclopedia Judaica*. These vast repositories of material provide a wealth of information about all aspects of Jewish life and thought. Nonetheless, very often students, particularly those with more general queries, find these works overwhelming (as well as difficult to gain access to if they are much in demand in the library).

Aware of these difficulties, I suggested they look at a number of single-volume encyclopedias and dictionaries of Judaism, but many of these works failed to meet their needs, since they tend to be highly selective in their choice of entries. Increasingly I came to see that what was needed was a single-volume comprehensive dictionary which contains basic information about Judaism and the Jewish people. Such a handy reference book would not take the place of the standard multi-volume reference works, but it could serve as first point of entry into the world of Judaica.

This volume, *The Blackwell Dictionary of Judaica*, was thus designed to fill a gap in the types of reference books available to students as well as to teachers and more general readers. The book has approximately 7,000 entries overall, containing nearly half a million words. Most of the articles are fairly short, since the work aims to provide readers with a vast array of information in concise, clear and accessible form. Although all aspects of Jewish civilization are covered (the Dictionary also embraces familiar Yiddish terms), my main criterion for inclusion has been reference-worthiness. My intention is that this dictionary should provide the type of information most commonly sought by students of Jewish life and thought.

Any scholar working in Jewish studies owes an enormous debt to those excellent lexicographers who have already published reference works in the field. All of the following have been consulted in checking and cross-checking the information contained in this Dictionary: Geoffrey Wigoder, *The New Standard Jewish Encyclopedia* (London: W. H. Allen, 1977); *Jewish Encyclopedia* (New York: Funk and Wagnalls, 1901–5); *Encyclopedia Judaica* (Jerusalem: Keter, 1972–); Yacov Newman and Gavriel Sivan, *Judaism A–Z: Lexicon of Terms and Concepts* (Jerusalem: Department for Torah Education and Culture in the Diaspora of the World Zionist Organization, 1980); Raphael Jehudah Zwi Werblowsky and Geoffrey Wigoder, eds, *The Encyclopedia of the Jewish Religion* (London: Phoenix House, 1967); Glenda Abramson, ed., *The Blackwell Companion to Jewish Culture* (Oxford: Blackwell, 1989); Geoffrey Wigoder, ed., *The Encyclopedia of Judaism* (New York: Macmillan, 1989); David Bridger and Samuel Wolk, eds, *The New Jewish Encyclopedia* (New York: Behrman House, 1976); and Leo Rosten, *The Joys of Yiddish* (London: W. H. Allen, 1968). I should also like to thank the advisers (whose names are listed on p. vi), as well as Glenda Abramson, for their helpful advice in planning the Dictionary. Thanks are due to Stephan Chambers,

Alyn Shipton and Caroline Richmond of Blackwell Publishers for their help and encouragement. In addition I should like to thank my copy-editor, Rosemary Roberts, who carefully read the entire manuscript and offered numerous suggestions; the book gained immeasurably from her dedication. I should also mention the librarians, particularly Cynthia Shiloh at the Institute of Jewish Affairs, who helped both me and my clerical assistant, Michael Durnin, in checking birth and death dates for many of the biographical entries. Finally, I owe so much to my wife Lavinia for her enormous help with this book; I couldn't have written it without her.

Notes on the Use of the Dictionary

1 Alphabetization

Entries are ordered alphabetically according to their bold headings (see section 3 below), ignoring spaces, hyphens, apostrophes, accents, and all bracketed material, up to the comma, and then in the same way after the comma. Where two headings are identical (ignoring bracketed material) the entries are ordered chronologically or, if that is not possible, in order of importance, and distinguished by lower-case roman numerals. The prefixes "Mac" and "Mc" are alphabetized as "Mac", and "St." is alphabetized as though it were spelled out. Headings containing numerals are ordered as though the numerals were spelled out. Entries on people are entered under surname, forename, or particle, according to prevalent usage for each individual; a cross-reference entry is generally included to lead the reader to the form of the name under which the article may be found.

2 Usages

General style In matters of orthography, terminology, and punctuation the Dictionary generally follows American practice.

Place names An effort has been made to identify small places by naming a larger place nearby, or by locating it within a state or area. Where a place name has changed in the course of history the name current at the time under discussion has been used. For the current names of cities the orthography of *The Times Atlas of the World: Comprehensive Edition* (London, 1987) has been adopted.

Dates In article headings the following abbreviations are used: b. = born; d. = died; fl. = flourished; *c.* = circa (about); cent. = century. The use of a question mark indicates uncertainty about the date or dates to which it is attached. Throughout the Dictionary BCE (before the common era) is used for dates before the year 1, and CE (common era), where necessary, for dates from the year 1 onward. References to historical periods or events (e.g., "the second Temple period," "the expulsion of the Jews from France") may occur without dates in the texts of entries; readers are referred to the chronology on p. xv.

Transliteration Hebrew words have been transliterated according to the Sephardi pronunciation. For purposes of tracing entries in the Dictionary readers should note that "ḥ" (not "ch") is used – hence "Ḥazzan" (not "Chazzan") – and "ph" (not "f") – hence "Sepher" (not "Sefer").

Titles of works Titles of works generally appear in italic type. For works written by a single identified author (i.e., not works of the Jewish religious tradition) an English-language title is used if a work has appeared in translation.

The Bible The words "Bible" and "Scripture" are used in this Dictionary to mean the Hebrew Bible; where the New Testament of the Christian Bible is mentioned, the reference makes this plain. References to books of the Bible are given in the following form: II Chronicles 5.2–6.7.

3 Article headings

People Only individuals whose lives and/or work are connected with Judaism and the Jewish people have been included. Articles begin with the name, in inverted form, in bold type. Brackets are used for alternative names. An asterisk precedes the name of any individual who was not a Jew or who, though born a Jew, converted from Judaism. Where two people bear the same name (ignoring bracketed material) the entries are ordered chronologically by date of birth and distinguished by lower-case roman numerals. The article heading is followed by years of birth and death, or an approximate period during which the individual flourished.

Terms, words, concepts, and topics Except where a heading is a Hebrew or an English word, all headings of entries on terms, words, concepts, and topics are followed by a parenthetical statement concerning language; foreign-language terms and words are translated, either in parentheses or (if the translation constitutes the definition) in the first sentence of the article. Wherever appropriate and possible an entry with an English headword is followed by the Hebrew equivalent in parentheses. The following examples illustrate these usages:

Abbreviations (Hebrew "rashei tevot").
Alter kocker (Yiddish). Crotchety, ineffectual old man.
Asmakhta (Aramaic: "support," "reliance").
Baal tashit ("Do not destroy").
Badhan. Merrymaker or entertainer.
Dienchelele (from Hebrew "dayyan kelili": general judge).

It is implicit in the subject of the dictionary that articles on terms, concepts, and topics include only information of relevance to Judaism and the Jewish people. No reference is made to this in the headings of entries: thus the article "Education" should be assumed to cover only Jewish education, the article "Parliament" only the history of Jews as members of parliaments. Similarly, the entries "Good," "Retribution," "Wisdom," etc. deal exclusively with the Jewish interpretation of those concepts.

Places Places are entered under the name in use at the time principally under discussion in the article. Where a place was simultaneously known under different names the alternative name is given in brackets following the bold heading: **Auschwitz** [Oswiecim]. Where a modern place stands on the site of an ancient city, the identity of the two is made clear in the first sentence of the article; a cross-reference is generally included to lead the reader from the modern place name to the name of the ancient site.

4 Definitions

Most entries begin with a definition. For entries on individuals the definition starts, where possible, with a nationality; nationalities have been determined on the basis either of the place of birth or of the principal place of activity, as seems appropriate. Entries on terms, concepts, and topics have been supplied with a definition where (a) they are sufficiently little known to need one, or (b) where it is important to distinguish between a commonly accepted interpretation and the Jewish interpretation of the heading.

5 Cross-references

Cross-references appear in large and small capitals. The large capital indicates the part of the heading under which the entry may be found; bracketed matter is excluded from cross-references. Cross-reference entries lead the reader from a heading s/he has looked up to the heading under which the information is entered. Cross-references within articles may appear in running prose, or at the ends of sentences or articles; in the latter case they are introduced by the words "see" or "see also" in italic type. Cross-references within articles are included only where significant additional information may be found elsewhere in the Dictionary.

Chronological Table

Patriarchal period	*c.* 1900–1600 BCE
Exodus from Egypt	*c.* 1250–1230 BCE
Period of the Judges	*c.* 1200–1000 BCE
Period of the united monarchy	*c.* 1030–930 BCE
Division of the kingdoms	*c.* 930 BCE
Destruction of the northern kingdom (Israel) by the Assyrians	722 BCE
Destruction of the southern kingdom (Judah) and of the Temple in Jerusalem by the Babylonians	586 BCE
Babylonian exile	586–538 BCE
Persian period	538–333 BCE
Return of the exiles	538 BCE
Rebuilding the Temple in Jerusalem	*c.* 520–515 BCE
Second Temple period	*c.* 515 BCE–70 CE
Ezra's and Nehemiah's reforms	*c.* 450–400 BCE
End of the era of prophecy	*c.* 450 BCE
Torah given scriptural status	*c.* 450 BCE
Hellenistic period	333–63 BCE
Prophets given scriptural status	*c.* 200 BCE
Maccabean rebellion and Hasmonean period	167–163 BCE
Hasmonean revolt	166–164 BCE
Roman period	*c.* 146 BCE–400 CE
New Testament written	*c.* 50–90
Jewish rebellion against Rome	66–70
Siege and destruction of Jerusalem and the second Temple	70
Mishnaic (Tannaitic) period	*c.* 100 BCE–200 CE
Bar Kokhba revolt	132–5
Hagiographa given scriptural status	*c.* 150
Mishnah compiled	*c.* 200
Talmudic (Amoraic) period	*c.* 200–600
Jerusalem Talmud compiled	*c.* 5th cent.

Babylonian Talmud compiled	*c.* 6th cent.
Medieval period	*c.* 600–1600
Period of the geonim	*c.* 600–1300
Karaism founded	*c.* 760
Expulsion of the Jews from France	1182
Crusades	1095–1291
Establishment of the Inquisition	*c.* 1230
Disputation of Tortosa	1413–15
Expulsion of the Jews from Spain	1492
Early modern period	*c.* 1550–1700
Establishment of the ghetto in Italy	1555
Modern period	*c.* 1700–present
Hasidism founded	*c.* 1735
Reform movement founded	*c.* 1850
Conservative movement founded	*c.* 1895
First Zionist Congress	1897
Modern orthodoxy founded	*c.* 1905
Reconstructionist movement founded	*c.* 1935
The Holocaust	1942–5
Founding of the State of Israel	1948

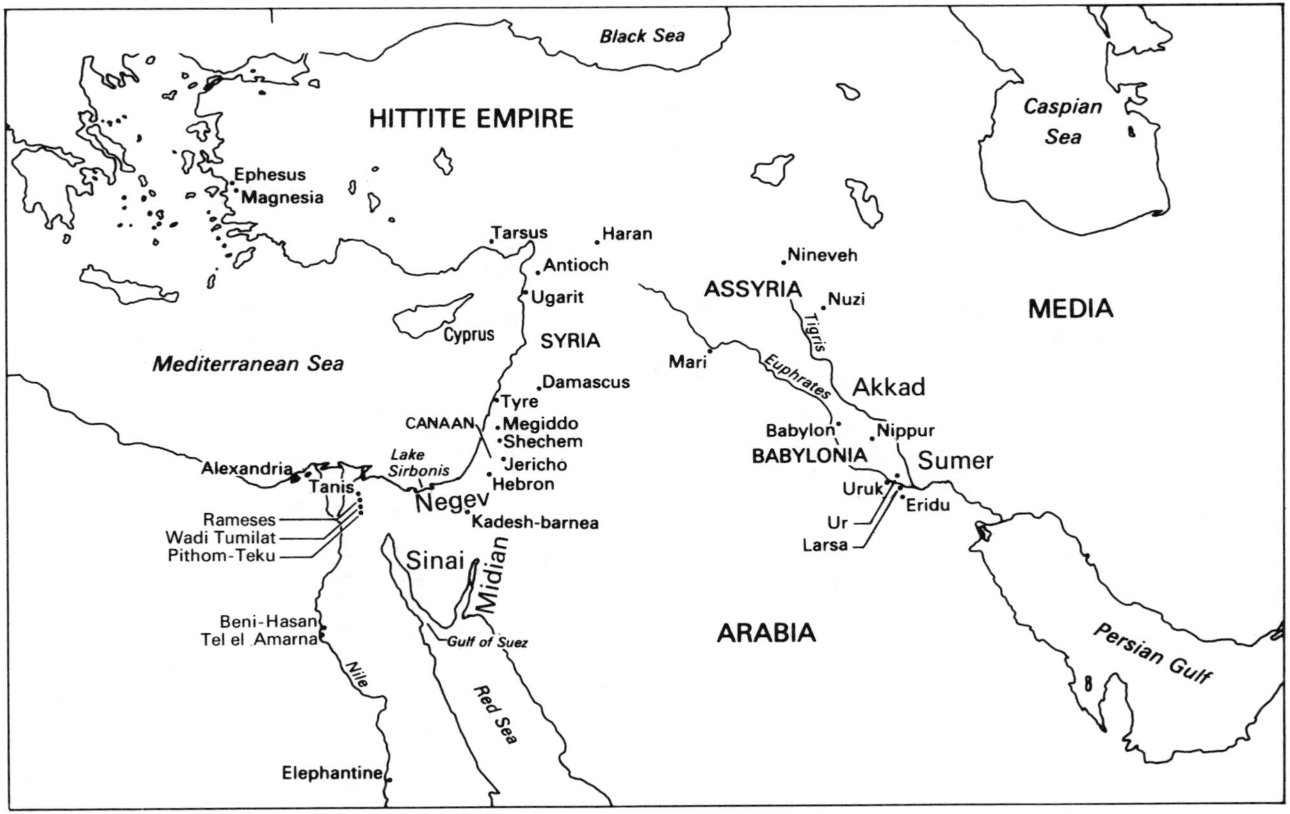

Map 1: The Ancient Near East

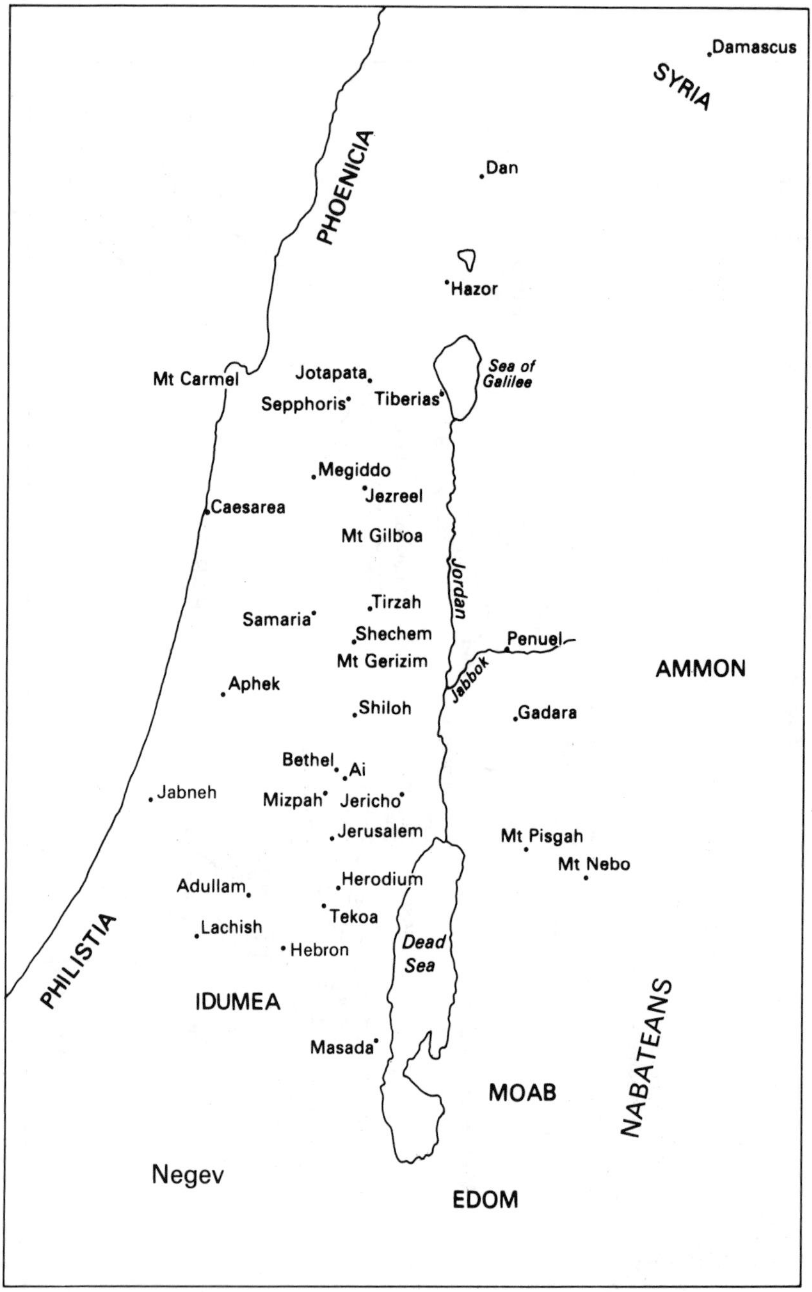

Map 2: Ancient Israel

A

Aaron (fl. ?13th cent. BCE). Israelite leader, elder brother of Moses. He and Moses freed the Jews from Egyptian bondage. He made the Golden Calf to placate the people when Moses did not come down from Mount Sinai (Exodus 32). When the Tabernacle was established, he and his sons became priests.

Aaron ben Elijah (?1328–1369). Karaite philosopher and exegete. Born in Nicomedia in Asia Minor, he lived in Constantinople. He used Maimonides' *Guide for the Perplexed* as a basis for his defense of Karaism in *The Tree of Life* (1346). He believed that the Mosaic law is immutable and should not be supplemented by rabbinic ordinances.

Aaron ben Jacob ha-Cohen of Lunel (fl. late 13th–early 14th cent.). French talmudist. When the Jews were expelled from France in 1306 he emigrated to Majorca. He wrote a compilation of Jewish law based on earlier legal works. This was abbreviated by an anonymous editor as *Kol Bo* (1490).

Aaron ben Joseph ha-Cohen Sargado (fl. 9th cent.). Babylonian gaon and head of the academy at Pumbedita from 942 to 960. He joined the campaign against Saadyah Gaon led by the exilarch David ben Zakkai. He wrote an Arabic commentary on the Torah.

Aaron ben Joseph ha-Levi [R'ah] (1235–1300). Spanish talmudist. He was a student of Naḥmanides in Barcelona. He wrote *Repair of the House* consisting of critical comments on *Law of the House* by Solomon ben Adret. In reply Adret wrote *Guard of the House*.

Aaron ben Joseph ha-Rofe (1250–1320). Crimean Karaite scholar and liturgical poet. His commentary on the Pentateuch, *Sepher ha-Mivḥar* (1293), was used by Karaites in the 14th and 15th centuries. Aaron's redaction of the Karaite liturgy was adopted by most Karaite congregations.

Aaron ben Moses ben Asher *see* BEN ASHER, AARON BEN MOSES.

Aaron [Abu Ahron] **ben Samuel** (fl. 9th cent.). Italian mystic. He left Baghdad and taught kabbalah in Italy. His pupil Moses ben Kalonymos of Lucca carried on his teaching in Germany. He is regarded as the father of kabbalistic study in Europe.

Aaron ha-Levi of Barcelona (fl. 14th cent.). Spanish talmudist. His *Book of Education* analyzes the 613 commandments.

Aaron Samuel ben Israel Kaidanover *see* KAIDANOVER, AARON SAMUEL.

Aaronson, Aaron (1849–1939). Palestinian leader. He studied agronomy in France and from 1895 worked as an expert for Edmond de Rothschild. During World War I he organized an underground intelligence service (Nili) in Palestine. He promoted Zionist concerns at the Paris Peace Conference in 1919.

Ab *see* Av.

Abba [Ba] (fl. late 3rd–early 4th cent.).

Babylonian amora. He was a disciple of Huna and Judah. In Tiberias he studied with Eleazar and Simeon ben Lakish. He frequently visited Babylonia and passed on Babylonian teachings in Israel.

Abba Arikha *see* RAV (ii).

Abbahu (279–320). Palestinian amora. He was the leader of the rabbis at Caesarea who were responsible for the redaction of the juridical parts of the Jerusalem Talmud.

Abba Mari ben Moses ha-Yarḥi [Don Astruc of Lunel] (fl. 13th–14th cent.). French scholar. He and Asher ben Jehiel persuaded Solomon ben Adret to issue a ban in 1305 prohibiting students under 30 from studying philosophy. Jacob ben Makhir ibn Tibbon issued a counter-ban. This controversy is discussed in Abba Mari's *The Offering of Zeal.*

Abba Sikra (fl. 1st cent.). Israelite Zealot leader. He helped Johanan ben Zakkai escape from Jerusalem when it was besieged by the Romans.

Abbaye [Naḥmani bar Kaylil] (278–338). Babylonian amora. He developed talmudic dialectic as head of the academy at Pumbedita. His arguments with Rava are recorded in the Babylonian Talmud. In his teaching Abbaye distinguished between the literal meaning of the biblical text ("peshat") and the figurative interpretation ("derash").

Abbreviations (Hebrew "rashe tevot"). Shortened word forms used extensively in the Talmud and subsequent rabbinic literature from as early as the 2nd century BCE; they also played an important role in rabbinic and mystical exegesis. The full form of the word is indicated by a dot, stroke, or double stroke over the first, second, or third letter; the other letters are eliminated. Abbreviating groups of words to form one word was also a common practice.

Abel. Son of Adam and Eve. He was a shepherd; his elder brother Cain was a farmer. When God favored Abel's sacrifice, Cain killed him out of jealousy. (Genesis 4.1–9)

Abenaes *see* IBN YAISH, SOLOMON.

Abendana, Isaac (1640–1710). English Hebrew scholar. He taught Hebrew at the universities of Cambridge and Oxford, and translated the Mishnah into Latin.

Abendana, Jacob ben Joseph (1630–1685). Dutch rabbinic scholar. He translated Judah ha-Levi's *Kuzari* and the Mishnah into Spanish.

Abiathar (fl. 11th–10th cent. BCE). Israelite, chief priest at Nob. He was loyal to David during Absalom's unsuccessful rebellion. At the end of David's reign he supported Adonijah's claim to become king in opposition to Solomon. Solomon later banished him from Jerusalem and transferred his priestly rights to Zadok. (I Kings 1.2; I Chronicles 15)

Abiathar ben Elijah ha-Cohen (1040–1109). Last Palestinian gaon. He left Palestine after quarreling with the Egyptian exilarch David ben Daniel. His travail is depicted in the *Scroll of Abiathar.*

Abib *see* AVIV.

Abigail (fl. 11th–10th cent. BCE). Israelite woman, wife of David. After the death of her husband, Nabal, she became David's wife. (I Samuel 25)

Abihu (fl. ?13th cent. BCE). Israelite priest, second son of Aaron. With his brother Nadab, he ascended Mount Sinai to behold God's revelation (Exodus 24.1–11). Later they made a fire sacrifice on the altar against God's command and were struck dead by fire as punishment (Leviticus 10.1–3).

Abijah (fl. 10th cent. BCE). King of Judah (914–912 BCE). He engaged in continuous battle with Jeroboam, King of Israel. (I Kings 15; II Chronicles 13)

***Abimelech (i)** (fl. ?19th–16th cent. BCE). King of Gerar in Palestine. He had friendly relations with Abraham and Isaac. (Genesis 20 and 26)

Abimelech (ii) (fl. 12th cent. BCE). Israelite king. Supported by the chiefs of Shechem, he ruled for three years before he was killed in a revolt. (Judges 9)

Abiram (fl. ?13th cent. BCE). Israelite rebel leader. With Dathan and Koraḥ, he led an unsuccessful revolt against Moses in the wilderness (Numbers 16).

Abishag (fl. 11th–10th cent. BCE). Shunamite woman who ministered to David. (I Kings 1.1–4)

Abishai (fl. 11th–10th cent. BCE). Israelite general. He was commander of David's army. He fought heroically and once saved David's life in battle. (II Samuel 21.16–17)

Abitur, Joseph ben Isaac ibn *see* IBN ABITUR, JOSEPH BEN ISAAC.

Ablution. In biblical and rabbinic usage, ritual washing. Women after menstruation or childbirth and converts during the conversion process completely immerse themselves in natural water or a ritual bath ("mikveh"). Priests wash their hands and feet during the Temple service. Individuals wash their hands before eating or praying, and after rising from sleep, touching a corpse, urinating, or defecating.

Abner ben Ner (fl. 11th cent. BCE). Israelite general. He was commander of Saul's army. He supported Ish-bosheth's claim to the throne when Saul died. Subsequently he became a member of David's court. He was killed by Joab. (I Samuel 3)

***Abner of Burgos** [Alfonso of Valladolid] (1270–1340). Spanish scholar. A convert to Christianity, he wrote anti-Jewish polemical tracts and engaged in disputes with Jewish scholars. He formulated an ideological justification for his conversion in *Epistle on Fate.*

Aboab, Immanuel (1555–1628). Spanish scholar. He wrote *Nomologia, o Discursos legales*, a defence of the divine origin of the Oral Law and the Jewish tradition.

Aboab, Isaac (i) (fl. 14th cent.). Spanish writer on ethics. He collected aggadic teaching and homiletical literature concerned with Jewish ethics in the *Candlestick of Light.*

Aboab, Isaac (ii) (1433–1493). Spanish rabbinic scholar. He is known as the last gaon of Castile. He was the head of the Toledo yeshivah.

Aboab, Isaac de Fonseca (1605–1693). Portuguese rabbi; he was the first rabbi in the western hemisphere. Born a Marrano in Portugal, he emigrated to Holland. In 1641 he traveled to Recife, Brazil. He later went to Amsterdam, where he was appointed ḥakham. He was a follower of Shabbetai Tzevi, and a member of the tribunal which excommunicated Benedict Spinoza.

Aboab, Samuel (1610–1694). Italian rabbi. He was an opponent of the Sabbetaians. He was among the rabbis who interrogated Nathan of Gaza in Venice in 1668. He wrote *Devar Shemuel.*

Abomination. In Jewish law, any of three kinds of abhorrent thing, grouped according to their gravity. "Toevah" is the worst, and consists of major sins such as idolatry and child-sacrifice. "Shikkutz" is less serious and applies to idolatrous usages and prohibited animals. "Piggul" is the least serious and refers to the flesh of a sacrifice which has become putrid.

Abortion. Termination of a pregnancy. The Bible stipulates liability for monetary compensation (as opposed to capital punishment) in the case of an attack on a pregnant woman that results in the loss of the unborn child (Exodus 21.22–3). The rabbis interpreted this to mean that full human rights extend only to a child who is born. Thus the Mishnah rules in favor of destroying a foetus if its continued existence endangers the mother's life (as long as the head or a greater part of the child has not yet emerged from the birth canal).

Abrabanel, Isaac ben Judah *see* ABRAVANEL, ISAAC BEN JUDAH.

Abrabanel, Judah *see* ABRAVANEL, JUDAH.

Abraham [Abram] (fl. ?19th–16th cent. BCE). Israelite patriarch. He left Ur and traveled to Canaan. God appeared to him and promised that his offspring would inherit the earth. The Lord made a covenant with Abraham and tested his faith by asking him to sacrifice his son Isaac. (Genesis 11.26–25.10)

Abraham, Apocalypse of. Pseudepigraphic book. It relates Abraham's conversion, destiny in heaven and the fate of all the nations.

Abraham, Testament of. Pseudepigraphic book. It depicts Abraham's initiation into the divine mysteries before his death and his ascent to heaven. *See* PSEUDEPIGRAPHA.

Abraham Abele of Gombin [Gombiner, Abraham Abele] (c. 1635–1683). Polish talmudist. His commentary on the Code of Jewish Law, *Magen Avraham*, influenced religious practice among the Ashkenazim.

Abraham bar Ḥiyya [Abraham Judaeus; Abraham Savasorda] (fl. 12th cent.). Spanish scholar. He established the foundations of Hebrew scientific terminology and transmitted Greco-Arabic science to the Christian world. His *Meditation of the Sad Soul* is an ethical treatise influenced by Neoplatonism.

Abraham ben Alexander Katz of Kalisk [Kalisher, Abraham] (1741–1810). Polish Ḥasidic rabbi. He represented popular elements of the Ḥasidic movement, but the odd customs of his followers evoked opposition. With Menaḥem Mendel of Vitebsk, he led a group of Ḥasidim from Russia to Palestine in 1777.

Abraham ben David of Posquières [Ravad] (1125–1198). French talmudist. His strictures on the writings of Maimonides, Alfasi and Zerahiah ben Isaac ha-Levi were widely read. He objected to Maimonides' *Mishneh Torah* because he believed such codes might take the place of talmudic study.

Abraham ben David Portaleone *see* PORTALEONE, ABRAHAM BEN DAVID.

Abraham ben Elijah of Vilna (1750–1808). Polish scholar. His edition of *Aggadat Bereshit* was the first complete history of midrashic literature. He wrote a critical index to 130 midrashim, *Rav Pealim*.

Abraham ben Ḥasdai ha-Levi *see* IBN ḤASDAI, ABRAHAM BEN SAMUEL HA-LEVI.

Abraham ben Isaac ben Garton (fl. 15th cent.). Spanish printer. He produced the first dated Hebrew book (Rashi's commentary on the Pentateuch) at Reggio di Calabria in 1475.

Abraham ben Isaac of Narbonne [Ravad II] (1110–1179). French talmudist. He was the spiritual leader of the Jews in Provence. He produced the first code of Jewish law in southern France, *Ha-Eshkol*.

Abraham ben Meir de Balmes *see* BALMES, ABRAHAM BEN MEIR DE.

Abraham ben Moses ben Maimon [Maimon, Abraham ben Moses] (1186–1237). Egyptian rabbinic scholar. He succeeded his father Maimonides as nagid of the Egyptian Jewish community. His *Comprehensive Guide for the Servants of God* is an encyclopedic work on the Jewish religion.

Abraham ben Nathan ha-Yarḥi (1155–1215). French talmudist. In his *Sepher ha-Manhig*, he describes synagogue practices in France, Germany, England, and Spain.

Abraham ben Samuel Ḥasdai *see* IBN ḤASDAI, ABRAHAM BEN SAMUEL HA-LEVI.

Abraham ben Samuel Zacut *see* ZACUTO, ABRAHAM.

Abraham ibn Daud *see* IBN DAUD, ABRAHAM.

Abraham ibn Ezra *see* IBN EZRA, ABRAHAM.

Abraham ibn Ḥasdai *see* IBN ḤASDAI, ABRAHAM BEN SAMUEL HA-LEVI.

Abraham Joshua Heshel of Apta [Apt [Opatov], Rabbi of] (1745–1825). Polish Ḥasidic leader. He opposed the maskilim for spreading heretical ideas among Russian Jewry. He recounted fantastic reminiscences about what he had witnessed in former incarnations as high priest, king of Israel, nasi, and exilarch.

Abraham Judaeus *see* ABRAHAM BAR ḤIYYA.

Abrahams, Israel (1858–1924). English scholar. He was reader in rabbinics at Cambridge University. With Claude Montefiore he founded (1888) and edited the *Jewish Quarterly Review*. His most important works were *Jewish Life in the Middle Ages, Studies in Pharisaism and the Gospels,* and *Hebrew Ethical Wills.*

Abraham Savasorda *see* ABRAHAM BAR ḤIYYA.

Abram *see* ABRAHAM.

Abramowitsch, Shalom Jacob [Sephorim, Mendele Mocher] (1836–1917). Russian Hebrew and Yiddish author. He was born in Belorussia. With Ḥayyim Naḥman Bialik and Yehoshua Hana Ravnitzky he translated the Pentateuch into Yiddish; he also wrote short stories. He is the father of prose literature in Hebrew and Yiddish.

Abrams, Lionel (b. 1931). South African artist. He was born in Johannesburg. He held his first exhibition in 1957. His interest in the Lubavitch movement in the early 1970s led to a four-year period of work on Jewish themes: he produced a series of pastel portraits of five generations of "Lubavitcher rebbes," and painted a number of traditional Jewish themes.

Abramsky, Chimen (b. 1917). British scholar of Russian origin. Born in Minsk, he emigrated to the UK, where he became professor of Hebrew and Jewish studies at University College, London. His publications include *Karl Marx and the English Labour Movement, First Illustrated Grace after Meals,* and *The Jews in Poland.*

Abravanel, David Dormido *see* DORMIDO, DAVID ABRAVANEL.

Abravanel [Abrabanel]**, Isaac ben Judah** (1437–1508). Portuguese biblical exegete and statesman. He was treasurer to Alfonso V of Portugal and served King Ferdinand and Queen Isabella of Castile. His writings include a commentary on the Bible, philosophical studies of an antirationalist nature, and theological treatises stressing the primacy of Judaism.

Abravanel [Abrabanel]**, Judah** [Leone Ebreo] (1460–after 1523). Portuguese philosopher. His *Dialoghi di amore* combines Judaism and Neoplatonism and stresses love as the foundation of the world.

Absalom (i) (fl. 10th cent. BCE). Israelite, son of David. He killed his brother Amnon who had raped his sister Tamar. He led an unsuccessful rebellion against David, in which his army was defeated and he was killed by Joab. (II Samuel 13–19)

Absalom (ii) (fl. 1st cent.). Israelite, Jewish patriot. He joined Menaḥem ben Judah in the revolt against Rome.

Abse, Dannie (b. 1923). Welsh poet and playwright. He was born in Cardiff. He published his first volume of poetry while still a medical student. His *Collected Poems, 1948–1976* draw together his roles as Jew, Welshman, British poet, doctor, bourgeois family man, bohemian observer, pragmatist, and mystic. In the collections *Way Out in the Centre* and *Ask the Bloody Horse* he displays an affinity with midrashic, Ḥasidic, and kabbalistic legends.

Abstinence *see* ASCETICISM.

Abu *see* ATTAR, ḤAYYIM BEN MOSES BEN.

Abu Ahron ben Samuel *see* AARON BEN SAMUEL.

Abudarham, David ben Joseph (fl. 14th cent.). Spanish talmudist. His commentary on synagogue liturgy, *The Book of Abudarham*, is based on numerous rabbinic sources.

Abu Imran of Tiflis *see* A-TIFLISI, ABU IMRAN.

Abu Issa al-Isfahani [Isfahani] (fl. 8th cent.). Persian, self-proclaimed Messiah. He claimed to be the Messiah ben Joseph, the last of the five forerunners of the Messiah ben David. He prohibited divorce, eating meat, and drinking wine. He recognized the prophecies of Jesus and Mohammed and decreed seven daily prayers. In a rebellion against the Abbasid rulers, he was killed in battle.

Abulafia, Abraham ben Samuel (1240–after 1291). Spanish kabbalist and pseudo-messiah. In 1280 he went to Rome to persuade Pope Nicholas III to help the Jews. He evoked hostility from Solomon ben Adret by prophesying his own messiahship and redemptive powers. He believed his kabbalistic practices, based on letter manipulation, enabled one to receive prophetic gifts and commune with God.

Abulafia, Ḥayyim ben Jacob (1580–1668). Palestinian talmudist. In 1666 he was one of the delegation who went to Gaza to investigate the authenticity of Nathan of Gaza's prophecies about Shabbetai Tzevi.

Abulafia, Meir ben Todros ha-Levi (?1170–1244). Spanish talmudist and poet. He wrote about halakhah, masorah, and the controversy over Maimonides' opinion on the subject of resurrection; he also composed Hebrew poetry.

Abulafia, Todros ben Joseph (1220–1298). Spanish kabbalist. He was the spiritual leader of the Jewish community in Castile. His *Oẓar ha-Kavod* combines kabbalistic doctrines of gnostic circles in Castile with those of the Gerona school.

Abulafia, Todros ben Judah (1247–after 1298). Spanish Hebrew poet. His poems throw light on contemporary conditions in Castile. His *Garden of Apologues and Saws* contains more than 1000 poems.

Abu Yakub al-Basir *see* JOSEPH BEN ABRAHAM HA-COHEN.

Academy. In Jewish usage a term applied specifically to a center of rabbinic scholarship. After the fall of Jerusalem (70 CE) the first academy was founded at Jabneh. In Babylonia the major academies were located at Sura, Nehardea, and Pumbedita. *See also* YESHIVAH.

Academy of the Hebrew Language. Israeli institution founded in 1953 to oversee the correct development of the Hebrew language.

Academy on High. The body of scholars in heaven. It is presided over by God and reserved for scholars after their death.

Accents ("neginot"). In liturgical texts a system of accents is used to aid cantillation. Accents are used in this context to indicate punctuation and stress, and to show the rise and fall of the chant.

Accident. Biblical laws of liability for damage caused by an accident are found in Exodus 21.28–36 and 22.4–5. The rabbis categorized the cases cited into four standard types of accident: the ox (representing injury caused in the course of normal activity); the pit (injury caused by a stationary thing); the crop-devouring animal (standing for accidents caused not in public places but on the private property of the person injured); and fire (representing consequential damage).

Achan (fl. 13th cent. BCE). Israelite. He took some of the consecrated spoil when Jericho was captured, and because of this sacrilege the Israelites were unable to capture Ai. Achan and his family were put to death as a punishment for his sin. (Joshua 7)

Acher, Mattathias *see* BIRNBAUM, NATHAN.

***Achish** (fl. 11th–10th cent. BCE). Philistine King of Gath. David took refuge with him when he fled from Saul. (I Samuel 21.10–15)

Achron, Joseph (1886–1943). American composer of Lithuanian origin. He was a founder of the Society for Hebrew Folk Music in St. Petersburg. He composed *Hebrew Melody* (1911), as well as violin concertos and string quartets inspired by Jewish motifs.

Acosta, Uriel (1585–1640). Spanish heretic. He lived first in Spain and later in Amsterdam and Hamburg. He wrote against the Jewish faith and was excommunicated. Before his death he published a brief autobiography, *Exemplar humanae vitae*.

Acre. Town in northern Israel. Its position on the coast made its occupation vital to every army waging war in Syria and Israel.

Acrostic. Literary device, in which successive verses of a text begin with the letters of the alphabet. Acrostics are found in the Bible (Psalms 34 and 37; Proverbs 31.10–31; Lamentations 1–4) and in many medieval liturgical compositions. They have mystical significance in kabbalistic literature.

Acsady, Ignac (1845–1906). Hungarian historian and writer. He fought for equal rights for Hungarian Jews. In 1883 he published *Jewish and Non-Jewish Hungarians after the Emancipation*.

Acts of the Pagan Martyrs *see* PAGAN MARTYRS, ACTS OF THE.

Adafina. Foods eaten by Jews on the Sabbath in medieval Spain. The Inquisition regarded the eating of special foods on the Sabbath as a sign of loyalty to Judaism.

Adam. First man. He was made in the image of God on the sixth day of creation. Eve was created out of one of his ribs. They were permitted to eat from all the trees in the Garden of Eden except the tree of the knowledge of good and evil. When they disobeyed God they were expelled from the Garden. Adam was condemned to a life of work; Eve was to suffer the pain of childbirth. (Genesis 1–3)

Adam and Eve, Book of the Life of. Pseudepigraphic work. It relates the lives of Adam and Eve after their expulsion from the Garden of Eden as well as their repentence, death, and resurrection.

Adam ha-Cohen *see* LEBENSOHN, ABRAHAM DOV.

Adam Kadmon. Primordial man. In kabbalistic literature he is the spiritual prototype of man. According to the Zohar, he is a manifestation of the sephirot. In Lurianic kabbalah he is a mediator between the En Soph and the sephirot.

***Adams, Hannah** (1755–1831). American writer. She was the author of *History of the Jews from the Destruction of Jerusalem to the Present Time* (1812).

Adar. 12th month of the Jewish year.

Addir bi-melukhah ("Mighty in kingship"). Opening words of an acrostic poem, based on Genesis Rabbah. It was introduced into the Passover Haggadah by Ashkenazic Jews in the Middle Ages.

Addir Hu ("Mighty is he"). Opening words of an acrostic prayer for the rebuilding of the Temple. It was introduced into the Passover Haggadah by Ashkenazic Jews in the Middle Ages.

Adler, Cyrus (1863–1940). American scholar. He was president of the Jewish Theological Seminary and Dropsie College, and served as editor of the *Jewish Quarterly Review*. His publications include *Lectures, Selected Papers, Addresses* and *I have Considered the Days*.

Adler, Elkan Nathan (1861–1946). English bibliophile. His library contained some 4500 Hebrew manuscripts. They are summarized in the *Catalogue of Hebrew Manuscripts in the Collection of E. N. Adler*.

Adler, Felix (1851–1933). American philosopher and educator. He founded the Society for Ethical Culture in 1876 and in 1902 was appointed professor of social ethics at Columbia University. He viewed ethical culture as a way of applying morality to modern life. An elaboration of his philosophy is contained in *An Ethical Philosophy of Life*.

Adler, Hermann (1839–1911). English rabbi. He was principal of Jews College. In 1891 he was elected chief rabbi. A selection of his sermons were published in *Anglo-Jewish Memories*.

Adler, Jacob (1855–1926). American actor of Russian origin. He began his acting career in Russia. In 1888 he went to the US where he became the most important actor on the Yiddish stage.

Adler, Nathan ben Simeon (1741–1800). German pietist. He founded a yeshivah in Frankfurt am Main. He conducted services in his home using Isaac Luria's prayerbook. A ban was imposed on these prayer meetings under threat of excommunication.

Adler, Nathan Marcus (1803–1890). English rabbi. Appointed chief rabbi in 1844, he modernized the British rabbinate and paved the way for the establishment of Jews College in 1855 and the United Synagogue in 1870. He wrote a commentary on *Targum Onkelos*.

Adler, Samuel (1809–1891). American Reform rabbi of German origin. He was born in Worms and settled in the US in 1857. An early European reformer, he became rabbi of Temple Emanuel in New York in 1857.

Adler, Samuel H. (b. 1928). American composer, conductor and educator of German origin. Born in Mannheim, he moved to the US in 1939. He was music director at Temple Immanuel in Dallas (1953–66), then became professor of composition at the Eastman School of Music in Rochester, New York. He has composed cantatas dealing with Jewish themes as well as synagogue services.

***Adler, Victor** (1852–1918). Austrian politician. He was born in Prague. Although he qualified as a physician he devoted his life to the cause of the working class. He was a member of the Austrian parliament from 1905 to 1918. He converted to Christianity and opposed the idea of Jewish nationhood.

Adler, Yankel (1895–1949). Polish painter. Born in Lódź, he taught in Düsseldorf and later lived in France and England. His style was based on Jewish folk traditions.

Adloyada. Purim festival. It is derived from the saying in the Talmud that one should revel on Purim until one no longer knows ("ad de-lo yada") the difference between the phrases "Blessed be Mordecai" and "Cursed be Haman."

Ad meah (ve-esrim) shanah ("[may you live] to a hundred (and twenty)"). Expression of good wishes on a birthday, especially that of an elderly person.

Admor. Title by which Ḥasidic rabbis are known. It is an abbreviation of "Adonenu, morenu, ve-rabbenu" ("Our lord, teacher, and master").

Adonai *see* GOD, NAMES OF.

Adonijah (fl. 10th cent. BCE). Son of David. When David was dying, Adonijah attempted to prevent Solomon from becoming king. But under the influence of Nathan the prophet, David decreed that Solomon should reign after him. When Adonijah desired to marry David's concubine Abishag, Solomon regarded this as an act of rebellion and had him executed. (I Kings 1–2)

Adoni-Zedek (fl. 13th cent. BCE). Canaanite king of Jerusalem. He reigned during the time of the Israelite conquest of Canaan. (Joshua 10.1–3)

Adon olam ("Lord of the world"). Opening words of a liturgical hymn, extolling the unity of God and expressing trust in his providence. It has been attributed to Solomon ibn Gabirol.

Adoption. The assumption of a parental relationship by one individual to another when the two are not natural parent and child. Although it is not a legal institution in Judaism, Jewish law provides for circumstances similar to those caused by adoption: a guardian may be appointed with authority to care for a child's welfare and property.

Adorno, Theodor Wiesengrund (1903–1969). German philosopher and sociologist. He taught at the University of Frankfurt (Frankfurt am Main) in 1931 and later lived in the US. In 1949 he returned to Germany, where he served as director of the Institute for Social Research in Frankfurt and professor of sociology and philosophy at the university. In his later works he discussed the nature of modern anti-Semitism.

Adoshem. Name of God. Derived from "Adonai" (Lord) and "Ha-Shem" (the name), it is used in liturgical contexts to avoid the speaking of God's name.

Adret [Abraham]**, Solomon ben** [Ibn Adret, Solomon ben Abraham; Rashba] (1235–1310). Spanish scholar. He studied under Naḥmanides and was later the leader of Spanish Jewry. His legal decisions were viewed as authoritative because of his stature as a scholar; they constitute a primary source of information about the history of the Jews of the period. He defended Judaism from Christian and Muslim detractors and disputed the messianic claims of Abraham ben Samuel Abulafia.

Adultery. In Jewish law, sexual intercourse between a married woman and a man other than her husband. It is prohibited in the Decalogue (Exodus 20.14; Deuteronomy 5.18) and is punishable by death (Leviticus 20.10; Deuteronomy 22.22). A special ritual is prescribed to determine whether a woman suspected of adultery is guilty (Numbers 5.12–31).

Adummim *see* ROSSI, AZARIAH BEN MOSES DEI.

Aelia Capitolina. Name given by the Romans to Jerusalem when they rebuilt it after the revolt led by Bar Kokhba in 135.

Afendopolo, Caleb ben Elijah (?1464–1525). Karaite scholar and poet. He lived most of his life in Kramariya near Constantinople. He wrote on biblical, theological, ethical, and scientific subjects, and composed liturgical poetry.

Afikomen [aphikoman]. Part of the middle mazzah. During the Passover seder, the leader breaks the middle mazzah into two. The larger part is the afikomen which is a symbolic reminder of the destruction of the Temple.

Afternoon service *see* MINḤAH (i).

***Agag** (fl. 11th cent. BCE). Amalekite king. He was captured in battle by Saul. Samuel regarded this as a transgression of God's command to destroy the Amalekites and killed Agag at Gilgal. (I Samuel 15)

Agam, Yakov (b. 1928). Israeli painter and sculptor. He was born in Rishon le Zion. He was the first to introduce geometical abstraction into Israeli art. From the early 1950s he produced experimental works involving techniques and concepts of his own invention, such as "simultaneous writing" in which superimposed words suggested multiple ideas to the viewer. In later works he used electrical motors to produce movement and change of composition, as well as light and sound effects. Some of his work contains traditional Jewish symbols.

Aggadah. Rabbinic teaching. It is an amplification of biblical narrative, history, ethics, and prophecy, and is found in midrashic literature and scattered throughout the Palestinian and Babylonian Talmuds. Unlike the halakhah, it is not authoritative. It contains parables, allegories, prayers, laments, polemics, stories, homilies, theology, ethics, and letter symbolism.

Aggadat Bereshit. Midrash on Genesis, based on other midrashim, particularly the Tanḥuma. It dates from around the 12th century.

Aggadat Ester. Midrash on the Book of Esther. Based on talmudic and midrashic sources, its origin is probably Yemenite. It originated not earlier than the 13th century.

Aggadat Mashiaḥ. Collection of homilies describing the messianic era. Composed of early legends, it was edited by Tobiah ben Eliezer.

Agla. Kabbalistic word made up of the initials of the Hebrew phrase "Atta gibbor le-olam adonai" (Thou art mighty forever, O Lord).

Agnon, Shemuel Yosef (1888–1970). Galician Hebrew writer. He settled in Palestine and published novels and short stories dealing with life in Galicia and Palestine. Regarded as the greatest epic writer of modern Hebrew literature, he was awarded the Nobel Prize. His writings include *The Bridal Canopy* and *A Guest for the Night*.

***Agobard** (779–840). Archbishop of Lyons. His opposition to the Jews arose from religious, political, and social motives. In 820 he attempted to convert local Jewish children by force.

Agrarian laws. A number of Biblical laws concerning agriculture are developed in the Talmud.

Agriculture. After the destruction of the second Temple, Jewish farmers lived in Palestine, Babylonia, Egypt, Arabia, Ethiopia, and various European countries. Modern Jewish farming originated in Russia at the beginning of the 19th century. In Israel agricultural settlements began in 1855 and continued to develop throughout the 19th and 20th centuries.

Agrippa I *see* HEROD AGRIPPA I.

Agrippa II *see* HEROD AGRIPPA II.

Agro-Joint [American Jewish Joint Agricultural Corporation]. Organization formed in 1928 by the American Jewish Joint Distribution Committee. It resettled in the Crimea and the Ukraine Russian Jews who had been barred by the Soviet government from practicing their trades.

Agudat ha-Sopherim ha-Ivriim. Palestinian organization established in 1921 in Tel Aviv to promote Hebrew literature. It was headed by Ḥayyim Naḥman Bialik.

Agudat ha-Sotzialistim ha-Ivriim. Jewish socialist union founded by A. S. Liebermann in London in 1876. Its members were tailors and cabinet-makers from Russia. It was criticized by British Jewish leaders and was disbanded the same year.

Agudat Israel. International organization of Orthodox Jews. It was founded in 1912 at Kattowitz in Upper Silesia. It sought to preserve Orthodoxy by adhering strictly to halakhah. Before the establishment of the State of Israel, it was anti-Zionist. In 1948 its representatives joined the Provisional Government of Israel, and it has continually had representatives in the Knesset.

Aguilar, Diego d' [Pereira, Moses Lopez] (1699–1759). Marrano financier. Born in Portugal, he settled in Vienna. He used his influence at court to assist Jews, preventing their expulsion from Moravia in 1742 and from Prague in 1744. When the Spanish Inquisition asked for his extradition, he went to London where he was active in the Sephardic community.

Aguilar, Grace (1816–1847). English writer. She was born in London. In 1842 she published *The Spirit of Judaism: In*

Defence of her Faith and its Professors. Her *Records of Israel: Two Tales* and *Women of Israel* presented idealized pictures of Jewish life in Spain and women in the Bible. Her own beliefs are contained in *The Jewish Faith, its Spiritual Consolation, Moral Guidance and Immortal Hope*. She also published popular novels dealing with Jewish life.

Agunah. A married woman whose husband's death is suspected but not proved. Since she is unable to prove that she is no longer married, she cannot remarry. Attempts have been made to liberalize the law, but no halakhically acceptable solution has been found.

Agur ben Jakeh. Compiler of proverbs. He is mentioned in Proverbs 30.

Agus, Jacob (1911–1986). American rabbi and philosopher of Polish origin. He was a rabbi in Cambridge (Massachusetts), Chicago, and Dayton (Ohio). Later he was appointed professor of religion at Temple University and was a member of the faculty of the Reconstructionist Rabbinical College. He also served as rabbi of Beth El Synagogue in Baltimore. His writings include *Modern Philosophies of Judaism*, *Guideposts in Modern Judaism*, *The Meaning of Jewish History*, and *Dialogue and Tradition*.

Ahab (fl. 9th cent. BCE). King of Israel (874–852 BCE). He was reproved by Elijah for seizing Naboth's vineyard. When his wife, Jezebel, introduced the worship of Baal into Israel, a struggle took place between Elijah and the prophets of Baal. Ahab was victorious over Ben-Hadad of Damascus and later formed an alliance with him against the Assyrians. (I Kings 16.29–22.40)

Aḥad ha-Am [Ginsberg, Asher] (1856–1927). Ukrainian Hebrew essayist. Born in the Ukraine, he lived in Odessa and Tel Aviv. He advocated spiritual Zionism, which he believed would lead to the founding of a national spiritual center. His writings include six volumes of collected essays.

Aḥa of Shabḥa (680–752). Babylonian scholar. When he failed to be appointed gaon of the academy at Pumbedita, he moved to Palestine. His *Book of Questions* contains lectures in Aramaic on weekly portions of the Torah.

Aḥaronim. Later rabbinic authorities.

***Ahasuerus (i).** King of Persia. He ruled from India to Ethiopia, according to the Book of Esther. Some scholars have identified him with Xerxes (486–465 BCE), the son of Darius I.

Ahasuerus (ii) *see* WANDERING JEW.

Ahavah rabbah ("Great love"). Opening words of the prayer preceding the Shema in the morning service of the Ashkenazi ritual. In the Sephardi ritual the opening words of the prayer are "Ahavat olam" ("Everlasting love"). This difference is based on a dispute between Rav and Samuel.

Ahaz (fl. 8th cent. BCE). King of Judah (743–727 BCE). When he introduced Assyrian cults into the Temple worship, he was criticized for doing evil in the eyes of the Lord. (II Kings 16.3–4)

Ahaziah (i) (fl. 9th cent. BCE). King of Israel (853–852 BCE). He was influenced by his mother, Jezebel, who introduced the cult of Baal into Israel. He was injured in a fall from an upper chamber in his palace and asked for an oracle from Baal-Zebub; Elijah reproved him and prophesied his death. (II Kings 1.2–17)

Ahaziah (ii) (fl. 9th cent. BCE). King of Judah (842–841 BCE). He and Jehoram, King of Israel, went to war against Hazael, King of Aram (II Kings 8.28–9; II Chronicles 22.5–6). When Jehoram was injured in battle, Ahaziah visited him in Jezreel. Both kings were assassinated by Jehu. (II Kings 9.27–8, II Chronicles 22.9)

Aḥdut ha-Avodah. Israeli socialist party. It was formed in 1919. After a number of alliances contracted with other socialist groups, in 1968 it finally merged with Mapai and Rafi to form the Israel Labor Party.

Aḥer *see* ELISHA BEN AVUYAH.

Aḥiasaph. Hebrew publishing house, active in Warsaw in 1893–1926. It was founded by Ben Avigdor and published important Hebrew works and translations, including a literary annual, *Luaḥ Aḥiasaph.*

Ahijah (fl. 11th cent. BCE). Chief priest at Shiloh during Saul's reign. He wore an ephod when Saul fought against the Philistines. (I Samuel 14.3)

Ahijah the Shilonite (fl. 10th cent. BCE). Israelite prophet. He prophesied during Solomon's reign and the concurrent reigns of Rehoboam and Jeroboam. (I Kings 11–14)

Aḥikar (fl. 8th–7th cent. BCE). Aramaic folk hero. He was chief cup-bearer, keeper of the royal signet, and chief administrator during the reigns of the Assyrian rulers Sennacherib and Esarhaddon. His sayings are recorded in the *Book of Aḥikar.*

Ahimaaz ben Paltiel (1017–1060). Italian chronicler and poet. In 1054 he compiled a genealogy of his family in rhymed prose, preserved in *The Ahimaaz Scroll.*

Ahimelech (fl. 11th cent. BCE). Israelite, priest of Nob. When David escaped from Saul, Ahimelech gave him bread and the sword of Goliath, which was kept in the Temple. Saul put him to death. (I Samuel 21–2)

Ahithophel (fl. 11th–10th cent. BCE). Adviser to David. He joined Absalom in his unsuccessful revolt against David. (II Samuel 15–17)

Ai. Ancient town north of Jerusalem. According to the Bible, it was destroyed by Joshua (Joshua 7–8) but archeologists have found no evidence of this destruction.

Aizman, David (1869–1922). Russian writer. He wrote about the Jewish poor and about revolutionary-minded Jewish intellectuals. An eight-volume edition of his work appeared in Russian between 1911 and 1919.

Akavia ben Mahalalel (fl. 1st cent). Palestinian scholar. He disagreed with other sages about legal issues. He was offered the position of president of the court on condition that he change his views; when he refused he was excommunicated.

Akdamut. Aramaic acrostic poem. It was written by Meir ben Isaac of Worms in the 11th century. It is recited by Ashkenazi Jews in the synagogue before the Torah reading on Shavuot.

Akedah ("binding"). Word used of Abraham's binding and intended sacrifice of Isaac (Genesis 22.1–19). According to rabbinic literature, akedah is a symbol of self-sacrifice in obedience to God. The passage from Genesis is read in the synagogue on the first day of Rosh ha-Shanah.

Akiva (50–135). Palestinian scholar, patriot, and martyr. He developed a method of biblical exegesis, systematized the Oral Law, and established an academy at Bene Berak. He believed that Simeon Bar Kokhba was the Messiah. He was imprisoned by the Romans for teaching Torah and was tortured to death.

Akiva, Alphabet of. Midrash attributed to Akiva. It is based on the letters of the Hebrew alphabet.

Akkadians. Semitic people who settled among the Sumerians in Mesopotamia. Sargon of Akkad established the first Akkadian empire in 2300 BCE.

Akkum. Worshipper of stars and planets. The word was originally applied to Chaldean star worshippers, but was later used to refer to all idolators and forms of idolatry.

Aknin, Joseph ibn Judah ibn *See* IBN AKNIN, JOSEPH BEN JUDAH.

Alav [*fem.* Aleha] **ha-shalom** ("Peace be on him [her]"). Phrase uttered when mentioning a deceased person.

Albalag, Isaac (fl. 13th cent.). Spanish translator and philosopher. He translated into Hebrew Al-Ghazzali's *Tendencies of the Philosophers*. He believed that there are two sources of knowledge: philosophical thought and prophetic intuition.

Albeck, Ḥanokh (1890–1972). German talmudist. He lectured on Talmud in Germany and later became professor of Talmud at the Hebrew University. His work covers almost all areas of talmudic research.

Albo, Joseph (fl. 15th cent.). Spanish philosopher. He was a pupil of Ḥasdai Crescas and participated in the Disputation of Tortosa (1413–14). His *Book of Dogmas* reduces the Jewish faith to three central principles: God's existence, divine revelation, and reward and punishment.

***Albright, William Foxwell** (1819–1971). American archeologist. He was professor of Semitic languages at Johns Hopkins University. His publications include *From the Stone Age to Christianity*, *Archaeology and the Religion of Israel*, *The Archaeology of Palestine*, and *The Excavation of Tell Beit Mirsim*.

Alchemy. The practice of chemistry with the aim of transmuting metals into gold. It was ascribed to Jews in ancient times. The Zohar contains hints of it in its views on metals. Jewish mysticism contributed the use of numerical and letter combinations to alchemical studies.

Alcimus (fl. 2nd cent. BCE). Judean high priest. He served as high priest during the Maccabean revolt (162–159 BCE). Appointed by the Syrian king Demetrius I to succeed Menelaus after the victories of Judah Maccabee, he favoured Hellenism.

Al-Damagani *see* DANIEL BEN MOSES AL-KUMISI.

Alenu ("It is our duty"). Opening words of a prayer proclaiming God's sovereignty and unity. It is ascribed to Rav. In the Middle Ages it was censored by Christians, who believed it contained an implied insult to Jesus. It is recited at the conclusion of the synagogue service.

Aleph. First letter of the Hebrew alphabet. Its numerical value is 1.

Aleph-baiz. The Hebrew ALPHABET.

Alexander (i) (80–49 BCE). Son of Aristobulus II, King of Judea. He was taken captive with his father by the Romans in 63 BCE. He later organized unsuccessful resistance in Judea.

Alexander (ii) (35–7 BCE). Son of Herod the Great. He and his brother Aristobulus were accused of plotting to kill their father. They were killed by strangulation.

***Alexander I** (1777–1825). Russian czar (1801–25). He appointed a committee to consider the situation of Russian Jewry. It produced a comprehensive piece of legislation to deal with Jewish affairs, the aims of which were to direct Jews toward employment in agriculture and industry, encourage secular education, and promote assimilation into Russian culture.

***Alexander II** (1818–81). Russian czar (1855–81). He attempted to integrate the Jews with the Russian people by extending the rights of certain groups within the Jewish community.

***Alexander III** (1845–94). Russian czar (1881–94). During his reign outbreaks of anti-Jewish violence took place. Legislation was passed which expelled Jews from Moscow and numerous villages; it also limited the number of Jews in secondary schools and universities.

Alexander, Haim (b. 1915). Israeli composer and pianist. He was born in Berlin but emigrated to Palestine in 1936. He taught at the Academy of Music in Jerusalem. In addition to composing choral, chamber, and orchestral works, he made a series of arrangements of traditional Jewish melodies.

***Alexander, Tiberius Julius** (fl. 1st cent.). Alexandrian official. He served in the Roman army and administration. He was procurator of Judea in 46–8. He was chief of staff to Titus in the siege of Jerusalem in 70.

Alexander Lysimachus (fl. 1st cent.). Alexandrian official. He was the brother of Philo. He served in the Roman fiscal administration in Egypt. A man of great wealth, he made a gift to the Temple so that its gates could be plated with gold and silver.

***Alexander the Great** (356–323 BCE). King of Macedonia. According to Flavius Josephus, he visited Jerusalem, honored the high priest, and granted privileges to the Jews in Palestine and the diaspora.

Alexander Yannai (fl. 2nd–1st cent. BCE). King of Judea and high priest (103–76 BCE). He added the coastal region to his kingdom. During his reign the Pharisees rebelled against him for violating Pharisaic law concerning Temple practice. A massacre took place and many leading Pharisees went into exile.

Alexandra (i) (fl. 1st cent. BCE). Daughter of Aristobulus II, King of Judea. She married Philippion, son of Ptolemy of Chalcis. Ptolemy had his son killed and married her.

Alexandra (ii) (d. 28 BCE). Daughter of Hyrcanus II. When her son Aristobulus was drowned, she accused Herod of murder. Herod had her executed after she attempted to seize power.

Alexandra, Salome *see* SALOME ALEXANDRA.

Alexandria. Egyptian port. In the Roman period Jews constituted a large proportion of the population. When the Jewish community attempted to obtain civic rights, riots broke out. In 66, under the influence of the revolt in Judea, further disturbances took place, which were suppressed by the Roman governor, Tiberius Julius Alexander.

Alfasi, David [David ben Abraham Alfasi] (fl. 10th cent.). Karaite grammarian and commentator. Originally from Fez, he settled in Palestine. He composed a Hebrew–Arabic lexicon of the Bible.

Alfasi, Isaac ben Jacob [Rif] (1013–1103). North African talmudist. He lived in Fez. He was the author of a code of Jewish law, *Sepher ha-Halakhot*, the most important code before the *Mishneh Torah* of Maimonides.

Alfayyumi, Jacob (fl. 12th cent.). Leader of the Yemenite Jewish community to whom Maimonides addressed his *Letter to the Yemen* in 1172.

***Alfonsi, Petrus** [Sephardi, Moses] (1062–1110). Spanish writer and translator. He converted to Christianity and wrote a polemic against Judaism in the form of a dialogue. His collection of pious anecdotes for preachers, *Training for the Clergy*, introduced oriental tales to European readers.

Alfonso de Spina *see* SPINA, ALFONSO DE.

Alfonso of Valladolid *see* ABNER OF BURGOS.

***Al-Ghazzali** (1058–1111). Persian Muslim theologian. He lived in Baghdad. His writings combine orthodox piety and the contemplative quest. He influenced Jewish philosophers such as Judah ha-Levi.

Al ha-nissim ("For the miracles"). Opening words of a thanksgiving prayer recited in the Amidah and Grace after Meals during Ḥannukah and Purim.

Al-Ḥarizi, Judah [Taḥkemoni] (1170–1235). Spanish Hebrew poet and translator. He traveled widely through Mediterranean countries. His *Taḥkemoni* consists of 50 narratives in rhymed prose; it throws light on the culture of the period and describes the scholars and leaders he met on his travels. He translated Maimonides' *Guide for the Perplexed* from Arabic into Hebrew.

Al ḥet ("For the sin"). Opening words of a confession of sins, recited on the Day of Atonement.

Alimony. Payment made to a divorced woman by her former husband. Although not a biblical ordinance, attempts were made in the rabbinic period to ensure the protection of divorced women. The ketubbah (marriage settlement) served as the basis of this remedy by providing for payment of a fixed sum from the husband's estate in the case of divorce.

Aliyah (i). The calling up of a member of the congregation to read the Torah in the synagogue. Originally each person called up read a section of the weekly portion; later a special reader was appointed for this purpose. Those who are called up read blessings instead.

Aliyah (ii) ("immigration"). Term used specifically of the immigration of the Jews to Israel. Three main waves took place, the first from 1882 to 1903, the second from 1904 to 1914, and the third from 1918 to 1923.

Aljama (Arabic "the gathering"). Jewish community, specifically the self-governing Jewish communities in medieval Spain; it also denotes the Jewish quarter of a city or town.

Alkabetz, Solomon ben Moses (1505–1584). Palestinian kabbalist and poet. Born in Salonica, he lived in Adrianople and Safed. He wrote on biblical and kabbalistic subjects. His Sabbath hymn "Lekhah dodi" ("Come, my beloved") is recited on Friday evenings.

Alkalai, Abraham ben Samuel (?1750–1811). Bulgarian codifier. He was the head of a yeshivah in Dupnitsa and later settled in Safed. His *Zekhor le-Avraham* contains the laws of the Shulḥan Arukh arranged alphabetically. He also wrote a collection of responsa, *Ḥesed le-Avraham.*

Alkalai, Isaac ben Abraham Alcalay (1881–1978). Yugoslav rabbi. He was chief rabbi of Yugoslavia, and the country's first Jewish senator. When the Germans invaded, he escaped to the US, where he became chief rabbi of the Sephardi congregations.

Alkalai, Judah Solomon Ḥai (1798–1878). Bosnian Zionist. He was born in Sarajevo. As rabbi to the Sephardi congregation in Semlin, near Belgrade, he encouraged Jewish settlement in Palestine. In 1874 he settled in Jerusalem. His writings supported a return to Israel on religious grounds.

Allegory. A narrative to be understood symbolically. Allegories are found in the Bible, biblical commentaries, and rabbinic texts. Philo interpreted the Bible allegorically, as did many medieval philosophers such as Maimonides and Solomon ibn Gabirol; the kabbalah also utilized allegorical interpretations of scripture. The technique of allegory is used by various modern Hebrew writers.

Allen, Woody (b. 1935). American film director and actor. He was born in Brooklyn. From the first his films used Jewish humor. Later he explored a range of American Jewish issues, including the role of the Jew in American life and Jewish paranoia and self-hatred.

Allgemeine Zeitung des Judentums. German Jewish journal. It was founded by Ludwig Phillipson in 1837. It was the first Jewish periodical to deal with Jewish affairs and encouraged Jewish emancipation and religious reform.

Alliance Israélite Universelle. International Jewish organization. It was founded in 1860 in Paris. Its aims were to defend Jewish civil and religious liberties, provide educational facilities, and protect Jews from attack.

Allon, Gedaliah (1902–1950). Russian historian. Born in Kobin, he emigrated to Palestine in 1924. He taught Talmud and Jewish history at the Hebrew University. His writings include *History of the Jews in Palestine in the Period of the Mishnah and the Talmud.*

Allon, Yigal (1918–1980). Israeli statesman and soldier. He was born at Kefar Tavor in Lower Galilee. He served in the Haganah and was a founder and commander of the Palmaḥ. In 1954 he was elected to the Knesset and served as minister of labor, 1961–8. After 1969 he was appointed deputy prime minister. His writings include *Curtain of Sand* and *Palmaḥ Campaigns.*

Allon-bachuth ("Oak of weeping"). Sacred tree near Bethel. Rebekah's nurse Deborah was buried under it. (Genesis 35.8)

Alman, Samuel (1877–1947). Russian liturgical composer. Born in Sobolevka, Podolia, he studied at Odessa and Kishinev and later settled in London. He served as choirmaster of London synagogues and Jewish choral groups. He wrote musical works for cantor, choir, chorus, and organ.

Almanzi, Joseph (1801–1860). Italian Hebrew poet and bibliophile. He was born in Padua. He wrote poems of a moralistic character, and collected thousands of Hebrew manuscripts.

Almemar [bimah, tebah]. Platform in the synagogue on which the reading desk stands. The Torah is read here. It is called "bimah" in Ashkenazi congregations and "tebah" in Sephardi congregations.

***Almohades.** Muslim sectarians. They arose in north Africa in the 12th century and conquered southern Spain between 1149 and 1174. They attempted to convert non-Muslims. African Jews fled to Egypt and Palestine, Spanish Jews emigrated to Christian Spain and southern France.

Almosnino, Moses (1515–1580). Greek scholar. He was born in Salonica. He was part of a delegation sent to Sultan Selim II to obtain the privileges and exemptions granted by Suleiman the Magnificent to the Salonican Jewish community. His writings include a description of Constantinople, *Extremos y grandezas de Constantinopla.*

Al-Mukammas, David ben Merwan [David ibn Merwan al-Mukammas] (fl. c. 900). Iraqi philosopher. He translated Christian commentaries on Genesis and Ecclesiastes and wrote on different religions and sects. His *Twenty Treatises* contains most of his theological and philosophical work. He was the first to introduce the methods of Arabic philosophy into the Jewish world.

Alnakawa, Ephraim (d. 1442). Spanish spiritual leader. He was born in Spain, and emigrated to north Africa in 1391, where he became spiritual leader of the Tlemcen Jewish community.

Alnakawa, Israel ben Joseph (d. 1391). Spanish writer. He composed an ethical treatise, *Candlestick of Light.* When the Toledans attacked the Jewish community of the city in 1391, he was dragged through the streets. He subsequently killed himself.

Aloni, Nissim (b. 1926). Israeli playwright and short-story writer. He was born in Tel Aviv. He was the first playwright to eschew the social realism characteristic of Israeli drama in the early 1950s. In 1963 he established his own theater in Tel Aviv. His plays synthesize Israeli consciousness and European cultural sources. The Sephardi working-class quarter in Tel Aviv is the setting for his short stories.

Alotin, Yardena. Israeli composer. Born in Tel Aviv, she was composer-in-residence at Bar-Ilan University in 1976. Much of her work has a Hebraic flavor.

Alphabet (Hebrew "aleph-bet"). The Hebrew alphabet consists of 22 consonants (see table), derived from the Canaanite alphabet. Until the first exile (6th century BCE) the alphabet was identical with that of the Phoenicians, but thereafter it was gradually replaced by letter forms based on an eastern Aramaic script. The square script now used developed during the first two centuries CE. Originally vowel sounds were not indicated by Hebrew script, but in time certain letters came to serve as vowel indicators (yod, vav, he). In the 7th to 9th centuries various systems were developed for indicating all vowels by means of new signs placed above and below the consonants. However, no vowel signs are given in the Torah scroll. Each letter in the Hebrew alphabet has a corresponding numerical value and combinations of letters are used in the Hebrew numbering system.

Hebrew letter form	*Hebrew letter name*	*English letter (or transliteration)*	*Numerical value*
א	aleph	' [smooth breathing]	1
ב	bet	b	2
ג	gimel	g	3
ד	dalet	d	4
ה	he	h	5
ו	vav	w	6
ז	zayin	z	7
ח	ḥet	kh	8
ט	tet	t	9
י	yod	y	10
כ	kaph	k	20
ל	lamed	l	30
מ	mem	m	40
נ	nun	n	50
ס	samekh	s	60
ע	ayin	' [rough breathing]	70
פ	pe	p	80
צ	tsadeh	ss	90
ק	koph	q	100
ר	resh	r	200
שׂ	sin	s	300
שׁ	shin	sh	300
ת	tav	t, th	400

Alroy, David [Ben Solomon, Menaḥem] (fl. 12th cent.). Leader of a messianic movement in Kurdistan. He was proclaimed Messiah among the Jews living in the mountains of the north-east Caucasus. He was subsequently murdered. He is the subject of *The Wondrous Tale of David Alroy* by Benjamin Disraeli.

Alshekh, Moses ben Ḥayyim (fl. 16th cent.). Palestinian biblical commentator and talmudist. Born in Adrianople, he settled in Safed. He was a halakhic authority, a teacher in talmudic academies, a preacher, and a member of the rabbinical court of Joseph Caro. He reworked his sermons into commentaries on most of the books of the Bible.

Altalena. Pseudonym of Vladimir Jabotinsky. The name was given to the ship used by the Irgun Tzevai Leumi to bring arms to Israel in June 1948.

Altar. In Jewish practice, a place of sacrifice. In the desert a bronze altar for burnt offerings and a gold altar for incense were located in the Tabernacle. Later they stood in Solomon's Temple.

Alter, Abraham Mordecai, of Gur (1864–1948). Polish leader of Agudat Israel. He urged his followers to participate in building Palestine, where he settled after World War II.

Alter, Isaac Meir, of Gur (1799–1866). Founder of a dynasty of Ḥasidic rabbis in Gur near Warsaw. He published numerous halakhic works.

Alter, Judah Aryeh Loeb, of Gur (1847–1905). Polish anti-Zionist. He persuaded Polish Ḥasidim not to join the Zionist movement.

Alter, Robert (b. 1935). American scholar. Born in New York, he became professor of Hebrew and comparative literature at the University of California, Berkeley. He has written on Hebrew and Jewish literature and the literary form and content of the Bible. His works include *The Art of Biblical Narrative*, *The Art of Biblical Poetry*, and *The Literary Guide to the Bible*.

Alter kocker (Yiddish). A crotchety, ineffectual old man.

Alterman, Nathan (1910–1970). Israeli Hebrew poet. Born in Warsaw, he settled in Tel Aviv in 1925. Influenced by French and Russian symbolists, he became the leading imagist poet of his generation. He also wrote satirical poetry related to political events. His collected works are contained in four volumes, *Kol Shirei Alterman.*

Al tikre ("Do not read"). Talmudic exegetical device, written before a biblical verse, which alters its meaning.

Altman, Nathan (1889–1970). Ukrainian painter, sculptor, and stage designer. He settled in St. Petersburg and became head of the city's section of the Department of Fine Arts. From 1918 to 1922 he developed a constructionist style. After 1929 he lived in France, but later returned to the USSR. His work was influenced by Jewish themes and includes paintings, sculptures, graphic art, and stage designs.

Altmann, Alexander (1906–1988). Rabbi and scholar of Hungarian origin. He served as rabbi in Berlin and taught philosophy at the Rabbinical Seminary there. In 1938 he settled in Manchester, England, where he founded the Institute of Jewish Studies. In 1959 he became professor of Jewish philosophy at Brandeis University. He wrote studies on Jewish philosophy and mysticism, including *Saadya Gaon: the Book of Doctrines and Beliefs, Isaac Israeli,* and *Studies in Religious Philosophy and Mysticism.*

Altschuler, David (fl. 18th cent.). Galician biblical exegete. He planned a commentary on the Prophets and Hagiographa based on the work of earlier commentators; his son Jahiel Hillel Altschuler continued the work. His commentary on Psalms, Proverbs, and Job was published in 1753–4.

Altschuler, Jahiel Hillel (fl. 18th cent.). Galician scholar. He completed the biblical commentary on the Prophets and Hagiographa (1780–82) begun by his father, David Altschuler.

Amalekites. A people of the Negev and the adjoining desert. They were the enemies of the Israelites from their days in the wilderness until the time of the early monarchy.

Amasa (fl. 11th–10th cent. BCE). Israelite commander. He led Absalom's army in the unsuccessful rebellion against David. After the suppression of this uprising, David appointed Amasa his general. He was later killed by Joab. (II Samuel 17–20)

Amatus Lusitanus (1511–1568). Portuguese physician. Born in Portugal of Marrano parents, he went to Antwerp, where he published a book on medicinal botany, *Index dioscorides.* He later taught medicine at the University of Ferrara and treated Pope Julius III. His major work was *Centuriae curationum* in seven volumes.

Amaziah (fl. 8th cent. BCE). King of Judah (796–780 BCE). He put to death the assassins who murdered his father Joash. He waged war against Edom and the Kingdon of Israel. (II Kings 14; II Chronicles 25)

Amen ("true," "truly"). Expression of affirmation made as part of blessings and prayers.

America–Israel Cultural Foundation. Fund-raising agency for educational and cultural institutions in Israel. It was founded in 1939 by Edward Albert Norman as the American Palestine Fund, Inc.

American Academy for Jewish Research. Learned society. It was formed in 1920 to foster Jewish scholarship and research. Its membership consists of fellows and associate members. It holds meetings and publishes an annual volume of proceedings.

American Association for Jewish Edu-

cation. Organization formed in 1939 to promote Jewish education. It publishes the *Pedagogic Reporter, Jewish Educational Newsletter, Audio Visual Review,* and *Jewish Education Register and Directory.*

American Council for Judaism. Anti-Zionist organization. It was formed in 1942 by Reform rabbis. It opposed the establishment of Israel and was critical of the Zionist domination of American Jewish life.

American Hebrew. Jewish weekly newspaper, published in New York. It was founded by Philip Cowen in 1879, and from the start favored Orthodoxy against Reform Judaism. Under the editorship of Isaac Landman it took an anti-Zionist position. In 1956 it combined with the *Jewish Examiner* to form the *American Examiner.*

American Israelite. Jewish weekly newspaper. It was founded by Isaac Mayer Wise in Cincinnati, Ohio, in 1854 and served as a platform for his ideas.

American Jewish Archives. Research center. It was established in 1947 at the Cincinnati campus of the Hebrew Union College–Jewish Institute of Religion. It collects research material on the history of the Jewish community in the western hemisphere and publishes the journal *American Jewish Archives.*

American Jewish Committee. Jewish defense organization. It was established in 1906 to protect the civil and religious rights of Jews throughout the world. It publishes the *American Jewish Year Book* (in conjunction with the Jewish Publication Society of America) and *Commentary* magazine.

American Jewish Conference. Relief organization. It was established in 1943 at the initiative of B'nai B'rith to deal with emigration to Palestine and the aftermath of the Holocaust. It was dissolved in 1949.

American Jewish Congress. Organization formed in 1918 to protect the civil, political, and religious rights of Jews throughout the world. In the 1930s it was a leading force in the anti-Nazi movement. Its publications include *Congress Bi-Weekly* and *Judaism.*

American Jewish Historical Society. Learned society. It was founded in 1892. Originally it was housed at the Jewish Theological Seminary, but in 1968 it moved to Brandeis University. Its publications include *American Jewish Historical Quarterly, Studies in American Jewish History,* and *American Jewish Communal Histories.*

American Jewish Joint Agricultural Corporation *see* AGRO-JOINT.

American Jewish Joint Distribution Committee [Joint Distribution Committee]. Organization formed in 1914 to provide relief and medical care for European and Palestinian Jews during World War I. After the war it aided eastern European Jewry, and in the period 1933–9 it assisted German Jewry. It carried on relief and rescue work during World War II. In post-war years it continued its relief activities world-wide.

American Zionist Council. Zionist organization. Formed in 1949, it represents nine national Zionist bodies in matters related to Zionism.

Am ha-aretz (*sing.*: "people of the land"). Term used in the Bible to refer to the masses of the Jewish people. In talmudic times it was applied to common people who did not observe rabbinic regulations and eventually came to mean an ignorant person.

Amichai, Yehuda (b. 1924). Israeli poet and novelist. Born in Germany, he settled in Palestine in 1936. His poetry reflects the changes in the Hebrew language during World War II and the Israeli War of Independence: he introduced airplanes, tanks, fuel trucks, and administrative contracts into Hebrew poetry. His writings include *Shirim: 1948–1962* and *Not of this Time, Not of this Place.*

Amidah ("Standing"). The prayer also known as the EIGHTEEN BENEDICTIONS.

Amiel, Moses Avigdor (1893–1946). Israeli rabbi and writer. After serving as a rabbi in Poland and Antwerp, he became chief rabbi of Tel Aviv in 1936. He established the first modern high school yeshivah in Tel Aviv. His writings include *Ha Middot le-Ḥeker ha-Halakhah, Derashot el Ammi,* and *Hegyonot el Ammi.*

Amittai (fl. c. 800). Italian Hebrew liturgical poet. Several piyyutim, signed Amittai, are credited to him, including the hymn "Lord I remember thee and am sore amazed." This is included in the concluding service for the Day of Atonement according to the Ashkenazi rite.

Amittai ben Shephatiah (fl. 9th cent.). Italian Hebrew liturgical poet. Several of his poems were incorporated into the Italian and Ashkenazi liturgies. His poems (more than 30 of which have been published) contain references to contemporary Jewish persecutions and Jewish–Christian disputations.

Amman *see* RABBATH AMMON.

Ammi bar Nathan (fl. late 3rd cent.). Palestinian amora. He and Assi headed the yeshivah at Tiberias. Together with Ḥiyya bar Abba, they acted as education inspectors in Palestine with authority to introduce reforms.

Ammonites. One of the tribes which emerged from the Syrio-Arabian desert during the second millennium BCE. They established a kingdom in Transjordan. After the Israelites occupied Canaan, they were frequently attacked by the Ammonites.

Amnon (fl. 11th–10th cent. BCE). Israelite, eldest son of David. He raped his half-sister Tamar. Her brother Absalom had him killed for this offense. (II Samuel 13)

Amnon of Mainz (fl. 10th cent.). German martyr. After attempts by the Bishop of Mainz to convert him, he asked for three days to consider the matter. When he failed to appear he was brought by force; his arms and legs were amputated and salt was poured on his wounds. On Rosh ha-Shanah he was carried to the synagogue, where he recited the hymn *U-Netannah Tokeph* ("Let us declare the mighty importance") and died. He later appeared to Kalonymus ben Meshullam in a dream and taught him the entire prayer. It is recited in synagogues on Rosh ha-Shanah.

Am Olam ("Eternal people"). Organization founded by Russian Jewish youth after the programs in 1881. They desired to emigrate to Palestine and the US; members of the group founded the New Odessa colony in Oregon and two colonies in South Dakota.

Amon (fl. 7th cent. BCE). King of Judah (642–640 BCE). His transgressions were greater than those of his father Manasseh (II Chronicles 33.23). He was assassinated by members of his court. (II Kings 21.23)

Amora ("scholar"). Term used specifically of Jewish scholars in Palestine and Babylonia in the 3rd–6th centuries. The amoraim expounded the Mishnah and interpreted Scripture. Some were noted for their expertise in halakhah, others were known for their aggadah. Their teachings are recorded in the Talmud and various midrashim.

Amorites. The inhabitants of Canaan before the Israelite conquest.

Amos (i) (fl. 8th cent. BCE). Israelite prophet. He prophesied during the reign of Jeroboam II. He was disturbed by the corruption in the country resulting from the exploitation of the poor. At Bethel he foretold the destruction of Israel; Amaziah, the priest of Bethel, told him to return to Judah, but he insisted on fulfilling his mission.

Amos (ii). Biblical book, one of the books

of the 12 Minor Prophets. It records the prophecies of Amos.

Amram (fl. 13th cent. BCE). Israelite, the father of Moses, Aaron, and Miriam. (Exodus 6.18, 20; Numbers 26.58–9)

Amram bar Sheshna (d. c. 875). Babylonian gaon. He was gaon of Sura. He wrote numerous responsa and the oldest surviving order of prayer: his *Seder Rav Amram* contains the text of the prayers for the entire year, as well as the laws and customs pertaining to the different prayers.

***Amraphel** (fl. ?19th–16th cent. BCE). King of Shinar in Mesopotamia. He was one of the kings who attacked the rulers of Sodom and were defeated by Abraham. (Genesis 14)

Amsterdam. City in the Netherlands. In the 16th and 17th centuries Jews flourished there owing to its climate of religious tolerance.

Amulet (Hebrew "kamia"). A charm carried about the person. In Jewish practice amulets are worn as protection against evil; they usually bear sacred letters or symbols, often the names of angels or demons written in geometric patterns. They were frequently worn in the talmudic and gaonic periods. Under the influence of later kabbalah they took the form of kabbalistic diagrams, biblical verses, and letter combinations, inscribed on paper, parchment, or metal.

***Anacletus II** (1090–1137). Italian cleric and anti-pope. He was a descendant of a converted Jewish financier. He was elected pope by a large number of cardinals after Innocent II had been elected by a rival group of cardinals.

Anagram. Literary device consisting of a word or phrase formed by the transposition of the letters of another word or phrase. It is found in medieval Hebrew and kabbalistic writings, and was frequently applied to divine and angelic names on amulets.

Anakim. One of the peoples who inhabited Canaan before the Israelite conquest. They were tall in stature. (Numbers 13.32–3)

Anan ben David (fl. 8th cent.). Babylonian biblical scholar, founder of the Karaites. When his younger brother was appointed exilarch, he founded his own sect which opposed the talmudic tradition. In his *Sepher ha-Mitzvot* he argued that the Bible was the sole basis of Judaism. He was strict in his application of biblical law.

Ananias (fl. 1st cent.). Israelite, high priest. Appointed by Herod of Chalcis, he was involved in the prosecution of Paul (Acts 24). He was killed by Jewish extremists at the outset of the rebellion against Rome in the late 60s.

Anatoli, Jacob ben Abba Mari (fl. 13th cent.). French translator and philosopher. Originally from Provence, he settled in Naples, where he was physician to Emperor Frederick II. He translated Arabic philosophical and astronomical works into Hebrew. His *Malmad ha-Talmidim* consists of popular sermons.

Anatomy. Anatomical facts, metaphors, and expressions are found in the Bible. Talmudic anatomy contains explanations of the normal and pathological structure of the body.

Anau, Phinehas Ḥai (1693–1768). Italian rabbi. He was rabbi in Ferrara. He became involved in a controversy about the correct pronunciation of the Priestly Blessing. His *Givat Pinḥas* is a collection of responsa.

Anav, Benjamin ben Abraham (c. 1215–c. 1295). Italian scholar and poet. His poetry is concerned with historical events. He also wrote treatises on Jewish law, notes on Rashi's biblical commentary, and a satire on rich Jewish families in Rome.

Anav, Jehiel ben Jekuthiel (fl. c. 1250–1300). Roman copyist and author. His

Maalot ha-Middot deals with ethical conduct and is based on midrashic and talmudic sources. The only complete extant manuscript of the Jerusalem Talmud was copied by him in 1289. He also wrote a liturgical poem about the burning of a Rome synagogue in 1268.

Anav, Judah ben Benjamin (fl. 13th cent.). Roman author. In 1280 he completed a treatise on the laws of ritual slaughter with special reference to Roman customs.

Anav, Zedekiah (fl. 13th cent.). Italian talmudist. His *Shibbolei ha-Leket* contains ritual law and regulations.

Ancient of Days *see* God, names of.

Ancient Order of Maccabeans *see* Maccabeans, ancient order of.

Andreas (i) *see* Elhanan (ii).

Andreas (ii) *see* Lukuas.

Anenu ("Answer us"). Prayer inserted on fast days in the Shema Kolenu blessing during the repetition of the Amidah in the morning and afternoon services.

Angel. Divine messenger. In Scripture angels are generally beneficient; they convey God's messages and carry out his will. In post-biblical literature they act as independent beings; in the Talmud and midrash they are depicted as participating in human affairs. Medieval philosophers often identified them with the higher intelligences of Aristotle. In the Zohar they occupy the seven heavenly halls. In Jewish liturgy their praise of God (based on Isaiah 6.1–3) is included in the kedushah, piyyutim, and seliḥot.

Angel of Death [Malakh ha-Mavet]. Divine being who takes the soul from the body. In the Bible the power of death is occasionally delegated to a messenger. In rabbinic sources the Angel of Death is depicted as a destroyer of human beings and is personified as Satan or represented as the Evil Inclination.

Anglo-Jewish Association. British organization founded in 1871 to protect Jewish rights. From 1878 it cooperated with the Board of Deputies of British Jews in the Conjoint Foreign Committee. In 1917 it opposed the Balfour Declaration, which supported the establishment of a Jewish homeland in Palestine, but later changed its attitude to Zionism. It publishes the *AJA Quarterly*.

Angoff, Charles (1902–1979). American novelist of Russian origin. He was editor of the *American Mercury* and the *Literary Review*. He wrote a series of autobiographical novels: *Journey to the Dawn, In the Morning Light, The Sun at Noon, Between Day and Dark, The Bitter Spring, Summer Storm, In Memory of Autumn,* and *Winter Twilight.*

Anilewicz, Mordecai (1919–1943). Polish Zionist. He was born in Wyszków. He became an active Zionist, and, as a member of Ha-Shomer ha-Tzair, was arrested by the Soviet authorities in 1939 for organizing the emigration of Jews to Palestine. As commander of the Jewish Fighting Organization, he led the uprising in the Warsaw Ghetto in April 1943.

Animals, treatment of. Cruelty to animals is forbidden in Scripture (Deuteronomy 22.4). Slaughter for food is permitted but must be humanely carried out (*see* Sheḥita). Rabbinic legislation applies the principle of care for animals to a wide range of circumstances.

Anim zemirot *see* Shir ha-kavod.

Aninut ("mourning"). Status of a bereaved person during the period between the death and burial of a relative. The mourner is exempt from daily prayer and should not eat meat or drink wine.

Anointing. Anointing with oil was practiced in ancient Israel to consecrate kings, priests, and sacred vessels. It was also performed on joyous occasions and feast days, as well as for medicinal purposes. The descendant of David who will redeem Israel is called "the Messiah" (the anointed one).

Anokhi, Z. I. *see* ARONSOHN, ZALMAN YITZ-ḤAK.

An-Ski, S. [Rapoport, Solomon Seinwil] (1863–1920). Russian author. He was born in Belorussia and settled in Paris in 1894. In 1905 he returned to Russia and joined the Social Revolutionary Party. He composed the party's hymn (*Di Shvue*) and wrote folk legends, Ḥasidic tales, and stories about Jewish poverty. His play *The Dybbuk* was translated into Hebrew by Ḥayyim Naḥman Bialik. His Yiddish works were published in 15 volumes.

Antek *see* CUKERMAN, YITZḤAK.

Anthropomorphism. The conception or representation of God as having human physical form or psychological characteristics. It is frequently found in the Bible. Rabbinic aggadah uses anthropomorphic imagery, as does the mystical tract *Shiur Komah*. Many medieval Jewish philosophers argued against conceiving of God anthropomorphically.

Anti-Defamation League. American civil rights organization. Founded in 1913 as part of B'nai B'rith, it fights anti-Semitism, fosters interfaith relations, and encourages civil rights reforms.

Antigonus II (fl. 1st cent. BCE). Israelite, last king of the Hasmoneans (40–37 BCE). When Pompey captured Jerusalem in 63 BCE, Antigonus was taken to Rome. In 40 BCE he captured Jerusalem, put to death Herod the Great's brother Phasael, and cut off Hyrcanus II's ears so he would be disqualified from the high priesthood. He then ruled as king and high priest. From 39 to 37 BCE Herod besieged his army in Judea and was eventually victorious. Antigonus was executed by the Romans.

Antigonus of Sokho (fl. early 2nd cent. BCE). Palestinian sage. Only one of his statements has been preserved: "Be not like servants who minister to their master in order to receive a reward, but be like servants who minister to their master not in order to receive a reward: and let the fear of Heaven be upon you." His pupils Zadok and Boethus interpreted it as a denial of the after-life and founded the Sadducees and Boethusians.

Antin, Mary (1881–1949). American author of Belorussian origin. Her autobiographical work *The Promised Land* contrasts her early life with her experiences in the US.

Antinomianism. Opposition to law. It was found in early Christianity, among the Sabbetaians, and in the Frankist movement. It is also a characteristic of Reform Judaism.

Antioch. Ancient city in Syria. In the 2nd and 1st centuries BCE it had a large Jewish population.

Antiochus, Scroll of. Hebrew account of the revolt of the Hasmoneans. It was probably written in the 7th century. It is used in the Italian and Yemenite ritual for Ḥanukkah.

***Antiochus III** (b. c. 242 BCE). King, ruler of the Seleucid empire (223–187 BCE). After capturing Jerusalem in 198 BCE, he restored the city, supplied funds for the Temple, and permitted Jews to form their own government.

***Antiochus IV Epiphanes** (fl. 2nd cent. BCE). King, ruler of the Seleucid empire (175–163 BCE). He attacked Jerusalem, killed thousands of Jews, and sold others into slavery. He desecrated the Temple and forced Jews to abandon their traditions. These acts provoked the revolt of the Hasmoneans.

Antipater I (fl. 1st cent. BCE). Edomite administrator, governor of Idumea. He was a convert to Judaism. He served under Alexander Yannai and Salome Alexandra.

Antipater II (fl. 1st cent. BCE). Edomite administrator, ruler of Judea (63–43 BCE). He supported Hyrcanus II in his war against Aristobulus II. Julius Caesar made him financial administrator of Judea in 44 BCE. He appointed his sons Phasael and Herod to administrative positions.

Antipater III (fl. 1st cent). Son of Herod the Great. When Herod executed his other sons, Alexander and Aristobulus, Antipater was made Herod's heir. He was executed when his plan to murder Herod was revealed.

Anti-Semitism. Hatred of the Jewish people. The term was coined by Wilhelm Marr in 1879 to designate anti-Jewish campaigns in Europe. It became a general term to denote all forms of hostility towards Jews through the centuries. *See also* CIVIL RIGHTS; DISABILITIES; DISCRIMINATION; EMANCIPATION.

***Antoninus Pius** (fl. 2nd cent.). Roman emperor (138–61). He rescinded Hadrian's legislation against Judaism. In the Talmud and midrash he is depicted in conversation with Judah ha-Nasi.

***Antonius Felix** *see* PROCURATOR.

Anusim *see* MARRANOS.

Aphikoman *see* AFIKOMEN.

Apikoros (Greek "Epicurean"). In Jewish usage, a heretic. The word is derived from the name of the Greek philosopher Epikouros (Epicurus), and refers to one who disobeys the commandments, derides the Torah, and defames rabbis.

Apocalypse. Revelation of the end of days and final judgement; any book purporting to reveal the last things. Such revelation is found in Jewish writings from the 2nd century BCE to the 2nd century CE, represented by the Apocrypha and Pseudepigrapha. It deals with the mysteries of the heavens, secrets of world government, the function of angels and evil spirits, details of the end of the world, and the soul's existence in Heaven and Hell.

Apocrypha. Collection of non-canonical Jewish writings from the period of the second Temple. It consists largely of historical and ethical works and contains I and II Esdras, Tobit, Judith, additions to Esther, the Wisdom of Solomon, Ecclesiasticus, Baruch with the Epistle of Jeremiah, The Song of the Three Holy Children, the History of Susanna, Bel and the Dragon, the Prayer of Manasseh, and I and II Maccabees.

Apologetics. Defensive argument or method of disputation. Judaic apologetics originated in response to pagan and Christian challenges. Medieval apologists defended the Jewish faith from external criticism as well as from doubts arising from comparisons with other cultural traditions. It also attempted to demonstrate the virtues of the Jewish faith to gentiles.

Apostasy. The abandonment of one's religion or principles. In Jewish usage the term is applied to conversion from Judaism to another religion. Jewish law differentiates between forced and voluntary conversion. The apostate is referred to as "mumar" (or "meshummad"). He remains a Jew, and no ceremony is required if he returns to Judaism. *See also* MUMAR.

Apostle. Emissary, one sent to preach. The mission of the apostle, originally a Jewish institution, was adopted into Christianity. Jesus sent out his twelve disciples to spread his message. They preached about the life and ministry of Jesus and exorcised spirits in his name.

Appelfeld, Aharon (b. 1932). Israeli writer. Born in Czernowitz, Bukovina, he settled in Palestine in 1947. His stories concern the Holocaust, which he often saw allegorically. They are collected in *Smoke, In the Fertile Valley, Frost upon the Land,* and *In the Wilderness.*

Apple, Raymond (b. 1935). Australian rabbi. Born in Melbourne, he served as a rabbi in England and later at the Great Synagogue, Sydney. He founded and ran the Christian–Jewish Study Group in

Sydney, and served as dayyan and registrar of the Sydney bet din.

Apt, Rabbi of *see* ABRAHAM, JOSHUA HESHEL.

Aptowitzer, Avigdor (1871–1942). Galician rabbinic scholar. He taught Talmud at the Hebrew Teachers College in Vienna from 1919 until 1938, when he settled in Jerusalem. He published studies on various aspects of rabbinic literature and Jewish history.

Aquila (fl. 2nd cent.). Translator of Roman origin. He participated in the rebuilding of Jerusalem and later converted to Christianity and then to Judaism. He translated the Bible into Greek.

Arakhin. Fifth tractate of the Mishnah. It deals with the valuation of persons, houses, fields, and objects vowed to the Sanctuary. (Leviticus 27.2–29)

Aram see ARAMEANS.

Arama, Isaac ben Moses [Isaac Arama] (1420–1494). Spanish rabbi, philosopher, and preacher. As rabbi of various Spanish communities, he delivered sermons on the principles of Judaism. He also engaged in public disputations with Christian scholars. After the Jews were expelled from Spain in 1492, he settled in Naples. His *Akedat Yitzḥak* is a philosophical commentary on the Pentateuch.

Aramaic. Any of a group of Semitic languages, but specifically the northwestern branch of that family of languages. Aramaic is found in the Bible (Daniel 2.4–7.28; Ezra 4.8–6.18; 7.12–26; Jeremiah 10.11), the Palestinian and Babylonian Talmud, and the Zohar. It became an international language from the period of the late Assyrian and Persian kingdoms (6th century BCE) and served as the vernacular language of Palestine for centuries. Biblical readings were translated into Aramaic in the synagogues.

Arameans. A Semitic people, natives of Aram (roughly modern Syria). They invaded the Fertile Crescent in the second half of the 2nd millennium BCE. They and the Israelites had a common ancestry (Genesis 10–22): the biblical patriarchs were their kinsmen.

Arba kanphot *see* TALLIT.

Arba kosot. The four cups of wine which are drunk at the Passover seder.

Arbitration. The adjudication of a dispute by a third party. In biblical times arbitration was based on a system of courts. The Talmud provides for nominated arbitrators who choose a chairman. In the Middle Ages Jewish tribunals acted as arbitrators. The Din Torah (decision by a rabbi or group of rabbis) became the common method.

Archa (Latin "chest"). Chest in which financial documents are stored. The word was used for an official archive set up in England in 1194 for the recording of all transactions in which Jews were involved. The Exchequer of the Jews in Westminster coordinated these records.

Archelaus *see* HEROD ARCHELAUS.

Archeology. The scientific study of the material remains of the past. The written biblical account of history has been supplemented by the excavation of ancient sites and the examination of texts from ancient Near Eastern cultures.

Archisynagogos (Greek). Head of a synagogue in the Roman and Byzantine empires. He arranged the service, administered the synagogue, and supervised Jewish community affairs. Roman law exempted him from physical servitude to the state and state taxes.

Archives. In the biblical period, laws, contracts, and political documents were kept in the Temple. Groups of Jews in the diaspora often maintained records, and many medieval Jewish communities did so. After the Emancipation of the Jews in the 18th century few records were kept. In the 19th and 20th centuries Jewish organizations collected extensive documentation.

Archivolti, Samuel (1515–1611). Italian Hebrew grammarian and poet. From 1568 he lived in Padua, where he was secretary of the community, principal of a yeshivah, and av bet din. His writings include a Hebrew grammar, *Arugat ha-Bosem*, and numerous poems and piyyutim. His poetry reflects the attitude of Jews to their Christian neighbors.

Ardon, Mordechai (1896–?). Israeli painter. Born in Poland, he settled in Palestine in 1933 and became director of the Bezalel School of Arts and Crafts in 1940. From 1952 to 1962 he was artistic adviser to the Ministry of Education.

Arendt, Hannah (1906–1975). American political and social philospher of German origin. Born in Hanover, she lived in Paris after Adolf Hitler came to power. In 1941 she escaped to the US. From 1963 to 1967 she taught at the University of Chicago, and then at the New School for Social Research. Her writings include *The Origins of Totalitarianism, Rachel Varnhagen: the Life of a Jewess, Between Past and Future, On Revolution, Eichmann in Jerusalem,* and *Men in Dark Times.*

Ari *see* LURIA, ISAAC BEN SOLOMON.

Aristeas, Letter of. Pseudepigraphic work. It was allegedly written by Aristeas to his brother Philocrates at the court of Ptolemy II Philadelphus. It describes the origin of the Septuagint and the virtues of the Jewish faith.

Aristobulus (c. 35–7 BCE). Son of Herod the Great. He and his brother Alexander were accused of plotting to kill their father. They were killed by strangulation.

Aristobulus I (fl. 2nd cent. BCE). King of Judah (104–103 BCE). Under the will of his father, John Hyrcanus I, he was to become high priest while his mother was to receive the throne. He put her in prison (where she died) and also imprisoned all his brothers except Antigonus; him he later put to death for treachery.

Aristobulus II (d. 49 BCE). King of Judea (67–63 BCE). He usurped the throne of his brother Hyrcanus II in 67 BCE and civil war broke out. In 63 both brothers urged their claims to the throne before Pompey. He ordered Aristobulus to surrender Jerusalem, but his supporters refused. Pompey besieged the city, captured the Temple, and took him prisoner. When Julius Caesar came to power, Aristobulus was released and given troops to attack Pompey's men, but he was poisoned before he could embark on this campaign.

Aristobulus III (d. 35 BCE). Hasmonean high priest. At the time he was due to become high priest, Herod the Great appointed Hananel in his place. Aristobulus' mother, Alexandra (daughter of Hyrcanus II), asked Cleopatra to intercede for him with Herod. Hananel was subsequently dismissed and Aristobulus appointed in his place. He was later drowned in the baths at Jericho by Herod's soldiers.

Ark (Hebrew "aron kodesh," "heikhal"). Cabinet in the synagogue containing the Torah scrolls. Among Ashkenazim it is called the "aron" or "aron kodesh." The Sephardim refer to it as the "heikhal." In Israel it is placed on the wall of the synagogue that faces the Temple mount. In other countries it faces Israel.

Ark of the Covenant. Chest in which the two Tablets of the Law were kept from the time of the Israelites' years in the wilderness. It is described in Exodus 25.10–22. Until the Temple was built, it was taken out from the Holy of Holies in times of national need. During the period of the first Temple it was never removed from the Holy of Holies. It is not mentioned among the vessels carried to Babylonia during the exile.

Arlosoroff, Ḥaim (1899–1933). Ukrainian Zionist leader. He lived in Germany, where he was active in the Ha-Poel ha-Tzair party. He emigrated to Palestine in 1924 and became editor of the monthly journal of Mapai. In 1931 he was elected to the executive of the Jewish Agency for Israel and headed its political department in Jerusalem. In 1933 he aided the emigration of German Jews to Palestine. His writings, *Kitvei Ḥaim Arlosoroff*, were published in seven volumes.

Armilus. Enemy of the Messiah. He is mentioned in apocalyptic midrash from the 7th century onward.

Arnshteyn, Mark (1879–1943). Polish Yiddish playwright. He initially wrote Polish plays on Jewish themes for the Warsaw stage. From 1912 to 1924 he directed and wrote for the Yiddish theater in Russia, Britain, and North and South America. After returning to Poland, he translated and directed popular Yiddish plays. He founded and directed the New Chamber Theater in the Warsaw Ghetto.

Aron kodesh *see* ARK.

Aronsohn, Zalman Yitzḥak [Anokhi, Z. I.; Onochi, Z. I.] (1878–1947). Hebrew and Yiddish author of Russian origin. Born in Belorussia, he lived in Argentina and later settled in Palestine. His stories describe Jewish life in eastern Europe. His collected works, *Between Heaven and Earth*, appeared in 1945.

Aronson, Solomon (1862–1935). Zionist leader and rabbi, of Ukrainian origin. He was chief rabbi of Kiev from 1906 to 1921. After the Russian Revolution, he sponsored the nationalist–religious Aḥdut Israel movement. In 1921 he escaped to Berlin and later emigrated to Palestine, where he served as chief rabbi to the community in Tel Aviv and Jaffa. He took an active part in the Mizraḥi movement.

Arpachshad. One of the sons of Shem. (Genesis 10.22)

Arragel, Moses (fl. 15th cent.). Spanish scholar. Together with Arias de Enciena (of the Franciscan order in Toledo), he translated the Bible into Spanish (with a commentary) in 1433.

Arrow Cross. Hungarian fascist and anti-Semitic organization, active from 1936. It was responsible for the death and deportation of thousands of Jews toward the end of World War II.

Artapanus (fl. 2nd cent. BCE). Hellenistic Jewish writer. He wrote *On the Jews*, the purpose of which was to demonstrate that the foundations of Egyptian culture were laid by Abraham, Jacob, Joseph, and Moses. Fragments of it are preserved in the writings of the Church Fathers.

***Artaxerxes I** (fl. 5th cent. BCE). King of Persia (465–425 BCE). He appointed Nehemiah Governor of Judah, with authority to fortify Jerusalem. (Nehemiah 2.1–8)

***Artaxerxes II** (fl. 5th–4th cent. BCE). King of Persia (404–359 BCE). Ezra began his mission during the seventh year of Artaxerxes' reign. (Ezra 7.7, 11, 21)

Artemion (fl. 2nd cent.). Leader of the Jewish uprising in Cyprus during the reign of Trajan (115–17).

Artificial insemination. The principles regarding this practice are based on the Talmud, which discusses whether a high priest may marry a woman who, though a virgin, was pregnant; the marriage was permitted, the pregnancy having resulted accidentally from the woman's bathing in water carrying human semen. According to most modern responsa, regardless of the circumstances of the donor and recipient, adultery cannot be deemed to have taken place; the child is therefore regarded as legitimate. Nonetheless Jewish religious authorities condemn the practice except in cases where the husband is the donor.

Arukh *see* NATHAN BEN JEHIEL OF ROME.

Aryeh Leib ben Samuel (1640–1718).

Polish rabbi. He served as rabbi in various Polish communities. In 1666 he met Shabbetai Tzevi in Constantinople. His *Shaagat Aryeh* is a collection of responsa.

Aryeh Leib of Shpola (1725–1812). Ukrainian Ḥasid. He was known as a miracle worker, and was called "Sabba" (grandfather) by his followers. He and Naḥman of Bratzlav engaged in a dispute over Sabbataism, which was continued by their disciples.

Aryeh Leib Sarahs (c. 1730–1791). Russian Ḥasidic tzaddik. He was the subject of various legends.

Asa (fl. 10th–9th cent. BCE). King of Judah (908–867 BCE). He restored the worship of the Lord in Jerusalem and built fortified cities in Judah (II Chronicles 14.5–6). There was warfare between the kingdoms of Israel and Judah during his reign.

Asaph ben Berechiah (fl. 11–10th cent. BCE). Israelite musician. He was one of the Levites appointed by David to supervise music in the Sanctuary. Psalms 50 and 73–83 are attributed to him. The sons of Asaph were singers in the Temple during the reign of the kings of Judah (10th–6th centuries BCE) and at the time of Ezra and Nehemiah.

Asaph the Physician (fl. 6th cent.). Syrian physician. He is allegedly the author of a Hebrew book on medicine, *Sepher Asaph ha-Rophe*. This work is a source of information about Jewish medical ethics, ancient Jewish remedies, and medical terminology.

Ascalon [Ashkelon]. Port in southern Israel. It was a center of Greek culture in the Hellenistic period.

Asceticism. Mortification of the flesh in pursuit of the spiritual. Apart from fasting for festivals, the practices of the Nazirites and Rechabites, and Ezekiel's abstinence, asceticism is not encouraged in the Bible. The rabbis considered it a sin. Nevertheless it was occasionally adopted by Jewish individuals and groups, such as the Essenes and the Therapeutae.

Asch, Sholem (1880–1957). Polish Yiddish author. He lived in the US, France, and Israel. In short stories, novels, and plays he depicted shtetl life in eastern Europe, as well as the American Jewish experience. His later novels deal with the Jewish–Christian idea of messianic redemption. His writings include *Motke the Thief, Kiddush ha-Shem, Three Cities, Salvation, East River, Moses, The Prophet, Mary, The Nazarene,* and *The Apostle.*

Ascher, Saul (1767–1822). German philosopher. In his early writings he encouraged Jews to abandon their traditional life-style in order to obtain civic emancipation. In *Leviathan, oder Ueber Religion in Ruecksicht des Judentums* he argued that the uniqueness of Judaism arises from its philosophical world-view rather than the revelation of divine law.

Ascoli, David (fl. 16th cent.). Italian writer. In *Apologia Hebraeorum* he protested against the anti-Jewish legislation of Pope Paul IV. He was imprisoned as a result.

Ascoli, Graziadio (1829–1907). Italian philologist. He was professor of linguistics at the University of Milan. He published studies of Hebrew, Latin, and Greek inscriptions on early medieval Jewish tombstones in southern Italy.

Asenath (fl. ?19th–16th cent. BCE). Israelite woman, wife of Joseph. She was the mother of Manasseh and Ephraim. (Genesis 41.50; 46.20)

Aseret Yeme Teshuvah *see* TEN DAYS OF PENITENCE.

Ashamnu ("We have trespassed"). Opening word of the acrostic alphabetical confession of sin recited on the Day of Atonement.

Ashdod. Ancient city in Israel, on a site

near the modern city of Jaffa. It was one of the five principal cities of the Philistines.

Asher (fl. ?19th–16th cent. BCE). Israelite, son of Jacob. His mother was Zilpah, Leah's handmaid (Genesis 30.12). One of the tribes of Israel was named after him.

Asherah. Canaanite goddess of fertility. Her cult penetrated into Judah through Maacah (wife of Asa). Jezebel encouraged the cult in Israel.

Asher ben Jehiel [Rosh] (1250–1327). German talmudist. He was a pupil of Meir of Rothenberg and became the spiritual leader of German Jewry. In 1303 he settled in Toledo. His responsa reflect the cultural life of Spanish and German Jews. In *Piske ha-Rosh* he recorded the decisions of earlier codifiers and commentators.

Ashi (335–427). Babylonian amora. He was head of the academy at Sura. With the help of other sages, he assembled and arranged in appropriate tractates the saying of earlier amoraim. He is credited with the redaction of the Babylonian Talmud.

Ashkelon *see* ASCALON.

Ashkenazi *see* LURIA, ISAAC BEN SOLOMON.

Ashkenazi, Berman (fl. 16th cent.). Polish rabbi. He was the author of *Matenot Kehunnah*, a commentary on Midrash Rabbah. His *Mareh Cohen* is a key to scriptural references to the Zohar.

Ashkenazi, Bezalel (c. 1520–1591). Palestinian talmudist. Born in Israel, he settled in Egypt, where he became chief of the Egyptian rabbis. After he excommunicated the nagid of Egyptian Jewry, this office was abolished. He later lived in Jerusalem, where again he was chief rabbi. He traveled extensively to collect money for the community and encourage immigration. His *Shittah Mekubbetzet* is a collection of medieval talmudic commentaries.

Ashkenazi, Jacob (1550–1626). Polish rabbinic scholar. He wrote (in Yiddish) the *Tz'enah u-Re'enah*, a compendium of rabbinic commentaries on the Pentateuch. His *Sepher ha-Maggid* is based on the Prophets and Hagiographa.

Ashkenazi, Tzevi [Ḥakham Tzevi] (1660–1718). Moravian talmudist. He traveled widely and became head of the rabbinic academy in Altona, then in 1710 he settled in Amsterdam, where he was head of the Ashkenazim. After a controversy concerning Nehemiah Ḥayyon, a follower of Shabbetai Tzevi, he resigned his position in 1714. He subsequently settled in Lwów. His *Ḥakham Tzevi*, after which he was known, is a collection of responsa.

Ashkenazim. One of the two main divisions of Jewry in the diaspora. The word comes from the Hebrew "Ashkenaz" (people of the north). Originally it was used of German Jewry, but later came to designate the Jews of northern France, Poland, Russia, and Scandinavia. Most American Jews are Ashkenazim. The Ashkenazim are distinguished from the Sephardim, the Jews of Spain, Portugal, and the Mediterranean countries. Aspects of liturgical practice and the pronunciation of Hebrew differ in the two groups. Until the 20th century Yiddish was widely spoken by the Ashkenazim.

Ashre ("Happy are those"). Opening words of verse 5 of Psalm 84. With Psalm 144.15, this verse is prefixed to Psalm 145 and recited in the morning and afternoon services.

Ashtoreth [Astarte]. Goddess of fertility worshipped by the Canaanites and the Phoenicians.

Asmakhta (Aramaic: "support," "reliance"). Talmudic term denoting a biblical text used to support a halakhah. It is also applied to a contract in which one of the parties binds himself to an unreasonable penalty.

Asmodeus. Evil spirit. His name is derived from Aeshma Daeva, the Persian god of anger. He first appears in the Book of Tobit. In the Talmud he is described as king of the demons. His name is invoked in spells and incantations in the kabbalah.

Assaf, Simḥah (1889–1953). Israeli historian and rabbinic scholar. From 1915 to 1919 he taught Talmud and was director of a yeshivah in Odessa. In 1921 he settled in Jerusalem. He later became a professor and rector at the Hebrew University and a member of the Israeli Supreme Court. He wrote many studies of the gaonic period, the history of Jewish law, medieval Jewish culture, and the history of the Jewish community in Palestine.

Asscher-Pinkhof, Clara (1896–1984). Dutch author. Born in Amsterdam, she lived there and in Groningen. She emigrated to Palestine in 1944. Her novels depict pre-war Holland, the experience of European Jewish children during the German occupation, and Israeli life.

Assembly of Jewish Notables. Convocation of French secular and religious Jewish leaders, called together by a decree of Napoleon in 1806. *See also* SANHEDRIN, GREAT.

Assi (fl. late 3rd–early 4th cent.). Palestinian amora. Born in Babylonia, he settled in Tiberias. He and Ammi bar Nathan were the most distinguished sages of their generation.

Assi, Rav (fl. early 3rd cent.). Babylonian amora. He was a contemporary of Rav and Samuel.

Assimilation. Word used specifically of the integration of Jews into another culture after the diaspora. In Hellenistic times many Jews were influenced by the civilization of the Greeks and Romans. In Muslim countries Jews were frequently attracted to various aspects of Islamic life and thought. During the Middle Ages anti-Jewish persecution and Jewish cohesiveness deterred Jews from assimilating, but since the 19th century assimilation has become a dominant aspect of Jewish life.

Assyrians. Ancient people of western Asia. In 721 BCE, under King Sargon, they destroyed the Kingdom of Israel and deported many Jews to Assyria. In 701 BCE King Sennacherib invaded Judah, conquered several cities, and besieged Jerusalem. (II Kings 15–19)

Astarte *see* ASHTORETH.

Astrology. Study of the influence of the stars on human events. It was condemned by the prophets (Isaiah 47.13; Jeremiah 10.2). During the talmudic period Jews believed that the stars influenced human destiny, and in the Middle Ages many rabbis and philosophers engaged in astrological studies, some serving as court astrologers. Kabbalistic literature shows familiarity with the discipline. A number of Jewish customs have an astrological basis.

Astronomy. Study of the heavenly bodies. It is not specifically referred to in the Bible. Apocryphal literature discusses astronomical questions such as the length of days, months, and years, and in the Talmud there are astronomical calculations for determining the new moon and the dates of festivals. In Islamic lands many Jews engaged in the science, and translated astronomical works from Arabic into Latin and Spanish. During the Renaissance Abraham Zacuto prepared astronomical tables, which were used by Spanish and Portuguese explorers.

Astruc Levi (fl. late 14th–early 15th cent.). Spanish rabbi. He participated in the Disputation of Tortosa in 1413–14.

Atarah ("crown"). Term applied since the

Middle Ages to the symbol used as one of the TORAH ORNAMENTS.

Athaliah (fl. 9th cent. BCE). Queen of Judah (842–836 BCE). When her son Ahaziah was murdered by Jehu she seized power and murdered all her rivals except Joash. Six years later she was killed when Joash was crowned king in the Temple. (II Kings 11.4–16; II Chronicles 23.1–5)

Athens. Greek city. During the reign of the Hasmoneans, it entered into friendly relations with the Jewish state. The Athenians honoured John Hyrcanus with a crown of gold and placed his statue in the Temple of Delos.

Athias, Isaac (fl. 16th–17th cent.). German rabbi. He was Ḥakham of the Sephardic community in Hamburg. His *Tesoro de preceptos* is a study of Jewish religious practices.

Athias, Joseph (fl. 17th cent.). Dutch publisher and printer. He founded a publishing house in Amsterdam. His first publication was a Sephardic prayerbook (1658). In 1659 he produced a commentary on the Pentateuch and in 1661 a Bible. In 1689 he announced that he had printed more than a million Bibles for England and Scotland.

Athrongaios *see* ETHRONGES.

A-Tiflisi, Abu Imran [Abu Imran of Tiflis] (fl. 9th cent.). Russian religious leader, founder of a dissident Karaite sect. He was born near Baghdad, and was taught by Ishmael al-Ukbari, who greatly influenced him. His followers were known as "Abu-Imranists" or "Tiflisists"; the sect persisted until the 12th century.

Atlan, Liliane (b. 1932). French dramatist and poet. She was born in Montpellier. She went into hiding during World War II. After the war she became interested in metaphysical issues. One of her plays, *Mister Fugue, or Earth Sick,* depicts the fantasies of children sent to the crematorium in the concentration camps.

Atonement. Reconciliation with God following repentance for sin. In the Bible it is connected with sacrifice (Leviticus 5.14). The rabbis emphasized the centrality of prayer, repentance, and charity. For sins committed against God, repentance is sufficient to earn atonement. If the sin involves injury to another person, restitution and forgiveness are necessary.

Attar, Ḥayyim ben Moses ben (1696–1743). North African kabbalist. Born in Morocco, he lived in Livorno and later settled in Jerusalem, where he founded the Midrash Keneset Israel Yeshivah. His *Or ha-Ḥayyim* is a commentary on the Pentateuch.

Attik Yomin *see* GOD, NAMES OF.

Auerbach, Berthold (1812–1882). German author. Born at Nordstetein in Würtemberg, he was an active supporter of Jewish Emancipation. He wrote short stories and novels, and translated Benedict Spinoza's works.

Auran *see* ELEAZAR (ii).

Auschwitz [Oswiecim]. Polish town near Kraków. It was the site of the largest concentration camp under the Nazis.

Auto-da-fé. Public ceremony at which the sentences of the Inquisition were announced in Spain and Portugal. After a procession through the streets, the condemned heretics were brought to the city square. A sermon was preached and the sentences were announced and carried out; the most severe penalty was public burning.

Autopsy *see* POST MORTEM.

Av [Ab]. Fifth month of the Jewish year.

Avadim. Minor tractate of the Talmud. It discusses laws concerning slavery.

Av bet din ("Father of the law court"). Title conferred on the president of an ecclesiastical court. During the period of the second Temple the title was given to the vice-president of the Supreme Court in Jerusalem. In gaonic times it designated the assistant to the gaon of the academies in Babylonia and Israel. From the 14th century a local rabbi, the head of a yeshivah, or the district rabbi of a large community used the title. In the modern period the head of a rabbinical court is called av bet din or rosh bet din.

Avele Zion ("Mourners for Zion"). Jews who mourned the destruction of the Temple and prayed for the redemption of Zion. In the Talmud they are known as "perushim" (abstainers) because they refused meat and wine. After the rise of Karaism they became important in Jewish life.

Avelut *see* MOURNING.

Avenger of blood (Hebrew "Goel hadam"). Next of kin of a murdered person who is responsible for avenging the murder. (Deuteronomy 19.6)

Averah ("transgression"). Word used specifically of the transgression of Jewish law.

***Averroes** (1126–1198). Spanish Muslim philosopher. He was born in Córdoba. His writings on Aristotle were translated into Hebrew. Some Jewish philosophers sought to harmonize his teaching with Judaism; others attempted to reconcile his views with those of Maimonides.

Av ha-raḥamim ("Father of mercy"). Opening words of a medieval dirge in memory of martyrs. It is recited among the Ashkenazim during Sabbath prayers.

***Avicenna** (980–1035). Arabic Muslim philosopher. He wrote on all branches of Aristotelian philosophy. He influenced Jewish philosophers such as Abraham ibn Daud, Levi ben Gershon, Abraham ibn Ezra, and Maimonides.

Avidan, David (b. 1934). Israeli poet. He was born in Tel Aviv. From the start his work was highly experimental, using composite words, loan words, and neologisms in Hebrew. He played an important role in the development of a modern style in Hebrew poetry.

Avidom, Menaḥem (b. 1908). Israeli composer. Born in Poland, he settled in Palestine in 1925, where he taught music. From 1945 to 1952 he was general secretary of the Israel Philharmonic Orchestra, and then became adviser on the arts to the Ministry of Tourism. He was appointed director-general of the Israeli Performing Rights Society in 1955, and was also chairman of the Israel Composers' League. His works include *Alexandra the Hasmonean* and the symphony *David.*

Avignon. City in southern France. The Jews were allowed to live there after they were expelled from the rest of France in the 14th century.

Avinoam, Reuben (1905–1974). Israeli poet and translator. Born in Chicago, he settled in Palestine in 1929, where he taught English at the Herzliah High School in Tel Aviv. In 1950 he became supervisor of English studies at the Israeli Ministry of Education and Culture. He published poetry, translations, and a collection of literary writings of those who died in the Israeli War of Independence.

Avinu malkenu ("Our father, our king"). Opening words of a prayer of supplication recited during the Ten Days of Penitence and on public fast days.

Aviv [abib] ("spring"). The word is also used to mean "period of the ripening of corn."

Avi-Yonah, Michael (1904–1974). Israeli archeologist and art historian. Born in Galicia, he emigrated to Palestine in 1919. He was professor of classical and Byzantine architecture at the Hebrew University. His writings concern the late-Hellenistic, Roman, and Byzantine periods, and the topography of Palestine.

Avni, Ahron (1906–1951). Israeli painter. Born in the Ukraine, he emigrated to Palestine in 1925. In 1936 he founded the Histadrut Seminary for Painting and Sculpture in Tel Aviv, of which he was director until his death. He painted members of the Haganah and later soldiers on the battlefield during the Israeli War of Independence.

Avodah ("service," "prayer"). Temple sacrificial service and ritual of the high priest on the Day of Atonement. It also refers to the Musaph service in the synagogue on the Day of Atonement.

Avodah Zarah. Eighth tractate of Nezikin in the Mishnah. It deals with idolatry.

Avon *see* SIN (ii).

Avot (i) [Pirke Avot] ("Ethics [Sayings] of the Fathers"). Ninth tractate of Nezikin in the Mishnah. It contains the teachings of sages from the 3rd century BCE to the 3rd century CE. It is part of the liturgy of the Ashkenazim and is studied on Sabbath afternoons in the summer. It is recited at home by the Sephardim on Sabbath days between Passover and Shavuot.

Avot (ii) *see* PATRIARCHS.

Avot de-Rabbi Nathan ("Fathers according to Rabbi Nathan"). Extra-canonical minor tractate of the Talmud attributed to Nathan the Babylonian. It is a commentary on Avot.

Avtalyon (fl. 1st cent. BCE). Palestinian scholar. He and Shemaiah constituted the fourth of the zugot in Palestine. He served as av bet din of the Sanhedrin.

Avukah. American students' Zionist organization. Formed in 1925, it engaged in educational and cultural activities. It was succeeded by the Intercollegiate Zionist Federation of America in 1945.

Axenfeld, Israel (1787–1866). Russian Yiddish writer. He was born in Nemirov. He originally was a follower of Naḥman of Bratzlav, but after contact with the maskilim, he became anti-Ḥasidic. He wrote 30 novels and plays which satirize Ḥasidic life.

Aydem. Son-in-law.

Ayin. 16th letter of the Hebrew alphabet. Its numerical value is 70.

Ayin ha-ra *see* EN HA-RA.

Ayllon, Solomon ben Jacob (1655–1728). Greek rabbi and kabbalist. He was born in Salonica. He became a follower of Shabbetai Tzevi. In 1689 he was appointed Ḥakham in London. He later served as rabbi to the Portuguese Jews in Amsterdam, where he came into conflict with Tzevi Ashkenazi.

Azar *see* RABINOWITZ, ALEXANDER SÜSSKIND.

Azariah *see* UZZIAH.

Azariah dei Rossi *see* ROSSI, AZARIAH BEN MOSES DEI.

Azazel. Name of the place or power to which the scapegoat was consigned on the Day of Atonement. On that day two of the goats in the Temple service were designated as sin offerings. The high priest cast lots and prescribed one for the Lord and the other for Azazel; the latter was sent into the wilderness and cast over a cliff.

Azharot ("exhortations"). Liturgical poems for Shavuot, in which the 613 commandments are enumerated. They were composed by many authors including Saadyah Gaon and Solomon ibn Gabirol.

Azriel of Gerona (fl. early 13th cent.). Spanish kabbalist. His work reflects the process whereby Neoplatonism permeated the kabbalistic tradition. He wrote a commentary on the ten sephirot, the Sepher Yetzirah, talmudic aggadot, and the liturgy, as well as several treatises on mysticism.

Azulai, Abraham (1570–1643). North African kabbalist. Born in Fez, he emigrated to Hebron. He wrote three treatises on the Zohar and a kabbalistic work, *Ḥessed le-Avraham.*

Azulai, Ḥayyim Joseph David (1724–1806). Palestinian emissary and writer. He was born in Jerusalem. He came to be regarded as the leading scholar of his generation, and also traveled abroad as an emissary of the Jewish community in Israel. His *Maagal Tov* is a literary diary covering the years 1753–78. His *Shem ha-Gedolim* contains 1300 brief biographies.

B

Ba *see* ABBA.

Baal. Canaanite god of fertility. He was portrayed as a man or bull. After the Israelites entered Canaan, they were influenced by Canaanite cults and engaged in the worship of Baal. The prophets protested against this idolatry.

Baal Dimyon *see* SHTIF, NOCHUM.

Baal ha-bayit ("head of the household"). The term is used in its literal sense, and also to denote a rich person or a married, taxpaying member of a congregation. The feminine form, "baalat bayit," refers to an efficient housewife.

Baal ha-Ḥotem *see* ISAAC BEN JOSEPH OF CORBEIL.

Baal ha-Turim *see* JACOB BEN ASHER.

Baal Kore ("Master of reading"). Title used by the Ashkenazim for the reader of the Torah portion in the synagogue.

Baal Makhshoves *see* ELYASHEV, ISIDOR.

Baal Nes ("Master of a miracle"). Miracle worker. The title was accorded to various individuals including Meir.

Baal Shem ("Master of the divine name"). Title accorded to one who works miracles by using divine names. In the medieval German Ḥasidic tradition, it was given to liturgical poets. Spanish kabbalists used the title from the middle of the 13th century, and during this period it also applied to writers of texts for amulets based on holy names. In the 17th and 18th centuries it referred to miracle workers who healed the sick.

Baal Shem, Elijah of Chełm *see* ELIJAH BEN JUDAH OF CHEŁM.

Baal Shem Tov, Israel ben Eliezer [Besht; Israel ben Eliezer] (1700–1760). Polish spiritual leader, founder of Ḥasidism. He was born in Podolia and lived in the Carpathian mountains. He emerged as a healer and spiritual leader and traveled about curing the sick and expelling demons and evil spirits; in the course of these journeys his influence grew. Prayer rather than study was his major approach to God. He attracted many followers and has remained the inspiration for Ḥasidim to the present day.

Baal Tekiyah ("Master of blowing"). Title accorded to the person who blows the shophar during synagogue services on Rosh ha-Shanah and Yom Kippur.

***Baal Zebub** [Beelzebub]. Canaanite deity. He was worshipped by the Philistines. When Ahaziah was ill he sent messengers to consult the deity (II Kings 1). He is spoken of as the chief of demons in the New Testament.

Baasha (fl. 10th–9th cent. BCE). King of Israel (906–883 BCE). He assassinated Nadab (son of Jeroboam I), proclaimed himself king, and killed all the members of the royal family. He lived at Tirzah. Throughout his reign he was at war with King Asa of Judah. (I Kings 15.16, 32)

Baba buch *see* BAVA-BUCH.

Babel, Isaac (1894–?1939). Ukrainian writer. He was born in Odessa. He served on the Romanian front after the Russian Revolution. From 1923 he devoted himself to literature and many of his stories contain Jewish themes. He was arrested and disappeared in 1939. His writing includes *Red Cavalry, Collected Stories,* and *The Lonely Years, 1925–1939.*

Babel, Tower of. Tower built by Noah's descendants in Shinar, intended to be high enough to reach Heaven. God frustrated this project and confused their tongues; as a result, there are diverse languages throughout the world (Genesis 11.1–9). Modern scholars note the similarity between this building and the Sumerian Ziggurat.

Babi Yar. Ravine outside Kiev in the Ukraine, where more than 30,000 Jews were murdered in September 1941. After 778 days of Nazi rule in Kiev more than 100,000 people were buried there. It is the subject of a poem (*Babi-Yar*) by Yevgeny Yevtushenko which was set to music by Dmitri Shostakovich.

Babylonia. Ancient country in western Asia between the Tigris and Euphrates rivers. It was settled by the Sumerians in the third millennium BCE; Sargon I founded the Akkadian dynasty there in the 24th century BCE. In the 19th century BCE the Amorites ruled over northern Babylonia. Later rulers of the country were the Hittites and Assyrians.

Babylonian Talmud *see* TALMUD.

Bacharach, Jair Ḥayyim (1638–1702). German talmudist. He served as rabbi in Koblenz and Worms. 13 scholars met under his leadership to study and prepare themselves for redemption. He collected writings connected with Shabbetai Tzevi. His *Ḥavvot Yair* consists of responsa demonstrating an extensive knowledge of secular subjects.

Bacher, Simon (1823–1891). Hungarian poet and translator. He lived in Budapest, where he was the treasurer of the Jewish community. He wrote poems in the florid style of the Haskalah and translated German and Hungarian poetry into Hebrew; his *Zemirot ha-Aretz* (Songs of the land) is an anthology of translations from Hungarian poetry. His translation of Gotthold Ephraim Lessing's *Nathan the Wise* appeared in Vienna in 1865.

Bacher, Wilhelm (1850–1913). Hungarian Semitic scholar. He was professor and head of the rabbinic seminary in Budapest, where he taught biblical exegesis, midrash, homiletics, and Hebrew poetry and grammar. He published on various aspects of Judaism; his works include studies of talmudic aggadah, Hebrew grammarians, medieval biblical exegesis, and Judeo-Persian literature.

***Bacon, Roger** (1214–1294). English philosopher and Hebraist. He viewed a knowledge of Hebrew as a prerequisite for the study of the Bible, and sought the aid of Jewish scholars in his learning of the language. He eventually prepared a Hebrew grammar.

Bader, Gershom (1868–1953). Polish Hebrew and Yiddish author. Born in Kraków, he lived in Lemberg from 1893 until 1912. He founded the first Yiddish daily in Galicia, the *Togblat,* in 1904. In 1896 he established the *Yidisher folks-kalender,* which he edited until 1912; in that year he settled in New York. His writings include a life of Jesus, a lexicon of Galician Jewish cultural figures, and a dictionary of talmudic abbreviations.

Badge, Jewish. Distinctive emblem or mark which Jews were forced to wear; it usually took the form of a cloth badge. From the 7th century Muslim rulers decreed that Jews should wear special clothing. The Fourth Lateran Council of 1215 laid down a similar order so that Jews could be distinguished from Christians. The badge was usually yellow. In medieval England it represented the two Tablets of the Law. In France and Spain it was a circular patch. In Germany it was a large yellow circle. Under the Nazi regime it was a yellow Star of David with the letter "J" (or the word "Jude") inside.

Badḥan. Merrymaker or entertainer. Medieval rabbinic literature refers to Jewish itinerant singers who entertained at weddings and at Ḥanukkah and Purim celebrations. They sang folk songs, told comic stories, and made jests based on scriptural verses and talmudic passages. In eastern Europe they acted as the professional wedding jesters and musicians.

Baeck, Leo (1873–1956). German rabbi and religious leader. He served as rabbi in Berlin, where he lectured on midrashic literature and homiletics at the Hochschule für Wissenschaft des Judentums. From 1933 he was president of the Reichsvertretung or representative body of German Jews. He was deported to Theresienstadt in 1943. After the war he settled in London, where he served as chairman of the World Union for Progressive Judaism. He was visiting professor at the Hebrew Union College. His writings include *The Essence of Judaism*.

Baer, Seligmann (1825–1897). German masorah scholar and linguist. He taught in the Jewish community school in Biebrich. Together with Franz Delitzsch he published the Psalms and other books of the Bible with masorah texts. His *Avodat Yisrael* (Service of Israel) became the standard prayerbook text for most subsequent editions of the siddur.

Baer, Yitzḥak (1888–1980). German historian. He was born in Halberstadt. He became professor of medieval history and head of the history department at the Hebrew University. His writings include studies of the Jews in Christian Spain and the period of the second Temple. He was one of the founders and editors of the Jewish historical review *Zion*.

Baghdad. Capital city of Iraq. From 762 it was the capital of the Abbasid dynasty. It attracted a large number of Jews and became the seat of the exilarch. By the end of the 9th century the academies of Sura and Pumbedita had been moved there.

***Bagoas** (fl. c. 400 BCE). Persian Governor of Judea. According to Josephus, when Johanan the high priest murdered Bagoas' brother Jeshua, Bagoas entered the Temple and imposed a fine on all offerings for seven years.

Baḥ *see* SERKES, JOEL BEN SAMUEL.

Bahir. Kabbalistic work. According to tradition it was composed by Neḥunyah ben ha-Kanah in the 1st century; modern scholarship believes it to have been compiled in Provence in the 12th century, though it incorporates ancient texts. It deals with letter mysticism and hints at the doctrine of the sephirot. Much of the terminology used in the book became part of the vocabulary of the kabbalah. It also contains a reference to the doctrine of the Transmigration of Souls.

Baḥur ("young man"). In the Bible it designates a fighting man. In rabbinic literature it refers to one who is unmarried. In the Middle Ages it was used of an advanced yeshivah student.

Baḥur, Elijah *see* LEVITA, ELIJAH.

Baḥya ben Asher ibn Halawa (fl. 13th cent.). Spanish exegete and kabbalist. He lived in Zaragoza where he was dayyan and preacher. In his commentary on the Torah he used literal, philosophical, homiletical, and mystical interpretations.

Baḥya ben Joseph ibn Pakuda [Ibn Bakuda; Ibn Pakuda, Baḥya] (fl. 11th cent.). Spanish moral philosopher. He lived in Zaragoza. In *Duties of the Heart* he examined the obligations of man's inner life, which he regarded as having equal importance with ritual and ethical observances; this work draws on Islamic mysticism and Neoplatonism.

Bailment. The making over of movable

property by the owner (bailor) to someone else (bailee) on the understanding that he will return it. Rabbinic law concerning bailment is based on Exodus 22.6–14 and sets out the duty of the bailee to restore the property in good condition. The Mishnah specifies four types of recipient: the unpaid guardian, the paid guardian, the hirer, and the borrower.

Baka *see* PEKIIN.

Bakkashah ("supplication"). A type of liturgical composition. It includes a wide range of prayers in prose or verse. Petitionary and abstract in content, they are used throughout the year. A number in the Sephardic prayerbook are to be recited before dawn as a prelude to the regular service.

***Balaam** (fl. 13th cent. BCE). Aramean prophet. He was asked by Balak, King of Moab, to curse the Israelites when they encamped in the steppes of Moab before entering the Promised Land. Riding on a donkey, he encountered an angel wielding a sword, and under divine inspiration he blessed Israel instead of cursing. (Numbers 22–3)

Balaban, Meir (1877–1942). Polish historian. He was born in Lemberg. He became director of the Taḥkemoni rabbinic seminary in Warsaw and lectured in Jewish history at the University of Warsaw. He was the founder of the historiography of Polish Jewry. His writings deal with the history of the Jews in Poland and Russia.

Balak (fl. 13th cent. BCE). King of Moab. When the Israelites approached his country, he asked the prophet Balaam to curse them, but, inspired by God, he blessed them instead. (Numbers 22–3)

Balfour, Arthur James, Lord (1848–1930). British statesman. In 1902–3 he took an interest in the Jewish question when Theodor Herzl conducted negotiations with Joseph Chamberlain and Lord Lansdowne. As foreign secretary he signed the Balfour Declaration in November 1917. His written works include *Speeches on Zionism.*

Balfour Declaration. British statement of sympathy with Zionism. It was signed by the foreign secretary, Lord Balfour, in November 1917. The document states: "His Majesty's government view with favour the establishment in Palestine of a national home for the Jewish people, and will use their best endeavours to facilitate the achievement of this object, it being clearly understood that nothing shall be done which may prejudice the civil and religious rights of the existing non-Jewish communities in Palestine, or the rights and political status enjoyed by Jews in any other country." *See also* PALESTINE MANDATE.

Balmes, Abraham ben Meir de (1440–1523). Italian physician and grammarian. He was born in Lecce. He became court physician to King Ferdinand I of Naples. He translated a number of medieval Arabic works from the Hebrew versions into Latin. His *Mikneh Avraham* is a standard work on Hebrew grammar.

Bal tashit ("do not destroy"). Biblical prohibition against destroying fruit-bearing trees when laying siege to a city (Deuteronomy 20.19–20). The Talmud extends the concept to cover any senseless destruction or waste.

Bamberger, Fritz (1902–1984). German philosopher. He was born in Frankfurt am Main. He was professor of philosophy at the College of Jewish Studies in Chicago from 1937 to 1942, then until 1961 was professor of intellectual history at the Hebrew Union College–Jewish Institute of Religion in New York. His writings include studies of Moses Mendelssohn and Benedict Spinoza.

Bamberger, Seligmann Bär (1807–1878). Leader of German Orthodoxy. He was born in Wiesenbronn. He served as rabbi in Würzburg, where he founded a teachers' training college. His writings were devoted to subjects of practical halakhah.

Bambus, Willi (1863–1904). German Zionist. He was a leading member of the Ezra society in Berlin, which supported agricultural settlements in Palestine. He was opposed to political Zionism. In 1901 he was a co-founder of the Hilfsverein der deutschen Juden. His writings include *Palaestina, Land und Leute, Die Kriminalität der Juden,* and *Die Juden als Soldaten.*

Ba-meh, madlikin ("With what may one kindle?"). Opening words of the second chapter of the Mishnah tractate Shabbat, which deals with the oils and wicks to be used for Sabbath lights and with what may be done on Fridays before the commencement of the Sabbath. The chapter is recited during the Friday evening service before or at the end of the Arvit prayer. The reading of the chapter was instituted during the gaonic period as a reminder of the duty of kindling the Sabbath lights, as a warning against unintentional desecration of the Sabbath by adjusting the lamp, and as a safeguard for latecomers to the synagogue so that they could catch up with the service.

Ban [excommunication]. In Jewish usage, the sentencing of an individual to exclusion or severance from the Jewish community. A short-term ban ("niddui") is used to cut off an individual from social and business contacts. A more severe ban ("ḥerem") involves a complete boycott of the individual (the cessation of personal, social, religious, and business contact) for an indefinite period. In the rabbinic period it was frequently employed against those Jews whose views were considered dangerous to the community, such as heretics or followers of sects not approved by the Jewish authorities. In the Middle Ages and afterwards it played an important role in Jewish life. Among those to whom the punishment was applied were Uriel Acosta, Benedict Spinoza, the followers of Shabbetai Tzevi, and Jacob Frank. In the modern period the practice of inflicting bans has largely fallen into disuse.

Banco, Anselmo del (d. c. 1532). Italian banker. He was the founder of the Jewish community in Venice. His financial assistance to the government and skill at negotiation led to the community's formal recognition.

Band, Arnold (b. 1929). American literary scholar. He was born in Boston. He served on the faculty of the University of California at Los Angeles from 1959, becoming professor of Hebrew literature and chairman of the Department of Comparative Literature. His publications include a study of Shemuel Yosef Agnon.

Bandes [Miller]**, Louis E.** (1866–1927). American Yiddish journalist. Born in Russia, he settled in the US, where he became a leader of the socialist movement. In 1890 he founded the Yiddish Marxist weekly *Die arbeiter zeitung,* and in 1897 helped to establish the labor daily newspaper *Forverts.* In 1905 he founded *Die varheit,* which later altered its ideology from socialism to Zionism.

Baneth, David Tzevi Hartwig (1893–1973). Israeli Arabist, son of Eduard Baneth. He was born in Krotoszyn, Poland. He settled in Palestine, where he became professor of Arabic language and literature at the Hebrew University. His writings concern the influence of Arabic thought on medieval Jewish philosophy.

Baneth, Eduard (1855–1930). Prussian talmudist. He was born in Liptó-Szent-Miklós, Hungary. He served as rabbi at Krotoszyn and lectured on Talmud at the Lehranstalt für die Wissenschaft des Judentums in Berlin. His work was concerned primarily with talmudic and rabbinic literature, the development of halakhah, and the Jewish calendar.

Baneth, Ezekiel (1773–1854). Hungarian rabbi. He was born in Alt-Ofen. He served as rabbi of Paks, Balassagyarmat, and Nyitra, and his yeshivah was attended by students from all over the country. He was a halakhic authority and an eloquent preacher.

Banishment. Exclusion from one's native soil. It was the punishment decreed by God for Adam (Genesis 3.23–4) and Cain (Genesis 4.14–16). In biblical times, those who killed by accident were banished to cities of refuge, where they were given asylum. During the period of the second Temple, banishment was imposed for misdeeds or political reasons. In the Middle Ages Jewish courts expelled individuals to protect the community.

Banking. During the 11th–13th centuries in Europe Jewish finance and credit were based on the resources of individuals and small groups. The growth of world currency markets in the 18th century gave rise to the private banks of Jewish families (Rothschild, Worms, Stern, Bischoffsheim), who financed international trade and industry. The revolutions of 1848 led to their decline. In the US in the early 19th century a number of banks were founded by Jewish merchants (Lazard, Erlanger, Guggenheim). In the 20th century, however, such Jewish banking firms lost their former significance owing to the rise of larger, more impersonal corporations.

Bank Leumi le-Israel. Bank established in Palestine in 1903 by the Jewish Colonial Trust as the Anglo-Palestine Company. It was the central bank of Palestinian Jewry. The Ottoman government closed it during World War I. From 1931 to 1951 it was known as the Anglo-Palestine Bank Ltd. It was subsequently incorporated in Israel as the Bank Leumi le-Israel Ltd, with a share capital and open reserves of I£5.25 million.

Bank of Israel. Israeli national bank. It was established in 1954 with capital of I£10 million and a reserve fund of I£10 million. It administers currency and regulates the credit and banking system in accordance with governmental policy.

Banu Kainuka [Kainuka]. One of three Jewish tribes in Medina, Arabia, in the 7th century. They engaged in commerce and worked as goldsmiths. When Mohammed failed to gain Jewish converts to Islam, they were attacked. They left Medina and migrated to Jewish centers in Wadi-i-Kura and Adhirat.

Banu Kuraiza [Kuraiza]. One of three Jewish tribes in Medina, Arabia, in the 7th century. They engaged in agriculture. One of the women in the tribe, Raihana, was married to Mohammed; when he accused them of treason, the men were executed and the women and children sold into slavery.

Banu-l-Nadir [Nadir Banu]. One of three Jewish tribes in Medina, Arabia, in the 7th century. They cultivated the soil, engaged in moneylending, and traded in weapons and jewels. They were besieged in their strongholds by Mohammed and surrendered. Their property was confiscated, and they founded settlements in Khaybar and Syria.

Baptism. Ablutionary rite symbolizing purification or consecration. In the Bible it was practiced by priests and laymen. Later it played an important role in the rites of the Essenes, Hemerobaptists, and Christians. Baptism by total immersion is a necessary rite for a convert to Judaism but it is also practiced by men and women as a means of purification.

Baptism, forced. Subjection to the Christian ritual of baptism. When Christianity became the religion of the Roman Empire, large numbers of Jews were forcibly baptized. From the time of Pope

Gregory I (590–604), this practice was condemned. Nevertheless baptism was frequently imposed on Jews through the centuries. *See also* CONVERSION, FORCED.

Bar (Aramaic: "son"). It occurs as a particle in many male personal names.

Barabbas (fl. 1st cent.). Palestinian rebel. According to the New Testament, he had been condemned to death at the same time as Jesus. He was reprieved when the governor, Pontius Pilate, allowed the Jewish population to choose one condemned man to be released.

Baraita (Aramaic: "external"). Any halakhah, halakhic midrash, historical or aggadic tradition not included in the Mishnah. The term is employed in the Babylonian Talmud to emphasize a view opposed to that in the Mishnah. A baraita is introduced by the formulae "Teno rabbanan" (The rabbis taught) and "Tanya, tena" (It was taught). The largest collection of extra-Mishnaic halakhot is the Tosephta.

Barak ben Abinoam (fl. 12th cent. BCE). Israelite commander. He served Deborah in the war against the Canaanites, doing battle at her instigation with King Jabin of Hazor (Judges 4–5).

Barash, Asher (1889–1952). Hebrew author of Galician origin. Born in Eastern Galicia, he emigrated in 1914 to Palestine, where he taught high school in Tel Aviv and Haifa. He wrote novels, short stories, poems, essays, and translations. His fictional works depict life among Galician Jewry and the pioneering efforts in Palestine.

Barcelona. Port in northeast Spain. It was the home of one of the most important Jewish communities in the medieval period. The Disputation of Barcelona between Naḥmanides and Pablo Christiani took place there in 1263. It was the home of Abraham bar Ḥiyya and Solomon ben Adret.

Barekhi naphshi ("Bless (the Lord), o my soul"). Opening words of Psalm 104, and the title by which it is known. The psalm glorifies God as creator and sustainer of nature. It is recited on Rosh Ḥodesh, and in some rites also on Sabbath afternoons between Sukkot and Passover.

Barekhu ("Bless"). The opening word of the synagogue formula of invitation to prayer. The entire phrase, "Barekhu et Adonai ha-mevorakh" (Bless ye the Lord who is (to be) blessed), is based on the biblical expression "Bless ye the Lord." It serves as the opening of both the morning and evening prayers in the synagogue and also functions as the introduction to the public reading of the Torah. It was also used for the zimmun (invitation to Grace), but was later replaced by the formula "Nevarekh" (Let us bless). When the reader chants "Barekhu," the congregation silently reads a prayer beginning "Yitbarakh." When the reader concludes the invitation, the congregation responds: "Blessed is the Lord who is (to be) blessed for ever and ever."

Bar Giora. Palestinian defense organization. Named after Simon Bar Giora, it was established in 1907 by Jewish immigrants. It was a forerunner of Ha-Shomer.

Bar Giora, Simon [Simeon] (fl. 1st cent.). Palestinian military leader in the war against Rome in 66–70. He fought in the battle at Beth-Horon in 66, in which the Jews defeated the Romans. He gathered together a band of patriots who attacked opponents of the revolt and Roman sympathizers. He opposed the moderate Jewish government in Jerusalem, which wished to come to terms with Rome. When Titus' forces reached Jerusalem in 70 he fought with the rebels against him. He eventually surrendered, was taken prisoner to Rome, and executed.

Bar-Hanina (fl. 4th cent.). Palestinian scholar. He lived in Bethlehem and was a teacher of Jerome. He introduced the

Church Fathers to rabbinic exegesis and influenced the translation of the Hebrew Scriptures into Latin.

***Bar-Hebraeus, Gregorius** (1226–1286). Syrian scholar of Jewish origin. He was appointed Archbishop of Mesopotamia and Persia in 1252. He wrote a Syriac grammar, commentaries on the Bible and Aristotle, and a history of the world.

Bar-Ilan [Berlin], **Meir** (1880–1949). Zionist leader of Russian origin. He was born in Volozhin. He represented the Mizraḥi movement at the seventh Zionist Congress in 1905. In 1926 he settled in Jerusalem, where he became President of the World Mizraḥi Center. Opposed to the Palestinian partition plan and the British White Paper of 1939, he advocated civil disobedience. After the establishment of the State of Israel he organized a group of scholars to examine the legal problems of the state in the light of Jewish law. He was editor of the Mizraḥi daily newspaper and organized the publication of the *Talmudic Encyclopaedia.*

Bar-Ilan University. Orthodox University near Tel Aviv. Named after Meir Bar-Ilan, it was founded in 1955. Its aim is to advance Jewish studies, as well as general science and research. It publishes the *Bar-Ilan Annual: Studies in Judaica and the Humanities.*

Bar Kappara (fl. 3rd cent.). Palestinian scholar. A disciple of Judah ha-Nasi, he was the author of a compilation of Jewish law. This collection explains obscure passages in the Mishnah and transmits traditions that differ from it. He valued natural science and encouraged the use of Greek, but was opposed to metaphysical speculation. He founded an academy in the south of Israel.

Bar Kokhba, Simeon [Bar Kosiba, Simeon; Ben Koziba] (d. 135). Palestinian military leader in the war against Rome in 132–5. At the outbreak of the war, Akiva proclaimed him Messiah; the appelation Bar Kokhba (Son of the Star) was given to him because of his messianic role. His forces captured Jerusalem, but in 133 the Romans counterattacked with an army of 35,000 under Hadrian and the commander Julius Severus. In 134–5 they besieged Bar Kokhba's stronghold, Betar, and he was killed.

Bar-Lev, Ḥayyim (b. 1924). Israeli military commander. Born in Vienna, he settled in Palestine in 1939. In 1946 he was in charge of blowing up the Allenby Bridge during the struggle with the British. In the War of Independence and the Sinai Campaign of 1956, he served as military commander of various units. In 1964 he was appointed head of the General Staff Branch at GHQ. From 1968 to 1971 he was chief of staff of the Israeli Defense Forces. In 1972 he became minister of commerce and industry.

Barminan ("Far from us"). Exclamation used by Sephardim to ward off misfortune. It is equivalent to the Ashkenazi phrase "Lo alenu" (Not on us), which is sometimes used among Ashkenazim to refer to a corpse.

Bar mitzvah ("Son of the commandment"). Term applied to the attainment of legal and religious maturity, also the occasion on which this status is assumed. At 13 a boy is obligated to fulfill all the commandments, and in the synagogue he may be called up to read the Torah and the Haphtarah. A special service is held at which he reads for the first time and the rabbi may deliver a sermon stressing his new obligations. After the service a festive kiddush frequently takes place. Reform congragations initially instituted a ceremony of confirmation as a substitute, but it is now adopted as an additional ceremony.

Barnett, Lionel David (1871–1960).

English orientalist. Born in Liverpool, he was Keeper of the Department of Oriental Printed Books and Manuscripts at the British Museum from 1908 to 1936. His writings include *Antiquities of India, Hindu Gods and Heroes,* and the English translations *A History of Greek Drama* and *Brahma-Knowledge.* He edited the Bevis Marks Synagogue records of the contributions made to history by members of the congregation.

Barnett, Richard David (1909–1986). English orientalist, son of Lionel David Barnett. He was born in London. He became head of the Department of Western Asiatic Antiquities at the British Museum, and from 1959 to 1961 he was president of the Jewish Historical Society of England. His publications include *Assyrian Palace Reliefs and their Influence on the Sculptures of Babylonia and Persia* and *Illustrations of Old Testament History.*

Baron, Devorah (1887–1956). Hebrew author of Russian origin. She was born in Belorussia and settled in Palestine in 1911. Childhood reminiscences and Jewish life in eastern Europe are major themes in her fiction. Her writings include *Sippurim, Le-Et Attah,* and *Parshiyyot. The Thorny Path* is a collection of her stories translated into English.

Baron, Salo Wittmayer (1896–1989). Galician Jewish historian. He taught history at the Jewish Teachers College in Vienna (1919–26), at the Jewish Institute of Religion in New York (1927–30), and at Columbia University (1930–62). He served as president of the American Academy for Jewish Research and as a member of other academic bodies. His writings include the multi-volume *Social and Religious History of the Jews.*

Baron de Hirsch Fund. Trust established by Baron de Hirsch in 1891 to help Jews flee from eastern Europe to the US. It subsidized a rural community, Woodbine, and an agricultural school in southern New Jersey and the Baron de Hirsch Trade School in New York.

Barondess, Joseph (1867–1928). American labor and communal leader. Born in the Ukraine, he emigrated to New York in 1888. He helped lead the cloakmakers' strike in 1890 and was sentenced to imprisonment as a result. He was active in the Socialist Labor Party and later in the Zionist movement. He was a founder of the American Jewish Congress and a member of the American Jewish delegation to the Versailles peace talks in 1919.

Barrenness. The inability of a woman to conceive and bear children. In rabbinic Judaism it is considered a misfortune since the procreation of children is the principal purpose of marriage. Talmudic law stipulates that a man is compelled to divorce his wife if his marriage is without issue after ten years; however, from the Middle Ages no compulsion has been exercised in such cases.

Barrios, Daniel Levi [Miguel] **de** (1635–1701). Spanish poet and playwright. He was born in Montilla of a Portuguese Marrano family. He served as a captain in the Spanish Netherlands, living in Brussels and Amsterdam. He was a follower of Shabbetai Tzevi. In his writing he initially emphasized classical and pagan allusions, but later stressed his Jewishness. His poems contain extensive information about contemporary Jewish life.

Barros Basto, Arturo Carlos de (1887–1961). Portuguese leader of the Marrano revival. He was born at Amarante near Oporto. He entered the military, and in the revolution of 1910 it was he who hoisted the Republican flag on the town hall of Oporto. After World War I he embraced Judaism and was active in the regeneration of the Marrano community. His periodical *Ha-Lappid* spread Jewish ideas among the Marranos. He also edited handbooks of religious guidance and wrote a history of Jewry in Oporto.

Barsimon, Jacob (fl. 17th cent.). Dutch emigrant, the first Jewish resident of New Amsterdam (New York). He arrived in the New World in July 1654 aboard the Dutch ship "Peartree." In 1655 he joined Asser Levy in petitioning for the right to stand guard instead of paying a special tax. The Dutch West India Company overruled Governor Peter Stuyvesant, who had rejected the petition.

Barth, Aaron (1890–1957). Israeli banker and Zionist leader. He was born in Berlin. He became active in the Mizraḥi movement in Germany; from 1921 to 1938 he was attorney for the Zionist Congress court and from 1946 its chairman. He settled in Palestine in 1933 and became director-general of the Anglo-Palestine Bank in 1947. His writings include *The Modern Jew Faces Eternal Problems,* in which he advocated a modern interpretation of Orthodoxy.

Barth, Jacob (1851–1941). German Semitic linguist. He was born in Flehingen, Baden. He taught Hebrew, biblical exegesis, and Jewish philosophy at the Orthodox Rabbinic Seminary in Berlin. From 1874 he also lectured on Semitic philology at the University of Berlin. He published studies on Semitic linguistics and edited grammatical, poetic, and historical texts.

***Bartolucci, Giulio** (1613–1687). Italian scholar. He was professor of Hebrew language and rabbinic literature at the Collegium Neophytorum in Rome, and *scriptor hebraicus* in the Vatican library. He compiled a comprehensive bibliography of Jewish books.

Bartov, Hanokh (b. 1926). Israeli novelist. Born in Petaḥ Tikvah, he served in the Jewish Brigade during World War II and in the Israeli army during the War of Independence. He was cultural attaché at the Israeli embassy in London from 1966 to 1968. His writings include stories, novels, plays, and journalism.

Baruch (i) (fl. 7th cent. BCE). Israelite, scribe of the Book of Jeremiah. He set down in writing all Jeremiah's prophecies and may have composed the biographical narrative about him. (Jeremiah 36.4)

Baruch (ii). Apocryphal book. The prose section relates how Baruch wrote the work in Babylon and read it to Jehoiachin and the exiles; they confessed their sins and sent money to Jerusalem to purchase sacrifices. The lyrical part consists of a hymn to the wisdom of the law, lamentations, and consolation.

Baruch, Apocalypse of. Apocalyptic work ascribed to Jeremiah's scribe Baruch. The Syriac version contains Baruch's visions on the eve of the destruction of Jerusalem and in its aftermath. The Greek version describes Baruch's journey through the heavens. The Ethiopic version contains stories of Baruch and Jeremiah at the period of the destruction of Jerusalem.

Baruch ben David Yavan (d. 1780). Polish financier. He exercised influence at the Polish court, by means of which he protected the Jewish community and discredited the Sabbetaians and the Frankist movement.

Baruch ben Samuel of Mainz (c. 1150–1221). German talmudist and liturgical poet. He was a dayyan of Mainz. His responsa were incorporated in his *Sepher ha-Ḥokhmah* (The book of wisdom). He wrote commentaries on several talmudic tractates, and piyyutim on persecutions of the Jews.

Baruch ben Samuel of Safed (d. 1834). Russian physician and rabbinic emissary. He settled in Palestine in 1819. In 1830 he went to the Yemen to find the Ten Lost Tribes of Israel.

Baruch of Medzibozh [Baruch of Tulchin] (1757–1810). Ukrainian Ḥasidic tzaddik. He was the grandson of the Baal Shem Tov, and regarded himself as the heir to his leadership. He held court in Medzibozh in a luxurious fashion and aroused the opposition of other Ḥasidic leaders. He believed the tzaddik could save the whole world. He was the first to institute payments to the tzaddik from the Ḥasidim.

Baruch of Shklov [Schick, Baruch] (1752–1810). Polish talmudist and scientist. He studied medicine in England and later lived in Berlin, where he wrote on astronomy, mathematics, and medicine. He was dayyan at Slutsk and physician to Prince Radziwiłł.

Baruch of Tulchin *see* BARUCH OF MEDZIBOZH.

Barukh ("blessed"). Opening word of a benediction, also of phrases and salutations deriving from benedictions. According to the Talmud, many benedictions beginning with the formula "Blessed art thou, o Lord our God, king of the universe" derive from the Men of the Great Synagogue, a group of around 100 sages who constituted a spiritual and legislative body in the period after the Prophets.

Barukh dayyan (ha-)emet ("Blessed be the true judge"). Benediction pronounced on hearing evil tidings. On hearing the report of a death, relatives are to recite the full formula: "Blessed art thou, o Lord our God, king of the universe, the true judge."

Barukh ha-ba ("Blessed is he who comes"). Greeting to a visitor or new acquaintance.

Barukh ha-shem ("Blessed be the name [of God]"). Expression of thanksgiving pronounced on hearing good tidings.

Barukh hu u-varukh shemo ("Blessed be he, and blessed be his name"). Response by the congregation to the mention of God's name in the first half of a benediction. The response to the second half is "Amen."

Barukh she-amar ("Blessed be he who spoke"). Benediction pronounced at the beginning of the section of the morning service called Pesuke de-Zimra (passages of song). In the Ashkenazi rite it is said at the beginning of the whole section. In the Sephardi rite verses and psalms are recited before it.

Barukh shem kevod malkhuto le-olam va-ed ("Blessed be his name whose glorious kingdom is eternal"). Benediction recited after the first verse of the Shema. It is spoken in an undertone, except on the Day of Atonement when it is recited aloud. According to the Talmud, when Jacob was dying he asked his sons if they believed in the one God; in reply they spoke the Shema, to which Jacob responded with this phrase.

Barukh she-petaroni ("Blessed be he who has relieved me"). Benediction pronounced by the father at his son's bar mitzvah. It refers to the father's being relieved of responsibility for his son's conduct. In Yiddish it became a familiar expression on getting rid of an annoying thing or person.

Bar-Yehuda, Yisrael [Idelson, Yisrael] (1895–1965). Israeli political leader. Born in Russia, he settled in Palestine in 1926. From 1949 he was a member of the Knesset. After the split in Mapam in 1954, he became a member of the Aḥdut ha-Avodah–Poale Zion party. From 1955 to 1959 he was minister of the interior, and from 1962 to 1965 minister of communications.

Barzillai (fl. 11th–10th cent. BCE). Gileadite who ministered to David. When David fled to Gilead because of Absalom's rebellion, Barzillai welcomed him with food and sustained him throughout his stay. He later sent his son to live in David's court in Jerusalem. (I Kings 2.7)

Basch, Victor (1863–1944). French philosopher. Born in Budapest, he was professor at the universities of Nancy,

Rennes, and Paris. He championed Alfred Dreyfus. In 1926 he served as president of the League for the Rights of Man. During World War II he was a member of the central committee of the French Résistance. His writings concern literature, philosophy, and political issues.

Bashyazi, Elijah (1420–1490). Turkish Karaite scholar. He was the ideologist of the Karaite rapprochement with the rabbis, and a codifier of Karaite law. His *Adderet Eliyahu* is a code of Karaite law.

Baskin, Leonard (b. 1922). American artist. He was born in New Jersey. He taught printmaking and sculpture at Smith College from 1953. He was influenced in his early years by Ben Shahn and many of his drawings and prints concern Jewish subjects.

Basle. City in northern Switzerland. During the Black Death Jews in the city were accused of poisoning the wells. 600 Jews were burned at the stake and 140 children were forcibly baptized. The first Zionist Congress was held there in 1897.

Basle, Council of. Church Council for disciplinary reform, held from 1431 to 1449. Among many other matters, it passed regulations aimed at cutting off personal relations between Jews and Christians and prohibited the study of the Talmud.

Basle Program. The official policy of the Zionist organization. It took its name from the city where the first Zionist Congress took place in 1897. It advocated the establishment of a Jewish homeland in Palestine, secured under public law.

Bass, Shabbetai ben Joseph (1641–1718). Polish cantor and publisher. He became the first Jewish bibliographer. When his parents were killed in a pogrom, he fled to Prague, where he served as an assistant cantor. From 1674 until 1679 he visited libraries in Poland, Germany, and Holland. His *Siftei Yeshenim* is a list in Hebrew of some 2200 items of Hebraica and Judaica.

Bassani, Giorgio (b. 1916). Italian writer. Born in Bologna, he lived in Ferrara until 1943, when he moved to Rome. He edited *Bolteghe oscure,* an international literary review, from 1948 to 1960. His *Garden of the Finzi-Continis* depicts an aristocratic Italian Jew unable to come to terms with Fascism.

Bassevi [von Treuenberg]**, Jacob** (1570–1634). Court Jew. He engaged in large-scale trading and business transactions. In 1622 Friedrich II granted him a coat-of-arms. As head of the Jewish community in Prague he took an active role in Jewish communal life and defended the Jews from persecution.

Bastard *see* MAMZER.

Bathing. In Jewish practice, specifically a means of ritual purification. It was a daily requirement for those who participated in Temple services. Groups such as the Essenes made it a cult. In post-biblical times it was of less significance. The kabbalists and several Ḥasidic sects revived the practice. *See also* IMMERSION; MIKVEH.

Bath-Sheba (fl. 11th–10th cent. BCE). Israelite woman, wife first of Uriah then of David. When David, from his rooftop, saw her bathing, he had Uriah her husband killed in battle by placing him in the front lines. Bath-Sheba was the mother of Solomon. (II Samuel 11–12; I Kings 1–2)

Bat kol ("daughter of a voice"). Rabbinic expression referring to a divine voice, sometimes heard to give heavenly approval to halakhic decisions.

Batlan ("man of leisure"). Talmudic term referring to a man who has spare time for communal business such as synagogue attendance. In Yiddish usage it denotes a man who is lazy and shiftless and cannot make his way in the world.

Bat mitzvah ("Daughter of the commandment"). Ceremony for girls corresponding to a boy's bar mitzvah. A girl reaches her religious majority at the age of 12 years and one day. The ceremony celebrating this occasion differs widely. In some congregations girls read from the Torah; in others they recite the Haphtarah and conduct certain prayers.

Baum, Oscar (1883–1941). Czech author. He was a member of the Prague circle of Max Brod and Franz Kafka. He lost his sight as a boy and therefore dictated his short stories. His *Die böse Unschuld* (1913) documents Jewish life in Bohemia against the background of the Czech nationalist struggle. His last novel, *Das Volk des harten Schlafes* (1937), portrays Jewish life in the early years of Nazi rule.

Bava ("gate"). Word used to denote a section of a book. The first tractate of the Mishnah order of Nezikin was divided into three such sections: Bava Kamma, Bava Metzia, and Bava Batra.

Bava Batra ("The last gate"). Third section of the first tractate of the Mishnah order of Nezikin. It deals with real estate, usurpations, hereditary succession, and legal documents.

Bava-buch [Baba buch]. Yiddish adaptation made at the beginning of the 16th century by Elijah Levita of the Anglo-French romance *Sir Bevis of Hampton*. The Yiddish phrase "bobemeise" (grandmother's tale) is probably derived from this.

Bava Kamma ("The first gate"). First section of the first tractate of the Mishnah order of Nezikin. It deals with the four principal types of damage to property and personal injury (Exodus 21.33; 22.5 ff).

Bava Metzia ("The middle gate"). Second section of the first tractate of the Mishnah order of Nezikin. It deals with found property, the laws of chattels, bailment, sales, interest, fraud, hiring, and partnership.

Bavli, Hillel (1863–1961). American Hebrew poet and educator of Lithuanian origin. He settled in the US in 1912 and taught modern Hebrew literature at the Jewish Theological Seminary. He was one of the first Hebrew poets to deal with the American milieu. His poems have been collected in several volumes. He translated Dickens's *Oliver Twist* and Shakespeare's *Antony and Cleopatra* into Hebrew.

Beadle *see* SHAMMASH.

Beard. The Bible explicitly forbids cutting the corners of the beard (Leviticus 19.27). The Talmud regards the beard as the ornament of the face, and mystics ascribed esoteric significance to it. In Europe the emphasis shifted from the obligation to wear a beard to the prohibition of shaving; however, it is permitted to clip it using scissors or an electric shaver with two cutting edges.

***Beck, Karl Isidor** (1817–1879). Hungarian born poet. His writing gave voice to the Hungarian people's struggle against the Austrian Empire, and is filled with despair over the state of Jewry and the world. Although he was baptized in 1843 he continued to be haunted by the fate of the Jewish people. After the failure of the Hungarian uprising in 1848, in which he was deeply involved, he renounced his radical activities and made peace with the Austrian government.

Bedersi, Abraham ben Isaac (c. 1230–c. 1300). French Hebrew poet. He lived most of his life in Perpignan. His poems and satires contain numerous historical details and provide an insight into the contemporary cultural scene. His *Ḥotam Tokhnit* was the first dictionary of Hebrew synonyms in the Bible.

Bedersi, Jedaiah [Jedaiah ha-Penini] (c. 1270–c. 1340). French philosopher and poet. He lived in Perpignan and Barcelona. His *Examination of the World* is an ethical work stressing the worthlessness of the world and indicating the way to attain eternal happiness. Among his poems is the prayer *Eleph Alaphim,* each word of which begins with the letter aleph. His *Apologetic Letter* addressed to Solomon ben Adret vindicates philosophical studies.

Bedikah ("examination"). Word used in connection with various kinds of inspection. It is applied especially to the examination of a slaughtered animal to ensure that it was not suffering from a serious disease.

Beelzebub *see* BAAL ZEBUB.

Be'er, Haim (b. 1945). Israeli poet and novelist. He served in the chaplaincy corps of the Israeli army. He published poems and short stories from an early age. His collection of poems *Shashuim Yom-Yom* (Day to day delights) portrays a religious upbringing in Jerusalem in the early years of the State of Israel. His novel *Notzot* (Feathers) depicts the memories of an Orthodox boy from Jerusalem who, as a soldier, served in a burial unit at the Suez Canal. *Et Hazamir* (The time of trimming) is a political satire about the religious nationalist movement.

Beer-Hofmann, Richard (1866–1945). Austrian poet and playwright. Born in Vienna, he emigrated to New York in 1939 after the Nazi occupation of Austria. Much of his work deals with Jewish themes. In a trilogy of biblical plays he sought to restate in modern terms the Hebraic position on fundamental questions of human existence.

Beersheba. City in the Negev, southern Israel. In biblical times it was the southernmost administrative and religious center of Palestine. It was settled by repatriated Jews after the return from Babylon. (Nehemiah 11.27, 31)

Be-ezrat ha-shem ("With the help of the name [of God]"). Expression of pious hope or trust, uttered or written at the beginning of letters.

Begin, Menaḥem (1913–1992). Israeli statesman. He was the leader of Betar in Poland. In 1942 he emigrated to Palestine and became commander of the Irgun Tzevai Leumi. From 1944 to 1948 he led the Irgun's underground war against the British. In 1948 he founded the Ḥerut party. He led the Likud party to victory in the general election of 1977 and became prime minister. His writings include *The Revolt* and *White Nights*.

Behab *see* MONDAYS AND THURSDAYS.

Behar, Nissim (1848–1931). Palestinian educator, the founder of modern Hebrew education in Palestine. He was born in Jerusalem. He organized schools in the Near East on behalf of the Alliance Israélite Universelle, and from 1882 to 1887 he directed their school in Jerusalem, where he introduced Hebrew as a spoken language. He later settled in the US and directed the National Liberal Immigration League from 1906 to 1924.

Behemoth. Creature depicted in Job 40.15–24. It ate grass, lived in a shady marsh, and could swallow the waters of the Jordan river.

Beilis, Menaḥem Mendel (1874–1934). He was the victim of a blood libel charge in Russia in 1911, having been accused of the ritual murder of a 12-year-old boy. In 1913 a trial was held and he was acquitted. This event was the subject of the novel *The Fixer* by Bernard Malamud.

Bein, Alex (b. 1903). German historian of Zionism. Born in Steinach, he served on the staff of the German State Archives from 1927 to 1933. In 1933 he settled in Palestine, where he became director of the General Zionist Archives. In 1956 he became state archivist of Israel. He published works on Zionism and anti-Semitism.

Bein ha-arbayim *see* TWILIGHT.

Bein ha-Mezarim *see* NINE DAYS; THREE WEEKS.

Bein ha-shemashot *see* TWILIGHT.

Bekhorot ("Firstlings"). Fourth tractate of the Mishnah order of Kodashim. It deals with laws relating to first-born animals and men.

Bekhor Shor, Joseph ben Isaac [Joseph Bekhor Shor] (fl. 12th cent.). French scholar. He lived at Orléans. His commentary on the Torah was based on a literal and rationalistic understanding of the text. He opposed the allegorization of the commandments, and the Christological interpretation of Scripture.

Bekiin *see* PEKIIN.

Bel. Babylonian deity. He was the chief god of the Babylonians.

Bel and The Dragon. Apocryphal book. It contains two stories about Daniel's exposure of the falsity of pagan cults. In *Bel* he reveals the footprints of the priests who secretly remove the sacrifices placed before the idol Bel. In *The Dragon* he causes the death of a dragon worshipped by the Babylonians by feeding it a mixture of pitch, fat, and hair.

Belial. Term denoting subversive individuals. In rabbinic and apocryphal literature it is often synonymous with Satan.

Beli en ha-ra ("without the evil eye"). Expression used to ward off the supposed ills resulting from praise or from the admission of good fortune. In Yiddish it is "kinanhora". *See also* EN HA-RA.

Belkin, Samuel (1911–1976). American rabbi and educator of Polish origin. He settled in the US in 1929. In 1943 he became president of the Rabbi Isaac Elchanan Theological Seminary and Yeshiva College. At Yeshiva he launched an extensive program of academic and physical expansion. In 1945 the college became Yeshiva University. He published studies on Philo, rabbinic literature, and traditional Jewish thought.

Belkind, Israel (1861–1929). Zionist leader of Belorussian origin. He was a leader of the first Bilu group to go to Palestine in 1882. He founded the first Hebrew school in Jaffa in 1889 and an agricultural school for orphans of the 1903 Kishinev pogroms. After World War I he established another agricultural school for orphans of the Ukrainian pogroms. He was the author of Hebrew, Yiddish, and Russian textbooks on Jewish subjects.

Bellow, Saul (b. 1915). American novelist. Born in Quebec, he lived in Montreal and Chicago. Many of his novels deal with Jewish life. *The Victim* (1947) is a treatment of anti-Semitism. *The Adventures of Augie March* (1953) deals with the experience of a Jewish boy from Chicago during the depression of the 1930s. And *Herzog* (1964) portrays a Jewish professor who attempts to relate humanistic values to the modern world.

Belsen *see* BERGEN-BELSEN.

***Belshazzar** (fl. ?6th cent. BCE). King of Babylon. According to the Book of Daniel he was the last king of Babylon. During a feast when vessels stolen from the Temple at Jerusalem were used, a mysterious hand wrote "Mene mene tekel upharsin" on a wall. Daniel interpreted this as prophesying the downfall of the kingdom. That night Belshazzar was killed. (Daniel 5)

Belteshazzar *see* DANIEL.

Belz. Town in eastern Galicia. From 1816 to 1856 Shalom ben Eleazar Rokeaḥ lived there and founded a Ḥasidic dynasty. He was succeeded by his son, Joshua, grandson Isachar Dov, great-grandson Aaron (who settled in Israel in 1944), and great-great-grandson Isachar Dov.

Bełżec. Polish village in the Lvov district. It was the site of a Nazi death camp.

Belzer [Spivak], **Nissan** (1824–1906). Ukrainian cantor. He was active in Belz, Kishinev and Berdichev. He was a leading ḥazzan and also wrote liturgical compositions.

Be-Midmar *see* NUMBERS (ii).

Ben ("son"). It occurs as a particle in many male personal names.

Benaiah ben Jehoiada (fl. 11th–10th cent. BCE). Israelite commander. He was one of David's warriors; after David's death he supported Solomon and became commander of his army. (I Kings 2)

Ben-Ammi [Rabinowicz, Mordecai] (1854–1932). Russian author. He became a maskil and organized Jewish defense in Odessa. He emigrated to Geneva and later settled in Palestine. His stories portray traditional Jewish life.

Benamozegh, Elijah (1822–1900). Italian rabbi and theologian. He was born in Livorno and served there as rabbi and professor of theology at the rabbinic school. In his writings he presented a systematic exposition of the doctrines of Judaism and defended the kabbalah.

Ben Asher, Aaron ben Moses (fl. first half of 10th cent.). Palestinian masoretic scholar. He lived in Tiberias. He produced a biblical manuscript incorporating vocalization and accentuation, which formed the basis for the accepted Hebrew text of the Bible. He also wrote grammatical works in the tradition of the scholars of Tiberias.

Ben-Avi, Ittamar (1882–1943). Palestinian Hebrew journalist. He initially wrote for Hebrew periodicals edited by his father, Eliezer Ben-Yehuda. During World War I he lived in the US, but later he returned to Palestine, where he founded the daily newspaper *Doar ha-Yom*. From 1924 he was editor of *The Palestine Weekly*.

Ben Avigdor [Shalkovitz, Leib; Shelkowitz, Abraham Leib] (1867–1921). Polish Hebrew writer and publisher. He lived in Warsaw, where he founded the series of small booklets called "Penny Books," which contained Hebrew belles-lettres. These introduced European literary trends into Hebrew literature. In 1893 he established the Aḥiasaph publishing company and later the Tushiyyah company, which published hundreds of Hebrew books. He founded the children's weekly *Olam Katan* in 1901, and the Aḥisepher publications in 1913.

Ben Azzai, Simeon (fl. early 2nd cent.). Palestinian rabbinic scholar. He lived in Tiberias. He was one of four sages who engaged in esoteric speculation (thereby entering Pardes); and according to tradition he was one of the ten martyrs who died during the Hadrianic persecutions.

***Bendemann, Eduard** (1811–1899). German painter. He was born in Berlin. He converted to Christianity in 1835 and later was appointed professor at the Academy of Fine Arts in Dresden. In 1859 he became director of the Academy in Düsseldorf. Some of his paintings depict biblical scenes.

Bender, A. P. (1863–1937). South African minister. He was the minister of the Cape Town Hebrew Congregation from 1895 to 1937. He inaugurated various educational, social, and cultural activities, and aided eastern European immigrants.

Bene Akiva ("Sons of Akiva"). Palestinian religious and pioneering movement. Founded in 1929, it affiliated with Ha-Poel ha-Mizraḥi. Its motto, "Torah and Labor," is well represented by the institutions of the yeshivah and the kibbutz.

Bene Berak. Ancient Palestinian city, north-east of Jaffa. It was the seat of Akiva's academy in the 1st–2nd centuries.

Bene Betera ("Sons of Bathyra"). Group of Palestinian scholars, active in the 1st century BCE. They were associated with the appointment of Hillel as president of the Sanhedrin.

Bene Binyamin ("Sons of Benjamin"). Palestinian farmers' association, active from 1921 to 1939. It promoted economic and cultural activities, as well as security and self-defense. Its motto is "To preserve the existing and to rebuild the destroyed." It was responsible for founding numerous agricultural settlements throughout Palestine.

***Benedict XIII** (fl. 14th–15th cent.). Spanish cleric and anti-pope. During his period in Avignon (1394–1411) he expressed hostility toward Jews and Judaism. In 1413 he presided over the Disputation of Tortosa. Subsequently he issued a bull condemning the Talmud and imposing restrictions on all aspects of Jewish life.

Benediction [blessing] (Hebrew "berakhah"). Formula of blessing or thanksgiving used in public and private services. Benedictions constitute a central part of synagogue and individual prayer. The phrase "Blessed art thou, o Lord" is incorporated into every benediction. The rabbis taught that a man should recite a hundred blessings daily. *See also* EIGHTEEN BENEDICTIONS.

Benedikt, Moritz (1849–1920). Austrian journalist. From 1881 he was editor of the *Neue Freie Presse* in Vienna. He was an anti-Zionist and would not allow Theodor Herzl to publish anything in support of Zionism in his newspaper.

Benei Adam *see* SON OF MAN.

Benei Elohim *see* SON OF GOD.

Bene Israel ("Sons of Israel"). Jewish community in India. Its members claim that their ancestors left Galilee because of the persecution under Antiochus IV Epiphanes in the 2nd century BCE. They retained many aspects of the Jewish tradition. Despite emigration to Israel, a small community of Jews still survives in India.

Bene Mosheh ("Sons of Moses"). An exclusive group of Ḥovevei Zion. It was founded in 1859 by Aḥad ha-Am and Joshua Barzilai because of dissatisfaction with the Zionist leadership. It established Hebrew schools and a publishing house in Warsaw. Its aim was to bring about a spiritual renaissance among the Jewish people and the return to Israel.

Benet, Mordecai (1753–1829). Bohemian rabbi and talmudist. In 1789 he was appointed chief rabbi of Moravia. He had a broad secular knowledge and was temperate in his attitude toward Reform Judaism and the Haskalah. He wrote several works of responsa.

Ben-Gurion, David (1886–1973). Israeli statesman and prime minister. Born in Poland, he joined the Zionist movement and settled in Palestine in 1906. He was among the labor leaders who founded the Aḥdut ha-Avodah party in 1919 and Mapai in 1930. From 1921 to 1935 he was general secretary of the Histadrut. He was chairman of the Zionist executive and the Jewish Agency executive from 1935 to 1948. In April 1948 he became head of the provisional government in which he served as prime minister and minister of defense. In 1956 he was responsible for the Sinai Operation. His writings include speeches, articles, and memoirs.

Ben-Hadad I (fl. 10th–9th cent. BCE). King of Aram (908–886 BCE). He was an ally of King Baasha of Israel until King Asa of Judah bribed him to attack the Northern Kingdom. (I Kings 15.16–21)

Ben-Hadad II (fl. mid-8th cent. BCE). King of Aram. He waged war against King Ahab of Israel, but was defeated and captured. He was later freed by Ahab, with whom he allied himself in the war against Shalmaneser III of Assyria. He subsequently defeated Ahab. (I Kings 22.1–40)

Ben-Hadad III (fl. late 9th–early 8th cent. BCE). King of Aram. He was defeated by King Jehoash of Israel, who recaptured the towns previously ceded to Aram. (II Kings 13.25)

Ben-Haim, Paul (1897–1984). Israeli composer. Born in Munich, he settled in Tel Aviv in 1933. He helped to create the eastern Mediterranean school of composition. His compositions evoke the pastoral atmosphere of the Israeli countryside and the youthful spirit of the people. They include *Hymn from the Desert, Sweet Psalmist of Israel, Liturgical Cantata, Vision of a Prophet, Three Psalms,* and *Kabbalat Shabbat.*

Benjacob, Isaac Eisik (1801–1863). Lithuanian Hebrew author and bibliographer. He lived in Vilnius. He published an edition of the Bible incorporating Moses Mendelssohn's German translation. His *Otzar ha-Sepharim* lists and describes about 8500 Hebrew manuscripts and 6500 Hebrew books.

Benjamin (i) (fl. ?19th–16th cent. BCE). Israelite, youngest son of Jacob. The tribe of Benjamin occupied territory between Ephraim and Judah, which included Jerusalem.

Benjamin (ii) [Israel ben Joseph Benjamin] (1818–1864). Romanian explorer and writer. He journeyed in the Near East, Asia, north Africa, and North America. He attempted to discover the Ten Lost Tribes of Israel and published an account of his travels. His *Drei Jahre in Amerika* is the first comprehensive account of Jewish communities in the US.

Benjamin, Judah Philip (1811–1884). American lawyer and statesman. He was born in the Virgin Islands. He was elected to the US Senate in 1852. In 1861 he became attorney-general of the Confederate government and he later served as secretary of state until the collapse of the Confederacy. After the Civil War he settled in England, where he had a distinguished career as a barrister.

Benjamin ben Moses Nahavendi [Nahavendi, Benjamin] (fl. 9th cent.). Persian Karaite scholar. He lived in Nahavend in Persia, where he established a community that observed Karaite principles and methods of biblical study. He was the first Karaite author to write in Hebrew, and was responsible for the use of the name "Karaites" to designate the members of the sect (in place of the former "Ananites").

Benjamin of Tudela (fl. second half of 12th cent.). Spanish traveler. A resident of Tudela, he set out on his travels in about 1167 and returned in 1172 or 1173. He visited France, Italy, Greece, Syria, Palestine, Iraq, the Persian Gulf, Egypt, and Sicily. His *Book of Travels* is an important source for Jewish history of the period.

Ben Kalba Sabbua (fl. 1st cent.). Israelite, citizen of Jerusalem. He was active during the Roman conquest in 70. According to the Talmud, he possessed sufficient grain to feed Jerusalem for several years, but this was destroyed by the Zealots.

Ben Koziba *see* BAR KOKHBA, SIMEON.

Ben Naphtali, Moses ben David (fl. 10th cent.). Palestinian masoretic scholar. He lived in Tiberias. Like his contemporary Aaron ben Moses Ben Asher, he edited the punctuation and accentuation of the Hebrew Bible. His version differs only in small details in about 850 instances from Ben Asher's text.

Ben-Ner, Yitzḥak (b. 1937). Israeli writer. He was born in Kfar Yehoshua. His novel *Eretz Rehokah* (A distant land) contrasts an idyllic portrayal of New Zealand with contemporary Israeli life. His other writings include *Shekiah Kafrit* (Rustic sunset) and *Protokol.*

Bensew, Judah Löb *see* BEN-ZEEV, JUDAH LÖB.

Bensh (Yiddish: "Bless"). Expression used in saying grace after meals or blessing children. It is also used in connection with the prayer for the new moon, the benediction recited by a person who has had a perilous escape, and the kindling of Sabbath and festival lights.

Ben Sira [Jesus ben Sira] (fl. 2nd cent.

BCE). Palestinian sage. He lived in Jerusalem. He was the author of the apocryphal book known as Ecclesiasticus or The Wisdom of Ben Sira.

Ben Sira, Alphabet of. Medieval work containing folklore, proverbs, and aphorisms arranged alphabetically. It recounts the story of the life, adventures, and teaching of Ben Sira.

Ben Solomon, Menaḥem *see* ALROY, DAVID.

Bentov, Mordekhai (b. 1900). Israeli politician. Born in Poland, he settled in Palestine in 1920. He was editor of the Mapam daily from 1943 to 1948. In the 1948 provisional government he served as minister of labor and reconstruction. He sat in the Knesset as a member for Mapam from 1949 to 1965, then from 1966 to 1969 he was minister of housing. He published books and articles on politics and economics.

Ben-Tzevi, Yitzḥak *see* BEN-ZVI, YITZḤAK.

Benveniste, Abraham (1406–1454). Spanish rabbi. He was rabbi to the court in Castile and financial agent to John II of Aragon. In 1432 he was appointed chief justice and tax superintendent of Castilian Jewry. In the same year he convened a synod at Valladolid which encouraged Jewish education, the correct administration of Jewish courts, and equitable tax apportionment.

Benveniste, Ḥayyim ben Israel (1603–1673). Turkish rabbinic codifier. He was born in Constantinople and served as a rabbi in Smyrna. He was opposed to the Sabbetaian movement. His *Keneset ha-Gedolah* is a guide to the halakhah embodying decisions made after the completion of the Shulḥan Arukh.

Benveniste, Immanuel (fl. 17th cent.). Netherlands printer of Hebrew texts. Active in Amsterdam, he printed the Midrash Rabbah, Mishnah, Alfasi's *Halakhot,* and the Talmud.

Ben-Yehudah [Perelmann], **Eliezer** (1858–1922). Hebrew writer and lexicographer of Lithuanian origin. He went to Paris in 1878 to study medicine and in 1879 he published articles encouraging Jewish settlement in Palestine. In 1881 he emigrated to Jerusalem, where he edited Hebrew journals. He advocated the acceptance of Hebrew as a spoken language and in 1890 founded the Hebrew Language Council of which he was chairman. He wrote a comprehensive dictionary of ancient and modern Hebrew (*see* DICTIONARIES, HEBREW).

Ben-Zeev [Bensew], **Judah Löb** (1764–1811). Polish Hebrew grammarian. Born in Poland, he lived in Berlin, Breslau, Kraków, and Vienna. His writings included a Hebrew grammar, a biblical lexicon, and an introduction to the Bible, as well as Hebrew poetry.

Ben-Zion, Simḥah [Gutmann, Simḥah Alter] (1870–1932). Hebrew author. He was born in Bessarabia and settled in Palestine in 1905. He wrote short stories as well as novels, and translated German classics into Hebrew.

Ben-Zvi [Ben-Tzevi], **Yitzḥak** [Shimshelevitz, Yitzḥak] (1884–1963). Israeli statesman. Born in the Ukraine, he was one of the pioneers of the Poale Zion movement in Russia. In 1907 he settled in Palestine, where he was active in the Jewish defense movement. He was a founder of the Aḥdut ha-Avodah party in 1919, of Histadrut in 1921, and of Mapai in 1930. He succeeded Chaim Weizmann as president of the state in 1952. His wife, Rachel Yanait (1886–1979), was involved with the Palestinian labor movement, Jewish self-defense, and agricultural training for women.

Berab, Jacob (1474–1546). Talmudist of Spanish origin. He lived in north Africa before settling in Safed. He initiated a plan to reintroduce ordination (semikhah) in order to establish an authoritative Jewish leadership and reconstitute the Sanhedrin. This project was opposed by Levi ibn Ḥaviv. A controversy ensued and the plan failed.

Berakhah *see* BENEDICTION; THANKSGIVING.

Berakhah Aḥaronah ("Last blessing"). The shorter form of Grace after Meals. It is recited after eating food other than bread prepared from the five primary grains, after drinking wine, and after eating food characteristic of Israel. (Deuteronomy 8.8)

Berakhot ("Blessings"). First tractate of the Mishnah order of Zeraim ("Seeds"). It consists of nine chapters dealing with blessings and prayer in general.

Berdichev. City in the Ukraine. In the 18th and 19th centuries it was an important Jewish center. In the latter part of the 18th century it was a focus of Ḥasidic life and in the following century it became a center of Haskalah.

Berdichevsky [Bin-Gorion]**, Micah Joseph** (1865–1921). Ukrainian Hebrew writer. He lived in Breslau and Berlin. In his writings he attacked the limited scope of Hebrew literature, the inadequacy of Haskalah, the ideology of Aḥad ha-Am, and Ḥibbat Zion. Influenced by Nietzsche, he called for a reevaluation of Judaism and Jewish history and the expansion of the canons of Hebrew literary taste. His fiction depicts Jewish towns of eastern Europe at the end of the 19th century and the life of eastern European Jewish students in the cities of central and western Europe.

Berechiah (fl. 4th cent.). Palestinian amora. His aggidic sayings are found mostly in the midrashim and the Jerusalem Talmud. In his homilies he stressed the virtues of charity and the uniqueness of the Jewish people.

Berechiah ben Natronai ha-Nakdan (fl. 12th–13th cent.). French translator and writer. He lived in Normandy and England. His *Fox Fables* were collected largely from non-Jewish sources. He translated into Hebrew the *Quaestiones naturales* of Abelard of Bath and wrote ethical treatises. He has been identified with Benedictus le Puncteur, who lived in Oxford at the end of the 12th century.

Berechiah of Nicole (d. 1278). English financier and scholar. In 1255 he was arrested in connection with the murder of Hugh of Lincoln, but was later released.

Berenice I (fl. late 1st cent. BCE). Judean woman, daughter of Salome. She married her cousin Aristobulus. After his death she married Theudion, brother-in-law of Herod the Great. She was the mother of Herod Agrippa I and Herodias.

Berenice II (b. 28). Judean woman, eldest daughter of Herod Agrippa I. She married her uncle Herod of Chalcis. After his death in 48 she was suspected of incest with her brother Herod Agrippa II and was induced to marry Polemon II of Cilicia. In 60 she rejoined Herod Agrippa and supported his efforts to suppress the revolt against Rome. She fled with him to the protection of the Romans and became the mistress of Titus. Because of the adverse reaction of the Roman populace, she was forced to part from Titus.

Bererah ("choosing"). In rabbinic law a term used of a situation in which the facts or legal implications of a case will become known only at a future time. According to the Talmud, there are two types of bererah: in the first the condition of doubt is due to an individual but the situation is certain; in the second the situation itself is uncertain. In the first category the outcome may depend either on the individual or on the intention or action of others.

Bereshit *see* GENESIS.

Bereshit Rabbah *see* GENESIS RABBAH.

Bereshit Rabbati. Midrash on Genesis. Composed by Moses ha-Darshan of Narbonne in the 11th century, it was quoted by Raymund Martini as *Midrash Bereshit Rabbah Major* in the 13th century.

Bergelson, David (1884–1952). Ukrainian writer. He initially wrote in Russian and Hebrew but later published Yiddish novels, plays, and stories. His works depict Russian Jewish urban life in the early 20th century. After living in Berlin for 11 years, he returned to the USSR, where he published realistic novels with a pro-communist emphasis.

Bergen-Belsen. Nazi concentration camp near Hanover. It was established in July 1943.

Bergman, George (1900–1979). Australian historian and biographer. He was born in Germany, where he worked as a lawyer. In 1933 he went to France and he served in the Foreign Legion in World War II. After moving to Australia he entered the public service and wrote about Australian Jewish history. He was the co-author of *Australian Genesis: Jewish Convicts and Settlers.*

Bergmann, Samuel Hugo (1883–1975). Czech philosopher. He was born in Prague. He was active in the Czech Zionist movement and in 1920 he settled in Palestine. He directed the National and University Library in Jerusalem and from 1928 he taught philosophy at the Hebrew University, where he was rector from 1936 to 1938. His writings include *Faith and Reason: an Introduction to Modern Jewish Thought* and *Philosophy of Solomon Maimon.*

Bergner, Herz (1907–1970). Australian Yiddish novelist. He emigrated from Galicia to Australia in 1938 and settled in Melbourne. From 1928 he published Yiddish short stories in Europe, Israel, Australia, and the US. His later novels and short stories deal with Jewish immigrants in Australia.

Bergner, Yosl (b. 1920). Israeli painter. Born in Vienna, he grew up in Warsaw. In 1937 he emigrated to Australia and in 1951 settled in Israel. His paintings depict the emotional world of early Russian settlers in Palestine.

Berit Ivrit Olamit ("World Hebrew Union"). International movement to promote spoken Hebrew and Hebrew culture. It was founded in 1931 in Berlin and held world congresses in Jerusalem in 1950 and 1955. Its publications include *Am va-Sepher* and *Megillat ha-Sepher.*

Berit Shalom ("Peace Covenant"). Society founded in 1926 to promote peace between Arabs and Jews in Palestine. It was founded by Arthur Ruppin and recommended an Arab–Jewish state based on equal rights. It was replaced by Iḥud in 1940.

Berkovits, Berel (b. 1949). English rabbi. He was born in London. He became the executive administrator of the London bet din. His publications include *Commentary of Ramban on Torah* and *Pesach in the Modern Home.*

Berkovits, Eliezer (b. 1900). American rabbi of Transylvanian origin. He served as a rabbi in Berlin, Leeds, and Sydney. He later settled in the US, where he was chairman of the department of Jewish philosophy at the Hebrew Theological College in Chicago. His writings include studies of religious faith after the Holocaust.

Berkovitz, Yitzḥak Dov (1885–1967). Hebrew and Yiddish author and translator of Belorussian origin. He lived in the US and settled in Palestine in 1928. His early writing deals with Jewish life in eastern Europe and Jewish immigrants in the US. His later work includes *Menakhem Mendel beretz Yisrael* and *Yemot Hamashiah.* He translated from Yiddish into Hebrew the writings of Sholem Aleichem.

Berkowitz, Henry (1857–1924). American Reform rabbi. He served as a rabbi in Philadelphia from 1892 to 1921. He founded the Jewish Chautauqua Society in 1893.

Berl, Emmanuel (1892–1976). French journalist. He was born in Paris. He published novels, essays, and pamphlets, and after World War II he wrote essays about the State of Israel. Influenced by the work of Gershom Scholem, he also resumed his pre-war studies of mysticism.

Berl Broder *see* BRODER, BERL.

Berlin. City in Germany. Jews settled there at the end of the 13th century but the Jewish community was dispersed in 1510. Settlement recommenced at the end of the 17th century. The period of the Enlightenment was ushered in there by Moses Mendelssohn in the 18th century. In the 19th century it became a major center of Reform Judaism.

Berlin, Sir **Isaiah** (b. 1909). English philosopher of Latvian origin. From 1957 he was professor of social and political theory at Oxford University and wrote widely on philosophical and political subjects. He supported Israel and Zionism. He also served as a governor of the Hebrew University.

Berlin, Isaiah ben Judah Loeb [Pick, Isaiah] (1725–1799). German talmudist. He was born in Hungary and lived in Berlin and Breslau. He wrote on a wide range of rabbinic literature. His emendations have been added to editions of the Talmud since 1800.

Berlin, Meir *see* BAR-ILAN, MEIR.

Berlin, Naphtali Tzevi Judah [Ha-Natziv] (1817–1893). Lithuanian talmudist. He was born in Mir and was head of the yeshivah at Volozhin for 40 years. He was one of the first rabbis to support Zionism. His *Haamek Sheelah* concerns the *Sheiltot* of Aḥa of Shabḥa.

Berlin, Saul (1740–1794). German rabbi. He served as rabbi of Frankfurt an der Oder but later retired from the rabbinate and settled in Berlin. He wrote a volume of responsa containing radical views which he attributed to Asher ben Jehiel and his contemporaries.

Berliner, Abraham (1833–1915). German literary historian. Born in Posen, he taught Jewish history and literature at the Berlin Rabbinical Seminary. His publications include an edition of Rashi's commentary on the Pentateuch, studies of medieval Bible commentators, an edition of *Targum Onkelos,* studies of Jewish life in the Middle Ages, and a history of the Jewish community of Rome.

Berlin Rabbinical Seminary [Rabbinerseminar für das Orthodoxe Judentum]. Orthodox rabbinical institute, founded by Azriel Hildesheimer in 1873. It was closed in 1938 by the Nazis.

Berlinski, Herman (b. 1910). American composer, conductor, and organist. Born in Leipzig, he emigrated to the US in 1946. He held positions at Temple Emanuel in New York and the Washington Hebrew Congregation. He was also professor of comparative history of sacred music at the Catholic University of America. His compositions include *The Burning Bush* (1957), *Avodat Shabbat* (1958), and *Job* (1971).

Berman, Hannah (1883–1955). English novelist and translator of Lithuanian origin. She translated novels by Sholem Aleichem and I. A. Lisky as well as Yiddish short stories. She also wrote two novels in English, which describe Jewish life in Lithuania under the rule of Nicholas I.

Bermann, Issachar (fl. 17th–18th cent.). German actor. He was a pioneer of the Yiddish folk theater, founding a Yiddish drama group in Frankfurt am Main in 1708.

Bermant, Chaim (b. 1929). British writer of Polish origin. After settling in the UK, he worked as a schoolteacher, economist, television writer, and journalist. His writings include *Jericho Sleep Alone, Diary of an Old Man, Israel, Troubled Eden: an Anatomy of British Jewry, The Cousinhood: the Anglo-Jewish Gentry, Point of Arrival: a*

Study of London's East End, Coming Home, and *The Jews.*

Bermuda Conference. Anglo-American conference on refugees held in Bermuda in April 1943. Its primary concern was to consider methods of rescuing the victims of Nazi persecution.

Bernays, Isaac (1792–1849). German rabbi. He was born in Mainz and served as rabbi in Hamburg from 1821. In his struggle against Reform Judaism, he denounced the Reform prayerbook. His modern approach to Orthodoxy influenced his disciple Samson Raphael Hirsch.

Bernfeld, Simon (1860–1940). Galician scholar. He was appointed chief rabbi of Belgrade in 1886. In 1894 he settled in Berlin, where he wrote on Jewish history and philosophy.

Bernstein, Ignaz (1836–1909). Polish Yiddish folklorist. As a rich merchant of Warsaw, he traveled for 35 years through Europe, north Africa, and Palestine, collecting Yiddish proverbs, which he published in several volumes.

Bernstein, Leonard (1918–1990). American composer and conductor. He was born in Lawrence, Massachusetts. He became director and conductor of the New York Philharmonic. His many works on Jewish subjects include the symphonies *Jeremiah* and *Kaddish.*

Ber of Bolechov [Birkenthav, Ber] (1723–1805). Galician writer. As one of the first maskilim, he took part in a debate with the Frankists at Lvov in 1759. He wrote a polemic against the Sabbetaians and the Frankists. His memoirs are a major source for the study of the economic and cultural conditions of Galician Jews in this period.

Ber of Liubavich *see* LIUBAVICH.

Ber of Mezhirich *see* DOV BER OF MEZHIRICH.

Bershadski, Isaiah (1817–1908). Russian Hebrew novelist. He was born in Belorussia and lived in Russia. His novel *To No Purpose* (1899) depicts Jewish life in the Pale of Settlement, and *Against the Stream* describes the collapse of traditional Russian Jewish life.

Berthold, Paul *see* PAPPENHEIM, BERTHA.

Bertinoro, Obadiah of (c. 1450–1510). Italian scholar. In 1485 he went to Palestine and settled in Jerusalem, where he founded a yeshivah. He was recognized as the chief halakhic authority in Palestine and Egypt. His writings include a commentary on the Mishnah, in which he incorporated the explanations of the Talmud as well as medieval commentators.

Beruryah (fl. 2nd cent.). Palestinian scholar. She was the wife of Meir. She is the only woman in Talmudic literature whose views on legal matters were recognized by contemporary scholars.

Besamim ("spices"). They are used in the Havdalah ceremony at the end of the Sabbath.

Besht *see* BAAL SHEM TOV, ISRAEL BEN ELIEZER.

Be-siman tov ("in good omen"). Expression of congratulation. It is the Sephardic equivalent of "mazzal tov."

Bet. Second letter of the Hebrew alphabet. Its numerical value is 2.

Betar. Youth organization of the Zionist Revisionist Party, formed in Latvia in 1923 and spread to other countries. It played an important role in Zionist education, teaching Hebrew language and culture, and self-defense. Its members set up the National Workers Organization in Palestine, founded settlements, and held prominent positions in the Irgun Tzevai Leumi. It was led by Vladimir Jabotinsky until 1940 when Menaḥem Begin became its leader.

Bet din ("house of judgment"). Rabbinic law court. In the Temple period the Sanhedrin, which was made up of 70 or 71 scholars, decided on questions of religious law and approved judges. After the destruction of the Temple, the Sanhedrin became the central religious authority for all Jews. With the decline of Palestinian Jewry, the Sanhedrin was abolished and every Jewish community had a local court, which exercised authority over community matters. After Jewish Emancipation in the 19th century the authority of the bet din was limited to voluntary arbitration and ritual matters.

Bet ha-midrash *see* BET MIDRASH.

Bet ha-mikdash *see* SANCTUARY; TEMPLE (i).

Bet ḥayyim ("house of the living"). Term used of a cemetery.

Bethel. Ancient city of the Israelites near Jerusalem. Abraham erected an altar near the site (Genesis 12.8), and it was the scene of Jacob's dream (Genesis 28). After the conquest of Canaan, the Tabernacle and Ark were placed there (Judges 20.26–7). Its importance as a center of pilgrimage declined after Solomon built the Temple in Jerusalem. Jeroboam set up a shrine there with the image of a calf which was denounced by the prophets (I Kings 12.25–33). *See also* LUZ.

Bet Hillel and Bet Shammai. Two schools of sages during the 1st century. They differed in their decisions concerning more than 300 legal issues. Bet Shammai generally adopted a stricter interpretation. Rabbinic scholars subsequently accepted the majority of opinions of Bet Hillel.

Bethlehem. Town near Jerusalem. It was the birthplace of David and Jesus.

Bet midrash [bet ha-midrash] ("house of study"). Rabbinic school, where Jews gather for study, discussion, and prayer. In the second Temple period the Great Bet Midrash stood in the Temple hall. In the Talmud the term is used of an academy presided over by a legal scholar. Later most synagogues had a bet midrash.

Betrothal [engagement]. In Jewish law betrothal creates no matrimonial relationship, and either party may retract the promise of marriage; however, an aggrieved party can claim reimbursement for loss suffered and demand compensation. It is customary to draw up the terms of a betrothal in a document called the "tenaim," which specifies the penalties payable by the defaulting party.

Bet Shammai *see* BET HILLEL AND BET SHAMMAI.

Bettelheim, Bruno (1903–1990). American psychologist and educator. He was born in Vienna. In 1938 he was transported to the Dachau concentration camp and then to Buchenwald. In 1939 he was released and settled in the US. He was principal of the University of Chicago's Orthogenic School for children with severe psychological problems and professor of educational psychology at the University. His psychological theories were based on his experiences in the concentration camps. His *The Children of the Dream* is an analysis of the rearing of kibbutz children.

Bet Yoseph *see* CARO, JOSEPH.

Betzah ("Egg"). Seventh tractate of the Mishnah order of Moed. It deals with laws relating to festivals, and contains a list of differences of opinion between Bet Hillel and Bet Shammai.

Beur *see* MENDELSSOHN, MOSES.

Bezalel (fl. ?13th cent. BCE). Israelite craftsman who constructed and decorated the Ark of the Covenant. (Exodus 36.2)

Bezalel School of Arts and Crafts. Art school founded in Jerusalem by Boris Schatz in 1906. It initially concentrated on arts and crafts but later emphasized design.

Bezem, Naftali (b. 1924). Israeli artist. He was born in Essen, Germany, and went to Palestine in 1939. In 1947 he was a teacher of painting in the detention camps in Cyprus. A number of his works deal with biblical and Jewish themes. After the death of his son (caused by a booby trap) in Jerusalem, he worked in Paris, where he painted a series of pessimistic paintings.

Bialik, Ḥayyim Naḥman (1873–1934). Russian Hebrew poet, essayist, storywriter, and translator. He was born in Zhitomir and lived in Volozhin, Odessa, Korostyshev, Sosnowiec, and Warsaw. In 1924 he settled in Palestine. His poetry is infused with Jewish hopes, memories, and national aspirations; written in a simple lyric style, it uses Hebrew metrics and biblical parallelism. His essays trace the course of Jewish culture, the state of Hebrew literature, and the development of language and style. Together with Yehoshua Ḥana Ravnitzky he published *Sepher ha-Aggadah*, which classified midrashic material according to subject matter.

Bibago, Abraham ben Shemtov (fl. 15th cent.). Spanish philosopher and writer. He was born in Aragon and became head of the yeshivah in Zaragoza. He engaged in disputations with Christian scholars at the court of Juan II, King of Aragon. His *The Path of Faith* examines the principal tenets of Judaism. He also wrote commentaries on Aristotle's works.

Bible [Old Testament; Scripture]. The Hebrew Scriptures. It consists of 24 books, divided into three sections: Torah (Pentateuch), Neviim (Prophets), and Ketuvim (Hagiographa). The Torah contains Genesis, Exodus, Leviticus, Numbers, and Deuteronomy. The Prophetic books are subdivided into the Former Prophets (Joshua, Judges, I and II Samuel, and I and II Kings) and the Latter Prophets, which are further divided into the Major Prophets (Isaiah, Jeremiah, and Ezekiel) and the 12 Minor Prophets (Hosea, Joel, Amos, Obadiah, Jonah, Micah, Nahum, Habakkuk, Zephaniah, Haggai, Zechariah, and Malachi). The Hagiographa consists of Psalms, Proverbs, Job, the Song of Songs, Ruth, Lamentations, Ecclesiastes, Esther, Daniel, Ezra, Nehemiah, and I and II Chronicles. Early translations of the Bible are the Targum (Aramaic), Peshitta (Syriac), Septuagint (Greek), and Vulgate (Latin).

Bible, lost books of the. Works cited in the Bible which have not survived. The principal lost books are the *Book of the Wars of the Lord*; the *Book of Jashar*; the *Chronicles of the Kings of Israel* and the *Chronicles of the Kings of Judah*; the *Book of the Words of Solomon*; and the *Words of Iddo the Seer*.

Bible, translations of the. The Aramaic TARGUM was the earliest translation of the Hebrew Scriptures, followed by the Greek SEPTUAGINT in the 3rd century BCE. The Syriac translation, the PESHITTA, was made in the 2nd century CE and St. Jerome created the first Latin version, the VULGATE, in the 4th century. Saadyah Gaon translated the Bible into Arabic in the 10th century, and Spanish and Yiddish editions were produced from the 15th century onwards.

Bible commentaries. There are two basic types of commentary on the Bible: peshat (literal) and derash (homiletical). Biblical interpretation is regarded as falling into three periods: (1) before the age of the geonim (until the 6th century); (2) from the gaonic period to the Haskalah (6th–18th centuries); and (3) from the Haskalah to modern times. In the earliest period principles of exegesis were formulated by Hillel and later expanded by Ishmael. Commentators of the second period include Saadyah Gaon, Abraham ibn Ezra, Rashi, David Kimḥi, and Naḥmanides. Prominent among the commentators of the third period are Moses

Mendelssohn, Samuel David Luzzatto, and Abraham Kahana.

Biblical criticism. Critical study of the Hebrew Bible. Higher, or literary, criticism deals with questions of authorship, date of composition, style, and the literary aspects of Scripture. Lower, or textual, criticism is concerned with textual matters and attempts to establish the true wording of the Bible.

Bibliography. The study, listing, and description of books. Jewish bibliography makes two principal categories of works: Hebraica (works written or printed in Hebrew) and Judaica (works by or about Jews in other languages).

Bickerman, Elias J. (1897–1981). American historian. He was born in Kishinev in the Ukraine. He taught at the University of Berlin from 1929 to 1932, when he emigrated to France. He later settled in the US, where he taught at the New School for Social Research, the Jewish Theological Seminary, the University of Judaism in Los Angeles, and Columbia University. His published writings cover ancient history, law, religion, epigraphy, chronology, and the political history of the Hellenistic world.

Bikkure ha-Ittim ("First fruits of the times"). Title of a Hebrew literary and scientific annual, published in Vienna from 1821 to 1832. It served as a forum for Haskalah literature.

Bikkur ḥolim *see* SICK, VISITING THE.

Bikkurim (i) ("First fruits"). 11th and last tractate of the Mishnah order of Zeraim. It deals with the offering of the first fruits in the Temple (Exodus 23.19; Deuteronomy 26.1–11) and contains a description of the ceremony associated with it.

Bikkurim (ii) *see* HARVEST FESTIVALS.

Bilhah (fl. ?19th–16th cent. BCE). Israelite woman, concubine of Jacob. She was the mother of Dan and Naphtali. Rachel, whose servant she was, gave Bilhah to Jacob when she herself proved to be barren. (Genesis 30.18; 32.25–6)

Biltmore Program. Official policy adopted by the Zionist conference meeting at the Biltmore Hotel in New York in May 1942. It denounced the British White Paper of 1939 and demanded open immigration to Palestine and the founding of a Jewish commonwealth.

Bilu (Hebrew initials of Isaiah 2.5 "House of Jacob, come ye and let us go"). Russian Zionist youth group. It was formed in Khar'hov in 1882 in response to the pogroms of 1881 in southern Russia and pioneered the return to Israel. A small group of men and women from its ranks reached Jaffa in the summer of 1882. Its name is made up of the initial letters of the phrase "Bet Yaakov lekhu venelkhah."

Bimah ("elevated place"). Platform in the synagogue on which the reading desk stands. The Torah is read here. Alternative names are "almemar," or among Sephardi Jews "tebah."

Binder, A. W. (1895–1966). American composer. He was born in New York. He became instructor in Jewish music at the Jewish Institute of Religion in 1921 and music director at the Stephen Wise Free Synagogue the following year. In 1948 he was appointed professor of Jewish liturgical music at the Hebrew Union College–Jewish Institute of Religion. He wrote synagogue services and songs, Hebrew and Yiddish songs, cantatas, and oratorios, as well as chamber and orchestral music.

Binding of Isaac *see* AKEDAH.

Bin-Gorion, Micah Joseph *see* BERDICHEVSKY, MICAH JOSEPH.

Biographies. The Book of Nehemiah, Josephus' apologetic *Vita*, and hagiographic works are the only works of biography and autobiography produced in ancient times. The first true Jewish biography is of Saadyah Gaon by his two sons at the request of Ḥasdai ibn Shaprut. Biographical writing was almost unknown in medieval Hebrew literature, but after the Enlightenment biographical works began to make their appearance. In modern times biography has become a common genre of Jewish literature.

Birkat ha-Ḥammah *see* SUN, BLESSING OF THE.

Birkat ḥa-Ḥodesh *see* NEW MOON, BLESSING OF THE.

Birkat ha-Mazon *see* GRACE AFTER MEALS.

Birkat ha-Minim. 12th benediction of the Amidah; it is actually a curse concerning minim (heretics). Instituted by Gamaliel II, it was composed or copied from earlier sources by Samuel ha-Katan.

Birkenthav, Ber *see* BER OF BOLECHOV.

Birkot ha-Torah. Blessings recited before studying the law, and before and after being called to the public reading of the Torah. Special blessings are also recited before and after the reading of the Haphtarah and the reading of the *Scroll of Esther* on Purim.

Birnbaum, Eduard (1855–1920). Polish liturgical composer and cantor. He was born in Kraków and served as cantor in Beuthen and Königsberg. He composed liturgical works, catalogued synagogue melodies thematically, and collected references to music in rabbinic texts.

Birnbaum, Nathan [Acher, Mattathias] (1864–1937). Austrian political philosopher. He was born in Vienna. An advocate of Jewish nationalism, he cooperated with Theodor Herzl and served as general secretary of the World Zionist Organization. However, after the Third Zionist Congress in 1899 he became an opponent of the Zionist movement. He regarded cultural and political autonomy in the diaspora as the means of attaining Jewish national existence. He was a convenor of the conference at Czernowitz in 1908, which proclaimed Yiddish as a national language. Later he embraced Orthodoxy.

Birnbaum, S. A. (1891–1990). British paleographer and Yiddish philologist of Austrian origin. He was born in Vienna. He lectured in Yiddish at Hamburg University from 1922 to 1933, when he emigrated to England. He taught Yiddish and Hebrew paleography at the London School of Oriental Studies and the School of Slavonic and East European Studies. He wrote for Yiddish newspapers and journals and published works on Yiddish grammar. His major work is in the field of paleography.

Birobidjan. Autonomous region of the USSR in eastern Siberia. In 1928 the Soviet government allotted it for Jewish settlement and instituted Yiddish as an official language.

Birth *see* CHILDBIRTH.

Birth control. According to the midrash, this practice goes back to the wicked generations before the Flood. In Genesis birth control is referred to in connection with Onan who spilled his seed on the ground (Genesis 38.9–10). The Talmud and responsa deal with the subject in detail. Birth control methods may be used only by the wife; the highest preference is for oral contraceptives.

Birthright. In ancient Jewish law the privilege of the first-born son to lead the family and receive a double share of the inheritance. It was an ancient practice reflected in the Bible. Talmudic law provides for the disposal of property in accordance with parental preference, so that the biblical inheritance laws should not be applied. *See also* FIRST-BORN.

Biur *see* MENDELSSOHN, MOSES.

Biur Hametz ("Elimination of leaven"). Household ceremony at which all leaven is burnt on the morning before Passover begins. It follows the search for leaven the previous evening.

Black Death. Plague which killed a large

portion of the population of Europe in the 14th century. Jews were accused of causing the disease by poisoning wells, and were attacked throughout Europe.

Black Hundreds. Name given to the local branches of the Union of Russian People, an organization formed after 1905 to suppress the liberal movement in Russia. The Black Hundreds were anti-Semitic and were largely responsible for the pogroms of the succeeding years.

Black Jews. A number of black Jewish congregations exist in New York. Claiming descent from the Falashas, the main group was organized in 1930 by Wentworth A. Matthew.

Blank, Samuel Leib (1893–1962). American Hebrew novelist and author of short stories, of Ukrainian origin. He lived in Bessarabia and settled in the US in 1922. His writings depict Jewish farmers in Bessarabia, the pogroms in the Ukraine, and immigrant life in the US.

Blankfort, Michael (1907–1982). American novelist, playwright, and screenwriter. He was born in New York. He taught psychology at Bowdoin College and Princeton, and worked as a clinical psychologist. He subsequently was a freelance novelist, dramatist, and screenwriter. His novel *The Juggler* portrays the disturbance and eventual recovery of a Holocaust survivor in Israel. *Behold the Fire* deals with the Nili, a secret group of Palestinian Jews who served as spies for the British.

Blaser, Isaac ben Moses Solomon (1837–1907). Lithuanian rabbi and educator. He was born in Vilnius. A disciple of Israel Salanter, he served as rabbi in St. Petersburg and later settled in Kovno, Lithuania, where he headed the advanced talmudic academy. He helped to found the yeshivah of Slobodka. In 1904 he emigrated to Palestine and settled in Jerusalem. He made an important contribution to the Musar movement in his emphasis on acquiring piety by emotional meditation on works of musar.

Blasphemy. Insult directed against religious belief or sacred things. Speaking contemptuously of God is forbidden in the Bible and was punishable by death (Leviticus 24.10–23). This punishment was later replaced by excommunication. The Mishnah restricts the definition of blasphemy to cases in which the name of God is pronounced.

Blau, Amram (1894–1974). Palestinian religious leader. He was born in Jerusalem. He was a founder of the anti-Zionist Ḥevrat Ḥayyim and refused to recognize the State of Israel when it was established in 1948. When Ḥevrat Ḥayyim was reconstituted as the ultra-Orthodox sect Neturei Karta he became its leader. After his first wife's death he married a proselyte, Ruth Ben-David.

Blau, Lajos (1861–1936). Hungarian talmudist. He was a professor and director of the Jewish Theological Seminary of Budapest. He served as editor of the *Hungarian Jewish Review* and was a founder of the Hebrew Review *Ha-Tzopheh*. He wrote on Jewish history and literature.

Blemish. In Jewish law a physical or moral defect that disqualifies a person for the Temple service or an animal for sacrifice. Any of 12 physical defects debars a priest from performing his duties (Leviticus 21.16–23); rabbinic law extends this list to 142. Moral blemishes also render a priest unfit. Biblical law lists defects that make an animal unsuitable for sacrifice (Leviticus 22.20–25), and rabbinic law lists 73. An animal set aside for idolatrous worship is also forbidden.

Blessing *see* BENEDICTION.

Blessing of children. In the Bible importance is attached to parental blessing; however, the custom of blessing children on the Sabbath eve is a later innovation. The formulae used are "God make thee as Ephraim and Manasseh" for boys, and "God make thee as Sarah, Rebekah, Rachel, and Leah" for girls. This is followed by the Priestly Blessing. Both hands are placed on the head of the child while saying the blessing. Among the Sephardim the blessing is also given after the father or child has performed a religious duty in the synagogue. There are special formulae for specific occasions (such as the eve of the Day of Atonement).

Blessing of the New Moon *see* NEW MOON, BLESSING OF THE.

Bloch, Ernest (1830–1959). American composer of Swiss origin. He was professor of composition at the Geneva Conservatory. In 1917 he settled in the US, where he served as director of the San Francisco Conservatory of Music. His works include *Trois poèmes juifs* (1913), *Israel Symphony* (1912–16), the rhapsody *Shelomoh* (1915–16), and *Avodat ha-kodesh* (1930–33).

Bloch, Ernst (1885–1977). German philosopher. He was born in Ludwigshafen. He served as professor at Tübingen. His *Erbschaft dieser Zeit* criticizes the mentality that made possible the subduing of Germany by the Nazis. In other writings he criticized Theodor Herzl's concept of Zionism.

Bloch, Jean-Richard (1884–1947). French author. He was born in Paris. When the Germans occupied France, Bloch escaped to Moscow, but later returned. His writings deal with the place of Jewry in contemporary society. His novel *Lévy* (1911) concerns the effects of the Dreyfus case on a Jewish family in a provincial French town. In *& Co.* (1918) he describes a Jewish cloth merchant from Alsace, who moves to a small town in western France.

Bloch, Joseph Samuel (1850–1923). Austrian rabbi. He was born in Galicia. He served as a lecturer in the Vienna bet midrash. In 1882 he accused August Rohling of perjury for his allegation that Jews practiced ritual murder. Rohling sued Bloch, but later withdrew his suit. Bloch was a member of the Austrian parliament. In 1885 he established the Union of Austrian Jews to Combat Anti-Semitism. His *Israel and the Nations* (1922) is a defense of Judaism.

Blois. Town in central France. In 1171 it was the scene of the first charge to be brought against Jews in Europe for ritual murder. 31 Jews were found guilty and were burnt at the stake.

Blondes, David (fl. late 19th–early 20th cent.). Lithuanian barber. He was accused of wounding a girl in order to use her blood for ritual purposes. He was convicted of injurious intent and sentenced to prison. On appeal in 1902 he was acquitted of all charges.

Blood. In the Bible blood is spoken of as life itself (Leviticus 17.11, 14; Deuteronomy 12.23). The prohibition against consuming it is one of the seven laws given to Noah (Genesis 9.4); Jewish law prescribes that blood must be drained from a slaughtered animal before it is eaten. Blood was sprinkled on the altar during the Temple sacrifice as a symbol of atonement.

Blood avenger. One who takes revenge for the murder of a relative by killing the murderer. In the Bible, blood vengeance is permitted without punishment only in cases of accidental manslaughter; the slayer could seek asylum in any of the six Cities of Refuge (Deuteronomy 19.1–10). Intentional murder was to be punished by the regular processes of law (Exodus 21.12–14; Deuteronomy 19.11–13). The Talmud outlines various rules on the subject.

Blood libel [ritual murder libel]. Allegation that Jews murder non-Jews to obtain blood for Passover or other rituals. In Christian countries Jews were accused of murdering children at Easter to use their blood in the preparation of matzot or in the seder rites. This led to trials and massacres of Jews in the Middle Ages and the early modern period.

Bloom, Harold (b. 1930). American literary critic and editor. He was born in New York and taught at Yale. In his literary work he has been influenced by the kabbalah and by Martin Buber. His publications include *Kabbalah and Criticism, Poetry and Repression,* and *Agon: Towards a Theory of Revisionism.*

Bloom, Hyman (b. 1913). American painter. He was born in Bounoviski, Lithuania, and emigrated to the US in 1920. Following the Depression he was employed by the Federal Arts Project in Boston. Early in his career he painted works dealing with European Jewry and he later returned to themes of the synagogue and Jewish observance.

Bloomgarden, Solomon [Jehoash; Yehoash] (1870–1927). American Yiddish poet and author of Lithuanian origin. He emigrated to the US in 1890. He wrote dramas, poems, fables, folktales, and stories, and translated the Bible into Yiddish. With C. D. Spivak he compiled a dictionary of Hebrew and Aramaic elements in the Yiddish language.

Blovstein, Rachel *see* RACHEL (ii).

Blue, Lionel (b. 1930). English rabbi and writer. He was born in London. He served as convener of the Reform bet din in London, and taught at Leo Baeck College. His publications include *To Heaven with Scribes and Pharisees, A Taste of Heaven, A Backdoor to Heaven, Simply Divine, Bolts from the Blue, Blue Heaven,* and *The Guide to the Here and Hereafter.*

Blum, Léon (1872–1950). French statesman. He first worked as a literary critic and author. He was premier in the Popular Front government of 1936–7, vice-premier from 1937–8, and premier in 1938. In 1943 he was handed over to the Germans, who deported him to Buchenwald, but he survived the war and was liberated in 1945. In 1946–7 he was head of an interim government and he became vice-premier in 1948. He was active in Jewish affairs and served on the council of the Jewish Agency.

Blumenfeld, Kurt Yehudah (1884–1963). German Zionist leader. He was born in Treuburg. He was one of the founders of Keren ha-Yesod and was president of the German Zionist Federation from 1923 to 1933. In that year he settled in Palestine and became a member of the Keren ha-Yesod directorate.

Blumenfeld, Simon (1907–1989). English novelist, journalist, and playwright. His novels include *Jew Boy, Phineas Kahn,* and *They Won't Let you Live.* Later he turned to journalism and drama. After the war he held various editorial jobs before working for the theatrical magazine *Stage.*

Blumenkranz, Bernhard (b. 1913). French historian. He lectured on the social history of the Jews at the École Pratique des Hautes Études in Paris and was president of the French Commission on Jewish Archives. His writings deal with Jewish–Christian relations in the Middle Ages and the history of the Jews in medieval France.

Blumenthal, Nissan (1805–1903). Ukrainian cantor. He was chief cantor at the Brody Synagogue in Odessa, where he founded a choir school to develop choral singing in four voices. He introduced melodies from German classical music into the liturgy.

B'nai B'rith ("Sons of the Covenant"). International Jewish service organization. It was founded in New York in 1843. Its aims are social, moral, educational, and philanthropic. During 1880–1920 it helped in the settlement and integration of immigrants to the US. A number of subsidiary sections have been formed: women's chapters were established in 1897, the Anti-Defamation League in 1913, the Hillel Foundation in 1923, youth organizations in 1924, the Vocational Service Bureau in 1938, and the Department of Adult Education in 1948. It has lodges and chapters in 45 countries.

Board of Delegates of American Israelites. American defense agency founded in 1859. It raised funds for the relief of persecuted Jews in Morocco, Tunisia, Persia, Italy, Russia, and Palestine. In the US it petitioned President Lincoln for support against General Ulysses S. Grant's order expelling Jews from occupied areas of the Confederacy. It was absorbed by the Union of American Hebrew Congregations in 1878.

Board of Deputies of British Jews. Representative body of British Jewry. It was formed in 1760. Membership was initially based on the synagogues of London and the provinces, but representatives of other communal organizations were later added. It aims to safeguard Jewish interests with regard to both religious practice and secular matters.

Boaz (i). Israelite landowner, husband of Ruth. When Ruth came to glean in his fields, Boaz saw and admired her devotion to her widowed mother-in-law Naomi. As a kinsman of Elimelech (Ruth's father-in-law), Boaz undertook to marry her. (Ruth, 2–4)

Boaz (ii) *see* JACHIN.

Bobemeise (Yiddish: "grandmother's tale," "incredible story"). The word is derived from the title of the chivalric romance that Elijah Levita adapted from *Buovo d'Antona* (the Italian version of *Sir Bevis of Hampton*); Levita's work appeared as *Bovo d'Antona* and was subsequently printed as *Bove-bukh.* In later editions it was titled *Bove-mayse.* The Yiddish word for grandmother ("bobe") led to the substitution of *Bobe-mayse* for *Bove-mayse.*

Bodek ("examiner"). Official who inspects a slaughtered animal to ensure that it is ritually acceptable. A licensed ritual slaughterer is referred to as "shoḥet u-vodek."

Bodo (fl. 9th cent.). French churchman, who converted to Judaism. Originally a deacon of the palace of Louis the Pious, he went to Spain in 838 and adopted Judaism under the name Eleazar. He engaged in religious debate with Paolo Alvarez of Córdoba, a Christian layman.

Body. The belief in the duality of body and soul is not found in Scripture. In rabbinic literature, however, the body is regarded as the seat of passion and the cause of sin, though both body and soul are accountable for misdeeds. The human body is viewed as the possession of God, of which human beings are simply custodians. At death the body must be kept inviolable; hence Orthodox Jews are opposed to cremation, dissection, embalming, or any other violation of the body's integrity. The doctrine of the resurrection of the body is a central aspect of rabbinic eschatology.

Boethusians. Jewish religious and political sect, active in the 1st century BCE. It was named after Boethus, a disciple of Antigonus of Sokho (or possibly after the high priest Simeon ben Boethus). Its adherents denied the belief in the resurrection and an after-life.

***Bogrov, Grigori** (1825–1885). Russian author. He wrote historical novels which were critical of Jewish leadership, and advocated reform. He was baptized before his death.

Böhm, Adolf (1873–1941). Bohemian Zionist historian and leader. He lived in Vienna, where he advocated practical work in Palestine. He wrote about Palestinian financial and agrarian problems, edited *Palästina,* the German monthly for Palestinography, and wrote a history of Zionism.

Bolechov, Ber of *see* BER OF BOLECHOV.

Bologna. City in northern Italy. It became a center for loan-bankers in the 14th century and in the 15th and 16th centuries sustained one of the most important Jewish communities in Italy. The Jews were expelled from Bologna in 1569.

***Bomberg, Daniel** (d. between 1533 and 1549). Hebrew printer. He was born in Antwerp. He founded a Hebrew publishing firm in Venice in 1516, which published about 200 books, including the first complete editions of the Palestinian and Babylonian Talmuds, the Tosephta, and the Rabbinic Bible. His pagination of the Talmud has become standard.

Bomberg, David (1890–1957). English painter. He was born in Birmingham and lived in the east end of London. A number of his paintings were influenced by scenes in the Whitechapel area. From 1923 to 1927 he lived in Palestine and later traveled widely. He returned to England and taught at the Borough Polytechnic in London from 1945 to 1953. His paintings include *Ghetto Theatre, The Talmudist,* and *Hear, O Israel.*

***Bonaparte, Napoleon** *see* NAPOLEON I.

Bonastruc de Porta *see* NAḤMANIDES.

Bonfils, Joseph ben Samuel [Tov Elem; Tuv Elem] (fl. 11th cent.). French talmudist. He was born in Narbonne and lived at Limoges and Anjou. He wrote religious poems, biblical and talmudic commentaries, and codifications of Jewish law.

Book of Creation *see* SEPHER YETZIRAH.

Book of Life. A book kept in Heaven, in which the names of the righteous are inscribed. The belief in the existence of heavenly ledgers is alluded to several times in the Bible. In the Mishnah, Akiva describes the heavenly book in which all human actions will be written down until the Day of Judgment; the same belief is expressed in the liturgy of the high holy days.

Bookplate. Label pasted into a book indicating its owner. Bookplates made by Christian Hebraists are known from the early 16th century. The earliest known bookplate made for a Jew was that of Isaac Mendes of London engraved by Benjamin Levi in 1746. In the 19th and 20th centuries Jewish bookplates often used Jewish symbols and motifs.

Books. Books were originally written in the form of a scroll, but under Roman influence the volume with leaves was adopted. Older Hebrew books were small, but in many cases larger volumes were created by binding a number together. In the Middle Ages illumination was common in Hebrew books such as the Passover Haggadah. In the early modern period Amsterdam and cities in Italy and eastern Europe became important centers for the production of Hebrew books.

Books, burning of. The attack on Jewish literature in the Middle Ages began with the Disputation of Paris in 1240; the Talmud was condemned and cartloads of Hebrew books were burned. Similar incidents took place in other cities. In 1553 thousands of volumes of Jewish literature were burned in Rome; this example was followed throughout Italy. In 1757 copies of the Talmud were burned in Poland after a disputation with the Frankists. On 10 May 1933 throughout Germany Nazis burned vast numbers of Jewish books.

Books, prohibited. The proscription of Jewish literature by the Roman Catholic Church began in the 13th century at the time of the Disputation of Barcelona. In 1564 the Council of Trent published the *Index librorum prohibitorum,* which listed, among other things, the Talmud and its glosses, annotations, interpretations, and expositions. In the Jewish community itself attempts were made to ban the writings of Maimonides (13th century), Immanuel ben Solomon of Rome (16th century), and Azariah dei Rossi (16th century).

Booth *see* TABERNACLE.

Boraisha, Menaḥem (1888–1949). American Yiddish poet of Polish origin. He emigrated to the US in 1914. His poem *Polyn* expresses the tense relationship between Jews and Poles. He published a number of collections, including *A ring in der keyt*, *Zamd*, a book of lyrics, one of which is on Theodor Herzl, and *Zavl rimer*, a rhymed chronicle exposing the horror of the post-war Russian pogroms. His *The Wayfarer* is a spiritual autobiography.

Borchardt [Hermann]**, Georg** (1871–1943). German author and art historian. He was born in Berlin and lived there until 1933, when he emigrated to Holland. After the Nazi invasion he was deported to Auschwitz, where he died. He published essays on fine art, sketches, novels and short stories. His fictional works portray cultivated Berlin Jews in the 19th century and modern Jewish intellectual life.

Borochov, Dov Ber (1881–1917). Ukrainian Socialist Zionist leader and writer. He was a founder of Poale Zion in 1906 and served as secretary of the World Confederation of Poale Zion. Having left Russia, he was from 1914 a spokesman for the American Poale Zion and for the World and American Jewish Congress movements. He later returned to the USSR. He analyzed the economic and social situation of the Jewish people along Marxist lines, and argued for their settlement in Palestine.

Borowitz, Eugene (b. 1924). American theologian. He was born in New York. He became a professor of education and Jewish religious thought at the Hebrew Union College–Jewish Institute of Religion in 1962. He is the author of numerous books about contemporary Jewish thought and has served as visiting professor at various universities, including Princeton, Columbia, and Harvard.

Boscovitch, Alexander Uriah (1907–1964). Israeli composer. He was born in Cluj, Transylvania, and conducted the Jewish Goldmark Orchestra there. In 1938 he settled in Palestine, and later became a music critic for the daily paper *Ha-Aretz*. He advocated the development of a nationalist school of composition in which the composer would represent the new reality of life in Palestine.

Bostanai ben Ḥanina (fl. 7th cent.). Babylonian exilarch. He was the first exilarch after the Arab conquest and his office was confirmed by the caliph Omar. He was appointed a member of the Council of State, and married a daughter of Chosroes, the former Persian king.

Botany. The study of plants. The Bible mentions about 100 types of plant. The Mishnah refers to 180 species in connection with various aspects of Jewish law. Maimonides presented a systematic classification of plants in his *Mishneh Torah*. In the Middle Ages Jewish scholars translated Greek studies of botany. The earliest scientific description of plants by a Jewish scholar is in the *Colloquies* by the 16th-century Marrano physician Garcia d'Orta.

***Brafman, Jacob** (c. 1825–1879). Russian scholar. He was born in Kletsk. He converted to Christianity, joining the Greek Orthodox Church, and served as teacher of Hebrew at the government theological seminary in Minsk. Later he was censor of Hebrew and Yiddish books in Vilnius and St. Petersburg. His *The Book of the Kahal* is a translation into Russian of the minutes of the kehillah of Minsk; it describes how Jews acquire power over gentiles and it was used to justify anti-Jewish acts.

Brahinski, Mani Leib *see* MANI LEIB.

Brainin, Reuben (1862–1939). American Hebrew and Yiddish author of Russian origin. He was born in Belorussia and lived for a time in Vienna and Berlin. At the beginning of the 20th century he encouraged the infusion of humanistic themes and new literary forms into Hebrew literature. From 1909 he lived in the US and Canada. During his later years he devoted himself to journalism, through which means he supported Jewish settlement in the Russian province of Birobidjan. He edited a number of Hebrew and Yiddish periodicals.

Bramson, Leon (1869–1941). Russian communal worker and writer. He was born in Kovno. He was active in the Society for the Dissemination of Enlightenment among the Jews, and served as director of the Jewish Colonization Association from 1899 to 1906. During World War I, the Russian Revolution, and the Civil War, he was an organizer of the Central Committee for the Relief of Jewish War Sufferers. When he left Russia in 1920 he worked in western Europe on behalf of ORT.

Brandeis, Louis Dembitz (1856–1941). American lawyer and Zionist leader. He was born in Louisville, Kentucky. He served as a justice in the Supreme Court from 1916 to 1939, its first Jewish member. He was active in American Zionism and the World Zionist Organization. Brandeis University was named after him.

Brandeis University. Non-sectarian, Jewish-sponsored university. It was founded in 1948 in Waltham, Massachusetts, and named in memory of Louis Dembitz Brandeis.

Brandes, Georg (1842–1927). Danish literary critic and writer. He was born in Copenhagen. He advocated the acceptance by Jews of the work of Ibsen, Björnsen, Strindberg, and Nietzsche. His writings include *Main Currents of Nineteenth-century Literature* and studies of Lassalle, Disraeli, Shakespeare, Goethe, Voltaire, Michelangelo, and Julius Caesar. Although he defended Dreyfus, he did not embrace Zionism until after World War I.

Brandstätter, Mordecai David (1844–1928). Galician Hebrew novelist. He was a successful manufacturer and owing to the circles in which he moved became interested in Haskalah. He contributed stories about Ḥasidic life in Galicia to the Hebrew journal *Ha-Shaḥar*. In his writing he ridiculed the Ḥasidim and the materialism of Galician Jewry. He later joined the Ḥibbat Zion movement and extolled Zionism in his stories.

Brann, Marcus (1849–1920). Polish historian. He was appointed successor to Heinrich Graetz at the Breslau Rabbinical Seminary. He wrote studies of Jewish history, literature, and bibliography, and served as co-editor of *Germania Judaica*, a topographical encyclopedia of German Jewish history.

Brasch, Rudolph (b. 1912). Australian rabbi, broadcaster, and author. He was born in Berlin. After holding pulpits in England, Ireland, and South Africa, he emigrated to Australia in 1949. He served as rabbi of the Liberal Synagogue in Sydney. His publications include *How did it Begin: Customs and Superstitions and their Romantic Origins*, *The Renegade in Rabbinic Literature*, *The Irish and the Jews*, *The Star of David*, *The Eternal Flame*, *The Judaic Heritage*, *Australian Jews of Today and the Part they have Played*, and *Thank God I'm an Atheist*.

Bratislava [Pressburg]. Czech city, capital of Slovakia. Jewish martyrs were recorded there in the 13th century and during the next two centuries Jews were serfs of the king. The Jews were expelled from the city in 1526 by Maria of Habsburg. From the 18th to the 20th centuries the community was a center of rabbinic learning.

Braudes, Reuben Asher (1851–1902). Lithuanian Hebrew novelist and reformer. He was born in Vilnius and lived in Odessa, Warsaw, and Lemberg, where he edited the monthly journal *Ha-Boker Or*. He later lived in Romania and Vienna. His novel *Two Extremes* depicts the limitations of Haskalah and Orthodoxy, and endorses Jewish nationalism. His writings, which advocate social and religious reform, reflect the intellectual changes taking place in eastern European Jewish society at the end of the 19th century.

Brauer, Erich (b. 1929). Austrian painter. He was born in Vienna. From 1938 to 1945 he was interned in a concentration camp. After the liberation he traveled extensively, and lived in Austria and Israel. His paintings depict crimes against the Jews, such as pogroms and the Holocaust.

Braunstein, Menaḥem Mendel [Mibashan] (1858–1944). Romanian Hebrew writer. He was one of the founders in Jassy of Doresh le-Zion, an organization which sought to revive the movement of Romanian Jews to Palestine. He edited the newspaper *Jüdischer Volksfreund* and taught Hebrew subjects in Jewish schools throughout Romania. He published a history of the Jewish people, as well as poems and stories for young people. He settled in Palestine in 1914.

Breach of trust. Biblical laws dealing with this topic relate to BAILMENT. A bailee suspected of misappropriating the property entrusted to him must take an oath that he has not "put his hand on his neighbor's goods" (Exodus 22.10). By analogy, others suspected of wrongdoing are obligated to take a similar oath. If a bailee falsely denies possession of the bailment and his deception is proved, he is rendered untrustworthy and is debarred thereafter from taking an oath or acting as a witness.

Bread. In the Bible and hence in Jewish life bread is regarded as the most important element of a meal. The blessing of bread takes precedence over that of any other solid food. The full Grace after Meals is recited only when bread has formed part of the meal.

Breaking of the Vessels. Kabbalistic term used to describe the primordial catastrophe that took place during creation. According to Isaac Luria, divine light emanated from Adam Kadmon into creation. It burst the vessels which were to contain it and many divine sparks fell and were captured by the realm of darkness. As a result, the cosmos is in need of repair ("tikkun") and restoration.

Breastplate. Sacred object worn by the high priest (Exodus 28.15ff). It consisted of a square gold frame in which were set 12 gems of different colors representing the tribes of Israel. It also held the Urim and Thummim. The term is now applied to the silver ornament placed in front of the cover of the Torah scroll in Ashkenazi congregations.

Brenner, Yoseph Ḥayyim (1881–1921). Hebrew author and editor of Ukrainian origin. He edited the *Bund* newspaper in Homel in 1898. His sketches of Jewish poverty in Russia appeared in 1900 and were followed by his novels *In Winter* and *Around the Point*. From 1904 to 1907 he lived in London, where he published the journal *Ha-Meorer,* which criticized Jewish political life. Later he lived in Lemberg, where he edited *Revivim*. In 1909 he settled in Palestine and became a leader of the workers' movement; his stories of this period describe contemporary Palestinian life. In 1919 he became the editor of the journal *Ha-Adamah.* He was murdered by Arabs.

Breslau Rabbinical Seminary [Jüdisch-Theologisches Seminar]. Founded in 1854, with funds left by Jonas Fränckel, it was the first rabbinical seminary in Germany; its first president was Zacharias Frankel. It was closed by the Nazis in 1938.

Breuer, Isaac (1883–1946). Leader of Orthodox Jewry, of Hungarian origin, son of Solomon Breuer. He lived in Frankfurt am Main, where he was active in Jewish organizations. When Agudat Israel was founded in 1912 he became one of its ideologists. He settled in Jerusalem in 1936 and he served as president of Poale Agudat Israel. He published works on Judaism and Jewish problems.

Breuer, Solomon (1850–1926). German rabbi. He served as rabbi in Frankfurt am Main and founded the Association of Orthodox Rabbis in Germany. He was president of the Free Union for the Advancement of Orthodoxy and co-founder of the Agudat Israel movement. In 1890 he founded and directed a yeshivah. With Phinehas Kohn he published the periodical *Jüdische Monatshefte* from 1913 to 1920.

Bribery. Bribery is condemned in the Bible and Talmud, where it is considered particularly in relation to judges. A judge is disqualified from adjudicating in a case if he receives a favor. When judges were given a salary, they were paid a year in advance to discourage the accepting of bribes. However, the Talmud regards the bribery of non-Jewish rulers, officials, and judges as legitimate in view of their prejudice against Jews.

Bridegroom of Genesis *see* SIMḤAT TORAH.

Bridegroom of the Law *see* SIMḤAT TORAH.

Brigade, Jewish *see* JEWISH BRIGADE.

Brill, Jehiel (1836–1886). Hebrew journalist of Russian origin. He settled in Palestine, where he edited the journal *Ha-Levanon* in 1863–4; the periodical reappeared under his editorship in Paris in 1865, and later in Mainz from 1872 to 1882. It supported Jewish law and the Jerusalem rabbis, and attacked Haskalah and religious reform. After the Russian pogroms of 1881, Brill returned to Palestine and helped to found the colony of Ekron. As a result of a dispute he left the country and settled in London, where he founded the Yiddish newspaper *Ha-Shulamit.* He also published editions of several medieval texts.

Brill, Joel ben Judah Loeb *see* LOEWE, JOEL BEN JUDAH LOEB.

Brill, Joseph [Iyyov of Minsk] (1839–1914). Russian Hebrew author. He was born in Gorki. He published critical essays as well as satirical feuilletons and parodies modeled on midrashic and talmudic texts.

Bris [brit milah] *see* CIRCUMCISION.

Broche (Yiddish: "blessing"). A prayer of thanksgiving or praise.

Brod, Max (1884–1968). Austrian author and composer. He was born in Prague. He was a founder of the National Council of Jews of Czechoslovakia and became active in the Zionist movement. In 1939 he settled in Tel Aviv, where he worked as a music critic and drama adviser to the Ha-Bimah theater. His writings include a trilogy of historical novels, a story of the Israeli War of Independence, and studies of Judaism. He was the discoverer and biographer of Franz Kafka, whose works he edited. His musical compositions include *Requiem Hebraïcum* and Israeli dances.

Broder [Margulies], **Berl** (1815–1868). Galician composer. He organized the first troupe of professional Yiddish folk singers; they toured Galicia, Hungary and Romania in the 1860s and sang many of his songs.

Broderson, Moses (1890–1956). Russian Yiddish poet and theater director. He was born in Moscow and lived in Łódź from 1918 to 1938. He was a journalist, poet, and writer of songs for children. He founded a number of small theaters and wrote modest plays and librettos for operas. He was confined to a Siberian labor camp from 1948 to 1955; his wife, Sheyne Miriam Broderson, described their years of misery in *My Tragic Road with Moshe Broderson.*

Brodetsky, Selig (1888–1954). British mathematician and Zionist leader, of Ukrainian origin. He was professor of mathematics at the University of Leeds from 1920 to 1949 and served as president of the Board of Deputies of British Jews from 1939 to 1949. In that year he became president of the Hebrew University, but he returned to England in 1952.

Brodie, Sir **Israel** (1895–1979). English rabbi. He was born in Newcastle upon Tyne. He served as senior minister in Melbourne, Australia, from 1923 to 1937. After several years as a senior chaplain in the British Army (1944–8) he was appointed chief rabbi of the British Commonwealth and continued in that office until 1965.

Brodski, Iosif [Joseph] **Aleksandrovich** (b. 1940). Russian poet. After having been arrested several times, he left the USSR in 1972, and settled in the US. His publications include the poem *Isaak i Avraam,* which deals with the sacrifice of Isaac. He also wrote a poem about the Jewish cemetery near Leningrad.

Brody, Heinrich (1868–1942). Hebrew scholar of Hungarian origin. He was appointed chief rabbi of Prague in 1912. He settled in Palestine in 1933 and was appointed head of the Schocken Institute for Hebrew Poetry. He was co-founder and editor of the *Zeitschrift für hebraïsche Bibliographie* and edited the poems of Judah ha-Levi, Moses ibn Ezra, and Immanuel of Rome.

Bródy, Sándor (1863–1924). Hungarian novelist and playwright. He prepared the ground for the development of Hungarian prose in the 20th century. A number of his stories and plays introduce Jewish characters: his collection of short stories *Misery* was the first work of Hungarian literature to describe the Jewish worker, and his play *Timár Liza* portrayed the decadence of assimilated Jews in Hungary.

Brokerage. The function of an intermediary acting for another in a legal transaction. According to Jewish law, the broker acts as an agent. Since he is paid for his services, he is liable for the loss or theft of the property of the person retaining him, and for personal negligence. In cases of dispute, the broker may clear himself by taking an oath if there are no witnesses and he insists that he was authorized to accept the terms realized. The marriage broker ("shadḥan") acts as a go-between in arranging marriages.

Broner, Esther (b. 1930). American novelist, playwright, and essayist. She was born in Detroit, and taught at Wayne State University and Sarah Lawrence College. Her novels include *Her Mothers, Unafraid Women,* and *A Weave of Women.* She is also the co-author with Naomi Nimrod of *A Woman's Passover Haggadah.*

Brooks, Mel (b. 1926). American film director, writer, and actor. He was born in New York, and first worked as a comedian in the Borscht Belt of New York's Catskill Mountain resorts. Later he was one of a team of comedy writers for *The Sid Caesar Show* and *Your Show of Shows.* He also wrote, directed, produced, and acted in a number of films. He is one of those comic writers and performers who see humor as a traditional Jewish response to adversity and a way of effacing anger.

Brown, Saul *see* PARDO, SAUL.

Bruggen, Carry van (1881–1932). Dutch novelist and philosopher. She was born in Smilde near Amsterdam. She displayed an ambivalent and occasionally antagonistic attitude to Jewish tradition and nationalism. Her novels include *The Little Jew*.

Brüll, Nehemiah (1843–1891). German scholar. He was rabbi of the Reform synagogue in Frankfurt am Main from 1870. He founded and edited the journal *Jahrbücher für jüdische Geschichte und Literatur*, in which he published Jewish studies.

Brunner, Constantin [Wertheimer, Leopold] (1862–1937). German philosopher. He lived in Potsdam until 1933, and then emigrated to the Netherlands. His philosophy was influenced by Plato and Spinoza. As part of his theory of society he opposed Zionism and argued for the assimilation of the Jews.

Brussels. Capital of Belgium. Jews lived in Brussels from the 13th century. The community suffered during the Black Death in 1348 and in 1370 a massacre took place when the Jews were accused of desecrating the host in a Brussels church. The community was reconstituted in the 19th century when it became the administrative center of Belgian Jewry.

Bubbe (Yiddish). Term of endearment.

Buber, Martin (1878–1965). Austrian theologian, grandson of Solomon Buber. He was born in Vienna. He joined the Zionist movement and became editor of *Die Welt* in 1901. He founded the Jewish National Council in Berlin during World War I and in 1916 established the monthly journal *Der Jude*. With Franz Rosenzweig he translated the Bible into German. From 1924 to 1933 he taught at the University of Frankfurt am Main and then became head of the Jüdisches Lehrhaus in Frankfurt. He settled in Palestine in 1938 and became professor of social philosophy at the Hebrew University. His writings include *I and Thou*, *For the Sake of Heaven*, *Between Man and Man*, *Tales of the Ḥasidim*, *The Prophetic Faith*, and *Two Types of Faith*.

Buber, Solomon (1827–1906). Galician rabbinic scholar. He was born in Lemberg and was a governor of the Austro-Hungarian Bank and the Galician Savings Bank. He published scholarly editions of midrashim, edited works by medieval scholars, and wrote on the history of the Jews in Poland.

Bubkes (Yiddish). Something trivial, worthless, absurd, or foolish.

Bublick, Gedaliah (1875–1948). American Yiddish journalist and Zionist leader. He was born in Russia. In 1900 he helped to lead a group of 50 Jewish families to Argentina. He settled in New York in 1904, where he became editor of the Yiddish *Jewish Daily News*. He was a founder of the American Jewish Congress and served as president of the Mizraḥi Organization of America from 1928 to 1932.

Buchenwald. Town in Germany near Weimar. In 1937 the Nazis established a concentration camp there to provide labor for factories in central Germany.

Büchler, Adolf (1867–1939). Historian and theologian of Hungarian origin. He became principal of Jews College in London in 1907. His writings include studies of the second Temple period, rabbinic literature of the 1st century, and the history of the synagogue.

Budapest. Capital of Hungary. Jews settled there in the 12th century, but were expelled during the Black Death in 1348. From the 15th century the Jewish community in the city grew in importance. A Jewish congregation was established there in 1821 and a rabbinical seminary in 1877. The Jewish population flourished during the early 20th century.

Budko, Yoseph (1888–1940). Polish painter and graphic artist. He was born in Płońsk then lived in Berlin from 1910 to 1933, when he settled in Jerusalem. He served as director of the Bezalel School of Arts from 1935. His work was influenced by eastern European Jewish life and scenes in Jerusalem.

Bul *see* MARHESHVAN.

Bulan (fl. 8th cent.). King of the Khazars. After a religious debate in Khazaria on the merits of Christianity, Islam, and Judaism, he and his servants converted to Judaism.

Bund. Jewish socialist party. It was founded in Vilnius in 1897. Its first branches were nearly all in Poland and Lithuania, but it soon spread to Jewish centers in Russia. It functioned as a trade union and political party. Though outlawed in czarist Russia, it became part of the Russian Socialist Party when the branches of that body were officially recognized. The influence of Bund increased after the revolution of 1905, and similar parties emerged in Galicia, Romania, and the US. A world federation of socialist parties under the name Bund was established in 1947.

Bunin, Ḥayyim Isaac (1875–1943). Belorussian author and teacher. He settled in Warsaw in 1929. A follower of the Ḥabad movement, he published studies of Ḥabad Ḥasidism. His *Mishneh Ḥabad* describes Ḥabad doctrines and applies them to modern life.

Burglary. In Scripture house-breaking by night is regarded as a more serious offence than ordinary theft since danger to life is assumed to be involved (Exodus 22.1). The houseowner is exonerated if he kills a thief who breaks in at night, but not if the burglary takes place during the day. The Talmud states that the burglar must restore the stolen article or its equivalent without an additional fine.

Burial. In ancient times the dead were buried in earthen graves or caves cut in rock. Whenever possible burial took place on the day of death. Bodies were sometimes dressed in costly garments, but later it became standard practice to bury the dead in a plain linen garment. Coffins consisted of a simple wooden casket. Eventually the Ḥevra kaddisha ("holy brotherhood") was organized in every Jewish community to provide for the rites of burial; its members help to read the deathbed confession ("viddui"), wash and dress the corpse, carry out the burial service and actual burial, and provide the special meal for the mourners.

Burla, Yehudah (1886–1969). Israeli novelist. He was born in Jerusalem. He became head of the Arab Department of the Histadrut, an envoy of Karen Hayesod to Latin American countries, and director of Arab affairs in the Israeli Ministry of Minorities. He wrote stories and novels depicting the life of the Middle Eastern Sephardim.

Burning Bush. The desert shrub from which God appeared to Moses at the foot of Mount Horeb. The bush was aflame but was not consumed. (Exodus 3.2–4)

Burning of books *see* BOOKS, BURNING OF.

Burnt offering *see* SACRIFICE.

Buttenwieser, Moses (1862–1939). American biblical scholar of German origin. He became professor of biblical exegesis at the Hebrew Union College in 1897. He wrote studies of the Prophets, Psalms, and Job.

Buxtorf, Johannes (i) (1564–1629). Swiss Hebraist. He was professor of Hebrew at the University of Basle. He edited *Biblia Hebraica Rabbinica* (the Hebrew Bible with rabbinic commentaries) and compiled the *Bibliotheca Rabbinica* (a rabbinic bibliography). He also wrote a Hebrew grammar and a Hebrew and Aramaic lexicon (*see* DICTIONARIES, HEBREW).

Buxtorf, Johannes (ii) (1599–1664). Swiss Hebraist, son of Johannes Buxtorf (i). He was professor of Hebrew and biblical exegesis at the University of Basle.

He wrote studies of the Hebrew alphabet and Hebrew pronunciation, and translated Maimonides' *Guide for the Perplexed* and Judah ha-Levi's *Kuzari* into Latin.

Byzantine rite. Liturgical rite of the Jews of the eastern Roman Empire. It was contained in the *Maḥzor Romania,* which was printed in the 16th and 17th centuries. Eventually it was superseded in Turkey and the Balkans by the Sephardi rite.

C

***Caballeria, Pedro** [Bonafos] **de la** (c. 1450). Spanish financial official. He lived and worked in Aragon. He converted to Christianity and wrote the anti-Jewish work *Zelus Christi adversus Judaeos.*

Caceres, Abraham (fl. 18th cent.). Dutch composer of Portuguese origin. He was the leading musician of the Portuguese community of Amsterdam. In 1726 he provided music for the consecration of the Ḥonen Dal synagogue in The Hague.

Caceres, Francisco [Joseph] **de** (b. c. 1580). Spanish Marrano writer. After leaving Spain, he lived in France and Amsterdam. His writings include *Nuevos fieros españoles, Dialogos satýricos,* and *Visión deleytable y sumario de todas las sciencias.*

Caceres, Jacob de *see* CACERES, SIMON DE.

Caceres, Joseph de *see* CACERES, FRANCISCO DE.

Caceres, Samuel de (1628–1660). Dutch scholar. He was the spiritual leader of the Jewish community in Amsterdam. He edited and revised a Spanish translation of the Bible.

Caceres, Simon [Jacob] **de** (d. 1704). English merchant. He was born in Amsterdam and settled in London before 1656. He lived openly as a Jew and urged Marranos in London to practice Judaism. He advised Cromwell during the conquest of Jamaica. He was one of the signatories of a petition organized by the Jews of London requesting freedom of worship, and he helped with the acquisition of the first congregational cemetery in 1657.

Caesarea. Ancient city on the Mediterranean coast of Israel. It was a flourishing port in the Hellenistic period. Herod the Great received it from Augustus and transformed it into a large city with a safe harbor; he called it Caesarea in the emperor's honor. When Judea became a Roman province, Caesarea was its capital. Vespasian made it a Roman colony. It had a large Jewish community in the 3rd–4th centuries.

Caftan *see* KAFTAN.

Cagoudards ("Hooded Men"). French secret anti-Semitic organization. It was uncovered in 1937. It aimed at overthrowing the Republic and establishing a dictatorship.

Cahan, Abraham (1860–1951). American Yiddish journalist and author. He was born in Lithuania and settled in the US in 1882. He organized the first Jewish tailors' union and founded Yiddish periodicals to propagate his theories of socialism and Americanization. From 1897 he was editor-in-chief of the Yiddish newspaper the *Forverts.* His novel *The Rise of David Levinsky* portrays the urban immigrant experience in America.

Cahan, Israel Meir *see* ḤAPHETZ ḤAYYIM.

Cahan [Cohen], **Yaakov** (1881–1961). Hebrew author of Russian origin. He taught at the Institute for Jewish Studies in Warsaw from 1927 to 1933. The following year he settled in Palestine. He wrote lyrics, ballads, epic poems, folk stories, and novels. Many of his poems and ballads were influenced by Jewish folklore.

Caiaphas, Joseph (fl. 1st cent.). High priest. Appointed by the procurator Valerius Gratus, he also served under Pontius Pilate. The New Testament portrays him as largely responsible for the prosecution of Jesus (Matthew 26).

Cain. Eldest son of Adam and Eve. When God accepted the animal sacrifice of Abel his brother but rejected his offering, Cain killed Abel (Genesis 4).

Cairo. Capital of modern Egypt. Jews lived in Old Cairo (Fostat) from the period of the Arab invasions in the 1st century. The city was the most important center of Egyptian Jewry. It served as the seat of the local exilarchs in the 11th–12th centuries and later of the nagid.

Caleb (fl. ?19th–16th cent. BCE). Israelite, one of the 12 spies sent to explore Canaan. He and Joshua were the only two spies to bring back a favorable report; as a result Caleb was allowed to enter the Promised Land. He captured Hebron and expelled its inhabitants, the Anakim. (Numbers 13–14; Joshua 14–15)

Calendar (Hebrew "luaḥ"). The Jewish calendar consists of 12 months, calculated according to the lunar cycle. The months are Nisan, Iyyar, Sivan, Tammuz, Av, Elul, Tishri, Marheshvan (Ḥeshvan), Kislev, Tevet, Shevat, and Adar. In a leap year there are two months of Adar. The numbering of years in the Jewish calendar is calculated from the creation of the world, which coincides with 3760 BCE. The year 5000 began on 1 September 1239. To calculate the Jewish year since 1240, 1240 should be deducted from the year of the Common Era (CE) and 5000 added. For dates in September–December another year is added.

Calendar, reform of the. The irregularity of the Gregorian calendar has led to a movement to reform it: a year of 364 days would be kept; a "blank" day every year (two "blank" days in a leap year) would not be reckoned part of any week. This change would cause the Sabbath to fall on different days of the week every year. The American League for Safeguarding the Fixity of the Sabbath is a Jewish organization which has taken action opposing this change.

Calf, Golden *see* GOLDEN CALF.

Calf worship. Calves or young bulls were regarded as symbols of strength and fertility by ancient Semitic peoples. Traces of calf worship are found in the account of the Golden Calf (Exodus 32) and the golden calves set up at Dan and Bethel by Jeroboam (I Kings 12.28–30).

***Caligula** (fl. 1st cent.). Roman emperor (37–41). He gave Herod Agrippa I the tetrarchy of north-east Palestine and the title of king. Caligula's insistence on being worshipped as a deity scandalized the Jewish community and their reaction led to anti-Jewish disturbances in Alexandria. Philo led a delegation of Alexandrian Jews sent to intercede with the emperor for protection.

Calisher, Hortense (b. 1911). American writer of short stories and novels. She was born in New York. Her numerous publications include *The Rabbi's Daughter*.

Calo, Maestro *see* KALONYMOS BEN KALONYMOS.

Camps *see* CONCENTRATION CAMPS; DETENTION CAMPS; IMMIGRANT CAMPS.

Canaan [Promised Land]. The land promised by God to the Israelites (Genesis 17.8; Exodus 6.4). The name is used variously in the Bible to refer either to an extensive area comprising all of Palestine and Syria, or simply to the strip of land along the eastern shore of the Mediterranean. Before the Israelite invasion, Canaan was divided into small city states, each of which was under the rule of a king.

Canaan, Mount. Mountain north-east of Safed in Upper Galilee; it is more than 3250 feet high.

Canaanites. A group of ancient peoples, inhabitants of the land of Canaan. According to tradition they were the descendants of Canaan, son of Ham. They occupied the area between the Nile and the Euphrates (Genesis 10.15–19) and appear to have been a mixture of Horites, Hittites, and Hebrews, originating in the Hyksos period. They were either eliminated or assimilated by the Israelites, Philistines, and Arameans.

Canadian Jewish Congress. Representative body of Canadian Jewry. It was founded in 1919 to assist eastern European Jewry, and was reorganized in 1934 to combat Nazism. It serves to safeguard the rights and welfare of Jews in Canada and throughout the world.

Candelabrum *see* MENORAH.

Candles. In Jewish practice the lighting of candles characterizes both joyful and sorrowful occasions. As a symbol of joy it is a feature of the Sabbath and of feast days; this custom was instituted by the Pharisees during the period of the second Temple. The lighting of candles on these occasions (accompanied by the appropriate blessing) is the prerogative of the principal woman in the household. Candles are also placed by the head of a deceased person, and are used during the week of mourning for the dead, on the anniversary of a death, and on the eve of the Day of Atonement.

Canetti, Elias (b. 1905). Austrian novelist, essayist, and dramatist. He was born in Ruse in Bulgaria. He was a freelance writer and translator and in 1938 he went to London, where he settled. His works include *Auto da Fé, Crowds and Power, The Tongue Set Free, the Torch in my Ear,* and *The Play of the Eyes*. In 1981 he received the Nobel Prize for Literature.

Canopy *see* ḤUPPAH.

Cantarini, Isaac Cohen (1644–1723). Italian rabbi and physician. He lived in Padua and his *Pahad Yitzḥak* describes the anti-Jewish outbreaks in the city in 1684. His *Vindex Sanguinis* is a refutation of the blood libel charge.

Cantillation. Musical or semi-musical chanting of a liturgical text in the Jewish synagogue tradition; *see* ACCENTS; CANTOR; ḤAZZAN.

Cantonists. Name given to conscripts between the ages of 12 and 18 in czarist Russia. The system of conscription was in force from 1805 to 1856 and Jews became subject to it from 1827. Many Jewish boys were conscripted with the intention of converting them to Christianity. From the age of 18 military service for Jewish males lasted for 25 years. Jewish communal leaders who were responsible for selecting recruits frequently filled their quota with children from poor homes; they were trained outside the Pale of Settlement and sent to distant lands.

Cantor (Hebrew "ḥazzan"). In Jewish worship the synagogue official who leads the worshippers in prayer and is in charge of the music. In the ancient Temple the liturgy was intoned by priests and Levites. In the synagogue service a prominent member of the community conducted the prayers. During the Middle Ages more complex music, known as "cantorial" music (ḥazzanut), came into fashion, and the office of cantor was established. Further musical developments in the 18th century had an impact on cantors, who studied musical composition and instrumental playing. In the 19th and 20th centuries outstanding cantors included Joseph Rosenblatt, Zavel Kwartin, Mordecai Hershman, David Roitman, Aryeh Leib Rutman, Mosheh Kusevitsky, and Leib Glanz.

Capernaum (Hebrew "Kephar Naḥum"). Ancient village in Palestine on the north-west shore of the Sea of Galilee. In the New Testament it is mentioned as the place of residence chosen by Jesus on the shore of the lake (Matthew 4.13; 9.1). He preached there and at least five of his disciples were fishermen from the village. A Judeo-Christian community continued there into talmudic times.

Caphtor. Place of origin of the Philistines (Genesis 10.14) before they penetrated southern Palestine. It is generally thought to have been Crete.

***Capistrano, John of** (1386–1456). Italian Franciscan monk. He was one of the preachers who inspired anti-Jewish feeling in Sicily, Italy, and central Europe in the middle of the 15th century. He was responsible for the burning of Jews in Breslau in 1453.

Capital punishment. The death penalty was decreed by biblical law for murder, sexual crimes (such as adultery and incest), blasphemy, idolatry, desecration of the Sabbath, witchcraft, kidnapping, and dishonor of parents. According to talmudic law, it may not be carried out unless two eye-witnesses testify to the crime; in addition, the perpetrator must have previously been warned concerning the crime and its punishment. The Bible specifies three types of capital punishment: stoning, burning, and hanging. Rabbinic law also specifies slaying by the sword and strangulation. Capital punishment was rarely imposed under Jewish law and many rabbis advocated its abolition. In the diaspora Jews were subject to the laws and punishments of the lands in which they lived, and particular forms of execution were inflicted on them because of their race and faith. In the Middle Ages they were frequently executed by being hung by the heels; it was also common practice to exacerbate the punishment by stringing up dogs on either side of the condemned person.

Cappadocia. Ancient province of Asia Minor. It was under Roman rule from the 1st century BCE. Jews are first mentioned there in the 2nd century BCE. They were in close contact with Palestine and a number moved there to settle in Jaffa, Sepphoris, and Tiberias.

Capsali, Elijah (1483–1555). Cretan rabbi and historian. He was head of the Jewish community in Crete. His *Seder Eliyahu Zuta* contains a survey of the history of Jewry in the Ottoman Empire down to his day, as well as an amount of Spanish Jewish history. His *Divrei ha-Yamim le-Malkhut Venezia* depicts the condition of the Jews in Venice and the Venetian dominions; it is a central source for the social, cultural, and political history of north Italian Jewry in the early 16th century.

Capsali, Moses (1420–1496/1497). Turkish rabbi. He was born in Crete. He served as a rabbi in Constantinople under Byzantine rule. After the conquest of the city by the Turks in 1453, he was the most important rabbi in the Ottoman Empire and became the spiritual and communal leader in the city.

Captives *see* RANSOM.

***Caracalla, Marcus Antoninus Aurelius** (fl. 3rd cent.). Roman emperor (211–17). Like his father, Septimus Severus, he favored the Jewish community. He has been identified with Antoninus, a friend of Judah ha-Nasi. He extended Roman citizenship to all free residents of the Roman Empire, including Jews.

Cardozo, Abraham (1626–1706). Spanish Marrano physician and mystic. He was born in Rio Seco. He became an adherent of Shabbetai Tzevi, supporting him even after his apostasy; he expounded Sabbetaian doctrines in a number of published works. His theology was based on gnostic dualism; he disparaged the value of the hidden First

Cause and placed supreme importance on the God of Israel.

Cardozo, Isaac (1604–1681). Portuguese Marrano physician and philosopher. He was physician at the Royal Court of Madrid. Persecuted by the Inquisition, he fled to Venice where he embraced Judaism; he later settled in Verona. In his *Philosophia Libera* he opposed the teachings of the kabbalah and Shabbetai Tzevi. His *Las excelencias y calumnias de los Hebreos* describes ten virtues of the Jewish people and refutes ten calumnies.

Caricatures. The earliest caricatures of Jews are Roman terracotta figures. An early example in modern times is found in an English Exchequer Roll of 1233. At the close of the Middle Ages caricatures were common in Germany and with the invention of printing they circulated in engraved form. In England the readmission controversy (1655–6) and the "Jew Bill" (1773) gave rise to a new wave of popularity and a similar effect was produced in France by the Dreyfus case. Anti-Jewish caricatures were widely circulated throughout the 19th century in Germany and reached a climax during the Nazi period.

Carigal, Raphael Ḥayyim Isaac (1733–1777). Palestinian rabbi and emissary. He was born in Hebron. He served as an emissary to Jewish communities in the Near East, Europe, and the US; there he became a friend of Ezra Stiles (later president of Yale University), with whom he maintained an extensive correspondence.

Carlebach, Azriel (1908–1956). Israeli journalist. He was born in Leipzig. He was secretary of the International Sabbath League. After serving as a foreign correspondent for several newspapers, he founded and edited *Maariv*, the most important Hebrew newspaper in Israel.

Carlebach, Joseph (1882–1942). German rabbi and educator. After teaching in Jerusalem, he founded a Hebrew high school in Kovno, Lithuania. He then succeeded his father, Solomon Carlebach, as rabbi of Lübeck. He became chief rabbi of Altona and later of Hamburg. He published commentaries on the Song of Songs, the Prophets, and Ecclesiastes, as well as a study of Levi ben Gershon.

Carmel, Mount. Mountain ridge in northwest Israel, running from the Samarian Hills to the Mediterranean. It was the site of Elijah's victory over the prophets of Baal (I Kings 18.19ff) and of his residence (II Kings 4.25).

Carmi, Tcharney (b. 1925). Israeli poet and literary historian. He was born in New York, but in 1946 he left the US for France, where he worked with Jewish war orphans. In 1947 he emigrated to Palestine. His publications include *There are No Black Flowers, Snow in Jerusalem,* and *At the Stone of Losses.* He edited the *Penguin Book of Hebrew Verse*, and was one of the editors of *The Modern Hebrew Poem Itself.* In addition he has translated numerous classic works into Hebrew.

Carmoly, Eliakim (1802–1875). German rabbi, writer, and editor. He was born in Alsace. He served as a rabbi in Brussels in 1832 and later settled in Frankfurt am Main, where he published articles about ancient manuscripts and books. His other publications include a work on the Ten Lost Tribes, descriptions of his travels in Palestine, a genealogy of the Rapoport family, and a coronation poem in praise of Louis-Philippe of France. He was a pioneer in the study of Jewish medicine and Jewish physicians.

Caro [Karo]**, Joseph** (1488–1575). Spanish talmudic codifier. He was born in Toledo, then settled in Turkey after the expulsion of the Jews from Spain in 1492. In 1536 he left Turkey for Safed, where he was the head of a large yeshivah. His *Bet Yoseph* (House of Joseph) is a commentary on Jacob ben Asher's *Arbaah Turim*. He also compiled its classical abbreviation, Shulḥan Arukh (The prepared table). His codes were criticized by Ashkenazi scholars, who claimed that they ignored French and German traditions. Nevertheless, the Shulḥan Arukh (printed with Moses Isserles' strictures) became the authoritative code for Orthodox Jewry.

Carpentras. French town about 14 miles north-east of Avignon. It was the principal Jewish community of the Comtat Venaissin, where Jews were allowed to reside after their expulsion from the rest of France in the 14th century.

Carrière des Juifs (French: "Jewish area"). Term applied in Avignon and the Comtat Venaissin to the ghetto. Local Jews referred to it by the Hebrew term "mesillah."

Carrion, Santob de (fl. 14th cent.). Spanish poet. His *Proverbios morales* is a collection of aphorisms dedicated to King Pedro of Castile. It is the principal work by a medieval Jew to enter Spanish literature. Santob de Carrion has been identified with the Hebrew poet Shem Tov ibn Ardutial.

Cartography. The science of map making. Cartography flourished in the Middle Ages in Majorca, where Abraham Cresques was "Master of Maps and Compasses" to the Infant Juan of Aragon. The work of Abraham Cresques and his son Judah included the Catalan Atlas. About 1500 Judah Abenzara of Alexandria and Safed produced important maps. The first Jewish map of Palestine with Hebrew lettering appeared in Amsterdam in the 17th century.

Carvajal, Antonio Fernandez (c. 1590–1659). Portuguese merchant. He settled first in the Canary Islands and later in Rouen. He eventually lived in London, where he engaged in trade with the East and West Indies. He organized a foreign information service for Oliver Cromwell. He was head of the crypto-Jewish community at the time that Manasseh ben Israel requested the readmission of the Jews to England (1655–6).

Casablanca. Port on the Atlantic coast of Morocco. Jews lived there from the 8th century. The city was destroyed by the Portuguese in 1468 and its Jewish community was dispersed. In 1750 the Rabbi Elijah Synagogue was built. In 1830 there was an influx of Jewish merchants from Mogador, Rabat, and Tetuán. The Alliance Israélite Universelle founded a school there in 1897. By 1912 it had become an important center for the Jews of Morocco.

***Casmir III** (1310–1370). King of Poland (1333–70). He welcomed Jewish refugees from Germany and extended the privileges enjoyed by Polish Jews. His mistress, Esterka, who bore him children, was the daughter of a Jewish tailor in Opoczno.

Caspi, Joseph ben Abba Mari (1280–c. 1340). French commentator, philosopher, and grammarian. He was born in L'Argentière and lived at Tarascon in southern France. He wrote commentaries on Maimonides' *Guide for the Perplexed.* As a follower of Aristotle and Averroes, he equated their teaching with Judaism. He evoked the opposition of many rabbis who regarded his views as heretical.

Cassel, David (1818–1893). German scholar. He was born in Silesia. He lectured at the Hochschule für die Wissenschaft des Judentums in Berlin. His publications include a history of Jewish literature, German translations of the Apocrypha and Judah ha-Levi's *Kuzari*, and critical editions of classical texts.

***Cassel, Paulus Stephanus** (1821–1892). German theologian and historian. After he converted to Christianity in 1855, he was librarian at the Royal Erfurt Library, and was elected as a conservative member to the Prussian

Landtag. From 1868 to 1891 he served as a researcher at the Christuskirche in Berlin and as a missionary for the London Society for Promoting Christianity among the Jews. His publications include an account of Jewish history based on non-Jewish sources, and studies of the Books of Judges, Ruth, and Esther, as well as the *Targum Sheni* to Esther.

Cassin, René (1887–1976). French statesman. He was born in Bayonne. He was professor of law at the universities of Lille and Paris, and French delegate to the League of Nations from 1924 to 1938. He served as National Commissioner for Justice and Education under De Gaulle (1941–3), head of the Conseil d'État (from 1944), and French delegate to the UN General Assembly (1946–51). He was awarded the Nobel Peace Prize in 1968. He also served as president of the Alliance Israélite Universelle.

***Cassius Dio** (c. 150–235). Roman historian. His narrative of the Jewish war of 66–70 complements Josephus' history. He also described the Jewish rebellions against Trajan and Hadrian.

Cassuto, Moses David [Umberto] (1883–1951). Italian biblical scholar. He was born in Florence and became chief rabbi there and director of the Collegio Rabbinico Italiano. He was professor of Hebrew at the University of Rome, and from 1939 professor of Bible at the Hebrew University. He was editor-in-chief of the *Biblical Encyclopaedia* and prepared the *Jerusalem Bible* for publication. His other publications include studies of Italian Jewish history and Immanuel of Rome, and catalogs of the Hebrew manuscripts in Florentine libraries.

Castel, Moshe (b. 1909). Israeli painter. He was born in Jerusalem. He was a member of the New Horizons group of Israeli painters. Judaism and Israel were dominant themes in his art. He produced a stained-glass window for the synagogue of the SS *Shalom* in 1956. His later paintings are reminiscent of ancient steles, in which writing is incorporated into the subject matter.

Castelnuovo-Tedesco, Mario (1895–1965). American composer of Italian origin. He was a member of an old Florentine family. He settled in Hollywood, where he wrote film music. In 1925 he found a notebook of Jewish melodies in his grandfather's house, which encouraged him to write Jewish compositions; his works on Jewish subjects include *La danza del Rè David, Tre corali su melodie ebraiche, The Prophets, Sacred Service, Ruth, Jonah, Naomi and Ruth,* and *Saul.*

Castration. According to Scripture, castrated animals were unfit to be used as sacrifices on the altar (Leviticus 22.24). Any man who was crushed or maimed in his private parts was not allowed to enter into the assembly of the Lord or to marry within the Jewish congregation (Deuteronomy 23.2). In the Talmud and the codes the prohibitions were extended to cover any man, domestic animal, beast, or bird whose reproductive organs were impaired, as well as any man who had been impotent and was then castrated.

Castro, Abraham de (fl. 16th cent.). Egyptian financial administrator. He was director of the mint in Cairo and supervisor of economic affairs in Egypt. When the Egyptian pasha (in revolt against Sultan Suleiman I) ordered Castro to issue a new coinage bearing his name, Castro refused. He escaped to Constantinople and informed the sultan of the pasha's rebellion; as a result the pasha was put to death. Egyptian Jews commemorate the date of the pasha's execution (28 Adar) as a feast day (Purim of Egypt).

Castro, Balthasar Orobio de (1620–1687). Spanish philosopher and physician. He was imprisoned and tortured by the Spanish Inquisition. He later went to Toulouse where he practiced Judaism. He wrote polemical works in Latin and Spanish, including a critique of Spinoza's writings.

Castro, Benedict Nehemias de (1597–1684). German physician of Portuguese origin. He practiced medicine in Hamburg from 1625, and in 1645 became physician to the Queen of Sweden. He served as president of the Portuguese congregation in Hamburg and was a follower of Shabbetai Tzevi.

Castro, David Henriques de (1832–1898). Dutch historian. He published a study of the Sephardi cemetery in Ouderkerk and a bicentennial history of the Amsterdam synagogue.

Castro, Jacob de (1758–1824). English comedian. He was born in London. He acted in traditional Purim plays and in 1786 joined Philip Astley's troupe known as "Astley's Jews." In 1803 he was appointed manager of the Royal Theatre, London. His *Memoirs* cast light on English Jewish life.

Castro, Moses de (fl. 16th cent.). Egyptian rabbi. He settled in Jerusalem in 1530. He opposed Jacob Berab's initiative to reintroduce Jewish ordination into Palestine.

Castro Tartas, Isaac de (c. 1625–1647). Portuguese Marrano martyr. He was the son of Portuguese New Christians (i.e., Jews converted to Christianity), who settled in Tartas in southern France. He lived in Amsterdam and Brazil before moving to Bahia. There he lived outwardly as a Catholic, but his pretense was detected and he was arrested. He was condemned and burned alive in Lisbon in 1647. He recited the Shema before he died, and his memory inspired many Marranos in the diaspora.

Catacombs. Subterranean tunnels with side recesses for tombs. The practice of burying the dead in catacombs originated with the Palestinian Jews. Catacombs are found in Rome, elsewhere in Italy, and in north Africa. They were also used by the early Christians in Rome.

Catechism. Instruction in religious doctrine by question and answer; a book containing such instruction. The first published Jewish catechism was Abraham Jagel's *Lekaḥ Tov*. During the period of Emancipation, many catechisms were published and occasioned religious controversy.

Catechumens, House of. Hostel in Rome for Jewish converts to Christianity. It was established in 1548 with the support of the Roman Jewish community. Similar institutions were founded in other Italian cities. The potential convert received instruction for 40 days; if he then refused baptism he was allowed to return to the ghetto.

***Catharine I** (1683–1727). Empress of Russia (1725–7). In May 1727 she expelled all Jews resident in Little Russia.

***Catharine II** (1729–1796). Empress of Russia (1762–96). Her Jewish policy was both lenient and coercive. Although Jews were allowed to register in the merchant and urban classes, permission to do so was restricted to Belorussia. This marked the beginning of the Pale of Settlement. During her last years Catharine prevented the extension of Jewish settlement and prohibited Jewish residence in rural areas.

Cattaui, Joseph Aslan (1861–1942). Egyptian politician, nephew of Moses Cattani. He was an official in the ministry of public works, directed a sugar factory, and set up other industrial plants. In 1915 he became a member of the Egyptian delegation to London to negotiate the independence of Egypt. In 1924 he was appointed minister of finance, and in the following year minister of communications. He served as a senator (1927–36) and as president of the Jewish community of Cairo.

Cattaui, Moses (1850–1924). Egyptian communal leader. He was president of the Jewish community of Cairo, and during the last year of his life was elected to the Egyptian parliament. He was decorated by the Egyptian and Austrian governments.

Cejtlin, Hillel *see* ZEITLIN, HILLEL.

Celan, Paul (1920–1970). German poet. He was born in Czernowitz and after the war lived in Bucharest, where he worked as a translator. In 1947 he escaped and went to Vienna and Paris, continuing to translate and also teaching languages. Several of his poems commemorate the victims of the Holocaust.

Celibacy *see* ASCETICISM.

Cemetery. In ancient times cemeteries consisted of a series of caves cut in rock; later the dead were buried in graves (*see* BURIAL). According to Jewish law, cemeteries are to be located far from human habitation. A special benediction is recited on entering a cemetery, and no priest may enter one. Buildings for discharging burial rites are usually attached. Graves are visited on anniversaries, fast days, and during the month preceding Rosh ha-Shanah.

Censorship. Censorship of Jewish literature began in the Middle Ages. After the Disputation of Paris in 1240 the Talmud was condemned and burned. As a result of the Disputation of Barcelona in 1263 Jews were ordered to delete references to Jesus from Maimonides' *Code.* A papal bull of 1554 specified that works other than the Talmud could be owned by Jews only if they contained no blasphemies against Christianity. Subsequently in most of Italy Hebrew books could not be kept unless they had been approved by a Christian censor. The Jewish Synod at Ferrara instituted a form of pre-censorship in 1554 to ensure that nothing objectionable was published. Similar censorship existed in the Austrian dominions in the 17th and 18th centuries, and in Russia after 1790.

Census. The Bible discourages the counting of the population. Nonetheless the first census of the Jewish people took place at Mount Sinai following the Exodus from Egypt (Exodus 38). Another census was conducted at Shittim in Moab before the Israelites entered the Promised Land (Numbers 26). The last census mentioned in the Bible took place at the close of David's reign (II Samuel 24). Estimates of the Jewish population since biblical times have generally been speculative, but they have become more reliable in recent years.

Central British Fund for Jewish Relief and Rehabilitation. Charitable organization. It was founded in 1933 as the Central British Fund for German Jewry. It was the main British Jewish organization for the relief of refugees from Nazi persecution.

Central Conference of American Rabbis. Reform rabbinic association. It was founded in 1889 by Isaac Mayer Wise as the successor of the Reform rabbinic councils of Germany in the 1840s, and similar groups in Philadelphia (1869) and Pittsburgh (1885). Its membership is composed of more than 900 rabbis, mostly from the US and Canada, but also from Argentina, Australia, Brazil, Curaçao, France, Guatemala, Israel, Netherlands, South Africa, the UK, and the Virgin Islands. It is involved in social action, church and state relations, interfaith activities, the military chaplaincy, and religious education. It publishes its own prayerbook, as well as the *Journal of Reform Judaism.*

Central Sephardic Jewish Community of America, Inc. Sephardic organization in Greater New York. It was founded in 1941 by Nissim Ovadia, who was succeeded by Isaac Alcalay. It has established cultural and religious centers, Talmud Torahs, and a home for the aged.

Central-Verein Deutscher Staatsbürger Jüdischen Glaubens ("Central Union of German Citizens of the Jewish Faith"). German organization founded in Berlin in 1893. It aimed to combat anti-Semitism, protect Jewish civic and social status, unite all Jews, and foster German patriotism. To further its purposes it established the publishing house Philo Verlag. In 1935 it changed its name to Central-Verein der Juden in Deutschland. It was dissolved by the Nazis in 1938.

Central Yiddish Culture Organization [CYCO]. American cultural organization, founded in 1935 in New York. It coordinates the cultural activities of the Workman's Circle, the Jewish National Worker's Alliance, the Yiddish Writers Union, and other groups. It took over the *Yiddish Encyclopaedia* in 1940 and continued it in Yiddish and English. In 1943 it established a Yiddish publishing house.

Central Yiddish School Organization [CYSHO]. Polish educational organization. Founded in 1921, it stimulated the growth of Yiddish schools and coordinated their curricula. It sponsored a teachers' seminary and a network of schools.

Centre de Documentation Juive Contemporaine ("Center for Contemporary Jewish Documentation"). French research organization. It was founded by Isaac Schneersohn in 1943 in occupied France with the aim of gathering documents dealing with the Nazi persecution of the Jews. After the liberation of France, it published documentary works and information during the trials of Nazi war criminals. It was primarily responsible for the monument to the unknown Jewish martyr dedicated in Paris in 1956.

Ceremonial laws. Observances prescribed by Jewish law, such as rites connected with the Sabbath and festivals, dietary laws, circumcision, marriage, death, etc. Jewish sources emphasize the practical importance of such observances, and the laws concerning them were codified by such Jewish scholars as Maimonides, Jacob ben Asher, and Joseph Caro. Today, while Conservative Judaism encourages modifications of the legal system where relevant, Reform Judasim regards many ceremonial laws as outmoded.

Ceremonial objects. They are used in the synagogue and at home on the Sabbath and festivals, as well as during ceremonies marking life-cycle events. They include Torah scrolls, Torah cases and covers, Torah crowns, Torah breastplates, pointers, Arks, curtains for the Ark, lamps, spice boxes, Sabbath candlesticks, kiddush cups, Sabbath tablecloths, Ḥannukah menorahs, Esther scroll cases, seder plates, etrog containers, chairs of Elijah, wedding rings, wedding canopies, and mezuzahs.

Cerfberr, Herz (1726–1794). Alsatian Jewish leader. He worked as an army contractor and employed many Jews in his factories. In 1780 he asked Moses Mendelssohn to help him in his efforts to improve the position of the Jews in Alsace. He commissioned a translation into French of Christian Wilhelm von Dohm's book encouraging Jewish emancipation. This resulted in the appointment of a commission to report to the king concerning the legal position of the Jews. As a consequence the poll tax for Jewry was abolished.

Chagall, Marc (1887–1985). French artist of Russian origin. He was born in Vitebsk and studied in St. Petersburg and Paris. In May 1914 he had a one-man show in Berlin. In 1917 he was appointed commissar for fine arts in Vitebsk and director of the Free Academy of Art. Later he became designer for the Chamber State Jewish Theater. He settled in France in 1923, and emigrated to New York in 1941, but later returned to France. Eastern European Jewish life is a dominant theme in his work.

Chair of Elijah. Symbolic chair set aside for the prophet Elijah at the circumcision ceremony. It is positioned to the right of the sandak and the child is placed for a moment in the chair before being moved to the sandak's lap for the circumcision to be carried out.

Chajes, Tzevi Hirsch (1805–1855). Galician rabbi and scholar. He was a rabbi at Zolkiev (1829–52) and Kalisz (1852–5). He was influenced by Naḥman Krochmal and corresponded with leading maskilim of Galicia and Italy (such as Solomon Judah Rapoport, Samuel David Luzzatto, and Isaac Samuel Reggio). Although he introduced modern critical methods into talmudic and cognate studies, he was a defender of Orthodoxy. He wrote on the principles of the Written and Oral Law, the Targums and midrash, and the Talmud.

Chajes, Tzevi Peretz (1876–1927). Galician rabbi and scholar, grandson of Tzevi Hirsch Chajes. He taught at the Collegio Rabbinico Italiano in Florence and at the University of Florence. In 1912 he was appointed chief rabbi at Trieste. From 1918 until his death he was chief rabbi of Vienna. He served as chairman of the Zionist Actions Committee from 1921 to 1925. He published studies of biblical exegesis, archeology, the Talmud, and Hebrew poetry.

Chaldeans. Ancient Semitic people who migrated to southern Mesopotamia at the end of the second millennium BCE. Eventually they became the ruling class of the Neo-Babylonian Empire. In classical sources southern Mesopotamia became known as Chaldea.

***Chamberlain, Houston Stewart** (1855–1927). English writer. He settled in Bayreuth, where he became a friend of Richard Wagner, whose daughter he married. He believed that the Jews were a mongrel race whose existence was a crime against humanity. His *Foundations of the 19th Century* served as the basis of National-Socialist ideology.

Chanting *see* CANTILLATION; CANTOR.

Chao. Family name of the principal family of native Chinese Jews in Kaifeng. The surname was conferred on the physician Yen Ch'eng in 1423.

Chao Yng Ch'eng (d. 1657). Chinese civil servant. He was born in Kaifeng. He entered public service as a mandarin and served at Fukien (1650–53), and in Hukwang (1656–7). He was largely responsible for rebuilding the Kaifeng synagogue in 1653. Although he was regarded as a Confucian mandarin when in Fukien, he lived as a religious Jew when in Honan, his home province.

Chapbook. A small, cheap book of popular ballads, stories, etc. Chapbooks were a regular feature of eastern European Jewish life in the 19th and 20th centuries. Vast numbers of poorly printed works of popular appeal were sold in markets and streets by itinerant peddlers. They included miraculous tales about Ḥasidic rabbis, ethical treaties, religious works, and instructions on divination. With the development of Yiddish literature, cheap novels were distributed in the same fashion.

Chaplain. A priest or clergyman attached to an institution or ministering to a military group or professional body. The first known Jewish military chaplains are those appointed in the US Army during the Civil War. In World War I American chaplains served full-time, and during World War II a chaplaincy committee of the National Jewish Welfare Board was organized. Military chaplaincy services also exist in other countries. In Israel the chaplaincy plays an active role in army life. A Jewish chaplaincy system for hospitals and prisons is organized in most western countries.

Chariot mysticism *see* MAASEH MERKAVAH.

Charity (Hebrew "tzedakah").The giving of money or material goods to help the poor and needy. In the Bible it is spoken of as an obligation, and involves offering succor to the widow, the orphan, the stranger, and the aged. The Mishnah assumes a well-defined system of organized relief. The rabbis stipulated that the highest form of charity is that in which the donor and recipient are unknown to one another. Maimonides believed that the best kind of charity involved helping the needy person to support himself in some occupation. By the Middle Ages philanthropic institutions were firmly established in the Jewish community. In the 19th and 20th centuries Jews took an active part in a wide range of Jewish charitable work. In modern times the development of state welfare activities has significantly altered the nature of Jewish philanthropy, the state having assumed some of the traditional functions of charity, such as care of the aged and destitute.

***Charlemagne** (742–814). Frankish king (from 768) and Holy Roman Emperor (800–814). He patronized the Jews and encouraged their immigration into the empire, granting them security of life and property, freedom of religion, and exemption from excise taxes. He employed Jews in his court and on official missions.

Charles, Gerda (b. 1915). English novelist. She was born in Liverpool. Her novels deal with various Jewish themes and include *The True Voice, The Slanting Light, A Logical Girl, The Crossing Point,* and *The Destiny Waltz.*

Charney, Daniel (1888–1956). Belorussian Yiddish poet and journalist. He was born in Minsk. He suffered from illness from early childhood and when he attempted to emigrate to the US in 1925 he was refused entry because of ill-health, and was forced to return to Europe. He finally settled in New York after the rise of Nazism. His stories, fables, and articles (including a series on the conditions of Jews in Lithuania, Latvia, and Poland) were printed in newspapers in Russia, Poland, and the US.

Charney, Samuel *see* NIGER, SAMUEL.

Chasanowitsch, Leon [Schub, Kasriel] (1882–1925). Labor Zionist leader, of Lithuanian origin. He was born near Vilnius. He became active in Labor Zionism in 1905 and in 1908 was forced to flee from the Russian police to Galicia. He served as secretary of the world Poale Zion movement from 1913 to 1919. He published studies on the Polish and Ukrainian pogroms and represented Labor Zionism at international socialist congresses.

Chastity. Abstinence from sexual commerce. The biblical emphasis on sexual purity is linked with the condemnation of idolatry. Four of the 12 curses in Deuteronomy 27 are directed against those guilty of sexual sins. The rabbis listed adultery with idolatry and murder as the cardinal sins which must not be committed under pain of death. Sexual commerce outside marriage is forbidden by Jewish law; early marriage was seen as the best safeguard against sexual impurity.

Chayefsky, Paddy (1923–1981). American playwright. He was born in New York. His work draws on Jewish life and tradition. His *The Tenth Man* is based on the legend of the dybbuk and *Gideon* was inspired by the biblical account of the Hebrew judge's victory over the Midianites.

Chazanovitz, Joseph (1844–1919).

Lithuanian Zionist. He practiced medicine in Grodno, Białystock, and Yekaterinoslav. He was one of the first members of Ḥovevei Zion. He helped to establish a central Jewish library in Jerusalem, which became the basis of the Jewish National Library.

Chazars *see* KHAZARS.

Chedorlaomer (fl. ?19th–16th cent. BCE). King of Elam. With his confederates, he overcame five Canaanite kings in southern Palestine. He was defeated by Abraham, who recaptured the spoil and liberated Lot (Genesis 14.1–16).

Chelkias (fl. 2nd–1st cent. BCE). Egyptian general. In 102 BCE he and his brother Ananias (Hananiah) commanded Cleopatra's forces in Palestine against her son, Ptolemy Lathyrus, King of Cyprus. It was owing to their influence that Cleopatra confirmed Alexander Yannai's rule over Palestine.

Chełm. Town in Poland, 30 miles south-east of Lublin. Jews settled there in the 12th century. In the Cossack massacres of 1648 many Jewish inhabitants were slaughtered. The natives of the town, who are portrayed as fools, figure in many anecdotes of Jewish folk humor.

Chełmno. Town in Poland, 125 miles north-west of Warsaw. It was the site of a Nazi concentration camp.

Chemosh. God of the Moabites. Solomon built a shrine to him (I Kings 11.7, 33), which stood for 400 years until it was destroyed by Josiah (II Kings 23.13).

***Cherethites and Pelathites.** David's bodyguard of foreign mercenaries (II Samuel 8.18).

Cherniakov [Tcherniakov; Tchernikhovski]**, Adam** (1881–1942). Polish labor leader. He was head of the organization of Jewish craftsmen in Poland after World War I. Under Nazi occupation, he was chairman of the council of the Warsaw Ghetto. In 1942, when confronted by a demand to supply the names of Jews for deportation he committed suicide. His diary is an important historical source about the Warsaw Ghetto.

Cherub. Supernatural being, or image of such a being, depicted variously in the Bible as a winged figure with human, animal, or bird's head and body. The cherubim guarded the gates to the Garden of Eden (Genesis 3.24). In the Tabernacle images of cherubim were placed on either side of the Ark, forming the throne of God (Exodus 25.18–20; 37.7–9). Later such images were located in the Holy of Holies in the Temple. Ezekiel describes four cherubim carrying the divine throne (Ezekiel 1). In post-biblical literature they are identified with angels.

Chief rabbi. Principal rabbinical authority of a national or provincial Jewish community. Chief rabbis were appointed in various countries in the Middle Ages. In modern times Napoleon desired to set up consistories presided over by a grand rabbi. In Germany before unification the chief rabbinate existed in various provinces. In England the chief rabbi represents British Jewry. In Israel there are two chief rabbis from the Ashkenazi and Sephardi communities. Not all countries, however, have a chief rabbi: the US is a notable example.

Childbirth. In biblical literature birth pangs are viewed as the legacy of Eve's disobedience. Rabbinic literature contains discussion of problems connected with birth. Superstitious practices connected with birth, including the wearing of amulets, were known in talmudic times and the Middle Ages and are condemned in rabbinic literature. A special prayer of thanks is recited in the synagogue after childbirth.

Children's villages *see* YOUTH VILLAGES.

Child sacrifice. It was practiced as a religious act in Moab and Canaan. The account of the binding of Isaac (Genesis 22) illustrates that child sacrifice was not required of the ancient Israelites. The Mosaic code specifically prohibits such a practice, laying down in its place symbolic and vicarious redemption or consecration to the service of God.

***Chmielnicki** [Khmelnitzki], **Bogdan** (1593–1657). Ukrainian Cossack leader. He led an uprising against Polish rule in the Ukraine in 1648, which resulted in the destruction of hundreds of Jewish communities. These events shocked the Jewish world and gave rise to a wave of messianic longing, culminating in the widely held conviction that Shabbetai Tzevi was the Messiah. Later Chmielnicki became hetman of the autonomous Ukraine and initiator of its unification with Russia.

Chocrón, Isaac (b. 1932). Venezuelan novelist and dramatist. His publications include *Break in Case of Fire, The Fifth Circle of Hell,* and *Wild Animals.*

Choir. A choir of Levites participated in the services of the first Temple. After the destruction of the Temple, the rabbis prohibited all music as a sign of mourning. In Babylonia the ceremony for the installation of the exilarch included singing by a choir. In the Renaissance synagogue choirs were introduced and by the 19th century choirs were accepted in many western synagogues. Also in the 19th century Ḥasidic groups introduced unaccompanied congregational singing. Reform congregations have used mixed choirs and an organ in the synagogue service.

Cholent. Dish made of beans, eaten by the Ashkenazim for the Sabbath midday meal. Prepared on Friday afternoon, it is placed in the local baker's oven to cook overnight; it is taken home to be eaten after the Sabbath service. The Sephardim prepare a similar hot dish for the Sabbath called "hamin."

Chomsky, William (1896–1977). American educator of Russian origin. He settled in the US in 1913. From 1922 he was on the faculty of Gratz College and from 1954 he lectured at Dropsie College. He wrote about Jewish education, stressing the importance of classical Hebrew language and literature.

Chorin, Aaron ben Kalman *see* ḤORIN, AARON BEN KALMAN.

Chosen people. The belief that the Jews were the chosen people of God is based on the covenant between God and Abraham (Genesis 15). The covenant was renewed on Mount Sinai, but the Jews' election was now made conditional on their observance of the Torah (Deuteronomy 7.6); Israel is spoken of in Exodus as a kingdom of priests and a holy nation (Exodus 19.6). The prophets taught that election is based on righteousness. In the Mishnah and Talmud the role of Israel as the teacher of all nations is emphasized. The Jewish idea of chosenness does not imply superiority, but rather the obligation to fulfill religious and moral duties.

***Chosroes** [Khosroes] **II** (fl. 6th–7th cent.). King of Persia (590–628). With Jewish support led by Benjamin of Tiberias, he conquered Palestine, defeating the Byzantines, in 614. After 15 years the Persian army was forced by the Byzantine emperor to withdraw.

Chouraqui, Nathan André (b. 1917). Israeli author and politician. He was born in Algeria. From 1959 to 1963 he was an adviser to David Ben-Gurion on the immigration to Israel of ethnic minorities. He was later deputy mayor of Jerusalem (1965–9). His publications include *Between East and West: a History of the Jews of North Africa.*

***Christiani, Pablo** (fl. 13th cent.). French Dominican monk. He was born in Montpellier. He converted to Christianity and joined the Dominican Order. In 1263 a public disputation took place in

Barcelona between him and Naḥmanides in the presence of King James I of Aragon. In 1269 he persuaded Louis IX of France to compel Jews to listen to his sermons and to wear the Jewish badge.

Christianity. A Jewish sect of followers of Jesus Christ emerged in Palestine in the 1st century. They believed that Jesus was the Messiah and had brought about the Kingdom of God. The New Testament preserves traditions about Jesus' life and teaching, and the epistles of Paul and others addressed to scattered Jewish Christian communities. The early church accepted Jesus as God incarnate, regarded the Hebrew Scriptures as authoritative, and developed its own traditions. Christianity quickly spread from the Jewish to the gentile community and over the centuries became a world religion with its own theology, liturgy, moral code, and way of life. Because of their failure to recognize Jesus as Messiah and their role in his death, Jews have frequently been persecuted by Christians. (*See also* POPES.)

Chronicles (Hebrew "Divre ha-Yamim"). The name of two biblical books in the Hagiographa. They contain genealogical lists of the Israelite tribes from Adam to the time of David (1 Chronicles 1–9); an account of David's rule (I Chronicles 10–29); an account of Solomon's reign (II Chronicles 1–9); and a history of the Kingdom of Judah to its destruction by the Babylonians (II Chronicles 10–36).

Chronology. The establishing of the proper sequence of past events. The Bible uses events such as the Flood, the reigns of kings, and the Babylonian exile to establish dates. Subsequently Jewish dates were fixed according to the number of years that have traditionally elapsed since creation (*see* CALENDAR). In Western countries Jews use the abbreviations BCE (before the Christian or Common Era) and CE (Christian or Common Era) instead of BC and AD.

***Chrysostom, John** (347–407). Patriarch of Constantinople. His *Homilies against the Jews* was one of the first attempts to stimulate Christian anti-Semitism.

Chuetas. Name given to the Marranos of Majorca, who were descended from the victims of forced baptism in 1391 and 1435. They were subjected to inquisitional persecutions in the 17th century.

Church *see* CHRISTIANITY; POPE.

Church councils. Ecclesiastical assemblies. During the history of the church such assemblies have been much concerned with Jewish matters. It was the task of regional councils to enforce local anti-Jewish regulations, while general councils were concerned with an overall policy toward the Jewish community. The Council of Nicaea in 325 widened the breach between Christianity and Judaism. The Third Lateran Council in 1179 enacted restrictive measures against Jews, and the Fourth Lateran Council of 1215 decreed that Jews must wear a Jewish badge. In the 15th century the Council of Basle condemned the Talmud and recommended conversionist sermons. The Second Vatican Council (1962–5) declared that the Jewish people cannot be blamed for the death of Jesus.

Church Fathers. Teachers and writers of the early Christian church. They flourished from the period following that of the New Testament writers until the 7th century. Some were familiar with aggadah; others quoted extracts from Hellenistic Jewish writers. Many facts of Jewish history are recorded in their writings. Frequently they engaged in polemics against Judaism.

Churchill White Paper *see* WHITE PAPER, CHURCHILL.

Churgin, Pinkhos M. (1894–1957). Scholar of Belorussian origin. He emigrated to Palestine in 1907 and later settled in the US. He was professor of Jewish history and literature at Yeshiva University and dean of its teachers' institute. In 1955 he emigrated to Israel and became head of Bar-Ilan University. He published studies of the Targumim and the history of the second Temple period.

***Chwolson, Daniel** (1819–1911). Russian orientalist of Lithuanian origin. He was born in Vilnius. He converted to Christianity in 1855. He was professor of Hebrew, Syriac, and Chaldaic philology at the University of St. Petersburg and at the Russian Orthodox and Roman Catholic theological academies in the same city. He defended the Jewish community against anti-Semitic allegations and intervened with Russian authorities on their behalf. He published studies of the Sabians, Syriac inscriptions, Jesus' trial, and the Semitic peoples.

***Cicero, Marcus Tullius** (106–3 BCE). Roman statesman. In 59 BCE he defended Flaccus, who was accused of seizing gold contributed by the Jews to the Temple when he was proconsul of Asia. He described Judaism as a barbaric superstition and criticized the Jews for their involvement in public assemblies.

Circumcision (Hebrew "bris," "brit milah"). The removal of the foreskin of the penis. In Jewish practice circumcision is carried out at a ceremony which also includes the naming of the child and is held when he is eight days old. It is a sign of the covenant between God and the Jewish people and is performed according to instructions given to Abraham (Genesis 17.11–12). The child to be circumcised is first placed in the Chair of Elijah. Then the sandak holds the child in his lap and the mohel carries out the circumcision. Blessings over a cup of wine follow the operation while the child is given his name. Male converts must also undergo circumcision.

Cities of refuge. Moses assigned six cities as places of refuge for those who accidentally committed manslaughter (Numbers 35.13; Deuteronomy 19.9). There the person was free from persecution by an avenger.

Citron *see* ETROG.

City of David. Title used generally as a synonym for JERUSALEM. More precisely it means that area which constituted the city in David's time.

Civil courts. According to Jewish law, Jews are prohibited from having recourse to non-Jewish courts of justice. In the 2nd century Tarphon applied such a prohibition even in cases where the dispensation of justice was identical with that of Jewish courts. Medieval Jewish authorities insisted that Jews bring their disputes only before their own courts. Such a prohibition has been largely abandoned in the modern period; the only occasion on which systematic attempts are made to avoid recourse to civil courts is when a dispute affects the internal regulations of the community.

Civil rights. The personal rights of the individual citizen, usually upheld by law. In ancient Israel civil rights were enjoyed only by those belonging to a tribe. Later some Jews became citizens of Greek cities or obtained Roman citizenship and enjoyed the rights that accompanied such a status. The Edict of Caracalla in 212 gave citizenship to all free members of the Roman Empire except those recently conquered. Subsequently, Jews were excluded from full citizenship in Christian lands. During the Middle Ages they were royal dependants. In the Western world the acquisition of full civil rights by the Jews began in the 18th century (*see* EMANCIPATION). *See also* MINORITY RIGHTS.

Classical literature, Jews in. Hellenistic writers regarded Judaism as a barbarous religion and interpreted the Jewish rejection of the Greek deities as atheism. They mocked circumcision, the dietary laws, and the Sabbath. A number of Roman writers such as Cicero, Juvenal, and Tacitus also criticized Judaism and the Jewish people.

***Claudius I** (10 BCE–54 CE). Roman emperor (41–54). His accession was due largely to the aid of Herod Agrippa, whom he subsequently appointed King of Judea. In 44, on Herod Agrippa's death, he placed Judea under a procurator. He gave Herod Agrippa's son (Herod Agrippa II) regions of northern Palestine to rule in 49. In 49–50 he expelled a number of Jews from Rome because of Jewish–Christian conflict.

Clean animals. Animals which, according to Jewish law, may be eaten and whose milk may be drunk. Detailed descriptions of clean and unclean animals are given in Leviticus 11.1–47 and Deuteronomy 14.3–20.

Cleanliness *see* ABLUTION; MIKVEH; PURITY, RITUAL.

Coat of arms. The heraldic bearings of a family or person. The midrash describes the flags of the 12 tribes of Israel, some of which became family badges in the Middle Ages (*see* FLAG). Priestly families used the symbol of hands spread in blessing on tombstones. From the 16th century many Italian Jewish families had distinctive badges. Coats of arms are found among Jews only from the 17th century.

Cochin [Malabar]. Name of both a city and a former state on the Malabar Coast in south-west India. The Jews of the area consist of the so-called White Jews (Jewish exiles from Europe), Black Jews (Indian Jews) and Freedmen (manumitted slaves). The Jewish community dates back to the 10th–11th centuries; it flourished under Dutch rule in the 17th and 18th centuries and continues in independent India, though its numbers have been heavily reduced.

Codes *see* LAW, CODES OF.

Coffin. In the Bible there is a reference to the use of a coffin for the body of Joseph (Genesis 50.26). During the Hasmonean period Jews collected the bones of the dead in sarcophagi. The use of coffins dates only from the second Temple period. *See also* BURIAL; CEMETERY.

Cohen *see* PRIEST.

Cohen, Abraham (1887–1957). English scholar. He was born in Reading. He served as minister to the Birmingham Hebrew Congregation and was the first minister to preside over the Board of Deputies of British Jews. He edited the Soncino Books of the Bible.

Cohen, Albert (1895–1981). French novelist. He was born in Corfu. He wrote poems and novels about modern Jewry, including *Solal of the Solals, Mangeclous,* and *Belle du Seigneur;* he also edited the journal *Revue juive*. He served as an official in international organizations in Geneva.

Cohen, Alfred Morton (1859–1949). American lawyer. He was born in Cincinnati. He was president of B'nai B'rith from 1925 to 1938 and chairman of the Board of Governors of the Hebrew Union College from 1918 to 1937.

Cohen, Boaz (1899–1968). American rabbinic scholar. He was born in Bridgeport, Connecticut. He served as chairman of the Rabbinical Assembly of America from 1945 to 1948. His *Kunteres ha-Teshuvot* is an annotated bibliography of rabbinic responsa of the Middle Ages. He published biographies of Israel Friedlaender, Louis Ginzberg, and Alexander Marx, and studies of comparative law.

Cohen, Francis Lyon (1862–1934). English rabbi and scholar. He was born in Aldershot. He served as senior Jewish chaplain to the Australian army from 1914 to 1934. He edited collections of Jewish music including *A Handbook of Synagogue Music for Congregational Singing* and *The Voice of Prayer and Praise.*

Cohen, Henry (1863–1952). American

rabbi. He was born in London. He became rabbi of Temple Beth Bnai Israel in Galveston, Texas. He was involved in numerous humanitarian activities.

Cohen, Hermann (1842–1918). German philosopher. He was born in Coswig. He was professor of philosophy at the University of Marburg until 1912 and later taught at the Hochschule für Wissenschaft des Judentums. In 1880 he began to resume his hitherto lapsed links with Judaism and to defend the Jewish people and tradition. His writings include *Religion der Vernunft aus den Quellen des Judentums.*

Cohen, Israel (1879–1961). English writer. He was born in Manchester. From 1922 he was secretary of the Zionist Organization in London, on whose behalf he visited Jewish communities in Egypt, Australia, China, Manchuria, Japan, Java, and India. His writings include *Jewish Life in Modern Times, The Zionist Movement, A Short History of Zionism,* and *Theodor Herzl: Founder of Political Zionism.*

Cohen, Jeffrey (b. 1940). English rabbi and writer. He was born in Manchester. He served various congregations and lectured at Jews College and Glasgow University. His publications include *Understanding the Synagogue Service, A Samaritan Chronicle, Festival Adventure, Understanding the High Holyday Services, Yizkor, Horizons of Jewish Prayer,* and *Moments of Insight.*

Cohen, Naphtali ben Isaac (1649–1719). German rabbi and kabbalist. He served as rabbi at Ostrog, Posen, and Frankfurt am Main, where he was known as a practical kabbalist. He resigned his post when it was alleged that his kabbalistic experiments were responsible for the destruction of the Frankfurt Ghetto by fire. He died at Constantinople on his way to Palestine. He was an opponent of the Sabbetaians.

Cohen, Raphael *see* RAPHAEL BEN JEKUTHIEL COHEN.

Cohen, Sir **Robert Waley** [Waley Cohen] (1877–1952). English Jewish communal leader. He was managing director of the Shell Transport and Trading Company and chairman of the Palestine Corporation. He served as president of the United Synagogue and vice-president of the Board of Deputies of British Jews.

Cohen, Shabbetai *see* SHABBETAI BEN MEIR HA-COHEN.

Cohen, Shalom ben Jacob [Ha-Cohen, Shalom] (1772–1845). German Hebrew poet of Polish origin. He joined the circle of maskilim in Berlin. In 1809 he revived the journal *Ha-measseph,* then in 1821, after settling in Vienna, he founded the annual *Bikkure ha-Ittim.* He later lived in Hamburg. He wrote poems on biblical themes and Jewish textbooks.

Cohen, Tobias [Tobias the Doctor] (1652–1729). Turkish physician and author, of German origin. He was born in Metz. He served as court physician in Turkey until he was 62. He then went to Jerusalem to concentrate on the study of Torah. His *Maaseh Tovyah* is an encyclopedia dealing with theology, astronomy, cosmography, geography, botany, and medicine; it also contains references to Shabbetai Tzevi.

Cohen, Yaakov *see* CAHAN, YAAKOV.

Cohn, Haim (b. 1911). Israeli lawyer. He was born in Lübeck and settled in Palestine in 1930. From 1953 to 1960 he was attorney general and contributed to the founding of the Israeli legal and judicial system. He was minister of justice in 1952–3, and in 1960 was appointed a justice of the Israeli Supreme Court. His publications include *Foreign Laws of Marriage and Divorce* and *The Trial and Death of Jesus.*

Cohn-Sherbok, Dan (b. 1945). American rabbi and theologian. He was born in Denver. He served as a Reform rabbi in congregations in the US, England, Australia, and South Africa. In 1975 he was appointed to the Faculty of Humanities at the University of Kent at Canterbury, England. His writings include *The Jewish Community of Canterbury, On Earth as it is in Heaven: Jews, Christians and Liberation Theology, The Jewish Heritage, Jewish Petitionary Prayer: a Theological Exploration, Holocaust Theology, Rabbinic Perspectives on the New Testament,* and *Issues in Contemporary Judaism.*

Cohon, Samuel Solomon (1888–1959). American theologian. He was born in Minsk. He became professor of theology at the Hebrew Union College in 1923. He was active in the Central Conference of American Rabbis and served as the principal draftsman of the Columbus Platform, the statement of principles of Reform Judaism. He was an editor of the *Union Haggadah* and the *Rabbis' Manual,* and his writings include *What we Jews Believe.*

Coins. The basic unit of weight and therefore the basic coin in the Bible was the shekel. Hasmonean coins (135–37 BCE) carry Hebrew inscriptions and certain symbolic images (lulav, etrog, chalice, palm). In the war against Rome (66–70) Jewish patriots issued silver shekels bearing Hasmonean symbols. Many of the coins circulated by Simeon Bar Kokhba (132–5) were defaced Roman issues, altered to show the rebuilt Temple. Subsequently Jews used the coinage of the countries in which they lived, until the establishment of a Jewish homeland in the 20th century.

College of Jewish Studies. American educational institution. It was founded in Chicago in 1924 by the Chicago Board of Jewish Education to foster Jewish studies and train teachers. From 1965 it served other colleges and universities as a department of Judaic studies.

Collegio Rabbinico Italiano [Istituto Convitto Rabbinico]. Italian rabbinical seminary. Established in Padua in 1829, it was the earliest modern rabbinical seminary. It was closed in 1871, revived in Rome in 1887, transferred later to Florence, and eventually returned to Rome. Although it was closed during the Fascist period, it reopened in 1955. It published *Rivista Israelitica* (1904–15) and the *Annuario di Studi Ebraici* (1935–69).

Colon, Joseph (c. 1420–1480). Italian rabbinic scholar. He was born in France. He served as rabbi in various Italian communities, including Pavia, which he made the center of Italian talmudic learning. After his death his responsa were collected and published. His decisions had considerable influence on later Italian halakhah.

***Columbus, Christopher** (1451–1500). Explorer of Italian origin, discoverer of America. He was possibly of Marrano extraction. He boasted about his connection with King David and was interested in Jewish and Marrano society. His name was not unknown among Italian Jews of the late medieval period. On his journeys he used nautical instruments perfected by Jews such as Joseph Vecinho and nautical tables drawn up by Abraham Zacuto.

Comité des Délégations Juives ("Committee of Jewish Delegations"). International representative body of Jews. It was founded in Paris in March 1919 to represent Jewish claims at the Paris Peace Conference. With Leo Motzkin at its head, it presented a demand for Jewish rights in various countries (primarily in central and eastern Europe), and was partly successful. Arrangements for the Jews were made in the Treaty of Sèvres (1920) agreed with Turkey, and the Minorities Treaty agreed with the small eastern European states. The Comité remained in existence during the next few decades to protect Jewish rights.

Financed primarily by the Zionist Organization, it was succeeded by the World Jewish Congress. It published books and pamphlets on Jewish concerns.

Comité Représentatif des Israélites de France *see* CRIF.

Commandment *see* MITZVAH.

Commandments, 613 *see* 613 COMMANDMENTS.

Commandments, Ten *see* TEN COMMANDMENTS.

Commentators *see* BIBLE COMMENTARIES; TALMUD COMMENTARIES.

Commerce. In biblical times Solomon encouraged international commerce. After his reign, it did not flourish again until the Maccabean period. With the rise of Islam, Jews served as middlemen in trade between the Islamic world and countries in Christian Europe. In the Middle Ages Jews were excluded from merchant guilds. Later, Marranos developed trade between Europe, America, and the Levant. With the Industrial Revolution and the rise of capitalism, Jews became widely involved in banking, foreign trade, and railway construction. In the 19th and 20th centuries Jews have engaged in the whole spectrum of commercial activities.

Committee for Jewish Claims on Austria. International legal aid organization. Founded in 1953, it attempted to improve benefits to Jewish victims of Austrian Nazism. In 1955 in concluded a settlement of Jewish indemnification claims with the Austrian government.

Communal affairs. In ancient Israel the Jews were able to control communal affairs in their own country. After the Babylonian exile, the synagogue became the focus of religious life. The patterns of institutional development which evolved during the exile served as the foundation of Jewish communal structures in many other countries. In the Hellenistic world nearly all Jewish communities modeled their organization on that of Greek cities. In the Roman Empire the Jews, like all other subjects, were permitted to establish and maintain religious organizations and municipal corporations. In Babylonia the Jewish community was headed by a dynasty of exilarchs. In other countries the head of the community was often a nagid. In the Middle Ages Jewish communities had authority over their own internal affairs. After the Emancipation Jews were granted full citizenship rights and no longer exercised jurisdiction over their own civil life.

Communism. Political movement which aims to achieve through revolution the proletarian control of society and public ownership of the means of production. It is based on the writings of Karl Marx. At the time of the Russian Revolution, nearly all Jewish socialist parties opposed communism, while the communist movement regarded Zionism as a tool of imperialism. Nevertheless some leaders of the Russian Communist Party were of Jewish origin and in several countries Jews took an active role in promoting communism.

Community Center *see* JEWISH COMMUNITY CENTER.

Community council. Local body elected by the Jewish community to govern some aspects of its life. Community councils are an adaptation of the European kehillah to the requirements of Jewish life in the US. They represent the variety of views in the community, and their activities include philanthropy, community relations, education, and internal Jewish affairs.

Compassion. In the Bible God is frequently described as compassionate. Human beings must imitate this divine attribute in their dealings with one another and their treatment of animals. Rabbinic Judaism enlarged this biblical concept, regarding compassion as of primary importance.

Comtat Venaissin. Former papal territory in south-east France, including the town of Avignon. Ceded by France in 1274 to the Holy See, it became a distinct territory. Jews first settled in the area in the 12th century. It became a haven of refuge for the Jews after their expulsion from the rest of France in the 14th century. The four major Jewish communities of this area were Avignon, Cavillon, Carpentras, and L'Isle. The territory reverted to France in 1791.

Comtino, Mordecai ben Eliezer (1420–before 1487). Turkish rabbinic scholar and scientist. He was born in Constantinople and became one of the leaders of the Hebrew cultural movement there. Two of his hymns were incorporated into the Karaite liturgy.

Concentration camps. The term is applied specifically to the prison camps established after the accession to power of the National Socialists in Germany in 1933. Initially they were intended for the detention of opponents of the new regime, then individuals were sent there on orders of the Gestapo. Later entire groups (particularly those racial groups condemned under the Nazis' Aryan policies) were arrested and committed to the camps, which grew to about 1000 in number. In six major camps (Auschwitz, Treblinka, Bełżec, Maidanek, Sobibor, and Chełmno) the mass extermination of millions of victims was carried out in specially constructed gas chambers.

Concordances *see* DICTIONARIES, BIBLE.

Conference of Presidents of Major American Jewish Organizations. Founded in 1954, it exchanges information and speaks on behalf of the Jewish community. It is composed of representatives of more than 20 national religious and secular bodies.

Conference on Jewish Material Claims against Germany. International aid agency. It was founded in 1951 to secure funds for the relief, rehabilitation, and resettlement of the Jewish victims of Nazism. It has sponsored the establishment of educational and research institutions, community and youth centers, synagogues, homes for the aged, children's and youth homes and kindergartens, summer camps, and medical institutions.

Conference on Jewish Social Studies. American scholarly body. It was formed in 1933 by Morris Raphael Cohen and Salo Wittmayer Baron with the aim of creating an association of scholars to assemble reliable data about Jews in the modern world. It sponsors studies in Jewish demography, the history and nature of anti-Semitism, and the problems of Jews in other countries. It publishes the journal *Jewish Social Studies*.

Conference, rabbinical *see* RABBINICAL CONFERENCE.

Confession of faith *see* SHEMA.

Confession of sin. The Bible mentions the efficacy of public and individual confession of sin. Sin offerings accompanied by prayer played an important role in the Temple sacrificial service. In the synagogue the confession of sins was part of the liturgy for daily services and the Day of Atonement. At death a special confession ("viddui") is prescribed.

Confirmation *see* BAR MITZVAH; BAT MITZVAH.

Conforte, David (1618–c. 1690). Greek rabbi and literary historian. He was born in Salonica. He founded a bet midrash in Jerusalem, and served as rabbi in Cairo. His *Kore ha-Dorot* is a chronicle of authors and works from post-talmudic times until the 17th century.

Congratulations. The most common expressions of congratulation among the Ashkenazim are "mazzal tov" (good luck) and "mazzal u-verakhah" (luck and blessing). Among the Sephardim the expression "be-siman tov" (in good omen) is used. On performing a religious duty, the form of congratulation among the Ashkenazim is "yeyasher koaḥ" (may he increase your strength). Among the Sephardim it is "ḥazak u-varukh" (be strong and blessed). As a toast the expression "le-ḥayyim" (to life) is used. A birthday greeting is "ad meah (ve-esrim) shanah" [may you live] to a hundred (and twenty)).

Congress *see* ZIONIST CONGRESSES.

Congress for Jewish Culture. American cultural organization. It was founded in New York in 1948 with the aims of preserving Jewish cultural activity, fostering Jewish education through the support of Yiddish and Yiddish–Hebrew schools, and assisting in the publication of literary and scholarly works in Yiddish. It publishes a Yiddish periodical, *Zukunft,* and helps Jewish institutions in various countries.

Congress of Berlin. Conference convoked by Bismarck in 1878. Among the issues discussed was the position of the Jews in the Balkan states.

Congress of Vienna. Conference held in 1814–15 to discuss the organization of Europe after the Napoleonic Wars. One of the topics debated was the status of Jewry. A resolution was passed whereby the Confederate Diet of the proposed German Federation was instructed to bestow citizens' rights on the Jewish community.

Coniah *see* JEHOIACHIN.

Conjoint Foreign Committee *see* ANGLO-JEWISH ASSOCIATION.

Conscription. Compulsory military service. During the tribal period in ancient Israel, all able-bodied men were to serve in the military from the age of 20 (Numbers 1.3). The kings retained the power of conscription (II Kings 25.19). In the 4th century Jews were legally excluded from the forces of the Roman Empire and in the Middle Ages they were forbidden to bear arms. During the French revolutionary wars, Jews were like other citizens liable to conscription in most European countries. Before 1827 in Russia Jews paid a tax in lieu of military service; subsequently they had to perform military service (*see also* CANTONISTS). After Jewish Emancipation the Jews were subject to conscription on the same basis as their fellow citizens.

Consecration. The making holy of someone or something, thus the dedication of a person or thing for a special use or function. Ceremonies of consecration, involving anointing with oil, are mentioned in the Bible in connection with kingship and priesthood. Vessels used in the Tabernacle were similarly anointed. The rededication of the altar by the Maccabees is commemorated by Ḥanukkah. In post-biblical times consecration ceremonies took place when synagogues were established. The bar mitzvah marks the consecration of a boy to the observance of the commandments.

Conseil Représentatif du Judaisme Traditionnel de France *see* CRIF.

Conservative Judaism. Religious movement which arose in the middle of the 19th century in Europe and the US. Reacting against Orthodox and Reform Judaism, its founders believed that the traditional forms and precepts of Judaism are valid but permitted some modifications of the halakhah. In the US it has its own rabbinical school (Jewish Theological Seminary of America), rabbinical association (Rabbinical Assembly of America), and congregational organization (United Synagogue of America). It has become a major force both there and in other countries.

Consistory. Official organization of Jewish congregations in France. The system was introduced by Napoleon in

1808. Each local consistory represented Jews of a particular area and sent delegates to Paris to the Central Consistory, which was responsible for the maintenance of the chief rabbinate and the rabbinical seminary. It has remained the official French Jewish representative organization.

Consolation *see* MOURNING.

***Constantine I** (c. 274–337). Roman emperor (312–37). He was the first Christian emperor. His edict of toleration issued at Milan in 312 gave civil rights and toleration to Christians. In 315 he made decrees that canceled Jewish exemptions from municipal office and prohibited interference with Jewish converts to Christianity. His legislation initiated legal discrimination against Jewry.

Constantinople. City, formerly capital of the Byzantine and Ottoman empires; renamed Istanbul, it is the capital of modern Turkey. During the Byzantine period, the Jewish community in Constantinople suffered continuous persecution. After the city was captured by the Turks in 1453 the Jewish community increased and in the early and late Ottoman periods there was a chief rabbi resident in the city. The Hebrew printing presses of Constantinople were famous from the end of the 15th century.

Consultative Council of Jewish Organizations. International body founded in New York in 1946 by the American Jewish Committee, the Anglo-Jewish Association, and the Alliance Israélite Universelle. It advises on problems connected with human rights and issues related to the Jewish community.

Contract. A formal agreement between two or more parties. In Jewish law a contract cannot be enforced by a bet din unless there has been a symbolic acquisition of rights before two proper witnesses, through a process known as "kabbalat kinyan" (acquiring possession). In this act obligation is effected by one of the parties' taking up or pulling at a garment or another object (such as a handkerchief) belonging to the other person. Contracts between Jews which violate Jewish law are invalid. There is no standard form of contract except in the cases of marriage and divorce.

Controversies, religious. The oldest post-biblical controversy concerned the Samaritans' adherence to the Pentateuch. In Hellenistic times Pharisees and Sadducees differed about the status of the Oral Law and belief in the after-life. The Karaite movement, in the 8th century, rejected the Oral Law and the rabbinic tradition. In the 17th and 18th centuries traditionalists engaged in controversy with the Sabbetaians and the Frankists, and in the 18th century there was a schism between the Ḥasidim and Mitnaggedim. In modern society there is a wide gulf between Orthodox and non-Orthodox Judaism (the Reform, Conservative, and Reconstructionist movements).

Conversion, forced. Compulsory submission to the practice of a religion other than one's own. The forcible conversion of Jews was common after the rise of Christianity and Islam. During the 4th–6th centuries conversion to Christianity took place throughout the Roman Empire and it later became state policy in the Byzantine Empire. In the 14th–15th centuries it was carried out in the Iberian Peninsula; this resulted in the emergence of a class of crypto-Jews (Marranos). Forced conversion to Islam occurred in the Arabian peninsula during Mohammed's lifetime, and in the 12th century it was imposed by the Almohades in north Africa and Spain. In the 17th–19th centuries forced conversion to Islam in Persia gave rise to another group of crypto-Jews (Jedid Al-Islam). *See also* BAPTISM, FORCED.

Conversos (Spanish and Portuguese: "the converted"). Term used to designate Jewish converts to Christianity in Christian Spain and Portugal. It was also applied to their descendants.

Convert from Judaism *see* APOSTASY.

Convert to Judaism *see* PROSELYTE.

Cooperatives. The cooperative movement began among Jews in Palestine at the end of the 19th century. Its pioneers were the vintners' association and the Pardes society, which exported citrus. Later, credit cooperatives were established and the movement spread to other fields of economic activity including transport, agriculture, and industry. At the beginning of the 20th century Jewish cooperatives were formed in eastern and central Europe. They provided financial credit to merchants, shopkeepers, craftsmen, and farmers. This movement was destroyed during World War II.

Coordinating Board of Jewish Organizations. International body formed in 1947. It is composed of B'nai B'rith, the Board of Deputies of British Jews, and the South African Board of Deputies.

Copland, Aaron (1900–1991). American composer. He was born in Brooklyn. He served as head of the composition department of the Berkshire Music Center in Tanglewood from 1940 to 1965. His compositions include symphonies, ballets, film scores, orchestral works, and operas. His chamber work *Vitebsk* is based on a Jewish melody.

Copper Scroll. One of the Dead Sea Scrolls; it is made of copper and was discovered in 1952. Its contents include an inventory of the Qumran community's treasures and the places where they were hidden when its headquarters were abandoned in the 1st century.

Córdoba. City in Andalusia, southern Spain. In the 10th century, when it was the capital of the western Caliphate, it became a center of Jewish culture. This was largely the result of the activity of Ḥasdai ibn Shaprut, physician and diplomat in the service of the caliph; he attracted Jewish philosophers, poets, and scholars to the city. Maimonides was born there.

Cordovero, Moses ben Jacob [Ramak; Remak] (1522–1570). Palestinian kabbalist, of Spanish origin. He was the most important kabbalist in Safed before Isaac Luria. His first systematic work, *Pardes Rimmonim,* covers a wide range of kabbalistic problems. He also wrote a second systematic work, *Elimah Rabbati,* and a commentary on the Zohar.

Corporal punishment. Physical punishment is one of the oldest forms of punishment in Jewish law. According to the Bible 40 lashes were the maximum that could be inflicted for any single offense. Three judges were to be present at the time of punishment: one ordered it, another counted the lashes, and a third read the relevant passage from Deuteronomy (28.58–9). The rabbis decreed that corporal punishment should be administered only in Palestine, except for the offense of disobedience. Maimonides enumerated 207 cases for which corporal punishment was specified.

Corpse. According to biblical law a dead body renders all persons and things which come into contact with it ritually unclean. Special purification by the ashes of the Red Heifer (Numbers 19) was required before a person contaminated in this way was rendered fit again to enter the Sanctuary or eat sanctified food. In rabbinic law the restrictions concerning contact with a corpse applied only to a priest.

Cossacks *see* CHMIELNICKI, BOGDAN; HAIDAMAKS.

***Costa, Isaac de** (1798–1860). Dutch writer and poet. The son of a distinguished Sephardi family in Amsterdam, he converted to Christianity in 1822. He published studies of Jews in Spain, Portugal, and the Netherlands. His *Israel and the Gentiles* is a history of the Jewish people written from a Christian point of view. Many of his poems have biblical themes.

Costa, Uriel da (1585–1640). Portuguese rationalist. He was born in Oporto into a Marrano family. After moving to Amsterdam in c. 1615 he returned to Judaism, but he was later excommunicated because of his heretical views about rabbinic doctrine and practice. His subsequent attack on the Bible led to a second ban.

Costume *see* DRESS.

***Coughlin, Charles Edward** (1891–?). American Roman Catholic priest. He came from Michigan. In the 1930s he used radio broadcasts to spread anti-Semitic feeling and distrust of organized labor.

Council of Four Lands (Hebrew "Vaad Arba Aratzot"). Autonomous institution for the self-government of Polish-Lithuanian Jewry. It was established in the middle of the 16th century and functioned until 1764. It represented Jewish communities in four provinces (Major Poland, Minor Poland, Red Russia, and Lithuania).

Council of Jewish Federations and Welfare Funds. Association of American Jewish community organizations. Founded in 1932, it conducts studies of Jewish communities and compiles statistics for various areas of local Jewish service. It publishes annual surveys, budget digests, and reports dealing with campaigning, public relations, and business management services.

Council of Lithuania. Autonomous institution for the self-government of Lithuanian Jewry. Initially Lithuania was one of the provinces represented in the Council of Four Lands. In 1623 a separate Council was formed, made up of representatives and rabbis of Brzesć, Grodno, and Pinsk; later Slutsk and Vilnius were added. The Council operated until 1764.

Council *see* SYNOD.

Counting of the Omer *see* OMER, COUNTING OF THE.

Court Jews. Individuals who served as financial or other agents of European rulers. Court Jews were a feature of the absolutist state, especially in central Europe, from the end of the 16th century. They enjoyed special privileges, were exempt from wearing the Jewish badge, and were allowed to live anywhere. Many became extremely wealthy. Because of their position, they were often influential in obtaining rights for their fellow Jews.

Courts *see* BET DIN; CIVIL COURTS; SANHEDRIN (i); TRIBUNAL.

Covenant. Binding agreement between persons, nations, or parties. In the Bible a covenant was effected by a ceremony such as passing between the two halves of a sacrificed animal (Genesis 15.9–11). The covenant made between God and individuals or nations was always accompanied by an external sign: the covenant made with Noah was symbolized by a rainbow (Genesis 9.13); the covenant with Abraham by the act of circumcision (Genesis 17.10); and the covenant with the children of Israel by the institution of the Sabbath (Exodus 31.13). God made a covenant with the house of Aaron to ensure them the priesthood (Numbers 25.12–13). He also made a covenant with David to establish that the monarchy would continue through his descendants (II Samuel 23.5).

Covering of the head. According to Jewish law married women must cover their hair; head-coverings for men were originally required only when special respect was to be shown. Babylonian Jewry, however, placed emphasis on the covering of the head by men and this practice was later adopted in other countries; Islamic influence contributed to its adoption in Spain. In France and Germany as late as the 12th century men could be called up to read the Torah bareheaded. In the 17th century David ha-Levi of Ostrog found a religious basis for this practice in the proscription of gentile customs among the Jews. In the modern period Orthodox Jewish men cover their heads at all times as a sign of humility before God; the covering takes the form of a skull cap known as "kipah" or "yarmulke." Conservative Jews, as well as some Reform Jews, cover their heads during prayers.

Covetousness. The envious desire to possess what belongs to another person. It is forbidden by the tenth commandment (Exodus 20.17). According to the rabbis, the violation of the tenth commandment is a transgression of the entire Decalogue.

Cowen, Joseph (1868–1932). English Zionist. He was the founder and leader of the Zionist movement in England. He encouraged the creation of the British Zionist Federation in 1899. In 1902 he accompanied Theodor Herzl during his audience with the Turkish sultan. He served as director of the Jewish Colonial Trust.

Cowen, Philip (1853–1943). American journalist and author. He was born in New York. In 1879 he founded the weekly *American Hebrew*, which he edited and published for 27 years. From 1905 he served as an official of the US Immigration Service at Ellis Island, and in 1906 he went to Russia on a special mission to report on the causes of immigration from eastern Europe.

Cracow *see* KRACÓW.

Crafts. Craftsmen are referred to in the Bible in connection with the construction of the Tabernacle and the Temple. They included workers in brass, iron, gold, silver, linen, and wood; refiners; smiths; potters; masons; and stone-cutters. In the Talmudic period craftsmanship was regarded highly. In the Middle Ages Jews engaged in wool and silk weaving, dyeing, goldsmithery, and glass manufacture. In modern times Jews have been active in such crafts as tailoring, diamond cutting, shoe-making, and working with furs.

Creation. According to biblical and rabbinic Judaism, God created the cosmos (*see also* GENESIS). The biblical depiction of the creation resembles creation myths in the Babylonian religion. The rabbis of the Talmud accepted gnostic ideas of creation, while many rabbinic scholars believed in *creatio ex nihilo*. Speculations about the nature of the visible universe ("maaseh bereshit") and the transcendental world ("maaseh merkavah") are found in Jewish mysticism. Medieval Jewish philosophy was influenced by the Ptolemaic conception of the cosmos. The Zohar propounds various theories about the nature of creation, which were later modified by Isaac Luria.

Creation, Book of *see* SEPHER YETZIRAH.

Creed. Authoritative statement of religious belief. Judaism does not contain a creedal formulation, but a number of Jewish thinkers have drawn up articles of faith. Philo set out five essential beliefs, and Maimonides listed 13 PRINCIPLES OF FAITH. Other scholars such as Ḥasdai ben Abraham Crescas and Joseph Albo proposed different formulations. Some scholars believed it to be impossible to separate out the essential beliefs of Judaism.

Creizenach, Michael (1789–1842). German educator and proponent of Reform. He was born in Mainz and founded a Jewish boys' school there based on the principles of Reform Judaism. In

1825 he was appointed teacher and preacher at the Philanthropin high school in Frankfurt am Main. With Isaac Marcus Jost he edited the Hebrew periodical *Zion*. In his writings he attempted to show that since talmudic Judaism represented a reform of biblical Judaism, Reform Judaism is a legitimate approach to the Jewish tradition.

Cremation. Disposal of a dead body by burning. It is forbidden by Orthodox Judaism, though some modern Orthodox authorities permit the ashes of a person who has been cremated to be interred in a Jewish cemetery. Reform Judaism permits cremation and its rabbis officiate at cremation ceremonies.

Crémieu(x). French family originating from the village of Crémieu in Dauphiné. Its members included many rabbis at Avignon and Carpentras in the 17th–18th centuries.

Crémieux, Isaac-Adolphe (1796–1880). French lawyer and statesman. He fought for the abolition of the oath *more judaico*. In 1843 he was elected president of the Central Consistory of French Jews. On several occasions he intervened with the government in an attempt to gain protection of Jewish rights in other countries. From 1864 to 1880 he served as president of the Alliance Israélite Universelle.

Crémieux Decree. Decree issued for the French government on 24 October 1870 by Isaac-Adolphe Crémieux. It conferred French citizenship on the Jews of Algeria. The Vichy Government abrogated the decree in 1940, but it was restored in 1943 by General de Gaulle.

Crescas, Ḥasdai ben Abraham (c. 1340–c. 1412). Spanish rabbi and theologian. He was born in Barcelona and was active as a merchant and communal leader there. In 1367 he was imprisoned on a charge of desecrating the Host, but was later released. With the accession of John I in 1387 he became associated with the royal household of the Court of Aragon. He later settled in Zaragoza, where he served as rabbi. In 1391 his son was killed in anti-Jewish riots in Barcelona, which he described in a Hebrew account. His *Light of the Lord* is a refutation of Maimonides.

Cresques, Abraham (fl. 14th cent.). Majorcan cartographer. He was Master of Maps and Compasses to the King of Aragon. In 1375–7 he and his son Judah made the *Catalan Atlas*, which was sent as a gift to the king of France. In 1381 they were granted royal protection and exemption from wearing the Jewish badge.

***Cresques, Judah** [Ribes, Jaime] (fl. 14th–15th cent.). Majorcan cartographer, son of Abraham Cresques. He made maps for John I and Martin of Aragon. During the anti-Jewish outbreaks in Spain in 1391, he converted to Christianity and changed his name to Jaime Ribes. He settled in Barcelona in 1394. From 1399 he is referred to in documents as "magister cartarum navegandi."

Cresson, Warder [Israel, Michael Boaz] (1798–1860). American religious zealot and Zionist. He was born in Philadelphia and emigrated to Palestine, where he converted to Judaism. On his return to the US he was declared insane by a court, but successfully appealed against the decision. He returned to Jerusalem as Michael Boaz Israel and undertook propaganda campaigns against Christian missionary groups and on behalf of the agricultural colonization by Jews of Palestine. Many of his writings were published in the journal *The Occident*.

CRIF [Comité Représentatif des Israélites de France]. French organization founded in Lyons in 1943 to represent the principal Jewish institutions. On a similar model Orthodox Jews in France established CRJTF (Conseil Représentatif du

Judaisme Traditionnel de France) in 1952.

Crime. In Jewish law no distinction is made between ritual and secular offences in respect of procedure and punishment. However, various degrees of seriousness of offense are recognized. In rabbinic law a distinction is made between civil law and criminal law.

Criticism, biblical *see* BIBLICAL CRITICISM.

CRJTF [Conseil Représentatif du Judaisme Traditionnel de France] *see* CRIF.

***Cromwell, Oliver** (1599–1658). English political and military leader, Lord Protector of England (1653–8). Manasseh ben Israel presented petitions to him concerning the return of the Jews to England, and in December 1655 Cromwell convened the Whitehall Conference to consider the problem. The conference was dissolved when it appeared that readmission would be recommended only on the most unfavorable conditions. Cromwell subsequently adopted an informal arrangement for the Jews' return.

Crown [official] **rabbi.** Rabbi appointed by the secular authority to represent the Jewish community in dealings with the state. In medieval England he was called the "Presbyter Judaeorum," in Spain "Rab de la Corte," in Portugal "Arrabi-Mor," and in Sicily "Dienchelele." In 19th-century Russia the crown rabbi was appointed to carry out the government's requirements regarding registration and various regulations. He functioned alongside local rabbis.

Crucifixion. Execution by fastening the condemned to a wooden cross, usually by binding or nailing the hands and feet; the position of the body resulted in death by suffocation. It was common among the Greeks and Romans but unknown in Jewish law. The practice was introduced into Palestine by the Romans, and many Jews were punished in this way. In the New Testament Jesus was sentenced by Pontius Pilate to be crucified.

Crusade. Any of the military expeditions undertaken by the Christian powers of Europe in the Middle Ages to win back the Holy Land from the Muslims. The crusades provoked religious passion and anti-Jewish sentiment and resulted in the massacre of many Jewish communities. During the preparations for the First Crusade (1096–9) Jews in northern France and the Rhineland were killed. Similar attacks took place in Prague and later in Salonica. When Jerusalem was captured in 1099 Jews and Karaites were slaughtered. During the Second Crusade (1147–9) outbreaks of violence again occurred in France and the Rhineland, and in the course of the Third Crusade (1189–92) Jews in England were attacked.

Crypto-Jews. Jews who, while remaining covertly faithful to Judaism, outwardly practiced another religion, which they were forced to accept. The phenomenon arose frequently after the forced conversions under the Visigoths in Spain in the 7th century, and under the Alhomades in north Africa and Spain in the 12th century. Other groups of crypto-Jews were the Neofiti in southern Italy from the end of the 13th century to the 16th, and the Conversos (or Marranos) in Spain after the persecutions of 1391 and the expulsion of 1492, and in Portugal after 1497. In Majorca such Jews were known as the Chuetas. In Persia in the 19th century forcible conversion to Islam gave rise to a group known as the Jedid Al-Islam.

Cukerman, Yitzḥak [Antek] (1915–1981). Polish communal leader in the Warsaw Ghetto. He was one of the four commanders of the Jewish Fighting Organization set up in Warsaw on July 22 1942. During the ghetto uprising in April 1943 he took part in the battle against the Germans. He helped to organize the Jewish National Council, a Jewish underground resistance movement among Jews hiding on the Aryan side of the ghetto boundary. He emigrated to Israel in 1946 and served as a prosecution witness at the Eichmann trial in 1961.

***Cumberland, Richard** (1732–1811). English playwright. His *The Jew* presents a Jewish usurer in a positive light, in contrast to the image of the Jew in Shakespeare's *The Merchant of Venice*. His other works include a comic opera, *The Jew of Mogador*, and a novel, *Nicholas Pedroza*, which depicts the life of the Marranos.

Cuneiform. Script employed in the writing of several ancient languages of Mesopotamia and Persia, including Sumerian and Akkadian. The wedge-shaped characters were incised on tablets with a stylus.

Cup of Elijah. Cup of wine placed on the table at the Passover seder which is not drunk. It is prepared to welcome the prophet, who visits every Jewish home on the Passover night.

Cups. In the Jewish tradition the drinking of wine plays an important role. The cup of benediction is an essential element of all joyous occasions (such as circumcisions, weddings, and the kiddush). At the Passover seder four cups of wine are drunk.

Curse. An appeal to a supernatural power to bring harm on a person or group; also a profane expression of anger. The Bible prohibits cursing God, one's parents, authorities, and the deaf. The Talmud expresses belief in the efficacy of curses. The uttering of a curse is permitted in some cases if it is done for religious reasons. Any curse involving God's name is forbidden.

Cush (i). Son of Ham (Genesis 2.13; 10.6–8).

Cush (ii). Ancient kingdom in north-east Africa.

Custom. Many Jewish regulations are not based on the written or oral law but are binding because they are customarily observed. Different customs developed among Jews in the diaspora, which accounts for variant practices in the Jewish communities of different countries. These variations have been noted by codifiers. Joseph Caro, for example, cited the customs of Spanish Jewry in the Shulḥan Arukh while Moses Isserles in his glosses to this work refers to the customs among the Ashkenazim.

CYCO *see* CENTRAL YIDDISH CULTURE ORGANIZATION.

***Cyril** (fl. 5th cent.). Bishop of Alexandria (c. 412–44). His animosity toward the Jews led to the expulsion and destruction of the Alexandrian Jewish community.

***Cyrus II** (fl. 6th cent. BCE). King of Persia (559–529 BCE). According to the Bible God appointed him to rebuild Jerusalem. In 538 BCE Cyrus granted permission to the Jews to return to Jerusalem and rebuild the Temple. (Ezra 1.1–44; II Chronicles 36.22–3).

CYSHO *see* CENTRAL YIDDISH SCHOOL ORGANIZATION.

***Czacki, Tadeusz** (1765–1813). Polish statesman and historian. From 1786 to 1792 he served in the Polish treasury and was responsible for supervising Jewish affairs in the country. He sought to ameliorate the position of the Jewish population. He wrote a comprehensive history of Polish Jewry.

D

Dachau. Town near Munich, Bavaria, where the first concentration camp was established by the Nazi regime in March 1932. It served as a model for other camps, and was the first in which doctors and scientists experimented on prisoners.

Da Costa, Isaac (1721–1783). American merchant and shipping agent. He was born in London and emigrated to Charleston, South Carolina, in the late 1740s. He was a founder in 1749 of Congregation Beth Elohim, where he served as cantor. Later he settled in Philadelphia, where he helped establish Congregation Mikveh Israel.

Dagesh. Diacritical mark in Hebrew, taking the form of a dot in a consonant. It indicates one of two things: that the consonant (e.g., bet, gimel, dalet, kaph, pe, tav) is to be pronounced with a hard sound; or that the consonant, which is written once, is to be pronounced as though it were doubled (this does not apply to aleph, he, ḥet, ayin, resh). In every case the dagesh is written inside the letter form.

***Dagon.** Canaanite god of seed and vegetation. The Philistines worshipped him as their god and set up temples to him in Gaza (Judges 16.23) and Ashdod (I Samuel 5.1–7). After the battle on Mount Gilboa the Philistines exposed the body of Saul in the temple of Dagon and his weapons at the sanctuary of Ashtaroth (I Samuel 31.10, 12; I Chronicles 10.10).

Dahia al-Kahinah (fl. 8th cent.). Queen of judaizing Berber tribes of the Aurez mountains in Algeria. She led her tribes successfully against Muslim invaders.

Dahlberg, Edward (1900–1977). American novelist. Born in Boston, he lived a vagabond existence and eventually settled in Europe. His novels *Bottom Dogs* and *From Flushing to Calvary* reflect his early childhood experiences. His *Those who Perish* deals with the impact of Nazism on a small American Jewish community. His later works include *Can these Bones Live*, *Flea of Sodom*, *The Sorrows of Priapus*, and *Truth is More Sacred*.

Daiches, David (b. 1912). English literary critic, nephew of Samuel Daiches. He was born in Sunderland. He taught at the universities of Chicago, Cornell, Cambridge, and Sussex. His *Two Worlds: an Edinburgh Jewish Childhood* depicts his rebellion against Orthodox Judaism personified by his father. His interest in Hebrew matters is reflected in *The King James Version of the English Bible*.

Daiches, Israel Ḥayyim (1850–1937). British Orthodox rabbi and scholar. He was born in Darshunishek, Lithuania, and eventually settled in England, where he served as a rabbi in Leeds. He founded the Union of Orthodox Rabbis of England. His writing includes annotations on the Jerusalem Talmud, responsa, and sermons.

Daiches, Samuel (1878–1949). British rabbi and scholar, son of Israel Ḥayyim Daiches. He was born in Vilnius. He served as rabbi in Sunderland, England, and later became a lecturer in the Bible, Talmud, and midrash at Jews College. He took an active part in the work of B'nai B'rith, the Anglo-Jewish Association, the Board of Deputies of British Jews, the Jewish Agency, and Jewish relief organizations. His published works include studies of Babylonian antiquity and its influence on Judaism, the Psalms, the Talmud in Spain, and Jewish divorce law.

Dainow, Tzevi Hirsch [Maggid of Slutsk] (1832–1877). Russian preacher. He was born in Slutsk. He advocated combining Torah with the Haskalah, and upheld the efficacy of manual labor and the need for educational reform. He was active on behalf of the Society for the Promotion of Culture among the Jews of Russia. Due to opposition to his views, he emigrated to England and settled in London, where he preached to Russian and Polish immigrants.

Dalet. Fourth letter of the Hebrew alphabet. Its numerical value is 4.

***Dalman, Gustaf Hermann** (1855–1941). German scholar. Associated with the Missionary Church Brotherhood, he became professor at the Institutum Judaicum in Leipzig in 1895. From 1902 to 1917 he served as director of the German Evangelical Institute for Antiquity in Jerusalem. Later he was professor at the Institute of Palestinology in Greifswald. He wrote studies in the fields of theology, Semitics, historical geography and topography, and Palestinian folklore.

Damascus. Capital of Syria. During the period of the reign of the kings of Judah it was the capital of Aram-Dammesek. Many of its Jews were killed in the revolt against Rome in 67, but it continued to harbor a Jewish population throughout succeeding centuries. In the 9th–10th centuries it was a Karaite center. After the Damascus Affair in 1840 many Jews left the city.

Damascus Affair. In 1840 a superior of the Franciscan convent in Damascus and his servant disappeared. Leading Jews were tortured and a confession of murder was obtained. This led to a campaign against the Jewish community. Through the intervention of Sir Moses Montefiore and Isaac-Adolphe Crémieux, the murder charge was dropped and the Jewish survivors of the unrest were released.

Dan. Israelite, fifth son of Jacob and the firstborn of Bilhah, Rachel's maid (Genesis 30.1–6). One of the 12 tribes of Israel took this name.

Dan, Joseph (b. 1935). Israeli scholar. He was born in Bratislava, Czechoslovakia, and went to Palestine in 1938. He taught at the Hebrew University, where in 1983 he was appointed the Gershom Scholem Professor of Kabbalah. His publications include *Ideological Movements and Conflicts in Jewish History.*

Danby, Frank *see* FRANKAU, JULIA.

***Danby, Herbert** (1889–1953). English Hebraist. He served as librarian and canon of the Anglican Cathedral of St. George in Jerusalem. In 1936 he was appointed professor of Hebrew at Oxford. His writings include an English translation of the Mishnah as well as a translation of parts of Maimonides' *Mishneh Torah.*

Dance. In ancient Israel meals, wine festivals, weddings, funerals, and ceremonials were accompanied by dancing. In the Maccabean period the Jews adopted Greek and Roman dances. During the Middle Ages almost every Jewish community in France, Germany, and Poland had a wedding house, where dancing took place. With the rise of Ḥasidism in the 18th century, dance assumed great religious importance for the Jewish masses. Many folk dances have evolved in modern Israel.

Danger. The biblical verses "Only take heed to yourself and keep your soul diligently" and "Take good heed to your souls" (Deuteronomy 4.9, 15) were interpreted in rabbinic sources as constituting a commandment prescribing the duty of personal safety and the avoidance of danger to life. The Talmud contains a long list of prohibitions for the purpose of preventing danger to life. The duty of preserving life takes precedence over and annuls all commandments, with the exception of the sins of idolatry, immorality, and the shedding of innocent blood.

Daniel [Belteshazzar]. Biblical book in the Hagiographa. It relates the story of Daniel, a Judean exile in Babylon (where he was known as Belteshazzar), and the miraculous experiences that occurred to him and his friends at the courts of Nebuchadnezzar, Darius the Mede, and Belshazzar. The second half of the book contains visions of the rise and fall of empires from Babylon to Macedon and beyond. Daniel is also the hero of the story of Susanna and the Elders and two other tales in the book of *Bel and the Dragon*.

Daniel ben Moses al-Kumisi [Al-Damagani] (fl. 9th–10th cent.). Karaite scholar and leader of the Avele Zion (Mourners of Zion). He was born in Damghan in northern Persia, and was the first eminent Karaite scholar to settle in Jerusalem. His *Pitron Sheneim-Asar* is a commentary on the Minor Prophets, which contains criticism of the rabbinate.

Daniel Sieff Research Institute *see* WEIZMANN INSTITUTE.

Danzig, Abraham ben Jehiel Michael (1748–1820). Polish rabbinic scholar. He was born in Danzig and served as dayyan in Vilnius from 1794 to 1812. His *Ḥayye Adam* (Human life) and *Ḥokhmat Adam* (Human wisdom) contain succinct presentations of parts of the Shulḥan Arukh.

Danziger, Itzchak (1916–1978). Israeli sculptor. He was born in Berlin and he settled in Palestine in 1923. He later taught at the Haifa Technion. His early sculptures achieved a balance between Near Eastern sculpture and a modern concept of human form. He was awarded the Israeli Prize for Sculpture in 1968.

***Darius I** (fl. 6th–5th cent. BCE). King of Persia (522–486 BCE). He permitted Zerubbabel and the Jews who returned to Jerusalem to resume reconstruction of the Temple.

Darmesteter, Arsène (1846–1888). French philologist, brother of James Darmesteter. He was born at Château-Salins. He was appointed lecturer in French language and literature at the Sorbonne in 1877 and also taught at the École Rabbinique. He was a founder of the Société de Études Juives and the *Revue des Études Juives*. His writings include a dictionary of 11th-century French, based on medieval Jewish commentators, and a dictionary of Rashi's French glosses in his commentaries on the Bible and the Talmud.

Darmesteter, James (1849–1894). French orientalist, brother of Arsène Darmesteter. He was born at Château-Salins. He became professor at the Collège de France. He translated the sacred books of the Zoroastrian religion into French and English and published material concerning the relationship between Zoroastrianism and Judaism.

Darmstadt Haggadah. Illuminated codex of the Passover evening service, produced in western Germany in about 1430. It is one of the most beautiful Jewish illuminated manuscripts of the Middle Ages.

Darshan ("Expounder [of Scripture]"). Title conferred on a preacher. Originally one given this title expounded both halakhically and aggadically on the biblical text. In the Middle Ages the term was used for a professional preacher. In some eastern European communities a person was appointed to be the official darshan of the community. An alternative title, given to both the official and the itinerant preacher, was "maggid."

Dathan (fl. ?13th cent. BCE). Israelite rebel leader, head of a family of the tribe of Reuben. He and Abiram, also of the tribe of Reuben, joined Koraḥ in his rebellion against Moses, whom they attacked for assuming the leadership; as descendants of Jacob's eldest son, they claimed the leadership for themselves. Later they were swallowed up by the earth. (Numbers 16)

Daube, David (1909–1989). British jurist and biblical scholar. He was born in Freiburg, Germany. He taught at the universities of Cambridge, Aberdeen, and Oxford, and at the University of California at Berkeley. He wrote studies of biblical and rabbinic law, the New Testament and rabbinic Judaism, and various themes in Scripture.

Daughter(s) of Zion. Biblical phrase referring to Jerusalem or the Jewish people.

Davar. Israeli daily newspaper of the Histadrut. It was first published in 1925 under the editorship of Berl Katznelson. It was the first daily of the Israeli labor movement, and has been concerned with the problems of the yishuv, Zionism, international socialism, and world politics.

Daven. Term used among the Ashkenazim, meaning "to pray."

David (fl. 11th–10th cent. BCE). King of Israel (c. 1001–986 BCE). David's life is divided into three main phases: the first when Saul was alive; the second when he was king in Judah (c. 1008–1001 BCE); the third when he was king over all Israel. A warrior king, he succeeded in uniting the tribes of Israel and created a kingdom that dominated surrounding peoples and attained power and riches. The Psalms were supposed to have been written by him. The account of his life appears in I Samuel 16ff., II Samuel, I Kings 1–2, and I Chronicles 10ff.

David, City of *see* JERUSALEM.

David, Star [Shield] **of** *see* MAGEN DAVID.

David, Tomb of. According to the Bible, David was buried in Jerusalem, to the south-east of the present area of Siloam (I Kings 2.10). Later kings of the Davidic dynasty were also buried there.

David ben Abraham Alfasi *see* ALFASI, DAVID.

David ben Judah he-Ḥasid (fl. 14th cent.). Spanish kabbalist, grandson of Naḥmanides. He wrote commentaries on the Zohar and the order of the prayers, and a treatise on the mysteries of the alphabet.

David ben Samuel ha-Levi (1586–1667). Polish rabbi and halakhic authority. He was born in the Ukraine. He established his own bet midrash in Kraków, and later served as a rabbi in Posen and Ostrog, where he maintained a yeshivah. During the Chmielnicki pogroms (1648–9), he escaped to a fortress in Ulick. In 1654 he was appointed rabbi of Lwów. His *Ture Zahav* (*Taz*) is a commentary on the Shulḥan Arukh.

David ben Solomon ibn Zimra *see* ZIMRA, DAVID BEN SOLOMON IBN AVI.

David ben Zakkai I (fl. 10th cent.). Babylonian exilarch (917–40). He appointed Saadyah ben Joseph gaon of Sura, but later quarreled with him and had him deposed. The supporters of Saadyah attempted to appoint a new exilarch, Josiah-Ḥasan. After a bitter dispute the two parties reached a compromise.

David de Caderousse *see* DAVIN DE CADEROUSSE.

David ibn Merwan al-Mukammas *see* AL-MUKAMMAS, DAVID BEN MERWAN.

David of Karlin *see* FRIEDMANN, DAVID BEN SAMUEL.

Davidson, Israel (1870–1939). American Hebrew scholar. He was born in Lithuania and emigrated to the US in 1888. He became professor of medieval Hebrew literature at the Jewish Theological Seminary. His *Thesaurus of Medieval Hebrew Poetry* lists in alphabetical order the initial words of more than 35,000 poems and prayers from post-biblical times to the Haskalah period.

Davin [David] **de Caderousse** (fl. 15th cent.). French dyer. He was the first Jew to attempt the printing of Hebrew. He lived in Avignon, where he met a Christian goldsmith (Pocop Waldvogel) from Prague. He promised to teach Waldvogel the art of dyeing, in return for which Waldvogel was to give him 27 iron letters of the Hebrew alphabet as well as instruments for printing. This arrangement broke down, and no specimen of the earliest Hebrew printing press has survived.

Davka ("exactly"). Hebrew and Yiddish term used to emphasize the accuracy of a fact or to draw attention to something unexpected. It also indicates obstinacy.

Day. The Mishnah divides the day into 24 hours. Depending on the time of year, an hour was of different duration since the period of daylight, however long or short, was divided into 12 hours. In the talmudic period more sophisticated methods for dividing time came into use.

Dayan, Moshe (1915–1981). Israeli military commander and politician, son of Shemuel Dayan. He was born in Deganyah Alef. During the War of Independence in 1948 he commanded the defense of Jewish settlements in the Jordan Valley. In 1952 he was appointed chief of operations at GHQ and later became commander-in-chief. In 1959 he was elected to the Knesset as a member of the Mapai party. Later he was elected to the Sixth Knesset representing Rafi. He conducted the Six Day War in 1967 and the Yom Kippur War in 1973 as minister of defense.

Dayan, Shemuel (1891–1968). Israeli pioneer and politician. He was born in the Ukraine and settled in Palestine in 1908. He was a founder of Deganyah and Nahalal and a leader of the moshavim cooperative settlement organization. He represented Mapai in the Knesset from 1949 to 1959. His writings include *Nahalal*, *Moshav Ovedim*, *Pioneers in Israel*, and *Man and the Soil*.

Day of Atonement [Yom Kippur]. Solemn fast day observed on 10 Tishri (Leviticus 23.32). To keep it one must refrain from work and cleanse oneself from sin (Leviticus 16.30). It ends the Ten Days of Penitence. In biblical times on the Day of Atonement the high priest entered the Holy of Holies dressed in white linen. The synagogue service contains prayers for forgiveness.

Day of Judgment. The occasion of the last judgment by God at the end of the world, when he will decide the final fate of all individuals. The Bible refers to an eschatological Day of Judgment. The Mishnah states that the judgment of the world is continuing and takes place at four different periods during the year. In the Jewish liturgy the New Year (on 1 Tishri) is considered an annual day of judgment for all people. Decrees are finally sealed on the Day of Atonement.

Day of the Lord. The time when God will punish the wicked and justice will triumph. The term is found in various prophetic passages, the prevailing feature of which is a dramatic sense of doom. The usual message is that the Day of the Lord is near.

Days of Awe *see* YAMIM NORAIM.

Dayyan. Title conferred on the judge in a rabbinical court. The title is confined to the members of the bet din (other than its head, who is referred to as "av bet din" or "rosh bet din"). Sometimes elders of the community or guild functionaries were given the title. In England the title is accorded to members of the official religious law courts, particularly that of the chief rabbi.

Dayyenu ("It would have satisfied us"). Refrain of a song of thanksgiving in the Passover Haggadah. The song enumerates 15 stages of the redemption of the Jews from Egyptian bondage.

Dead, Prayers for the *see* KADDISH.

Dead Sea. Lake between Israel and Jordan. It is also known as the Sea of the Arabah, the East Sea, the Sea of Sodom, the Sea of Lot, and the Sea of Death.

Dead Sea Scrolls. Collection of ancient manuscripts found between 1947 and 1956 in caves in various areas west of the Dead Sea. They are written in Hebrew and Aramaic and date mainly from c. 150 BCE to 68 CE, when the monastic community at Qumran, which owned them, was destroyed by the Romans. They contain fragments of nearly every book of the Bible, as well as copies of the book of Isaiah. Fragments have also been found of the Apocrypha and Pseudepigrapha. In addition, they contain the plan of a struggle between the Sons of Light and the Sons of Darkness, religious hymns, the rule by which the sect was governed, details of a hidden treasure, and minute descriptions of the Temple. Many scholars believe they were written by the Essenes. They are housed in the Shrine of the Book in Israel.

Deaf, imbeciles, and minors. Individuals who fall into any of these three categories are deprived of legal rights in Jewish law, since they are viewed as lacking understanding and being incapable of exercising responsibility. The Talmud decrees that they cannot claim property, their business transactions are invalid, and they are debarred from acting as witnesses.

Death. The last act of a dying Jew is to recite a special confession of sin ("viddui") and the Shema. After death the body is washed and watched until it is buried. According to the Bible, the dead continue to exist in Sheol. The concept of resurrection and reward and punishment in the after-life became a central tenet of Pharisaic Judaism.

Death penalty *see* CAPITAL PUNISHMENT.

Deborah (i) (fl. 12th cent. BCE). Israelite woman, judge and prophetess. She promoted the war of liberation from the oppression of Jabin, King of Canaan (Judges 4). She was the author of the Song of Deborah (Judges 5), which describes the battle and victory of the Israelites over the Canaanites.

Deborah (ii). American German-language weekly publication. Edited by Isaac Mayer Wise, it was published in Cincinnati from 1855 to 1900.

Debt. Biblical law contains many ordinances to ease the burden of debt: a creditor may not charge interest; debts are automatically canceled every seven years; and chattels may not be taken in lieu of payment of a debt. Eventually these provisions were modified to facilitate credit; Hillel introduced the prosbul to overcome the cancelation of debts in the Sabbatical year, and the rabbis decreed that chattels could become security.

Decalogue *see* TEN COMMANDMENTS.

Decapolis (from Greek: "ten cities"). League of ten Hellenized cities, including Damascus, in north-eastern Palestine. It was established by Pompey in 63 BCE and governed by Rome.

Dedication. In Jewish religious practice a liturgical ceremony is performed to dedicate a building for a sacred purpose or a plot of land for a cemetery. The dedication of a sanctuary dates from the biblical period. In post-biblical times the Temple was rededicated by Judah Maccabee and this occasion is celebrated by the festival of Ḥanukkah. Ceremonies for the dedication of other sacred buildings are of later origin. The order of service for the dedication of a cemetery includes the recitation of penitential prayers at the morning service on the day of dedication.

Deed (Hebrew "shetar," "sepher"). In Jewish law a document witnessed by two individuals which confirms the conveyance of property, marriage contract, and bill of divorce on the occasion of a marriage. In the Bible it is known as a "sepher," but in rabbinic sources it is referred to as a "shetar" or "get." The "shetar ḥov" is a sealed bond acknowledged by two witnesses; it makes liable for seizure all property held by the giver of the bond at the time of its signature.

De Haan, Jacob Meijer (1852–1895). Dutch painter. He was born in Amsterdam, where he ran a biscuit factory with his brothers. They also formed a string quartet which gained a reputation throughout the Netherlands. A disciple of Gauguin, he was a popular painter of Jewish subjects.

Deinard, Ephraim (1846–1930). Bibliographer and Hebrew author of Latvian origin. He worked for much of his life as a bookseller in Odessa. In 1897 he tried unsuccessfully to found an agricultural settlement in Nevada. In 1913 he settled in Palestine, but he was expelled three years later by the Turks. He then returned to the US and continued his bibliographic work. His writings include: *Or Mayer: Catalogue of Old Hebrew Manuscripts and Printed Books of the Library of the Hon. Mayer Sulzberger of Philadelphia*, and *Koheleth America*, a list of Hebrew books published in America between 1735 and 1926. He also wrote polemical books and pamphlets on a variety of Jewish topics.

De Lange, Nicholas (b. 1944). English scholar. He was born in Nottingham. He became lecturer in rabbinics at Cambridge University in 1971. His publications include *Judaism*, *Apocrypha*, *Jewish Literature of the Hellenistic Age*, and *Atlas of the Jewish World*.

Delilah (fl. 12th–11th cent. BCE). Philistine woman, mistress of Samson. She persuaded Samson to tell her the secret of his strength, which lay in his hair (as a Nazirite he abstained from cutting his hair). While Samson was asleep she cut his hair so that he could be taken captive by the Philistines, who blinded and enslaved him. (Judges 16)

***Delitzsch, Franz** (1813–1890). German theologian and Judaist. He was born in Leipzig and taught at the universities of Leipzig, Rostock, and Erlangen. He translated the New Testament into Hebrew and in 1880 established the Institutum Judaicum in Leipzig for the training of missionary workers among Jews. His writings include a history of Jewish poetry and commentaries on several books of the Bible. He defended the Jewish community against anti-Semitic attacks.

***Delitzsch, Friedrich** (1850–1922). German orientalist. He was a professor of Semitic languages and Assyriology in Leipzig, Breslau, and Berlin. He published studies of Babylonian culture and the world of the Bible, and a critical account of Judaism and the Jews.

Della Reina, Joseph *see* REINA, JOSEPH DELLA.

Della Torre, Lelio (1805–1871). Italian rabbi and scholar. He was born in Cuneo in Piedmont. He became professor of Talmud at the Padua Rabbinical College. He published volumes of Hebrew poetry, sermons, and a commentary on the Pentateuch; he also translated and annotated the Psalms, and rendered the prayers according to Ashkenazi custom into Italian.

Delmedigo, Elijah ben Moses Abba (c. 1460–1497). Greco-Italian philosopher and talmudist. He was born in Crete and emigrated to Italy, where he served as head of the yeshivah in Padua. He engaged in a bitter controversy on a halakhic question with Judah Mintz, the rabbi of Padua. Subsequently he left Italy and returned to Crete, where he completed his major work, *The Examination of Religion*.

Delmedigo, Joseph Solomon ben Elijah [Medigo, Joseph Solomon ben Elijah del] (1591–1655). Cretan rabbi, philosopher, mathematician, and astronomer. He studied astronomy and mathematics under Galileo at the University of Padua, then traveled widely, visiting Egypt, Turkey, Poland, Germany, Holland, and Bohemia. He wrote studies of religious, metaphysical, and scientific topics.

Demai. Third tractate in the Mishnah order of Zeraim. It deals with the requirements for tithing produce in cases where there is doubt whether proper tithes have been given.

Dembitz, Lewis Naphtali (1833–1907). American lawyer. He was born in Prussia and emigrated to the US in 1849. Initially he was involved with Reform Judaism, but later joined the Conservative movement and helped to establish the Jewish Theological Seminary. He contributed articles on Talmudic jurisprudence and liturgy to the *Jewish Encyclopedia*, and prepared the translations of Exodus and Leviticus for the revised English Bible. He also wrote *Jewish Services in Synagogue and Home*.

Dembitzer, Ḥayyim Nathan (1820–1892). Polish talmudist and historian. He was born in Kraków and became a dayyan there. He was active in financial support of the old yishuv in Palestine. He published works on responsa literature, the tosaphists, and talmudic and rabbinic literature; he also wrote biographies of the rabbis of Lwów/Lemberg and neighboring communities.

***Demetrius I** (fl. 2nd cent. BCE). King of Syria (162–150 BCE). His general, Bacchides, was victorious over Judah Maccabee in 160 BCE. Demetrius became embroiled with Attalus II of Pergamon and Ptolemy V of Egypt, who joined forces against him in support of the pretender to the Syrian throne, Alexander Balas. He was later defeated in battle.

***Demetrius II** (fl. 2nd cent. BCE). King of Syria (145–138 BCE). He expelled Alexander Balas and confirmed Jonathan the Hasmonean as high priest. Tryphon rose against him in the name of Alexander Balas' son and Demetrius II was imprisoned. He later regained the kingdom only to lose it once more through revolution.

Democracy. Government by the people or their elected representatives. Ancient Israel was not a democracy though the Bible does lay down principles for governing the people. Political democracy was not possible for the Jews in the diaspora, since they lived under alien rule. In medieval Jewish communities authority was generally invested in the wealthy, but the rights of the poor were respected. In the 19th century European Jewry supported the institution of democratic government. In modern Israel the Vaad Leumi and later the Knesset were organized on a democratic basis.

Democratic Fraction. The name taken by a group of delegates at the Fifth Zionist Congress in 1901. It included Chaim Weizmann and Martin Buber. It encouraged nationalism, cultural activity, democracy in the leadership of the Zionist movement, and concern for youth. It disappeared after the election of the Zionist Council at the congress.

Demonology. The study of demons or demonic beliefs. The Bible and rabbinic sources refer to various demonic beings. In the kabbalah there is a dichotomy between the demonic and the divine spheres. Demons also play a role in Jewish folklore and legend. Amulets and magic formulae were used to protect Jews from their evil influence.

Denunciation. In Jewish law it is a serious offence for one Jew to denounce another Jew to gentile authorities, except where a criminal act has been committed. A prayer for condemnation of such slanderers was included in the daily Amidah prayer from the 1st century.

Derash *see* MIDRASH.

Derekh eretz ("way of the land"). Desirable behavior, in keeping with accepted social and moral standards. It includes rules of etiquette and polite behavior. In rabbinic sources it refers to normal human behavior, worldly occupation, and correct conduct.

Derekh Eretz Rabbah. Minor tractate appended to the Babylonian Talmud at the end of Nezikin. It includes laws relating to forbidden marriages, moral sayings, rules of conduct, and a list of practices that are dangerous to life.

Derekh Eretz Zuta. Minor tractate appended to the Babylonian Talmud at the end of Nezikin. It consists of exhortations to self-examination and modesty, and extols temperance, resignation, gentleness, patience, respect for the elderly, and forgiveness.

Derenbourg, Hartwig (1844–1908). French orientalist, son of Joseph Derenbourg. He lectured in Arabic at the École des Langues Orientales Vivants in Paris, and on oriental languages at the École Rabbinique. In 1885 he became professor of Arabic at the École des Hautes Études. He wrote studies of Arabic grammar, literature, and religion, and of Semitic manuscripts and inscriptions.

Derenbourg, Joseph (1811–1895). French orientalist. He worked as a domestic tutor in Amsterdam in 1835–8, and then settled in Paris. In 1852 he became corrector at the Imprimerie Nationale, and also catalogued the Hebrew manuscripts at the Bibliothèque Nationale. In 1877 he was appointed to a chair for rabbinic Hebrew language and literature at the École Pratique des Hautes Études. He published studies of oriental languages and inscriptions as well as works on various Jewish subjects.

Derenbourg, Tzevi Hirsch (fl. 18th cent.). German Hebrew writer. He was born in Offenbach and went to Mainz in 1789, where he kept a restaurant and was a private tutor of Hebrew. His *Yoshevei Tevel* is a didactic moral drama.

Derush. Homiletic or aggadic interpretation.

***Derzhavin, Gavriil** (1743–1816). Russian administrator. His investigation of the Jewish problem influenced Russian policy and the status of the Jews in Russia from the beginning of the 19th century until the end of the czarist regime. He recommended that the Jews be divided into four estates according to income and place of residence. In addition he suggested that the steppes of Astrakhan and New Russia should be made available for Jewish agricultural colonization.

Desecration of the host. The defilement of the consecrated bread or wafer used in the Christian sacrament of the Eucharist. After the recognition by the Fourth Lateran Council in 1215 of the doctrine of transubstantiation (according to which the bread becomes the body of Christ), the accusation that Jews defiled or tortured the host became common in Europe. It was the pretext for a number of Jewish massacres, the first of which took place in Belitz in 1243; other outbreaks occurred in Paris in 1290, in Brussels in 1370, and in Segovia in 1410.

Desecration of the name *see* ḤILLUL HA-SHEM.

De Spinoza, Benedict *see* SPINOZA, BENEDICT.

Detention camps. They were set up in the 1940s by the British administration for Jewish immigrants who entered Palestine in contravention of the Mandatory regulations; they were also used for those accused of political offenses. From January 1940 immigrants were confined to Athlit; from August 1946 most were sent to Cyprus. Alleged members of Jewish terrorist organizations were sent to camps at Latrun and in Kenya and Eritrea.

Determinism. The philosophical doctrine that all acts, choices, and events are determined by causal necessity or by God's decree. Judaism combines a belief in free will with a belief in divine foreknowledge. In the Middle Ages a number of Jewish theologians discussed how these concepts could be compatible.

Deutero-Isaiah *see* ISAIAH (ii).

Deuteronomy (Hebrew "Devarim"). Biblical book, the fifth book of the Torah. It contains Moses' review of events after the giving of the law on Mount Sinai; his ethical exhortation and a summary of divine legislation; his final speeches; his farewell song and blessing; and an account of his death.

Deuteronomy Rabbah (Hebrew "Devarim Rabbah"). Aggadic midrash on the book of Deuteronomy. It is part of Midrash Rabbah. It consists of 27 expositions each beginning with a halakhic statement. It draws upon tannaitic literature, the Palestinian Talmud, Genesis Rabbah, and Leviticus Rabbah.

Deuterosis. Term applied by the Byzantine emperor Justianian to rabbinic interpretation, which he forbade to be incorporated into the synagogue liturgy.

Deutsch, Bernard Seymour (1884–1935). American lawyer and communal leader. He was born in Baltimore. In 1933 he was elected president of the Board of Aldermen of New York in 1933. He was president of the American Jewish Congress and led campaigns with Stephen Samuel Wise to arouse public opinion on behalf of the rights of German Jews.

Deutsch, Emanuel Oscar Menaḥem (1829–1873). British orientalist. He was born in Upper Saxony. He became assistant in the oriental department of the British Museum in 1855. He wrote studies of Phoenician inscriptions, the Targumim, the Samaritan Pentateuch, and the Jewish background of Jesus.

Deutsch, Gotthard (1859–1921). American historian and theologian of Moravian origin. He became professor of Jewish history and philosophy at the Hebrew Union College, Cincinnati, in 1891. In 1901 he succeeded Isaac Mayer Wise as editor of *Deborah*. He published studies of Jewish history and served as editor of the modern Jewish history division of the *Jewish Encyclopedia*.

Deutsch, Leo (1855–1941). Russian revolutionary. He was born in Tylchin. In 1877 he led a revolt of Ukrainian peasants. He was exiled to Siberia in 1884 but escaped in 1901. Later he moved to the US, where he edited a workers' journal, but he returned to Russia in 1917. In 1923 he published in Berlin a study of Jews in the Russian revolutionary movement.

Deutsch, Moritz (1818–1892). German cantor and teacher of Moravian origin. He became second cantor of the Liberal Temple in Vienna. He later served as chief cantor of the Reform synagogue in Breslau. He taught cantorial music at the Breslau Theological Seminary for 30 years and composed original arrangements of liturgical music.

Deutscher, Isaac (1907–1967). British historian and political scientist. He was born in Kraków. He was a member of the Communist Party in Poland, but was expelled, and in 1939 went to London, where he was on the editorial staff of the *Economist* and the *Observer*. Later he devoted himself to historical research. He wrote political biographies of Stalin and Trotsky and published works on Stalin, Soviet Russia, and Communism. His *The Non-Jewish Jew and Other Essays* describes the contributions of such Jews as Spinoza, Freud, Marx, and Trotsky.

Devarim *see* DEUTERONOMY.

Devekut ("cleaving [to God]"). Spiritual state of communion with God, achieved during prayer and meditation. The term is based on the phrase "love the Lord your God . . . and cleave unto him (Deuteronomy 11.22). Usually devekut is described as the highest step on a spiritual ladder. It plays an important role in the kabbalah.

Devir. Israeli Hebrew publishing house. It was founded in Berlin in 1922 by Ḥayyim Naḥman Bialik, Shemaryahu Levin, and Yehoshua Ḥana Ravnitzky. It later acquired the rights of Moriah in Odessa. In 1924 it moved to Tel Aviv and published works of Hebrew literature and scholarship.

Devotion (Hebrew "kavvanah"). The Bible and rabbinic literature stress that observances and prayer must be conducted with inner devotion and steadfast INTENT ("kavvanah"). The concept of devotion is of particular importance in the kabbalah, since prayer can influence the upper realms ("sephirot"). Kabbalists maintain that devotion in prayer can be attained by the mystical action of combining the letters of God's name.

Devotional literature. In Jewish religious practice devotional literature consists of the traditional Jewish liturgy; services for prayer meetings (such as Joseph Jedidiah Carmi's hymn collection); private meditations for various occasions (such as those collected by Nathan Hannover in *Shaare Zion*); and pious writings such as Solomon ibn Gabirol's *Keter Malkhut*. In addition, many devotional handbooks have been published, such as *Prayers and Meditations* by Hester de Rothschild.

Dhimma (Arabic). Legal term used in Muslim lands to denote the relationship between protector and protected. It fixed the legal status of Jews and Christians and involved mutual obligations. The Muslim government agreed to protect the life and property of non-Muslims, exempted them from military service, and guaranteed them religious freedom. Those who were protected were under the obligation to pay the poll tax, not to insult Islam, not to convert Muslims, and not to betray the Muslim government.

Dhu Nuwas (fl. 6th cent.). Arabian king. He was the last ruler of the Himyarite kingdom (d. 525). He converted to Judaism and took the name Yusuf when he ascended the throne. When the Christian city of Najarn surrendered to his forces, he encouraged the inhabitants to embrace Judaism; on their refusing to do so, he killed a large number.

Dialectics *see* PILPUL.

Dialects. Jewish dialects fall into two groups. The first consists of local dialects of the language of the country in which the speakers live (Judeo-Aramaic, Judeo-Arabic, Judeo-Persian, Judeo-German, Judeo-Italian, Judeo-Provençal); these differ from the vernacular by preserving old forms of speech or the addition of Hebrew words. The second group consists of languages of the Jews of particular regions, which continue to be spoken when they migrate to another country (Yiddish, Ladino).

Diamond, David (b. 1915). American composer. His compositions include violin concertos, symphonies, chamber music, ballets, film scores, and choral music. His *Ahavah* for narrator and orchestra is based on Jewish themes.

Diaries. As a source of information on Jewish history, diaries are a comparatively recent phenomenon. The first significant diary is *Maagal Tov* (1753–78) by Ḥayyim Azulai, which records details of his travels in the Holy Land. Other important diaries include the record of his travels by Sir Moses Montefiore, the diaries of Theodor Herzl, which describe his Zionist activities, and the numerous diaries of Holocaust victims.

Diaspora. The dispersion and settlement of the Jews outside Palestine after the Babylonian captivity. When the Temple was destroyed in the 6th century BCE large numbers of Jews settled in Babylonia. From the Hellenistic period onward Jews lived in many lands, including Islamic and Christian countries. In the Middle Ages Jews in northern and western Europe were much persecuted and often expelled from the countries in which they lived. Eventually they gravitated to eastern Europe, then to the US; many also sought to return to Palestine. The establishment of the State of Israel and the emigration there of many Jews have profoundly affected Jewish life in the diaspora.

Dibbuk [dybbuk]. Evil spirit, which enters into a person. It cleaves to the soul, causes mental illness, talks through his mouth, and represents an alien personality. It can be exorcised by conjuring the divine name; such exorcism was practiced in the circle of Isaac Luria and later by wonder-workers and Ḥasidic tzaddikim. A play entitled *The Dybbuk* was written by S. An-Ski.

Dick, Isaac Meir (1814–1893). Polish Yiddish author. He was born in Vilnius. As an exponent of the Haskalah, he advocated reforms in Jewish life. He was the first popular writer of Yiddish fiction, producing more than 300 stories and short novels, which introduced sentimental and realistic story-telling into Yiddish literature. He also popularized knowledge of the Bible, wrote on the Passover Haggadah, and composed a popular version of the Shulḥan Arukh.

Dictionaries, Bible [concordances]. The first dictionary of the Hebrew Scriptures was Blasius Ugolini's *Thesaurus antiquitatum sacrarum* (1744–69). This was followed by *Dictionnaire historique et critique, chronologique, géographique et littéraire de la Bible* by Auguste Calmet, which was published in 1772. The development of oriental archeology led to the publication of the *Encyclopaedia biblica* (1899–1903); *Dictionary of the Bible* (1898–1904); and *Dictionnaire de la Bible* (1891–1912). The first Jewish Bible dictionary was the *Entziklopedia Mikrait* (1950–68). The *Encyclopaedia Judaica* (1972–), a comprehensive work in many volumes, also contains numerous entries on biblical subjects.

Dictionaries, Hebrew. The first Hebrew dictionary was written in 912 by Saadyah ben Joseph. Others followed in the 10th–11th centuries. In the 13th century Tanḥum Yerushalmi composed a dictionary of mishnaic Hebrew. Non-Jewish Hebrew lexicography began with Johannes Buxtorf's *Lexicon Hebraicum* (1607) and *Lexicon Chaldaicum, Talmudicum et Rabbinicum* (1639). Biblical lexicography was placed on a new basis by Wilhelm Gesenius' *Handwörterbuch* (1810–12). The first dictionary to include Hebrew of all periods was Eliezer Ben-Yehudah's *Thesaurus totius Hebraitatis* (1910–52).

Dienchelele (from Hebrew "dayyan kelili": general judge). Judicial office instituted in Sicily in 1396 by King Martin I of Aragon. The holder of the office was judge and final court of appeal in cases tried according to Jewish law. Joseph Abenafia held the office until 1407. He was followed by Rais of Syracuse and then by a succession of physicians. The position was abolished in 1447.

Diesendruck, Tzevi Hirsch Wolf (1890–

1940). American philosopher and scholar of Galician origin. He taught at the Jewish Pedagogium in Vienna (1918–27), the Jewish Institute of Religion in New York (1927), the Hebrew University (1928–30), and the Hebrew Union College, Cincinnati (1930–40). He published Hebrew translations of Plato's writings and wrote studies of Maimonides' philosophy.

Dietary laws (Hebrew "kashrut"). The Bible and rabbinic legislation permit certain foods for consumption; they are referred to as "kasher" (fit). They prohibit other foods, including meat from birds and animals which are "unclean" or not ritually slaughtered; certain parts of animals (such as the sinew of the hip); meat and milk products eaten together; any kind of fish that does not have both fins and scales. They also deal with the preparation of food: for example, since Jews may not consume blood in any form, all meat must be soaked and salted before it is eaten. Although no reason is given in Scripture or rabbinic literature for these prohibitions, various explanations have been advanced: that dietary restrictions in themselves regulate holiness in everyday life, encourage self-discipline, and keep Jews separate from gentiles, and that abstention from the particular foods named prevents disease. *See also* KASHRUT.

Dillon, Abraham Moshe (1883–1934). American Yiddish poet. He was born in Russia and emigrated to the US in 1909. As a poet he was affiliated with the New York impressionistic movement of Yunge. His writings include *Gele bleter* and *Lider fun A. M. Dillon*.

Din ("judgment"). The word is used in the context of secular or religious law to refer to a legal decision or lawsuit.

Dinaburg, Ben Zion *see* DINUR, BENZION.

Dina de-malkhuta dina (Aramaic: "the law of the country is law"). The halakhic rule that the law of the country is binding; in certain cases the law of the country is to be preferred to Jewish law. It was laid down in the 3rd century by the sage Samuel, who imbued Babylonian Jewry with the consciousness that they must be reconciled with the government of the Sassanid kingdom.

Dinah (fl. ?19th–16th cent. BCE). Israelite woman, daughter of Jacob and Leah (Genesis 30.21). She was raped by Shechem. Jacob's sons Simeon and Levi avenged their sister by slaughtering the male population of the town of Shechem, carrying off their women and children, and taking their goods and livestock as spoil (Genesis 34).

Dinesohn, Jacob (1856–1919). Russian Yiddish novelist. He was born in the district of Kovno. His first Yiddish novel, *For the Parents' Sins*, was banned by the Russian censor. His second, *The Beloved and the Pleasant, or The Black Youth* sold more than 200,000 copies. In 1885 he settled in Warsaw. He was the pioneer of the Yiddish sentimental novel and also helped to modernize elementary Jewish education by founding secular schools.

Din torah ("judgment of the law"). A judicial hearing conducted in accordance with Jewish law.

Dinur, Benzion [Dinaburg, Ben Zion] (1884–1973). Israeli historian and educator of Ukrainian origin. He emigrated to Palestine in 1921. From 1923 to 1948 he taught at the Jewish Teachers' Training College in Jerusalem, of which he later became head. In 1948 he was appointed professor of modern Jewish history at the Hebrew University. He was elected to the first Knesset (1949–51) as a Mapai delegate and from 1951 to 1955 was minister of education and culture. He edited the Jewish historical quarterly *Zion* and wrote on Jewish and Zionist history.

***Dio Cassius** *see* CASSIUS DIO.

Disabilities. In Jewish usage the civil and social disadvantages suffered by Jews as a result of restrictive laws and customs. Before the 18th century rights accorded to Jews were limited. In most parts of Europe Jewish disabilities ranged from extreme severity to minimal deprivation. After the Enlightenment Jews aspired to rights which they had previously been denied. As an indirect result of the French Revolution they gained full legal equality. In modern times Jews have been given full civil rights under the law.

Discipline Scroll [Manual of Discipline]. One of the Dead Sea Scrolls. It describes the organization and some of the beliefs of the Dead Sea sect that originally owned the scrolls.

Discrimination. The singling out of an individual or group for special treatment on the basis of race, religion, color, or national origin. Before the modern period anti-Jewish legislation was enacted by civil and religious authorities. Modern anti-Semitism is generally not enshrined in law but finds expression in nonlegislative discriminatory patterns.

Diskin, Yehoshua Leib (1817–1898). Russian rabbi and halakhist. He was born in Grodno and served as a rabbi in various Russian cities. He opposed the religious authorities, was imprisoned, and in 1887 emigrated to Palestine. He settled in Jerusalem, where he served as a rabbi and was in the vanguard of Orthodox activism. He founded an orphanage and directed the Ohel Moshe yeshivah.

Dispensation. Permission to dispense with or modify rules to relieve hardship. In rabbinic practice it is referred to as "giving a heter" (permission). It is generally limited to laws having only rabbinic validity or arising from custom.

Displaced persons. Individuals forced or deported from their homes, especially as a result of war. The term is applied particularly in Jewish parlance to those deported to other lands by the Nazi regime in World War II. After the war the United Nations specialized agency, the Relief and Rehabilitation Administration, assisted the repatriation of displaced persons. In 1947 this body was replaced by the International Refugee Organization. Between 1948 and 1950 the majority of the 450,000 Jews in camps for displaced persons emigrated from Europe to Israel, the US, and elsewhere.

Disputation. Formal debate between the adherents of different philosophies or religious faiths. Disputations took place between Jews and philosophers during the Hellenistic period. With the growth of Christianity, Jews engaged in debate with Christian theologians about such subjects as the Virgin Birth, the nature of messianic prophecies, and the divinity of Jesus. In the Middle Ages disputations between Jewish and Christian scholars (such as the Disputation of Paris in 1240 and the Disputation of Barcelona in 1263) commonly resulted in the formal condemnation and burning of the Talmud.

***Disraeli, Benjamin,** Earl of Beaconsfield (1804–1881). English statesman and novelist. His father, Isaac d'Israeli, quarreled with the London Sephardi community and had his children baptized. Disraeli was already an established novelist when he was elected to parliament in 1837 as a Tory. In 1868 he became prime minister. Although he was defeated in the next general election, he became prime minister again in 1874. In 1876 he was created Earl of Beaconsfield. Jewish figures and themes appear in several of his novels.

D'Israeli, Isaac *see* ISRAELI, ISAAC D'.

Divination. The art or practice of discerning future events or unknown things. All forms of pagan divination, including augury, soothsaying, charming, and conjuring the spirits of the dead, are prohibited in the Bible. Yet despite this denunciation they were occasionally used. Prophecy and prophetic dreams were approved by God, as was the use for divinatory purposes of the Urim and Thummim and the ephod. In the rabbinic period the belief in omens and oracles flourished despite official disapproval.

Divorce (Hebrew "get"). The dissolution of a marriage. It is effected in Jewish law by a bill of divorce termed "sepher keritut" in Scripture (Deuteronomy 24.3) or "get" in the Talmud. This bill is written by the husband and handed to his wife in the presence of witnesses. Biblical law stipulates that divorce is permitted if the husband finds an "unseemly thing" in his wife (Deuteronomy 24.1). This phrase was diversely interpreted by rabbinic authorities. Although the power of divorce is vested in the husband, Jewish divorce laws have developed in the direction of establishing greater equality between husband and wife.

Divre ha-Yamim *see* CHRONICLES.

Dizengoff, Meir (1861–1937). Politician of Russian origin. He was born in Bessarabia. He became active in Russian revolutionary circles and later in the Hovevei Zion movement. In 1892 he was sent by Baron Edmond de Rothschild to establish a bottle factory in Palestine. He returned to Russia, but in 1905 went back to Palestine and settled in Jaffa. He was a founder of Tel Aviv and became its first mayor in 1921. He published his memoirs, *With Tel Aviv in Exile*, in 1931.

***Döblin, Alfred** (1878–1957). German poet and novelist. He was born in Stettin and became a psychiatrist. His first novels were expressionist in nature. In 1933 he fled from Germany to France and then to the US. In his novels of this period he criticized Jewish assimilationists and Zionists. In 1940 he converted to Catholicism. After World War II he returned to Germany, where he continued his literary activity.

Doeg the Edomite (fl. 11th cent. BCE). Edomite court official and adviser to Saul. He was the only one to inform the king of the assistance extended by Ahimelech, one of the priests of Nob, to David when he fled from Saul. On Saul's orders, Doeg put to death 85 of the priests of Nob (I Samuel 22).

Dogma. A religious doctrine or system of doctrines proclaimed as true by the religious authority. Abstract dogmas are not found in the Bible, but when Judaism came into contact with the Greek world such formulations began to be proposed. Philo was the first to lay down articles of faith. Karaism and the rise of Islam brought about further attempts to establish the essential beliefs of Judaism. Maimonides' 13 principles of the Jewish faith became influential in the Middle Ages. Other scholars such as Ḥasdai ben Abraham Crescas and Joseph Albo also proposed formulations of the doctrines of Judaism.

***Dohm, Christian Wilhelm von** (1751–1820). German writer. As royal archivist in Berlin, he was among the first to advocate the improvement of the civil status of the Jews. His *On the Improvement of the Jews as Citizens* was undertaken at the request of Moses Mendelssohn. In this work he argued that the inferior status of European Jewry was due to Christian prejudice, and he urged that the Jewish community be granted equal rights.

Dolitzki, Menaḥem Mendel (1856–1931). American Hebrew and Yiddish writer of Russian origin. He was born in Białystok. He was Hebrew secretary to Kalonymos Ze'ev Wissotzky in Berlin from 1882 to 1892, when he emigrated to the US and settled in New York. In his early works he described the sufferings of Jewish people in Russia; later he wrote poems of yearning for Zion. He also published a biography of Wissotzky. In the US his descriptions of Jewish persecution in Russia appeared in the journal *Ha-Ivri*.

Domain. Ownership and control of the use of land; the land thus owned and controlled. In rabbinic literature a distinction is made between public and private domain. For purposes of the rules of Sabbath observance, there are four types: private, where carrying is permitted; public, such as streets, where carrying is forbidden; semi-private, such as fields, where carrying is forbidden; and semi-public. In cases of ritual uncleanness, a private domain is one where there are fewer than three persons; where there are three or more the domain is public. In cases of claims for damages, a public domain is any place or road where there is public access; in such cases the person who causes injury is liable to pay compensation.

Dome of the Rock *see* OMAR, MOSQUE OF.

***Dominicans.** Roman Catholic order of preaching friars. It was founded by St. Dominic in 1216 and engaged in activities against the Jews. The friars delivered conversionist sermons and censored Hebrew books; Dominicans also engaged in disputations with Jews and participated in the Inquisition. The deteriorating status of the Jewish community from the 13th century onward was due largely to the propaganda of the Dominicans.

Domus Conversorum. Home for converted Jews in London. It was established in 1232 in New Street by Henry III. After the Jews were expelled in 1290, it received apostates who went to England to live.

Don Astruc of Lunel *see* ABBA MARI BEN MOSES HA-YARḤI.

***Donin, Nicholas** (fl. 13th cent.). French Franciscan monk. He was a pupil of Jehiel ben Joseph of Paris, who excommunicated him for his heretical ideas. He joined the Franciscan order and compiled a list of 35 accusations against the Talmud. He was the main instigator of the Disputation of Paris in 1240, as a consequence of which 24 cartloads of copies of the Talmud were burned in 1242.

Dönmeh. Judeo-Muslim sect formed in the 17th century by a group of Shabbetai Tzevi's followers. Like Shabbetai Tzevi, they converted to Islam, but they retained many Jewish observances as well as their belief in him as the Messiah. Eventually the sect divided into several groups based largely in Salonica.

Donnolo, Shabbetai (913–c. 982). Italian physician. He was born in Oria. He traveled widely and served as physician to the Byzantine governor in Calabria and to church officials. He wrote a commentary on the Sepher Yetzirah. His *Book of Remedies* was the first Hebrew treatise on medicine written in Christian Europe.

Don Profiat *see* IBN TIBBON, JACOB.

Dori, Ya'akov (1899–1973). Israeli military leader. He was born in Odessa and was taken to Palestine in 1906. From 1931 to 1939 he was commander of the Haganah in the Haifa district. In September 1939 he became the first chief of staff of the Haganah. With the establishment of the State of Israel, he became chief of staff of the Israeli Defense Forces. He was president of the Haifa Technion from 1951 to 1965.

Dormido, David Abravanel (fl. 17th cent.). One of the founders of the modern English Jewish community. Born in Spain, he was arrested by the Inquisition in 1627 and eventually escaped to Bordeaux. In 1640 he reached Amsterdam. He accompanied Samuel Soeiro, the son of Manasseh ben Israel, to London in 1654, where he petitioned Oliver Cromwell to readmit the Jews to England. When the Jewish community was organized in 1663, he served as its presiding warden.

D'Orta, Garcia (c. 1500–1568). Portuguese Marrano scientist and physician. He was born in Castelo de Vide, and taught at Lisbon University. In 1534 he left Portugal for India, where he served in Goa as a physician to Portuguese viceroys, Christian dignitaries, and the Muslim ruler. His *Coloquios dos simples e drogas he cousas medicinais da India* laid the foundation for the study of tropical diseases. He was posthumously condemned by the Inquisition.

Dosa ben Saadyah (930–1017). Babylonian communal leader and head of the academy of Sura. 71 years after the death of his father, Saadyah ben Joseph, he became gaon of Sura. He wrote a biography of his father, responsa, commentaries on the Talmud, and philosophical works.

Dosh *see* GARDOSH, KARIEL.

Dositheus (fl. 1st cent.). Samaritan pseudo-messiah. He was the founder of a sect that resembled Judaism.

Doubrovsky, Serge (b. 1928). French critic and novelist. In a number of works of fiction (*Fils, Un amour de soi, La vie l'instant*) he discussed his Jewish past and origins, World War II, and the treatment of Jews in France during the Nazi period.

Doubt. In Jewish law a state of doubt exists in cases where the law is undecided or where the facts are uncertain. A code of procedures and criteria has been evolved, according to which each instance is to be resolved. The basic guide to be followed is the general rule that doubts affecting biblical law are to be decided in conformity with the stricter view, while those involving rabbinic law are to be resolved according to the more lenient position. Exceptions to this rule concern doubts in monetary matters (decided according to the lenient view) and cases involving danger to life (decided according to whatever policy will most effectively remove the danger).

Dov Ber of Mezhirich [Ber [Maggid] of Mezhirich] (c. 1710–1772). Russian Ḥasidic teacher. Originally a folk preacher (maggid), he became a disciple of the Baal Shem Tov, after whose death he became the leader of the Ḥasidim. He transferred the movement from Medzhibozh to Mezhirich and under his leadership it spread into the Ukraine, Lithuania, and central Poland. Many of his homilies are included in works written by his disciples. He provided Ḥasidism with a speculative–mystical system based on the kabbalah.

Dowry. Property a wife brings to her husband at marriage. The Bible mentions gifts brought by the husband to the bride and also by the wife to the husband. In talmudic times, the practice of giving a dowry was well established. The dowry is recorded in the marriage contract. It reverts to the wife upon divorce or the death of her husband.

Drabkin, David *see* REMEZ, DAVID.

***Drach, David Paul** (1791–1865). French scholar. He was born in Strasbourg. In 1819 he was appointed head of the Paris Jewish School, but in 1823 he was baptized into the Catholic Church. He worked in Paris as an expert in Hebrew and took part in the publication of the Venice Bible. From 1832 to 1842 he served as librarian of the Congregation for the Propagation of the Faith in Rome and published poems in honor of the pope and the cardinals. Returning to Paris, he collaborated with the Abbé J. P. Migne in the publication of his *Patrologia* and edited Origen's *Hexapla*. He also published books and pamphlets justifying his conversion.

Drachman, Bernard (1861–1945). American Orthodox rabbi. He was born in New York and served as an Orthodox rabbi there and in Newark, New Jersey.

He was the first Orthodox rabbi to preach in the vernacular in the US and was one of the founders of the Jewish Theological Seminary, where he taught from 1887 to 1902. He later taught at Yeshiva College and from 1908 to 1920 served as president of the Union of Orthodox Jewish Congregations. He translated Samson Raphael Hirsch's *Nineteen Letters of Ben Uziel* into English.

Drama *see* THEATER.

Dream. In the Bible dreams are frequently regarded as divine communications. Joseph and Daniel were noted for their ability to interpret dreams. In the Talmud various views are presented about the significance of dreams. Interest in dreams continued through the Middle Ages to modern times, especially among the kabbalists and Ḥasidim.

Dreck (Yiddish). Excrement, trash, cheap things, works of art of any kind that are of inferior quality.

Dreidel [trendel] (Yiddish). Spinning top. The word is applied specifically to a traditional Jewish toy which bears the initial letters of the Hebrew words: "A great miracle happened there." It is spun in a game played at Ḥanukkah.

Dress. In biblical times the dress of the Jews was similar to that of neighboring peoples, and during the Hasmonean period Greek and Roman costumes became prevalent among the Jewish upper classes. Later the wearing of fringes (tzitzit) on four corners of a garment differentiated Jews from gentiles. From the Middle Ages Jews were often forced to wear the JEWISH BADGE or other distinctive clothing. In north Africa the prohibition of bright colours in Jewish dress resulted in the evolution of the black robe and skull-cap. But in eastern Europe the wearing of fur-trimmed hat (streimel) and a long kaftan reflected local customs. In certain Mediterranean areas, Jews wore Spanish fashions introduced by Sephardi exiles in 1492.

Dreyfus, Alfred (1859–1935). French soldier. He was born in Alsace. He became a captain on the general staff of the French army in 1892. In 1894 he was accused of treason, found guilty, and sentenced to life imprisonment. He protested his innocence and was eventually exonerated, but the case plunged France into a state of virulent anti-Semitism for a decade. The so-called Dreyfus Affair deeply influenced Theodor Herzl and contributed to the development of Zionism. Dreyfus' *The Letters of Captain Dreyfus to his Wife* and *Five Years of my Life* depict his ordeal.

Dreyfus, Ferdinand-Camille (1851–1905). French journalist. He was a founder of the liberal newspaper *La nation* and general secretary of *La grande encyclopédie*. He was twice elected to the Chamber of Deputies. He fought several duels with anti-Semites.

Dreyfus, George (b. 1928). Australian composer and arranger. He was born in Wuppertal, Germany, and went to Australia in 1939. A number of his works reflect his Jewish background.

Dreyfus Affair *see* DREYFUS, ALFRED.

Drink offering. Offering of wine added to all sacrifices in the Temple. The quantities varied from a fourth part of a hin of wine for a lamb, a third part of a hin for a ram, and half a hin for a bullock (Numbers 15.5–9).

***Driver, Samuel Rolles** (1846–1914). English bible scholar and Hebraist. He was appointed professor of Hebrew at Oxford in 1883. He wrote studies of Hebrew grammar and commentaries on biblical books, and collaborated with F. Brown and C. A. Briggs in producing the *Hebrew and English Lexicon of the Old Testament*.

Dropsie College for Hebrew and Cognate Learning. American postgraduate institution for research in Jewish and related branches of learning. It was established in Philadelphia in 1907 through the will of Moses Aaron Dropsie. After World War II the college added departments of Jewish philosophy, Hebrew language and literature, the history of Semitic civilization, and comparative religion. In addition, a school of education and the Institute for Israel and the Middle East were established. It has published the *Jewish Quarterly Review* since 1910.

***Drumont, Edouard-Adolphe** (1844–1917). French anti-Semitic activist. In 1886 he published *La France juive*, which describes France as subjugated to the Jews in political, economic, social, and cultural spheres. In 1889 he founded the Anti-Semitic League and the journal *La libre parole*.

Drunkenness. According to the Talmud a person under the influence of alcohol is legally responsible for his actions unless he has reached the state of oblivion attributed to Lot. A drunken person is not allowed to conduct a religious service. However, on Purim a person is permitted to become so intoxicated that he is unable to distinguish between the expressions "Blessed be Mordecai" and "Cursed be Haman."

Druyanow, Alter (1870–1938). Polish Hebrew writer and Zionist leader. He was born in Druya in the district of Vilnius. He was a member of the Ḥibbat Zion movement and secretary of its Odessa committee from 1890 to 1905. He lived in Palestine in 1906–9 and from 1923. He edited the Zionist organ *Ha-Olam* and wrote a history of Ḥibbat Zion. He also published a collection of Jewish folk humor, *The Book of Jokes and Witticisms*.

Druze. A member of a religious sect in Syria and Lebanon, having certain characteristics in common with Muslims. In the 12th century Benjamin of Tudela was one of the first Europeans to describe the Druze people and their religion. A number live in modern Israel and have cooperated with the Israeli forces during and since the War of Independence. They have their own religious courts which administer Druze law.

Dualism. Religious or philosophical doctrine. The term is used of two different beliefs. (1) The belief in a cosmic struggle between the powers of good and evil. This doctrine was taught in the ancient religion of Persia and later by gnostics. The rabbis condemned those who recognized two divine powers. Dualistic trends affected some Jewish theologians and is found in Jewish mysticism. (2) The belief in a radical opposition of matter and spirit. Stemming from Greek thought, this belief influenced Philo as well as medieval Jewish philosophy.

Dubinsky, David (1892–1982). American labor leader. He was born in Belorussia, and emigrated to the US in 1910. He became president of the International Ladies Garment Workers' Union in 1932, and vice-president of the American Federation of Labor in 1934. After World War II he was a founder of the International Confederation of Free Trade Unions. He was a supporter of Israel, and in particular the Histadrut.

Dubno, Solomon (1738–1813). Dutch Bible scholar and Hebrew poet of Ukrainian origin. He lived in Amsterdam and Berlin, where he served as a tutor for Moses Mendelssohn's son. He helped with Mendelssohn's German translation of the Bible and commentary. He eventually returned to Amsterdam, where he published a commentary on the Torah as well as Hebrew poetry.

Dubnow, Simon (1860–1941). Russian historian. Born in Belorussia, he lived in St. Petersburg, Odessa, Vilnius, Berlin, and Riga. He wrote a ten-volume history of the Jewish people, a history of the Jews in Russia and Poland, and a history of Ḥasidism. In his writings he propounded the doctrine of national autonomy. He believed that the Jews are a nation spiritually and should aspire to social and cultural, rather than political, independence.

***Dühring, Eugen** (1833–1921). German anti-Semitic writer. He was born in Berlin. He was one of the initial proponents of modern anti-Semitism, attacking the Jews in his book *Die Judenfrage als Frage des Rassencharakters*. His writing had an important influence on the development of German anti-Semitism in the 1880s.

Dujovne, Leon (1899–1984). Argentine philosopher and communal leader. He was born in Russia and went to Argentina as a child. He taught at the University of Buenos Aires and published studies of Benedict Spinoza and Martin Buber. He also translated the writings of a number of medieval Jewish philosophers into Spanish. He served as president of the Sociedad Hebraica Argentina and the Instituto de Intercambio Cultural Argentina–Israel.

Duker, Abraham Gordon (1907–1987). American educator and historian. He was born in Poland and went to the US in 1923. From 1956 to 1962 he was president of the Chicago Spertus College of Judaica. In 1963 he became director of libraries and professor of history and social institutions at Yeshiva University. He wrote studies of Polish–Jewish relations and American Jewish sociology.

Dukes, Leopold (1810–1891). Hungarian historian. He was born in Pressburg. He visited libraries in Europe and uncovered many unknown medieval works. His research covered aggadic literature, Bible exegesis, medieval Jewish literature, Hebrew grammar and masoretic texts, and talmudic maxims and truisms. He translated Rashi's Torah commentary into German and published studies of the poetry of Solomon ibn Gabirol and Moses ibn Ezra.

Dukhan. Platform. According to talmudic literature, it refers variously to: the place in the Temple where the Levites sang while the sacrifice was being offered; the place where the priests stood while reciting the Priestly Blessing; the place where the Priestly Blessing was recited in the synagogue after the destruction of the Temple; or the platform where teachers sat while teaching children.

Dunash ben Labrat [Ibn Labrat, Dunash] (c. 920–990). Iraqi Hebrew poet and grammarian. He was born in Baghdad, studied at Fez, and later settled in Córdoba. He applied Arabic forms of Hebrew to poetry and laid the foundation for medieval Hebrew poetry. He wrote 200 criticisms of Menaḥem ben Saruk's dictionary, the *Maḥberet*. This led to a controversy which influenced the development of Hebrew philology and grammar.

Dunash ben Tamim (c. 860–after 955/6). North African scholar. He wrote studies of philology, mathematics, astronomy, and medicine, as well as a commentary on the Sepher Yetzirah.

Dünner, Joseph Hirsch (1833–1911). Dutch rabbi and talmudist. He was born in Kraków. He was appointed director of the rabbinical seminary in Amsterdam in 1862. In 1874 he became chief rabbi of the Ashkenazi community in the city, and later a leader of the Mizraḥi party. He published glosses to 19 tractates of the Talmud as well as an enquiry into the origin of the Tosephta.

Dura-Europos. Ancient city on the Euphrates. It was excavated by a Franco-American expedition from 1928 to 1932. The ruins of a synagogue built in the 3rd century were discovered on the site. Its walls were covered with frescos depicting scenes from the Bible.

Duran, Profiat [Ephodi] (fl. 13th–14th cent.). Spanish scholar and polemicist. He was born in Perpignan. He was forcibly converted to Christianity in 1391 but later reverted to Judaism. He wrote two polemical tracts against Christianity, a Hebrew grammar, a commentary on Maimonides' *Guide for the Perplexed*, and a history of the persecutions and expulsions of the Jews from the destruction of the second Temple until his own time.

Duran, Simeon ben Tzemaḥ [Rashbatz] (1361–1444). North African rabbinic scholar, philosopher, and scientist. He was born in Majorca and worked as a physician and surgeon in Palma. After the massacre there in 1391 he settled in Algiers, where he served as chief rabbi. His writings include an encyclopedic philosophical work, *Magen Avot*. His responsa deal with religious and legal problems as well as grammar, philology, exegesis, literary history, philosophy, kabbalah, mathematics, and astronomy.

Duran, Solomon ben Simeon [Rashbash] (c. 1400–1447). North African scholar, son of Simeon ben Tzemaḥ Duran. He was born in Algiers. He joined his father's bet din at an early age and became the head of the yeshivah. His *Milḥemet Mitzvah* is a defense of the Talmud against the accusations made by the apostate Joshua Lorki (Geronimo de Santa Fé).

Duress. According to Jewish law, a person is responsible for his actions only if they are initiated and performed by his own free will. However, compulsion may be used as an extenuating circumstance only where it takes the form of physical violence or threat to the life of the individual concerned. The compulsion to commit idolatry, murder or engage in an adulterous or incestuous act is to be resisted even if it involves the loss of one's life. A divorce granted under duress is invalid, and a woman who is forced to agree to marriage is considered unwed by law. Oaths or vows made under duress are invalid. Similarly a gift given under duress may be rescinded. But a sale or purchase made under duress remains valid, and not withstanding the circumstances an injury caused under duress to someone else must be compensated.

Durkheim, Émile (1858–1917). French sociologist. He was born in Épinal. He became professor of sociology at the University of Bordeaux in 1887, and in 1902 he was appointed professor of sociology and education at the Sorbonne. He founded and edited *L'année sociologique* and wrote numerous sociological works including *The Elementary Forms of the Religious Life*. Although he did not write directly on Jewish topics, his work reflects his Jewish background.

Duschak, Moritz (1815–1890). Moravian rabbi, teacher, and writer. He served as a rabbi in Aussee and Gaya. From 1877 he occupied the post of preacher and teacher in Kraków. He published studies on talmudic topics and Jewish scholarship.

Dushkin, Alexander (1890–1976). American educator. He was born in Poland and was taken to the US in 1901. He was director of Chicago's Board of Jewish Education (1923–34) and executive director of the Jewish Education Committee in New York (1939–49). From 1962 he headed the Department of Jewish Education in the Diaspora at the Hebrew University Institute of Contemporary Jewry. He published numerous studies of Jewish education.

Duty. An action that a person is obliged to perform for God or another person. Jewish law recognizes different kinds of duty. "Ḥovah" (an obligation) is distinct from "mitzvah," which can signify both duty and a commendable action ("reshut"). According to Baḥya ibn Pakuda a distinction should be made between the duties of the limbs (involving ceremonial and practical obligations), and the duties of the heart (involving the spiritual life).

Dybbuk *see* DIBBUK.

Dyeing. The dyeing of cloth is mentioned in the Bible. The craft developed considerably during mishnaic and talmudic times and in the Middle Ages the Jewish trade in dyestuffs also expanded greatly. In the modern period Jews continued to practice this profession in the Near East.

Dymov, Ossip [Perelmann, Joseph] (1878–1959). Russian Yiddish author and playwright. He was born in Białystok. He first wrote fiction in Russian, blending symbolism, irony, and wit. His plays deal with Jewish suffering and experience. After he emigrated to the US in 1913 he wrote for the Yiddish theater.

E

Easter. Christian festival celebrating the resurrection of Jesus. During the Middle Ages Jews were frequently attacked at Easter time to avenge Jesus' death. Owing to the proximity of Passover, these massacres were frequently connected with blood libel accusations.

East Sea *see* DEAD SEA.

Eban, Abba (b. 1915). Israeli statesman and diplomat. He was born in Cape Town. He lectured in Arabic at Cambridge University from 1938 to 1940. After World War II he settled in Israel. He was a member of the Jewish Agency delegation to the UN (1947–8) and then represented Israel at the UN (1948–9) before serving as Israeli ambassador to the US (1950–59). He was president of the Weizmann Institute from 1958 to 1966. Elected to the Knesset as a Mapai delegate, he was successively minister of education and culture (1960–63), deputy prime minister (1963–6), and foreign minister (1966–74).

Ebed-Melech (fl. 6th cent. BCE). Cushite eunuch. He persuaded Zedekiah, King of Judah, to rescue Jeremiah from the pit into which he had been thrown. Jeremiah later predicted that Ebed-Melech would be saved when disaster befell Jerusalem. (Jeremiah 38.7–13; 39. 15–18)

Eber. Great-grandson of Shem and ancestor of Abraham (Genesis 10.21ff; 11.14ff).

Ebionites [Nazarenes]. Judeo-Christian sect active in Palestine in the 2nd–4th centuries. They observed the Mosaic law, believed Jesus was the Messiah, considered poverty a basic principle, and held property in common.

Ebreo, Leone *see* ABRAVANEL, JUDAH.

Ecclesiastes (Hebrew "Kohelet"). Biblical book, one of the five scrolls in the Hagiographa. The name Ecclesiastes is Greek, meaning "convoker," and is a rendering of the Hebrew word "Kohelet," by which the author is referred to. The book discusses the meaning of life: the central theme is that all is futile, but the last few verses are optimistic and pious. The work is read in the synagogue during Sukkot.

Ecclesiastes Rabbah (Hebrew "Kohelet Rabbah"). Post-talmudic midrash on the book of Ecclesiastes. It is an exegetical midrash which gives a chapter-by-chapter and verse-by-verse exposition of Ecclesiastes. It is based on various older midrashic works.

Ecclesiasticus [Wisdom of Ben Sira]. Apocryphal book. It was written by Ben Sira and translated into Greek by his grandson in 132 BCE. It contains moral maxims, as well as liturgical poems and psalms.

Éclaireurs Israélites *see* SCOUTS.

École Rabbinique de France *see* SÉMINAIRE ISRAÉLITE DE FRANCE.

Edels, Samuel Eliezer [Maharsha] (1555–1631). Polish talmudist. He was born in Kraków and settled in Posen, where he married the daughter of Moses

Ashkenazi Heilpern. His mother-in-law Edel (by whose name he became known) supported him and his disciples for 20 years. He was later a rabbi in Chełm, Lublin, and Ostrog, where he founded a yeshivah. His *Ḥiddushe Halakhot* is a talmudic commentary which is included in most editions of the Talmud.

Eden, Garden of. The abode of Adam and Eve (Genesis 2–3). They were excluded from the garden because they disobeyed God and ate the forbidden fruit. In rabbinic literature the Garden of Eden is the place where the righteous dwell after death.

Eder, Montagu David (1865–1936). English psychoanalyst and physician. He was born in London. He was a founder of the Psychoanalytical Association in England; he also established a children's clinic and edited the journal *School Hygiene*. He was active in Zionist affairs and served on the Zionist Commission in Palestine from 1918 to 1921. He later served on the World Executive Committee of the Zionist Organization in Jerusalem and London.

Edidin, Ben M. (1899–1948). American educator. He was prominent in Jewish educational activities in New York. He wrote several textbooks on Jewish and Zionist education.

Edom. Ancient kingdom in south-east Palestine, between the Dead Sea and the Gulf of Aqaba. In the Talmud Edom symbolized oppressive governments, especially Rome. In the Middle Ages it symbolized Christian Europe.

Edomites. Ancient people of Semitic origin. Traditionally descendants of Esau, they lived by hunting and were enemies of the Israelites. They fought Saul and were defeated by David. Later they gained their independence and frequently engaged in war with Israel. They were conquered by John Hyrcanus, who forcibly converted them to Judaism.

Education. The Bible stipulates that divine precepts must be taught to the people, especially children. The religious revival under Ezra in the 5th century BCE centered on the regular reading of and instruction in the Torah (Ezra 7.1–10.44). In the rabbinic period there was a comprehensive educational system for Jewish boys. Synagogues had a bet sepher for elementary study and a bet midrash for advanced learning. In the Babylonian academies Jewish scholarship reached great heights. Subsequently yeshivot were established throughout the Jewish world which carried on the tradition of Jewish learning (*see* YESHIVAH). In the modern period traditional Jewish religious educational institutions have been established, as well as neo-Orthodox religious schools and day schools. All these institutions are, in their different ways, committed to perpetuating Jewish learning. *See also* HEDER; TALMUD TORAH; UNIVERSITIES.

Eduyyot. Seventh tractate in the Mishnah order of Nezikin containing a great variety of laws. Its purpose is to put on record the testimonies of later sages on the legal pronouncements and controversies of earlier authorities.

Efros, Israel (1891–1981). American Hebrew scholar. He was born in the Ukraine and emigrated to the US in 1905. He was professor at Johns Hopkins University, Buffalo University, Hunter College, and Dropsie College. In 1955 he settled in Israel and served as rector and later honorary president of Tel Aviv University. He published studies of medieval Jewish philosophy, translated *Hamlet* into Hebrew and Ḥayyim Naḥman Bialik's poetry into English, co-authored an English–Hebrew dictionary, and wrote volumes of poetry.

Eger, Akiva ben Moses (1761–1837). German rabbi. He was born in Eisenstadt and served as a rabbi at Märkisch-

Friedland in 1791, and from 1814 at Posen, where he established a yeshivah. As one of the foremost rabbinic authorities in Europe, he opposed the Reform movement. He published glosses on the Mishnah and the Talmud, as well as numerous responsa.

Eger, Akiva ben Simḥa Bunem (c. 1720–1758). German rabbi and author. He was born in Halberstadt and served as rabbi of Zuelz in Upper Silesia. In 1756 he became head of the yeshivah of Pressburg. He was one of the foremost talmudic scholars of his generation. He published novellae on the Talmud and responsa.

Eger, Judah Leib (1816–1888). Polish Ḥasidic leader. He was born in Warsaw and led a Ḥasidic congregation in Lublin. After the death of Menaḥem Mendel of Kotsk in 1859, he assumed the role of tzaddik and propounded his own teaching. He spent much time in prayer, devoting himself to it with fervor accompanied by weeping and loud cries. His teachings on the law and festivals were arranged by his son Abraham in *Torat Emet* and *Imrei Emet.*

Eger, Samuel Levin ben Judah Leib (1769–1842). German talmudist. He was born in Halberstadt and served as rabbi of Braunschweig. An opponent of the Reform movement, he insisted on the retention of Hebrew in prayer. He wrote talmudic novellae, homiletic discourses, and responsa.

Eger, Solomon ben Akiva (1786–1852). Polish rabbi and communal leader. He was born in Lissa and served as rabbi of Kalisz and Posen. He encouraged Jews to move away from commerce into farming, solicited contributions for Palestine, and campaigned for the emancipation of the Jews in his own country. He was an opponent of the Reform movement. He published notes on the Talmud and Isaac ben Jacob Alfasi's code.

Eglah aruphah. Heifer sacrificed on the occasion of an unsolved murder (Deuteronomy 21.1–9). The elders of the community nearest to the place where the corpse is discovered must break the heifer's neck, wash their hands over it, and profess their innocence.

***Eglon** (fl. 12th cent. BCE). King of Moab. He assembled the Ammonites and the Amalekites, and with them attacked Israel and subdued the land for 18 years. He was killed by Ehud. (Judges 3)

Egypt. Country in north-east Africa. The history of the Jewish people from its beginnings has been linked with Egypt. The patriarchs visited the country, and early Jewish history is connected with the bondage of the Jews there and the Exodus. Throughout the period of the monarchy there were constant Judeo-Egyptian contacts. With the conquest of Egypt by Alexander the Great, a large number of Jewish immigrants settled there. In later centuries there was a continual Jewish presence in the country.

Eḥad mi yodea ("Who knows one?"). Opening words of a medieval Hebrew riddle of numbers, appended to the Passover Haggadah in certain rites.

Ehrenburg, Ilya Grigoryevich (1891–1967). Russian author and journalist. He was born in Kiev. He was exiled from 1908 to 1917 for revolutionary activities. On his return to Russia in 1917 he opposed the Bolsheviks and he again left the country in 1921. He returned once more in 1941 and became a spokesman for Stalin. He wrote against Nazi anti-Semitism and Zionism. He was awarded the Stalin Prize in 1942 for his novel *The Fall of Paris* and in 1948 for *The Storm.* His autobiography appeared in six volumes.

Ehrenkranz, Benjamin Wolf [Zbahrz, Velvel of] (1819–1883). Galician Yiddish and Hebrew poet. He traveled to various European cities as a singing bard. His poems were concerned with nature and man, poverty and wealth, and the struggle of light and darkness (symbolizing the opposition of the maskilim and the Ḥasidim). Much of his poetry employs parody and satire. His collected poems appeared between 1865 and 1878.

Ehrenpreis, Marcus (1869–1951). Swedish rabbi and author. He was born in Lemberg, and served as rabbi in Djakovo, Croatia, from 1896 to 1900. He later became chief rabbi of Sofia, and from 1914 of Stockholm. At the request of Theodor Herzl he translated the invitation to the First Zionist Congress into Hebrew; he acted as a consultant on cultural matters at Zionist congresses. He translated modern Hebrew literature into Swedish, founded a Jewish–Swedish journal, and edited a Jewish encyclopedia in Swedish.

Ehrenstein, Albert (1886–1950). Austrian poet and author. He was born in Vienna. He lived in Berlin, traveled widely in Europe, and eventually settled in New York in 1941. His poetry was pessimistic in character and occasionally bears witness to a yearning for the oriental world; he published several volumes of Chinese poetry in his own free adaptations, as well as narrative works and essays.

Ehrlich, Arnold Bogumil (1848–1919). American biblical exegete of Polish origin. He was born in Włodawa near Lublin. He worked as a librarian in the Semitics department of the Berlin Royal Library. At the age of 30 he settled in the US. He helped Franz Delitzsch to translate the New Testament into Hebrew and later published Hebrew and German commentaries on the Bible.

Ehrlich, Joseph (1842–1899). Austrian writer. He was born in Brody, Galicia. He worked as a poet and journalist in Vienna. His autobiography, *My Life's Way*, describes the life of the Jewish community in Brody in the 1840s and 1850s.

Ehud (fl. 12th cent. BCE). Judge of the tribe of Benjamin. He delivered Israel from Eglon, King of Moab. Under the pretext of having a secret message for the king, he drew a dagger and killed him. This ended Moabite rule over Israel for several generations. (Judges 3)

Eibeschütz, Jonathan (c. 1690–1764). Bohemian talmudist and kabbalist. He was head of a yeshivah in Prague and became the rabbi at Metz in 1741. From 1750 he officiated in turn at Altona, Hamburg, and Wandsbeck. He was accused of being a follower of Shabbetai Tzevi but denied the charge. He was one of the greatest talmudic scholars of his time.

Eichelbaum, Samuel (1894–1967). Argentine playwright and short story writer. He was born in Domínguez, Entre Ríos. His play *El Judío Aarón* is based on a Jewish theme, and his short story *Una buena cosecha* is set in Rosh Pinnah, Israel.

Eichenbaum, Jacob (1796–1861). Polish Haskalah poet, educator, and mathematician. He was born in Krystianopol, Galicia. He was married at 11, but divorced when his father-in-law suspected him of secular leanings. He married again in 1815, lived in Zamość, and later settled in Odessa, where he established a Jewish school. In 1844 he was appointed director of the Kishinev Jewish school, and in 1850 inspector of the Zhitomir Rabbinical Seminary. A collection of poems by him was one of the first books of poetry published in the Haskalah period.

***Eichmann, Karl Adolph** (1906–1962). Austrian Nazi official. He was born in Solingen. He became director of the Center for Jewish Emigration of the German Reich in 1939. In 1941 he was appointed head of the Gestapo section that dealt with Jewish affairs and the expulsion of populations. Later the same year he was placed in charge of the liquidation of Jewry throughout Europe. In

1960 he was brought to trial in Israel for crimes against humanity, and sentenced to death.

'Eid *see* WITNESS.

Eighteen Benedictions (Hebrew "Shemoneh Esreh") [Amidah; Tephillah]. The principal prayer in the Jewish liturgy. It consists of blessings and prayers on the following subjects: (1) the commemoration of the patriarchs; (2) the mightiness of God in natural phenomena; (3) the sanctification of God (*see* KEDUSHAH); (4) understanding; (5) penitence; (6) forgiveness; (7) redemption; (8) healing; (9) the harvest; (10) the ingathering of the exiles; (11) the restoration of the judges; (12) the destruction of the heretics; (13) the rewarding of the righteous; (14) the rebuilding of Jerusalem; (15) the restoration of the Kingdom of David; (16) the acceptance of prayer; (17) the restoration of Temple service; and (18) thanksgiving. It ends with the blessing of priests and a prayer for peace. The benedictions were written at various times between 100 BCE and 100 CE and were gathered together in their final form by Rabban Gamaliel II. The first three and the last three benedictions are recited at every service; the intermediate ones are used only on weekdays. *See also* SILENT PRAYER.

Einhorn, David (1809–1879). American reform rabbi of German origin. He was born in Bavaria and succeeded Samuel Holdheim as chief rabbi of Mecklenburg-Schwerin. In 1855 he became rabbi of the Har Sinai Congregation of Baltimore, and he later served as rabbi of Kenesseth Israel in Philadelphia and Congregation Adath Israel in New York. He was the leader of the extreme Reform wing of American Jewry. His *Olat Tamid* served as the model of the *Union Prayer Book* of the Reform movement.

Einhorn, Ignaz [Horn, Éduard] (1825–1875). Hungarian Reform rabbi and economist. He was born in Nove Mesto. He organized the Society for the Reform of Judaism in Pest in 1847; later he served as rabbi of the society's first Reform Temple. He also helped to found the Society for the Propagation of Hungarian Language and Culture, and edited the first Jewish–Hungarian yearbook. After the suppression of the Hungarian uprising in 1849 he settled in Paris, where he published works on economic problems. In 1867 he returned to Budapest and was elected to the Hungarian parliament.

Einhorn, Moses (1896–1966). American physician and editor. He was born in Russia, and was taken to Palestine in 1908. He was forced to emigrate by the Turkish authorities in 1916 and later settled in the US. He was head of the gastroenterological department of the Bronx Hospital in New York. In 1926 he founded (with Asher Goldstein) the Hebrew medical journal *Ha-Rophe ha-Ivri*.

Einstein, Albert (1879–1955). German physicist. He was born in Ulm. He worked in the patent office at Berne and later was professor at the University of Prague and at the Prussian Academy of Science in Berlin. In 1921 he received the Nobel Prize for Physics, in recognition of his work on relativity, quantum physics, and Brownian motion. In 1933 he settled in the US and became professor of theoretical physics at the Princeton Institute for Advanced Studies. He was an active supporter of Zionism and served as a trustee of the Hebrew University.

Eisendrath, Maurice Nathan (1902–1973). American Reform rabbi. He was born in Chicago, and served as rabbi in Charleston, South Carolina, and Toronto. In 1943 he became president of the Union of American Hebrew Congregations. He was active in interfaith activities and social action. His publications include *Spinoza*, *Never Failing Stream*, and *Can Faith Survive?*.

***Eisenmenger, Johann Andreas** (1654–1704). German writer. He was born in Mannheim. He studied midrash and Talmud with Jewish scholars for 19 years. In 1700 he published *Entdecktes Judentum*, which maligned the Jews and collected rabbinic quotations critical of Christianity. After its publication the intervention of the Jewish community resulted in its withdrawal, but a second edition was published in 1711.

Eisenstadt, Benzion (1873–1951). American rabbi and Hebrew writer of Belorussian origin. He settled in the US in 1903. He published lexicographic and biographical works on contemporary rabbis and writers.

Eisenstadt, Meir ben Isaac [Maḥaram Ash] (c. 1670–1744). Polish rabbinic authority. He served as rabbi in Szydłowiec, Poland, and later settled in Worms, where he became head of a yeshivah. When the French occupied Worms in 1701 he went to Prossnitz, Moravia, where he served as rabbi. In 1714 he was appointed rabbi of Eisenstadt and its seven communities, where he established a yeshivah. His *Panim Meirot* contains responsa and novellae on the Talmud.

Eisenstein, Ira (b. 1906). American rabbi. He was born in New York. He led the Society for the Advancement of Judaism, and subsequently served as rabbi to Anshe Emet synagogue in Chicago. Later he became president of the Reconstructionist Foundation and editor of the *Reconstructionist*. In 1968 he was appointed president of the Reconstructionist Rabbinical College. His writings include *Creative Judaism, What we Mean by Religion,* and *Judaism Under Freedom.*

Eisenstein, Judah David (1854–1956). American Hebrew writer and editor of Polish origin. He emigrated to the US in 1872, where he became a coal manufacturer. He was a founder in 1880 of Shoḥarei Sefat Ever, the first Hebrew society in the US. He published in Hebrew a Jewish encyclopedia in ten volumes (*Otzar Yisrael*) as well as several anthologies of Jewish literature.

Eisler, Moritz (1823–1902). Moravian educator and historian of Jewish philosophy. He founded and served as president of an organization for the support of disabled Jewish teachers and their widows and children. His *Lectures on Jewish Philosophy in the Middle Ages* was one of the first attempts to summarize and present the main systems of medieval Jewish philosophy.

Ekhah *see* LAMENTATIONS.

Ekron. Ancient city in Palestine, the most northerly of the five Philistine cities in Palestine. Its local god was Baal Zebub.

El *see* GOD, NAMES OF.

Elah (fl. 9th cent. BCE). King of Israel (883–882 BCE), son of Baasha. He was murdered, while in a state of intoxication, by Zimri, the captain of his chariots. His murder arose from the army's dissatisfaction with his indifference to the campaign against the Philistines near Gibbethon.

El Al. Israeli airline. It was established in 1948, initially to facilitate the transporting of Jewish immigrants. It eventually became a major world airline.

Elamites. Ancient people, the inhabitants of a kingdom to the east of Babylonia. The Elamites are described by the Bible as the descendants of Shem (Genesis 10.22). Chedorlaomer, King of Elam, attacked the kings of southern Canaan in the neighborhood of the Dead Sea and was in turn defeated by Abraham (Genesis 14). Elamites participated in Sennacherib's siege of Jerusalem in 704 BCE (Isaiah 22.6). Ashurbanipal transferred part of the population of Elam to Samaria after 639 BCE (Ezra 4.9–10).

Elath [Epstein]**, Eliahu** (b. 1903). Israeli diplomat. He was born in Russia and settled in Palestine in 1924. From 1934 to 1945 he was director of the Middle East section in the Jewish Agency's Political Department, and from 1945 to 1948 head of its Political Office in Washington. In 1949 he served as ambassador in Washington, and was then ambassador in London (1950–59). He was president of the Hebrew University from 1962 to 1968. His writings include *Israel and its Neighbours*.

Elazari-Volcani [Volkani; Wilkanski; Wilkansky]**, Yitzḥak Avigdor** (1880–1955). Israeli agronomist. He was born in Lithuania and settled in Palestine in 1908, where he became one of the leaders of the Ha-Poel ha-Tzair party. He founded and directed workers' farms at Ben Shemen and Ḥulda from 1909 to 1918, and in 1921 he established the Agricultural Experiment Station at Ben Shemen. He was appointed professor of agricultural economics at the Hebrew University in 1938.

Elbogen, Ismar (1874–1943). American scholar. He was born in Schildberg, in the Posen district. He began teaching Jewish history and biblical exegesis at the Collegio Rabbinico Italiano in Florence in 1899. In 1903 he joined the faculty of the Hochschule für die Wissenschaft des Judentums in Berlin. In 1938 he emigrated to New York, where he was appointed research professor at the Jewish Theological Seminary, Hebrew Union College, Jewish Institute of Religion, and Dropsie College. He published studies in Jewish history and the history of Jewish liturgy.

El Brit *see* GOD, NAMES OF.

Eldad (fl. 13th cent. BCE). Elder of Israel. He was one of the 70 Israelite elders appointed by Moses to aid him in governing the people (Numbers 11.16ff). He and Medad aroused the suspicion of Joshua by prophesying within the camp, but their conduct was approved by Moses (Numbers 11.26–9).

Eldad ha-Dani (fl. 9th cent.). Traveler. His origins are obscure. He claimed to belong to the tribe of Dan and asserted that the tribes of Dan, Naphtali, Gad, and Asher formed an independent kingdom in Africa. He visited Jewish communities in north Africa and Spain. The Kairouan community sought the opinion of the gaon Tzemaḥ about the halakhic practices described by him.

Elder. In Jewish usage, one of the members of the governing body of the nation or community. In biblical times the elders helped to rule the Israelites; Moses appointed 70 elders to aid him in this task (Numbers 11.16ff). The elders served as judges and representatives of the people until the second Temple period. In the Middle Ages the title "zaken" (elder) was given to communal councillors in some areas.

Elders of Zion, Protocols of the. Forged document, purporting to prove the existence of international Jewish aspirations to attain world power; it has been widely used to inspire anti-Semitic feeling. It was first published in Russian at the beginning of the 20th century. After the Russian Civil War, the work was introduced into western Europe by Russian émigrés. It describes a plan supposed to have been made by a conference of leaders of world Jewry to attain global domination and the overthrow of Christian society. The *Protocols* circulated in many countries, played a part in Nazi propaganda, and continues to be reprinted.

Eleazar (i) (fl. 13th cent. BCE). Israelite, third son of Aaron (Exodus 6.23). After his father's death, he was appointed high priest (Exodus 20.28; Deuteronomy 10.6). The priestly family of Zadok traced its descent from him.

Eleazar (ii) [Auran] (fl. 2nd cent. BCE). Hasmonean warrior and brother of Judah Maccabee. At the battle of Bet

Zechariah, he stabbed an elephant of the enemy's army, believing that its rider was Antiochus Eupator, the Syrian ruler. He was killed when the animal fell on him.

Eleazar (iii) (fl. 2nd cent. BCE). Judean martyr. During the religious persecution instigated by Antiochus Epiphanes in 167 BCE, he chose death rather than submit to eating pork (II Maccabees 16.18–31; IV Maccabees 5–6).

Eleazar ben Arakh (fl. 1st cent.). Palestinian tanna. He was the most outstanding of the inner circle of the five disciples of Johanan ben Zakkai. He engaged in mystical speculation concerning the divine chariot ("merkavah"). He later settled in Emmaus.

Eleazar ben Azariah (fl. 1st–2nd cent.). Palestinian tanna. He traced his ancestry back ten generations to Ezra. When Rabban Gamaliel II was temporarily deposed as nasi, Eleazar ben Azariah was chosen to succeed him; the school at Jabneh, the center of rabbinic learning, was opened to all who wished to study, and no longer restricted (as it had been under Gamaliel) to those considered worthy. According to tradition, Eleazar ben Azariah went on a mission to Rome with Rabban Gamaliel II. He was both a halakhist and an aggadist.

Eleazar ben Dinai (fl. 1st cent.). Palestinian Zealot leader. He ravaged Judea for 20 years until he was captured by the procurator Felix and sent to Rome.

Eleazar ben Hananiah (fl. 1st cent.). Palestinian scholar. He was a leader of the school of Shammai.

Eleazar ben Jair (fl. 1st cent.). Palestinian Zealot leader. After the assassination of Menaḥem ben Judah in 66, he led Jewish forces to the fortress of Masada and held it for seven years. When it was surrounded by the Romans, he persuaded the Jews to kill one another in order to avoid capture.

Eleazar ben Judah of Worms [Eleazar Rokeaḥ] (c. 1165–c. 1230). German talmudist, kabbalist, and liturgical poet. Born in Mainz, he spent most of his life in Worms. He witnessed the murder by crusaders of his wife and children. He published works on halakhah, liturgical poetry, theology, ethics, and exegesis. His *Sepher ha-Rokeaḥ* was intended to educate the common reader in the details of halakhic law. He was the last major scholar of the Ḥaside Ashkenaz movement.

Eleazar ben Parta (fl. 2nd cent.). Palestinian tanna. He was one of the sages arrested by the Romans for contravening Hadrian's decree forbidding the public teaching of Torah and observance of the commandments. Although the offense carried the death penalty he was miraculously delivered from execution.

Eleazar ben Pedat (fl. 3rd cent.). Palestinian amora. He was born in Babylonia and settled in Palestine. After the death of Johanan in 279, he was appointed head of the council in Tiberias. He was a major exponent of the Oral Law and a prolific aggadist.

Eleazar ben Shammua (fl. 2nd cent.). Palestinian tanna. He was one of the last pupils of Akiva. After Simeon Bar Kokhba's revolt (132–5) he was ordained by Judah ben Bava. Several of his teachings were incorporated into the Mishnah by his pupil Judah ha-Nasi. He is included among the Ten Martyrs of the Hadrianic persecutions.

Eleazar ben Simeon (i) (fl. 1st cent.). Palestinian Zealot leader. He played an important role in the war against Cestius Gallus. He was responsible for the entry of the Idumeans to Jerusalem and the subsequent massacre of the opponents of the Zealots. He fought against John of Giscala until the beginning of the siege of the city by Titus.

Eleazar ben Simeon (ii) (fl. 2nd cent.). Palestinian tanna. He was the son of

Simeon ben Yoḥai, with whom he escaped from the Romans by hiding in a cave for 13 years. He engaged in halakhic controversy with Judah ha-Nasi as well as in halakhic and aggadic discussions with other scholars. He eventually accepted a position in the Roman administration as an official responsible for the apprehension of thieves and robbers.

Eleazar Rokeaḥ *see* ELEAZAR BEN JUDAH OF WORMS.

Election *see* CHOSEN PEOPLE.

Elegy *see* KINAH.

El Elyon ("Most high God"). Name of God, used only in Genesis 14.18; it occurs in the description of Melchizedek, a priest in the time of Abraham.

Elephantine [Yeb]. Ancient fortress town on the western bank of the Nile, opposite Aswan. It was on the border between Ethiopia and Egypt, and from the end of the Egyptian royal period (c. 590 BCE) to the end of the Persian period (333 BCE) a military garrison of Jewish soldiers was stationed there. The temple used by the Jews in the town was destroyed by an Egyptian mob, but was later rebuilt. The episode is depicted in Elephantine papyri.

El erekh appayim ("O God, slow to anger"). Opening words of the seliḥah prayer recited in the synagogue during the morning service on Mondays and Thursdays before the reading of the law. It is omitted on the New Moon, the eve of Passover, the Ninth of Av, Ḥanukkah, and Purim.

Elhanan (i) (fl. 10th cent. BCE). Israelite warrior. According to II Samuel 21.19 he killed Goliath; in I Chronicles 20.5 it is stated that he killed Lahmi, the brother of Goliath.

Elhanan (ii) [Andreas]. Legendary Jewish pope. According to tradition he was the son of Simeon the Great of Mainz. Kidnapped by monks, he was baptized, educated in a monastery, and became a priest. Eventually he was elected pope. When he discovered his Jewish origins he threw himself from a tower; another tradition relates that he reverted to Judaism.

Eli (fl. 11th cent. BCE). Israelite, head priest in the Sanctuary at Shiloh during the period of the Judges. When Elkanah made an annual pilgrimage to Shiloh, his wife, Hannah, made a vow in the presence of Eli and received the assurance that her prayer for a son would be answered (I Samuel 1.11ff). After her son, Samuel, was weaned Hannah brought him to Eli to serve in the Sanctuary. Eli's family was subsequently deprived of the priesthood (I Kings 2.26–7) because of the immoral conduct of Eli's sons, Hophni and Phinehas (I Samuel 2.11–36; 3.11–14).

Eliakim *see* JEHOIAKIM.

Eliashib (fl. 5th cent. BCE). Israelite, high priest in the time of Ezra and Nehemiah. He and his priestly colleagues were responsible for rebuilding the wall guarding the north-western approach to the Temple Mount: their portion was the Tower of Hananel, the Tower of the Hundred, and the Sheep Gate (Nehemiah 3.1).

Eliezer (i) (fl. ?19th–16th cent. BCE). Israelite, steward of Abraham's household (Genesis 15.2). He was to have been Abraham's heir in the absence of any offspring. But when Abraham complained to God that material goods were of little use to him since he had no children to whom to bequeath them, God responded with the promise of a son (Genesis 15.4ff). Eliezer was identified by the rabbis with the servant sent by Abraham to find a wife for Isaac.

Eliezer (ii) (fl. 13th cent. BCE). Israelite, second son of Moses (Exodus 18.4).

Eliezer (iii) (fl. 9th cent. BCE). Israelite, prophet of Mareshah. He denounced

Jehoshaphat's alliance with Ahaziah (II Chronicles 20.37).

Eliezer ben Hyrcanus (fl. 1st–2nd cent.). Palestinian tanna. He was a pupil of Johanan ben Zakkai and teacher of Akiva. After the destruction of the Temple in 70 he was among the important scholars of the great bet din of Jabneh. Later he established an academy at Lydda. He was a member of a delegation to Rome led by the nasi to obtain concessions for the Jews. He also traveled to Antioch on behalf of the scholars.

Eliezer ben Joel ha-Levi [Rabiyah] (1140–1225). German scholar. He wandered from place to place, visiting Bonn, Worms, Würzburg, Mainz, Metz, Cologne, and Regensburg. He refused to accept rabbinic office in order not to derive material benefit from his learning. Eventually he accepted the rabbinate of Cologne in 1200. His *Sepher ha-Rabiyah* contains halakhot and legal decisions according to the order of the tractates in the Talmud, and also responsa.

Eliezer ben Nathan of Mainz [Raben] (c. 1090–c. 1170). German scholar. He lived in Slavic countries, then settled in Mainz. His *Sepher ha-Raban* (also called *Even ha-Ezer*) is the first complete book emanating from the German Jewish community to have survived. It contains responsa, and various extracts and halakhic rulings following the order of the talmudic tractates. He was also the first commentator on liturgical poetry in Germany. Some of his own piyyutim were influenced by the terrors of the First Crusade.

Eliezer ben Yose ha-Galili (fl. 2nd cent.). Palestinian tanna. He was one of the last pupils of Akiva and was among those who reestablished the academy in Jabneh, and then in Usha after the Hadrianic persecutions. He wrote the *Baraita of the Thirty-Two Rules*, which enables the aggadah to be expounded like the halakhah by fixed hermeneutical rules. He was one of the greatest aggadists of his time.

Eliezer of Touques (fl. 13th cent.). French tosaphist. He edited most of the tosaphot incorporated in standard editions of the Babylonian Talmud. The disciples of Meir of Rothenburg used his tosaphot extensively, and it was through them that his versions became accepted in France and Germany.

Elijah [Elijah the Tishbite; the Tishbite] (fl. 9th cent. BCE). Israelite prophet. He prophesied during the reigns of Ahab and Ahaziah. He attempted to restore the purity of the worship of the God of Israel when Ahab's wife, Jezebel, introduced the cult of Baal into the country. In a contest with the prophets of Baal, he emerged victorious (I Kings 18). According to II Kings 2.1–11, Elijah did not die but was carried to heaven in a chariot of horses and fire. In the rabbinic tradition he is viewed as the harbinger of the Messiah. At the Passover seder a glass of wine is traditionally poured for him.

Elijah, Apocalypse of. Apocryphal work. It describes the archangel Michael's account to Elijah of the end of Rome, the destruction of the wicked, the last judgment, and the heavenly Jerusalem.

Elijah, Chair of *see* CHAIR OF ELIJAH.

Elijah Baal Shem *see* LOANS, ELIJAH BEN MOSES.

Elijah Baḥur *see* LEVITA, ELIJAH.

Elijah Be'er ben Shabbetai [Elijah Sabot] (fl. 14th–15th cent.). Italian physician. He taught at the University of Padua, and was in the service of several popes (Innocent VII, Martin V, and Eugene IV) as well as Italian rulers. He was summoned to England in 1410 to attend on Henry IV.

Elijah ben Judah of Chełm [Baal Shem, Elijah of Chełm] (1514–1583). Polish rabbi and kabbalist. He was known for his miracle cures by means of charms and amulets. According to legend, he created a golem.

Elijah ben Solomon Zalman [Vilna Gaon] (1720–1797). Lithuanian talmudist. After traveling throughout Poland and Germany he eventually settled in Vilnius. He encouraged the translation of works on natural science, but was opposed to philosophy and the Haskalah. He also led the opposition to the Ḥasidic movement and was regarded as the spiritual leader of the Mitnaggedim. He wrote commentaries on the Bible; annotations on the Talmud, midrash, and Zohar; and works on mathematics, the geography of Palestine, and Hebrew grammar. In his studies of halakhah he sought to establish critical texts of rabbinic sources; he avoided pilpul and based his rulings on the plain meaning of the text.

Elijah Sabot *see* ELIJAH BE'ER BEN SHABBETAI.

Elimelech (fl. 12th–11th cent. BCE). Israelite, husband of Naomi and father of Mahlon and Chilion. Owing to the famine during the time of the Judges, he crossed over from Judah to Moab, where he and his sons died. Following their deaths, his wife Naomi returned to Judah with her daughter-in-law Ruth. (Ruth 1.1–3; 2.1, 3; 4.3, 9)

Elimelech of Lizensk (1717–1787). Galician rabbi. He was one of the founders of Ḥasidism in Galicia. A disciple of Dov Ber of Mezhirich, he is regarded as the theoretician and creator of practical tzaddikism. His *Noam Elimelekh* describes the role of the tzaddik in the Ḥasidic movement; it stresses the holiness and perfection of the tzaddik and his influence in the earthly and spiritual realms.

***Eliot, George** [Evans, Mary Anne] (1819–1880). English novelist. She was a friend of the talmudic scholar Emanuel Deutsch, and began to study Hebrew and show an interest in Jewish topics at an early age. Her *Daniel Deronda* is a Zionist novel, which influenced a number of Zionist thinkers and Hebrew writers.

Eliphaz. Israelite, the eldest son of Esau and his wife Adah (Genesis 36.2–4).

Eliphaz the Temanite. One of the three friends of Job (Job 2.11).

Elisha (fl. 9th cent. BCE). Israelite prophet. He prophesied during and after the reign of Jehoram. He was the disciple and successor of Elijah. He foretold Hazael's accession to the Syrian throne, and anointed Jehu king over Israel.

Elisha ben Avuyah [Aḥer] (fl. 2nd cent.). Palestinian tanna. He was born in Jerusalem. He came to doubt the unity of God, divine providence, and reward and punishment, and ultimately renounced Judaism. Although befriended by Meir, the rabbis dissociated themselves from him and referred to him as Aḥer (the other). He was the subject of several historical novels including *As a Driven Leaf* by Milton Steinberg.

***Elisheva** [Zhirkhova, Yelizaveta] (1888–1949). Russian Hebrew poet. She was attracted by the movement for Jewish national renaissance and her poems are full of yearning for the beautiful and noble qualities of Judaism. She also wrote literary criticism of Hebrew literature. She settled in Palestine in 1925.

Eliya, Joseph (1901–1931). Greek poet and scholar. He was born in Janina and taught French at the Alliance Israélite Universelle school there. He wrote poetic love songs dedicated to Rebekah and also produced Greek translations of Isaiah, Job, the Song of Songs, Ruth, and Jonah, as well as the works of medieval and modern Jewish writers.

***Elizabeth Petrovna** (1709–1762). Empress of Russia (1741–62). She decreed the expulsion of the Jews from Russia in 1742.

Eli Zion. Acrostic elegy for the fast day of the Ninth of Av. Written in the Middle

Ages, it consists of 12 stanzas, each closing with the refrain "Wail, Zion and its cities, as a woman in labor pains, and like a maiden that dons sackcloth to mourn for the husband of her youth." It is sung by the congregation standing.

Elkan, Benno (1877–1960). German sculptor. He was born in Dortmund, went to Paris in 1905, and returned to Germany in 1911. In 1933 he settled in England. His seven-branched candelabrum embellished with biblical scenes was presented by members of the British Parliament to the Israeli Knesset.

Elkanah (fl. 11th cent. BCE). Israelite, father of Samuel (I Samuel 1.1ff).

Elkasaites. Judeo-Christian sect connected with the Essenes. They existed from the 2nd century in the Transjordan. They emphasized ritual purification, encouraged procreation, and regarded Jesus as one of a series of reincarnations of the Messiah. Under persecution they feigned conversion to paganism.

Elkin, Stanley (b. 1930). American short story writer and novelist. A number of protagonists in his writings are Jews.

Elkus, Abram Isaac (1867–1947). American lawyer. He was born in New York. He served as special US attorney to prosecute bankruptcy in 1908. In 1911 he was counsel for the New York State Factory Investigating Commission. He was ambassador in Turkey from 1916 to 1919, and then president of the New York Free Synagogue until 1927.

El male raḥamim ("O God, full of compassion"). Opening words of the prayer for the dead. It is recited at a funeral service, on the anniversary of a death, on visiting the grave of a relative, and after being called up for the reading of the law. In some Ashkenazi rites it is also part of the memorial service on festivals and the Day of Atonement. It originated in Jewish communities of western and eastern Europe, where it was recited for the martyrs of the crusades and the Chmielnicki massacres.

El melekh ne'eman ("O God, faithful, king"). Phrase interposed between the Ahavah benediction and the recitation of the Shema. Its initial letters form the word "Amen." It was introduced either in order to preface the Shema with the idea of divine kingship, or to bring the total number of words in the Shema to 248 (to correspond with the 248 members of the human body according to the rabbis). It is recited only when the Shema is said in private.

Elohim *see* GOD, NAMES OF.

El Olam *see* GOD, NAMES OF.

Elon, Amos (b. 1926). Israeli journalist and writer. He was born in Vienna and emigrated to Palestine as a child. He was a journalist, editorial writer, and columnist for *Ha-Aretz*. His books include *Journey through a Haunted Land*, *The Israelis: Founders and Sons*, and *A Certain Panic*. He also wrote a biography of Theodor Herzl and a play entitled *Herzl*.

Elon Moreh. Place near Shechem in Israel, regarded as sacred by the ancient Israelites. It was associated with Abraham (Genesis 12.6–7).

El Shaddai *see* GOD, NAMES OF.

Elul. Sixth month of the Jewish year. It immediately precedes the High Holiday season and has become the traditional month of penitence and spiritual preparation. The shophar is sounded after the morning service on weekdays throughout the month.

Elvira. Town in Andalusia, Spain. The church council convened there at the beginning of the 4th century issued canons forbidding marriage between Jews and Christians, prohibiting Jews from keeping Christian concubines, preventing them from entertaining Christian clergy, and forbidding them to bless fields belonging to Christians.

Elyashar, Jacob Saul ben Eliezer

Jeroham (1817–1906). Palestinian Sephardi rabbi. He was born in Safed. He was appointed dayyan in Jerusalem in 1853 and became head of the bet din in 1869. In 1893 he became Sephardi chief rabbi of Palestine. He wrote thousands of responsa to questions from Ashkenazim and Sephardim throughout the world.

Elyashev, Isidor [Baal Makhshoves] (1873–1924). Russian Yiddish and Hebrew critic. He devoted himself to Yiddish journalism in Russia and Poland and later in Berlin. He was the founder of modern aesthetic criticism in Yiddish.

Emanation. Philosophical theory explaining the origin of the universe as a flowing out from a primary source. It was taken over from Neoplatonists by Arab philosophers, and passed into medieval Jewish philosophy and kabbalah. In kabbalistic literature it is an essential part of the concept of the ten sephirot.

Emancipation. In Jewish usage the word is applied to the removal, particularly in the Western world in the 18th–20th centuries, of restrictions imposed on Jews. From the 4th century the Holy Roman Empire imposed a system of discrimination against Jews, which was intensified in medieval Europe. Jewish emancipation stemmed from utopian political and social thought in the 18th century. In the 19th and 20th centuries Jews have been granted full civil equality in nearly all countries where they live. (*See also* CIVIL RIGHTS.)

Embezzlement. The fraudulent conversion to one's own use of money or property in one's care. It differs from theft in that the possession of the property by the embezzler is lawful. According to Jewish law, if the embezzler denies his fraud on oath, and it is later proven, he must restore the property plus one fifth of its value. In addition he is required to offer the sacrifice of a guilt offering.

Emden, Jacob Israel [Yavetz] (1697–1776). Danish halakhic authority. He was born in Altona. He served as rabbi at Emden from 1728 to 1733, when he returned to Altona and set up a printing press. He regarded Sabbetaianism as a danger to Judaism and engaged in a prolonged dispute about this movement with Jonathan Eibeschütz. He wrote studies on halakhic subjects as well as polemical pamphlets.

Emes, Der. Russian Yiddish daily paper. Started in 1918 by the Yevsektzia, it was published until 1940. It was the official organ of the Russian Communist Party relating to Jewish affairs.

Emet ("truth"). In biblical and rabbinic Hebrew the word signifies honesty, loyalty, truthfulness, and right action. God is often described as the God of truth in the Bible (Psalm 31.6), the Talmud, and later Jewish philosophical writings; traditionally truth is understood as one of the 13 attributes of God. In medieval philosophical literature "emet" is used as a logical term.

Emet ve-emunah ("True and trustworthy"). Opening words of the blessing immediately following the Shema in the evening service.

Emet ve-yatziv ("True and valid"). Opening words of the prayer immediately following the Shema in the morning service.

Emigdirect. Office established by the Jewish Emigration Conference in Prague in 1921 to assist and organize Jewish emigration from Europe. In 1935 it merged with ORT.

En ("well"). It occurs commonly as a component of place names in biblical and modern times.

Encyclopedias. General surveys of knowledge were written by Jewish scholars in the Middle Ages. In the 18th century Isaac ben Samuel Lampronti produced a talmudic encyclopedia, *Paḥad Yitzḥak.*

In 1870–84 Jacob Hamburger published the *Real-Encyklopädie für Bibel und Talmud*. The first comprehensive Jewish encyclopedia was the American *Jewish Encyclopedia* published between 1901 and 1906. This was followed by encyclopedic works in Russian, Hebrew, and German. From 1939 to 1943 the *Universal Jewish Encyclopaedia* appeared, which served as the basis for a Spanish work, *Enciclopedia Judaica Castellana*. The *Encyclopaedia Hebraica* appeared in 1949, and the *Encyclopaedia Judaica* began publication in 1972.

Endeks. Polish anti-Semitic political party. Its members played a leading role in the elimination of Jews from Polish economic and intellectual life in the 1930s.

End of days *see* ESCHATOLOGY.

En Dor. City in the territory of Issachar, south of Mount Tabor, occupied by the Manasseh tribe (Joshua 17.11). Gideon's triumph over the Midianites took place there (Psalm 83.11). Saul visited a witch in the city, who divined the future through the medium of a ghost (I Samuel 28.7).

Enelow, Hyman Gershon (1877–1934). American Reform rabbi and scholar. He was born in Lithuania and went to the US as a youth. He served as a rabbi in Kentucky and at Temple Emanuel in New York from 1912 to 1934. He was president of the Central Conference of American Rabbis from 1927 to 1929. His writings include *The Synagogue in Modern Life*, *The Faith of Israel*, and *A Jewish View of Jesus*. He also edited Israel Alnakawa's *Menorat ha-Maor* as well as the *Midrash of 32 Hermeneutic Rules* ascribed to Eliezer ben Hyrcanus.

Engagement *see* BETROTHAL.

En Gedi. Desert town on the western shore of the Dead Sea. It is mentioned in the Bible in connection with Joshua's invasion of Canaan (Joshua 15.62). David hid there from Saul (I Samuel 24.1–2). Its vineyards were famous in biblical times (Song of Songs 1.14).

Engel, Yoel (1868–1927). Russian composer. He was music critic of the journal *Russkiye Vedomosti* for 20 years. In 1900 he began to adapt Jewish folk songs. In 1912 he took part with S. An-Ski in an expedition to southern Russia to collect folk songs among the Jewish population. He later contributed the music to An-Ski's play *The Dybbuk*. He settled in Tel Aviv in 1924, where he composed Hebrew songs.

En [ayin] **ha-ra** ("evil eye"). A look or glance believed to have the power of inflicting harm or injury. Although a belief in the evil eye is not found in the Bible, it occurs in rabbinic literature and kabbalistic lore. Many practices developed for averting its power, including reading the Scriptures, wearing amulets, and reciting incantations.

En k-Elohenu ("There is none like our God"). Opening words of an ancient hymn, which is sung during the Sabbath additional service. In its original form it was an acrostic constituting the word "Amen."

Enlightenment *see* HASKALAH.

Enoch (i). Son of Cain and father of Irad. The world's first city was named after him. (Genesis 4.17ff)

Enoch (ii). Father of Methuselah (Genesis 5.18–24). According to Genesis he "walked with God; then he was no more for God took him" (Genesis 5.23). This verse was traditionally interpreted to mean that he did not die naturally but was transported to heaven on account of his righteousness. Several apocalyptic books are centered on his decease. Early Christians utilized this interpretation to expound Jesus' immortality. In later Jewish legend he was identified with the angel Metatron.

Enoch (iii). Apocryphal work, translated in the 10th or 11th century from Greek into Slavonic. It describes Enoch's ascent, his journey through the seven heavens, his return to earth, his address to his son, and his second ascent.

Enoch (iv). Apocalyptic work of Ethiopic origin, one of the most important of the apocalyptic works. Dating from the period of the second Temple, it contains accounts of visions, messianic yearnings, and moral discourses.

En Soph ("Infinite"). The name given to the divine infinite in kabbalistic thought. Early kabbalists conceived of the En Soph as the absolute perfection in which there is no distinction or plurality. It does not reveal itself and is beyond all thought. In kabbalistic teaching creation is bound up with the manifestation of the hidden God as En Soph.

En Yaakov ("Fountain of Jacob"). Popular compilation of aggadic passages from the Babylonian and Palestinian Talmuds. It was compiled by Jacob ibn Ḥaviv, and first published in 1515–16.

Ephah. Ancient Hebrew dry measure. It is equivalent to a tenth of a ḥomer, and is itself ten times as large as an omer. The size of the ephah differed in biblical and mishnaic times.

Ephod. Upper garment worn during sacred rites in ancient Israel. In the Bible the word is usually used of the ornamented vestment which the high priest wore over the blue robe. To this he bound the breastplate with the Urim and Thummim. Although soothsaying and divination were prohibited, the ephod and the Urim and Thummim were to be used as a means of seeking God's counsel. By the beginning of the second Temple period, consultation of the ephod no longer took place.

Ephodi *see* DURAN, PROFIAT.

Ephraim (fl. 19th–16th cent. BCE). Israelite, younger son of Joseph. His name became that of one of the tribes of Israel and of the more northern of the two Israelite kingdoms. During the period of the Judges, the tribe of Ephraim claimed priority. When the northern tribes seceded after Solomon's death, the first king of the northern kingdom of Israel (Jeroboam I) belonged to this tribe. The prophets later referred to the House of Judah and the House of Ephraim.

Ephraim, Mount. Area occupied by the tribe of Ephraim in the hill regions from Bethel northward. During the time of Solomon, the name was used of the entire region occupied by the tribes of Ephraim and Manasseh.

Ephraim ben Isaac of Regensburg (1110–1175). German tosaphist and liturgical poet. As a youth he lived in France, where he was among the first pupils of Jacob ben Meir Tam. He wrote piyyutim which reflect the hardships suffered by the Jews of Germany in the Regensburg massacre of 1137 and during the Second Crusade (1146–7).

Ephraim ben Jacob of Bonn (1132–c. 1175). German liturgical poet and commentator. When Joel ben Isaac ha-Levi left Bonn, Ephraim ben Jacob succeeded him as av bet din. He also taught in Mainz and Speyer. He wrote the *Book of Remembrance* and dirges on the sufferings of Jews during the Second Crusade. He also composed liturgical poems for the festivals, responsa, tosaphot, and commentaries on benedictions and various customs.

Ephraim ben Shemariah (c. 980–1060). Egyptian rabbi. He was leader of the Palestinian community in Fostat (Old Cairo). Although he was engaged in commerce, he bcame the community's rabbi in about 1020. He corresponded with the gaon Solomon ben Judah for many years.

Ephraim Moses Ḥayyim of Sodilkov *see* MOSES OF SODILKOV.

Ephraim Veitel Heine (1703–1775). German court jeweler and community leader. In 1745 he was appointed court jeweler to the King of Prussia. Three years later he was elected head of the Berlin Jewish community. He built a school for the children employed in his factories and set up an educational foundation.

***Ephron.** Son of Zohar, from whom Abraham purchased the cave of Machpelah and the field east of Mamre (Genesis 23; 25.9; 49.29–30; 50.13).

Ephron, Elia (1847–1915). Russian publisher. With P. Brockhaus he founded the Brockhaus–Ephron publishing house, which published a general Russian encyclopedia in 86 volumes. It also participated in the publication of the 16-volume Russian–Jewish encyclopedia, *Yevreyskaya Entziklopedia.*

Epicurean *see* APIKOROS.

Epiphanes, Antiochus *see* ANTIOCHUS IV EPIPHANES.

Epitaph. Inscription on a tomb. Commemorative inscriptions marking places of Jewish burial are known from the first Temple period. In the second Temple period sarcophagi and ossuaries generally bore the names of the deceased. From the period of Roman and Byzantine domination in Palestine many epitaphs have been preserved, usually bearing the name of the dead in Hebrew or Greek. In the Middle Ages Jewish epitaphs were invariably in Hebrew. In the 16th century elaborate rhymed epitaphs were frequently used. By the next century Spanish and Portuguese communities in Venice, Amsterdam, London, and New York had introduced the use of Spanish in epitaphs and eventually the use of the vernacular became a common practice.

Epitropos (Greek: "trustee," "guardian"). Term applied in the Talmud to one who cares for the property of minors, the deaf, or someone of unsound mind; *see* DEAF, IMBECILES, AND MINORS.

Epstein, Abraham (1841–1918). Austrian rabbinic scholar of Russian origin. He traveled to western Europe in 1861, where he met some of the leading figures in Jewish scholarship. Eventually he sold his shares in the family business and devoted himself to research. In 1876 he settled in Vienna, where he wrote studies on a wide range of Jewish topics.

Epstein, Eliahu *see* ELATH, ELIAHU.

Epstein, Isidore (1894–1962). English rabbi and scholar. He was born in Lithuania and emigrated first to France and then (in 1911) to England. He served as rabbi in Middlesbrough from 1921 to 1928. In 1928 he began teaching Semitics at Jews College, and he became principal there in 1948. His publications include *Studies in the Communal Life of the Jews of Spain, as Reflected in the Responsa of Rabbi Solomon ben Adreth and Rabbi Simeon ben Zemach Duran; Faith of Judaism*; and *Judaism.* He also supervised the English translation of the Babylonian Talmud.

Epstein, Sir **Jacob** (1880–1959). British sculptor. He was born in New York and settled in England in 1905. His works include a number of sculptures on Jewish themes.

Epstein, Jacob Nahum (1878–1952). Israeli talmudist. He was born in Brest-Litovsk. He became a lecturer at the Hochschule für die Wissenschaft des Judentums in Berlin in 1923, and in 1925 he was appointed professor of talmudic philology at the Hebrew University. He published studies on the Mishnah and Talmud and edited the journal *Tarbitz* from 1930 to 1952.

Epstein, Louis M. (1887–1949). American Conservative rabbi. He was born in Lithuania and emigrated to the US in 1904. He was appointed rabbi of Kehilath Israel in Brookline, Massachusetts, in 1925. He served as president of the Rabbinical Assembly and chairman of its committee on Jewish law. His writings include *The Jewish Marriage Contract,*

Marriage Laws in the Bible and Talmud, and *Sex Laws and Customs in Judaism.*

Epstein, Yitzḥak (1862–1943). Writer and teacher of Belorussian origin. He settled in Palestine in 1886. From 1908 to 1915 he directed the Alliance Israélite Universelle school in Salonica. After World War I, he returned to Palestine and engaged in educational activities. He was a pioneer in teaching Hebrew by the direct method. He wrote studies on Hebrew language problems and Arab–Jewish relations, and a Hebrew textbook, *Ivrit be-Ivrit.*

Epstein, Zalman (1860–1936). Russian Hebrew essayist and critic. He was born in Belorussia and moved to Odessa in 1876, where he lived for 30 years. Later he lived in St. Petersburg, Warsaw, and Moscow; he eventually settled in Palestine in 1925. He published studies on Zionism and the settlement of Palestine as well as Hebrew and general literature. He also wrote a number of poetic sketches.

Eretz Yisrael *see* ISRAEL, LAND OF.

Erev ("evening"). The word is used specifically to refer to the evening of the Sabbath and festivals.

Erikson, Erik Homberger (b. 1902). American psychoanalyst. He was born in Frankfurt am Main and emigrated to the US in 1933. He taught at Harvard, Yale, and the University of California. In 1960 he was appointed professor of human development and psychiatry at Harvard. His publications include *Childhood and Society,* in which he discusses anti-Semitism and the role of Jews in society.

Erlanger, Camille (1863–1919). French composer. In addition to operas, orchestral music, and songs, he composed *Le juif polonais.*

Erter, Isaac (1791–1851). Galician Hebrew satirist. He was born in Koniuszek and lived in various cities before settling in Brody in 1831. In addition to his literary work, he was active in Haskalah circles. *The Watchman of the House of Israel* consists of five satires on Jewish society in Galicia and Poland in the first half of the 19th century.

Erusin *see* MARRIAGE.

Eruv (*lit.* "mixing"). Term applied to various symbolical acts which facilitate the accomplishment of otherwise forbidden acts on the Sabbath and festivals. These include carrying burdens on the Sabbath (permitted through Eruv Ḥatzerot – amalgamating individual holdings), walking further than the permitted 2000 cubits beyond the inhabited area of the town (through Eruv Teḥumim – amalgamating boundaries), and cooking for the Sabbath on a festival day falling on Friday (through Eruv Tavshilin – amalgamating meals).

Eruvin. Second tractate in the Mishnah order of Moed. It deals with the laws of Eruv. The last chapter is a collection of laws concerning the Sabbath.

***Esarhaddon** (fl. 7th cent. BCE). King of Assyria (680–669 BCE). He was the son of Sennacherib. He made 22 western vassals (including Manasseh, King of Judah) drag beams and timber for the construction of his palace, and stone statues of protective deities. According to the Bible, Manasseh was taken in chains to Babylonia by the army officers of the king of Assyria but was later allowed to return to his kingdom. (II Chronicles 33.11–12)

Esau. Israelite, firstborn son of Isaac and Rebekah and twin brother of Jacob. After Jacob obtained Esau's birthright and the firstborn's blessing, Esau became Jacob's enemy and Jacob fled to Haran. When he returned 20 years later, his brother greeted him affectionately (Genesis 35ff). The Bible identifies him with Edom (Genesis 36.1). In the Talmud, he was associated with wickedness and violence.

Eschatology. Theology, biblical exegesis, or doctrine concerning the end of days;

all eschatological theology supposes a fundamental alteration of the present world by divine intervention. Initially Jewish eschatology was an expression of faith in a glorious future for the nation after a period of suffering. Later it was introduced by the Hebrew prophets into their teaching; they added moral content and threatened catastrophe in the absence of repentance. Such expectations were subsequently transformed into apocalyptic beliefs, which regarded the end as a sign of the coming of the Messiah, who would bring about the ingathering of the exiles, the Kingdom of God, and the Day of Judgment when the righteous would receive eternal reward and the wicked would be punished.

Esdras. The name of two apocryphal books ascribed to Ezra; they are known as III Esdras and IV Esdras (the books of Ezra and Nehemiah are regarded as I Esdras and II Esdras). III Esdras describes the history of Israel from the time of Josiah to the reading of the law by Ezra. IV Esdras (also known as the Apocalypse of Ezra) discusses the problem of human suffering, the fate of Israel, and the advent of the Messiah.

Eshbaal *see* ISH-BOSHETH.

Eshet ḥayil ("a woman of valor"). The phrase occurs in Proverbs 31.10; this verse and succeeding verses are recited in the Jewish home on Friday evenings before the Kiddush by the head of the house.

Eshkol. German publishing house. It was founded in Berlin in 1923 by Nahum Goldmann and Jacob Klatzkin. Its publications of Jewish encyclopedias in Hebrew and German had to be abandoned after the Nazis came to power.

Eshkol, Levi (1895–1969). Israeli politician. He was born in Oratov, in the Ukraine, and settled in Palestine in 1914. After World War I he became director-general of the Ministry of Defense. He represented Mapai in the Knesset from 1949. In 1951 he joined David Ben-Gurion's government as minister of agriculture and development and the following year he became minister of finance. In 1963 he succeeded Ben-Gurion as prime minister, remaining in office until his death.

Esnoga. Term for "synagogue" among the Sephardim.

Espinoza, Benedict *see* SPINOZA, BENEDICT.

Espinoza, Enrique (1898–1987). Argentine writer, editor, and journalist. He was born in Kishinev and was taken to Argentina as a child. He edited monthly literary reviews in the 1920s. In 1928 he helped to found the Argentine Writers' Association. From 1935 he lived in Chile. His writings include *Ruth y Noemi, El angel y el leon, El Castellano y Babel, Cuadernos de oriente y occidente.*

Essenes. Monastic Jewish sect in Palestine at the close of the second Temple period. Their main group was located on the north-western shore of the Dead Sea. Their religious outlook was closer to that of the Pharisees than the Sadducees, but they had their own specific beliefs and observances. They withdrew from everyday life to their own communities, where emphasis was placed on meticulous ritual purity. The Dead Sea Scrolls illuminate their beliefs and practices.

***Esterhazy,** Count **Marie Charles Ferdinand Walsin-** (1847–1923). French military officer. He sold military secrets to Germany. When the leak was discovered, Alfred Dreyfus was suspected and condemned. The supporters of Dreyfus accused Esterhazy, but he was tried and acquitted. After the suicide of Colonel Henry, one of Dreyfus' accusers, Esterhazy fled to London.

Esterka (fl. 14th cent.). Mistress of Casmir III, King of Poland (1333–70). According to tradition, she bore children to

Casmir, influenced Jewish policy, and was the victim of a pogrom after his death. She is the subject of several Hebrew and Yiddish works.

Esther (i) [Hadassah]. Israelite woman, wife of Ahasuerus, King of Persia, and niece of Mordecai. Through her intervention, the plan of Haman (the prime minister) to annihilate the Jewish community was thwarted.

Esther (ii). Biblical book relating the story of the deliverance of the Jews from Persia. It is part of the Hagiographa and was composed around 350 BCE. The scroll ("megillah") of Esther is read in its entirety on the festival of Purim.

Esther (iii). Apocryphal book containing additions to the biblical Book of Esther. It consists of six passages found in the Septuagint but not in the Hebrew text.

Esther (iv) [Lifschitz, Malkah] (1880–1943). Russian writer and communist leader. She was born in Minsk. She edited Bundist periodicals after the revolution of 1905. She was one of the main promoters in the Bund of Jewish education in Yiddish. After the Russian Revolution in February 1917 she became a member of the central committee of the Bund. From 1921 to 1930 she was a leader of the Yevsektzia. She published a Yiddish edition of Lenin's writings, and edited the Moscow Yiddish daily *Emes*.

Esther, Fast of. Fast on 13 Adar, the day before Purim. If the fast falls on a Sabbath, it is observed the preceding Thursday.

Esther Rabbah. Midrash on the Book of Esther. Initially it was divided into six sections: later editions have ten sections, the last being subdivided into five smaller ones. The work consists of two different midrashim: Esther Rabbah I (sections 1–6) and Esther Rabbah II (sections 7–10).

Estimate. In Jewish usage a term found in connection with a special type of vow regarding a money-offering in the Temple. One could vow to give a sum equivalent either to one's own or another's "value." A vow involving "value" is called "arakhin." Such value is estimated on a scale depending upon the age of the person (Leviticus 25).

Estori ha-Parḥi *see* FARḤI, ESTORI.

Eternal light *see* NER TAMID.

Ethan the Ezrahite (fl. 10th cent. BCE). Israelite sage, spoken of as one whom Solomon surpassed in wisdom (I Kings 5.11). Psalm 89 is attributed to him.

Ethical literature *see* MUSAR.

Ethical will. Verbal or written testament, expressing the ethical instructions of a deceased person to his family. Such wills are described in the Bible, Apocrypha, and Talmud. During and after the Middle Ages, they became a common feature of Jewish life.

Ethics. A code of moral behavior; also the philosophical study of the values governing human conduct. It is a fundamental aspect of biblical teaching that Jews have the free choice to live moral lives in accordance with God's law. The first systematic presentation of Jewish ethics was made by Philo. Ethics also pervade rabbinic literature, and theoretical and practical ethics were developed by medieval Jewish philosophers. Kabbalistic thought also influenced the evolution of Jewish ethics. In the 19th century the Musar movement particularly encouraged moral reflection.

Ethics of the Fathers *see* AVOT (i).

Ethnarch. The ruler of a people. The title "ethnarch" was given to Hyrcanus II and his sons by Julius Caesar in 47 BCE. It was also used to designate the head of the Jewish community at Alexandria.

Ethronges [Athrongaios] (fl. 1st cent. BCE–1st cent. CE). Palestinian rebel and pretender to the Judean throne. After the death of Herod the Great in 4 BCE he claimed the Judean throne. Supported by his four brothers, he began a campaign of guerilla warfare aimed at Romans and royalists. He was defeated after an attack near Emmaus.

Etrog [citron]. Citrus fruit eaten on Sukkot. It was a popular Jewish symbol used on coins and graves, and in the decoration of synagogues during the second Temple period. Silver boxes for the etrog were a common object of Jewish ritual art.

Ettinger, Akiva Yaakov (1872–1945). Zionist leader of Belorussian origin. He went to London as an adviser on settlement matters during the negotiations over the Balfour Declaration. He settled in Palestine in 1918 and served as director of the agricultural settlement department of the Jewish National Fund until 1924. From 1924 to 1932 he played a prominent role in the purchase of land and the drafting and implementation of Jewish settlement plans. He wrote many articles on agriculture and settlement in Palestine.

Ettinger, Solomon (1803–1856). Polish Yiddish poet and dramatist. He was born in Warsaw and settled in Zhdanov near Zamość. He wrote parables, satirical ballads, epigrams, poems, and dramas. His *Serkele* portrays an ambitious woman who pursues power and wealth.

Ettlinger, Jacob (1798–1871). German rabbi and champion of neo-Orthodoxy. In 1826 he was appointed district rabbi for the districts of Ladenburg and Ingolstadt and settled in Mannheim, where he founded a yeshivah. He was appointed chief rabbi of Altona in 1836. He wrote numerous studies of Jewish law.

Etzel *see* IRGUN TZEVAI LEUMI.

Etz ḥayyim ("tree of life"). Expression found in Proverbs 3.18; it is applied to the wooden staves on which the Torah scroll is rolled.

Euchel, Isaac (1756–1804). German Hebrew author and Bible commentator of Danish origin. He became a leader of the Haskalah in Germany. He was born in Copenhagen and in 1787 settled in Berlin, where he managed the printing press of the Jüdische Freischule. His writings include a comedy satirizing Orthodoxy, a study of Moses Mendelssohn, a translation of and commentary on the Book of Proverbs, and a German translation of the prayerbook.

Eulogy, funeral. Funeral or memorial oration. From ancient times it was a custom to praise and lament the dead. Talmudic literature also contains funeral orations. In later times a eulogy ("ḥesped") was recited at the funeral. Among the Sephardim the eulogy consists of a talmudic discourse after the expiration of the 30 days' mourning period ("sheloshim").

Euphemism. An inoffensive word substituted for one which is indelicate, blasphemous, or taboo. Euphemisms are found in the Bible and in rabbinic literature. Typical examples include "house of the living" to mean a cemetery and the use of the verb "to know" to indicate sexual commerce.

Euphrates. River in western Asia. According to Genesis 2.14 it was one of the four branches of the river that watered the Garden of Eden. It was also the northern boundary of the land promised to Israel (Genesis 15.18; Deuteronomy 11.24; Joshua 1.4). In talmudic times and afterwards many Jewish communities lay along the Euphrates. On its lower course were the centers of Babylonian scholarship Sura, Nehardea, and Pumbedita.

***Eusebius** (260–339). Church Father. He was born in Caesarea and was appointed its bishop in c. 313. His *Praeparatio evangelica* demonstrates the superiority of Judaism over pagan Hellenism. In *Demonstratio evangelica* he criticizes Jews for distorting Scripture and neglecting the New Testament. His writings contain numerous quotations from otherwise lost Alexandrian Jewish authors.

Eve. First woman. She was created out of Adam's rib, and lived with him in the Garden of Eden. Seduced by the snake into eating the forbidden fruit of the tree of knowledge of good and evil, she persuaded Adam to eat as well. This act of disobedience was punished by their expulsion from Eden. Eve was condemned to suffer in childbirth and to be subservient to her husband. She was the mother of Cain, Abel, and Seth. (Genesis 2–4)

Evel Rabbati [Semaḥot]. Minor tractate included in the Babylonian Talmud. It deals with death and mourning. It was written in Palestine during the tannaitic period with later accretions from the amoraic and gaonic eras.

Evel Zutrati [Semaḥot of Rabbi Ḥiyya]. Minor tractate included in the Babylonian Talmud. It contains discourses on mourning customs.

Even ha-Ezer *see* JACOB BEN ASHER.

Evening service *see* MAARIV.

Even Shetiyyah. Rock projecting on the summit of the Temple hill in Jerusalem. According to tradition the world was founded on this rock, and Isaac was bound there for sacrifice. The Mishnah states that the Ark and the Tables of the Law were placed upon it in the first Temple, and in the second Temple it supported the censer. The Mosque of Omar is now built upon it.

Even-Shoshan, Avraham (b. 1906). Hebrew educator of Russian origin. He was born in Minsk and emigrated to Palestine in 1925. From 1954 to 1968 he was director of the Bet ha-Kerem Teachers' Institute in Jerusalem. He published stories, poems, and plays for children, translated children's books into Hebrew, and compiled a Hebrew dictionary.

Ever min ha-ḥai ("A limb from the living"). Prohibition based on Deuteronomy 12.23 against eating a limb taken from a living animal, beast, or bird. It is one of the seven Noachian Laws.

Évian, Conference of. Conference on refugees held at Évian-les-Bains on the shore of Lake Geneva in 1938. It was called by President Roosevelt in July 1938 to discuss the organization of the emigration and resettlement of refugees, as well as those persecuted because of their race and religion. It established an Inter-Governmental Committee for Refugees.

Evidence. Data on which to base proof or establish the truth. Biblical law calls for the testimony of at least two witnesses in criminal cases (Deuteronomy 19.15; 17.6). Rabbinic law limits suitable witnesses by disqualifying usurers, gamblers, individuals of improper character, non-Jews, slaves, women, and minors. In civil cases documents are acceptable where witnesses are not available.

Evil. According to the Bible, evil entered the world when Adam ate the forbidden fruit in the Garden of Eden (*see* FALL OF MAN). Human beings, whose behavior is guided by both good and evil inclinations according to rabbinic sources, are granted FREE WILL to choose which they will follow. In the Talmud and in medieval Jewish philosophy the existence of evil posed numerous theological dilemmas. Medieval Jewish mysticism viewed evil as grounded in the manifestations of the divine essence in the form of ten sephirot. Modern Jewish theologians have grappled with the religious perplexities caused by the death of six million Jews at the hands of the Nazis.

***Evil-Merodach** (fl. 6th cent. BCE). Son of Nebuchadnezzar II and King of Babylonia (562–560 BCE). According to the Bible, he freed Jehoiachin, King of Judah, from prison (II Kings 25.27–30; Jeremiah 52.31–4).

Evolution. Theory formulated by Charles

Darwin that plant and animal species evolve through successive generations, and that lower forms of life thereby become the ancestors of higher forms. Initially traditional Judaism rejected this view, but some Orthodox writers have attempted to reconcile the biblical account of creation with the theory of evolution by interpreting the six days of creation figuratively.

***Ewald, Georg Heinrich August** (1803–1875). German theologian and biblical scholar. He was professor at Göttingen (1827–37; 1848–67) and Tübingen (1838–48). He wrote about Hebrew and Arabic grammar, biblical texts, and the history of the Jews.

Exchequer of the Jews. Medieval English government department for Jewish affairs. The Exchequer controlled the system of chests ("archae") in which all moneylending transactions were registered. In addition most legal cases in which Jews were concerned were heard by the Exchequer. It also handled revenues from the Jewish community. *See also* PRESBYTER JUDAEORUM.

Excommunication *see* BAN.

Execution *see* CAPITAL PUNISHMENT.

Exegesis *see* BIBLE COMMENTARIES.

Exilarch (Aramaic "resh galuta"). Head of the Jewish community in Babylonia during the 1st–13th centuries. The office was hereditary and its holder was traditionally a member of the House of David. He was recognized by the royal court, served as chief tax collector among the Jews, appointed judges, and exercised criminal jurisdiction in the Jewish community. There were close ties as well as frequent conflicts between exilarchs and the geonim.

Exile *see* DIASPORA; GALUT; GOLAH; GOLUS.

Exile, Babylonian. Exile of the Jews in Babylonia in the 6th century BCE. The period of exile began with the destruction around 585 BCE of the Kingdom of Judah by Nebuchadnezzar and ended with the return of the Jews from captivity in c. 538 BCE. Encouraged by the prophecies of Jeremiah and Ezekiel, the Jewish exiles maintained their Jewish identity, worshipped in the synagogue, and generally prospered under foreign rule.

Exiles, ingathering of the. During the Babylonian exile Ezekiel prophesied the return of the exiles to their native land. He addressed himself first to Judean exiles and then extended his prophecy to include the exiles of the northern kingdom. The belief that the exiles would be restored became a central aspect of rabbinic belief and was an important theme of the liturgy. In modern times the concept of the ingathering of the exiles ("kibbutz galuyyot") is often used to designate the immigration of Jews in the diaspora to the State of Israel.

Exodus (i). The flight of the Israelites from Egypt. It is a central event in the history of the Jewish people. With the accession of a new king who did not know Joseph (Exodus 1.8), the Jews in Egypt were reduced to slavery. Under the leadership of Moses, they were delivered from their bondage and escaped their pursuers on dry land when the Red Sea miraculously parted. The Exodus was the prelude to the years in the wilderness during which the Jews sought the Promised Land.

Exodus (ii) (Hebrew "Shemot"). Biblical book, second book of the Pentateuch. It consists of 40 chapters. Chapters 1–17 describe the oppression of the Israelites by the Egyptians, the rise of Moses, the ten plagues, and the Exodus from Egypt. Chapters 18–24 give details of the divine revelation and legislation and the covenant between God and Israel. The episode of the Golden Calf and subsequent events are contained in chapters 25–40.

Exodus 1947. Name of the ship that attempted to carry more than 4000 Jewish refugees to Palestine under the auspices of the Haganah in 1947. It was seized by the British in the Mediterranean, and the refugees were forcibly returned to Hamburg.

Exodus Rabbah (Hebrew "Shemot Rabbah"). Midrash on the Book of Exodus. It consists of two different midrashim: Exodus Rabbah I (sections 1–14), and Exodus Rabbah II (sections 15–52).

Exorcism. The driving out of an evil spirit. The practice is mentioned in the Apocrypha, New Testament, and the Talmud. Magical formulae were used to bring about the expulsion of evil spirits, and amulets were employed to ward off their influence. Exorcism was commonly performed by kabbalists and Ḥasidim, who were anxious to rid individuals of the souls of the dead who possessed them.

Exploration. In the early biblical period the Jewish world comprehended Egypt, Chaldea, and Babylon; this was extended by Solomon's trading expeditions. In the diaspora Jews came into contact with Greece, western Asia, and the lands of the Roman Empire. Under the rule of Byzantium and Islam Jews traded with India and China. Later they pioneered routes from north Africa to the Niger. The major contribution of Jews to voyages of exploration at the close of the Middle Ages was the production of maps and nautical instruments. Some sources suggest that Christopher Columbus was of Jewish descent.

Expulsions. Throughout their history in the diaspora the Jewish people have been subjected to expulsion from the places in which they settled, as part of a general pattern of persecution. As early as 139 BCE Jews were driven out of Rome. In the Middle Ages Jews who refused to convert to Christianity were expelled from England (1290), France (1306, 1322, 1394), and Germany (1348–50). Professing Jews were excluded from Andalusia in 1484 and expelled from Spain and Spanish dominions in 1492. This was followed by the expulsion from Portugal (1497), Navarre (1498), Provence (1512), and Naples (1541). In 1569 they were expelled from the smaller centers of the papal dominions in Italy and France. In the 18th century Jews were expelled from Little Russia (1727, 1739, 1742), and in the 19th from areas outside the Pale of Settlement.

Extermination camps *see* CONCENTRATION CAMPS.

Eydoux, Emmanuel (b. 1913). French author. He was born in Marseilles. He taught Jewish history and thought in an ORT school and was active in the Marseilles Jewish community. He wrote poems, as well as plays and books on the history of Judaism.

Ezekiel (i) (fl. 6th cent. BCE). Israelite prophet. He prophesied among the Babylonian exiles from 592 to 570 BCE. After the destruction of Jerusalem, he consoled and encouraged those in captivity.

Ezekiel (ii). Biblical book, the third of the books of the Latter Prophets. The first chapter contains a description of the divine chariot ("merkavah") which served as the basis of later mystical speculation. Chapters 1–24 of the book contain prophecies of destruction before the fall of Jerusalem; chapters 25–32 prophesy catastrophes that will befall the gentiles; chapters 33–9 contain words of consolation for Israel; and chapters 40–48 record visions of the restored Temple and kingdom.

Ezekiel, Jacob (1812–1899). American communal leader. He was born in Philadelphia and moved to Baltimore and then to Richmond, Virginia, where he was active in Jewish affairs. He fought against legislation which discriminated against Jews. Later he moved to Cincinnati, where he served as secretary to the board of governors of the Hebrew Union College.

Ezekiel, Moses Jacob (1844–1917). American sculptor. He served in the Civil War, only later becoming a sculptor. His *Religious Liberty* is a large marble group commissioned by the B'nai B'rith for the Centennial Exposition of 1876.

Ezion Geber. Place at which the Israelites camped on their way to Canaan (Numbers 33.35–6). At the head of the Gulf of Aqaba, it later served as a port from which Solomon's ships sailed to Ophir (I Kings 9.26). After being captured by Edom, it was recovered by Jehoshaphat, who attempted to renew the gold route between there and Ophir (I Kings, 22.49).

Ezra (i) (fl. 5th cent. BCE). Israelite prophet. He served as a scribe in the Persian government. Later he received permission from Artaxerxes I to lead the Jewish exiles back to Jerusalem. Together with Nehemiah, he persuaded the people to return to the Torah, observe the Sabbath and sabbatical year, pay Temple dues, and refrain from intermarriage. The story of Ezra is contained in the books of Ezra and Nehemiah.

Ezra (ii). Biblical book, part of the Hagiographa. It relates the story of the Jews' return from exile in Babylon from the return of Zerubbabel to Judah in the 6th century BCE until after the return of Ezra.

Ezra, Apocalypse of *see* ESDRAS.

Ezrat Nashim ("women's court"). Court in the Temple beyond which women were not permitted to pass. Later the term was applied to the section of the synagogue where the women sit during the service.

F

Fable (Hebrew "mashal"). Short moral tale in which the characters are usually animals. Fables are frequently found in midrash and the Talmud. In the Middle Ages popular collections of fables were produced by Jewish authors, who based their writing on Arab sources. Some modern Jewish writers have published fables as well.

Fackenheim, Emil (b. 1916). Canadian theologian. He was born in Halle, Germany. He emigrated to Canada in 1940, where he became professor of philosophy at the University of Toronto. His major work concerns the religious response to the Holocaust. His writings include: *God's Presence in History, The Jewish Return into History,* and *To Mend the World.*

Fair. A gathering held regularly for the sale of goods. The gathering of large numbers of Jews at the annual fair held in Lublin and at the early summer fair at Jarosław was responsible for the development of the Council of the Four Lands in the 16th century. In western Europe fairs were frequently held in Jewish quarters on Purim.

Faith, confession of *see* SHEMA.

Faith, 13 principles of *see* CREED; 13 PRINCIPLES OF FAITH.

Faitlovitch, Jacques (1881–1955). Polish researcher and activist on behalf of the Falashas. He went to Ethiopia in 1904 and spent 18 months among the Falashas. He published *Notes of a Voyage among the Falashas* and organized committees in Italy and Germany to raise money for their education. Later he continued with his activities on the Falashas' behalf in the US and Israel, and published books on their literature.

Falaquera, Shemtov ben Joseph [Ibn Falaquera] (c. 1225–1295). Philosophical author. Born in Spain, he lived there and in the border provinces of Spain and France. His writings include a defense of Maimonides' *Guide for the Perplexed,* a compilation of ethical aphorisms, an introduction to the study of the sciences, an encyclopedia of the sciences, and translations of sections of Solomon ibn Gabirol's *Fountain of Life.*

Falashas. Black ethnic group of Ethiopia, which claims to be of Jewish origin. They follow a form of the Jewish religion based on the Bible, the Apocrypha, and other post-biblical Scripture. They claim to have originated from the notables of Jerusalem who accompanied Menelik, the son of King Solomon and the Queen of Sheba, when he returned to his country. In the mid-1980s there was a secret airlift of about 20,000 Falashas to Israel, and a further large airlift took place in 1991.

Falk, Ḥayyim Samuel Jacob (c. 1708–1782). English mystic. He was born in Podolia and settled in England in about 1742. He was reputed to be a miracle-worker and became known as the Baal Shem of London.

Falk, Jacob Joshua ben Tzevi Hirsch

(1680–1756). Polish rabbi and halakhic authority. He was born in Kraków and lived and worked in Lwów before serving as rabbi in the communities of Tarnów, Kurów, and Lesko. In 1717 he became rabbi of Lwów; from 1730 to 1734 he was rabbi of Berlin, and he later became rabbi of Metz and Frankfurt am Main. His *Penei Yehoshua* is an outstanding work of novellae on the Talmud.

Falk, Joshua ben Alexander ha-Cohen [Walk, Joshua] (1555–1614). Polish educationist and communal leader. He was born in Lublin. He devoted his life to teaching and took an active part in the Council of the Four Lands. His *Bet Yisrael* is a commentary on Jacob ben Asher's *Turim*. In *Sepher Meirat Enayim*, he amended and interpreted part of the text of the Shulḥan Arukh. He also wrote responsa as well as commentaries on the Pentateuch and Talmud.

Fall of man. Adam's state of disobedience and the state of innate sinfulness into which all mankind is born as a consequence of his sin. According to rabbinic teaching, death, labor, and pain were brought into the world when Adam ate the forbidden fruit in the Garden of Eden, and his sin doomed all human beings to death. The acceptance of the Torah on Mount Sinai restored man's original state, but this was again lost by the worship of the Golden Calf. Christian theology maintains that human beings suffer from original sin because of Adam's disobedience.

False witness. The biblical injunction against bearing false witness (Exodus 20.13) embraces all types of slander, defamation, and misrepresentation. In Jewish law evidence must be presented by two witnesses at least if a case is to be proved. If a second pair of witnesses state in court that the first pair were with them at the time of the criminal act and not at the scene of the crime, the testimony of the second pair of witnesses incriminates that of the first pair; this is refered to as "hazammah."

Familianten (German). Term applied to Jews in Bohemia, Moravia, and Silesia who were legally allowed to marry. The maximum number of families with this privilege (limited to the eldest son) was fixed by law in 1726. In 1789 they numbered 8600 in Bohemia and 5400 in Moravia. The Familiantengesetz was abrogated in 1849, revived in 1853, and abolished in 1859.

Family. In biblical times Jewish families were based on polygamy and included all male descendants and dependants. Talmudic literature reflects a monogamous society and the idealization of family life. It was the duty of the father to educate his sons and prepare them for a useful trade. Monogamy became firmly established in northern Europe as a result of the takkanah of Gershom in the 11th century. Family solidarity and loyalty are regarded as central virtues and strengths of the Jewish tradition.

Fano, Jacob (fl. 16th cent.). Italian scholar and poet. He lived in Cento, Ferrara, and Bologna. His elegy on the Marrano martyrs of Ancona of 1555 provoked church authorities. He was punished and his book was burned.

Fano, Joseph (c. 1550–1630). Italian communal leader. He was on familiar terms with the dukes of Mantua and Ferrara and occasionally acted as their intermediary. Some time before 1628 he was raised to the rank of Marquis of Villimpenta. He was the first Jew to be ennobled in Europe.

Fano, Menaḥem Azariah (1548–1620). Italian rabbi and kabbalist. He was active in Ferrara, Venice, Reggio nell'Emilia, and Mantua. He published a collection of 130 responsa and also wrote works on the kabbalah, prayer, and the transmigration of the soul.

***Farabi, Abu Nasr Muhammad Al-** (c. 870–c. 950). Babylonian Muslim philosopher. He spent most of his life in Baghdad and played a major role in the dissemination of ancient philosophy in the Islamic world. He influenced medieval Jewish philosophers, including Maimonides.

Farband Labor Zionist Order. Zionist educational and aid organization in the US and Canada. It was formed in 1913. It established Zionist-oriented Jewish schools, and helped to found the Jewish Teachers' Seminary and People's University. It has also been active in relief and fund-raising for the Histadrut.

Farbstein, David Tzevi (1868–1953). Swiss lawyer and Zionist. He was born in Warsaw and settled in Zurich in 1894. He served as a member of the Swiss parliament after World War I until 1939. He was the first president (from 1920) of the Keren ha-Yesod in Switzerland. When the State of Israel was founded, he suggested that its legislation be based on the model of the Swiss republic. He wrote studies of Judaism, Zionism, and law.

Farbstein, Joshua Heschel (1870–1948). Polish communal leader. He was born in Warsaw. He was president of the Zionist Organization in Poland from 1915 to 1918. A founder of Mizraḥi in Poland, he was its president from 1918 to 1931; he was also president of the Keren ha-Yesod in Poland and of the Warsaw Jewish community from 1926 to 1931. He moved to Jerusalem, where he led the Community Council from 1938 to 1945.

Farḥi [Parḥi], **Estori** [Estori ha-Parḥi] (1280–?1355). Palestinian topographer. Born in Provence, he lived in various cities in Spain, and later settled in Palestine. His *Kaphtor va-Pheraḥ* presents the results of his travels throughout Palestine: it establishes the names of Palestinian towns and villages, describes the geography and natural history of the country, and identifies ancient sites.

Farḥi, Ḥayyim Mu'Allim (c. 1760–1820). Palestinian statesman. He entered the service of Aḥmad al-Jazzar Pasha in Damascus and was responsible for Palestine's treasury affairs. He participated in the city of Acre's stand against Napoleon in 1799. Later he was imprisoned, but was restored under Al-Jazzar's successor, Suleiman Pasha (ruled 1805–18). He acted as the protector of the Jews of Palestine.

Farrisol, Abraham (c. 1451–c. 1525). Italian biblical scholar, geographer, and polemicist. He was born in Avignon and lived in Ferrara and Mantua, working as a cantor and copyist. He represented Judaism before the Duke of Ferrara in a religious dispute with two Dominican monks. He wrote a commentary on the Torah, Ecclesiastes and Job, a defense of Judaism, and the first modern Hebrew work on geography.

Fascism. Any right-wing nationalist ideology with an authoritarian and hierarchical structure, opposed to democracy and liberalism. Often linked with an anti-Semitic program, it belongs to the political right and embraces nationalism, militant anti-Marxism, and veneration of the state. Specifically the political regime of Benito Mussolini in Italy in the 1920s–1940s.

Fast. Abstention from eating all or certain foods. Fasting may be undertaken individually as a sign of mourning or in expiation of sin; the community as a whole observes a number of traditional fast days: 3 Tishri, the Fast of Gedaliah commemorating the assassination of Gedaliah; 10 Tishri, the Day of Atonement; 10 Tevet, commemorating the siege of Jerusalem begun by Nebuchadnezzar; 13 Adar, the Fast of Esther; 14 Nissan, the Fast of the First-born, commemorating the last of the ten plagues of Egypt; 17

Tammuz, commemorating the breaching of the walls of Jerusalem by Nebuchadnezzar and by Titus; and 9 Av, commemorating the destruction of the first and second Temples. The major fast days, the Day of Atonement and the Ninth of Av, last from sunset to sunset and involve abstention from eating, drinking, sexual intercourse, and the wearing of footgear. Other fasts last from sunrise to sunset and involve abstinence only from food and drink.

Fast, Howard (b. 1914). American author. He was born in New York. He wrote novels about American history, injustice, and oppression. He also published books on Jewish themes, including *Haym Solomon: Son of Liberty*, *Picture Book of History of the Jews*, *My Glorious Brothers*, and *Moses, Prince of Egypt*.

Father. According to the Jewish faith, the father has legal obligations toward his children. Conversely children are obligated to honor and respect their father (and mother). A father's legal responsibility generally ends when his children attain their majority.

Fear of God. It is regarded as the basis of religious awareness. Thus Proverbs states that fear of God is the beginning of knowledge (Proverbs 1.7), and of wisdom (Proverbs 10.10).

Feast of Lights *see* Ḥanukkah.

Feast of Tabernacles *see* Sukkot.

Feast of the Commandment *see* Seudat mitzvah.

Feast of Unleavened Bread *see* Passover.

Feast of Weeks *see* Shavuot.

Feasts *see* Holy days.

Feder, Tobias Guttman (1760–1817). Galician Haskalah scholar. He was born in Przedbórz and later wandered through Galicia, Poland, and Russia. He wrote plays and satires, as well as studies in linguistics and grammar, and was one of the pioneers of Hebrew literary criticism.

Fefer, Itzik (1900–1952). Ukrainian Yiddish poet. He was born in Shpola. He made his debut as a Yiddish poet in 1920 and became prominent in Soviet Yiddish literature. The majority of his poems are propaganda for the Communist Party. He also wrote poetry about Birobidjan, the Jewish autonomous region in eastern Siberia. He was arrested in 1948 in the Stalinist anti-Jewish purges.

Feh (Yiddish). Expression of disgust.

Feierberg, Mordecai Ze'ev (1874–1899). Russian Hebrew author. He wrote essays and lyrical novels. In his novels he expressed the plight of eastern European youth at the end of the 19th century, who were disillusioned with the Haskalah movement but were unable to accept traditional Judaism.

Feigenbaum, Benjamin (1860–1932). American Yiddish writer and activist. He was born in Warsaw. He became a militant atheist and agitator for socialism. He settled in London in 1887, where he published pamphlets on socialism, then in 1891 he emigrated to the US. He attempted to win support for socialism and atheism among Jewish workers and in 1900 became general secretary of the Workmen's Circle.

Feinberg, Abraham L. (1899–1986). American Reform rabbi. He was born in Bellaire, Ohio. He served congregations in Niagara Falls, New York, Denver, and Toronto. He was an advocate of liberal social causes, a supporter of nuclear disarmament, and an opponent of the Vietnam War. His works include *Storm the Gates of Jericho* and *Hanoi Diary*.

Feinberg, Avshalom (1889–1917). Palestinian writer and leader of the Nili. He was born in Gedera. He founded the Nili movement with Aaron Aaronsohn. He was shot and killed by Bedouin on a journey to Egypt. His writings depict the world of the first generation born in Jewish settlements in Palestine.

Feiwel, Berthold (1875–1937). German

Zionist leader. He was born in Moravia. He was a close associate of Theodor Herzl and helped to organize the first Zionist Congress in 1897. In 1901 he became editor-in-chief of the central organ of the Zionist Organization, *Die Welt*. He translated Hebrew and Yiddish works into German and was a founder of the Judischer Verlag in Berlin. In 1933 he settled in Palestine.

Feldman, Louis (1896–1975). South African Yiddish writer. He was born in Lithuania and went to South Africa in 1910, where he worked as a businessman. His publications include *Jews in South Africa, Oudtshoorn: the Jerusalem of Africa, Jews in Johannesburg*, and *Israel as I see it*.

Felix Libertate ("Happy through Freedom"). Dutch society formed in Amsterdam in 1775 to promote Jewish emancipation. After the national assembly granted emancipation, it demanded a revision of the statutes of the Amsterdam Jewish community. When these demands were rejected by the leaders of the Jewish community, the Adath Jessurun congregation was founded. These two rival communities engaged in bitter dispute. In 1808 the Adath Jessurun congregation was reunited with the old community by a decree of King Louis Bonaparte.

Fels, Mary (1863–1953). American Zionist. She was born in Bavaria and was taken to the US in 1869. She organized the Joseph Fels Foundation in 1925 to promote human welfare through education and cultural exchange, particularly between the US and Palestine.

Felsenthal, Bernard (1822–1908). American rabbi. He was born in Germany and settled in the US in 1854. He served as rabbi in Chicago from 1861 to 1887. He was a founder of the Jewish Publication Society of America and the American Jewish Historical Society.

Feminism. In all areas of Jewish life feminism has brought marked changes in Jewish consciousness. Outside the Orthodox world, women have been ordained as rabbis, trained as cantors, and have taken a leading role in Jewish communal life. Within Orthodoxy a number of women wish to see changes in the status of women in the Jewish community.

Fence around the law (from Hebrew "seyag": fence). Preventive rabbinic ordinance enacted to safeguard traditional practices. In the Mishnah one of the three precepts of the Men of the Great Synagogue is the prescription to make fences around the law. The practice consisted of producing stringent regulations to safeguard the original commandments.

***Ferdinand and Isabella.** Spanish king and queen (respectively 1452–1516, 1451–1504). Initially they adopted a tolerant attitude toward their Jewish subjects. Later they were determined to eradicate the sin of heresy which had spread among the Conversos. In 1480 the Spanish Inquisition was established and in 1492 the Jews were expelled from Spain.

Ferrara. City in central northern Italy. Privileges enjoyed by the Jews living there are recorded in 1275. During the Renaissance it fostered one of the most important Jewish communities in Italy. After 1492 Spanish refugees were welcomed in the city, and Portuguese Marranos arrived there in the middle of the 16th century. When the ghetto system was introduced in 1597, the city continued to be a center of Jewish cultural life.

***Ferrer, Vicente** (c. 1350–1419). Spanish Dominican monk. He advocated conversion to Christianity and his preaching provoked mass demonstrations and anti-Jewish outbursts at the beginning of the 15th century. In 1412 he helped to formulate the laws of Valladolid, which were directed against the Jews. He wrote over 6000 sermons.

Ferrer Saldin *see* ZERAHIAH LEVI.

Festival prayers. An extra prayer (Musaph) is added on festivals to the regular morning prayer; it corresponds to and describes the additional sacrifice offered on these days in the Temple. Appropriate verses are read from the Torah and the Prophets. Special commandments such as blowing the shophar have given rise to special festival prayers, and it has become customary to recite piyyutim in honor of the festival. The festival prayerbook is referred to as the Maḥzor.

Festivals *see* HOLY DAYS.

***Fettmilch, Vincent** (d. 1616). German anti-Jewish communal leader. In 1614 the population of Frankfurt am Main attacked the ghetto, and Jewish defenders rushed to join women and children who were hiding in the cemetery. When it was surrounded by Fettmilch and his followers, the Jewish community was forced to leave the city. On 10 March 1616 Fettmilch was hanged, and the Jewish community celebrated the date annually as the Purim of Vincent.

Feuchtwanger, Lion (1884–1958). German historical novelist. He was born in Munich. He wrote plays as a young man and in 1926 his novel *Jud Süss* was published. Eventually he settled in the US. His novel *The Oppermanns* deals with a German Jewish family during the rise of Nazism. He also wrote a historical trilogy on the life of Josephus.

Feuerberg, Mordecai Ze'ev (1874–1899). Ukrainian Hebrew writer. He was born in Novograd Volynskiy. His literary career began in 1896, when he went to Warsaw. He broke with his Ḥasidic background and wrote short stories about the conflict between traditional Judaism and modern secular culture.

Feuerstein, Avigdor *see* HA-MEIRI, AVIGDOR.

Fez. City in north central Morocco. Its Jewish community dates from the 9th century and produced many rabbinic scholars. Persecutions were instigated against the Jews there by the Almohades in the 12th century and the Marabout movement during the 13th century, as a consequence of which Jews were allotted a special quarter of the city (the Mellah). Refugees from Spain joined the community in 1391 and after 1492.

Fichman, Yaakov (1881–1958). Palestinian Hebrew poet, critic and literary editor. He was born in Bessarabia and lived in various cities in Russia and western Europe before settling in Palestine in 1912. He edited literary periodicals, anthologies, and textbooks, and wrote poetry.

Fiedler, Leslie A. (b. 1917). American writer and critic. He was born in Newark, New Jersey. He taught at the University of Montana and the State University of New York at Buffalo. Jewish themes have played an increasing role in his later work. His writings include *Image of the Jew in American Fiction* and *The Jew in the American Novel.*

Fifteenth of Av (Hebrew "Tu b'Av"). Day of rejoicing marking the beginning of the vintage; it was observed during the period of the second Temple. Girls dressed in white danced and sang in the vineyards and wood offerings were brought to the Temple.

Fifteenth of Shevat (Hebrew "Tu bi-Shevat"). The date on which the new year begins for the purposes of tithing fruit. It is celebrated as Hamishah Asah bi-Shevat ("New year for trees"). A different system of tithing is applied to fruit harvested before and after this date. It is celebrated by eating special fruits particularly oranges and lemons, which have a special place in Israel's horticulture. In modern Israel the day is celebrated by tree-planting.

Filipowski, Herschell Phillips (1816–1872). British Hebraist, editor, and actuary. He was born in Lithuania and emigrated to London in 1839, where he taught at a Jewish school. He was the editor of the Hebrew annual *Ha-Asif* from 1847 to 1849. In 1851 he founded a Jewish antiquarian society for the purpose of publishing medieval Hebrew texts on which he wrote various studies. In 1862 he printed a pocket edition of the prayerbook. His *Biblical Prophecies* discusses the Jewish view of prophecy and messianism.

Finaly case. Robert and Gerald Finaly were the subjects of a legal struggle in France from 1950 to 1953. Their parents died in a Nazi concentration camp, and they were baptized in 1948. Despite the decision of a French court to award custody of the boys to their nearest relative, they disappeared in 1953 and were later traced to Spain. Ten individuals were arrested for kidnapping, and the children were returned to France. They later emigrated to Israel.

Finance *see* BANKING; MONEYLENDING.

Finding of property. The Bible stipulates that lost property must be returned to its owner (Exodus 23.4; Deuteronomy 22.3). The person who finds lost property must make a public announcement. In ancient Israel announcements were made over a period covering the festival celebrations. Later they were made in the synagogue. Proper identification should be made by the owner of lost property. No reward should be claimed for its return, but the finder is entitled to reimbursement for expenses in caring for it. If the owner does not claim the property the finder is regarded as the owner. The subject is discussed in the talmudic tractate Bava Metzia.

Fineman, Irving (1893–?). American novelist. He was born in New York and worked as an engineer until 1929, when he turned to writing. Of his later novels, *Jacob* and *Ruth* deal with biblical themes. He also wrote a biography of Henrietta Szold, *Woman of Valor*.

Fines. The Bible imposes a fine payable to the injured party as the punishment for wrongdoing in four cases: (1) 50 shekels for ravishing a virgin: (2) 50 shekels for seducing a virgin; (3) 100 shekels for falsely accusing one's wife of prenuptial unchastity; (4) 30 shekels for the killing of a slave by an ox. Later the rabbinical courts imposed fines payable to the community fund for a number of public offenses. In addition, Jewish communities stipulated fines as punishment for refusing communal office or synagogue honors, and for absence from religious services or communal meetings.

Finkelstein, Louis (b. 1895). American Conservative rabbi, scholar, and educator. He was born in Cincinnati. He began teaching at the Jewish Theological Seminary in 1920 and later became provost, president, and chancelor there. He served as president of the Rabbinical Assembly from 1928 to 1930. He wrote and edited books and articles on general problems in religion, sociology, culture, and ethics. His publications include *Pharisees, Jews: their History, Culture, and Religion,* and *Jewish Self-Government in the Middle Ages.*

Finta (Spanish: "fine"). The assessment of dues payable to the Sephardi congregation by its members.

Finzi, Angelo Mordecai (d. 1476). Italian banker and scientist. He lived in Bologna and Mantua. He wrote studies on mathematics and astronomy, translated various works on mathematics, geometry, and astronomy into Hebrew, explained recently invented astronomical instruments, and published treatises on grammar and mnemonics.

Finzi, Isaac Raphael (1728–1812). Italian preacher. He served as a rabbi in Padua and was widely acclaimed as a preacher. He was a member of the French Sanhedrin in 1806 and served as its vice-president.

Finzi, Solomon (fl. 16th cent.). Italian rabbinical scholar. He served as a rabbi in Forlì and Bologna. His methodological work *Mafteaḥ ha-Gemara* was reprinted in 1697 in Helmstedt with a Latin translation and notes, and again reprinted in the 18th century in *Clavis Talmudica maxima*.

Firkovich, Abraham (1786–1874). Palestinian Karaite leader of Polish birth. He engaged in bitter disputes with rabbinic authorities. In 1830 he accompanied Simḥah Bobowich to Palestine, where he collected numerous manuscripts. When, in 1839, the governor general of the Crimea addressed a series of questions dealing with Karaite origins to Bobowich, he recommended Firkovich, who initiated archeological expeditions to the Crimea and the Caucasus to uncover ancient tombstones and manuscripts. Firkovich's travels and discoveries are described in his *Avnei Zikkaron*.

First-born. In biblical times special privileges and a double share of the father's inheritance belonged to the first-born son (Deuteronomy 21.17). *See also* BIRTHRIGHT.

First-born, Fast of the. Fast observed by first-born sons on the day before Passover. It stems from the desire to express gratitude for the saving of the first-born Israelites during the tenth plague of Egypt (Exodus 13.1ff). Eventually it became a custom to finish the study of a Talmud tractate on the morning before Passover, when a festive banquet was arranged in the synagogue. Since first-born sons were allowed to partake of this meal, they were not obliged to fast.

First-born, redemption of the (Hebrew "Pidyon ha-Ben"). The Bible stipulates that every first-born son belongs to God (Exodus 13.11–16). Redemption is achieved by the payment to the priests of 5 shekels, or its equivalent in goods, on the 31st day after the birth of a son. Redemption does not apply to the first-born of priests or Levites. The ceremony of the redemption of the first-born takes place on the 31st day after birth; a sum is paid to a cohen and this act is accompanied by the recital of special prayers.

First fruits. The Bible decrees that the first choice fruits of the harvest should be brought to the Temple and the declaration in Deuteronomy 26.5–10 be recited. The third chapter of the Mishnah tractate Bikkurim deals with this custom.

***Firuz** (fl. 5th cent.). Sassanid king of Persia (459–83). He used the alleged murder of two magi at Isfahan in 468 as a pretext for persecuting the Jews. Half of the local Jews were killed, and the exilarch, Huna bar Zutra, was sentenced to death.

Fischel, Harry (1865–1948). American philanthropist. He was born in Russia and emigrated to the US in 1885. He settled in New York, where he was active as a businessman in the construction and real estate industry. He was associated with a number of Jewish institutions, and endowed the Harry Fischel Foundation for Research in Talmud in Palestine.

Fiscus judaicus. Fund of the Roman Empire into which was paid the money from the tax levied on the Jews by Vespasian after the destruction of the second Temple. During the reign of Domitian its exaction was especially harsh. The tax continued to be collected until the 4th century.

Fish. The Bible decrees that man is to exercise dominion over the fish as well as over other living things (Genesis 1.28). Fish are divided into clean and unclean creatures: "These you may eat, of all that are in the waters. Everything in the waters that has fins and scales ... you may eat. But anything in the seas or the rivers that has not fins and scales ... is an abomination to you." (Leviticus 11.9–11)

Fishberg, Maurice (1872–1934). American physician and anthropologist. He was born in Russia and emigrated to the US in 1889. He was professor of clinical medicine at New York University and Bellevue Hospital Medical College. His publications include *The Jews: a Study of Race and Environment.*

Fishman, Jacob (1878–1946). American Yiddish editor and Zionist leader of Polish origin. After he emigrated to the US he was active in Zionist societies that pre-dated those founded under the influence of Theodor Herzl. He was a founder of the Zionist Organization of America. He coedited the New York Yiddish dailies *Tageblat* (1893–1914) and *Varhayt* (1914–16). Later he served as managing editor of the *Jewish Morning Journal.*

Fishman, Yehudah Leib *see* MAIMON, YEHUDAH LEIB.

***Fita y Colomer, Fidel** (1838–1918). Spanish historian. He published studies on the history of Spanish Jewry in the proceedings of the *Real Academia de la Historia.*

Five Books of Moses *see* TORAH.

Five Scrolls. Name given to five books of the Hagiographa, which are read on particular festivals: the Song of Songs on Passover; Ruth on Shavuot; Lamentations on the Ninth of Av; Ecclesiastes on Sukkot; and Esther on Purim.

Flag. According to the Bible each of the 12 tribes of Israel had its own banner (Numbers 2). The midrash describes them as having the colors of the 12 stones in the high priest's breastplate. The Maccabees are said to have carried a banner on which were inscribed the initial letters of the words "Who is like you among the gods, O Lord?" The flag adopted by the Zionist movement (and later by the State of Israel) consisted of a Shield of David with two broad blue horizontal stripes on a white background.

Flagellation *see* FLOGGING.

Flavius Josephus *see* JOSEPHUS, FLAVIUS.

Flayshig (Yiddish: "made of meat"). Meats, poultry, or foods prepared with animal fats. They may not be eaten with dairy foods.

Fleckeles, Eleazar ben David (1754–1826). Bohemian rabbi and author. He was born in Prague and served as a rabbi there; he was also head of a large yeshivah and president of a three-man rabbinate council. When the Frankists made their appearance in the city in 1800, he led the opposition to them. He published a collection of sermons on halakhic and aggadic themes, as well as a volume of responsa.

Fleg, Edmond (1874–1963). French poet, playwright, and essayist. He lived in Paris, where he worked as a theater critic and playwright. Jewish themes are found throughout his work. His writings include: *Écoute Israel, Pourquoi je suis Juif, Ma Palestine, L'anthologie juive,* and *Jésus, raconté par le Juif Errant.*

Fleisher, Ezra (b. 1928). Israeli poet and scholar. He was born in Transylvania and emigrated to Israel in 1960. He became a lecturer on medieval Hebrew literature at Bar Ilan University, and then at the Hebrew University. His writings include *Mershalim* and *Be-Heḥalek Laylah.*

Flesh. In the Bible the term refers variously to the body as a whole; humanity; the impressionable side of human nature; and an item of food. Initially flesh was forbidden as food (Genesis 1.29–30), but it was later permitted as long as it was not torn from a living creature. According to Jewish law only certain kinds of animals may be eaten (*see* CLEAN ANIMALS), and they must be slaughtered and prepared in specific ways. Rabbinic teaching does not encourage mortification of the flesh or the view that flesh is inherently sinful.

Flexner, Bernard (1865–1945). American lawyer and Zionist leader. He was born in Louisville, Kentucky, and practiced law in Kentucky, Chicago, and New York. He was concerned with social welfare and labor problems as well as the Zionist movement. In 1919 he was counsel to the Zionist delegation at the Paris Peace Conference. He later served as president and chairman of the board of the Palestine Economic Corporation.

Flogging. Harsh beating, especially with a whip. Punishment by inflicting stripes is prescribed in Deuteronomy 25.1–3. Although the Bible decrees a maximum of 40 stripes, the rabbis interpreted this as a maximum of 39. Two-thirds were administered on the back, and one-third on the chest. It was the normal punishment for actively transgressing the negative commandments; it was also viewed as sufficient punishment for severe violations of laws, for which the traditional punishment was "karet" (cutting off). There is no physical punishment for failure to observe the positive commandments; nonetheless the rabbis were empowered to administer such punishment for the good of the community when they saw fit.

Flood. The Flood was brought about by God to destroy human beings because of their wickedness (Genesis 6–9). Noah was commanded to make an ark in which to place his family as well as males and females of all living creatures. Eventually the waters abated, and God promised not to destroy mankind again.

Florence. City in central Italy. In the 15th century Jews were invited to establish loan banks there for the benefit of the poor. Duke Cosimo I introduced the Jewish badge and established the ghetto in 1571. The Florentine Jews were emancipated in the 19th century and the city became a center of Jewish spiritual activity. The Collegio Rabbinico Italiano flourished there from 1899 to 1930.

Foa, Eleazar Naḥman (d. after 1641). Italian rabbi and kabbalist. He lived at Reggio nell'Emilia and became chief rabbi of the duchy of Modena. He was head of Ḥevrat ha-Aluvim, which sponsored the printing of a commentary on the Haggadah. He also wrote a philosophic and kabbalistic commentary on the Torah.

Foa, Moses Benjamin (1729–1822). Italian bibliophile and bookseller. Living in Reggio nell'Emilia, he supplied books to the ducal library at Modena and became one of the most important booksellers of his day. He wrote a Hebrew grammar and copied several Hebrew manuscripts.

Folkisten [Volkisten]. Polish Jewish political party. Formed in 1919, it advocated Jewish national and cultural autonomy in Poland, as well as equal rights for Jews. Its organ was the Yiddish monthly *Das folk*.

Folklore. The traditions of a people as expressed in popular beliefs, customs, stories, songs, and practices. The Bible records folklore reflecting the civilization of the ancient Near East. Rabbinic literature contains Jewish folklore, influenced by the cultural environment in which the Jews lived. The scientific study of Jewish folklore began at the close of the 19th century.

Fonseca, Daniel de (1672–c. 1740). Turkish physician and diplomat. He was born in Portugal. Although he was brought up as a Christian and even became a priest, he adhered to Judaism in secret. He was pursued by the Inquisition and fled to France. In 1702 he arrived in Constantinople, where he embraced Judaism. He later became medical attendant to Prince Mavrocordato at Bucharest. After returning to Constantinople, he became physician to the sultan, and eventually settled in Paris.

***Ford, Henry** (1863–1947). American industrialist. He was a pioneer of mass production in the automobile industry. He held strong anti-Semitic views and published a series of articles based on the Protocols of the Elders of Zion in the *Dearborn Independent.*

Forgery. The false making or altering of a document in an attempt to defraud. To aid the detection of alterations to legal documents, rabbinic legislation established the type of paper and ink which could be used. When it was suspected that an entire document was a forgery, it could be submitted for certification by a court. Forgery is viewed as a sin, but there is no prescribed punishment for it. At worst the person involved is not allowed to serve as a witness in other cases.

Forgiveness. According to the Bible, it is one of God's attributes (Exodus 34.6); to be forgiven by God human beings must repent of their sins and resolve to improve their ways. Forgiveness for sins committed against others cannot be obtained until the wrong is righted and pardon sought from the injured party. The final sections of the tractate Yoma in the Talmud deal with repentance and the ritual of the Day of Atonement.

Formstecher, Solomon (1808–1889). German philosopher and rabbi. He was born in Offenbach and served as rabbi there from 1842. He was active in the Reform movement and edited *Der Freitagabend* and *Die Israelitische Wochenschrift.* His *Die Religion des Geistes* presents a basis for the aims of the Emancipation and Reform movements in Judaism.

Forverts. American Yiddish daily newspaper. Founded in New York in 1897, it was the organ of the Jewish labor movement and the Jewish socialists. Its most famous editor was Abraham Cahan.

Foundation Fund *see* KEREN HA-YESOD.

Four Parashiyyot *see* PARASHIYYOT, FOUR.

Four species. Term applied to the four plants used during Sukkot, as stipulated in Leviticus 23.40: "And you shall take on the first day [of Sukkot] the fruit of goodly trees, branches of palm trees, and boughs of thick trees, and willows of the brook." The four species are the etrog, palm, myrtle, and willow, which are held or waved during the festival.

Fox, Brian Douglas (b. 1943). Australian rabbi. He was born in London and went to New Zealand in 1953. He served as a rabbi in Melbourne, Australia, and at Temple Emanuel in Sydney, and founded the King David School (Melbourne) and the Emanuel School (Sydney). He was awarded the Order of Australia (AM).

Fram, David (b. 1903). South African Yiddish poet. He was born in Lithuania and became a member of the Yung Vilne school of poets. In 1927 he settled in South Africa, where he published poems about Jewish life in Lithuania. His later poetry deals with South Africa, but is rooted in the tradition of Lithuanian Jewry. He served as editor of the Johannesburg Yiddish periodical, *Der yidisher ekspres.*

Frances, Immanuel ben David (1618–c. 1710). Italian Hebrew poet. He was born in Livorno. He led an unsettled life, wandering from town to town and suffering many misfortunes, including the death of his family. He later served as a rabbi in Florence. He wrote love poems, satirical epigrams, polemics against the Shabbetaians, and religious poetry.

Frances, Jacob ben David (1615–1667). Italian poet. He was born in Mantua. Some of the poetry attributed to him has also been ascribed to his brother, Immanuel ben David. Both men opposed the Shabbetaians.

Franck, Adolphe (1809–1893). French philosopher and writer. He was born at Liocourt. He taught philosophy at several lycées and lectured at the Sorbonne. He was later appointed to the Collège de France as professor of ancient philosophy and then professor of natural and international law. He served as president of the Alliance Israélite Universelle. His writings include *The Kabbalah, or The Religious Philosophy of the Hebrews.*

Franck, Henri (1888–1912). French poet. He was born in Paris. He wrote philosophical essays, literary criticism, and poetry. His poem *La danse devant l'Arche* seeks to harmonize biblical inspiration with the French Cartesian tradition; in this work he saw himself as a new David dancing before the Ark of the Covenant.

Franco-Mendes, David (1713–1792). Dutch Hebrew writer. He was born in Amsterdam and became a leading Hebrew poet there. He engaged in trade and served as honorary secretary of the Amsterdam Spanish and Portuguese community. Besides poetry, he wrote plays, articles, biographies of famous Sephardi Jews, and responsa.

Frank, Anne (1929–1945). Dutch diarist. Her family fled from Germany to Amsterdam in 1933. When deportations of Jews from Holland began in 1942, she and her family went into hiding. In December 1944 she was deported to Bergen-Belsen, where she died. Her diary about her experiences while hiding from the Nazis was published in 1947.

***Frank, Hans** (1900–1946). German politician. During the last years of the Weimar Republic, he was the Nazis' leading lawyer. In 1939 he became governor general of the occupied Polish territories and was subsequently responsible for the mass deportation of Polish Jewry to the Nazi concentration camps.

Frank, Jacob (1726–1791). Polish communal leader, founder of the Frankist movement. He was born in Podolia. He was regarded as the successor to Shabbetai Tzevi. His mystical festivities were alleged to be accompanied by sexual orgies. He and his followers were excommunicated in 1756. The Frankists later renounced the Talmud, and debates were held between Frankists and rabbis, which concluded with the baptism of members of the Frankist sect. When the Polish authorities discovered that the Frankists revered Frank as their lord, he was tried and secluded in a monastery. He was released by the Russians in 1772 and settled at Offenbach, which became the center of his movement.

Frankau, Julia (1859–1916). English novelist and critic. She used the pseudonym Frank Danby for her fiction. Her novel *Dr. Philips: a Maida Vale Idyll* is a story of London Jewish life. She edited a weekly publication, *Jewish Society*, from 1889 to 1901.

Frankel, David ben Naphtali Hirsch (1707–1762). German rabbi and scholar. He served as a rabbi at Dessau and Berlin, and wrote a commentary on the Palestinian Talmud.

Frankel, William (b. 1917). English journalist. He was born in London. He was editor of the *Jewish Chronicle* from 1958 to 1977.

Frankel, Zacharias (1801–1875). German rabbi and scholar. He was born in Prague. He served as rabbi at Litomerice and Teplice and became chief rabbi of Dresden in 1836. In 1854 he became director of the Breslau Rabbinical Seminary. He founded the positivist–historical school which later influenced Conservative Judaism in the US. At the second Reform rabbinical conference at Frankfurt am Main in 1845 he protested against the gradual abolition of Hebrew in the liturgy and withdrew from the conference. He published studies of halakhic issues, the history of the oral tradition, and the methodology of the Mishnah and the Talmud. He also founded and edited the *Monatsschrift für Geschichte und Wissenschaft des Judentums*.

Frankenthaler, Helen (b. 1928). American painter. She was born in New York. Her work includes ark curtains for the Temple of Aaron Congregation in St Paul, Minnesota.

Frankfurt am Main. City in western Germany. The Jewish community there dates from the 12th century. From the 14th century Jews were engaged in financial transactions, and a ghetto was established in the city in 1458. In the 17th century Jews suffered persecution, and their economic position deteriorated steadily from that time. Recognition of Jewish citizenship was given in 1824, and full equality was granted to the Jews in 1864. Throughout its history the community produced important rabbis and scholars.

Frankfurter, Felix (1882–1965). American jurist. He was born in Vienna and was taken to New York at the age of 12. He served as professor at Harvard Law School (1914–39), and associate justice of the US Supreme Court (1939–62). In 1919 he was the legal adviser to the Zionist delegation at the Paris Peace Conference, and later maintained an interest in the establishment of a Jewish national home in Palestine.

Frankists *see* FRANK, JACOB.

Frankl, Ludwig August, Ritter von Hochwart (1810–1894). Austrian poet. He was born in Bohemia. He was appointed secretary and archivist of the Vienna Jewish community in 1838 and in 1842 he started to edit the literary periodical *Sonntagsblätter*. Half a million copies of his revolutionary poem *Die Universität* were circulated, and it was set to music 28 times. In 1856 he founded the Lamel school in Palestine, which offered a secular as well as a religious education for children. In 1876 he founded the Vienna Jewish Institute for the Blind and was ennobled.

Frankl, Victor E. (b. 1905). Austrian psychiatrist. He was a prisoner at Auschwitz and other concentration camps. His experiences led to the formulation of his existential psychotherapeutic approach (known as logotherapy), which is described in *Man's Search for Meaning*.

Franklin, Arthur Ellis (1857–1938). English banker and art collector. He served as chairman of the Routledge publishing firm, president of the Jewish Religious Education Board, and vice-president of the board of Deputies of British Jews. His collection of Jewish ritual art is in the Jewish Museum in London.

Franklin, Jacob Abraham (1809–1877). English editor and communal leader. He founded and edited the journal *Voice of Jacob* as a forum for anti-Reform opinion. He was active in communal organizations and left most of his fortune to endow educational projects, including the publication of Jewish textbooks.

Franks, Jacob (1688–1769). American merchant. He was born in London and settled in New York in 1708. In 1712 he married Abigail Bilhah Levy, the daughter of one of New York's richest Jews. He was active in the congregational affairs of Shearith Israel in New York. He served as president of the congregation in 1729, and was a founder of the congregation's Mill Street synagogue.

Franzos, Karl Emil (1848–1904). Austrian novelist and journalist. He was born in Czortkow. He worked as a journalist for several newspapers and in 1873 he began publishing in the *Neue Freie Presse* tales about the life of eastern European Jewry. His writings include *Der Pojaz*, *Aus Halb-Asien*, and *Die Juden von Barnow*.

Fraternal [friendly] **societies.** Mutual aid organizations, particularly active in the US. Jewish societies, whose aim was to foster fellowship, relieve distress, and provide life insurance and sickness and death benefits, originated in the 19th century. Initially many were composed of immigrants from the same areas. The oldest and largest is B'nai B'rith.

Fraternity. American collegiate social society for men. The female equivalent is the sorority. Jewish fraternities and sororities were formed when existing college and university societies refused to accept Jewish members.

Fraud. Deliberate deception or cheating in order to gain an advantage. In Jewish law fraud annuls a contract, and the injured party is entitled to damages. The Bible contains numerous laws against the use of false weights and measures. A purchaser must be informed of any blemish in an object before it is sold or the transaction is fraudulent. If a false description is given, the buyer has the right to have the contract annulled and his money refunded.

Freed, Isadore (1900–1960). American composer, organist, pianist, and educator. He was born in Brest-Litovsk, Belorussia, and went to the US as a child. He taught at music schools in Philadelphia and New York, and at the Hartt School of Music in Hartford, Connecticut. He also served as an organist and choir director in several temples. His work includes the book *Harmonizing the Jewish Modes.*

Freedom. Although slavery existed in biblical times, the freedom of the individual and nation was of supreme value to the Jews. Biblical law provides for the release of even the gentile slave in the Jubilee year. During the Passover seder freedom is the central theme. The political and social concept of freedom was spiritualized in later theological writings.

Freehof, Solomon (1892–1990). American Reform rabbi and scholar. He was born in London and was taken to the US in 1903. He served as professor of liturgy at the Hebrew Union College, and was later a rabbi in Chicago and at Congregation Rodeph Shalom in Pittsburgh. In 1955 he was appointed head of the Responsa Committee of the Central Conference of American Rabbis. He published numerous volumes of responsa.

Freeland League. Non-Zionist resettlement organization. It was established in Europe and reorganized in the US in 1935. Its founder was Ben Addir and its aim was to create a Jewish settlement in an unoccupied area for Jews who could not or would not go to Israel. The league published English, Yiddish, and Spanish periodicals.

Freemasonry. Widespread secret order, founded in London in 1717 to promote brotherliness and mutual aid. Some of the words and phrases used in its rituals are derived from Hebrew terms, and Solomon's Temple plays a role in its symbolism. In the 18th century Jews became members in Holland, England, France, Germany, and the US. Freemasonry was established in Palestine before World War I.

Free Sons of Israel. American Jewish fraternal society. It was founded in New York by German Jews in 1849. Its early lodges adopted biblical names.

Free will. The human ability to make choices that are not predetermined. The Bible stresses the ability of each individual to choose between good and evil. The concept of punishment and reward is based on this principle. According to the Talmud, God is omniscient but human beings have the power to choose their own way of living. Although rabbinic sources do not discuss the apparent contradiction between free will and divine omniscience, it was examined by medieval Jewish philosophers.

Free-will offering. An offering made spontaneously rather than as the result of an obligation or a vow. Jews often made such gifts to the Temple. According to Leviticus, a free-will offering might be a burnt offering or a peace offering (Leviticus 22.18, 21).

Freidus, Abraham Solomon (1867–1923). American librarian and bibliographer. He was born in Riga, Latvia, and lived in Paris, Palestine, and London, before settling in New York in 1889. In 1897 he was appointed first chief of the Jewish Division of the New York Public Library. He developed a classification scheme used for Judaica.

Freier, Recha (1892–1984). German youth leader. She was born in Norderney. In 1932 in Berlin she founded the Youth Aliyah movement to aid Jewish young people to prepare for agricultural life. After 1933 she organized agricultural training outside Germany and directed pupils to Palestine, where she settled in 1941.

Freiheit [Morning Freiheit]. American Yiddish daily newspaper published in New York. It was founded in 1922 as the organ of Jewish communists in the US.

Freimann, Aron (1871–?). German scholar, son of Israel Meir Freimann. He was born in Filehne, in the province of Posen. He worked at the municipal library in Frankfurt am Main, where he assembled a large collection of Judaica and Hebraica. After the Nazis came to power, he emigrated to the US. Between 1939 and 1945 he served as consultant to the New York Public Library. He was the author and editor of books and articles about Jewish history, culture, and bibliography.

Freimann, Avraham Ḥayyim (1889–1948). Jurist and rabbinic scholar of Moravian origin. He served as a magistrate at Königsberg and county judge at Braunsberg. In 1944 he began lecturing on Jewish law at the Hebrew University in Jerusalem. In 1947 he was appointed head of an advisory committee for Jewish law on personal status in the proposed Jewish state. He published studies of medieval rabbinics and Jewish law in modern Israel, and also wrote a work which deals with changes in Jewish marriage laws after the talmudic period.

Freimann, Israel Meir (1830–1884). Polish rabbi. He served communities in the province of Posen and published a critical edition of the *Ve-Hizhir* midrashic work.

Freimann, Jacob (1866–1937). German rabbi, scholar, and editor. He was born in Kraków. He served as a rabbi at Kanitz in Moravia and Holleschau (1890–1913). In 1913 he became chief rabbi of Posen. In 1928 he joined the rabbinate of the Berlin Jewish community and he later lectured on rabbinics and Jewish history at the Berlin Rabbinical Seminary. He published studies in medieval rabbinic literature.

Frenk, Azriel Nathan (1863–1924). Polish journalist and historian. He was born in Wodzisław. He began to write for the Jewish press in Warsaw in 1884, publishing articles about current events, stories about Ḥasidic life, and studies of Jewry in Poland.

Fress (Yiddish). To eat gluttonously.

Freud, Sigmund (1856–1939). Austrian psychologist, founder of psychoanalysis. He was born in Freiberg. He worked as a neuropathologist and clinical neurologist in Vienna and as a result of his work and research formulated a new approach to understanding the human mind. In addition to numerous psychoanalytical studies, he published *Moses and Monotheism*. He was a member of the Jewish community in Vienna and was a loyal member of the local B'nai B'rith.

Friedberg, Abraham Shalom [Har-Shalom] (1838–1902). Polish Hebrew writer, editor, and translator. He was born in Grodno, Belorussia, and after wandering from town to town in southern Russia returned to his native city in 1858. After the pogroms of 1881 he joined the Ḥibbat Zion movement. In 1886 he went to Warsaw, where he was an editor of the first Hebrew encyclopedia, *Ha-Eshkol*. His *Memoirs of the House of David* is a series of stories embracing Jewish history from the destruction of the Temple to the beginning of the Haskalah period in Germany.

Friedberg, Bernhard (1876–1961). Israeli scholar and bibliographer. He was born in Kraków and moved to Frankfurt am Main in 1900. In 1904 he set up his own publishing firm. He later entered the diamond trade and moved to Antwerp. In 1946 he settled in Tel Aviv. He published Jewish biographies, family histories, and a series of works on the history of Hebrew printing. His *Beit Eked Sepharim* is a bibliographical lexicon.

Friedenwald, Aaron (1836–1902). American ophthalmologist. He was born in Baltimore. He was a professor at the College of Physicians and Surgeons in Baltimore. He was active in the Baltimore Hebrew Orphan Asylum, the Jewish Theological Seminary of America, the Federation of American Zionists, and the American Jewish Historical Society.

Friedenwald, Harry (1864–1950). American ophthalmologist, son of Aaron Friedenwald. He was born in Baltimore and taught at the Baltimore College of Physicians and Surgeons. He was president of the Federation of American Zionists from 1904 to 1918. In 1911 and 1914 he went to Palestine, where he was a consultant for eye diseases in several hospitals. His writings include the *The Jews and Medicine* and *Jewish Luminaries in Medical History*.

Friedlaender, Israel (1876–1920). American scholar and communal leader. He was born in Kovel, Poland, and grew up in Warsaw. He became lecturer in Semitics at the University of Strasbourg, then in 1904 was appointed professor of Bible at the Jewish Theological Seminary of America. He also taught at Dropsie College in Philadelphia and was active in Jewish communal life. He published studies of Islamic sects, Judeo-Arabic literature, and Jewish influences on Arabic folklore, and translated Simon Dubnow's *History of the Jews in Russia and Poland*.

Friedland, Abraham Hyman (1891–1939). American writer and educator. He was born in Hordok, near Vilnius, and emigrated to the US in 1906. In 1911 he founded the National Hebrew School in New York. He later served as superintendent of the Cleveland Hebrew Schools, and in 1924 became director of the Cleveland Bureau of Jewish Education. He wrote poems, short stories, and articles, and edited educational texts.

Friedlander, Albert (b. 1927). British rabbi. He was born in Berlin. He has served as senior lecturer and dean of the Leo Baeck College in London and rabbi of Westminster Synagogue. His writings include *Out of the Whirlwind*, and *Leo Baeck*.

Friedländer, David (1750–1834). German communal leader and author. He was born in Königsberg and settled in Berlin in 1770, where he established a silk factory. He was a founder and director of the Jewish Free School in Berlin and led the fight for equal rights for Prussian Jewry. After the death of Moses Mendelssohn, he was the leader of the German Jewish Enlightenment movement. He championed extreme religious reform.

Friedländer, Michael (1833–1910). British educator and writer. He was born in Jutrosin in the province of Posen. He served as the head of the Talmud Torah school in Berlin from 1862, and was principal of Jews College in London from 1865 to 1910. He took an active part in the communal and cultural life of Anglo-Jewry. His writings include *Jewish Religion, Textbook of the Jewish Religion,* and *Jewish Family Bible.*

Friedlander, Moritz (1844–1919). Hungarian educator and writer. He became secretary of the Israelitische Allianz and worked in Galicia assisting the emigration of Russian Jews to the US. With the help of Baron Maurice de Hirsch and his wife, he established and supervised more than 50 schools for boys and girls in Galicia. He wrote studies of the relationship of Hellenism and Christianity to Judaism.

Friedländer, Saul (b. 1932). Israeli historian. He was born in Prague, lived in France from 1939 to 1948, and then emigrated to Israel. He later taught at the Institut des Hautes Études Internationales in Geneva, and he was appointed professor of history and international relations at the Hebrew University in 1969. His writings include *Hitler et les États-Unis, 1939–41, Prelude to Downfall: Hitler and the United States,* and *Pius XII and the Third Reich.*

Friedman, Bruce Jay (b. 1930). American novelist. He was born in the Bronx and in his novels satirized middle-class American Jewish life. His works include *Stern, A Mother's Kisses,* and *The Dick.*

Friedman, Elisha Michael (1889–1951). American economist. He acted as economic consultant to several US governmental agencies. He was an active Zionist and a supporter of the Hebrew University. His *Survival or Extinction* is a discussion of the Jewish problem.

Friedman, Lee Max (1871–1957). American lawyer and historian. He was born in Memphis, Tennessee. He was professor of law at Portia Law School in Boston and vice-president of the school. He served as president and later honorary president of the American Jewish Historical Society. He published studies on various aspects of Jewish history.

Friedmann, David Aryeh (1889–1957). Israeli critic and editor. After studying medicine at Moscow University, he emigrated to Palestine in 1925, where he practiced ophthalmology. He published studies on Hebrew and world literature, art criticism, and the history of Jewish medicine.

Friedmann, David ben Samuel [David of Karlin] (1828–1917). Lithuanian rabbi and halakhic authority. He was born in Biała, and served as rabbi of Karlino near Pinsk from 1868. His *Piskei Halakhot* is an exposition and summary of matrimonial law. In his *Emek Berakhah* he discussed the conditions under which a religious ban should be imposed. Although he initially was active in the Ḥibbat Zion movement, he later became an opponent of Zionism.

Friedmann, Meir *see* ISH-SHALOM, MEIR.

Friedmann-Yellin, Nathan *see* MOR, NATHAN.

Friendly societies *see* FRATERNAL SOCIETIES.

Frigeis, Lazaro de (fl. 16th cent.). Italian physician. He was a friend of the anatomist Andrea Vesalius in Padua and supplied the Hebrew names for some of the anatomical structures described in Vesalius' work, *De humani corporis fabrica.* These terms were taken from the Hebrew translation of the *Canon* of Avicenna and from the Talmud.

Fringes *see* TZITZIT.

Frischmann, David (1859–1922). Polish Hebrew and Yiddish writer. He was born in Zgierz, near Lódź. His first works were written in the spirit of the Haskalah; later writings include satires, stories, critical essays, and poems. He also published translations of European literature and worked in journalism. He served as editor of several periodicals and anthologies and contributed to the Hebrew press.

Fromm (Yiddish). Strict in religious observance.

Fromm, Erich (1900–1980). American psychoanalyst and social philosopher. He was born in Frankfurt am Main and worked at the Institute for Social Research there from 1929 to 1932. After the Nazis came to power, he emigrated to the US and taught at Bennington College, the National University of Mexico, Michigan State University, and New York University. Much of his writing was influenced by Jewish sources. His publications include *The Art of Loving* and *You shall be as Gods*.

Frug, Simon Samuel (1860–1916). Ukrainian Yiddish poet. He was born in Kherson province. He published three volumes of Russian poetry and was the first poet to treat Jewish themes in Russian verse. Later he published Yiddish songs and ballads. In his Zionist lyrics he pleaded for a return of the Jews to productive labor in their ancestral homeland.

Frumkin, Aryeh Leib (1845–1916). Palestinian rabbinic scholar and writer, of Lithuanian origin. He visited Palestine in 1867 and 1871 and began research for a history of the rabbis and scholars of Jerusalem. He returned to Europe and served as a rabbi at Ilukste in Latvia. Later he became a farmer–scholar in Ptaḥ Tikvah, Palestine, where he established a yeshivah. In 1894 he settled in London, but he eventually emigrated to Palestine. His *Seder Rav Amran* is a siddur with notes and a commentary.

Frumkin, Israel Dov (1850–1914). Palestinian journalist. He was born in Belorussia and was taken to Jerusalem when he was nine. He edited the Jerusalem periodical *Ḥavatzelet* from 1870 to 1910. From the mid-1880s his journalistic writings attacked the Ḥibbat Zion movement.

Fuchs, Daniel (b. 1909). American novelist, short story writer, and screenwriter. He was born in New York. He taught elementary school in Brooklyn and wrote several novels during summer vacations. His *Summer in Williamsburg* depicts the lives and fantasies of several poor Jewish families.

Fuchs, Ernst (b. 1930). Austrian painter. He was born in Vienna and became a member of the Viennese school of Fantastic Realism. Some of his paintings include allusions to the kabbalah, Hebrew script, and biblical themes.

Fuchs, Eugen (1856–1923). German jurist. He was an executive member of the German Barristers' Association and wrote legal studies. He led the anti-Zionist Central-Verein Deutscher Staatsbürger Jüdischen Glaubens.

Fulvia (fl. 1st cent.). Roman proselyte. She sent presents of purple and gold to the Temple which were never delivered. When her husband reported the matter to the emperor, Tiberius expelled all the Jews from Rome in the year 19. Thousands of young Jews were drafted into military service and sent to fight the brigands in Sardinia.

Funeral *see* BURIAL.

Funeral eulogy *see* EULOGY, FUNERAL.

Fünn, Samuel Joseph (1818–90). Lithuanian Hebrew writer. He was born in Vilnius and was a founder of the first Jewish school in the city. He taught the Bible and Hebrew there, and later taught at the local rabbinical school. In 1856 he was appointed inspector of the government Jewish schools in the Vilnius district. In 1863 he opened a printing press in Vilnius, which enabled him to publish *Ha-Karmel*, a journal which he edited and to which he contributed studies of Russian Jewry. He wrote a biographical lexicon of notable Jews and a Hebrew dictionary.

Fürst, Julius (1805–1873). Polish Hebraist, bibliographer, and historian. He settled in Leipzig, where he taught at the university. His publications include a bibliography of Jewish books and books on Judaism, a history of Karaism, a Bible concordance, a Hebrew and Aramaic lexicon, and a history of Jewish literature.

Fürstenthal, Raphael Jacob (1781–1855). German author and translator. He wrote poetry and translated Maimonides' *Guide for the Perplexed,* Baḥya ibn Pakuda's *Hovot ha-Levavot,* and Isaac Aboab I's *Menorat ha-Maor* from Hebrew into German. He also translated Jewish liturgical works.

Furtado, Abraham (1756–1817). French politican and communal leader. Of Portuguese descent, he lived in Bordeaux. He was elected president of the Assembly of Jewish Notables convened by Napoleon, and acted as secretary of the Paris Sanhedrin. He published *Mémoire d'Abraham Furtado sur l'état des Juifs en France jusqu'à la Révolution.*

G

Gabbai ("collector"). Communal official. In biblical times the title was used for one who collected dues and charitable contributions, but from the Middle Ages it applied to any communal official.

***Gabinius, Aulus** (fl. 1st cent. BCE). Roman governor of Syria (57–55 BCE). He put into effect Pompey's decision to diminish the territory of Judea, dividing the country into five districts and rehabilitating the Greek cities which the Hasmoneans had destroyed. He also prevented Aristobulus II and his son Alexander from seizing power in Judea.

Gabirol, Ibn *see* IBN GABIROL, SOLOMON.

Gabriel. Archangel. With Michael, he is the only angel mentioned by name in the Bible (Daniel 8–10). In rabbinic literature he is referred to as a leader of the angelic host and one of the highest angels in the celestial hierarchy.

Gad (i). Israelite, son of Jacob and Zilpah (Genesis 30.10–11). His tribal territory lay to the east of the Jordan. The tribe of Gad flourished during the rule of Saul and David.

Gad (ii). Israelite prophet. He was one of the three prophets during the days of King David. He joined David when he fled from Saul to Adullam, and persuaded him to return to Judah (I Samuel 22.5). He remained at the court of David in Jerusalem (II Samuel 24.11–14; I Chronicles 21.9–30), and was one of the organizers of the Levitical service in the Temple (II Chronicles 29.25).

Gad (iii). Ancient Semitic god of fortune. He was worshipped by the Jews in Babylonia (Isaiah 65.11).

Gad (iv). Name given to the tribal territory of Gad, the son of Jacob and Zilpah. It lay to the east of the Jordan. After the split in the kingdom, Gad belonged to the northern kingdom and was subject to Syrian attacks. In 732 BCE the region was devastated by Tiglath-Pileser III and most of its inhabitants were exiled (II Kings 15.29).

Gadi *see* JOHANAN.

Gadna. Israeli youth movement. It was established by the Haganah in 1939 and was taken over by the Israeli government in 1949. It trains its members in the knowledge of Israel's geography and topography, physical fitness, marksmanship, scouting, field exercises, and teamwork.

Gaḥal. Israeli political party. It was established in 1965 by an alignment of the Liberal and Ḥerut parties.

Galante, Abraham (1873–1961). Turkish scholar. He was born in Bodrum. He was first a teacher and inspector in the Jewish and Turkish schools of Rhodes and Smyrna. Later he lived in Egypt, where he edited the Ladino newspaper *La vara.* He encouraged the acculturation of Turkish Jewry to its homeland, and fought for Jewish rights. Eventually he returned to Istanbul where he became a professor at the university. He wrote studies of Jewish history in Turkey.

Galante, Abraham ben Mordecai (fl.

16th cent.). Palestinian kabbalist. He was born in Rome and settled in Safed. He wrote a commentary on the Zohar.

Galante, Moses ben Jonathan (1620–1689). Palestinian rabbi. He studied in Safed and later moved to Jerusalem, where he was a leading rabbi and head of a yeshivah. Influenced by the Sabbetaians, he and other rabbis went to Gaza to seek purification of the soul from Nathan of Gaza. He accompanied Shabbetai Tzevi to Smyrna and Constantinople. He wrote responsa and commentaries on the Torah.

Galante, Moses ben Mordecai (fl. 16th cent.). Palestinian talmudist and kabbalist. He was born in Rome. He became a disciple of Joseph Caro and his teacher in the field of kabbalah was Moses ben Jacob Cordovero. From 1580 he served as av bet din in Safed. He wrote responsa, an index of biblical passages interpreted in the Zohar, and a homiletic and kabbalistic commentary on Ecclesiastes.

***Galich, Alexander** (1919–1977). Ukrainian poet, songwriter, and dramatist. He was born in Yekaterinoslav. In the 1960s he was baptized into the Russian Orthodox Church, and was later expelled from the Writers' Union. In 1974 he left the USSR and settled in Munich then Paris. His works include comic ballads, and songs and poems on the Holocaust and the Stalinist camps.

Galilee. The northernmost region of Israel. It was separated from Israel by Tiglath-Pileser III of Assyria in 732 BCE. In 104 BCE it was reunited to Judea by Aristobulus I. Later it became the main center of Judaism in Palestine. It was the seat of the patriarchate and talmudic academies were founded in its cities of Tiberias and Sepphoris. From the 16th–17th centuries Safed in Galilee was an important rabbinic and kabbalistic center.

Galilee, Sea of. Lake on the River Jordan, referred to variously in the New Testament as the Sea or Lake of Gennesaret, Kinneret, or Tiberias. It was an important center of the fishing and salting industries during the second Temple period.

Galili, Israel (1910–1986). Israeli Labor and Haganah leader. He was born in the Ukraine and was taken to Palestine at the age of four. In 1924 he was among the founders of the youth wing of the Histadrut. He joined the central command of the Haganah in 1941 and from 1945 to 1947 he was one of the principal organizers of underground armed activities in Palestine; in 1947 he was appointed head of Haganah's territorial command. He served as deputy minister of defense in the provisional government in 1948. From 1966 to 1970 he was minister without portfolio in the Israeli government, responsible for the information services.

Galitzianer. A Jew from Galicia.

Gallico, Abraham Jagel ben Hananiah [Jagel, Abraham] (fl. 16th cent.). Italian writer on ethics. He served as mint-master to the Prince of Correggio. His *Valley of Vision* is an imitation of Dante's *Divine Comedy*. He also wrote *Lekaḥ Tov*, the first Jewish catechism.

Galut ("exile"). The word is used to refer to the condition of the Jewish people in the diaspora and has connotations of alienation, degradation, and persecution.

Galveston Plan. Project initiated in the US by Jacob Henry Schiff in 1907, and funded by him. Its purpose was to divert European Jews immigrating to the US from the eastern to the southwestern states. It was named for Galveston in Texas, where the project was first established. Between 1907 and the outbreak of World War I the project had arranged the settlement of 10,000 immigrants.

Gamaliel the Elder (fl. 1st cent.). Palestinian elder, grandson of Hillel. He was president of the Sanhedrin and, according to Acts, Paul was one of his pupils. He maintained close contact with Jews in Palestine and the diaspora. He was responsible for many takkanot.

Gamaliel II (fl. 1st–2nd cent.). Palestinian elder. He was president of the Sanhedrin at Jabneh and strengthened the new center there. He consolidated Jewish law and sought to unite the Jewish people around the Torah. He provoked a revolt against his authority and Eleazar ben Azariah was appointed nasi in his place. Later he was reinstated.

Gamaliel III (fl. 3rd cent.). Palestinian elder, son of Judah ha-Nasi. He was appointed nasi in the first half of the 3rd century.

Gambling. Judaism is traditionally opposed to gambling. Although the tendency of rabbinic law is to forbid all forms of gambling, a distinction is made between those who indulge in it as a pastime and those who are professional gamblers. Professional gamblers are viewed as untrustworthy and may not act as witnesses.

Gamoran, Emanuel (1895–1962). American educator. He was born in Russia and was taken to the US in 1907. In 1923 he became the education director of the Commission of Jewish Education of the Union of American Hebrew Congregations. He also served as president of the National Council for Jewish Education (1927–8). His writings include *Changing Conceptions in Jewish Education.*

Gam zo le-tovah ("This is also for the good"). Expression of resignation to divine providence. It was frequently uttered by Nahum of Gimzo.

Gan Eden *see* HEAVEN.

Ganef [gonif] (Yiddish). Word used variously to mean thief, clever person, dishonest businessman, shady character, prankster.

Gans, David ben Solomon (1541–1613). Bohemian chronicler, astronomer, and mathematician. He was born in Lippstadt, Westphalia. He studied with Moses Isserles in Kraków and later settled in Prague, where he was in contact with Johann Kepler and Tycho Brahe. He wrote works on astronomical and mathematical problems, Jewish and general history, the calendar, and the geography of Israel.

***Gans, Eduard** (1798–1839). German jurist and historian. Together with Leopold Zunz and Moses Mosher, he founded in 1819 the Society for Jewish Culture and Learning, of which he became president. In 1820 he was appointed a lecturer at the University of Berlin. He converted to Christianity in 1825 and became a professor at the university. He wrote studies of law, edited Hegel's lectures on the philosophy of history, and founded the journal *Jahrbücher für Wissenschaftliche Kritik.*

Ganzfried, Solomon (1804–1886). Hungarian rabbi and author. He was born in Ungvar. He served as rabbi of Brezewicz and later head of the bet din of Ungvar. His *Kitzur Shulḥan Arukh* is an abridgement of the Shulḥan Arukh.

Gaon. Religious leader of the Babylonian Jewish community in the post-Talmudic period (6th–11th centuries). The geonim were the heads of the leading academies at Sura and Pumbedita. The title "gaon" (literally "eminence," "pride") derives from their position as "rosh yeshivat gaon Yaakov" (head of the academy which is the pride of Jacob). In the 12th–13th centuries the title was also used by the heads of academies in Baghdad, Damascus, and Egypt. It eventually became an honorific title for any rabbi who had a great knowledge of Torah.

Garden of Eden *see* EDEN, GARDEN OF.

Gardner, Herb (b. 1934). American playwright. He was born in Brooklyn. His plays deal with Jewish characters and include *The Goodbye People, I'm Not Rap-*

paport, and *Who is Harry Kellerman and Why is he Saying those Terrible Things about me?*

Gardosh, Kariel [Dosh] (b. 1921). Israeli cartoonist. He was born in Budapest. He emigrated to Israel in 1948, and joined the staff of the paper *Maariv* as editorial cartoonist. Signing himself "Dosh," he created the figure of Little Israel, a young boy who became the popular symbol of the State and its people. He also illustrated books and wrote short stories and plays. He has exhibited in Israel and other countries.

***Garstang, John** (1876–1956). British archeologist. He was professor of archeology at the University of Liverpool (1907–41) and director of the British School of Archaeology in Jerusalem (1919–26). His work in the Middle East began in 1900–08, when he conducted excavations in Egypt, Nubia, Asia Minor, and northern Syria; in 1930–36 he worked at Jericho. He published studies of Hittite history and the historical topography of Palestine and the Bible, and excavation reports.

Gartel (Yiddish: "girdle"). Girdle made of black silk or wool. It is worn by Ḥasidim at prayer, in fulfillment of the injunction to make a division between the upper and lower halves of the body when praying. It is also symbolic of the injunction to gird one's loins in the service of God.

Gary, Romain (1914–1980). French novelist. He was born in Vilnius, moved to Poland when he was seven, and in 1926 settled in Nice. He served in the French diplomatic service and was consul-general in Los Angeles from 1956 to 1960. His *A European Education* includes elements of Jewish interest. In *The Dance of Genghis Cohn*, he tells the story of a Jewish comedian shot by the Nazis who haunts his executioner. Jewish characters frequently appear in his novels.

Gaster, Moses (1856–1939). British rabbi and scholar. He was born in Bucharest and taught Romanian language and literature in the university there from 1881 to 1885. Later he settled in England, where he taught Slavonic literature at Oxford University. In 1887 he was appointed Haham of the English Sephardi community. From 1891 to 1896 he was principal of Judith Montefiore College in Ramsgate. He was active in Ḥibbat Zion and later in the Zionist movement. He published studies of Romanian literature, comparative and Jewish folklore, Samaritan history and literature, rabbinic scholarship, liturgy, Anglo-Jewish history, and biblical studies.

Gaster, Theodor Herzl (b. 1906). American educator and scholar, son of Moses Gaster. He was born in London. He taught comparative religion at Dropsie College in Philadelphia and at other universities in the US. His writings include: *Passover: its History and Traditions*, *Purim and Hanukkah in Custom and Tradition*, *Thespis: Ritual, Myth, and Drama in the Ancient Near East*, *Festivals of the Jewish Year*, *Holy and Profane*, and *New Year: its History, Customs, and Superstitions*.

Gath. Philistine city in the southern coastal plain of Palestine, one of the Philistines' five principal cities. It was the home of Goliath (I Samuel 17.52). It was captured by David (I Chronicles 18.13) and conquered by the Assyrian king Sargon in the 8th century BCE.

Gaza. Ancient city on the southern coastal plain of Palestine. It was captured by the Philistines in the 12th century BCE and became the most important of their five coastal cities (I Samuel 6.17) Although allotted to the tribe of Judah (Joshua 15.47), it remained in Philistine hands. It was the place of the imprisonment and death of Samson (Judges 16). In 720 BCE it was annexed by Tiglath-Pileser III of Assyria. Alexander the Great recolonized it as a Hellenistic city. In 198 it was annexed by Antiochus III of Syria, but it was later recaptured by Alexander Yannai.

Gaza Strip. Area of land (including the modern city of Gaza) extending from the eastern border of Egypt northward along the Palestinian coast for 22 miles. Since the War of Independence sovereignty over the territory has been in dispute and the area has been the scene of frequent fighting.

Geber, Hana (b. 1910). American sculptor. She was born in Prague and eventually settled in New York. Her sculptures deal with Jewish themes. She has also produced mezuzot, spice holders, kiddush cups, and Ḥannukah lamps.

Gebirtig, Mordecai (1877–1942). Polish Yiddish poet. He was born in Kraków and worked as a carpenter. Regarded as a Yiddish bard, he composed the words and melodies for his songs, which were collected in 1936 in a volume edited by Menachem Kipnis. His most famous song, *Our Town is Burning*, was written in 1938 under the impact of the pogrom in Przytyk.

Gedaliah (fl. 6th cent. BCE). Babylonian governor of Judah. He was appointed after the destruction of the first Temple in 586 BCE, and resided at Mizpah. He was murdered by Ishmael ben Nethaniah, who hoped to overthrow Babylonian rule; Gedaliah's supporters fled to Egypt, taking Jeremiah with them (II Kings 25.25–6; Jeremiah 41.1ff).

Gedaliah, Fast of. Fast kept on 3 Tishri (after Rosh ha-Shanah) to commemorate the assassination of Gedaliah.

Gedud ha-Avodah [Labor Battalion]. Commune of Jewish workers in Palestine. It was founded near Tiberias in 1920 by 80 members of the Third Aliyah, who were disciples of Joseph Trumpeldor; it undertook pioneering work building roads throughout the country. In 1928 it split and its surviving members joined Ha-Kibbutz ha-Meuḥad in 1929.

Gefilte fish (Yiddish). Fish cakes or fish loaf made of various types of fish.

Gehazi (fl. 9th cent. BCE). Israelite, servant of Elisha. In the story of the wealthy Shunammite woman (II Kings 4.8–37), he acted as Elisha's faithful messenger and loyal protector. However, he is depicted as greedy and cunning in the story of Naaman; after trying to deceive Elisha he was cursed with the leprosy of which Naaman was cured (II Kings 5). In the story of the woman from Shunem and the King of Israel (II Kings 8.1–6) he told the king about the great deeds which Elisha had performed.

Gehinnom [Valley of Hinnom]. Valley to the south-west of Jerusalem. During the period of the monarchy it was the site of a cult that involved the burning of children (II Kings 23.10; Jeremiah 7.31; 32.35). In rabbinic Judaism the name is used to refer to the place of torment for the wicked after death.

Geiger, Abraham (1810–1874). German Reform leader and scholar. In 1832 he became rabbi in Wiesbaden, where he reformed the synagogue services and published the *Wissenschaftliche Zeitschrift für jüdische Theologie*. In 1837 he convened the first meeting of Reform rabbis. He later became rabbi in Breslau, where he established a school for religious studies and led a group that worked on Hebrew philology. He participated in subsequent Reform synods and from 1863 served as rabbi in Frankfurt am Main. In 1870 he became rabbi of the Berlin congregation, and he helped to establish the Hochschule für Wissenschaft des Judentums in the city. His works include studies of the Bible, the Sadducees and Pharisees, Jewish history, mishnaic Hebrew, and Maimonides.

Geiger, Lazarus (1829–1870). German philosopher and philologist, nephew of Abraham Geiger. He was born in Frankfurt am Main and later taught at the

Jewish educational institute Philanthropin there. His writings include *Ursprung und Entwicklung der menschlichen Sprache und Vernunft* and *Der Ursprung der Sprache.*

Geiger, Ludwig (1848–1919). German literary historian, son of Abraham Geiger. He studied at his father's Hochschule in Berlin, and in 1880 was appointed professor of German literature and cultural history at Berlin University. He made contributions to Renaissance and Reformation studies, German-Jewish history, and research on Goethe. From 1909 he edited the Jewish newspaper *Allgemeine Zeitung des Judentums.*

Gelber, Natan Mikhael (1891–1966). Austrian historian and Zionist leader. He was born in Lemberg. He was general secretary of the eastern Galician delegation of the Vaad Leumi in Vienna (1918–21), and later became secretary of the Austrian Zionist Organization. In 1934 he emigrated to Palestine where he worked in the head office of Keren ha-Yesod in Jerusalem. He published books and articles on Jewish history and contemporary Jewish life.

Gelilah. The rolling up of the Torah scroll after its reading in the synagogue.

Gélleri, Andor Endre (1907–1945). Hungarian novelist. He was born in Budapest and worked as a dyer and locksmith. His writings include *The Laundry, Thirsty Apprentices, Hold Street, The Harbor,* and *Lightning and Evening Fire.* Jewish figures appear in many of his works.

Gelman, Aryeh Leon (b. 1887). American journalist and Zionist leader. He was born in Russia and went to the US at the age of 23. He was the principal of various Hebrew schools in St. Louis, and later served as editor and publisher of the Yiddish *St. Louis Jewish Record.* He was president of the American Mizraḥi movement from 1935 to 1939 and subsequently was editor of various Mizraḥi publications in New York.

Gelt (Yiddish). Money.

Gemara. Commentary on the MISHNAH; together, the Mishnah and Gemara make up the TALMUD. Traditionally the Mishnah is printed in the center of the page with the Gemara surrounding it.

Gemar ḥatimah tovah ("A final good sealing"). Traditional greeting during the period between Rosh ha-Shanah and the Day of Atonement; it is sometimes used until Hosha-na Rabbah. It alludes to the belief that on the New Year a person's fate is inscribed in the Book of Life and on the Day of Atonement the decree is sealed.

Gematria (? from Greek "geometria": geometry). Method of biblical exegesis based on the numerical value of Hebrew words. It appeared among tannaim in the 2nd century. Later it was used in midrashic sources, and in kabbalistic writings from the 12th century onward.

Gemilut ḥasadim ("doing kindness"). Charity in the broadest sense. It encompasses the various duties of sympathetic consideration toward others.

Genealogy. The study of the relationships and descent of an individual, family, or group. Genealogical material is found in the Pentateuch and the Book of Chronicles, which demonstrates the descent of the Jewish people from the patriarchs. The priests claimed descent from Aaron. Although genealogies were maintained during the period of the second Temple, the practice declined in talmudic times. Nonetheless the patriarchs in Palestine and the exilarchs in Babylonia were believed to have descended from David. In the medieval period and later descent from distinguished scholars was valued in the Jewish community.

General Archive of German Jews. Central repository for the archives of

German Jewish communities, established in 1906 in Berlin.

General Zionists. Zionist party. When the first parties were established in the Zionist movement in the late 19th century, those Zionists who did not join any faction were known as General Zionists. In 1929 Isaac Ignacy Schwarzbart established the World Union of General Zionists. This body eventually split into various groups. In Israel too General Zionists divided into separate factions.

Genesis (Hebrew "Bereshit"). First book of the Bible. It describes the creation of the world and the beginning of humankind (1.1–6.8); gives an account of the ten generations to Abraham including the episode of the Flood (6.9–11.32); and tells the stories of Abraham (12–20), Abraham and Isaac (21.1–25.18), Esau and Jacob (25.19–36.43), Jacob and his sons (37.1–47.27), and Jacob and Joseph (47.28–50.26).

Genesis Rabbah (Hebrew "Bereshit Rabbah"). Midrash on the Book of Genesis. It is the first work in the Midrash Rabbah, comprising 101 sections. Each is headed by a quotation from Genesis, followed by interpretative aggadot. It was produced by Palestinian amoraim.

Genesis Zutarta *see* JUBILEES, BOOK OF.

Genevah *see* THEFT.

Genizah (*lit.* "hiding"). Repository, usually associated with a synagogue, for books or ritual objects which have become unusable. Ritual objects and books containing the name of God cannot be destroyed and were therefore buried when they wore out. The genizah might be a cave or plot of land, or part of a house. The practice fell into disuse after the Middle Ages.

Gennesaret, Sea of *see* GALILEE, SEA OF.

Genocide. The deliberate killing of a nationality, race, or ethnic group. The word was first used by Raphael Lemkin in a report to the Fifth International Conference for the Unification of Penal Law held in 1933 in Madrid. In the UN convention on the Prevention and Punishment of the Crime of Genocide, it signifies a coordinated set of acts intended to destroy a national, ethnic, racial, or religious group. It is frequently applied to the Holocaust.

Gentile [heathen]. Any person (especially a Christian) who is not a Jew. According to Jewish law, a person whose mother is not Jewish is considered a non-Jew, regardless of whether the father is Jewish. (American Reform Judaism however has decreed that if a person is born of either a Jewish mother or father, that individual is Jewish.) The seven Noachian laws are binding on a gentile. A righteous gentile is entitled to enter into the after-life.

Gentili, Gershom ben Moses (1683–1700). Italian rabbinic scholar, son of Moses ben Gershom Gentili. He was the author of *Yad Ḥaruzim*, a Hebrew rhyme lexicon; it contains an introduction, 12 rules for Hebrew usage in poetry, and an appendix containing a poetical formulation of the 613 commandments.

Gentili, Moses ben Gershom (1663–1711). Italian scholar. He was born in Trieste. He served as rabbi in Venice and was the author of *Melekhet Maḥashevet*, a philosophical commentary on the Torah. His *Ḥanukkat ha-Bayit* deals with the construction of the second Temple.

Geography. The study of the natural features of the earth's surface and man's response to them. The first systematic geographic work in Hebrew was written by Abraham bar Ḥiyya in the 12th century. Travel books also appeared at this time. In the Middle Ages Jewish cartographers of Majorca produced maps for explorers. The first modern Hebrew geographical textbooks were published in the 18th century.

George, Manfred (1893–1965). American journalist and editor. He was born in

Berlin. He worked as a newspaper editor and writer in Germany until the Nazis came to power; he then moved to Prague and later emigrated to the US. In New York he took over the newsletter (*Aufbau*) of the German-Jewish New World Club.

Ger *see* PROSELYTE.

Gerchunoff, Alberto (1884–1950). Argentine journalist and writer. He was born in Russia and was taken to Argentina as a child. In 1908 he joined the staff of the daily *La nación* with which he was associated for over 40 years. His *The Jewish Gauchos of the Pampas* contains a collection of articles describing the life of Jewish colonists in Entre Ríos at the beginning of the 20th century. Following the rise of Hitler, he became an ardent Zionist.

Gerim ("Proselytes"). Minor tractate appended to the Talmud. It contains halakhic statements concerning conversion and the acceptance of proselytes.

Gerizim, Mount. Mountain in the Hills of Ephraim, 30 miles north of Jerusalem. When the Israelites entered Canaan, a ceremony was held there; the assembled gathering blessed all who observed the law, while those opposite on Mount Ebal cursed those who violated it (Deuteronomy 11.29–30; 27.11–13; Joshua 8.30–35). Mount Gerizim was venerated by the Samaritans and Sanballat built a temple there, which constituted their religious and political center. Later Antiochus Epiphanes converted the temple to the worship of Zeus. It was destroyed by John Hyrcanus in 129 BCE.

Gerona. City in Catalonia, north-east Spain. An important Jewish community existed there from the 11th century. It suffered in the persecutions of 1391, but continued to exist until the expulsion of the Jews from Spain in 1492.

Gerondi, Isaac ben Zerachiah (fl. 13th cent.). Spanish Hebrew poet. About 20 of his liturgical poems survive.

Gerondi, Jacob ben Sheshet (fl. 13th cent.). Spanish kabbalist. He lived in Gerona. He wrote *Meshiv Devarim Nekhoḥim*, in which he formulated kabbalistic meanings of the essence of the Torah, the creation of the world, divine providence, and retribution.

Gerondi, Jonah ben Abraham (fl. 13th cent.). Spanish talmudist. While living in Montpellier, he signed the ban that led to the burning of the works of Moses Maimonides. He subsequently vowed to go on a pilgrimage to Palestine to seek forgiveness, but was induced to remain in Toledo to direct a yeshivah. He wrote novellae on talmudic tractates as well as ethical treatises.

Gerondi, Nissim ben Reuben [Nissim, Rabbenu Gerondi; Ran] (fl. 14th cent.). Spanish talmudist, physician, and astronomer. He lived in Barcelona, where he played an important role in communal life. He wrote commentaries on the writings of Isaac ben Jacob Alfasi and on numerous talmudic tractates.

Gerondi, Samuel ben Meshullam (fl. ?12th–13th cent.). Spanish scholar. He lived in Gerona. He wrote a code of laws, *Ohel Moed*, which have practical applications.

Gerondi, Zerachiah ben Isaac (fl. 12th cent.). Italian rabbinic scholar and poet. He was born in Gerona and settled in Lunel. His *Sepher ha-Maor* is a critical examination of the writings of Isaac ben Jacob Alfasi. In *Sepher ha-Tzava* he provided an introduction to talmudic methodology. He also composed liturgical poems.

Geronimo de Santa Fé *see* LORKI, JOSHUA.

Gershom ben Judah (c. 960–1028). German talmudic scholar and spiritual leader. He was born in Metz and lived in Mainz, where he conducted a yeshivah. He issued legal decisions and takkanot, laid the foundations for a commentary on the Talmud, transcribed and corrected the Mishnah and the *Masorah Gedolah* of the Bible, and composed seliḥot and piyyutim.

Gershom ben Solomon (fl. 13th cent.). Provençal scholar. He lived in Béziers. His *Shalman* gives the halakhic rulings of the Talmud according to the order of the halakhot of Isaac ben Jacob Alfasi, and approximating to the order of Maimonides in his *Mishneh Torah*.

Gersonides *see* LEVI BEN GERSHON.

Gerushin ("driving out"). In Jewish law, a term denoting divorce. Among the kabbalists in the 16th century it also designated peregrinations undertaken in order to share the exile of the Shekinah and gain mystical illumination.

Gerusia (Greek: "old people"). Council of elders. According to Josephus, the earliest Jewish gerusia dates back to biblical times. During the Hellenistic period, the Jewish gerusia served as a legislative, judicial, and representative body. It eventually evolved into the Sanhedrin of Jerusalem. A similar body existed in Alexandria.

***Gesenius, Wilhelm** (1786–1842). German orientalist, lexicographer, and Bible scholar. He was born at Nordhausen. He became professor of theology at the University of Halle in 1811. His writings include a comparative and critical grammar, the lexicon *Thesaurus philologicus-criticus*, a history of the Hebrew language and script, and a Hebrew dictionary.

***Gessius Florus** *see* PROCURATOR.

Get *see* DIVORCE.

Geullah ("Redemption"). The name of several benedictions in the liturgy. It designates one of the petitions in the weekday Amidah; the benediction giving thanks for the redemption from Egypt, with which the central part of the Passover Haggadah is concluded; and the benediction following the Shema in the Shaḥarit and Maariv prayers.

Gevalt (Yiddish). Cry of fear, amazement, astonishment, or protest, or a cry for help.

Gezelah *see* ROBBERY.

Gezer. Ancient town in Palestine, northwest of Jerusalem. The Canaanite King of Gezer was vanquished by Joshua (Joshua 10.33). The Egyptian pharaoh gave the town to Solomon as dowry for his daughter. It was later captured from Rehoboam by Pharaoh Shishak and later still was taken by Simon the Hasmonean. Jews lived there during the period of the first and second Temple.

Gezerah ("decree"). In Jewish law a technical term for a rabbinic prohibition; it is distinct from a positive enactment (takkanah). In a non-legal context it came to denote an evil or anti-Jewish decree; by extension it also referred to anti-Jewish persecutions and pogroms.

Gezer Calendar. Hebrew inscription of the late 10th century BCE, found on a table at Gezer. Written in Canaanite script, it consists of a list of agricultural seasons and the work associated with them.

Ghazzati, Nathan Benjamin *see* NATHAN OF GAZA.

Ghetto. Area of a city in which Jews were required to live. The term derives from the foundry ("ghetto") in Venice where Jews were segregated in 1517. The institution was established in cities and towns throughout Europe. The ghetto enjoyed a degree of autonomy and had its own spiritual and intellectual life, but the segregation of the Jews in their own quarter was frequently accompanied by forced baptism, the wearing of the Jewish badge, occupational restrictions, and conversionist activities. Ghettos largely disappeared after the Emancipation of the Jews in the 19th century, but the system was reimposed in some cities (notably Warsaw) under Nazi rule.

Ghetto benches. In Polish universities between the wars special benches were instituted for Jewish students to separate them from others. Jewish students refused to accept such segregation, and serious clashes occurred.

Ghirondi, Mordecai Samuel (1799–1852). Italian scholar and biographer. He was born in Padua and taught theology at the rabbinical college there; he became the city's chief rabbi in 1831. His writings include a biographical dictionary of Jewish scholars and rabbis.

Giants. The Bible refers to races of giants, the Nephilim, Anakim, and Gibborim (Genesis 6.4; Numbers 13.28). Other giants mentioned in the Bible include Goliath (I Samuel 17) and Ishbi-benob (II Samuel 21.16).

Gibeath Benjamin. The principal city of the territory of the tribe of Benjamin (Joshua 18.24; Judges 19–20) and Saul's royal city.

Gibeon. Ancient city north of Jerusalem (Joshua 18.25; 21.17). Solomon offered sacrifices and was visited by a divine vision there (I Kings 3.14).

Gibeonites. Canaanite tribe. During the Israelite conquest they feared they might be destroyed. By pretending not to be Canaanites they tricked Joshua into a treaty that would save them (Joshua 9). When their deceit was discovered, Joshua forced them into servitude (Joshua 9.27). Gibeonites were among the returning exiles from Babylon; they resettled the city and helped to build the walls of Jerusalem (Nehemiah 7.25; 3.7).

Gideon [Jerubaal] (fl. 12th cent. BCE). Judge of the tribe of Manasseh. He defeated the Midianites near En Harod. When offered the kingship of Israel he refused, out of loyalty to the principle that God is the King of Israel (Judges 6–8). In Judges 6.32 he is referred to by the name Jerubaal.

Gideon, Miriam (b. 1906). American composer and educator. She was born in Greeley, Colorado, and grew up in Boston. She taught at Brooklyn College, City College of the City University of New York, the Cantors Institute of the Jewish Theological Seminary, and the Manhattan School. Her works on Jewish themes include: *Friday Evening Service*, *Sabbath Morning Service*, *Adon Olam*, *Psalm 84*, *Biblical Masks*, and *Aetet Hashahar*.

Gikatilla, Isaac (fl. 10th cent.). Spanish Hebrew poet and grammarian. A student of Menaḥem ben Saruq, he took part in the controversy on grammar between his teacher and Dunash ben Labrat. He lived at Lucena.

Gikatilla, Joseph ben Abraham (1248–c. 1325). Spanish kabbalist. He was born in Medinaceli, Castile, and lived in Segovia. His *Ginnat Egoz* is an introduction to the mystic symbolism of the alphabet, vowel points, and the divine names. In his *Shaare Orah* he explained kabbalistic symbolism and the designations of the ten sephirot.

Gikatilla [Ibn Gikatilla]**, Moses ben Samuel** (fl. 11th cent.). Spanish liturgical poet and grammarian. He was born in Córdoba and lived in Zaragoza. He wrote poetry as well as studies of Hebrew grammar and Bible exegesis.

Gilbert, Martin (b. 1936). English historian. He was born in London. He has been a fellow of Merton College, Oxford, and visiting Professor at the Hebrew University and Tel Aviv University. His publications include *Exile and Return: a Study in the Emergence of Jewish Statehood*, *The Holocaust*, *Auschwitz and the Allies*, *The Jews of Hope*, *The Plight of Soviet Jewry Today*, *Jerusalem: Rebirth of a City*, and the *Jewish History Atlas*.

Gilboa. Mountain ridge in Israel, west of the Jordan. It was the site of the Philistine victory over the Israelites when Saul and three of his sons were killed (I Samuel 31.1–6).

Gilboa, Amir (1917–1984). Israeli poet. He was born in Radzywilow, Volhynia, and went to Palestine in 1937, where he worked initially as a laborer. He began to publish poetry while serving in the Jewish Brigade during World War II. Some of his poems concern biblical characters.

Gilgal. The name of several holy places in ancient Israel. It was the site of the first camp of the Israelites after they crossed the Jordan; Joshua set up 12 commemorative stones there (Joshua 4.19–20). After celebrating their first Passover in Canaan at Gilgal, the Israelites born in the desert were circumcised (Joshua 5.2–10). Samuel judged Israel there, and Saul was crowned king at Gilgal (I Samuel 10.8; 7.16; 11.14–15). Later the idolatrous cult practiced there aroused the fury of the prophets (Hosea 4.15; Amos 4.4; 5.5).

Gilgamesh Epic. Ancient Babylonian creation story. It parallels certain elements of the biblical narrative, such as the story of the Flood.

Gilgul *see* METEMPSYCHOSIS.

Gimel. Third letter of the Hebrew alphabet. Its numerical value is 3.

Ginsberg, Allen (b. 1926). American poet. He was born in Newark, New Jersey. His work includes *Kaddish.*

Ginsberg, Asher *see* AḤAD HA-AM.

Ginsberg, Harold Louis (b. 1903). American biblical scholar and Semitist. He was born in Montreal. He became professor of Bible at the Jewish Theological Seminary of America in 1941. He wrote studies of biblical philology, history, and religion. In addition, he contributed to Aramaic linguistics and was a pioneer in the interpretation of Ugaritic texts and their application to the Bible.

Ginzberg, Louis (1873–1953). American talmudic scholar. He was born in Kovno, Lithuania, and emigrated to the US. He joined the staff of the *Jewish Encyclopedia* as editor of the rabbinic department. In 1903 he was appointed professor of Talmud at the Jewish Theological Seminary. His writings deal with the origins of aggadah, halakhah, and the literature of the geonim. In *The Legends of the Jews* he collected together legends, maxims, and parables from midrashic literature.

***Ginsburg, Christian David** (1831–1914). British biblical scholar. He was born in Warsaw. He converted to Christianity in 1846 and settled in England, where he wrote studies of the masoretic text of the Bible; his *The Massorah* contains the original text of the masorah as well as additional notes. He also published standard editions of the Hebrew Bible, contributed to a new critical Hebrew Bible text, wrote commentaries on several books of the Bible, and produced studies of the Karaites and kabbalistic literature.

Ginsburg [Günzburg]**, Jekuthiel** (1889–1957). American mathematician and Hebrew writer. He was born in Russia and emigrated to the US in 1912. In 1930 he was appointed professor and head of the department of mathematics at Yeshiva College. His publications include studies of the Jewish contribution to mathematics.

Ginzburg, Natalia (b. 1916). Italian novelist and playwright. She was born in Palermo and studied in Turin. The characters in her novels include many Jews. Her works include *Family Sayings*, a psychological novel based on the author's recollections of her own family and the events of her youth.

Ginsburg, Saul (1866–1940). Russian author and historian. He was born in Minsk. In 1903 he established the first Yiddish daily in Russia. Later he devoted himself to the study of the cultural history of the Jews in Russia. He left the USSR in 1930 and settled in Paris, later moving to New York. Together with Peretz Marek he published *Jewish Folk Songs.*

His *Historical Works* contains material on 19th-century Russian Jewry.

Girdle *see* GARTEL.

Girgashites. Ancient people, one of the groups who inhabited the land of Canaan (Genesis 15.21; Deuteronomy 7.1; Joshua 3.10; Nehemiah 9.8). They were one of the peoples the Israelites dispossessed when they entered Canaan (Joshua 24.11).

Gittelsohn, Roland (b. 1910). American rabbi. He was born in Cleveland. He was rabbi at the Central Synagogue of Nassau County in Long Island from 1936 to 1953, then served as rabbi of Temple Israel in Boston. In 1968 he became president of the Central Conference of American Rabbis. His writings include *Modern Jewish Problems*, *Little Lower than the Angels*, *Man's Best Hope*, *My Beloved is Mine*, and *Fire in my Bones*.

Gittin. Sixth tractate of the order Nashim in the Mishnah. It deals with the laws of divorce (Deuteronomy 24.1–4).

Glanz, Leib (1898–1964). American cantor and composer. He was born in Kiev and held cantorial positions at Kishinev and in Romania before emigrating to the US in 1926. He served as cantor of the Ohev Shalom Synagogue in Brooklyn and of Heikhal Sinai Synagogue and the Shaarei Tefillah Synagogue in Los Angeles. In 1954 he settled in Israel and became chief cantor of the Tiferet Ẓevi Synagogue in Tel Aviv. He founded the Tel Aviv Institute of Religious Jewish Music.

Glaser, Eduard (1855–1908). Bohemian explorer and Arabist. He was born in Deutsch-Rust. He made four journeys to Arabia between 1883 and 1894, discovering many geographical locations, numerous inscriptions, archeological remains, and Arabic manuscripts.

Glatstein, Jacob (1896–1971). American Yiddish poet, novelist, and critic. He was born in Lublin and emigrated to the US in 1914. He helped to inaugurate Inzikhist, an introspective school of American Yiddish poetry. He later became one of the most important elegists of eastern European Jewish life. He was also a columnist for the New York Yiddish daily, and contributed to various periodicals.

Glatzer, Nahum Norbert (1903–1990). American scholar, teacher, and editor. He was born in Lemberg. He became professor of Jewish philosophy and ethics at the University of Frankfurt am Main in 1932. In the next year he left Germany and settled in Palestine, where he taught at Bet Sepher Reali in Haifa. From 1938 he lived in the US, and became professor of Near Eastern and Judaic Studies at Brandeis University in 1956. He was also a director of the Leo Baeck Institute. His writings include studies of talmudic history, the history of 19th-century Jewry, and the life and thought of Franz Rosenzweig.

Gleanings (Hebrew "leket"). Useful remnants of the crop left in the field after harvesting. In biblical times the gleanings were left for the poor (Leviticus 19.9–10; 23.22; Deuteronomy 24.19–21) in the corners of the field (*see* PEAH (i)). The regulations for gleaning are found in the tractate Peah in the Talmud.

Glicenstein, Enrico (1870–1942). American sculptor, painter, and printmaker. He was born in Poland, lived in Munich, settled in Italy in 1897, and finally emigrated to New York in 1928. He produced 60 plates to illustrate an edition of the Book of Samuel. A Glicenstein Museum containing his library was established in Safed, Israel.

Glick, Hirsch (1922–1944). Lithuanian Yiddish poet. He was born in Vilnius and was influenced in his writing by the Yiddish poets of the Yung Vilne group. He edited and published four issues of the poetry review *Yungvald*. His *Lider un poemes* were published posthumously in 1953. His poem *Mir zaynen do* became the battle song of the Vilnius partisan fighters in World War II.

Glick, Saul Irving (b. 1934). Canadian composer, conductor, and music producer. He was born in Toronto. He taught theory and composition at the Royal Conservatory of Music in Toronto and at York University. From 1962 to 1986 he was a music producer for the CBC. In 1969 he became the choir director of Beth Tickvah Synagogue in Toronto. His works include *Hashirim Asher l'Yisrael*, *Kedusha*, *Sing unto the Lord a New Song*, *Deborah*, *Music for Passover*, Yiddish Suite, *Suite Hebraïque*, *Sonate Hebraïque*, Psalm for Orchestra, and Sonata for Orchestra "Devequt."

Glickson, Mosheh (1878–1939). Palestinian author and Zionist leader, of Lithuanian origin. He edited the weekly *Ha-Am* in Moscow, as well as the miscellanies *Olamenu* and *Massuot* published in Odessa during World War I. In 1919 he settled in Palestine and was the chief editor of *Ha-Aretz* from 1922 to 1937. He wrote studies of Aḥad ha-Am and Maimonides.

Gloss. A short explanation or interpretation of a word or phrase added to a text or manuscript. Commentators on the Bible and Talmud frequently explain words by giving equivalents in the vernacular language (written using Hebrew script). Such glosses are an important source for knowledge of French, Italian, German, and Greek.

Glückel of Hamelin (1646–1724). German Yiddish writer. She lived mainly in Hamburg. After her husband's death, she wrote her memoirs in Yiddish. They are an important source of information about German Jewish life, court Jews, the impact of Shabbetai Tzevi, and the history of Yiddish.

Glueck, Nelson (1900–1971). American archeologist. He was born in Cincinnati. He was director of the American School of Oriental Research at Jerusalem (1932–3, 1936–40, 1942–7), and at Baghdad (1933–4). In 1947 he was elected president of the Hebrew Union College. His writings include *Explorations in Eastern Palestine*, *The Other Side of the Jordan*, *The River Jordan*, *Rivers in the Desert*, and *Deities and Dolphins: the Story of the Nabateans*.

Gnessin, Uri Nisan (1881–1913). Ukrainian Hebrew author. He was born in Starodub, but lived an unsettled life, wandering from city to city and often enduring hardship. He published poems, literary criticism, stories, translations, and sketches. He was among the first Hebrew writers to explore the alienation and uprootedness of Jews in modern society.

Gniessin, Michael Fabianovich (1883–1957). Russian composer. He was born in Rostov-na-Donu. He was professor of composition at the Moscow Conservatory (1923–35), taught composition at the Leningrad Conservatory (1935–45), and later headed the composition department at the music school in Leningrad which bore his and his sister's name. He published books on composition, aesthetics, and Jewish music, and a study of Rimsky-Korsakov. In addition he pioneered the new Russian symphonic style in his music, and the use of the folk music of the peoples of the USSR. Many of his works have Jewish titles.

Gnosticism. Religious movement characterized by a belief that through intuitive knowledge of spiritual truth the spiritual element of man could be released from its bondage in matter. It flourished in the Hellenistic period and later. Gnostics believed that the material world is the result of a primeval fall and was created by an intermediary fallen from the divine realm. Gnosticism contained oriental mythological elements combined with Greek philosophy. Gnostic dualism was regarded by the rabbis as a heresy and condemnation of such heretics ("minim") is contained in rabbinic sources. Gnosticism influenced later Jewish mysticism.

God. Divine creator and ruler of the universe. The belief in God is the foundation of the Jewish faith, and the ground of the legal system. The Bible depicts creation and God's activity in ancient Israelite history. Medieval Jewish philosophers attempted to prove the existence of God and investigated the nature of the divine attributes. Kabbalists explored the hidden depths of the Godhead, and God's activity in the world.

God, attributes of. The Bible ascribes certain traits to God, such as mercy, justice, and benevolence. In addition he is described as possessing human physical characteristics. Medieval Jewish philosophers debated whether these should be understood literally or figuratively. Some philosophers, such as Maimonides, decreed that only negative attributes (e.g., incorporeality) are permissible. Others, such as Ḥasdai Crescas, disagreed. In rabbinic sources God is described as omnipotent, omniscient, incorporeal, and all-good. *See also* 13 ATTRIBUTES.

God, names of. Because it was forbidden to pronounce the tetragrammaton (YHVH, pronounced Yahweh), substitutions and circumlocutions were adopted to refer to God. Various Hebrew terms are used in the Bible; other names arose as a result of rabbinic, philosophical, and kabbalistic usage. Such names include El (God); El Elyon (most high); El Olam (eternal God); El Shaddai (God almighty); El Brit (God of the covenant); Elohim (God); Adonai (Lord); Yhwh (God of Israel); Yahweh Zeva'ot (Lord of hosts); Ha-Shem (the name); Shem ha-Mephorash (the ineffable name); Kedosh Yisrael (the holy one of Israel); Ha-Makom (the place); Shekhinah (divine presence); Ha-Kadosh Barukh Hu (the holy one, blessed be he); Ha-Gevurah (the strength); Ha-Raḥaman (the merciful); Attik Yomin (Aramaic: Ancient of Days).

***Goebbels, Josef** (1897–1945). German Nazi leader. In 1933 he became minister of propaganda. He was among the initiators of the Final Solution, the plan that was to lead to the extermination of the Jews.

Goel ha-dam *see* AVENGER OF BLOOD.

***Goering, Hermann** (1893–1946). German Nazi leader. He joined the Nazi party in 1922, and became the first leader of its Sturmabteilung (storm troops). He later formed the Gestapo. He was involved in every phase of the destruction of European Jewry.

Gog and Magog. Apocalyptic figures. They are mentioned in Ezekiel 38–9 in the vision of the end of days. Ezekiel describes the war of the Lord against Gog of the land of Magog. According to rabbinic sources the wars of Gog and Magog will precede the coming of the Messiah.

Goido, Isaac (1868–1925). American Hebrew and Yiddish author. He published a number of popular Yiddish editions in Vilnius. In 1894 he settled in New York, where he was active as a theater critic and dramatist; among his works is a history of Yiddish drama.

Goitein [Koitein]**, Shelomoh Dov** (b. 1900). Israeli orientalist. He was born in Burgkunstadt, Germany, and emigrated to Palestine in 1923. In 1928 he became a member of the faculty of the Institute of Oriental Studies at the Hebrew University, where from 1947 he was professor. From 1957 to 1970 he was professor of Arabic at the University of Pennsylvania. He published works on the religious institutions of Islam, the culture of the Jews of Yemen, and texts from the Cairo Genizah.

Golah ("exile"). The word is used to refer to the condition of the Jewish people in the diaspora.

Gold, Herbert (b. 1924). American novelist. He was born in Cleveland. He taught at the University of California at Berkeley. His novels deal with the search for love between men and women and children and parents. A number of his novels deal with American Jewish life.

Gold, Michael (1893–1967). American communist author and journalist. He was born in New York. He worked as a copy editor on the socialist *Call* and contributed articles and poetry to *Masses*. Later he was editor of the communist *Liberator* and of *New Masses*. He also worked with the left-wing New Playwrights' Theater. His novel *Jews Without Money* is an account of Jewish immigrant life in New York.

Gold, Ze'ev (1889–1956). American rabbi and leader of religious Zionism. He was born in Poland and became rabbi in Juteka. In 1907 he emigrated to the US, where he served several congregations and was in the forefront of Zionist workers. He was president of the American Mizraḥi from 1932 to 1935, when he settled in Palestine. He later became head of the country's Department for Torah Education and Culture.

Goldberg, Abraham (1883–1942). American journalist and Zionist leader. He was born in Russia and settled in New York in 1901. He was co-founder of Poale Zion in the US, and editor of its newspaper, *Freie shtimme*. He became editor of the New York Zionist journal *Dos yiddishe folk* in 1909. In 1920 he was appointed editor of the Hebrew monthly *Ha-Toren*.

Goldberg, Dov Ber (1801–1884). French scholar of Polish origin. He devoted himself to the publication of editions of Jewish manuscripts housed in European libraries. He traveled widely, visiting libraries in Europe and England, and from 1852 lived in Paris. He wrote numerous articles in Hebrew periodicals.

Goldberg, Isaac Leib (1860–1935). Lithuanian Zionist leader and philanthropist. After studying at the Kovno yeshivah, he settled in Vilnius. He was one of the first members of the Ḥibbat Zion movement, and founded the Ohavei Zion society in Vilnius. In 1908 he established a farm at Hartuv and purchased the first plot of land on Mount Scopus for the future Hebrew University. In 1919 he settled in Palestine.

Goldberg, Isaiah N. *see* YAKNEHAZ (ii).

Goldberg, Leah (1911–1970). Israeli Hebrew poet and critic. She was born in Königsberg and lived in Russia until after the Revolution, when she settled in Kovno, Lithuania. In 1935 she emigrated to Tel Aviv. In 1952 she was invited to organize the Department of Comparative Literature at the Hebrew University, where she became a professor. She published poetry, literary criticism, translations, children's works, a novel, and a play.

Golden, Harry Lewis (1902–1981). American author, editor, and publisher. He was born in New York. He was sentenced to five years' imprisonment for running a Wall Street gambling house. Later he became the editor of the *Carolina Israelite*. His publications include *Only in America*, *For 2 Cents Plain*, and *Enjoy*.

Goldenberg, Eliezer (1846–1916). Russian socialist. He was arrested while a student in St. Petersburg, but escaped to London. Together with Aaron Samuel Liebermann he was a founder of the Society of Hebrew Socialists.

Golden Book. Zionist roll of honor, instituted in 1902. It is kept at the headquarters of the Jewish National Fund in Jerusalem.

Golden Calf. Idol constructed by Aaron

at the behest of the Israelites when Moses was absent on Mount Sinai. Moses later burnt it and ground it to dust. (Exodus 32)

Golden rule. Term applied to the exhortation to treat others as one would wish to be treated oneself. The injunction of Jesus in the gospels "Do unto others as you would have them do unto you" (Matthew 7.12) is a positive formulation of a principle laid down earlier by the sage Hillel.

Goldenthal, Jacob (1815–1868). Austrian orientalist. He was born in Brody. He was principal of the Jewish school in Kishinev. Then in 1846 he settled in Vienna and taught oriental languages, rabbinics, and literature at the University of Vienna. He published studies of medieval Jewish literature and philosophy, as well as the first Hebrew textbook for the study of Arabic.

Goldfaden, Abraham (1840–1908). Ukrainian Yiddish poet. He established the first modern Yiddish theatrical company in Romania in 1876. By 1880 his troupe was giving performances throughout Russia. When in 1883 the Russian government banned performances in Yiddish, Yiddish theaters were established in Paris, London, and New York. In 1887 Goldfaden moved to New York, but he returned to Europe to produce and direct performances. He wrote 60 plays, many of which are in the form of operas or operettas.

Goldhar, Pinchas (1901–1947). Australian Yiddish writer. He was born in Lódź and in 1928 settled in Melbourne, where he operated a dye-shop. He edited the first Yiddish weekly in Australia. His stories describe the integration of Polish-Jewish immigrants into Australian life.

Golding, Louis (1895–1958). English novelist. He was born in Manchester. He joined an ambulance unit during World War I and served in Macedonia and France. During the 1920s he traveled widely and his novels reflect his experiences. His *Magnolia Street* is the first of a cycle of novels about Anglo-Jewish life. In *The Glory of Elsie Silver* he depicted his response to Nazism and his sympathy for Zionism. He also wrote *The Jewish Problem* and *Hitler through the Ages*.

Goldman, Emma (1869–1940). American anarchist. She was born in Kovno, Lithuania, and emigrated to the US in 1885. Her lectures and journal (*Mother Earth*) aimed to illustrate the injustice of American society. In 1919 she was deported to the USSR. She eventually fled Russia, disillusioned with the suppression of the individual. Her writings include *Anarchism and Other Essays*, *My Disillusionment in Russia*, *My Further Disillusionment in Russia*, and *Living my Life*.

Goldman, Solomon (1893–1953). American Conservative rabbi. He was born in Volhynia and was taken to the US as a child. He was rabbi of the Anshe Emet Synagogue of Chicago from 1929. He was known as an orator, scholar, communal leader, and Zionist. His publications include *A Rabbi Takes Stock*, *The Jew and the Universe*, *Crisis and Decision*, *Undefeated*, *The Book of Books*, *In the Beginning*, and *From Slavery to Freedom*.

Goldman, William (b. 1910). English novelist. He was born in London. His publications include *East End my Cradle*, *Light in the Dust*, *A Tent of Blue*, *A Start in Life*, and *A Saint in the Making*.

Goldmann, Nahum (1895–1982). American statesman and Zionist leader. He was born in Lithuania and was taken to Germany as a child. In 1925 he helped to found the Eshkol publishing house in order to produce the *Encyclopaedia Judaica*. Together with Stephen Samuel Wise, he organized the World Jewish Congress in 1936; he became chairman of its executive board and later its president.

He was also president of the Zionist Organization. He played an important role in negotiating the reparations agreement with Germany after World War II. In 1962 he left the US and became an Israeli citizen.

Goldschmidt, Lazarus (1871–1950). German orientalist and bibliophile. He was born in Lithuania and lived in Berlin, later emigrating to London. His early studies dealt with the Ethiopian language and literature. He published an edition of the Sepher Yetzirah, a Hebrew translation of the Koran, and a translation of the Babylonian Talmud into German.

Goldschmidt, Meir Aaron (1819–1887). Danish novelist and journalist. He was born in Vordingborg, Zealand, and settled in Copenhagen, where he founded *Corsaren*, a satirical weekly. From 1847 to 1859 he published the periodical *Nord og syd*. He wrote novels and plays dealing with Jewish subjects.

Goldsmid, Albert Edward Williamson (1846–1904). English communal leader, nephew of Isaac Goldsmid. A soldier by profession, he adopted Judaism later in life. He was a leading member of the Ḥovevei Zion and administered the Jewish colonies in Argentina in 1892–4. He may have been the model for the protagonist in George Eliot's *Daniel Deronda*.

Goldsmid, Sir **Isaac Lyon** (1778–1859). English communal leader. In his business life he financed railway construction. Prominent in the struggle for Jewish Emancipation in England, he was one of the founders of University College, London. He also played a role in the establishment of the Reform synagogue. He was made a baronet in 1841 and in 1846 he was created Baron de Palmeira by the King of Portugal.

Goldstein, Israel (1896–1986). American Conservative rabbi and Zionist leader. He was born in Philadelphia and served as a rabbi of Congregation B'nai Jeshurun in New York. He was president of the Jewish National Fund of America and the Zionist Organization of America. He also served as a member and officer of various Jewish, interfaith, and public organizations. In 1961 he settled in Israel, where he was world chairman of the Keren ha-Yesod–United Israel Appeal. He wrote a history of his congregation in New York and also published collections of sermons and essays.

Goldziher, Ignaz (1850–1921). Hungarian scholar. He was born in Székesfehérvár. He became lecturer at the University of Budapest in 1872. He served as secretary of the Budapest Neolog Jewish community for 30 years, becoming professor of religious philosophy at the Budapest Rabbinical Seminary in 1900. Four years later he was appointed professor at the university. He published studies of pre-Islamic and Islamic culture, the religious and legal history of the Arabs, and their ancient and modern poetry.

Golem. An artificially created being, usually human, brought to life through a magical act or the use of holy names. The concept is connected with the magical exegesis of the Sepher Yetzirah and the idea of the creative power of Hebrew letters. The Talmud records stories of the creation of a golem, and they are found as well in Jewish literature from the 12th century. German Ḥasidim of the 12th–13th centuries viewed the creation of a golem as a symbolic ecstatic experience following a solemn ceremony. From the 15th century a golem was regarded as a real creature able to perform specific tasks.

Golgotha (from Hebrew: "place of a skull"). Place outside Jerusalem, northwest of the city walls, where Jesus was crucified (Matthew 27.33).

Goliath. Philistine giant from the city of

Gath, who was killed by David in combat (I Samuel 17). Another tradition relates that he was slain by Elhanan the Bethlehemite (II Samuel 21.19).

Goll, Iwan (1891–1950). Franco-German poet and author. He was born in Saint-Dié, Vosges. He was initially active in German expressionist circles, but during World War I he moved to Switzerland. Later he settled in Paris, where he established the magazine *Surréalisme*. After living for a period in the US, he returned to Paris in 1947. Jewish themes frequently appear in his poetry.

Gollancz, Sir **Hermann** (1852–1930). British rabbi and teacher, brother of Israel Gollancz. He was born in Bremen and settled in London. He officiated at the Bayswater Synagogue (1892–1923) and taught Hebrew at University College, London (1902–24). He published critical editions and translations of Hebrew, Aramaic, and Syriac texts. He was the first British rabbi to receive a knighthood.

Gollancz, Sir **Israel** (1864–1930). English literary scholar, brother of Hermann Gollancz. He was a lecturer in English at University College, London (1892–5), and then at Cambridge University. In 1903 he became professor of English at King's College, London. He published studies of Shakespeare and early English literature and philology. He served on the council of Jews College for several years.

Gollancz, Sir **Victor** (1893–1967). English publisher and writer. He founded his own publishing house in 1928 and later helped to establish the Left Book Club, whose aim was to expose Nazism; during World War II he campaigned for the National Committee for Rescue from Nazi Terror. From 1945 he endeavored to secure the admission of Jewish refugees to Palestine. His writings include *The Brown Book of the Hitler Terror*, *My Dear Timothy*, *More for Timothy*, and *The Case of Adolf Eichmann.*

Golomb, Eliyahu (1893–1945). Palestinian Zionist. He was born in Belorussia and settled in Palestine in 1909. At the outbreak of World War I he helped to form an independent Jewish defense force. From 1921 he was a member of the Haganah Committee of the Histadrut and the following year he was sent abroad to purchase arms. Beginning in 1931, he attempted to establish a broad popular basis for the Haganah. He was one of the founders of the Palmaḥ.

Golus (Yiddish). Diaspora. The word has connotations of restricted freedom and oppression.

Gombiner, Abraham Abele *see* ABRAHAM ABELE OF GOMBIN.

Gomel, Blessing of *see* HA-GOMEL.

Gomorrah *see* SODOM.

Gonif *see* GANEF.

Good. According to the Bible, goodness is defined in terms of what is pleasing to God, one of whose attributes is absolute goodness. Human beings are granted FREE WILL to choose to do good or EVIL. Rabbinic psychology sees each person as driven by both good and evil inclinations ("yetzer ha-tov," "yetzer ha-ra").

***Goodenough, Erwin Ramsdell** (1893–1965). American scholar. He was born in Brooklyn. He began teaching history at Yale University in 1923. He published numerous studies of Hellenistic Judaism, including *Jewish Symbols in the Greco-Roman Period.*

Goodman, Paul (1875–1949). British Zionist leader. He was born in Estonia and went to England in 1891. He served as secretary of the Spanish and Portuguese Congregation, and held various positions in the Zionist movement in London. His publications include *The Synagogue and the Church*, *History of the Jews*, *Moses Montefiore*, *Zionism in England*, and *The Jewish National Home.*

Goodman, Percival (b. 1904). American architect. He was born in New York and became professor of architecture at Columbia University. He designed numerous synagogues in the US.

Goor, Yehudah (1862–1950). Israeli educator and lexicographer. He was born in Belorussia and emigrated to Palestine in 1887. He was a co-founder of the first Hebrew Teachers' Association in Palestine, and was one of the pioneers of the Ivrit be-Ivrit method of teaching Hebrew. He wrote manuals on the study of Hebrew, Jewish history, natural sciences, and the geography of Palestine, and translated classical literature into Hebrew. He also published several dictionaries, including the *Dictionary of the Hebrew Language*.

Gordin, Jacob (1853–1909). American Yiddish playwright and journalist. He was born in the Ukraine. He taught at a russified Jewish school in Yelizavetgradka, and in 1880 he founded the Spiritual Biblical Brotherhood. In 1891 he emigrated to the US, where he worked as a Yiddish journalist and wrote more than 100 Yiddish plays.

Gordis, Robert (b. 1908). American rabbi and biblical scholar. He was born in New York. He served as rabbi of Temple Beth El in Rockaway Park, New York, from 1931 until his retirement in 1968. From 1940 he was a professor of Bible at the Jewish Theological Seminary. He has served as editor of the journal *Judaism* and president of the Rabbinical Assembly and Synagogue Council of America. He has published studies of wisdom literature, biblical poetry, and the masorah.

Gordon, Aaron David (1856–1922). Palestinian Hebrew writer. He was born in Troyanov, Russia. He held a post in the financial management of Baron Horace Günzburg's estate for 23 years. In 1904 he emigrated to Palestine, where he worked as an agricultural laborer. In his writings he emphasized that self-realization can be attained only through settlement on the land.

Gordon, David (1831–1886). Hebrew journalist and editor. He was born in Podmerecz and settled in Sergei, where he worked as a teacher. In the mid-1850s he emigrated to England, where he taught Hebrew and German. In 1858 he moved to Lyck, where he was assistant editor and later editor of the Hebrew weekly *Ha-Maggid*. He became one of the leading members of Ḥibbat Zion in the 1880s. He published several books and contributed to Hebrew and Yiddish journals.

Gordon, Lord **George** (1751–1793). English convert to Judaism. He was president of the United Protestant League and was implicated in the serious anti-Catholic riots of 1780; as a result he was tried for high treason but was acquitted. In 1787 he was circumcised and assumed the name Israel ben Abraham. He was later tried for libel and was imprisoned in Newgate, London, where he surrounded himself with foreign Jews.

Gordon, Judah Löb (1831–1892). Lithuanian Hebrew poet, writer, critic, and allegorist. He was born in Vilnius, and taught in various government schools in the Kovno province. Later he became critical of Jewish religious life. In 1872 he went to St. Petersburg as secretary to the Jewish community and director of the Society for the Promotion of Culture among the Jews in Russia. Although his early poetry was romantic in character, his later work was full of disillusionment and despair. He is regarded as the creator of Hebrew realist poetry.

Gordon, Michel (1823–1890). Lithuanian Hebrew and Yiddish poet. He was born in Vilnius. He was influenced by the Haskalah circle of Abraham Dov Lebensohn. He wrote Hebrew books and articles as well as Yiddish songs; his later poetry is pessimistic in character.

Gordon, Samuel Löb (1865–1933). Palestinian writer and biblical scholar. He was born in Lithuania and emigrated to Palestine in 1898, where he taught at the boys' school in Jaffa. In 1901 he settled in Warsaw and established a Hebrew school for boys. In 1924 he returned to Palestine. He composed a commentary on the Bible, contributed poems, articles, and translations to Hebrew periodicals, and wrote for children.

Gordonia. Pioneer Zionist youth movement, based on the philosophy of Aaron David Gordon. It was founded in 1923 in Galicia and became an international movement. Its principles were to educate its members in humanistic values, build a homeland, create a working nation, and bring about the renaissance of Hebrew culture and self-sufficiency. Members of the movement founded several settlements in Palestine.

Goren, Shelomo (b. 1917). Israeli rabbi of Polish origin. After settling in Palestine he joined the Haganah and fought in the War of Independence. He became Chief Chaplain of Haganah and was later responsible for the organization of the military chaplaincy and regulations for religious observance in the army. In 1961 he received the Israel Prize for the first volume of his comprehensive commentary on the Jerusalem Talmud. He was elected Ashkenazi chief rabbi of Tel Aviv–Jaffa in 1968 and of Israel in 1972.

Gospels. Four books of the New Testament, which describe the life and ministry of Jesus. Matthew, Mark, and Luke are referred to as the "synoptic Gospels"; the fourth gospel, that of John, is regarded by most scholars as the latest.

Gottheil, Gustav (1827–1903). American Reform rabbi, liturgist, and Zionist leader. He was born in Pinne, in the Posen district. He was a teacher to the Reform congregation in Berlin from 1855 to 1860, and served as rabbi of the progressive Congregation of British Jews in Manchester, England, from 1869 to 1873. He then emigrated to New York, where he became co-rabbi at Temple Emanu-El. He published a hymnal and a devotional compilation.

Gottheil, Richard James Horatio (1862–1936). American orientalist, son of Gustav Gottheil. He was born in Manchester, England, and was taken to New York in 1873. From 1886 he taught Semitic languages at Columbia University; he also served as director of the Oriental Department of the New York Public Library from 1896. He was an active Zionist, and served as president of the American Federation of Zionists from 1898 to 1904. He published studies of Zionism and of Semitic languages.

Gottlieb, Adolph (1903–1974). American painter. He lived in New York and Tucson, Arizona, and created works of art for various synagogues.

Gottlieb, Jack (b. 1930). American composer and conductor. He taught at Loyola University and the Institute of Judaic Arts at Warwick, New York. He was appointed music director of Congregation Temple Israel in St. Louis in 1970, then in 1973 became composer-in-residence at the Hebrew Union College in New York. His compositions include *Love Songs for Sabbath, New Year's Service for Young People,* and *Verses from Psalm 118.*

Gottlieb, Maurycy (1856–1879). Polish painter. He was born in Galicia and lived in Lemberg, Vienna, Munich, and Kraków. Many of his paintings are based on Jewish themes.

Gottlober, Abraham bär (1810–1899). Hebrew and Yiddish writer and poet. He was born in Starokonstantinov and was taken to Tarnopol, Galicia, at the age of 17. Influenced by the Haskalah, he developed a hostility toward orthodoxy and Ḥasidism. During a period when he was living in Podolia, he wrote in Yiddish and Hebrew. From 1830 to 1850 he lived in Bessarabia, Berdichev, and Kremenetz. Later he became an instructor in Talmud at the rabbinical seminary in Zhitomir. He published poems, dramas, stories, memoirs, translations, and studies of the history of the Karaites, kabbalah, and Ḥasidism.

Gottschalk, Alfred (b. 1930). American communal leader. He was born in Oberwessel, Germany. He served as president of the Hebrew Union College–Jewish Institute of Religion and professor of Bible and Jewish thought. His publications include studies of Aḥad ha-Am.

Gottschalk, Max (1889–1976). Belgian social scientist. He was born in Liège. He joined the Institute of Sociology of the Free University of Brussels as research professor in 1923. During World War II he taught at the New School for Social Research in New York but when the war was over he returned to the institute in Brussels. He served as president of the International Association of Social Progress and of the Brussels National Center of Jewish Studies.

Goudchaux, Michel (1797–1862). French banker and politician. He was born in Nancy. He worked as a banker and founded a working-class newspaper, *Le national*. After the revolution of 1848 he was mayor of his district of Paris, member of the general council of the department of the Seine, and paymaster general in Strasbourg. He later became minister of finance in the Second Republic, and was vice-president of the National Assembly in 1849.

Goudsmit, Samuel (1884–1954). Dutch author. He was born in Kampen, at the mouth of the river IJssel. His publications include *Dievenschool*, *In de grote leerschool*, *Jankefs jongste*, *Jankefs oude sleutel*, *Simcha, de knaap uit Worms*, and *De gouden kroon van Beieren*.

Government, Prayer for. The duty to pray for the welfare of the civil authorities was first stated in the Book of Jeremiah (Jeremiah 29.7); the idea was reinforced by the Mishnah. In the synagogue prayers for the government became a regular feature from the 14th century. The prayer now used has a fixed form and is usually recited on the Sabbath after the reading of the law (*see* HA-NOTEN TESHUAH).

Governor of Judea *see* PROCURATOR.

Goy (Yiddish). Non-Jew. Originally it was used to characterize a whole nation, but it came to be applied to any individual who is not a Jew.

Grace after Meals (Hebrew "Birkat ha-Mazon"). Prayer consisting of four benedictions, recited after a meal where bread is eaten. If bread is not eaten, a shorter form of grace is recited. The benedictions praise God for providing food, express gratitude for his blessings, ask him for mercy and support, and thank him for his goodness.

Grace before Meals. Prayer consisting of one or more benedictions recited before a meal or before the separate courses of a meal. The rabbis instituted separate blessings for various species of food. The blessing for bread ("Who brings forth bread from the earth") is based on Psalm 104.14; when recited at the beginning of the meal, it exempts one from the obligation to recite additional blessings for other courses.

Grade, Ḥayyim (1910–1982). Lithuanian Yiddish poet and novelist. He was born in Vilnius and became leader of the Yung Vilne literary movement. During World War II he lived in Soviet Russia, later settling in Poland. He subsequently moved to Paris, where he was active in revivifying Yiddish cultural life. Eventually he emigrated to New York, where he was associated with the Yiddish daily *Jewish Morning Journal*. His poetry reflects Jewish life in eastern Europe.

Graetz, Heinrich (1817–1891). German historian and biblical scholar. He was born in Xions, in the district of Posen. He lectured in Jewish history and the Bible at the Jewish Theological Seminary of Breslau; in 1869 he was made an honorary professor at the university there. His multi-volume *History of the Jews* influenced subsequent Jewish historians.

Grammarians. The study of Hebrew grammar was fostered by the Masoretes. The development of Arabic philology in the 8th and 9th centuries served as a model for Hebrew scholars such as Saadyah ben Joseph in Babylonia and Menaḥem ben Saruk and Dunash ben Labrat in Spain. Other medieval scholars, such as Judah ben David Ḥayyuj of Fez, Jonah ibn Janaḥ of Córdoba, Abraham ibn Ezra, and David Kimḥi, made further contributions to the study of Hebrew grammar. The scientific study of Hebrew began in the first half of the 19th century with Wilhelm Gesenius' *Elementarbuch*.

Granada. City in southern Spain. It became an important Jewish center in the 11th century, when it was the residence of Samuel ibn Nagrela. In 1066 the Jewish community suffered a massive pogrom, and it was destroyed in 1090. During the Almohad regime (1148–1212) only Jews who had converted to Islam were allowed to live there. The Jews began to return to Granada when the Muslim Nasrid dynasty (1232–1492) came to power. In 1492 the edict of expulsion of the Jews from Spain was signed in the city.

Grand Sanhedrin *see* SANHEDRIN, GREAT.

Granott, Avraham (1890–1962). Israeli economist of Bessarabian origin. He became secretary of the Jewish National Fund in 1919. After settling in Jerusalem in 1922 he became the fund's managing director, and later chairman of its board of directors and president. He was elected to the Knesset in 1949 and served as chairman of its finance committee. He published studies of agrarian reform.

Gratz. American company of shippers owned by the brothers Barnard Gratz (1738–1801) and Michael Gratz (1740–1811). The Gratz brothers were born in Poland and later moved to London from where they emigrated to the US. They formed a partnership as shippers and traders, and as part of their business they sold kosher meat to the West Indies. They helped to found the first Philadelphia synagogue. They supplied goods to the Continental Army during the Revolution. After the war they became involved in a struggle for equal rights for Jews in Pennsylvania.

Gratz, Rebecca (1781–1869). American philanthropist. She is reputed to have been the model for Rebecca in Walter Scott's novel *Ivanhoe*. She lived in Philadelphia, where she aided in founding the Female Hebrew Benevolent Society, the Hebrew Sunday School Society, and the Philadelphia Jewish Foster Home and Orphan Asylum.

Gratz College. American teachers' training college. In 1856 Hyman Gratz bequeathed approximately £150,000 to Mikveh Israel Congregation to establish a college for the education of Jews residing in Philadelphia. The college, the first Jewish teachers' training college in the US, was opened in 1897. It now offers courses leading to teachers' diplomas and bachelors' and masters' degrees.

Graves *see* BURIAL; CATACOMBS; EPITAPH; TOMBS.

Grayzel, Solomon (1896–1980). American historian and editor. He was born in Minsk, Belorussia. He taught Jewish history at Gratz College from 1929. In 1939 he became editor-in-chief of the Jewish Publication Society of America.

From 1966 he taught Jewish history at Dropsie College. He published studies of the relationship of Christians and Jews during the Middle Ages.

Great Assembly (Hebrew "Keneset Gedolah"). Religious body active at the beginning of the second Temple period. It embodied Jewish leadership and served as the supreme authority in religious matters. According to tradition, it was composed of 120 prominent Jewish scholars. It has been identified with the great assembly of the people in the Temple court presided over by Ezra, which accepted the authority of the Torah (Nehemiah 8–9).

Great Hallel *see* HALLEL HA-GADOL.

Great Sanhedrin *see* SANHEDRIN, GREAT.

Green, Gerald (b. 1922). American novelist. He was born in Brooklyn. His publications include *To Brooklyn with Love, An American Prophet, The Legion of Noble Christians,* and *Holocaust.*

Greenberg, Ḥayyim (1889–1953). American Zionist leader, essayist, and editor. He was born in Todoristi in Russia. He edited the Russian Jewish weekly *The Dawn*, before moving in 1921 to Berlin, where he edited *Haolam,* the official weekly of the World Zionist Organization. He had settled in the US by 1924, when he became editor of the Yiddish Zionist publication *Farn folk*. In 1934 he was appointed editor of the labor Zionist monthy the *Jewish Frontier*. During World War II he served as head of the American Zionist Emergency Council and after the war he was director of the Department of Education and Culture of the Jewish Agency in America. He published studies espousing Zionism.

Greenberg, Joanne (b. 1932). American novelist. She was born in Brooklyn. She served as adjunct professor at the Colorado School of Mines. Her novels include *The King's Persons, I Never Promised you a Rose Garden, The Monday Voices, In this Sign, Founders Praise,* and *A Season of Delight.*

Greenberg, Leopold Jacob (1861–1931). English editor and Zionist. He was born in Birmingham. He served as Theodor Herzl's representative in his dealings with the British government. In 1907 he and a group of his friends acquired the *Jewish Chronicle*, and he was appointed its editor-in-chief. He was a founder of a number of publications, including *The Jewish Year Book.*

Greenberg, Uri Tzevi (1894–1981). Israeli poet. He was born in Galicia and was taken as a child to Lemberg. After World War I he became a leader of a group of Yiddish expressionist poets. In 1924 he emigrated to Palestine, where he became a spokesman for the Revisionist movement. His *Book of Indictment and Faith* is an attack on the Jewish Agency's policy of self-restraint, and a defence of his conception of fighting Jewish youth; he supported underground movements that struggled against the British. He was a Ḥerut member in the first Knesset (1949–51). After World War II he published poems about the destruction of European Jewry.

Greenstone, Julius Hillel (1873–1955). American educator and author. He was born in Lithuania and emigrated to the US in 1894. In 1905 he joined the faculty of Gratz College, where he taught Jewish education and religion, and from 1933 to 1948 he was principal of the college. His writings include *The Jewish Religion* and *The Messiah Idea in Jewish History.* For 20 years he contributed a popular column to the Philadelphia weekly *Jewish Exponent.*

Greetings. The general greeting "Shalom aleikhem" (Peace be with you) is answered by "Aleikhem shalom" (With you be peace). The word "Shalom" is also frequently used alone. On the Sabbath the expression "Shabbat shalom" (A Sabbath of peace) is used. On festivals the common greeting is "Gut yomtov" (Good festival) or its equivalents "Ḥag sameaḥ" or "Moadim le-simḥah." The greeting for the New Year is "Le shanah tovah tikkatevu" (May you be inscribed for a good year). On the ninth of Av and in a house of mourning greetings are discouraged. On the completion of a religious duty, the Ashkenazim say "Yishar koaḥ" (May your strength increase), while the Sephardim say "hazak barukh" (Be strong, blessed).

Gregger. Small rattle, with a toothed wheel that rotates against a wooden tongue. It is sounded in the synagogue on Purim when the name of Haman is mentioned during the reading of the Scroll of Esther.

***Grégoire, Henri** (1750–1831). French Catholic priest. He led the campaign for the civic emancipation of the Jews before and during the French Revolution. In his *Essay on the Physical, Moral and Political Reformation of the Jews* he suggested that Jews should be westernized and integrated within French society.

***Gregory I** (fl. 6th–7th cent.). Pope (590–604). He complained of the obduracy of the Jews and ensured that canonical restrictions against them should be obeyed. Nonetheless he insisted that Jews must be protected in the enjoyment of their legal rights. His approach became the official policy of the papacy.

Greidiker, Ephraim (fl. 18th cent.). Polish jester. Influenced by German and Italian motifs, his jokes resembled those of the German folk hero Till Eulenspiegel.

Greiner, Leo (1876–1928). Austrian author. He wrote poems and plays, edited literary journals, and compiled anthologies.

Grinshpan, Yosl (1902–1934). Canadian Yiddish poet. He is known for two works, *Tsvishn vent* and *Lider un poemes*.

Grodno. Town now in Belorussia. In the 17th century it was one of the three chief communities of Lithuania (with Brest-Litovsk and Pinsk).

Grodzinski, Ḥayyim Ozer (1863–1940). Lithuanian talmudic scholar. In 1887 he was appointed one of the dayyanim of the bet din of Vilnius. He was one of the initiators of the Vilnius Conference of 1909, which resulted in the formation of the Orthodox Keneset Israel organization. He was also a sponsor of the conference of rabbis at Grodno in 1924, which founded the Council of the Yeshivot. He was an opponent of Zionism and secular education for Jews. His responsa were published in three volumes.

Gronemann, Sammy (1875–1952). German author and Zionist leader. He was born in Strasburg, West Prussia. He settled in Tel Aviv in 1936. An active Zionist, he was a member of the Zionist Action Committee in Germany and president of the Zionist Congress court. His novels depict the eastern European Jewish milieu; he also wrote comedies, which were adapted for the Hebrew stage.

Gross, Charles (1857–1909). American historian. He was born in Troy, New York. He became professor of history at Harvard University. He published studies on medieval English administrative and economic history, and on the Exchequer of the Jews in England in the Middle Ages.

Gross, Haim (b. 1904). American sculptor and graphic artist. He was born in Galicia, studied in Budapest, and went to Vienna in 1920. In 1921 he emigrated to the US. His work is dominated by Judaic and biblical themes.

Gross, Heinrich (1835–1910). Bavarian rabbi and scholar. He was born in Szenicze, Hungary. He served as a rabbi in Gross-Strelitz, then (from 1870) in Augsburg, Bavaria. He wrote studies of the lives of French rabbis and their communities in the Middle Ages. His *Gallia*

Judaica is a geographic dictionary of France according to rabbinic sources.

Grossman, David (b. 1954). Israeli novelist. He was born in Jerusalem and worked as an editor and broadcaster on Israeli radio. His publications include *The Smile of a Lamb*, *See Under Love*, and *The Yellow Wind*.

Grossman, Elias Mandel (1898–1947). American artist. He was born in Poland and emigrated to the US in 1911. His works are based on Jewish life.

Grossman, Meir (1888–1964). Israeli Zionist leader. He was born in Russia. He lived in Copenhagen during World War I, where he began the publication of a Yiddish daily. At the suggestion of Vladimir Jabotinsky, he published a periodical, *Di Tribune*, which promoted the cause of a Jewish legion. After the Russian Revolution, he helped to establish the Jewish Correspondence Bureau. In 1934 he settled in Palestine. Initially a leader of the Revisionist and Jewish State parties, he joined the General Zionists in 1953. From 1948 to 1961 he was a member of the executive of the Jewish Agency.

Grossman, Vasily Semyonovich (1905–1964). Russian writer. He was born in Berdichev and moved to Moscow as a young man. He later worked as a chemical engineer in the coal mines of Donbas. His trilogy *Stepan Kolchugin* includes Jewish themes. His *Cartea neagră* provides documentary evidence of Nazi crimes committed against Jews in Soviet territory.

***Grotius, Hugo** (1583–1645). Netherlands statesman, jurist, theologian, and historian. His report *Remonstrantie* described the conditions under which Jews could be allowed in the United Provinces. In his scholarly writings, he quoted from Josephus, Philo, medieval Jewish commentators, the Targum, Talmud and midrash. He was on friendly terms with Manasseh ben Israel.

Group Theater. American Jewish theater company formed in 1931. It was influenced by Yiddish theater and remained active until 1941.

Grumberg, Jean-Claude (b. 1939). French dramatist. He was born in Paris and first worked in a tailor's shop. His plays include *Dreyfus*.

Grünbaum, Max (1817–1898). German folklorist and philologist. He was born in Seligenstadt. He became director of the Hebrew Orphan Asylum in New York in 1858, but in 1870 he returned to Europe and settled in Munich, where he engaged in research about Jewish folklore. He wrote studies of Jewish folklore and the structure and evolution of the Yiddish language, as well as a chrestomathy of Judeo-Spanish. He is regarded as one of the founders of Yiddish philology.

Grünbaum, Yitzḥak (1879–1970). Israeli Zionist leader and author of Polish origin. He was born in Warsaw, where he later edited several newspapers. During World War I he lived in St. Petersburg, but he returned to Warsaw, where he became the leader of Polish Zionism. In 1919 he was elected to the Sejm. In 1933 he became a member of the executive of the Jewish Agency and settled in Palestine. As a representative of the General Zionist Party, he was minister of the interior in 1948–9. He published studies on Polish and Zionist history.

Grünthal, Yoseph *see* TAL, YOSEPH.

Grunwald, Max (1871–1953). Israeli rabbi and folklorist of German origin. He was born in Hindenburg. He served as a rabbi in Hamburg (1895–1903) and Vienna (1905–35), then in 1938 settled in Jerusalem. He wrote studies of the communities he served and of Jewish folklore.

Grynszpan, Herschel (1921–?). German Jewish activist. He was born in Hanover and moved to Paris in 1938. He killed Ernst vom Rath, a German embassy official in Paris, in order to arouse public opinion in the West about Nazi persecution. This event served as a pretext for the pogroms of 9–10 November 1938 (Kristallnacht) against Jews.

Guardian *see* EPITROPOS.

Güdemann, Moritz (1835–1918). Austrian rabbi and historian. He was born in Hildesheim, Prussia. He served as rabbi in Magdeburg (from 1862) and Vienna. In 1869 he became head of the Vienna bet din, and subsequently chief rabbi. He wrote a study of trends and institutions in medieval Jewish life from the viewpoint of the non-Jewish environment. He was a leader of the opposition to Theodor Herzl's Zionism.

Guilds. Associations of artisans. Guilds are mentioned in the Bible and were established by the beginning of the second Temple period (Nehemiah 3.8, 31–2). In the Mishnaic period (2nd and 3rd centuries) guilds existed throughout the Jewish world, but Jews were excluded from Christian guilds in European cities in the Middle Ages. In eastern Europe a body of Jewish guilds developed from the 17th century.

Guilt offering. Sacrifice to atone for sin. Biblical ordinances concerning guilt offerings (Leviticus 5.14 ff; 7.1–7) usually decree that a ram be sacrificed.

***Gumplowicz, Ludwig** (1838–1909). Austrian sociologist. He was born in Kraków. He taught at the University of Graz from 1862. He converted to Christianity, but maintained an interest in Jewish affairs. He exercised an important influence on the development of sociology as a science.

Günzburg, Baron **David** (1857–1910). Russian scholar and orientalist, son of Horace Günzburg. He was born in Kamenets-Podolskiy. He published studies on oriental subjects and linguistics and medieval Arabic poetry. He was active in the St. Petersburg Jewish community and the Society for the Promotion of Culture Among the Jews in Russia. In 1908 he established the Jewish Academy, where he taught rabbinics and Arabic literature.

Günzburg, Baron **Horace** (1833–1909). Russian communal leader, son of Joseph Yozel Günzburg. He was born in Zvenigorodka in the province of Kiev, and became active as a banker in St. Petersburg. During the blood libel case in Kutais in 1878 he encouraged Daniel Chwolson to write a book about the history of blood libel. In 1881–2 he attempted to establish an organization of Russian Jews. Later he headed the Jewish community in St. Petersburg and the Society for the Promotion of Culture Among the Jews in Russia.

Günzburg, Jekuthiel *see* GINSBURG, JEKUTHIEL.

Günzburg, Baron **Joseph Yozel** (1812–1878). Russian banker and communal leader. He was born in Vitebsk and settled in Paris in 1857. In 1859 he founded the Joseph Yozel Günzburg Bank in St. Petersburg. He was active in attempts to improve the situation of Russian Jewry. As a founder of the Society for the Promotion of Culture Among the Jews in Russia, he provided scholarships for Jewish youth to encourage higher education.

Günzburg, Mordecai Aaron (1795–1846). Lithuanian Hebrew author and educationalist. He was born in Salantai and settled in Vilnius in 1835. Together with Solomon Salkind, in 1841 he founded the first modern Jewish school in Lithuania, where he served as headmaster. As a spokesman for the Vilnius Haskalah, he published studies of French and Russian history, translations, and an autobiography (*Aviezer*).

Günzburg, Pesaḥ (1894–1947). Palestinian writer and journalist. He was born in Volhynia and lived in the US (1912–14), Scandinavia (1914–17), and London (1917–22), before settling in Palestine. He published poems and stories, as well as translations from English and the Scandinavian languages into Hebrew.

Günzburg, Shimon (1890–1944). Palestinian poet and critic. He was born in Volhynia and lived in the US from 1912 and in Palestine from 1933. He wrote poetry and edited the plays and letters of Moses Ḥayyim Luzzatto.

Gunzenhauser. The name of two German printers, Joseph ben Jacob Gunzenhauser (d. 1490) and his son Azriel ben Joseph Gunzenhauser (fl. 15th cent.), active in Naples. They moved to Naples from Gunzenhausen in south Germany and set up a Hebrew press. From 1487 to 1492 they produced various books, including a Hagiographa with rabbinical commentaries, Avicenna's medical *Canon*, and Abraham ibn Ezra's commentary on the Pentateuch.

Günzig, Azriel (1868–1931). Polish rabbi and scholar. He was born in Kraków and served as a rabbi in Czechoslovakia and Antwerp. He edited and published the literary journal *Ha-Eshkol* from 1899 to 1913. He wrote about the history of the Haskalah in Galicia.

Guph *see* PRE-EXISTENCE.

Guri, Ḥayyim (b. 1922). Israeli poet, novelist, and journalist. He was born in Tel Aviv and spent his early years in the Palmaḥ. In 1947 he went to Europe as an aliyah official. His writings include volumes of poetry and novels, dealing with Holocaust survivors and memories of his Tel Aviv childhood. He has also made a documentary film about the Holocaust.

Gush Emunim (Hebrew "The bloc of the faithful"). Israeli spiritual and political movement. Founded in 1974, it aims to implement its conviction that the creation of a Jewish state constitutes the beginning of redemption. It actively supports the settlement of areas liberated in the Six Day War.

Guston, Philip (1913–1980). American painter. His work was mainly abstract and was strongly affected by the horrors of the Holocaust.

Gutmacher, Elijah (1796–1874). Polish Zionist. He was born in Borek. He served as a rabbi in Pleschenitsy and Grodzisk Wielkopolski. His studies of the kabbalah led him to the view that the Jewish return to Palestine was necessary to purify Jewry from the pollution of exile. He took part in the Thron conference in 1860, which discussed the problems of Palestinian colonization, and worked with Tzevi Hirsch Kalischer to encourage Jewish settlement in Palestine. He was the author of various rabbinic studies.

Gutman, Naḥum (1898–1980). Israeli artist. He was born in Romania and was taken to Palestine at the age of seven. He designed scenery for the Ohel Theater in 1935, and created a mosaic for the chief rabbinate building in Tel Aviv in 1961. He also wrote children's stories.

Gutmann, Simḥah Alter *see* BEN-ZION, SIMḤAH.

Guttmann, Jacob (1845–1919). German rabbi and historian. He was born in Beuthen, Silesia. He served as rabbi in Hildesheim from 1874 to 1892 and in Breslau from 1892. From 1910 he was president of the German Rabbinical Assembly. He published studies of medieval Jewish philosophers and the relation between Christian scholasticism and medieval Jewish philosophy.

Guttmann, Julius (1880–1950). Israeli philosopher and historian of German origin. He lectured in philosophy at the University of Breslau (from 1910) and in

Jewish philosophy at the Hochschule für die Wissenschaft des Judentums in Berlin (from 1919). In 1934 he settled in Jerusalem, where he became professor of Jewish philosophy at the Hebrew University. He published sociological studies of Jewry, philosophical investigations, and explorations of the history of Jewish philosophy.

Guttmann, Michael (1872–1942). Hungarian talmudic scholar. He lectured on Jewish law at the Budapest Rabbinical Seminary from 1907 to 1921. He was then rabbi and professor of Talmud and halakhah at the Breslau Jewish theological seminary (1921–33), of which he became head in 1933. He published studies of rabbinic literature and began work on a talmudic encyclopedia.

H

Haapalah. Movement dedicated to aiding the MAAPILIM.

Ha-Aretz. Israeli daily newspaper. On 18 June 1919 the first issue of *Hadashot ha-Aretz* was published in Jerusalem. Later its name was changed to *Ha-Aretz*. From 1922 to 1937 Mosheh Glickson served as editor, and the paper moved to Tel Aviv. It was subsequently edited by Gershom Schocken. It has brought together Hebrew writers and scholars in Israel and abroad.

Ḥabad. Ḥasidic movement. The name is based on the initials of the words "hokhmah" (wisdom), "binah" (understanding), "daat" (knowledge). Ḥabad was founded in the late 18th century by Shneour Zalman of Lyady, who was opposed by the Ḥasidic leaders of Volhynia and the mitnaggedim led by the Vilna Gaon. His teaching is contained in the *Tanya* in which he developed a theosophical doctrine based on the kabbalah of Isaac Luria. Originally the movement was centered in Belorussia, but after World War I it spread to other regions.

Habakkuk. Biblical book, one of the books of the 12 Minor Prophets. It records the prophecies of Habakkuk, who was active in the 7th century BCE. It consists of three chapters containing a protest against injustice in the world, a complaint about the victory of the Chaldeans, God's reply, a prayer, and a description of the Day of the Lord.

Habermann, Avraham Meir (1901–1980). Israeli bibliographer and scholar of medieval Hebrew literature. He was born in Galicia. After serving as librarian at the Schocken library in Berlin, he emigrated to Palestine in 1934, where he was director of the Schocken library in Jerusalem until 1967. From 1957 he taught medieval literature at Tel Aviv University and at the Graduate Library School of the Hebrew University. He wrote studies of Jewish bibliography, the history of Hebrew poetry, and medieval Hebrew poetry.

Ḥabib, Jacob *see* IBN ḤAVIV, JACOB.

Ha-Bimah. Hebrew theater company. It was formed in Moscow in 1917 by amateur actors. They staged their première in October 1918. Owing to the opposition of the Yevsektzia, their subsidy was withdrawn. From 1926 the company toured Europe and the US and it eventually made its base in Palestine. In 1945 its own building was opened. Its repertory includes Israeli and Jewish plays, as well as classical and modern works.

Habiru. Ancient people living in the Fertile Crescent in the second millennium BCE. The name appears in the Tel el Amarna tablets and other documents. Some scholars identify this group with the ancient Hebrews.

Ha-Bonim. International organization of Zionist youth movements. It was founded in Great Britain in 1929 to undertake youth education. Later it spread to South

Africa, India, Australia, the US, and Holland. The movement has helped to establish settlements in Israel.

Ha-Cohen, Mordecai ben Hillel (1856–1936). Hebrew author of Russian origin. He was born in Belorussia. He began publishing articles in Hebrew periodicals when he was 18. In 1875 he moved to St. Petersburg, where he wrote a comprehensive survey of Jewish agriculturalists in modern Russia. In 1881 he joined the Ḥibbat Zion movement, and he later formed two societies for promoting settlement in Palestine. He moved to Palestine himself in 1907 and was one of the founders of Tel Aviv. He played an active role in the economic and cultural life of the yishuv.

Ha-Cohen, Shalom *see* COHEN, SHALOM BEN JACOB.

Hadad (i). God of several early Semitic peoples. He was one of the chief gods of the Amorites, and later of the Canaanites. He is identified with Baal whom Elijah denounced on Mount Carmel (I Kings 18).

Hadad (ii). The name of several Edomite kings (Genesis 36.35; I Kings 11.14–25; I Chronicles 1.46, 50).

***Hadadezer** [Hadarezer] (fl. 11th cent. BCE). King of Aram-Zoba. He led a coalition of Syrian states, which was defeated by David (II Samuel 10.7–19; I Chronicles 19.6–19).

Ḥadash. In Jewish law, a term used to describe the new grain ripening in spring. It could not be eaten until a sheaf of the first fruits from the new harvest was offered by the priests in the Temple on the second day of Passover.

Hadassah (i). Alternative name for Esther (Esther 2.7).

Hadassah (ii) [Women's Zionist Organization of America]. It was founded in 1912 by Henrietta Szold to raise the standard of health in Palestine, to encourage Jewish life in the US, and to foster the Jewish ideal. In Israel it sponsors medical training, research, care, and special education. Its members in the US participate in fund-raising and Jewish educational activities.

Hadassi, Judah ben Elijah (fl. 12th cent.). Turkish Karaite scholar. He lived in Constantinople. He wrote *Eshkol ha-Kopher*, an encyclopedic survey of Karaite belief and knowledge. It explains the mitzvot and the halakhot, and the reasons for their observance in accordance with specific commandments.

Ḥad Gadya ("An only kid"). Aramaic song chanted at the end of the Passover seder. It was adapted from a German folk song, itself based on a French nursery rhyme. It was included in the service so that children would not fall asleep before the end of the seder. The verse is as follows:

A father bought a kid for two zuzim.
A cat came and ate the kid.
A dog bit the cat.
The dog was beaten by a stick.
The stick was burned by fire.
Water quenched the fire.
An ox drank the water.
A shoḥet slaughtered the ox.
The shoḥet was killed by the Angel of Death, who was punished by God.

Ha-Doar. American Hebrew weekly journal. It was founded in New York in 1922 under the editorship of Mordekhai Lipson. Menaḥem Ribalow was later its editor for 30 years.

***Hadrian** (fl. 2nd cent.). Roman emperor (117–38). Initially he was not hostile to the Jews, but later he decided to erect a gentile city on the site of the destroyed Jerusalem. This act was one of the central causes of the Jewish revolt (132–5), which was crushed by Hadrian's commander, Julius Severus. Subsequently Hadrian issued restrictive edicts against the study of Torah and the practice of Judaism (including circumcision).

Ha-Emet. Austrian Hebrew journal. The first Hebrew socialist periodical, its three issues were published in Vienna in 1877 under the editorship of Aaron Samuel Liebermann.

Ḥag ("festival") *see* HOLY DAYS.

Haganah. Underground military organization of the yishuv in Palestine. It succeeded Ha-Shomer in 1920 and operated until 1948, when its members transferred to the Israeli army, Tzeva Haganah le-Israel. In 1931 the movement split and a minority formed the Irgun Tzevai Leumi. The Haganah carried out underground training within individual settlements, organized illegal immigration, and manufactured equipment. In 1941 military commando units (the Palmaḥ) were established. After World War II, Haganah's operations were directed against the British in order to secure the removal of the anti-Zionist White Paper of 1939. From 1947 it concentrated on defense against Arab attack.

Hagar (fl. ?19th–16th cent. BCE). Egyptian woman, maidservant of Sarah and mother of Ishmael. Since Sarah was barren, Hagar became Abraham's wife. When Hagar discovered she was pregnant, she fled to the desert to escape Sarah's anger, but she later returned. After Sarah had a son, Abraham banished Hagar, but she and her son were miraculously rescued in the wilderness. (Genesis 16)

Hagbahah ("lifting"). Term used in a liturgical context to mean the raising of the Torah scroll in the synagogue before or after the reading so that the congregation can see the writing.

Ha-Gevurah *see* GOD, NAMES OF.

Haggadah, Passover. Ritual service performed in the home on the first Passover evening (or on the first two evenings in the diaspora). Originally a narrative of the Exodus from Egypt, it consists of a set form of benedictions, prayers, midrashic comments, and Psalms, recited in the course of a festive meal. The order of the Passover Haggadah became an established custom and is recorded in the Mishnah. Later it took on a more elaborate form which is contained in the prayerbooks of Amram Gaon (8th century) and Saadyah ben Joseph (10th century). It has become the subject of various commentaries as well as manuscript illuminations.

Haggai. Biblical book, one of the books of the 12 Minor Prophets. It records the prophecies of Haggai, which date from the second year of the reign of Darius I, King of Persia (c. 520 BCE). They deal with the construction of the Temple, the restoration of the nation, and the greatness of Zerubbabel.

Ḥagigah. 12th tractate in the Mishnah order of Moed. It deals with the laws related to peace offerings made during the festivals, festival sacrifices, pilgrimage, and ritual purity connected with sacred objects belonging to the Temple.

Hagiographa (Hebrew "Ketuvim": *lit.* writings). The third section of the Hebrew Scriptures. It contains: Psalms, Proverbs, Job, the Song of Songs, Ruth, Lamentations, Ecclesiastes, Esther, Daniel, Ezra, Nehemiah, and I and II Chronicles.

Ḥagiz, Jacob (1620–1674). Palestinian scholar, son-in-law of Moses Ḥagiz. He lived in various communities in Italy as a youth. In 1658 he emigrated to Jerusalem, where he became head of the Bet Yaakov yeshivah. He was an opponent of Shabbetai Tzevi. His writings include a commentary on the Mishnah, a study of talmudic methodology, and responsa.

Ḥagiz, Moses (1672–?1751). Palestinian scholar and kabbalist. He was born in Jerusalem. He left Palestine in 1694 to collect money to found a yeshivah; he traveled to Egypt, Italy, Prague, and Amsterdam, where together with Tzevi

Ashkenazi he struggled against Sabbetaianism. Later he lived in Altona, and eventually settled in Safed. His writings include novellae on the Shulḥan Arukh, ethical works, and responsa.

Ha-Gomel ("Blessing of Gomel"; from Hebrew "gomel": he who makes recompense). Thanksgiving benediction recited by those who have been saved from danger. It should ideally be said in the presence of ten men (two of whom should be rabbis) within three days of the person's delivery from danger. It is customary to recite the blessing after being called to the reading of the Torah in the synagogue on Monday, Thursday, or the Sabbath. After the benediction is said, the congregation responds: "He who hath shown thee kindness, may he deal kindly with thee for ever."

Ḥag sameaḥ ("Joyful feast"). Greeting used on a religious holiday.

Hague, The. City in Holland. Sephardi and Ashkenazi Jews settled there in the 17th century. In the 18th century Portuguese Jews built their synagogue in the city. Several Portuguese families played an important role in the city's social and intellectual life.

Haham *see* Ḥakham.

Haidamaks ("those who move on") [Cossacks]. Ukrainian paramilitary group. Active between 1708 and 1770, chiefly in the provinces of Kiev and Podolia, the Haidamaks often chose Poles and Jews as defenseless targets for their marauding attacks. In 1768 they massacred thousands at Uman. Eventually they were suppressed by the Russian and Polish authorities.

Haifa. Port in north-east Israel. After the 1st century it was the home of various Jewish scholars. In 1071 the Jerusalem academy was temporarily transferred there. In 1100 the Jews defended the city against the crusaders.

Haifa Technion. Israeli technological university. It was founded in 1912 on the initiative of the Hilfsverein der Deutschen Juden and with funds from Jacob Schiff and the Wissotsky estate in Moscow. In 1953 it moved to a campus on Mount Carmel.

Hai Gaon (939–1038). Babylonian gaon, son of Sherira Gaon. Initially he assisted his father in administering and teaching in the academy at Pumbedita. He was appointed head of the bet din in 986 and gaon in 998. Under his leadership the Pumbedita academy became a center of Jewish learning; he was the last gaon of Pumbedita. He issued thousands of responsa covering numerous areas of halakhic literature. In addition, he wrote a commentary on several tractates of the Talmud, poetry, and a treatise on commercial transactions.

Haim, Victor (b. 1935). French playwright. He was born in Asnières. In 1954, he went to Paris, where he supported himself as a journalist. Some of his work integrates Jewish and universal themes.

Haimish (Yiddish). Informal, cosy, warm, or unpretentious.

Haint. Polish Yiddish daily newspaper. It was founded in Warsaw in 1908 by Samuel Jacob Jackan, who was its first editor. From 1920 it was edited by Abraham Goldberg, and after 1933 by an editorial board. During World War I it became a Zionist organ. It ceased publication when the Germans invaded Poland in 1939.

Ha-kadosh barukh hu ("The holy one, blessed be he"). Expression used in rabbinical literature in order to avoid mentioning God's name in non-liturgical contexts.

Ḥakham [Haham] ("Sage"). Title given to rabbinic scholars. Originally it was inferior to the title "rabbi." Later it was used to designate the third in rank after the nasi and the av bet din of the Sanhedrin. Sephardi Jews subsequently used the title for their local rabbis. In England the title "Haham" is applied to the rabbi of the Spanish and Portuguese congregation in London.

Ḥakham Bashi ("Chief sage"). Title of the chief rabbi of the Turkish empire. In 1836 the Ottoman authorities confirmed the first Ḥakham Bashi in Constantinople. The title was also used of chief rabbis in provincial towns.

Ḥakham Tzevi *see* ASHKENAZI, TZEVI.

Hakhnasat kallah ("bringing in the bride"). The rabbis decreed that it is a duty to provide a dowry for brides and to rejoice at their weddings. This term is popularly applied to the provision of a dowry for poor brides. During the Middle Ages and later, communal societies (known as Hakhnasat Kallah societies) were organized for this purpose.

Hakhnasat oreḥim ("entertaining wayfarers," "hospitality"). The obligation to provide for travelers and strangers is a central commandment of the Jewish faith. Such hospitality is mentioned in the Bible in the narratives about Abraham, Laban, Jethro, and Rahab. In rabbinic literature it is frequently extolled. During the Middle Ages and later the custom arose of providing special lodging for the vagrant poor in a guest house.

Hakhsharah ("preparation"). Intellectual and physical training for settlement in Israel. In the pioneering movements in the diaspora the word was applied especially to training in physical labor (such as farming).

Ha-Kibbutz ha-Artzi ha-Shomer ha-Tzair. Union of socialist kibbutzim in Israel. It was formed in 1927 by the first collective settlements established by Ha-Shomer ha-Tzair. Its members see themselves as the nucleus of the future socialist society in Israel.

Ha-Kibbutz ha-Dati. Union of religious kibbutzim in Israel. It was established in 1935 by members of the Ha-Poel ha-Mizraḥi. Its members combine religious practice with the principles of collective living.

Ha-Kibbutz ha-Meuḥad. Union of kibbutzim in Israel. It was founded in 1927 by pioneers of the Third Aliyah, including groups that had earlier belonged to Gedud ha-Avodah. It was associated with the development of the Palmaḥ. In 1951 a split occurred between its Mapai members and those associated with Aḥdut ha-Avodah.

Hakkaphot ("circuits"). In liturgical and ceremonial use the term used for the circular route taken repeatedly by a procession. On the Feast of Tabernacles during the Hoshanah service, the reader and members of the congregation walk around the Torah carrying the lulav and etrog. This recalls the procession made in biblical times around the altar in the Temple. On Hosha-na Rabbah a similar circuit is made seven times. On the Feast of the Rejoicing of the Law, repeated hakkaphot take place. In Sephardi and Ḥasidic communities, mourners walk around a coffin seven times. In some communities the bride encircles the bridegroom several times before the wedding ceremony.

Ha-Koaḥ. Jewish sports society. It was founded in Vienna in 1909 as a soccer club, but it developed into an Austrian Jewish sports federation that espoused Zionist ideals. It was refounded in Palestine in 1942.

Ha laḥma anya ("This is the bread of affliction"). Opening words of the introductory paragraph of the seder service. It is an invitation to all who are hungry to come and partake of the Passover meal.

Halakhah (*lit.* "walking"). The body of law comprising the rules and ordinances of Jewish religious and civil practice; it is identified with the Oral Law. It was first formulated by the scribes and was later refined and developed by rabbinic authorities. The law was passed down in this form from generation to generation, but eventually it became necessary to formulate it systematically. The most important early collection of halakhah was the Mishnah edited by Judah ha-Nasi. The next great compilation was the Talmud. After the talmudic period, the geonim interpreted and developed law in their responsa.

Halakhot Gedolot. Codification of talmudic law arranged according to the order of the tractates. It was compiled in Babylonia during the 8th century by Simeon Kayyara. It was the first work that enumerated the 613 commandments.

Halakhot Pesukot. The first known halakhic work of the geonim. It was written in Babylonia in the 8th century and is attributed to Yehudai Gaon. It confines itself to those halakhot that have a practical application. They are arranged according to their subject matter.

Halberstamm, Ḥayyim (1793–1876). Polish rabbinic scholar. He was born in Tarnogrod, and was appointed rabbi of Nowy Sadz in Galicia in 1830. He became drawn to Ḥasidism and founded the Sanzer dynasty of Ḥasidic rabbis. He was the head of a yeshivah in Zanz which attracted both Ḥasidim and mitnaggedim. In 1869 he was involved in a dispute with the Sadagora Ḥasidim. He published works on talmudic subjects as well as responsa.

Halberstamm, Solomon Zalman Ḥayyim (1832–1900). Polish Hebrew scholar and bibliophile. He was born in Kraków and became a successful merchant in Bielsko-Biała, Poland, where he collected rare books and manuscripts. In 1890 he published a catalog of his manuscripts.

Halevai ("May it be so"). Expression voicing a wish for a desirable outcome to any project, situation, or circumstances.

Halévy, Élie (1760–1826). French Hebrew writer and poet. He was born in Fürth, Bavaria, and moved to Paris, where he served as cantor, secretary of the Jewish community, and teacher. From 1817 to 1819 he edited and published a weekly journal, *L'Israélite français*. His *Teachings of Religion and Ethics* is a textbook for Jewish religious instruction. His poem *Ha-Shalom* commemorates the cease-fire between France and England in 1802.

Halévy, Isaac (1847–1914). Polish rabbinic scholar. Born in Ivenets, he lived in various cities including Pressburg, Homburg, and Hamburg, where he served as Klausrabbiner. His *Dorot ha-Rishonim* is a history of the Oral Law from biblical times to the period of the geonim.

Halévy, Jacques François Fromental (1799–1862). French composer, son of Élie Halévy. He was born in Paris, and taught at the Paris Conservatoire from 1816, becoming professor of counterpoint and fugue in 1833, and professor of composition in 1840. He composed operas, cantatas, and ballets. His opera *La Juive* is the story of a Renaissance prince in love with a Jewess.

Halévy, Joseph (1827–1917). French orientalist and Hebrew writer. He was born in Turkey and later taught in Bucharest. In 1868 he visited Ethiopia to study the Falashas. Later he explored southern Arabia and discovered numerous Sabean inscriptions. In 1879 he taught Ethiopic at the École Pratique des Hautes Études in Paris and became the librarian of the Société Asiatique. In 1893 he founded the *Revue semitique d'épigraphique et d'histoire ancienne*, to which he contributed articles on epigraphy and biblical studies. He was an ardent Hebraist and Zionist.

Halévy, Léon (1802–1883). French writer and dramatist, son of Élie Halévy. He was born and lived in Paris. He became assistant professor of French literature at the École Polytechnique in 1831 and head of the antiquities department of the Ministry of Education in 1837. His writings include *Résumé de l'histoire des juifs anciens* and *Résumé de l'histoire de juifs modernes*.

Ḥalitzah (*lit.* "drawing off"). Ceremony performed when a man refuses to marry his brother's childless widow (Deuteronomy 25.9–10). It involves her removing her brother-in-law's shoe and reciting the formula: "So shall be done to the man who will not build his brother's house." Without undergoing this ceremony, she is forbidden to remarry. The ceremony has become obligatory in Israel, where marriage between a man and his brother's widow is not permitted.

Halkin, Abraham (b. 1903). American orientalist and educator, brother of Simon Halkin. He was born in Russia and was taken to the US in 1914. From 1928 to 1950 he was a lecturer in Semitic languages at the City College of New York, and latterly professor of Hebrew. He also taught at the Jewish Theological Seminary from 1929 to 1970. He edited Maimonides' *Epistle to Yemen,* and published studies of Judeo-Arabic literature and history.

Halkin, Shemuel (1897–1960). Russian Yiddish poet. He was born in Belorussia. He published a book of lyrics in 1922 and later Yiddish translations of English, American, and Russian classics, as well as poetry and plays about Jewish history. Initially he supported Zionism and was criticized for his advocacy of Jewish nationalism.

Halkin, Simon (1898–1987). American Hebrew poet, novelist, and educator, brother of Abraham Halkin. He was born in Russia and emigrated to the US in 1914. He taught at the Hebrew Union College School for Teachers in New York from 1925 to 1932, when he settled in Palestine. He returned to the US in 1939 and became professor of Hebrew literature at the Jewish Institute of Religion in New York. In 1949 he was appointed professor of modern Hebrew literature at the Hebrew University. He wrote novels and works of literary criticism, and made translations.

Ḥallah (i) ("dough offering"). In the Bible the word is used of a portion of dough given to the priest (Numbers 15.17–21). It now refers to a special Sabbath loaf.

Ḥallah (ii). Ninth tractate in the Mishnah order of Zeraim. It deals with the setting aside of the Ḥallah ("dough offering").

Hallaph *see* SHEḤITA.

Hallel ("Praise"). In Jewish liturgical use the name of the group of Psalms 113–18. These psalms are expressions of thanksgiving and joy for divine redemption. They are recited in two forms. The full Hallel, consisting of Psalms 113–18, is chanted in the synagogue on Sukkot, Ḥanukkah, the first day of Passover, Shavuot, and Israeli Independence Day; it is also recited at the Passover seder. The half Hallel, consisting of the full Hallel except Psalm 115.1–11 and Psalm 16.1–11, is recited on the new moon and the last six days of Passover.

Hallel ha-Gadol ("Great Hallel"). In Jewish liturgical use the name given to Psalm 136. It is recited at the Sabbath and at festival morning services as well as the last day of Passover.

Hallelujah ("Praise ye the Lord"). Word used as the refrain at the beginning and end of certain psalms. It was also the congregational response in the Hallel ha-Gadol during the talmudic period.

Halper, Ben Zion (1884–1924). American Hebraist, Arabist, and editor. He was born in Lithuania and emigrated to Germany, from there to England, and finally to the US. From 1913 he taught at Dropsie College in Philadelphia, becoming professor of cognate languages in 1923. He served as editor of the Jewish Publication Society of America from 1916 to 1924. He published studies of Hebrew and Arabic, an anthology of post-biblical Hebrew literature, and a catalog of documents from the Cairo Genizah.

Halpern, Leivick *see* LEIVICK, H.

Halprin, Rose Luria (1896–1978). American Zionist leader. She was born in New York. She served as president of the women's Zionist organization Hadassah from 1932 to 1934 and 1947 to 1951. From 1934 to 1939 she was Hadassah's correspondent in Palestine. In 1947 she was elected to the Executive of the Jewish Agency for Israel, on which she served for over 20 years; in 1968 she became chairman of the American section of the Jewish Agency.

Halter, Marek (b. 1932). French artist and writer. Born in Warsaw, he escaped from the Warsaw Ghetto and lived in Soviet Uzbekistan. In 1945 he returned to Poland, but later moved to Paris, where he was appointed director of the Centre du Judaisme. His writings include *The Book of Abraham.*

Ḥalukkah ("distribution"). Financial support given to the inhabitants of Palestine by Jews in the diaspora. This type of charity flourished during the period of the tannaim, and from the 13th century the Jewish academies established in Palestine were supported in this fashion. Those sent from Palestine to collect money were known as "meshullaḥim" or "shadarim"; during the 17th and 18th century such emissaries were sent from Jerusalem, Hebron, Safed, and Tiberias. The system of ḥalukkah continued into the 20th century.

Ḥalutz ("pioneer"). Word used particularly of Jewish settlers in Palestine before the establishment of the State of Israel.

Halvah. Middle Eastern sweetmeat of which sesame is a principal ingredient.

Ham. Son of Noah. Because of his unseemly behavior toward Noah, his descendants, the Canaanites, were cursed and condemned to servitude (Genesis 9.20ff.). He was the father of Cush, Put, Mizraim, and Canaan.

Ha-Mabbit. Austrian Hebrew weekly literary journal. It was edited by Peretz Smolenskin in Vienna from February to October 1878.

Hamadān. City in western Iran. It has been identified with Ecbatana, where Cyrus II issued his decree permitting the Jews to rebuild the Temple in Jerusalem (Ezra 6.2). According to tradition, Hamadan was founded by Queen Sushan-Dukht, the Jewish wife of Yazdegerd I, in the 5th century. Later it became one of the cultural centers of Persian Jewry.

Ha-Maggid. The first Hebrew newspaper, it was founded in 1856 in Lyck under the editorship of Eliezer Lipmann Silbermann. It appeared weekly until it ceased publication in 1903. It supported the Haskalah and was the first organ of Ḥibbat Zion.

Ha-Makom yenaḥem ("May God comfort you"). Opening words of the expression of consolation addressed to mourners before they leave the cemetery after a burial. The formula is also used by visitors to a house of mourning during Shivah when taking leave of the mourners.

Haman. Persian official in the court of Ahasuerus. He plotted to kill all Jews, but his plans were defeated by Esther. He was hanged on a gallows which he had prepared for Mordecai. He became the object of hatred among the Jews, and a symbol of villainy. The story of these events is recorded in the Book of Esther, and in memory of them the Jews celebrate the festival of Purim.

Hamantash (Yiddish: "Haman's hat"). Triangular cake filled with poppy seeds or prune jelly. It is eaten during Purim.

Ha-Mavdil [Mavdil] ("The one who distinguishes"). Hymn sung in the Havdalah ceremony at the close of the Sabbath. It begins: "May he who makes a distinction between holy and profane pardon our sins; may he multiply our offspring as the sand and as the stars in the night." It was probably composed for the concluding service of the Day of Atonement.

Hamburg. City in northern Germany on the River Elbe. Wealthy Marranos from Spain and Portugal lived there in the 16th century. In the 17th century the three neighboring Ashkenazi congregations of Hamburg, Altona, and Wandsbeck were united. Important Jewish scholars lived there from the 17th century.

Hamburger, Jacob (1826–1911). German rabbi and scholar. He was born in Poland and served as a rabbi in Neustadt and Mecklenburg-Strelitz. His *Real-Encyklopaedie für Bibel und Talmud* was later expanded into a three volume *Real-Encyklopaedie des Judentums.*

Hamburger, Michael (b. 1924). British poet. He went to England in childhood as a refugee from Nazi Germany. His works include *Treblinka.*

Ha-Measseph. German Hebrew monthly journal; it was the first secular Hebrew monthly. It was founded at Königsberg in 1783 by young maskilim and was subsequently published in Berlin, Altona, Dessau, and Breslau. It gave the name "Meassephim" to a literary school of the Jewish Enlightenment. It ceased publication in 1829.

Ha-Meiri [Feuerstein]**, Avigdor** (1890–1970). Israeli poet, novelist, and translator. He was born in the Carpathian region of Russia and settled in Palestine in 1921. He published poems, stories, translations, and critical articles. His writings include *The Great Madness* and *Hell Below.*

Hamelin, Glückel of *see* GLÜCKEL OF HAMELIN.

Ha-Melitz. Russian Hebrew weekly newspaper; it was the first Hebrew paper in Russia. It was founded by Alexander Zederbaum in Odessa in 1860. In 1871 it transferred to St. Petersburg, where it appeared until 1904. It advocated Haskalah, Jewish agricultural settlement in Russia, occupation in trades, and educational advancement, and upheld religious values. Later it became the organ of Ḥibbat Zion in Russia.

Ḥametz *see* LEAVEN.

Ha-Mevasser (i). Galician Hebrew weekly journal. It appeared in Lemberg from 1861 to 1866.

Ha-Mevasser (ii). Hebrew political and literary weekly. It was edited by Vladimir Jabotinsky and appeared in Constantinople in 1910–11.

Ḥamishah Aser bi-Shevat *see* FIFTEENTH OF SHEVAT.

***Hammurabi** (fl. 18th cent. BCE). Babylonian king (1792–1750 BCE). There are important resemblances between his legal code and biblical legislation.

Hamnuna (fl. 4th cent.). Babylonian amora. He was born in Harpania in Babylonia and lived in Harta of Argiz near Baghdad. He was a pupil and colleague of Ḥisda.

Hamnuna Saba (fl. 3rd cent.). Babylonian amora. He was a pupil of Rav and succeeded him as head of the academy at Sura.

Hamnuna Zuta (fl. 4th cent.). Babylonian amora. His confession of sin, which he recited on the Day of Atonement, is included in the liturgy for this holy day.

Ha-Motzi [Motzi] ("Who brings forth"). Title of the blessing over bread. The blessing is: "Blessed art thou o Lord our

God, king of the universe, who brings forth bread from the earth."

Ha-Nagid *see* SAMUEL IBN NAGRELA.

Hanamel (fl. 1st cent. BCE). Israelite high priest (37–36 BCE, and again in 34 BCE). He was born in Egypt. He was appointed high priest by Herod who passed over Aristobulus III, the brother of Mariamne. Owing to the protests of Alexandra and Mariamne, Herod deposed Hanamel and appointed Aristobulus III. But after Aristobulus was murdered, Hanamel was restored to office.

Hananel ben Ḥushiel (d. 1055). Babylonian rabbinic scholar. He was born in Kairovan. He was given the title "chief among the rabbis" by the Babylonian academies. He wrote commentaries on the Babylonian Talmud and the Pentateuch.

Hananiah (fl. 2nd cent.). Babylonian tanna. In his youth he lived in Palestine, but later he settled in Babylonia, where he remained until his death. He was the greatest scholar in Palestine at the time of the Hadrianic persecutions. He established the calendar in exile, which was followed by the Jews of Babylonia. After Hadrian's death, the Sanhedrin was reconstituted and called on him to recognize its authority. He agreed and exhorted all Babylonian congregations to recognize the Palestinian Sanhedrin.

Hananiah ben Ḥakhinai (fl. 2nd cent.). Babylonian tanna. He lived in Palestine and was one of those who debated before the sages in Jabneh. He studied with Akiva in Bene-Berak for 12 years. Later he resided in Sidon. According to tradition, he was one of the Ten Martyrs under the Hadrianic persecutions.

Hananiah ben Teradyon (fl. 2nd cent.). Babylonian tanna. He was head of the yeshivah of Siknin in Galilee. He was sentenced to death for teaching the Torah in defiance of Hadrian's decree forbidding religious instruction. He was burned at the stake wrapped in a Torah scroll.

Ha-Natziv *see* BERLIN, NAPHTALI TZEVI JUDAH.

Handler, Simon *see* HEVESI, SIMON.

Hanging. According to the rabbis hanging was not used as a method of capital punishment but only as a posthumous ignominy. This treatment was applied only to a person executed for blasphemy or idolatry, and the body was to be buried on the same day.

Ḥanina bar Ḥama (fl. 3rd cent.). Palestinian scholar. He was born in Babylonia and emigrated to Palestine, settling in Sepphoris, where he was a pupil of Judah ha-Nasi. He earned a living by trading in honey, and also practiced medicine. He was a noted aggadist.

Ḥanina ben Dosa (fl. 1st cent.). Palestinian tanna. He lived in extreme poverty and was noted for his piety and his ability to perform miracles; his prayers for the sick had great efficacy. According to tradition, a divine voice proclaimed daily: "The whole world is fed by the merits of Ḥanina my son, but Ḥanina himself is satisfied with a measure of carobs from one Sabbath eve to the next."

Ḥankin, Yehoshua (1864–1945). Palestinian Zionist pioneer. He was born in the Ukraine and went to Palestine in 1882. In 1897 he negotiated for the purchase of land in the Jezreel Valley, but not until 1909 was the sale completed. In 1915 he was exiled to Anatolia by the Turkish authorities, but he returned to Palestine three years later. In 1920 he purchased a second tract of land in the Jezreel Valley, on which many agricultural settlements were established. From 1932 he served as director of the Palestine Land Development Corporation. He wrote *Jewish Colonization in Palestine*.

Hannah (fl. 11th cent. BCE). Israelite

woman, wife of Elkanah and mother of Samuel. She was barren and in praying for a child she vowed to dedicate any son she had to the Temple. When her son Samuel was born she left him with Eli the priest to serve in the Temple. (I Samuel 1–2)

Hannah and her seven sons *see* MACCABEES (i).

Hannover, Nathan Nata (fl. 17th cent.). Polish preacher, kabbalist, lexicographer, and chronicler. During the Chmielnicki massacres, he left his birthplace in Volhynia and wandered through Poland, Germany, and the Netherlands. In 1653 he went to Italy. In 1662 he was appointed president of the bet din and head of the yeshivah in Jassy, Walachia. Later he moved to Moravia. He published sermons, a Hebrew–German–Latin–Italian lexicon, a kabbalistic prayerbook, and an account of the Chmielnicki persecutions.

Ha-Noar ha-Oved ("Working youth"). Israeli youth movement. It was founded in Palestine in 1926, as part of the Histadrut, to foster educational activities among working youth and improve their wages and working conditions. It first kibbutz was established in 1933. In 1959 it merged with an organization called Habonim-ha-Tenuah ha-Meuḥedet.

Ha-Noar ha-Tziyyoni ("Zionist youth"). International Zionist youth movement. It was founded in eastern Europe and in the early 1930s was established as an international organization with headquarters in Poland. During this period it organized kibbutzim in Palestine. After the creation of the State of Israel its members helped to form the Progressive Party.

Ha-noten teshuah ("He who gives salvation"). Opening words of the PRAYER FOR GOVERNMENT recited during the Sabbath and festival morning service.

Ḥanukkah ("Dedication") [Feast of Lights]. Eight-day festival (starting on 25 Kislev) commemorating the victory of Judah Maccabee over Antiochus Epiphanes and the rededication of the Temple. It is associated with the miracle of the cruse of oil which kept the candelabrum burning for eight days in the Temple. During the festival one light is kindled every night in an eight-branched menorah until all eight are burning.

Ha-Olam. Hebrew weekly journal. A central organ of the World Zionist Organization, it was published from 1907 to 1950. It appeared in Cologne (1907–8), Vilnius (1908–12), Odessa (1912–14), London (1919–20, 1924–36), Berlin (1923–4), and Jerusalem (1936–50).

Ha-Oved ha-Tziyyoni ("The Zionist worker") [Liberal Workers Movement]. Israeli labor movement. It was founded as a faction of Histadrut in 1935 by pioneer immigrants from eastern Europe who belonged to the General Zionists youth movement. In 1948 it helped to establish the Progressive Party, and it later became part of the Independent Liberal Party.

Hapamim *see* SHEWBREAD.

Hapax legomenon (Greek: "word used only once"). Term applied to a word of which only one use is recorded. There are about 1300 in the Bible. Saadya ben Joseph and other medieval grammarians wrote studies of them.

Ḥaphetz Ḥayyim [Cahan [Kahan], Israel Meir] (1835–1933). Lithuanian talmudist and communal leader. He was born in Poland and became one of the leaders of eastern European Orthodox Jewry. He founded and was the head of a yeshivah at Radin, Lithuania, and was active in Agudat Israel. The name by which he is commonly known derives from his ethical and religious treatise *Ḥaphetz Ḥayyim*.

Haphtarah ("conclusion"). Section from the prophetic books of the Bible read in the synagogue on the Sabbath, festivals, and the afternoon of fast days after the reading from the Torah. The haphtarah is chosen because of its relevance to the Torah portion or the specific festival. It is chanted according to a system of cantillation and benedictions are read before and after it.

Ha-Poel ("The worker"). Israeli workers' sports organization. Affiliated to the Histadrut, it was founded as an association in 1926. It sponsors sports championships and organizes recreation and sporting activities at places of work.

Ha-Poel ha-Mizraḥi. Religious Zionist labor movement. It was established in Palestine by religious pioneers in 1922 in order to cultivate the land and inspire religious practice. It began as part of the Mizraḥi movement, and established employment bureaus, welfare institutions, economic enterprises, and cooperative settlements. It formed part of most Israeli coalition governments from 1948. In 1955 it amalgamated with Mizraḥi.

Ha-Poel ha-Tzair (i). Palestinian Zionist labor party. Founded in 1905, it encouraged agricultural settlement and the rights of Jewish labor, but opposed the class struggle. In 1930 the party merged with Aḥdut ha-Avodah to form Mapai.

Ha-Poel ha-Tzair (ii). Israeli newspaper of the labor movement; it was the first labor paper in Palestine. Founded in 1907, it ceased publication in 1970.

Ha-Raḥaman *see* GOD, NAMES OF.

Haran (i) (fl. ?19th–16th cent. BCE). Israelite, brother of Abraham. He lived at Ur of the Chaldees (Genesis 11.26–31).

Haran (ii). Ancient town in north-west Mesopotamia. It is mentioned in Genesis in connection with the patriarchs. Assyrian inscriptions mention a settlement of the Habiru people in the vicinity of Haran.

Harby, Isaac (1788–1828). American writer, teacher, and Reform leader. He was born in Charleston, South Carolina, and worked on various newspapers there. He helped to establish the Reformed Society of the Israelites, of which he became president in 1827.

Ha-Reuveni, Ephraim (1881–1953). Israeli botanist. He was born in the Ukraine and settled in Palestine in 1906. He founded the Museum of Biblical and Talmudical Flora in 1912 which was later transferred to the Hebrew University; he was appointed lecturer in biblical botany at the Hebrew University in 1935. He published (with his wife Ḥannah) studies of the flora of Palestine.

Harkavy, Albert (1835–1919). Russian orientalist. He was born in Belorussia. He became head of the department of Jewish literature and oriental manuscripts at the Imperial Library in St. Petersburg in 1877. He published studies of the Khazars, the Karaites, and the history and languages of Russian Jewry. His writings on the ancient Jewish tombstones in the Crimea exposed the fabrications of Abraham Firkovich.

Harkavy, Alexander (1863–1939). American Yiddish lexicographer and writer. He was born in Belorussia and emigrated to the US in 1881. He first joined a collective agricultural colony, but after it failed he lived in numerous cities, including Paris, New York, Montreal, and Baltimore. He published textbooks and dictionaries for immigrants, including the *Yiddish–English–Hebrew Dictionary*.

Ḥaroset. Paste made of fruit, spices, wine, and matzah meal, eaten at the Passover seder. The bitter herb is dipped into ḥaroset to make it less harsh. Ḥaroset symbolizes the mortar which the Israelites used during their slavery in Egypt.

Har-Shalom *see* FRIEDBERG, ABRAHAM SHALOM.

Hart, Aaron (1670–1756). British rabbi.

He was born in Breslau. He emigrated to England and was appointed rabbi of the Ashkenazi community in London in 1705. He is regarded as the first chief rabbi of Great Britain. His *Urim ve-Tummim* (1707) was the first book printed entirely in Hebrew in London.

Hartog, Numa Edward (1846–1871). English mathematician. He was senior wrangler in mathematics at Cambridge. His inability to graduate because of his Jewish origin occasioned the abolition of religious tests imposed on university students in England.

Harvest festivals. In biblical times there were three harvest festivals: the Omer festival during Passover, when the offering of barley flour was brought to the Temple; Shavuot, the festival of the first fruits ("bikkurim") seven weeks later when the wheat ripened; and Sukkot, the feast of the ingathering, which concluded the entire harvest.

Ḥasdai *see* IBN ḤASDAI, ABRAHAM BEN SAMUEL HA-LEVI.

Ḥasdai Crescas *see* CRESCAS, ḤASDAI BEN ABRAHAM.

Ḥasdai ibn Shaprut *see* IBN SHAPRUT, ḤASDAI.

Ha-Shaḥar. Austrian Hebrew journal. It was published and edited in Vienna by Peretz Smolenskin from 1868 to 1884. It awakened Zionist consciousness among the maskilim and contributed to the development of Hebrew literature.

Ha-Shem ("the name"). Term referring to God, used to avoid mentioning his name. It is found in phrases such as "Barukh ha-Shem" (Blessed be God), "Be ezrat ha-Shem" (With the help of God), and "Im yirtze ha-Shem" (God willing).

Ha-Shiloaḥ. Hebrew literary, social, and scientific monthly. Founded by Kalonymos Ze'ev Wissotzky in 1896, it was first edited by Aḥad ha-Am in Odessa and printed in Berlin and Kraków until after the Russian revolution of 1905. From 1907 to 1919 it was edited and printed in Odessa, and from 1920 to 1926 in Jerusalem. The journal was devoted to Zionism, Jewish scholarship, and belles lettres.

Hashkamah ("early rising"). Early morning service held before the official morning prayers.

Hashkava (*lit.* "lay to rest"). The name given by the Sephardim to the memorial prayer. It corresponds to the Yizkor prayer in the Ashkenazi rite.

Hashkivenu ("Cause us to lie down [in peace]"). Opening word of the second benediction following the evening Shema. It is a prayer for protection and peace during the night.

Ha-Shomer. Association of Jewish watchmen in Palestine, active between 1909 and 1920. It was founded by pioneers who had been involved in revolutionary movements and Jewish self-defense in Russia. It defended Jewish settlements and struggled for the employment of Jewish workers. Its members spoke Arabic, wore Arab and Circassian dress, and carried modern weapons; they played an important role in the life of the yishuv. Later its functions were taken over by the Haganah.

Ha-Shomer ha-Dati. Religious pioneering youth movement. Founded in Warsaw in 1929, it was active in eastern Europe and the US. It was affiliated with Ha-Poel ha-Mizraḥi, and later become incorporated into Bene Akiva.

Ha-Shomer ha-Tzair. Zionist-socialist youth organization. Established in Galicia in 1913, it was reorganized in Vienna in 1917. Its members were influenced by revolutionary ferment, German youth movements, and the activities of Ha-Shomer. Many of them emigrated to Palestine in 1919–21 and espoused Marxist ideals. In the diaspora, the movement adopted scouting practices and prepared for pioneering activities. It advocated the joint organization of Arab and Jewish workers, and favored a binational state to solve the Palestinian problem. In 1948 it participated in the formation of Mapam.

Hasideans. Religious sect active in Palestine during the persecutions of Antiochus Epiphanes in the 2nd century BCE. Its members suffered martyrdom rather than desecrate the Sabbath. They were involved in the Hasmonean revolt, but ceased to support the Maccabees when their political aims became clear. Some scholars believe that they were the antecedents of the Pharisees.

Ḥaside Ashkenaz ("Pious men of Germany"). German medieval religious movement. The first centers of the movement were Regensburg and the communities of Speyer, Worms, and Mainz. Its central figures included Samuel ben Kalonymus he-Ḥasid, his son Judah ben Samuel he-Ḥasid, and Eleazar ben Judah of Worms. The teachings of these pietists (Ḥasidim) are collected in *Sepher Ḥasidim*. They advocated asceticism and the expurgation of sin by doing penance and practicing physical mortifications and fasting. They fostered humility by rejecting honors and accepting insults. They based their moral judgments on ethical considerations rather than strictly talmudic teaching.

Ḥaside umot ha-olam ("pious ones of the nations of the world"). Expression used to designate righteous gentiles who have a share in the world to come. According to Maimonides, these are the pious gentiles who adhere to the seven Noachian Laws.

Ḥasidism. Religious and social movement founded by the Baal Shem Tov in Volhynia and Podolia in the 18th century. He taught that all are equal before God, purity of the heart is superior to study, and devotion to prayer and God's commandments is of fundamental importance. He was succeeded by Dov Ber of Mezhirich, who systematized Ḥasidic teaching. Although the Ḥasidim were bitterly opposed by the talmudists (mitnaggedim), the movement spread throughout eastern Europe and beyond. The great centers of Ḥasidism were wiped out during World War II, but several dynasties emigrated to the US, among them the Lubavicher and the Satmar. They established their own training colleges and schools, and through them the movement continues to exert an important influence on world Jewry.

Haskalah ("Enlightenment") [Maskil]. Hebrew social, spiritual, and literary movement, which developed in the last quarter of the 18th century and continued to around 1880. It began in Germany and spread to Austria, Poland, and Russia. Its proponents (maskilim) believed that the Jews should reform their schools, learn the language of the land in which they lived, increase their knowledge of secular subjects, and adopt the manners of their gentile neighbors. The movement was challenged by leaders of orthodox Jewry, who regarded such innovations as a threat to the Jewish tradition.

Haskamah ("approbation"). Authorization prefixed to Hebrew books. Its use was established after the decision of the rabbinical synod of Ferrara in 1554 that Hebrew books should be approved by local Jewish authorities so as to avoid censorship by the civil authorities. Later the Haskamah was sought by an author as a seal of approval for his scholarship and the orthodoxy of his writings. Among the Sephardim, the term has come to refer to a communal regulation.

Hasmoneans. Priestly dynasty founded in the 2nd century BCE by Mattathias of Modiin. He and his five sons (Judah Maccabee, Jonathan, Simon, John, and Eleazar) led a revolt against the Hellenizing policy of Antiochus Epiphanes.

In 164 BCE they captured Jerusalem and rededicated the Temple. The Hasmonean dynasty of rulers lasted until 37 BCE.

Ḥasseneh. Wedding.

Ḥas ve-shalom ("Forebear and [hold] your peace"). Expression of apprehension used to restrain another from discussing an unwanted event.

Ha-Talmi, Yehoshua *see* RABBI BINYAMIN.

Ḥatam Sopher *see* SOPHER, MOSES.

Ḥatan. Bridegroom.

Ḥatan Bereshit *see* SIMḤAT TORAH.

Ḥatan Torah *see* SIMḤAT TORAH.

Ḥataph. In Hebrew a phonetic sign, consisting of two vertically placed dots, used to modify vowels. It appears alone to give a short "e" or to shorten other vowel sounds (ḥataph patah; ḥataph segol; ḥataph kamatz).

Ha-Tekuphah. Hebrew literary, scientific, and social journal. It appeared between 1918 and 1950. Volumes 1–3 were published in Moscow, volumes 4–23 in Warsaw, 24–5 in Berlin, 26–9 in Tel Aviv, and 30–35 in New York.

Ha Tenuah ha-Meuḥedet. Israeli pioneering youth movement. It was organized in 1950 by Mapai supporters who had split from Maḥanot ha-Olim. It joined the international Ha-Bonim organization in 1951.

Ha-Tikvah ("Hope"). Anthem of the Zionist movement and national anthem of the State of Israel. The poem was written by Naphtali Herz Imber in 1878 and was first published in 1886. The words are:

As long as deep in the heart
The soul of a Jew yearns,
And towards the East
An eye looks to Zion,
Our hope is not yet lost,
The hope of two thousand years,
To be a free people in our land,
The land of Zion and Jerusalem.

The melody echoes a Sephardi hymn and a tune in Smetana's *Vltava*.

Ha-Toren. American Hebrew journal. It was published in New York between 1913 and 1925. Its editors included Shemaryahu Levin, Yitzḥak Dov Berkovitz, Reuben Brainin, and Simon Bernstein. It dealt with current issues and literary topics.

Hatraah ("warning"). The Talmud stipulates that a person may not be sentenced to capital or corporal punishment for a crime unless a warning has previously been given against committing the crime. This legislation was enacted to ensure that the person sentenced was being punished for an act committed willfully. If no specific warning had been given, the sentence was commuted to imprisonment.

Hatred. Scripture commands that a person should not hate another (Leviticus 19.17). However, hatred of evildoers and enemies of God is allowed. The rabbis emphasized the duty of hating the sin rather than the sinner.

Hattarat Horaah *see* ORDINATION.

Ḥatta't *see* SIN OFFERING.

Hatvani, Lajos (1880–1961). Hungarian writer, literary critic, and journalist. He was born in Budapest. He was a founder of the literary periodical *Nyugat* and served as the editor of the journal *Pesti Napló* before and during World War I. At the outbreak of the Communist Revolution in 1919 he went to Vienna, but he later returned to Budapest. He spent World War II in England and returned to Hungary in 1947. In his writings he dealt with the problem of the Hungarian attitude toward the Jews, as well as Jewish assimilation and nationalism.

Ha-Tzephirah. Polish Hebrew journal. It was founded by Ḥayyim Selig Slonimski and appeared in Warsaw from 1862 to 1931. In 1879 Naḥum Sokolow joined the editorial board and in 1904 became the journal's editor. The aim of *Ha-Tzephirah* was to disseminate knowledge of the natural sciences and mathematics in Hebrew circles. After World War I it became the organ of the Polish Zionist organization.

Ha-Tzevi. Palestinian Hebrew journal. It appeared in Jerusalem from 1884 to 1900 and in 1909–10 under the editorship of Eliezer Ben-Yehudah. It opposed religious fanaticism and encouraged the use of spoken Hebrew. It was the first modern political journal in Palestine.

Ha-Tzohar *see* REVISIONISM.

Ha-Tzopheh (i). Polish Hebrew daily newspaper. It appeared in Warsaw between 1903 and 1905.

Ha-Tzopheh (ii). Israeli daily newspaper. It was founded by Meir Bar-Ilan in Tel Aviv in 1937. It became an organ of Mizraḥi and Ha-Poel ha Mizraḥi.

Ha-Tzopheh ba-Eretz ha-Ḥadashah. American Hebrew journal. It was the first Hebrew periodical published in the US. It was founded and edited by Tzevi Hirsch Bernstein and appeared between 1871 and 1876.

Ha-Tzopheh le-Ḥokhmat Israel. Hungarian Hebrew scholarly quarterly. Edited by Ludwig Blau, it appeared in Budapest from 1921 to 1931.

Ḥavatzelet. Palestinian Hebrew periodical. It first appeared in Jerusalem in 1863 and renewed publication in 1870; from 1873 its editor was Israel Dov Frumkin. Initially it opposed fanaticism and the ḥalukkah system, and from the mid-1880s it rejected Zionist settlement on religious grounds. It ceased publication in 1911.

Havdalah ("Differentiation"). Ceremony marking the termination of the Sabbath. It consists of blessings recited over wine, spices, and flame. The central blessing refers to the distinctions between the holy and profane, light and darkness, Israel and the nations, and the Sabbath and the other days of the week.

Ḥaver ("companion"). In the Talmud the term refers to the individual members of associations of pietists who appeared in the 2nd century BCE. They ate only tithed produce, strictly observed laws of ritual purity, and kept apart from the am haaretz. Subsequently the term came to refer to rabbinic scholars. It is now used to denote a friend.

Havlagah ("self-restraint"). Name given to the policy adopted by the Jewish Agency and the Haganah during the Arab revolt of 1936–9 in Palestine. It involved self-defense and forbade attacks on Arabs not known to be implicated in the outbreaks.

Ḥavurah kaddisha *see* ḤEVRA KADDISHA.

Ha-Yom. Russian Hebrew daily newspaper. It was the first paper of its kind in Russia. It appeared in St. Petersburg from 1886 to 1888, and was published and edited by Judah Leib Kantor with the assistance of David Frischmann and Judah Löb Katzenelson.

Ḥayyim ben Isaac of Volozhin (1749–1821). Lithuanian talmudist. After the death of the Vilna Gaon, he became the leader of Lithuanian Jewry. He founded the Volozhin yeshivah in 1802 to counteract the influence of the Ḥasidim and the Haskalah movement.

Ḥayyon, Nehemiah (c. 1655–c. 1730). Kabbalist. He was born in Safed and became a rabbi at Uskub. Later he wandered from place to place and eventually joined the Sabbetaian movement. He then lived in Italy, Prague, and Berlin. He published kabbalistic studies, and advocated a new form of Sabbetaianism based on the doctrine of the Trinity, comprising the First Cause, the Infinite, and the Holy Father (who was identified with Shabbetai Tzevi). He was involved in a controversy in Amsterdam, and his works were criticized and banned by European rabbis. He finally settled in north Africa.

Ḥayyuj, Judah ben David (c. 945–c. 1000). Spanish Hebrew grammarian. He was born in Fez but arrived in Córdoba in 960 and lived most of his life in Spain. He wrote a study of Hebrew punctuation, a philological commentary on the biblical books from Joshua to Ezekiel, and two treatises on Hebrew verbs. A translation of his grammatical works from Arabic into Hebrew by Moses Gikatilla was the first of its kind.

***Hazael** (fl. 9th–8th cent. BCE). Syrian King of Aram-Damascus (c. 842–798 BCE). He usurped the throne from Ben-Hadad II (II Kings 8.7–15) and attacked Israel, injuring Joram (II Kings 8.28–9). He later overran the entire territory of Israel. He threatened Jerusalem, retreating from the city only on the payment of a tribute by Joash, King of Judah (II Kings 12.19; II Chronicles 24.23–4).

Ḥazak ("Be strong"). Greeting. It is based on Moses' address to Joshua: "Be strong and of good courage" (Deuteronomy 31.7; 31.23). At the Torah reading in the synagogue a full version is recited when one of the Five Books of Moses is completed ("Be strong, be strong, and let us be strengthened"). In the Sephardi rite the person who returns to his seat after having been called up to the reading of the Torah is greeted with the expression: "Be strong and blessed."

Ḥazakah ("taking hold"). Legal term expressing (1) the mode of acquiring ownership; (2) the means of proving ownership or property rights; (3) the presumption of the existence of particular facts. In the first case ḥazakah creates a new legal reality; in the latter two cases it is instrumental in proving or presuming an already existing state of affairs.

Ḥazal. Word formed by the initials of the phrase "Hakhameinu zikhronam li-verakhah" ("our sages of blessed memory"). This expression refers to the teachers of the talmudic period.

Hazammah *see* FALSE WITNESS.

Ḥazars *see* KHAZARS.

Hazaz, Ḥayyim (1898–1973). Israeli writer. He was born in Zidorovichi and in his youth moved from one Russian city to another. During and after the Russian Revolution, he worked on the Hebrew daily *Ha-Am* in Moscow. In 1921 he went to Constantinople, and then lived in Paris and Berlin. He emigrated to Palestine in 1931 and settled in Jerusalem. In his novels he depicted Jewish life in different eras in various countries.

Ḥazer. Swine, objectionable person.

Ḥazon Ish *see* KARLITZ, AVRAHAM YESHAYAHU.

Hazor. Ancient city in Upper Galilee. Jabin, King of Hazor, led the forces of a league of Canaanite cities against Joshua, who burned Hazor (Joshua 11.10–13). It was later rebuilt by Solomon (I Kings 9.15). In 732 BCE it was conquered by Tiglath-Pileser III (II Kings 15.29).

Ḥazzan. Title given at different times to those performing certain liturgical or communal functions. In talmudic times the ḥazzan was a communal official, who performed certain duties in the synagogue. During the period of the geonim the term was used of the permanent representative of the congregation ("sheliaḥ tzibbur"). When piyyutim became part of the liturgy, the ḥazzan was the one who recited them and provided suitable melodies. In the Middle Ages the role developed into that of leading and chanting the service and the title became synonymous with CANTOR.

Ḥazzanut *see* CANTOR.

He. Fifth letter of the Hebrew alphabet. Its numerical value is 5. As an abbreviation, the letter stands for the name of God.

Health. The biblical command "Only take heed to yourself and keep your soul diligently" (Deuteronomy 4.9) is understood as enjoining care for one's health and physical well-being. Rabbinic law prohibits actions that endanger health (*see* DANGER). Many Jewish laws contribute to physical welfare and HYGIENE, for example those forbidding any mutilation of the body such as tattooing.

Heathen *see* GENTILE.

Heaven [Paradise] (Hebrew "Gan Eden"). The abode of God, where he is surrounded by his court and by the souls of the righteous. In the Bible the location of Heaven is said to be the upper part of the universe, or the firmament dividing the upper from the lower waters. Later the word came to be used as a cognate for "God" (as is reflected by such expressions as "the fear of Heaven," "the kingdom of Heaven," "for the sake of Heaven"). Rabbinic literature refers to a plurality of heavens, where the various orders of the angelic host reside. It is the place where the righteous ascend after death. *See also* KINGDOM OF HEAVEN.

Heave offering. Offering made to the Sanctuary or to the priests. It refers to tithes, to the dough offering made to the priests (*see* ḤALLAH (i)), and to the half-shekel that had to be contributed to the Sanctuary.

Hebraists, Christian. Christian scholars and theologians have studied Hebrew for various purposes from the early days of the church. Jerome knew Hebrew and consulted Jews when he was preparing the Vulgate version of the Bible. In the Middle Ages the Dominicans encouraged the study of Hebrew as an aid in their controversies with Jews. The Franciscan Nicholas de Lyra used the works of the French scholar Rashi in his biblical commentaries. In 1305 the Council of Vienna established chairs of Hebrew at several universities, and during the Renaissance Italian humanists began to study Hebrew. In Germany reformers advocated the study of Hebrew as an instrument for the understanding of the Bible. From the 17th century numerous Christian Hebrew scholars appeared in Europe, Britain, and the US.

Hebrew. Hebrew belongs to the Canaanite branch of Semitic languages. It was used by the ancient Israelites until about 500 years after the Babylonian exile. Mishnaic Hebrew, an altered form of biblical Hebrew, was used by the tannaim from the 2nd century BCE to the 2nd century CE. Eventually it was superseded by Aramaic and Greek. In about 500 a literary revival of Hebrew began, which lasted throughout the Middle Ages. From 900 to 1400 Jews in north-western Europe wrote in Hebrew, while in Muslim countries (including Spain) Arabic was used; in eastern Europe Jews spoke and wrote in Yiddish. Though Hebrew continued in use as a religious language, for other purposes Jews used the vernacular. The Haskalah revived the use of Hebrew, and it was later adopted as the language of modern Israel. *See also* ALPHABET; SCRIPT.

Hebrew Academy *see* HISTADRUT IVRITH OF AMERICA.

Hebrew Immigration Aid Society *see* HIAS.

Hebrew Language Council *see* VAAD HA-LASHON HA-IVRIT.

Hebrew literature. Biblical literature embraces various types of literary form, including narrative, poetry, prophecy, and law. During the second Temple period, the related writings collected together as the Apocrypha and Pseudepigrapha appeared. In the tannaitic and amoraic periods (roughly covering the 2nd century BCE to the 5th century CE) rabbinic literature consisted of the Mishnah, midrash, the Tosephta, and the Palestinian and Babylonian Talmuds. In the gaonic period (6th–12th centuries) much Hebrew writing took the form of legal lectures, collections, and inquiries; liturgical poems (piyyutim) and collections of midrashim were also written. Medieval rabbinic scholars wrote studies of grammar and works of lexicography, poetry, exegesis, philosophy, science, and mysticism. The modern period witnessed an efflorescence of Hebrew literature by followers of the Haskalah, and Hebrew was used for writings of every kind. With the establishment of the State of Israel, modern Hebrew became the literary language of the country.

Hebrews. Name given to various groups of Jews. In the Bible it is used of the descendants of Eber, grandson of Shem (Genesis 10.24), and of the people who came from beyond the River Euphrates. Abraham is referred to as "the Hebrew" (Genesis 14.13). Later the term was used interchangeably with "Israelites" (Exodus 9.1). Some scholars identify the people known as Habiru with the Hebrews. The word "Hebrew" was frequently used in place of "Jew" in the 19th century, but in Europe "Israelite" was more common.

Hebrew Teachers College. American college for Jewish studies. It was founded in Boston in 1921 under the deanship of Nissan Touroff. In 1951 it moved to Brookline, Massachusetts. It maintains a high school, a department of adult studies, and an undergraduate program.

Hebrew Theological College. American Orthodox rabbinical school. It was founded in Chicago in 1922 as an extension of the Hebrew high school Yeshiva Etz Chaim. It was the first rabbinical school to require courses in the Bible and Jewish philosophy and history, in addition to rabbinics.

Hebrew Union College. American Reform rabbinical seminary. It was founded in Cincinnati in 1875 by Isaac Mayer Wise. In 1950 it combined with the Jewish Institute of Religion in New York (founded 1922). A Los Angeles branch was chartered in 1954, and a Jerusalem campus opened in 1963. The college trains rabbis, offers a doctoral program in various aspects of Jewish studies, and confers degrees in Jewish music, religious education, and communal service.

Hebrew University. Israeli university. The proposal to establish a Hebrew university was made by Hermann Tzevi Schapira at the First Zionist Congress in 1897. In 1914 an area of land was purchased on Mount Scopus to the east of Jerusalem, and the foundation stones were laid in 1918. The university was officially opened in 1925. From 1925 to 1935 Judah Leon Magnus served as chancellor. The university has faculties in many fields, now housed on several sites. It grants undergraduate and graduate degrees in a wide variety of subjects.

Hebron. Ancient city of Judah. Abraham bought a plot of land in Hebron (the cave of Machpelah) in which to bury Sarah (Genesis 13.18). The city was assigned by Joshua to Caleb, and subsequently became a Levitical city and a city of refuge (Joshua 20.7). David reigned there before transferring the capital to Jerusalem (II Samuel 2.11).

***Hechler, William H.** (1845–1931). British Zionist. He was born in Benares, India. After serving as a missionary in Lagos, Nigeria, he became the tutor of the children of Friedrich Grand Duke of Baden. He was then appointed chaplain to the British embassy in Vienna (1885) and remained there until 1910. He eventually settled in London. He attempted to establish a relationship between the grand duke and Theodor Herzl, and, through the grand duke, between Herzl and the German Kaiser, Wilhelm II. He wrote *The Restoration of the Jews to Palestine.*

Hecht, Ben (1893–1964). American novelist and playwright. Born in New York, he grew up in Racine, Wisconsin. He wrote plays and novels, including *Jew in Love*. In the 1940s he became an advocate of the Palestinian underground organization Irgun Tzevai Leumi. His *A Guide for the Bedeviled* is an analysis of anti-Semitism.

Ḥeder ("school"). The word is applied particularly to a school dedicated to teaching children the rudiments of Judaism. Many synagogues have a ḥeder attached to them.

Hedyot *see* LAYMAN.

He-Ḥalutz ("The pioneer"). International association of Jewish youth. Its aim was to train young people so as to fit them to settle in Israel. The first He-Ḥalutz group was founded in the US in 1915 by David Ben-Gurion and Yitzḥak Ben-Tzevi. In eastern Europe the association was inspired by Joseph Trumpeldor after World War I. A world organization was established in 1924. He-Ḥalutz supplied pioneer labor in Palestine, particularly in agriculture. In the 1920s and 1930s the pioneering ideal spread to affiliated youth movements.

Heidenheim, Wolf Benjamin (1757–1832). German Hebrew grammarian, masoretic scholar, exegete, and commentator on the liturgy. He was born in Heidenheim. In 1800 he published the first volume of a nine-volume edition of the maḥzor. He also published other works in the field of liturgy.

Heijermans, Hermann (1864–1924). Dutch playwright and novelist. He was born in Rotterdam. He published short stories, novels, and plays. In his play *Ahasverus* he expressed concern for the fate of Jewry. His novels *Sabbath* and *Diamantstad* and the play *Ghetto* contrast the narrowmindedness of the inhabitants of the Amsterdam Ghetto with the liberal attitudes of Dutch Christians.

Heikhal *see* HEKHAL.

Heilprin, Jehiel ben Solomon (1660–1746). Lithuanian talmudic scholar and historian. He served as a rabbi in Glussk, and in 1711 was appointed head of the yeshivah in Minsk. His *Seder ha-Dorot* contains a chronology of events and personages to 1696, an alphabetical list of tannaim and amoraim, and a catalog of post-talmudic Hebrew authors and books.

***Heine, Heinrich** (1797–1856). German poet and essayist. He was born in Düsseldorf and settled in Berlin, where he published his first book of poetry. Influenced by Moses Mendelssohn and Leopold Zunz, he joined the Society for the Culture and Science of Judaism. In 1825 he embraced Christianity, but later he expressed regret for leaving the Jewish faith. In many of his works, such as *The Rabbi of Bacherach* and *Hebrew Melodies*, he exhibited an interest in Judaism. He later lived in Paris, where he worked as a journalist and poet. He influenced the development of the Haskalah movement as well as Hebrew and Yiddish poetry.

Heinemann, Yitzḥak (1876–1957). Israeli humanist and philosopher. He was born in Frankfurt am Main. From 1919 to 1938 he lectured in Jewish philosophy and literature at the Jewish Theological Seminary in Breslau. In 1939 he settled in Jerusalem. His writings deal with Hellenistic and medieval Jewish philosophy.

Heir *see* BIRTHRIGHT; FIRST-BORN; INHERITANCE.

Hekdesh. Property sanctified to God. It consisted of (1) property owned by the Temple; (2) animals, wine, oil, or flour set aside for sacrificial purposes; and (3) property set aside as a gift to the Temple. Such property was not to be handled by a person who was in a state of ritual impurity, and no benefit was to be derived from it. If anyone accidentally made use of it, he was obligated to offer a special sacrifice ("korban meilah") to the Temple. Hekdesh could be redeemed by payment of its value plus a fifth to the Temple treasury. The concept fell into disuse with the destruction of the Temple.

Hekhal [heikhal] ("shrine," "temple"). The forward part of the central Temple building in Jerusalem (I Kings 7; II Chronicles 4). Among the Sephardim, the term denotes the Ark in the synagogue.

Hekhalot, Books of. Collections of mystical midrashim of the amoraic and gaonic periods, attributed to Ishmael ben Elisha. They contain descriptions of the ascent to Heaven to behold the divine chariot ("merkavah"), heavenly places ("hekhalot"), and the throne of glory. Embracing ecstatic experiences and hymns in praise of God, some of this material has been incorporated into the Ashkenazi High Holy Day liturgy.

Helena (fl. 1st cent.). Parthian queen, wife of Monobaz I, King of Adiabene. She and her sons Izates II and Monobaz II converted to Judaism through the influence of Ananias, a Jewish merchant. She spent the latter part of her life in Jerusalem, where she built herself a palace. When a famine raged in Israel she bought food for the people. She also made gifts to the Temple, and was fastidious in the observance of Jewish law. She was interred in a mausoleum north of the city.

Ḥelev ("fat"). In the Bible the word refers specifically to certain portions of the intestinal fat of oxen, sheep, and goats sacrificed on the altar (Leviticus 3.3–17); this was forbidden as food.

Hell *see* GEHINNOM.

Hellenism. The principles, ideals, and way of life associated with classical Greek civilization. Hellenism spread over the Mediterranean and the Middle East from the 4th century BCE. At this time Palestine was under Greek rule and Judea was surrounded by numerous Hellenized cities. In addition the Jewish diaspora was expanding into Egypt, Cyrenaica, Syria, and Asia Minor, which were all under Hellenistic influence. By the Mishnaic period, Jewish life in Palestine and the diaspora was largely dominated by Hellenistic influences.

Heller, Bernhart (1871–1943). Hungarian Arabist and literary scholar. He was born in Nagybicse. He taught languages at high schools in Budapest and became director of the Jewish High School; in 1922 he was appointed professor of Bible at the Rabbinical Seminary. He published studies of ancient Jewish literature, Jewish folk literature, and Muslim legends.

Heller, Chaim (1878–1960). American rabbinic and biblical scholar. He was born in Białystok, Poland, and served as rabbi in Łomża. In 1917 he settled in Berlin, where he established a new type of yeshivah for research on the Bible and Talmud. In 1929 he joined the faculty of the Isaac Elchanan Theological Seminary in New York. He wrote studies of Syriac and Samaritan translations of the Bible and of halakhic issues. He also published an edition of Maimonides' *Book of the Commandments*.

Heller, James (1892–1971). American Zionist and communal leader, son of Maximilian Heller. He was rabbi of Isaac Mayer Wise Temple in Cincinnati and president of the Labor Zionist Organization of America.

Heller, Joseph Elijah (1888–1957). British Hebrew writer. He was born in Lithuania and lived in Russia and Germany. In 1938 he moved to London, where he edited the Zionist organization's journal, *Tarbut,* and taught. He published studies of Jewish and general philosophy, and translated several of Plato's dialogues into Hebrew.

Heller, Maximilian (1860–1929). American rabbi and Zionist. He was rabbi of Temple Sinai in New Orleans, and a prominent Zionist in the American Reform movement.

Heller, Yom Tov Lipmann (1579–1660). Bavarian talmudist. He became dayyan in Prague at the age of 18. In 1629 he was fined for libeling the state and Christianity and was forbidden to act as a rabbi in Prague. Later he served several communities. During the Chmielnicki massacres of 1648–9 he lived in Kraków, where he composed pentitential psalms and commemorative prayers for those who died. His *Tosephot Yom Tov* is a commentary on the Mishnah. He also wrote studies of religious subjects as well as works on mathematics and natural science.

Helsingfors Conference. Conference of Russian Zionists held at Helsinki in December 1906 and chaired by Jehiel Tschlenow. It encouraged Jewish nationalism, autonomy in Jewish national life, and respect for the Jewish religion, and affirmed that the ultimate goal of Zionism was a Jewish settlement in Palestine.

Heman (fl. 11th–10th cent. BCE). Levite musician. He and his sons were among those who performed at the dedication of the Temple (II Chronicles 5.12).

Heman the Ezrahite. Sage. He is named in the Bible as one of the great sages who was surpassed in wisdom only by Solomon (I Kings 5.11). Psalm 88 is attributed to him.

Hemerobaptists. Jewish sect. They practiced ablution at the beginning of the day. These "bathers at dawn" referred to by the Church Fathers may be identical with the "tovele shaḥarit" mentioned in the Talmud.

Henriques, Sir **Basil Lucas Quixano** (1890–1961). English social reformer and communal leader, son of Henry Straus Quixano Henriques. He was born in London. With the help of his wife he established the St. George's Jewish Settlement in London after World War I. He served as a magistrate and later as chairman of the East London Juvenile Court. He visited boys' homes and prisons, suggested reforms, and took an interest in Jewish offenders. After World War II he headed the anti-Zionist Jewish Fellowship. He wrote *The Indiscretions of a Warden, The Indiscretions of a Magistrate,* and *The Home Menders.*

Henriques, Henry Straus Quixano (1864–1924). English lawyer, communal worker, and historian. He served as president of the Board of Deputies of British Jews from 1922 to 1925. He wrote *The Jews and the English Law* and *Jewish Marriages and the English Law.*

Hep! Hep!. Rallying cry against the Jews. The expression originated during the crusades and is derived from the initials of the phrase: "Hierosolyma est perdita" (Jerusalem is lost). It was also used during the anti-Jewish riots that broke out in 1819 in Germany.

Ḥephetz ben Yatzliaḥ (fl. 10th cent.). Persian scholar. He was active in Mosul. His *Sepher ha-Mitzvot* interprets the 613 commandments according to talmudic sources.

Hephker ("ownerless"). In Jewish law it denotes any goods or chattels that have no owner. In most cases such goods are ownerless because they have been renounced or because they are unclaimed. The law stipulates that anyone may acquire such property by taking possession of it. In Yiddish the word means lawlessness.

Herberg, Will (1906–1977). American writer. He was active in the Young Communist League and edited Communist Party publications. In the 1940s he renounced communism and developed Jewish interests. His writings include *Judaism and Modern Man* and *Protestant, Catholic, and Jew.*

***Herbert of Bosham** (fl. 12th cent.).

English Hebraist. He wrote a commentary on the Psalms derived from the work of the French scholar Rashi and other rabbinic commentators. He was one of the first Christian exegetes to use Jewish sources.

Ḥerem ("separated out"). Term used in various senses to do with prohibitions and bans. In biblical times it applied to the prohibition against making use of spoils taken during war; these were destroyed. In the rabbinic period it came to mean the most serious form of ban, or excommunication, used as a punishment for individuals who committed offences harmful to Jewry (*see* BAN).

Heresy. Opinion or doctrine contrary to the orthodox tenets of a religion. Since Judaism does not have an official formulation of dogma, it has no clear definition of heresy. Nevertheless, rabbinic Judaism regards as heretics those who renounce the teaching of the Torah, and refers to them by such terms as "min" (sectarian), "apikoros" (epicurean), "kopher" (freethinker), and "mumar" (one who has changed). The punishment of heretics was justified as a means of preventing them from leading others into sin. In the Middle Ages heresy was punished by excommunication ("ḥerem").

***Herford, Robert Travers** (1860–1950). English theologian. He was a Unitarian minister and served as librarian of Dr. Williams Library, London. His writings include *Christianity in Talmud and Midrash*, *Pharisaism*, *What the World Owes to the Pharisees*, *The Pharisees*, and *Talmud and Apocrypha: A Comparative Study of the Jewish Ethical Teaching in the Early Centuries*. He also produced an edition of the *Pirke Avot* with a commentary.

Herman, Joseph (b. 1911). British painter. He was born in Warsaw and moved successively to Brussels, France, and Glasgow; in 1944 he settled in Wales. His work of 1938–43 depicts the world of his Jewish childhood.

Hermann, Georg *see* BORCHARDT, GEORG.

Hermeneutics, talmudic. System or method of interpreting Scripture according to talmudic principles. Various collections of rules (referred to as "middot" in rabbinic sources) governing the methodology of exegesis existed in the rabbinic period: the seven rules of Hillel; the 13 rules of Ishmael ben Elisha; and the 32 rules of Eliezer ben Yose ha-Galili. In addition Nahum of Gimzo developed a system of interpretation based on the assumption that the marking on every letter has a specific meaning; this was later developed by Akiva.

Herod I [the Great] (fl. 1st cent. BCE). King of Judea (37–4 BCE), son of Antipater II. He was appointed Governor of Galilee by his father in 47 BCE. When he successfully crushed a Galilean revolt, he was censured by the Great Sanhedrin. Later he was appointed tetrarch of Judea and subsequently king. As ruler he constructed a Greek theater and amphitheater in Jerusalem, transformed Samaria into a Greco-Samaritan city, built the port of Caesarea, and rebuilt the Temple in Jerusalem. During his reign he dealt harshly with any whom he believed to constitute a threat to his power; he put many people to death, including his wife Mariamne and her sons.

Herod Agrippa I (10 BCE–44 CE). King of Judea (41–4), son of Aristobulus and Berenice and grandson of Herod the Great. Educated in Rome, he served as market overseer in Tiberias and later returned to Rome, where he became a friend of Caligula. After being imprisoned for treachery, he was freed by Caligula, who appointed him King of Judea. He was sympathetic to the Pharisees and observant of Jewish law.

Herod Agrippa II (28–92). King of Judea (50–92), son of Herod Agrippa I. He was the last king of the house of Herod. During the Jewish revolt against Rome, he sided with the Romans. When Titus became emperor, he served under him. According to the New Testament, he was indifferent to the spread of Christianity (Acts 25–6).

Herod Antipas (20 BCE–c. 40 CE). Tetrarch of Galilee and the Judean Transjordan, son of Herod the Great. He founded Tiberias in honor of the emperor. His forbidden marriage to Herodias (wife of his half-brother Philip) evoked the hostility of the population; John the Baptist was put to death when he denounced the marriage. During the reign of Caligula, Herod Antipas was accused of plotting against Rome and was exiled to Gaul.

Herod Archelaus (fl. 1st cent. BCE to 1st cent. CE). Israelite, ruler of Judea (4 BCE–6 CE). He was a son of Herod the Great and under Herod's will he was appointed king. When he went to Rome to ratify this appointment, the Jewish community protested. The emperor, Augustus, abolished the title of king, but confirmed him as ruler of Judea, Idumea, and Sumeria. He was later removed from office and exiled to Gaul.

Herodians. Faction loyal to the house of Herod. According to the New Testament, they conspired with the Pharisees against Jesus (Matthew 22.16; Mark 3.6; 12.13).

Herodias (fl. 1st cent.). Judean queen, wife of Philip, the son of Herod the Great and Mariamne II. She bore Philip a daughter, Salome. In 31 she was divorced from her husband and married his half-brother Herod Antipas. This marriage violated Jewish law and angered the Jewish population. John the Baptist, who led the opposition, was imprisoned and, according to the New Testament, was killed at the request of Salome.

Herod of Chalcis (d. 48). King of Chalcis (41–8), son of Aristobulus and grandson of Herod the Great and Mariamne. He was granted the kingdom of Chalcis in 41. After the death of Herod Agrippa I in 44, he was given charge of the Temple administration and treasury and invested with the ability to appoint high priests.

Herschell [Hirschel]**, Solomon** (1762–1842). English rabbi. He was born in London. He served as a rabbi in Prussia, then in 1802 became rabbi of the Great Synagogue in London. He was recognized as chief rabbi by the Ashkenazi communities throughout Britain.

Herschmann, Mordechai (1888–1940). American cantor. Born in the Ukraine, he served as a cantor in Zhitomir, and in 1913 became chief cantor of Vilnius. In 1920 he emigrated to the US, where he became cantor of Beth El Temple in Brooklyn. Later he made concert tours in Europe, Palestine, and the US.

Hertz, Henri (1878–1966). French poet, novelist, and critic. He was born in Norgent-sur-Seine. As a journalist, he discussed Jewish problems. In 1925 he became General Secretary of the French Zionist organization, France-Palestine. His story *Ceux de Job* explores the aspirations and despair of the Jewish nation, and his poetry pursues themes of revolt against the Jewish condition.

Hertz, Joseph Herman (1872–1946). British rabbi. He was born in Slovakia and in 1884 was taken to New York. He served as a rabbi in Syracuse, New York, and Johannesburg, South Africa. In 1911 he returned to the US and became rabbi of Congregation Oraḥ Ḥayyim in New York. In 1913 he was appointed chief rabbi of Great Britain. He was critical of Russian anti-Jewish policies and liberal Judaism. He supported Zionism and later struggled against Nazism. His writings include the *Book of Jewish Thoughts* and commentaries on the Pentateuch and the Prayer Book.

Hertzberg, Abel (1893–?). Dutch author

and lawyer. He was born in Amsterdam. He became the editor of *De joodsche wachter,* the journal of the Dutch Zionist Federation. His publications include *Amor fati* and *Brieven ann mijn kleinzoon.*

Ḥerut. Israeli political party, associated outside Israel with the Ḥerut Federation of Zionist Revisionists. It was founded in 1948 by members of the Irgun Tzevai Leumi, the Revisionist Party, and the Betar movement; it was later led by Menaḥem Begin. It advocates a State of Israel on both banks of the Jordan, the mass ingathering of exiles, and liberalism in political and economic policies.

***Herz, Henriette** (1764–1847). German society leader, wife of Marcus Herz. She held a salon in her home in Berlin which attracted many of the leading figures in society; both Moses Mendelssohn and Solomon Maimon were frequent guests. She belonged to the Tugenbund, a youth group dedicated to encouraging ethical values. In 1817 she was baptized through the influence of Friedrich Schleiermacher.

Herz, Marcus (1747–1803). German physician and philosopher. He was born in Berlin, and became a doctor at the Jewish Hospital there. He published philosophical works and corresponded with Immanuel Kant. As a friend of Moses Mendelssohn, he promoted the welfare of Prussian Jewry.

Herzfeld, Levi (1810–1884). German Reform rabbi and historian. He was born in Ellrich. A spokesman for moderate Reform, he was one of the conveners of the first Reform Rabbinical Conference in Braunschweig, and participated in the two following conferences. He and Ludwig Philippson headed the Institut zur Förderung der Israelitischen Literatur from 1860 to 1873. He wrote studies of the history of the second Temple and the Jews in antiquity.

Herzl, Theodor (1869–1904). Austrian writer and journalist, founder of political Zionism. He was born in Budapest. From 1891 to 1895 he was the Paris correspondent for the *Vienna Neue Freie Presse.* In his play *Das neue Ghetto* he criticized Jewish assimilation, and after the Dreyfus case he wrote *Der Judenstaat* ("The Jewish state"), in which he advocated the establishment of a Jewish homeland. He convened the First Zionist Congress in Basle in 1897, at which the World Zionist Organization was established; Herzl was elected its president. He subsequently began negotiations with world leaders to create a Jewish state.

Herzog, Yitzḥak ha-Levi (1888–1959). Israeli rabbinic scholar. He was born in Poland and was taken by his family to Leeds, England, when he was nine. He served as a rabbi in Belfast (1916–19) and Dublin (1919–36), where he was chief rabbi of the Irish Free State. He became chief rabbi of Palestine in 1937. During World War II he attempted to rescue Jews from persecution in Europe, and after the war he traveled throughout Europe to find orphaned Jewish children. He published studies of the institutions of Jewish law and the Talmud as well as responsa.

Heschel, Abraham Joshua (1907–1972). American theologian. He was educated in Berlin, then in 1938 deported by the Nazis to Poland; he later emigrated to England. From 1940 he taught philosophy and rabbinics at Hebrew Union College in Cincinnati; in 1945 he was appointed professor of Jewish ethics and mysticism at the Jewish Theological Seminary of America. He wrote studies of medieval Jewish philosophy, the Bible, kabbalah, Ḥasidism, and the philosophy of religion.

Ḥeshvan *see* MARḤESHVAN.

Ḥesped *see* EULOGY, FUNERAL.

Hess, Moses (1812–1875). German socialist. He was born in Bonn. In 1841 he helped found the socialist daily *Rheinische Zeitung,* of which Karl Marx became editor. Subsequently he lived in Belgium, Switzerland and Paris. In 1862 he published *Rome and Jerusalem* which espoused Zionist ideals. Later he engaged in the work of the Alliance Israélite Universelle. His other publications include *The Holy History of Humanity* and *The European Triarchy*.

Hessaḥ daat (*lit.* "removal of the mind"). Expression conveying the idea of a lack of attentiveness in performing religious duties which require mental awareness. Because of this lack, such actions become invalid. The duties in which alertness is required include the separation from one's produce of the heave offerings due to the priests, the maintaining of the laws regarding ritual uncleanness, and the preparation of the ashes of the Red Heifer.

Ḥessed ve-emet *see* ḤEVRA KADDISHA.

Hessen, Julius (1871–1939). Russian historian. He was born in Odessa. His scholarly and communal activities were concerned with the emancipation of Russian Jewry. He served as the secretary of the Union for Full Equality of the Jewish People in Russia in 1905–6. Later he initiated the publication of the Russian Jewish encyclopedia and served as its general secretary. His publications include studies of the history of the Jewish people in Russia.

Ḥet (i). Eighth letter of the Hebrew alphabet. Its numerical value is 8.

Ḥet (ii) *see* SIN (ii).

Ḥever ha-Kevutzot. Organization of Palestinian Jewish collective villages. Founded in 1926, it consisted of kevutzot that wished to avoid over-centralization. In 1951 it merged with the dissident minority of Ha-Kibbutz ha-Meuḥad to form Iḥud ha-Kevutzot veha-Kibbutzim.

Hevesi [Handler]**, Simon** (1868–1943). Hungarian scholar and rabbi. In 1894 he was appointed rabbi of Kassa, and later became chief rabbi of Budapest. From 1905 he was lecturer in homiletics and Jewish philosophy at the Budapest Rabbinical Seminary. His publications include a Hungarian translation of the liturgy.

Ḥevra [Havurah] **Kaddisha** ("Holy brotherhood"). Mutual benefit society. The term now applies to associations devoted to visiting the sick, burying the dead, and comforting the bereaved. Among the Sephardim such a society is generally called Ḥessed ve-Emet ("Kindness and truth").

Ḥevra Talmud Torah *see* TALMUD TORAH.

Hexapla *see* ORIGEN.

***Heydrich, Reinhard** (1904–1942). Nazi leader. After the Nazis' accession to power, he became head of the Gestapo. He was responsible for the transportation of millions of Jews to the concentration and extermination camps.

Heymann, Isaac (1818–1906). Russian cantor and composer. He served as cantor in Filehne, Graudenz, and Gnesen. He was later appointed chief cantor of the Great Synagogue of the Amsterdam Ashkenazi congregation.

Hezekiah (i) (fl. 8th–7th cent. BCE). King of Judah (715–687 BCE). Unlike his father Ahaz, he attempted to free Judah from Assyrian influence. He removed pagan images and altars from the Temple and renewed the religion of ancient Israel. These reforms were supported by Isaiah. When Hezekiah led a league of states against Assyria, Sennacherib invaded Judah, but did not occupy Jerusalem. As a consequence, Hezekiah was forced to pay tribute to the Assyrians.

Hezekiah (ii) (d. c. 1058). Babylonian exilarch and gaon. He served as exilarch from 1021. When Hai Gaon died in 1038 Hezekiah succeeded him as gaon and head of the academy at Pumbedita.

Hezir. Israelite priestly family. It is mentioned as active in Jerusalem during the time of David (I Chronicles 24.15).

HIAS [Hebrew Immigration Aid Society]. American organization for aiding Jewish immigrants. It was created in New York in 1902, by the merger of the Hebrew Sheltering House Association and the already existing Hebrew Immigration Aid Society, to assist Jewish immigrants to the US. After World War I, agencies were established in eastern Europe. In 1954 the society merged with the United Service for New Americans and the Overseas Migration Service of the American Jewish Joint Distribution Committee to form the United HIAS Service.

Ḥibbat Zion ("Love of Zion"). International Zionist movement. It grew up in the 1860s and served as the focus of early Zionist aspirations from the middle of the 19th century, before the establishing of political Zionism. It had widespread appeal among the Jewish masses of Russia and Romania, and similar groups existed in western Europe and the US. Its adherents (called Ḥovevei Zion) provided Theodor Herzl with wide popular support for his policies. When the World Zionist Organization was founded in 1897, the members of Ḥibbat Zion joined the new movement.

Ḥibbut ha-kever ("torture in the grave"). Belief that a person who has not lived a righteous and devout life is subjected to torture in the grave after burial unless he remembers his name; his tormentors are the Angel of Death and other demonic beings. To avert this judgment it was recommended that one learn by heart a biblical verse beginning and ending with the initial and terminal letters of one's name. The concept is found in eschatological aggadic passages and was developed by the kabbalists.

Hicem. Emigration association. It was established in 1927 by HIAS, ICA and Emigdirect, and its name was made up from those of the founding agencies. In 1934 Emigdirect severed its connections, and the association was then known as HIAS-ICA. It served as an information and assistance office for Jews who left Europe.

Ḥiddekel *see* TIGRIS.

Ḥiddushim *see* NOVELLAE.

Ḥidka, Feast of Rabbi. Light meal eaten in addition to the three Sabbath meals. It is named after Rabbi Ḥidka, who asserted that four meals should be eaten on the Sabbath.

Higger, Michael (1898–1952). American talmudic scholar. He was born in Lithuania and emigrated to the US in 1915. He served as a consultant to the law committee of the Rabbinical Assembly of America. He edited minor treatises of the Talmud and compiled all of the baraitot and the non-Mishnaic tannaitic statements found in the Babylonian and the Palestinian Talmuds.

High Commissioner of Palestine. Title of the head of the British Mandatory administration in Palestine. He was empowered to promulgate ordinances to ensure peace and order, and his powers included those of pardon and reprieve.

High holy day. Term applied to the festivals of New Year and the Day of Atonement. The Ten Days of Penitence that fall between the two festivals are often known as the "high holy day period."

High place. Place of worship built on a hill or mountain. Worship at such places was widespread until the establishment of the Temple in Jerusalem. They were eventually removed by Hezekiah and Josiah.

High priest. Title given to the chief priest of the Jews from ancient times until the destruction of the second Temple in the year 70. It is first found in reference to Aaron and his descendants, who were anointed with holy oil (Leviticus 21.10; Numbers 35.25, 28; Joshua 20.6). Later the title was applied to the chief priest of the first and second Temple. In addition to the priestly garments (breeches, tunic, girdle, and miter), the high priest wore a robe, ephod, breastplate, and frontlet; attached to the breastplate were the Urim and Thummim. On the Day of Atonement he wore white linen. The high priest was the principal officiant in the Temple and was entitled to be present at all sacrifices; among his responsibilities was the administration of the treasury. He also administered the divine oracle and the Urim and Thummim. He was the sole celebrant on the Day of Atonement, when he entered the Holy of Holies to offer incense. The office of high priest was brought to an end by the destruction of the second Temple.

Hildesheimer, Azriel (1820–1899). German rabbi, scholar, and leader of Orthodox Jewry. Born in Halberstadt, he served as secretary to the community there. In 1851 he became rabbi of the Austro-Hungarian community of Eisenstadt, where he set up a yeshivah. In 1869 he became a rabbi in Berlin and he later established a rabbinical seminary there. Together with Samson Raphael Hirsch, he was a leader of the Orthodox Jewish community of Germany. He assisted the victims of Russian pogroms from 1882, and was a supporter of the Jews in Palestine. His publications include an edition of the Halakhot Gedolot.

Hildesheimer, Meier (1864–1934). German rabbi, son of Azriel Hildesheimer. From 1899 he was a preacher at the Adass Jisroel Synagogue in Berlin. Subsequently he became executive director of the rabbinical seminary founded in Berlin by his father. He represented Orthodox German Jewry in numerous Jewish organizations. He published several studies on Jewish subjects and edited a collection of some of his father's writings.

Hilfsverein der Deutschen Juden ("German Jews Aid Society"). Society founded in Berlin in 1901 and active until 1941. It extended financial aid to Jews, and assisted Jewish emigration from eastern Europe. After 1933 it helped Jews to leave Germany. It maintained schools in Palestine and the Balkan countries from 1903 to 1918, and after World War I supported Jewish schools in eastern Europe. It also helped to establish the Haifa Technion.

Ḥillazon. Rare sea creature found on the Mediterranean coast. It is mentioned in the Talmud as the source of the blue dye used for the fringes of the tallit.

Hillel (fl. 1st cent. BCE). Palestinian rabbinic scholar. He was born in Babylonia and settled in Palestine, where he studied with Shemaiah and Avtalyon. He was later appointed president of the Sanhedrin. Together with Shammai, he was the last of the pairs (zugot) of scholars. He formulated seven hermeneutical rules for scriptural interpretation, and he was also the originator of the golden rule: "Do not do unto others that which you would not have them do unto you." He was the founder of the school known as Bet Hillel (*see* BET HILLEL AND BET SHAMMAI).

Hillel II (fl. 4th cent.). Palestinian patriarch (nasi) (330–65). After the revolt of the Jews against the emperor Gallus in 351–2, the Roman government attempted to restrict the privileges of the nasi. Hillel II agreed to limit his authority and functions. He later corresponded with the emperor Julian. In 358 he published a system of intercalation to equalize the solar and lunar years.

Hillel ben Samuel (fl. 13th cent.). Italian physician, talmudic scholar, and philosopher. He lived in Rome, Naples, and finally Capua, where he practiced medicine. He played a major role in the controversies of 1289–90 concerning the philosophical writings of Maimonides, whom he defended. His *Tagmule ha-*

Nephesh explores the nature of the soul and the concept of reward and punishment in the hereafter.

Hillel Foundation. Charitable foundation, established in 1923 and supported by B'nai B'rith. It administers funds given by the Jewish community to maintain university and college student organizations which offer religious, cultural, and communal services to Jewish students. It is active in the US, Canada, Israel, the UK, South Africa, Australia, Switzerland, and the Netherlands.

***Hiller, Ferdinand** (1811–1885). German composer. From 1828 to 1835 he was active as a music teacher and pianist in Paris. He subsequently converted to Christianity and held various positions in Germany and Italy. He founded the Conservatory of Cologne in 1850 which he directed. His compositions include the oratorios *The Destruction of Jerusalem, Saul,* and *Rebecca,* and settings of the Psalms.

Hillesum, Etty (1914–1943). Dutch writer. She was born in Middelburg. She was active in the left-wing, anti-Fascist movement and in 1942 she began work at an office of the Jewish Council in Amsterdam. Later she was transferred to the Dutch transit camp, where she was assigned to care for people who were to go to extermination camps. She herself was killed in Auschwitz. Her letters describe life in the transit camp.

Ḥillul ha-Shem ("desecration" or "profanation of the name"). Expression used to designate any action that desecrates God's name. Such action must be avoided not only because it is itself a sin and is forbidden by the third of the Ten Commandments, but also because it sets a bad example to others. The phrase has also come to denote any action likely to bring disgrace on Judaism or the Jewish people. It is the opposite of kiddush ha-Shem.

Ḥilphai *see* Ilpha.

Hilsner, Leopold *see* Polna case.

***Himmler, Heinrich** (1900–45). Nazi leader. He served as head of the SS, chief of the German police, and minister of the interior. He was responsible for the transportation of millions of Jews to the concentration and extermination camps.

Hinneni he-ani ("Behold the poor [in good works]"). Opening words of a prayer recited at the beginning of the additional service on Rosh ha-Shanah and the Day of Atonement, according to the Ashkenazi rite.

Hinnom, Valley of *see* Gehinnom.

***Hiram (i)** (fl. 10th cent. BCE). Phoenician king, ruler of the city of Tyre. He supplied Solomon with cedars and firs for the building of the Temple. He also contributed to the building of palaces for Solomon and his wife. His navy sailed with Solomon's fleet to Ophir to gather gold, timber, and precious stones. (I Kings 5, 7, 9)

***Hiram (ii)** (fl. 10th cent. BCE). Craftsman in metals. He cast the objects for Solomon's Temple (I Kings 7.13–45; II Chronicles 2.12–13; 4.11–16).

Hiring and letting (Hebrew "sekhirut"). Transactions in which parties contract for the use of property or the labor and skill of an individual. In Jewish law the hiring of one who offers a personal service is governed firstly by the relationship between master and servant, or employer and employee, as specified in the Talmud, and secondly by the specific terms of the contract. Hiring and letting of property is subject to the same laws as selling. The liability of the lessee extends to damage caused by neglect but not to that caused by normal use; due notice of the cessation of the arrangement must be given to the lessee if no date of termination of the lease is stated in the contract.

Hirsch, Baroness **Clara** *see* HIRSCH, MAURICE DE.

Hirsch, Emil Gustav (1851–1923). American rabbi, scholar, and civic leader. Born in Luxembourg, he went to the US in 1866. He served as a rabbi in Baltimore and Louisville, and to the Chicago Sinai Congregation. He taught rabbinic literature and philosophy at the University of Chicago, and served as the editor of the section on the Bible in the *Jewish Encyclopedia.* He was a spokesman for the radical wing of Reform Judaism.

Hirsch, Baron **Maurice de** (1831–1896). German financier and philanthropist. He was born in Munich, moved to Brussels in 1851, and later settled in Paris. In 1873 he made contributions to the Alliance Israélite Universelle to establish Jewish schools in Turkey, and in 1891 he set up the Jewish Colonization Association (ICA) to establish agricultural colonies in Argentina and elsewhere. He also founded the Hirsch Fund, the purpose of which was to open agricultural and crafts schools in Galicia, and the Baron de Hirsch Fund in New York for the technical and agricultural training of immigrants. His philanthropic activities were continued by his wife Baroness Clara de Hirsch after his death.

Hirsch, Samson Raphael (1808–1888). German rabbi and writer. He was born in Hamburg. He served as a rabbi at Oldenburg and Emden, and as chief rabbi of Moravia (from 1846); from 1851 he was a rabbi in Frankfurt am Main. He was the founder of neo-Orthodoxy, which attempted to combine European culture with loyalty to traditional Judaism. His writings include *Nineteen Letters on Judaism* and *Horeb: Essays on Israel's Duties in the Diaspora.* He was the leader and foremost exponent of Orthodoxy in Germany in the 19th century.

Hirsch, Samuel (1815–1889). American Reform rabbi. He was born in Prussia. He served as a rabbi in Dessau and as chief rabbi of Luxembourg before emigrating to the US; there he became rabbi of the Reform congregation Keneseth Israel in Philadelphia. In his *Die Religionsphilosophie der Juden* he depicted Judaism as an evolving religious system.

Hirschbein, Peretz (1880–1948). American Yiddish dramatist and novelist. He was born in Poland and lived in Warsaw from 1904. His first drama, *Miriam* (which is written in Hebrew), is the story of a prostitute. In 1908 he organized a dramatic group in Odessa to produce Yiddish plays. From 1912 to 1917 he wrote a series of folk dramas, which were later staged at the New York Yiddish Art Theater. He eventually settled in the US, where he wrote numerous works, including the Yiddish novel *Babylon,* describing Jewish life in America.

Hirschel Levin *see* LEVIN, HIRSCHEL.

Hirschel, Solomon *see* HERSCHELL, SOLOMON.

Hirschfeld, Georg (1873–1942). German playwright and novelist. Dissatisfied with a career in his father's factory in Berlin, he began to write plays. His *Die Mütter* depicts life among the Jewish bourgeoisie. A later play, *Agnes Jordan,* deals with Berlin Jewish society.

Hirschfeld, Hartwig (1854–1934). British orientalist. He was born in Thron, Prussia, and went to England in 1889. He first taught at Montefiore College in Ramsgate, then in 1901 became librarian and later professor of Semitic languages at Jews College, London. His publications include an edition of the *Kuzari* by Judah ha-Levi, a Hebrew translation of the *Book of Definitions* by Isaac ben Solomon Israeli, studies of the Koran, and works on Arabic and Hebrew philology and bibliography.

Hirsch Ostropoler *see* OSTROPOLER, HIRSCH.

Hirszenberg, Samuel (1865–1908).

Polish artist. He taught at the Bezalel School of Arts and Crafts in Jerusalem in his later years. His paintings were influenced by Jewish sentiment.

Ḥisda (c. 217–309). Babylonian amora. He was born in Kafri. He became wealthy as a brewer in 294 and rebuilt the academy of Sura at his own expense. During the last 10 years of his life he was the academy's head. Numerous aggadic sayings are ascribed to him, many on the topic of health and hygiene. He and Huna were known as the pious men of Babylonia.

Histadrut. Israeli federation of trade unions, founded in 1920. The basic units in the organizational hierarchy are the workers' committee in the place of employment, the trade union, the labor council, and the national organization. The federation's central institutions consist of the conference, the council, and the executive. Every member of the Histadrut enters the Ḥevrat Ovedim ("Workers' company"), the cooperative society of all the workers. The Histadrut includes manual and white-collar urban and rural workers, wage-workers, and independent earners. It maintains the Amal network of schools and vocational training, a Hebrew cultural center, artistic activities, newspapers and journals, a correspondence course institute, and a publishing house.

Histadrut ha-Ovedim ha-Leumit ("National labor federation"). Workers' organization in Palestine. Founded in Jerusalem in 1934, it was established as a result of a clash between Revisionist workers and the Histadrut. Its purpose was to unite all national workers loyal to the principle of the creation of the Jewish state in all of Palestine. Its symbol was a blue and white flag, and its anthem was *Ha-Tikvah.*

Histadrut Ivrith ("Hebrew federation") **of America.** American Hebrew cultural organization. Its purposes are to encourage the knowledge and use of Hebrew, the publication of Hebrew books and periodicals, and an interest in Hebrew culture. Shemaryahu Levin was its first president in 1917–18. The organization pursued its aims by founding a Hebrew newspaper, establishing its own publishing house, creating a youth organization, and sponsoring Hebrew theater. In 1954 it established the Hebrew Academy, which organizes lectures in Hebrew.

History and historiography. The Hebrew Scriptures give an account of the early history of humanity as well as a detailed narrative of Jewish history. Accounts of the Hasmonean revolt are contained in the Apocrypha, and Josephus' *Jewish Wars* depict the Jewish revolt of 66–73 and the siege of Jerusalem. Medieval Jewish historiography was restricted to histories of tradition and stories of persecution. During the Renaissance historical interest in Jewish events revived and it has continued into the modern period. In the 19th and 20th century numerous Jewish scholars have engaged in historical research, and their writings cover all periods of Jewish history.

Hitaḥdut [Mifleget ha-Avodah ha-Ziyyonit ("United Zionist labor party")]. Socialist Zionist party. It was formed in 1920 by the union of the Palestinian Ha-Poel ha-Tzair and the diaspora Tzeire Zion groups. It was active in central and eastern Europe, and supported the founding of the Gordonia movement. It amalgamated in 1932 with Poale Zion.

***Hitler, Adolf** (1889–1945). Nazi leader. He was born in Austria. He joined the National Socialist German Workers' Party after World War I. In 1933 he became German chancelor and imposed a totalitarian regime on the state. During

World War II, precipitated by his imperialist ambitions, he put into effect the so-called "Final Solution" to what he regarded as the Jewish problem; millions of Jews were transported from their homes in German-occupied territory to be murdered in ghettos and camps.

Hittites. Ancient people of Asia Minor. The Bible connects them with the Canaanites (Genesis 10.15) and indicates that they dwelt in Palestine. Abraham purchased the cave of Machpelah from them, and Esau took wives from their number. They were one of the seven peoples whom the Israelites conquered in their invasion of Canaan.

Ḥivi al-Balkhi (fl. 9th cent.). Persian biblical commentator. He was born in Balkh. He wrote a polemical work containing 200 criticisms of the Bible, for which he was rebuked by both Rabbanite and Karaite scholars; among those who criticized his work was Saadyah Gaon.

Hivites. Ancient people, inhabitants of Canaan. The Bible names them as one of the seven nations inhabiting Canaan when the Israelites invaded the country (Joshua 11.3). Those Hivites living in four important towns were exempt from Israel's war against the seven nations by means of a sacred treaty (Joshua 9.19).

Ḥiyya (fl. 2nd cent.). Palestinian tanna. He was born in Babylonia. He studied with Judah ha-Nasi and became an important halakhist. He and his pupil Hoshaiah were responsible for a collection of baraitot.

Ḥiyya bar Abba (fl. 3rd–4th cent.). Palestinian amora. He was born in Babylonia and settled in Palestine, where he was the outstanding pupil of Johanan. He was appointed by Judah ha-Nasi II as his emissary to the diaspora.

Hobson, Laura (1900–1986). American novelist. She grew up in Long Island and studied at Cornell University. Her novels include *The Trespassers, Gentleman's Agreement, First Papers,* and *Consenting Adult.*

***Hochhuth, Rolf** (b. 1931). German playwright. In his play *The Deputy* he condemned Pope Pius XII for his failure to denounce Hitler's policy toward the Jews.

Hochschule für die Wissenschaft des Judentums. German center for the scientific study of Judaism, and rabbinical seminary. It was established in Berlin in 1872. Initially it adopted the name Hochschule ("College") to indicate its high academic standard, but the government degraded its title to Lehranstalt ("Institute") in 1883. After World War I its name reverted to Hochschule but was again changed to Lehranstalt by the Nazis in 1934. Its faculty included important German Jewish scholars and attracted foreign scholars, Jewish students from Berlin University, and Christian students of Judaica. During the Nazi period it became a center for adult education. It was closed in 1942.

Hod, Mordekhai (b. 1926). Israeli military leader. He was born in Deganyah. He became commander of the Israeli Air Force in 1966. He was in charge of the air strike at the beginning of the Six-Day War in 1967 which destroyed the Egyptian, Jordanian, and Syrian air forces.

Hoffmann, David (1843–1921). German biblical and talmudic scholar. He was born in Verbo. He taught rabbinics at the Hildesheimer Rabbinical Seminary in Berlin, where he later became rector. He was regarded as the supreme halakhic authority of German Orthodox Jewry, and in 1918 he was awarded the title "professor" by the German government. He opposed the Reform movement andattacked the Wellhausen school of biblical criticism. His publications include commentaries on parts of the Pentateuch and an introduction to tannaitic midrashim.

Hofjude *see* COURT JEWS.

Hofsteyn, David (1889–1952). Ukrainian Yiddish poet. He wrote poems that acclaimed the achievements of the Communist Revolution of 1917. Later he protested against the banning of Hebrew and the persecution of Hebrew writers. He left the USSR but returned in 1926. When Israel became a state in 1948, he was an enthusiastic supporter; as a consequence he was arrested, transported to Siberia, and executed.

Höhe Rabbi Löw *see* JUDAH LÖW BEN BEZALEL.

Ḥokhmah *see* LOGOS; WISDOM.

Holdheim, Samuel (1806–1860). German Reform leader. He was born in Kempno near Posen. He served as a rabbi in Frankfurt an der Oder, Mecklenburg-Schwerin, and (from 1847) Berlin. He advocated radical reform at rabbinical conferences in Braunschweig (1844), Frankfurt am Main (1845), and Breslau (1846).

Holdsworth, Mrs. *see* STERN, GLADYS BRONWYN.

Ḥol ha-moed ("weekday of the festival"). Name given to each of the days between the first and last days of the Passover and Sukkot festivals. The first and last days are holy days but on the intermediate days essential work may be done; however, no marriages may take place and mourning is forbidden.

Holidays *see* HOLY DAYS.

Holiness (Hebrew "kedushah"). The Hebrew word for holiness denotes separation, in particular separation for holy purposes. As an aspect of moral life holiness is stressed in Leviticus 19: "You shall be holy for I, the Lord your God, am holy." In ceremonial practice it is connected with the dietary laws, laws of ritual purity, and spirituality. Special holiness is attributed to the Temple, Priests, and Levites. Holiness is demanded of the entire people, who are referred to as a "holy people"; the land of Israel is known as the "Holy Land."

Holocaust. The word originally meant a sacrificial burnt offering, but has come to mean great destruction or loss of life, especially by fire. It is used specifically of the extermination of 6 million Jews during the Nazi era. This chapter of history is also referred to as the Catastrophe, the Shoah (calamity), and the Ḥurban (destruction).

Holophernes *see* JUDITH.

Holy City *see* JERUSALEM.

Holy days. In the Bible the following holy days are mentioned: the three pilgrim festivals Passover, Shavuot, and Sukkot, which in biblical times were harvest festivals as well as commemorations of historical events; and the days of solemnity, which are New Year and the Day of Atonement. On all holy days work is forbidden. (The first and last days of Passover and Sukkot are holy days when work is not allowed, but some work is permitted on the intermediate days; *see* ḤOL HA-MOED.) In the diaspora other than in the Reform community holy days (except the Day of Atonement) are observed for two days (*see* SECOND DAY OF FESTIVALS); Reform Judaism limits observance to one day. Work may take place on the post-biblical festivals of Ḥanukkah and Purim, which are the best-known and most frequently observed of the many minor festivals.

Holy Land *see* ISRAEL, LAND OF; PALESTINE.

Holy of Holies *see* TABERNACLE; TEMPLE.

Holy places. In modern Jewish tradition the principal holy places are the Western (or Wailing) Wall (a relic of the Temple of Herod) and the graves of biblical figures or famous sages from the mishnaic period until the present day.

Holy Spirit (Hebrew "Ruaḥ ha-Kodesh"). In the Bible the Hebrew term means literally "divine spirit" (Isaiah 63.

10–11; Psalm 51.13). In rabbinic literature it refers to "divine inspiration"; the criterion for determining the biblical canon was whether each book had been inspired by the Holy Spirit. According to rabbinic sources, the communication to an individual of the Holy Spirit takes place only after long religious discipline resulting in spiritual ascent.

Ḥomah u-migdal ("stockade and tower"). Name given to the pattern of settlements adopted in Palestine from 1936 to 1945. The camps were constructed in one day from pre-fabricated parts, with a watchtower and stockade. This construction enabled the settlers to meet Arab attack but at the same time did not contravene the rules laid down under the British Mandate.

Homberg, Herz (1749–1841). Bohemian educationist and leading figure of the Haskalah. He was born in Lieben near Prague. He served as tutor to Moses Mendelssohn's son in 1779. In 1782 he moved to Vienna, and later in the 1780s taught at the Jewish school in Trieste. In 1787 he became superintendent of German-language Jewish schools in Galicia and assistant censor of Jewish books; he subsequently was censor of Hebrew books in Vienna. From 1814 he was government inspector of Jewish schools in Bohemia. He advocated the reform of Jewish education, the teaching of Hebrew grammar and German, and the purging of Jewish literature of superstition and hatred of the gentiles.

Ḥometz Botel. The removal of leaven from the house before Passover.

Homicide *see* MURDER.

Homiletics. The art of preaching. Traditionally sermons began with a biblical verse which was illustrated in turn by another biblical verse and so on; eventually the preacher returned to his original text and expounded an ethical teaching or a ritual act prescribed by Jewish law. The preliminary biblical verses were chosen from sections of the Pentateuch, Prophets, and Hagiographa associated with the week (*see* HAPHTARAH; LAW, READING OF THE). The use of a scriptural verse at the beginning of a sermon has continued to the present day.

Ḥoni ha-Meaggel ("Honi the Circle-Drawer") (fl. 1st cent. BCE). Palestinian miracle worker. His name originated from his habit of drawing a circle around himself, which he refused to leave until his prayer was granted. According to the Talmud, his prayers for rain were efficacious. During the war between Aristobulus II and Hyrcanus II, he was seized by the supporters of Hyrcanus and told to curse Aristobulus and his army; when Ḥoni ha-Meaggel refused to comply, he was stoned to death.

Hophni (fl. 11th cent. BCE). Israelite priest, son of Eli. The Bible describes Hophni and his brother Phinehas as following an evil way and they died in battle against the Philistines (I Samuel 2–4).

Hora. Israeli folk dance. It was originally from the Balkans, but became popular in Palestine after World War I.

Horayot ("Decisions"). Tenth tractate of the Mishnah order of Nezikin. It deals with decisions in matters of religious law made in error by the high priest or the Sanhedrin (Leviticus 4.1–21).

Horeb. Mountain in Arabia, at the foot of which Moses saw the Burning Bush (Exodus 3). The name replaces Sinai in Deuteronomy, and the two mountains have become identified. Horeb has been used as the name for various religious journals.

Ḥorin [Chorin]**, Aaron ben Kalman** (1766–1844). Hungarian Reform leader. He was born in Hranice and became rabbi of Arad in 1789. In 1803 he published *Emek ha-Shaveh*, which attacked those customs he believed had no basis in Judaism. He subsequently put his reforms into practice, and also endeavored to improve the social and cultural status of Hungarian Jewry. He was bitterly criticized by the Orthodox for his views.

Horites [Hurrians]. Ancient people from south of the Caucasian mountains, who invaded Palestine in the 17th century BCE. They were responsible for transmitting Sumero-Akkadian culture to the Hittites. Their territory was conquered by the Edomites. (Genesis 14.6; 36.20–30; Deuteronomy 2.12, 22)

Horkheimer, Max (1895–1973). German sociologist. He was born in Stuttgart. He became professor of social philosophy at the University of Frankfurt am Main in 1930. He emigrated to Paris in 1933 and the following year went to the US. From 1945 to 1947 he served as chief research consultant to the American Jewish Committee. In 1948 he returned to Germany and re-established the Institut für Sozialforschung in Frankfurt, which had been closed under Nazi rule. After 1954 he taught at the University of Chicago.

Horn *see* SHOPHAR.

Horn, Éduard *see* EINHORN, IGNAZ.

Horodetzky, Shemuel Abba (1871–1957). Israeli scholar of Ḥasidism and Jewish mysticism. He was born in Malin. After going as a delegate to the eighth Zionist Congress in 1907, he remained in the West, living from 1908 to 1938 in Switzerland and Germany. In 1938 he settled in Tel Aviv. He published studies of mysticism, Ḥasidism, and the history of Polish Jewry, as well as biographies of medieval rabbis.

Horovitz, Bela (1898–1955). British publisher. He was born in Budapest. He set up the Phaidon Verlag in Vienna in 1923, then in 1938 transferred his publishing activities to London. In 1944 he founded the East and West Library, which published books of Jewish interest.

Horovitz, Israel (b. 1939). American playwright. He was born in Wakefield, Massachusetts. His plays include *Today, I am a Fountain Pen, A Rosen by Any Other Name,* and *The Chopin Playoffs.*

Horovitz, Marcus (1844–1910). German Orthodox rabbi, historian, and halakhist. He was born in Hungary. He served as an Orthodox rabbi to the Frankfurt am Main general community after Reform had eliminated all Orthodox institutions. His publications include *Frankfurter Rabbinen,* a study of the rabbis who served the Frankfurt community.

Horovitz, Saul (1859–1921). German talmudic scholar. He was born in Hungary. He became lecturer in religious philosophy and homiletics at the Breslau Rabbinical Seminary in 1896; later he served as religious tutor at the seminary. He wrote studies of Jewish and Islamic philosophy, and began to publish critical editions of the halakhic midrashim.

Horowitz, David (1899–1979). Israeli economist. He was born in Galicia and settled in Palestine in 1920. From 1935 to 1948 he was director of the Economic Department of the Jewish Agency. From 1948 to 1952 he served as director general of the Ministry of Finance. After he left his ministry post he worked to establish the Bank of Israel, of which he became the first governor in 1954. He published studies of economics and finance.

Horowitz, Eleazar (1803–1868). Austrian rabbi. He was born in Bavaria. He officiated as rabbi in Vienna from 1828. He engaged in disputes with anti-Semites and successfully advocated the abolition of the Jewish Oath. He contributed to Hebrew periodicals.

Horowitz, Isaiah (c. 1565–1630). Scholar and kabbalist. He was born in Prague. He became av bet din of Dubno in 1600, and av bet din and head of the yeshivah of Ostraha in 1602. He later served as av bet din of Frankfurt am Main and rabbi of Prague. After the death of his wife, he settled in Jerusalem, where he became the rabbi of the Ashkenazi community. His *Two Tablets of the Covenant* is a study of Jewish laws and customs influenced by the kabbalah. He was known as "Sheloah," a name derived from the title of this work (*Shene Luḥot ha-Berit*).

Horowitz, Jacob Isaac [Rabbi of Lublin] (fl. 18th–19th cent.). Polish Ḥasidic rabbi. Originally from Galicia, he moved to Lublin at the turn of the century. He was believed by the Ḥasidim to be possessed of the Holy Spirit and was referred to as "Ha-Hozeh" (the seer). He published studies of the Bible, stressing the importance of the tzaddik.

Horowitz, Leopold (1839–1917). Slovakian painter. He lived in Warsaw from 1869 to 1893, and then in Vienna. He painted the Austrian royal family as well as scenes from Jewish life.

Horowitz, Moses ha-Levi (1844–1910). American Yiddish playwright. He organized a Yiddish company in 1878, which performed plays throughout Europe. In 1886 he settled in New York, where he wrote for the Yiddish stage. He introduced operetta into the repertory of the American Yiddish theater.

Horowitz, Phinehas (1730–1805). German rabbi. He was born in Czortkow, Poland, and served as a rabbi in Witkowo and Lachowicze. In 1771 he became a rabbi in Frankfurt am Main. He was an opponent of the Haskalah movement and criticized Moses Mendelssohn's German translation of the Pentateuch and its commentary. His *Haphlaah* consists of novellae on parts of the Talmud.

Hos, Dov (1894–1940). Labor leader in Palestine. He was born in Belorussia and emigrated to Palestine in 1906. At the beginning of World War I he was a founder of the Jaffa Group, which promoted military training. In 1919 he joined the Aḥdut ha-Avodah Party and became a member of its executive committee. He was also active in the Histadrut and the Haganah. From 1935 to 1940 he served as deputy mayor of Tel Aviv.

Hosea (i) (fl. 8th cent. BCE). Israelite prophet. He exhorted the Israelite nation to concentrate on religious and moral reform rather than dabble in international politics. Nonetheless he adopted a compassionate stance, using his own matrimonial difficulties as a symbol for God's love for his wayward people.

Hosea (ii). Biblical book, one of the 12 books of the Minor Prophets. It records the prophecies of Hosea.

Hoshaiah Rabbah (fl. c. 200). Palestinian amora. He was the head of an academy at Sepphoris which was later transferred to Caesarea. He was a noted halakhist and aggadist, and the author of the opening homily of Midrash Rabbah.

Hosha-na ("Save now"). Words used as the refrain in the liturgical poems recited during Sukkot in the daily procession around the synagogue; they are taken from Psalm 118.25. They also refer in popular usage to the willow branch used in the Sukkot ritual.

Hoshanah Rabbah. Seventh day of the Sukkot festival. According to rabbinic teaching, God's decrees are sealed on this day. It became a widespread practice to spend the night before the festival in prayer. In biblical times on this day seven circuits were made around the altar in the Temple. Now seven circuits are made around the bimah of the synagogue; the Torah scrolls and branches of lulav, etrog, myrtle, and willow are carried in the procession. When the seventh circuit is completed the willow branches are beaten.

Hoshanot. Prayers recited during the Hakkaphot (circuits) of the Sukkot festival. They consist of brief lines, each of which opens and concludes with the response "Hoshana" (O deliver) spoken by the congregation. They address God by different epithets and beseech his deliverance. Originally these were prayers for rain recited on Sukkot. Some of the Hoshanot were composed by liturgical poets such as Eleazar Kallir.

Hoshea (fl. 8th cent. BCE). King of Israel (732–724 BCE). He was the last king of Israel. He secured the throne after his revolt against Pekah (II Kings 15.30). He later rebelled against Assyria and was imprisoned by Shalmaneser IV, who then captured Samaria (II Kings 17.1–6).

Ḥoshen Mishpat *see* JACOB BEN ASHER.

Hospitality *see* HAKHNASAT OREḤIM.

Hospitals. There are references to Jewish hospitals in the Middle Ages; in this context a hospital was not only a place where the sick were nursed and might be kept in quarantine but also a place where poor travelers could lodge. Hospitals in the modern sense developed only in the last few hundred years. Portuguese Jews established a hospital in London in 1747, and others were founded in Metz and Berlin in the 18th century. The first Jewish hospital in the US was the Jews Hospital in New York, founded in 1852. Subsequently Jewish hospitals have been established in numerous countries.

Host, Desecration of the *see* DESECRATION OF THE HOST.

Ḥovah *see* DUTY.

Ḥovevei Zion *see* ḤIBBAT ZION.

Howe, Irving (b. 1920). American literary and social critic. He was born in New York and taught English literature at Brandeis University and Hunter College. He wrote studies of English and American novelists and Yiddish literature. His works include *A Treasury of Yiddish Stories* and *A Treasury of Yiddish Poetry*.

Hübsch, Adolph (1830–1884). American rabbi and orientalist. He was born in Liptó-Szentmiklós in Hungary and served as a rabbi in Miawa and Prague. In 1886 he was appointed head of Congregation Ahawath Chesed in New York. He published an edition of the Syriac Peshitta on the Five Scrolls.

***Hugh of Lincoln** (fl. 13th cent.). English boy, alleged victim of a ritual murder. His body was found in a well in the Jewish quarter of Lincoln at Passover time in 1255. Under torture Copin, a member of the Jewish community, confessed that he had killed the child for ritual purposes. He was executed and about 90 other Jews were tried in London, 18 of whom were put to death. The child Hugh came to be regarded as a martyr and was canonized.

Ḥukkat ha-goy ("law of the gentile"). Expression used of any non-Jewish practice that a religious Jew would seek to avoid.

Huldah (fl. 7th cent. BCE). Israelite prophetess. She is the only prophetess mentioned in the biblical account of the period of the monarchy (II Kings 22.14–20). She prophesied God's judgement on the nation after Josiah's death.

Ḥullin ("profane matters"). Third tractate of the Mishnah order of Kodashim. It is also called Sheḥitat Ḥullin ("Slaughtering for profane use"). It discusses the laws of ritual slaughtering and other regulations connected with the preparation of animal food.

Ḥumash (from Hebrew root "h-m-sh": five). The Five Books of Moses (*see* TORAH).

Humility. According to the Talmud the verse "And what doth the Lord require of thee but to do justly, to love mercy, and to walk humbly with thy God" (Micah 6.8) contains within it the entire Torah. Humility is viewed as the greatest Jewish virtue.

Humor. The Bible contains many examples of satire and irony, and the Talmud and midrash contain humorous parables and anecdotes. A number of medieval works such as the Taḥkemoni contain humorous passages. In addition

Jewish figures such as Motke Ḥabad, Sheike Fifer in Lithuania, and Hershel Ostropoler in southern Russia were noted for their wit. In the modern period Sholem Aleichem and Mendele Mocher Sephorim are known as humorous storytellers, and Ephraim Kishon was a leading comic author in Israel. Jewish humor is today found in a wide variety of fields: literature, film, theater, television, and radio.

Huna (d. c. 297). Babylonian amora. He became a leading authority in his time and served as the head of the academy at Sura from 256. His invitation "He who is hungry, let him come and eat" is quoted in the Passover seder service.

Ḥuppah ("canopy"). The word is used specifically of the canopy used in the marriage ceremony. Originally it referred to the bridal chamber, of which the modern canopy is a symbolic representation. In some communities a tallit is held as a ḥuppah over the bride and groom. In the Talmud the term indicates the legal domain of the man, to which the woman becomes subject on her marriage.

Hurrians *see* HORITES.

Hurwicz, Saul Israel (1860–1922). Russian Hebrew author. He was born in Uvarovichi and became a merchant and banker. He moved to Berlin after the 1905 revolution, but having returned to Russia in 1914 he lost his fortune in the Communist Revolution of 1917. Eventually he moved back to Berlin, where he became a prominent figure among émigré Hebrew writers. With Ḥayyim Naḥum Bialik, he directed the Kelal Publishing House. He contributed stories and articles to Hebrew journals, and established his own periodical, *He-Atid.*

Hurwitz, Henry (1886–1961). American editor and Jewish educationist. Born in Lithuania, he went to the US at the age of five. In 1906 he organized the Harvard Menorah Society, and in 1913 established the Intercollegiate Menorah Association, of which he was president and chancelor. In 1915 he founded the *Menorah Journal,* a magazine of Jewish opinion.

Hushai the Archite (fl. 11th–10th cent. BCE). Friend of David (I Chronicles 27.33). During David's flight from Jerusalem, Hushai sought to join his forces, but David persuaded him to offer allegiance to Absalom; the purpose of the plan was to oust Ahithophel as Absalom's adviser and obtain information of use to David in his struggle against Absalom (II Samuel 15.32–7). Hushai succeeded and was able to create an opportunity for David to escape (II Samuel 17.5–16).

Ḥushi, Abba (1898–1969). Israeli labor leader. He was born in Galicia and emigrated to Palestine in 1920. He served as secretary of the Haifa Labor Council (1938–51), as Mapai member of the Knesset (1949–51), and as Mayor of Haifa (1951–69).

Ḥushiel ben Elhanan (fl. 10th–11th cent.). North African talmudist. He was head of the academy of Kairouan. According to tradition, he was one of the four shipwrecked scholars from Bari who were ransomed in various communities. He developed new methods of study, stressing the importance of the Palestinian Talmud and the halakhic midrashim.

Husik, Isaac (1876–1939). American historian of Jewish philosophy. He was born in Russia and moved to Philadelphia in 1888. From 1898 to 1916 he taught at Gratz College in Philadelphia, later becoming professor of philosophy at the University of Pennsylvania. His publications include *A History of Medieval Jewish Philosophy.*

***Hussein** (b. 1935). King of Jordan (1953–). He was born in Amman. In 1967 he signed a military alliance with Abdel Nasser of Egypt, which precipitated the Six-Day War. Jordan lost considerable territory to Israel and suffered extensive casualties in the conflict. Hussein's position was subsequently threatened by support for Arab terrorist organizations operating from Transjordan.

***Hussein, Hajj Mohammed Amin el-** (1893–1976). Arab leader. He was born in Jerusalem and was active in the Arab nationalist movement from 1919. He was sentenced to prison for his role in the 1920 anti-Jewish riots in Jerusalem, but was reprieved in 1921. In the same year Sir Herbert Samuel, the British High Commissioner, appointed him Mufti (expounder of Muslim law) of Jerusalem. The following year Hussein was appointed chairman of the Supreme Muslim Council. He helped to organize the anti-Jewish riots of 1929 and 1936. In 1940 he moved to Iraq, where he took part in a pro-German coup in 1941. He collaborated with Nazi Germany during the war. In 1946 he settled in Cairo, and directed the Palestine–Arab war against the yishuv.

Ḥutzpah (Yiddish). Impudence.

Ḥutzpit ha-Meturgeman (fl. 2nd cent.). Palestinian tanna. He was the mouthpiece ("meturgeman") of Rabban Gamaliel of Jabneh. In the Tosephta he is described as one of the four elders who studied under Eliezer ben Azariah in Sepphoris. According to midrashic tradition, he was one of the Ten Martyrs executed under the Hadrianic persecutions of c. 135.

Ḥuyayy ibn Akhtab (d. 627). Arabian tribal leader. He was chief of the Banu Nadir tribe in Hejaz. After the expulsion of his tribe from Medina in 626, he attempted to organize Mohammed's enemies. His daughter was later captured, adopted Islam, and became one of Mohammed's wives.

Hyamson, Albert Montefiore (1875–1954). English administrator. From 1917 to 1919 he edited the *Zionist Review*. He served as Chief Immigration Officer in Palestine under the British Mandate, returning to England in 1934. He was president of the Jewish Historical Society of England from 1945 to 1947. He published studies of Palestine and Zionism as well as a history of the Jews of England.

Hyamson, Moses (1862–1949). American rabbi and scholar. Born in Lithuania, he was taken to England at the age of five. He served as a rabbi in England, Wales, and the US. He taught the codes of Jewish law at the Jewish Theological Seminary of America from 1915 to 1940. His writings include translations of Maimonides' *Mishneh Torah* and Baḥya ben Joseph ibn Pakuda's *Duties of the Heart.*

Hygiene. Many biblical prescriptions (such as those concerning circumcision, ablution, and isolation of the sick) promote personal cleanliness. The Talmud amplifies these laws. In the Middle Ages such regulations ensured that the Jewish community had a relatively high level of hygiene.

Hyksos. Semitic and Horite peoples who controlled Egypt from 1655 to 1570 BCE. Some scholars associate the migration of the Hyksos with that of the Israelite patriarchs, and their expulsion from Egypt with the Exodus.

Hypocrisy. According to the Talmud a hypocrite is a person who says one thing in his heart and another with his lips. Hypocrisy was condemned by the rabbis.

Hyrcanus II (fl. 1st cent. BCE). Judean high priest and ethnarch, elder son of Alexander Yannai and Salome Alexandra. He succeeded his mother to the Judean throne but was driven out and had the high priesthood wrested from him by his brother Aristobulus II. With the help of Antipater, he resolved to overcome Aristobulus. The brothers appealed for arbitration to Pompey, who preferred

Hyrcanus. After conquering Aristobulus and his supporters, Pompey appointed Hyrcanus high priest with limited political authority. Following Pompey's death Hyrcanus supported Julius Caesar, who elevated him to the position of ethnarch. When Judea was invaded by the Parthians, he was taken captive. He subsequently returned to Judea, where he was accused of treason by Herod the Great and executed.

Hyrcanus, John *see* JOHN HYRCANUS.

I

Ibn Abitur, Joseph ben Isaac (fl. 10th–11th cent.). Spanish scholar. After Moses ben Enoch's death in Córdoba, his place as rabbi and head of the yeshivah there was taken by his son Enoch. Ibn Arbitur attempted to displace Enoch, causing a split in the community. He was forced into exile and traveled to north Africa, Pumbedita, and Damascus. He wrote an Arabic commentary on the Talmud, a Hebrew commentary on the Psalms, and liturgical poetry.

Ibn Adret, Solomon ben Abraham *see* ADRET, SOLOMON BEN.

Ibn Aknin, Joseph ben Judah (1150–1220). North African philosopher and poet. He was born in Barcelona and moved to north Africa, where he lived as a crypto-Jew. He wrote studies of Jewish law and philosophy. He should not be confused with Maimonides' disciple Joseph ben Judah ibn Shimon who is also referred to as Ibn Aknin.

Ibn Avi Zimra, David ben Solomon *see* ZIMRA, DAVID BEN SOLOMON IBN AVI.

Ibn Bakuda *see* BAḤYA BEN JOSEPH IBN PAKUDA.

Ibn Balam, Judah ben Samuel [Judah ibn Balam] (fl. 11th cent.). Spanish biblical commentator and Hebrew grammarian. He was born in Toledo and lived in Seville. He wrote biblical commentaries, a study of the stylistic devices in the Bible, and works on Hebrew verbs and particles.

Ibn Barun, Isaac ben Joseph (fl. 11th–12th cent.). Spanish Hebrew grammarian and lexicographer. He lived in Zaragoza and Málaga. He wrote Hebrew poetry, and developed the comparative linguistic studies begun by Judah ibn Kuraish, Dunash ben Tamim, and Jonah ibn Janaḥ.

Ibn Daud, Abraham (c.1110–1180). Spanish historian, philosopher, physician, and astronomer. He was born in Córdoba and settled in Toledo. His *Emunah Ramah* ("Sublime faith") is a philosophical treatise based on Aristotelian principles. In this work he explores central problems connected with God, the soul, prophecy and creation, and free will. His *Sepher ha-Kabbalah* ("Book of tradition") relates the history of talmudic scholarship to his own day.

Ibn Ezra, Abraham (1089–1164). Spanish poet, grammarian, biblical commentator, philosopher, astronomer, and physician. Born in Toledo, he lived in Spain and later journeyed to Italy, France, England, and Palestine. He wrote poetry, Bible commentaries, grammatical works, philosophy, and astrological studies.

Ibn Ezra, Moses (b. c.1055–after 1135). Spanish Hebrew poet and philosopher. He was born in Granada and became a friend of Judah ha-Levi. After the Almoravides captured Granada in 1090 he led a wandering life. He wrote poetry, an examination of the methodology and meter of Hebrew and Arabic poetry, an

Arabic philosophical work based on Neoplatonism, and penitential prayers (seliḥot).

Ibn Falaquera *see* FALAQUERA, SHEMTOV BEN JOSEPH.

Ibn Gabirol, Solomon [Gabirol] (c. 1021–c. 1056). Spanish poet and philosopher. He was born in Zaragoza. He wrote secular and religious poetry and philosophical studies. His poem *Keter Malkhut* ("Crown of divine kingship") has been incorporated into the liturgy. Two of his philosophical works have survived: *Mekor Ḥayyim* ("Source of life") and *Tikkun Middot ha-Nephesh* ("Improvement of the moral qualities"). His philosophical investigations are based on Neoplatonic principles.

Ibn Gikatilla *see* GIKATILLA, MOSES BEN SAMUEL.

Ibn Ḥasan, Jekuthiel ben Isaac (d. 1039). Spanish statesman and philanthropist. He served as vizier in the Muslim state of Zaragoza. He was a patron of Solomon Ibn Gabirol, who wrote three dirges in his memory after he had been deposed and executed.

Ibn Ḥasdai, Abraham ben Samuel ha-Levi [Abraham ben Samuel Ḥasdai; Abraham ben Ḥasdai ha-Levi; Abraham ibn Ḥasdai; Ḥasdai] (fl. 13th cent.). Spanish translator and Hebrew poet. He lived in Barcelona. He translated numerous Arabic works into Hebrew, and was an ardent defender of Maimonides.

Ibn Ḥaviv, Jacob [Ḥabib] (?1445–1515/16). Spanish rabbinic scholar. He was born in Zamora in Castile, and became head of a yeshivah in Salamanca. When the Jews were expelled from Spain in 1492, he went to Portugal and later settled in Salonica, where he was one of the leading scholars. His *En Yaakov* is a compilation of aggadic sections of the Palestinian and Babylonian Talmuds.

Ibn Ḥaviv, Levi (c. 1480–1545). Palestinian rabbinic scholar, son of Jacob ibn Ḥaviv. He lived in Salonica. He completed his father's talmudic compilation, *En Yaakov*. Later he moved to Palestine, where he became chief rabbi in Jerusalem. He was an opponent of Jacob Berab's plan to revive rabbinic ordination.

Ibn Janaḥ, Jonah (fl. 11th cent.). Spanish Hebrew grammarian and lexicographer. Born in Córdoba, he settled in Zaragoza, where he was a physician. He wrote studies of biblical exegesis and Hebrew philology. His *Sepher ha-Dikduk* includes a list of roots of Hebrew words, interpreted in the light of biblical and rabbinic literature and compared with other Semitic languages. It was translated from Arabic into Hebrew by Judah ibn Tibbon.

***Ibn Killis, Yakub ben Yusuf** (930–91). Egyptian statesman. He was born in Baghdad and first settled in Palestine. Later he went to Egypt and converted to Islam. He served several caliphs, and as vizier reorganized the administrative system of the Fatimid caliphate.

Ibn Kuraish, Judah (fl. 10th cent.). North African philologist. He was born in Morocco and became a physician. He wrote an Arabic letter to the Jewish community in Fez, protesting against the elimination of the recitation of the Aramaic Targum. In this letter he laid the foundation for a method which was later of considerable help in solving problems of biblical vocabulary.

Ibn Labrat, Dunash *see* DUNASH BEN LABRAT.

Ibn Latif, Isaac ben Abraham (c. 1220–1290). Spanish philosopher, kabbalist, and physician. He spent the latter part of his life in Palestine. He established a new method of kabbalah based on Aristotelian philosophy and natural science. He also used a kabbalistic terminology derived from philosophy and mathematics.

Ibn Migas, Joseph ben Meir ha-Levi (1077–1141). Spanish talmudic scholar.

He served as the head of a yeshivah in Lucena, as a successor to Isaac Alfasi. He wrote novellae to the Talmud and numerous responsa.

Ibn Nagrela [Nagdela] *see* SAMUEL IBN NAGRELA.

Ibn Pakuda, Baḥya *see* BAḤYA BEN JOSEPH IBN PAKUDA.

Ibn Polegar, Isaac ben Joseph [Ibn Pulgar; Ibn Pulkar] (fl. 14th cent.). Spanish theologian. He wrote a polemical reply to the anti-Jewish tract, *Minḥat Kenaot*, written by the convert Abner of Burgos. This work, *Ezer ha-Dat*, attempts to reconcile faith and philosophical reason.

Ibn Sahulah, Isaac ben Solomon (fl. 13th cent.). Spanish Hebrew writer. He worked as a physician at Guadalajara. He wrote a kabbalistic commentary on the Song of Songs, and a book of fables, *Meshal ha-Kadmoni* ("Easterner's parable").

Ibn Shahin *see* NISSIM BEN JACOB BEN NISSIM.

Ibn Shaprut, Ḥasdai [Shaprut] (c. 915–c. 970). Spanish statesman and physician. He served at the courts of the caliphs Abder-Raḥman III and Ḥakam II at Córdoba, and was employed on various foreign missions. He supported Jewish scholars and scholarship and defended Jewish communities. He wrote a well-known letter to the king of the Khazars expressing his joy at their independent Jewish kingdom. His scholarly activities included collaboration in translating a work of Dioscorides into Arabic.

Ibn Shaprut, Shemtov ben Isaac [Shaprut] (fl. 14th–15th cent.). Spanish scholar and physician. In 1375 he conducted a disputation in Pamplona with the future Pope Benedict XIII. He wrote a polemical work to combat apostasy (*Even Boḥan*), a commentary on Avicenna, a supercommentary to Ibn Ezra's Bible commentary, and a philosophical explanation of talmudic aggadah.

Ibn Shemtov, Joseph ben Shemtov (c. 1400–c. 1460). Spanish philosopher. He served in the Castilian court of King John II and his successor Henry IV. In 1452 he was sent to Segovia to suppress an anti-Semitic movement. Later he wandered around the country giving lectures. His *Kevod Elohim* is a theological study which seeks to find a compromise between Maimonides and the anti-philosophical views of contemporary Jewish scholars.

Ibn Shemtov, Shemtov (c. 1380–c. 1441). Spanish kabbalist. In *Sepher ha-Emunot* he criticized rationalists from Abraham ibn Ezra through Levi ben Gershom and Isaac Albalag. He was sharply opposed to the views of Maimonides and was particularly incensed by his *Guide for the Perplexed.*

Ibn Tibbon, Jacob [Don Profiat] (c. 1230–1312). French astronomer, physician, writer, and translator. He was born in Marseilles and lived at Montpellier, where he taught medicine at the university. He translated Euclid, Averroes, and Al Ghazzali from Arabic into Hebrew. In addition he produced astronomical tables, which were translated into Latin and used by Dante for his *Divine Comedy*. He was a defender of Maimonides.

Ibn Tibbon, Judah ben Saul [Tibbon] (c. 1120–after 1190). Spanish physician and translator. Born in Granada, he settled in Lunel, France. He translated such Jewish works as Saadyah Gaon's *Beliefs and Opinions*, Baḥya's *Duties of the Heart*, and Judah ha-Levi's *Kuzari* from Arabic into Hebrew.

Ibn Tibbon, Moses ben Samuel [Tibbon] (d. c. 1283). French writer and translator. He lived in Marseilles, where he practiced medicine. He translated philosophical and scientific works from

Arabic into Hebrew, and also wrote commentaries on the Bible and rabbinical studies.

Ibn Tibbon, Samuel ben Judah [Tibbon] (c. 1150–c. 1230). French translator, scholar, and physician. After traveling widely, he settled in Marseilles. He translated Maimonides' *Guide for the Perplexed* from Arabic into Hebrew in collaboration with the author. He also translated other writings of Maimonides and wrote philosophical commentaries on the Bible.

Ibn Tzaddik, Joseph ben Jacob (c. 1075–c. 1149). Spanish philosopher and poet. From 1138 he served as a dayyan at Córdoba. His philosophical study *Olam Katon* explores cosmology, the nature of man, and his relation to the external world. This work was influenced by Neoplatonism and Aristotelian concepts.

Ibn Verga, Joseph (d. c. 1559). Turkish scholar, son of Solomon ibn Verga. When the Jews were expelled from Spain in 1492, he fled to Lisbon with his father. Later he emigrated to Turkey, where he served as a rabbi and dayyan in Adrianople. He published his father's *Shevet Yehudah,* a collection of narratives describing persecutions and disputations, together with supplementary material. He also wrote a study of talmudic principles.

Ibn Verga, Solomon (fl. 15th–16th cent.). Spanish historiographer. After the conquest of Málaga in 1487, he was sent by Spanish Jewish communities to raise funds for ransoming Jews captured there. When the Jews were expelled from Spain in 1492, he settled in Lisbon. From 1497 he was compelled to live as a Converso, but he later emigrated to Italy. His *Shevet Yehudah* is a narrative describing the persecution of the Jews from the destruction of the second Temple until his own time. It was published with additions by his son Joseph ibn Verga.

Ibn Yaḥia, David ben Joseph [Yaḥia] (1465–1543). Portuguese rabbi, grammarian, and philosopher. Born in Lisbon, he became a leader of Portuguese Jewry and an adviser to the kings of Portugal. In 1525 he was appointed rabbi of Naples. After the Jews were expelled from Naples in 1540 he settled in Imola. He wrote studies of grammar and philosophy as well as poetry.

Ibn Yaḥia, David ben Solomon (c. 1440–1524). Portuguese biblical commentator and grammarian. He was born in Lisbon and served as a rabbi there. Later he lived in Naples and Constantinople. He wrote biblical commentaries, grammatical and legal studies, and a commentary on Maimonides' *Guide for the Perplexed.*

Ibn Yaḥia, Gedaliah ben Joseph (1515–1587). Italian historiographer and talmudist. He was born in Imola and lived in various cities in Italy before settling in Alexandria. His *Shalshelet ha-Kabbalah* consists of a history of the Jewish people, scientific tractates, and a chronicle of events from creation to the 16th century.

Ibn Yaḥia, Jacob Tam (d. 1542). Portuguese scholar and physician, son of David ben Solomon ibn Yaḥia. He served as a rabbi and as court physician in Constantinople. He was the author of numerous responsa and completed *Tehillah le-David,* a study of the principles of Judaism begun by his father.

Ibn Yaḥia, Joseph (1494–1534). Italian biblical commentator and philosopher. He was born in Florence and moved with his family to Imola. He wrote biblical commentaries, a commentary on talmudic sayings, and studies of eschatology and the commandments.

Ibn Yaish, Solomon [Abenaes] (d. 1603). Turkish statesman and merchant. Born a Portuguese Marrano, he reverted to Judaism in Turkey. He later became

Duke of Mytilene and was the organizer of the Anglo-Turkish alliance against Spain.

Ibn Zabara [Zabara]**, Joseph** (c. 1140–c. 1200). Spanish Hebrew poet. He was born in Barcelona and worked as a physician there. His *Sepher Shaashuim* ("Book of amusements") contains a literary account of his journey to several countries, together with stories and proverbs.

Ibn Zeraḥ, Menaḥem (d. 1385). Spanish codifier. He was injured in the attack on the Jews of Navarre in 1328, and afterwards settled in Toledo. His *Tzedah la-Derekh* is a handbook of essential Jewish laws for the use of Jews at the royal court.

***Ibrahim, Pasha** (1789–1848). Muslim ruler of Syria and Palestine (1832–41), of Greek origin. He invaded Syria and Palestine in 1831; Acre and Damascus finally fell to his forces in the following year. During his rule, the Jewish community was generally secure.

ICA *see* JEWISH COLONIZATION ASSOCIATION.

Ichabod (fl. 11th cent. BCE). Israelite, son of Phinehas and grandson of Eli. Phinehas' wife was in labor when news reached her of the capture of the Ark by the Philistines and the death of Phinehas, his brother Hophni, and Eli. She died in childbirth after naming her son Ichabod, which means "there is no glory." (I Samuel 4.10–22)

Icor. American organization founded in 1924 to promote Jewish colonization in the USSR. It was run by Jewish communists. After 1928 it encouraged the development of Birobidjan, conducting a fund-raising campaign for agricultural machinery and cultural activities. Its activities had ceased by the end of World War II.

Idelsohn, Abraham Zvi (1882–1938). American musicologist, of Lithuanian origin. He served as cantor in Leipzig, Regensburg, and Johannesburg, and later settled in Jerusalem. There he worked as a cantor and music teacher at the Hebrew Teachers College. He later became professor of Jewish music at the Hebrew Union College in Cincinnati. He was the founder of modern Jewish musicology and one of the pioneers of ethnomusicology. His publications include a *Thesaurus of Hebrew Oriental Melodies*, *Jewish Music in its Historical Development*, and *Jewish Liturgy*.

Idelson, Yisrael *see* BAR-YEHUDA, YISRAEL.

Idolatry. The worship of idols. Although biblical Judaism was opposed to idol-worship, the ancient Israelites engaged in idolatrous practices, which evoked the hostility of the prophets. Rabbinic law in the Mishnah treatise Avodah Zarah deals with prohibitions concerning contact with idolators. The Rabbis forbade commercial transactions with an idolator before an idolatrous holiday in order to preserve the Jew from even indirect involvement in the festivities. It was also prohibited to sell or lease land or houses in Palestine to an idolator, to sell him animals, or eat with him. Further, it was forbidden to eat his bread, oil, or wine.

***Ignatiev, Nicolai** (1832–1908). Russian minister of the interior. He was responsible for the formulation and enforcement of Russia's anti-Jewish policy, the principal manifestation of which were the so-called May Laws of 1882.

Ignatov, David (1885–1954). American Yiddish author. He was born in the Ukraine and was active in the revolutionary movement in Kiev in 1903–6 before he emigrated to the US. He was one of the founders of the eastern European literary group Di Yunge, and edited various literary journals. He was one of the creators of the modern Yiddish novel and also reworked Ḥasidic tales and medieval Jewish fables. His stories describe the lives of Jewish workers in the US.

Igrat Bat-maḥlat. Name of an evil spirit of the night. According to the Talmud, it was rendered powerless by Abbaye.

Iḥud. Jewish organization founded to foster cooperation between Jews and Arabs in Palestine. It was established in 1942 as the successor of Berit Shalom and advocated the creation of a binational Jewish–Arab state. It has promoted the rights of the Arab minority, the return of refugees, and territorial concessions by Israel.

Iḥud ha-Kevutzot Ve-he-Kibbutzim. Organization of Israeli collective villages. It was formed in 1951 by the merger of the kibbutzim that favored Mapai policies (which seceded from Ha-Kibbutz ha-Meuḥad) and Ḥever ha-Kevutzot.

Ikor, Roger (1912–1986). French novelist. He was born in Paris and became a teacher there. His novel *The Sons of Avrom* is a depiction of Jewish immigrant life in Paris during the early decades of the 20th century.

Ikriti, Shemariah (1275–1355). Italian philosopher and biblical commentator. He was brought up in Crete and spent most of his life in Italy. In 1352 he went to Spain on an unsuccessful mission to reconcile Karaites and Rabbinites; he was accused of messianic pretentions and died in prison. His works include a philosophical commentary on the Bible, a cosmological polemic, and a study of talmudic legends.

Illegitimacy. In Jewish law the status of a child who is the product of any union prohibited in the Bible. Such a person is designated a "mamzer." He or she may not marry an Israelite (or Jew), except one of the same status, but is allowed to marry a proselyte. The children of mamzerim share the same prohibition with regard to marrying a true Israelite. These restrictions still pertain.

Illuy (Hebrew). Outstanding scholar or genius. The word is usually applied to a young talmudic scholar of extraordinary ability.

Ilpha [Ḥilphai] (fl. 3rd cent.). Palestinian amora. He was an aggadist and miracle worker.

Images *see* IDOLATRY.

Imbeciles *see* DEAF, IMBECILES, AND MINORS.

Imber, Naphtali Herz (1856–1909). American Hebrew poet. He was born in Galicia and went to Palestine in 1882, where he served as secretary and adviser on Jewish affairs to Laurence Oliphant (1882–8). He then returned to Europe and wandered as far as India, where he was wooed by missionaries; he was later accused of converting to Christianity. In 1892 he went to the US. His first volume of poems contained *Tekvatenu,* which (as *Ha-Tikvah*) later become the anthem of the Zionist movement and ultimately the Israeli national anthem.

Imber, Samuel Jacob (1889–c. 1942). Galician Yiddish poet. He was born in the Ukraine. He became the pioneer and mentor of a generation of Galician Yiddish poets. His poetic romance *Esterke* recounted the 14th-century story of the love of the beautiful daughter of a Jewish blacksmith for the Polish King Casmir. After World War I he founded the literary monthly *Nayland.*

Imitation of God. According to the rabbis, God's attributes should be seen as models for human behavior. Human beings are to imitate his qualities of mercy, compassion, and loving-kindness. The doctrine of the imitation of God was important in the moral teaching of the kabbalistic mystics.

Immanuel ben Solomon of Rome (c. 1261–after 1328). Italian poet and rabbinic commentator. He was born in Rome and lived in various cities in Italy. He wrote philosophical commentaries on the Bible, poetry, and hymns; he introduced Spanish metrical forms into Italy and the sonnet form into Hebrew. His *Maḥberot Immanuel* contains poems on love, wine, and friendship, riddles, epigrams, epistles, elegies, religious poems, and an account of a journey through Hell and Paradise. The piyyut *Yigdal*, which is included in the daily prayerbook, is an adaptation of one of his poems in this work.

Imma Shalom (fl. 1st–2nd cent.). Palestinian woman, wife of Eliezer ben Hyrcanus and sister of Rabban Gamaliel II. She was praised for her learning and religious devotion. She is one of the few women mentioned in talmudic literature.

Immersion. The statement "He shall bathe his flesh in water" (Leviticus 15.16) is interpreted as referring to the total immersion of the body in a ritual bath ("mikveh") or flowing river water. Ritual immersion is the means of eliminating ritual impurity. In all cases the body must be scrupulously clean before immersion. Orthodox practice stipulates that women of childbearing age should practice immersion after menstruating, and that proselytes should immerse themselves as a sign of adopting Judaism. Among the very pious it is the custom to prepare for festivals by immersion, and some groups practice it daily before the morning prayer. Vessels that have been rendered unclean also require cleansing by this means, as do new or used vessels which have been purchased from a non-Jew. *See also* MIKVEH.

Immigrant camps. Temporary accommodation for immigrants to Israel awaiting permanent settlement. The first such camps were established by the Jewish Agency in 1948 in Raananah to receive arrivals from detention camps in Cyprus.

Immigration *see* ALIYAH (ii).

Immortality of the soul. The eternal existence of the soul after death. In the Bible the dead are depicted as living a shadow-like existence in Sheol. According to rabbinic literature human beings are described as having a body and a soul, which are parted at death but reunited in the resurrection of the dead. After the Day of Judgment, the righteous enter into Heaven (Gan Eden) and the wicked are punished in Hell (Gehinnom). In modern times this traditional view of physical resurrection, reward, and punishment has been replaced in various branches of Judaism by belief in the immortality of the soul.

Imprisonment. The rabbis legislated for imprisonment as punishment in the case of certain offenses for which no other penality is prescribed in Scripture; it was also to be used in special circumstances. The Talmud stipulates three sets of circumstances in which imprisonment is appropriate: to punish the incorrigible offender who has already received corporal punishment for transgressing a prohibition involving excision or cutting off from the community; to punish someone who is guilty of murder but on whom the court cannot pronounce a death sentence because of legal technicalities; and to punish a person found guilty of murder by hiring an assassin.

Impurity *see* PURITY, RITUAL.

Im yirtzeh ha-shem ("If the name [God] wills"). Pious expression used in discussing future events.

Incense. Gum, spice, or other substance producing a sweet smell when burned. In biblical times the burning of incense accompanied all sacrifices in the Temple except the sin offering of the poor and the meat offering of the leper. It was burned by the high priest in the Holy of Holies on the Day of Atonement. Its ingredients are prescribed in Exodus 30.34–8 and elaborated in the Talmud.

Incest. Sexual relationships between close kindred. Leviticus 18.6–18 lists prohibited sexual relationships between members of a family. The Talmud added other unions to those already defined as incestuous.

Incunabula. Early printed books, especially those dating from before 1500. Approximately 150 Hebrew incunabula are known, about two-thirds of which were printed in Italy. The leading printers of early Hebrew books were the Soncino family.

Indemnity. Security against or compensation for damage or loss. In Jewish law financial compensation and restitution are due if a person is injured or his property damaged. In cases of injury, indemnity consists of payment for the injury itself, the pain suffered, the medical expenses incurred, the loss of earnings arising, and the indignity suffered. Since Jewish law states that two punishments may not be given for a single offense, a person who pays an indemnity should receive no further punishment. Offenses punishable by the payment of an indemnity are not classified as criminal.

Independence Day *see* YOM ATZMAUT.

Independent Liberal Party *see* PROGRESSIVE PARTY.

Index librorum prohibitorum *see* BOOKS, PROHIBITED.

Informer. One of the greatest crimes a Jew could commit against other Jews was to denounce them to the secular authorities. The attitude of the Talmud towards such individuals was one of extreme hostility. During the Middle Ages the incidence of betrayal by informers increased as a result of political and social conditions; the handing over of information to non-Jewish authorities about the lives, property, and religious beliefs of Jews often had calamitous results. In response Jewish leaders and scholars tried offenders and imposed sentences on them.

Ingathering Festival *see* SUKKOT.

Inheritance. In biblical times the Jews adopted the principle of the right of primogeniture. The case of Zelophehad's inheritance determined that daughters should inherit if there were no sons (Numbers 27.8–11). According to the rabbis, the order of legal heirs is: (1) sons and their descendants (the first-born receiving a double portion); (2) daughters and their descendants; (3) the father; (4) brothers and their descendants; (5) sisters and their descendants; (6) the father's father; (7) the father's brothers and their descendants; (8) the father's sisters and their descendants; (9) the father's father's father; and so on.

Innocence. In Jewish law a person is presumed innocent until proven otherwise. Neither hearsay nor circumstantial evidence are allowed to overturn this presumption, and self-incrimination has no validity.

***Innocent III** (fl. 12th–13th cent.). Pope (1198–1216). He confirmed the existing papal bulls that protected the Jews, but he also renewed all the former restrictive legislation against them. He was responsible for the decrees enacted at the Fourth Lateran Council in 1215 which discriminated against the Jewish community.

Inquisition. Ecclesiastical tribunal of the Catholic Church dedicated to investigating and suppressing heresy. It was established in the 13th century under Innocent III. Initially it concerned itself only incidentally with Jews, but in Spain from 1478, operating under royal auspices and according to a papal bull, it dealt with Marranos. The first auto-da-fé was held at Seville in 1481 and in 1483 Tomas de Torquemada became inquisitor-general. In 1540 the inquisition spread to Portugal, and later it was introduced into Spanish and Portuguese dependencies overseas.

Insanity. According to the rabbis symptoms of insanity include going out alone at night, sleeping in a cemetery, and destroying what is given to one; in addition a generally confused and irresponsible attitude are considered evidence of the condition. In Jewish law an insane person is exempt from all religious obligations and punishments, his dealings have no legal validity, and he cannot marry. Any man who becomes insane after marriage cannot give his wife a bill of divorce, but a woman who becomes insane after marriage can be divorced (although the rabbis forbade such an act on humanitarian grounds).

Inscriptions *see* SCRIPT.

Inspiration. Divine influence affecting a written or spoken utterance. In Jewish sources the Holy Spirit or the "Shekinah" is depicted as descending or resting upon human beings. Jewish philosophers in Alexandria compared the effect of divine inspiration on man with a lyre, the strings of which are moved by wind. Rabbinic sources distinguish between the verbal inspiration of the Pentateuch and the lesser forms of inspiration found in other biblical books; the Pentateuch is regarded as the result of the highest form of inspiration, every letter, vowel, and musical accent being of divine origin.

Institute for the Study of Hebrew Poetry. Scholarly institution dedicated to collecting, examining, and editing poetic and liturgical material. It was founded in Berlin in 1931 by Salman Schocken and was directed by Heinrich Brody until 1942. It moved to Jerusalem in 1934.

Institutum Judaicum (i). Name given to a number of German educational institutions dedicated to the study of Judaism and missionary activity. They were originally connected with the faculties of Protestant theology at German universities. The first one was established at Halle in 1728. In 1886 Franz Delitzsch founded an Institutum Judaicum to train probationers in theology for missionary work among the Jews at Leipzig University. Delitzsch died in 1890 and was succeeded by Gustav Dalman. The Institutum Judaicum in Leipzig was closed by the Nazis in 1935, but was reopened in Vienna and later transferred to Munster.

Institutum Judaicum (ii). German educational institution dedicated to Jewish studies in the context of Christianity. It was founded in Berlin in 1883 by H. L. Strack. Later it was associated with the faculty of the university under the direction of Hugo Gressman. It published studies in the area of post-biblical Judaism and Talmud.

Insult. In Jewish law an insult is viewed as an injury and must be compensated. Where bodily injury occurs, the insult involved is viewed as an additional factor in determining the damages. According to the rabbis, a person who insults another in public has no share in the world to come.

Intent. The Hebrew word "kavvanah" refers to a state of mental concentration which bestows religious intention on an act; in the medieval period it came to mean specific devotional intention as well as mystical meditation (*see* DEVOTION). The term denoting intention in the legal sense is "zadon." Intent must be proven for an individual to be culpable; when it is lacking, the Bible prescribes compensatory ritual obligations in place of punishment in certain cases.

Intercollegiate Menorah Association *see* MENORAH MOVEMENT.

Intercollegiate Zionist Federation of America [IZFA] *see* STUDENT ZIONIST ORGANIZATION.

Intermarriage. In Jewish usage marriage between a Jew and a non-Jew. Intermarriage was rare before the Emancipation of Jewry, but increased in the 19th century with the establishment of civil marriages. Although intermarriage is forbidden by Jewish law, a number of

Reform rabbis in the US are willing to participate in mixed-marriage ceremonies.

International Refugee Organization. Temporary agency of the UN established in Geneva in 1947. It was entrusted with the care of refugees and displaced persons.

Irgun Tzevai Leumi [Etzel]. Jewish underground organization in Palestine; its alternative name is derived from the initial letters of the formal title. Founded in 1937 by members of Betar and Revisionists in the Haganah, its purpose was to retaliate against Arab attacks. When the White Paper advocating joint Jewish–Arab rule in Palestine was published in 1939, Irgun Tzevai Leumi attacked the British authorities in the country and was subsequently outlawed by the Mandatory government. The Jewish Agency dissociated itself from the activities of the organization. Its leader David Raziel was killed in 1941 and was succeeded by Menaḥem Begin. In 1944 the Irgun Tzevai Leumi renewed its anti-British activities, and later it carried out attacks on Arab villages. When the State of Israel was proclaimed, its members joined the Haganah.

Isaac (i) (fl. ?19th–16th cent. BCE). Israelite, son of Abraham and Sarah. He was born when Abraham was 100 years old (Genesis 21.5). He was the heir of the Abrahamic tradition and covenant (Genesis 17.19; 21.12). In order to test him, God ordered Abraham to sacrifice Isaac, but the boy was saved at the final moment (Genesis 22). Isaac married Rebekah, who bore him two sons, Esau and Jacob.

Isaac (ii) (fl. 8th–9th cent.). Jewish merchant of Aachen. In 797 he was appointed by Charlemagne as guide and interpreter to an official delegation to Harun al-Rashid. When Charlemagne's ambassadors died on the way, Isaac completed the journey and was received by Charlemagne in audience when he returned after four years.

Isaac, Jules (1877–1963). French historian. He was born in Rennes. His *Cours d'histoire* served as a textbook in French schools and colleges. In 1936 he was appointed inspector-general of education for France. After his family was killed by the Nazis, he wrote about the Christian roots of anti-Semitism in *Jésus et Israel* and *Genèse de l'antisémitisme.*

Isaac Arama *see* ARAMA, ISAAC BEN MOSES.

Isaac ben Abba Mari (?1120–?1190). Franco-Spanish rabbinic scholar. Active in Provence and Spain, he corresponded with the important scholars of his generation. His *Sepher ha-Ittur* is a compilation of the main halakhic laws that have practical application. It was regarded as the authoritative code until the appearance of Jacob ben Asher's *Tur*, which superseded it.

Isaac ben Abraham Troki *see* TROKI, ISAAC BEN ABRAHAM.

Isaac ben Joseph of Corbeil [Baal ha-Ḥotem] (fl. 13th cent.). French codifier. His *Sepher Mitzvot Katan* contains a compendium of halakhah, together with ethical homilies, parables, and aggadot. This work, known from its initials as *Semak,* received recognition from scholars in France and Germany.

Isaac ben Meir of Düren (fl. 14th cent.). German codifier. His *Sepher Shearim* (also known as *Sharre Dura* or *Issur ve-Hetter*) served as the authoritative code for dietary laws until the publication of the Shulḥan Arukh.

Isaac ben Moses of Vienna [Isaac Or Zarua] (c. 1180–c. 1250). Bohemian halakhic authority. He became known as Isaac Or Zarua from the title of his halakhic work *Or Zarua.* This study is arranged on the basis of the Talmud, and contains commentaries on talmudic subjects, together with earlier codifications and responsa. It also includes material about medieval Jewish life in Germany, France, and Italy.

Isaac ben Samuel of Acre (fl. 13th–14th cent.). Spanish kabbalist. In 1291 he left Acre for Italy, and then went to Spain, where he met Moses de Leon. His publications include a commentary on Naḥmanides' mysticism, a mystical diary, a commentary on the Sepher Yetzirah, and a study of the composition of the Zohar.

Isaac ben Samuel of Dampierre (d. c. 1185). French tosaphist. He lived in Ramerupt, assisting his teacher and uncle, Jacob Tam. Later he settled in Dampierre. Together with Jacob Tam, he was a central figure in the activity of the tosaphists.

Isaac ben Sheshet Perfet [Ribash] (1326–1408). Spanish rabbi and halakhic authority. He was born in Barcelona. After the persecution of the Jews in 1391, he left Spain and settled in Algiers, where he served as a rabbi. He wrote numerous responsa, which exercised considerable influence on later halakhah and contain information about popular customs in Spain and north Africa. He also wrote commentaries on talmudic tractates and the Pentateuch, as well as poetry.

Isaac Elhanan *see* SPEKTOR, ISAAC ELHANAN.

Isaac Elhanan Yeshiva *see* YESHIVA UNIVERSITY.

Isaac Judaeus *see* ISRAELI, ISAAC BEN SOLOMON.

Isaac Or Zarua *see* ISAAC BEN MOSES OF VIENNA.

Isaacs, Abraham Samuel (1852–1920). American rabbi, writer, and educator. He taught Hebrew and German at New York University between 1885 and 1906. He served as a preacher at the East 86th Street Synagogue in New York and rabbi of the B'nai Jeshurun Congregation in Patterson, New Jersey. In 1878 he became editor of the *Jewish Messenger* and continued in that post until the journal merged with the *American Hebrew* in 1903. His publications include *A Modern Hebrew Poet: The Life and Writings of Moses Chaim Luzzatto* and *What is Judaism?*.

Isaacs, Rufus Daniel *see* READING.

Isaacs, Samuel Myer (1804–1878). Preacher and communal leader. He was born in the Netherlands and first settled in London, where he served as principal of an orphan asylum. He emigrated to the US in 1839. He was the first cantor and preacher of Congregation B'nai Jeshurun in New York. Later he became rabbi of Congregation Shaarei Tefila. He founded the first English-language Jewish weekly in the US, *The Jewish Messenger,* which supported the abolition of slavery and opposed Reform Judaism. In 1859 he was one of the organizers of the Board of Delegates of American Israelites, which advocated Jewish civil and religious rights.

Isaac the Blind (fl. 12th–13th cent.). Franco-Spanish kabbalist, son of Abraham ben David of Posquières. He was one of the earliest kabbalists in Provence and Spain. He transmitted his teachings orally and wrote a commentary on the Sepher Yetzirah. He has been referred to as the "father of the kabbalah."

***Isabella** *see* FERDINAND AND ISABELLA.

Isaiah (i) (fl. 8th cent. BCE). Israelite prophet. He prophesied in Jerusalem from the death of Uzziah until the middle of Hezekiah's reign (740–701 BCE). He protested against unrighteousness and demanded justice for the poor and downtrodden. He opposed all treaties with neighboring states and insisted that the people should put their trust in God. He proclaimed that the nation would be punished through Assyrian conquest and domination, but that a remanent of the people would return and continue the covenant.

Isaiah (ii). Biblical book, one of the books of the Latter Prophets. It contains the account of Isaiah's prophecies. Most scholars believe that the Book of Isaiah should be divided into two sections, chapters 1–39 and 40–66; they are believed to have been written by different authors, Isaiah and Deutero-Isaiah.

Isaiah, Ascension of. Early Christian apocalyptic work containing the Jewish apocryphon, the *Martyrdom of Isaiah.* In this work Isaiah's death is viewed as foreshadowing the coming of Jesus and the early history of the Church. The latter part of the book describes the scenes witnessed by Isaiah during his ascent to the seven heavens.

Isfahani *see* ABU ISSA AL-ISFAHANI.

Ish-bosheth [Eshbaal] (fl. 11th cent. BCE). Israelite prince, son of Saul. After Saul and his other sons died in battle, Ish-bosheth was proclaimed king by Saul's general, Abner (II Samuel 2.8–9). Abner led the war against David (II Samuel 2.12–17; 3.6), but eventually abandoned Ish-bosheth. According to II Samuel 4, Ish-bosheth was murdered by Rechab and Baanah.

Ishmael (fl. ?19th–16th cent. BCE). Israelite, son of Abraham and Hagar. After Hagar conceived, she was treated harshly by Sarah; she fled to the wilderness, but eventually returned. After the birth of Isaac, she and her son, Ishmael, were expelled by Abraham at Sarah's request (Genesis 21). According to tradition, Ishmael was the ancestor of the Arabs.

Ishmael ben Elisha (fl. 2nd cent.). Palestinian tanna. He lived at Kephar Aziz, south of Hebron. He disputed with Akiva about halakhic and aggadic matters, and expanded to 13 the seven hermeneutical rules laid down by Hillel. He was also one of the leading aggadists of the period. According to legend, he was one of the martyrs who was killed in the persecutions that followed the Bar Kokhba revolt. Many mystical statements and literary works were ascribed to him.

Ishmael ben Nethaniah (fl. 6th cent. BCE). Israelite soldier. After the destruction of Jerusalem by the Babylonians, he fled to Baalis, King of the Ammonites. When the Babylonians made the Israelite Gedaliah King of Judah, he gathered the scattered remnants of the people together and prepared to govern them. Ishmael murdered him and endeavoured to take the remaining Jewish community to Ammon, but was thwarted by Johanan ben Kareah. (Jeremiah 40–41)

Ishmaelites. Ancient people who lived in northern Arabia between Egypt and the Assyrian border. According to tradition, they are the Arab descendants of Ishmael, the son of Abraham and Hagar.

Ishmael of Akbara (fl. 9th cent.). Babylonian sectarian. He was the founder of the Akbaraites who seceded from the Karaite community. He did not recognize the masoretic emendations in the text of the Bible. He permitted the consumption on the Sabbath of food cooked or gathered on that day by non-Jews, and the use of the income of a business which operated seven days a week.

Ish-Shalom [Friedmann]**, Meir** (1831–1908). Austrian scholar. He was born in Slovakia. He taught midrash at the Vienna Rabbinical Seminary and published editions of midrashic and aggadic literature.

Isidor, Lazare (1814–1818). French rabbi. He was born in Lixheim, Lorraine. He served as rabbi of Pfalzburg and Paris, and later as chief rabbi of France. During his time at Pfalzburg he refused to allow a member of the congregation of Saverne to pronounce the Jewish oath, *more judaico.* He was subsequently prosecuted, defended by Adolphe Crémieux, and acquitted.

***Isidore of Seville** (c. 560–636). Spanish theologian and encyclopedist, Archbishop of Seville. Born in Cartagena, he moved to Seville as a child. His *Contra Judaeos* attempts to demonstrate the fallacies of the Jewish faith, and provides evidence for the truth of Christianity in all the books of the Bible.

Islam [Mohammedanism]. Monotheistic faith conveyed by the prophet Mohammed to the Arabs. It derives from the Koran, the sacred book of the faith, the contents of which are believed to have been revealed by God to Mohammed; it later developed through oral tradition ("ḥadith"). The original legislation of Islam was similar to Jewish halakhah. In the Koran biblical personages such as Abraham, Noah, Moses, David, Solomon, and the prophets play an important role. According to Islam, the Jews are the "People of the Book" who should enjoy religious freedom. Islam had a profound influence on Jewish thought, particularly in the Middle Ages when Jewish and Muslim thinkers came into contact with one another.

Israel. Name used variously in Jewish history for the territory of the Jews and for the Jewish people. The name was given to Jacob after his struggle with the angel: "Your name shall be called no more Jacob but Israel, for you have striven with God and with men and have prevailed" (Genesis 32.28–9). It is also used for the descendants of Jacob. With the division of the kingdom during the reign of Rehoboam (930 BCE), the southern kingdom was known as "Judah" and the northern kingdom as "Israel." Subsequently the name "Israel" was used in books of the Bible written after the end of the northern kingdom and in rabbinic literature to denote the Jewish people as a whole. When a Jewish homeland was established in 1948 it was called the State of Israel.

Israel, Kingdom of [Samaria]. The northern kingdom of the two kingdoms into which Palestine was divided after the revolt led by Jeroboam I against Rehoboam in 930 BCE. The seceding tribes, led by Ephraim, were Issachar, Zebulun, Naphtali, Asher, Dan, Reuben, Gad, and part of Manasseh. During two centuries Israel had 19 kings. It was eventually captured by the Assyrians in 721 BCE. (I Kings 12–II Kings 17)

Israel, Land of [Canaan; Eretz Yisrael; Holy Land; Jeshurun; Promised Land]. Name of the land promised by God to Abraham and his descendants. The area is indicated in the patriarchal covenant (Genesis 15.18–19). Other boundaries are described in Numbers 34.2–12 and other biblical books, as well as in talmudic sources. It is viewed as an inalienable divine gift to the Jewish people. Love of the land is expressed in the Bible, the Talmud, the liturgy, religious thought, and Jewish law.

Israel, Michael Boaz *see* CRESSON, WARDER.

Israel, State of. From the beginning of World War II, the creation of a Jewish state was the primary aim of Zionists. Although the Balfour Declaration of 1917 supported the creation of a Jewish homeland in Palestine, the British document known as the 1939 White Paper effectively rejected this proposal. After the end of the war the United Nations discussed the Palestinian problem. A plan to partition Palestine into areas for Arabs (Jordan) and Jews (Israel) was endorsed by the General Assembly of the United Nations on 29 November 1947. On 14 May 1948 in Tel Aviv David Ben-Gurion read out the Israeli Scroll of Independence. In the years that followed Israel has repeatedly been at war with those of its Arab neighbors who have not recognized the legitimacy of the state.

Israel ben Eliezer *see* BAAL SHEM IOV, ISRAEL BEN ELIEZER.

Israel ben Joseph Benjamin *see* BENJAMIN (ii).

Israel ben Samuel Ashkenazi of Shklov (d. 1839). Palestinian talmudic scholar of Lithuanian origin. He was born in Shklov, and during his years in Lithuania was entrusted with the publication of the Vilna Gaon's commentaries. He later settled in Safed. In 1816 he was chosen to succeed Menaḥem Mendel of Shklov, the leader of the Kolel ha-Perushim, in Safed. After an earthquake in 1837, he moved to Jerusalem. His *Peat ha-Shulḥan* supplements the Shulḥan Arukh with a codification of laws relating to life in Palestine, which had been omitted by Joseph Caro.

Israel ben Shabbetai of Kozienice [Kozienicer Maggid] (c. 1737–1814). Polish Ḥasidic leader and scholar. He lived in Kozienice in central Poland. He was known for his ability to perform miraculous cures by means of prayers and the use of amulets. According to tradition, the failure of Napoleon's Russian expedition of 1811 was due to Israel ben Shabbetai's prayers.

Israeli, Isaac ben Joseph (fl. 14th cent.). Spanish astronomer. He lived in Toledo and is known for his *Yesod Olam,* which deals with the geometrical problems of the earth in the Ptolemaic system of the universe.

Israeli, Isaac ben Solomon [Isaac Judaeus] (c. 855–c. 955). Physician and philosopher. He was born in Egypt. At about the age of 50 he moved to Kairouan, where he served as court physician. He wrote eight medical works, including treatises on pharmacology, fevers, and ophthalmology, as well as studies of logic and psychology. He was one of the first Jewish medieval philosophers, and attempted to reconcile Jewish theology with Neoplatonism.

Israeli, Isaac d' (1766–1848). English author. He was the son of an Italian-born merchant. His first essays were among the earliest Jewish contributions to English literature. His writings include *Curiosities of Literature* and *Commentary on the Life and Reign of Charles I.* In 1813 he was fined by the Sephardi synagogue in London for refusing to serve as warden. He resigned from the congregation and had his children baptized. Benjamin Disraeli, later prime minister and Earl of Beaconsfield, was his son.

Israelites *see* ISRAEL.

Israelitische Allianz zu Wien. Austrian Jewish organization. It was founded in Vienna in 1873 as a branch of the Alliance Israélite Universelle, but shortly became an independent society. It struggled for equal rights for Jews, established relief agencies, and organized educational institutions. In 1938 it was abolished by the Nazis.

Israelitische Rundschau *see* JÜDISCHE RUNDSCHAU.

Israelitisch-Theologische Lehranstalt *see* VIENNA RABINNICAL SEMINARY.

Israel Labor Party. It was founded in 1968 by the reunion of Mapai with Aḥdut ha-Avodah and Rafi.

Israel Land Development Company. It was founded in 1908 by the World Zionist Organization as the Palestine Land Development Company. Its aim was to purchase land from the Arabs for the Jewish National Fund and for private investors. At the time of the establishing of the State of Israel in 1948 nearly half of all Jewish-owned land had been acquired through the company.

Israel Museum. Israeli national museum, opened in Jerusalem in 1965. It comprises the Bezalel Museum, the Billy Rose Garden of modern sculpture, the Samuel Bronfman Biblical and Archeological Museum, and the Shrine of the Book.

Israel of Ruzhin *see* RUZHIN, ISRAEL OF.

Israels, Jozef (1824–1911). Dutch painter. He was born in Groningen, and earned his living in Amsterdam by painting portraits and historical subjects, including scenes from Jewish life and history. In 1855 he settled in Zandvoort, and later he moved to The Hague.

Isru Ḥag ("Bind the festival offering"). Name given to the semi-festal days occurring after the festivals of Passover, Shavuot, and Sukkot; on these days no applications or confessions are said, and fasting and funeral eulogies are forbidden.

Issachar (fl. ?19th–16th cent. BCE). Son of Jacob and Leah. His birth was considered by Leah to be a sign of divine favor after a long period of barrenness, as a reward for her having given her handmaid to Jacob (Genesis 30.18). Issachar was the ancestor of the tribe bearing his name.

Isserlein, Israel ben Pethahiah (1390–1460). German rabbi and talmudist. He was born in Regensburg and served as rabbi in Marburg and Wiener-Neustadt, where he was the leading halakhic authority of his time. His responsa were collected together in *Terumat ha-Deshen.*

Isserles, Moses [Rema] (c. 1525–1572). Polish codifier. He was born in Kraków, where he later founded and maintained a yeshivah. When Joseph Caro's code, *Bet Yoseph*, appeared, Isserles wrote the *Darkhe Mosheh,* which explained the views of Ashkenazi scholars. After the abridgement of Caro's code, the Shulḥan Arukh, was published, Isserles wrote the *Mappah,* which incorporated Ashkenazi practice. It was through these additions to the Shulḥan Arukh that the code was eventually accepted as authoritative among the Ashkenazim. He also wrote studies of philosophy and kabbalah.

Istanbul *see* CONSTANTINOPLE.

Istituto Convitto Rabbinico *see* COLLEGIO RABBINICO ITALIANO.

Italia, Salom (c. 1619–c. 1655). Italian engraver, etcher, and draftsman. He was born in Mantua, but lived and worked in Amsterdam. He produced engraved portraits and book illustrations, as well as copper-plate borders for the Ketubbah and Megillah.

Ithamar (fl. ?13th cent. BCE). Israelite, youngest son of Aaron. During the wanderings of the Israelites in the wilderness he was assigned special duties as leader over all the Levites (Exodus 31; 38.21). The house of Eli traced descent to him (I Samuel 14.3; I Chronicles 24.3).

ITO *see* JEWISH TERRITORIAL ORGANIZATION.

Itzig, Daniel Jaffe [Jaffe, Daniel] (1723–1799). German financier, leader of the Berlin Jewish community. He minted coins on behalf of the Prussian state during the Seven Years' War. In 1797 he was appointed court banker and inspector of road construction. He was also the chief representative of Prussian Jewry and responsible for the foundation of the Jewish Free School.

Ivrit be-Ivrit ("Hebrew in Hebrew"). Method of teaching Hebrew by speaking the language. It was first practiced in about 1874 in an Alliance Israélite Universelle school in Constantinople at the initiative of Nissim Behar. In 1883 he introduced his method into Palestine, where it was adopted by various Jewish educational institutions under the leadership of Eliezer Ben-Yehudah. It was later widely accepted in many Jewish schools outside Palestine.

Iyyar. Second month of the ancient Israelite calendar, and eighth month of the modern Jewish calendar. 5 Iyyar is Israeli Independence Day. The Second (or Little) Passover (celebrated in the Temple period by those who could not observe Passover in the usual month of Nisan) falls on 14 Iyyar, and Lag Ba-Omer on 18 Iyyar.

Iyyov of Minsk *see* BRILL, JOSEPH.

Izates II (fl. 1st cent.). King of Adiabene (c. 35–60). In his youth he was sent by his father to the court of Abnerigos, King of Mesene. There he was attracted to Judaism, as was his mother, Helena. His conversion to the Jewish faith aroused considerable opposition in Adiabene. On the occasion of a famine in Palestine, both he and his mother sent assistance to the hungry. He sent five of his sons to Jerusalem to be educated.

IZFA [Intercollegiate Zionist Federation of America] *see* STUDENT ZIONIST ORGANIZATION.

Izmir *see* SMYRNA.

J

Jabbok. Tributary of the River Jordan, flowing into it on the eastern side. Jacob wrestled with an angel on a ford of the Jabbok (Genesis 32). The river marked the frontier between the territories of the Ammonites and the Amorites (Deuteronomy 2.31–7; 3.16).

Jabès, Edmond (b. 1912). French writer and poet. He was born in Cairo and settled in Paris in 1957. His works, most of which are theological, include *The Book of Questions* and *The Book of Resemblances.*

Jabesh Gilead. Israelite city in Gilead, east of the Jordan, in the territory of the half tribe of Manasseh. It flourished during the period of the Judges and the monarchy. Its inhabitants did not join the expedition of the Israelite tribes against Benjamin; as a punishment the city was destroyed, the population killed, and the young women seized and given to the Benjamites (Judges 21). In the 11th century BCE Saul saved the city from the Ammonites. After Saul's death in a battle with the Philistines, the citizens of Jabesh-Gilead sought out his body and the bodies of his sons and buried them (I Samuel 31.11–13; I Chronicles 10.11–12).

Jabin (fl. ?13th cent. BCE). King of the Canaanite city of Hazor, and leader of the Canaanite alliance against the Israelites in their quest for the Promised Land. According to the Bible, he was killed after the battle of Merom, and Hazor was destroyed (Joshua 11.10–13).

Jabneh [Jamnia; Yavneh]. Ancient city located on the coastal plain to the south of Jaffa; the modern town of Yebnah stands on the same site. Jabneh was fortified by Uzziah as a barrier against the Philistines (II Chronicles 26.6). During the second Temple period it was Hellenized, and by the time of the accession of Alexander Yannai (103 BCE), it was a Hasmonean city. Pompey attempted to revive it as a gentile town (63 BCE) and it became the seat of an imperial procurator. In the first Jewish war, it was occupied by Vespasian, but after the fall of Jerusalem (70 CE) the Sanhedrin was reconstituted at Jabneh under Johanan ben Zakkai and the city flourished as the center of Jewish life in Palestine until the time of the Bar Kokhba revolt (132).

Jabotinsky, Vladimir (1880–1940). Russian Zionist leader, soldier, and writer. He was born in Odessa. He first worked as a foreign correspondent in Berne and Rome. After returning to Odessa, he formed a Jewish self-defense group there. During World War I he advocated the recruiting of Jewish regiments to fight on the Palestinian front, and after the war he supported the maintainance of a Jewish legion in Palestine to protect Jews from Arab hostility. In 1920 he organized a Jewish self-defense unit in Jerusalem, for which he was arrested, tried, and punished by a British military tribunal. In 1925 he formed the World Union of Zionist Revisionists, and from 1936 he urged the evacuation of eastern European Jewry to Palestine. He was the spiritual father and head of the Jewish underground movement Irgun Tzevai Leumi, founded in 1937. Besides his military activities, he was also a translator, writer, and poet.

Jachin. The name of one of the two pillars set up by Solomon at the entrance to the Temple in Jerusalem (I Kings 7.15–22); the other was called Boaz.

Jackson, Bernard (b. 1944). British lawyer. He was born in Liverpool and later taught law there, at the polytechnic and the university; he has also taught at the University of Kent. His publications include *Theft in Early Jewish Law*, *Essays in Jewish and Comparative Legal History*, and *Semiotics and Legal History*. He has served as the president of the Jewish Law Association and editor of the *Jewish Law Annual*.

Jacob [Israel] (fl. ?19th–16th cent. BCE). Israelite, son of Isaac and Rebekah. He bought the birthright of his brother Esau in exchange for food when Esau was faint with hunger, and later succeeded in securing the blessing Isaac intended to bestow on Esau. Fearing his brother's anger, Jacob left home and went to Haran, where he married Rachel and Leah, the daughters of his uncle Laban; by them and their handmaids Bilhah and Zilpah he had 12 sons and a daughter. After many years he made his way back to Canaan; during the journey he wrestled with an angel at a ford on the River Jabbok. In his old age, during a time of famine in Canaan, he was reunited with his youngest son, Joseph, who had been sold into slavery by his brothers and had become Pharoah's chief minister in Egypt. (Genesis 25–50)

Jacob, Benno (1862–1945). German rabbi and biblical scholar. He was born in Breslau. He served as a rabbi in Göttingen and Dortmund before settling in Hamburg and then (in 1939) in England. He published studies of the Pentateuch, defending it against the claims of modern biblical criticism, and claimed that "higher criticism" of the Bible was anti-Semitic. He was also opposed to Zionism, viewing it as a secularization of Judaism and a basis for Jewish atheism.

Jacob ben Asher [Baal ha-Turim] (c. 1270–c. 1343). Spanish codifier, son of Asher ben Jehiel. He was born in Germany and went with his father to Spain in 1303. He lived first in Barcelona and later in Toledo. His code, *Arbaah Turim*, contains the decisions found in both versions of the Talmud, and those of the geonim, as well as those given in earlier commentaries and codes. The work is divided into four parts: "Oraḥ Ḥayyim" deals with daily conduct, including prayers, Sabbaths, and holidays; "Yoreh Deah" lays down dietary laws; "Even ha-Ezer" covers personal and family matters; and "Ḥoshen Mishpat" describes civil law and administration.

Jacob ben Jacob Moses of Lissa (d. 1832). Polish talmudist. He served as a rabbi at Kalisz, Lissa, and Stryy. He was opposed to the Reform movement and to Ḥasidism. His *Derekh ha-Ḥayyim* is a compendium of Jewish practice.

Jacob ben Meir Tam [Rabbenu Tam] (c. 1100–1171). French tosaphist, grandson of Rashi and brother of Samuel ben Meir. He lived at Ramerupt, and later settled at Troyes, where the first conference of French rabbis met under his leadership. His *Sepher ha-Yashar* contains many of his tosaphot and novellae. He wrote studies of grammar and biblical interpretation, and composed liturgical poetry.

Jacob ben Moses ha-Levi Mölln [Mölln, Jacob ben Moses] (c. 1360–1427). German codifier. He served as a rabbi in Mainz and later in Worms. He was a leading authority on Jewish customs and liturgy. His religious practices were recorded by his disciple Zalman of St. Goar in *Sepher Maharil*.

Jacob ben Reuben (fl. 12th cent.). Turkish Karaite biblical commentator. A native of Constantinople, he traveled to various countries to spread Karaism. His biblical commentary, *Sepher ha-Osher*, contains excerpts from Karaite authors.

Jacob ben Samson (fl. 12th cent.). French historian and scholar, pupil of Rashi. According to the tosaphists, he was the author of *Seder Olam*, a chronology of the tannaim and amoraim.

Jacob ben Wolf Kranz [Jacob of Dubno; Maggid of Dubno] (c. 1740–1804). Polish preacher and scholar. He was active in Poland and Galicia, and at Dubno in the Ukraine. His writings were published posthumously.

Jacob ben Yakar (d. 1064). German rabbi. He was a teacher of Rashi and the head of a yeshivah at Worms. He was known for his humility. He wrote glosses on several talmudic tractates.

Jacob Hebraeus *see* ROSALES, JACOB.

Jacobi, Frederick (1891–1952). American composer. He was assistant conductor at the Metropolitan Opera House in New York and taught composition at the Juilliard School of Music from 1936 to 1951. Many of his works are based on Jewish themes.

Jacob Isaac of Przysucha (1766–1814). Polish tzaddik. He inaugurated a Ḥasidic approach to Judaism based on the speculative study of the Torah and Ḥasidism. He was, however, opposed to the more popular form of Ḥasidism, with its belief in miracles.

Jacob Joseph of Polonnoye (d. 1782). Ukrainian Ḥasidic scholar. He was a rabbi at Sharagrod, but left his position after he became a follower of the Baal Shem Tov. Later he served as a rabbi at Rashkov, Nemirov, and Polonnoye. His *Toledot Yaakov Yoseph* is a primary source for the teachings of the Baal Shem Tov; it led the Vilna Gaon to issue a ban against the Ḥasidim. His other works include the biblical commentaries *Ben Porat Yoseph*, *Tzaphenat Paneaḥ*, and *Ketonet Passim*.

Jacob Joshua ben Tzevi Hirsch Falk (1680–1756). Polish talmudist. He served as a rabbi in several Polish and German cities; his yeshivah at Lwów became the centre of rabbinic learning in Poland. In 1730 he became a rabbi in Berlin and later in Frankfurt am Main, though he resigned the latter post because of his support for the rabbinical scholar Jacob Emden. His *Pene Yehoshua* contains novellae on the Talmud.

Jacob of Dubno *see* JACOB BEN WOLF KRANZ.

Jacobowski, Ludwig (1868–1900). German poet and author. He was born in Strelno, in the Posen district, and lived in Berlin. He edited a newspaper, wrote several volumes of poetry, and published a number of novels. He was a significant Jewish figure in the last decade of 19th-century German literature; his writings sought to create a synthesis of Judaism with German culture.

Jacobs, Joseph (1854–1916). British historian, folklorist, and scholar. Born in Australia, he settled in England, where he became active as an author and journalist. He was the founder (in 1896) and editor of the *Jewish Year Book*. His studies of medieval Anglo-Jewish history included *Jews of Angevin England*. In 1900 he settled in the US, where he was an editor of the *Jewish Encyclopedia* and taught at the Jewish Theological Seminary.

Jacobs, Louis (b. 1920). English rabbi and scholar. He was born in Manchester and served as a rabbi there and, later, in London. From 1959 to 1962 he was a tutor at the Jews College, but he was disqualified by Chief Rabbi Brodie as a candidate for the post of principal of the college because of his religious views. He subsequently founded the New London Synagogue, where he served as rabbi. He wrote on halakhic issues, Jewish theology and philosophy, and Jewish mysticism. His publications include *We have Reason to Believe*, *Principles of the Jewish Faith*, and *A Jewish Theology*.

Jacobson, Dan (b. 1929). British novelist. He was born in Johannesburg, lived in Israel, and later settled in London. His novels deal with the problems of apartheid in South Africa and of Jewish identity in the modern world.

Jacobson, Howard (b. 1942). English novelist. He was born in Manchester. After a period spent in Australia as a lecturer in English literature at Sydney University, he returned to Britain to teach at Cambridge; he also worked as a publisher and retailer. In 1975 he became a lecturer in English at Wolverhampton Polytechnic. His novels deal with Jewish characters.

Jacobson, Israel (1768–1828). German Reform leader. He was born in Halberstadt. He was president of the Jewish consistory in Westphalia, where he worked for the reform of Jewish education and the synagogue liturgy. In 1801 he founded the Jacobson School for Jewish and Christian pupils in Seesen, Braunschweig. He set up a Reform synagogue in Seesen in 1810. Later he moved to Berlin, where he held Reform services in his home.

Jacobson, Victor (1869–1935). Russian Zionist leader and diplomat. He was born in Simferopol in the Crimea. From 1899 he was a member of the Zionist General Council. In 1903 he opposed the Uganda Scheme and was one of the organizers of the Khar'kov Conference in opposition to Theodor Herzl. He served as head of the Beirut office of the Anglo-Palestine Company from 1906, and later directed its branch in Constantinople. During World War I he ran the Zionist office in Copenhagen and subsequently he represented the Zionist organization and the Jewish Agency in Paris and at the League of Nations.

Jacoby, Johann (1805–1877). Prussian politician. He was born in Königsberg. He advocated Jewish religious reform and emancipation. In 1848 he was elected to the Prussian Landtag, and in the following year to the German Nationalversammelung in Frankfurt am Main. From 1863 he served in the Prussian House of Representatives.

Jael (fl. 12th cent. BCE). Kenite woman, wife of Heber the Kenite. After the army of Jabin of Hazor was defeated by the Israelites, the commander Sisera sought refuge in her tent. She killed him in his sleep (Judges 4–5).

Jaffa *see* JOPPA.

Jaffe, Daniel *see* ITZIG, DANIEL JAFFE.

Jaffe, Joseph (1865–1938). American Yiddish poet. Born in Lithuania, he settled in New York in 1892. His poetry deals primarily with the theme of love.

Jaffe, Leib (1876–1948). Russian Zionist leader and writer. He was born in Grodno in Belorussia. He participated in the First Zionist Congress in 1897 and those following it. He edited Zionist periodicals in Russia, and later was called to Moscow to edit the monthly journal of the Zionist Organization. He subsequently moved to Lithuania, where he was elected president of the Zionist Organization and edited its newspaper.

In 1920 he emigrated to Palestine, and became editor of the daily paper *Haaretz*. As a writer he published Zionist literature in Russian, Russian anthologies of Hebrew poetry, and a selection of world poetry on Jewish nationalist topics.

Jaffe, Meir ben Israel (fl. 15th cent.). German copyist and book binder. He wrote a Haggadah (now in Cincinnati) at the end of the 15th century. In 1468 the Nuremberg Council invited him to go to Nuremberg to bind a copy of the Pentateuch.

Jaffe, Mordecai ben Abraham (c. 1535–1612). Talmudist, kabbalist, and communal leader. He was born in Prague. He studied in Poland under Solomon Luria and Moses Isserles, then returned to Prague, where he became head of a yeshivah. Later he settled in Venice but he eventually moved back to eastern Europe and was appointed av bet din and head of the yeshivah of Grodno (now in Belorussia). He subsequently lived in Lublin, Kremenets, Prague, and Posen. He was the author of *Levush Malkhut*, a comprehensive code of Jewish law which provoked widespread criticism.

Jaffe, Tzevi Hirsch (1853–1929). Russian mathematician. He wrote studies of mathematical theory and invented a calculating machine. He was also a talmudic scholar and an authority on the Jewish calendar.

Jagel, Abraham *see* GALLICO, ABRAHAM JAGEL BEN HANANIAH.

Jair (i) (fl. ?13th–12th cent. BCE). Israelite hero. During the Israelites' wanderings in the wilderness he captured a group of villages from the Amorites (Numbers 32.41).

Jair (ii) (fl. 12th cent. BCE). Israelite judge. He flourished in the generation preceding Jephthah and judged Israel for 22 years (Judges 10.3–5).

Jakobovits, Immanuel, Lord (b. 1921). British rabbi. He was born in Königsberg. He served as a minister in several London synagogues and became chief rabbi of Dublin in 1949. From 1958 he was a rabbi at the Fifth Avenue Synagogue in New York. In 1966 he was appointed Chief Rabbi of the United Hebrew Congregations of the British Commonwealth. He was subsequently knighted, and eventually created a peer. His publications include *Jewish Medical Ethics*.

Jamnia *see* JABNEH.

Janco, Marcel (1895–1984). Israeli painter. He was born in Bucharest. Early in his career he was involved in Dadaism in Paris, but he left the movement and returned to Romania, where he worked as an architect. In 1941 he settled in Palestine and began to paint works that reflect the colors of the landscape and its picturesque aspects. In 1947 he was a founder member of the New Horizons group. Later he established Ein Hod, an artists' village outside Haifa.

Janner, Barnett, Lord (1892–1982). Welsh politician and communal leader. He served as a member of parliament – as a Liberal from 1931 to 1935 and as a Labour member from 1945 to 1970. He was also president of the Zionist Federation of Great Britain and Ireland (1950), and of the Board of Deputies of British Jews (1955–64). He was subsequently knighted and then created a life peer.

Janner, Greville (b. 1928). Welsh politician and communal leader, son of Barnett Janner. He was born in Cardiff. He became a barrister and has served as a Labour member of parliament. He has worked in various Jewish communal bodies and has written and contributed to a number of books.

Janowsky, Oscar (b. 1900). American historian. He was born in Poland and was taken to the US in 1910. In 1948 he became professor of history at New York

City College. His writings include *The Jews and Minority Rights (1898–1919)*, *The American Jew: a Composite Portrait*, *The American Jew: a Reappraisal*, *The Education of American Jewish Teachers*, and *Foundations of Israel*.

Japheth. Son of Noah. With his brothers, Shem and Ham, he traveled with Noah in the ark. After the Flood, Noah planted a vineyard; the Bible recounts the story of Noah's drunkenness and of Shem and Japheth covering him with a garment as he lay naked in his tent (Genesis 9).

Japheth ben Ali ha-Levi (fl. 10th cent.). Palestinian Karaite scholar. He lived in Jerusalem. He wrote biblical commentaries, a translation of the Bible into Arabic, and polemical tracts against Saadyah Gaon.

Jaques, Heinrich (1831–1894). Austrian lawyer and politician. He was born in Vienna, and worked as a lawyer and banker. In 1879 he entered the Reichsrat as a German Liberal. He published a tract on Jewish Emancipation.

Jashar, Book of [Sepher ha-Yashar]. Ancient work, one of the lost books mentioned in the Bible (Joshua 10–13; II Samuel 1.18; I Kings 8.53). It contained poems about individuals and events from the time of Joshua to the beginning of the monarchy (1250–1000 BCE). A medieval composition of biblical legends, based on midrashim to the Pentateuch, was known by the same title.

Jason (fl. 2nd cent. BCE). Israelite, high priest. He bribed Antiochus IV to depose his brother, Onias III, so that he could become high priest. But later he was dismissed from the high priesthood by the king, and Menelaus, who offered Antiochus IV a large sum of money, was appointed instead. Jason's Hellenizing policy contributed to the Hasmonean revolt (166–164 BCE), which freed Judea from the rule of the Seleucids.

Jastrow, Marcus (1829–1903). American rabbi and philologist. He was born in Rogasen, in the Posen district. After serving as preacher to the progressive German congregation in Warsaw, he became a rabbi in Worms. In 1866 he emigrated to the US and was appointed rabbi at Rodeph Shalom in Philadelphia. His publications include *Dictionary of the Targumim, the Talmud Babli and Yerushalmi, and the Midrashic Literature*.

Jastrow, Morris (1861–1922). American orientalist, son of Marcus Jastrow. Born in Poland, he was brought up in the US. He taught Semitics at the University of Pennsylvania, where he became research professor of Assyriology. He wrote studies of biblical and Assyriological topics.

Jawitz, Ze'ev (1847–1924). Polish historian. He settled in Palestine in 1888, and worked as a teacher and writer. He left Palestine in 1894 and moved in succession to Vilnius, Germany, and London. His *Toledot Yisrael* is a 14-volume history of the Jews.

Jebusites. Ancient people, inhabitants of Canaan before the conquest of the territory by the Israelites. The Jebusites lived in the hill region around Jerusalem. Although the Israelites under Joshua conquered a coalition led by the Jebusites, Jerusalem itself was not taken until the time of David (II Samuel 5.6–7).

Jeconiah *see* JEHOIACHIN.

Jedaiah ha-Penini *see* BEDERSI, JEDAIAH.

Jedid al-Islam ("New Muslims"). Name of a group of crypto-Jews, resident in Meshed, Persia. Their ancestors converted to Islam in response to persecution by the Muslims in 1839. The Jedid al-Islam lived as Muslims but secretly observed Jewish customs.

Jeduthun (fl. 11th cent. BCE). Israelite seer and singer of David's household (II Chronicles 35.15). He was head of a family of singers whom David singled out from the Levites (I Chronicles 25.1).

Psalms 39, 62, and 77 are attributed to him.

Jehiel ben Joseph of Paris (d. c. 1265). French talmudist and tosaphist. He was the leading Jewish protagonist in the Disputation of Paris (1240) held at the court of Louis IX, which originated from the charges of the apostate Nicholas Donin. As a result of this disputation, copies of the Talmud were burned in Paris in 1242. Jehiel ben Joseph continued to lead the Jewish academy in Paris, but in 1260 he moved to Palestine and settled in Acre, where he opened a yeshivah.

Jehiel Michal of Zloczov [Maggid of Zloczov] (c. 1731–1786). Galician Ḥasidic leader. He was born in Brody and served as a preacher there and, later, in Zloczov. He was one of the early propagators of Ḥasidism in Galicia; he was strongly opposed by the mitnaggedim. Toward the end of his life he settled in Yampol, Podolia. Miraculous tales are told of his asceticism and saintliness.

Jehoahaz (i) [Joahaz] (fl. 9th cent. BCE). King of Israel (c. 814–800 BCE), son of Jehu. During his reign, Aram turned Israel into a tributary nation, reduced her army, and controlled large parts of her territory (II Kings 13.1–9).

Jehoahaz (ii) [Shallum] (fl. 7th cent. BCE). King of Judah (609 BCE), son of Josiah. His name was originally Shallum (Jeremiah 22.11), but it was changed to Jehoahaz when he was made king after his father had been killed in the battle against Pharaoh Necho II at Megiddo. Three months later Necho II deposed Jehoahaz and put his elder brother Jehoiakim in his place (II Kings 23.33–4; II Chronicles 36.3–4). Jehoahaz died in captivity in Egypt (II Kings 23.29–34).

Jehoash (i) *see* JOASH (i) and (ii).

Jehoash (ii) *see* BLOOMGARDEN, SOLOMON.

Jehoiachin [Coniah; Jeconiah] (fl. 6th cent. BCE). King of Judah (597 BCE), son of Jehoiakim. He ascended the throne at the age of 18 during the rebellion against Babylon. He was exiled to Babylon by Nebuchadnezzar, together with his family and 10,000 captives (II Kings 24.12ff). He was released during the reign of Evil-Merodach (II Kings 24–5; II Chronicles 36.8–10).

Jehoiada [Joiada] (fl. 9th cent. BCE). High priest. After Athaliah assumed the throne and killed the royal family (II Kings 11.1), it was feared that the entire house of David would be eliminated. But Jehoiada's wife, Jehosheba, hid Joash, the baby son of King Ahaziah, in the Temple. Jehoiada later proclaimed Joash king, had Athaliah slain, and acted as regent until Joash was seven. Under Jehoiada's influence, the cult of Baal was prohibited and the Temple at Jerusalem restored (II Kings 12).

Jehoiakim [Eliakim; Joiakim] (fl. 7th–6th cent. BCE). King of Judah (608–598 BCE), son of Josiah. He was made king by Pharaoh Necho II in succession to his brother Jehoahaz (ii). During the first three years of his reign Judah was subject to Egypt. After Necho II was defeated in the battle of Carchemish in 605 BCE, Judah came under the Babylonian yoke; according to II Chronicles, Nebuchadnezzar bound him in fetters to take him to Babylon (II Chronicles 36.6ff). Jehoiakim was a vassal of Babylon for three years before he rebelled (II Kings 24.1), which brought about his downfall and death.

Jehonadab ben Rechab *see* RECHABITES.

Jehoram (i) [Joram] (fl. 9th cent. BCE). King of Israel (853–842 BCE), son of Ahab. He joined Jehoshaphat of Judah in the war against Mesha of Moab. He engaged in battle with Aram and was wounded in the battle of Ramoth-Gilead; while he was recuperating in Jezreel, Jehu assassinated him. (II Kings 8–9)

Jehoram (ii) [Joram] (fl. 9th cent. BCE).

King of Judah (851–843 BCE), son of Jehoshaphat of Judah. He was married to Athaliah who introduced the cult of Baal into Judah. During his reign, Edom rebelled against Judah and Judah was ravaged by the Philistines. (II Kings 8; II Chronicles 21)

Jehoshaphat (fl. 9th cent. BCE). King of Judah (874–850 BCE), son of Asa. He was the first king of Judah to make a treaty with Israel. He married his son Jehoram (ii) to Athaliah, the daughter of King Omri of Israel (II Kings 8.26). Together with Ahab, he waged war unsuccessfully against Aram. With Ahab's son Jehoram (i), he engaged in battle with Mesha of Moab.

Jehoshaphat, Valley of. According to the Bible, it is the place where God will gather all the nations to judge them (Joel 3.2, 12).

Jehovah. In the Vulgate and other versions of the Christian Bible, the form given to the Tetragrammaton (that is, the letters YHWH, used in Hebrew to refer to God). *See* GOD, NAMES OF.

Jehu (fl. 9th cent. BCE). King of Israel (c. 842–814 BCE). He was commander-in-chief to Jehoram (i) but conspired with the army against the king. With the assistance of Elisha, he eliminated the royal family (including Jehoram, Ahaziah of Judah, and Jezebel), as well as the priests of Baal, whose worship had flourished under Jehoram's reign. He fought unsuccessfully against Aram and paid tribute to Shalmaneser III of Assyria for protection from the Arameans. His dynasty continued for 100 years. (II Kings 9–11)

Jeiteles [Jeitteles]**, Alois** (1794–1858). Bohemian physician and poet, nephew of Baruch and Judah Jeiteles. Born in Brünn, he served as a physician there. In 1819 he published, with Ignaz Jeiteles, the short-lived Jewish periodical *Siona*. A cycle of his poetry was set to music by Beethoven.

Jeiteles [Jeitteles]**, Baruch** (1762–1813). Bohemian Hebrew writer and physician, brother of Judah Jeiteles. He maintained a yeshivah in Prague, but later became a supporter of the Haskalah movement. He wrote halakhic novellae as well as Hebrew poems and translations. In 1813 he persuaded leading individuals in the Prague community to open a hospital for wounded soldiers of all nationalities in the Jewish quarter.

Jeiteles [Jeitteles]**, Ignaz** (1783–1843). Bohemian writer, son of Baruch Jeiteles. He studied law at Prague University before moving to Vienna, where he worked as a merchant. With his cousin Alois Jeiteles he published the short-lived Jewish periodical *Siona* in 1819. He wrote studies of literature, philosophy, history, and statistics as well as poetry.

Jeiteles [Jeitteles]**, Judah** (1773–1838). Bohemian orientalist, brother of Baruch Jeiteles. He was one of the four chairmen of the Jewish community in Prague, where he supervised the German-language school. He was the first to use the word "Haskalah" for the Jewish Enlightenment movement. In 1830 he settled in Vienna. He contributed to Hebrew periodicals, and was the author of an Aramaic grammar in Hebrew.

Jellinek, Adolf (c. 1820–1893). Austrian preacher and scholar. He was born in Moravia and moved to Prague in 1838. He was a rabbi in Leipzig from 1845, and in Vienna from 1856, where he became a famous preacher. He published studies of the history of the kabbalah and medieval Jewish philosophy, editions of smaller midrashim in his *Bet ha-Midrash*, and bibliographical booklets on medieval Jewish history and literature.

Jephthah (fl. c. 12th cent. BCE). Israelite judge. When Gilead was threatened by the Ammonites, he went to war against them. Before he engaged in battle, he vowed to sacrifice to God whatever came first from his house should he return safely. To his grief he was met by his daughter, whom he subsequently sacrificed (Judges 11). Later he was victorious over the Ephramites.

Jerba. Island off the coast of Tunisia. According to legend, a Jewish population was found there from biblical times.

Jeremiah (i) (fl. 7th–6th cent. BCE). Israelite prophet. When he first emerged as a prophet he rebuked the nation for idolatry. After the religious revival that marked the reign of Josiah, Jeremiah warned the people to keep the newly made covenant with God. When Nebuchadnezzar became king in Babylonia, Jeremiah prophesied that he would conquer Judah. Later he foretold the defeat of Zedekiah and his anti-Babylonian alliance, and advocated surrender. After the fall of Jerusalem, he went to Egypt, where he condemned Egyptian Jewry for idol-worship.

Jeremiah (ii). Biblical book, one of the books of the Latter Prophets. It contains 52 chapters: chapters 1–18 contain prophecies from the time of Josiah; chapters 19–36 record prophecies and narrative from the reigns of Jehoiakim, Jehoiachin, and Zedekiah; chapters 37–44 consist of historical narrative; chapters 45–51 contain prophecies concerning other nations; and chapter 52 recapitulates the Book of Kings.

Jeremiah (iii) (fl. 4th cent.). Palestinian amora. He was born in Babylonia and became head of the academy at Tiberias. He engaged in halakhic discussions with most contemporary sages.

Jericho. Ancient city in the southern Jordan valley, 15 miles north-east of Jerusalem. A royal city of great antiquity (Deuteronomy 32.49), it was destroyed by Joshua (Joshua 6). It was left desolate, but was revived during the reign of Ahab by Hiel the Bethelite (I Kings 16.34).

Jeroboam I (fl. 10th cent. BCE). King of Israel (c. 928–907 BCE). During Solomon's reign, he was a superintendent of forced labor and led a revolt against the monarchy. After Solomon's death, he led a delegation representing the northern tribes, which met Rehoboam at Shechem. The delegation demanded changes in the system of labor; when its request was refused, the northern tribes declared their independence and appointed Jeroboam king. He first made his capital at Shechem, but later moved it to Penuel. He set up new shrines at Bethel and Dan, centered round the worship of golden calves. (I Kings 11–15; II Chronicles 10, 13)

Jeroboam II (fl. 8th cent. BCE). King of Israel (789–748 BCE), son of Joash. He was the greatest ruler of the dynasty of Jehu; during his reign the Northern Kingdom attained the height of its economic, military, and political power. His rule was marred by corruption, which was denounced by the prophets Amos and Hosea. (II Kings 14)

***Jerome** (c. 340–420). Christian ascetic and scholar, one of the Church Fathers. He was born at Stridon in Dalmatia, and eventually settled in Bethlehem, where he directed a monastery. There he studied Hebrew with several Jewish teachers, and translated the Bible from Hebrew into Latin. This translation (together with his translation of the New Testament from Greek into Latin) was accepted as the official version of the Bible by the Catholic Church, and is known as the "Vulgate." He also wrote biblical commentaries and biographical studies.

Jerubaal *see* GIDEON.

Jerusalem [City of David; Holy City; Salem]. Capital of Israel. In the time of Joshua, Adoni-zedek, King of Jerusalem, was defeated by the Israelites at Aijalon (Joshua 10). Yet his city remained an independent enclave between the tribal areas of Benjamin and Judah. It was later captured by David and became the capital of a united Israel (II Samuel 5.6–8; I Chronicles 11.4–6). By transferring the Ark of the Covenant there, David made it also the religious center of Israel. Solomon enlarged the city by adding the Palace and the Temple. After his death, it remained the capital of Judah and the Davidic dynasty until it was destroyed by the Babylonians in the 6th century BCE. Subsequently Jewish exiles returned and rebuilt the Temple. The Temple and the city were devastated a second time by the Romans in the 1st century. In modern times Jerusalem has again become the capital of the Jewish state.

Jerusalem, Wilhelm (1854–1923). Austrian philosopher. He was born in Drenic, Bohemia. He became a schoolmaster and later taught philosophy and pedagogics at the University of Vienna; between 1894 and 1902 he also taught at the Jüdisch-Theologische Lehranstalt in Vienna. He wrote studies of the psychology of language and thought, the theory of consciousness, and problems of logic.

Jerusalem Post. Israeli English-language newspaper. It was founded as the *Palestine Post* by Gershon Agron in 1932, and became the *Jerusalem Post* in 1950, under which name it continues to be published. It played an important role as the organ of the official Jewish agencies under the British Mandate.

Jerusalem Talmud *see* TALMUD.

Jeshua ben Damna (fl. 1st cent.). Israelite, high priest (c. 61–3). He was appointed by Herod Agrippa II but after a short period of office was displaced by Joshua ben Gamla. At the end of the Roman siege of Jerusalem (70 CE) he fled for refuge to the Romans, together with other members of priestly families.

Jeshua ben Judah (fl. 11th cent.). Palestinian Karaite scholar. He lived in Jerusalem. His principal works are an Arabic translation of the Pentateuch with a philosophical commentary, a study of the law of incest, and philosophical tracts.

Jeshurun. Poetic name for Israel, used several times in the Bible (Deuteronomy 32.15; 33.5,26; Isaiah 44.2).

Jesofowicz, Michael (d. 1531). Lithuanian financier and communal leader. In 1514 Sigismund I appointed him "elder and judge" of Lithuanian Jewry, chief collector of dues, and the Jewish representative at court. In 1525 he was ennobled.

Jesse (fl. 11th–10th cent. BCE). Israelite, father of David. He lived in Bethlehem, but later settled in Moab for fear of Saul. The royal house of David is referred to in the Bible as growing from the root of Jesse (Isaiah 11.1, 10).

Jesurun, Isaac (fl. 17th cent.). Dalmatian merchant. He was a merchant at Ragusa, where he was accused in 1622 of the ritual murder of a Christian girl. His suffering is described in Hebrew and Spanish accounts. Banished for his supposed crime, he died in Palestine.

Jesurun, Reuel (fl. c. 1575–1634). Portuguese Marrano. He was born in Lisbon. In 1599 he traveled to Rome, intending to join a Christian monastic order; but on the journey he was persuaded to return to Judaism, and went back to Lisbon. In 1604 he settled in Amsterdam, where he worked as the administrator of the Talmud Torah rabbinical school. His *Diálogo dos montes* is a dramatic poem in praise of Judaism.

Jesus (fl. 1st cent. BCE–1st cent. CE). Palestinian religious leader, founder of Christianity. According to the New Testament, he grew up in Galilee and was baptized by John the Baptist. He performed various miracles and announced the coming of the Kingdom of God. He was arrested and crucified by order of the Roman procurator, Pontius Pilate, at the instigation of the Jewish authorities. His followers believed that he rose from the dead and ascended to Heaven. They formed the core of the earliest Christian Church, and actively spread the good news about Jesus, whom they believed to be the Messiah (hence the addition to his name of "Christ": the anointed one). According to Christian belief, Jesus was God Incarnate and is restored to the Godhead in the form of the Trinity.

Jesus ben Sira *see* BEN SIRA.

Jethro [Reuel] (fl. ?13th cent. BCE). Midianite, father-in-law of Moses. Moses married Jethro's daughter Zipporah, and Jethro appointed him as shepherd of his flocks (Exodus 2.16–21; 3.1). After the Exodus, Jethro advised Moses on the reorganization of the judicial system (Exodus 18). In Scripture Jethro is also referred to as Reuel.

Jew. Member of the Jewish community. The word is derived from the Latin "Judaeus," which itself is from the Hebrew "Yehudah," meaning "Judah." Traditionally Jewish identity is dependent on maternal descent or conversion to Judaism. The term is also used to denote ethnic origin without reference to religious observance. *See also* ISRAEL.

Jew Bill. Name by which the Jewish Naturalization Bill, debated in the English parliament in 1753, was commonly known. The bill, which was passed in May 1753, facilitated the naturalization of foreign Jews and encouraged immigration. It gave rise to considerable opposition and was repealed in December 1753.

Jewish Academy of Arts and Sciences. American learned society. Its members are Jews distinguished in the arts and professions. Founded in 1927, it sponsors public meetings, publishes papers, and encourages research.

Jewish Agency for Israel. The executive and representative body of the World Zionist Organization. Until the establishment of the State of Israel in 1948, it played a major role in the relations between those seeking to establish a Jewish homeland in Palestine and world Jewry. Thereafter it relinquished many of its activities to the government of Israel, but it has continued to be responsible for immigration, land settlement, youth work, and other functions financed by voluntary Jewish contributions from abroad.

Jewish Agricultural Society. American charitable organization, founded in New York in 1900 to provide eastern European immigrants to the US with agricultural training. It was a subsidiary of the Baron de Hirsch Fund and stressed self-supporting agricultural activities. It published a monthly journal, the *Jewish Farmer*.

Jewish Braille Institute of America. Charitable organization founded in 1931 to help the blind. It formulated a Yiddish Braille alphabet in 1945, and in 1950 published a Hebrew Braille Bible.

Jewish Brigade. Jewish infantry brigade of the British Army. It was established in September 1944 at the request of the Jewish Agency. Its headquarters were set up in Egypt under Brigadier A. P. Benjamin, but were later moved to Italy. It went into action in February 1945 in northern Italy and was then stationed on the Italian–Yugoslav border. In September 1945 it was transferred to Belgium and Holland. The brigade finally returned to Palestine and was disbanded in February 1946.

Jewish Chautauqua Society. American educational and interfaith organization. It was established in 1893 by Henry Berkowitz. It sends speakers to summer camps and universities, sponsors resident lectureship programs on university campuses, and donates Jewish reference books to university libraries. Since 1939 it has been sponsored by the National Federation of Temple Brotherhoods.

Jewish Christians (i) [Nazarenes]. Initially they were followers of Jesus under the leadership of James, the brother of Jesus. They observed Jewish practices and opposed Paul's policy of attracting gentiles who did not accept Jewish law. Eventually they became a minority sect within the Christian community.

Jewish Christians (ii). Term applied by Christians to Jews who have adopted the Christian faith while continuing to stress their Jewish identity.

Jewish Chronicle. English Jewish newspaper. It first appeared in 1841 under the editorship of D. Meldola and M. Angel. It is the oldest Jewish periodical in existence.

Jewish Colonial Trust. Bank of the Zionist Organization. It was incorporated in London on 20 March 1899, in accordance with a decision made at the First and Second Zionist Congresses. In 1902 it began to operate through its offshoot, the Anglo-Palestine Bank. In 1955 it became an Israeli company. It assisted in the colonization of Palestine and participated in the establishment of the Workers' Bank, the Palestine Electric Co., and other institutions.

Jewish Colonization Association [ICA]. Philanthropic society. Founded in 1891 by Baron Maurice de Hirsch, its aim was to assist Jews to emigrate from countries where they were oppressed. The society was incorporated in London and initially had its offices in Paris; the headquarters transferred to London in 1949. Hirsch's original intention was to bring about a mass emigration of Jews from European countries, where they were persecuted, to Argentina. Later the association concentrated its efforts on assisting Jewish communities in Europe.

Jewish Community Center. American-Jewish communal institution with branches throughout the US. It has its origins in young people's literary societies established in the US from the 1840s, which came to be known as the Young Men's Hebrew Association (YMHA) or Young Women's Hebrew Association (YWHA). It sponsors recreational programs, health education, and Jewish culture, and its activities include physical education, arts and crafts programs, drama, music, lectures, forums, and concerts. Membership is open to both Jews and non-Jews.

Jewish Conciliation Board of America. Tribunal for adjudicating Jewish disputes. Founded in 1930, it functions as a voluntary social service agency in New York; cases are heard by a panel consisting of a lawyer, a rabbi, and a businessman.

Jewish Cultural Reconstruction. International agency founded after World War II to deal with Jewish cultural and religious property seized by the Nazis and recovered by the US military government. It was established in New York in 1947 by world Jewish organizations, and operated in Germany from 1948 to 1951.

Jewish Daily Forward *see* FORVERTS.

Jewish Education Committee of New York. American community service agency supporting Jewish education in New York. Founded in 1939, it aims to increase the number of children receiving Jewish education and to improve Jewish teaching. It services Orthodox, Conservative, Reform, Hebrew, and Yiddish schools.

Jewish Historical Society of England. Learned society established in London in 1893 to foster the study of Jewish history. It is equipped with a library of English Judaica and has published volumes of *Transactions, Miscellanies*, and various Jewish studies.

Jewish Information Bureau. American

charitable organization providing information on Jewish affairs and community interests. It was founded in New York in 1932 by Bernard Richards, and is supported by voluntary contributions. It maintains a reference library and publishes *The Index*.

Jewish Institute of Religion *see* HEBREW UNION COLLEGE.

Jewish Labor Committee. American community agency within the labor movement, established in 1934. It supported Jewish labor institutions in European countries, assisted the anti-Hitler underground movement, aided victims of Nazism, combated anti-Semitism, and supported the foundation of Israel.

Jewish Legion. Body of Jewish volunteers who fought in the British Army in World War I to liberate Palestine from Turkish rule. The concept orginated in Zionist circles in Europe and the US. British military authorities permitted the creation of the Zion Mule Corps which served in Gallipoli in 1915–16. In 1917 the first Jewish fighting battalion (the 38th Royal Fusiliers) was established; it left for Palestine in 1918, where it was reinforced by Jews who had enrolled in the US and Canada (the 39th Battalion) and the liberated areas of southern Palestine (the 40th Battalion).

Jewish Memorial Council. British institution which aims to foster Jewish education and improve the Jewish ministry. It was created in London after World War I as the Jewish War Memorial.

Jewish National Fund [Keren Kayemet le-Israel]. Fund established by the Zionist Organization for the purchase and development of land. It was founded at the Fifth Zionist Congress in 1901, according to principles laid down by Hermann Schapira. It aimed to purchase and supervise the care of land in Palestine and to prevent land speculation there. It began to acquire land in 1904 and engaged in large-scale activity from 1921. When the State of Israel was established in 1948 it owned 235,523 acres.

Jewish oath [more judaico]. Oath imposed on Jews involved in legal proceedings with non-Jews. It was current from the Middle Ages in central and eastern Europe. The oath was sworn on the Sepher Torah (or tephillin), and invoked curses upon any who took it in vain. It was abolished in 1846 through the efforts of Isaac-Adolphe Crémieux. Although it disappeared in Germany in the 19th century, it continued to be used in eastern Europe.

Jewish Occupational Council. American organization founded in 1939 to coordinate the efforts of local and national institutions in aiding Jewish immigrants. It is concerned with vocational guidance, rehabilitation, and employment, and may assist its clients through psychological testing.

Jewish Publication Society of America. Organization which supports the publication of English-language books on Jewish subjects. Founded in 1888, it was the successor of two similar societies created in the 19th century. It has published works in all fields of Jewish literature.

Jewish Quarterly Review. Scholarly journal. It was founded in England by Israel Abrahams and Claude G. Montefiore in 1888. In 1910 it was adopted by Dropsie College in Philadelphia as an official publication.

Jewish Reconstructionist Foundation *see* RECONSTRUCTIONISM.

Jewish Restitution Successor Organization [JRSO]. Agency established in 1948 in the American zone of Germany to recover unclaimed Jewish property. Corresponding organizations were subsequently established in the British zone in 1950 (the Jewish Trust Corporation) and in the French zone in 1952.

Jewish Science. American movement whose aims were to promote a religious renaissance among Jews. Founded in 1921 by Morris Lichtenstein, it stressed the spiritual dimensions of Judaism, the essential goodness of God, and the efficacy of prayer. After Lichtenstein's death, his wife, Tehilla Lichtenstein, became the leader of the movement.

Jewish Socialist Verband of America. Organization formed in 1921 to promote democratic socialism and the strengthening of Jewish life, based on Yiddish culture. It was originally identified with Jewish leaders of the needle-trade unions and the Workmen's Circle, and found an outlet for its ideas in the daily paper *Forverts*. It publishes the Yiddish monthly *Der vecker*.

Jewish State Party. Zionist party. Founded in Poland in 1933, it broke away from the Revisionists when they left the Zionist Organization. Eventually it was reunited with the Revisionists when they rejoined the Zionists.

Jewish Teachers' Seminary and People's University. American educational organization. Founded in New York in 1918, it prepares teachers for Yiddish and Hebrew schools in the US and sponsors adult education.

Jewish Telegraphic Agency. International Jewish news agency. It was founded in 1914 in The Hague; its headquarters were later transferred to London and then to New York.

Jewish Territorial Organization [ITO]. International body dedicated to the procuring of land for Jewish settlements on an autonomous basis. It was founded in Basle in 1905 by members of the Seventh Zionist Congress, after the rejection of the scheme to establish a Jewish homeland in Uganda, and was led initially by Israel Zangwill. Its head office was in London and branches of the organization were established in Europe, America, Australia, and South Africa. After the Balfour Declaration of 1917 some of the ITO's leaders returned to the Zionist Organization, and the ITO was dissolved in 1925.

Jewish Theological Seminary of America. Educational institution of Conservative Judaism. Founded in 1886, its first classes were held at the Shearith Israel synagogue in New York, where students were taught by Sabato Morais and Henry Pereira Mendes. From 1902 presidents have been Solomon Schechter, Cyrus Adler, Louis Finkelstein, G. D. Cohen, and Ismar Schorsch. In 1947 a branch of the seminary was opened in California (the University of Judaism). The institution educates rabbis, teachers, cantors, and synagogue administrators.

Jewish War Memorial *see* JEWISH MEMORIAL COUNCIL.

Jewish War Veterans of the USA. War veterans organization. It was founded in 1896 by Jewish veterans of the Civil War as the Hebrew Union Veterans Organization. In 1917 it amalgamated with the Hebrew Veterans of the War with Spain. The present name was adopted in 1929. It maintains the National Shrine to the Jewish War Dead in Washington, DC, and veterans' service offices throughout the US.

Jewish Welfare Board *see* NATIONAL JEWISH WELFARE BOARD.

Jews *see* ISRAEL; DIASPORA.

Jews College. British Orthodox rabbinical seminary. Founded in London in 1855 by Nathan Marcus Adler, it initially trained English-speaking ministers and laymen, and educated boys in a Jewish secondary school. The secondary school was closed in 1879, but the college continued to train rabbis, cantors, laymen, and teachers. It has provided leadership for British Orthodox Jewry, and produces a series of publications under its own name.

Jezebel (fl. 9th cent. BCE). Israelite woman

of Sidonite origin, wife of Ahab, and daughter of Ethbaal, King of Sidon. She introduced her native cult of Baal worship into Israel, thereby arousing the anger of Elijah. In I and II Kings she is portrayed as a callous woman who unjustly brought about the death of Naboth and persecuted the prophets (I Kings 16–II Kings 9). She was killed in Jehu's revolt against the monarchy.

Jezreel (i). Ancient city, situated at the foot of Mount Gilboa. It was the winter resort of Omri, King of Israel; Joram and his mother Jezebel were killed there by Jehu (II Kings 9).

Jezreel (ii). Ancient city in Judah (Joshua 15.56).

Jezreel, Valley of. Plain and valley of northern Israel, dividing the mountains of Samaria and Carmel from those of Lower Galilee.

Joab (fl. 10th cent. BCE). Israelite commander-in-chief, nephew of David. When David became king Joab was appointed head of the army. He defeated the Ammonites and led the campaign against Absalom. During the revolt of Sheba, son of Bichri, he was replaced as commander-in-chief by Amasa, whom he later murdered. He supported Adonijah's claim to succeed David, and was put to death by Solomon in accordance with David's wishes. (II Samuel 2–3, 10–11, 14, 17–21; I Kings 1–2; II Chronicles 11, 18–21, 27)

***Joachim, Joseph** (1831–1907). German violinist of Hungarian origin. He was born in Köpcsény and moved with his family to Budapest. He studied under Felix Mendelssohn, and later led Liszt's orchestra at Weimar. From 1854 to 1864 he was concertmaster and conductor of the Royal Hanoverian Orchestra. During this period he converted to Christianity. In 1866 he settled in Berlin, where he was director of the Hochschule für Musik, and founded the Joachim Quartet. His compositions, mainly for violin, include *Hebrew Melodies*.

Joahaz *see* JEHOAHAZ (i).

Joash (i) [Jehoash] (fl. 9th cent. BCE). King of Judah (835–798 BCE). His grandmother, Athaliah, seized the throne and murdered all members of the house of David when Joash was a year old. He was rescued by his aunt Jehosheba, wife of the high priest Jehoiada. Jehoiada later crowned him king, had Athaliah put to death, and acted as regent until Joash became king when he was seven. Joash restored the Temple, but he later deviated from following Jewish law. During his reign, Judah was invaded by Hazael of Aram. Joash was killed by conspirators. (II Kings 11–14)

Joash (ii) [Jehoash] (fl. 9th cent. BCE). King of Israel (801–785 BCE). After Aram was defeated by the Assyrians, he recaptured several towns ceded by his father Jehoahaz. When Amaziah of Judah attempted to free his country from Israelite domination, Joash captured Jerusalem, plundered the Temple and royal treasures, and reduced the country to vassaldom (II Kings 13.10–13).

Job (i). Biblical book, part of the Hagiographa. It tells the story of Job, a righteous man, who questioned God's justice in allowing him to suffer. His friends argued that his suffering was a result of wickedness, but Job refused to accept their explanation. God eventually spoke from a whirlwind and stressed Job's finite knowledge compared with his designs for the universe.

***Job (ii).** Non-Jewish hero in Israelite folklore. The Bible portrays him as just a non-Jew; he is classed with Noah and Daniel in Ezekiel 14.14.

Job, Testament of. Greek Pseudepigraphic book, which reveals the secrets and last wishes of Job. In this work Job suffers various trials set by Satan, but is comforted by his belief that the righteous will be rewarded in the afterlife.

Jochebed (fl. ?13th cent. BCE). Israelite woman, wife of Amram and mother of Moses, Aaron, and Miriam (Exodus 6.20).

Joel. Biblical book, one of the 12 Minor Prophets. Its four chapters depict a plague of locusts (chapters 1–2) and describe the Day of the Lord, when God will rescue the Jewish people from captivity and punish their enemies in the Valley of Jehoshaphat (chapters 3–4).

Joel, Manuel (1826–1890). German rabbi and scholar. He was born in Birnbaum, Poznania. In 1854 he joined the faculty of the Breslau Rabbinical Seminary, and ten years later he became rabbi of the Breslau community. In the rabbinical assemblies of Kassel and Leipzig, he advocated moderation in Reform practice. He published studies of Ibn Gabirol, Maimonides, Ḥasdai Crescas, and Levi ben Gershom; he also wrote a two-volume work on comparative religion.

Joezer (fl. 1st cent. BCE–1st cent. CE). High priest, son of Boethus. He was a brother of Herod's wife, Mariamne, and of Eleazar, who also served as high priest. He played a role in pacifying the people when they resisted the attempts of Quirinius (governor of Syria) to conduct a census in Judea.

Johanan [Gadi] (fl. 2nd cent. BCE). Israelite fighter, son of Mattathias the Hasmonean. He and his brothers fought in the uprising against the Syrians. He was killed while on a mission to the Nabateans.

Johanan bar Nappaḥa (c. 180–c. 279). Palestinian amora. He was born in Sepphoris. He studied with Judah ha-Nasi, and was the brother-in-law of Simeon ben Lakish. He founded his own academy in Tiberias. His teachings constitute a major part of the Jerusalem Talmud.

Johanan ben Kareaḥ (fl. 6th cent. BCE). Israelite military commander, active in Judah at the time of the destruction of the first Temple (Jeremiah 40–43). He supported Gedaliah and warned him of Ishmael ben Nethaniah's treachery; after Gedaliah's murder, he prevented Ishmael from carrying away prisoners. Out of fear of Babylonian reprisals, he went to Egypt along with other exiles including Jeremiah.

Johanan ben Nuri (fl. 2nd cent.). Palestinian tanna. Living in poverty, he influenced the formulation of laws and customs of the Jews in Galilee. He is often mentioned in the Mishnah as taking part in debates with Akiva.

Johanan ben Zakkai (fl. 1st cent.). Palestinian tanna. He was the leading sage at the end of the second Temple period and in the years following the destruction of the Temple. During the rebellion against Rome (66–70), he was among the peace party in Jerusalem. According to legend, he was carried out of the city in a coffin, approached Vespasian, and predicted his accession to the imperial throne; as a reward, he was allowed to continue his teaching. He founded an academy at Jabneh, which became the seat of the Sanhedrin after the fall of Jerusalem.

Johanan ha-Sandelar (fl. 2nd cent.). Palestinian tanna. He was born in Alexandria and became a pupil of Akiva. After Hadrian's reign (117–38), which saw widespread persecution of the Jews, and the death of Akiva at Caesarea, Johanan transmitted Akiva's teachings.

Johlson, Joseph (1773–1851). German scholar and teacher. He taught at the Philanthropin school in Frankfurt am Main from 1813 to 1830. He based the teaching of Hebrew on the mastery of grammar and established a systematic plan for teaching Judaism. He published textbooks about Jewish history in biblical times, a biblical dictionary, and a German translation of the Bible.

John Hyrcanus (fl. 2nd cent. BCE). High priest and ethnarch (135–104 BCE), son of Simon the Hasmonean. After the murder of his father and his two brothers by Ptolemy, he escaped to Jerusalem. In 135–134 BCE Antiochus Sidetes captured Jerusalem, and John Hyrcanus was confirmed as high priest. Later he threw off Syrian domination, attacked the Samaritans, destroying their temple on Mount Gezirim, and forced the Idumeans to convert to Judaism. Although initially allied with the Pharisees, he subsequently drew closer to the Sadducees.

John of Giscala (fl. 1st cent.). Palestinian fighter, leader of the revolt against Rome (66–70). He was born in Giscala. He conducted retaliatory raids against the Syrians after they had destroyed his native city. In 66 when Josephus arrived as commander in Galilee, a controversy arose between the two military leaders: John suspected Josephus of disloyalty and advocated his removal. After Galilee was conquered by Vespasian, John fled to Jerusalem. He took control of the Temple from the Zealots, who subsequently fought under his command during Titus's siege. He was later captured by the Romans, sentenced to life imprisonment, and died in a Roman prison.

John the Baptist (fl. 1st cent.). Palestinian religious leader, forerunner of Jesus. He preached repentance, proclaimed the coming of the messianic age, and practiced baptism of those who accepted his preaching; Jesus was among those whom he baptized. He was put to death by Herod Antipas at the behest of Herodias, his wife, whose marriage to Herod John the Baptist had condemned.

Joiada *see* JEHOIADA.

Joiakim *see* JEHOIAKIM.

Joint Distribution Committee *see* AMERICAN JEWISH JOINT DISTRIBUTION COMMITTEE.

Jolowicz, Heymann (1816–1875). German reform leader and writer. He was a preacher in various German towns. Belonging to the radical element of the Reform movement, he wrote on Jewish theology and, together with David Cassel, translated Judah ha-Levi's *Kuzari* into German.

Jonadab *see* RECHABITES.

Jonah (i). Biblical book, one of the 12 Minor Prophets. It relates God's command to Jonah, son of Amittai, to go to Nineveh and proclaim judgment upon its inhabitants for their wickedness. On a sea voyage Jonah was swallowed by a great fish and eventually spewed out on dry land. As a result of his prophecy, the inhabitants of Nineveh repented of their evil ways.

Jonah (ii) (fl. 4th cent.). Palestinian amora. He and Yose were heads of the academy in Tiberias. Discussions between these sages are contained in the Palestinian Talmud.

Jonah Gerondi *see* GERONDI, JONAH BEN ABRAHAM.

Jonah ibn Janaḥ *see* IBN JANAḤ.

Jonathan (i) (fl. 11th cent. BCE). Israelite prince, eldest son of Saul. He was a devoted friend of David. Together with Saul, he was killed in a battle against the Philistines on Mount Gilboa. The news of their deaths caused David to compose his famous lament (II Samuel 1.17–27).

Jonathan (ii) (fl. 2nd cent. BCE). Israelite head of state (160–143 BCE), youngest son of Mattathias. Together with his brother Judah Maccabee, he fought in the battles at the beginning of the Hasmonean revolt (166–164 BCE). On the death of his brother, he took over the leadership of the anti-Syrian campaign. Alexander Balas (a contender with Demetrius I for the Syrian throne) conceded to him the title of high priest and recognized him as

Governor of Judah. He was captured by the Syrian leader Tryphon at Acre and killed.

Jonathan ben Amram (fl. 2nd–3rd cent.). Palestinian sage. A pupil of Judah ha-Nasi, he lived during the period between the tannaim and the amoraim. The halakhot quoted by him concern laws of levitical cleanness.

Jonathan ben David ha-Cohen of Lunel (c. 1135–after 1210). French talmudic scholar. He was active in Provence. He defended Maimonides in the controversy about him encouraged by Meir Abulafia. He wrote commentaries on the Mishnah, the Talmud, and Alfasi's Code.

Jonathan ben Eleazar (fl. 3rd cent.). Palestinian amora. He is the Jonathan ben Eleazar mentioned in the Talmud and midrash. Of Babylonian origin, he went to Palestine in his youth and became a pupil of Simeon ben Yose ben Lakunya. He lived in Sepphoris and was one of the great aggadists of his time.

Jonathan ben Uzziel (fl. 1st cent. BCE–1st cent. CE). Palestinian translator. He was an outstanding pupil of Hillel and was responsible for the first translation of the biblical books of the prophets into Aramaic.

Joppa. Ancient port on the coast of Israel, 35 miles north-west of Jerusalem; the modern city of Jaffa stands on the same site. In the biblical period Joppa marked the boundary of the territory of the Philistines. During the reign of Solomon, the cedars of Lebanon used to rebuild the Temple were floated by sea to Joppa on their way to Jerusalem. The city belonged to the Phoenicians from 538 to 333 BCE, and during the Hellenistic period (to *c* 60 BCE) it was an independent city with a non-Jewish population. In the 2nd century BCE Judas Maccabee avenged an attack on the Jewish community there; his brothers Jonathan and Simon took Joppa and replaced the population with Jews. The city was the principal Jewish port until the destruction of Jerusalem in 70.

Joram *see* JEHORAM (i) and (ii).

Jordan. River flowing from the foothills of Mount Hermon in the Lebanon through lakes Huleh and Galilee and into the Dead Sea.

Jordan, Hashemite Kingdom of *see* TRANSJORDAN.

Joselman [Josel] **of Rosheim** [Loanz, Yoseph ben Gershom] (1480–1544). German writer and communal leader. In 1510 he was elected warden and leader by the Alsatian Jewish communities. He represented German Jewry before secular authorities and interceded for the Jewish community in times of danger. In 1532 he attempted to curb the activities of the pseudo-messiah Solomon Molcho. Later he defended the Jews against the charges made by Martin Luther.

Joseph (fl. ?19th–16th cent. BCE). Israelite, 11th son of Jacob and first-born of Rachel. As his father's favorite son, he aroused the anger of his brothers, who sold him into slavery in Egypt. He was bought as a slave by Potiphar, a high official. Later he was imprisoned on a false charge made by Potiphar's wife. After interpreting Pharaoh's dreams, he achieved high office in Egypt. Eventually he was reconciled with his brothers and reunited with his father, after which his family settled in the Goshen region. (Genesis 37–50)

***Joseph II** (1741–1790). Emperor of Germany (from 1765) and King of the Romans (from 1764). In 1782 he introduced the Toleranzpatent, which ameliorated the situation of Austrian Jewry.

Joseph, Morris (1848–1930). English Reform rabbi. He served as minister at the West London Synagogue for nearly 20 years. He also taught homiletics at Jews College in 1891–2. His writings include *Judaism as Creed and Life*, *The Ideal* *in Judaism, The Message of Judaism,* and *The Spirit of Judaism.*

Joseph abu Jacob *see* JOSEPH BEN ABRAHAM HA-COHEN.

Joseph bar Ḥiyya (fl. 9th cent.). Babylonian gaon. He was gaon of Pumbedita (828–33). During the controversy between the exilarch David ben Judah and his brother Daniel, Joseph bar Ḥiyya and Abraham ben Sherira presided over the academy at Pumbedita. When peace was restored, Joseph renounced the office of gaon and temporarily resumed the position of av bet din at Pumbedita.

Joseph Bekhor Shor *see* BEKHOR SHOR, JOSEPH BEN ISAAC.

Joseph ben Abraham ha-Cohen [Joseph abu Jacob; Abu Yakub al-Basir] (fl. 11th cent.). Babylonian or Persian Karaite scholar. He traveled widely, seeking converts to Karaism. Despite his blindness, he wrote religio-legal and philosophical works.

Joseph ben Gorion (fl. 1st cent.). Palestinian military leader. He participated in the revolt against Rome. His name was associated with the authorship of the Hebrew historical narrative, *Josippon.*

Joseph ben Isaac ha-Levi (fl. 17th cent.). Bohemian philosopher of Lithuanian origin. He lived in Prague, where he taught medieval religious philosophy. He wrote a commentary on Maimonides' *Guide for the Perplexed*, which was published by Yom-Tov Lipmann Heller with his own introduction and annotations. Joseph ben Isaac's *Ketonet Passim* treats the basic ideas of the *Guide.*

Joseph ben Isaac Kimḥi *see* KIMḤI, JOSEPH.

Joseph ben Jacob bar Satya (fl. 10th cent.). Babylonian gaon. In 930 he was appointed gaon of Sura by the exilarch David ben Zakkai after the exilarch had become embroiled in a dispute with Saadyah Gaon. Saadyah was later reinstated but Joseph ben Jacob resumed the post after Saadyah's death. Some time after 943 he left Sura and settled in Basra.

Joseph ben Jacob ibn Tzaddik *see* IBN TZADDIK, JOSEPH BEN JACOB.

Joseph ben Joshua ha-Cohen (1496–c. 1575). Italian historian. He was brought up in Italy and practiced medicine in Genoa. His *History of the Kings of France and Turkey* describes the struggle between Christians and Muslims from the time of the crusades. In *Valley of Weeping* he recounts the trials of the Jews in the Middle Ages.

Joseph ben Judah ibn Aknin *see* IBN AKNIN, JOSEPH BEN JUDAH.

Joseph ben Mattathias *see* JOSEPHUS, FLAVIUS.

Joseph ben Nathan [Official, Joseph] (fl. 13th cent.). French writer, son of Nathan ben Joseph Official. He was born of a family who had close relations with the local nobility, and he himself was in the service of the Archbishop of Sens as a financial agent. His *Sepher ha-Mekanne* recounts the religious arguments he and his circle had with the Christian community.

Joseph ben Shemtov *see* IBN SHEMTOV, JOSEPH BEN SHEMTOV.

Joseph ben Tanḥum Yerushalmi (b. 1262). Egyptian Hebrew poet. At the age of 15 he composed a collection of poems in imitation of Moses ibn Ezra. On his father's death in 1291 he composed a lamentation in which he mentions the conquest of Acre by the crusaders. He was the most representative Hebrew poet of Egypt in the 13th century.

Joseph della Reina *see* REINA, JOSEPH DELLA.

Josephon *see* JOSIPPON.

Josephs, Wilfred (b. 1927). English composer. He was born in Newcastle upon Tyne. He has composed operas, ballets, vocal and choral works, and chamber and instrumental music. His compositions on Jewish themes include the *Jewish Requiem* (1963).

Josephus, Flavius [Flavius Josephus; Joseph ben Mattathias] (c. 38–after 100). Palestinian historian and soldier. He was born in Jerusalem. In 64 he went to Rome on a mission to secure the release of several priests. At the outbreak of the Jewish rebellion against the Romans in 66 he was appointed commander of Galilee, and, when the Romans attacked the province in 67, he directed the resistance. He surrendered to the Romans after Jotapata was captured; he accompanied Vespasian and Titus during the siege of Jerusalem. After the Roman victory he lived in Rome. His writings include *The Jewish War, The Antiquities of the Jews, Against Apion*, and an *Autobiography*.

Joshua (i) (fl. ?13th cent. BCE). Israelite leader. As Moses' successor, he was assigned the task of leading the people in the conquest of Canaan. He commanded the Israelites in the war with the Amalekites (Exodus 17.14–16). Later he was one of the 12 spies sent to reconnoiter the land of Canaan. After the Israelites had crossed the Jordan, Joshua led them to victory over the alliance of southern kings, and then the northern kings. He subsequently brought the Tabernacle to Shiloh and divided the newly won territory among the 12 tribes.

Joshua (ii). Biblical book, one of the books of the Former Prophets. It describes Joshua's conquests and the division of the land of Canaan among the 12 tribes of the Israelites.

Joshua ben Gamla (d. 69/70). High priest. He married one of the wealthiest women in Jerusalem (Martha, daughter of Boethus). He established a universal system of education throughout Palestine. An opponent of the Zealots at the time of the Jewish rebellion against Rome, he was put to death by the Idumeans.

Joshua ben Hananiah (fl. 1st–2nd cent.). Palestinian tanna. During the siege of Jerusalem (70), he helped his teacher, Johanan ben Zakkai, to escape. Favored by the Romans, he traveled repeatedly to Rome on national missions to aid the Jewish cause. After the death of Gamaliel II he became av bet din at the Jabneh academy. His polemical debates with Christians are recorded in rabbinic literature. For some time he had a school in Pekiin.

Joshua ben Jehozadak (fl. 6th cent. BCE). High priest. He went to Jerusalem with Zerubabel. Encouraged by Zechariah and Haggai, he set up the altar as the first step in the restoration of the Temple. His descendants remained in office until the time of the Hasmoneans.

Joshua ben Korḥa (fl. 2nd cent.). Palestinian tanna. He studied under Johanan ben Nuri and Eleazar ben Azariah. He laid down the rule that where there is a difference of opinion the stricter view should be adopted with regard to a biblical injunction, but the more lenient view where the injunction is of rabbinic provenance. He engaged in disputations with sectarians and non-Jews.

Joshua ben Levi (fl. 3rd cent.). Palestinian amora. He was born in Lydda and later taught there, also concerning himself closely with communal needs. He was involved in affairs affecting the community in its relations with the Roman authorities, and traveled on various missions to Caesarea and Rome. He was a master of the aggadah, and some of his sayings are recorded in the Mishnah.

Joshua ben Peraḥyah (fl. 2nd cent. BCE). Palestinian leader, head of the Sanhedrin. Together with Nittai the Arbelite, he formed the second of the pairs ("zugot") of sages. The Babylonian Talmud records that he was a teacher of Jesus.

Joshua Heshel ben Jacob of Lublin (1595–1663). Polish rabbi. Born in Lublin, he succeeded his father as rabbi of the community in 1650. Later he succeeded Yom-Tov Lipmann Heller as rabbi of Kraków. Subsequently he moved to Vienna and sought to exert pressure on the government in the interests of Jewry. He eventually returned to Poland, where he continued his educational activities. He was a noted halakhic authority.

Joshua Lorki *see* LORKI, JOSHUA.

Josiah (fl. 7th cent. BCE). King of Judah (640–609 BCE), son of Amnon. He was proclaimed king while still a child after his father was assassinated. His reign was marked by a great religious revival: he removed foreign cults and reestablished monotheism. During the restoration of the Temple, Hilkiah, the high priest, announced the discovery of a Book of the Law; this prompted Josiah to convene an assembly of the people, during which he made a covenant with God. He also discontinued worship in the high places and centralized it in the Temple at Jerusalem.

Josiah ben Zakkai (fl. 10th cent.). Babylonian exilarch. He was appointed exilarch after his brother David was deposed from office by Saadyah Gaon. The caliph intervened in David's favor; Josiah was then banished to Chorassan, where he died.

Josippon [Josephon]. Hebrew historical narrative, describing the period of the second Temple. Written in southern Italy in the 10th century, it was ascribed to Joseph ben Gorion. It is based on Josephus' writings.

Jost, Isaac Marcus (1793–1860). German historian. He was born in Bernburg. He served as head of a private high school in Frankfurt am Main; from 1835 he taught at the Philanthropin high school in Frankfurt, and in 1853 he founded an orphanage for Jewish girls there. He published a Pentateuch for young people, a vocalized Mishnah text with translations and notes, a textbook of English, a dictionary of Shakespeare, and a manual of German style. He was a pioneer in modern Jewish historiography and a supporter of the Reform movement.

Jotham (i) (fl. c. 12th cent. BCE). Israelite, youngest son of Gideon. He was the sole survivor of Abimelech's massacre in which all his brothers died (Judges 9). He escaped to Mount Gerizim where he denounced the Shechemites for accepting Abimelech as king (Judges 9.8–15).

Jotham (ii) (fl. 8th cent. BCE). King of Judah (c. 742–735 BCE), son of Uzziah. He defeated the Ammonites in battle (II Chronicles 27.5), and during his reign the country enjoyed considerable prosperity. He made repairs and additions to buildings in the Temple area in Jerusalem (II Chronicles 27.3; II Kings 15.35).

Journey, Prayer on Setting out on a. The offering of prayers in preparation for traveling is enjoined in the Talmud. Different versions of the prayer exist for land, sea, and air journeys; they include appropriate Bible verses.

Joy. According to the Bible (Psalm 100.2), joy is a prerequisite for true worship. Special occasions of joy include circumcision, bar mitzvah ceremonies, weddings, the Sabbath, and festivals. Among the Ḥasidim it is a central feature of prayer.

JRSO *see* JEWISH RESTITUTION SUCCESSOR ORGANIZATION.

Jubal. Musician, son of Lamech. He is regarded as the father of all who handle the harp and pipe (Genesis 4.19–21).

Jubilee *see* SABBATICAL YEAR.

Jubilees, Book of [Genesis Zutarta; Lesser Genesis]. Pseudepigraphic work. Dating from the middle of the second Temple period, it contains the secret revelation of the Angel of the Divine Presence to Moses on his second ascent to Mount Sinai. Some scholars believe it may have originated in an early Essene group.

Judah (fl. ?19th–16th cent. BCE). Israelite, fourth son of Jacob and Leah. When the sons of Jacob turned against Joseph, the 11th son, Judah convinced them to sell Joseph to traveling Ishmaelites rather than leave him to die in a pit (Genesis 37). Judah later received Jacob's patriarchal blessing (Genesis 49.8). David belonged to the tribe of Judah and his accession to the throne assured its supremacy. When the Israelite kingdom split after Solomon's death, the tribe of Judah supported Rehoboam and became predominant in the south.

Judah, Kingdom of. The southern kingdom of the two kingdoms into which Palestine was divided after the revolt led by Jeroboam I against Rehoboam in 930 BCE. The monarchy passed peacefully from father to son in the Davidic house, except during the usurpation of Athaliah in the 9th century BCE. In the 8th century the reigns of Hezekiah and Josiah were associated with religious revival. In 586 BCE the Kingdom of Judah was conquered by the Babylonians and many Jews were deported. Later in the century a number of Babylonian exiles returned to Judah to rebuild the Temple and renew Jewish life; the kingdom was thus restored, and it continued to exist as a province under a succession of foreign hegemonies.

Judah al-Ḥarizi *see* AL-ḤARIZI, JUDAH.

Judah bar Ezekiel (d. 299). Babylonian amora. He was the founder of the academy at Pumbedita, and was an authority on halakhah. His teachings are extensively quoted in the Babylonian and Jerusalem Talmuds.

Judah ben Asher (1270–1349). Spanish rabbi and talmudist, of German origin. He was born in Cologne, but left Germany with his family as a consequence of anti-Jewish outbreaks in 1283, and settled in Toledo. In 1321 he was appointed his father's successor as rabbi of the Toledo community and later became the head of the bet din and the Toledo yeshivah. His *Zikhron Yehudah* comprises 83 responsa. In *Iggeret Tokheḥah* he offered a testament to his children containing ethical sayings, an account of his family history, and instruction in the method of learning.

Judah ben Barzillai al-Bargeloni (fl. 11th–12th cent.). Spanish rabbi. He was rabbi of the community in Barcelona. He wrote numerous halakhic studies, incorporating summaries of talmudic discussions and gaonic material, as well as a commentary on the Sepher Yetzirah.

Judah ben Bathyra I (fl. 1st cent.). Babylonian tanna. He lived in Jerusalem in his youth, but left Palestine before the destruction of the Temple and settled in Nisibis in Babylon.

Judah ben Bathyra II (fl. 2nd cent.). Babylonian tanna, perhaps the grandson of Judah ben Bathyra I. He was born in Rome and studied in Palestine. Subsequently he went to Babylon and settled in Nisibis. At the time of the Hadrianic persecutions, he was regarded as an authority of equal rank with Akiva.

Judah ben Bava (fl. 1st–2nd cent.). Palestinian tanna. He was a leading sage in Jabneh, renowned for his piety. During the Hadrianic persecutions he was put to death by the Romans for ordaining five scholars, in transgression of the law forbidding ordination.

Judah ben Ilai (fl. 2nd cent.). Palestinian tanna. Born in Usha, he was a pupil of his father and of Tarphon and Akiva. His account of their teachings was used by Judah ha-Nasi in compiling the Mishnah. He was the original author of the *Siphra* and was a renowned aggadist. After the Hadrianic persecutions, he helped to establish the academy at Usha.

Judah ben Isaac [Sir Léon of Paris] (1166–1224). French tosaphist, grandson of Rashi. He became the head of the Paris bet midrash, which was reopened when the Jews returned to France following their expulsion in 1182. He composed tosaphot to nearly all the Talmud, based on the teachings of Isaac ben Samuel of Dampierre.

Judah ben Jehiel *see* LEON, JUDAH MESSER.

Judah ben Kalonymos (d. 1196/1199). German scholar. He lived in Speyer. His *Yiḥuse Tannaim va-Amoraim* provides biographical details of talmudic rabbis and outlines their views.

Judah ben Samuel he-Ḥasid of Regensburg (c. 1150–1217). German rabbi and mystic. He lived in Speyer and later settled in Regensburg. He was one of the most important scholars of the Middle Ages in the fields of ethics and theology, and was the main teacher of the Ḥaside Ashkenaz movement. His writings include magical treatises and the *Book of Divine Glory*, a commentary on the prayers of the Jewish liturgy. He was also the principal author of the *Sepher Ḥasidim*. His teachings were popularized by Eleazar ben Judah of Worms.

Judah ben Simon (fl. 4th cent.). Palestinian amora. He was a leading aggadist.

Judah ben Tabbai (fl. 1st cent. BCE). Palestinian sage. With his colleague Simeon ben Setaḥ, he formed the third of the pairs ("zugot") of sages during the time of Alexander Yannai.

Judah ha-Levi [Zionides] (before 1075–1141). Spanish Hebrew poet and philosopher. Born in Toledo, he lived in various towns in Christian and Muslim Spain, where he was active as a physician. Eventually he left Spain for Palestine. He wrote about 800 poems, including eulogies and laments, covering such topics as love, Jewish festivals, personal religious experience, and longing for Zion. His philosophical work *The Kuzari* describes a disputation conducted before the King of the Khazars by a rabbi, a Christian, a Muslim, and an Aristotelian philosopher.

Judah ha-Nasi (fl. c. 2nd–3rd cent.). Palestinian communal leader, son of Simeon ben Gamaliel II. He lived most of his life in Galilee, first at Bet Shearim and then at Sepphoris. He was known as "Rabbenu ha-Kadosh" (our holy teacher), and is referred to in rabbinic literature as "Rabbi." He served as the political and religious head of the Jewish community in Palestine. His major contribution was the redaction of the Mishnah.

Judah Ḥasid ha-Levi (?1660–1700). Lithuanian Shabbetaian preacher. He was born in Dubno. He was maggid in Szydłowiec, and was active in preparing the people for the second appearance of Shabbetai Tzevi in 1706. He traveled throughout the communities and urged total repentance, mortifications, and fasts. He and hundreds of followers set out for Palestine to await the Messiah. He died a few days after arriving in Jerusalem in 1700.

Judah ibn Balam *see* IBN BALAM, JUDAH BEN SAMUEL.

Judah Löw ben Bezalel [Höhe Rabbi Löw; Maharal] (c. 1525–1609). Bohemian rabbi, talmudist, moralist, and mathematician. He served as chief rabbi of Moravia from 1553 to 1573, and later settled in Prague. There he founded a yeshivah, organized circles for the study of the Mishnah, and regulated the statues of the ḥevra kaddisha. Revered for his piety and asceticism, he was active in all aspects of communal life, particularly education. He wrote studies of halakhah, aggadah, ethics, philosophy, and homiletics, as well as rabbinic commentaries. According to legend, he was the creator of the Prague golem.

Judah Maccabee (fl. 2nd cent. BCE). Palestinian rebel leader, third son of Mattathias the Hasmonean. He succeeded his father as leader of the revolt against Antiochus IV Epiphanes. After occupying Jerusalem in 164 BCE he purified the Temple and assisted Jewish communities in Transjordan and Galilee. He was later killed in battle at Elasa. He is celebrated as the prototype of Jewish heroism. *See also* MACCABEES.

Judah Nesiah (fl. 3rd cent.). Palestinian nasi, son of Gamaliel III. He was the first nasi to settle in Tiberias. He was assisted by Johanan bar Nappaḥa and Resh Lakish.

Judah the Galilean (d. c. 6). Palestinian Zealot leader. He was born in Gamala in the Golan. He participated in the disturbances in the country following the death of Herod the Great. He was the head of a band of rebels active around Sepphoris, who had seized control of the armory in Herod's palace there. Though the rebels were defeated, Judah escaped. Together with Zadok the Pharisee he founded the Zealots, and opposed the census conducted in Judea by Quirinius.

Judaism. The Jewish religion originated with God's call to Abraham (Genesis 12). The Jewish faith has undergone numerous developments. Throughout its history various groups (Sadducees, Pharisees, Karaites, Hasidim, Conservative Jews, Reform Jews, etc.) have claimed that their beliefs and practices are authentically Jewish. In the Middle Ages Maimonides formulated 13 principles of the Jewish faith, which are widely recognized as the central tenets of Judaism. In modern times the Jewish community is fragmented along religious lines. Groups ranging from the ultra-Orthodox to the most liberal all claim to represent valid manifestations of Judaism.

Judas Maccabaeus *see* JUDAH MACCABEE.

Judea. Latin form of the name Judah. It was the name of the vassal kingdom in Palestine which came under Roman rule in 63 BCE. The kingdom was renamed Palaestina in 135. The name Judea is also applied to the southern part of Palestine (as opposed to the central area, Samaria, and the northern area, Galilee).

Judea capta (Latin: "Judea taken"). Phrase inscribed on a coin issued by Vespasian after the fall of Jerusalem in the 1st century.

Judenrein (German: "free of Jews"). Term applied by the Nazis to an area from which Jews had been expelled.

Judenstaat, Der *see* HERZL, THEODOR.

Judeo-. Prefix used in the names of various Jewish DIALECTS.

Judge. Before the settlement in Canaan, elders of the Israelite community acted as judges; later leaders, priests, and prophets assumed this position. The prophet Samuel administered justice (I Samuel 7.15–17), but after the creation of the monarchy this responsibility passed to the king (II Samuel 12:1–16; 15:2). According to the Book of Chronicles, David appointed 6000 Levites as officers and judges (I Chronicles 23.4). Jehoshaphat's court in Jerusalem consisted of judges selected from among the priests, Levites, and heads of houses (II Chronicles 19.8–11). During the period of the second Temple, the Great Sanhedrin in Jerusalem consisted of 71 judges; in addition lesser Sanhedrins of 23 judges sat in towns. Courts of three judges also settled civil disputes. In the Middle Ages and subsequently, tribunals of rabbis sat as judges in religious cases.

Judges (Hebrew "Shophetim"). Biblical book, one of the books of the Former Prophets. It describes the period of the Judges from the death of Joshua until before the time of Eli and Samuel. Chapters 1–3.6 consists of an introduction; chapters 3.7–16.31 recount stories about the Judges (particularly Othniel, Ehud,

Deborah, Gideon, Jephthah and Samson); and chapters 17–21 relate the incident of the statue stolen by the Danites, and the story of the concubine of Gibeah.

Judgment *see* DIN.

Judgment, Day of *see* DAY OF JUDGMENT.

Jüdische Rundschau. Weekly journal of the German Zionist Organization. It was founded as the *Israelitische Rundschau* in 1896 and was published in Berlin. The name was changed in 1902 and the journal appeared as the *Jüdische Rundschau* until 1938, when it was discontinued.

Jüdischer Verlag. German publishing house. Founded in Berlin in 1902, it was taken over by the Zionist Organization in 1907. It published over 300 books on Jewish and Zionist topics before it was liquidated by the Nazis in 1938.

Jüdische Wissenschaft *see* WISSENSCHAFT DES JUDENTUMS.

Jüdisch-Theologisches Seminar *see* BRESLAU RABBINICAL SEMINARY.

Judith. Apocryphal book. It recounts the story of Judith, a Simeonite woman, living in Bethulia in northern Samaria. During the siege of the city by the Assyrians she succeeded in beheading their general, Holophernes, as a result of which the besieging army took flight.

Judith Montefiore College. English rabbinical seminary. It was founded in Ramsgate in 1869 by Sir Moses Montefiore in memory of his wife.

Jud Süss *see* OPPENHEIMER, JOSEPH.

***Julian the Apostate** (331–363). Roman emperor (361–63). He was opposed to Christianity and supported paganism. In his writings he regarded the Jews favorably and in 362 announced his intention of restoring the Temple in Jerusalem, though this plan was eventually abandoned.

***Julius Caesar** (c. 100–44 BCE). Roman leader. After the battle of Pharsalia (48 BCE) he received help from Hyracanus II and Antipater during the Alexandrian War (47 BCE). Later he confirmed Hyrcanus as hereditary high priest and ethnarch, and Antipater as procurator of Judea. He also safeguarded Jewish worship in Asia and Rome.

Jung, Leo (1892–1987). US Orthodox rabbi, of Moravian origin. He became rabbi of Congregation Kenesseth Israel in Cleveland in 1920, and later of the Jewish Center in New York. He was professor of ethics at Yeshiva University from 1931 and later at Stern College for Women. In 1935 he was appointed chairman of the New York State Advisory Board for Kashrut Law Enforcement. He was also a member of the supreme council of the Agudath Israel organization. He started the series known as the Jewish Library in 1928 and himself edited eight of its early volumes.

Jus gazaga ("law of right by usage"; from Latin "jus": law, and Hebrew "ḥazakah": right by usage). Term used in Italy during the ghetto period (16th–18th centuries) to denote a tenant's rights. It applied to houses occupied but not owned by Jews.

Jus talionis (Latin: "law of retaliation"). Law exacting equality of punishment and crime; it is embodied in the phrase "an eye for an eye, a tooth for a tooth." The law is stated three times in Scripture: Exodus 21.24, Leviticus 24.20, and Deuteronomy 19.21. According to rabbinic interpretation, these prescriptions were not to be taken literally; instead financial compensation was allowed.

Juster, Jean (c. 1886–1916). French lawyer and historian, of Romanian origin. He became an advocate at the Paris Court of Appeal. His major work was *Les juifs dans l'empire romain: leur condition juridique, économique et sociale.*

Justice. The Hebrew words for justice ("tzedek," "tzedakah," and "mishpat") denote various types of just action. Justice is a cardinal principle of biblical ethics, based on a recognition of human rights and their protection. According to the rabbis, justice should be tempered with mercy, in imitation of God's nature and activity. The concept of justice is a central feature of biblical and rabbinic law.

***Justinian** (fl. 6th cent.). Emperor of the Eastern Roman Empire (527–65). He prosecuted all non-Orthodox Christians including the Jews. His intolerant legislation concerning the Jews fixed the status of the Jew in Byzantine society for the next 700 years. According to his proclamations, Jews were not allowed to serve in civil or military posts, own Christian slaves, give evidence against Christians, or celebrate Passover at the same time as Easter. He also issued an edict regulating the synagogue service and forbidding rabbinic expositions, and he outlawed synagogues in Africa.

Justus of Tiberias (fl. 1st cent.). Historian. He was a contemporary of Josephus and opposed his actions in Galilee during the Jewish rebellion against Rome (66–70). With his father and others Justus was arrested and taken to Tarichaea. Later he fled to Beirut, where he became the private secretary of Herod Agrippa II. He wrote a chronicle of the war against Rome, which takes a different stance from Josephus' history.

K

Kabak, Ahron Avraham (1880–1944). Lithuanian writer. Born in Smorgon in the province of Vilnius, he lived in Turkey, Palestine, Germany, France, and Switzerland. In 1921 he settled in Palestine, where he taught at the Jerusalem Reḥavyah Gymnasium. His novel *By Herself* was regarded as the first Zionist novel in Hebrew literature. His other novels include *Daniel Shafranov*, *Victory*, *Shelomo Molkho*, *Between the Sea and the Desert*, *The Narrow Path*, *History of One Family*, *The Empty Space*, *In the Shadow of the Gallows*, and *Story without Heroes*.

***Ka'b Al-Aḥbār** (fl. 7th cent.). Yemenite scholar. Though born a Jew, he converted to Islam. He was one of the followers of the caliph Omar when he entered Jerusalem. At Omar's request, Ka'b Al-Aḥbār pointed out the site where the Temple had stood. Many teachings of the rabbis and words of the aggadah are attributed to him in Muslim literature.

Kabbalah ("mysticism"). The body of esoteric teachings of Judaism and Jewish mystical literature, particularly from the 12th century onward. The kabbalah draws on early rabbinic mystical traditions about the divine chariot ("maaseh merkavah") and the mysteries of creation ("maaseh bereshit"); it is concerned with esoteric doctrines about God and creation, the problem of evil, the soul, and the mystic way. Important kabbalistic texts include the Bahir, the Shiur Komah, the Sepher Yetzirah, and the Zohar. In the 16th century, kabbalistic speculation was transformed by the teachings of Moses Cordovero and Isaac Luria. In Lurianic kabbalah the term "tzimtzum" refers to the process whereby God contracts himself to form a vacuum in which creation can take place; the concept of "tikkun" (cosmic repair) is also associated with Lurianic kabbalah. Kabbalistic thought also profoundly influenced the Sabbetaian movement. In modern times kabbalistic theories are subscribed to by various Ḥasidic groups.

Kabbalat Shabbat ("Reception of the Sabbath"). Synagogue service marking the inauguration of the Sabbath. The Sabbath begins at nightfall; it is customary to prepare for it by bathing, putting on festive clothes, and reciting various prayers and hymns.

Kabronim (from "kavar": to bury). Gravediggers in the Jewish community.

Kaddish [Prayers for the Dead]. Doxology in Aramaic, recited at the end of individual sections of the funeral service and at its conclusion. There are four forms: the complete kaddish; the half kaddish; the scholars' kaddish ("kaddish de-rabbanan"); and the mourners' kaddish, which is recited by close relatives of the deceased at the end of the service. All four forms of the kaddish are recited standing, facing Jerusalem. In some communities the entire congregation stands; in others only the mourners. The prayer consists of praise and glorification of God, and expressions of hope for the establishment of God's kingdom on earth.

Kadimah. Austrian Jewish students' association. Established in Vienna in 1882, it was influenced by Peretz Smolenskin. It struggled against assimilation, encouraged Jewish nationhood, and fostered the settlement of a national homeland in Palestine. Similar associations were subsequently founded in western Europe.

Kadoorie, Sir **Ellis** (1865–1922). Hong Kong philanthropist. He was born in Baghdad and settled in Hong Kong. He bequeathed funds for the building of two agricultural schools for Jews and Arabs, one at Tulkarm and one near Mount Tabor. He also contributed to the Anglo-Jewish Association for Education.

Kadoorie, Sir **Elly Silas** (1867–1944). Hong Kong businessman, brother of Ellis Kadoorie. He was born in Baghdad and settled in Hong Kong, developing business interests in Shanghai and other cities. He was an active Zionist and served as president of the Palestine Foundation fund in Shanghai, established agricultural schools in Palestine, and contributed to the construction of the Hebrew University.

Kafka, Franz (1883–1924). German novelist of Czech origin. He was born in Prague and worked in a law office and then an insurance company, pursuing his writing in his spare time. His short stories (including *Metamorphosis*) were published in his lifetime. At his death he instructed his friend Max Brod to burn his remaining manuscripts; but Brod succeeded in publishing three novels, *The Trial*, *The Castle*, and *America*. Some commentators interpret Kafka's works as reflecting the Jew's isolation in society.

Kaftan [caftan]. Long gown or undertunic. It was worn by oriental and eastern European Jews.

Kahal. Congregation. In eastern Europe the term was applied to the Jewish community, which had autonomous rights and was responsible for such civil matters as taxation.

Kahan, Israel Meir *see* ḤAPHETZ ḤAYYIM.

Kahana (i) (fl. 2nd–3rd cent.). Babylonian amora. He and Assi were prominent scholars when Rav returned from Palestine to Babylonia. Later Kahana emigrated to Palestine, where he joined some of the last tannaim.

Kahana (ii) [Kahana, pupil of Rav] (fl. 3rd cent.). Babylonian amora. It is recorded that he read the weekly Bible portion at Rav's academy. After executing a person who had threatened to denounce a fellow Jew to the Persian authorities, he fled from Babylonia to Palestine. There he joined the academy of Johanan.

Kahana (iii) [Kahana, pupil of Rava] (fl. 4th cent.). Babylonian amora. He taught at the academy of Pum Nahara; among his pupils was Ashi, the redactor of the Babylonian Talmud.

Kahana (iv) (d. c.414). Babylonian amora. He succeeded Rafram ben Papa as head of the academy of Pumbedita from 396.

Kahana, Aharon (1905–1967). Israeli painter and ceramic artist. He was born in Stuttgart and lived in Berlin and Paris before settling in Palestine in 1934. In 1947–8 he was a founder member of the New Horizons group of artists. Initially his work was influenced by biblical themes, but later his painting became more abstract. Subsequently he returned to figurative painting.

Kahana, Avraham (1874–1946). Russian biblical scholar and historian. He emigrated to Palestine in 1923, where he served as as librarian at the Sha'ar Zion Library in Tel Aviv. From 1903 he worked on an edition of the Hebrew Bible, which was published with a critical commentary and introduction. He also edited the Apocrypha, wrote historical studies, published biographical works, and contributed to Hebrew linguistics.

Kahana, David *see* KOGAN, DAVID.

Kahane, Meir (d. 1990). Israeli rabbi and politician, of American origin. He was ordained at the Mirrer Yeshiva, and received a law degree at the New York Law School. He was the founder of the Jewish Defense League, the Jewish Identity Center, and the organization Shuva. His publications include *Never Again*, *Time to go Home*, *The Story of the Jewish Defense League*, and *Why be Jewish?*.

Kahanovitz, Phinehas [Der Nister] (1884–1952). Russian Yiddish author. He is chiefly known for his realistic historical novel of Ukrainian Jewish life, *House of Crisis*, the first volume of which appeared in 1939.

***Kahle, Paul** (1875–1965). German orientalist, masoretic scholar, and minister. He was born in East Prussia. After serving as a pastor in Cairo he taught at the universities of Halle, Giessen, and Bonn. From 1923 he was director of the Oriental Institute at Bonn. Later he settled in Oxford. He made pioneering contributions to the understanding of the emergence and development of the masorah, basing his studies on material from the Cairo Genizah. He also wrote articles on Muslim holy places in Palestine, and published studies of the Dead Sea Scrolls.

Kahn, Bernhard (1876–1955). German-American community leader. He was born in Sweden, but spent much of his life in Germany, where he became involved in Jewish affairs. He was appointed secretary-general of the Hilfsverein der Deutschen Juden in 1904. In 1921 he became director of the refugee department of the American Jewish Joint Distribution Committee (JDC), and later the JDC's European director, as well as managing director of the American Joint Reconstruction Foundation. In 1939 he emigrated to the US, where he served as honorary chairman of the JDC European Council.

Kahn, Zadok (1839–1905). French rabbi. He was born in Mommenheim, Alsace. He became director of the Talmud Torah of the École Rabbinique in Metz. In 1866 he became assistant to Chief Rabbi Isidore Lazare of Paris, whom he succeeded in 1868, and in 1889 he became chief rabbi of France. He was active in the Ḥibbat Zion movement, and served as president of the Société des Études Juives. He served as editor of the French translation of the Hebrew Bible, and assisted Isidore Singer in preparing the American *Jewish Encyclopedia*.

Kaidanover, Aaron Samuel [Aaron Samuel ben Israel Kaidanover; Maharshak] (1614–1676). Polish talmudist. He was active as a religious leader in Polish and German Jewish communities. His publications include talmudic novellae, sermons, and responsa.

Kaidanover, Tzevi Hirsch (d. 1712). Lithuanian writer, son of Aaron Samuel Kaidanover. He was imprisoned for four years in Vilnius on a false charge. After his release he published his father's writings in Frankfurt-am-Main. He was himself the author of an ethical treatise, *Kav ha-Yashar*, which he also translated into Yiddish.

Kai-Feng-Fu. Town in central China. It was the seat of the Chinese Jewish community. In 1652 Chao Yng Ch'eng rebuilt the synagogue there, which had been destroyed by floods.

Kainuka *see* BANU KAINUKA.

Kairouan. Town in north Africa. Jews settled there after its foundation in the 7th century. It subsequently became the leading Jewish intellectual center in the West. After the rise of the Almohades in the 12th century, the Jewish community in Kairouan went into decline.

Kalam (Arabic: "theology"). The name given to a tradition of Arabic scholastic theology which arose in the 8th century. It profoundly affected Jewish philosophy in the Middle Ages and influenced both Karaite and rabbinic thinkers.

Kalich, Bertha Rachel (1875–1939). American actress. She was born in Poland and settled in New York in 1895. In her youth she appeared at the Bucharest National Theater and later in the Romanian Imperial Theater. After emigrating to the US she became the first Yiddish-speaking actress to be recognized in the English-language theater; she also appeared in Yiddish repertory.

Kalischer, Tzevi Hirsch (1795–1874). German rabbi and Zionist pioneer. He was born in Lissa, in the Posen district, and settled in Thorn in 1824. An opponent of Reform Judaism, he advocated Jewish settlement in Palestine, and in *Derishat Zion* argued for the establishment of a Jewish agricultural society there. In 1864 he was responsible for the founding in Berlin of the Central Committee for Palestine Colonization. He believed that Jewish redemption would come about through human endeavor before the coming of the Messiah. His publications deal with rabbinic topics and Zionism.

Kalisher, Abraham *see* ABRAHAM BEN ALEXANDER KATZ OF KALISK.

Kalisky, René (1936–1981). Belgian writer. He was born in Brussels and worked as a journalist. Many of his essays and dramas deal with Jewish topics.

Kallah (i). Bride.

Kallah (ii) ("Bride"). Minor tractate appended to the fourth order, Nezikin, in the Babylonian Talmud. The tractate is known in two versions. The shorter version consists of one chapter and deals with betrothal, marriage, chastity, and moral purity. The longer version, known as Kallah Rabbati, discusses betrothal and marriage, and also amplifies Derekh Eretz Rabbah and Derekh Eretz Zuta.

Kallah (iii). During the talmudic and gaonic periods, the name given to courses of study which took place at the Babylonian academies of Sura and Pumbedita in the months of Elul and Adar (the so-called "kallah" months, when agricultural work was minimal and students had time to meet for study and discussion). During each kallah month a specific tractate of the Talmud was studied.

Kallah Rabbati *see* KALLAH (ii).

Kallen, Horace Meyer (1882–1974). American philosopher. He was born in Berenstadt, Silesia, and was taken to the US in 1887. He taught at the New School for Social Research in New York from 1919–1952, and was an active member of the Jewish community. His publications include *The Book of Job as a Greek Tragedy*, *Zionism and World Politics*, and *Judaism at Bay*.

Kallir, Eleazar (fl. ?7th cent.). Hebrew poet. He lived in Tiberias. He was the greatest and most prolific of the early composers of piyyutim, writing examples for all the main festivals, special Sabbaths, weekdays of festive character, and fasts.

Kalmanovitch, Zelig (1881–1944). Lithuanian Yiddish writer, philologist, and translator. He was born in Latvia and settled in Vilnius in 1929, where he joined the YIVO Institute and served as editor of its journal. In 1943 he was deported to a concentration camp in Estonia, where he was killed the following year. He published studies on Yiddish philology, the influence of Hebrew on Yiddish syntax, and Yiddish dialects. He also translated various works into Yiddish.

Kalonymos ben Kalonymos [Maestro

Calo] (1286–after 1328). French Hebrew author and translator. He lived in various French cities and also in Rome. He translated philosophical and scientific works from Arabic into Hebrew and Latin for King Robert of Naples. His *Even Boḥan* is an ethical study in rhymed prose. In *Masekhet Purim* he presented a satirical parody of a talmudic tractate.

Kalonymus. German family which flourished from the 9th to the 13th century. One of the most prominent Jewish families in Germany, it flourished in cities near the Rhine. Its members included rabbis, preachers, poets, teachers, authors, moralists, theologians, and communal leaders.

Kal va-Ḥomer ("Light and heavy"). The name given to the first principle of rabbinic HERMENEUTICS in the systems of Hillel and Ishmael ben Elisha. It consists of an *a fortiori* argument.

Kamatz. Sign used to indicate two vowel sounds in Hebrew. "Kamatz gadol" is sounded as an "a" in Sephardi pronunciation and as "o" in Ashkenazi pronunciation. "Kamatz katan" is sounded as an "o" and occurs only in closed, unstressed syllables. The sign, which resembles a capital T in the Roman alphabet, is written below the consonant preceding the vowel sound.

Kamia *see* AMULET.

Kaminer, Isaac (1834–1910). Ukrainian Hebrew writer. He was born in Lewkiow in the Ukraine and from 1854 to 1859 taught at the government school for Jews in Zhitomir. Later he served as a physician in Kiev. He wrote verse satires for the Hebrew socialist papers, criticizing supporters of the Haskalah, the Ḥasidim, and rich communal leaders. After the pogroms of the 1880s he joined the Ḥibbat Zion movement.

Kaminka, Armand Aharon (1866–1950). Austrian scholar. He was born in Berdichev in the Ukraine. He served as a rabbi at Frankfurt an der Oder, and then as preacher at the Reform temple in Prague. After a period as rabbi to the Jewish community in Esseg, Slavonia, he moved to Vienna, where he became secretary of the Israelitische Allianz. In 1924 he founded Maimonides College, and from 1924 lectured on the Talmud and Jewish philosophy at the University of Vienna. After the annexation of Austria by Hitler in 1938, Kaminka settled in Palestine. His works include biblical and rabbinic studies, translations of Greek and Latin classics into Hebrew, and poetry.

Kaminski, Esther Rachel (1870–1925). Polish Yiddish actress, wife of Abraham Isaac Kaminski. She toured Poland acting in her husband's theater company. In 1909–11 she appeared in the US, and in 1913 played in London and Paris.

Kaminski, Ida Kaminska (1899–1980). Polish Yiddish actress, daughter of Esther Rachel Kaminski and Abraham Isaac Kaminski. As a child she acted in her father's company, and later became the outstanding actress on the Yiddish stage in Poland. She left Poland in 1968 after anti-Semitic disturbances.

Kammerknechtschaft (German: "servitude to the [imperial] chamber"). Term applied to the juridical status of Jews in medieval Germany as serfs to the Holy Roman Emperor. The emperor exercised exclusive jurisdiction over the Jews and the right to exact a poll tax.

Kanah, Book of. Kabbalistic work on the commandments. Composed in Spain during the 14th century, it was written in the form of a commentary on the commandments, containing the author's own mystical interpretation.

Kaniuk, Yoram (b. 1930). Israeli author. He was born in Tel Aviv. His publications include *The Acrophile*, *The Last Jew*, and *Confessions of a Good Arab*.

Kann, Jacobus Henricus (1872–1945).

Dutch banker and Zionist. He was born in The Hague and became the owner and manager of his family's bank (Lissa & Kann) from 1891. As an aide to Theodor Herzl, he was one of the founders of the Jewish Colonial Trust in 1899. He was an active participant in the Zionist Congresses and was elected to the Zionist Organization's executive in 1905. Later he worked on various projects in Palestine.

Kantor, Judah Leib (1849–1915). Lithuanian journalist. He was born in Vilnius. After working as an editor on Jewish newspapers in Berlin and St. Petersburg, in 1886 he founded the first Hebrew daily, *Ha-Yom*, which he edited until 1888. He later served as crown rabbi in Libau (1890–1904), Vilnius (1905–8), and Riga (1909–15).

Kaph. 11th letter of the Hebrew alphabet. Its numerical value is 20.

Kaplan, Eliezer (1891–1952). Russian Labor Zionist. He was born in Minsk. He was one of the founders of the Tzeire Zion in Russia in the early years of the 20th century. He became active in the Labor Zionist movement in Europe, and from 1923 in Palestine. He was a member of the executive of the Jewish Agency from 1933, and served as head of its finance department until the establishment of the State of Israel in 1948. He then became Israeli minister of finance, and later was appointed deputy prime minister.

Kaplan, Jacob (b. 1895). French rabbi and author. He was born in Paris. He held rabbinical positions in Mulhouse, Alsace, and Paris. During the German occupation of France he worked with the Résistance movement. In 1950 he became chief rabbi of Paris, and in 1955 was appointed chief rabbi of France. He was a lecturer at the Institut d'Études Politiques and a member of the Académie des Sciences Morales et Politiques in Paris. His writings include *Le Judaïsme et la justice sociale*, *Racisme et Judaïsme*, *French Jewry Under the Occupation*, *Le Judaïsme dans la société contemporaine*, and *Témoignages sur Israël*.

Kaplan, Mordecai Menaḥem (1881–1983). American rabbi and founder of the Reconstructionist movement. He was born in Lithuania and at the age of nine emigrated with his family to the US. After his ordination he became rabbi of the Kehillath Jeshurun synagogue in New York. In 1909 he became dean of the Teachers Institute of the Jewish Theological Seminary of America in New York. Later he taught homiletics, midrash, and philosophy of religion at the seminary's rabbinical school. He developed a concept of Judaism known as RECONSTRUCTIONISM, and in accordance with his ideas in 1922 set up a congregation known as the Society for the Advancement of Judaism. He also established the Jewish Reconstructionist Foundation, which published *The Reconstructionist* magazine. His writings include *Judaism as a Civilization*, *The Meaning of God in Modern Jewish Religion*, and *The Future of the American Jew*.

Kaplansky, Shelomoh (1884–1950). Israeli Zionist labor leader, of Polish origin. He was born in Białystok and lived in Vienna from 1903 to 1912. After moving to London, he was chairman of the finance and economics committee of the Zionist Executive (1919–21). From 1927 to 1929 he was a member of the Zionist Executive in Jerusalem and the director of its Settlement Department. He then served as an emissary of the Zionist labor movement to the British Labour Party (1929–31). In 1932 he was appointed director of the Haifa Technion.

Kapparah ("atonement"). In Jewish practice the custom of transferring the sins of a person symbolically to a bird. In a ceremony performed on the eve of the

Day of Atonement, a fowl is swung over the head of an individual, who prays that by its death it will serve as his substitute and bear his sins. The following prayer is said during the ceremony: "This is my substitute, my vicarious offering, my atonement; this cock [or hen] shall meet death, but I shall find a long and pleasant life of peace."

Kappel, Alexander *see* MUKDONI, ALEXANDER.

Kara, Abigdor ben Isaac (d. 1439). Bohemian rabbi, kabbalist, and poet. He lived in Prague. There he witnessed the massacre of the Jewish community in 1389 as a result of the accusation that they had desecrated the Host; he wrote an elegy to commemorate their sufferings. His other writings include rabbinic studies and kabbalistic works. He also engaged in polemical debates with Christians. According to legend, he was a favorite of Wenceslaus IV, King of Bohemia, and played an important role in his court.

Kara, Joseph ben Simeon (c. 1060–c. 1130). French Bible commentator. He lived in Troyes and Worms. He took part in theological discussions with Christians, wrote commentaries on most of the books of the Bible, and commented extensively on the piyyutim.

Karaites. Jewish sect founded at the beginning of the 8th century and active in and around Persia. The Karaites denied the talmudic–rabbinical tradition. The most ancient Karaite text is the *Sepher ha-Mitzvot* of Anan ben David, the founder of the movement. In this work he interpreted the Bible literally and attempted to deduce from it a code of life without reference to the Oral Law. During the following centuries various Karaite groups flourished in Persia, Babylonia, Palestine, Egypt, and elsewhere. Karaite scholars produced polemical works, grammars, Bible commentaries, and codes. From the 12th century the movement went into decline.

Karavan, Dani (b. 1930). Israeli sculptor. He was born in Tel Aviv. He produced abstract forms for decorative walls including the Assembly Hall of the Knesset. His large-scale sculptures include *The Monument to the Negev Brigade.*

Kardos, Gyorgy (b. 1925). Hungarian writer. He settled in Palestine but later returned to Budapest, where he was active as a freelance writer. He wrote three novels about his post-war experiences in the Middle East.

Karkasani [Qirqisani]**, Abu Yusuf Yakub** [Jacob; Kirkisani, Jacob] (fl. 10th cent.). Babylonian Karaite scholar. He came from Karkasan near Baghdad. He was the most important proponent of Karaism of his age. His *Book of Lights and Watch-Towers* is a systematic code of Karaite law. In *Book of Gardens and Parks* he commented on the non-legal parts of the Torah.

Karlin. Suburb of Pinsk. It was the seat of a Ḥasidic dynasty from the mid-18th century until World War II, and became the center of Lithuanian Ḥasidism.

Karlitz, Avraham Yeshayahu [Ḥazon Ish] (1878–1953). Israeli rabbi and codifier, of Russian origin. He was born in the province of Grodno and lived in Vilnius. Later he settled at Bene Berak in Palestine, where he founded a yeshivah. Writing under the name Ḥazon Ish, he became one of the most important modern codifiers.

Karni, Yehuda (1884–1949). Hebrew poet of Russian origin. He was born in Pinsk. After settling in Palestine, he served on the editorial board of the daily *Ha-Aretz* from 1921. In his *Shirei Yerushalayim*, Jerusalem is presented as the eternal symbol of the people and their destiny. In later writings he lamented the victims of the Holocaust.

Karo, Joseph *see* CARO, JOSEPH.

Karpeles, Gustav (1848–1909). German literary historian. He was born in Einwanowitz, Moravia. He edited the *Allgemeine Zeitung des Judentums* in Berlin from 1890 and also played an important role in establishing and running the Association of Societies for Jewish History and Literature. He wrote various literary studies, including a history of Jewish literature.

Kashe (Yiddish: "a difficult question"). A problem, talmudic query, or question.

Kasher *see* DIETARY LAWS; KASHRUT.

Kasher, Menaḥem (1895–1983). American rabbi and halakhist. He was born in Warsaw. In 1925 he went to Palestine, and founded the yeshivah Sefat Emet in Jerusalem. From 1939 he lived in the US. His *Torah Shelemah* is an encyclopedia of the Talmud and midrash, in which all relevant material in the Oral Law is collected according to the scriptural verse to which it applies.

Kashrut ("dietary laws"). The body of regulations governing Jewish diet. The laws enumerated in the Pentateuch were developed in the Oral Law and by rabbinic legislation. In the Talmud the tractate Ḥullin deals with the dietary laws, as does the section "Yoreh Deah" in the Shulḥan Arukh. Only food which is fit to be eaten in accordance with Jewish law ("kasher" or "kosher") may be consumed. Food which is "terephah" (unfit) is forbidden. The laws of kashrut deal with animals that are fit for consumption, methods of slaughter, the preparation of meat, the eating of milk and meat products together, vegetable foodstuffs, Passover regulations, and so on. *See also* DIETARY LAWS.

Kassovsky [Kossovsky]**, Ḥayyim Yehoshua** (1873–1960). Israeli rabbinic scholar. His writings include concordances of the Bible, Targum Onkelos, the Mishnah, the Tosephta, and the Babylonian Talmud.

Kastein, Joseph [Katzenstein, Julius] (1890–1946). German writer and biographer. Born in Bremen, he lived in Switzerland and in 1933 settled in Palestine. He wrote poems, plays, tales, novels, and studies of Jewish figures.

Katsh, Abraham (b. 1908). American educator. He was born in Poland and emigrated to the US in 1925. He joined the staff of New York University in 1933 and taught Hebrew education and culture. From 1957 he served as director of the university's Hebrew language and literature section, and from 1962 was director of its Institute of Hebrew Studies. In 1967 he became president of Dropsie College. His writings include *Judaism in Islam*.

Kattowitz Conference. First conference of the Ḥibbat Zion movement, held at Kattowitz (now Katowice) in 1884. 22 delegates came to the conference from Russia and ten from other countries. In his opening address Leo Pinsker emphasized that Jews should return to work on the land. A permanent committee of members of the group was created with its headquarters at Odessa, and a subcommittee was established in Warsaw.

Katz, Ben-Tziyyon (1875–1958). Israeli journalist and author, of Russian origin. In 1903 he founded and edited the Hebrew periodical *Ha-Zeman*, which appeared first at St. Petersburg and later at Vilnius. In 1916 he established a Hebrew weekly *Ha-Am*, in Moscow. After World War I he settled in Berlin, and in 1931 moved to Palestine, where he continued his work in Hebrew journalism. He published studies of Russian Jewish history.

Katz, Mané *see* MANÉ-KATZ.

Katz, Menke (1906–1991). American Yiddish poet. He was born in Tsvintsyan, Lithuania, and emigrated to the US in 1920. His publications include *Three Sisters*, *Burning Village*, *My Grandmother*

Moyne Speaks, *Safad*, and *Aspects of Modern Poetry: a Symposium.*

Katz, Steven T. (b. 1944). American scholar. He was born in Jersey City, New Jersey. He taught at Dartmouth College and in 1984 became professor of Jewish studies at Cornell University. His publications include *Jewish Mysticism*, *Jewish Ideas and Concepts*, and *Post-Holocaust Dialogs*.

Katzenellenbogen, Meir *see* PADUA, MEIR.

Katzenelson, Isaac (1886–1944). Polish Hebrew poet and playwright. He was born in Korelichi and later lived and taught in Łódź. He was one of the pioneers of the modern Hebrew theater. During World War II he was active in Warsaw and other cities. His works of this period describe the catastrophe that befell European Jewry.

Katzenelson, Judah Löb Benjamin (1864–1917). Russian physician, writer, and scholar. He was born in Chernigov in the Ukraine. He practiced medicine in St. Petersburg and his medical writings contributed to the formulation of a Hebrew terminology in medicine. A supporter of the Haskalah, he was a lecturer at the Institute of Jewish Studies in St. Petersburg and later its head. He was one of the editors of the Russian Jewish encyclopedia, and also wrote articles, stories, and fables.

Katzenstein, Julius *see* KASTEIN, JOSEPH.

Katznelson, Berl (1887–1944). Palestinian labor leader. He was born in Belorussia and emigrated to Palestine in 1909. He became an ideologist of the labor movement there. He was one of the founders of the Aḥdut ha-Avodah party in 1919, and of the Histadrut in 1920. He served in various positions in the Zionist Organization and edited various labor journals, including the Histadrut daily *Davar*. He was a founder of Mapai in 1930.

Kaufman, Shirley (b. 1923). American poet and translator. She was born in Seattle. Her poetry deals with Jewish themes, and her publications include *The Floor Keeps Turning*, *Gold Country*, and *From One Family to Another*.

Kaufmann, David (1852–1899). Hungarian scholar. He was born in Kojetein, Moravia. He taught Jewish history, religious philosophy, and homiletics at the new rabbinical seminary in Budapest. He published studies of Jewish history, medieval Jewish philosophy, history of religion, and the history of Jewish art.

Kaufmann, Isidor (1854–1921). Hungarian painter. He was born in Arad. He traveled throughout Galicia, Poland, and the Ukraine, making sketches of shtetl life. He was a pioneer in the depiction of eastern European Jewish life.

Kaufmann, Yeḥezkel (1889–1963). Israeli biblical scholar and philosopher. He was born in Russia and settled in Palestine in 1920, where he later became professor of Bible studies at the Hebrew University. In *A History of the Israelite Faith* he challenged numerous theories of biblical criticism.

***Kautzsch, Emil Friedrich** (1841–1910). German scholar. He taught at Leipzig, Basle, Tübingen, and Halle. He published a revision of Gesenius's Hebrew grammar, philological studies, works on the Apocrypha and apocalyptic literature, and a critical translation of the Bible into German.

Kavvanah *see* DEVOTION; INTENT.

Kayserling, Meyer (1829–1905). German rabbi and historian. He was born in Hanover. He served as a rabbi in Switzerland and later in Budapest. He published studies of Jewish history, literature, and religion, and a seminal study of Marrano history.

Kayyara, Simeon [Simeon ha-Darshan; Simeon Kahira] (fl. 9th century). Babylonian scholar. He was the compiler of the Halakhot Gedolot.

Kedar. Arab herdsman, founder of an ancient tribe, related to the Ishmaelites (Genesis 25.13). The Sons of Kedar were noted for the size of their flocks; they were also skilled archers (Isaiah 21.17). During the Babylonian exile, they lived in southern Judah.

Kedeshah. Sacred harlot. Cultic prostitution was regarded as an abomination and condemned under Jewish law (Deuteronomy 23.18), but it probably did not disappear until the end of the first Temple period. In the Bible both male and female prostitutes are mentioned (I Kings 14.24).

Kedosh Yisrael *see* GOD, NAMES OF.

Kedushah ("Sanctification"). The name given in the Mishnah to the third of the Eighteen Benedictions; in later rabbinic literature the title is used for an addition to the third blessing, in which the congregation responds to the cantor's introduction and alternates with his text by reciting prayers of praise to God. The Kedushah prayer takes different (sometimes amplified) forms, depending on the various liturgical traditions and the occasion on which it is used. *See also* HOLINESS.

Kehillah. Congregation. The term is applied to a Jewish community or to the congregation in the synagogue.

Kehillah movement. Name given to an attempt made in the early 20th century to form central community organizations in the US modeled on the kehillah of eastern Europe. In 1908 steps were taken in New York to form a representative body composed of delegates from Jewish organizations. Under Judah Leon Magnes, it directed community affairs in the areas of education, sociology, religion, industrial problems, and public relations. Following this innovation, other Jewish communities in the country established Jewish community councils.

Kelal Israel ("the whole of Israel"). Term used to mean the body of all Jewish people. The unity of the Jewish nation is viewed as a spiritual reality as well as a social concept.

Kelim ("Vessels"). First tractate in the Mishnah order of Tohorot. It deals with the laws of ritual purity affecting different kinds of vessels (Leviticus 11.32; Numbers 19.14; 31.20).

Kellner, Leon (1859–1928). Austrian scholar and Zionist. He was a specialist in English literature, and, after teaching in high schools, became a lecturer in literature at the University of Vienna. From 1904 to 1914 he was a professor at the University of Czernowitz. When World War I broke out, he returned to Vienna, and he later served as an English expert in the office of the Austrian president. He was one of Theodor Herzl's advisers and published a selection of Herzl's writings as well as the first part of a biography of Herzl.

Kelm, Maggid of (1828–1899). Lithuanian preacher. He studied under Israel Salanter at Kovno, and later became the envoy and preacher of the Musar movement. He traveled throughout the Pale of Settlement and also lived in London.

Kemelman, Harry (b. 1908). American novelist. His novels deal with an amateur detective, Rabbi Small, who solves murders by using talmudic logic. His publications include *Friday the Rabbi Slept Late*, *Saturday the Rabbi went Hungry*, and *Someday the Rabbi will Leave*.

Kemph, Franz (b. 1928). Australian artist and printmaker. He was born in Melbourne. He became president of the Contemporary Art Society of the South Australian School of Art, and later head of the graphic art department at the school. Influenced by the Ḥabad movement, he became a practicing Jew. His work contains biblical and Ḥasidic themes.

Kene-hora ("No evil eye"). Expression used to ward off the evil eye.

Keneset Gedolah *see* GREAT ASSEMBLY.

Keneset Israel ("congregation of Israel"). In rabbinic literature the phrase refers to the whole Jewish community. In modern times it was used as a title by the official Jewish community in Palestine when it was organized as a corporate entity in 1927. When the provisional council of the State of Israel was convened in 1948, the Keneset Israel was abolished and its powers transferred to the state.

Kenites. Ancient tribe which inhabited the Negev and the Sinai desert. They were among the early peoples living in Canaan (Genesis 15.19). Because of the kindness the Kenites had shown to Israel during the Exodus (I Samuel 15.6), Saul gave them friendly warning before he attacked the neighboring Amalekites.

Kenizzites. Ancient tribe which inhabited the Promised Land (Genesis 15.19).

***Kennicott, Benjamin** (1718–1783). English Hebraist. A theologian at Oxford, he collated biblical manuscripts in order to produce a "scientific" text of the Hebrew Bible (for illustration, see jacket).

Kephar Naḥum *see* CAPERNAUM.

Kepher avodah ("work village"). A type of transitional settlement in Israel in which immigrants were placed on their arrival. The inhabitants were employed by the Jewish National Fund to develop the land; they built their own homes and received agricultural training. The kephar avodah then formed the nucleus for a permanent village.

Kerem Ḥemed ("Vineyard of delight"). Hebrew annual publication issued by Galician proponents of the Haskalah. It was published in Vienna, Prague, and Berlin from 1833 to 1856 and served as a forum for Eastern and Western Jewish scholars and authors.

Keren ha-Yesod [Foundation Fund; Palestine Foundation Fund]. Financial arm of the Zionist Organization. It was founded at the Zionist conference held in London in July 1920. Its objectives were to do everything necessary to establish a Jewish national home in Palestine, and to invest all contributions, loans, and legacies. It became in 1929 the central financial instrument of the enlarged Jewish Agency. After 1948 many of the agency's activities passed to the government of Israel, and the Keren ha-Yesod concentrated its resources on financing immigration, settlement, and absorption.

Keren Kayemet le-Israel *see* JEWISH NATIONAL FUND.

Keriat Shema al ha-mittah *see* NIGHT PRAYER.

Keritot ("Excisions"). Seventh tractate in the Mishnah order of Kodashim. It deals with the biblical punishment of "karet" (cutting off, that is temporary or permanent excommunication from the community) and lists the offenses to which it applies.

Keri u-khetiv ("read and written"). In rabbinic studies a term used of corrections to those words that are regarded as deviations from the original biblical text. Over 1300 such corrections were transmitted orally and later noted by the Masoretes in the margins of Bible manuscripts; these manuscripts were not used in synagogues.

Kerovah (from Aramaic "kerova": precentor). Name given to several types of piyyut that form part of the Amidah prayer. They were written for Sabbaths, festivals, Purim, and fast days. On Sabbaths and festivals they generally extend over the first three blessings. At other times they extend over all the Eighteen Benedictions.

Kesten, Hermann (b. 1900). German novelist. He was appointed literary adviser to the Berlin publishing house of Kiepenheuer in 1927. In 1933 he left

Germany and became active in European refugee circles; he later settled in the US. After the collapse of Fascism in Italy he went to Rome. In *Spanish Fire* he re-created the period of the Jewish expulsion from Spain in the late 15th century. His *Die fremden Götter* portrays the return to Judaism of a father and daughter under the Nazis.

Kestenberg, Leo (1882–1962). Israeli pianist and music educator, of Hungarian origin. He served as music counselor at the Ministry of Culture in Berlin, and from 1933 directed the Czech Society for Musical Education. He arrived in Palestine in 1938, where he became the general manager of the Palestine Orchestra. In 1945 he founded the Music Teachers' Training College in Tel Aviv, of which he became the director.

Ketav *see* SCRIPT.

Ketav Sopher *see* SCHREIBER, ABRAHAM SAMUEL BENJAMIN.

Keter malkut ("crown of royalty"). The mark of the sovereignty of God, recognized by angels and men in worshipping him. It is also the name given by Solomon ibn Gabirol to his poem in praise of God, which is recited after the evening service on the Day of Atonement.

Keter Torah ("crown of law"). Symbol of learning in the form of a crown. The cover of the Scrolls of the Law is often embellished with a silver crown.

Ketubbah ("writing"). Document recording the financial obligations a bridegroom undertakes towards his bride. Written in Aramaic, it contains various clauses which follow a stereotyped formula. The tractate Ketubbot in the Talmud deals with the document and its preparation. It was frequently engrossed on parchment with illuminated borders; the art of illuminating ketubbot is especially associated with Italy.

Ketubbot ("Marriage contracts"). Second tractate in the Mishnah order of Nashim. It deals with the money to be received by the wife in case of divorce or widowhood. In addition it contains a discussion of a father's rights regarding his daughter, as well as the mutual rights and duties of a husband and wife.

Ketuvim *see* HAGIOGRAPHA.

Kevutzah ("group"). Cooperative agricultural group in Israel, working a common farm on national land. The earliest such group was Deganyah (1910). The kevutzah was responsible for health, housing, and education; unlike the kibbutzim, its members excluded outside wage-workers. The kevutzot initially belonged to an organization called Ḥever ha-Kevutzot; this later merged with an association of kibbutzim to form Iḥud ha-Kevutzot Ve-he-Kibbutzim.

Khazars [Chazars; Hazars]. Turkish or Finnish tribe which settled in the lower Volga region. From the 8th to the 10th centuries the Khazar state extended westward as far as Kiev. In the 8th century a Judaizing movement manifested itself among the people and their king, Bulan, and thousands of nobles converted to Judaism. The central theme of Judah ha-Levi's *Kuzari* is the legendary disputation which resulted in this conversion. Ḥasdai ibn Shaprut believed that the Khazars were one of the Ten Lost Tribes of Israel; according to tradition, he entered into correspondence with their king, Joseph, in the 10th century.

Khmelnitzki, Bogdan *see* CHMIELNICKI, BOGDAN.

Khosroes II *see* CHOSROES II.

Kibbitzer (Yiddish). Person who offers unsolicited advice, busybody.

Kibbush avodah ("conquest of labor"). Concept formulated in the early 20th century by pioneers in Palestine. The phrase is used principally to mean the acquisition of the skills of productive manual labor. It also refers to the process of obtaining work with Jewish employers.

Such practices were central objectives of the Ha-Shomer movement and the Histadrut, which organized bodies (such as Yakhin and Solel Boneh) to encourage the employment of Jewish labor.

Kibbutz ("gathering in"). Collective village in Israel. Similar to the kevutzot, kibbutzim originated during the Third Aliyah (1918–21). During this period the kevutzah concept was broadened to incorporate industry, wage labor, and the removal of restrictions on the size of the group. Inspired by social ideas, the kibbutz movement has played a pioneering role in the economic, political, and cultural activities of the country, and has contributed significantly to Israeli national security.

Kibbutz galuyyot ("ingathering of the exiled communities"). The name given to the ideal of reuniting the Jewish people. It originated with the Babylonian exile (6th century BCE), and was intensified after the destruction of the second Temple (70 CE). Linked to messianic aspirations, it was one of the aims of pseudo-messiahs such as Serenus, Shabbetai Tzevi, and Judah Ḥasid. In modern times it became a central concept of Zionism and Israeli political philosophy.

Kibbutznik. Member of a kibbutz. The word is Hebrew with a Russian suffix.

Kichel (Yiddish). A small, plain biscuit.

Kiddush ("Sanctification"). The name of a prayer recited over a cup of wine in the home or the synagogue to consecrate the Sabbath or a festival.

Kiddush ha-Shem ("sanctification of the [divine] name"). Descriptive term originally used of acts of martyrdom; later it was also applied to other acts of righteousness that reflect well on Jews and Judaism in the eyes of non-Jews. When a Jew willingly suffers death rather than violate God's commandments, he achieves Kiddush ha-Shem; if he fails to do so, he is guilty of Ḥillul ha-Shem.

Kiddushin ("Betrothals"). Seventh tractate in the Mishnah order of Nashim. It deals with the regulations regarding betrothal (including prohibited marriages). *See also* BETROTHAL; MARRIAGE.

Kiddush Levenah *see* MOON, BLESSING OF THE.

Kidnapping. According to the Bible kidnapping is a capital offense (Exodus 21.16; Deuteronomy 24.7). The Talmud states that the eighth commandment of the Decalogue refers to kidnapping rather than stealing property. To be liable to capital punishment for kidnapping four conditions must obtain: the kidnapper must have taken the kidnapped person into his possession or domain; he must have sold him as a slave; he must have sold him to a stranger; and he must have treated his victim as a slave before selling him. Each condition must have been attested by at least two witnesses.

Kidron. Valley to the north-east of Jerusalem. It separates the city from the Mount of Olives.

Kiev. Capital of the Ukraine. Jewish merchants visited the town in the 9th and 10th centuries. The Jewish population there increased during the next centuries, but was destroyed by the Tartars in 1240. Subsequently a Rabbinite and Karaite community existed in the city. The Jews were expelled in 1495 and 1619, but in 1708 Peter the Great decreed that they might trade there, and Kiev became one of the largest Russian Jewish communities. In 1881 and 1905 it was the scene of pogroms, and in 1913 the Beilis ritual murder trial took place there.

Kike. A disparaging and offensive term for a Jew.

Kilayim ("Diverse kinds"). Fourth tractate in the Mishnah order of Zeraim. It deals with the prohibitions concerning the mingling of different species of plants and animals, and of different textiles in fabric for clothing (Leviticus 19.19; Deuteronomy 22.9).

Ki lo naeh ("For to him it is befitting"). Opening words of an alphabetic eulogy chanted at the end of the Passover seder service in the Ashkenazim liturgy.

Kimḥi, David [Redak] (?1160–?1235). French grammarian and exegete, son of Joseph Kimḥi. He was a teacher in Narbonne, Provence, where he was also active in public life. During the Maimonidean controversy of 1232, he undertook a journey to Toledo to gain the support of Judah ibn Alfakhar for the adherents of Maimonides. His *Mikhlol*, which assembled the researches of Spanish Jewish grammarians and philologists, consists of a Hebrew grammar and biblical dictionary. He also wrote biblical commentaries, which combine Spanish speculative, philological, and philosophical traditions with the rabbinic midrashic method of exegesis and the interpretations of Rashi.

Kimḥi, Dov (1889–1961). Israeli author, translator, and editor, of Galician origin. He was born in Jasło, Galicia, and emigrated to Palestine in 1908. He settled in Jerusalem, where he taught at the Reḥaviah Gymnasium. He wrote novels, short stories, and essays, and produced numerous translations.

Kimḥi, Joseph [Joseph ben Isaac Kimḥi] (c. 1105–c. 1170). Spanish grammarian, exegete, translator, and polemicist. As a refugee from the Almohad persecutions in Spain, he settled in Narbonne, Provence. His writings include grammars, commentaries on biblical books, religious poems, and translations from Arabic. His *Sepher ha-Berit* was one of the first anti-Christian polemical works written in Europe.

Kimḥi, Moses (d. c. 1190). French grammarian and exegete, son of Joseph Kimḥi. He was active in Narbonne, Provence. His *Mahalakh Shevile ha-Daat* was the first printed Hebrew grammar (1489); translated into Latin, it was used by Christian scholars during the period of the Reformation. He was also the author of commentaries on Proverbs, Ezra, and Nehemiah as well as liturgical poems.

Kinah ("lamentation") [Elegy]. Dirge for the dead. Kinot were recited at funerals and on other days of mourning in biblical, mishnaic, and talmudic times. In the Middle Ages the term was applied to a special type of piyyut for the Ninth of Av, dealing with the loss of the Temple and national independence, contemporary persecutions, and the hope for the coming of the Messiah and redemption. The most famous author of kinot was Eleazar Kallir.

Kindling of lights. Lights are kindled by the housewife at the beginning of Sabbaths and festivals. This act is obligatory: if no woman is present, it must be done by a man. Before the lighting takes place, an appropriate blessing is recited. Other occasions for the kindling of lights are Ḥanukkah, the anniversary of the death of a near relative, and the Day of Atonement.

Kingdom of Heaven. Eschatological concept concerning a future state of perfection in the world. After the divine judgment the sinful order of the world will come to an end and God will create a new Heaven and a new earth, in which all creatures will be at peace with one another (Daniel 7.13–14). Eventually this notion was linked to the concept of the Messiah.

Kings. The name of two biblical books, which form part of the group known as the Former Prophets. They relate the history of Israel and Judah from the death of David until the liberation of Jehoiachin during the Babylonian captivity.

Kings and kingship. The Israelite monarchy replaced tribal chiefs of the earlier period, and from the 11th to the 10th centuries BCE ruled over the entire kingdom. In 931 BCE the nation divided into two kingdoms (Judah and Israel) with their own dynasties. With the destruction of these kingdoms (Israel in 722 BCE, Judah in 586 BCE), Israelite kingship came to an end. Under the Hasmoneans (2nd–1st centuries BCE) the monarchy was restored for a brief period but Jewish movements of the 1st–2nd centuries CE produced claimants to messianic kingship. The positions, rights, and limitations of the king are elaborated in the Mishnah (Sanhedrin 2.2–5), as well as in Maimonides' *Mishneh Torah.*

Kinneret, Lake of [Lake] *see* GALILEE, SEA OF.

Kinnim ("Bird nests"). 11th tractate in the Mishnah order of Kodashim. It deals with the regulations for the bringing of an offering after childbirth (Leviticus 12.8) and for the offerings made by the poor who might commit the offenses listed in Leviticus 5. It also treats cases where sacrifices are interchanged.

Kinyan *see* SALE.

Kipnis, Menachem (1878–1942). Polish singer, folklorist, and writer. He was born in Ushomir, in the Ukraine, and moved to Warsaw in 1901. From 1912 to 1932 he toured Poland, Germany, and France, appearing with his wife, Zimra Seligsfeld, in lecture-recitals of Jewish folk songs. These he published in numerous collections; he also published articles on various aspects of Jewish music.

Kirchheim, Raphael (1804–1889). German scholar. He was born in Frankfurt am Main and became a partner in a banking house. Initially he was an opponent of Reform Judaism, but under the influence of Abraham Geiger he became a supporter. His publications include editions of various medieval Hebrew works.

Kirkisani, Jacob *see* KARKASANI, ABU YUSUF YAKUB.

Kirschen, Ya'akov (b. 1938). Israeli cartoonist. He was born in Washington DC and grew up in Brooklyn. In 1968 he settled in Israel. He created "Dry Bones," a daily political comic strip which appeared in the *Jerusalem Post.*

Kisch, Alexander (1848–1917). Austrian rabbi and scholar. He was born in Prague. He served as a rabbi in Brüx, Bohemia (1874–7), Zurich (1877–81), Jungbunzlau, Bohemia (1881–6), and Prague (1886–1917). In Zurich he founded the first Swiss-Jewish weekly. In 1899 Franz Joseph I awarded him a gold medal for 25 years' service as a military chaplain. He was the first rabbi in Austria to be appointed a government professor of religion and inspector of religious education. His writings include studies of Bohemian Jewish history.

Kisch, Frederick Hermann (1888–1943). British soldier and Zionist. He was born in India. He joined the Indian Army and was posted to Baluchistan in World War I. Later he was appointed to the Directorate of Military Intelligence at the War Office, working in the section covering Russia, Persia, China, and Japan. He was a member of the British delegation to the Paris Peace Conference (1919–21). In 1923 he became a member of the Zionist Executive in Jerusalem and head of its Political Department. Later he advised the Jewish community on security matters. During World War II he returned to active service in the British Army.

Kisch, Guido (1889–1986). American legal historian. He was born in Prague. He taught the theory and history of law at the universities of Leipzig, Königsberg, Halle, and Prague. After emigrating to the US in 1935 he taught history at the Jewish Institute of Religion in New York. In 1962 he moved to Basle, where he taught at the university. He published studies on medieval law and German Jewry. He was also the founder and editor of the periodical *Historia Judaica*.

Kishka (Yiddish). Sausage containing a mixture of meat, flour, and spices.

Kishon. River that rises in Mount Tabor, traverses the Valley of Jezreel, and enters the Mediterranean two miles north of Haifa. On its banks near Mount Carmel Elijah slaughtered the priests of Baal (I Kings 18.40).

Kishon, Ephraim (b. 1924). Israeli humorist. He was born in Hungary and moved to Israel in 1949. From 1952 he wrote a column in the newspaper *Maariv*, which dealt with political and social issues. He published books, plays, film scripts, satires, and articles reflecting Israeli life.

Kislev. Ninth month of the Hebrew calendar. Historic days during the month are: 1 Kislev, the announcement of a series of public fasts in Judea in the intercession for rain in years of drought; 3 Kislev, the anniversary of a Hasmonean victory over the Greeks (164 BCE); 7 Kislev, the anniversary of the death of Herod the Great; 21 Kislev, the "Day of Gerizim," which commemorates the legendary decision by Alexander the Great in favor of erecting the Temple in Jerusalem (against the Samaritan claim for siting it on Mount Gerizim); 25 Kislev, the beginning of the festival of Ḥanukkah.

Kiss, Joseph (1843–1921). Hungarian poet. He was born in Mezocsat. After the publication of several volumes of his poetry, he became acknowledged as a leading figure in Hungarian literature. In his writings he described social change, moral degeneration, and the breakdown of traditional Jewish family life. The theme of anti-Semitism is a prevailing motif throughout his work.

Kissing. The rabbis disapproved of kissing except in the case of a kiss given to a man when appointing him to a position of honor, a kiss given at meeting or parting, and a kiss exchanged between relatives. Sacred objects (such as fringes, the Scroll of the Law, the mezuzah, a religious book that has fallen to the ground) are kissed as a sign of respect. Among the Sephardim, children kiss their parents' hands after receiving the parental blessing. Oriental Jews kiss the hand of the Ḥakham in salutation.

Kitaj, R. B. (b. 1932). American painter. He was born in Cleveland and later lived in England. From the 1970s he became concerned with Jewish identity as a conscious and subconscious impulse. His paintings include *The Murder of Rosa Luxemburg*, *The Jew Etc.*, and *If Not, Not.*

Kittel (Yiddish). White shroud-like garment worn by the officiant and many members of the congregation during the prayer service on the high holy days, and by the cantor at the musaph service on Shemini Atzeret and the first day of Passover. It is also worn by the person conducting the seder on Passover, and by the groom during the marriage ceremony. In some communities it is called a "sargenes."

***Kittel, Rudolph** (1853–1929). German Protestant theologian and Bible scholar. He taught at the universities of Tübingen (1879–81), Stuttgart (1881–8), Breslau (1888–98), and Leipzig (1898–1924). A follower of the Wellhausen school of biblical criticism, he published studies of the Jews in biblical times. He also translated into German several books of the Bible, the Apocrypha, and apocalyptic literature. Together with other scholars, he published a critical edition of the Hebrew Bible (*Biblia Hebraica*).

***Klaczko, Julian** (1825–1906). Polish author, critic, and historian. Raised in the atmosphere of the Lithuanian Haskalah, he wrote poetry in Hebrew and

Polish. In 1840 he moved to Germany and then settled in Paris. After converting to Catholicism, he continued to live in France from 1849 to 1869. Subsequently he served in the Galician and imperial Austrian parliaments. From 1888 he lived in Kraków.

Klatzkin, Jacob (1882–1948). German Hebrew editor and philosopher. He was born in Bereza Kartuskaya, Russia. He worked in Germany as a writer for Hebrew periodicals. After World I, he and Nahum Goldmann founded the publishing house Eshkol, which produced the *Encyclopaedia Judaica* under Klatzkin's editorship. With the rise of the Nazis to power in Germany, Klatzkin moved to Switzerland. He published studies of Hermann Cohen and Baruch Spinoza, as well as his own philosophical works.

Klaus(e) (German: "enclosure"). Term used from the 16th century in central and eastern Europe to refer to an institution (usually with a synagogue attached) where the Talmud was studied by adults. The Ḥasidim applied the same name to their synagogues.

Klausner, Yoseph Gedaliah (1874–1958). Israeli literary critic, historian, and Zionist. Born in Olkienik, near Vilnius, he was raised in Odessa. At the age of 28 he moved to Warsaw, where he became editor of the literary monthly *Ha-Shiloaḥ*. In 1919 he emigrated to Palestine, where he was active in the Academy of the Hebrew Language. Appointed to the chair of Hebrew literature at the Hebrew University, he subsequently became professor of the history of the second Temple. His publications include histories of modern Hebrew literature, the second Temple period, and the idea of the Messiah, studies of Jesus and Paul, philological works, monographs on Hebrew authors, and philosophical works. From 1950 he served as editor-in-chief of the *Encyclopaedia Hebraica*.

Klein, Abraham M. (1909–1972). Canadian poet and author. He was born in Montreal, and became a partner in a law firm. He is regarded as the first outstanding Jewish contributor to Canadian literature. In addition to writing his own poetry, he made numerous translations of Hebrew and Yiddish poems. His publications include *Hath not a Jew*, *The Hitleriad*, *Poems*, and *The Rocking Chair*. His work was influenced by Jewish themes, talmudic erudition, and Yiddish folklore.

Klein, Shemuel (1886–1940). Hungarian historian and geographer of Palestine. He served as a rabbi in Dolnja Tuzla, Bosnia (1909–13), and Ersekujvar (1913–28). In 1929 he became professor of historical topography of Palestine at the Hebrew University. In his writings he used the Talmud and midrash as primary sources of information on the country's topography and the history of its settlement.

Kleinbaum, Mosheh *see* SNEH, MOSHEH.

Klop (Yiddish). To hit (also a blow), to blab.

Klotz (Yiddish). A clumsy person, a bungler.

Kluger, Solomon ben Judah Aaron (1785–1869). Austrian rabbinic scholar. He was also known as the Maggid of Brody. He initially lived in Rava, where he worked as a shopkeeper. He then became rabbi at Kolki. From there he went to Josefov, and in 1820 to Brody. An opponent of the maskilim, he wrote hundreds of responsa and numerous books.

Klutznick, Philip Morris (b. 1907). American communal leader and diplomat. He was born in Kansas City, Missouri. He held a succession of appointments connected with community planning: in 1935–6 he was a special assistant on housing to the US attorney-general, in 1938–41 general counsel for the Omaha Housing Authority, and in 1944–6 federal housing commissioner. From 1961 to 1963 he served as ambassador to the United Nations Economic and Social Council. He held several positions in Jewish organizations, including international president of B'nai B'rith, general chairman of the United Jewish Appeal, and vice-president of the Jewish Welfare Board.

Knaydl (Yiddish). A dumpling made of matzo meal.

Knesset ("assembly"). The parliament of Israel. It consists of a single chamber of 120 members, who are elected by proportional representation for a four-year term. It is the supreme authority in the state. Created in 1949, the Knesset initially met in Tel Aviv but later moved to Jerusalem.

Knishes (Yiddish). Little dumplings. It is also used figuratively as a term of abuse.

Kobrin, Leon (1873–1946). American Yiddish dramatist and novelist. He was born in Russia, and emigrated to the US in 1892, where he worked in a sweatshop. His stories and plays describe Jewish life in the US during the period of immigration, depicting the problems of nationalism, assimilation, and relations between parents and children.

Kodashim ("Holy things"). Fifth order of the Mishnah. It deals with the laws of ritual slaughter, sacrifice, and other topics connected with the Temple ritual.

Koenig, Leo (1889–1970). British Yiddish author, critic, and journalist. He was born in Odessa. He wrote art criticism for leading Yiddish periodicals in Paris, before moving to London in 1914; he then worked for the Yiddish press in England and abroad. In 1952 he settled in Haifa.

Koestler, Arthur (1905–1983). English author. Born in Budapest, he traveled widely, settling in England in 1940. Initially a communist in the 1930s, he later repudiated communism. His works include novels, essays, and reminiscences. *Thieves in the Night* portrays kibbutz life in Palestine, and *Promise and Fulfilment* deals with Zionism.

Kogan [Kahana]**, David** (1838–1915). Ukrainian scholar. He was born in Odessa. He wrote numerous studies of Jewish history and literature, including *History of the Kabbalists, Sabbataians and Ḥasidim.*

Kohelet *see* Ecclesiastes.

Kohen Tzedek ben Joseph (fl. 10th cent.). Babylonian gaon. He was gaon of Pumbedita from 917 to 936. He was appointed gaon by the exilarch David ben Zakkai I, but the scholars of the academy refused to recognize him and elected Mevasser Kahana instead. As a result both men served simultaneously as geonim, but after Mevasser's death in 926 Kohen Tzedek ben Joseph assumed the post alone.

Kohler, Kaufmann (1843–1926). American Reform leader. He was born in Fürth in Bavaria and emigrated to the US in 1869. He served as rabbi of the Congregation of Beth El in Detroit, Sinai Congregation in Chicago, and Temple Beth El in New York. He was a leading figure at the Pittsburgh Conference of Reform Jews in 1885, at which the Pittsburgh Platform (a statement of the tenets of American Reform Judaism) was adopted. In 1903 he became president of the Hebrew Union College. His publications include *Jewish Theology*.

Kohler, Max James (1871–1934). American attorney and communal leader. He was born in Detroit. He served as assistant US district attorney in the southern district of New York from 1894 to 1898, and then entered private law as a defender of the legal and public rights of immigrants, naturalized citizens, and aliens. His writings include *Immigration and Aliens in the United States: Studies of American Immigration Laws and the Legal Status of Aliens in the United States.*

Kohler, Rose (1873–1947). American sculptor and painter, daughter of Kaufmann Kohler. Her works include busts and portraits of Jewish leaders, as well as a medallion entitled *The Spirit of the Synagogue.*

Kohn, Abraham (1807–1848). Ukrainian rabbi. He was born in Bohemia, and served as a rabbi in Hohenems. In 1844 he became a preacher in Lemberg, where his reforms aroused the opposition of Orthodox Jews. When he and his son died from food poisoning, Orthodox leaders were arrested, but they were later released for lack of evidence.

Kohn, Samuel (1841–1920). Hungarian rabbi and scholar. He was born in Baja, Hungary. He served as a rabbi in Budapest from 1866 to 1905, when he was appointed chief rabbi of Hungary. He was one of those responsible for the establishment of the Jewish Theological Seminary in Budapest. He published works on the Samaritans, and the history of the Jews in Hungary.

Kohut, Adolph (1848–1917). German journalist and writer, of Hungarian origin. He was the editor of several German papers. He published studies of history, culture, and Jewish affairs, as well as a history of the Jews in Germany.

Kohut, Alexander (1842–1894). American rabbi and scholar, of Hungarian origin. He served as a rabbi in Stuhlweissenburg, and later became chief rabbi of Fünfkirchen. In 1885 he left for the US, where he served as rabbi of Congregation Ahavath Chesed in New York. He helped to establish the Jewish Theological Seminary, where he taught midrash and talmudic methodology. His *Arukh ha-Shalem* is a lexicon of talmudic terms based on the talmudic dictionary of Nathan ben Jehiel.

Kohut, Rebekah (1864–1951). American educator and community leader, wife of Alexander Kohut. She was born in Kaschau. From 1897 to 1901 she was president of the New York Council of Jewish Women, and in 1914 was appointed head of the employment bureau of the Young Women's Hebrew Association. In 1942 she became president of the World Congress of Jewish Women. Her writings include *My Portion, More Yesterdays,* and *George Alexander Kohut: his Memoir.*

Koigen, David (1879–1933). Ukrainian philosopher and sociologist. He lived in Germany until 1912, when he returned to Russia. In 1921 he was appointed professor of philosophy and sociology at the Ukrainian University in Kiev. His writings include studies of the Jewish experience in history and culture.

Koitein, Shelomoh Dov *see* GOITEIN, SHELOMOH DOV.

***Kokowzoff, Pavel** (1861–1942). Russian orientalist. He was born in Pavlovsk. In 1894 he became professor of Hebrew at St. Petersburg University, succeeding his teacher Daniel Chwolson. He wrote studies of Aramaic, Syriac, Turkish, and Ethiopic manuscripts and epigraphic material, and also published an edition of the 10th-century correspondence between Ḥasdai ibn Shaprut and the Khazar king Joseph.

Kol Bo ("Compendium"). Anonymous medieval Jewish legal codification. It contains 148 sections dealing with such topics as blessings, prayer, the synagogue, the meal, the Sabbath and festivals, marriage, money, vows and oaths, laws relevant to the land of Israel, forbidden foods, the redemption of the first-born son, visiting the sick, and mourning.

Kollek, Theodor (b. 1911). Israeli politician. He was born in Vienna. In 1934 he emigrated to Palestine, where he became a member of kibbutz En Gev. From 1940 to 1947 he served in the political department of the Jewish Agency. He then (1947–8) represented the Haganeh in the US and in 1951–2 served as Israel's minister plenipotentiary in Washington DC. He was director of the Israeli prime minister's office from 1952 to 1964, and chairman of the Israel Government Tourist Corporation from 1956 to 1964. In 1965 he was elected Mayor of Jerusalem.

Kol Nidre ("All vows"). Opening words (and hence title) of the formula for the annulment of vows, recited on the eve of the Day of Atonement. The custom of annulling all personal vows and oaths made unwittingly or rashly during the preceding year originated in the early gaonic period. The practice gave rise to the accusation among non-Jews that a Jewish oath was not to be trusted. In the 12th century Jacob Tam changed the formula to refer to vows of this nature that might be made in the forthcoming year. It has become the most beloved ritual of the Day of Atonement.

Kompert, Leopold (1822–1886). Austrian novelist. He was born in Bohemia. In 1840 he moved to Hungary, where he became editor of the German-language literary periodical *Pannonia* published in Pressburg. Later he settled in Vienna, where he worked as a journalist. His writings deal with eastern European Jewish life, mixed marriage, and anti-Semitism. He was active in Jewish affairs and Viennese civic life, taking a special interest in education and the welfare of orphans.

Konrád, György (b. 1933). Hungarian author. He was born in Berettyóújfalu in eastern Hungary. His writings include *The Loser.*

Kook, Avraham Yitzḥak (1865–1935). Palestinian rabbinic scholar of Latvian origin. He was born in Greiva, Latvia, and served as rabbi of Zaumel and Bauska, before emigrating to Palestine in 1904. An ardent Zionist, he became chief rabbi of the Ashkenazi community in Palestine in 1921. He believed that the return to Palestine marked the beginning of divine redemption. His writings include *Orot* (on holiness in the new-born nationalism), *Orot ha-Teshuvah* (on repentance), and *Halakhah Berurah* (on halakhic issues).

Koph. 19th letter of the Hebrew alphabet. Its numerical value is 100.

Kops, Bernard (b. 1926). English playwright and novelist. He was born in the East End of London, which became the subject of his work. His writings include *The World is a Wedding*, *Yes from No-Man's Land*, *By the Waters of Whitechapel*, and *The Hamlet of Stepney Green.*

Kopytman, Mark (b. 1929). Israeli composer, of Russian origin. He went to Israel in 1972, and became a professor of composition at the Rubin Academy of Music in Jerusalem. Some of his work is influenced by traditional Jewish cantillation.

Korah (fl. 13th cent. BCE). Levite, kinsman of Moses. Together with Dathan, Abiram of the tribe of Reuben, and 250 Israelite leaders, he rebelled against Moses and Aaron (Numbers 16). As a punishment, the earth opened and swallowed them (Numbers 26.11).

Koran. The holy book of Islam. It contains the teachings of Mohammed, delivered during his prophetic ministry. The Koran reflects Jewish ideas and religious law, and embodies biblical traditions.

Korban meilah ("special sacrifice") *see* HEKDESH.

Korczak, Janos (1879–1942). Polish author, educator, and communal leader. He was born in Warsaw, where he worked as a physician and became concerned with the plight of the poor; his early writings depict the condition of homeless orphans in the cities. In 1911 he became head of a Jewish orphanage in Warsaw. He published theoretical studies about pedagogical method, as well as children's books. With the rise of Hitler, he became Poland's non-Zionist representative on the Jewish Agency. In 1942 he was deported to a concentration camp, where he was killed.

Kornfeld, Joseph Saul (1876–1943). American rabbi and diplomat, of Austro-Hungarian origin. He went to the US as a child. He served congregations in Pine Bluff, Arkansas; Montreal; and Columbus, Ohio, where he became active in civic affairs. He was appointed American ambassador to Persia in 1921. In 1925 he became rabbi of the Collingwood Avenue Temple in Toledo, Ohio.

Kornfeld, Paul (1889–1942). German playwright. He was born in Prague. He wrote tragedies, comedies, and an historical drama, *Jud Süss*. He was deported by the Nazis and died in the Łódź ghetto.

Kosher *see* KASHRUT.

Kossovsky, Ḥayyim Yehoshua *see* KASSOVSKY, ḤAYYIM YEHOSHUA.

Kotel Maaravi *see* WESTERN WALL.

Kovner, Abba (1918–1987). Lithuanian resistance fighter and Hebrew poet. Born in Sevastopol', he grew up in Vilnius. He was a commander of the Vilnius ghetto and fought the Germans as leader of the partisan groups in the surrounding forests. In 1945 he settled in Palestine, but he was imprisoned in Egypt by the British when he attempted to return to Europe to continue Jewish rescue work. His poems and novels deal with Jewish partisans during the Nazi period and Israel's War of Independence.

***Kovner, Abraham Uri** (1842–1909). Russian Hebrew author. He was born in Vilnius. He published a collection of essays, *Ḥeker Davar*, in 1865, which condemned Haskalah literature, and in *Tzeror Peraḥim* he attacked Hebrew as a dead language. In 1870 he settled in St. Petersburg, where he contributed weekly articles to the Russian journal *Golos*. Condemned to exile in Siberia for a criminal offense, he later adopted Christianity. His last years were spent in Łomża, Poland, where he worked as a government official.

Kozakov, Mikhail (1897–1954). Russian author. He was born in the Ukraine. His novel *The Fall of the Empire* deals with the last years of imperial Russia and the Revolution. Some of his early stories describe life in a Jewish shtetl in the Pale of Settlement. His novella *The Person Kissing the Ground* deals with Russian anti-Semitism.

Kozienicer Maggid *see* ISRAEL BEN SHABBETAI OF KOZIENICE.

Krakauer, Leopold (1896–1954). Israeli architect and designer, of Austrian origin. He was born in Vienna. He helped to design the parliament building in Belgrade. In 1924 he emigrated to Palestine, settling in Jerusalem. He designed public buildings and private houses, and later concentrated on town planning. He also produced drawings of the countryside around Jerusalem.

Kraków [Cracow]. City in southern Poland. Its Jewish community developed from the 14th century. Many outstanding rabbis and scholars flourished there, as well as intellectual leaders, during the 16th–18th centuries. In the 18th century Jewry in the city was initially opposed to Ḥasidism and the Haskalah, but both movements eventually gained supporters. From 1890 Zionism played an important role in Kraków's Jewish life.

Kramer, Jacob (1892–1962). British painter. He was born in the Ukraine; his family emigrated to England in 1900 and settled in Leeds. His paintings include *The Day of Atonement*, and *Hear our Voice, O Lord our God.*

Kranz, Jacob ben Wolf *see* JACOB BEN WOLF KRANZ.

Krauskopf, Joseph (1858–1923). American Reform rabbi. He was born in Prussia and settled in the US in 1872. He served congregations in Kansas City and Philadelphia. A leader of radical reform, he was an important figure in the national organizations of Reform Judaism. He established the National Farm School in Doylestown, Pennsylvania, and in 1917 was appointed to direct food conservation among Jews for the US Food Administration.

Krauss, Samuel (1866–1948). Austrian historian, philologist, and talmudic scholar, of Hungarian origin. He taught the Bible and Hebrew at the Jewish teachers' seminary in Budapest. In 1906 he was appointed to teach the Bible, history, and liturgy at the Vienna Rabbinical Seminary (the Israelitisch-Theologische Lehranstalt); later he became head of the seminary and rector. When the Nazis came to power, he fled to England. He published studies in the fields of philology, history, the Bible, the Talmud, Christianity, and medieval literature.

Krechtz (Yiddish). To grunt in pain, to fuss or complain (also a sound of complaint), to make gasping noises.

Krein, Alexander (1883–1951). Russian composer, brother of Grigori Krein. He studied at the Moscow Conservatory, where he served as professor (1912–17). He was then secretary of the Russian Board of Education (1918–20), and a member of the board of the State Publishing Department (1918–27). He was one of the leaders of the Jewish musical movement and an active member of the Society for Jewish Folk Music. His music contains Jewish traditional folk motifs.

Krein, Grigori (1885–1955). Russian composer and violinist, brother of Alexander Krein. He studied in Moscow and later in Leipzig. From 1926 to 1934 he lived in Paris and later in Tashkent. A number of his compositions have a Jewish content.

Kreitman, Esther (1891–1954). Polish Yiddish author, sister of Israel Joshua Singer and Isaac Bashevis Singer. She was born in Biłgoraj, Poland. Her publications include *Der sheydem-tants*, *Brilyantn*, and *Yikhes*.

Krementzky, Johann (1850–1934). Austrian Zionist leader. He was born in Odessa; he settled in Vienna in 1880 and built several factories. An ardent Zionist, he became an adherent of Theodor Herzl; he served as a member of the Zionist Executive and the Zionist General Council and was appointed director of the Jewish National Fund.

Krenk (Yiddish). An illness.

Kreplach (Yiddish). Triangular or square dumpling containing chopped meat or cheese. It is usually served in soup.

Krimchaks. The original Orthodox Jews of the Crimea. They spoke a Turkish dialect, wore Turkish dress, and adopted many Turkish customs.

Kristallnacht (German: "night of broken glass"). Name given to the night of 9–10 November 1938 on which the Jewish community of Germany was attacked by the Nazis and their sympathizers. The onslaught was provoked by the assassination of Ernst vom Rath, Third Secretary of the German embassy in Paris, by a Jewish youth named Herschel Grynszpan. Throughout Germany, synagogues and Jewish-owned property were devastated and Jewish people attacked.

Krochmal, Abraham (d. 1888). Galician-born writer and scholar. He lived in Lemberg, Brody, Odessa, and Frankfurt am Main. In Galicia and Odessa he moved in Haskalah circles. He wrote studies of the Talmud and the Bible, philosophical works on Judaism, and articles advocating religious reform.

Krochmal, Naḥman (1785–1840). Galician philosopher and historian. He was born in Brody, and lived in Zolkiew in Galicia. Later he returned to Brody, and eventually moved to Tarnopol. He was a leading figure in the Haskalah movement and the founder (in the 1830s) of Wissenschaft des Judentums. His *Guide to the Perplexed of the Time* is a philosophical investigation of the course of Jewish history.

Kroměříž. Town in central Moravia (now in Czechoslovakia). In 1322 the Bishop of Kroměříž was granted the privilege of keeping one Jew in the town, and soon a Jewish community was established under his protection. Although the Jewish population was nearly destroyed during the Thirty Years War (1618–48), it flourished in the latter half of the 17th century. Kroměříž consequently became the seat of the county rabbinate.

Kubbutz. Vowel sound in Hebrew. It is generally sounded "oo," as in "foot," but in some traditions it is sounded like the German "ü."

Kugel (Yiddish). Pudding of noodles or potatoes.

Ku Klux Klan. American secret society. It flourished in the South during the Civil War and was revived in the 20th century. During the 1920s it mounted a campaign against blacks, Jews, and Catholics. Its members wore sheets covering their heads and bodies and burned crosses. The society re-emerged during the civil rights struggle in the 1960s.

Kulisher, Michael (1847–1919). Russian historian, ethnographer, and communal worker. He studied at the rabbinical seminary in Zhitomir in the Ukraine, and at the law faculty of the University of St. Petersburg. From 1869 to 1871 he was on the editorial board of the Russian Jewish newspaper *Den*. He published a life of Jesus as well as studies of gentile attitudes to the Jews.

Kumin, Maxine (b. 1925). American poet and writer. She was born in Philadelphia. She taught at Tufts, Columbia, and Princeton universities. Some of her poetry deals with her Jewish identity.

Kumran *see* QUMRAN.

Kumsitz ("come and sit"). Expression used in modern Hebrew to denote an impromptu party.

Kuntras (medieval Hebrew). Notebook. The word was applied by the tosaphists to Rashi's commentary on the Talmud. It was also used in France as a general term for collected commentaries.

Kuppah. Poor box. Jews contribute to the poor box in the synagogue or at home on joyful, sad, and solemn occasions, and at weekday services. The distribution of the collection was formerly supervised by a group of overseers. The term has come to refer to general relief.

Kuraiza *see* BANU KURAIZA.

Kuranten. The first Yiddish periodical. It appeared twice weekly in Amsterdam in 1686–7.

Kurzweil, Baruch (1907–1972). Israeli literary critic. He was born in Moravia, and emigrated to Palestine in 1939. He was appointed professor of modern Hebrew literature at Bar-Ilan University in 1955. His writings include *On the Novel*, *Our New Literature: Continuation or Revolution?*, *Bialik ve-Tchernichovsky*, *Massot al Sippurei S.Y. Agnon*, and *Between the Vision and the Absurd.*

Kusevitsky, Mosheh (1899–1966). Polish cantor. He served as chief cantor at the main synagogue in Warsaw. From 1947 he lived in the US and made concert tours abroad.

Kushner, Harold (b. 1935). American rabbi. He has served congregations in New York and Massachusetts. His publications include *When Bad Things Happen to Good People*.

Kutim (i). Talmudic term for the Samaritans. The word was also used to denote any individual or group that rejected the Oral Law.

Kutim (ii) ("Samaritans"). Minor tractate appended to the Talmud, which deals with the relationships between Samaritans, gentiles, and Jews.

Kutscher, Eduard Yechezkel (1909–1971). Israeli linguist. He was born in Topoltshani, Slovakia, and went to Israel in 1941. He taught at the Hebrew University and later at Bar-Ilan University, specializing in Hebrew and Semitic languages. His publications include *The Language and Linguistic Background of the Isaiah Scroll, and History of the Hebrew Language.*

Kuzari *see* JUDAH HA-LEVI.

Kvell (Yiddish). To beam with pride and pleasure, to enjoy, to gloat.

Kvetch (Yiddish). To fuss, to complain, to squeeze, to delay, to shrug, to exert. It can also refer to someone who complains, works slowly, or uses alibis for a lazy performance.

Kvitko, Leib (1890–1952). Russian Yiddish writer. He worked in various cities in the Ukraine as a dyer, shoemaker, porter, and stevedore. In 1920 he settled in Germany, but he later returned to the USSR. He was arrested in the Stalinist purges in 1949, and executed with other Yiddish writers in 1952. He wrote novels and poetry, as well as stories for children.

Kwartin, Zavel (1874–1953). American cantor and composer. He was born in the Ukraine. He served as a cantor in synagogues in Vienna, St. Petersburg, and Budapest, before emigrating to the US in 1919. He became cantor at Temple Emanuel in Borough Park, Brooklyn. He moved to Palestine in 1926, but later returned to the US.

L

Laaz. In medieval Jewish commentaries a word in a foreign language, transliterated into Hebrew script and used as a gloss. In Rashi's commentaries on the Bible and the Talmud there are thousands of such glosses. The origin of the word "laaz" is unknown.

Laban (fl. ?19th–16th cent. BCE). Israelite herdsman, brother of Rebekah and father of Leah and Rachel. He was a breeder of sheep and goats. He gave his sister Rebekah in marriage to Isaac (Genesis 24). Later he consented to the marriage of his daughter Rachel to Jacob, but deceived Jacob by substituting her sister Leah; he finally gave Rachel to Jacob as a wife in exchange for a further seven years of labor (Genesis 29).

Labor. The Bible and Talmud praise physical work for its moral and spiritual value. The Bible prescribes fair treatment of laborers (Deuteronomy 24.14) and makes obligatory their payment on the day of work (Leviticus 19.13). These passages serve as the basis for further mishnaic and talmudic legislation concerning the relationship between employer and laborer. In modern times the Haskalah and Ḥibbat Zion movements stressed the importance of manual labor.

Labor Battalion *see* GEDUD HA-AVODAH.

Labor movement *see* SOCIALISM; TRADE UNIONS.

Labor Zionism *see* POALE ZION.

Lachish. City in Judah, south-west of Jerusalem. It was captured from the Canaanites by Joshua and fortified by Rehoboam. Under Hezekiah it was besieged in 701 BCE by Sennacherib; this siege is represented on reliefs found at Nineveh. Nebuchadnezzar destroyed the city in 588 BCE, but it continued to exist and passed into Persian hands.

Lachish Letters. A series of communications, inscribed on clay tablets, sent in 589 BCE to Ya'ush, an army commander stationed in Lachish, when the Babylonians threatened the city. Fragments survive.

Lachover, Yeruḥam Fishel (1883–1947). Israeli literary scholar. He was born in Chorzele, Poland. He began his literary career as a critic in 1904, and in 1908 moved to Warsaw, where he edited several journals and miscellanies. He settled in Palestine in 1927. His publications include a history of modern Hebrew literature and a biography of Bialik.

Ladino. Judeo-Spanish dialect. It is spoken by the Sephardim of Mediterranean countries and written in Hebrew script.

***Lagarde, Paul de** (1827–1891). German orientalist. He was a professor at Göttingen from 1869. He published studies of the Septuagint, and editions of the Targum to the Prophets and Hagiographa. He encouraged the emigration of Jews from Germany.

Lag Ba-Omer. The 33rd day of the Omer period. It falls on 18 Iyyar. According to tradition, a plague among the pupils of Akiva ended on this date, and it is thus called the "Scholars' Feast." It has been celebrated as a semi-holiday since the time of the geonim. Kabbalists observed this day as the anniversary of the death of Simeon ben Yoḥai.

Laguna, Daniel Israel Lopez (1653–1723). Jamaican Marrano poet. As a child he was taken to Peyrehorade in the south of France. Later he was arrested by the Inquisition in Spain. He settled in Jamaica, where he practiced Judaism. In about 1720 he moved to London but he eventually returned to Jamaica. During his time in London he published a paraphrase of the Psalms in Spanish verse forms.

Lake Kinneret *see* GALILEE, SEA OF.

Lambert, Mayer (1863–1930). French scholar. He was born in Metz. He lectured on Arabic, Syriac, and Hebrew at the École Rabbinique and taught Hebrew at the École Normale Orientale of the Alliance Israélite Universelle. In 1903 he began teaching Hebrew and Syriac at the École Pratique des Hautes Études. His publications include studies of Hebrew grammar and the writings of Saadyah Gaon.

Lamdan. Talmudic scholar.

Lamdan, Yitzḥak (1899–1954). Hebrew poet. He was born in Milnov, in the Ukraine, and witnessed the Ukrainian pogroms after World War I. In 1920 he emigrated to Palestine, where he initially worked as a laborer. From 1934 he published and edited the literary monthly *Gilyonot*. His poem *Masadah* reflects the spirit of the pioneers of the 1920s.

Lamech. Patriarch. He was the son of Methushael (Genesis 4.18), and the father of Jabal, Jubal, Tubal-Cain, and Naamah (Genesis 4.20–22); according to Genesis 5, he was also the father of Noah. His wives were Adah and Zillah (Genesis 4.19). He was the father of the founders of nomadism, and of those who invented the musical arts and metalworking; he also composed a song (Genesis 4.23–4) which is an example of early Hebrew poetry.

Lamed. 12th letter of the Hebrew alphabet. Its numerical value is 30.

Lamed, Louis *see* LOUIS LAMED LITERARY FOUNDATION.

Lamed vav. 36 righteous men. According to tradition, 36 righteous men live in every generation, and on their continued existence the world depends. Each one is referred to as a "lamed-vovnik" or "nistar" (secret saint).

Lämel, Simon von (1776–1845). Bohemian merchant. He established a wool factory in Prague and was ennobled in 1812 for his services to Austria during the Napoleonic Wars. He was a benefactor of various Jewish causes.

Lamentations [Ekhah]. Biblical book, the third of the five scrolls in the Hagiographa. It contains elegies and mourning over the destruction of Judah, Jerusalem, and the Temple by the Babylonians. It is read in the synagogue on the Ninth of Av.

Lamentations Rabbah [Ekhah Rabbati]. Aggadic midrash on the Book of Lamentations. It contains homiletical interpretations of the text as well as aggadot about the destruction of the Temple. It was produced by Palestinian amoraim.

Lamm, Norman (b. 1927). American scholar. He was born in Brooklyn. He became professor of philosophy and president of Yeshiva University. His publications include *A Hedge of Roses*, *The Royal Reach*, *Faith and Doubt*, *Torah Lishmah*, and *The Good Society*. He has also served as the editor of the Library of Jewish Law and Ethics.

Lampronti, Isaac ben Samuel (1679–1756). Italian talmudist. Born in Ferrara, he taught in the Talmud Torah of the

Italian and Sephardi community in the city. Later he became head of the yeshivah there. His *Paḥad Yitzḥak* is a talmudic encyclopedia.

Lamps. Lamps and the symbol of light play an important role in Jewish tradition. In biblical times a menorah was placed in the Tabernacle and the Temple; smaller lamps were used for houses and public buildings. The eight-branched Ḥanukkah lamp was produced in a variety of forms from the Middle Ages. In the synagogue the ner tamid ("eternal light") is kept constantly burning before the Ark. The custom of lighting a lamp during mourning and on the anniversary of a parent's death is based on Proverbs 20.27. *See also* SABBATH LAMP.

Landau, Adolph (1842–1902). Russian journalist, educator, and publisher. He was born in Lithuania. He contributed to the Russian liberal press, and in 1871 began to publish a literary-historical anthology, the *Jewish Library*. In 1881 he founded the monthly journal *Voskhod*, later adding a weekly supplement in which he attacked Ḥibbat Zion, Zionists, and those who hated Jews.

Landau, Ezekiel ben Judah (1713–1793). Bohemian Halakhic authority. He was born in Opatów, Poland, and served as dayyan of Brody and rabbi of Yampol. In 1754 he became rabbi of Prague and the whole of Bohemia. He attempted to mitigate the conflict between Jacob Emden and Jonathan Eibeschütz, fought against the Sabbetains, and opposed Ḥasidism. He objected to Moses Mendelssohn's German translation of the Bible. His *Noda bi-Yhudah* contains over 800 responsa.

Landau, Jacob (1892–1952). Austrian journalist and publisher. He was born in Vienna. In 1914 he established the Jewish Correspondence Bureau, a news agency, in The Hague. He later moved his offices to London and renamed the organization the Jewish Telegraphic Agency. Branch offices were opened in Berlin, Warsaw, Prague, Paris, New York, and Jerusalem, and headquarters were subsequently established in New York. In 1940 he helped to found the Overseas News Agency.

Landau, Judah Leo (1866–1942). South African rabbi, scholar, poet, and playwright, of Galician origin. He served as minister of the North Manchester Hebrew Congregation (1900–04) before moving to Johannesburg to become rabbi of the Johannesburg Hebrew Congregation. In 1915 he became chief rabbi there and professor of Hebrew at Witwatersrand University. He wrote Hebrew poems and plays, as well as studies of modern Hebrew literature.

Landau, Zisho (1889–1937). American Yiddish poet, of Polish origin. He settled in New York, where he published an *Anthology of Yiddish Poetry in America until 1919*. Deeply affected by Jewish suffering during World War I, he reverted to Jewish themes in his later poetry.

Landauer, Gustav (1870–1919). German philosopher and writer. The son of a wealthy Karlsruhe merchant, he was attracted to anarchism in his youth and was twice imprisoned for political agitation. In 1918 he became editor of the theatrical periodical *Masken* published in Düsseldorf. When the Bavarian Soviet Republic was proclaimed in 1919, he accepted an invitation to become minister of public instruction. Following the overthrow of the government, he was murdered by counter-revolutionary soldiers in Munich. He published novels and philosophical and literary essays, and translated foreign literature into German.

Landauer, Samuel (1846–1937). German orientalist and bibliographer. He was born in Hürben. He taught oriental languages at the University of Strasbourg from 1875, and in 1905 he became director of the state and university library. Later he settled in Augsburg. He published the Arabic original of Saadyah Gaon's *Emunot ve-Deot*, as well as a standard edition of the works of the Persian poet Firdausi.

Landesmann, Heinrich [Lorm, Hieronymus] (1821–1902). German author. Born in Nikolsburg, he lived in Leipzig, Berlin, Vienna, Dresden, and Brünn. Although he was both deaf and blind, he published fiction, works of philosophy, and poetry. His novel *Gabriel Solmar* depicts a Jew's disillusionment with Emancipation and his return to the Jewish community.

Landlords and tenants *see* TENANT.

Landman, Isaac (1880–1946). American rabbi, of Russian origin. He emigrated to the US in 1890 and served as a Reform rabbi in New York. He edited the *American Hebrew* as well as the *Universal Jewish Encyclopedia*. From 1906 to 1916 he served as executive secretary of the National Farm School.

Landrabbiner. In Germany, a rabbi appointed (or recognized) by government. The term was used from the 17th century, and applied to rabbis who were invested with authority over a political region.

Landsberg, Yitzḥak *see* SADEH, YITZḤAK.

Landshath, Eliezer (1817–1887). German liturgical scholar and historian. He was born in Lissa. He worked as a bookseller and later was superintendent of the cemetery of the Berlin Jewish community. His *Ammude ha-Avodah* is a history of Jewish liturgical poets and their works.

Landsmannschaft (German: "compatriots' organization"). Aid organization for immigrants from eastern Europe. Such organizations were formed in the US, Israel, Latin America, the UK, South Africa, and elsewhere, and were given names according to the place of origin of their members. They were established to deal with social, economic, and cultural problems, and provided a social framework for mutual assistance.

Landstone, Charles (1891–1978). British dramatist and novelist. He was taken to London from Vienna at the age of four. He was a founding member of the Jewish Drama League and later its secretary. He reviewed fiction for the *Jewish Chronicle* and subsequently became its theater critic. His publications include *The Kerrels of Hill End*, and *I Gatecrashed*.

Langer, Jiří (1894–1943). Czech poet and author. After a visit to Palestine in 1913, he stayed for some time at the court of the Rokeaḥ dynasty of Ḥasidic rabbis in Galicia. Returning to Prague, he led a religiously observant life, became a teacher at a Jewish school, and wrote Hebrew poetry. In various studies he applied Freudian theories to the interpretation of certain aspects of Jewish literature and ritual. His *Nine Gates* is a volume of Ḥasidic tales.

Languages of the Jews. Hebrew is the original language of the Jews, but from the time of the first exile in the 6th century BCE, Jews have spoken the vernacular of the peoples among whom they lived in the diaspora. In some places, however, special DIALECTS (such as Ladino and Yiddish) developed and Jewish communities never abandoned Hebrew as a holy language and the language of the liturgy. With the founding of the State of Israel, modern Hebrew has become the language of the Jewish nation.

Lanzmann, Claude (b. 1925). French writer and film maker. He was born in Paris. He produced the film *Shoah* on the subject of the Holocaust.

Lara, David Cohen de (1602–1674). German philologist, lexicographer, writer, and translator. He was born in

Lisbon, and became ḥakham of the Spanish-Portuguese community in Hamburg. He later lived in Amsterdam and then returned to Hamburg. His *Keter Kehunnah* deals with talmudic words which do not appear in the *Arukh* of Nathan ben Jehiel of Rome. He also translated ethical works from Hebrew into Spanish.

La-Shanah ha-Baah bi-Yerushalayim *see* NEXT YEAR IN JERUSALEM.

Lasker, Eduard (1829–1884). German Liberal politician. He was born in Posen. He took part in the Revolution of 1848. During 1853 he went to England to study the system of British parliamentary government. He was elected to the Prussian parliament in 1865, and later led the Liberal Party in the Reichstag. He was a champion of Jewish rights.

Lasker-Schüler, Else (1869–1945). German poet. She first emigrated to Switzerland then later settled in Palestine. Her writings express affection for eastern European Jews and their rabbis; her Jewish poems include *Hebräische Balladen.*

Laski, Neville Jonas (1890–1969). English barrister and communal worker. He served as president of the Board of Deputies of British Jews from 1933 to 1939. He was also chairman of the administrative committee of the Jewish Agency for Palestine, and vice-president of the Anglo-Jewish Association. His publications include *Jewish Rights and Jewish Wrongs* and *The Laws and Charities of the Spanish and Portuguese Jews Congregation of London.*

Laskov, Ḥayyim (b. 1919). Israeli military commander. He was born in Borisov, Belorussia, and moved to Palestine in 1925. In 1944 he served with the Jewish Brigade Group in Italy. He joined the permanent staff of the Haganah in 1947, later becoming commander of the Israeli Air Force. After the Sinai Compaign against Egypt in 1956 he was appointed commanding officer of the southern command of the Israeli forces, and in 1958 fifth chief of general staff. In 1961 he became director general of the ports authority.

Lateran Council. Name given to a series of ecclesiastical synods held in the Lateran in Rome. The Third Lateran Council (1179) reinforced older restrictive church legislation regarding the Jews. The Fourth Lateran Council (1215), under Pope Innocent III, strengthened anti-usury laws, excluded Jews from public office, and enforced the wearing of the Jewish badge.

Latif, Ibn *see* IBN LATIF, ISAAC BEN ABRAHAM.

Latke (Yiddish). A potato pancake.

Latrun. Historical site at a crossroads in the southern Ayalon Valley, where the Judean Hills meet the Shephelah (the coastal plain). In the Middle Ages the crusaders' stronghold of Le Toron des Chevaliers was situated there. It was the scene of battle during the Israeli War of Independence in 1948. It was a no-man's land until it was taken by Israel in the Six-Day War in 1967.

Latteiner, Joseph (1853–1935). American Yiddish dramatist. He was born in Romania, and emigrated to New York in 1884. Initially he chose biblical subjects for his plays, but later turned to contemporary sources. He produced more than 80 plays, comedies, and musicals.

Lattes, Bonet (fl. 15th–16th cent.). Italianrabbi, astronomer, and physician. He was born in southern France, and later settled in Rome, where he served as rabbi and dayyan of the community. He foretold the coming of the Messiah in 1505. In 1513 Johannes von Reuchlin asked Lattes to use his influence with Pope Leo X to support him in his controversy with the Dominicans.

Lattes, Dante (1876–1965). Italian writer,

journalist, and educator. From 1896 he worked for the paper *Corriere Israelitico* in Trieste. Subsequently he helped to found the weekly *Israel* in Florence and *La rassegna mensile di Israel.* He also taught Hebrew language and literature at the Institute for Oriental Languages in Rome. He translated the work of writers of the Jewish national revival movement into Italian, and also produced commentaries on the Torah, the Prophets, and the Psalms.

Lattes, Isaac ben Jacob (fl. 14th cent.). French rabbi and physician. He was active in Provence. His *Kiryat Sepher* explains passages of the Oral Law, the process of transmission of the oral tradition, and the basis of the Mishnah and Tosephta. This work also lists the 613 commandments in the order of their appearance in the Torah and interprets them according to Maimonides.

Lattes, Isaac Joshua ben Immanuel (d. c. 1570). Italian rabbi. He was born in Provence, and emigrated to Italy, where he became a rabbi. He lived in Rome, Bologna, Mantua, Venice, and Ferrara. He wrote responsa and poetry, and was associated with the printing of the Mantua edition of the Zohar.

Lattes, Judah ben Jacob (fl. 13th cent.). French scholar. He was educated at Béziers. His *Baal Asuphot* is a collection of rabbinical decisions and responsa.

Lattes, Moses (1846–1883). Italian scholar. He wrote works on Italian Jewish history, talmudic lexicography, and the historical writings of Elijah Capsali.

Latzky-Berthold, Jacob Wolf (1881–1940). Ukrainian socialist leader. He was born in Kiev. He became involved in socialist activities and became minister for Jewish affairs in the government of the independent Ukraine in 1918. In 1920 he settled in Berlin, but he later returned to Riga, where he edited the Yiddish daily newspapers *Dos folk* and *Frimorgn.* In 1935 he moved to Palestine.

Lauterbach, Jacob Zallel (1873–1942). American rabbinic scholar. He was born in Galicia, and went to New York in 1903. After working on the staff of the *Jewish Encyclopedia*, he served as a rabbi in Peoria, Illinois; Rochester, New York; and Huntsville, Alabama. In 1911 he became professor of Talmud at the Hebrew Union College. His publications included an edition of the *Mekhilta de-Rabbi Ishmael* with an English translation.

Lavadores (Ladino). The name used by the Sephardim for members of the communal burial society (Ḥevrah Kaddisha).

Laver. Basin for ritual ablutions required of priests. In biblical times lavers were provided in the Tent of Meeting and in the Temple. They are used for washing the priests' hands before the priestly blessing in some synagogues.

Lavon [Lubianiker]**, Pinḥas** (1904–1976). Israeli labor leader. He was born in eastern Galicia, and was one of the organizers of Gordonia in Galicia and Poland. In 1929 he settled in Palestine, where he was secretary of Mapai in 1938–9, and later general secretary of the Histadrut. He served in the government as minister without portfolio (1950–52) and minister of defense (1953–4). He was involved in a dispute within Mapai (known as the "Lavron Affair"), which led to a split in the party.

Lavry, Marc (1903–1967). Israeli composer and conductor. He was born in Riga, and was active as a conductor in Riga, Saarbrücken, and Berlin. In 1935 he settled in Palestine, where he conducted at the Opera Amamit and for the Palestine Broadcasting Service. In 1949 he became director of the music section of the Kol Zion la-Golah broadcasting service. Later he settled in Haifa. His compositions include an opera, a

Sabbath morning service, symphonic poems, oratorios, and music for the stage.

Law. The rules by which Jewish life is governed. The ultimate source of Jewish law is the Pentateuch, the Five Books of Moses. In addition the Oral Law was passed on from generation to generation. Discussions of the law were recorded in the Mishnah and Talmud, and decisions concerning it were collected in the codes. Later decisions based on individual laws are known as responsa. *See also* LAW, CODES OF; LAW, READING OF THE; LAW, SCROLL OF THE; LAW, TABLETS OF THE; NOACHIAN LAWS; ORAL LAW; RESPONSA; TORAH; WRITTEN LAW.

Law, codes of. The earliest compilations of Jewish law are the gaonic codes: Halakhot Pesukot and Halakhot Gedolot. In these works the order of the laws is based on the talmudic sequence. The later code of Isaac Alfasi, *Sepher ha-Halakhot* (11th–12th centuries), gives a synopsis of talmudic law, omitting legislation which is not applicable in post-Temple diaspora life. The *Mishneh Torah* of Maimonides includes all talmudic law. The code of Asher ben Jehiel, *Piske ha-Rosh* (13th–14th centuries), follows Alfasi's code with the addition of the views of later authorities. His son Jacob ben Asher compiled the *Arbaah Turim*, which formed the basis for the Shulḥan Arukh of Joseph Caro. Moses Isserles added supplementary notes (*Mappah*) to this code, incorporating Ashkenazi practices. Every generation produced posekim (religious leaders), who interpreted the meaning of the law in practice and thus contributed to its codification.

Law, Oral *see* ORAL LAW.

Law, reading of the. The practice of reading passages from the Torah in the synagogue. The entire Pentateuch, divided into 54 sections ("sedarot"), is read in the course of a year, concluding on Shemini Atzeret, in accordance with the Babylonian rite. (In Palestine the complete reading took three years.) Originally congregants read the section to themselves, but eventually a special reader read it aloud (though the Yemenites still keep to the older tradition). Three people are called up to say blessings before and after the readings on Mondays, Thursdays, Ḥanukkah, Purim, fast days, and Sabbath afternoons; four on New Moons and intermediate days of the festivals; five on festivals; six on the Day of Atonement; and seven on Sabbaths.

Law, Rejoicing in the *see* SIMḤAT TORAH.

Law, Scroll of the (Hebrew "Sepher Torah"). The form in which the Pentateuch (Torah) is used for public reading in the synagogue. The law is written by a "sopher" (scribe) on strips of vellum or parchment, which are sewn together to form a roll; each end is attached to a wooden stave and is rolled towards the middle. The Scroll of the Law is kept in the synagogue in the Ark.

Law, Tablets of the. Two stone tablets on which were inscribed the Ten Commandments, received by Moses from God on Mount Sinai. When Moses descended from the mountain and found the people worshipping the Golden Calf, he shattered the tablets. Later he reascended Mount Sinai, where he received the Commandments a second time. The Tablets of the Law were placed in the Ark of the Covenant.

Laws of Noah *see* NOACHIAN LAWS.

Layman. In Temple times the word "hedyot" was used to refer to a commoner who held no special office (as opposed to a member of the royal family or the priesthood). It was also used to refer to an ignorant or ill-mannered person, or an unskilled worker. After the destruction of the Temple, such distinctions disappeared, though priests retained a limited number of exclusive functions and were subject to various restrictions. In modern times the term "layman" designates the members of a congregation in contrast to officiants.

Layton, Irving (b. 1912). Canadian poet. He was born in Romania, and was taken to Montreal as a child. He later worked in a library and taught in Jewish parochial schools. In some of his poetry he used biblical imagery to illustrate contemporary issues.

Lazare, Bernard (1865–1903). French writer. He was born in Nîmes. He lived in Paris, where he was involved in Jewish affairs and worked on a number of Jewish periodicals. In *Anti-Semitism, its History and Causes* he argued that anti-Semitism could help to bring about the advent of socialism by teaching hatred of Jewish capitalism. After the Dreyfus Affair he changed his views.

Lazaron, Morris Samuel (b. 1888). American Reform rabbi. He was born in Savannah, Georgia. He served as a rabbi in Wheeling, West Virginia, and later to the Baltimore Hebrew Congregation. He was a founder and vice-president of the American Council for Judaism.

Lazarus, Emma (1849–1887). American poet. She was born into a New York Sephardi family. She wrote poetry, tragedies, and numerous essays, as well as translating the works of medieval Spanish Jewish poets. Her sonnet *The New Colossus* was inscribed on the Statue of Liberty in New York. Her writings include *Songs of a Semite* and *By the Waters of Babylon.*

Lazarus, Moritz (1824–1903). German philosopher and psychologist. He was born in Filehne, in the district of Posen. He became professor of philosophy at the University of Berne, and later rector of the university. In 1868 he moved to Berlin, where he lectured in psychology, political science, and education at the military academy, and then became professor at the University of Berlin. Later he taught at the Hochschule für die Wissenschaft des Judentums in Berlin. His writings include *Ethik des Judentums.*

Lazarus, Sidney *see* LEE, SIDNEY.

League for Safeguarding the Fixity of the Sabbath *see* CALENDAR, REFORM OF THE.

League of Nations. International organization for the establishment of world peace and cooperation among nations. Founded in 1919, until its demise during World War II it exercised theoretical supervision over British Mandatory rule in Palestine, and played a role in the protection of Jewish minorities in the diaspora.

Leah (fl. ?16th cent. BCE). Israelite woman, elder daughter of Laban and wife of Jacob. She was married to Jacob as a result of Laban's trickery in substituting her for her sister Rachel (Genesis 29.23–5). She gave birth to Reuben, Simeon, Levi, Judah, Issachar, Zebulun, and Dinah (Genesis 29.32–5; 30.14–21).

Leaven (Hebrew "ḥametz"). Fermenting dough made from flour and used as a raising agent in making bread. It was forbidden for use as a meal offering in most of the Temple sacrifices and is prohibited during Passover.

Leaven, search for. On the evening preceding Passover a search is made by candlelight in Jewish households so that all foodstuffs containing yeast may be destroyed. This practice commemorates the institution of the Passover, when God commanded that no leaven be kept in the Israelites' households (Exodus 12.15; 13.7). In modern times small pieces of bread are placed in various parts of the house so that the search is not in vain. After the search the bread is burned and an Aramaic formula is recited.

Lebensohn, Abraham Dov [Adam ha-Cohen] (1794–1878). Lithuanian Hebrew poet. He was born in Vilnius, where he became a successful broker. He was a central figure in the Haskalah movement in Lithuania, and an outstanding poet; his poetry was collected in *Shire Sephat Kodesh*. With Isaac Benjacob he published a Bible edition – Mikrae Kodesh – with Moses Mendelssohn's German translation – *Biur*– and his own notes. In 1847 he became a teacher of Hebrew, Aramaic, and biblical exegesis at the government rabbinical school of Vilnius.

Lebensohn, Micah Joseph [Michal] (1828–1852). Lithuanian Hebrew poet of the Haskalah. He was born in Vilnius. His publications include a Hebrew translation of part of Virgil's *Aeneid*, but later he turned to subjects from Hebrew literature. His poems were published in *Songs of the Daughter of Zion* and the posthumous collection *Lyre of the Daughter of Zion*.

Lee, Sir **Sidney** [Lazarus, Sidney] (1859–1926). English literary historian. From 1913 to 1924 he was professor of English literature and language at London University. He was editor of the *Dictionary of National Biography* and published a study of Jews and crypto-Jews in Shakespearean England.

Leeser, Isaac (1806–1868). American rabbi and author. He was born in Westphalia, and went to America in 1824. From 1829 he officiated as ḥazzan to the Mikveh Israel congregation in Philadelphia. He was editor of a monthly newspaper, *The Occident*, and founded the first Jewish Publication Society of America. He published the first American translation of the Bible and edited various prayerbooks.

Lefin, Mendel *see* LEVIN, MENDEL.

Legacy *see* INHERITANCE.

Legend *see* AGGADAH.

Legion, Jewish *see* JEWISH LEGION.

Legislation *see* LAW, CODES OF.

Le-hakhis. To anger or provoke.

Le-havdil. To distinguish between higher and lower status (of a person or category).

Le-ḥayyim ("To life"). Hebrew expression accompanying a toast.

Leḥi *see* LOḤAME ḤERUT YISRAEL.

Lehman, Herbert Henry (1878–1963). American banker, politician, and statesman. He worked for his father's banking and investment firm, Lehman Bros. During his political career he served as Democratic lieutenant-governor of New York State (1928–32), governor of New York State (1932–42), and director-general of the United Nations Relief and Rehabilitation Agency (1943–6). From 1949 to 1957 he was US Senator for New York. He was active in Jewish and general social welfare, and a member of the American Jewish Committee.

Lehman, Irving (1876–1945). American jurist. He was born in New York. He served as state justice in the Supreme Court until 1924 and then as judge on the New York State Court of Appeals (1924–45). He was president of the Jewish Welfare Board (1921–40), honorary vice-president of the American Jewish Committee (1942), and a supporter of development projects in Palestine.

Lehmann, Behrend (1661–1730). German court Jew. He was born in Essen. He was a financial adviser to Augustus II of Saxony, who became King of Poland. He used his influence to improve the position of the Jewish community.

Lehmann, Marcus (1831–1890). German rabbi, scholar, and writer. He was born in Verden. From 1854 he served as a rabbi in Mainz, where he founded the weekly *Israelit*, the principal voice of German Orthodoxy. Lehmann became one of the leaders and spokesmen of modern German Orthodox Jewry. He wrote historical novels, short stories, and Sabbath lectures, and made a German edition of the Haggadah.

Lehranstalt für die Wissenschaft des Judentums *see* HOCHSCHULE FÜR DIE WISSENSCHAFT DES JUDENTUMS.

Lehrer, Leibush (1887–1965). American Yiddish writer and educator. He was born in Poland. After living in Belgium from 1906 to 1909 he emigrated to the US. He helped to develop the Shalom Aleichem schools and founded and directed the Yiddish-speaking Camp Boiberik. He taught in the Teachers Seminary of the Shalom Aleichem Folk Institute in New York, and from 1921 to 1947 was director of the Shalom Aleichem Secondary School. He wrote studies of literature, psychology, education, and Judaism.

Leib, Mani *see* MANI LEIB.

Leib, Yehudah *see* LEVANDA, LEV.

Leibowitz, Yeshayahu (b. 1903). Israeli scientist and writer. He was born in Riga. He emigrated to Palestine in 1935 and became professor of organic chemistry, biochemistry, and neurophysiology at the Hebrew University. He has written studies of Maimonides, Jewish Orthodoxy, and Israeli politics.

Leibzoll (German: "body tax"). Tax levied on Jews by states in central Europe from which they were normally excluded. By paying the tax a Jewish person could gain access to a ticket of passage or of limited residence, which guaranteed his safety. The Leibzoll was abolished in Prussia in 1787, in Bavaria in 1799, and in most other German states at the beginning of the 19th century. The Russian form of the tax ("Geleitzoll": escort tax) was abolished in 1862.

Leivick [Leyvick]**, H.** [Halpern, Leivick] (1886–1962). American Yiddish poet and dramatist. He was born in Igumen, Belorussia. He was active in revolutionary politics and was exiled to Siberia as a result. He escaped to the US in 1913, where he worked in a sweatshop and as a paper-hanger. His writings include *Der goylem, Shmates, In Treblinka bin ich nit geven,* and *Di chasene in fernvald.*

Lekaḥ Tov ("Good teaching"). Midrashic commentary on the Torah and the Five Scrolls of the Hagiographa (Song of Songs, Ruth, Lamentations, Ecclesiastes, and Esther). It was composed by Tobiah ben Eliezer of Castoria in the 11th century.

Lekert, Hirsh (1879–1902). Russian revolutionary. A bootmaker by trade, he was a member of the Jewish socialist party, the Bund, in Dvinsk, Kovno, Yekaterinoslav, and Vilnius. He was executed for shooting the Governor of Vilnius because he had ordered the flogging of 26 demonstrators on 1 May 1902.

Leket *see* GLEANINGS.

Lekhah dodi ("Come, my beloved"). Opening words of a song of greeting for the Sabbath, written by Solomon Alkabetz in the early 16th century in Safed. It is customary, while reciting the final verse, to turn toward the synagogue entrance and bow.

Leku nerananah ("O come, let us exult"). Opening words of Psalm 95, and hence of the group of six psalms (95–9 and 29) which are recited in the Ashkenazi rite for the inauguration of the Sabbath at the beginning of the Friday evening service. These six psalms describe God's grandeur in nature and his righteous judgment of the world. The custom of reciting these psalms was introduced by kabbalistis in Safed in the 16th century.

Lel Shimmurim ("Night of watching"). The first night of Passover. Because it was believed that no danger could befall on this night it was the custom to leave the doors unbolted and to omit the recital of the night prayer.

Lelyveld, Arthur (b. 1913). American Reform rabbi and community leader. He was born in New York. He served as national director of the B'nai B'rith Hillel Foundations from 1947 to 1956, and later as rabbi of Fairmount Temple in Cleveland. From 1966 he was president of the American Jewish Congress, and he was also appointed general chairman of the Jewish Welfare Fund campaign of Cleveland. He wrote *Atheism is Dead*, a response to radical theology.

Lemberg *see* Lvov.

Lemon, Hartog (c. 1750–1823). Dutch physician and protagonist of Jewish rights. Living in Amsterdam, he was a central figure in the Felix Libertate society, which struggled for Jewish rights. He served as a deputy in the second national assembly of the Batavian Commonwealth, and was a delegate to the Napoleonic Sanhedrin in Paris in 1807.

Leningrad *see* St. Petersburg.

Lensky, Ḥayyim (1905–?1942). Russian Hebrew poet. He was born in Slonim, a district of Grodno in Russia, and lived in Moscow and Leningrad. In Moscow he wrote poems which he sent to literary periodicals in Palestine. Later he was sentenced to imprisonment in Siberia for writing in Hebrew, but in 1937 he was transferred to a forced-labor camp near the Soviet–Mongolian border. Although he returned to Leningrad on his release, he was again arrested; he is assumed to have died in captivity. His poetry describes his childhood and Siberian exile as well as his faith in the Jewish people.

***Leo X** (1475–1521). Italian pope (1513–21). His pontificate was a happy one for the Jewish community. In 1514 he reconfirmed the privileges of the Jews in the papal territory of Comtat Venaissin in France. He authorized the establishment of a Hebrew press in Rome and approved the printing of the Talmud.

Leo Baeck College. English rabbinical seminary, founded after World War II in London and named for the German rabbi and religious leader Leo Baeck. It trains Liberal and Reform rabbis, and offers higher degrees in Judaica.

Leo Baeck Institute. Scholarly institution founded by the Council of Jews from Germany in 1955 in Jerusalem, and named for the German rabbi and religious leader Leo Baeck. It collects material on the history of the Jewish community in Germany and other German-speaking countries, and sponsors research in the same areas. It has branches in Jerusalem, London, and New York.

Leon, Judah Messer [Judah ben Jehiel; Messer Leon] (fl. 15th cent.). Italian rabbi and author. He was the head of a yeshivah in Mantua. He engaged in a controversy with Joseph Colon which split the Jewish community there. Subsequently he lived in Venice, Bologna, Ancona, and Naples, where he was the head of the yeshivah. His writings include *Nophet Tzuphim*, a Hebrew work based on the rhetorical rules of Aristotle, Cicero, and Quintilian.

Leone Ebreo *see* Abravanel, Judah.

Leon of Modena *see* Modena, Leone.

Léon of Paris *see* Judah ben Isaac.

Leon Templo, Jacob Judah Aryeh [Temple, Judah] (1603–1675). Dutch rabbi and scholar. He was born in Hamburg. He officiated at Middelburg in the Netherlands, and taught in Amsterdam from 1643. He constructed a model of Solomon's Temple and published an accompanying exposition in Spanish, which was translated into several languages. He also produced a model and exposition of the Tabernacle.

Leontopolis. Ancient Egyptian city; its site is 6 miles north of modern Cairo. Jewish soldiers were stationed there under the high priest Onias IV after the outbreak of the Maccabean revolt in the second century BCE. Onias erected a temple to God in the city; it was closed by the Romans in 73 CE.

Leprosy. In the Bible the term "tzoraat" refers to an affliction of the skin which renders the person unclean. (The word is also applied to a blemish on the surface of an object, which similarly makes it unfit for ritual or sacred use.) Signs of leprosy are described in Leviticus 13. A person pronounced leprous by a priest is quarantined; when cured, the leper must undergo a service of cleansing and must bring offerings to the Temple. According to the rabbis, the disease is the result of scandalmongering and evil talk. The laws concerning leprosy are contained in the talmudic tractate Negaim.

Leshon ha-ra ("tongue of evil"). Expression denoting SLANDER or unfounded malicious gossip.

Lesser Genesis *see* JUBILEES, BOOK OF.

***Lessing, Gotthold Ephraim** (1729–1781). German dramatist, philosopher, and critic. A supporter of the Enlightenment, he was a friend of Moses Mendelssohn, who was the inspiration of his play *Nathan der Weise*. This work presented Judaism in a positive light.

Lessing, Theodor (1872–1933). German philosopher. He was born in Hanover. He converted to Lutheranism in 1908 and was appointed instructor at the Technische Hochschule in Hanover. He published studies of Schopenhauer, Wagner, and Nietzsche. Later he returned to Judaism, and expressed his views in *Jewish Self-Hate*. Towards the end of his life he lived in Marienbad, where he was murdered by the Nazis.

Lestschinsky, Jacob (1876–1966). German scholar. He was born in Horodicz in the Ukraine, and left the USSR in 1921 for Berlin. In the 1920s he helped to establish the Institute for Research into Contemporary Jewry and Judaism. He was a pioneer in the study of the sociology, economics, and demography of Jewish life and published studies of eastern European Jewry.

Letteris, Meir ha-Levi (?1800–1871). Galician Hebrew poet, writer, and editor. He was born in Zolkiew. He worked as a copy-reader in Vienna, Pressburg, and Prague. He published books of Hebrew poetry, translations, and collections of Hebrew literature. Among his editions of Hebrew texts was the Bible, which he prepared for the British and Foreign Bible Society.

Letter of Aristeas *see* ARISTEAS, LETTER OF.

Letters. A notable group of letters from the biblical period are the so-called Lachish Letters, inscribed on potsherds in the 6th century BCE (before the fall of Israel). Letters in Aramaic, dating from the 5th century BCE, were discovered at the site of the Jewish military colony at Elephantine. Official letters are included in the Books of Maccabees and the writings of Josephus, and a number of Hebrew letters written during the Bar Kokhha revolt survive. In the Middle Ages rabbinic responsa were written in the form of letters. Large numbers of Hebrew letters are preserved from the 16th century. From the 18th century onward Jews commonly wrote letters in the vernacular.

Levanda, Lev [Leib, Yehudah] (1835–1888). Russian author. He was born in Minsk, where from 1854 to 1860 he taught at a government Jewish school. In 1860 he became the Jewish adviser to the governor-general of Vilnius. After the pogroms of 1881 Levanda became a supporter of the Ḥovevei Zion. His writings include Russian stories depicting Jewish life in the Pale of Settlement.

Levanon, Mordekhai (1901–1968). Israeli painter of Transylvanian origin. He went to Palestine in 1921 and he worked as an agricultural laborer. From 1922 he studied painting in Jerusalem and Tel Aviv. His works include paintings of Jerusalem, the Sea of Galilee, and Safed.

Levayah. Funeral.

Leven, Narcisse (1833–1915). French

public figure. He was born in Germany, and moved to Paris as a child. He was secretary to Isaac-Adolphe Crémieux during the Franco-Prussian War, and later practiced law. One of the founders of the Alliance Israélite Universelle, he served successively as its secretary, vice-president, and president. He was also president of the Jewish Colonization Association. His writings include *Cinquante ans d'histoire: l'Alliance Israélite Universelle.*

Levertin, Oscar Ivar (1862–1906). Swedish poet and literary critic. He was born in Gryt. He became a professor of literature at the Academy of Stockholm. Some of his poems and stories deal with Jewish themes.

Levi (fl. ?19th–16th cent. BCE). Israelite, third son of Jacob and Leah. He was the founder of the tribe of Levites. He and Simeon, his brother, killed the men of Shechem who raped their sister, Dinah (Genesis 34); because of this act they were rebuked by Jacob, who foretold that their descendants would be scattered throughout Israel (Genesis 49.7).

Levi, David (1742–1801). English Hebraist and polemicist. He was born in London, and worked as a hatter. He published translations of the Pentateuch for use in the synagogue, a Hebrew grammar and dictionary, and polemics in defense of Jews and Judaism.

Lévi, Israel (1856–1939). French rabbi. He was born in Paris. He began teaching Jewish history at the École Rabbinique in 1892, and the Talmud and rabbinic literature at the École Pratique des Hautes Études in 1896. In 1886 he became editor of the *Revue des Études Juives.* From 1919 to 1938 he was the chief rabbi of the French Central Consistoire. He published studies of the Bible, Apocrypha, Talmud, midrash, and Jewish history.

Levi, John (b. 1934). Australian rabbi. He was born in Melbourne, where he served as rabbi of Temple Beth Israel. He has been active in various Jewish communal organizations, and was appointed a Member of the Order of Australia. His publications include *The Forefathers*, and *Australian Genesis.*

Levi, Primo (1919–1987). Italian author. He was born in Turin, and trained as a chemist. His works, many of which describe his experiences in Auschwitz, include *If This is a Man* and *The Truce.*

Lévi, Sylvain (1863–1935). French Indologist. He was born in Paris. He taught at the Sorbonne, the École des Hautes Études, and the Collège de France. He also served as president of the Alliance Israélite Universelle and the Société des Études Juives. His publications include studies of Buddhism.

Levias, Caspar (1860–1934). American orientalist and lexicographer, of Lithuanian origin. He was an instructor in Semitic languages at the Hebrew Union College (1895–1905) and then (1910–20) principal of the Plaut Memorial Hebrew Free School in Newark, New Jersey. His writings include *A Grammar of the Aramaic Idiom Contained in the Babylonian Talmud.*

Leviathan. Sea monster described in Job 40–41. The aggadah and Apocrypha identify it with the male and female sea animals made by God on the fifth day of Creation; when they threatened to destroy the world, God emasculated the male but preserved the female. In the future God will make war on leviathan and the righteous will participate in the struggle. A similar legend is found in Ugaritic sources.

Levi bar Sisi (fl. 2nd–3rd cent.). Palestinian and Babylonian amora. A pupil of Judah ha-Nasi, he settled in Nahardea in Babylonia. His baraitot are mentioned in the Talmud.

Levi ben Abraham ben Ḥayyim (c. 1245–c.1315). French talmudist and philosopher. He was born in Villefranche-de-Conflent, and lived in various towns in southern France, earning his living as a teacher. His book *Livyat Ḥen* deals with various branches of science, and includes his theological and philosophical views. He was persecuted by opponents of Maimonides because of his rational interpretation of miracles as well as his allegorical biblical exegesis.

Levi ben Gershon [Gersonides; Ralbag] (1288–1344). French philosopher, mathematician, astronomer, biblical commentator, and talmudist. He was born at Bagnols-sur-Cèze, and lived in Orange and Avignon. His *Milḥamot Adonai* deals with the immortality of the soul, prophecy, omnipotence, providence, astronomy, the Creation, and miracles. He also wrote a study of the 13 hermeneutical rules of Rabbi Ishmael, and works on arithmetic, geometry, harmonic numbers, and trigonometry. In addition he produced commentaries on Aristotle, Averroes, and the Bible.

Levi ben Japheth (fl. 10th–11th cent.). Palestinian Karaite scholar. He lived in Jerusalem. His *Book of the Precepts* deals with Karaite law.

Levi-Bianchini, Angelo (1887–1920). Italian naval officer and member of the Zionist Commission. He was born in Venice. He lectured at the naval academy and the military school in Turin. He was appointed to the Zionist Commission and traveled to Palestine in 1918. In 1920 he helped to obtain the approval of the Italian Foreign Office for the British Balfour Declaration and the Mandate on Palestine, which was ratified at the San Remo Conference.

Levi Isaac of Berdichev (c. 1740–1810). Polish Ḥasidic leader. A pupil of Dov Ber of Mezhirich, he was a rabbi in Zhelikhov, Pinsk, and Berdichev. He founded Ḥasidism in central Poland, consolidated the movement in Lithuania, and expanded it in the Ukraine. His *Kedushat Levi* contains his teachings.

Levin, Hanoch (b. 1943). Israeli playwright. He was born in Tel Aviv. His plays include *You and I and the Next War*, *Ketchup*, *Queen of the Bathtub*, *Solomon Grip*, and *Yaacobi and Leidental*. In 1988 he became house playwright at Israel's Cameri Theater.

Levin [Loebel]**, Hirschel** [Hirschel Levin; Lyon, Hart] (1721–1800). German rabbi and author. He was born in Galicia. He served as rabbi at the Great Synagogue in London from 1756 to 1763, then officiated in Halberstadt, Mannheim, and Berlin. He opposed Naphtali Herz Wesseley's reforms in Jewish education, and was an advocate of Moses Mendelssohn's German translation of the Hebrew Bible, *Biur*.

Levin, Judah Leib [Yehalel] (1844–1925). Russian Hebrew socialist poet and writer. In 1870 he became a tutor and secretary to the Brodskis, Jewish sugar magnates of Kiev. Between 1874 and 1880 he contributed poetry to the literary monthly *Ha-Shaḥar*, which introduced socialist themes into Hebrew literature. After the pogroms of 1881 he joined Ḥibbat Zion as one of its founding members in Kiev. Later he settled in Tomashpol', where he continued his literary work. He published his memoirs in 1910. He eventually returned to Kiev.

Levin, Mayer (1905–1981). American novelist. He was born in Chicago, and became a reporter for the Chicago *Daily News*. In his writings he retold stories of the Ḥasidim and depicted his own generation of Chicago Jews. He also wrote various histories of Israel for young people and published books on the synagogue and the Jewish way of life. In 1958 he settled in Israel.

Levin [Lefin; Satanower]**, Mendel** (1749–1826). Russian author, translator, and educator, and a leading figure in the Haskalah movement. He was born in Satanev, Podolia. From 1780 to 1784 he lived in Berlin, where he met Moses Mendelssohn, through whom he came into contact with the leaders of the Haskalah. Later he lived in various Russian centers and became one of the chief advocates of the Haskalah in Galicia. His publications include studies of natural sciences, translations of classics, and a Yiddish translation of various books of the Bible.

***Levin** [Varnhagen von Ense]**, Rachel** (1771–1833). German socialite. She was born in Berlin. Her home there was a meeting place for literary, intellectual, and social leaders. She married Karl August Vernhagen von Ense, and converted to Protestantism.

Levin, Shemaryahu (1867–1935). Russian Zionist leader and author. He was born in Svisloch', Belorussia. He served as a rabbi in Grodno (1896–7) and Yekaterinoslav (1898–1904), and a preacher in Vilnius (1904–6). At the Sixth Zionist Congress he was one of the leaders of the opposition to the project to found a Jewish homeland in Uganda. Later he represented Vilnius in the Russian Duma. He left the USSR and lived first in Berlin, then, during World War I, in the US, where he promoted Zionism. From 1922 he worked in Berlin for the Devir Publishing Company. He finally moved to Palestine, and was one of the founders of the Haifa-Technion.

Levin, Yitzḥak Meir (1894–1971). Israeli activist and politician, leader of the Agudat Israel movement. He was born in Gora, Poland. He served in various offices in Agudat Israel. In 1940 he settled in Palestine, where he was active in rescue operations to help Jews escape from Nazi-controlled Europe. He was appointed minister of social welfare in the first Knesset. In 1954 he became president of the World Actions Committee and chairman of the World Executive of Agudat Israel.

Levinas, Emmanuel (b. 1905). French philosopher, of Lithuanian origin. He became head of the École Normale Orientale of the Alliance Israélite Universelle in Paris, and taught at the University of Paris at Nanterre. His writings include *De l'existence à l'existant, En découvrant l'existence avec Husserl et Heidegger, Totalité et infini, Difficile liberté,* and *Quatres lectures talmudiques.*

Levinsohn, Isaac Ber (1788–1860). Russian Hebrew author. He was born in Kremenetz in Volhynia, and lived in Radzivilov and later in various towns in eastern Galicia. He was one of the founders of the Haskalah movement in Russia and from 1820 to 1823 he spread its ideas as a private tutor. His writings extol the virtues of the Enlightenment and manual labor, and seek to combat anti-Semitism. His publications include *Teudah be-Yisrael, Bet Yehudah,* and *Zerubbabel.*

Levinthal, Bernard (1865–1952). American Orthodox rabbi, of Lithuanian origin. He emigrated to the US in 1891 and became rabbi of Congregation B'nai Abraham in Philadelphia. He served as head of the United Orthodox Hebrew Congregations of Philadelphia and president of the Union of Orthodox Rabbis of the United States and Canada. In addition he helped to establish the Mizraḥi Organization of America.

Levinthal, Israel Herbert (1888–1978). American rabbi. He served as rabbi of the Brooklyn Jewish Center from 1919. Active in the Zionist movement, he was president of the Rabbinical Association of America. His writings include *Judaism: an Analysis and an Interpretation, Point of View: an Analysis of American Judaism,* and *Judaism Speaks to the Modern World.*

Levinthal, Louis (b. 1892). American communal leader. He practiced law in

Philadelphia, eventually becoming judge in the Philadelphia Court of Common Pleas. He served as president of the Zionist Organization of America, chairman of the Board of Governors of the Hebrew University, and president of the Jewish Publication Society of America.

Levirate marriage. The marriage of a man with his brother's childless widow. Such a marriage is prescribed if the deceased brother has left no offspring (Deuteronomy 25.5). Release from the obligation of such a marriage may be obtained through performance of the ceremony of Ḥalitzah (Deuteronomy 25.7–10). Regulations governing levirate marriage are contained in the tractate Yevamot in the Talmud.

Levita, Elijah [Baḥur, Elijah] (1468–1549). Italian Hebrew philologist, grammarian, and lexicographer. He was born in Neustadt but spent most of his life in Italy, where he taught Hebrew. Numerous Christian humanists, such as Cardinal Egidio da Viterbo, were his students. He also served as a proof-reader for the Protestant Hebraist Paul Fagius in Isny. He wrote studies of Hebrew grammar, lexicographical works, and a Yiddish–Hebrew dictionary. In addition he composed Hebrew and Yiddish poetry and produced various Yiddish translations.

Levites. The descendants of the tribe of Levi. Moses consecrated them to serve in the Tabernacle and instruct the people; they were therefore in attendance upon the priests. Each family of Levites was assigned specific duties. The Book of Chronicles records that David divided them into separate groups with different functions in the Temple. According to Jewish law, the Levite is regarded as second only to the priest in the line of those who may read the law.

Levitical cities. Name given to the 48 towns which God commanded Moses to set apart for the tribe of Levi (Numbers 35). They included the six cities of refuge. Joshua 21 records the decisions made by each of the other 11 tribes as to which cities should be assigned to the Levites.

Leviticus (Hebrew "Va-Yikra"). Biblical book, the third book of the Pentateuch; it was formerly known in Hebrew as Torat ha-Kohanim ("Law of the Priests"). It contains laws given to Moses concerning sacrifice, impurity, moral instruction, and social legislation. Chapters 1–7 deal with sacrificial laws; chapters 8–10 with the installation of priests; chapters 11–16 with physical purity and unclean animals; chapter 17 with prohibitions against eating meat that has not been sacrificed; chapters 18–22 with moral instruction; chapter 23 with festivals; chapter 24 with regulations concerning the Tabernacle; chapter 25 with sabbatical and jubilee years; chapter 26 with blessings for observance and curses for non-observance of the law; and chapter 27 with valuations and devotion to sacred usage.

Leviticus Rabbah [Va-Yikra Rabbah]. Homiletical midrash, the third part of the Midrash Rabbah. It dates from the 5th–6th centuries in Palestine. It contains 37 chapters dealing with topics based on the opening verses of the weekly Torah readings, according to the triennial cycle (*see* LAW, READING OF THE).

Levontin, Zalman David (1856–1940). Russian banker and pioneer of Jewish settlement in Palestine. He was born in Belorussia. In 1882 he went to Palestine, where he purchased land and founded the town of Rishen-le-Zion in the Judean coastal plain. He subsequently served as branch bank manager in various towns in the Pale of Settlement. In 1901 he was summoned by Theodor Herzl to become one of the directors of the Jewish Colonial Trust in London. Two years later he returned to Palestine to establish the Anglo-Palestine Bank which he directed.

Levy, Asser (d. 1681). Dutch merchant and landowner. He was among the first Jews to arrive in New Amsterdam in 1654, and became the most prominent member of the Jewish community there, defending the rights of the Jews in the New World.

Levy, Benjamin (c. 1650–1704). British merchant, founder of the Ashkenazi community in London. The son of Levy Moses of Hamburg, he arrived in London in about 1670. In 1697, in the course of the reorganization of the Royal Exchange, he became one of the 12 original Jewish brokers of the City of London. In 1696 he purchased a cemetery for the Ashkenazi community.

Levy, Jacob (1819–1892). German rabbi and lexicographer. He was born near Poznán in Poland. He served as rabbi of Rosenberg, Upper Silesia, but then for a period devoted himself to scientific work. In 1857 he became assistant rabbi in Breslau, and later was appointed to the Breslau court to administer the Jewish oath. In 1878 he was appointed lecturer at the Mora-Salomon Leipziger Foundation. He compiled dictionaries of the Targum and of the Talmud and midrash.

Levy, Louis Edward (1846–1919). American chemist, inventor, and newspaper editor. He was born in Pilsen, Bohemia, and was taken to the US at the age of eight. He published and edited the *Philadelphia Evening Herald*, the *Mercury*, and the *Jewish Year*. He was a leader of the Philadelphia Jewish community and served as president of the Association for Relief and Protection of Jewish Immigrants. His writings include *The Russian Jewish Refugees in America*.

Levy, Moritz Abraham (1817–1872). German scholar. He taught Semitic paleography and epigraphy at the Breslau Synagogen-Gemeinde. He wrote textbooks on the Jewish history and religion, and a history of Jewish coins.

Levy, Reuben (1891–1966). English orientalist. He was born in Manchester. He was a lecturer in Persian language and literature at Oxford University (1920–23), then (1923–6) taught biblical literature at the Jewish Institute of Religion in New York. He later became professor of Persian at Cambridge University. He edited and translated classical Persian and Arabic texts, wrote textbooks about Persian language and literature, and published studies of Islam.

Lewandowski, Louis (1821–1894). German choral director and composer. He was born in Wreschen, near Posen. After moving to Berlin he served as conductor of the choir at the Old Synagogue in the Heidereutergasse, and later at the New Synagogue. He also served as a singing teacher at the Jewish Free School and the Jewish Teachers Seminary. His compositions had a profound influence on Western Ashkenazi synagogue music, and his style was transferred to numerous Conservative and Reform congregations in the US.

Lewin, Benjamin Manasseh (1879–1944). Israeli rabbinic scholar, educator, and authority on gaonic literature. He was born in Gorodets, Russia. In 1912 he went to Palestine, where he was a teacher and later head of the religious schools network, Netzaḥ Yisrael. His *Otzar ha-Geonim* is a collection of the teachings of the geonim of Sura and Pumbedita.

Lewin, Judah Leib (1894–1971). Russian rabbi. Born in Yekaterinoslav, he became the rabbi of Grishino, and later of Yekaterinoslav. He then returned to Grishino, where he worked as a religious scribe. In 1957 he was appointed principal of the yeshivah of the Moscow Great Synagogue; after the death of Solomon Schliefer he became the rabbi there.

Lewinski, Elhanan Löb (1857–1910).

Russian Hebrew writer and Zionist leader. He was born in Podberezye, Russia. He traveled to Palestine after the pogroms of 1881 and returned an ardent Zionist. He settled in Odessa and in 1896 became the representative in Russia of the Palestinian Carmel wine company. He was a founder of the Moriah publishing house and supported literary enterprises. He also served as treasurer and preacher in the Zionist synagogue in Odessa. His writings were published in various journals.

Lewis, Bernard (b. 1916). English orientalist. He was born in London. He was appointed assistant lecturer at the University of London in 1938. During World War II he served in the army and was seconded to the Foreign Office. In 1949 he became professor of Near and Middle Eastern history in the School of Oriental and African Studies at London University. He published studies of Arab and Turkish history and translated Hebrew prose and poetry into English.

Lewisohn, Ludwig (1883–1955). American author and translator. Born in Berlin, he was taken to Charleston, South Carolina, in 1890. He was professor of German at Ohio State University (1911–19), and from 1948 professor of comparative literature at Brandeis University. Between 1924 and 1940 he lived in Paris. His writings include novels on Jewish subjects: *The Island Within* and *The Last Days of Shylock.* He also wrote books dealing with Judaism and Zionism, including *Israel, Mid-Channel, Theodor Herzl: A Portrait for this Age, The American Jew: Character and Destiny*, and *What is the Jewish Heritage?*.

Lewy, Israel (1841–1917). German rabbi and scholar. He was born in Inowrocław, Poland. He became a lecturer in Talmud at the Hochschule für die Wissenschaft des Judentums in Berlin, then in 1883 took up an appointment at the Breslau Rabbinical Seminary. He published studies of Talmudic literature.

Lexicography *see* DICTIONARIES, BIBLE; DICTIONARIES, HEBREW; ENCYCLOPEDIAS.

Leyvick, H. *see* LEIVICK, H.

Libation. A drink offering or sacrifice. In biblical times oil and wine were used in nearly all sacrificial ceremonies. Oil was usually offered with the meal offering. Every animal oblation was accompanied by a wine libation, different measures being prescribed for the various types of animals (Numbers 15.1–16).

Liberal Judaism *see* REFORM JUDAISM.

Liberal Party. Israeli political party. It was formed by a merger of the General Zionists with the Progressive Party in 1961.

Liberal Workers Movement *see* HA-OVED HA-TZIYYONI.

Liberman, Serge (b. 1942). Australian novelist and editor. He was born in Fergana in Uzbekistan, and went to Australia in 1951. He became the editor of the *Melbourne Chronicle.* His publications include *Ethnic Australia, Jewish Writing from Down Under, Joseph's Coat: An Anthology of Multicultural Writing*, and *Bibliography of Australian Judaica.*

Libin, Solomon (1872–1955). American Yiddish writer. He was born in Russia, and emigrated to London in 1891, later moving to New York. He wrote hundreds of stories about early immigrant life and the suffering of sweatshop workers. In addition he wrote about 50 plays.

Libraries. Jewish libraries existed in the academies of Babylonia after the completion of the Talmud. The first great Jewish private library was that of Samuel ibn Nagrela; private libraries continued to exist throughout the Middle Ages and during the Renaissance. In modern times various scholars have established important collections of Jewish books and manuscripts. In addition Hebrew libraries are found in such institutions as the British Museum, the Vatican, the Palatine Library, the Bibliothèque Nationale in Paris, the Bodleian Library in Oxford, the University Library in Cambridge, the Hebrew University in Jerusalem, the Jewish Theological Seminary in New York, the Hebrew Union College in Cincinnati, and Jews College, London.

Lichtenstein, Hillel (1815–1891). Hungarian rabbi. He served as rabbi in Margarethen, Kolozsvar, Szikszó (1865–7), and Kolomyya in Galicia. He was an ardent critic of religious reform.

Lichtenstein, Morris (1889–1938). American rabbi. He emigrated from eastern Europe to the US in 1907. He inaugurated the Jewish Science movement in opposition to Christian Science.

***Lidzbarski, Mark** (1868–1928). German Semitic philologist. He was born in Płock in the Russian part of Poland, and in adulthood converted to Protestantism. In 1896 he began lecturing in oriental languages at the University of Kiel. In 1907 he took up an appointment at the University of Greifswald, and in 1917 one at the University of Göttingen. He was the founder of Semitic epigraphy, and also published various studies and texts of the gnostic Mandeans.

Lieberman, Saul (1898–1983). American scholar. He was born in Motol, near Pinsk, Belorussia, and settled in Jerusalem in 1928. In 1931 he was appointed lecturer in Talmud at the Hebrew University. He also taught at the Mizraḥi Teachers Seminary, and was dean of the Harry Fischel Institute for Talmudic Research. In 1940 he became professor of Palestinian literature and institutions at the Jewish Theological Seminary where he later served as dean and rector of the rabbinical school. He published studies of Jewish Hellenism, editions of the Tosephta, and works on the Palestinian Talmud.

Liebermann, Aaron Samuel (1845–1880). Lithuanian socialist and Hebrew writer. He was born in Lunna, Lithuania, and became secretary of the Jewish community of Suwalki. Later he lived in Vilnius, where he worked with an insurance company and as a draftsman. From 1872 he was a leader of a local revolutionary group. He subsequently joined socialist circles in Berlin and became a pioneer of Jewish socialism. He lived successively in London (where he worked as a typesetter), Vienna (from where he was expelled to Germany), London again, and finally the US. He published various works about socialism.

Liebermann, Max (1847–1935). German painter. He was born in Berlin, and lived in various cities, including Paris (1873–7). His work includes *Judengasse*, a series of paintings of street scenes in the Jewish quarter of Amsterdam.

Liebman, Joshua Loth (1907–1948). American Reform rabbi. He was born in Hamilton, Ohio. He served as a rabbi in Lafayette, Indiana, and as an instructor at the Hebrew Union College. Later he was rabbi to congregations in Chicago and Boston, where he also taught at Boston University and at Andover-Newton Theological Seminary. He published the book *Peace of Mind.*

Liebmann, Jost (c. 1640–1702). Prussian court Jew. He was court jeweler and mint-master to Friedrich Wilhelm and Friedrich III of Brandenburg. Toward the end of the 17th century he was one of the richest Jews in Prussia. The owner of the only synagogue in Berlin, he played an important role in the Jewish community.

Lieme, Nehemiah de (1882–1940). Dutch economist and Zionist leader. He was involved in life insurance and education for Dutch workers. In 1913 he became chairman of the Dutch Zionist Federation, and from 1919 to 1921 he served as president of the Jewish National Fund.

Liessin, Abraham (1872–1938). American Yiddish poet and editor. He was born in Minsk, and went to the US in 1897, where he became an active socialist. From 1913 he was editor of *Zukunft*, a Yiddish literary and cultural monthly. In his writings he described the heroes and martyrs of the Jewish past.

Life. The Bible teaches that life is God's supreme blessing. According to the rabbis, all laws (except those that deal with idolatry, bloodshed, and forbidden sexual liaisons) can be suspended if there is danger to life. Human life is viewed as infinitely valuable, and thus one is prohibited from hastening death. Rabbinic law also prohibits euthanasia.

Lifschitz, Joshua Mordecai (1829–1878). Russian Yiddish lexicographer and author. He propounded the idea of a secular Jewish culture based on Yiddish. His writings include a Yiddish–Russian dictionary.

Lifschitz, Malkah *see* ESTHER (iv).

Lifshitz, Nehama (b. 1927). Israeli Yiddish and Hebrew singer. Born in Kaunas, Lithuania, she went to Uzbekistan during World War II. In 1946 she returned to Soviet Lithuania and studied at the Vilnius conservatoire. She later traveled throughout the USSR giving concerts of Yiddish songs. In 1969 she emigrated to Israel.

Light. It is the symbol of life, blessing, peace, knowledge, understanding, redemption, the soul, and goodness. According to Genesis, it was God's first creation (Genesis 1.3–4). Light played an important role in kabbalistic mysticism. Its symbolic importance is reflected in the frequent use of candles and candelabra.

Lights, Feast of *see* ḤANUKKAH.

Lights, kindling of *see* KINDLING OF LIGHTS.

Likkute Amarim *see* TANYA (ii).

Likkud. Right-wing political party in Israel made up of a group of smaller parties. It was established in 1973, and in elections in 1977 gained a victory, emerging as the largest party in the Knesset; its leader, Menaḥem Begin, then took office as prime minister.

Lilien, Ephraim Moses (1874–1925). German artist. He was born in Drohobycz, Galicia. He first worked in Munich as a cartoonist, later in Berlin as a book illustrator. An active Zionist, he was a founder and editor of the Berlin publishing house Jüdischer Verlag. In 1902 he published *Juda*, a volume of ballads on Old Testament themes with his illustrations. He was a member of the committee formed to establish the Bezalel School of Arts and Crafts in Jerusalem. Among his works are a group of etchings that include impressions of Palestine.

Lilienblum, Moses Leib (1843–1910). Russian Hebrew writer, critic, and political journalist. He was born in Kėdainiai, near Kovno. He was initially attracted to the Haskalah and encouraged religious reform, but in his autobiography, *Ḥattot Neurim* (1876), he criticized the impracticality of the Haskalah movement and expressed his socialist ideas. After the pogroms of 1881 he became an advocate of Zionism and a leader and ideologist of Ḥibbat Zion; he published articles in Hebrew, Yiddish, and Russian.

Lilienthal, Max (1813–1882). American educator and rabbi, of Russian origin. He was born in Munich, Bavaria. He served as director of the Jewish school of Riga. In 1841 the czarist government invited him to initiate the creation of state schools for Jews. Encountering opposition from the Jewish community, he eventually realized that this proposal was aimed at the conversion of Jewry. He left Russia and settled in the US, becoming rabbi of the Bene Israel Congregation in Cincinnati.

Lilith. Female demon. She is mentioned in Isaiah 34.14, and is depicted in the Talmud as having a human face, long hair, and wings. In mystical sources she was the queen of demons and the consort of Satan-Samael. In kabbalistic literature she is the symbol of lust and temptation. It was common to protect women who were giving birth from her power by fixing amulets over their beds.

Lincoln. English city. In the Middle Ages there was a large Jewish community there. In 1255 Jews in the town were accused of a ritual murder (of the boy who became known as Hugh of Lincoln and was later canonized) and 18 Jews were executed.

***Lincoln, Abraham** (1809–1865). American president. He was the first president to be officially involved in questions of Jewish equality and anti-Jewish discrimination.

Lind, Jacob (b. 1927). Austrian writer. Born in Vienna, he went to the Netherlands in 1938. During the Nazi period he worked as a gardener, and escaped deportation by acquiring false papers and finding employment in Germany. He lived in Palestine after the war, and later settled in London. His publications include *Soul of Wood*, and *Counting my Steps*.

Linetzki, Isaac Joel (1839–1935). Ukrainian Yiddish author. He was born in Podolia. Living in Odessa, he became a spokesman for the radical wing of the Haskalah. He published various works including *Dos poylische yingel*, which criticized Jewish life and satirized the Ḥasidim.

Lion of Wrath. Character mentioned in the Dead Sea Scrolls in the commentaries on Nahum and Hosea. He took vengeance on his enemies by crucifying them. He has been identified with Alexander Yannai, who crucified 800 rebels in the 1st century BCE.

Lipchitz, Jacques (1891–1973). American sculptor. He was born in Lithuania and in 1925 became a French citizen. He left Paris in 1940 and settled in the US. In his work he often utilized biblical episodes and themes taken from Jewish life and history.

Lipkin, Israel *see* SALANTER, ISRAEL.

Lipmann, Yomtov ben Solomon *see* MÜHLHAUSEN, YOMTOV LIPMANN.

Lippe, Karpel (1830–1915). Romanian Zionist, of Galician origin. He was born in Stanislav, Galicia. He became a physician in Jassy, Romania. Active in Ḥibbat Zion, he was one of the initiators of the Zionist idea. In 1911 he returned to Galicia. He published scientific studies, Jewish apologetics, works on the rights of Romanian Jews, and poetry.

Lipschütz, Israel ben Gedaliah (1782–1860). German rabbinic scholar. He was a rabbi in Wronki, Dessau and Colmer, and Danzig. His *Tiferet Israel* is a commentary on the Mishnah.

Lipschütz, Jacob (1838–1922). Russian author. He was born in Vilkomir. He became the secretary and chief assistant of Isaac Elhanan Spektor, the rabbi at Kovno, and opposed the Haskalah and Zionism. His *Zikhron Yaakov* is a book of reminiscences which casts light on Russian Jewish history.

Lipsky, Louis (1870–1963). American Zionist leader, journalist, and author. He was born in Rochester, New York. He founded the Zionist periodical *The Maccabean* in 1901, and also edited the *American Hebrew*. From 1922 to 1930 he was president of the Zionist Organization of America. He was a founder of Keren ha-Yesod, the Jewish Agency, and the American and World Jewish congresses. His writings include *Thirty Years of American Zionism*.

Lipton, Seymour (b. 1903). American

sculptor. He trained as a dentist and practiced in New York before devoting himself to sculpture. Some of his works are based on Jewish motifs.

Liptzin, Solomon (b. 1901). Israeli literary scholar. He was born in Satanov, Russia, and taken to the US at an early age. He was professor of German at City College, New York. Later he settled in Israel. His writings include *Peretz, Eliakum Zunser, The Flowering of Yiddish Literature, The Maturing of Yiddish Literature,* and *The Jew in American Literature.*

Lisbon. Capital of Portugal. The Jewish community was established there under the Moors, and developed after the Christian recapture of the city in the 12th century. The Jews were active as physicians, astronomers, and tax-farmers. The forced conversion of Lisbon's Jewish inhabitants took place in 1497, and the city became a center for Marranos. From the 16th to 18th centuries the Portuguese Inquisition was active there.

Lisitzky, Ephraim E. (1885–1962). American Hebrew poet and educator, of Russian origin. He was born in Minsk. He emigrated to the US and settled in New Orleans, where he became the principal of the city's Hebrew school. He wrote Hebrew poetry about American Indians as well as Jewish themes.

Literature *see* HEBREW LITERATURE; YIDDISH LITERATURE.

Liturgy. The Jewish liturgy dates back to worship in the Temple in ancient Israel, when prayers were recited during the sacrificial ritual. During the Babylonian exile sacrifice was replaced by prayers recited in public assemblies. In time the Jewish liturgy followed a fixed pattern of three daily services: Shaḥarit (morning service), Minḥah (afternoon service), and Maariv (evening service). An additional prayer (Musaph) was recited on Sabbaths and festivals, and a special prayer (Neilah) was recited at the conclusion of the service on the Day of Atonement. The central prayers of the Jewish liturgy are the Shema and the Amidah or Eighteen Benedictions. Prayers recited on weekdays and the Sabbath are contained in the siddur (the prayerbook); those recited on festivals are found in the maḥzor (the festival prayerbook). The prayer structure is based on the threefold division of adoration, thanksgiving, and petition. There are two versions of the Jewish liturgy: the Ashkenazi ritual is used by eastern European Jewry and the Sephardi ritual by Jews of Spanish and Portuguese origin, as well as a number of oriental Jewish communities.

Litvak. Lithuanian Jew.

Litvakov, Moses (1875–?1938). Russian Yiddish writer. He was born in Cherkassy in the Ukraine. He wrote in Russian, Hebrew, and Yiddish on social and literary issues. After the revolution of 1905 he became a member of the central committee of the territorialist Socialist–Zionist Party. He edited periodicals in Vilnius, and after 1917 he contributed to Yiddish journals in Kiev. In 1919 he joined the Communist Party and became a leader of Moscow's Yevsektzia. From 1924 he edited *Emes*, the Yiddish organ of the Communist Party. He was arrested in the Stalinist purges of 1937 and died in prison.

Litvinoff, Emanuel (b. 1915). English poet. He was born in London. He wrote poetry and novels, including *The Last Europeans*, which deals with the position of Jews in the diaspora.

Litvinovsky, Pinḥas (b. 1894). Israeli painter. He was born in the Ukraine. He settled in Palestine and studied at the Bezalel School of Arts and Crafts in Jerusalem; later he studied at the St. Petersburg Academy. After returning to Jerusalem in 1919 he participated in the first group exhibitions of Palestinian artists there from 1923, and in Tel Aviv from

1926. In his paintings he utilized various styles to depict traditional Jewish themes.

Liubavich. Russian village near Mohilev. It was the center of Ḥabad Ḥasidism. Dov Ber, the successor of Shneour Zalman of Lyady, settled there. He was succeeded as leader of the sect by Menaḥem Mendel Shneersohn, also known as Menaḥem Mendel of Liubavich, whose descendants lived there until 1916. In that year Shalom Dov Shneersohn went to Rostov-na-Donu.

***Lloyd George, David** (1863–1945). British statesman. He was prime minister (1916–22) of the government which issued the Balfour Declaration of sympathy with Zionism in 1917.

Loans. According to Jewish law, whoever borrows money must return it at a fixed time. Otherwise the lender may recover the value of the loan in the form of the borrower's property. If the loan is made by a promissory note, it may even be recovered from property sold by the debtor after the date of the note. Originally a Sabbatical Year canceled all debts, but the sage Hillel instituted the prosbul, a legal document which allowed the collection of debts to be postponed until after the Sabbatical Year. According to the Bible loans with interest are forbidden; nonetheless, permission was given to charge interest under certain conditions.

Loans [Loanz]**, Elijah ben Moses** [Elijah Baal Shem] (1564–1636). German kabbalist. He was born in Frankfurt am Main, and served as a rabbi in Fulda, Hanau, Friedberg, and Worms. He was a writer of kabbalistic amulets and incantations. His *Rinnat Dodim* is a kabbalistic commentary on the Song of Songs.

Loanz, Yoseph ben Gershom *see* JOSELMAN OF ROSHEIM.

Loch in kop (Yiddish: "hole in the head"). Expression used to designate something which is not needed.

Locker, Berl (1887–1972). Israeli Labor Zionist leader. He was born in Galicia and became the editor of the Lemberg Labor Zionist newspaper. Before World War I he organized the Poale Zion party in the Austrian Empire, and from 1916 he ran the world office of Poale Zion at The Hague. From 1931 to 1936 he was a member of the executives of the Zionist Organization and the Jewish Agency in London. He settled in Palestine in 1936 and served as a member of the executive of Histadrut. From 1948 to 1956 he was chairman of the Jewish Agency in Jerusalem. He wrote articles in Yiddish, German, Hebrew and English.

Lod *see* LYDDA.

Łódź. City in central Poland. Jews settled there in the 18th century and played a part in the textile industry. After the Russian pogroms of 1881, the community increased in size. In the 20th century it was a Jewish cultural center.

Loeb, Isidore (1839–1892). French rabbi and scholar. He was a tutor in Bayonne and Paris, and later served as a rabbi at St.-Étienne. In 1869 he was appointed secretary of the Alliance Israélite Universelle. From 1878 he taught Jewish history at the École Rabbinique. He wrote studies of biblical and talmudic literature, medieval historiography, and Jewish history in Spain and France.

Loeb, Sarahs *see* ARYEH LEIB SARAHS.

Loebel, Hirschel *see* LEVIN, HIRSCHEL.

Loeb of Spola *see* ARYEH LEIB OF SHPOLA.

Loewe, Heinrich (1867–1950). German Zionist and scholar of Jewish folklore. He was born in Wanzleben. He founded Jung Israel, the first Zionist group in Germany, in 1892, and edited various Zionist publications. From 1899 he worked as a librarian in the University of Berlin, where he became a professor in 1915. In 1933 he settled in Palestine and worked as a librarian in Tel Aviv. He published studies in the field of Jewish folklore.

Loewe, Herbert Martin James (1882–1940). English orientalist. He was born in London. He taught rabbinic Hebrew at Oxford, rabbinics at Cambridge (1931), and Hebrew at the University of London. He published studies of rabbinics and Jewish history. With C. G. Montefiore, he edited the *Rabbinic Anthology*.

Loewe, Joel ben Judah Loeb [Brill, Joel ben Judah Loeb] (1762–1802). German Hebrew writer, grammarian, and exegete. He was born in Berlin, and joined Moses Mendelssohn's Haskalah movement. In 1791 he was appointed principal of the Wilhelms-Schule in Breslau. He published an introduction and commentary to Mendelssohn's German translation of the Psalms, a scientific grammer of biblical Hebrew, and epigrams in the style of the Book of Proverbs. He also translated the Passover Haggadah into German.

Loewe, Louis (1809–1888). British orientalist. He was born in Zülz, Germany, and settled in England. In 1837 he visited Egypt (where he deciphered various inscriptions) and Palestine. From 1839 he was Sir Moses Montefiore's secretary, as well as the director of the oriental department of the Duke of Sussex's library. He was principal of Jews College in 1856–8, and later served as principal of Ohel Moshe vi-Yhudit, the theological seminary founded by Montefiore. He published works on the life of Montefiore and on oriental languages.

Loewisohn, Solomon (1788–1821). Austrian Hebrew poet and scholar. He was born in Hungary, and settled in Vienna, where he worked as a proofreader. He was one of the outstanding Hebrew authors of the Haskalah movement. His *Melitzat Yeshurun* is an exposition of biblical poetry, and his Meḥkere Aretz is the first modern lexicon of biblical geography.

Logos (Greek: "the word"). The Word of God, by which the universe was created. It was understood by Philo as divine reason, the mind of God manifested in and through the created universe. It is linked to the concept of memra (also meaning "word") in Targum literature. In Proverbs, Job, and various apocryphal books the concept of divine wisdom ("ḥokhmah") shares some of the qualities of the logos. It later became a central feature of Christian theology. In kabbalistic literature concepts similar to the logos are found in the doctrine of the sephirot.

Loḥame Ḥerut Yisrael ("Fighters for the Freedom of Israel") [Lehi; Stern Gang]. Revolutionary Jewish organization in Palestine. It split from the Irgun Tzevai Leumi in 1940. After its founder, Avraham Stern, was killed, the group was led by Yisrael Scheib, Nathan Mor, and Yitzḥak Shamir. Among its actions were the murders of the British minister in the Middle East, Lord Moyne, in 1944, and Count Bernadotte in 1948.

London. Capital of the UK. A Jewish community existed in the city in the 12th century, and became the largest Jewish population in the country during the Middle Ages. At the coronation of Richard I in 1189 there was an attack on London Jewry. Another pogrom took place during the Barons' Wars in the 13th century, and ritual murder accusations were made against Jews in the city in 1238, 1244, and 1276. After the Jews were expelled from England in 1290, a house for converts existed in London, as well as a secret Marrano community. Under the Commonwealth, Marranos settled there, and through the efforts of Manasseh ben Israel they formed a Sephardi community. They were followed by Askhenazi Jews, who established a synagogue in 1690. In the modern period,

London has continued to be the center of English Jewish life.

London, Meyer (1871–1926). American lawyer and socialist leader. He was born in Poland, and went to the US in 1891. In 1914 he was elected to the House of Representatives as a socialist from the imigrant district on the Lower East Side in New York. He opposed the US entry into World War I, and had little sympathy with Zionism.

Lonzano, Menaḥem di (1550–before 1624). Palestinian linguist, poet, and kabbalist. Born in Constantinople, he emigrated to Jerusalem and later moved to Safed; 40 years later he went to Turkey and Italy, returning to Jerusalem in 1618. He wrote studies of the masoretic text of the Bible, Hebrew grammar, prosody, and lexicography. His *Shete Yadot* contains original writings and midrashic literature.

Lookstein, Joseph Hyman (1902–1979). American rabbi, of Russian origin. He went to the US as a child. He served as a rabbi of Kehilath Jeshurun Congregation in New York and professor of homiletics and sociology at Yeshiva University. In 1958 he became president of Bar-Ilan University in Tel Aviv.

Lopez, Aaron (1731–1782). American merchant shipper. He was born in Portugal, and settled in Newport, Rhode Island, in 1752. There he became a leader of the Yeshuat Israel Congregation. He built up an extensive transatlantic mercantile empire and became Newport's leading merchant. A supporter of the rebel cause, he moved to Leicester, Massachusetts, when the British captured Newport.

Lopez, Roderigo (1525–1594). British Marrano physician. Originally from Portugal, he settled in London during the reign of Queen Elizabeth. He was appointed physician to the Earl of Leicester and to Queen Elizabeth. In 1594 he was arrested, found guilty of plotting to poison the Queen, and executed.

Lorca, Joshua de *see* LORKI, JOSHUA.

Lord of hosts *see* GOD, NAMES OF.

***Lorki** [de Lorca]**, Joshua** [Geronimo de Sante Fé] (d. c. 1419). Spanish physician and writer. He was born in Lorca, Spain. He converted to Christianity in 1412 and assumed the name Geronimo de Sante Fé. He became a physician to anti-Pope Benedict XIII. He initiated the Disputation of Tortosa (1413–14) in which he was a participant; subsequently he traveled widely, attempting to convert Jews to Christianity.

Lorm, Hieronymus *see* LANDESMANN, HEINRICH.

Lost property *see* FINDING OF PROPERTY.

Lost Tribes of Israel *see* TEN LOST TRIBES OF ISRAEL.

Lot (fl. ?19th–16th cent. BCE). Israelite, nephew of Abraham. The Bible depicts his sojourn in Sodom, escape from the city, and the disaster that befell his wife who looked back at the destruction of Sodom and became a pillar of salt. After the devastation of the city, Lot lived in a cave with his two daughters, who plied him with wine and, when he was drunk, committed incest with him; each daughter bore him a son, Ammon and Moab (Genesis 19).

***Lothar, Ernst** (1890–1974). Austrian writer and stage director. He was born in Brünn, Moravia, and became a civil servant. He was later active as a theater critic and director. Although he converted to Catholicism, he had to leave Austria in 1938. He lived in the US, but later returned to Vienna. His publications include *The Angel and the Trumpet*, which discusses intermarriage.

Lots *see* PURIM.

Louis Lamed Literary Foundation. American literary organization. It was founded by Louis Lamed in Detroit in 1939 to foster Hebrew and Yiddish literature. It made annual awards for new works in both languages.

Louvish, Simon (b. 1947). Israeli author. He was born in Glasgow, and moved to Israel in 1949. His publications include *A Moment of Silence*, *The Therapy of Avram Blok*, and *The Death of Moishe Ganef*.

Love (Hebrew "ahav"). In the Bible the term "ahav" refers to love of all kinds – that of men and women as well as moral and spiritual relationships. In rabbinic literature, the concept of the love of God is a central religious value. In the Middle Ages it acquired a mystical significance.

Löw, Eleazar (1758–1837). Polish rabbi. He was born in Wodzisław, and became dayyan there. Later he was rabbi of Pilica, Třešt, Pilsen, Liptovsky Mikuláš, Slovakia, and Santo. An opponent of religious reform, he published studies of the halakhah.

Löw, Immanuel (1854–1944). Hungarian rabbi and scholar, son of Leopold Löw. He was rabbi of Szeged. From 1927 he represented non-Orthodox communities in the Upper Chamber of the Hungarian parliament. He published works in the field of Hebrew and Aramaic philology as well as the *Flora of the Jews*.

Löw, Leopold (1811–1875). Hungarian scholar. He served as a rabbi in several Hungarian communities. From 1850 he officiated at Szeged. He was an extreme reformer and engaged in controversy with the Orthodox. He wrote studies of the history of Hungarian Jewry. In addition he was the publisher of a journal of Jewish studies (*Ben Ḥananiah*) from 1858 to 1867.

***Lowdermilk, Walter Clay** (1888–1974). American agronomist. He was a professor of soil conservation at the Haifa-Technion from 1954 to 1957. His *Palestine, Land of Promise* formulated a plan for the irrigation of Palestine by utilizing its rivers and subterranean water resources.

Löwenberg, Jacob (1856–1929). German poet. He was a teacher in Hamburg. By stressing Jewish themes in his writing, he reacted against German anti-Semitism. His *Vom goldnen Überfluss* is an anthology of modern German poets.

Lowenthal, Marvin (1890–1969). American author. He was born in Bradford, Pennsylvania. He organized the Zionist movement on the West Coast. From 1924 to 1929 he was the European editor of the *Menorah Journal*, and during this period wrote about literature, politics, and Zionism. He served on the Zionist Advisory Commission (1946–9), and was editor of the *American Zionist* (1952–4). He translated and edited *Memoirs of Glueckel of Hameln*, and edited *Henrietta Szold: Life and Letters*.

Lox (Yiddish). Smoked salmon.

Lozowick, Louis (1892–1973). American painter, graphic artist, and art critic. He was born in Ludovinka, a small village in the Kiev district, and went to the US in 1906. He published articles in the *Menorah Journal* on the works of Jewish artists. His *Hundred American-Jewish Painters and Sculptors* is a comprehensive study of modern American Jewish art.

Luaḥ *see* CALENDAR.

Luaḥ Aḥiasaph *see* AḤIASAPH.

Luaḥ Eretz Israel. Hebrew literary almanac. It was published in Jerusalem from 1896 to 1915 by Abraham Moses Luncz. It contained ethnographic, cultural, and biographical information about Palestine.

Lubianiker, Pinḥas *see* LAVON, PINḤAS.

Lublin. City in eastern Poland. Jews lived in the city from the 15th century. Jewish merchants participated in the Lublin fairs, and it was one of the four meeting places of the Council of Four Lands. It became a flourishing Jewish center with a famous printing press and yeshivah. Most Jews were expelled from Lublin in the 18th century, but they returned to the center of the city in 1862, and reestablished an important Jewish community.

Lublin, Meir ben Gedaliah of [Maḥaram Lublin] (1558–1616). Polish talmudist. He was born in Lublin, and became head of the yeshivah there (1582–7). He later served as dayyan and head of the yeshivah at Kraków. From 1595 to 1613 he was a rabbi in Lemberg, and he was then appointed rabbi and head of the yeshivah in Lublin. His *Meir Ene Ḥakhamim* contains novellae on the entire Talmud. His responsa were published in *Manhir Ene Ḥakhamim.*

Lublin, Rabbi of *see* HOROWITZ, JACOB ISAAC.

Lublinski, Samuel (1868–1910). German playwright, literary historian, and philosopher of religion. He was born in East Prussia. As a young man he was apprenticed to a bookseller in Italy, and he eventually devoted himself to literature. He lived in Berlin, Dresden, and Weimar. His writings include *Jüdische Charaktere bei Grillparzer, Hebbel, und Otto Ludwig, Die Enstehung des Judentums*, and *Der urchristliche Erdkreis und sein Mythos.*

Lucena. Town in southern Spain. During the Moorish period it was called the "Jews' Town," and became an important center of Jewish cultural and intellectual life. In the 12th century many Jewish inhabitants were forced to convert to Islam.

Ludomir, Maid of. Ukrainian Ḥasidic leader. Her real name was Hannah Rachel and she was the daughter of Monesh Werbermacher. After an illness, she followed Ḥasidic customs, built her own synagogue, and observed the religious duties of men (putting on tallit and tefillin when she prayed). She later emigrated to Palestine where she continued her mystical studies and practiced rituals designed to hasten the coming of the Messiah.

***Lueger, Karl** (1844–1910). Austrian politician. He was born in Vienna. He qualified as a lawyer and was elected to parliament in 1885. In 1893 he united the different Christian factions into the Christian Social Party, which he led until his death. He became mayor of Vienna in 1897. His administration pursued various discriminatory policies against the Jewish community.

Luftmensch (German). Rootless person. The expression was introduced by Max Nordau to describe the Jews in eastern Europe, who lived by peddling and minor speculation.

Lukács, György (1885–1971). Hungarian philosopher and literary critic. He was born in Budapest, where he later became commissar of education. When Hitler came to power he fled to the USSR. After World War II he returned to Hungary, was elected to parliament, and was appointed a professor of aesthetics and cultural philosophy at the University of Budapest. He published Marxist interpretations of literature and was influenced by the socialist views of Moses Hess.

Lukuas [Andreas] (fl. 1st cent. BCE–1st cent. CE). Cyrenian rebel leader. He led the revolt of the Jews of Cyrene against Rome in 115. After invading Egypt, he was defeated.

Lulav. Palm branch. According to Leviticus, it is to be used ceremonially on the feast of Sukkot, together with the etrog, myrtle, and willow (Leviticus 23.40). It is the custom to carry them during the recital of the Hallel and the Hoshanot. At particular points in the recitation the lulav is shaken in all directions.

Lunchitz, Solomon Ephraim (d. 1619). Czech talmudist. He was the head of the yeshivah in Lwów. From 1604 he served as chief rabbi in Prague. He contributed to talmudic study and composed liturgical poems.

Luncz, Abraham Moses (1854–1918). Palestinian author, publisher, and editor. He was born in Kovno, and emigrated to Jerusalem in 1869. Although he became blind, he published 12 volumes of a yearbook about Palestine, as well as a literary almanac, which appeared from 1895 to 1915; he also edited geographical works on Palestine.

Lunel, Armand (1892–1977). French novelist. He was born in Aix-en-Provence and taught philosophy in Monaco. He wrote novels about Provençal life, including portrayals of the region's Jewish inhabitants. He also wrote the librettos for Darius Milhaud's *Esther de Carpentras*, and the oratorio *David*.

Luria, Isaac ben Solomon [Ari; Ashkenazi] (1534–72). Palestinian kabbalist. He was born in Jerusalem and educated in Egypt. From 1570 he lived in Safed. His kabbalistic teachings were received by his disciples orally; they were later recorded by his pupil Ḥayyim Vital in *Etz Ḥayyim, Peri Etz Ḥayyim*, and *Sepher ha-Gilgulim*. His kabbalistic theories profoundly influenced the development of Jewish mysticism. In his teaching he propounded doctrines about divine contraction ("tzimtzum"), the shattering of the vessels ("shevirat ha-kelim"), and cosmic repair ("tikkun").

Luria, Solomon ben Jehiel [Maharshal] (?1510–1574). Polish codifier. He officiated in communities in Lithuania and Poland. His *Yam shel Shelomoh* was critical of the Shulḥan Arukh, which according to Luria relied on the codifiers instead of being based on the Talmud.

Lusitano, Salusque *see* Usque, solomon.

***Luther, Martin** (1483–1546). German Protestant reformer. The Reformation in Christendom is normally dated from 1517, when he nailed the so-called 95 Theses to the door of the church in Wittenberg. Initially Luther condemned the persecution of the Jews, but when he realized that the Jewish community would not convert to Christianity, he grew hostile to the Jewish population. His anti-Jewish attitudes were expressed in various tracts including *On the Jews and their Lies*. Despite such views, Luther was attached to the Hebrew Bible, which he translated into German.

Luz. Ancient city near Jerusalem, renamed Bethel by the Israelites (Genesis 28.19). At the beginning of the period of the Judges it was captured by the Israelites. The person who delivered the city to the Israelites went to the land of the Hittites, where he built another city of the same name (Judges 1.26).

Luz, Kadish (1895–1972). Israeli labor leader. He was born in Bobruisk, Belorussia, and served in the Russian army during World War I. He was a founder of the organization of Jewish soldiers in Russia and of the Zionist pioneer movement. He settled in Palestine in 1920. From 1951 to 1969 he was a Mapai member of the Knesset. He was minister of agriculture (1955–9) and speaker of the Knesset (1959–69).

Luzki, Joseph Solomon ben Moses (d. 1844). Crimean Karaite scholar. He was born at Kukizow, near Lemberg, and lived at Lutsk, Volhynia. In 1802 he moved to Yevpatoriya in the Crimea, where he became rabbi of the Karaites. He went with Simḥah Babovich to St. Petersburg to obtain exemption for the Karaites from military service. In 1831 he settled in Palestine, but he later returned to Yevpatoriya. He wrote religious poems, studies of Hebrew grammar, and Bible commentary.

Luzki, Simḥah Isaac ben Moses (d. 1766). Crimean Karaite writer and bibliographer. He was born in Lutsk, and lived in Chufut-Kale in the Crimea, where he became head of a bet midrash. He was a copyist of early Karaite manuscripts, and wrote various studies of theology, philosophy, halakhah, and kabbalah. His *Oraḥ Tzaddikim* is a history of the Karaites and Karaite literature.

Luzzatti, Luigi (1841–1927). Italian statesman and economist. He was born in Venice, where he founded a mutual aid society for the gondoliers. Expelled from the city as a revolutionary, he went to Milan where he became professor of economics at the Istituto Tecnico; he was later appointed professor of constitutional law at the University of Padua. In 1869 he became general secretary to the Ministry of Agriculture, Industry, and Commerce, and from 1871 he served in parliament in various posts, becoming prime minister in 1910. He acted on behalf of oppressed European Jews, and supported Zionist activities in Palestine.

Luzzatto, Moses Ḥayyim [Ramḥal] (1707–1746). Italian kabbalist, Hebrew poet, and writer. He was born in Padua. He engaged in mystical practices and gathered around himself a group of disciples. He believed he was in communion with a maggid who dictated secret doctrines to him. His messianic claims provoked the hostility of the rabbis. Forced to leave Italy, he settled in Amsterdam and subsequently went to Palestine. He wrote kabbalistic studies, ethical works, theological investigations, poetry, and verse drama. He is regarded as the father of modern Hebrew literature.

Luzzatto, Samuel David [Shadal] (1800–1865). Italian scholar, philosopher, biblical commentator, and translator. From 1829 he was professor at the Padua Rabbinical College. He wrote studies of the Bible, Hebrew grammar and philology, Jewish liturgy, Hebrew poetry, and philosophy. In addition he edited the poems of Judah ha-Levi, translated parts of the Bible into Italian, and composed poetry in Hebrew in the traditional Italian style. He was opposed to the kabbalah and criticized several Jewish philosophers including Maimonides, Ibn Ezra, and Spinoza. His correspondence with other Jewish scholars is of historical importance.

Luzzatto, Simone (1583–1663). Italian rabbi. Born in Venice, he served as rabbi there for 57 years. His *Socrate* espouses the view that human reason is impotent unless aided by revelation. In another work he argued for Jewish toleration largely on economic grounds. He also wrote a treatise defending the authority of tradition and the Oral Law.

Lvov [Lwów, Lemberg]. City in the Ukraine, formerly the capital of Galicia. Jews lived in the city from the 13th century. During the Chmielnicki massacre in the 17th century, the community suffered great losses. From 1759 the Jews were confined to a ghetto, but in 1867 they were permitted to reside in other areas. Many outstanding rabbis and leaders of the Haskalah lived there. From 1880 it became the center of the Zionist movement.

Lvovich, David (1882–1950). American communal worker. He was born in southern Russia, and was a founder of the Jewish socialist party SS. From 1921 he lived in Berlin, and later settled in Paris (1932–9). He then went to the US where he worked for ORT; he had already served as the vice-chairman of its World Federation since 1921. After World War II he organized occupational training in displaced persons' camps in Europe.

Lwów *see* Lvov.

Lydda. Ancient town on the coastal plain of Israel; the modern town of Lod occupies the same site. According to I Chronicles 8.12, it was built by the tribe of Benjamin. During the second Temple period it grew in significance. After the Jews participated in the revolt of 66–70, it was devastated by the Romans. Later it became the seat of a rabbinical academy.

Lying. The act of lying is forbidden in the Bible (Leviticus 19.11) and the bearing of false witness is specifically prohibited in the ninth commandment. The talmudic scholar Jonah of Gerona (d. 1263) lists nine types of lies: (1) untruths spoken in business; (2) deceit without causing harm; (3) lying with desire for benefit; (4) deliberate falsification of facts heard; (5) a promise made with the intention of not keeping it; (6) a promise which is not kept; (7) leading another to believe, falsely, that one has done him a favor; (8) priding oneself on qualities one does not have; and (9) the falsehoods of children.

Lyon, Hart *see* LEVIN, HIRSCHEL.

Lyons. French city on the River Rhône. In the 9th century various restrictions were imposed on the Jewish community there, and during the Middle Ages Jews were repeatedly expelled (1251–1420). In the 18th century Jews from the papal territory of the Comtat Venaissin in France began to settle there.

***Lyra, Nicholas de** (c. 1270–1349). French exegete. He published Bible commentaries in Latin, based largely on those of Rashi.

***Lysias** (d. 162 BCE). Syrian general. He was appointed ruler of the western sector of the Seleucid empire by Antiochus IV Epiphanes in 165 BCE. Charged with crushing the revolt of Judah Maccabee (I Maccabees 3.31–7), he was defeated at Bet Tzur. He subsequently invaded Judea, defeated Judah at Bet Zechariah, and besieged Jerusalem. He granted the Jewish community religious freedom and autonomy on condition that they acknowledge Seleucid suzerainty.

***Lysimachus** (fl. 1st cent. BCE). Alexandrian Hellenistic author. His writings are colored by anti-Jewish views. According to Josephus, he maintained that the Jews were expelled from Egypt because they were lepers.

M

Maabarah ("transit camp"). Temporary village of a type constructed in Israel during the mass immigration that began in 1948. From 1950 it was replaced by the kephar avodah.

Maamad. One of the non-priestly Israelites who attended the Temple sacrifice. The whole people was divided into 24 groups of priests, levites, and Israelites, who were assigned specific times to attend in the Temple. The groups of Israelites sent only a few representatives (the maamadot) to be present at the sacrifices; the rest assembled in their own towns at the appointed time to read prayers and the first chapter of Genesis. In the post-Talmudic period the practice of reading these selections was partially retained. *See also* MAHAMAD.

Maapilim. Term applied to Jews who attempted to reach Palestine despite obstacles, in particular those who defied the restrictions imposed by the British Mandatory government. From 1934 transports were arranged by the Polish organization He-Ḥalutz and the Revisionists. Immigration began in 1938, but the British were quick to counter it by restrictive legislation.

Maariv [evening service]. The service of evening prayer. According to tradition, it was ordained by Jacob. The Talmud relates a controversy about whether it is obligatory or optional; in time it became required. The service includes the Shema, its blessings, and the Eighteen Benedictions. During the medieval period, poems called "maaravot" were composed for it.

Maaseh (Yiddish from Hebrew). A far-fetched story.

Maaseh bereshit ("work of creation"). Mystical tradition concerning the Creation. Based on Genesis 1, it depicts the creation of the universe according to mystical doctrines. These views are expressed in the Sepher Yetzirah, in which the cosmos is said to have been created out of 32 secret paths of wisdom (consisting of 10 basic numbers, sephirot, and the 22 letters of the Hebrew alphabet).

Maaseh Book. Name given to any of several collections of mostly miraculous stories, which provide ethical instruction. Derived from the Talmud as well as medieval folklore, they were written in Yiddish. A comprehensive English edition of the stories was published in 1934 by Moses Gaster. Similar collections were found among Mediterranean Sephardi communities under the title *Maaseh Nissim*.

Maaseh merkavah ("work of the chariot") [chariot mysticism]. Mystical doctrine, based on the vision of the divine chariot in Ezekiel 1. It describes the mystic's ascent to Heaven, his visions of the divine palaces, and personal experience of the divine presence. It formed the basis of a complex of speculations, homilies, and visions connected with the throne of glory and the divine chariot. *See also* HEKHALOT, BOOKS OF.

Maaser *see* TITHE.

Maaserot ("Tithes"). Seventh tractate in the Mishnah order of Zeraim. It deals with the tithe given to the Levites (Numbers 18.21).

Maaser Sheni ("Second tithe"). Eighth tractate in the Mishnah order of Zeraim. It deals with tithes eaten in Jerusalem (Deuteronomy 14.22–7) and how they can be redeemed for money.

***Macalister, Robert Alexander Stewart** (1870–1951). Irish archeologist. He was the director of fieldwork operations for the Palestine Excavation Fund from 1898 to 1909 and in 1924. His most important excavations took place at Gezer, Marissa, and Ophel in the Davidic City of Zion. He later became professor of Celtic archeology at Trinity College, Dublin. He was one of the pioneers of Palestinian archeology.

***Macaulay, Thomas Babington,** Lord (1800–1859). English statesman and historian. Elected to parliament in 1830, he made a maiden speech in the House of Commons supporting the removal of political disabilities affecting Jews in England. He argued the same case in the *Edinburgh Review* of January 1831.

Maccabaeans, Ancient Order of. British benefit society, composed of supporters of Zionism. Founded in 1896 by Ephraim Ish-Kishor, it aims to assist members in distress, provide free medical aid, and offer support. Its organization displays masonic features. It has 25 branches; the principal officers are called "Grand Commander," "Grand Treasurer," and "Grand Secretary."

Maccabee. Name given to Judah, son of Mattathias, who led the revolt against Syria in 168 BCE (*see* JUDAH MACCABEE). It was also applied to the Hasmonean dynasty, which lasted for about 120 years from the 2nd century BCE.

Maccabees (i) [Hannah and her seven sons]. Name given in Christian tradition to the seven children of Hannah martyred by Antiochus Epiphanes when they refused to commit idolatry. Shrines to their memory, and to Hannah's, were established throughout the Christian world.

Maccabees (ii). Name of four apocryphal works (of which the first two only are included in the Apocrypha). I Maccabees covers the period of 40 years from the accession of Antiochus Epiphanes in 175 BCE to the death of Simeon the Hasmonean in 135 BCE. II Maccabees focuses on the life and times of Judah Maccabee. III Maccabees is unrelated in subject matter to the other books: it explains why the Jews in Egypt have a Purim-like festival in the summer; it may have been grouped with I and II Maccabees because it relates a persecution of the Jews by a Hellenistic king and their miraculous deliverance. IV Maccabees depicts the story of the martyrs of the persecution preceding the Maccabean revolt in 168 BCE; it is a philosophical sermon on the theme of pious reason.

Maccabi. World union of Jewish athletic organizations. In 1895 branches were established in Berlin, Constantinople, Bucharest, and St. Petersburg. Berlin became the union's headquarters, but they later moved to London, and then to Tel Aviv. The quadrennial Maccabiah is held under its auspices.

Maccabiah. International games held every four years in Israel under the auspices of Maccabi. It was conceived by Joseph Yekutieli, who advocated the idea from 1921. The first Maccabiah was held in Tel Aviv in 1932. The games are open to Jewish athletes from all countries.

Maccoby, Hyam (b. 1924). English historian and librarian. He was born in Sunderland. He has served as librarian and lecturer at Leo Baeck College in London.

His publications include *Revolution in Judaea, Judaism on Trial, The Sacred Executioner, The Mythmaker,* and *Early Rabbinic Writings.*

***McDonald, James Grover** (1886–1964). American diplomat. He was born in Coldwater, Ohio. He first taught history at the University of Indiana. He then served as chairman of the American Foreign Policy Association (1919–33), League of Nations high commissioner for refugees from Germany (1933–5), and as a member of the Anglo-American Commission of Inquiry in Palestine. He was the first US minister (later ambassador) to Israel.

Macdonald White Paper *see* WHITE PAPER OF 1939.

Machaerus. Transjordanian fortress; now a ruin (Al-Mukāwir), its site is 14 miles south-west of Madaba. It was erected by the Hasmonean king Alexander Yannai around 80 BCE. Destroyed by Gabinus (57–54 BCE), it was rebuilt by Herod the Great. According to Christian tradition, John the Baptist was executed there. It served as a Zealot stronghold during the Jewish revolt against the Romans (66–70) and was captured by Lucius Bassus in 72 CE.

Macher (Yiddish). Important person, active member of an organization.

Machetunim (Yiddish). Members of the extended family of one's spouse.

Machpelah. Site near Hebron consisting of a field containing a cave. It was purchased by Abraham from Ephron the Hittite as a burial plot for Sarah (Genesis 23). Abraham, Isaac, Rebekah, Jacob, and Leah were also interred there.

Mack, Julian William (1866–1943). American judge and Zionist leader. He was born in San Francisco. He began his career as a professor of law at Northwestern University, Illinois (1895–1902). He served as a judge in the circuit court of Cook County, Illinois, in the Chicago juvenile court, and in the US commerce court; in 1913 he was appointed to the US circuit court of appeals. He was president of the Zionist Organization of America (1918–21) and was the first president of the American Jewish Congress. He was also the first chairman of the Comité des Délégations Juives at Versailles (1919).

McMahon Letters. Name given to a series of letters exchanged in 1915 between Sir Henry McMahon, British commissioner in Egypt, and Sherif Hussein of Mecca and his son Feisal, later King of Iraq. They contained a promise of British support for Arab independence in exchange for an Arab revolt against the Turks. Although the letters do not explicitly mention Palestine, the Arabs claimed that it was included in the area designated for independence, but this was denied by McMahon in 1937.

Madaba Map. Ancient map of Palestine, dating from the 6th century. It was executed in mosaic on a pavement in the Byzantine church of Madaba in the Transjordan in 1884.

Maestro Calo *see* KALONYMOS BEN KALONYMOS.

Maestro Vidal Blasom *see* MOSES OF NARBONNE.

Magdala. City on the western shore of the Sea of Galilee. It was one of four large towns in Galilee during the second Temple period, and the home of Mary Magdalene (Mark 15.40; Matthew 27.56). It was captured by Titus during the Roman War in 67. After the destruction of the Temple, the priests of the family of Ezekiel settled in the town.

Magdeburg. City in eastern Germany, 80 miles south-west of Berlin. Its Jewish community was among the oldest in Germany. In 965 Emperor Otto the Great placed the Jews of Magdeburg under the protection of the archbishop. In 1349 the Jewish community was decimated by the Black Death. The Jews were expelled from the city in 1493.

Magen Avot ("A shield of our forefathers"). Opening words of an abbreviated form of the seven benedictions of the Friday evening Amidah. It is recited by the cantor after the Amidah.

Magen David ("Shield of David"). The name given in Judaism to the symbol consisting of two superimposed triangles forming a star (it is also known as the Star of David). Although it was used in the synagogue at Capernaum as early as the 3rd century, it was not commonly adopted as a Jewish symbol until much later. From the 13th century the name figures in practical kabbalah, and the symbol (believed to have magical properties) is found in association with the pentagram (or Star of Solomon). The Magen David occurs in a Jewish context in Prague in the 17th century. In the 19th century it was adopted by the First Zionist Congress as its symbol, and it appears on the flags of the Zionist Organization and the State of Israel. The Nazis employed a yellow six-pointed star as a Jewish badge.

Magen David Adom ("Red Shield of David"). Israeli first-aid society. It was founded in Tel Aviv in 1930 as the medical wing of the Haganah.

Maggid ("preacher"). Popular preacher. Such preachers spoke both on Sabbaths and on weekdays. Frequently they described the torments of hell to bring their congregations to repentance. But they also preached words of comfort and hope, and the promise of Messianic redemption. The Ḥasidim, in particular, produced many preachers who helped to spread the teachings of the Ḥasidic movement in Poland and Russia.

Maggid of Dubno *see* JACOB BEN WOLF KRANZ.

Maggid of Kelm *see* KELM, MAGGID OF.

Maggid of Mezhirich *see* DOV BER OF MEZHIRICH.

Maggid of Slutsk *see* DAINOW, TZEVI HIRSCH.

Maggid of Zloczov *see* JEHIEL MICHAL OF ZLOCZOV.

Magic. The art of influencing events by the occult control of natural and spiritual forces. In the Bible sorcery, witchcraft, and magic are prohibited (Exodus 22.17). Nonetheless the Bible, Talmud, and later Jewish literature abound with examples of magical practices. Magical activities connected with divine names, the names of angels, permutations and combinations of Hebrew letters, and scriptural quotations flourished under the influence of kabbalah. In the medieval period Jewish magicians were widely known.

Magister Judaeorum (Latin: "Master of the Jews"). Title given to a French palace official during the Carolingian period (8th–9th centuries). He was appointed by the sovereign to supervise and protect the Jewish community.

Magnes, Judah Leon (1877–1948). American rabbi and educator. He was born in San Francisco. He was the rabbi of Temple Israel in Brooklyn, and later assistant rabbi of Temple Emanu-El in New York. He was also president of the kehillah in New York. In 1922 he emigrated to Palestine, where he helped build up the Hebrew University; when the university opened in 1925 he became its chancellor, and he was its president from 1935. He inspired the founding of the peace movement Berit Shalom and its successor, Iḥud.

Magnus, Katie, Lady (1844–1924). English author, wife of Sir Philip Magnus. She published traditional and historical tales for young readers. Her works include *Outlines of Jewish History* and *Jewish Portraits*.

Magnus, Laurie (1872–1933). English

writer, son of Sir Philip Magnus and Lady Katie Magnus. He wrote various studies of Judaism, including *Aspects of the Jewish Question, Religio laici Judaici,* and *The Jews in the Christian Era and their Contribution to its Civilisation.* From 1917 he served as editor of the anti-Zionist *Jewish Guardian.* He was active in Jewish communal life.

Magnus, Philip, Sir (1842–1933). English Reform minister and politician. He was born in London. He served as minister of the West London Synagogue of British Reform Jews from 1866 to 1880. He lectured in applied mathematics at University College, London, and in 1880 he became the organizing secretary and director of the City and Guilds of London Institute. From 1906 to 1922 he served as London University's member of parliment. He was knighted in 1886 and created a baronet in 1917. He played an important role in Anglo-Jewish affairs.

Magog *see* GOG AND MAGOG.

Magonet, Jonathan (b. 1942). English rabbi, educator, and biblical scholar. He was born in London. He has served as principal of the Leo Baeck College and published a number of works on the Bible, including *Studies in Literary Techniques in the Book of Jonah.*

Maḥal. Name given to overseas volunteers in the Israel Defense Army during the War of Independence. They came largely from English-speaking countries, France, Holland, and Switzerland. The term is derived from the initials of the words "Mitnaddeve ḥutz la-aretz" (overseas volunteers).

Mahamad. In Sephardi communities the name given to the governing body of the congregation of the synagogue. During the 18th and 19th centuries the term was also applied to the executive body of an autonomous Jewish community. The word is an alternative transliteration of the Hebrew word more often rendered "maamad."

Mahanaim. Place in Gilead where Jacob met a group of angels (Genesis 32.3). It was on the border between the territories of the half-tribe of Manasseh and the tribe of Gad (Joshua 13.26, 30). It served as David's capital during Absalom's rebellion (II Samuel 13–19).

Maḥanot ha-Olim ("Camps of the ascenders"). Palestinian pioneer youth movement. It was founded in 1927 by pupils of the Herzliyyah secondary school in Tel Aviv and established several kibbutzim.

Maharal *see* JUDAH LÖW BEN BEZALEL.

Maharam *see* SCHIFF, MEIR.

Maḥaram Ash *see* EISENSTADT, MEIR BEN ISAAC.

Maḥaram Lublin *see* LUBLIN, MEIR BEN GEDALIAH OF.

Maḥaram Padua *see* PADUA, MEIR.

Maharil *see* JACOB BEN MOSES HA-LEVI MÖLLN.

Maharsha *see* EDELS, SAMUEL ELIEZER.

Maharshak *see* KAIDANOVER, AARON SAMUEL.

Maharshal *see* LURIA, SOLOMON BEN JEHIEL.

Mahler, Eduard (1857–1945). Hungarian orientalist, mathematician, and astronomer. He was born in Cziffer. He taught oriental history and languages at Budapest University, becoming professor there in 1914. In 1912 he was appointed director of the Egyptological Institute in Budapest and in 1922 director of the Oriental Institute. His *Handbuch der jüdischen Chronologie* established the systems of the different Jewish calendars and chronologies in the light of ancient Near Eastern and medieval calculations.

Mahler, Raphael (1899–1977). Galician historian. He was born in Nowy Sadz in eastern Galicia. He served as a teacher in Jewish secondary schools in Poland. In 1937 he went to the US and taught in various educational institutions in New

York. In 1950 he went to Israel, where he lectured on the history of Israel at Tel Aviv University; he was appointed professor there in 1961. He wrote various works about Jewish history from a Marxist perspective, including a history of the Jews in modern times, and studies of the Jews in Poland, the Karaites, and Galician Jewry.

Maḥloket ("division"). Used figuratively, it signifies dissension as well as difference of opinion. Dissension was condemned by the rabbis, but differences of opinion based on principle were a central feature of rabbinic discussion.

Mah nishtannah? ("Why is it different?"). First of the four questions recited at the Passover seder.

Mahomet *see* MOHAMMED.

Maḥoza. Town in Babylonia, and important Jewish center in the early centuries CE. The Jewish community there was active in commerce and lived in a luxurious fashion. The town was mentioned for the first time as a center of study after the destruction of the academy of Nehardea in 259. In the 4th century the academy of Pumbedita and its scholars moved to Maḥoza; Rava was the head of the academy from 338 to 352. Destroyed by the Emperor Julian in 363, Maḥoza was rebuilt and became the capital of the independent area established by the exilarch Mar Zutra in the 6th century.

Mah Tovu ("How goodly"). Opening words of a prayer recited by Ashkenazim upon entering the synagogue. It consists of biblical verses taken from the Psalms. In the Sephardi ritual Psalm 5.8 is recited on entering and Psalm 5.9 on leaving the synagogue.

Maḥzor. Festival prayerbook. Initially the term was applied to the collection of prayers for the entire year in chronological order. In later usage it came to refer to the festival prayerbook as distinct from the daily prayerbook ("siddur"). It contains additional prayers ("piyyutim") to those of the liturgy, written by various poets. Both the Ashkenazi and the Sephardi versions of the prayerbook are based on the oldest maḥzor, the Maḥzor Vitry, compiled in the 11th century by Simḥah ben Samuel of Vitry, a pupil of Rashi.

Maidanek. Nazi concentration camp, three miles from Lublin. It was established in the autumn of 1941 as a prisoner-of-war camp. In 1942 it was enlarged and gas chambers and crematoria were installed. In that year Jews from Slovakia, Bohemia, France, and Greece were transported there; they were later followed by large numbers of Polish Jews.

Maimon, Abraham ben Moses *see* ABRAHAM BEN MOSES BEN MAIMON.

Maimon, Solomon (1754–1800). Polish philosopher. Born in Sukoviboeg, Poland, he was a child prodigy in the study of rabbinical literature. He initially supported his family by working as a tutor. In his spare time he studied Jewish philosophy and kabbalah, adopting the name Maimon in honor of Maimonides. He later left his home and went to Berlin, where he was a member of Moses Mendelssohn's circle. He subsequently lived in various cities, returning to Berlin in 1786. His work was praised by Immanuel Kant, and he published various studies of philosophical subjects.

Maimon [Fishman]**, Yehudah Leib** (1876–1962). Israeli rabbi and leader of Mizraḥi. He was born in Bessarabia, where he served as a rabbi amd became active in the Zionist movement. In 1913 he moved to Palestine. After World War I he arranged for the executive of the World Center of Mizraḥi to be based in Palestine and became its head. He was a member of the executive of the Jewish Agency from 1935 to 1948, and Israeli minister for religious affairs from 1948 to 1951; concurrently he was a Mizraḥi delegate to the Knesset (1949–51). He wrote on folklore, and talmudic and Zionist subjects. He was also the director of the Mosad ha-Rav Kook which he initiated.

Maimon ben Joseph (d. 1165/70). Spanish rabbi and dayyan, father of Maimonides. He served as a dayyan in Córdoba, and wrote an Arabic commentary on the Bible. In 1148 he left Spain with his family because of persecution by the Almohades after their conquest of the city. For about ten years he wandered through Spain and possibly also Provence. In about 1160 he emigrated to Fez, Morocco; he later moved to Palestine, where he died. His writings include *Iggeret ha-Neḥamah*, a guide for forced converts to Islam.

Maimonides [Moses ben Maimon; Rambam] (1135–1204). North African philosopher and halakhist. He is commonly referred to by the name Maimonides, though his given (Hebrew) name was Moses ben Maimon; the name Rambam is derived from the title Rabbi Moses ben Maimon. He was born in Córdoba, but left the city with his family in 1148 when it was captured by the Almohades. After years of wandering, they settled in Fez. During this period he wrote treatises on the Jewish calendar, logic, and halakhah. In 1168 he completed his commentary on the Mishnah. From 1170 to 1180 he worked on the *Mishneh Torah* (also known as *Yad Ḥazakah*), a compilation of the halakhah. In 1190 he completed his philosophical study, the *Guide for the Perplexed* (*Moreh Nevukhim*), which evoked a controversy that lasted for a century; the work was accused by some of excessive rationalism, which might lead to heresy, while others supported Maimonides' views. He also wrote medical studies and became physician to the Sultan of Egypt. Maimonides exercised a profound influence on Jewish scholarship: his codification of Jewish law remained a standard guide to halakhah and he is perceived as the principal Jewish philosopher of the Middle Ages.

Maintenance. Rabbinic law decrees that on marrying a man assumes responsibility for feeding, clothing, and housing his wife, as well as other duties. If the husband neglects these obligations his wife may borrow in his credit and he is liable for the debt. By blameful conduct a wife forfeits her maintenance rights.

Mainz. City in western Germany, about 20 miles south-west of Frankfurt am Main. Jews may have lived there in Roman times. From the 10th century it became the principal Jewish community in northern Europe. In 1012 Jews were expelled from the city, but they soon returned. The Jews received the protection of the Archbishop of Mainz from the crusaders, and in 1209 the emperor granted the archbishop official rights over the Jews. At the time of the Black Death (1349) a massacre of the Jewish population took place. Expulsion edicts were subsequently issued in 1438, 1462, and 1470–71. From the 12th century the Jewish community in Mainz united with those in Speyer and Worms. These three towns were called "Shum" after their Hebrew initials.

Maisler, Binyamin *see* MAZAR, BINYAMIN.

Majority (i). According to the Bible the decision of the majority does not excuse the individual for wrongdoing and a person should not follow the majority in doing evil (Exodus 23.2). On this basis the rabbis stress that a majority should be followed only in doing good.

Majority (ii) *see* BAR MITZVAH; BAT MITZVAH.

Makhir ben Abba Mari (fl. ?14th cent.). French exegete. His *Yalkut ha-Makhiri* is a collection of aggadot on the books of the Prophets and the Hagiographa.

Makhshirim ("Predisposings"). Eighth tractate in the Mishnah order of Tohorot. It deals with the laws of ritual impurity in connection with foods which are liable to become impure when wet (Leviticus 11.34, 38).

Maki [Ha-Miphlagah ha-Kommunistit ha-Yisra'elit]. Israeli Communist Party. It was formed in 1965 when the PALESTINE COMMUNIST PARTY split into two (the other new party formed at that time was Rakaḥ).

Makkeph. Hyphen. In Hebrew two, three, or four words may be connected by hyphens. The vocalization of some words alters when they are followed by a makkeph.

Makkot ("Stripes"). Fifth tractate in the Mishnah order Nezikin. It deals with the rules that govern flogging (Deuteronomy 25.1–3), false witnesses (Deuteronomy 19.15–21), and the cities of refuge (Numbers 35.9–28).

Malabar *see* COCHIN.

Malachi (i) (fl. 5th cent. BCE). Israelite prophet. He protested against the transgression of ritual laws concerning sacrifice and tithes, and also condemned mixed marriages and divorce. His eschatology embraced a vision of the Day of the Lord preceded by the coming of Elijah. According to rabbinic tradition, he was the last of the prophets.

Malachi (ii). Biblical book, one of the books of the 12 Minor Prophets. It records the prophecies of Malachi.

Malakh ha-Mavet *see* ANGEL OF DEATH.

Malamud, Bernard (1914–1986). American novelist. He was born in New York. He taught at Oregon State University and Bennington College. A number of his novels deal with Jewish themes, including *Idiots First*, *The Assistant*, and *The Fixer*.

Malben. American charitable organization for the care of aged, sick, and handicapped immigrants in Israel. It was formed in 1950 by the American Joint Distribution Committee to relieve the Israeli government of responsibility for the maintenance of infirm immigrants. It has established old-age homes, hospitals, TB sanitoriums, sheltered workshops, and rehabilitation centers.

Malbim, Meir Leibush (1809–1879). Rabbinic scholar. He was born in Volochisk, and lived in Warsaw and Łęczyca. In 1839 he became rabbi of Wreschen, and then moved to Kempen. In 1858 he became chief rabbi of Romania. He attacked the Reform movement, was forced to leave the country, and subsequently wandered throughout Europe. He wrote a commentary on the Bible.

Malkhuyyot ("Sovereignty"). The name of the first of the three sections of the additional Amidah service on Rosh ha-Shanah (the others are Zikhronot and Shopharot). It deals with the theme of God's sovereignty.

Malsin *see* MOSER.

Malter, Henry (1864–1925). American rabbi and scholar. He was born in Bonze, Galicia. He became the librarian of the Jewish community in Berlin. In 1900 he went to the US, where he taught medieval Jewish philosophy, the Bible, and rabbinic law and literature at the Hebrew Union College, and served as the rabbi of Shearith Israel Congregation in Cincinnati. In 1909 he became a professor of talmudic literature at Dropsie College. His writings include *Saadia Gaon: his Life and Works*.

Mammeloshen (Yiddish: "mother tongue"). Colloquial expression for Yiddish.

Mamran [mamrem] (Hebrew, ? from Latin "membrana": parchment). Promissory note. First mentioned in the 12th century, the term came by the 16th century to mean the particular kind of promissory note used by Jewish merchants in their internal trade. It was a simple document. On one side was the signature of the debtor; the amount owed and the date that payment was due were written on the other side. Since it did not bear the name of the creditor, the mamran could be transferred from one person to another.

Mamre. In ancient times, an oak grove near Hebron. It was a dwelling place of Abraham (Genesis 13.18). There he learned of Lot's captivity and met the three angels (Genesis 14.13; 18.1).

Mamrem *see* MAMRAN.

Mamzer ("bastard"). Offspring of any sexual relationship forbidden in Jewish law (that is, incest or congress between a married woman and a man who is not her husband); the offspring of an unmarried woman is not a mamzer. A marriage between a mamzer and a legitimate Jew is prohibited, but two mamzerim may marry. The offspring of a mamzer and legitimate Jew is also a mamzer. *See also* ILLEGITIMACY.

Man *see* MANKIND.

Man, Son of *see* SON OF MAN.

Manasseh (i) (fl.?19th–16th cent. BCE). Israelite, first son of Joseph and Asenath (Genesis 41.50–51). One of the 12 tribes of Israel was named after him.

Manasseh (ii) (fl. 7th cent. BCE). King of Judah (698–643 BCE), son of Hezekiah. He ascended to the throne at the age of 12 (II Kings 21.1). He revoked his father's reforms and reintroduced pagan practices. According to II Kings 21.11–17, the destruction of the Temple was due to his unrighteousness. He paid tribute to Esarhaddon and Assurbanipal of Assyria. According to II Chronicles 33.11–19 he was taken captive to Babylon.

Manasseh, Prayer of. Apocryphal book consisting of a penitential psalm supposedly by Manasseh, King of Judah. According to II Chronicles 33.11 ff. Manasseh repented of his sins when he was taken to Babylonia. In this prayer he praises God's compassion for the repentant. The prayer was written by an unknown author before the beginning of the Christian era.

Manasseh ben Israel (1604–1657). Dutch rabbi. Born a Marrano in Madeira, he was taken to Amsterdam as a child. He succeeded Isaac Uziel as preacher to the Neveh Shalom congregation in 1622. In 1626 he founded the earliest Hebrew printing press in Amsterdam and proceeded to publish numerous works in Hebrew, Spanish, and Latin. He represented Jewish scholarship in the Christian world, corresponded with various gentile scholars, and was a friend of Grotius and Rembrandt. In 1655 he presented a petition to Oliver Cromwell to allow the Jews to return to England.

Manasseh ben Joseph of Ilye (1767–1831). Lithuanian talmudic scholar. He was born in Smorgon, and became a disciple of the Vilna Gaon. He was versed in both rabbinic and secular studies. In his writings he challenged the Talmud as well as Rashi's understanding of the Mishnah. An advocate of halakhic change, he was persecuted by the Orthodox. He later worked as a private teacher in Russia and Galicia, where he became acquainted with the maskilim.

Mandate, Palestine. Enabling legislation passed by the League of Nations in 1922 to create conditions in which a Jewish homeland could be established in Palestine. In 1917 the British government issued the BALFOUR DECLARATION undertaking to support the creation of a Jewish national home in Palestine. After considerable delay the Palestine Mandate was approved by the Council of the League of Nations in 1922. It stated that the Mandatory power (Britain) was responsible for placing the country under the political, administrative, and economic conditions that would secure the creation of a homeland, but also that the civil and religious rights of all those who lived in Palestine must be protected. In addition, it provided for the establishment of a Jewish Agency, a recognized public body to advise and assist in the administration of Palestine. Finally, the Mandate made provisions to facilitate Jewish immigration. The Mandate ceased to operate on 15 May 1948 with the withdrawal of the British administration.

Mandelkern, Solomon (1846–1902). German Hebrew poet and scholar, of Polish origin. He was born in Mlynow. He served as assistant to the government-appointed rabbi of Odessa from 1873 to 1880, then settled in Leipzig, where he devoted himself to research. A supporter of Ḥibbat Zion, he attended the First Zionist Congress at Basle in 1897. His publications include *Hekhal ha-Kodesh* (a Bible concordance), a history of Russia, a history of Russian literature, and a German–Russian dictionary.

Mandelstam, Osip (1891–?1938). Russian poet. He was born in Warsaw, and lived in Leningrad. In 1934 he was arrested and exiled to the eastern USSR, where he died in a prison camp. His writing is filled with Jewish self-hatred.

Mandelstamm, Benjamin (1805–1886). Lithuanian Hebrew author, brother of Leon Mandelstamm. He was born in Zagare. In the 1840s he settled in Vilnius, where he adopted an extremist stance in the Haskalah circles in which he moved. Critical of Russian Jewish life, he advocated governmental intervention to forbid the printing of the Talmud, remove kabbalistic and Ḥasidic works from circulation, and dissolve the traditional ḥeder system.

Mandelstamm, Leon (1819–1889). Russian writer, of Lithuanian origin, brother of Benjamin Mandelstamm. He was born in Zagare. He studied at St. Petersburg University and was the first Jew to enrol in a Russian university. In 1846 he was appointed to take charge of Jewish affairs in the ministry of education and to establish a network of governmental schools for Jews; he also supervised the Jewish ḥeder and Talmud Torah schools, and prepared Jewish textbooks. His work obliged him to travel throughout the Pale of Settlement. Dismissed from his post in 1857, he lived in Germany, where he engaged in trade and contracting. He eventually returned to Russia and lived in St. Petersburg.

Mandelstamm, Max Emanuel (1839–1912). Russian ophthalmologist and Zionist, of Lithuanian origin, nephew of Benjamin and Leon Mandelstamm. He was born in Zagare. He opened a clinic in Kiev, where his practice flourished, and lectured in ophthalmology at Kiev University. A founder of the Ḥibbat Zion movement in Russia, he became an associate of Theodor Herzl. At the Seventh Zionist Congress, he participated in the Founding Conference of the Jewish Territorial Organization. He was the head of the emigration office established by the Territorialists in Kiev to organize the emigration of Jews to Galveston, Texas *see* GALVESTON PLAN).

Mané-Katz (1894–1962). French artist. He was born in Russia, moved to France in 1921, and later lived in the US. His early subjects included biblical scenes and figures from the ghetto. There is a museum dedicated to his paintings in Haifa.

***Manetho** (fl. 3rd cent. BCE). Greco-Egyptian historian. He was born in Sebennytos, Egypt, and served as a priest in Heliopolis. His history of Egypt gives an account of the expulsion of the Hyksos from Egypt. He wrote that they crossed the desert on their way to Syria, and in Judea built a town called Jerusalem. Although he did not mention the Jews by name, scholars believe he was referring to them. He also mentioned Osarsiph, a former priest of Heliopolis and the leader of a group of lepers, whom he identified with Moses.

Manger, Itzik (1901–1969). Yiddish poet, dramatist, and novelist. He was born in Czernowitz, and lived in Germany as a child. He learned Yiddish in Romania and published ballads and plays, which were influenced by German lyricists and such writers as Eliakum Zunser. During and after World War II he lived in London, later moving to the US. He finally settled in Israel.

Mani Leib [Brahinski, Mani Leib] (1883–1953). American Yiddish poet and journalist. He was born in Russia and emigrated to the US in 1905. He served on the editorial staff of *Forverts* from 1916 to 1953 and edited a number of journals of the Yiddish literary movement Di Yunge. He translated several Russian novels into Yiddish and published poems in Di Yunge's periodicals and anthologies. His ballads and tales for children were sung and recited in Yiddish schools.

Mankind. According to the Bible, men and women are part of God's creation. They have responsibility for all created things, and are free moral agents. Through the covenant with Israel, God created a special bond between himself and human beings. The Bible views the human person as an indivisible whole, but the rabbis assert that each individual consists of a body and soul and is driven by both a good and an evil inclination. The kabbalah envisages humans as closely linked to the divine and their life as vital to the entire cosmos.

Mankowitz, Wolf (b. 1924). English author. He was born in London, where he became an antique dealer. He wrote various books inspired by his childhood in the East End of London. His publications include *A Kid for Two Farthings*, *Make me an Offer*, *The Boychick*, and *The Mendelman Fire*.

Mann, Jacob (1888–1940). American scholar. He was born in Galicia. He studied in London, and subsequently taught history at the Hebrew Union College in Cincinnati. He utilized genizah material in a series of studies on the history and literature of the gaonic period. His publications include *The Jews of Palestine and Egypt under the Fatimids*, *Texts and Studies in Jewish History and Literarure*, and *The Bible as Read and Preached in the Old Synagogue*.

Manna. Food eaten by the Israelites in the desert (Exodus 16.4–35). It was discovered on the ground every morning except the Sabbath; a double portion was left on the day before the Sabbath. It was thin and white, and tasted like honey cake.

Manne, Mordecai Tzevi (1859–1886). Lithuanian Hebrew lyric poet and artist. He was born near Vilnius, and studied art there. In 1880 he became a student at the Academy of Arts in St. Petersburg, and began to write poems and articles. He later went to Warsaw, where he designed the covers for anthologies of works by Naḥum Sokolow and Saul Phinehas Rabinowitz. His poem *Masat Nafshi* expresses his longing for Palestine.

Mannheimer, Isaac Noah (1793–1865). Austrian preacher and liturgist. He was born in Copenhagen, where he taught religion and held services for adherents of Reform Judaism. In 1824 he became a preacher at the new Seitenstetten Synagogue in Vienna. He later adopted a more Conservative approach to Reform Judaism, and created a moderate Reform liturgy; he also translated the prayerbook and the festival prayers into German. In 1848 he was elected to the Reichstag, where he advocated Jewish rights.

Man of Lies. Character who is described in the Dead Sea Scrolls as the opponent of the Teacher of Righteousness. He is said knowingly to have perverted the meaning of the law.

Mantino, Jacob (d. 1549). Italian physician and translator, of Spanish origin. He practiced medicine in Bologna, Verona, and Venice. During the debate on the annulment of the marriage of Henry VIII of England and Catharine of Aragon, he opposed Henry's supporters. He thus earned the gratitude of Pope Clement VII, by whose influence he was appointed lecturer in medicine at Bologna University. In 1533 he was invited by the pope to Rome, where he took a stand against the messianic claims of Solomon Molcho. The following year he was appointed personal physician to Pope Paul III, and became professor of practical medicine at the Sapienza in Rome. His scholarly work included translations of philosophical works from Hebrew into Latin.

Mantua. City in northern Italy. There was a Jewish settlement there in the 12th century. In the 14th century groups of Jewish loan-bankers from Italy and Germany were authorized to operate in the city. The Jewish community flourished during the Renaissance: a printing press was established in 1476, and Leone de' Sommi led a Jewish theater group at court; Jewish musicians, including Salomone de' Rossi, and enlightened scholars, such as Azariah dei Rossi, also lived in the city. A ghetto was imposed on the Jewish community in 1612, but Mantua nevertheless continued to be an important Jewish center.

Manual of Discipline *see* DISCIPLINE SCROLL.

Manufacturers' Association of Israel. Israeli organization, representing the interests of industrialists. Founded in 1923, it aims to improve production and efficiency, protect home industries, encourage investment, and organize exhibitions by local manufacturers.

Manuscripts. Early manuscripts of Hebrew sources include the Dead Sea Scrolls, manuscripts from the Cairo Genizah, and the Nash Papyrus. The oldest complete manuscript of the Hebrew Bible is the Codex Petropolitanus from the 10th century. Numerous Hebrew manuscripts of European origin have survived from the 12th century onward, containing all kinds of literature. With the advent of Hebrew printing in 1475 manuscripts ceased to play such an important role. Great collectors of Hebrew manuscripts include David Oppenheim, G. B. de' Rossi, Elkan Nathan Adler, David Kaufmann, and David Solomon Sassoon. Important collections are held in the libraries of Oxford and Cambridge universities, the British Museum, the Bibliothèque Nationale, the Vatican and Parma Libraries, and the library of the Jewish Theological Seminary of America.

Maot ḥittim ("wheat monies"). Collections made before Passover to ensure that there is a supply of flour for unleavened bread for the poor. The maot ḥittim was a compulsory community tax from the period of the Talmud. In modern times the term denotes a collection of charitable donations to provide for all the holiday needs of the poor at Passover.

Maoz tzur ("O fortress, rock [of my salvation]"). Opening words of a hymn sung in the Ashkenazi ritual in the synagogue and at home after the kindling of the Ḥanukkah lights. The song originated in Germany in the 13th century and was composed by a poet named Mordecai.

Mapai. Israeli labor party. It was formed in 1930 by the union of Ha-Poel ha-Tzair with Aḥdut ha-Avodah. In the diaspora, the World Conference of Poale Zion merged with the Tzeire Zion in 1931, and Mapai entered the Second International.

In 1935 it became the most important party in the Zionist Organization. In 1965 the party split and dissidents led by David Ben-Gurion founded the Rafi party. In 1968 Mapai merged with Aḥdut ha-Avodah and Rafi to form the Israel Labor Party.

Mapam. Israeli socialist party. It was formed in 1948 by the fusion of Ha-Shomer ha-Tzair and Aḥdut ha-Avodah–Poale Zion. Marxist in orientation, it stressed the importance of class conflict and initially sought an alliance with the Soviet bloc. In 1954 Aḥdut ha-Avodah–Poale Zion seceded from Mapam, and later a small group under Mosheh Sneh also broke away and joined Maki.

Maphtir ("one who concludes"). Term referring both to the person who concludes the reading in the synagogue and to the reading itself. The maphtir first reads a portion of the Torah (usually a repetition of the last three verses of the portion assigned for the day) and then the HAPHTARAH.

Mappah ("cloth"). The fabric strip used as a binder round a Torah scroll. The term is also used of the decorated cover of the reading desk in the synagogue. The term was used by Moses Isserles as the title of his commentary on the Shulḥan Arukh.

Mappik. The dagesh (diacritical mark) inside the letter at the end of a word. It shows that the letter is sounded as h.

Mapu, Abraham (1808–1867). Lithuanian Hebrew novelist. He worked as a children's tutor and lived in various towns, including Slobodka, Georgenberg, Kovno, Rossyieny, and Vilnius. His *Ahavat Tziyyon* is a historical romance set in the period of Hezekiah. In *Alyit Tzavua* he satirized contemporary Lithuanian Jews. His other novels include *Ashmat Shomron* and *Ḥozeh Ḥezyonot.*

Mar ("Master"). Title given to some Babylonian amoraim and especially to exilarchs.

Marbitz Torah *see* RABBI (i).

Marcus, David [Stone, Mickey] (1902–1948). American soldier. He was born in New York. He served in the US Attorney-General's Office, and later as Commissioner of Correction in New York. He joined the army, and was appointed head of its War Crimes Branch. In 1948 he was David Ben-Gurion's military adviser, taking the name Mickey Stone. In the same year he became commander of the Jerusalem front. He was killed by a sentry during the Israeli War of Independence.

Marcus, Jacob Rader (b. 1896). American rabbi and historian. He was born in Connellsville, Pennsylvania. He taught history from 1920 at the Hebrew Union College, where he founded the American Jewish Archives. He published numerous studies of American Jewry.

Marcus, Ralph (1900–1956). American scholar of Hellenistic Judaism. He was born in San Francisco. He taught at the Jewish Institute of Religion at Columbia University, and at the University of Chicago. He edited, translated, and annotated four volumes of the works of Josephus and two of those of Philo in the Loeb Classical Library series.

Marduk *see* MERODACH.

Margolin, Eliezer (1874–1944). Australian military commander. He was born in Belgorod, Russia. He moved to Palestine in 1892 and settled in Reḥovot. In 1900 he went to Austrialia and he served in the Australian army during World War I, later commanding the Second Battalion of the Jewish Regiment. In 1919 he became commander of the Jewish Legion. When the legion was dismantled, he became commander of the Jewish unit of the Palestine Defense Force. Subsequently he returned to Australia.

Margoliouth, David Samuel (1858–1940). English classical scholar and orientalist. He was born in London, and became a professor of Arabic at Oxford University. He published studies in the fields of Islamic history and literature, and edited medieval Arabic texts. His writings include *The Origin of the "Hebrew Original" of Ecclesiasticus*, and *Relations between Arabs and Israelites prior to the Rise of Islam.*

***Margoliouth, George** (1853–1952). English bibliographer. He converted to Christianity and became a priest. He was in charge of the Hebrew, Syriac, and Ethiopic manuscripts in the British Museum from 1891 to 1914. His publications include *The Liturgy of the Nile, The Palestine Syriac Version of the Holy Scriptures*, and *Catalogue of the Hebrew and Samaritan Manuscripts in the British Museum.*

Margolis, Max Leopold (1886–1932). American biblical and Semitic scholar. He was born in Russia, and went to the US in 1889. He taught at the Hebrew Union College, and in 1897 went to the University of California at Berkeley to teach Semitic languages. He then returned to the Hebrew Union College, but resigned in 1910, to become professor of biblical philology at Dropsie College. He supervised the translation of the Bible published by the Jewish Publication Society of America, and collaborated with Alexander Marx on the *History of the Jewish People.*

Margoshes, Samuel (1887–1968). American Yiddish journalist. He was born in Galicia, and went to the US in 1905. He engaged in communal, educational, and relief activities before, during, and after World War I. Later he served as editor of the New York Yiddish daily, *Dertog* (1926–42). He supported Zionism in the US and took an active role in the American Jewish Congress and Zionist activities.

Margulies, Berl *see* BRODER, BERL.

Marḥeshvan [Ḥeshvan]. Second month of the Jewish year (eighth of the civil year); it is often shortened to Ḥeshvan. The name dates from post-exilic times and replaced the earlier name Bul (I Kings 6.38).

Mari. Ancient Mesopotamian city; its site is close to the modern town of Tell Ḥarīrī. Archeological and epigraphical discoveries made there cast light on the history of Mesopotamia and Upper Syria, as well as on the formative stages of Israelite history.

Mariamne (?60–29 BCE). Israelite queen, daughter of Alexander (son of Aristobulus II) and granddaughter of John Hyrcanus. She was the second wife of Herod the Great, though she hated him because he had killed nearly all the members of her family, and had replaced her own dynasty (the Hasmoneans) with his own. Herod eventually put her to death.

Mariamne II (d. c. 20 BCE). Israelite queen, daughter of the high priest Simeon ben Boethus. She was the third wife of Herod the Great. Her son, also Herod, was designated to succeed to the throne after Antipater III (Herod the Great's son by his first wife, Doris). Although Mariamne knew of Antipater's intentions to kill his father, she held her peace because of the succession. When Antipater's plot was discovered, Herod divorced her and expunged her son's name from his will.

Marinoff, Jacob (1869–1964). American Yiddish poet and editor. He was born in Russia. He moved to London, where he worked in a tailor's shop (1891–93), then emigrated to the US and settled in Denver. From 1895 he contributed poems to Yiddish periodicals. He was a co-founder of the journal *Der groyser kundas* in 1909 and served as its editor.

Markfield, Wallace (b. 1926). American

novelist. He was born in Brooklyn. His publications include *To an Early Grave*, *Teitelbaum's Window*, and *You could Live if they Let you*.

Markish, David (b. 1938). Israeli novelist, of Russian origin. He settled in Israel in 1972 and has worked as a novelist and journalist. His publications include *The World of Simon Ashkenazy*, *The Jewters*, *The Dog*, *In the Shade of the Great Rock*, and *The Crimson Well*.

Markish, Peretz (1895–1952). Ukrainian Yiddish poet, novelist, and playwright. Born in Volhynia, he left Russia in 1921 and lived in Poland and France. From 1921 to 1926 he wrote poetry about the anti-Jewish pogroms in the Ukraine. In 1926 he returned to the USSR, where he published epic poems and novels. He was accused of Jewish nationalism and executed.

Markon, Isaac Dov Ber (1875–1949). Russian scholar and librarian. Born in Rybinsk on the Volga, he was a professor of Jewish studies at the University of St. Petersburg, and later professor at the Belorussian University at Minsk. In 1926 he settled in Berlin. Expelled from Germany in 1938, he went to Holland and then England, where he joined the Montefiore College in Ramsgate. His publications deal with Karaite history and literature and associated topics.

Marks, David Woolf (1811–1909). English Reform minister. He served as the minister of the London Reform synagogue for nearly 70 years.

Marks, Simon, Baron (1888–1964). English industrialist and philanthropist. He was born in Manchester. He became chairman of the board of Marks and Spencer Ltd. chain-stores in 1917. He was an active Zionist and served as secretary of the Zionist delegation to the Versailles Peace Conference. Later he became chairman of the Keren ha-Yesod Committee, vice-president of the Zionist Federation, and a member of the executive of the Zionist Organization.

Marmorek, Alexander (1865–1923). French bacteriologist and Zionist leader. He was born in Mielnice, Galicia. He became assistant and later senior researcher at the Pasteur Institute in Paris. He was an associate of Theodor Herzl, and served as a member of the Zionist General Council at the first 11 Zionist congresses. He was a co-founder of the Paris Zionist monthly *L'écho Sioniste*.

Marmorek, Oscar (1863–1909). Austrian architect and Zionist leader. He was born in Skala, Galicia. He built important buildings in Vienna and Austria, and designed synagogues based on old Jewish architecture. After the publication of Theodor Herzl's *Der Judenstaat*, Marmorek joined Herzl and was elected to the executive of the Zionist Organization at the first six Zionist congresses. He was a co-founder of the Zionist weekly *Die Welt*.

Marmorstein, Arthur (1882–1946). British rabbi, scholar, and teacher. He was born in Miskolc, Hungary, and served as a rabbi at Jamnitz, Czechoslovakia. From 1912 he taught at Jews College in London. His publications embrace a wide range of Jewish topics and include *Doctrine of Merits in Old Rabbinic Literature* and *Old Rabbinic Doctrine of God*.

Maror ("bitter herb"). Generic term for a bitter-tasting herb. The children of Israel were commanded to eat maror with unleavened bread at the Passover celebration in remembrance of the bitterness of slavery (Exodus 12.8; Numbers 9.11). A bitter herb is still eaten during the Passover seder.

***Marr, Wilhelm** (1818–1904). German writer. He was born in Hamburg and published various anti-Jewish works. In 1879 he introduced the word "anti-

Semite" into the political vocabulary by founding the League of Anti-Semites.

Marranos (Hebrew "Anusim": the coerced) [New Christians]. Term applied in Spain and Portugal to the descendants of baptized Jews suspected of adhering to Judaism. They became numerous in Spain after the Jewish massacres of 1391 and after the Dominican campaign at the beginning of the 15th century. It was partly to deal with such individuals that the Inquisition was introduced into Spain in 1480. Similarly in Portugal the forced conversions in 1497 led to an increase in the number of Marranos, whose heretical tendencies were suppressed by the Inquisition, introduced in 1540. Many Marranos fled to Italy, north Africa, and Turkey, and large groups later settled in the Netherlands, the West Indies, and North America.

Marriage. The Bible stipulates that it is necessary for the human race to reproduce and ensure its continuance. Thus the first commandment of God to man in the Bible is "be fruitful and multiply" (Genesis 1.22); men are obligated to marry to fulfil this commandment. According to Judaism there are two stages in the marriage ceremony: betrothal ("erusin" or "kiddushin") and marriage ("nissuim"). Betrothal is the ceremony at which a woman is promised as the wife of the betrother. The ceremony must take place before witnesses and can be contracted in three ways: by money; by deed; or by sexual intercourse (committed in private but with the knowledge of the witnesses). The second stage is "marriage," which involves bringing the woman into the home in order to live a marital life with her. Until the 10th century, when monogamy became legally binding, the Jews practiced polygamy. In modern Jewish tradition marriage continues to be a social, moral, and religious ideal.

Mar Samuel *see* SAMUEL (iii).

Marshalik (Yiddish). Name given to a jester at eastern European weddings. He sang humorous songs and announced the gifts in verse.

Marshall, Louis (1856–1929). American lawyer and communal leader. He was born in Syracuse, New York, and became a partner in the New York legal firm of Guggenheimer, Untermyer, and Marshall. He was the chief spokesman for the German-Jewish elite in Jewish affairs. In 1912 he became president of the American Jewish Committee. He also served as president of Temple Emanu-El in New York, and chairman of the board of directors of the Jewish Theological Seminary. During World War I he was president of the American Jewish Relief Committee.

***Marti, Karl** (1855–1925). Swiss biblical scholar. He taught at Basle University and later became a professor of Semitic philology in Berne. His publications include critical studies on the books of Jeremiah and Zechariah, and a concise grammar of biblical Aramaic.

Marti, Raymund *see* MARTINI, RAYMUND.

Martin, David (b. 1915). Australian poet and novelist. He was born in Hungary. He fought in the Spanish Civil War, then lived in London from 1938. In 1949 he moved to Sydney, where he became editor of the *Sydney Jewish News*. His novel *The Shepherd and the Hunter* deals with the Palestine problem in the 1940s, and *Where a Man Belongs* discusses various aspects of modern Jewish life.

***Martinez, Ferrand** (fl. 14th cent.). Spanish priest, Archdeacon of Écija. In sermons preached in public in Seville, he demanded that the synagogues in the city should be destroyed and the Jews confined to their own quarter. He later secured the right of jurisdiction over the Jews of Seville and its environs, and demanded their expulsion. As a result of his agitation, riots broke out throughout Castile and spread to Aragon.

***Martini** [Marti], **Raymund** (1220–1285). Spanish Dominican friar and polemicist. He was born in Subirat, Catalonia. He participated in the Disputation of Barcelona in 1263, which involved debates between Naḥmanides and representatives of the Church. In 1264 he was appointed a member of the first censorship commission to examine Jewish books. His *Pugio fidei* is an anti-Jewish polemic.

Martyrs. Prominent among early Jewish martyrs were the seven sons of Hannah, killed by Antiochus IV Epiphanes during the Hasmonean revolt (166–164 BCE). In the early rabbinic period the Ten Martyrs were killed during the Bar Kokhba revolt of 132 BCE. According to rabbinic Judaism a martyr is someone who dies willingly for the Jewish faith and thereby achieves the sanctification of the divine name ("Kiddush ha-Shem"). During the Middle Ages regulations governing the ways in which martyrs should comport themselves and the benedictions they were to recite were formulated by the rabbis.

Martyrs Forest. Plantation in the Judean mountains to commemorate the Jews who perished under the Nazis. It was initiated in 1951 by the Jewish National Fund, which succeeded in planting a memorial forest of six million trees.

Marx, Alexander (1878–1953). German historian, bibliographer, and librarian. He was born in Elberfeld, Germany, and emigrated to the US in 1903. He served as librarian and taught history at the Jewish Theological Seminary. He published studies of bibliography and history, and collaborated with Max Margolis on the *History of the Jewish People*.

***Marx, Karl** (1818–1883). German social philosopher, founder of modern communism. He was born in Trier, and converted to Protestantism at the age of six. He was the editor of the Cologne daily, *Rheinische Zeitung*. He moved to Paris in 1843, and then went to Brussels. In 1848 he and Friedrich Engels published *The Communist Manifesto*. In 1849 he settled in London, where he wrote *Das Kapital*. In his writings he expressed hostility towards Jews and Judaism.

Mar Zutra *see* ZUTRA, MAR.

Masada. Stronghold on a rock near the Dead Sea. It was the refuge of Herod the Great in 40 BCE, when it was unsuccessfully besieged by Antigonus Mattathias. Herod later built a palace there. In the Jewish war against Rome (66–70) and afterwards, it served as a Zealot fortress; in 73 a garrison of nearly 1000 Jews committed suicide there rather than be captured by the Romans.

Masekhet [massekhet] (*lit.* "woven fabric"). Term applied to a traetate of the Mishnah or Talmud. *See also* MEKHILTA.

Mashal *see* FABLE.

Mashgiaḥ ("supervisor"). Overseer who supervises the observance of the laws of kashrut.

Mashiaḥ *see* MESSIAH.

Mashiv ha-ruaḥ u-morid ha-gashem ("who causes the wind to blow and the rain to fall"). Phrase in the Amidah prayer added to the second of the benedictions. It is recited during the winter season from the last day of Sukkot until the last day of Passover. A variant ("who causes the dew to descend") is recited during the summer months in Israel; elsewhere it is used in the Sephardi ritual only.

Maskil *see* HASKALAH.

Masliansky, Tzevi Hirsch (1856–1943). Polish-American preacher. He was born in Slutsk, Belorussia, and taught at the Polish Talmud Torah and at the yeshivah of Pinsk. Active in Ḥibbat Zion, he left the country in 1894, and undertook a lecture tour of central and western

Europe. In 1895 he settled in New York where he helped to popularize Zionism through Friday evening sermons at the Educational Alliance on East Broadway.

Masorah [massorah]. Body of rules, principles, and traditions developed in the 6th–9th centuries by textual scholars, known as "masoretes," in order to preserve the authentic text of the Hebrew Bible. The masoretes divided the biblical text into words and sentences as well as into segments of verse length. They added vowel signs to the Hebrew words and cantillation marks indicating the articulation and inflections of the text for chanting. They also indicated those cases where the written form of the word ("ketiv") differs from the pronunciation or even the actual word used when the text is read aloud ("keri"). In addition they corrected spellings. The accepted text of the Bible is that determined by Aaron ben Asher of the Tiberias school of Masoretes.

Massadah. Israeli publishing house. Founded by Meir and Berakhah Peli in Tel Aviv in 1931, it has published encyclopedias and the works of Yoseph Klausner, David Shimoni, and Asher Barash.

Massekhet *see* MASEKHET.

Massorah *see* MASORAH.

Matate. Theater company founded in Tel Aviv in 1928. It produced plays which satirized various aspects of life in Israel. It was disbanded in 1954.

Mater synagogae *see* PATER SYNAGOGAE.

Mathematics. Jews engaged in mathematical studies from the early medieval period. In the 12th century such scholars as Abraham ibn Ezra and Abraham bar Ḥiyya made important contributions, and later Jacob ben Maskhir, Levi ben Gershon, and Immanuel ben Jacob of Tarascon added their discoveries. In the 15th century Simeon ibn Motot invented the pure equation of the 3rd and 4th degrees and solved the problem of asymptotes. Modern mathematics is indebted to the work of numerous Jewish mathematicians.

Matmid ("one who persists"). A scholar devoted to the study of the Talmud.

Matriarchs. The wives – Sarah, Rebekah, Leah, and Rachel – of the three patriarchs.

Matrimony *see* MARRIAGE.

Matsa, Joseph (1919–1986). Greek scholar and Hebrew folklorist. He was born in Ioannina and taught Greek literature at a high school there. His publications include *The Hebrew Songs of the Jannina Jews* and *The Names of the Jews of Ioannina.*

***Matsas, Nestoras** (b. 1932). Greek author, painter, and film director. Born in Athens, he was baptized into the Greek Orthodox Church during the Nazi occupation. Some of his stories and novels deal with Jewish themes.

Mattan Torah ("giving of the law"). Term applied to the giving of the law by God to Moses on Mount Sinai.

Mattaniah *see* ZEDEKIAH (i).

Mattathias (fl. 2nd cent. BCE). Israelite priest and rebel leader. He was priest of Modiin and led the uprising of the Hasmoneans against Antiochus IV in 166–164 BCE. He led the revolt in the Judean hills, waging war on the Syrians. He was succeeded by his son Judah Maccabee.

Mattathias ha-Yitzhari (fl. 14th–15th cent.). Spanish scholar. A pupil of Ḥasdai Crescas, he wrote a commentary on Psalm 119, a commentary on Avot, and homiletical explanations of the Pentateuch. He played a role in the Disputation of Tortosa in 1413–15, representing the Zaragoza community.

Mattuck, Israel Isidor (1883–1954). British Liberal rabbi, of Lithuanian origin. He went to the US as a child and served as a rabbi in Far Rockaway, New York, and Lincoln, Nebraska. In 1911 he became the leader of the Liberal Jewish Synagogue in London. He served as chairman of the World Union of Progressive Judaism. His writings include *What are the Jews?*, *Essentials of Liberal Judaism*, *Jewish Ethics*, and *Thoughts of the Prophets*.

Matyah ben Harash (fl. 2nd cent.). Palestinian tanna. He left Palestine after the Hadrianic persecutions of 135–8 and settled in Rome, where he founded a rabbinical academy.

Matzah *see* PASSOVER.

Matzevah. Monument. The word is usually used of a gravestone.

Mausoleum. Large stately tomb. Tombs marked by freestanding monuments were common in Palestine in the Hellenistic period. From the Middle Ages mausoleums were rare in Jewish communities, but they were reintroduced in the 19th century in the US.

Mavdil *see* HA-MAVDIL.

Maybaum, Ignaz (1897–1976). British Reform rabbi and theologian. Born in Vienna, he was a rabbi in Bingen, Frankfurt an der Oder, and Berlin. In 1939 he settled in England and served as a rabbi in London. He also lectured on theology and homiletics at Leo Baeck College. His writings include *Synagogue and Society*, *Jewish Mission*, *Jewish Existence*, *The Future of the Jewish Diaspora*, and *The Face of God after Auschwitz*.

Mayer, Leo Ari (1895–1959). Israeli orientalist. He was born in Stanislav in the Ukraine. He moved to Palestine in 1921 and became inspector of antiquities, and librarian and keeper of records for the Department of Antiquities. From 1932 to 1958 he was professor of Near Eastern art and archeology at the Hebrew University. He published works on Islamic art, costume, epigraphy, and numismatics.

Mayer, Sigmund (1831–1920). Austrian merchant and writer. He was born in Pressburg, Hungary. He became active in efforts to defend Jewish interests in Austria. His publications include *A Jewish Merchant* and *The Viennese Jews: Commerce, Culture, and Politics*.

May Laws. A group of laws, enacted on 3 May 1882 by the Russian government, to prohibit Jews from living or acquiring property except in the Pale of Settlement. This legislation resulted in local expulsions, overcrowding, and economic restrictions. The May Laws were officially revoked in 1917.

Mayzel [Meisel]**, Naḥman** (1887–1966). Polish Yiddish writer. From 1921 he edited Yiddish periodicals in Warsaw. He emigrated to New York in 1937 and became the central figure of the Yiddish cultural society Yiddisher Kultur Farband, and editor of its monthly journal, *Yiddisher kultur*. He wrote studies of Jewish life in Poland and Russia. In 1964 he settled in Israel.

Mazar [Maisler]**, Binyamin** (b. 1906). Israeli archeologist and historian. He was born in Ciechanowiec in Poland, and settled in Palestine in 1929. In 1951 he became professor of the history of the Jewish people in the biblical period and the archeology of Palestine at the Hebrew University. In 1952 he became rector of the university, and the following year president. He directed various archeological excavations. His publications include numerous archeological studies, a historical atlas of the country, and a history of Palestine up to the period of the monarchy.

Mazzal. Constellation. By astrological association the term refers to luck.

Mazzal tov ("Good luck"). Phrase used as a greeting on festive occasions.

Mazzik ("one who causes harm"). In Jewish folklore a demon; it is synonymous with "shed" (demon), and "ruaḥ" (evil spirit). It connotes the dangerous and harmful nature of demons.

Meal offering (Hebrew "minḥah"). A sacrificial offering made with flour. The various types of meal offering are described in Leviticus 2. Made with oil and seasoned with salt, they were either unbaked, baked in an oven or on a griddle, cooked, or parched with fire. Part was left on the altar, and the rest was given to the priests.

Meassephim. Name adopted by the contributors to the Hebrew monthly, *Ha-Measseph*. The journal was founded in 1783 by Isaac Euchel, M. M. Bresselau, and the Friedländer brothers. It was published in Königsberg (1784–6), Berlin (1788–90), Breslau (1794–7), and in Berlin, Altona, and Dessau (1809–11). It published poetry, essays, interpretations of biblical passages, explanations of grammar, historical studies, and book reviews.

Mechaieh (Yiddish). Pleasure, enjoyment.

Medad *see* ELDAD.

Medals. The midrash contains a fanciful account of medals struck to honor the patriarchs. The first modern medal was made for the physician Benjamin ben Elijah Beer in the 16th century. In the 16th century medals were made for important Jewish families. A medal with a portrait and Hebrew inscription was struck in 1735 when Eliezer Brody was appointed rabbi of Amsterdam. At the end of the 18th century medals were made on historic occasions or to honor important figures. A number of Jews were awarded medals for their services to the Jewish community by the governments who had employed them to further the causes of Emancipation and integration. In modern times medals have been issued in Israel by the coins and medals department of the Prime Minister's Office.

Media. Ancient Asiatic country in the eastern and north-eastern region of Mesopotamia. According to the Bible, the Medes were the sons of Japheth. They cooperated with the Babylonians in the 6th century, but in spite of this alliance they were defeated by Cyrus II of Persia.

Medicine. The Bible records the existence of physicians during the period of the first Temple (Jeremiah 8.22), and the Talmud contains extensive medical information. In the Middle Ages Jews often served as court physicians, and Jewish scholars translated Greco-Arabic medical treatises. Jewish physicians of this period included Asaph, Shabbetai Donnolo, Isaac Israeli, and Maimonides. In the Renaissance noted Jewish physicians were active in western Europe, but various restrictions meant that there were fewer prominent Jewish physicians in the 17th–18th centuries. After the Emancipation Jews made major contributions to medical science.

Medigo, Joseph Solomon ben Elijah del *see* DELMEDIGO, JOSEPH SOLOMON BEN ELIJAH.

Medina (i). Country or neighborhood.

Medina (ii). Ancient town in the fertile valley of the Hejaz in northern Arabia. When Mohammed settled there in 622 it had the largest Jewish community in that region of Arabia. The Jews formed three tribes: Banu-l-Nadir, Banu Kainuka, and Banu Kuraiza. Several years after Mohammed's arrival, all the Jews there were expelled or massacred.

Medini, Ḥayyim Hezekiah (1832–1904). Palestinian rabbi. He was born in Jerusalem. From 1867 to 1899 he was a rabbi in Karasubazar in the Crimean peninsula. He subsequently moved to Palestine and settled in Hebron, where he founded a yeshivah. His *Sede Ḥemed* is a halakhic encyclopedia.

Medzibozh. Village in Podolia, Russia. When the Baal Shem Tov settled there in the 18th century, it became a center of the Ḥasidic movement.

Megged, Aharon (b. 1920). Israeli writer and editor. He was born in Włocławek, Poland, and went to Palestine in 1926 with his family. In 1950 he settled in Tel Aviv, where he edited the journal *Ba-Sha'ar* and was a founder of the literary magazine *Massa*. From 1960 to 1971 he was Israel's cultural attaché in London. His stories and novels depict modern life in Israel.

Megiddo. Ancient fortified town in the Valley of Jezreel in Israel. It was the scene of numerous battles, including Deborah's victory over the Canaanites in the 12th century BCE and Josiah's defeat by the Egyptians (7th century BCE). Encounters also took place there in the reign of Tilgath Pileser III (8th century BCE) and during the Jewish war against the Romans (66–70).

Megillah (i). Scroll. Parchment scrolls were the traditional form of books in the ancient world. Letters were also written on scrolls. Biblical books used in the synagogue still take this form, notably the Scroll of the Law from which the Torah portions are read. In its plural form, "megillot," the word is used specifically to refer to five biblical books: the Song of Songs, Ruth, Lamentations, Ecclesiastes, and Esther.

Megillah (ii) ("Scroll"). Tenth tractate in the Mishnah order of Moed. It deals with the reading of the Scroll of Esther on Purim and enumerates scriptural readings for special Sabbaths, festivals, and fast days. It also contains regulations for the care of synagogues and holy objects.

Megillat Taanit ("Scroll of the fast"). Early tannaitic work compiled at the beginning of the 1st century. It lists the 36 days that commemorate miracles and joyous events and on which it is forbidden to fast.

Meḥitzah ("partition"). Screen in the synagogue separating men from women during public prayer. In Jewish law it is also a technical term for the partition, fence, or wall which creates a separate domain.

Meḥuttan. Relative by marriage. The term also denotes a wedding guest.

Meijer, Jacob (b. 1912). Dutch historian, author, and poet. He was born in Winschoten, and taught history at the Jewish Lyceum in Amsterdam in 1941–3. He was deported to Bergen-Belsen in 1944. After the war he taught history in Amsterdam, and later in Haarlem. He published studies of the pre-war history of the Jews of the Netherlands.

Me'il ("mantle"). The term used for the richly embroidered cloth covering in which a Scroll of the Law is wrapped.

Me'ilah (i) *see* SACRILEGE.

Me'ilah (ii) ("Trespass"). Eighth tractate in the Mishnah order of Kodashim. It deals with the laws concerning trespass in the sense of using things consecrated for holy use in a profane way (Leviticus 5.15–16).

Meir (fl. 2nd cent.). Palestinian tanna. A pupil of Akiva, he was a member of the Sanhedrin at Usha after the Hadrianic persecutions. He was sometimes known as RABBI MEIR BAAL HA-NES. His Mishnah was one of the main sources of the Mishnah of Judah ha-Nasi. His wife, Beruryah, was also an outstanding scholar.

Meir [Meyerson]**, Golda** (1898–1978). Israeli politician. She was born in Kiev, and emigrated to the US in 1906. In 1921 she settled in Palestine. Active in Labor Zionism, she held important positions in the Histadrut and the Jewish Agency. After the establishment of the State of Israel in 1948, she was appointed minister to Moscow. In 1949 she was elected to the Knesset as a member for Mapai. Later she was minister of labor in sucessive governments, and from 1956 to 1966 she served as foreign minister. She was prime minister from 1969 to 1974.

Meir, Yaakov (1856–1939). Palestinian rabbi. Born in Jerusalem, he was a Zionist and advocated the revival of spoken Hebrew. In 1906 he was elected Ḥakham Bashi. From 1908 to 1919 he served as chief rabbi of Salonica, and in 1921 he became Sephardi chief rabbi in Palestine.

Meir Baal ha-Nes, Rabbi ("Rabbi Meir the miracle worker"). Appellation applied to Meir because of miracles he performed. Traditional charity boxes in the diaspora for collecting funds for poor Jews in Palestine were called after him.

Meir ben Gedaliah of Lublin *see* LUBLIN, MEIR BEN GEDALIAH OF.

Meir ben Isaac Nehorai (fl. 11th cent.). German religious poet. He lived in Worms and wrote hymns, including the acrostic poem Akdamut. According to tradition he was killed by the crusaders in 1096.

Meir ben Samuel (c. 1060–c. 1135). French tosaphist, son-in-law of Rashi. He lived with Rashi in Troyes, but later moved to Ramerupt where he founded a bet midrash. He wrote commentaries to the Talmud. Halakhic statements by him were quoted by his son Jacob Tam in his writings.

Meiri, Menaḥem ben Solomon, of Perpignan (1249–1316). French talmudist. He was born in Perpignan. He was a participant in Solomon ben Adret's polemic against Maimonides, which led to Adret's excommunicating any person who read philosophical works in his youth. Later Meiri disassociated himself from Adret, and supported freedom of thought for the scholars of every country. He wrote studies of halakhah, customs, ethics, and philosophy. His *Bet ha-Behirah* is a commentary on the Talmud.

Meir of Przemyslany (1780–1850). Polish Ḥasidic leader. He was a miracle worker. Thousands of Ḥasidim went to receive his blessing and hear his teaching.

Meir of Rothenburg (c. 1215–1293). German teacher, scholar, tosaphist, and communal leader. He was born in Worms. He became the outstanding rabbinic authority of his generation. He was imprisoned by Emperor Rudolf I at Ensisheim in 1286 for attempting to settle in Palestine; refusing to be ransomed lest European rulers begin to blackmail other communities in a similar way, he died a prisoner. His body was ransomed 14 years later. He wrote numerous responsa, as well as tosaphot and novellae to 18 tractates of the Talmud.

Meir Shepheyah *see* SHEPHEYA.

Meisel, Mordecai Marcus (1528–1601). Bohemian financier, philanthropist, and communal leader. He was a court banker to the Austrian imperial house, and built the Meisel Synagogue in Prague in 1597; he also financed the building of a hospital, a bet midrash, and a mikveh. In addition he sent money to Jerusalem and granted loans to the Jewish communities in Kraków and Poznán.

Meisel, Naḥman *see* MAYZEL, NAḤMAN.

Meisels, Dov Berush (1798–1870). Polish rabbi and patriot. He settled in Kraków, where he opened a bank, and was later elected rabbi of the city; rabbi Saul Landa and his followers did not, however, recognize this election and established their own bet din. Opposed to the Haskalah, Meisels played a major role in the life of the Kraków Jewish community. In 1846 he was elected to the senate of the Kraków Republic and two years later to the Austrian parliament. In 1856 he became chief rabbi of Warsaw. He participated in the events leading to the Polish rebellion of 1863. His writings include a commentary on Maimonides' *Sepher ha-Mitzvot.*

Mekhilta (*lit.* "measure"). Term applied to various midrashic works. It is also used as a synonym for "masekhet" (tractate of the Mishnah or Talmud).

Mekhilta de-Rabbi Ishma'el. Tannaitic midrash on Exodus. It consists largely of a halakhic commentary on Exodus 12–23.19, and concludes with two sections on the Sabbath (related to Exodus 31 and 35).

Mekhilta de-Rabbi Simeon ben Yoḥai. Tannaitic midrash on Exodus.

Mekhulleh (*lit.* "destroyed"). Bankrupt.

Mekitze Nirdamim ("Rousers of the slumbering"). Society dedicated to publishing medieval Hebrew literature, founded in Germany by E. L. Silbermann and others in 1862. Its headquarters were transferred to Jerusalem in 1934.

Melamed, Samuel Max (1885–1938). American writer and journalist. He was born in Lithuania, and in 1914 settled in the US, where he edited periodicals including the *American Jewish Chronicle.* His writings include *Der Staat in Wandel der Jahrtausende*, *Psychologie des Jüdischen Geistes*, and *Spinoza und Buddha.*

Melammed ("teacher"). Private teacher or assistant in a ḥeder.

Melavveh Malkah. The meal eaten at the close of the Sabbath. Kabbalistic and Ḥasidic influence has led to the practice of prolonging the meal (and thus delaying the end of the Sabbath) by the singing of melodies.

Melchett *see* MOND.

***Melchizedek** (fl. ?19th–16th cent. BCE). King of Salem (Genesis 14.18–20). After Abraham's victory over the four kings who had captured Lot, Melchizedek welcomed Abraham, gave him bread and wine, and blessed him.

Meldar. Sephardi term for the reading of sacred literature.

Meldola, David (1797–1853). English rabbi, son of Raphael Meldola. He succeeded his father as presiding rabbi of the Sephardi community in London. He was a founder of the *Jewish Chronicle* and opposed the Reform movement.

Meldola, Raphael (1754–1828). British rabbi. He was born in Livorno. In 1804 or 1805 he became Ḥaham of the Sephardi community in London. In this capacity he reformed Jewish educational institutions, introduced a choir into the synagogue, and cooperated with Solomon Hirscher, the Ashkenazi chief rabbi. He published a handbook of the laws of marital life, as well as sermons, memorial poems, and a catechism.

Melitzah. In biblical Hebrew the word means "aphorism." During the Middle Ages it referred to an elegant literary style. In modern times it denotes a literary technique, popular during the Haskalah period, based on the artistic combination of phrases from the Bible.

Mellaḥ. The name given to the Jewish quarter in Moroccan cities.

Melnikoff, Avraham (1892–1960). Israeli sculptor. He was born in Russia, studied sculpture in Chicago, and in 1918 emigrated to Palestine. His work includes a monument to the soldier and pioneer Joseph Trumpeldor and his comrades.

Meltzer, Shimshon (b. 1909). Israeli poet. He was born in Tluste, and settled in Palestine in 1933. Initially he taught in a school in Tel Aviv, and later he engaged in editorial work. From 1959 he was on the editorial staff of the Zionist Library publications produced by the Jewish Agency. He published poems and ballads combining Ḥasidic tales and motifs. He also translated Yiddish literature into Hebrew.

Mem. 13th letter in the Hebrew alphabet. Its numerical value is 40.

Memmi, Albert (b. 1920). French author and sociologist. He was born in Tunis. He fought with the Free French during World War II, and later became head of a psychology institute in Tunis. In 1966 he became a professor at the École Pratique des Hautes Études. His writings, which concern north African Jewry, include *Pillar of Salt, Agar: Portrait of a Jew*, and *The Liberation of the Jew*.

Memorbuch (German: "book of memory"). A type of community prayerbook, once common in Jewish communities in central Europe. It consisted of a collection of prayers, a necrology of distinguished persons, and a martyrology.

Memorial service *see* YIZKOR.

Memra *see* LOGOS.

Menaḥem (fl. 8th cent. BCE). King of Israel (c. 746/7–737 BCE). He seized the throne after assassinating Shallum, son of Jabesh. When the Assyrian king Tiglath-Pileser III invaded Israel, Menaḥem was forced to pay him tribute (II Kings 15.19).

Menaḥem ben Judah (fl. 1st cent.). Israelite rebel leader, son of Judah the Galilean. He led the group known as the Sicarii in the war against Rome (66–70), successfully attacking the stronghold of Masada, and gaining victory over the Romans in Herod's palace. Later he antagonized Eleazar ben Hananiah and his followers, who killed him.

Menaḥem ben Saruk (c. 910–c. 970). Spanish Hebrew lexicographer. He was born in Tortosa. He served as the secretary of Ḥasdai ibn Shaprut, but was dismissed and persecuted for his heretical views. His *Maḥberet*, the first Hebrew dictionary, was attacked by Dunash ben Labrat.

Menaḥem ibn Zeraḥ *see* IBN ZERAḤ, MENAḤEM.

Menaḥem Mendel of Chernobyl (1730–1789). Ukrainian Ḥasidic rabbi. Initially he engaged in ascetic practices and fasting. After studying with the Baal Shem Tov, he became a maggid, spreading Ḥasidism in Russia and the Ukraine. He collected money for ransoming Jewish captives and for other charitable ends. He emphasized the importance of the spiritual state known as "devekut" and upheld the position of the tzaddik.

Menaḥem Mendel of Liubavich [Shneersohn, Menaḥem Mendel] *see* LIUBAVICH.

Menaḥem Mendel of Przemyslany (fl. 18th cent.). Palestinian Ḥasidic leader. A pupil of the Baal Shem Tov, he went to Palestine in 1764 and settled in Tiberias. He was an extreme enthusiast among the first generation of Ḥasidic leaders, and emphasized the importance of prayer.

Menaḥem Mendel of Rymanov (fl. 18th–19th cent.). Galician Ḥasidic rabbi. His preaching attracted thousands of Ḥasidim to visit him in Rymanov, Galicia. During the Napoleonic Wars, he predicted the coming of the Messiah.

Menaḥem Mendel of Vitebsk (1730–1788). Polish Ḥasidic leader. A disciple of Dov Ber of Mezhirich, he became the head of a congregation in Minsk. In 1772 he went with Shneour Zalman to defend the Ḥasidic movement to the Vilna Gaon, but the Vilna Gaon refused to meet them. In 1773 he settled in Gorodok in Belorussia and later moved to Palestine, where he became the leader of the Ḥasidic community. He subsequently settled in Tiberias. He taught that God is present through the process of contraction ("tzimtzum"), whereby he makes a space in which creation can take place. His writings include *Peri ha-Aretz, Peri ha-Etz, Etz Peri*, and *Likkutei Amarim*.

Menaḥem the Essene (fl. 1st cent. BCE). Israelite seer. He prophesied that Herod would become king but that he would act unjustly and be punished. Later Herod questioned Menaḥem about how long he would reign.

Menaḥot ("Meal offerings"). Second tractate in the Mishnah order of Kodashim. It deals with the preparation of the meal offering (Leviticus 2.1–14; 5.11–13), as well as the shewbread (Leviticus 24.5–9), and the two loaves brought to the Temple on the Feast of Weeks (Leviticus 23.17).

Mendel, David *see* NEANDER, JOHANN AUGUST WILHELM.

Mendele Mocher Sephorim *see* ABRAMOWITSCH, SHALOM JACOB.

Mendelssohn, Erich (1887–1953). Israeli architect. He was born in Allenstein, Germany. From the 1920s he was a member of the revivalist movement in European architecture. He left Germany in 1933 and worked in Britain and Palestine. Beween 1934 and 1939 he designed various buildings in Palestine, including the Anglo-Palestine Bank in Jerusalem, the Hadassah hospital on Mount Scopus, and the government hospital in Haifa. He subsequently built a number of synagogues in American cities.

***Mendelssohn** [Mendelssohn-Bartholdy]**, Felix** (1809–1847). German composer, grandson of Moses Mendelssohn. He was baptized, and later converted to Christianity. His compositions include the oratorio Elijah; he was also responsible for the revival of Bach's *St. Matthew Passion.*

Mendelssohn, Moses [Biur] (1729–1786). German philosopher. He was born in Dessau. He lived in Berlin, where he studied philosophy, mathematics, Latin, French, and English, and became a partner in a silk factory. In 1754, with the help of Gotthold Ephraim Lessing, he began to publish philosophical studies and in 1763 was awarded the first prize of the Prussian Royal Academy of Sciences for his philosophical work. He became embroiled in a dispute about Judaism, and from 1769 devoted his literary work to issues dealing with the Jewish faith. He published a German translation of the Pentateuch with a Hebrew commentary (*Biur*). His *Jerusalem* is an analysis of Judaism and a defense of tolerance. He was the hero of Lessing's *Nathan der Weise.*

Mendes, Gracia *see* NASI, GRACIA.

Mendes, Henry Pereira (1852–1937). American Sephardi rabbi. He was born in Birmingham, England, and served as a rabbi to the new Sephardi congregation of Manchester from 1874 to 1877. He then emigrated to New York, where he served as a rabbi to the Shearith Israel congregation. He was a founder of the Union of Orthodox Congregations of America, the Jewish Theological Seminary, and the New York Board of Jewish Ministers. He wrote about Jewish and general topics for the weekly paper *American Hebrew.* His works include *Looking Ahead, Bar Mitzvah, Esther and Harbonah, Jewish Religion Ethically Presented, Jewish History Ethically Presented, Mekor Ḥayyim: Mourners' Handbook*, and *Derekh Ḥayyim: Way of Life.*

Menelaus (fl. 2nd cent. BCE). High priest. He obtained the priesthood in 171 BCE by means of bribery. An extreme Hellenizer, he supported the persecution of the Jews by Antiochus IV Epiphanes. At the beginning of his tenure of office, he plundered the Temple. Later he lost favor in the Seleucid court and was put to death on the advice of Lysias.

Mene mene tekel u-pharsin. The phrase, in an unknown language, that appeared miraculously on the wall during Belshazzar's feast (Daniel 5.25). It was interpreted by Daniel to mean that the king's deeds had been weighed and were found wanting. He explained the words as follows: *Mene*: "God has numbered the days of your kingdom and will bring it to an end"; *tekel*: "You have been weighed in the balance and found wanting"; *pharsin*: "Your kingdom has been divided and given over to the Medes and Persians."

Menes, Abraham (1897–1969). American Jewish historian. He was born in Grodno, Poland, and founded a branch of the socialist party the Bund there; he later became vice-chairman of the Grodno Jewish community. In 1920 he moved to Berlin, and he subsequently settled in Paris, where he contributed to the *Yiddish Encyclopedia*. In 1940 he moved to the US. He published studies of the economic and social aspects of Jewish history.

Menorah. Candelabrum. The golden seven-branched menorah stood in the Tabernacle and the Temple. The menorah from the second Temple was taken to Rome by Vespasian and is depicted on the Arch of Titus there. The term also refers to the eight-branched Ḥannukah lamp.

Menorah Movement. American cultural organization. It developed out of the Menorah Society, founded at Harvard in 1906 to promote Jewish culture. Similar societies were subsequently founded in other colleges and universities in the US and Canada. In 1913 the Intercollegiate Menorah Association was established. The *Menorah Journal* was edited by Henry Hurwitz, who served as chancelor of the association from its beginning. The association was disbanded after his death in 1961.

Mensh (Yiddish). Literally a human being; but colloquially an honorable person, someone of consequence.

Menstruation *see* NIDDAH.

Mephibosheth (fl. 11th cent. BCE). Name given to Meribaal, the son of Jonathan, in the Book of Samuel. When he was five his father was killed (I Samuel 4.4) and he fled with his nurse; in the haste of the journey he was dropped and the accident left him lame. When David was established in Jerusalem he restored Mephibosheth to favor. During Absalom's rebellion, Mephibosheth remained in Jerusalem, while his servant Zoba accompanied David. When the uprising was quelled, Mephibosheth pleaded that he had been misled by Zoba and David treated him leniently.

Merchant. During the biblical period, although mercantile commerce was well developed, the Jews appear not to have acted as merchants; nor, according to Josephus, were Jews of his time engaged in trade. However, Jewish merchants are documented in Alexandria and elsewhere in the Roman Empire. During the Middle Ages, the Jews played an increasingly important role in international trade, but after the Crusades, these activities were curtailed and in western Europe they turned instead to moneylending. In eastern Europe the Jews continued to act as merchants, as did Marranos in northwest Europe and America. In the modern period, Jewish merchants have been active throughout the world.

Meribaal *see* MEPHIBOSHETH.

Merits, doctrine of. The belief that by performing works commanded by God a person may obtain divine favor, which benefits himself and his descendants.

Merits of the fathers. According to Jewish doctrine, the blessings secured for their descendants by parents who perform worthy deeds. In particular the merits of the patriarchs (Abraham, Isaac, and Jacob) are believed to have obtained benefits for future generations.

Merkavah mysticism *see* MAASEH MERKAVAH.

***Merodach** [Marduk]. Babylonian deity. In Babylonian myth he was the opponent of the monster Tiamat. He was regarded as creator of the world and of human beings. As king of the gods, he determined the fate of humans at the beginning of the year.

***Merodach-Baladan** (fl. 8th cent. BCE). King of Babylon (722–710 BCE). During Hezekiah's reign he sent envoys to Judah to establish political links with the Israelites in opposition to Assyria (II Kings 20.12).

Merom, Waters of. Lake supplied by the Jordan. Its shores were the site of Joshua's victory over the alliance of northern kings led by Jabin of Hazor (Joshua 11.5).

Meron. Town in Upper Galilee. It was

conquered by the Assyrian king Tiglath-Pileser III in 732 BCE. During the war with Rome (66–70 CE) it was fortified by Josephus. The tomb of Simeon ben Yoḥai and his son Eliezer at Meron made the town a place of pilgrimage on Lag Ba-Omer, the traditional date of Simeon's death.

***Mesha** (fl. 9th cent. BCE). King of Moab. According to II Kings 3.4, he was a sheep breeder. He was subjugated by Ahab, but after Ahab's death, he revolted and ceased to pay the tribute that had been exacted from him (II Kings 3.4–5; II Kings 1.1). Jehoram, the son of Ahab, conducted a military campaign against Moab, in alliance with Jehoshaphat of Judah and the King of Edom. Their campaign was successful until they besieged Kir-Hareseth, whereupon Mesha sacrificed his son and the invading armies retreated (II Kings 3). Mesha then attempted to regain the land he had lost. An account of his victories is recorded on the Moabite Stone.

Mesharet. The accent marks in Hebrew which indicate minor pauses.

Meshuga (Yiddish). Crazy.

Meshullaḥ (*lit.* "shadow"). Emissary. The term is applied particularly to emissaries sent to raise funds for a charitable institution. In the early rabbinic period the rabbinical academies in the Four Holy Cities of Palestine (Jerusalem, Hebron, Safed, and Tiberias) sent emissaries known as "shadar" to Jewish communities in distant lands. Because they traveled widely meshullaḥim performed a useful function in linking communities throughout the world. Their accounts of their journeys serve as important historical sources.

Meshullam ben Menaḥem of Volterra *see* VOLTERRA, MESHULLAM.

Meshummad. Convert to Christianity, apostate; *see* APOSTASY.

Messer Leon *see* LEON, JUDAH MESSER.

Messiah [Mashiaḥ]. Anointed one. In the Bible the term refers to kings, high priests, and any individual who had a divine mission. After the exile the prophetic vision of God's kingdom was associated with the ingathering of Israel under an annointed scion of the House of David. During the period of Roman rule, the expectation of a messiah who would free the Jews gained prominence. During this period various false messiahs appeared, including Jesus, whom the Jews refused to accept because he did not fulfill the role laid out for the Messiah in the Hebrew Scriptures. In the 2nd century Simeon Bar Kokhba was viewed as the Messiah. In the 5th century a pseudo-messiah, Moses, appeared in Crete. Other false messiahs included: Abu Issa al-Isfahani (8th century), Serene (8th century), Yudghan (8th century), David Alroy (12th century), Abraham Abulafia (11th–12th centuries), Moses Botarel (14th century), Asher Lamlein (16th century), Solomon Molcho (16th century), Shabbetai Tzevi (17th century), and Jacob Frank (18th century).

Metatron. The most important angel in aggadic and kabbalistic literature. He was identified with the Angel of the Presence and with Enoch after he ascended to Heaven. He served as the scribe of the divine court, the keeper of celestial secrets, and the heavenly archetype of man.

Meteg. Short vertical line placed on the left of a vowel sign in Hebrew (*see* VOCALIZATION). It denotes a secondary emphasis in a word (or series of words joined by a MAKKEPH).

Metempsychosis (Hebrew "gilgul"). The migration of a soul from one body after its death to another. In kabbalistic Judaism the doctrine of the transmigration of souls appears in the Bahir and the Zohar. Eventually it became a commonly accepted belief among mystics and played an important role in Ḥasidic lore. *See also* PRE-EXISTENCE.

Methuselah. Patriarch, son of Enoch, father of Lamech, and grandfather of Noah (Genesis 5.21–5). According to the Bible, he lived 969 years (Genesis 5.25–7).

Metivta (Aramaic). Yeshivah.

Metsieh (Yiddish). Bargain, nothing to brag about.

Meturgeman (Aramaic: "interpreter"). The title given to the spokesman for a talmudic rabbi. It was customary for sages to deliver their lectures through him: the rabbi spoke to the meturgeman who then addressed the assembled congregation.

Mexican Indian Jews. Proselytes living in Mexico, who appear to be descendants of members of the Christian sect of Iglesia de Dios.

Meyerson, Golda *see* MEIR, GOLDA.

Mezhirich. Village in Volhynia, Russia. It was the residence of the Ḥasidic leader Dov Ber in the 18th century. After the death of the Baal Shem Tov in 1760, it became the center of Ḥasidism.

Mezumman (*lit.* "ready cash"). The word is used to refer to one of the quorum of three people whose presence is necessary for the public recitation of Grace after Meals.

Mezuzah (i) ("doorpost"). Parchment scroll placed in a container which is fixed to the doorpost of a room in a Jewish house; every doorway in the house carries a mezuzah. On the scroll are written verses from Deuteronomy (6.4–9 and 11.13–21). The practice is prescribed by Deuteronomy 11.20: "You shall write [these words] upon the door posts of your house and upon your gates."

Mezuzah (ii) ("Doorpost"). One of the seven minor talmudic tractates. It deals with regulations regarding the writing and use of the mezuzah.

Mi addir al ha-kol ("He who is mighty above all"). Opening words of a hymn recited before the wedding service in the Ashkenazi rite.

Mibashan *see* BRAUNSTEIN, MENAḤEM MENDEL.

Micah (i) (fl. 8th cent. BCE). Israelite prophet. He lived in Judah, where he defended the people against the oppression of the ruling classes. He prophesied the destruction of the country and exile to Babylon, and also predicted the coming of a king of the House of David who would bring peace to the world.

Micah (ii). Biblical book, one of the books of the 12 Minor Prophets. It records the prophecies of Micah.

Michael. Archangel. With Gabriel he is the only angel mentioned by name in the Bible (Daniel 10.13). He is a divine messenger who executes God's judgments. In the Apocrypha and aggadic literature he is the guardian angel of Israel, the chief opponent of Satan, and the keeper of the celestial keys.

Michal (i) (fl. 10th cent. BCE). Israelite princess and queen, daughter of Saul and wife of David. She helped her husband to escape from Saul's messengers, who had been sent to kill him. Subsequently she was given in marriage to Paltiel son of Laish, but was eventually restored to David. When David danced in front of the Ark, she rebuked him. She died childless (I Samuel 18–19; II Samuel 16; I Chronicles 15).

Michal (ii) *see* LEBENSOHN, MICAH JOSEPH.

Microcosm. A miniature representation or version of something. In ancient philosophy humankind was regarded as a model or epitome of the universe. During the Middle Ages it was asserted that there is a correspondence between the human organism and the cosmos. In Jewish thought this concept is found in midrashic and philosophical works, such as

Olam Katon by Joseph ibn Tzaddik, as well as in kabbalistic texts.

Middot (i) ("Measures"). Tenth tractate in the Mishnah order of Kodashim. It deals with the architecture, organization, and dimensions of the second Temple.

Middot (ii) *see* HERMENEUTICS, TALMUDIC.

Middot tovot *see* VIRTUES.

Midian [Midianites]. Bedouin tribe related to Abraham (Genesis 25.2). They traveled with caravans of incense from Gilead to Egypt and other countries. After he had killed the Egyptian, Moses fled from Pharaoh to the land of Midian and married the daughter of Jethro. Later the princes of Midian cooperated with Moab against Israel (Numbers 21.29). According to the Book of Judges, the Midianites subsequently plundered the Valley of Jezreel but were repulsed by Gideon (Judges 6).

Midrash ("study," "interpretation") [derash, ("enquiry," "exposition")]. Interpretation of biblical texts. The interpretive approach known as "midrash halakhah" aims to define the full meaning of biblical law; "midrash aggadah" seeks to derive a moral principle, lesson, or theological concept from Scripture. The rabbis formulated various rules to deduce hidden or new meanings. Rabbinic literature is replete with midrashic expositions.

Midrashic literature. The body of rabbinic writings concerning the interpretation of biblical texts. It dates from the tannaitic period (beginning c. 100 BCE) to the 10th century. Of works connected with the Bible, the best known is Midrash Rabbah on the Pentateuch and the five megillot. The Tanḥuma contains discourses on the portion of the law read weekly in the synagogue. Other homiletic works on the Bible include *Shoḥer Tov* on Psalms, and works on Proverbs and Samuel. Midrashim relating to festivals and special Sabbaths are called "pesiktot." The *Pesikta de-Rav Kahana* and *Pesikta Rabbati* contain homilies for special occasions. *Avot de-Rabbi Natan* is an expansion of the Mishnaic tractate Avot. *Derekh Eretz Rabbah* deals with ethical teachings, and *Derekh Eretz Zuta* advises scholars about religious and pedagogic duties. The *Tanna de-ve-Elyahu* contains moral advice. *Seder Olam* is a work of historical aggadah, and *Pirke de-Rabbi Eliezer* contains numerous stories about biblical events. The *Yalkut Shimoni* is a collection of aggadic literature. In addition, there are large numbers of separate midrashim on books of the Bible, and short midrashim on various topics.

Midrash Rabbah. Collection of aggadic midrashim on the Pentateuch and the five megillot. It consists of: Genesis Rabbah, Exodus Rabbah, Leviticus Rabbah, Numbers Rabbah, Deuteronomy Rabbah, Song of Songs Rabbah, Ruth Rabbah, Lamentations Rabbah, Ecclesiastes Rabbah, and Esther Rabbah.

Midrash Shoḥer Tov *see* PSALMS, MIDRASH ON.

Midrash Tanḥuma *see* TANḤUMA.

Mielziner, Moses (1828–1903). American Reform rabbi and scholar. He was born in Czerniejewo, and served as a preacher and teacher in Waren. From 1857 to 1865 he was head of the Jewish school in Copenhagen. He emigrated to the US, where he served as a rabbi in New York and later became a professor of Talmud and rabbinic literature at the Hebrew Union College. His writings include *Introduction to the Talmud, The Jewish Law of Marriage and Divorce and its Relation to the Law of the State,* and *The Introduction of Slavery among the Ancient Hebrews.*

Miesas, Matisyohu (1885–1945). Galician Yiddish semiologist. He was born in Pshemeshl, Galicia. At a language conference held at Czernowitz in 1908 he gave a paper on the scientific analysis of

Yiddish; this was the first such study to be written in the language itself. His publications include *Entstehungsursache der jüdischen Dialekte*, *Die jiddische Sprache*, and *Die Gesetze der Schriftgeschichte*.

Mifleget ha-Avodah ha-Ziyyonit *see* HITAḤDUT.

Miggo (*lit.* "since"). In talmudic studies the word denotes a type of legal proof.

Migration. The first major migration of the Jewish people was the deportation of Israelites to Babylonia after the destruction of the first Temple in the 6th century BCE; the Jews returned from exile in the 5th century BCE. The destruction of the second Temple in the 1st century CE precipitated a new wave of migration to Mesopotamia, Asia Minor, and Egypt. In later centuries Jews emigrated from Palestine to southern Italy, and then into France and Germany; from the Byzantine Empire up the valley of the Danube into central Europe; and under the Arabs from Mesopotamia and Egypt through Morocco into Spain. Later western European Jewry moved from northern Europe into Poland, and from Spain to the Ottoman Empire. In the modern period Jewry has shifted from Europe to the US and Israel.

Mikhoels, Solomon (1890–1948). Russian Yiddish actor. He was born in Dvinsk. He became the chief actor in Alexander Granovsky's drama group, and later succeeded him to the directorship of the Jewish State Theater in Moscow. During World War II he visited western countries on behalf of the Jewish Anti-Fascist Committee. He was assassinated by the Soviet secret police.

Mikulov. Town in southern Moravia (now Czechoslovakia). It had a sizable Jewish community by the 15th century, and became the leading center of Moravian Jewry. It was the home of a number of noted rabbis and contained a famous yeshivah.

Mikvaot ("Ritual baths"). Sixth tractate in the Mishnah order of Tohorot. It deals with regulations about ritual bathing (Leviticus 14.8; 15.5).

Mikveh. Ritual bath. According to Jewish law, individuals as well as various objects have to be immersed and ritually cleansed on certain occasions. The water in the mikveh must come from a natural spring or river. Such immersion renders a person ritually clean who has had contact with the dead or a defiled object, or who has become impure through an unclean flow from the body (it is, for example, practiced by women after menstruation). In addition, ritual bathing is undertaken by pious individuals to add to their spirituality, and is prescribed for proselytes. Ritual cleansing is also used for vessels. *See also* IMMERSION.

Mikveh Israel. Israeli agricultural school near Tel Aviv. It was founded in 1870 by Charles Netter on behalf of the Alliance Israélite Universelle and was the first Jewish agricultural undertaking in Palestine in the modern period.

Milah *see* CIRCUMCISION.

Milchig (Yiddish). Milk foods; they may not be eaten with or after meat dishes.

Milcom *see* MOLOCH.

Milhaud, Darius (1892–1974). French composer. He was born in Aix-en-Provence. He served as secretary to the French minister in Brazil in 1917–18. After returning to Paris, he wrote a wide variety of musical compositions including *David*, *Service sacré*, *Poèmes Juifs*, *Chants populaires Hébraïques*, *La création du monde*, and *Le candelabre à sept branches*. In 1940 he settled in the US, where he was appointed professor at Mills College in California. Later he was a professor of composition at the Paris Conservatory.

Military titles. In biblical times the following titles were used: "sar" (commander), "sar tzava" (commander-in-chief), "sar gedud" (unit commander), "sar ha-rekhev" (captain of chariots), "sare alaphim, [meot], [ḥamishim], [asarot]" (captain of a thousand, a hundred, fifty, ten). The terms "sar ha-tabbaḥim" (captain of the bodyguard) and "shalish" (charioteer) are also found. In modern Israel various other military titles are employed.

Milk. The halakhic restrictions on the consumption of milk are that it be drawn from a permitted animal, and that milk or milk products not be mixed or cooked with meat or meat products.

Millennium. A thousand years. In Jewish usage the word is applied specifically to the thousand-year period after the coming of the Messiah; this period, also referred to as the "Days of the Messiah," will precede the last Judgment and the inauguration of the Kingdom of Heaven.

Miller, Arthur (b. 1915). American novelist and playwright. He was born in New York. His early works included *Focus*, a novel about anti-Semitism. He later wrote *Incident at Vichy*, which concerns the arrest of Frenchmen, including Jews, during the Nazi occupation of France.

***Milman, Henry Hart** (1791–1868). English clergyman. He was the Dean of St. Paul's Cathedral in London from 1849. His writings include *A History of the Jews*.

Minhag. Custom. The word is used of customs that became binding and assumed the force of halakhah. It also refers to local traditions and liturgical rites which developed in different Jewish communities.

Minḥah (i) [afternoon service]. The service of afternoon prayer. It was instituted in place of the afternoon Temple offering. On the Sabbath and fast days a portion of the Torah is read during the service.

Minḥah (ii) *see* MEAL OFFERING.

Minim ("heretics"). Talmudic term for heretical sects. It was applied to various groups, including early Christians and gnostics.

Minister. In Jewish usage, an Orthodox Jewish spiritual leader in the British Commonwealth, functioning as a rabbi.

Minkowski, Maurice (1881–1930). Polish artist. Although he was deaf and dumb, he was an important chronicler of traditional Jewish life during the czarist period.

Minkowsky, Phinehas (1859–1924). Ukrainian cantor. He was born in Belaya Tserkov. He officiated at Kishinev, Kherson, and New York, and later became the chief cantor of the Brody Synagogue in Odessa. He introduced a modern form of service, which utilized an organ and a choir. He taught at the Jewish Conservatory in Odessa and published studies of Jewish music. In 1923 he settled in the US.

Minor Prophets *see* PROPHET.

Minority rights. Before and during World War I, various Jewish bodies struggled to protect the religious and civil rights of Jews in eastern Europe. At the Versailles Peace Conference in 1919, they obtained the agreement of the principal allied powers that special treaties should be made with the successor states of the Austro-Hungarian and Czarist empires and the enlarged states of south-eastern Europe. Later a project to include an article in the covenant of the League of Nations concerning minority rights came to nothing. However, treaties were concluded with Poland, Romania, Hungary, Austria, Lithuania, and Latvia. In addition, it was agreed that any member of the Council of the League of Nations had the right to bring an infringement of minority rights to the attention of the Council. The United Nations Charter encourages respect for human rights without distinction on grounds of race, religion, or language. *See also* CIVIL RIGHTS.

Minors *see* DEAF, IMBECILES, AND MINORS.

Minsk. Town in Belorussia. Jews began to settle there in the 16th century, and in 1579 they received a charter from King Stephen Batory of Poland. During the Chmielnicki uprising, the Jews endured persecution, and they were expelled from Minsk in 1654. The town was the scene of disputes between the mitnaggedim and the Ḥasidim, and between traditionalists and the maskilim. In the 20th century Minsk became a center of activities by Jewish revolutionaries and communists.

Minyan ("number"). Term applied to the group of ten male Jews (13 years or older) who constitute the minimum number for communal worship.

Minyan man. A Jew who, for payment, attends synagogue services regularly to ensure that there is a minyan.

Minz *see* MÜNZ.

Mir. Small town in Grodno Oblast, Belorussia. Jews settled there in the 17th century. Its yeshivah was founded in 1815 and achieved an international reputation. During World War II its student body was transferred to Shanghai. Later the yeshivah moved to Brooklyn, New York, and became the Mirrer Yeshivah Central Institute. Some of its scholars subsequently joined the Mir Yeshivah in Jerusalem.

Mirabeau, Gabriel-Honoré de Riqueti, Comte de (1749–1791). French statesman. Influenced by Jews who supported the Enlightenment, he wrote a book about Moses Mendelssohn (*Sur Moses Mendelssohn: sur la réforme politique des Juifs*) and advocated Jewish emancipation.

Miracle. Extraordinary event attributed to divine intervention. In the Bible such occurrences are referred to as "signs" and "wonders." The Talmud records miracles performed by men of God or brought about through their merits. In Jewish philosophy attempts were made to give a rational account of miraculous occurrences.

***Mirandola, Giovanni Pico della** [Pico della Mirandola] (1463–1494). Italian humanist. He studied Hebrew under Elijah del Medigo and became convinced that the kabbalah provided an access to the truths of Christianity. His writings mark the beginning of the study of Hebrew as an academic discipline by Christian scholars.

Miriam (fl.?13th cent. BCE). Israelite woman, sister of Moses. According to Exodus 2.2–8, she advised Pharaoh's daughter, who had discovered the hiding place of the baby Moses, to call a Hebrew nurse for Moses and succeeded in having his mother engaged to care for him. Later, when she and Aaron challenged Moses' exclusive right to speak in the name of the Lord (Numbers 12), she was stricken with leprosy, but she was healed by Moses, who interceded with God on her behalf.

Mirrer Yeshivah Central Institute *see* MIR.

Miseh. An abnormal or violent death.

Mi she-berakah ("He who blessed"). Opening words of a benediction recited on behalf of one called up for the reading of the Torah. After each reading it is customary for the cantor to ask God's blessing on the reader, his family, and anyone he wishes to have mentioned. In many congregations the person called up for the Torah reading makes an offering for the synagogue or to charity. Additional forms of this prayer are recited after the birth of a son, after the birth and naming of a daughter, by the bridegroom before his wedding, and on behalf of a sick person.

Mishegoss (Yiddish). An irrational belief, nonsense.

Mishkovsky, Zelda (1914–1984). Israeli poet. She was born in Chernigov in the Ukraine. She emigrated to Jerusalem at the age of 11, and taught in a religious school for girls. Her poetry contains ultra-Orthodox and modern sensibilities. She became known by her forename alone.

Mishnah ("Repetition," "Study," "Teaching"). Early rabbinic legal code. Compiled by Judah ha-Nasi in the 2nd century, it is divided into six orders: (1) Zeraim ("Seeds"), dealing with laws regarding agriculture; (2) Moed ("Set feast"), regarding the laws of the Sabbath and festivals; (3) Nashim ("Women"), describing the laws of marriage, divorce, and vows; (4) Nezikin ("Damages"), treating civil and criminal violations; (5) Kodashim ("Holy things"), setting out the laws concerning ritual slaughter, sacrifices, and consecrated objects; and (6) Tohorot ("Purities"), dealing with the laws of ceremonial purity.

Mishneh Torah *see* MAIMONIDES.

Mishpokhe (Yiddish). Family, relatives.

Mission. In a religious context, the sending out of persons to bring about the spread of religion. Medieval church bodies devoted to conversionist propaganda were the prototypes for Christian mission among the Jews. The earliest organizations to adopt this policy were established in the 17th century in the Netherlands. Later they spread to Germany, where the Institutum Judaicum was founded at Halle in 1728. In England the London Society for Promoting Christianity among the Jews was founded in 1809. Educational and medical facilities set up by these institutions in Europe and Near Eastern countries pursued similar ends. In recent years such activities have diminished and have been replaced by a more sympathetic attitude toward Judaism.

Mitnagged ("opponent"). The term "mitnaggedim" is applied specifically to opponents of the Ḥasidic movement. The Vilna Gaon gave the impetus to the development of opposition to Ḥasidism. His antagonism was based on the pantheistic tendencies of the Ḥasidim, their use of the Sephardi liturgy, their belief in tzaddikim, and the creation of Ḥasidic synagogues. Because of the ban issued against the Ḥasidim by the Vilna Gaon, Shneour Zalman of Lyady was arrested and held in the St. Petersburg fortress in 1798. After he was released, the conflict abated. During the 19th century the two groups were generally reconciled.

Mittwoch, Eugen (1876–1942). German orientalist. He was born in Schrimm. He helped Paul Nathan to set up a school system in Palestine under the auspices of the Hilfsverein der deutschen Juden. He taught at the universities of Berlin and Greifswald, and in 1919 became a professor at the Seminary for Oriental Languages in Berlin, where he was eventually appointed director. In 1933 he directed the office of the Joint Distribution Committee in Berlin and in 1939 moved to England. He published studies of the influence of Jewish prayer on the liturgy of Islam; Hebrew epigraphy; and Islamic art and politics. He was also one of the editors of an edition of the works of Moses Mendelssohn.

Mitzvah ("commandment"). In Jewish law commandments are either positive ("mitzvat aseh") or negative ("mitzvah lo taaseh"). According to tradition, there are 613 commandments in the Torah, and various scholars enumerated them. The Talmud differentiates between two types of commandment: "mishpatim," ordinances that would have been deducible even if Scripture had not prescribed them; and "ḥukkim," commandments that could not have been logically derived. Medieval scholars referred to the first type as rational ("sikhliyyot") and the second as revealed ("shimiyot"). The term "mitzvah" is also applied to a good deed. *See also* DUTY; 613 COMMANDMENTS; TEN COMMANDMENTS.

Mixed marriage *see* INTERMARRIAGE.

Mizpah. Ancient place in the territory of Benjamin. Samuel gathered the Israelites there for prayer before they went into battle against the Philistines (I Samuel 7.5). After their victory, he visited Mizphah annually to judge the people. Later it was in the Kingdom of Judah and served as the residence of Gedaliah when he was governor. Judah Maccabee and his men also assembled there before engaging in battle.

Mizraḥ ("east"). Decorated parchment or metal plate, hung on a wall to indicate, for the purposes of prayer, the direction of Jerusalem.

Mizraḥi (from "merkaz ruḥani": spiritual center). Religious Zionist organization. It was founded in 1902 and its first conference took place in Pressburg. It encouraged a program of religious Zionism within the framework of the Zionist movement. Since the establishment in 1948 of the State of Israel, it has formed part of successive Israeli governments. It also engaged in religious education at all levels, created an organization for yeshivot, established the Mosad ha-Rav Kook publishing society, maintained economic enterprises (including banks and a house-building company), and ran an organization to deal with refugee rabbis. Its women's section sponsors kindergartens, social welfare, and children's homes in Israel. In 1955 it joined with Ha-Poel ha-Mizraḥi to form the National Religious Party. The World Center of Mizraḥi and Ha-Poel ha-Mizraḥi is the highest body of the religious Zionist movement and acts as the executive of both bodies.

Mizraḥi, Elijah (c. 1450–1526). Ottoman rabbinic authority. He was born in Constantinople, and became the foremost rabbinic authority in the Ottoman Empire. He adopted a more tolerant attitude to the Karaites than other rabbinic scholars. He wrote various responsa, a super-commentary on Rashi's commentary to the Pentateuch, and a mathematical treatise.

Mnemonic. Device to aid memory. A common Hebrew type of mnemonic is the combination of the initials of a sequence of words to form an actual word or a meaningless word-like construction. Psalms and proverbs were sometimes written as alphabetic acrostics (*see* ACROSTIC).

Moab. Ancient kingdom in southern Transjordan. According to Genesis 19.37 the Moabites were descended from Lot. During the patriarchial period, they settled in land which they had captured from the Rephaim (Deuteronomy 2.10–11). Initially divided into small tribes, they later united into a single kingdom. Their ruler Balak summoned Balaam to curse the Israelites (Numbers 22). David conquered the country (II Samuel 8.2) which remained under the suzerainty of the northern kingdom until the rebellion of Mesha (II Kings 3.4ff.). During the reign of the Assyrian king Tiglath-Pileser III, it became an Assyrian province. It was later conquered by the Hasmoneans.

Moabite Stone. Stone set up by King Mesha of Moab to commemorate his successful revolt against Joram of Israel (II Kings 3.4ff.). It records Omri's subjection of Moab and the country's liberation from Israel.

Moadim le-simḥah ("Holidays for rejoicing"). Greeting used among the Sephardim on religious holidays. The reply is: "Hagim u-zemanim le-sason ("Festivals and festal periods for joy").

Mocatta, Frederick David (1828–1905). English philanthropist, scholar, and communal leader. He was active in the Charity Organization Society and the Jewish Board of Guardians. An observant Jew, he was a member of Orthodox as well as Reform synagogues. He donated his library to University College, London, and the Jewish Historical Society of England. His writings include *The Jews and the Inquisition.*

Mocatta Library. Library of Jewish history and English Judaica, housed at University College, London. The basis of the collection is part of the library of Frederick David Mocatta.

Modeh ani ("I give thanks"). Opening words of the prayer said upon waking in the morning.

Modena. City in north-central Italy. Jews lived there from the 14th century. Under the ducal house of Este, Jewry flourished, but in the 17th century the ghetto system was introduced. In the 17th–18th centuries Modena had an important Jewish community and was a center of kabbalistic study and of support for Palestinian settlement.

Modena, Aaron Berechiah (fl. 17th cent.). Italian kabbalist. He composed collections of material for liturgical use. His *Maavar Yabbok* contains prayers for the sick and the dead in addition to regulations concerning mourning.

Modena, Leone [Leon of Modena] (1571–1648). Italian rabbi, scholar, and writer. Born in Venice, he initially became an elementary teacher and preacher there. In his autobiography, *Ḥayyei Yehudah*, he listed the various occupations he resorted to throughout his life. He was regarded by Christian scholars as the most distinguished Jewish scholar of his day. His writings include sermons, as well as polemics against the Oral Law, the kabbalah, and Christianity.

Modiin [Modiim]. Village in the toparchy of Lydda. It was the home town of Mattathias the Hasmonean and his descendants. The Hasmonean revolt began there.

Moed ("Set feast"). Second order of the Mishnah. Its tractates deal with laws concerning the Sabbath, festivals, and fast days.

Moed Katan ("Minor festival") [Mashkin ("One may irrigate")]. 11th tractate in the Mishnah order of Moed. It deals with the nature of work permitted during the intermediate days of the feasts of the Passover and Tabernacles, as well as mourning on holy days.

Moetzet ha-Poalim ("Workers' councils"). Supreme authority in a given locality of the Israeli federation of trade unions, the Histadrut. It oversees the enterprises and institutions that serve the workers, and encourages their economic consolidation. It is elected by the local workers and in turn elects the secretariat and the local Histadrut court.

Moetzet ha-Poalot. Women workers' council. Formally established in 1922 as part of the Histadrut, its roots go back to the pioneering movement of the second Aliyah. It is concerned with social services and with the problems of working women, including retirement age, maternity benefits, vocational training, and career advancement. It maintains day nurseries, children's residential homes, kindergartens, youth clubs, summer camps, agricultural high schools, community centers, girls' vocational high schools, women's hostels, special training courses, and women's clubs.

Mogilev *see* MOHILEV.

***Mohammed** [Mahomet] (c. 570–632). The prophet of Islam. He publicly proclaimed the revelations made to him through the intermediation of the angel Gabriel. These were eventually written down in the Koran. He viewed the Hebrew Scriptures with respect, and initially believed there was no essential difference between his teaching and Judaism. Hoping to convert Jews to the new faith, he incorporated certain features of Judaism into Islam. When he realized he would not succeed, he adopted a hostile attitude to the Jews of Medina.

Mohammedanism *see* ISLAM.

Mohel *see* CIRCUMCISION.

Mohilev [Mogilev]. City in Belorussia. In 1654 Jews living there were expelled or massacred by the Russians. Jewish captives from the city formed the basis of the Moscow community. In the 17th–18th centuries the city became a center of the Sabbetaian movement. After Mohilev was annexed to Russia in 1772, the Jewish community organization was abolished and a poll-tax was imposed.

Mohilever, Samuel (1824–1898). Polish rabbi and religious Zionist. He was born in Glebokie, in the district of Vilnius, and became a rabbi there in 1848. Later he served in Szaki, Suwałki, and Radom. From 1874 he actively supported Jewish settlement in Palestine, and his views on this influenced Baron Edmond de Rothschild and Baron de Hirsch. He formed the first society of Ḥovevei Zion in Warsaw, and later supported Theodor Herzl. In 1884 he was the honorary president of the Kattowitz Conference.

Mohr, Abraham Menaḥem Mendel (1815–1868). Galician Hebrew scholar and maskil. He was born in Lemberg. His writings, in Hebrew and Yiddish, include a geography of Palestine and its Jewish inhabitants, Purim plays, and editions of *Mikveh Yisrael* by Manasseh ben Israel and *La-Yesharim Tehillah* by Moses Ḥayyim Luzzatto. He also published a Yiddish newspaper.

Moïse, Penina (1797–1880). American poet, hymn writer, and teacher. She was born in Charleston, South Carolina, and became the superintendent of the Beth Elohim Congregation's Sunday school there. She was the author of the first American Jewish hymnal. Her hymns and poetry were published as *Secular and Religious Works* in 1911.

Moissis, Asher (1899–1975). Greek author, translator, and communal leader. He was born in Trikkala. He became a lawyer and participated in Jewish communal and Zionist affairs. In 1917 he founded the Zionist monthly *Israel*, which he also edited. In the 1930s he published books on Jewish subjects, particularly Greco-Jewish relations through the ages. He served as president of the Jewish National Fund (1930–38), the Salonika Jewish community (1934–6), and the Greek Zionist Federation (1936–8). Later he was president of the Central Council of Jewish Communities in Greece (1944–9), and from 1948 served as honorary consul of Israel in Athens.

Molcho, Solomon (c. 1500–1532). Italian kabbalist and pseudo-messiah. He was born in Lisbon of Marrano parents, and his given name was Diogo Pires. He became secretary to the King of Portugal's council and recorder at the Court of Appeals. After meeting David Reveni he circumcised himself and took his Hebrew name. He lived for a time in Salonika, where he studied kabbalah, then returned to Italy. Believing himself to be the Messiah, he preached about the coming of messianic redemption. Although he obtained the protection of Pope Clement VII against the inquisition, he was accused by an inquisitional court of Judaizing (trying to persuade converts to Christianity to return to Judaism) and was condemned to be burned at the stake. He was reprieved on this occasion but was condemned again after refusing to convert to Christianity and was burned in 1532. Many Jews and Marranos in Italy refused to believe that he had died, and thought he had been saved once more.

Moldova, György (b. 1934). Hungarian writer. He was born in Budapest. He began his career by writing film scripts, but was also obliged to do manual work. Some of his writings deal with the situation of Hungarian Jews during World War II and in the post-war years.

Molech *see* MOLOCH.

Mölln, Jacob ben Moses *see* JACOB BEN MOSES HA-LEVI MÖLLN.

Moloch [Molech; Milcom]. Canaanite deity. The Canaanites sacrificed first-born children to Moloch by passing them through fire. This practice was forbidden in Scripture (Leviticus 18.21; 20.3–5). Nevertheless in Jerusalem altars were built to Moloch at Topheth in the valley of Hinnom (Jeremiah 7.31; 19.1–5; II Chronicles 28.3).

Molodowski-Lew, Kadia (1894–1975). American Yiddish poet and novelist. She was born in Lithuania. She participated in the publications of the Kiev Yiddish Group after 1917, but soon moved to Warsaw to teach in Yiddish schools. In 1935 she settled in New York. Her verse reflects her experiences in Europe, America, and Israel. After the establishment of the State of Israel, she wrote lyrics expressing joy at the restoration of Zion. She also wrote novels, short stories, and plays, depicting Jewish life in Poland as well as biblical and historical themes.

Momigliano, Arnaldo (1908–1987). Italian historian. He was born in Caraglio. He taught in Rome, Turin, Pisa, London, and Chicago. He wrote studies about ancient history, the Maccabees and Judaica, and the history of the second Temple period. His publications include *Alien Wisdom: the Limits of Hellenisation.*

***Mommsen, Theodor** (1817–1903). German classical scholar and historian. A liberal member of the Prussian and German parliaments, he was active on behalf of Russian Jewry and consistently opposed anti-Semitism. Nevertheless he encouraged Jews to abandon their separateness and assimilate into contemporary German life.

Monasticism. The conventual life is practically unknown among the Jews. Celibacy is discouraged in Judaism, and ascetic tendencies have been generally counteracted by the social orientation of the Jewish faith. The only Jewish monastic communities date from the late second Temple period; they include the Essenes and the Therapeutae.

Monatsschrift für Geschichte und Wissenschaft des Judentums. German scholarly monthly publication which appeared from 1851 to 1939. It was founded in Dresden by Zacharias Frankel, and dealt with various Jewish subjects; after 1861 it was published mostly from Breslau.

Mond, Alfred Moritz, 1st Baron Melchett (1868–1930). English industrialist and statesman. He entered his father's firm, which later became Imperial Chemical Industries. He was elected to parliament as a Liberal in 1906, and was appointed commissioner of works, and later minister of health. He subsequently became a member of the Conservative Party. He was made a baron in 1928. A dedicated Zionist and contributor to Zionist causes, he helped to found the Jewish Agency in 1929 and became the chairman of its council.

Mond, Henry, 2nd Baron Melchett (1898–1949). English Zionist and communal leader, son of Alfred Moritz Mond. He was brought up in the Christian faith but converted to Judaism after the rise of Hitler. An ardent Zionist, he succeeded his father as chairman of the council of the Jewish Agency. He also served as the president of the World Union of Maccabi.

Mondays and Thursdays. These days of the week are characterized liturgically by the reading of the law and the recitation of additional penitential and supplicatory prayers during the morning service. In addition they are also the preferred days for voluntary fasts. The three voluntary fasts, known as "Behab" (Monday, Thursday, and Monday), are observed shortly after the feasts of the Passover and Tabernacles and are intended to atone for unintentional sins and levity during the festive season.

Money *see* COINS.

Moneylending. The exacting of interest on a loan to a fellow citizen is prohibited in the Torah but it is permitted when the borrower is a stranger (Deuteronomy 23.20–21). Despite this exception, there was a tendency to forbid any lending at interest in biblical times. In the Middle Ages Jews were frequently approached for loans; as they were excluded from trade and craftsmen's guilds in northern Europe, moneylending became a common Jewish activity, which performed an important function in medieval society. In southern Europe moneylending was the profession of a small Jewish minority. In central and northern Italy, the employment of Jews as municipal moneylenders was responsible for the establishment of new Jewish communities in the 13th–14th centuries. With the removal of civil and economic restrictions on Jewry in modern society, moneylending ceased to be concentrated in Jewish hands.

***Monis, Judah** (1683–1764). American Hebraist. He is believed to have been born in Algiers or Italy. He was educated in Livorno and Amsterdam, and later settled in the US, where he was admitted as a freeman of New York in 1715. In 1722 he was baptized in the hall of Harvard College at Cambridge, Massachusetts. In the same year he was appointed instructor of Hebrew at the college. His essays are an apology for and defense of his new faith. His *Dickdook Leshon Gnebreet: a Grammar of the Hebrew Tongue* was published in 1735.

Monobaz II (fl. 1st cent.). King of Adiabene, eldest son of Helena and Monobaz I. He succeeded his younger brother Izates II to the throne. He was a convert to Judaism and settled in Jerusalem with his mother.

Monogamy *see* MARRIAGE; POLYGAMY.

Monotheism. The belief that there is only one God. Jewish monotheism is enshrined in the Shema (confession of faith): "Hear, o Israel, the Lord our God, the Lord is one" (Deuteronomy 6.4). The doctrine of Jewish monotheism describes God as holy, transcendent, immanent, eternal, omnipresent, omniscient, omnipotent, and all-good. As creator of the universe, he is also a redeemer of humanity, just, compassionate, and merciful, and ready to answer the prayers of humankind. In the Middle Ages Jewish theologians discussed a wide range of issues connected with this concept of God.

Monsky, Henry (1890–1947). American communal leader, of Russian origin. He lived in Omaha, Nebraska, where he was active in Jewish and communal organizations. An ardent Zionist, he was the principal organizer of the American Jewish Conference of 1943. In 1945 he served as a consultant to the US delegation to the United Nations Organizing Conference in San Francisco. He was president of the Supreme Lodge of B'nai B'rith from 1943 until his death.

Montagu, Edwin Samuel (1879–1924). English politician, son of Samuel Montagu. He was elected to parliament in 1906, and served as parliamentary under-secretary of state for India from 1910 to 1914. In that year he became financial secretary to the Treasury, and in 1916 Chancellor of the Duchy of Lancaster and minister of munitions. From 1917 to 1922 he was secretary of state for India. He was an opponent of Zionism and the Balfour Declaration.

Montagu, Ewen Edward Samuel (1901–1985). English lawyer and communal leader, grandson of Samuel Montagu. He was judge-advocate of the fleet and chairman of the Middlesex Quarter Sessions. He served as president of the United Synagogues (the federation of Ashkenazi synagogues in the UK) from 1954 to 1962.

Montagu, Lilian Helen (1873–1963). English social worker and magistrate, daughter of Samuel Montagu. She founded the West Central Girls' Club in London in 1893. Together with Claude Goldsmid Montefiore, she established the Jewish Religious Union in 1902, and the World Union for Progressive Judaism in 1926.

Montagu, Samuel, 1st Baron Swaythling (1832–1911). English banker and commual leader. He was born in Liverpool. In 1853 he founded the merchant bankers Samuel Montagu and Company. He served as the Liberal member of parliament for Whitechapel from 1885 to 1900. In 1894 he was made a baronet, and in 1907 a baron. He was the leader in Britain of Orthodox Russian Jewish immigrants, and in 1887 founded the Federation of Synagogues. He traveled to Palestine, Russia, and the US on behalf of Jewry, but was an opponent of Zionism.

Montefiore, Claude Joseph Goldsmid (1858–1938). English theologian and leader of Liberal Judaism. He studied at Balliol College, Oxford, and the Hochschule für Wissenschaft des Judentums in Berlin. In 1888 he founded the scholarly journal the *Jewish Quarterly Review*. He was a founder of the Jewish Religious Union in 1902 which led to the establishment in 1926 of the Liberal Jewish Synagogue in London. In 1926 he was elected president of the World Union for Progressive Judaism. With Baron von Hugel, he founded the London Society for the Study of Religion. An opponent of Zionism, he served as president of the Anglo-Jewish Association. His writings include *Aspects of Judaism, The Synoptic Gospels, Liberal Judaism, Outlines of Liberal Judaism*, and *Rabbinic Literature and Gospel Teaching*. With Herbert Loewe he edited *A Rabbinic Anthology*.

Montefiore, Francis Abraham (1860–1935). English Sephardi leader. A supporter of Theodor Herzl he was active in Ḥibbat Zion and served as chairman of the English Zionist Federation.

Montefiore, Sir **Moses** (1784–1855). British communal leader. He was born in Livorno, but grew up in London, where he worked as a broker. An observant Jew, he maintained his own synagogue in Ramsgate from 1833; he was an opponent of Reform Judaism. In 1837 he was sheriff of the City of London, and he was the first Jew to be knighted in Britain. He went on a mission to the Levant with Isaac-Adolphe Crémieux in 1840 at the time of the Damascus Affair, and he intervened with their governments on behalf of the Jews of Russia, Morocco, and Romania. He visited Palestine on several occasions and worked to improve the conditions under which the Jewish community lived there. From 1838 to 1874 he was president of the Board of Deputies of British Jews.

Months. The months of the Jewish year are Nisan, Iyyar, Sivan, Tammuz, Av, Elul, Tishri, Heshvan, Kislev, Tevet, Shevat, and Adar. *See also* CALENDAR.

Montor, Henry (1905–1982). American Zionist, of Canadian origin. He was assistant editor of the journal *New Palestine* from 1926 to 1930. He served with the United Palestine Appeal (1930–39), and was then executive vice-president of the United Jewish Appeal (1939–50). Later he was vice-president and chief executive of the American Financial and Development Corporation for Israel.

Montpellier. City in southern France, the principal town of the Languedoc. Jews lived there from the 11th century. It was the home of many important rabbis, and the ban proclaimed there against Maimonides because of the excessive rationalism of his *Guide for the Perplexed* began the Maimonidean controversy. In 1306 and 1394 the Jewish community was expelled from Montpellier, but Marranos settled in the city in later centuries.

Moon, Blessing of the (Hebrew "Kiddush levenah"). Prayer of thanksgiving recited at the appearance of the new moon. According to tradition, a quorum ("minyan") of ten adult men is required to perform this rite, which usually takes place at the close of the Sabbath in the synagogue courtyard on any day between the 3rd and 15th days of the lunar month (when the moon is waxing).

***Moore, George Foot** (1851–1931). American scholar. He was professor of Hebrew at Andover Theological Seminary from 1883. In 1904 he became professor of the history of religion at Harvard University. He published studies of the Hebrew Bible and tannaitic Judaism. His writings include *Judaism in the First Centuries of the Christian Era: the Age of the Tannaim.*

Mor [Friedmann-Yellin]**, Nathan** (b. 1913). Israeli public figure. He was born in Poland, and settled in Palestine in 1941. He joined the underground terrorist movement Loḥame Ḥerut Yisrael, which he headed from 1943. After the assassination of Count Bernadotte in 1948, he was sentenced to prison, but he was freed under the terms of the general amnesty of February 1949. He represented the Fighters' Party in the first Knesset. Later he was active in Semitic Action, which supported the idea of a Jewish–Arab federation.

Morais, Sabato (1823–1897). American rabbi. He was born in Livorno. At the age of 22 he became assistant ḥazzan to the Spanish and Portuguese congregation in London. In 1851 he became ḥazzan to the Mikveh Israel Congregation in Philadelphia. A leading opponent of Reform, he was an Abolitionist during the Civil War. In 1856 he helped to establish the Jewish Theological Seminary and he then served as president of its faculty.

Mordecai (fl. 5th cent. BCE). Persian palace official at Shushan during the reign of Ahasuerus. His niece Esther was part of the king's harem. Through her Mordecai informed the king of an assassination plot against him. Later, when Mordecai refused to bow to the vizier Haman, the vizier resolved to avenge himself on the Jewish population; his plan was frustrated by Esther, Haman was hanged, and Mordecai assumed Haman's position as chief minister. These events are recorded in the Book of Esther.

Mordecai ben Hillel (fl. 13th cent.). German codifier. He lived in Nuremberg, where he died a martyr's death in the Rindfleisch massacres along with his wife and five children. His *Sepher Mordekhai* is a compendium in the style of the tosaphot, dealing with talmudic problems. He also wrote responsa and liturgical poetry.

Moreh Nevukhim *see* MAIMONIDES.

More judaico *see* JEWISH OATH.

Morenu ("Our teacher"). Title accorded to distinguished rabbis. Introduced in Germany in the 14th century, it spread to other countries.

Morgenstern, Julian (1881–1976). American biblical scholar. He was born in St. Francisville, Illinois. He served as a rabbi in Lafayette, Indiana, and later taught at the Hebrew Union College, where he became president in 1922. He published studies of a wide range of biblical topics.

Morgenthau, Henry (1856–1946). American financier and diplomat. He was born in Mannheim, Germany, and settled in the US in 1865. Initially he practiced law, but then became active in real estate and banking. From 1913 to 1916 he was US ambassador to Turkey. Later he led a commission to investigate the condition of Jews in Poland. He was active in secular as well as Jewish religious and philanthropic work.

Morgenthau, Henry, Jr. (1891–1967). American agriculturalist and politician, son of Henry Morgenthau. He was born in New York. He became chairman of the Agricultural Advisory Commission in 1928, and in 1934 was appointed secretary to the Treasury. He was active in a wide variety of Jewish organizations.

Moriah. Area of Palestine. On one of its mountains Abraham was ready to sacrifice his son (Genesis 22.2–4). The Bible identifies Mount Moriah as the place where Solomon built the Temple (II Chronicles 3.1).

Morning benedictions. Series of blessings. In talmudic times they were recited on waking. The gaonim later transferred them to the beginning of the synagogue service, where they are followed by the reading of passages from the Written and Oral Laws and by other prayers.

Morning Freiheit *see* FREIHEIT.

Morning Journal. American Yiddish daily newspaper. It was founded in 1901 by Jacob Saphirstein, and its editor was Peter Wiernik. It was an organ of American Orthodoxy. In 1928 it absorbed the Yiddish daily *Yidishes tageblatt*, and in 1954 it merged with *Der tog*.

Morning service *see* SHAḤARIT.

Morpurgo, Rachel (1790–1871). Italian Hebrew poet. She was born in Trieste. Her poetry, which shows the influence of Samuel David Luzzatto, describes autobiographical and family incidents. Written in the style of Spanish and Italian Hebrew religious poetry, it depicts Jewish historical values and traditions.

Morpurgo, Salomone (1860–1942). Italian philologist and librarian. From 1884 to 1942 he was director of the Biblioteca Riccardiana in Rome. He also served as head of the Biblioteca Marciana in Venice, which he transferred to the Palazzo della Zecca, and of the National Library in Florence (1905–23). His studies included an investigation of the medieval Italian version of the legend of the Wandering Jew.

Morpurgo, Samson (1681–1740). Italian rabbi and physician. He was born in Gradisca d'Isonzo, in Friuli. He became a member of the bet din of the kabbalist Joseph Fiametta in 1709, and he later served as a rabbi in Ancona. He had contacts with all the great scholars of his generation, and his skills as a doctor were widely recognized. In 1713 he was involved in the polemics of the rabbis against Nehemiah Ḥayyon. He published a polemic against the priest Luigi Maria Benetelli, who wrote an anti-Semitic work. He also wrote numerous responsa and a philosophical commentary on Jedaiah Bedersi's *Beḥinat Olam*.

Mortara, Marco (1815–1894). Italian rabbi and scholar. From 1842 he served as rabbi of Mantua. An advocate of reform, he published books on the principles of Judaism and a new edition of the prayerbook. He produced a catalog of the manuscripts in the library of the Mantua community, and a list of Jewish scholars who lived in Italy from the 1st to the 19th centuries.

Mortara Case. In 1858 the Jewish child Edgardo Mortara, who had been baptized, was abducted by the papal police and taken to the House of Catechumens in Rome. Napoleon III protested against the abduction, and Sir Moses Montefiore went to Rome in 1859 and attempted (unsuccessfully) to secure the child's release. Eventually Mortara became a canon in Rome and a professor of theology.

Morteira, Saul Levi (c. 1596–1660).

Dutch rabbi and scholar, of Venetian origin. He became Ḥakham of the Beit Ya'akov community in Amsterdam, and founded the Keter Torah Yeshivah there. He was a member of the bet din that excommunicated Benedict Spinoza. His *Givat Shaul* is a collection of sermons. He also wrote responsa and Jewish apologetics.

Mosad Bialik. Israeli institute for the publication of Hebrew books. It was founded in Jerusalem in 1935 by the Jewish Agency. It has published a biblical encyclopedia, comprehensive collections of Hebrew classics, and works of Jewish scholarship.

Mosad ha-Rav Kook ("Rabbi Kook Foundation"). Israeli religious cultural institution. It was founded in Jerusalem in 1937 in cooperation with the Jewish Agency by the World Center of Mizraḥi. It publishes and subsidizes the publication of religious books and issues the monthly review *Sinai*.

Moscow. City on the Moskva River, capital of the USSR, and of the Russian SFSR. Decrees forbidding Jewish settlement there were issued in 1490, 1549, 1610, and 1667. When Belorussia was annexed to Russia in 1772, Jewish merchants began to settle in Moscow. Between 1826 and 1856 a ghetto was established in the city. Subsequently the community expanded and became a center of the Ḥovevei Zion. In 1891 thousands of Jewish workers were expelled from Moscow and sent to the Pale of Settlement. After the 1917 Revolution, the Jewish population of Moscow increased, and it became the most important Jewish center in the USSR.

Mosenthal, Solomon Hermann von (1821–1877). German author. He was born in Kassel. He wrote poems, stories, melodramas, and opera libretti. His works include the play *Deborah* and a volume of stories about Jewish life.

Moser ("betrayer"). Term used among the Ashkenazim to refer to an informer who denounces fellow Jews to the secular authority. In southern Europe the equivalent term is "malsin."

Moses (fl. ?13th cent. BCE). Lawgiver, leader of the Israelites, and prophet. He was born in Egypt to Amram and Jochebed, who hid him in a basket among the reeds of the Nile to escape Pharaoh's decree to slaughter all new-born Jewish males. He was found by Pharaoh's daughter, who raised him in the royal household. In early manhood he killed an Egyptian whom he discovered beating a Hebrew. He fled to Midian and became a shepherd to the local priest Jethro, whose daughter, Zipporah, he married; she bore him two sons. While keeping Jethro's sheep on Mount Horeb he encountered God, who spoke to him from the burning bush and commanded him to free the Hebrew slaves. He interceded with Pharaoh who eventually released the Hebrews after ten plagues had afflicted Egypt. Moses led the people across the Red Sea, which miraculously parted to let them pass, and guided them for 40 years in the desert. On Mount Sinai he received God's revelation of the law, embodied in the Ten Commandments written on tablets of stone. Before his death he appointed Joshua his successor.

Moses, Adolph (1840–1902). American rabbi, of Polish origin. He emigrated to the US in 1870, and served as rabbi to the Reform congregation in Louisville from 1881 until his death. With Isaac S. Moses and Emil G. Hirsch, he edited the German-language weekly *Zeitgeist*. A collection of his writings appeared posthumously as *Yahvism and Other Discourses*.

Moses, Assumption of. Apocryphal work. It relates the address given by Moses to Joshua in the form of a prophecy. It also includes a history of Israel to the time of Herod. In an additional section, which is now lost, the death of Moses and the war between Satan and the archangel Michael over his body are depicted.

Moses, Blessing of. Title given to Deuteronomy 33, which records the blessing of the tribes of Israel by Moses before his death. Poetic in form, this text consists of a blessing for each tribe (except Simeon) and a blessing for the entire people.

Moses, Seat of. Term used of a place in the synagogue which cannot be identified with certainty. According to Matthew 23.2 it was the seat occupied by the scribes and Pharisees. Some scholars maintain that it was either the place of the rabbi, or the stand where the Sepher Torah was placed.

Moses, Song of [Haazinu]. Title given to the speech made by Moses before his death; it is recorded in Deuteronomy 32. It foretells the disasters that will occur if the Torah is disobeyed, and describes God's love for Israel. It is also known by its initial word "Haazinu" (Hearken).

Moses ben Enoch (fl. 10th cent.). Spanish scholar. In the story of the Four Captives in *The Book of Tradition*, Abraham ibn Daud relates that four rabbis (including Moses ben Enoch) were captured by Saracen pirates after they sailed from Bari in southern Italy in 972. Moses ben Enoch was ransomed in Córdoba, and was appointed rabbi of the community.

Moses ben Isaac di Rieti [Rieti, Moses of] (1388–c. 1460). Italian physician, philosopher, and poet. He worked as a physician at Rieti until 1422, and then lived in Perugia, Narni, Fabriano, and Rome, where he was a rabbi and physician to Pope Pius II. His *Mikdash Me'at* is a moral and philosophical poem in *terza rima*; it contains a vision of Paradise, and an account of Jewish scholars down to his own time. He also wrote medical and other philosophical studies.

Moses ben Jacob of Coucy (fl. 13th cent.). French scholar. An itinerant preacher, he began his ministry in Spain in 1236, where he preached sermons that attracted a huge audience. Later he visited other countries, and participated in the Disputation of Paris in 1240. His *Sepher Mitzvot Gadol* (also known as *Semag*) contains the Oral Law presented as groups of positive and negative commandments. His other writings include the *Tosaphot Yeshanim* and a commentary on the Torah.

Moses ben Jacob of Russia (1449–1520). Ukrainian talmudic author. He was born in Seduva, Lithuania. He lived in Kiev, where he pursued his studies as a biblical exegete, talmudist, poet, linguist, and kabbalist. When the Tartars attacked the city in 1482 he escaped, but his children were taken captive to the Crimea; after ransoming them, he returned to Kiev. In 1495 the Jews of Lithuania and the Ukraine were expelled, and he was forced to wander. In 1506 he was himself taken captive by the Tartars and was ransomed by the Jews of Salkhat. He then settled in Kaffa, where he became rabbi and head of the community. His writings include a liturgy according to the Crimean rite.

Moses ben Maimon *see* MAIMONIDES.

Moses ben Naḥman *see* NAḤMANIDES.

Moses ben Shemtov de León (1250–1305). Spanish kabbalist. He lived in Guadalajara and, from 1290 in Avila. He wrote some 20 kabbalistic works and is known for his revelation of the Zohar: according to kabbalistic tradition, the book (attributed to Simeon ben Yoḥai) was sent by Naḥmanides from Palestine to Spain, where it reached Moses ben Shemtov, who made it known.

Moses ha-Darshan [Narboni, Moses] (fl. 11th cent.). French scholar. He lived in Narbonne. His writings, notably commentaries on the Bible, influenced Rashi.

Moses of London (fl. 13th cent.). English grammarian, halakhist, and Jewish scholar. His *Darkhe ha-Nikkud veha-Neginah* is a treatise on Hebrew punctuation and accentuation.

Moses of Narbonne [Maestro Vidal Blasom] (fl. 14th cent.). French philosopher, translator, and physician. His commentary on Maimonides' *Guide for the Perplexed* is based on an Aristotelian–Averroistic perspective.

Moses of Sodilkov [Ephraim Moses Ḥayyim of Sodilkov] (c. 1737–c. 1800). Ukrainian Ḥasidic leader, grandson of Israel Baal Shem Tov. He studied under Dov Ber of Mezhirich, and lived as a rabbi and preacher in Sodilkov in Volhynia. His *Degel Maḥaneh Ephraim* is based on the doctrines of the Baal Shem Tov and teaches that the goal of Ḥasidism is humility and self-evaluation. The role of the tzaddikim is to reprove and reform those who are negligent, and to elevate the people through prayer and religious teaching.

Moshavah ("settlement"). Agricultural village of a type established in Palestine from around 1880. Each household owns and farms its own land. The institution originated during the first Aliyah, and the earliest settlements of this kind were Petaḥ Tikvah and Rishon le-Zion. The majority of moshavot are plantation colonies, growing citrus fruits. A number founded since the 1930s cooperate in marketing and supply.

Moshav ovedim ("workers' settlement") [moshav]. Cooperative village of a type established in Palestine from 1907. Its inhabitants possess individual homes and smallholdings but cooperate in the purchase of equipment, the sale of produce, and mutual aid. The land is normally purchased by the Jewish National Fund. The first experiments of this type were at Beer Yaakov, En Ganim, and Naḥlat Yaakov. During the third Aliyah (1918–23) a reaction against the earlier type of settlement, the kevutzah, led to the foundation of larger moshave ovedim. After the establishment of the State of Israel, moshave ovedim became the most common form of workers' village.

Moshav shituphi ("cooperative settlement"). Agricultural village of a type established in Palestine from 1936 onwards. The members possess individual homesteads, but the agricultural operation and entire economic life of the community are conducted as a single cooperative unit. The land is normally owned by the Jewish National Fund. The form of the settlement is intermediate between the kibbutz (in which everything is commonly owned) and the moshav ovedim (in which only equipment and the proceeds of agricultural trade are shared).

Moshav zekenim. Old people's home.

Moss, Celia (1819–1873). English writer. Together with her sister Marian Moss (1821–1907), she wrote *The Romance of Jewish History* and *Tales of Jewish History*.

Mosse, Rudolf (1843–1920). German publisher and philanthropist. He was born in Oraetz. He founded an advertising business in 1867, and several years later established the *Berliner Tageblatt*, one of Germany's leading newspapers. In 1880 he acquired the *Allgemeine Zeitung des Judentums*. His activities on behalf of the community included the setting up of a hospital in Graetz and the founding of an educational institute in Wilhelmsdorf.

Mosul. City in northern Iraq. Jews settled there when Shalmaneser IV, King of Assyria, conquered Samaria in the 8th century BCE. In the 13th century it had the largest Jewish community in Iraq and served as the seat of the exilarch.

Mother. According to the Bible and the Talmud, the mother has equal rights with the father in the moral and ethical sphere to the respect and deference of her children. The duty of honoring both parents is enjoined by the fifth of the Ten Commandments. Similarly the punishment for smiting or cursing parents applies to such actions against the mother as well as against the father. In valid Jewish marriages the child is accorded the status of the father, but in mixed marriages (between a Jew and a gentile) the child receives the status of the mother. The child of an unmarried Jewish woman is regarded as Jewish in every respect; the concept of bastardy applies only to the children of prohibited relationships (*see* MAMZER). The mother is the symbol of home and family life for which she is responsible. In Jewish tradition the four matriarchs (Sarah, Rebekah, Rachel, and Leah) are to be revered equally with the three patriarchs (Abraham, Isaac, and Jacob).

Motke Ḥabad [Rakover, Mordecai] (fl. 18th cent.). Lithuanian jester. He was a famous figure among Lithuanian Jewry.

Motta, Jacob de la (1789–1845). American physician and communal leader. He was born in Savannah, Georgia. He served as an army surgeon in the War of 1812. He was prominent in Jewish communal life in Savannah and later in Charleston, South Carolina.

Motzi *see* HA-MOTZI.

Motzkin, Leo (1867–1933). Ukrainian Zionist leader. He was born in Brovary, near Kiev. In 1887 he helped to found the Russian Jewish Scientific Society in Berlin, which included Jewish students from Russia and Galicia who supported the Ḥibbat Zion movement. A follower of Theodor Herzl, he was active in the Zionist movement; in 1901 he joined the Democratic Fraction, formed at the Fifth Zionist Congress. During World War I he directed the Zionist bureau in Copenhagen, and in 1919 he acted as secretary and president of the Comité des Délégations Juives at the Paris Peace Conference. In 1925 he was appointed chairman of the Zionist Executive; he served in this capacity and as head of the organization of European National Minorities until his death in 1933. His publications include a history of Russian pogroms.

Mount of Olives [Mount Scopus]. Mountain to the east of Jerusalem. According to II Samuel 15.30, 32, David worshipped on "the Ascent of the Olives"; the name "Mount of Olives" appears first in Zechariah 14.4. During the second Temple period, the mountain's summit served as the first post in a chain of beacons to Babylonia by means of which the Jews in exile were reminded of the religious events in the Jewish calendar. According to the New Testament Jesus was arrested at the foot of the mountain, and his ascension took place from its summit.

Mount Sinai. Mountain in the wilderness of Horeb on the Sinai peninsula. The Book of Deuteronomy identifies Mount Sinai with Mount HOREB and they are thus sometimes confused. The Israelites camped at the foot of Mount Sinai after the Exodus from Egypt (Exodus 19.1), and Moses ascended the mountain to receive the Ten Commandments (Exodus 20.1–24.8). According to rabbinic tradition, Moses received both the Written Law and the Oral Law there.

Mount Zion. Hill on the south-west side of Jerusalem. It was originally the site of a Jebusite fortress, which was captured by David (II Samuel 5.6–7). In poetic writings "Zion" is often used as a synonym for "Jerusalem."

Mourners for Zion *see* AVELE ZION.

Mourning (Hebrew "avelut"). Mourning customs during the biblical period involved the rending of garments, wearing sackcloth, sitting on the ground, placing earth and dust on the head, and weeping; other practices were added during the talmudic period. In contemporary practice mourning begins after the burial of a close relative. The bereaved person puts on special garments, takes off his shoes, remains in the home for seven days of mourning (SHIVAH) sitting on a low stool, refrains from attending the synagogue except on the Sabbath, and reads Scripture. No work may be done and sexual intercourse is forbidden. It is the duty of friends and relatives to visit the mourner during this period. Parents are mourned intensively for 30 days (SHELOSHIM), during which the hair and beard are left uncut and no weddings or joyful ceremonies may take place; a lesser state of mourning continues until 12 months after the burial. In post-talmudic times some alterations to these mourning customs took place, but most continued to be observed. A major innovation was the kindling of a lamp during the mourning period, and the recitation of the KADDISH prayer for 11 months after the burial of a parent or child, and each year on the anniversary of the death.

Mowshay, Ben *see* SUMMERFIELD, WOOLFE.

Mufti *see* HUSSEIN, HAJJ MOHAMMED AMIN EL-.

Mühlhausen, Yomtov Lipmann [Lipmann, Yomtov ben Solomon; Yomtov Lipmann] (fl. 14th–15th cent.). Bohemian scholar, philosopher, kabbalist, and polemicist. He lived in Prague, where he participated in a disputation with the apostate Peter (Pesaḥ) who alleged that the Jews blasphemed Christian beliefs. 80 Jews were martyred as a consequence, but Mühlhausen was saved. His *Sepher Nitzaḥon* contains a depiction of this disputation.

Mukachevo [Munkacs]. City in the Ukraine, formerly in Hungary. Jews settled there in the 18th century. The city attracted a large number of Polish Ḥasidim and became the center of the orthodoxy of the notable Ḥasidic family Spira.

Mukdoni [Kappel]**, Alexander** (1877–1958). American Yiddish essayist and theater critic. He was born in Lyakhovichi in Belorussia. After World War I he edited the Yiddish daily *Nayes* produced in Kovno. In 1922 he settled in the US, where he wrote for the Yiddish daily *Jewish Morning Journal*. He wrote stories, essays, and memoirs.

Muktzeh ("[things] set aside"). Objects that a Jew must not handle on the Sabbath or festivals. The Talmud specifies several categories of forbidden objects: (1) money and tools, the nature of which renders them unfit for use on the Sabbath or festivals because of their connection with forbidden work; (2) objects not normally used; (3) objects that were not in existence or were inaccessible at the beginning of the Sabbath or festival; (4) objects that at the beginning of the Sabbath or festival were being used as a support or base for others which it is forbidden to use.

Müller, Joel (1827–1895). Moravian rabbinic scholar. He was born at Mährisch Ostrau and served as a rabbi there, and later in Leipa, Bohemia. After teaching religion in Vienna, he took up a post at the Berlin Hochschule für die Wissenschaft des Judentums. He published studies of gaonic and French responsa.

Müller-Cohen, Anita (1890–1962). Austrian social worker. She was born in Vienna. She served as a relief worker in Galicia and Bukovina during World War I. She established hospitals for mothers, day nurseries, medical services for children, and institutions for the care of the aged. After the war she helped returning soldiers to readjust to civilian life and established milk stations for undernourished children in Austria. She also directed the placement of orphans in

Jewish homes. In 1936 she settled in Tel Aviv.

Mumar. Apostate. Although an apostate is regarded as a sinner under Jewish law and is denied certain rights and privileges, he still retains his status as a Jew. A distinction is made between a "mumar le-hakis" (who violates a precept in a spirit of rebellion and denial of its divine authority) and a "mumar le-te'avon" (who violates the precept because he is unable to withstand temptation). The Talmud classifies apostates in various categories: (1) one who violates a single commandment; (2) one who regularly violates a particular precept; and (3) one who violates the whole Torah.

Muni, Paul [Weissenfreund, Muni] (1895–1967). American actor. He began acting at the age of 12 in Chicago and in 1918 joined the Yiddish Art Theater in New York. He appeared in numerous plays on Broadway as well as in films.

Munich. City in western Germany. Jews lived there from the 13th century and engaged in moneylending. In 1285 Jews were burned in the synagogue as a result of a blood libel charge against a member of the community. The Jewish population suffered grievously during the Black Death in the 14th century. In the 15th century an allegation was made that the community was guilty of desecrating the Host: expelled in 1440, the Jews did not return to Munich until the 18th century.

Muñiz, Angelina (b. 1936). Mexican novelist, of French origin. She was a lecturer in literature at the Colegio de México and the Universidad Autónoma de México. Her publications include *Morada interior, Tierra adentro, La guerra del unicornio,* and *Huerto cerrado, huerto sellado.* Her works deal with Jewish cultural and religious themes.

Munk, Salomon (1803–1867). French orientalist. He was born in Glogau, Silesia. He settled in Paris in 1828, where he took charge of Semitic manuscripts at the Bibliothèque Nationale. In 1840 he joined the delegation to Egypt led by Sir Moses Montefiore and Isaac-Adolphe Crémieux, and intervened in the Damascus Affair. He became blind in 1850, but was nevertheless appointed professor of Hebrew and Syriac literature at the Collège de France in 1864. His writings include studies of Hebrew and Arabic literature of the Golden Age of Spain, as well as an edition of the Arabic text of Maimonides' *Guide for the Perplexed.*

Munkacs *see* MUKACHEVO.

***Münster, Sebastian** (1489–1552). German Hebraist and reformer. He was born in Ingelheim. He taught Hebrew at Heidelberg, and became professor of Hebrew at Basle University in 1528. One of the outstanding Christian Hebraists of the 16th century, he edited the Hebrew Bible, translated the Gospel of Matthew into Hebrew, wrote grammars of biblical Aramaic and rabbinic Hebrew, and translated the grammatical works of Elijah Levita into Latin.

Münz [Minz]**, Judah** (c. 1409–1509). German rabbi. After the Jews were expelled from Mainz in 1461, he settled in Padua, where he founded a yeshivah and taught philosophy at the university; he remained in Italy for the rest of his life. He wrote numerous responsa and engaged in a polemic with Elijah Delmedigo.

Münz [Minz]**, Moses** (c. 1750–1831). Hungarian rabbi. He was born either in Podolia or in Galicia. He served as a rabbi in Vishravitz and Brody, then in 1789 was appointed rabbi of Alt-Ofen, where he represented the Jewish community at royal ceremonies. In 1793 he became chief rabbi of the entire Pest region. Initially tolerant of reformers, he later became antagonistic towards them. He wrote responsa and published (with annotations) the *Peri Ya'akov of* Jacob ben Moses.

Murabaat. Site of four caves near the Dead Sea where important archeological finds were made in 1951–2. During the Bar Kokhba revolt (132–5) the caves were the headquarters of Yeshua ben Gilgola, and remains of the period, as well as items of correspondence with Bar Kokhba, were discovered there. Other documents found included Bible fragments and manuscripts pertaining to the Roman military post established after the caves were captured from the rebels.

Murder [homicide]. According to Hebrew law, the penalty for premeditated murder, witnessed by two individuals who warned the perpetrator of the seriousness of the crime before it was committed, is beheading. Yet the law requires such meticulous proof of the details of the act that, for practical purposes, it became impossible to impose capital punishment. Under these circumstances, the guilty person was sentenced to imprisonment. When the murder was not premeditated, the killer could flee to one of the cities of refuge.

Musaph ("additional sacrifice"). Service comprising an additional Amidah which is recited on those days when an additional sacrifice was formerly offered in the Temple (Sabbaths, New Moons, the three pilgrim festivals, New Year, and the Day of Atonement). It can take place at any time of day before the seventh hour.

Musar. In biblical Hebrew the word is used variously to mean punishment or chastisement and instruction. Later it came to signify morals, ethics, and moral instruction. In the Middle Ages a distinct branch of literature developed, known as "musar literature," which dealt with moral and ethical matters. In the modern period the word has connotations of sermonizing and denotes a type of literature of edification.

Musar movement. Movement for ethical education in the spirit of the halakhah. It began in the 19th century among Orthodox groups in Lithuania; its founder, Israel Salanter, stressed the need to develop inner piety, and his followers encouraged the study of traditional ethical literature. Throughout Lithuania musar institutions were established, and the movement became influential among the yeshivot. A number of yeshivot were established by leaders of the movement at Chełm, Slobodka, and Novahardok.

Muselman (German: "Muslim"). The word became a colloquial term for the victims of the concentration camps in the Nazi period; it may have originated as a reference to their posture of squatting with expressionless faces.

Museums. Jewish museums are a relatively new phenomenon resulting from the development of scholarly research into Judaica in western and eastern Europe and the US at the end of the 19th century and beginning of the 20th. From this period exhibitions of Judaica began to be organized, and the interest generated led to the founding of numerous Jewish museums throughout the world, notably in Europe (Vienna, Frankfurt am Main, Gdańsk, Berlin, London, and Paris), the US (New York), and Israel (Jerusalem and Tel Aviv).

Music. In early biblical history Jewish music and musical instruments are frequently mentioned. In the Temple the Levites organized the performance of the service, and trained singers, players, and conductors. After the Babylonian exile, a decline in instrumental music took place, and with the destruction of the second Temple, Jewish music was restricted to chanting in the synagogue. Services were sung in traditional chant by the ḥazzan (or cantor), who might, however, embellish the melodies. Jewish musical life in eastern Europe culminated in the worship of the Ḥasidim, which placed emphasis on ecstatic religious music. In modern times there has been a resurgence of interest in the development of music in the Jewish world, and many works have been written for the concert hall that take Jewish events as their subjects, or use Hebrew words or melodies.

Muslims. Adherents of ISLAM.

***Mussolini, Benito** (1883–1945). Founder of Italian Fascism. When it was first established in the 1920s his movement was not hostile towards the Jewish community. But his alliance with Hitler resulted in his adopting anti-Semitic policies.

***Mussolino, Benedetto** (1809–1888). Italian statesman. He was born in Pizzo. He served as a member of the Italian parliament, and was later a senator. In *Gerusalemme ed il popolo Ebreo*, he advocated the return of the Jews to Palestine.

Myrtle. One of the four species of plant, branches of which are used ceremonially on the feast of Sukkot; see LULAV.

Mysticism *see* KABBALAH.

N

Naaman (fl. 9th cent. BCE). Syrian commander-in-chief. He suffered from leprosy and was sent by his king to search for a cure in Israel. After Elisha had cured him he was overtaken on his return journey to Damascus by Elisha's servant Gehazi, who obtained gifts from him by pretending that Elisha would distribute them to the poor. When Elisha discovered this deception, he inflicted Naaman's leprosy on Gehazi. (II kings 5)

Nabal (fl. 11th–10th cent. BCE). Israelite landowner, husband of Abigail. He was a wealthy man, the owner of thousands of sheep and goats in Carmel. When ten young followers of David visited him he received them inhospitably. David gathered a band of 400 together to take revenge on Nabal, but was appeased by Abigail. However, Nabal did not escape: he was killed by God a few days later, and David married Abigail. (I Samuel 25)

Nabateans. Ancient Semitic people, who lived in the territory of Edom. During the period when the Selelucid Empire was in decline (2nd century BCE) they extended their sphere of influence to the north to include Damascus. They came into conflict with Alexander Yannai, and were subdued by the Romans in 63 BCE. In 106 CE their country was annexed and became the Provincia Arabia.

Nablus *see* SHECHEM.

Naboth (fl. 9th cent. BCE). Israelite landowner. He possessed a vineyard, which Ahab coveted. When Naboth refused to give it up, Ahab's queen Jezebel plotted to bring about his downfall. She persuaded the local elders to honor Naboth and then to bring false evidence of blasphemy against him. Eventually he was stoned to death. This act led Elijah to predict the downfall of Ahab. (I Kings 21; II Kings 9)

Nadab (i) (fl. ?13th cent. BCE). Israelite priest, eldest son of Aaron. With his brother Abihu, he ascended Mount Sinai to behold God's revelation (Exodus 24.1–11). Later they made a fire sacrifice on the altar against God's will and were struck dead by fire as punishment (Leviticus 10.1–3).

Nadab (ii) (fl. 10th cent. BCE). King of Israel (907–906 BCE), son and successor of Jeroboam I. He and the House of Jeroboam were assassinated by Baasha (I Kings 15.25–31).

Nadel, Arno (1878–1943). German poet and musicologist. He was born in Vilnius. He became conductor of the choir at the synagogue in Pestalozzistrasse in Berlin, and later was the musical supervisor of the Berlin synagogues. He published poetry, collected synagogue music and eastern European Jewish folk songs, painted portraits and landscapes, and composed music.

Nadir, Banu *see* BANU-L-NADIR.

Nadir, Moshe [Reiss, Isaac] (1885–1943). American Yiddish writer. He was born in eastern Galicia, and emigrated to New

York in 1898. He contributed to numerous literary publications, and wrote poetry, drama, and essays.

Nagdela, Ibn *see* SAMUEL IBN NAGRELA.

Nagid ("prince"). Head of the Jewish community in Islamic countries (except under Abbasid rule, 750–1258, when the Jews were led by the exilarch). From the 10th century there was a nagid in Spain, Kairouan, Egypt, and Yemen, and from the 16th century to the 19th in Morocco, Algeria, and Tunisia; the office was discontinued in the 19th century.

Nagrela, Ibn *see* SAMUEL IBN NAGRELA.

Naḥal (from Hebrew "Noar Ḥalutzi Loḥem": Fighting pioneer youth). Unit of the Israel Defense Forces. During their term of military service, the soldiers in this unit are prepared for their future membership in cooperative agricultural settlements. They are recruited from youth movements, Youth Aliyah, pioneer youth organizations abroad, and the army.

Naḥal Mizrayim. The largest of the wadis of the Negev and Sinai. It runs down to the Mediterranean to the east of El Arish in the Sinai Peninsula. According to the Bible, the southern boundary of the Land of Israel followed its course (Numbers 34.5; Joshua 15.4).

Naḥal Sorek ("Brook of Shorek"). Valley in Judah, where Delilah lived (Judges 16.4). Samson was captured there by the Philistines.

Nahavendi, Benjamin *see* BENJAMIN BEN MOSES NAHAVENDI.

Nahem ("Comfort"). The name of a prayer, instituted by Palestinian amoraim, which is recited in the Amidah of the afternoon service on the Ninth of Av. It consists of a supplication for comfort for those who mourn Zion, and a prayer for the rebuilding of the city.

Naḥman bar Jacob (fl. 3rd–4th cent.). Babylonian amora. He was born in Nehardea, and married into the family of the exilarch. When Nehardea was destroyed by the Palmyrenes in 259, he went to Shekanzib, but after it was rebuilt he returned to Nehardea, where he taught and served as a dayyan. The Talmud contains many of his halakhic and aggadic statements.

Naḥmani bar Kaylil *see* ABBAYE.

Naḥmanides [Bonastruc de Porta; Moses ben Naḥman; Ramban] (1194–1270). Spanish talmudist, kabbalist, and biblical commentator. He is commonly known by the name Naḥmanides, though his Hebrew name was Moses ben Naḥman and his Spanish name Bonastruc de Porta; the name Ramban is derived from the title Rabbi Moses ben Naḥman. He served as rabbi of Gerona. In 1263 he was challenged by Pablo Christiani to a religious disputation, which took place in Barcelona in the presence of King James I (1213–1276). Later he was tried for blasphemy and forced to leave Spain. From 1267 he lived in Palestine, settling in Acre. Naḥmanides was regarded as the foremost Spanish talmudist of his day. Among his works are *Torat ha-Adam*, which deals with the rites of mourning, and a popular Bible commentary.

Naḥman of Bratzlav (1772–1811). Ukrainian Ḥasidic leader, great-grandson of the Baal Shem Tov. He was born in Medzhibozh and lived in Medvedevka in the province of Kiev, where he attracted numerous disciples. In 1798 he went to Palestine, but he later settled in Zlatopol in the province of Kiev, where he engaged in controversy with Aryeh Leib of Spola. In 1802 he moved to Bratslav. His various journeys are described in works by his disciple Nathan Sternhartz. In 1810 he settled in the Ukrainian city of Uman. In his teachings he emphasized simple faith and prayer, and developed the theory of the tzaddik as the intermediary between man and God.

Nahoum, Haim (1873–1960). Turkish

rabbi and scholar. He went to Abyssinia in 1907 to investigate the Falashas. From 1908 to 1920 he served as Ḥakham Bashi of Turkey, and from 1923 he was chief rabbi of Cairo; he was later appointed chief rabbi of Egypt. He also served as a member of the Egyptian Senate (1930–34).

Nahshon (fl. ?13th cent. BCE). Israelite, chief of the tribe of Judah during the Exodus and the wanderings in the desert; he was the brother-in-law of Aaron. According to rabbinic tradition, he was the first Israelite to embark on the crossing of the Red Sea during the flight from Egypt.

Nahum. Biblical book, one of the books of the 12 Minor Prophets. It records the prophecies of the Israelite prophet Nahum (fl. 7th century BCE) concerning the fall of Nineveh.

Nahum of Gimzo (fl. 1st–2nd cent.). Palestinian tanna. His system of exegesis was based on the view that in the Torah the untranslated Hebrew particle "et" signifies that the word it precedes should be given a wide rather than a narrow connotation. This method was developed by his pupil Akiva. He was known for his saying "gam zo le-tovah" (this is also for good) when confronting misfortune; this has been understood as the basis for the name "Gimzo."

Naiditsch, Isaac (1868–1949). Russian philanthropist and Zionist. He was born in Pinsk, and lived in Moscow, where he was an alcohol industrialist. An ardent Zionist, he contributed to Hebrew periodicals. At the beginning of World War I he was a founder and director of the Central Committee for the Relief of Jewish War Sufferers. After the Russian Revolution, he became a strong supporter of Hebrew culture. Later he emigrated to France, but he fled to the US during the Nazi occupation. He returned to Paris in 1941. He was a friend and adviser of Chaim Weizmann.

Najara, Israel ben Moses (c. 1555–c. 1625). Syrian Hebrew poet. Born in Damascus, he was secretary to the Jewish community there. In 1587 he published two collections of hymns, *Zemirot Yisrael* and *Mesaḥeket ba-Tevel,* in Safed. Later he served as a rabbi in Gaza.

Nakdanim ("punctuators"). Name given to a group of scholars (active from the 9th to the 14th centuries), who provided biblical manuscripts with vowels and accents. Successors of the masoretes, they lived in the Orient and in England, France, and Germany.

Nakhes (Yiddish). Pleasure.

Name, change of. The Bible contains a number of accounts of God's changing a person's name (Abram to Abraham; Sarai to Sarah; Jacob to Israel). According to the Talmud, a person's name is customarily changed if the individual is dangerously ill; this was regarded as a means of misleading the Angel of Death. The change is conferred at a short ceremony in which charity is given on behalf of the invalid, a blessing is recited, and a formula is read announcing the additional name. A prayer is then recited asking renewed life for the person with the new name.

Names. Biblical names in the early period were based on Hebrew roots and often (for reasons which are not known) incorporated the name of Baal (e.g., Ishbaal). Later monotheistic attitudes were reflected in names based on such prefixes as El- or Jeho- (Eliezer, etc.), and in suffixes such as -el, -eli, or -jahu. At the end of the second Temple period, Greek names were often used in conjunction with Hebrew, and Aramaic forms were found in Palestine and Babylonia. In the Middle Ages vernacular equivalents (often based on the blessings of Jacob or Moses) were used alongside Hebrew names. Although surnames appeared in Italy and Spain in the medieval period, patronymics were generally employed in Jewish communities. Surnames in the modern sense were used in western European countries and in the US from the 18th century. Surnames were often patronymic, geographical or occupational in character. In the 19th century, it was usual for Jews to adopt names of a non-Jewish nature, whereas in Israel in the 20th century the opposite process has taken place.

Names of God *see* GOD, NAMES OF.

Namier, Sir **Lewis Bernstein** (1888–1960). British historian and Zionist. He was born in eastern Galicia. He was professor of modern history at Manchester University from 1931. An ardent Zionist, he served as political secretary of the Jewish Agency from 1929 to 1931. He wrote studies of the social–political structure of England in the 18th century, the 1848 revolutions, the Habsburg monarchy, and the events leading up to World War II.

Namir, Mordekhai (1897–1975). Israeli politician. Born in Bratolinbovka, Ukraine, he settled in Palestine in 1924. From 1929 to 1935 he was the director of the statistical section of the Histadrut, and in 1936–43 he served as secretary-general of the Tel Aviv Workers' Council. After the establishment of the State of Israel in 1948 he held diplomatic posts in Bulgaria, Czechoslovakia, Romania, and the USSR. From 1951 he served in the Knesset, and became minister of labor; he was also the first mayor of Tel Aviv.

Naomi (fl. 12th–11th cent. BCE). Israelite woman, wife of Elimelech. With her husband and sons (Mahlon and Chilion), she left Bethlehem for Moab during a famine. After several years, during which time Elimelech and her sons died, she returned with Ruth, her daughter-in-law, whom she helped to marry the Israelite landowner Boaz.

Naphtali (fl. ?16th cent. BCE). Israelite, sixth son of Jacob, and second son of Bilhah, Rachel's maid (Genesis 30.7). The tribe of Naphtali was named after him.

Naphthali, Peretz (1888–1961). Israeli economist. He was born in Germany. He served as economic editor of the *Frankfurter Zeitung* (1921–6) and manager of the Labor Movement's Economic Research Bureau in Berlin (1926–33). He settled in Palestine in 1933 and directed the Workers' Bank from 1938 to 1949. He was then elected a Mapai member of the Knesset; during his ten years in parliament (1949–59) he was minister without portfolio (1951–2; 1955–9), and minister of agriculture (1952–5).

***Napoleon I** [Napoleon Bonaparte] (1769–1821). French military leader and emperor. In 1806 he convoked an Assembly of Jewish Notables in Paris which discussed problems submitted by the authorities regarding Jewish affairs. The delegates insisted on their religious rights, but recognized the authority of civil law. Napoleon subsequently convoked a Sanhedrin which met from 9 February to 9 March 1807. In 1808 he set up a central Jewish communal administration which worked through consistories at local level. His admission of Jewry to civil rights advanced the cause of Jewish Emancipation.

Narboni, Moses *see* MOSES HA-DARSHAN.

Narbonne. Town in southern France, close to the Mediterranean coast. Jews lived there from the 5th century, but were expelled in the 7th century by Wamba, the Visigoth king. In the Middle Ages, a Jewish king served as head of the Jewish community there. Narbonne was a prominent Jewish center until the Jews were expelled from France in 1306.

Nardi, Naḥum (1901–1977). Israeli composer. He was born in Kiev. After studying the piano and composition at the Kiev, Warsaw, and Vienna conservatories, he emigrated to Palestine in 1923 where he gave piano recitals and began composing. His work was inspired by Arab bedouin and peasant songs as well as Sephardi and Yemenite melodies.

Nash [nosh] (Yiddish). Snack.

Nashim ("Women"). Third order of the Mishnah. It deals with betrothal, marriage, divorce, the relationship between husband and wife, vows, and the law of the Nazirite.

Nashn [noshen] (Yiddish). To eat a little something between meals.

Nash Papyrus. A papyrus fragment of the 2nd century BCE on which 24 broken lines of text in square Hebrew script are inscribed. The text, which accords closely with the Septuagint, consists of the Ten Commandments, followed by the beginning of the Shema. It was taken from Egypt by W. L. Nash and published in 1903.

Nasi ("prince"). The title accorded in the Talmud to the president of the Sanhedrin. He served as spiritual head, and subsequently political representative of the Jewish people. The second in authority to the nasi was the av bet din ("president of the court"). From the 2nd century CE the nasi was recognized by the Roman authorities as Patriarch of the Jews. Later the title was used in some places to designate the lay leader of the Jewish community.

Nasi [Mendes]**, Gracia** (c. 1510–1569). Portuguese Marrano stateswoman and patroness. She was born in Portugal (as Beatrice de Luna), and married the banker Francisco Mendes. On his death she went to Antwerp in 1537. Fearing religious persecution, she escaped to Venice in 1545, but she was denounced and imprisoned there. Released in 1549, she moved to Ferrara, where she was known as a Jewess and became a patron of writers. She also controlled an underground organization which rescued Marranos from Portugal. In 1553 she went to Constantinople, where she became known as Gracia Nasi. Joined by her nephew Joseph Nasi, she became the leader of Turkish Jewry. She built synagogues, helped fugitive Marranos, and began a project for the colonization of Tiberias.

Nasi, Joseph, Duke of Naxos (c. 1524–1579). Portuguese statesman, active in Turkey. He was born a Marrano in Portugal, under the name Joao Micas. He accompanied his aunt Gracia Mendes (*see* NASI, GRACIA) when she went from Lisbon to Antwerp in 1537, but when in 1545 she fled to Italy, he remained behind to settle her affairs. In 1554 he joined her in Constantinople, where he embraced Judaism publicly and married her daughter, Reyna. He became an intimate of Selim, the heir to the Turkish throne. In 1561 he obtained from the sultan the lease of Tiberias and control of an adjacent area, which he developed as a Jewish center. He was eventually created Duke of Naxos and the Cyclades.

***Nasser, Gamal Abdul** (1918–1970). Egyptian military leader and politician. In 1948, as an officer in the Egyptian army, he invaded Palestine. After becoming prime minister of Egypt in 1954, he organized anti-Israel activities. When the Egyptian forces were defeated in the Sinai Campaign in 1956 Nasser (by now president of Egypt) expelled stateless Jews from the country and curtailed the activities of Egyptian Jewry. In 1967 he headed an Arab coalition against Israel, but their forces were defeated in the Six-Day War.

Nassy, David (fl. 18th cent.). Caribbean physician and communal leader. He was born in Surinam, and became president of the Jewish community there. His *Essai historique sur la colonie de Surinam* is a record of the Jewish role in the colony's history. Eventually he settled in Philadelphia and became the first Jewish physician to practice in the city. In 1795 he returned to Surinam, where he went into business. Later he published a tract supporting the emancipation of Dutch Jewry.

Nathan (i) (fl. 11th–10th cent. BCE). Israelite prophet. He prophesied during David's reign and declared to David that his royal dynasty would be established perpetually. Yet he prevented David from building a Temple in Jerusalem and accused him of plotting the death of Uriah the Hittite. Subsequently he was instrumental in securing Solomon's succession. According to I Chronicles 29.29, he wrote an account of David's reign.

Nathan (ii) (fl. 2nd cent.). Palestinian tanna and son of the exilarch. He went to Palestine to study, but was forced to leave during the Hadrianic persecutions. Later he returned and became president of the court at Usha. An expert judge in civil suits, he was opposed to the fixing of the calendar outside Palestine. The *Avot de-Rabbi Natan* is attributed to him.

Nathan, Sir **Frederick Lewis** (1861–1933). English soldier and chemist. He joined the Royal Artillery in 1879. He became an explosives expert and during World War I organized munitions manufacture. He was president of the Institution of Chemical Engineers from 1925 to 1927. From 1905 to 1926 he served as commandant of the Jewish Lads' Brigade.

Nathan, Isaac (?1790–1864). Australian composer, singer, and writer. He was born in Canterbury, England, and began a career as a singer, composer, and music teacher in London in 1810. He was a friend of Lord Byron who at his request wrote *Hebrew Melodies,* which Nathan set to music. In 1841 he emigrated to Australia and settled in Sydney. He was Australia's first resident professional composer.

Nathan, Paul (1857–1927). German philanthropist and public figure. He was the editor of the Berlin liberal publication *Die Nation* and the founder of the Hilfsverein der Deutschen Juden. He was active at international Jewish conferences on emigration and the relief of Jewish victims of persecution and war. During the trial of Menaḥem Mendel Beilis in 1913 on a blood libel charge Nathan helped to organize Beilis's defense outside Russia. Opposed to the Zionist movement, he advocated assimilation as a solution to anti-Semitism. After World War I, he fostered agricultural settlement among Russian Jewry.

Nathan, Robert (1894–1985). American novelist. He was born in New York. He wrote a number of novels which deal with Jewish themes, such as *Jonah, Road of Ages,* and *A Star in the Wind.*

Nathan ben Isaac of Baghdad [Nathan the Babylonian] (fl. 10th cent.). Babylonian chronicler. He lived in Baghdad and his *Akhbar Baghdad* is a book on the Jews of the city. This work is an important source for the history of Babylonian Jewry in the 10th century. It contains an account of the organization of the gaonic academies in Mesopotamia as well as the disputes that occurred during this period.

Nathan ben Jehiel of Rome [Arukh] (1035–c. 1110). Italian lexicographer. He was also called "Baal he-Arukh" after the title of his lexicon. He was taught by his father, the head of the yeshivah in Rome; when his father died, he and his two brothers in turn succeeded him in that office. Nathan's *Baal he-Arukh* (by which name he was also sometimes known) is a lexicon of the Talmud and the midrashim.

Nathan ben Joseph Official (fl. 13th cent.). French talmudist. He engaged in religious controversies with Christians.

These disputes were recorded by his son Joseph in his *Yosef ha-Mekanne*.

Nathan der Weise *see* LESSING, GOTTHOLD EPHRAIM.

Nathan of Gaza [Ghazzati, Nathan Benjamin] (1643–1680). Palestinian religious leader, disciple of Shabbetai Tzevi. He was born in Jerusalem, and lived in Gaza, where he engaged in a kabbalistic study and practices. He met Shabbetai Tzevi in Gaza and proclaimed him to be the Messiah. After Shabbetai Tzevi converted to Islam, Nathan traveled throughout the Balkans and Italy, developing and preaching the theology of Sabbetaianism, which was based on Lurianic kabbalah. He was expelled by the rabbis of Venice, and returned to the Balkans. He died at Uskub near Salonica.

Nathansen, Henri (1868–1944). Dutch playwright. He was born in Hjørring, Jutland, and trained as a lawyer. In 1909 he became the stage director of Copenhagen's Royal Theater. Many of his plays deal with Jewish issues. In 1919 he protested against the persecution of Polish Jewry and later he called for the Copenhagen Jewish community to counteract Nazi anti-Semitism. In 1943 he fled to Sweden.

Nathanson, Mendel Levin (1780–1868). Danish merchant and journalist. He was born in Altona, and moved to Copenhagen at the age of 12. From 1798 he was a wholesale draper. In 1838 he became editor of the newspaper *Berlingske Tidende*. He worked for the emancipation of the Jews and helped to establish the Jewish Free School for boys in Copenhagen in 1805 and later a similar school for girls. He wrote a history of the Jews of Denmark.

Nathan the Babylonian *see* NATHAN BEN ISAAC OF BAGHDAD.

National and University Library [National Library]. Israeli library. Its holdings developed from a small collection begun in 1884. The library was established in Jerusalem and later received a large collection of books from Joseph Chazanowitz. It passed under the control of the World Zionist Organization in 1920, and of the Hebrew University in 1925. In 1930 it was transferred to Mount Scopus, and a second library was established on the university's campus in Jerusalem.

National Committee for Labor Israel. American organization assisting the Israeli federation of trade unions, Histadrut. It was founded as the National Labor Committee for the Organized Jewish Workers in Palestine. It is supported by US trade unions, labor Zionist groups, and branches of the Workermen's Circle.

National Community Relations Advisory Council. American agency coordinating planning and policy making among Jewish organizations and community councils.

National Conference of Christians and Jews. American organization founded in 1928 to promote interfaith relations. Its membership comprises Catholics, Protestants, and Jews. Centered in New York, it has numerous branches promoting cultural, religious, and educational activities.

National Council for Jewish Education. American organization founded in New York in 1926 to encourage the development of Jewish education and educators. Its membership is composed of Orthodox, Conservative, and Reform Jews.

National Council of Jewish Women. American welfare organization founded in 1893 by Hannah Greenebaum Solomon. It fosters human welfare in the Jewish and general community locally, nationally, and internationally through a wide range of service, educational, and social activities.

National Council of Young Israel *see* YOUNG ISRAEL.

National Federation of Hebrew Teachers and Principals. American educational organization. It was founded in 1944 as the Hebrew Teachers Federation. It maintains a placement bureau, protects the rights of teachers and principals, and cooperates with other Jewish educational bodies in the US.

National Federation of Jewish Men's Clubs. American organization of men's social clubs and brotherhoods, founded in 1929. Its members are all affiliated to Conservative Jewish congregations.

National Federation of Temple Brotherhoods. American organization of men's social clubs attached to Reform congregations. Founded in 1923, it is affiliated with the Union of American Hebrew Congregations.

National Federation of Temple Sisterhoods. American women's charitable organization. It was founded in 1913 as the women's subsidiary of the Union of American Hebrew Congregations, and its member groups are all attached to Reform congregations. It maintains youth activities programs, subsidizes institutes for the training of Reform teachers, and is the patron body of the Jewish Braille Institute of America.

National Foundation for Jewish Culture. American organization founded in 1960 by the Council of Jewish Federations and Welfare Funds. It aims to promote Jewish studies and cultural programs in the US and it supports Judaica courses in universities and other educational institutions.

Nationalism. In biblical times the ancient Israelites inhabited the Promised Land and established a monarchy. Forced into exile by the Babylonians in 586 BCE, many Jews never returned to Israel but made their homes elsewhere. Palestine ceased to be a Jewish center after the destruction of the Temple by the Romans in 70 CE and the crushing of the Bar Kokhba rebellion in 132. Through much of the period of the diaspora the desire for a Jewish homeland permeated the religious and artistic expressions of Jews in all parts of the world. This nationalistic feeling was grounded in the practice of the Jewish faith, such as the annual celebration of Passover which promised the return to the homeland in the greeting "Next year in Jerusalem!" The return to Zion was fostered by numerous writers, such as Moses Hess, Judah Loeb Pinsker, Theodor Herzl, and Aḥad ha-Am. According to Zionist ideology, Jewish persecution would cease only when Jews were secure in their own land. After 2000 years of living in the diaspora with no country of their own the Jews reestablished a Jewish state in modern Israel in 1948. *See also* ZIONISM.

National Jewish Hospital. Hospital in Denver, Colorado, established in 1899. It offers care for victims of tuberculosis and chest diseases, irrespective of race, religion, or nationality.

National Jewish Welfare Board [Jewish Welfare Board]. American organization of community centers for Jewish servicemen. Founded in 1917, it cares for the welfare of Jewish members of the armed forces and those in Veterans Administration hospitals. During and after World War II, it was a member of the United Service Organizations. Through its Commission on Jewish Chaplaincy it provides chaplains for the armed services. Its centers make available educational services and recreational facilities for servicemen, prayerbooks, and materials to chaplains.

National Refugee Service. American welfare organization for refugees from Nazi persecution. Established in 1939, it set up a program of relief, economic rehabilitation, resettlement, and integration to help European Jews to adjust to life in the US.

National Religious Party. Israeli political party. It was founded in 1956 after the merger in 1955 of Mizraḥi and Ha-Poel ha-Mizraḥi; other religious political bodies also joined the party. It emphasizes legislation based on Jewish law, economic policies based on the country's needs, and religious services provided through governmental and public institutions. Together with the Histadrut ha-Poel ha-Mizraḥi ("Workers and trade union organization"), it represents the religious Zionist movement in Israel.

National Socialism *see* NAZISM.

Natore Karta ("Guardians of the city"). Israeli organization of Orthodox Jewish zealots. It was formed as a separate body in 1937 when a group of like-minded Orthodox Jews seceded from Agudat Israel. The Natore Karta oppose political Zionism, refuse to cooperate with non-Orthodox Jews, and do not recognize the State of Israel.

Natronai bar Hilai (fl. 9th cent.). Babylonian gaon of the academy at Sura (853–6). He was one of the most prolific writers of responsa among the geonim in the 9th century. His responsum to a query from the Lucena Jewish community as to how to fulfill the rabbinic dictum to recite 100 benedictions daily became the basis of the prayerbook.

Natronai bar Nehemiah (fl. 8th cent.). Babylonian gaon of the academy at Pumbedita (719–30). He married into the family of the exilarch. He was known for his severity with scholars in the academy, some of whom left for Sura, returning to Pumbedita only after his death.

Natural law. The law of nature or the moral sense innate in the human mind, as opposed to that which results from revelation or legislation. The NOACHIAN LAWS may be construed as natural laws. In addition there are many rabbinic dicta which assume the existence of natural law. Medieval Jewish philosophers argued that God did not intend morality to be left to the vagaries of human reason; he therefore revealed a number of laws that are part of natural law (such as the prohibition against murder); he also revealed those rituals and precepts which would not otherwise occur to human beings. Non-philosophical Jewish theologians maintain that the purpose of the Torah is to lift the Jews above natural law.

Nature. Although the biblical writers recognized the regular workings of nature (as Psalms 104 and 148 show), they were primarily concerned with God's supervision of the universe. According to the rabbis, the regularity of natural phenomena is an expression of God's will, just as are miraculous occurrences.

Naumbourg, Samuel (1815–1880). German musicologist. He was born in Dennelohe, near Ansbach. He became the first ḥazzan at the synagogue in the rue Notre-Dame-de-Nazareth in Paris in 1845. Two years later he published two volumes of *Zemirot Yisrael*, which contain musical settings of the entire liturgical cycle. His *Agudas Shirim* is a collection of traditional synagogue melodies.

Navigation. Under Solomon the ancient Israelites collaborated with the Tyrians in maritime journeys (I Kings 9.26–8). During the period of the second Temple, the symbols on Hasmonean coins suggest maritime knowledge, and from this time onward there seems to have been an interest in sea journeys. Naval engagements took place in the Mediterranean and the Sea of Galilee during the war of 66–70, and in the Mediterranean in the war of 132–5. During the Middle Ages Jewish merchants owned ships and a number of Jews were expert cartographers; others invented important navigational instruments. In modern times the State of Israel has established a navy and a merchant fleet.

Navon, Joseph (1852–1934). Palestinian philanthropist. He was born in Jerusalem and became a merchant banker. He helped settlers in Palestine and supported popular housing schemes in Jerusalem. In 1888 he received a concession to construct a railway from Jaffa to Jerusalem. He settled in Paris in 1894.

Naxos, Duke of *see* NASI, JOSEPH.

Nazarenes *see* EBIONITES; JEWISH CHRISTIANS (i).

Nazareno, Eli *see* SILVA, FRANCISCO MALDONADO DA.

Nazareth. Town in Galilee. According to the New Testament, it was the place where Jesus was brought up (Matthew 2.23; Luke 2.39, 51).

Nazarite *See* NAZIRITE.

Nazir ("Nazirite"). Fourth tractate in the Mishnah order of Nashim. It deals with the biblical prescriptions concerning Nazirite vows (Numbers 6.1–21).

Nazirite [Nazarite]. Jewish ascetic bound by a vow. The Nazirite is prohibited from drinking wine, cutting his hair, and contracting impurity by contact with a dead body (Numbers 6.2). The vow was usually taken for a limited period, but could also be for life (as in the case of Samuel and Samson). Taking the Nazirite vow was common in biblical times, but the practice ultimately disappeared.

Nazism (from German "Nationalsozialistische Deutsche Arbeiterpartei": National Socialist German Workers' Party). German fascist political movement. It was formed from the German Workers' Party (founded 1919) and led by Adolf Hitler (1921–45). Its ideology was based on nationalism, racism, and the supremacy of the state over the individual. Inherently anti-Semitic, the movement whipped up popular sentiment against Jewish people, claiming, among other things, that they were responsible for the defeat of Germany in World War I. When the party came to power various anti-Jewish laws were passed, such as the Aryan decree (1933) and the Nuremberg Laws (1935). In 1942 the Nazis adopted the "Final Solution" to the Jewish problem, which had as its goal the annihilation of the Jewish people. By 1945 it is estimated that six million Jews, together with other "inferior" peoples, had been exterminated in Nazi concentration camps. After World War II Nazi leaders were sentenced to death for genocide and the party was banned, but the philosophy of National Socialism survives in various fascist organizations in Europe.

***Neander, Johann August Wilhelm** [Mendel, David] (1789–1850). German church historian. Of Jewish birth, he was a convert to Christianity. He became a professor of church history at Berlin University, and in 1847 opposed the admission of Jews to the university. During the Damascus Affair, he argued that the murder charge against members of the Jewish community was a falsehood.

Neapolis *see* SHECHEM.

Nebbish (Yiddish). Interjection, expressing sympathy. The word also refers to an ineffectual or unfortunate person.

Nebo, Mount. Mountain in the extreme north-west of the mountains of Moab. It was from there that Moses saw the Promised Land before he died (Deuteronomy 34.1–3).

***Nebuchadnezzar** (fl. 7th–6th cent. BCE). King of Babylon (605–562 BCE). After his victory over the Assyrian–Egyptian alliance at Carchemish, he conquered lands from the Euphrates to the Egyptian frontier, including Judah. After Judah revolted he took Jerusalem in 597 BCE, replaced the reigning king Jehoiachin with Zedekiah, and carried captives back to Babylonia. Later Zedekiah rebelled, and Nebuchadnezzar invaded Judah again. In 586 BCE he captured the Temple and destroyed it, and expelled the Jews from Jerusalem. (II Kings 24–5)

***Nebuzaradan** (fl. 6th cent. BCE). Babylonian soldier, captain of Nebuchadnezzar's bodyguard. He commanded the armies which in 586 BCE) captured Jerusalem, destroyed the Temple, and expelled the Jewish inhabitants.

***Necho II** (fl. 7th–6th cent. BCE). King of Egypt (c. 609–593 BCE). At the Battle of Megiddo he defeated Josiah of Judah. He deposed Jehoahaz (the successor of Josiah), exiled him to Egypt (II Kings 23.31–5; Jeremiah 22.10–12), and replaced him with Jehoiakim. He was defeated at Carchemish by Nebuchadnezzar.

Necromancy. The art of divination by summoning and questioning the spirits of the dead. Although forbidden in Scripture (Leviticus 19.31; 20.6; Deuteronomy 18.11), it was widely practiced in ancient Israel.

Nedarim ("Vows"). Third tractate in the Mishnah order of Nashim. It deals with regulations regarding vows as well as their annulment and interpretation.

Nederlandsch Israelitisch Seminarium. Dutch Ashkenazi rabbinical seminary. Its establishment dates back to the founding of a yeshivah in 1708. In 1834 it became a state institution.

Nedoveh (Yiddish). A charitable contribution.

Negaim ("Plagues of leprosy"). Third tractate in the Mishnah order of Tohorot. It deals with the laws concerning leprosy (Leviticus 13–14).

Negev. Semi-desert region in southern Israel. David's conquest of the Amalekites and of Edom (I Samuel 30; II Samuel 8) opened up Elath and the copper mines there to the Israelites under Solomon, which led to the development of maritime trade. The division of the kingdom in 930 BCE led to the decline of Judean power in the Negev. Under Uzziah, roads in the Negev were developed (II Chronicles 26.10). After the fall of Jerusalem in 586 BCE the Edomites moved into southern Judah, and the territory was occupied by the Nabateans.

Neginot *see* ACCENTS.

Negligence. In Jewish law an artisan or laborer is guilty of negligence when work is performed badly, when instructions are disregarded, or when materials are destroyed. In such cases full compensation is required of the artisan or laborer by the person who has commissioned the work. Jewish law also recognizes categories of negligence arising from intention and accident; in such cases the ordinary compensation does not apply (in the former it would be too lenient a penalty, in the latter too severe).

Nehardea. Babylonian town situated on the Euphrates at its junction with the Malka River. It was established by the Jews exiled to Babylonia in the time of Jehoiakim in the 6th century BCE; they built a synagogue there called Shaf Yeyativ. Nehardea was the seat of a famous academy, and of the exilarch and his bet din. In 259 the academy was destroyed and most of its scholars moved to the academy at Pumbedita.

Nehemiah (i) (fl. 5th cent. BCE). Israelite, Governor of Judah. He was a cupbearer to the Persian king Artaxerxes I, of whom he asked permission to go to Jerusalem. The king agreed, and appointed him Governor of Judah. Nehemiah organized the repair of the walls of Jerusalem, and initiated various social and religious reforms. Later he returned to Susa, but subsequently settled in Jerusalem. He and Ezra took steps to discourage the Israelites from contracting mixed marriages.

Nehemiah (ii). Biblical book, part of the Hagiographa. It relates the events of the life of Nehemiah, Governor of Judah, and includes part of the story of the prophet Ezra.

Neher, André (1913–1988). French scholar. He was born in Alsace, and became professor of Jewish studies at the University of Strasbourg. He wrote works dealing with prophecy and with the teachings of Judah Löw ben Bezalel.

Neḥunyah ben ha-Kanah (fl. 1st cent.). Palestinian tanna. He was born in Emmaus in Judea. His students included Ishmael ben Elisha, who was influenced by his method of interpreting Scripture. He adopted the interpretive principle of "kelal u-pherat" (a general followed by a particular), in opposition to the system of Nahum of Gimzo. A number of mystical works are ascribed to him, including the Bahir and the acrostic prayer *Anna be-koaḥ.*

Nehushtan. The name of the brass serpent which King Hezekiah broke into pieces in an attempt to reform its cult (II Kings 18.4). According to tradition, it was created by Moses to prevent the fiery snakes from biting the people (Numbers 21.6–9; II Kings 18.4). It probably stood in the Temple court.

Neilah ("Closing"). The name of a prayer originally recited daily one hour before sunset and the closing of the Temple; it was also said on all public fast days and on the Day of Atonement. It now survives only as a service on the Day of Atonement; the Neilah concludes the rite for the day, symbolizing the closing of the gates of Heaven after the Day of Judgment.

Nekamah *see* VENGEANCE.

Nemerov, Howard (b. 1920). American writer. He was a student at Harvard, and later taught at Bennington College, Hollins College, Brandeis University, and Washington University in St. Louis. He also served as consultant in poetry to the Library of Congress. Some of his work deals with Jewish subjects.

Németh, Andor (1891–1953). Hungarian writer. He studied at the University of Budapest, and became the press attaché of the Hungarian Soviet Republic in Austria. From 1919 to 1926 he lived in Vienna, but then returned to Budapest. He settled in France in 1939, but in 1947 returned finally to Hungary. His writings include *Kafka ou le mystère juif.*

Nemoy, Leon (b. 1901). American scholar and librarian. He was born in Buta, Russia. He was the librarian successively at the Society for the Propagation of Knowledge in Odessa, at the Academic Library in Odessa, and at the University Library of Lwów. In 1923 he settled in the US and was appointed curator of Hebrew and Arabic literature at Yale University library. He published numerous studies of the Karaites.

Neofiti (Italian: "neophytes"). The name given to the Jews forcibly converted to Christianity in southern Italy from the end of the 13th century. While living outwardly as Christians, many of the Neofiti remained secretly attached to Judaism.

Neo-Hebrew literature *see* HEBREW LITERATURE.

Neoplatonism. Late Greek philosophy combining Platonism with Oriental elements, expounded by Plotinus, Porphyry, and Proclus. In the Middle Ages it had an important impact on the writings of Jewish theologians, including Isaac Israel, Solomon ibn Gabirol, Baḥya ibn Pakudah, Abraham bar Ḥiyya, Joseph ibn Tzaddik, and Abraham ibn Ezra. The kabbalah was also influenced by Neoplatonic ideas.

Nephesh *see* SOUL.

Nephilim. The offspring of the sons of God and the daughters of men (Genesis 6.4). The Israelite spies sent by Moses used the term to refer to the inhabitants of the land of Canaan (Numbers 13–33).

***Nero** (37–68). Roman emperor (54–68). During his reign the Jewish revolt against Rome began in Jerusalem (66), which ended with the destruction of the Temple (70).

Ner tamid ("eternal light"). The name given to the light which is kept burning constantly in the synagogue. It is a symbolic reminder of the golden seven-branched candelabrum, or menorah, which burned continuously in the Temple; originally this was placed in a niche in the Western Wall, but later was suspended in front of the Ark. The ner tamid has been interpreted alternatively as the symbol of God's presence and as the spiritual light emanating from the Temple. In ancient times it was created by a wick burning in olive oil, but in the modern period an electric light is used.

Nesekh. Wine intended or used for heathen worship; by extension, any wine made by a gentile. Wine produced by a non-Jew was always suspected of having been sanctified for a libation or a similar ceremonial act. In modern times the ban on drinking gentile wine ("setam yeinam": their wine) is still binding. The prohibition also extends to unbottled wine that is no more than touched by a gentile; wine which has not been touched by a gentile before the bottle was sealed is kosher.

Neshamah *see* SOUL.

Neshamah yeterah ("extra soul"). According to tradition, God gave Adam a higher soul which elevated him on the Sabbath. This soul is given to all Jews during the Sabbath. The smelling of spices at the Havdalah service is meant to provide comfort for the loss of this extra soul when the Sabbath comes to an end.

Netanyah. Israeli coastal town, north of Tel Aviv. Founded in 1929 by the descendants of Galilean settlers, it has become a seaside resort.

Nethinim. Temple servants, the descendants of conquered Canaanites. David assigned them to the Levites for menial service in the Temple. They were exiled with the Jews to Babylonia in 586 BCE, but returned under Zerubbabel and Ezra and were given a special quarter in Jerusalem (Ezra 2.58; 8.20; Nehemiah 3.26). They accepted Ezra's covenant that the Jews should keep the Torah, but were debarred from the Jewish community.

Netter, Charles (1826–1882). French philanthropist. He was born in Strasbourg. He went into business in Lille, Moscow, and London, and in 1851 settled in Paris, where he engaged in various public activities. One of the founders of the Alliance Israélite Universelle, he served as its treasurer. He established the Mikveh Israel Agricultural School near Jaffa, and was its first director (1870–73). He was also active in Jewish philanthropic work in Europe.

Neubauer, Adolph (1831–1907). British bibliographer, of Hungarian origin. He went to Oxford in 1868 to complete the catalog of Hebrew manuscripts in the Bodleian Library, which had been begun by Moritz Steinschneider; he later became a sublibrarian. His writings include a series of medieval Hebrew chronicles, as well as studies of the geography of the Talmud.

Neugeboren, Jay (b. 1938). American author. He was born in Brooklyn, and taught in the New York public schools and at Stanford University and SUNY. He later became writer-in-residence at the University of Massachusetts. His publications include the novels *The Stolen Jew,* and *Before my Life Began.*

Neuman, Abraham Aaron (1890–1970). American rabbi, historian, and educator. He was born in Brezan, Austria, and emigrated to the US in 1898. He taught history and later became president of Dropsie College. He was active in the Zionist movement. His writings include *The Jews of Spain, Cyrus Adler, a Biography,* and *Landmarks and Goals.*

Neumann, Emanuel (1893–1980). American Zionist leader. He was born in Libau, Latvia, and was taken to the US as an infant. He founded the youth movement Young Judea in 1909, and served as education director of the Zionist Organization of America. He subsequently was director of the Keren ha-Yesod in the US (1921–5) and chairman of the executive committee of the United Palestine Appeal (1925–8). In 1929–30 he was president of the Jewish National Fund in the US; he then moved to Palestine, where he worked for the Jewish Agency in Jerusalem (1931–41). He was also president of the Zionist Organization of America (1947–8, 1956–8). In 1954 he founded the Herzl Foundation and served as its president. He was elected president of the World Union of General Zionists in 1963.

Neumann, Robert (1897–1975). Austrian author. He was born in Vienna. After working as a chocolate manufacturer he went to sea. He wrote poetry, parodies, and anti-Nazi novels. After the war he settled in Switzerland, where he wrote documentary works dealing with the Nazi period.

Neumann, Solomon (1819–1908). German physician and public worker. He engaged in work on medical statistics and public hygiene. His refusal in 1845 to take the special form of medical oath for Jews led to its abolition in Prussia. Besides his professional work he was active in Jewish communal activities and was a patron of scholarship.

Neumark, David (1866–1924). American Reform scholar, of Galician birth. He was a rabbi in Rakonitz, Bohemia, and later professor of Jewish philosophy at the Veitel-Heine-Ephraimschen Lehranstalt in Berlin. In 1907 he emigrated to the US and became professor of philosophy at the Hebrew Union College. His writings include a *History of Jewish Philosophy* and *Essays in Jewish Philosophy.*

Neusner, Jacob (b. 1932). American scholar. He was born in Hartford, Connecticut. He taught at Columbia University, the University of Wisconsin, Dartmouth College, Brown University, and the University of Southern Florida. An expert in rabbinics, he has published more than 300 books and received numerous scholarly awards. In 1968–9 he served as president of the American Academy of Religion.

Nevelson, Louise (1899–1988). American sculptor. She was born in Kiev, and emigrated to the US in 1905. Her work includes *Six Million,* a work in memory of the victims of the Holocaust.

New Christians *see* MARRANOS.

Newman, Louis Israel (1893–?). American rabbi and writer. He was rabbi of Temple Rodeph Shalom in New York, and taught at the Jewish Institute of Religion. He published *Jewish Influence on Christian Reform Movements, The Jewish People, Faith and Life,* and *The Ḥasidic Anthology.*

Newmann, Barnett (1905–1970). American painter and sculptor. He was born in New York. Jewish themes are found throughout his oeuvre in such works as *Covenant, Abraham,* and *Adam.*

New Moon *see* ROSH ḤODESH.

New Moon, Blessing of the (Hebrew "Birkat ha-Ḥodesh"). Formula for announcing the day or days on which Rosh Ḥodesh (the beginning of the lunar month) may be celebrated. It is recited after the reading of the Torah on the Sabbath preceding the new moon, by a reader holding a Torah scroll. The Ashkenazi rite is more complex than the Sephardi and includes a formal announcement, a supplication for national redemption, and a prayer for a prosperous month.

Newspapers *see* PRESS.

New Testament. The name given to the collection of writings that make up the Christian Scriptures. It contains the gospels of Matthew, Mark, Luke, and John, the Acts of the Apostles, the Epistles and the Book of Revelation.

New Year (i) *see* ROSH HA-SHANAH (i).

New Year (ii). The opening Mishnah of the treatise *Rosh ha-Shanah* lists four dates for New Year in the Jewish calendar: 1 Nisan is regarded as New Year for the purpose of dating the reigns of kings, for ordering religious festivals, and for counting the months; 1 Tishri (Rosh ha-Shanah) is the start of the agricultural year, and from this date the years are counted to establish the observance of Sabbatical and Jubilee years; cattle are tithed according to a year beginning on 1 Elul; and fruit is tithed according to a year starting on 15 Shevat.

New year for trees *see* FIFTEENTH OF SHEVAT.

New York. American city on the eastern seaboard of the US at the mouth of the Hudson River. Its Jewish community dates from the 17th century. In the 1820s and 1830s European immigrants greatly increased the size of the Jewish population. By the end of the century 250,000 Jews resided there, and by 1940 2 million. New York now has the largest Jewish community in the US with a vibrant religious and cultural life.

Next Year in Jerusalem (Hebrew "La-Shanah ha-Baah bi-Yerushalayim"). Expression of communal hope, uttered at the end of the Passover seder service by all participants; in some communities it is also used as the conclusion to the services on the Day of Atonement. Its purport is to remind Jews of the coming era of the Messiah when all nations will look to Jerusalem.

Nezikin ("Damages") [Yeshuot ("Deeds of help")]. Fourth order of the Mishnah. It deals with money matters, damages decided by the courts, criminal law, and oaths. It also contains an ethical treatise, *Pirke Avot* (*see* AVOT (i)).

***Nicanor** (fl. 2nd cent. BCE). Syrian officer sent by the general Lysias to fight against Judah Maccabee. Judah defeated and killed him at Bet Horon in 161. This victory is commemorated on 13 Adar as Nicanor Day.

Nicanor, Gate of. During the period of the second Temple, the name given to the gate leading to the Temple court.

***Nicholas I** (1796–1855). Russian czar (1825–55). He attempted to assimilate the Jewish community by introducing military service for Jews in 1827. His government supported the maskilim against Orthodoxy and also instituted a state system of Jewish schools in the 1840s. At the end of the 1840s legislation was passed forbidding traditional Jewish clothing. Hundreds of similar anti-Jewish laws were enacted during Nicholas's reign.

***Nicholas II** (1868–1918). Russian czar (1894–1917). He regarded Jews as a major influence on the revolutionary movement. During his reign a number of pogroms took place, as well as the trial, on a charge of ritual murder, of Menaḥem Mendel Beilis.

***Nicholas of Damascus** (fl. 1st cent.). Greek historian, philosopher, dramatist, and statesman. He was the private secretary of Herod the Great and friend of the Emperor Augustus. He wrote a universal history from ancient times to Herod's reign, a biography of Augustus, and an autobiography. His writings were used as a source by Josephus.

Niddah ("Menstruous woman"). Seventh tractate in the Mishnah order of

Tohorot. It deals with the ritual uncleanness created by menstruation (Leviticus 15.19–24) and childbirth (Leviticus 12.1–5).

Niemirover, Jacob Isaac (1872–1939). Romanian chief rabbi. He was born in Lemberg, and served as rabbi of Jassy. He became rabbi of the Sephardi community of Bucharest in 1911 and later chief rabbi of Romania. In 1926 he was elected to the Romanian senate, where he served as the representative of Romanian Jewry. Active in educational and Zionist circles, he also served as president of the order of B'nai B'rith in Romania. He wrote studies of various Jewish topics.

Nieto, David (1654–1728). British rabbi and philosopher. He was born in Venice. He served as a rabbi in Livorno, and in 1702 became Ḥaham of the Sephardi community in London. He wrote about the Inquisition and also produced anti-Sabbetaian polemics. His *Matteh Dan* is a philosophical defense of Judaism.

Niger, Samuel [Charney, Samuel] (1883–1955). American Yiddish literary critic. He was born in Russia, and began his career contributing to various Russian literary magazines. In 1909 he went to Berlin; several years later he edited a Yiddish monthly, *Di yidishe velt,* in Vilnius. In 1919 he emigrated to the US and settled in New York, where he became literary editor of *Der tog*. His studies of Yiddish literature appeared in various volumes.

Niggun ("air"). Type of traditional song, cultivated particularly among the Ḥasidim.

Night (Hebrew "leilah"). The Jewish day is reckoned from sunset to sunset; the period from sunset until sunrise constitutes night. The night is traditionally divided into three or four watches. According to Jewish law, certain activities (such as starting a court session or signing a document) may not be carried out at night.

Night of watching *see* LEL SHIMMURIM.

Night Prayer (Hebrew "Keriat Shema al ha-mittah": *lit.* the reading of the Shema on the bed). Prayer recited before going to sleep. The central part of the prayer is the first paragraph of the Shema; the rest consists of blessings and prayers taken from the evening service. The talmudists and later authorities, including kabbalists, added other prayers and scriptural texts to the Shema to form the Night Prayer liturgy. The substance of the Night Prayer is based on a saying of Joshua ben Levi that he who wishes to sleep should recite a certain portion of the Shema and the blessing to God.

Nikkur ("separating the fat"). The act of removing the fat of animals brought for sacrifice in the Temple. According to Leviticus, fat taken from a sacrificial offering may not be eaten (Leviticus 7.25); generally it was burnt on the altar (Leviticus 3.3–4). Most of the forbidden fats could be easily removed, since much animal fat forms a separate solid surrounded by a membrane. However some threads of fat run through the lean tissue and these had to be removed by a process known as "porging." Only someone familiar with this technique might undertake the preparation of an animal for sacrifice.

Nili. Underground intelligence organization, active in Syria and Palestine under Turkish rule during World War I. Its name was formed from the Hebrew initials of the words "The glory of Israel will not die" from I Samuel 15.29. Led by Aaron Aaronson, it transmitted information to British warships off the Palestinian coast. The Turks arrested a number of its members.

Nîmes. Town in southern France, about 70 miles north-west of Marseilles. Jews settled there in the 10th century, and by the 12th century it had become an important Jewish center. The Jewish community was expelled in 1306 and 1394, but eventually resettled there in the 18th century.

Nimrod. Son of Cush and grandson of Ham (the son of Noah) (Genesis 10.8–12; I Chronicles 1.10). A mighty hunter, he is said to have ruled over Babylon, Uruk, Akkad, Calah, and Nineveh.

Nine Days (Hebrew "Bein ha-Mezarim": *lit.* "between the straits"). In the Ashkenazi rite a penitential period during the later part of the THREE WEEKS of mourning that lead up to the fast of the NINTH OF AV. For the three-week period no festivities are celebrated, nor do marriages take place. During the period of Nine Days, pious Jews abstain from meat and wine. On the Sabbath before the Ninth of Av a prophetic portion is read from Isaiah (Isaiah 1. 1–27).

Nineveh. Ancient city situated on the left bank of the Tigris, capital of the Assyrian Empire. Jonah was sent there by God, and successfully persuaded its citizens to repent.

Ninth of Av (Hebrew "Tisha b'Av"). Fast day commemorating the destruction of the first and second Temples and other Jewish tragedies. In the synagogue service Lamentations is read and dirges (kinot) are recited. A three-week period of mourning, which includes the NINE DAYS of penitential observance, lead up to the fast day.

Nir'ah *see* REVELATION.

Nirim. Kibbutz in the West Negev in southern Israel. A mosaic floor from a synagogue of the Byzantine period was discovered there.

Nisan. First month of the religious year (it is the seventh month of the civil year). In the Bible it is referred to as the month of aviv ("spring"). Passover occurs on 15 Nisan. No public mourning is permitted during the month, nor is the penitential taḥanun (the prayer for grace and forgiveness) recited during the daily prayers.

Nishmat ("The breath of every living thing"). Opening words of the doxology recited at the end of the Pesuke de-Zimrah on Sabbaths and festivals. It is referred to as the "Birkat ha-Shir" (Blessing of the song) in talmudic literature. During the Mishnaic period it was recited after the Hallel on the Passover seder night. It consists of three parts: the section known in Mishnaic days; a section which served as a thanksgiving for rain; and a gaonic addition. According to medieval legend, it was ascribed to the apostle Peter.

Nisibis. City in Mesopotamia; the modern town of Nesib in southern Anatolia stands on the same site. In the 1st century it was the center for the collection of gifts from the Babylonian Jews and their despatch to the Temple in Jerusalem. It was the seat of the academy of Judah ben Bathyra I. In 155–7 its Jewish population was massacred as a punishment for resisting the Romans. In the Middle Ages a Jewish community existed there.

Nissenbaum, Isaac (1868–1942). Polish rabbi, author, and Zionist. He was born in Bobruysk, Belorussia, and lived in Minsk, where he was an active Zionist. Later he became head of a secret nationalistic association formed by members of the yeshivah of Volozhin after it was closed. In 1894 he moved to Białystok, where he became secretary to Samuel Mohilever. After Mohilever's death, he preached about Zionism throughout Russia, Poland, Latvia, and Lithuania. In 1900 he settled in Warsaw, where he was active in the Mizraḥi organization. He wrote numerous works about Zionism.

Nissenson, Hugh (b. 1933). American novelist and short-story writer. He was born in New York. His work explores the difficulties of sustaining religious belief in modern society; his fictional publications include *My own Ground* and *Tree of Life*. In 1961 he reported on the trial of Eichmann for the magazine *Commentary*. His *Notes from the Frontier* is a memoir of visits to a kibbutz before and during the Six-Day War.

Nissim, Rabbenu Gerondi *see* GERONDI, NISSIM BEN REUBEN.

Nissim, Yitzḥak Raḥamim (1896–1981). Israeli rabbi. He was born in Baghdad, and settled in Jerusalem in 1925. In 1955 he was elected Rishon le-Zion, Sephardi chief rabbi of Israel. He published and edited volumes of responsa.

Nissim ben Jacob ben Nissim [Ibn Shahin] (c. 990–1062). North African talmudist. Born in Kairouan, he became head of the academy there after the death of Hananel. He had close contacts with Samuel ha-Naggid, and corresponded with Hai Gaon. His *Kitab Miftaḥ Maghalik al-Talmud* ("Key to the locks of the Talmud") is a commentary on the Talmud and its methodology.

Nister, Der *see* KAHANOVITZ, PHINEHAS.

Nittai the Arbelite (fl. 2nd cent. BCE). Palestinian sage, one of the ZUGOT. He served as president of the Sanhedrin when Joshua ben Peraḥyah was patriarch.

Noachian Laws [Laws of Noah]. A series of laws, derived from Genesis 9.4–7, which according to the rabbis are binding on all human beings. They prohibit idolatry, blasphemy, murder, adultery, robbery, and the eating of flesh cut from a living animal; they also require the establishment of courts of justice. According to tradition, gentiles can enter into the after-life as long as they observe these commandments.

Noah. Son of Lamech, father of Shem, Ham, and Japheth (Genesis 5.28–9; 6.10; I Chronicles 1.4). In the Bible he is described as a righteous and blameless man who walked with God (Genesis 6.9). At God's behest he built an ark, and placed in it members of his family, as well as representatives of the animal kingdom; when a great Flood came they were thus saved to perpetuate humankind and the animals. After the Flood, Noah disembarked from the ark and offered sacrifices to God, who blessed him and his sons and established a covenant with them (Genesis 6–9).

Noah, Mordecai Manuel (1785–1851). American newspaper editor, politician, and playwright. He was born in Philadelphia, and started his career as a clerk in the US Treasury. In 1809 he went to Charleston, South Carolina, where he edited the *City Gazette*. Later he became the editor of the *National Advocate* in New York and established the *New York Enquirer*. In 1841 he became a judge of the Court of Sessions. He was active in the congregations of Mikveh Israel in Philadelphia and Shearith Israel in New York. In 1825 he helped to purchase land on Grand Island near Buffalo, New York, which he planned to develop as a Jewish colony. After the failure of this project, he became an advocate of Palestine as a national home for the Jews.

No Amon. Ancient Egyptian city on the Nile. The temple of Rameses III was located there and contains illustrations of his campaign against the peoples of the sea on the borders of Palestine.

Nob. Town in the territory of Benjamin, built by the priests of the sons of Eli. When David escaped from Saul's court, he traveled by way of Nob (I Samuel 21). As a punishment for their assisting David, Saul had 85 priests of the town killed, as well as men, women, children, sucklings, oxen, asses, and sheep (I Samuel 22.18–19).

Nobel Prize winners. Since the prize was established in 1899, Jews in a variety of fields (World Peace, Literature, Physiology and Medicine, Chemistry, Physics, and Economics) have received the award. They include Henry Kissinger and Eli Wiesel (World Peace), Albert Einstein (Physics), Arthur Kornberg (Medicine), Melvin Calvin (Chemistry), and Isaac Bashevis Singer, Nelly Sachs, and many others (Literature).

Noch (Yiddish). Another, more, yet.

No-goodnik. An unethical, irresponsible, or undependable person. It is also used of someone who does not earn an honest living.

Nokhrim *see* STRANGER.

***Nöldeke, Theodor** (1836–1930). German orientalist. He was born in Harburg, and taught at the universities of Kiel and Strasbourg. He wrote studies of the Mandean language and of Semitic languages, Syriac grammars, and a history of the Koran.

Nomberg, Hirsch David (1876–1927). Polish writer. He was born in Mszczonów, near Warsaw, and from 1903 to 1905 he wrote for the Warsaw Hebrew paper *Ha-Tzopheh.* He published a collection of Hebrew stories in 1905; this was followed by five collections in Yiddish. A disciple of Isaac Leib Peretz, he helped resolve the struggle between Hebraists and Yiddishists at the Czernowitz Yiddish conference in 1908. After 1910 he engaged in politics and journalism. In 1916 he was a founder of the Polish People's Party, and later was a member of the Polish Sejm. He was also president of the Society for Jewish Writers and Journalists.

Nordau, Max [Zidfeld, Simeon] (1849–1923). Hungarian author and Zionist leader. He was born in Budapest. In 1880 he settled in Paris, where he practiced as a doctor. In 1883 he published *Conventional Lies of our Civilization*; this was followed by *Paradoxes, The Malady of the Century,* and *Degeneration.* An associate of Theodor Herzl, he participated in all the Zionist congresses until 1911. Later he was a political counselor to the president of the Zionist Organization, David Wolffsohn. After Wolffsohn's policy was rejected by the practical Zionists, Nordau joined the opposition circles within the Zionist movement, which worked against the cultural Zionism advocated by, among others, Aḥad ha-Am.

Norman, Edward Albert (1900–1955). American financier and philanthropist. He was born in Chicago, and entered his family's financial business. He served as president of the American Fund for Israel Institutions, president of the American Economic Commission for Palestine, national secretary for the American Jewish Committee, and director of the Joint Distribution Committee. In addition he was president of the Group Farming Research Institute.

Norsa [Norzi]**, Jedidiah Solomon ben Abraham** (1560–1616). Italian rabbi and biblical scholar. He was born in Mantua. He wrote a critical masoretic commentary on the Bible.

Norsa [Norzi]**, Raphael ben Gabriel** (1520–?1583). Italian rabbi. He served as rabbi at Ferrara and Mantua, and wrote various studies of ethical issues connected with religious questions.

Norwich. English city, about 100 miles east of London. In 1144 a ritual murder accusation was made against Jews there in connection with the death of William of Norwich. Although royal officers protected the Jews, they were attacked in 1190 and 1234–8.

Norzi *see* NORSA.

Nosh *see* NASH.

Noshen *see* NASHN.

Nossig, Alfred (1864–1943). Polish author, sculptor, and musician. He was born in Lemberg. He initially belonged to the circle of assimilationist Polish Jews, but later he became a supporter of Zionism and advocated the establishment of a Jewish state in Palestine. In 1908 he founded a Jewish colonization organization. He published studies about Jewish national problems, and his work on Jewish statistics served as the basis for the Jewish Statistical and Demographic Institute. He also produced sculptures with Jewish themes. He lived in Berlin, but was expelled to Poland when the Nazis rose to power; suspected of collaborating with the Nazis, he was sentenced to death by the Jewish underground.

Notables, Assembly of *see* SANHEDRIN, GREAT.

Notarikon (Greek). System of abbreviation by shortening words or writing only one letter of a word. The term is derived from the system of shorthand used by the notarii in Roman courts of justice. In Hebrew studies notarikon is one of the tools or methods of interpreting Scripture; it is the 30th of the 32 hermeneutical rules laid down in the *Baraita of 32 Rules*.

Novellae (Latin; Hebrew "ḥiddushim"). Commentaries on the Talmud and later rabbinic literature, which attempt to derive new principles or facts from the text. Novellae of the early French and German talmudists are incorporated into the tosaphot, but in Spain novellae were issued as separate works by such scholars as Naḥmanides, Solomon ben Adret, and Yomtov ben Abraham of Seville. From the 16th century Rashi's commentary and the tosaphot were printed in editions of the Talmud; this practice gave rise to new novellae which were printed either together with the Talmud or as separate works.

Novi Israel. Jewish Christian sect. Founded in 1881 in Odessa by Jacob Priluker, it sought to unite Reform Judaism with the beliefs of Greek Orthodox dissenters. Although the group acknowledged the authority of the Pentateuch, it rejected the Talmud, circumcision, and the food laws. In 1883 it united with the Spiritual Biblical Brotherhood of Jacob Gordin. Priluker became a Christian, and later emigrated to England. In 1884 the sect was revived in Kishinev by Joseph Rabinovich, who also, in 1888, became a Christian.

Novomski, Moissaye *see* OLGIN, MOSES JOSEPH.

***Nowack, Wilhelm** (1850–1928). German biblical scholar and theologian. He was a professor at the universities of Halle and Strasbourg. He published biblical commentaries, a textbook on Hebrew archeology, and translations of the Mishnaic tractates Shabbat and Eruvin.

Nu (Yiddish). An ejaculation used in many different contexts. It can express the emotions connected with a sigh, a frown, a grin, a grunt, or a sneer. It can be used fondly, acidly, tritely, or belligerently.

Nudnik (Yiddish). Bore, idiot.

Numbers (i). In Hebrew the letters of the ALPHABET stand also for numbers; this attribute of the language has given rise to the significance of numbers in some systems of Jewish thought. Although the Bible does not generally attribute a particular significance to numbers, talmudic literature used numbers mnemonically. In addition, rabbinic sources regard the occurrence of the same number in different contexts or events as indicating a connection between them. This concept was later developed in the tradition of biblical exegesis known as GEMATRIA. In mystical sources numbers were regarded as having special creative powers. The concept of the magical significance and uses of numbers was developed in the Jewish and (particularly) Christian traditions of the KABBALAH.

Numbers (ii) (Hebrew "Be-Midbar"). Fourth book of the Pentateuch. It traces the history of the Israelites in the desert after the Exodus.

Numbers Rabbah. Midrash on the Book of Numbers; it is part of the Midrash Rabbah. The first 14 sections comprise a late aggadic composition on Numbers 1–7. Sections 15–23 is largely the Midrash Tanḥuma.

Numerus clausus (Latin: *lit.* "closed number"). Term applied to the restricted number of persons who may be admitted to specific professions, higher education, professional associations, and positions of public office. Such restrictions frequently applied to Jews, particularly in czarist Russia.

Numismatics *see* COINS.

Nun. 14th letter of the Hebrew alphabet. Its numerical value is 50.

Nuñez, Hector (1521–1591). Portuguese physician and merchant. He became leader of the Marrano community in England. His overseas trading activities enabled him to supply valuable information to the English government.

Nuñez, Maria (fl. 16th cent.). Portuguese Marrano communal leader. With other Marranos she escaped from Portugal on a ship bound for the Netherlands. Captured by a British vessel, they were diverted to London. According to one account, Nuñez was presented to Queen Elizabeth, who took her on a tour of London. She eventually settled in Amsterdam, where she founded a community that became a haven for other Marranos.

Nun reversed. The letter nun written back to front. In the Hebrew Bible the character appears as a sign before or after Numbers 10:35–6, before Psalm 107.21–6, and before Psalm 40. Its significance is not known.

Nuremberg. City in Bavaria, south-west Germany. Jews lived in the city from the 12th century and by the 13th century a sizable community was established. Destroyed in the Rindfleisch persecutions of 1298, it reestablished itself only to suffer again in the massacres of 1349 that accompanied the depredations of the Black Death. Later the community was re-formed, and a famous yeshivah existed in the city.

Nuremberg Laws. A group of anti-Jewish laws passed by the Reichstag at Nuremberg on 15 September 1935. They excluded Jews from German citizenship and prohibited marital and extra-marital relations between Jews and non-Jews. The legislation defined a Jew as one who had at least two Jewish grandparents. Through a series of later decrees of a similar kind Jews were placed outside the German law and excluded from civil and economic life.

Nusakh (*lit.* "version"). Term used of the various rites of prayer in different communities of Judaism; for example, Nusakh Ashkenaz means the Ashkenazi rite or liturgy. It also refers to the different traditions of synagogal melody.

Nuzi. Ancient city in Mesopotamia; the modern town of Yoghlan Tepe in north-east Iraq stands on the same site. Excavations there have cast light on biblical traditions.

O

Oak of weeping *see* ALLON-BACHUTH.

Oath "more judaico" *see* JEWISH OATH.

Obadiah (i) (fl. 9th cent. BCE). Israelite official, governor of the house of King Ahab. He hid 100 prophets of God to save them from Jezebel's persecution (I Kings 18).

Obadiah (ii) (fl. 6th cent. BCE). Israelite prophet. His life spanned the Babylonian conquest of Judah, and he spoke out against the Edomites for having refused to assist Jerusalem in her time of need.

Obadiah (iii). Biblical book, one of the 12 books of the Minor Prophets. It records the prophecies of Obadiah. It is the shortest book in the Hebrew Bible.

Obadiah of Bertinoro *see* BERTINORO, OBADIAH OF.

Obermann, Julian (1888–1956). American orientalist. He was born in Warsaw. He taught Semitic languages at the University of Hamburg from 1919 to 1922. After emigrating to the US he became professor of Semitic philology at the Jewish Institute of Religion in New York, and later professor of Semitic languages at Yale University. In 1944 he was appointed director of Judaic research and editor of the Yale Judaica Series. He wrote works on Semitic philology and epigraphy, Old Testament and Ugaritic studies, Islamic culture, and Arabic philosophy.

Occupations. Throughout the biblical and second Temple periods the Israelites were largely farmers, herdsmen, and craftsmen. Jews in the diaspora engaged in trade and in skilled handicrafts such as glass-making, silk-weaving, and dyeing; in Muslim lands they mostly worked on the land. From the Middle Ages southern European Jews continued the traditional occupations of trade and handicrafts, while in northern Europe, many Jews became moneylenders. In Poland the majority of Jews were craftsmen, whereas in Salonica and other parts of the Turkish Empire they were employed as menials. In western Europe the Jews were involved in trade and commerce. With the Emancipation such concentration on particular occupations began to be eroded and in the modern period Jews have engaged in all kinds of work.

Odel (fl. 18th cent.). Polish matriarch, daughter of the Baal Shem Tov. She was the mother of several tzaddikim. In Ḥasidic literature she is presented as the ideal type of womanhood.

Odessa. Ukrainian city and seaport on the Black Sea. The Jewish community was established there in 1798 and became prominent in the city's development. Odessa was the center of Russo-Jewish assimilation and the focus in the Russian Empire of Jewish literary and nationalist life. The first secular school for Russian Jews was founded there, as well as the first Russian synagogue with a choir, the first Russian Jewish newspaper, and the first Hebrew newspaper in Russia. Many of the major figures of modern Hebrew literature were active in the city, which became a center of the Haskalah, Hebrew literature, and the Zionist movement. The Jewish community in Odessa suffered from numerous pogroms, notably in 1812, 1859, 1871, 1881, and 1905.

***Oesterley, William Oscar** (1866–1950). English Semitic scholar. He was born in Calcutta. He taught Hebrew and Old Testament exegesis at King's College, London, from 1926. In his writings he showed the talmudic influence on the form and content of the New Testament. He published studies of the Bible, the Apocrypha, Hellenistic Judaism, and Jewish history.

Ofek, Abraham (b. 1935). Israeli painter. He was born in Burgus, Bulgaria, and emigrated to Israel in 1949. He has taught at the Bezalel School of Arts and Crafts and at the University of Haifa. His paintings cover the walls of Kfar Uriah, the Jerusalem Central Post Office, the Agron and Stone schools in Jerusalem, the Tel Aviv University Library, and the entrance to the main building of the University of Haifa.

Official, Joseph *see* JOSEPH BEN NATHAN.

Official rabbi *see* CROWN RABBI.

***Og** (fl. ?13th cent. BCE). Amorite king, ruler of Bashan in the Transjordan. He attempted to interrupt the march of the Israelites under Moses, but was defeated in battle at Edrei (Numbers 21.33–5).

Ohalot ("Tents"). Second tractate in the Mishnah order of Tohorot. It deals with the ritual impurity caused by contact with a corpse (Numbers 19.13–20).

Ohel ("tent") **(i).** Structure over a grave. The Ḥasidim, in particular, venerate the tombs of their tzaddikim, visiting them on the anniversary of the death. An ohel is erected over the grave and a ner tamid is kept burning at its foot. It was formerly the practice to prostrate oneself upon the grave and place a note there asking for help.

Ohel ("Tent") **(ii).** Israeli workers' theater. It was founded in Tel Aviv in 1925 by the cultural committee of the Histadrut, but later became independent. Based in Tel Aviv, it closed in 1969.

Oholah and Oholibah. Sisters who represent Israel and Judah in an allegorical prophecy of Ezekiel (Ezekiel 23); their sexual promiscuity and depravity stand for the sins of the Israelites and their downfall for the fate of Israel and Judah.

Oil. Oil plays an important part in the ritual, ceremonial, and sacrificial practices of Judaism. Pure olive oil was used in the Sanctuary and Temple (Exodus 27.20), and among oriental Jews this is still the only oil that may be used to fuel the ner tamid in the synagogue. Rabbi Tarphon declared that only olive oil could be used for Sabbath lamps, but the general ruling is that any oil may be used. Oil was also used to annoint high priests and kings, and formed part of certain sacrificial offerings.

Okhlah ve-Okhlah. Early collection of masoretic notes to the Bible, dating from before the 10th century. They are arranged partly alphabetically and partly in the order of the books of the Bible.

Olam ha-zeh, olam ha-ba ("This world, the world to come"). Talmudic terms designating respectively earthly life and the after-life. "Olam ha-ba" refers to the eternal world of the spirit, to which the soul passes after death; it also is used of the period following the coming of the Messiah, when the world will be perfected (*see* KINGDOM OF HEAVEN).

Old people's home *see* MOSHAV ZEKENIM.

Old Testament *see* BIBLE.

Oleh (*lit.* "one who ascends"). The word is used specifically of an immigrant to Israel. It is also applied to a person visiting the Holy Land as a pilgrim for the observance of Passover, Shavuot, and Sukkot (Exodus 23.14–17).

Olgin, Moses Joseph [Novomski, Moissaye] (1876–1939). American journalist and translator. He was born near Kiev, and began his career as a teacher. In 1913 he moved to Vienna, where he was co-editor of the Bundist Yiddish weekly *Di tsayt*. He emigrated to the US and settled in New York in 1914. He was a staff member of the Yiddish daily paper *Forverts*, and later edited the Communist Yiddish daily *Freiheit* and the monthly *Der hamer*. He wrote about political affairs, literature, and the theater.

***Oliphant, Laurence** (1829–1888). English writer and traveler. He was born in the Cape of Good Hope. He was a member of Parliament from 1865 to 1867. During the Russo-Turkish War of 1878, he became interested in Palestine and advocated Jewish settlement there. He was in contact with Ḥovevei Zion societies, engaged in political negotiations in Constantinople, and finally himself settled in Haifa. His writings include *The Land of Gilead* and *Haifa, or Life in Modern Palestine*.

Olives, Mount of *see* MOUNT OF OLIVES.

Olman, Israel (1883–1968). Dutch composer and choirmaster. He studied music in Amsterdam and became choirmaster of the Santo Servicio choir of the Sephardi synagogue there. His compositions include *Jigdal, Populus Sion, Jerusalem* for performance in the synagogue, as well as liturgical works for Jewish choirs.

***Omar** (fl. 7th cent). Caliph (634–44). He conquered Palestine, Syria, Iraq, Persia, and Egypt. He formed a covenant with Jews and Christians in his dominions which assured them of protection in exchange for the payment of a poll tax and the observance of various restrictions of their civil rights.

Omar, Mosque of [Dome of the Rock]. Mosque in the Temple area in Jerusalem. It was built by Caliph Abd al-Malik in c. 738. According to tradition it is situated on the site of Mount Moriah, where Solomon built the Temple.

Omer ("Sheaf") **(i).** First sheaf cut during the barley harvest. It was offered in the Temple as a sacrifice on the second day of Passover (Leviticus 23.15). Until the sacrifice had been offered, it was forbidden to eat the new grain. The period of seven weeks between the second day of Passover and the feast of Shavuot is known as the COUNTING OF THE OMER.

Omer ("sheaf") **(ii).** Dry measure equal to the tenth part of an ephah.

Omer (iii). Israeli daily newspaper. It is written in Hebrew but with vowels included. It was founded in Tel Aviv in 1951 by the publishers of the daily *Davar* to help immigrants learn Hebrew.

Omer, Counting of the (Hebrew "Sephirat ha-Omer"). The counting of the 49 days from the second day of Passover, when the first sheaf of the barley harvest – the omer – was offered in the Temple, until the feast of Shavuot. The time of counting is referred to as the Sephirah period, during which mourning customs are practiced and marriages are forbidden. The kabbalists viewed the 49 days of the Counting of Omer as having mystical significance.

Omri (fl. 9th cent. BCE). King of Israel (c. 882–871 BCE). During his reign he transferred the capital of Israel from Tirzah to Samaria (I Kings 16.21–8). According to the Moabite Stone, he conquered Moab.

Onaah (*lit.* "overreaching"). In Jewish law a term meaning fraudulent representation or unfair profit. The biblical instruction "You shall not wrong one another" (Leviticus 25.14) was interpreted by the rabbis as pertaining to transactions in which the profit was so great that the overcharging was tantamount to fraud. They decreed that if the seller of movable goods overcharged the buyer by one-sixth or more of the market value of the goods the buyer had grounds for canceling the transaction. (The transaction could be regarded as fraudulent only if the seller concealed such profit.)

Onam ken ("Yes it is true"). Opening words of a penitential piyyut for the Kol Nidre service on the eve of the Day of Atonement in the Ashkenazi rite. It was composed by Yom Tov ben Isaac of Joigny in the 12th century.

Onan (fl. ?19th–16th cent. BCE). Second son of Judah and Shua (Genesis 38.2–4; 46.12; Numbers 26.19). After the death of his brother Er, his father instructed him to marry his childless sister-in-law, Tamar. He refused to fulfil his duty, and would not consummate the marriage. His conduct was viewed as abhorrent, and God took his life. (Genesis 38.8–10)

Oneg Shabbat ("Sabbath delight"). Name given to an educational or cultural gathering that takes place on Saturday afternoon. The term has come to refer to any celebration during the Sabbath.

Onias I (fl. 4th cent. BCE). High priest. According to I Maccabees 12.20–23, Areios I, King of Sparta, sent a letter to Onias I claiming that the Spartans and the Jews were both descended from Abraham.

Onias II (fl. 3rd cent. BCE). High priest, grandson of Onias I. He wished to free the Jewish people from the yoke of Ptolemaic Egypt; in pursuit of this aim he conspired with the enemies of Ptolemy III and withheld the payment of taxes. Ptolemy responded by threatening to expel the Jews from Judea, but was pacified through the intervention of Onias's nephew, Joseph son of Tobias.

Onias III (fl. 2nd cent. BCE). High priest, grandson of Onias II. Simeon, an official in the Temple, demanded from Onias the post of market commissioner, which was in his gift. When his petition was refused, Simeon revealed to Apollonius, the commander of the Syrian army, that the treasures of King Seleucus of Syria were being held in the Temple vaults. Seleucus then sent his chancellor Heliodorus to remove them. When his mission failed, Onias fell out of favor with his Syrian overlords. After Antiochus IV Epiphanes ascended the throne, Onias was summoned to Antioch and his brother Jason became high priest in his place. Later Jason was replaced by Menelaus, who was an extreme Hellenizer.

Onias IV (fl. 2nd cent. BCE). Son of Onias III. After he was ousted as high priest by Akimus, he went from Judea to Egypt. In 145 BCE Ptolemy VI Philometer granted him authority to build a temple in Leontopolis.

Onkelos (fl. 2nd cent.). Palestinian proselyte. He was a contemporary of Rabban Gamaliel II of Jabneh. He translated the Pentateuch into Aramaic (*see* TARGUM).

Onochi, Z. I. *see* ARONSOHN, ZALMAN YITZḤAK.

Opatoshu, Joshua [Opatovsky, Joseph] (1886–1954). American Yiddish novelist, of Polish origin. He settled in the US in 1907. From 1910 he contributed stories to periodicals and anthologies. Later he joined the staff of the New York Yiddish daily paper *Der tog*. His novels deal largely with Jewish life in Poland and America.

Opatov, Rabbi of *see* ABRAHAM, JOSHUA HESHEL.

Operation Ezra and Nehemiah. Code name for the airlift of 120,000 Jews from Iraq to Israel, carried out by the Jewish Agency and the Israeli government between May 1950 and October 1951.

Operation Magic Carpet. Code name for the airlift of 50,000 Jews from Yemen to Israel, carried out by the Jewish Agency and the Israeli government between autumn 1949 and autumn 1950.

Opferpfennig (German: "tribute penny"). Poll tax introduced in 1342 throughout the Holy Roman Empire by Emperor Louis IV, the Bavarian. All Jews over 12 years old who possessed 20 guilders or more were to pay one guilder annually. The tax was regarded as a continuation of the traditional Temple tax which the Jews had paid to the Roman authorities after the destruction of the second Temple.

Ophan. Name given to a type of piyyut, incorporated into the morning service for the Sabbath and feast days. Based on the description of the ophannim (traditionally identified with the cherubim) in Ezekiel 1, it describes the recitation of the doxology by the angels.

Ophel. Rocky site in Jerusalem, to the north of the original City of David. In ancient times it formed part of the eastern fortification of Jerusalem. According to Nehemiah (3.27), it was situated between the tower of the royal palace and the water gate, and in his day the Temple servants (Nethinim) lived there. The term is applied by modern archeologists to the whole area of the old City of David south of the Temple mount.

Oppenheim [Oppenheimer], **David** (1664–1736). German rabbi. He was born in Worms, and served as a rabbi in Nikolsburg and Prague. His library contained 7000 volumes, including 1000 manuscripts; they became the basis of the Hebrew section of the Bodleian Library in Oxford.

Oppenheim, Moritz Daniel (1799–1882). German painter. He was born in Hanau. In 1821 he went to Rome, where he was influenced by a Christian group known as the Nazarenes, who painted pictures based on the New Testament. Later he returned to Germany and settled in Frankfurt am Main. He painted biblical scenes and pictures on Jewish themes, including confrontations between Christians and Jews.

Oppenheim, Samuel *see* OPPENHEIMER, SAMUEL.

Oppenheimer, David *see* OPPENHEIM, DAVID.

Oppenheimer, Franz (1864–1943). German economist and sociologist. He was born in Berlin. From 1919 to 1929 he was a professor of sociology at the University of Frankfurt am Main. After Hitler's rise to power, he taught at the Hochschule für die Wissenschaft des Judentums in Berlin. In 1938 he settled in the US. He was associated with the Zionist movement, and the Merḥavyah cooperative settlement in Palestine was founded in accordance with his theories.

Oppenheimer, Joseph (c. 1698–1738). German financier. His father was a merchant in Heidelberg and collector of taxes from the Jews of the Palatinate. In 1732 Oppenheimer became the finance minister of Karl Alexander of Württemberg. After the duke's death in 1737 he was accused of stealing state finances and was hanged at Stuttgart; he refused to save his life by accepting baptism. His life was the subject of the novel *Jud Süss* by Lion Feuchtwanger.

Oppenheimer [Oppenheim], **Samuel** (1630–1703). Austrian financier and philanthropist. He was Leopold I's agent and financier, and was the first Jew to be allowed to settle in Vienna. He helped to finance Leopold's wars with the Turks and the War of the Spanish Succession. In 1697 he was accused of conspiring to murder Samson Wertheimer, but was acquitted. Among his benefactions were support for the poor, Jewish scholars, and Judah Ḥasid ha-Levi's movement for a Jewish settlement in Palestine.

Oppert, Jules (1825–1905). French philologist, orientalist, and archeologist. Born in Hamburg, he settled in France early in his life. He became an authority on Old Persian and Assyrian, and in 1851 he went on an expedition to explore Mesopotamia, where he identified the site of ancient Babylon. In 1874 he became professor of Assyrian philology and archeology at the Collège de France. He wrote studies on various aspects of oriental scholarship. He was an active member of various Jewish communal and scholarly bodies.

Oracle *see* URIM AND THUMMIM.

Oraḥ Ḥayyim *see* JACOB BEN ASHER.

Oral Law. According to tradition, the Oral Law was given to Moses on Mount Sinai (together with the Written Law). During the second Temple period, the Oral Law was upheld by the Pharisees (in opposition to the Sadducees). Later the Oral Law was studied in the academies, and was eventually written down in the Mishnah, compiled by Judah ha-Nasi (2nd century). After further centuries of discussion, the Oral Law was recorded in the Talmud (6th century). After the redaction of the Talmud, the Oral Law was further studied in talmudic academies. During the gaonic period, the Karaites rejected the authority of the Oral Law. Modern non-Orthodox Judaism (Reform, Conservative, Liberal) rejects the belief that the Oral Law was revealed to Moses on Mount Sinai, maintaining instead that it originated through discussion and interpretation over the centuries.

Ordeal, trial by. Judicial method for determining the validity of an accusation. It usually involved the infliction of a painful physical test upon the suspected person; if the victim emerged unscathed it was supposedly a sign of supernatural intervention and (in Jewish law) was seen as proof of innocence. In biblical times the test of bitter waters was imposed by the priest upon a "sotah" (a married woman suspected of adultery) (Numbers 5.11–31). In a ceremony involving a meal offering and ritual curses, a mixture of holy water and dust was administered to the woman; if her flesh swelled and became diseased she was guilty, but if she was unharmed she was innocent. This practice was eventually abolished by Johanan ben Zakkai.

Ordination (Hebrew "semikhah") [Hattarat Horaah ("Permission to lay down a decision"]. In Jewish usage, the conferring of the title "rabbi" on a man learned in Jewish law and the practice of religion. Traditionally teachers granted the title "rabbi" to learned pupils, who thereby earned the right to give decisions about ritual and legal matters. The Talmud traces the origin of this institution to Moses, who conveyed leadership to Joshua by placing his hands on Joshua's head. Initially Jewish ordination was confined to Palestine; in Babylonia scholars received the title "rav." A new form of ordination was established in the 14th century in Germany by Meir ha-Levi of Vienna. He required that all newly qualified candidates should receive a "ketav semikhah" (writ of ordination), and this practice spread to other countries. Later a distinction was made between ordination in the sense of granting "Hattarat Horaah" (permission to lay down a decision), and the conferring of the title "Morenu" (our teacher) as an honorary title. In modern times a candidate for the rabbinate undergoes a lengthy period of study in a seminary, at the end of which he is given the certificate of Hattarat Horaah; this usually includes the phrase "yoreh yoreh, yadin yadin" (he may surely give a decision and may surely judge). In some seminaries the graduation ceremony is described as "ordination" and may involve the laying on of hands.

Oren (from Latin "orare": to pray). Word

used among German Jews, meaning to pray.

Orgad, Ben-Zion (b. 1926). Israeli composer and educator. He was born in Germany, and in 1933 settled in Palestine, where he later became a superintendent of music education. His works are motivated by national ideology.

Organ. According to the Talmud there was an organ of ten pipes in the second Temple. In the 17th–19th centuries an organ was used in the principal synagogue in Prague. During the 19th century the use of the organ in synagogues became a point of conflict between Reform and Orthodox Jews: according to Orthodoxy, the organ is forbidden under the general ban on instrumental music in worship outside the Temple; its use also contravenes the rabbinic ordinance against playing a musical instrument on the Sabbath. The organ is now used in services of worship in Reform and Conservative synagogues.

Orient, Der. German weekly journal. It was founded by Julius Fürst, and was published from 1840 to 1851. It was the organ of German Jewish conservative groups.

Orientalists. An orientalist is one who studies the civilization and culture of Eastern (especially Asiatic) countries. In Jewish usage the term is applied principally to those studying the countries of the eastern Mediterranean, north Africa, and the Middle East. From the Middle Ages onward Jewish scholars studied Islamic theology, philosophy, and religious law. In the 19th and 20th centuries, Jewish philologists, archeologists, theologians, and philosophers have made important contributions to the study of oriental languages and civilizations.

***Origen** (184–253). Alexandrian Christian scholar, one of the Church Fathers. He was the first Christian scholar to study Hebrew. He visited Palestine, where he came into contact with Jewish scholars. His *Hexapla* is an edition of the Jewish Scriptures, containing the original Hebrew and a Greek transliteration. He also translated the Septuagint and the works of Aquila, Symmachus, and Theodotion into Greek.

Original sin. Christian doctrine that all human beings live in a state of sin because of Adam's transgression; according to this view, humanity can be redeemed only by the atoning death of Jesus. Jewish theology, however, maintains that humans are not born in a state of sinfulness, but that each person is motivated by innate evil and good inclinations.

Orlah ("Uncircumcised fruit"). Tenth tractate in the Mishnah order of Zeraim. It deals with the law forbidding the use of the fruit of trees or vineyards for the first three years after planting (Leviticus 19.23).

Orlinski, Harry (b. 1908). American biblical scholar. He was born in Toronto, Canada, and went to the US in 1931. He was professor of Bible at the Hebrew Union College from 1943, and served as president of the Society for Biblical Literature in 1969–70. He was also editor-in-chief of the Jewish Publication Society's translation of the Torah. His writings include *Understanding the Bible through History and Archaeology*.

Ornitz, Samuel (1890–1957). American author. He was born in New York, where he worked as a social worker from 1908 to 1920. An advocate of Jewish assimilation, he saw no virtue in Jewish immigrant life. His novels chiefly concern the Jewish immigrant generation of the 1880–1914 period and portray Jewish types in an unsympathetic light.

Orpah (fl. 12th cent. BCE). Moabite woman, wife of Chilion and sister-in-law of Ruth. When her mother-in-law, Naomi, returned home to Judah, Orpah was persuaded to remain behind in

Moab, while Ruth went with Naomi (Ruth 1).

Orphans. According to the Bible, caring for orphans is an important act of charity and a duty (Deuteronomy 14.29; 24.19–21). Rabbinic law provided for the support of orphans and granted them special privileges. During the Middle Ages the number of orphans increased, owing to frequent massacres of the Jewish community; many communities organized special bodies to care for their welfare. In the 19th century orphanages were established in many Jewish centers (such as the Jewish Orphanage in London).

ORT [Obshtchestvo Remeslenovo Truda (Russian: "Society for the Encouragement of Handicraft")]. Jewish organization for the development of skilled trades and agriculture. It was founded in Russia in 1880 at the instigation of Baron Horace Günzburg and others. Initially it created a network of vocational schools and cooperative workshops in Russia, but later its programmes were extended throughout Europe. In 1933 its head office was transferred to Paris, and ORT schools were established in South America, Canada, Australia, and elsewhere. In 1943 its head office moved to Geneva. After World War II, ORT established schools in displaced persons' camps in Germany and eastern Europe, and its activities were extended to Israel and north Africa.

Orthodoxy. Applied to a particular strand of religious thought and practice in Judaism, the term was first used in 1795. From the beginning of the 19th century it passed into common usage to denote traditional Judaism, which adheres to the belief in the divine origin of the Written and Oral Law and insists on strict adherence to the laws of the Shulḥan Arukh.

Osiris, Daniel (1825–1908). French financier and philanthropist. He was born in Bordeaux. His beneficiaries included the French state, the Institut de France, and the Jewish community.

Ossuary. Receptacle, usually in the form of a small chest, in which the bones of the dead are placed. The use of ossuaries is referred to in the Mishnah. Most surviving Jewish ossuaries originated in Palestine in the period from the 2nd century BCE to the 3rd century CE. They are decorated with geometrical patterns, rosettes, olive branches, palms, wreaths, columns, and chalices, and carry the names of the dead whose bones they contain inscribed in Hebrew, Aramaic, and Greek.

Ostracon (from Greek "ostrakon": potsherd). Fragment of pottery carrying an inscription. Such fragments were used for various purposes, among others as letters and receipts. Important finds of ostraca of Jewish interest have been made at Gezer, Samaria, Lachish, Elath, Elephantine, and Edfu.

Ostropoler, Hirsch (fl. 18th cent.). Polish Yiddish jester. He was born in Balta, Podolia, and lived at Medzibozh. He derived his name from Ostropol in Poland, where he was the shoḥet. He later wandered throughout Podolia. Booklets recording his tales and anecdotes were published posthumously.

Oswiecim *see* AUSCHWITZ.

Othniel (fl. ?13th cent. BCE). First judge of Israel. He was a hero of the tribe of Judah during the period of conquest. After capturing Debir for his brother Caleb, he received Caleb's daughter Achsah in marriage. Later he led the army which vanquished Cushan Rishathaim, King of Aram-Naharaim, who had enslaved Israel for eight years (Judges 3.8–11).

Otzar Neḥmad ("Thesaurus of delight"). Hebrew annual of Jewish studies, published by Isaac Blumenfeld in Vienna from 1856 to 1863.

Oxford. English city 50 miles west of

London, the seat of one of the oldest universities in the world. Jews lived there in the 12th century. Between the 14th and 19th centuries a number of Hebrew teachers worked in the city. The Oxford Jewish community was established in 1840, and Jews began to enter Oxford University in the 1850s; after the removal of religious tests in 1871, the number of Jewish students increased. The Bodleian Library of the university contains an important collection of Judaica and Jewish studies are pursued within the university and the Centre for Postgraduate Hebrew Studies.

Oy (Yiddish). Exclamation with a wide range of meanings. It may express surprise, fear, sadness, contentment, joy, relief, uncertainty, indignation, irritation, pain, revulsion, anguish, dismay, despair, regret, or outrage.

Oz, Amos (b. 1939). Israeli novelist. He was born in Jerusalem. His works include *Where the Jackals Howl, Elsewhere Perhaps, My Michael, Unto Death, Touch the Water, Touch the Wind, A Perfect Peace, In the Land of Israel,* and *The Black Box.*

Oze [Obshtchestvo Zdravookhranyenie Evreyev (Russian: "Jewish health society")]. Organization dedicated to the promotion of good health among the Jews. It was founded in 1912 at St. Petersburg, and after World War I, branches were established in various countries. Since 1946 it has also been active in Israel and north Africa. Its activities are centered on the maintenance of hospitals, sanatoria, dispensaries, and other similar institutions.

Ozick, Cynthia (b. 1928). American novelist. She was born in New York. Her writings include *The Pagan Rabbi and other Stories* and *The Messiah of Stockholm.*

P

Pablo Christiani *see* CHRISTIANI, PABLO.

Pacifico, David (1784–1854). Anglo-Portuguese merchant and diplomat. Born in Gibraltar, he was a British subject. He served as Portuguese consul in Morocco (1835–7) and Greece (1837–42). In a riot against the Jewish community of Athens, he was attacked and his house was destroyed. When his claim for compensation was refused, the British blockaded the port of Piraeus and captured 200 Greek ships. The Greek government then made financial reparations to Pacifico.

Pacifism *see* PEACE.

Padua. City in north-east Italy, west of Venice. Its Jewish community dates from the 13th century. From the 14th century Jews studied medicine in the university there, and in the 17th–18th centuries it was one of the few places in Europe where Jews could graduate as physicians. The Paduan ghetto was established in 1602. The Collegio Rabbinico Italiano was situated in the city between 1829 and 1871.

Padua [Katzenellenbogen], **Meir** [Maḥaram Padua] (1482–1565). Italian talmudist. He was born in Germany, studied in Poland, and served as a rabbi in Padua. An important codifier, he was frequently consulted about halakhic issues.

Pagan Martyrs, Acts of the. Title given to an Egyptian papyrus dating from the 2nd–3rd centuries. The work, which adopts an anti-Jewish stance, purports to describe the trial of Alexandrian Greek leaders by Roman emperors.

Pagis, Dan (1930–1986). Israeli scholar and poet. He was born in Bukovina, Romania. In his youth he was imprisoned by the Nazis. He settled in Israel in 1947 and later became professor of medieval Hebrew literature at the Hebrew University. He published studies of Hebrew literature; an annotated anthology of Hebrew love poetry of the 10th–18th centuries from Spain, Italy, Turkey, and the Yemen; and his own poetry.

Palache, Juda Lion (1886–1944). Dutch orientalist and teacher. He was born in Amsterdam, and in 1925 became professor of the Bible and Semitic languages at the University of Amsterdam. He also served as parnas (or head) of the Spanish and Portuguese congregation in the city. He published studies of Judaism, Islam, and comparative Semitic philology.

Palache, Samuel (d. 1616). Community leader. He was the first person to settle in Amsterdam as a declared Jew, and he obtained authorization for other Jews to settle there. In 1596 he gathered the first minyan in Amsterdam at his home for prayers on the Day of Atonement. He also built the first synagogue in the Netherlands. In 1608 he was appointed ambassador to The Hague by the Moroccan sultan Mulay Zidan, and in 1610 he negotiated an alliance between Morocco and the Netherlands – the first treaty of alliance between Christian and Muslim states. Later he assumed command of a small Moroccan fleet which seized some ships belonging to the King of Spain; he was charged with piracy, but was acquitted.

Pale of Settlement. Territory within the borders of czarist Russia where Jews were legally authorized to reside. It consisted of 25 provinces in Poland, Lithuania, Belorussia, Ukraine, Bessarabia, and the Crimea, and was established in 1791 by a decree of Catharine II. Permission to settle outside the Pale was given only to certain groups (including members of the liberal professions, Jews with a secondary school diploma, successful businessmen, skilled artisans, and former Cantonists). In 1882, under the May Laws, Jews were excluded from rural areas inside the Pale. In August 1915 the Pale was effectively abolished, though the laws concerning it remained in force until March 1917.

Paleography *see* ALPHABET; SCRIPT; WRITING.

Palestine. One of the names of the territory also known as Israel or the Holy Land. The name "Palestine" is derived from the Hebrew name "Peleshet"; in classical antiquity Palestine was called "Palestinian Syria," but in time "Syria" was omitted and the first element of the name adjusted accordingly. It is probable that the Romans imposed the name Palestine on the territory because of the strong Jewish associations connected with the name Judea. In modern times the name Palestine was changed to Israel with the founding of the Jewish state in 1948.

Palestine Communist Party. It was founded in 1919 and until 1948 viewed Zionism as a reactionary offshoot of British imperialism. Its aim was to liberate the Arab masses with the aid of Jewish workers. It split into two in 1965, resulting in the formation of Maki and Rakaḥ.

Palestine Economic Corporation. Public company incorporated in the US in 1926. It was the instrument of American private capital for the development of a Jewish homeland. Under its auspices Americans furnished financial support for productive enterprises in Palestine, including banking, credit, industry, and agriculture.

Palestine Electric Company. Company founded in 1923 by Pinḥas Rutenberg to supply electricity to the country. It established power stations in Haifa, Tel Aviv, and Tiberias, and in 1926 obtained a concession to produce hydroelectric power using the waters of the Yarmuk and Jordan rivers. A plant constructed at Naharayim was destroyed by the Arab legion during the war of 1948. The Israel Electric Corporation now oversees the electrical industry in Israel.

Palestine Exploration Fund. British organization dedicated to the exploration and study of the Holy Land. Founded in 1865, it produced the first modern map of Palestine, together with a complete archeological survey. It was active in the excavation of Jerusalem (1894–7), the city mounds of the Shephelah (1899–1900), the mound of Gezer (1902–9), Beth Shemesh (1911–12), and the Ophel in Jerusalem (1923–7). Later it was involved in excavations at Jericho. Its quarterly journal is an important source for Palestinian archeology and history.

Palestine Foundation Fund *see* KEREN HA-YESOD.

Palestine Jewish Colonization Association *see* PICA.

Palestine Land Development Company *see* ISRAEL LAND DEVELOPMENT COMPANY.

Palestine Mandate *see* MANDATE, PALESTINE.

Palestine Office. Zionist institution. Founded in Jaffa by the World Zionist Organization in 1908, it supervised practical work in Palestine. Under its director, Arthur Ruppin, it became the central institution of the Jewish community in Palestine. It financed settlement, organized a Hebrew school system, and looked after Palestinian Jewry's needs during World War I. After the war, it was dissolved and its activities were taken over by the Zionist Commission. The name "Palestine Office" then came to be applied to Zionist consulates in the diaspora responsible for the organization, regulation, and implementation of Jewish immigration to Palestine.

Palestine Post *see* JERUSALEM POST.

Palestinian Talmud *see* TALMUD.

***Pallière, Aimé** (1875–1949). French writer and theologian. He was born into a Catholic family, but lived the life of a Jew, though he did not convert to Judaism. He was a spiritual guide to the congregation of the Liberal synagogue in Paris and to members of the French Reform movement. He served as president of the World Union of Jewish Youth, and edited the periodical *Chalom*. Later in life he drew closer to Catholicism. His writings include *Le sanctuaire inconnu*, *Bergson et le Judaïsme*, and *L'âme juive et Dieu*.

Palmaḥ. The mobilized striking force of the Haganah. Established on 19 May 1941, it was an underground movement until 1948, when it became a part of the Israel Defense Army. It was commanded by Yitzḥak Sadeh (1941–3), Yigal Allon (1943–8), and Uri Brenner during the War of Independence. From 1945 to 1947 it struggled against the British. In November 1948 General Yaakov Dori, chief of general staff to the Israeli forces, ordered its disbanding.

Palmyra *see* TADMOR.

Pann [Pfefferman]**, Abel** (1883–1963). Israeli artist, of Russian origin. He trained in Vienna and Paris. In 1913 he moved to Palestine, where he was a teacher at the Bezalel School of Arts and Crafts. His paintings depict Bible stories and scenes of Israeli settlement life.

Pantheism. The doctrine that the universe is God and God the universe. All forms of pantheism are opposed to classical theism, which affirms the belief in a creator and a created order. Kabbalistic doctrines often exhibit pantheistic tendencies.

Pap, Karoly (1897–1945). Hungarian writer, son of the chief rabbi of Sopron. He served in the Hungarian Red Army, and later settled in Budapest. Some of his writings deal with the issue of Jewish identity and assimilation.

Papacy *see* POPE.

Pappa (c. 300–375). Babylonian amora. He studied under Rava and Abbaye. He founded an academy at Neresh, near Sura, which he directed. He frequently participated in halakhic disputes. Besides his scholarly activities, he engaged in the sale of poppy seeds and the brewing of date beer.

Pappenheim, Bertha (1859–1936). German communal leader. She was born in Vienna, where she was treated by the neurologist Joseph Breuer, who viewed her case as important in the development of psychoanalysis. Later she settled in Frankfurt am Main, where she became the headmistress of an orphanage. In 1904 she founded the relief organization Jüdischer Frauenbund and visited Galicia, Romania, and Russia to carry out its work. In 1914 she established and directed an institute near Frankfurt for unmarried mothers, prostitutes, and delinquent women. She translated Yiddish works into German and wrote under the name of Paul Berthold.

Pappus and Julianus (fl. 2nd cent.). Judean patriots. They were brothers. According to rabbinic tradition, they set up banks to assist wayfarers in Jerusalem. They were probably among the leaders of the Jewish revolt against Trajan (115–17), since they were captured by the Romans at Laodicea in Syria and executed.

Papyrus. Ancient Egyptian writing material made from an aquatic plant of the sedge family; also a manuscript written on this material. Aramaic papyri from Elephantine contain information about the Jewish garrison community there in the 5th century BCE. The majority of Egyptian papyri are written in Greek and date from the 2nd century BCE to the 7th century CE. They include petitions, proclamations, ordinances, records of court proceedings, wills, official correspondence, contracts, registers of people and property, tax lists, receipts, and private letters. Papyri of importance to Jewish studies include the Acts of the Pagan Martyrs and the Nash Papyrus.

Paradise *see* HEAVEN; PARDES.

Parah ("Heifer"). Fourth tractate in the Mishnah order of Tohorot. It deals with regulations concerning the congregational sacrifice of the red heifer (Numbers 19).

Parah adummah *see* RED HEIFER.

Paran. Desert in the Negev. It was the home of Ishmael after he and Hagar were cast out by Abraham (Genesis 21.21). During their wanderings the Israelites camped in the wilderness of Paran; it was from here that Moses sent 12 men into Canaan to spy out the land (Numbers 13.3, 26).

Parashah ("section"). Term applied to the entire weekly portion ("sidrah") of the Torah read in the synagogue on the Sabbath, or to one of the shorter passages into which the sidrah is divided; each of these shorter sections is read by a different person.

Parashiyyot, Four. Name given to the final portions (or "maphtir") of the Torah, read in the synagogue on the four Sabbaths preceding Passover. They are followed by an appropriate conclusion (haphtarah). The names given to the passages are Shekalim (Exodus 30.11–16); Zakhor (Deuteronomy 25.17–19); Parah (Numbers 19.1–22); and Ha Ḥodesh (Exodus 12.1–20). A second Scroll of the Law is used for the reading of these portions.

Pardes. Paradise. The Hebrew is derived from Greek "paradeisos." In the Middle Ages "pardes" was used as an acronym for the four types of biblical interpretation: "peshat" (literal); "remez" (allegorical); "derash" (aggadic); and "sod" (mystical).

Pardo, David (1718–1790). Palestinian rabbinical author and poet. He was born in Venice, and served as a rabbi in Spalato in Dalmatia and in Sarajevo. Between 1776 and 1782 he traveled widely, making his way to Palestine; he settled in Jerusalem, where he became head of a yeshivah. He wrote commentaries and novellae on tannaitic literature, as well as liturgical poetry.

Pardo [Brown]**, Saul** (d. 1708). American ḥazzan, also known as Saul Brown. He was the first ḥazzan of the Jewish community of New York, the Congregation Shearith Israel.

Parents. The duty of children to respect their parents is laid down in the Ten Commandments (Exodus 20.12) Leviticus 19.3) and is emphasized in rabbinic teaching. According to Jewish law, parents must be obeyed unless they order their children to transgress the Torah, or disagree with a son in his choice of a wife. The Talmud decrees that a son should not stand or sit in his father's place or contradict him. He should provide for his father's material needs in old age and take him where he needs to go. A father has the duty to support his children up to the age of six. He is permitted to chastise them, but only while they are minors. Both the father and mother are equal with regard to the duties owed them by their children.

Pareveh [parveh] (Yiddish: "neutral"). Food which is considered to be neutral in relation to milk and meat, and which therefore may be eaten with either.

Parḥi, Estori *see* FARḤI, ESTORI.

Parḥon, Solomon (fl. 12th cent.). Italian lexicographer. He was born in Qal'a, Spain, and became a pupil of Judah ha-Levi and Abraham ibn Ezra. He settled in Italy, where he wrote a biblical lexicon (*Maḥberet he-Arukh*) in 1160 at Salerno.

Paris. Capital of France. Jews settled there in Roman times, and a Jewish community existed in the city throughout the early Middle Ages. From the 12th century Parisian Jews faced persecutions, and between 1182 and 1198 the Jewish community was banished from France as a whole. In 1240 the Disputation of Paris was followed by a burning of the Talmud. Further expulsions of the Jews took place in 1306 and 1394. In the 17th century Jews from Bordeaux, Avignon, and Alsace settled in Paris, and a major influx of Jews occurred in the next century. At the end of the 19th century the Dreyfus Affair, centered in Paris, caused consternation among Jews and Christians alike and had far-reaching effects on French political and civil life.

Paris Peace Conference *see* VERSAILLES, TREATY OF.

***Parkes, James William** (1896–1977). English theologian and historian. From 1928 to 1934 he was study secretary of the International Student Service in Geneva, and in 1949–51 served as president of the Jewish Historical Society of England. He published works on anti-Semitism, the origins of Christianity, and the history of Palestine, including *The Conflict of the Church and the Synagogue, The Jew in the Medieval Community,* and *Arabs and Jews in the Middle East: a Tragedy of Errors.*

Parliament, members of. In spite of various restrictions and civil disabilities imposed on Jewish communities in many countries, Jews have served as members of parliament and in other political and legislative office since Emancipation in the 18th century. In 1775 Francis Salvador was elected to the Provincial Congress of South Carolina and later became a member of the General Assembly of that state. Jewish members were first elected to the Dutch National Assembly in 1797. In Italy Moses Formiggini represented Milan in the Legislative Assembly of the Cisalpine Republic, while in France Isaac-Adolphe Crémieux became the first Jewish member of the French Chamber of Deputies in 1842. Lionel Rothschild entered the British House of Commons in 1858, and his son Nathaniel Mayer Rothschild was the first Jew to sit in the House of Lords (1885). In South Africa Saul Solomon represented Cape Town in parliament from 1854. In Russia Jews were among the members of the first Duma, convened in 1906. In the US the first Jewish member of the House of Representatives was David L. Yulee (1845), who was also the first Jewish senator. In the 20th century Jews have been elected to parliamentary assemblies throughout the world and have held important positions in government. The parliament of Israel, the KNESSET, was created in 1949.

Parnas ("provider," "supporter"). Head of the Jewish community. Originally he was a lay leader, but later (especially among the Ashkenazim from the Middle Ages onward) he was elected to office as president of the community or synagogue. Election was usually for a term of one or three years, but it could occasionally be for life. In the Middle Ages and the early modern period, a system existed whereby several parnasim led the community in rotation. In modern times the term refers to the president of a community or a congregation.

Parnosse (Yiddish). Sustenance, livelihood.

Parokhet. The curtain used to veil the Sanctuary of the Tabernacle which served as a temple for the Israelites during the years in the wilderness. It was made by Bezalel of scarlet, purple, and fine linen with a woven design (Exodus 26.31). In modern times the term is used by the Ashkenazim to refer to the curtain hanging before the Ark in the synagogue.

Parsi. Adherent of ZOROASTRIANISM. The Parsis are descendants of Persians who fled to India from Muslim persecution in the 7th and 8th centuries.

Parthia. Iranic empire which flourished from the 3rd century BCE to the 2nd century CE. Its dominions included Mesopotamia, Babylonia, and Media, in all of which there were sizable Jewish populations. In 40 BCE the Parthians restored Antigonus Mattathias to the throne of Judah. Under Parthian rule the Jews, led by the exilarch, enjoyed a large degree of autonomy, and the rabbinical academies in Mesopotamia flourished.

Partisans. In Jewish usage a term applied to nationalist guerilla groups active in Europe during World War II. In many conquered countries Jews organized such groups, setting up family camps in the countryside the better to protect the defenseless members of the community, and attempting to carry out acts of sabotage against the occupying forces.

Partition (i) *see* MEḤITZAH.

Partition (ii). In 1937 the Peel Commission, a British royal commission appointed to examine the causes of Arab unrest in Palestine, recommended the division of the country into autonomous areas for Arabs and Jews. The proposal was accepted by the British government, but provoked differences of opinion within Zionist circles. The 18th Zionist Congress of 1937 empowered the executive of the Jewish Agency to negotiate the basis of a partition, but the Jewish Agency made further efforts to come to terms with the Arabs. In 1937 the Woodhead Commission was appointed by the British government to formulate practical proposals for partition. However, the notion of Jewish sovereignty gained support, and the Zionist movement demanded a Jewish state in Palestine. In 1946, after a report of the Anglo-American Joint Committee, the executive of the Jewish Agency agreed to enter into negotiations about partition, and the following year the UN Committee on Palestine formulated a program to bring about partition. The UN Assembly adopted this program, with minor amendments, on 29 November 1947.

Partnership. In Jewish law the concept of partnership in business includes joint ownership and commercial partnership. A partnership is formed by joint acquisition or through inheritance, and can be dissolved on demand. According to Maimonides, commercial partnership is a development of joint ownership: before a partnership can be established the parties to it must gain ownership of all the capital invested in the enterprise. But other authorities regard symbolic consent or verbal agreement as a sufficient basis for partnership.

Partos, Ödön (1909–1977). Israeli composer and violinist. He was born in Budapest. He became first violinist of the Lucerne Orchestra in 1924, and from 1936 to 1938 taught violin and composition at the conservatory in Baku. In 1938 he went to Palestine and joined the Palestine Orchestra as a viola player. He was appointed director of the Israel Conservatory and Academy of Music in Tel Aviv in 1953. His compositions include *Song of Praise* for viola and orchestra and the symphonic fantasy *En Gev.*

Parveh *see* PAREVEH.

Paschal lamb. The name given to the lamb sacrificed, in the Temple period, on the eve of Passover (14 Nisan). After the sacrifice the animal was roasted whole and eaten by the community. (Exodus 12.1–28, 43–9; Deuteronomy 16.1–8)

Pasken (Yiddish: "decide," "declare the law"). To give a ruling on a religious question.

Passfield White Paper *see* WHITE PAPER, PASSFIELD.

Passover (Hebrew "Pesaḥ") [Feast of Unleavened Bread]. The first of the three pilgrim festivals, beginning on 15 Nisan. It commemorates the Exodus from Egypt, and, according to tradition, the Hebrew name is derived from the verb "to pass over" (Exodus 12.13). The festival is observed for seven days (or eight days outside Israel). The first and last day (outside Israel the first two and last two days) are feast days; the intermediate period, HOL HA-MOED. All leaven ("ḥametz") is removed from the home on the evening before the festival; during the Passover period it is forbidden to eat or possess leaven, and only unleavened bread ("matzah") is eaten. During the period of the first and second Temples, the paschal lamb was slaughtered on the eve of the festival. After the destruction of the Temple, a home celebration ("seder") was instituted; this takes place on the first night of Passover and the Passover Haggadah is read. Passover is a major Jewish festival; in modern times even Jews who are not devout are likely to attend the seder service.

Passover, Second (Hebrew "Pesaḥ Sheni"). Passover sacrifice offered on 14 Iyyar by anyone who had been absent or ritually impure during Passover in the preceding month (Numbers 9.6–13).

Pastan, Linda (b. 1932). American poet. She was born in New York. A number of her poems deal with Jewish themes.

Patai, Joseph (1882–1953). Hungarian poet and editor. He was born in Gyöngyöspata, and taught at a Budapest high school. He published a Hebrew verse collection, anthologies of Hungarian poetry, Hungarian versions of Hebrew poetry, and memoirs. He was also the editor of a Zionist monthly. In 1938 he settled in Palestine.

Patai, Raphael (b. 1910). American anthropologist and biblical scholar, son of Joseph Patai. He was born in Budapest, and in 1933 moved to Palestine, where he became an instructor in Hebrew at the Hebrew University. In 1944 he founded the Palestine Institute of Folklore and Ethnology in Jerusalem and served as its director of research. In 1947 he settled in the US, where he taught anthropology at Dropsie College and later at Fairleigh Dickinson University. He published studies on the culture of the ancient Hebrews and the modern Middle East.

Paternity. Although it is impossible conclusively to prove the paternity of a child, it is of fundamental importance in Jewish civil and ritual law concerning inheritance, incest, forbidden marriages, and claims to the priesthood.

Pater synagogae (Latin: "father of the synagogue"). Title found in Greek and Roman inscriptions of Jewish origin in the classical period. It occurs in inscriptions discovered in the diaspora, particularly in Rome. The term "Mater synagogae" (mother of the synagogue) was also used. The nature of the office referred to by these titles is not known.

Patria. French ship. In 1940 in Haifa harbor, 1771 immigrants were transferred from the steamers *Milos* and *Pacific* to the *Patria* by the British Mandatory government for deportation to Mauritius. On 25 November 1940 an explosion took place resulting in the death of 202 immigrants and 50 crew. The explosion was the work of the Jewish resistance, which aimed at stopping the deportation. The survivors of the disaster were permitted to remain in Palestine; they were detained in a camp at Athlit until 1941, when they were released.

Patriarchate *see* NASI.

Patriarchs [avot]. Term applied in Judaism to the three progenitors of the Jewish people, Abraham, Isaac, and Jacob.

Patterson, David (b. 1922). English scholar. He was born in Liverpool. He was Cowley Lecturer in Post-Biblical Hebrew at Oxford University and President of the Oxford Centre for Postgraduate Hebrew Studies. His publications include *Abraham Mapu, The Hebrew Novel in Czarist Russia,* and *A Phoenix in Fetters.*

***Patterson, John Henry** (1867–1947). Irish soldier and author. He was born in Dublin. He worked as an engineer in East Africa, and served as a soldier in the Boer War. In 1915 he became the commander of the Zion Mule Corps; he went through the Gallipoli campaign with Joseph Trumpeldor and the Jewish volunteers from Palestine. Later he was associated with Vladimir Jabotinsky's efforts to form the Jewish Legion in Palestine. His writings include *With the Zionists in Gallipoli* and *With the Judeans in the Palestine Campaign.*

PATWA [Professional and Technical Workers' Aliyah]. Israeli organization whose purpose is to encourage and assist the settlement of professional and technical workers in Israel. It was founded by the Jewish Agency in 1943.

***Paul** [Saul of Tarsus] (fl. 1st cent). Early Christian evangelist. He was born in Tarsus in Asia Minor, and was a Roman citizen. He studied under Gamaliel the Elder. As a result of a vision he was converted to Christianity, changed his name from Saul to Paul, and traveled throughout the Mediterranean and Middle East as an "apostle to the gentiles." His epistles form a central part of the New Testament.

***Paul IV** (1476–1559). Pope (1555–9). A leading figure in the Counter-Reformation, he was hostile to the Jews. He was head of the Inquisition, and was responsible for the burning of the Talmud in 1553. In a Papal Bull of 14 July 1555 he proclaimed a number of discriminatory decrees against the Jewish community, which inaugurated the ghetto system. He was also responsible for the burning of a group of Marrano refugees in Ancona in 1556.

***Paul VI** (1897–1978). Pope (1963–78). He was born in Concesio in Italy. He became a cardinal in 1958. His personal intervention led to the approval of the Nostra Aetate declaration promulgated in 1965 by the Second Vatican Council; this dealt with non-Christian religions, including Judaism, and paved the way for improved Jewish–Catholic relations.

Paul of Burgos *see* SANTA MARIA, PAUL DE.

Payess (Yiddish from Hebrew "peah" (*sing.*), "peot" (*plural*)). Long ringlets of hair worn in front of the ears by Orthodox, Yemenite, and Ḥasidic Jewish men. The practice is based on Leviticus 19.27.

Paytanim *see* PIYYUT.

Pe. 17th letter of the Hebrew alphabet. Its numerical value is 80.

Peace (Hebrew "shalom"). The Hebrew word "shalom" carries connotations of wholeness. The ideal of peace was proclaimed by the prophets and the Messiah was heralded as the bringer of peace. The last of the Eighteen Benedictions is a prayer for peace. In spite of the emphasis placed on peace in Judaism, pacifism is not required of the Jewish people, since war is justified in certain circumstances. The word "shalom" is also used as a greeting.

Peace offering. Sacrifice of cattle or sheep, given as a thanksgiving, in fulfilment of a vow, or as a free-will offering (Leviticus 3; 7.11). The priests sprinkled the blood of the animal on the altar, sacrificed parts of the fat, and took their own portion. Those making the sacrifice then ate the remains.

Peah (i) ("corner"). Term used specifically of the corner of a field, in connection with the rules on gleaning. GLEANINGS are one of the obligatory gifts to the poor (Leviticus 19.9–10; 23.22), and the Bible specifies that they should be left at the corners of a field that is being harvested. The rabbis taught that at least one-sixtieth of the harvest should be left. In the event of a good crop or a large number of poor gleaners, the proportion should be increased.

Peah (ii) ("Corner"). Second tractate in the Mishnah order of Zeraim. It deals with the setting aside of the corners of the field for the poor (Leviticus 19.9–10, 23.22), as well as other dues owed to them (Deuteronomy 24.19–21).

Peel Commission. British royal commission of enquiry on Palestine. Chaired by Lord Peel, it was appointed on 7 August 1936 to study the causes of Arab riots in Palestine. Its report, made in 1937, recommended the partition of Palestine into a Jewish state, an Arab state, and a British Mandatory enclave.

Peerce, Jan (1904–1984). American singer. He was born in New York. He sang at Radio City Music Hall from 1932, and later performed in numerous operas. He also gave recitals of cantorial music and recorded cantorial works and Jewish folksongs.

Peixotto, Benjamin Franklin (1834–1890). American lawyer, diplomat, and communal leader, grandson of Moses Levy Maduro Peixotto. He was born in New York, and became a clothing merchant in Cleveland, Ohio. He was Grand Sar (president) of the B'nai B'rith in 1863–4. In 1866 he moved to New York to practice law. In 1870 he was appointed the first US consul in Bucharest, where he argued for Jews to be allowed to emigrate to the US. He was US consul in Lyons from 1877 to 1885.

Peixotto, Moses Levy Maduro (1767–1828). American merchant. From 1820 he was ḥazzan of New York's Congregation Shearith Israel.

Pekah (fl. 8th cent. BCE). King of Israel (735–732 BCE). He gained the throne by killing Pekahiah. He formed an alliance with Rezin of Aram-Dammesek and together they attacked Judah. King Ahaz of Judah appealed to the Assyrian king Tiglath-Pileser III, who invaded the allied kingdom, abolished Aram-Dammesek as a state, and stripped Israel of Galilee and Gilead. Pekah was later killed by Hoshea.

Pekahiah (fl. 8th cent. BCE). King of Israel (737–735 BCE). He reigned at the same time as Uzziah, King of Judah. According to II Kings 15.24, he did what was evil in the sight of the Lord. He was killed by Pekah who took his place on the throne.

Pekiin [Bekiin]. Village in Upper Galilee. It is probably identifiable with ancient Baka, mentioned by Josephus. According to tradition, Simeon ben Yoḥai and Eleazar hid from the Romans in a cave at Baka for 13 years, thus escaping the Hadrianic persecutions. Ancient remains of a synagogue from the 3rd–4th centuries have been found in the village.

Pelathites *see* CHERETHITES AND PELATHITES.

Peleshet *see* PALESTINE.

Peli, Meir (b. 1894). Israeli publisher of Russian origin. He and his brother Berakhah (b. 1897) emigrated to Palestine in 1921. They founded the Massadah Publishing Company which produced the *Encyclopedia Hebraica.*

Peloni almoni. An anonymous individual.

***Peñaforte, Raimon de** (1176–1275).

Spanish Dominican friar. A participant in the Disputation of Barcelona in 1263, he persuaded the Dominicans to study Hebrew for conversionist purposes. He introduced censorship and conversionist sermons into Aragon.

Penitence, Ten Days of *see* TEN DAYS OF PENITENCE.

Penitential prayers *see* SELIḤOT.

Pentateuch [Five Books of Moses] *see* TORAH.

Pentecost *see* SHAVUOT.

People of the Book. Term used in the Koran to denote the followers of religions dependent on Scripture (Jews and Christians).

Peot *see* PAYESS.

Pereira, Abraham Israel [Tomás Rodrigues] (d. 1699). Spanish religious leader and writer. He escaped from the Spanish Inquisition to the Netherlands, where he founded a Talmud Torah in Amsterdam. He also established the Ḥesed Abraham yeshivah at Hebron. A member of the Sabbetaian movement, he wrote *La certeza del camino* to encourage Marranos to repent in preparation for the Messianic age. He set out for Palestine to meet Shabbetai Tzevi but stopped in Italy.

Pereira, Moses Lopez *see* AGUILAR, DIEGO D'.

Péreire, Jacob Rodriguez (1715–1780). French educator and communal leader. He was born into a Marrano family in Berlangua, Spain, and went to France, where he embraced Judaism. He was a teacher of deaf mutes, and his work was recognized by Louis XV. He was also an inventor. Active in Jewish spheres, he was a counselor of the Sephardi community in Paris from 1749.

Perek Shirah ("Chapter of song"). Collection of scriptural verses in which the praise of God is uttered by different parts of creation. The notion that God is praised by all creation in its several ways is expressed in Psalm 148. This prompted the selection and putting together of a "hymnal of creation" consisting of scriptural verses that represent the praises of the universe offered to God. The Perek Shirah is recited as a private devotion after the morning service.

Perelmann, Joseph *see* DYMOV, OSSIP.

Peres, Shimon (b. 1923). Israeli politician, of Polish origin. He went to Palestine in 1934. He served as chairman of the Labor Party from 1977. He was acting prime minister in 1977 and prime minister of Israel in 1984–6. His publications include *From these Men*, *Tomorrow is Now*, and *The Next Phase*.

Peretz, Isaac Leib (1852–1915). Polish Yiddish and Hebrew poet and author. He was born in Zamość. Educated in the eastern European religious tradition, he also came into contact with modern learning. He practiced law and lived in Warsaw, where he was an employee in the Jewish Communal Bureau. He began writing at an early age, and eventually decided to use Yiddish as a means of making literary material available to the Jewish masses. He was a master of the Yiddish short story, in which he depicted the misery and virtues of Polish Jewry. He also wrote romantic and symbolic stories based on Jewish legend and mysticism, mystic dramas, and poetry, and edited a number of literary compilations.

Perizzites. Ancient Canaanite people, inhabitants of Palestine before the Israelite conquest (Genesis 13.7; 15.20; Judges 1.4).

Perjury. The act of swearing to a statement known to be false, or of giving false evidence while under oath. Perjury violates the third of the Ten Commandments and constitutes a desecration of God's name. It thus may bring devastation on the whole community. Jewish law does not require witnesses to swear to the truth of their evidence.

Perl, Joseph (1773–1839). Galician

Hebrew author and maskil. He was born in Tarnopol. He was initially attracted to Ḥasidism, but later embraced the Haskalah. In 1813 he established the first modern Jewish school in Galicia (in Tarnopol), which he directed. He encouraged the creation of Jewish agricultural colonies, and opposed the Ḥasidim in his satirical writings.

Perles, Felix (1874–1933). Austrian rabbi and scholar, son of Joseph Perles. He was active in the Zionist movement in Vienna. In 1899 he became a rabbi at Königsberg and taught at the university there. He wrote studies of Bible criticism, Hebrew and Aramaic lexicography, apocryphal and pseudepigraphical literature, medieval Hebrew poetry, liturgy, and Jewish dialects.

Perles, Joseph (1835–1894). German rabbi and scholar. He was born in Baja, Hungary. He served as rabbi in Posen, and later in Munich. He wrote studies of Syriac, medieval literature, biblical exegesis, and Hebrew and Aramaic lexicography and philology.

Pernambuco *see* RECIFE.

Perpetual Light *see* NER TAMID.

Persky, Daniel (1887–1962). American Hebraist, educator, and journalist. He was born in Minsk, and in 1906 moved to the US, where he worked for the Hebraist movement, which aimed to foster the Hebrew language and literature. From 1921 he taught at the Herzliah Hebrew Teachers' College in New York. He contributed articles to the Hebrew weekly *Hadoar*; a number of his books were based on these contributions. He also edited several children's magazines.

Pesaḥ *see* PASSOVER.

Pesaḥim ("Paschal lambs"). Third tractate in the Mishnah order of Moed. It deals with regulations regarding the Passover holiday.

Pesaḥ Sheni *see* PASSOVER, SECOND.

Pesha *see* SIN (ii).

Peshat. The term applied to the basic type of scriptural interpretation, concerned with the simple, literal meaning of the words.

Pesher ("interpretation"). The name given to a number of biblical commentaries found among the Dead Sea Scrolls. The term derives from the authors' method of introducing their commentaries with the phrase "pishro al" (its interpretation refers to). Pesharim have been found on the books of Habakkuk, Isaiah, Nahum, Micah, Hosea, and Psalms.

Peshitta (Syriac: "Simple"). Syriac translation of the Bible. It was called Peshitta because the text was translated directly from the Hebrew, in contrast to the Syrio-Hexapla, which is a literal translation from the Greek of the Septuagint in Origen's *Hexapla*. The Peshitta was begun in the 1st or 2nd century, and was intended for use by Jews in certain synagogues. By the 3rd century it had become the Bible of Syriac-speaking Christians.

Pesikta de-Rav Kahana. Collection of midrashic homilies for holidays and special Sabbaths. Attributed to Rav Kahanah, it is the oldest midrash termed "Pesikta" (Aramaic: "Section"); it is sometimes known by that title.

Pesikta Rabbati. Collection of midrashic homilies for holidays and special Sabbaths. Its contents are drawn from numerous sources though more than half of the homilies are of the Yelammedenu type.

Pesuke de-Zimrah ("Passages of songs"). The name given to a section of the Shaḥarit prayer recited between the morning blessings and the prayer that precedes the Shema. The ordering of these elements accords with the dictum that praise of God should precede prayer. The Pesuke de-Zimrah consists of Psalms 145–150, various verses, and the Song of Moses

(Exodus 14.30–15.18). They are introduced by the blessing "Barukh she-amar," and end with the blessing "Yishtabbaḥ" (which on Sabbaths and festivals is preceded by the doxology Nishmat). Among the Sephardim the Pesuke de-Zimrah are referred to as the Zemirot. In the Sephardi rite a different ordering is observed (some of the psalm verses precede the "Barukh she-amar") and on Sabbaths and festivals more psalms are added.

Pethahiah of Regensburg (fl. 12th cent.). German traveler. In about 1175 he set out on a journey, which took him to Tartary, Khazaria, Armenia, Kurdistan, Babylonia, Syria, and Palestine. An account of his experiences was recorded by Judah ben Samuel he-Ḥasid; it casts light on Jewish life, especially in Baghdad and the Holy Land.

***Petlura, Simon** (1879–1926). Ukrainian nationalist. He was born in Poltava. He was active in the Ukrainian Social Democratic Workers' Party, and later served in the provisional government of the independent Ukraine. From 1919 he was chairman of the government and also chief commander of the army. During the retreat of his forces before the Red Army in 1919, his units attacked Jews in the Ukraine. From 1924 he lived in Paris, where he was assassinated by Shalom Schwarzbard.

***Petrie,** Sir **William Matthew Flinders** (1853–1942). English Egyptologist. From 1893 to 1935 he was professor of Egyptology at University College, London. In 1926 he founded the British School of Archaeology in Egypt which supported excavations in Palestine. His publications include *Hyksos and Israelite Cities*, *Egypt and Israel*, and *Ancient Gaza*.

Petrograd *see* ST. PETERSBURG.

***Petronius Publius** (fl. 1st cent). Roman administrator, Governor of Syria (39–42). He was ordered by the Emperor Caligula to erect a statue of him in the Temple in Jerusalem. Because of the Jewish reaction, Petronius delayed putting this order into effect. Later he protected the Syrian Jewish community from attack by gentiles.

Petuchowski, Jacob (b. 1925). American scholar. He was born in Berlin. After emigrating to the US he taught at the Hebrew Union College from 1956, becoming Sol and Arlene Bronstein Professor of Judeo-Christian Studies. He is the author of numerous books including *Ever Since Sinai: a Modern View of the Torah*, *Prayerbook Reform in Europe*, *Understanding Jewish Prayer*, and *When Jews and Christians Meet*.

***Pfefferkorn, Johann Joseph** (1469–after 1521). Moravian apostate and anti-Jewish agitator. He was a butcher by trade. He was baptized at Cologne in 1504 and published a number of anti-Jewish tracts. In 1509 he was authorized by Emperor Maximilian to examine Jewish books in Germany and destroy any which blasphemed the Christian faith. As a result of various protests, the matter was referred to a group of scholars, including Johannes Reuchlin. Reuchlin's defense of the Talmud gave rise to a polemical dispute with Pfefferkorn. In 1520 the pope decided against Reuchlin, but the censorship of Jewish books was not revived and the Talmud was printed by David Bomberg.

Pfefferman, Abel *see* PANN, ABEL.

***Pfeiffer, Robert Henry** (1892–1958). American Bible scholar and Assyriologist. From 1922 he taught at Harvard University. He directed the excavations at Nuzi carried out by a team from Harvard and the Baghdad School. He later served as curator of the Harvard Semitic Museum. His writings include *Introduction to the Old Testament*, *History of New Testament Times, with an Introduction* *to the Apocrypha,* and *The Books of the Old Testament.*

Pharaoh. The title of the king in ancient Egypt. The word means "great house" and originally referred to the royal palace.

Pharisees ("separatists"). One of the three main sects of Judaism before the destruction of the Jewish state in 70 CE; the others were the Sadducees and the Essenes. It is probable that the Pharisees were the successors of the Hasideans. They adhered strictly to the Oral Law and were skillful interpreters of the Torah. They believed in resurrection and immortality, the existence of angels, divine providence, and the freedom of the will. The traditions of Pharisaic Judaism were continued by talmudic and later rabbis, and the Pharisees' teachings formed the basis of rabbinic Judaism.

Phasael (fl. 1st cent. BCE). Judean prince, son of Antipater II and brother of Herod the Great. He was appointed Governor of Jerusalem by Antipater when Herod became Governor of Galilee. Accompanied by Hyrcanus II, Phasael went to negotiate peace in the Parthian camp, but was imprisoned by the Parthians. According to tradition, he committed suicide. Herod called one of the towers on the wall of Jerusalem after him.

Philadelphia *see* RABBATH AMMON.

Philanthropin. Jewish school in Frankfurt am Main. It was founded by Sigismund Geisenheimer in 1804, and adopted a liberal religious attitude. It was closed before World War II.

Philanthropy *see* CHARITY.

Philately *see* STAMPS.

Philip (d. 34). Judean tetrarch, son of Herod the Great. He was educated in Rome. He was appointed tetrarch by the provisions of his father's will, and received the territories of Gaulanitis, Trachonitis, Bashan, and the city of Paneas. He married Salome.

Philippson, Franz (1851–1925). Belgian financier and communal leader, son of Ludwig Philippson. He was born in Magdeburg. He established a bank in Belgium in 1871; later he was president of the Belgian Congo railway company and a founder of the Belgian Congo Bank. He served as president of the Jewish community in Brussels and contributed to Jewish colonization in Argentina and Brazil.

Philippson, Ludwig (1811–1889). German rabbi and newspaper editor. He served as preacher to the Jewish community of Magdeburg and was instrumental in initiating Reform rabbinical synods in Germany. In 1837 he founded the *Allgemeine Zeitung des Judentums,* which he edited. He published a translation of the Bible, and helped found the Institut zur Förderung der Israelitischen Literatur.

Philippson, Martin (1846–1916). German historian and communal leader, son of Ludwig Philippson. He was born at Magdeburg. He taught at the University of Bonn, and later at the University of Brussels, where he became rector. Owing to anti-German attitudes in Brussels, he was forced to resign and settled in Berlin, where he became involved in Jewish affairs and served as head of the Lehranstalt für die Wissenschaft des Judentums. He published studies of modern history.

Philipson, David (1862–1949). American Reform rabbi. He was born in Wabash, Indiana, and served as a rabbi in Baltimore and Cincinnati. He was president of the Central Conference of American Rabbis, and taught at the Hebrew Union College. His writings include *The Reform Movement in Judaism, The Jew in English Fiction,* and *My Life as an American Jew.*

Philistines. Ancient people living on the south coast of Palestine. They dominated parts of Judah during the time of the

Judges. David conquered Philistia, and ended the period of Philistine domination.

Philo (c. 25 BCE–40 CE). Hellenistic philosopher. He lived in Alexandria. He combined Hellenistic thought with Jewish belief in Holy Scripture; his writings include a legal exposition, philosophical interpretation, and a commentary on the Pentateuch. In 40 CE he was a member of the Jewish deputation which traveled to Rome to make representations to the Emperor Caligula concerning anti-Jewish activities in Alexandria.

Philosophy. Jewish philosophical reflection about religious belief began with Philo of Alexandria who interpreted Judaism in Neoplatonic terms. Later Jewish writers were influenced by the revival of Greek philosophy by the Arabs. Prominent among such medieval thinkers were Saadyah Gaon, Solomon ibn Gabirol, Baḥya ibn Pakuda, Abraham ibn Daud, Maimonides, Levi ben Gershon, Ḥasdai ben Abraham Crescas, Joseph Albo, and Isaac Abravanel. The modern period of Jewish philosophy began with Moses Mendelssohn who was followed by such writers as Solomon Formstecher, Samuel Hirsch, Naḥman Krochmal, Solomon Ludwig Steinheim, Hermann Cohen, Franz Rosenzweig, Leo Baeck, Martin Buber, Abraham Heschel, and Mordecai Kaplan. In 1979 the Academy of Jewish Philosophy was founded in the US to promote Jewish philosophical study.

Philo Verlag. German publisher and bookseller. It was founded in Berlin in 1919 by Ludwig Holländer, who was followed as its director by Alfred Hirschberg. It published books, pamphlets, and periodicals on Jewish subjects. During the rise of Nazism, its publications were designed to strengthen Jewish morale and develop Jewish knowledge. The firm was liquidated by the Nazis in 1938.

Phinehas (i) (fl. ?13th cent. BCE). Israelite priest, grandson of Aaron. He slew Zimri and as a reward he and his descendants were granted the priesthood (Numbers 25); he was also given a holding on Mount Ephraim. Phinehas continued to officiate and was still in office at the time of the campaign against Benjamin (Judges 20.28). The Zadokites traced their ancestry to him.

Phinehas (ii) (fl. 11th cent. BCE). Israelite priest, second son of Eli. He and Hophni, his brother, officiated at Shiloh but were guilty of conduct unworthy of priests. While accompanying the Ark of the Covenant into battle against the Philistines, they were killed (1 Samuel 4).

Phinehas ben Abraham of Koretz (1726–1791). Lithuanian Ḥasidic rabbi. He lived in Volhynia, where he came under the influence of the Baal Shem Tov. An opponent of the tradition of legal interpretation known as "pilpul," he preached simplicity and humility.

Phinehas ben Jair (fl. 2nd cent.). Palestinian tanna, son-in-law of Simeon ben Yoḥai. He was a prominent halakhist.

Phoenicians. Ancient people, inhabitants of the region along the coast of Syria and Palestine. Their language was similar to Hebrew. The Phoenician Hiram of Tyre was an ally of Solomon, and Ethbaal of Sidon cooperated with Omri. In the 8th century BCE the Assyrians subdued most of the Phoenicians' cities. Later the country was incorporated into the Persian Empire, and in 64 BCE it was brought under Roman rule. The Phoenicians engaged in maritime trade. Their religious practice included the worship of Baal and Astarte, the sacrifice of children to Moloch, and the institution of religious prostitutes.

Phylacteries *see* TEPHILLIN (i).

Physicians *see* MEDICINE.

PICA [Palestine Jewish Colonization Association]. Colonization company. It was founded after World War I by ICA to administer colonies in Palestine supported by Baron Edmond de Rothschild; it was directed by James de Rothschild. In 1957 it ceased operating and transferred its property to the State of Israel.

***Picart, Bernard** (1673–1733). French artist and engraver. In 1710 he settled in Amsterdam. He made a series of etchings to illustrate the section devoted to Jewry in his *Cérémonies et coutumes religieuses de tous les peuples du monde*. He also engraved title-pages for several Hebrew works.

Pick, Isaiah *see* BERLIN, ISAIAH BEN JUDAH LOEB.

Pico della Mirandola *see* MIRANDOLA, GIOVANNI PICO DELLA.

Picon, Molly (b. 1898). American actress. She was born in New York. She played Yiddish roles on Second Avenue, acted at Kessler's Theater, and went on tour with her husband, Jacob Kalich. From 1942 she managed the Molly Picon Theater in New York. After World War II she visited displaced persons' camps, and toured widely. Subsequently she appeared in plays and films and on television. Her *So Laugh a Little* is a family biography.

Pidyon ha-Ben *see* FIRST-BORN, REDEMPTION OF THE.

Pig *see* SWINE.

***Pilate, Pontius** *see* PROCURATOR.

Pilgrimage. Journey made to a holy city or site for the spiritual benefit of the traveler. Jews made pilgrimage to Jerusalem for the festivals of Passover, Shavuot, and Sukkot until the destruction of the second Temple. In the Middle Ages, the institution was revived largely through Karaite influence. Special prayers were composed for pilgrims to recite in Jerusalem, as well as on visits to the graves of biblical figures and rabbinic sages.

Pilgrim festivals. According to Scripture, male Israelites were enjoined to make a pilgrimage to Jerusalem on the festivals of Passover, Shavuot, and Sukkot (Exodus 23.17; Deuteronomy 16.16), which therefore became known as "pilgrim festivals." All pilgrims were to offer a sacrifice and give the second tithe of their produce to the Temple (this had to be consumed in Jerusalem). In modern times there is no longer a formal obligation to go to Jerusalem on the pilgrim festivals. Special prayers, including the Hallel, are recited in the synagogue, and each festival has its own special liturgical characteristics, ceremonies, and customs.

Pilichowski, Leopold (1869–1933). Polish painter. Born in Zadzin, he lived in Łódź, Paris, and London. He painted work scenes of wool-dyers at Łódź, and shopkeepers and artisans in London's Whitechapel. He also executed portraits of Ḥayyim Naḥman Bialik, Albert Einstein, Aḥad ha-Am, Max Nordau, and Chaim Weizmann. His other works include *The Opening of the Hebrew University in Jerusalem*.

Pilpul (*lit.* "fine distinctions"). A tradition of interpretation of the Oral Law involving dialectical reasoning. It was occasionally carried to extremes of legal casuistry and its unrestrained use aroused the disapproval of various scholars. Nonetheless, the pilpul approach to the study of the law was developed by tosaphists and in yeshivot.

Pincus, Louis Arieh (1912–1973). Israeli lawyer and Zionist, of South African origin. He was a lawyer and served as chairman of the South African Zionist Socialist Party. In 1948 he moved to Israel, where he became a legal adviser and general secretary to the Ministry of Transportation. Later he was appointed managing director of El Al. In 1961 he became a member of the executive of the Jewish Agency. He was acting chairman at the 27th Zionist Congress, and served as chairman of the Board of Governors of Tel Aviv University.

Pines, Jehiel Michal (1843–1913). Russian author, Zionist, and yishuv leader. He was born in Ruzhany, Belorussia. He contributed to the Hebrew press, arguing against assimilation, and made plans to establish an agricultural school. He represented the Mazkeret Mosheh society in Palestine from 1878, and played an important role in the early stages of Jewish settlement. One of the founders of the Hebrew-speaking movement in Jerusalem, he opposed Ḥalukkah and fanaticism; his attitudes gave rise to conflict with rabbis in Jerusalem.

Pinhel, Duarte *see* Usque, Abraham.

Pinkas. Term applied to a Jewish communal register among the Ashkenazim. The word derives from a mispronunciation of the Greek word "pinaks," used in the Talmud to designate a writing tablet.

Pinsk. Town in the Brest oblast, Belorussia, formerly in Poland. There were Jews living there by the early 16th century. The Chmielnicki massacres of 1648–9 devastated the community, which suffered again during the Swedish wars of 1700. In the 18th century Pinsk was a center in the bitter conflict between the mitnaggedim and Ḥasidim.

Pinsker, Judah Loeb [Leon] (1821–1891). Russian Zionist. He was born in Tomaszów, Poland, and was one of the first Jews to enrol at Odessa University, where he studied law. Later he studied medicine at the University of Moscow, and returned to Odessa to set up practice in 1849. He was a founder of the first Russian Jewish weekly to which he contributed. Initially he was an advocate of the Haskalah movement, but after the wave of pogroms in 1881 he argued that only national, territorial rebirth could solve the Jewish problem. In his pamphlet *Auto-Emancipation* he called for the establishment of a Jewish territory, where the Jews could support and govern themselves. In 1884 he convened the Kattowitz Conference of Ḥovevei Zion where he was elected president of Hibbat Zion's presidium.

Pinsker, Simḥah (1801–1864). Galician scholar. He was born in Tarnów. He was the founder of the first successful modern Jewish school in Russia – in Odessa in 1826. He accumulated a collection of ancient Hebrew manuscripts, several of which were examined and described by the Karaite scholar Abraham Firkovich on a visit to Odessa. Eventually Pinsker moved to Vienna, where he published a history of Karaism and Karaite literature. He later returned to Odessa.

Pinski, David (1872–1959). American Yiddish dramatist and novelist. He was born in Mohilev on the Dnieper, and lived in Warsaw. In 1899 he emigrated to the US, where he wrote for the Yiddish stage. His early works deal with Jewish suffering in Russia, but later he wrote poetic and symbolic treatments of Jewish historic themes. His plays include *The Treasure, The Eternal Jew,* and *Shabbetai Tzevi.* He also wrote novels and short stories. Active in Jewish affairs, he served as president of the Jewish Workers' Alliance. Later he settled in Israel.

Pioneer *see* He-Ḥalutz.

Pioneer Women. International socialist Zionist women's organization. It originated as an American society, founded in New York in 1925 to provide social welfare services for women, young people, and children in Palestine; this body also encouraged American women to take an active role in the Jewish community and civic affairs. The World Union of Pioneer Women's Organizations has branches throughout the world. Through its sister organization, Moetzet ha-Paolot, it supports a network of social agencies in Israel.

Pirbright, Lord [Worms, Henry de, Baron] (1840–1903). British statesman. He was active in London Jewish communal life, serving as president of the Anglo-Jewish Association from 1874 to 1886. He was then Undersecretary of State for the colonies (1888–92).

Pirke Avot *see* Avot (i).

Pirke de-Rabbi Eliezer. Tannaitic midrash on Genesis and the first chapters of Exodus. The first two chapters consist of biographical details of Eliezer ben Hyrcanus, for whom the midrash is named.

Pisgah, Mount. A peak on the ridge of the Abarim mountains. According to Deuteronomy 3.17 it was on the eastern border of the Dead Sea, but it has also been identified with Mount Nebo (Deuteronomy 34.1). Balaam prophesied there (Numbers 23.14), and Moses saw the Promised Land from Pisgah before his death (Deuteronomy 3.27).

Pisher (Yiddish). An inexperienced young person, a nobody.

Pishon. One of four streams branching from the river that surrounded Eden (Genesis 2.11). It was identified with the Ganges in rabbinic sources.

Pithom. Ancient city in Egypt. Together with Rameses, it was one of the places where the Hebrews built storage cities for Pharaoh (Exodus 1.11).

Pittum ha-Ketoret ("The compound forming the incense"). Title of the baraita on the preparation of incense in the Temple. Among the Ashkenazim it is recited on Sabbaths and festivals at the end of the musaph prayer; in the Sephardi ritual it is recited every morning and afternoon. In mystic circles importance was attached to the meticulous recital of this text.

***Pius V** (fl. 16th cent.). Pope (1566–72). As Cardinal Ghislieri, he was responsible for the burning of the Talmud in Rome in 1554. Later as pope he continued his anti-Jewish policies, renewing some of the decrees originally passed by Paul IV. In a papal bull of 1569 he expelled the Jews from the Papal States except Rome and Ancona.

***Pius VI** (fl. 18th cent.). Pope (1775–9). In 1775 he issued an edict concerning the Jews, which renewed various restrictions against the Jewish community.

***Pius IX** (fl. 19th cent.). Pope (1845–78). Initially he adopted a liberal policy regarding the Jews, but later imposed repressive measures against the Roman Jewish community.

***Pius XI** (1857–1939). Pope (1922–39). He attempted to protect Jews in Fascist Italy against anti-Semitism. He also called upon the envoys accredited to the Holy See to provide immigration visas for the victims of racial persecution in Germany and Italy.

***Pius XII** (1876–1958). Pope (1939–58). He has been condemned for his failure to denounce unequivocally Hitler's policy toward the Jews. His attitude to the establishment of the State of Israel was cool. However, during his pontificate a significant change was made to the wording of the Catholic liturgy in the substitution of the phrase "unbelieving Jews" for "perfidious Jews."

Piyyut. Liturgical poem, specifically one added to a statutory prayer. Originating in Palestine, possibly in the 5th century, piyyutim were also composed in Babylonia, Germany, France, Spain, and Italy. The oldest known paytanim (authors of such poems) are Yose ben Yose, Yannai, and Eleazar Kallir; later important writers included Saadyah Gaon, Meshullam ben Kalonymos, Amittai ben Shephatiah, Rashi, Solomon ibn Gabirol, Judah ha-Levi, Solomon ben Judah ha-Bavli, Moses ben Kalonymos, Jekuthiel ben Moses, and Meir ben Baruch of Rothenburg. The chief groups of piyyutim are: the yotzer, inserted in the first blessing before the Shema in the morning service; the ophan, inserted in the middle of the same blessing; the zulat, inserted in the Emet ve-yatziv prayer said after the Shema in the morning service; and the kerovah, accompaning the first three blessings of the Amidah. Piyyutim for the evening service are known as "maaravot." Special groups of piyyutim were written for the Day of Atonement ("seliḥot") and the Ninth of Av ("kinot"). (For the form of piyyutim *see* POETRY.)

Plagues, Ten [Plagues of Egypt]. The afflictions suffered by the Egyptians because of Pharaoh's refusal to allow the Israelites to leave Egypt (Exodus 7.14–12.34). The waters of the Nile were turned to blood; infestations of frogs, lice, and flies occurred; the cattle were smitten with disease, and both men and animals with boils; a fierce hailstorm was sent; a swarm of locusts devastated the crops; for three days Egypt was blanketed in darkness; and finally the first-born were killed in the night.

***Plato** (428–347 BCE). Greek philosopher. His writing influenced Jewish scholars of the early rabbinic period (2nd–1st century BCE), both directly and indirectly through other philosophers such as Philo. In the Middle Ages a number of Jewish philosophers adopted Neoplatonic ideas.

Pledge. Object given to a lender as security for a loan. According to Scripture, vessels used for the preparation of food should not be used in this way. If the lender accepts as a pledge a garment in which the borrower sleeps, it must be returned to its owner at night. The principle of returning the pledge when its owner has need of it also applies to any object taken from a poor man as security for a loan (Deuteronomy 24.10–17).

***Plehve, Vyacheslav von** (1846–1904). Russian statesman. In 1881 he was appointed director of the police department of the ministry of the interior; later he served as deputy minister and from 1902 as minister of the interior. He adopted a systematic anti-Jewish policy in interpreting discriminatory legislation against Jews. In 1903 he was accused of being responsible for riots in Kishinev. In the same year he called for measures to be taken against the Zionist movement, which prompted Theodor Herzl to request a meeting with the Russian authorities. In 1905 Plehve was assassinated by E. S. Sazonov.

Plotst (Yiddish). To split, burst, or explode; figuratively to be aggravated beyond endurance.

Poale Agudat Israel. Israeli Orthodox religious labor party, of Polish origin. It was founded in Łódź in Poland in 1922 as an affiliate of Agudat Israel and is now a member of the World Union of Poale Agudat Israel. Its ideology is based on applying the social principles found in the Torah to daily life.

Poale Zion ("Workers of Zion") [Labor Zionism]. Socialist Zionist movement, originating in Russia at the beginning of the 20th century. Socialists participated in the First Zionist Congress in 1897. Several years later socialist Zionist groups were established. In Berlin around 1900 Nachman Syrkin helped to create the Ḥerut Federation of Zionist Revisionists. In Russia various groups of Zionist workers formed under the name Poale Zion and similar groups began to be formed in other European countries, in the US, and in Palestine. In 1907 the World Confederation of Poale Zion was formed. In the diaspora the movement struggled for the democratization of Jewish communal life, and sought to promote Jewish culture and education, and the pioneering movement. In Palestine it formed collective settlements, cooperatives, and the Histadrut. Eventually there emerged three groupings of socialist Zionists: one centered on Mapai, another on Mapam, and a third on Aḥdut ha-Avodah.

Podhoretz, Norman H. (b. 1930). American writer and editor. He was born in Brooklyn. In 1960 he became editor of the intellectual monthly *Commentary* published by the American Jewish Committee. His writings include *Doings and Undoings: the Fifities and After in American Writing*, *The Commentary Reader*, and *Making it*.

Poetry. Biblical poetry consists of epic poems, popular lyrical poetry, and prophecies. It is characterized by "parallelism," a technique in which the verse is divided into two halves, the second repeating the content of the first or forming an antithesis to it. Poetry is also found in the Dead Sea Scrolls and in the prayerbook. Throughout the medieval period liturgical poetry (piyyutim) was composed by numerous poets (paytanim); piyyutim are characterized by the use of rhyme, meters, strophic organization, refrains, and acrostics. Hebrew poetry was revived by the Haskalah movement, and has enjoyed a further renaissance in modern Israel.

Pogrom (Russian). Organized massacre of a body or class of people. The term has come to be used particularly of attacks against the Jews, carried out by the Christian population between 1881 and 1921; three waves of pogroms occurred, in 1881–4, 1903–6, and 1917–21. Such attacks involved destruction of property, looting, rape, bloodshed, and murder.

Polakevich, Mattathias *see* SHOHAM, MATTATHIAS.

Polemic. Controversial discussion or writing, expecially in theology. In talmudic literature there are references to Jewish polemics in the discussions between rabbis and heretics ("minim"). Christians also produced polemical literature aimed at convincing Jews of the truth of Christianity and proving the dogmas of the Trinity, The Virgin birth, and the Messiahship of Jesus. In the Middle Ages anti-Jewish polemics were encouraged by the Dominicans, and various public disputations between Christians and Jews took place, such as the Disputation of Paris (1240) and the Disputation of Barcelona (1263). In addition, Jewish writers produced polemics on particular subjects: of importance are the satirical letter of Profiat Duran, the *Sepher ha-Berit* by Joseph Kimḥi, the *Sepher Nitzaḥon* by Yomtov Lipmann Mühlhausen, and the *Ḥizzuk Emunah* by Isaac of Troki. Polemical works were also produced by Marranos.

Poliakov, Léon (b. 1910). French historian. He was born in St. Petersburg, and moved to France in 1920. He was on the staff of *Pariser Tageblatt* until 1939, then served in the French army during World War II. After the war he became head of the research department of the Centre de Documentation Juive Contemporaine, and in 1952 research fellow at the Centre National de la Recherche Scientifique. He was appointed to a post at the École Pratique des Hautes Études in 1954. His writings include a multivolume *History of Anti-Semitism*.

Pollak, Jacob (1460/1470–after 1522). Polish rabbi and halakhic authority. He was born in Bavaria, and became a rabbi in Prague, where he was a member of the bet din. Later he went to Kraków, where he opened the first yeshivah in Poland, and instituted the interpretive method known as "pilpul" (fine distinctions). In 1503 he was appointed by King Alexander as the rabbi of the whole of Poland.

Poll tax. A tax levied on every person. In biblical times a poll tax of half a shekel was imposed on all male Israelites (Exodus 30.12–16); during the period of the second Temple, this was an annual levy. The Romans imposed a poll tax which caused a rebellion led by Judah the Galilean. After the destruction of Jerusalem in 70, the voluntary contribution of half a shekel per year that Jews had formerly made for the upkeep of the Temple was transformed into the contribution *fiscus judaicus*, which was levied until the 4th century. During the Middle Ages the poll tax on the Jews was renewed by the Holy Roman Emperors in Germany under the name "Opferpfennig."

Polna case. Ritual murder case brought against the Jew Leopold Hilsner for the death of a Christian girl whose body was found in a wood near Polna, Bohemia, in 1899. Hilsner was found guilty of the murder and sentenced to death. Protestors led by Thomas G. Masaryk came to Hilsner's defense and the court of appeal overturned the verdict. In a retrial in 1900 Hilsner was again sentenced to death, but the Austrian emperor commuted the sentence to life imprisonment. In 1916 Hilsner was released under the terms of an amnesty.

Polygamy. In biblical times Jewish society was polygamous. However, certain passages in the Bible, such as the image of the housewife in Proverbs 31, appear to reflect the values of a monogamous community. In the Talmud monogamy is extolled. The takkanah of Gershom ben Judah (c. 1000), forbidding polygamy, gave formal sanction to the state of affairs that already existed among Ashkenazi Jewry. Among Spanish and oriental Jews polygamy continued to be accepted under religious law, though in modern times civil law enforces monogamy.

Pomi, David de (1525–1588). Italian physician, linguist, and philosopher. He was born in Spoleto. He was a rabbi and physician at Magliano, and later settled in Venice, where he published most of his works. Pope Pius IV gave him permission to attend Christians, but this concession was revoked by Pius V, though it was later restored by Pope Sixtus V. He published a treatise on gynecology, a historical defense of Jewish physicians, and a Hebrew–Latin–Italian dictionary (*Tzemaḥ David*) containing scientific and historical information.

***Pompey** (106–48 BCE). Roman general. He went to Syria in 65 BCE for the purpose of settling the dispute between Hyrcanus II and Aristobulus II over the throne of Judea. Supporting Hyrcanus, he captured Jerusalem and the Temple from the supporters of Aristobulus. He made Judea a tributary to Rome, and the period of independence under the Hasmoneans thus came to an end.

***Pontius Pilate** *see* PROCURATOR.

Pool, David de Sola (1885–1970). American rabbi, communal leader, and historian. He was born in London. After moving to the US he became minister of Congregation Shearith Israel in New York in 1907. He wrote studies in the fields of American Jewish history, religion, education, and Zionism, and edited and translated liturgical works.

Poor *see* POVERTY.

Pope. The title of the head of the Roman Catholic church, the Bishop of Rome. The pontificate was established in the 1st century, and throughout the history of the Jewish people in the diaspora the popes have, through legislation binding on Catholic Christendom, exercised far-reaching influence on the religious and civil rights of Jews. In the 6th century Gregory I (590–604) established the policy of protecting Jews under papal jurisdiction and encouraging their conversion to Christianity. In the Middle Ages Innocent III (1198–1216) encouraged the anti-Jewish legislation passed by the Fourth Lateran Council of 1215; Gregory IX (1227–41) enforced the Lateran legislation and took steps leading to the condemnation of the Talmud, but nevertheless issued several protective bulls. In the same century Innocent IV (1243–54) sentenced the Talmud in a papal bull, but also condemned the ritual murder libel. Benedict XIII (1394–1423) presided over the Disputation of Tortosa (1413–15). In spite of earlier moves to suppress the Talmud, in the 16th century Leo X (1513–21) permitted it to be printed. Under Paul IV (1555–9) the ghetto system was instituted. In the 18th century Pius VI (1775–9) renewed anti-Jewish measures. Discriminatory legislation was gradually reduced from the 19th century, and in the modern period the papacy has adopted a more positive attitude to Jewry.

Population *see* STATISTICS.

***Porcius Festus** *see* PROCURATOR.

Porge [purge]. To remove the sinews of the hind legs of an animal slaughtered according to ritual law.

Portaleone, Abraham ben David (1542–1612). Italian physician and author. He graduated from the University of Pavia in 1563, and later served as physician to the ducal house there. In 1591 he was given papal authorization to attend Christian patients. He wrote a Latin work containing guidance for physicians, and a study of the application of gold in medicine. His *Shields of the Mighty* is a study of the Temple and its service.

Posekim *see* LAW, CODES OF.

Possen *see* POZNAŃ.

Post mortem [autopsy]. An examination (usually medical or forensic) made after death. In Jewish law a post mortem must be carried out on all animals after slaughter to ensure the absence of physical defects and thus conformity with the dietary regulations. The halakhah objects to post-mortem operations on human beings, but this ruling may be overriden where such an examination might lead to the saving of other lives. Thus, for example, post mortems are allowed in cases of obscure or hereditary diseases, where the findings may yield information of value in the treatment of patients suffering from the same or similar diseases.

***Potiphar** (fl. ?19th–16th cent. BCE). Egyptian soldier, chief of Pharaoh's bodyguard. During his captivity in Egypt Joseph first served as Potiphar's slave, but later became his chief official. Eventually Joseph was imprisoned on a false charge of attempting to seduce Potiphar's wife (Genesis 37–9).

***Potiphera** (fl. ?19th–16th cent. BCE). Egyptian priest of the god On. He was the father of Joseph's wife Asenath.

Potocki, Count **Valentin** (d. 1749). Polish count. While studying in Paris, he became a friend of Zaremba, another Polish aristocrat; both men converted to Judaism. Zaremba settled in Palestine and Potocki lived in Ilya near Vilnius. Eventually he was put on trial as a proselyte, condemned, and burned to death. His grave became a place of pilgrimage for Jews and his life has been celebrated in various literary works.

Potok, Chaim (b. 1929). American novelist. He was born in New York. He taught at the University of Judaism in Los Angeles and the Jewish Theological Seminary. In 1965 he became editor of the Jewish Publication Society. His novels include *The Chosen, The Promise, My Name is Asher Lev, In the Beginning, The Book of Lights,* and *Davita's Harp.*

Pottery. The earliest pottery remains found in Palestine date from the Neolithic period. The Philistines were making pottery on the coastal plain in the 12th century BCE, and from the period of the monarchy the Israelites are known to have used earthenware storage jars with handles, and bowls. Greek glazed ware from the 7th century BCE has been found in the region, as has black-glazed and brown-slipped ware of the Hellenistic period. During the Roman era red-glazed pottery was imported, and later was imitated locally by Jewish craftsmen.

In the 4th century color-coated pottery was developed. The Talmud records numerous names for different types of vessels. The tractate Kelim in the Mishnah deals with the ritual cleanliness of earthen vessels.

Poverty. According to the Bible, poverty is an ever-present misfortune (Deuteronomy 15.11), and its relief is a religious duty. Although various institutions have been founded throughout history to sustain the poor, and the giving of alms is enshrined in Jewish law and practice, the Jewish tradition stresses that the aim of charitable giving and social welfare should be to help the poor to become self-supporting.

Poznań [Posen]. Town in Poland, about 180 miles west of Warsaw. Jews settled there in the 14th century. In 1399 an allegation that members of the Jewish community had desecrated the Host led to the martyrdom of the rabbi and 13 others. Anti-Jewish attacks occurred in 1468 and 1577; in 1687 an assault on the Jewish community was resisted. From 1532 to 1803 legislation restricted the size of the community to 49 dwelling houses. The city nevertheless became an important center of Jewish scholarship, and a Hebrew press operated there from the 16th century.

Poznanski, Samuel Abraham (1864–1921). Polish scholar. He served as a rabbi in Warsaw from 1897. He wrote studies of gaonic and Karaite history, edited medieval commentaries, and produced a biographical lexicon of Karaite literature.

Praag, Siegfried van (b. 1899). Dutch novelist. He was born in Amsterdam. He became a schoolteacher and settled in Brussels; later he lived in London, where he worked for the BBC. A number of his novels deal with Jewish topics and his later writings recall the Jewish life of Amsterdam that was destroyed by the Nazi invasion.

Practical Zionism *see* ZIONISM.

Praefectus Judaeorum ("Prefect of the Jews"). Title of the lay representative of Hungarian Jewry in the 15th–16th centuries.

Prague. Capital of Czechoslovakia. Jews settled there in the 10th century, but from as early as the 11th century, with the rise of the crusaders, they were subject to attack and harassment. During the 14th and 15th centuries the Jewish community in Prague was repeatedly attacked and expelled. In the 16th century, however, the position of Jewry improved and over the next 200 years the city had one of the largest and most important Jewish communities in central Europe. In 1848 Jews were granted full equality, and the ghetto was abolished four years later.

Prawer, Siegbert Salomon (b. 1925). British scholar. He was born in Cologne, and went to England in 1939. He taught at the University of Birmingham, and later became a professor of German at London University. In 1969 he was appointed Taylor Professor of German at the University of Oxford. His publications include *Heine's Jewish Comedy: A Study of his Portraits of Jews and Judaism.*

Prayer. The offering, in public worship or private devotion, of petition, confession, adoration, or thanksgiving to God; also the form of words in which such an offering is made. In the Bible prayers are mentioned as being made by individuals as well as in a cultic context. At the beginning of the second Temple period a formal pattern of daily worship, consisting of prayer, was determined by the Great Assembly: following the pattern of sacrifice, it took place in the morning (SHAḤARIT), afternoon (MINḤAH (i)), and evening (MAARIV), and an additional prayer (MUSAPH) was recited on Sabbaths and festivals. On the Day of Atonement a further prayer (NEILAH) was added. The original version of the prayer service included the EIGHTEEN BENEDICTIONS (or Amidah) and the SHEMA; over the centuries other prayers have been added. From the gaonic period compilations of prayers were made in the daily prayerbook ("siddur") and the festival prayerbook ("mahzor"). *See also* LITURGY.

Prayers for the Dead *see* KADDISH.

Preacher *see* MAGGID.

Preaching *see* HOMILETICS.

Predestination. The doctrine that all events are predetermined by God. The biblical doctrine of predestination was amplified by the rabbis. Human beings have FREE WILL, but God controls the course of history and directs it to its final culmination.

Pre-existence. The doctrine that souls and objects existed before the creation of the world or before they came into being on earth. The concept is found in Apocryphal literature and was believed by the Essenes. In the Talmud various sages asserted that souls pre-existed in an abode called "guph," that the Torah and the Messiah existed before creation, and that certain objects (such as the staff of Aaron) were pre-created. Some Jewish philosophers accepted the theory and it became a central kabbalistic doctrine associated with metempsychosis.

Preil, Gabriel (b. 1911). American Hebrew poet. He was born in Dorpat, Estonia, and went to the US in 1922. He published essays, translated Hebrew texts into English, and wrote Hebrew poetry.

Presbyter Judaeorum. Secular head of the Exchequer of the Jews in 13th-century England. He supervised the collection of taxes and fees for the Crown, was called on by the king to advise on Jewish matters, and was responsible for the administration of justice in the Jewish community. The names of six holders of the office are known: Jacob of London; Josce fil'Isaac; Aaron of York; Elias le Eveske; Hagin, son of Master Moses of Lincoln; and Cok Hagin, son of Deulecresse of London.

Press. The first Jewish newspapers were published in the 17th century to convey information to Jews who did not read the language of their countries of residence; the earliest known is the *Gazeta de Amsterdam*, which was founded in 1678. In the following century publications dealing with rabbinic matters appeared in various cities, among them Amsterdam and Ferrara. In 1783 the literary monthly *Ha-Measseph* was founded in Königsberg. In the 19th century many Jewish newspapers appeared in western Europe: among the most important were the British *Hebrew Intelligence* (1823, superseded by the *Jewish Chronicle* in 1841) and the French *Univers Israélite* (1846). In eastern Europe and in immigrant communities in the US and western Europe Yiddish papers were produced, including *Kol Mevasser* (1853). Both Hebrew and Yiddish papers proliferated until World War II, and although the Nazis suppressed the Jewish press in all the territories it took over, the number of Jewish newspapers multiplied rapidly after 1945. Today there are more than 500 Jewish papers published in the diaspora and more than 300 in the State of Israel.

Pressburg *see* BRATISLAVA.

Presser, Jacob (1890–1970). Dutch writer and historian. He was born in Amsterdam, and became professor of modern history at the university there. His writing includes *The Destruction of Dutch Jewry*.

Priesand, Sally (b. 1946). American rabbi. A graduate of the University of Cincinnati and the Hebrew Union College, she was the first woman to be ordained as a rabbi in the US.

Priest (Hebrew "cohen"). In Judaism the

position of priest is hereditary, and is based on descent from the family of Aaron. The duties of the priests were originally connected with the sacrificial service in the Temple at Jerusalem. The HIGH PRIEST served as the spiritual head of the people and in some cases was also the secular head of the community. After the destruction of the Temple (70 CE), the duties of the priest were limited to pronouncing the Priestly Blessing on festival days, redeeming first-born males on the 31st day after birth ("pidyon haben"), and taking precedence at functions such as the Torah reading. While theoretically the priesthood continues to exist the identity of those entitled to claim membership of it is obscure.

Priestly Blessing. Formula of words ordained by God and given to the priests by Moses for the blessing of Israel (Numbers 6.24–6): "The Lord bless you and keep you; the Lord make his face to shine upon you and be gracious to you; the Lord lift up his countenance upon you and grant you peace." It was recited by the priests in the Temple each day, and eventually became part of the synagogue liturgy.

Priluker, Jacob *see* NOVI ISRAEL.

Prilutski, Noyakh [Prylucki, Noah] (1882–1941). Polish Yiddish scholar and political leader. He was born in Berdichev, and grew up in Kremenetz. He was an activist in the campaign for Jewish access to higher education. In 1909 he set up a private law practice in Warsaw and founded a Yiddish daily newspaper. The following year he was elected to the Warsaw city council, and later he served as a member of the Polish parliament. He helped establish Yiddish-speaking schools in Poland, organized the country's first Yiddish cultural conference, and helped to set up schools and libraries in rural areas. He published various works on Yiddish scholarship. He later became professor of Yiddish at the University of Vilnius.

Primogeniture *see* INHERITANCE.

Printing. In the 15th century Davin de Caderousse studied the art of printing in Avignon. The first dated example of Hebrew printing was produced in 1475 at Reggio di Calabria. About 150 Hebrew incunabula were produced in Spain, Italy, and Portugal. The most important family in the early history of Hebrew printing was that of Soncino. Daniel Bomberg established Venice as a center of Hebrew printing, and in the 16th century other cities with important presses were located in Germany, Poland, and the Levant. In 1627 Manasseh ben Israel introduced Hebrew printing to Amsterdam, which became the major center in the 17th–18th centuries; this role moved to various cities in eastern Europe in the 19th century and has been taken over by Israel in the modern period.

Prinz, Joachim (1902–1988). American rabbi and communal leader. He was born in Burchartsdorf, Germany, and became the rabbi of the Berlin Jewish community in 1926. He attacked Nazism from the pulpit and was expelled from Germany. In 1939 he became rabbi at Temple B'nai Abraham in Newark, New Jersey. Active in Jewish affairs, he served as president of the American Jewish Congress from 1958 to 1966. His writings include *Wir Juden, Das Leben im Ghetto,* and *The Dilemma of the Modern Jew.*

Procurator. In the Roman Empire, a civil official of the emperor's administration, often appointed governor of a minor province. The Governor of Judea in the period 6–66 was a procurator. Subordinate to the Syrian legate, he was responsible for the imperial revenue, and for collecting taxes and excise duties. His residence was at Caesarea, the capital of the Roman province of Judea. There were 14 procurators: Coponius (6–9),

Marcus Ambibulus (9–12), Rufus Tinneius (12–15), Valerius Gratus (15–26), Pontius Pilate (26–36), Marcellus (36–7), Marullus (37–41), Cuspius Fadus (44–6), Tiberius Julius Alexander (46–8), Ventidius Cumanus (48–52), Antonius Felix (52–60), Porcius Festus (60–62), Albinus (62–4), and Gessius Florus (64–6).

Profanation. The desecration of holy things. Anyone committing such an act was required to bring a sacrifice and pay for the value of whatever was profaned with an increment of a fifth (Leviticus 5.14). If an animal donated for sacrifice was found to be unfit through a physical blemish, the donor could redeem it by paying the value of the animal plus the same increment. A house which had been consecrated to the sanctuary could also be redeemed (Leviticus 27.13–15). The priestly order was consecrated, and a priest was not allowed to marry a divorcee or harlot. The term is also used in a wider, non-cultic context, in such expressions as "profanation of God's name" (*see* Ḥillul ha-shem) and "profanation of the Sabbath."

Profiat Duran *see* Duran, profiat.

Progressive Party. Israeli liberal party. It was founded in 1948 by the progressive wing of the General Zionists, Ha-Oved ha-Tziyyoni, and the Aliyah Hadashah group. In 1961 it united with the General Zionists to form the Liberal Party, and in 1965 it was reconstituted as the Independent Liberal Party.

Prohibited books *see* Books, prohibited.

Promised Land *see* Canaan; Israel, land of.

Proof *see* Evidence.

Proops, Solomon ben Joseph (d. 1734). Dutch printer. His printed catalog, *Apirion Shelomah*, was the first of its kind in Hebrew.

Property. According to Jewish law property can come into an individual's possession through "meshikhah" (drawing an object toward oneself), "hagbahah" (raising an object), and "ḥazakah" (taking possession); it can also be acquired through what is accepted by local custom as achieving the transfer of property. All these methods lead to what is termed "kinyan" (possession). Change of ownership may also take place through inheritance. An individual has the right to abandon his property, which may then be taken over by another person. *See also* Finding of property.

Prophet (Hebrew "navi") [seer]. A person who speaks through divine inspiration, especially one through whom the divinity gives warning of the future and expresses his will. Prophets existed in the ancient Near East, and were of particular importance in ancient Israel. Several major periods of prophecy may be traced in biblical times: Mosaic prophecy (?13th century BCE), charismatic prophecy (including Deborah and Samuel) (12th century BCE), early solitary prophesy (including Elijah and Elisha) (9th century BCE), classical prophecy (including Amos, Hosea, and Isaiah) (8th–7th century BCE), later pre-exilic prophecy (including Micah and Jeremiah) (7th century BCE), and post-exilic prophecy (including Deutero-Isaiah, Nehemiah, and Ezra) (6th–5th centuries BCE). Some prophets predicted disaster; others provided words of comfort and consolation. Prophetic utterances were oral or written, and were sometimes demonstrated by symbolic actions. In Scripture the title "Former Prophets" applies to the historical books of Joshua, Judges, I and II Samuel, and I and II Kings. The books of the "Latter Prophets" are divided into the "Major Prophets," Isaiah, Jeremiah, and Ezekiel, and the "12 Minor Prophets," Hosea, Joel, Amos, Obadiah, Jonah, Micah, Nahum, Habakkuk, Zephaniah, Haggai, Zechariah, and Malachi.

Prosbul (Greek: *lit.* "for the court"). Legal document enabling a creditor to claim debts after the Sabbatical Year. (The Sabbatical Year gave automatic release from debts, as set down in Deuteronomy 15.) The prosbul was instituted by Hillel (1st century BCE). Since there was a tendency not to make loans as the Sabbatical Year approached, Hillel issued an enactment by which a lender would not lose his money if he made a declaration that he wished to collect his debts after the Sabbatical Year.

Proselyte (Hebrew "ger"). A convert, especially a gentile converted to Judaism. According to tradition candidates for conversion are to be warned of the dangers of becoming a Jew. During the second Temple period there was widespread proselytization around Judea, particularly in Galilee and Idumea. In Roman times the number of converts to Judaism became so great that Hadrian and later emperors forbade conversion. Similarly, it was a capital offense in Christian Europe in the Middle Ages, though this did not prevent some individuals from joining the Jewish faith, including Obadiah the Norman, active in Palestine and neighboring countries in the 12th century, and Robert of Reading, an English Dominican, who was burned at the stake in Oxford in 1222. In the modern period conversion to Judaism has become increasingly frequent; converts often join the non-Orthodox sects which are easier to enter than Orthodox Judaism. The essential rites of conversion are for the male cirumcision and "tevilah" (complete immersion in a ritual bath), and for the female tevilah. Reform Judaism has generally replaced these rites with a course of study and a religious ceremony of conversion.

Proskauer, Joseph Meyer (1877–1971). American lawyer and communal leader. He was born in Mobile, Alabama, and became a lawyer and later a judge. An associate of Alfred E. Smith, he worked with him in his 1928 presidential campaign. In 1935 he was a member of the New York Charter Revision Commission. He also served as president of the American Jewish Committee.

Prossnitz, Löbele (c. 1670–1730). Moravian preacher and miracle worker. Born in Uherský Brod, he settled in Prossnitz. He underwent a spiritual transformation, and studied the Mishnah, the Zohar, and kabbalistic writings. He claimed that in his study of kabbalah he was accompanied by the souls of Isaac Luria and Shabbetai Tzevi, and predicted the return of Shabbetai Tzevi in 1706. He was criticized by the Moravian rabbis, but continued to preach in Austria and Germany. Later he claimed to be the Messiah ben Joseph, the precursor of the Messiah ben David. He subsequently lived in Hungary.

Prostitution *see* KEDESHAH.

Prostration. The act of lying face down, as in submission. As a gesture of reverence, prostration was practiced in the Temple. Four types of obeisance are referred to in the Talmud: "berikhah" (bending the knee), "kidah" (bowing with the face to the ground), "keriah" (kneeling), and "hishta-ḥavvayah" (full prostration with outstretched hands and feet). The last was performed by the priests and people at 13 different places in the Temple when the high priest pronounced the Tetragrammaton during the service on the Day of Atonement. A form of prostration is still practiced by Ashkenazim during the recital of the Avodah on the Day of Atonement, and during the Aleinu prayer at New Year and on the Day of Atonement. A modified form (in which one is seated with the head resting on the arm) is performed when the Taḥanun prayer is recited in the presence of a Scroll of the Law.

Protestantism. The religion of any of the Western churches that are separated from the Roman Catholic Church and adhere substantially to the principles established by religious leaders at the Reformation. Some of the Reformation leaders studied Hebrew, and initially hoped to convert the Jewish community. When this failed, some, including Martin Luther, expressed hostility toward the Jews. Some Protestant parts of Germany excluded Jewry, as did other Protestant countries, but in England and Holland a more liberal attitude toward the Jews was encouraged.

Protest rabbis. Term applied by Theodor Herzl in 1897 to German rabbis who protested against the holding of the First Zionist Congress. Unable to prevent the conference from taking place, they published a statement in the *Berliner Tageblatt* that Zionism undermined the Jewish messianic hope.

Protocols of the Elders of Zion *see* ELDERS OF ZION, PROTOCOLS OF THE.

***Proust, Marcel** (1871–1922). French novelist. He was born in Paris. Although he was raised as a Catholic, he retained Jewish sympathies. His *A la recherche du temps perdu* contains three major Jewish characters: the actress Rachel, the intellectual Albert Bloch, and Charles Swann. The work also alludes to the Dreyfus Affair.

Proverbs (Hebrew "Sepher Mishlei"). Biblical book, part of the Hagiographa, consisting of a collection of moral maxims. The first section (chapters 1–9) contains an introduction and a depiction of wisdom. The second section (10.1–22.16) and the fifth (25–39) are ascribed to Solomon and consist of collections of sayings. The third section (22.17–24.22) and the fourth (24.23–24) consist of long stanzas on various themes. And the sixth section (chapter 30), attributed to Agur ben Jakeh, contains riddles, the sayings of King Lemuel, and a poem praising a virtuous wife.

Proverbs, Midrash to. Medieval midrash on the Book of Proverbs, based on material from earlier midrashic collections and mystical sources (such as the Hekhalot).

Providence. God, especially those attributes demonstrating his foreseeing care for his creatures. According to the Bible, God directs the course of human history and the destiny of his chosen people. During the medieval period, Jewish philosophers, including Saadyah Gaon, Judah ha-Levi, and Maimonides, discussed various issues connected with this doctrine.

Prylucki, Noah *see* PRILUTSKI, NOYAKH.

Psalm, daily. A different psalm is recited on each day of the week at the conclusion of the morning service. They are, on Sunday Psalm 24, on Monday Psalm 48, on Tuesday Psalm 82, on Wednesday Psalm 94, on Thursday Psalm 81, on Friday Psalm 93, and on Saturday Psalm 92. The practice, as well as the same choice of psalms, dates back to the Temple service, in which the Levites recited the daily psalm; the custom was continued in the synagogue after the destruction of the Temple.

Psalms (Hebrew "Tehillim"). Biblical book, part of the Hagiographa, containing 150 songs. It is subdivided into five books, beginning with Psalm 1, 42, 78, 90, and 107. Each section concludes with a benediction of thanksgiving. The psalms include poems of thanksgiving and praise, didactic songs, songs in honor of kings, war songs, songs connected with festivals and historical events, and songs concerning events in individual's lives. According to tradition, they are attributed to David.

Psalms, Midrash on. Collection of homilies on the Book of Psalms. It is popularly known as "Midrash Shoḥer Tov."

Psalms of Solomon. Pseudepigraphic book, thought to have been written in Palestine after the fall of Pompey in 48 BCE. It contains 18 poems attributed to Solomon, describing the desecration of the Temple by the enemy. It also condemns immorality and looks forward to the coming of the Messiah.

Pseudepigrapha. Collective title given to a group of works of Jewish religious literature written between the 2nd century BCE and the 2nd century CE. Like the books of the Apocrypha, these works were not included in the canon of the Hebrew Scriptures. They are primarily apocalyptic in content and comprise the Psalms of Solomon, the Testament of the Twelve Patriarchs, the Book of Jubilees, the Apocalypse of Baruch, the Book of Enoch, the Assumption of Moses, the Ascension of Isaiah, and the Sibyline Oracles.

Pseudo-Messiah *see* MESSIAH.

Psychology. The scientific study of behavior, or (more loosely) the mental make-up of an individual which gives rise to his actions. Various cases of mental disorder are described in the Bible. The Talmud specifies criteria for analyzing human behavior and identifies signs by which mental deficiency can be recognized. A number of medieval Jewish philosophers wrote about psychology, including Isaac ben Solomon Israeli, Baḥya ben Joseph ibn Pakuda, Solomon ibn Gabirol, Joseph ibn Tzaddik, Judah ha-Levi, Abraham ibn Daud, and Maimonides. Responsa literature also deals with mental diseases. In the 18th century the Ḥasidic movement introduced suggestive therapy. In the modern period a number of Jews (such as Kurt Lewin, Joseph Breuer, Sigmund Freud, Alfred Adler, and Otto Rank) have made important contributions to the development of psychology.

***Ptolemy I** [Ptolemy Soter] (fl. 4th–3rd cent. BCE). Egyptian ruler (323–283 BCE). Founder of the Ptolemic dynasty (323–30 BCE). He became satrap in 323 BCE, and king in 305 BCE. According to Josephus, he captured Jerusalem on the Sabbath in 320 BCE.

***Ptolemy II** [Ptolemy Philadelphus] (fl. 3rd cent. BCE). King of Egypt (283–246 BCE). He freed Jewish slaves and encouraged the translation of the Bible into Greek (Septuagint).

***Ptolemy III** [Ptolemy Euergetes] (fl. 3rd cent. BCE). King of Egypt (246–221 BCE). He adopted a positive attitude to the Jewish people. According to Josephus, after his victory over the Seleucids he offered incense at the Temple in Jerusalem.

***Ptolemy IV** [Ptolemy Philopator] (fl. 3rd cent. BCE). King of Egypt (221–203 BCE). According to III Maccabees, he went to Jerusalem to enter the Temple. God intervened, however, and Ptolemy was felled to the ground. In revenge, he ordered the Jews to be massacred in the Alexandrian arena by a horde of elephants, but the animals turned on the royal troops instead. This event was commemorated by the Jews as an annual feast day.

***Ptolemy V** [Ptolemy Epiphanes] (fl. 3rd–2nd cent. BCE). King of Egypt (203–181 BCE). He lost Palestine to Antiochus III at the battle of Paneas.

***Ptolemy VI** [Ptolemy Philometor] (fl. 2nd cent. BCE). King of Egypt (181–145 BCE). Although he invaded Palestine to intervene in disputes over the succession to the Syrian throne, he was not unfavorable to the Jewish community. According to II Maccabees 1–10, his mentor was a Jewish philosopher and biblical exegete, Aristobulus. Under Ptolemy VI, the high priest Onias IV built a temple at Leontopolis. Moreover, Ptolemy's military garrisons were commanded by two Jews, Onias and Dositheos.

***Ptolemy VIII** [Ptolemy Euergetes II] (fl. 2nd cent. BCE). King of Egypt (145–116 BCE). According to Josephus, the Jews were persecuted during his reign, but, notwithstanding this, the Egyptian Jewish community dedicated a synagogue to him. During his rule the grandson of Ben Sira went to Egypt, where he translated his grandfather's work into Greek.

***Ptolemy IX** [Ptolemy Lathyrus; Ptolemy Soter II] (fl. 2nd–1st cent. BCE). King of Egypt (intermittently 116–80 BCE). He attacked Alexander Yannai, but was driven back by his mother, Cleopatra III; later, however, Cleopatra planned an assault on Yannai in collaboration with Ptolemy IX.

***Ptolemy X** [Alexander I] (fl. 2nd–1st cent. BCE). King of Egypt (108–88 BCE). He had Jewish generals, who influenced him and his mother,Cleopatra III, to terminate his war with Alexander Yannai.

Puah (fl. ?19th–16th cent. BCE). Israelite midwife. She disobeyed Pharaoh's orders to kill all Hebrew male children at birth (Exodus 1.15).

Publishing. As early as the 15th century Jews were involved in trade and commerce in the written word. In that century Jewish booksellers in Naples exported large quantities of books, and in the next books produced by the Venetian Hebrew press were exported to Poland and Turkey; Hebrew books were also sold at the fair at Frankfurt am Main. Many works were published with the help of patrons or were subsidized by their authors. The first catalog of publications by a Jewish printer was produced by Manasseh ben Israel in Amsterdam in 1652. In the 19th century Jews entered into the general publishing field, and in the modern period there are numerous publishing firms throughout the world which produce books of Jewish interest.

Pulpit. Raised platform in a place of worship reserved for the preacher or other leader of the service. The traditional synagogue did not have a pulpit; the sermon was delivered from the ALMEMAR in the middle of the synagogue or from a position in front of the Ark. In the modern period pulpits are found in many synagogues and are often positioned close to the reading desk and the Ark.

Pumbedita. Town in Babylonia situated on the bank of the River Euphrates. The Jewish community was established there in the second Temple period and the town became a center for the study of the Torah. After Nehardea was destroyed in 259, an academy was founded at Pumbedita, which was the central religious authority for Babylonian Jewry until the middle of the 4th century. After the death of Rava in 352 and until the beginning of the 9th century the academy was second in importance to that at Sura, and it eventually moved to Baghdad (though it retained the name Pumbedita). Under Sherira Gaon and his son Hai Gaon the Pumbedita academy attained considerable distinction in the 10th–11th centuries. It closed in 1038.

Punctuation *see* VOCALIZATION.

Punishment. Biblical law makes provision for both physical and financial penalties for crime and wrongdoing. Physical penalties included stoning, burning, beheading, strangulation, and flogging, as well as exile. Material penalties included restitution, reparation for any loss inflicted, and financial compensation. All these penalties were supplemented by rabbinic law. Wilful violation of rabbinic prescriptions was dealt with by disciplinary flogging, and the punishment of excommunication enabled courts to apply pressure on those who would not respect its authority. *See also* RETRIBUTION.

Pupik (Yiddish). Navel.

Purification after childbirth. According

to Jewish law a mother is regarded as ritually impure for 33 days after the birth of a male child, and 66 days after the birth of a girl. After this period she must offer a sacrifice of purification (Leviticus 12.1–8). From the 15th century it was a custom among European Jews for a mother to visit the synagogue after recovering from childbirth. *See also* PURITY, RITUAL.

Purim ("Lots"). Festival, celebrated on 14 and 15 Adar, commemorating the rescue of Jewry through the mediation of Esther from the threat of annihilation planned by Haman. (The name derives from Haman's casting lots to fix a date for his massacre of the Jews.) The Book of Esther (Megillat Ester) is read in the synagogue on the eve and morning of Purim; whenever the name Haman is mentioned, rattles are sounded. An account of the story of Purim is inserted into the Amidah on that day, and a passage referring to the defeat of Amalek is read from the Pentateuch. It was customary in Jewish communities to wear fancy dress or masks at Purim, and plays were enacted based on the story of Esther (*see* PURIM PLAYS). In modern times a Purim carnival takes place in Israel.

Purim, special. Name given to any annual celebration instituted by a Jewish community or individuals to commemorate a deliverance from danger. The oldest special festival of this kind was the Purim of Narbonne, which celebrated a deliverance of the Jews of the town on 21 Adar 1236. The Purim of Zaragoza commemorated an event of 1380 or 1420, and there were other Purim celebrations in Cairo (23 Adar 1524), Buda (10 Elul 1684), and Livorno (22 Shevat 1743). In southern France celebrations in Avignon, Carpentras, and Cavaillon were called "the yom-tov ("good day," i.e. "festival") of the community."

Purim Katan. Name given to the 14th and 15th days of the first month of Adar in a leap year, when Purim is celebrated during the second month of Adar. Fasting and funeral eulogies are prohibited on Purim Katan, and the Taḥanun prayer is not recited.

Purim plays. The custom of presenting plays on the festival of Purim originated in Europe during the Middle Ages. The topic of the plays was the story of the Book of Esther. The earliest recorded Purim play took place in the Venice ghetto in 1531, and the oldest known text was written in Portuguese by Solomon Usque in 1559. It became the custom for itinerant actors to go from one community to another to perform the plays during the festival.

Purity, ritual. Biblical and Mishnaic law contain strict regulations on ritual purity (the prerequisite for worship) and impurity. Ritual bathing was regarded as sufficient to remove the impurity resulting from sexual intercourse or the emission of semen (Leviticus 15.16–18). PURIFICATION AFTER CHILDBIRTH required not only ritual bathing but also a sin offering and a burnt offering (Leviticus 12.6–8; 15.13–15, 28–30). Ritual impurity resulting from contact with a corpse required the sprinkling of water mixed with the ashes of the RED HEIFER (Numbers 19.17–19). After menstruation women had to offer sacrifices; in post-Temple times a ritual bath (MIKVEH) was required. After the destruction of the Temple, laws connected with the Temple cult were no longer carried out, but practices associated with menstruation and childbirth, impurity through contact with the dead, and ritual bathing for various other purposes persist. The term TOHORAH (purification) has been transferred to the ritual washing of a corpse before burial. *See also* IMMERSION.

Q

Qirqisani, Abu Yusuf Yakub *see* KARKASANI, ABU YUSUF YAKUB.

Queen of Sheba *see* SHEBA, QUEEN OF.

Querido, Israel (1872–1932). Dutch novelist. He was born in Amsterdam, and in his novels portrayed Jewish diamond workers and the life of poor Jews of his native city. He also wrote plays with biblical backgrounds (including *Saul en David*).

Querido, Jacob (c. 1650–1690). Greek religious leader. His sister became the last wife of Shabbetai Tzevi. After Shabbetai's death in 1676 she returned to Salonica and claimed that her brother was the recipient of her husband's soul. In 1683 there was a mass apostasy to Islam of a large group of Salonica families, who nevertheless continued to observe Sabbetaian and Jewish rites in secret. This group formed the nucleus of the Dönmeh sect. Taking the Turkish name Abdullah Yacoub, Querido became the most important leader of these sectarians.

Qumran [Kumran]. Ancient settlement on the north-west shore of the Dead Sea. Archeological excavations have revealed buildings believed to have been occupied by the community that produced the Dead Sea Scrolls (which were found in the nearby caves of Wadi Qumran).

R

Raaya Mehemena ("The faithful shepherd"). Kabbalistic work on the commandments, dating from the 14th century. It was later incorporated into the Zohar. It is called after Moses, the faithful shepherd, who revealed secret knowledge to the kabbalists.

Rabb, Maxwell Milton (b. 1910). American lawyer, government official, and communal leader. He was born in Boston. He served as associate counsel to President Eisenhower in 1953–4, and later as secretary to the cabinet. Active in Jewish affairs, he became chairman of the government division of the United Jewish Appeal.

Rabbah (i) *see* RABBATH AMMON.

Rabbah (ii) *see* RABBAH BAR NAḤMANI.

Rabbah bar bar Ḥanah (fl. 3rd cent.). Babylonian amora. He studied at the academy of Johanan ben Zakkai in Palestine. Later he returned to Babylonia, where he transmitted Johanan's teachings. Legends about his journeys are recorded in the tractate Bava Batra.

Rabbah bar Naḥmani [Rabbah] (c. 270–330). Babylonian amora. He studied under Huna at Sura and Judah bar Ezekiel at Pumbedita. Known for his interpretation of the Mishnah, he was knowledgeable about ritual purity. He was nicknamed Oker Harim ("uprooter of mountains") because of his dialectical ability.

Rabban. Variant of the title "rabbi." It was used as an honorific title during the Mishnaic period, especially for heads of the Sanhedrin.

Rabbanites *see* RABBINITES.

Rabbath Ammon [Rabbah]. Ancient city at the source of the River Jabbok; its site is now occupied by Amman, the capital of Jordan. Originally an Ammonite city, it was captured by David, but lost again by the Israelites after his death. It was later subject to Assyrian, Babylonian, and Persian domination. Under the Greeks, its name was changed to Philadelphia in honor of Ptolemy Philadelphus. From the time of Pompey, it was a city of the Decapolis, and under Trajan it was annexed to Provincia Arabia.

Rabbenu Tam *see* JACOB BEN MEIR TAM.

Rabbi ("My master") **(i)** [Marbitz Torah ("Teacher of the law"); Rav]. Title originally used during the 1st century to refer to ordained members of the Sanhedrin. It was employed only in Palestine until the 5th century; scholars in Babylonia were addressed by the equivalent title "rav." Later, Jews distinguished in learning were referred to as "rabbi," and the title was also conferred on the appointed spiritual heads of Jewish communities. Rabbis were not salaried until the 15th century. In large communities they maintained yeshivot, and various functions were performed under their supervision: dayyanim adjudicated lawsuits and arranged divorces, the shoḥet carried out ritual slaughter, and members of the community were purified by ritual bathing. In the eastern Mediterranean, the rabbi was called Marbitz Torah. In modern times rabbis have adopted pastoral, social, and educational responsibilities. A rabbi is appointed by a congregation to act as its spiritual leader, to organize services, to supervise the religious education of the young, to visit the sick and bereaved, and to preside over life-cycle events.

Rabbi (ii) *see* JUDAH HA-NASI.

Rabbi Binyamin [Ha-Talmi, Yehoshua; Radler-Feldman, Yehoshua] (1880–1957). Israeli journalist. He was born in Zborov, Galicia, and went to London in 1906. The following year he traveled to Palestine, where he worked as a laborer, and later served as secretary of Herzlia high school in Tel Aviv. In 1910 he moved to Jerusalem, where he taught high school. After World War I he was active in the Mizraḥi party, and edited the national monthly *Ha-Hed* (1926–53). He was a founder (in 1926) of Berit Shalom, a society that advocated a binational state for Jews and Arabs. He published numerous books, articles, and essays.

Rabbinerseminar für das Orthodoxe Judentum *see* BERLIN RABBINICAL SEMINARY.

Rabbinical Alliance of America. Orthodox organization, founded in 1944 to promote Torah Judaism (the belief in the total authority of the Torah) within the Jewish community. It supports the Yeshivah Torah Vadaath in Brooklyn.

Rabbinical Assembly. American organization of Conservative rabbis. Founded in 1901 in New York, it serves as an alumnus body for graduates of the Jewish Theological Seminary of America and seeks to promote the principles of Conservative Judaism.

Rabbinical conference. Synod of rabbis. In the 2nd century conferences were held at Lydda and Usha to deal with problems arising from the Bar Kokhba revolt of 132–5 and the persecution of the Jews under Hadrian. In the amoraic and gaonic periods conventions were held in the Middle East twice a year. In the Middle Ages a number of rabbinical conferences took place in western Europe, including an assembly at Troyes in 1165 and councils at Mayence in 1223 and 1245. At the beginning of the 19th century the Napoleonic Sanhedrin was convened, and in Germany rabbinical conferences were held from the mid-19th century onward. In modern times the rabbis of the various divisions of Judaism hold national and international conferences but there is no governing body of the worldwide Jewish community.

Rabbinical Council of America. Organization of Orthodox rabbis in North America, founded in 1923. It is the most powerful Orthodox group in the US.

Rabbinical court *see* BET DIN.

Rabbinical seminaries. After the Emancipation of Jewry, training institutions for rabbis were established in European countries: in Italy (Collegio Rabbinico Italiano, Padua, 1829), France (École Rabbinique de France, Metz, 1829), the Netherlands (Ashkenazi, 1834; Sephardi, 1837), Lithuania (Vilnius, 1847), the Ukraine (Zhitomir, 1847), England (Jews College, London, 1855), Germany (Breslau, 1854; Hochschule für Wissenschaft des Judentums, Berlin, 1872; Berlin, 1873), Hungary (Budapest, 1877), Austria (Vienna, 1893), Turkey (1898), and Poland (1928). In the US the following seminaries were founded from the late 19th century: Maimonides College (Philadelphia, 1867), Hebrew Union College (Cincinnati, 1875), the Jewish Theological Seminary of America (New York, 1886), the Isaac Elhanan Yeshiva (New York, 1896), the Jewish Institute of Religion (New York, 1922), and the Reconstructionist Rabbinical College (New York, 1968).

Rabbinites [Rabbanites]. Name given by the Karaites to their rabbinical opponents.

Rabbinovitz, Raphael Nathan (1835–1888). Galician talmudic scholar. He was born in Novo-Zhagory, in the Kovno district. He lived in Lemberg and Pressburg, and traveled widely. His *Dikduke Sopherim* consists of 16 volumes of variant readings from Talmud manuscripts. He also wrote a study of the printed editions of the Talmud.

Rabbinowitz, Israel Michael (1818–1893). French writer and scholar. He was born in Gorodets, Lithuania. He became a physician and settled in Paris, where he devoted himself to scholarship. He participated in the Kattowitz Conference of Ḥibbat Zion in 1884, and was head of the Benei Zion of Paris. In 1889 he went to Russia, and he eventually lived in London. His publications include *Législation civile du Talmud, Législation criminelle du Talmud, La médicine du Talmud*, and *Le traité des poisons de Maimonide*.

Rabbi of Lublin *see* HOROWITZ, JACOB ISAAC.

Rabbi Yose *see* YOSE BEN HALAPHTA.

Raben *see* ELIEZER BEN NATHAN OF MAINZ.

Rabin, Chaim (b. 1915). Israeli scholar. He taught at the University of Oxford and later was professor of Hebrew language at the Hebrew University. His major contribution is in the field of linguistics; his publications include a thesaurus of Hebrew words, and studies of Qumran Hebrew, Aramaic, biblical Hebrew, and modern Hebrew.

Rabin, Yitzḥak (b. 1922). Israeli soldier and diplomat. He was born in Jerusalem. He joined the Palmaḥ in 1940 and participated in underground activities against the British Mandatory government. In 1947 he became deputy commander of the Palmaḥ, and later chief of operations of the Southern Command; from 1956 to 1959 he was chief of operations of the Northern Command. He subsequently became head of the General Staff Branch, deputy chief of staff, and eventually chief of staff. In 1968 he was appointed Israeli ambassador to the US.

***Rabinovich, Joseph** (1837–1899). Bessarabian missionary. He was active in Kishinev. Initially attracted by the Haskalah, he joined Ḥibbat Zion in the 1880s and visited Palestine. In 1883 he founded a sect known as the Children of Israel of the New Testament, which accepted the tenets of Christianity while retaining Jewish nationalism and traditions; two years later he converted to Protestantism. His writings include *Prayers and Principles of Faith of the Children of Israel of the New Testament* and *Words of Comfort*.

Rabinovich, Ossip (1817–1869). Ukrainian journalist. He was born in Kobelyaki. In 1845 he settled in Odessa, where he was an adviser and pleader at the commercial court, and later a notary. He founded the first Russian weekly, *Rasviet*, in Odessa in 1860. He advocated reforms in Jewish life, the acceptance of Jews as Russian citizens, and the integration of Jewry into Russian society.

Rabinovitz, Solomon *see* SHOLEM ALEICHEM.

Rabinowicz, Mordecai *see* BEN-AMMI.

Rabinowitz, Alexander Süsskind (1854–1945). Palestinian Hebrew scholar, also known as Azar. He was born in Lyady, Belorussia. He taught in Poltava in the Ukraine, and became active in the Ḥibbat Zion movement. In 1906 he moved to Palestine, where he became a teacher and a librarian. He wrote stories, monographs, translations of world literature and Judaica into Hebrew, and textbooks.

Rabinowitz, Louis Isaac (1906–1984). South African rabbi. He was born in Edinburgh, and served as a rabbi in various London congregations. In 1945 he became chief rabbi of the United Hebrew Congregation of Johannesburg and the Federation of Synagogues of Transvaal and the Orange Free State. He also served as professor of Hebrew at the University of Witwatersrand. His writings include *The Social Life of the Jews of Northern France, Jewish Merchant Adventurers, Soldiers from Judea*, and *Far East Mission*.

Rabinowitz, Louis M. (1887–1957). American manufacturer and philanthropist. He was born in Rosanne, Lithuania, and moved to the US in 1901, where he established a corset-manufacturing company. He was active in Jewish community affairs.

Rabinowitz, Saul Phinehas [Shepher] (1845–1890). Polish Hebrew writer and Zionist leader, of Lithuanian origin. He lived in Warsaw, where he was initially attracted to Jewish nationalism and later to Zionism. After the pogroms of 1881, he helped to organize the emigration of Jewish refugees. He was secretary of the Kattowitz Conference of Ḥibbat Zion in 1884, and subsequently secretary of the movement's Warsaw office. He contributed to Hebrew journalism, edited the annual *Keneset Yisrael* in 1886–8, translated Heinrich Graetz's *History of the Jews* into Hebrew, and wrote studies of the Jews exiled from Spain in the 1490s.

Rabiyah *see* ELIEZER BEN JOEL HA-LEVI.

Rabshakeh ("Steward"). Title of the Assyrian army official and chief spokesman for Sennacherib's delegation to Hezekiah, which demanded the surrender of Jerusalem (II Kings 18.17).

Rachel (i) (fl. ?19th–16th cent. BCE). Israelite woman, daughter of Laban and wife of Jacob. Her father was a herdsman in Haran, for whom Jacob worked. Jacob wished to marry Rachel but was tricked into marrying her elder sister Leah. Subsequently Rachel also became his wife and bore him two sons, Joseph and Benjamin. (Genesis 29–35)

Rachel (ii) [Blovstein, Rachel] (1890–1931). Palestinian Hebrew poet, of Russian origin. In 1909 she emigrated to Palestine, where she worked as a laborer. Her poetry is imbued with love for the countryside of Palestine and the Jewish pioneers.

Rachel, Tomb of. According to Scripture, Rachel died and was buried on the way to Ephrath (Genesis 35.19). From the Byzantine period her tomb was identified as a site 5 miles south of Jerusalem. Another tradition places the tomb at Ramah, north of Jerusalem (Samuel 10.2; Jeremiah 31.15).

Rachmones (Yiddish). Compassion, pity.

Racialism. The belief that races have distinctive hereditary characteristics that render some intrinsically inferior to others. In the 19th century racial theories developed according to which the Jews were an inferior homogenous group. In Germany this doctrine became a central tenet of the anti-Jewish movement and was a fundamental doctrine of Nazism.

Radanites. Jewish merchants. In the 9th century they traveled between southern France and China. Their activities are known about from the writings of the Arab geographer Ibn Khordadbeh. The origin of the name is obscure: it may derive from a Persian expression meaning "knowing the way" or from the Latin Rhodanus (the name for the River Rhône).

Radbaz *see* ZIMRA, DAVID BEN SOLOMON IBN AVI.

Radler-Feldman, Yehoshua *see* RABBI BINYAMIN.

Rafi [Reshimat Poale Yisrael ("Israel workers list")]. Israeli political party. It broke away from Mapai in 1965 under the leadership of David Ben-Gurion. In 1968 it merged with Mapai and Aḥdut ha-Avodah to form the Israel Labor Party.

Ragoler, Elijah ben Jacob (1794–1850). Lithuanian talmudist. He was born in Sogindat in the Zamut region, and became known throughout Lithuania for his talmudic knowledge; he was also an expert on kabbalah. He served as rabbi of Slobodka in the Ukraine (1824–40) and later Kalisz in Poland. He was a fierce opponent of religious reform. He produced manuscript studies in all spheres of Torah study.

R'ah see AARON BEN JOSEPH HA-LEVI.

Rahab (fl. ?13th cent. BCE). Canaanite prostitute. She lived in Jericho and shielded the spies sent by Joshua (Joshua 2). As a reward she and her family were spared by the Israelites (Joshua 6).

Rain, prayer for. Petition in the musaph service on Shemini Atzeret, the last day of the festival of Sukkot. Liturgical poets (such as Eleazar Kallir) wrote special prayers to be recited on this occasion.

Rainbow. According to Scripture God set a rainbow in the clouds after the Flood as a sign that he would never again destroy the earth in that way (Genesis 9.8–17). The rabbis decreed that when a rainbow is seen, the following prayer is to be recited: "Blessed are thou, o Lord our God, king of the universe, who remembers the Covenant, is faithful to his Covenant, and keeps his promise."

Raisin, Max (1881–1957). American rabbi and author, of Polish origin. He served as rabbi of Congregation B'nai Jeshurun in Paterson, New Jersey, from 1921 to 1953. His writings include *Mordecai Manuel Noah: Zionist, Author, and Statesman, Israel in America, A History of the Jews in Modern Times*, and *Great Jews I have known*.

Rakah [Reshimah Komunist Ḥadashah ("New Communist list")]. Israeli communist party. It was formed as a result of a split in the Communist Party in 1965 (see MAKI).

Rakover, Mordecai see MOTKE ḤABAD.

Ralbag see LEVI BEN GERSHON.

Ramak see CORDOVERO, MOSES BEN JACOB.

Rambam see MAIMONIDES.

Ramban see NAḤMANIDES.

Rameses. Ancient Egyptian city in the Nile Delta. Jacob and his family settled there (Genesis 47.11, 27), and their descendants built storehouses for the Egyptian king in the city. It served as the point of departure for the Exodus (Exodus 12.37).

Ramḥal see LUZZATTO, MOSES ḤAYYIM.

Ram's horn see SHOPHAR.

Ran see GERONDI, NISSIM BEN REUBEN.

Ransom. It is the duty of a Jew to ransom a fellow Jew captured by slave dealers or robbers, or unjustly imprisoned. Jewish law specifies several rules for the ransoming of captives: (1) women should be given preference over men; (2) a person captured with his father and teacher may ransom himself first but is then bound to ransom his teacher, and then his father; (3) preference should be given to a scholar; (4) the court has the power to compel a husband to ransom his wife; (5) money set aside for charity or the building of a synagogue may be used to ransom captives; (6) a person who delays ransoming a captive is regarded as if he has spilled the captive's blood.

Raphael. Archangel and divine messenger. He had the special function of healing. He is first mentioned in the books of Enoch and Tobit. In the Talmud he is named as one of the three angels who visited Abraham after he had circumcised himself. Jewish traditions regarding Raphael were eventually taken over into Christian angelology and syncretistic magic.

Raphael, Frederic (b. 1931). British novelist and screenwriter. He was born in Chicago, and moved to England at the age of seven. Some of his novels deal with Jewish themes. His publications include *The Limits of Love, Lindmann, A Wild Surmise, Orchestra and Beginners, The Glittering Prizes,* and *Heaven and Earth.*

Raphael ben Jekuthiel Cohen [Cohen, Raphael] (1722–1803). Polish talmudist. He served as rabbi at Minsk (1757–63), Pinsk (1763–71), Posen (1772–6), and Altona (1776–99). An opponent of Moses Mendelssohn, he was critical of modernism. His *Torat Yekutiel* is a commentary on the first part of the Shulḥan Arukh.

Rapoport, Solomon Judah [Shir] (1790–1867). Galician rabbi. He was born in Lemberg. He was a rabbi in Tarnopol from 1837 to 1840, when he was appointed chief rabbi of Prague. He was attacked by the Ḥasidim and the ultra-Orthodox for his enlightened approach to Jewish study, which laid the foundation for the modern Jewish scholarship. He wrote studies of Jewish scholars of the gaonic period, began a talmudic encyclopedia, and translated European poetry into Hebrew. He was also known as Shir, a name derived from his initials.

Rapoport, Solomon Seinwil *see* AN-SKI, S.

Rappoport, (O.) Yehoshua (1895–1971). Australian Yiddish essayist, translator, and editor, of Polish origin. He was born in Białystok, and emigrated to Australia in 1947. He wrote about the Bible and the Talmud and translated works from Russian, German, French, and Hebrew into Yiddish. In Australia he was the editor of the newspaper *Yidishe neies.*

Rashba *see* ADRET, SOLOMON BEN.

Rashbam *see* SAMUEL BEN MEIR.

Rashbash *see* DURAN, SOLOMON BEN SIMEON.

Rashbatz *see* DURAN, SIMEON BEN TZEMAḤ.

Rashe tevot *see* ABBREVIATIONS.

Rashi [Solomon ben Isaac; Solomon [Saloman] Yitzḥak ben Isaac] (1040–1105). French rabbinical scholar. He was born in Troyes. After studying in the Rhineland he returned to Troyes, where he established a school. He published responsa, composed penitential hymns, and wrote commentaries on the Bible and the Talmud. His commentary on the Talmud established the correct text, defined numerous terms, and explained unusual words and phrases. His Bible commentary served as the basis for later interpretations of Scripture. Both works include numerous examples of the type of textual gloss known as a "laaz" – an explanatory word in French (or another language) transliterated into Hebrew script.

Rashi script. Semi-cursive form of Hebrew script, used in rabbinical commentaries, particularly that of Rashi.

Raskin, Saul (1886–1966). American artist. He was born in Nogaisk, Russia, and went to the US in 1904. He painted scenes of Jewish life on the East Side of New York and later in Palestine. He also illustrated various Hebrew texts.

Ras Shamra *see* UGARIT.

Rasviet. The name of three Russian Jewish weekly journals. The first appeared in Odessa in 1860–61; it was edited by Ossip Rabinovich and advocated Jewish enlightenment and equal rights. The second was published in St. Petersburg between 1879 and 1883 under the editorship of Alexander Zederbaum. The third was established in St. Petersburg in 1907 by Abraham Idelson; later it was published in Berlin (1921–33), and finally (1933–4) in Paris under the editorship of Vladimir Jabotinsky.

Ratisbon *see* REGENSBURG.

Ratosh, Yonatan (1909–1981). Israeli poet, of Russian origin. He emigrated to Palestine in 1921. His poetry portrays Hebrew youth as strong and heroic, in contrast to the downtrodden Jews of the diaspora. He is best known for his championship of the anti-Zionist nationalist ideology known as "Canaanism" and for his "Manifesto to Hebrew Youth."

Rav (i) *see* RABBI (i).

Rav (ii) [Abba Arikha] (fl. 3rd cent.). Babylonian amora, also known as Abba Arikha ("Abba the Tall"). He was born at Kafri in southern Babylonia. He went to Palestine, where he studied under Ḥiyya and joined the academy of Judah ha-Nasi. Later he returned to Babylonia; he declined the position of head of the Nehardea academy at Sura, which flourished for eight centuries. He and Samuel are the two sages whose teachings figure most prominently in the Talmud. According to tradition, he was the author of the Alenu prayer.

Rava (fl. 4th cent.). Babylonian amora. He was born in Maḥoza, and established an academy there when Abbaye became head of the academy at Pumbedita. After Abbaye's death, Rava succeeded him at Pumbedita, which he amalgamated with Maḥoza. His controversies with Abbaye were famous; with six exceptions the ordinances of halakhah were determined in accordance with his views.

Ravad *see* ABRAHAM BEN DAVID OF POSQUIÈRES.

Ravad II *see* ABRAHAM BEN ISAAC OF NARBONNE.

Ravenna. City in north-east Italy, close to the Adriatic coast. Its Jewish community was founded in the classical period. In 519 a synagogue was destroyed there by the Christian population. A number of Jews were living in the city in the early 13th century. After Ravenna came under Venetian rule in 1441, it was the scene of a synod of Italian Jewish communities in 1443. In the 16th century Jews were expelled from Ravenna as from other Italian cities.

Ravitsh, Melekh (1893–1976). Canadian Yiddish poet and essayist, of Galician origin. He was born in Radymno, eastern Galicia. He traveled widely, and in Warsaw during the 1920s he was a member of the poetic group known as Khalyastre. In 1941 he settled in Montreal, though he spent 1953–6 in Israel. In addition to poetry, he published a three-volume biographical work on Yiddish literary figures.

Ravnitzky, Yehoshua Ḥana (1859–1944). Palestinian Hebrew and Yiddish author and editor. He was born in Odessa. He became a member of a group of Ḥovevei Zion and was one of the founders of Bene Mosheh. In 1899 he was appointed editor of the Yiddish periodical *Der Yid*, and later was a co-founder of the publishing house Moriah. In 1922 he emigrated to Palestine, where he helped to establish the Devir publishing house. Together with Ḥayyim Naḥman Bialik, he published the *Sepher Aggadah*.

Rawidowicz, Simon (1897–1957). American philosopher, of Polish origin. He taught at Leeds University (1941–7), the Chicago College of Jewish Studies (1948–51), and Brandeis University (1951–7). He published studies of philosophical thinkers and subjects, as well as works on contemporary Jewish topics. From 1927 to 1930 he was co-editor of the scholarly journal *Ha-Tekuphah*; he was also editor of the scholarly and literary journal *Metzudah*, and a founder of Berit Ivrit Olamit.

Raymund Martini *see* MARTINI, RAYMUND.

Rayner, John (b. 1924). British rabbi. He was born in Berlin. He served as a rabbi at the South London Liberal Synagogue (1953–7) and the Liberal Jewish Synagogue (1961–89). He also taught at the Leo Baeck College. His publications include *Guide to Jewish Marriage*, *Judaism for Today*, and *The Jewish People: their History and their Religion*.

Raziel. Angel, guardian of divine secrets. His name occurs first in the Slavonic Book of Enoch and later in the Pseudepigraphia. He is connected with the "mysteries of God."

Raziel, Book of. Collection of mystical, cosmological, and magical Hebrew works. It contains mystical teachings, letter mysticism, descriptions of the heavens, angelology, magical recipes, and formulas for amulets.

Raziel, David (1910–1941). Palestinian underground fighter. He was born in Smorgon, near Vilnius, and went to Palestine with his parents at an early age. During the 1929 Arab riots he joined the Haganah. He was a founder (in 1937) and commander of the underground organization Irgun Tzevai Leumi. Captured by the British in 1939, he was later released. In 1941 he was killed in a German air-raid while on a mission for the British to Iraq.

Reading, (1st) Marquess of [Isaacs, Rufus Daniel] (1860–1935). English statesman. He was born in London. He entered parliament as a Liberal, and later became solicitor-general, attorney-general, and lord chief justice. He also served as ambassador to the US (from 1918), and Viceroy of India. In 1931 he was appointed foreign secretary. Besides his appointments of state he was chairman of the Palestine Electric Corporation.

Reading of the law *see* LAW, READING OF THE.

Real estate. Landed property. According to Jewish law it can be acquired by purchase, presumptive right, or deed. If intention is demonstrated or proved (*see* INTENT), all movable property within the area of the real estate is automatically transferred without a separate deed. Real estate can serve as security for a loan contracted by deed, but not for one contracted verbally. No oath may be taken on claims involving real estate, and the laws of bailment do not apply to it. Only if the purchase price exceeds the value of the land by more than half, can a claim of overcharging be brought against the seller. Real estate cannot be stolen, thus no matter how many times it may have been sold, and despite whatever improvements have been made to it, if it has been sold without the permission of the original owner it reverts to him and no compensation is due to those who have had possession of it in the interim.

Rebbe (Yiddish). Rabbi. The title is also accorded to a teacher, and among the Ḥasidim to their spiritual leader.

Rebbitsen. Wife of a rabbi.

Rebekah (fl. ?19th–16th cent. BCE). Israelite woman, wife of Isaac. When Abraham sent his servant Eliezer to Aram Naharaim to seek a wife for his son Isaac, Eliezer chose Rebekah. She bore Isaac twin sons, Esau and Jacob. (Genesis 24–8)

Rebellious son. According to the Bible, a son who rebels against his parents may be sentenced to death on their complaint (Deuteronomy 21.18–21). The rabbis redefined the law of the rebellious son so that it was inapplicable in practice.

Rebuke and reproof. According to the Bible it is a duty to rebuke or reprove one who violates a religious practice (Leviticus 19.17).

Recanati, Menaḥem ben Benjamin (fl. 13th–14th cent.). Italian kabbalist and halakhic authority. He lived in Recanati. He introduced German mysticism and the study of the Zohar into Italy.

Rechabites. Ancient Jewish sect, identified in Jeremiah 35. They traced their descent to Jehonadab (or Jonadab) ben Rechab (II Kings 10.15–17); according to the precepts laid down by Jehonadab, the Rechabites abstained from drinking wine, and were forbidden to own fields or vineyards and to build houses. Jeremiah was commanded by God to put them to the test by taking them to one of the chambers of the Temple and serving them wine; the Rechabites refused to drink and were rewarded by God for their steadfastness by a promise of his favor. After Nebuchadnezzar invaded Israel, they fled to Jerusalem.

Recife. City in north-west Brazil, capital of the state of Pernambuco. It had a Jewish community, largely of Marrano origin, for a brief period in the 17th century. From 1642 its rabbi was Isaac Aboab da Fonseca. The Jewish community came to an end with the Portuguese reconquest in 1654. The first 23 Jewish settlers in New Amsterdam came from there.

Reconstructionism. Religious and social movement, established by Mordecai Menaḥem Kaplan. According to Kaplan, Jewish theism should be rejected, and Judaism should be understood as an evolving religious civilization. He called for a reconstruction of Judaism, in which synagogues should serve as centers for all aspects of Jewish culture. His congregation, the Society for the Advancement of Judaism (formed in 1922) served as a vehicle for his thought. In 1935 he established the Jewish Reconstructionist Foundation in New York and began to publish the magazine *The Reconstructionist*. In 1954 a congregational organization was created, and the Reconstructionist Rabbinical College opened in 1968.

Records *see* ARCHIVES.

Redak *see* KIMḤI, DAVID.

Redemption. Religious quest for salvation. In the Bible it is spoken of primarily as a historical event, involving the entire nation. In the rabbinic period the concept underwent various transformations, involving the coming of the Messiah and the restoration of the world. Later redemption was understood in kabbalistic literature as involving a metaphysical change in the order of Creation, whereby the identity of the Godhead would be wholly restored in the universe. After the failure of the Sabbetaian movement, redemption was more widely understood in terms of personal salvation. In modern times, a purely secular concept of redemption has been related to the Zionist longing for a Jewish homeland.

Red heifer (Hebrew "parah adummah"). A young cow used for sacrifice in accordance with the instructions laid down in Numbers 19. The animal should be unblemished and should never have been yoked. Its ashes, mixed with water, formed a substance that would remove impurity created by contact with the dead. On the occasion of the institution of the sacrifice it took place outside the Israelite camp, and those who handled it required purification. Thereafter the red heifer was sacrificed in Jerusalem on the Mount of Olives.

Red Sea. A long narrow sea between Arabia and north-east Africa, linked to the Indian Ocean in the south and extending from the Strait of Aden to Suez and Elath. It has traditionally been identified with the "Reed Sea" (Yam Suph) crossed by the Israelites during the Exodus from Egypt (Exodus 13.18).

Red Shield of David *see* MAGEN DAVID ADOM.

Reformation. Religious movement in 16th-century Europe, which began as an attempt to reform Roman Catholicism but resulted in the split of Western Christendom and the establishment of Protestant Churches. Early reformers attached great importance to the text of the Hebrew Scriptures. Martin Luther initially hoped that Jewry would be converted to Christianity, but was disappointed by their unwillingness. In various writings he expressed his fierce hostility to the Jewish faith. The Reformation had little effect on the position of Jews. Many Protestant areas of Europe excluded them, but more liberal attitudes in Britain and the Netherlands eventually generated greater tolerance in the Protestant world.

Reform [Liberal] **Judaism.** Religious movement, established in Europe in the early 19th century. It began with the formation of synagogues by laymen such as Israel Jacobson. In the 1840s Reform rabbis convened rabbinical councils to determine the principles of the movement, which involved modifications of traditional belief and practice to meet contemporary needs. The first congregation in the US was Beth Elohim in Charleston, South Carolina; its synagogue was built in 1840. Reform Judaism in the US received its central impetus from Isaac Mayer Wise, who founded the Union of American Hebrew Congregations (1873), the Hebrew Union College (1875), and the Central Conference of American Rabbis (1889). Reform Judaism has become a central force in Jewish life, with congregations throughout the world. It advocates the harmonization of the Jewish tradition with modern life and culture.

Refuge, cities of *see* CITIES OF REFUGE.

Refugees. After World War I the protection of refugees was accepted as an international responsibility. In 1921 Dr. Nansen was appointed by the League of Nations as high commissioner for Russian and Armenian refugees; later this responsibility passed to the Nansen Office of the League. In 1933 another high commissioner of the League was appointed for Jewish and other refugees from Germany. In 1938 President Roosevelt convened a conference at Évian to arrange for the emigration and resettlement of refugees. During World War II the high commissioner for German refugees worked to help those who were outside the Nazi-occupied territories, and to improve conditions of emigration. In 1947 the League office and committee were replaced by an instrument of the United Nations.

Refusenik. Term used in the USSR for a dissident Jew.

Regensburg [Ratisbon]. City in southeastern Germany. Jews lived there from the 5th century and until the time of the crusades engaged in trade and moneylending. In 1096 crusaders forced Jews to be baptized, but the emperor Henry IV permitted them to resume their faith. In the Middle Ages Regensburg became an important center of Jewish scholarship, and the leading German Jewish community. But relations between Jews and Christians eventually deteriorated, and from 1452 the Jews were forced to wear the Jewish badge. In 1476 a blood libel charge was made by the local bishop. The Jews were expelled from Regensburg in 1519, by decree of the king, but a few families resettled there in 1695.

Reggio, Isaac Samuel [Yashar] (1784–1855). Italian scholar and mathematician. He was born in Gorizia. His inspiration led to the funding of the Collegio Rabbinico Italiano in Padua in 1829. He published an Italian translation of the Pentateuch with a commentary in Hebrew. In 1846 he became the rabbi of Gorizia. His writings include *Torah and Philosophy*.

Reggio nell'Emilia. Town in northern Italy. In 1413 Jewish loan bankers were summoned there to curb the usurious practices of Christian moneylenders. Later its Jewish community became one of the most important in Italy, but in the 17th century the Jews were confined to the ghetto.

Rehoboam (fl. 10th cent. BCE). King of Judah (930–908 BCE). He was the son of Solomon by his wife Naamah. When he refused to moderate his policy of taxation, the country split into the kingdoms of Israel and Judah; only the tribes of Judah, Simeon, and most of Benjamin remained loyal to Rehoboam. Subsequently Shishak of Egypt invaded Judah and plundered the Temple. (I Kings 11ff.)

Reich, Steve (b. 1936). American composer, conductor, and percussionist. He was born in New York, and lived in San Francisco, where he wrote music for the San Francisco Mime Troupe and presented concerts at the San Francisco Tape Music Center. His compositions include *Tehilim*, based on pseudo-biblical cantillation.

Reichsvertretung der Deutschen Juden. Representative body of German Jewry from 1933 to 1939. It was an organization to which all Jews were compulsorily subject; supervised by the ministry of the interior it was the instrument by means of which the Nazis implemented their policies. It promoted Jewish emigration from Germany and supported the Jewish school system and welfare organizations.

Reifmann, Jacob (1818–1895). Polish Hebrew scholar. He engaged in historical and philological research and corresponded with the major scholars of his time. His publications include studies of the Talmud and other areas of Judaica.

Reik, Ḥavivah (1914–1944). Palestinian resistance fighter, of Slovak birth. She joined Ha-Shomer ha-Tzair, and settled in Palestine in 1939. In 1944 she volunteered to join the allied forces as a parachutist. She was dropped in Poland, where she organized radio communications with the allies and Jewish partisan groups, and aided the escape of refugees. She was eventually captured and shot.

Reina, Joseph della (fl. 15th cent.). Palestinian kabbalist. According to tradition, he attempted to hasten the coming of redemption by breaking the power of the angel Samael, but his failure postponed the event. According to one legend he failed because he took pity on Samael. Another tradition holds that he was too preoccupied with the mystical combination of divine names to carry out the instruction to slay Samael.

Reinach, Joseph (1856–1921). French politician, brother of Solomon and Theodore Reinach. In 1881–2 he served as head of Léon Gambetta's cabinet, and he later served as a deputy (1893–8; 1906–14). He attempted to establish the innocence of Alfred Dreyfus, to which end he published a seven-volume history of the affair. He also wrote works on politics and history, including several on Gambetta.

Reinach, Salomon (1858–1932). French archeologist and historian, brother of Joseph and Theodore Reinach. He directed the excavations at Carthage in 1883, and three years later was appointed curator of the French national museums. He lectured at the Louvre School, and from 1902 directed the Musée des Antiquités Nationales de Saint-Germain-en-Laye. He was the author of authoritative works on ancient Greece and the history of religions. He served on the council of the Jewish Colonization Association and on the central committee of the Alliance Israélite Universelle.

Reinach, Theodore (1860–1928). French historian and numismatist, brother of Joseph and Solomon Reinach. After working as a lawyer, he edited the scholarly journals *La revue des études grecques* (1888–1907) and *La gazette des beaux arts* (1906–28). He taught at the Sorbonne (1894–1901), the École des Hautes Études (director of studies from 1903), and the Collège de France (professor of numismatics from 1924). He was a member of the Chamber of Deputies from 1906 to 1914. He was active in the Société des Études Juives, and some of his work deals with Hellenism and Judaism. He also edited the French translation of the works of Josephus.

Reines, Isaac Jacob (1839–1915). Lithuanian rabbi and Zionist. He officiated as a rabbi in various Lithuanian centers, evolving a method of talmudic study based on abstract rules of logic. In 1882 at a rabbinical conference in St. Petersburg, he advocated the introduction of secular studies into the syllabus of yeshivah training. He was one of the first rabbis to join the Zionist movement, and helped to found the religious Zionist Mizraḥi movement in 1902.

Reisen, Abraham [Reyzen, Avrom] (1876–1953). American Yiddish poet and story writer, brother of Zalman Reisen. He was born in Koydenev, Belorussia. Initially he wrote tales and simple lyrics. He advocated the recognition of Yiddish as the Jewish national language, and helped to convene the Yiddish Language Conference at Czernowitz in 1908. He traveled throughout Europe and America supporting Yiddish cultural activities. In 1914 he settled in New York, where he contributed to Yiddish papers and magazines.

Reisen, Zalman [Reyzen, Zalman] (1888–1941). Lithuanian Yiddish editor and scholar, brother of Abraham Reisen. He was born in Koydenev, Belorussia. In 1915 he moved to Vilnius, where he became a leader of the new Yiddish cultural movement. He edited the Yiddish daily *Vilner tog* (1919–39) and was a lecturer in Yiddish and Yiddish grammar at the Folk University and the Vilnius Yiddish Teachers' Seminary. His writings include a grammar of Yiddish, a study of the origins of modern Yiddish literature, and a biographical and bibliographical encyclopedia of Yiddish literature.

Reiss, Isaac *see* NADIR, MOSHE.

Rejoicing in the Law *see* SIMḤAT TORAH.

Release, Year of *see* SABBATICAL YEAR.

Religious parties. After the Fifth Zionist Congress in 1901, Isaac Jacob Reines founded a religious wing of the Zionist Organization, which he called Mizraḥi. In 1912 the Agudat Israel was formed in opposition to political Zionism. From each of these movements there emerged a socialist group, the Poel Mizraḥi and the Poale Agudat Israel; in addition a small extremist religious group, the Natore Karta, was formed in 1937 by members of Agudat Israel. The two Mizraḥi groups eventually merged as the National Religious Party, but the two Agudat parties have remained separate.

Religious Zionists of America. Zionist organization formed in 1957 from a merger of the American Mizraḥi and Ha-Poel ha-Mizraḥi.

Rema *see* ISSERLES, MOSES.

Remak *see* CORDOVERO, MOSES BEN JACOB.

***Rembrandt van Rijn** (1607–1669). Dutch painter. He lived in Amsterdam. Besides the biblical scenes that most artists of his age depicted, Rembrandt painted portraits of members of the Jewish community of Amsterdam.

Remez [Drabkin]**, David** (1886–1951). Israeli labor leader, of Russian origin. He settled in Turkey in 1911, and later in Palestine. He was active in the labor movement, serving as secretary-general of Histadrut (1926–36), chairman of the Vaad Leumi (1944–8), and a Mapai member of the Knesset. He served as minister of communications in 1948–50, and minister of education in 1950–51.

Remnant of Israel. The Bible demonstrates, through its account of history, that even when the nation or its leaders deserted the faith there remained a "remnant" whose faithfulness prevailed. The Bible teaches that after God destroys the sinners of Israel as a prelude to the Day of Judgment, he will leave the righteous remnant who will serve as his kingdom on earth. The concept is found in the biblical prophetic books from Amos (8th century BCE) onward.

Renaissance. The name given to the art, culture, science, and thought of the period in European history that marked the waning of the Middle Ages and the rise of the modern world. It is normally regarded as having begun in Italy in the 14th century. During the Renaissance Jewish scholars such as Elijah Delmedigo advocated Aristotelian ideas and translated classical texts. In Florence a number of Jews were part of the circle of Pico della Mirandola, who was largely responsible for the revival of the study of Hebrew; in this milieu the *Dialoghi di amore* by Judah Abravanel became a popular work. At the end of the period Salomone de' Rossi of Mantua was actively involved in the musical revival, and Leone de' Sommi influenced the development of the theater. In addition Jewish loan bankers patronized the arts, supported scholars, and commissioned illuminated manuscripts. However, the Counter-Reformation in the 16th century put an end to the artistic and intellectual commerce of the Jews with the non-Jewish community by the introduction of the ghetto.

***Renan, Ernest** (1823–1892). French orientalist and philosopher. He became professor of Hebrew at the Collège de France in 1862, but he was forced to leave this position after the publication of his *Life of Jesus* in 1863. Later he became administrator of the Collège de France. His writings include *History of the Origin of Christianity* and *History of the People of Israel*.

Rending of clothes. Mourning custom. It is first mentioned in the Bible in connection with Joseph (Genesis 37.29, 34). According to rabbinic law, it is obligatory after the death of a father, mother, son, daughter, brother, sister, wife, or husband. The tear must be a hand's breadth wide; when the dead person is a parent the rent should never be completely resewn. The rending of clothes is performed before the funeral when the Barukh dayyan emet blessing is recited.

Reparations. In international law the payment exacted by a victorious state from a defeated one to compensate for injury or damage caused. The related concept of restitution involves the restoration of property wrongly taken from the owner. Both reparation and restitution were exacted from Germany after the Nazi persecution of the Jews before and during World War II. In 1951 the Federal Republic of Germany agreed to make good material damage caused to Jewish property and to pay compensation for costs incurred in the integration of Jewish refugees in the various countries to which they had fled. The amount to be paid was set out in an agreement signed in 1952 by the German chancellor and the Israeli foreign minister.

Repentance (Hebrew "teshuvah"). The renunciation of sin, appeal for forgiveness, and return to righteous living. Repentance is a central idea in the Bible, and serves as the theme of the Ten Days of Penitence. On the Day of Atonement prayers focus on this doctrine. Forgiveness is dependent on true repentance and if another person has been wronged rectification and restitution must also take place. In the Middle Ages Jewish writers dealt extensively with this subject. During the modern period religious leaders have created movements (such as the Musar movement) that focus on moral improvement.

Rephaim. Ancient people who inhabited the Transjordan in the time of Abraham (Genesis 14.5).

Rephidim. Stopping place on the Israelites' journey between the Wilderness of Sin and the Sinai Desert (Numbers 33.14–15). While the people were encamped there Moses struck the rock at Mount Horeb. At Rephidim the Israelites under Joshua's leadership repelled an attack of the Amalekites (Exodus 17).

Reproof *see* REBUKE AND REPROOF.

Resh. 20th letter of the Hebrew alphabet. Its numerical value is 200.

Resh galuta *see* EXILARCH.

Resh kallah ("Head of the kallah"). Title of the second in authority to the gaon in the academies of Babylonia. He was especially active in the study courses (*see* KALLAH) that took place during the months of Adar and Elul.

Resh Lakish *see* SIMEON BEN LAKISH.

Reshut *see* DUTY.

Resistance movement *see* PARTISANS.

Responsa (Latin: "responses"; Hebrew "she'elot u-teshuvot"). Written replies ("teshuvot") given to questions ("she'elot") on all aspects of Jewish law by authorities from the time of the geonim to the present day. More than a thousand volumes of responsa have been written. Their influence is found in various codes, in novellae, and in compendia of the tosaphists.

Restitution *see* REPARATIONS.

Resurrection (Hebrew "tehiyat hametim"). The coming back to life of the dead. Belief in the resurrection of the dead is part of the Messianic hope. It became a central feature of post-exilic Judaism, particularly in Pharisaic circles; according to the Talmud, it is a central feature of the Jewish faith, and Maimonides included it among his thirteen principles of faith. In the modern period it has ceased to play as important a role in Jewish thought.

Retaliation. Retributive action whereby injury or wrong is returned in kind. The concept is expressed in Scripture: "Eye for eye, tooth for tooth, hand for hand, foot for foot, burn for burn, wound for wound, bruise for bruise" (Exodus 21.24–5; Leviticus 24.19–20; Deuteronomy 19.21). According to Jewish law, the one who has inflicted injury may compensate his victim financially and thus avert the literal application of this legislation.

Retribution (Hebrew "zedekah"). The just requiting of each person according to their actions. According to the Bible, divine justice is meted out according to merit: prosperity is seen as proof of righteous action, while misfortune is regarded as the result of wickedness. Rabbinic theology insisted that God's retribution was always tempered by mercy ("ḥesed"). At the same time, the rabbis extolled the vicarious suffering of righteous martyrs. In rabbinic literature the belief in reward and punishment in the after-life is combined with the doctrine of retribution.

Reuben (fl. ?19th–16th cent. BCE). Eldest son of Jacob and Leah. He opposed his brothers' plot to kill Joseph (Genesis 37). When Jacob learned of Reuben's incestuous relations with Bilhah, he transferred his rights as first-born to Joseph (Genesis 48–9).

Reubeni, David *see* REUVENI, DAVID.

***Reuchlin, Johannes von** (1455–1522). German Hebraist. He was born in Pforzheim, Baden. He served as a member of the Swabian League's supreme court from 1502 to 1513. In reaction to the criticisms of Hebrew literature by Johann Pfefferkorn, he wrote a defense of the Talmud; a long debate ensued in which Reuchlin was assailed by the Dominicans under Jacob van Hoogstraaten of Cologne, and in 1520 Pope Leo X gave a verdict against him. Subsequently he was professor of Greek and Hebrew at the University of Ingolstadt (1520–21) and of Hebrew at the University of Tübingen (1521–2).

Reuel *see* JETHRO.

Reuveni [Reubeni]**, David** (fl. 16th cent.). Italian adventurer. He claimed to be the son of a King Solomon and brother of a King Joseph, who ruled the lost tribes of Reuben, Gad, and half Manasseh in the desert of Habor. After traveling through

Palestine and Egypt, he appeared in Venice in 1523. Later he settled in Rome, and Pope Clement VII gave him letters of recommendation. In 1525–7 he lived in Portugal, where he was greeted by Marranos (including Solomon Molcho) who believed him to be the herald of the Messiah. In 1532 he and Molcho appeared before Charles V. Molcho was burned at the stake, and Reuveni was taken to Spain where he died. He left a diary which records these events.

Revel, Bernard (1885–1940). American educator and scholar. He was born in Kovno, Lithuania, and settled in the US in 1906. Initially he ran an oil-refining business in Oklahoma. In 1915, as rosh yeshivah, he reorganized the Isaac Elhanan Yeshiva, and in the following year founded the Talmudical Academy in New York. In 1928 he founded Yeshiva College which he directed as president. He wrote studies of Targum Jonathan, Josephus, Jubilees, the development of ancient exegesis, and Karaism.

Revelation (Hebrew "nir'ah"). Divine disclosure. The Bible account is concerned, essentially, with God's revelation of his nature and purposes to humankind. According to Scripture, God revealed himself to individuals, and on Mount Sinai provided the nation with a code of moral and ritual law. In the Middle Ages Jewish philosophers discussed the relationship between revelation and human reason. In modern times Reform Judaism has adopted the belief in progressive revelation, maintaining that revelation is a continual process throughout history.

Revisionism. Zionist political movement, founded in 1925 by Vladimir Jabotinsky under the name World Union of Zionist Revisionists or Ha-Tzohar. It advocated the establishment of a Jewish state on both sides of the Jordan. Initially it opposed the official Zionist policy toward British Mandatory rule, and encouraged political action. In 1935 the Revisionists seceded from the World Zionist Organization and formed the New Zionist Organization. The Irgun Tzevai Leumi and Loḥame Ḥerut Yisrael originated from the Revisionist section of the Haganah.

Revue des Études Juives. French Jewish scholarly periodical. It was founded in 1880, on the initiative of Zadoc Kahn and Isidore Loeb, and served as the organ of the Société des Études Juives. In 1961 it merged with *Historia Judaica.*

Reyzen *see* REISEN.

Reznikoff, Charles (1894–1976). American poet and lawyer. He was born in Brooklyn. He wrote several books on legal and social history, as well as poetry influenced by Jewish literary and liturgical traditions. Some of his work deals with the plight of urban Jews in the US.

Rhodes. Aegean island, off the west coast of Turkey. Its Jewish community dates from classical times, and by the Middle Ages it had grown to a considerable size. Under Turkish rule many Sephardi settlers arrived. In 1840 a ritual murder accusation was made, which was averted through the intervention of Sir Moses Montefiore. After Italy occupied the island in 1912, an attempt was made to establish it as a center for the diffusion of Italian Jewish culture.

Rhodes Armistice Agreements. A series of armistice agreements, signed at Rhodes in 1949 between Israel and Egypt, Lebanon, Jordan, and Syria, by which the military phase of Israel's War of Independence was ended. As a result, Israel gained more territory than had been allocated to the Jews under the partition plan of 1947.

Ribalow, Menaḥem (1895–1953). American Hebrew critic and editor. He was born in Chudnov, Volhynia. He studied in Odessa and began to publish poems and essays at an early age. In 1921 he emigrated to the US, where he became editor of the Hebrew weekly *Ha-Doar*, and edited anthologies of American Hebrew literature.

Ribash *see* ISAAC BEN SHESHET PERFET.

Ribes, Jaime *see* CRESQUES, JUDAH.

Riboyne shel o'lem (Yiddish). O God in Heaven! or God willing. The phrase is used as an expression of amazement or hope.

***Ricardo, David** (1772–1823). English economist. He was born in London. He was a member of the stock exchange until 1814, when he retired to devote his energies to economics. Although he left Judaism when he married a Quaker, he advocated the removal of Jewish disabilities.

Ricchi, Imanuel Ḥai (1668–1743). Italian rabbi, kabbalist, and poet. He was born in Ferrara and raised in Rovigo. At the age of 20 he traveled to various Italian cities. He was ordained a rabbi in 1717; the following year he emigrated to Palestine and settled in Safed, where he studied kabbalah. Because of a plague, he left the country and moved to Livorno. He later traveled to Smyrna, Salonica, Constantinople, and London, before returning to Palestine (1737) and finally Livorno. He wrote various kabbalistic works.

Richler, Mordecai (b. 1931). Canadian novelist and journalist. He was born in Montreal, and moved to London in the 1950s. His *Son of a Smaller Hero* and *The Apprenticeship of Duddy Kravitz* depict Jewish life in Montreal. In later novels he contrasted Jewish and gentile culture. *Joshua Then and Now* tells the story of a Canadian Jew obsessed with the desire to avenge his defeat in an encounter with an ex-Nazi.

Ridbaz, Yaakov [Slutzker Rav] (1845–1913). Russian rabbi. After serving as a rabbi in Russia, he lived in the US from 1900 to 1905. He subsequently emigrated to Palestine, where he founded and directed a yeshivah in Safed.

Riesser, Gabriel (1806–1863). German lawyer and politician. He was born in Hamburg. After he was refused permission to practice as a notary in his native city because of his faith, he published a series of memoranda and articles demanding civil equality for Jewry. He became an important advocate of Emancipation for German Jews. From 1832 to 1837 he edited *Der Jude*. He was elected to the parliament at Frankfurt am Main in 1848 and was a member of the 1850 "Union" parliament at Erfurt. In 1859 he became the first Jewish judge in Germany.

Rieti, Moses of *see* MOSES BEN ISAAC DI RIETI.

Rif *see* ALFASI, ISAAC BEN JACOB.

Righteousness. Uprightness, virtue, honesty, freedom from wickedness. According to Jewish teaching, a "tzaddik" (righteous man) is one who lives according to the divine law. Righteousness is a central theme of biblical legislation and prophetic teaching. Jewish tradition holds that in every generation there are 36 perfectly righteous men ("lamed vav") on whose account the world continues to exist. In rabbinic and medieval Hebrew the word "tzedakah" denotes almsgiving and charity.

Rimmonim ("pomegranates"). Word used by the Sephardim to refer to the finial ornaments on the wooden staves on which the Scroll of the Law is rolled. Originally these were shaped like pomegranates; later they were in the shape of towers.

Rindfleisch massacres. Name given to the series of attacks on Jews carried out in Franconia and the surrounding regions in 1298, following a ritual murder accusation at Röttingen. They were led by Rindfleisch, a Bavarian noble.

Ringelblum, Emanuel (1900–1944). Galician historian. He was born in Buchach, in eastern Galicia, and became a high-school history teacher. Active in the Poale Zion movement, he was sent by the American Jewish Joint Distribution Committee to Zbaszyń in 1938 to direct relief work and collect testimonies from Jews who had been deported there. During World War II he assembled a secret archive of events in the Warsaw Ghetto; it later came to light and constitutes an important source of information on what took place there.

Rishonim ("first ones"). Older authorities. The Talmud uses the term to distinguish the earlier from the later prophets, as well as the former from the later generations in the talmudic period. In modern times the term refers to all commentators and codifiers of talmudic law of the gaonic period, up to the time of the compilation of the Shulḥan Arukh (i.e., c. 600–1300 CE).

Rishon le-Zion. The title given to the Sephardi chief rabbi of the Holy Land.

Ritba *see* YOMTOV BEN ABRAHAM ISHBILI.

Ritual murder libel *see* BLOOD LIBEL.

Ritual purity *see* PURITY, RITUAL.

Ritual slaughter *see* SHEḤITA.

Robbery (Hebrew "gezelah"). The unlawful removal of another person's property. According to the Bible, the penalty for the crime of robbery is restitution of the property or its value; the latter provision pertains if the stolen property no longer exists, has been seriously altered, has been incorporated in a structure that will have to be demolished if it were removed, or is regarded by its owners as lost. A penitent robber should be treated leniently.

Robbins, Jerome (b. 1918). American choreographer. He was born in New York. He began his career as a dancer, appearing with the New York City Ballet. His choreography for Broadway shows includes *Fiddler on the Roof*.

Rödelheim. German town. Jewish settlement was first permitted there in 1290, but the first evidence of Jews having lived in the town dates from 1371. From the mid-18th century, Rödelheim had a Hebrew press, which published Haskalah literature; in the 19th century it was acquired by Wolf Heidenheim and Baruch Baschwitz, who produced editions of the Pentateuch and the liturgy. In 1925 the town was absorbed into Frankfurt am Main.

Rodgers, Bernard (1893–1968). American composer and educator. He was born in New York. He taught at the Hartt School of Music and at the Eastman School of Music. Some of his work was influenced by biblical themes.

Rodkinson [Frumkin] **Michael** (1845–1904). American Hebrew writer and editor. He was born in Dubrovno, Belorussia, and initially wrote tales of the Ḥasidim. He later moved to Königsberg, where he published Hebrew periodicals from 1876 to 1880. In 1889 he settled in the US and devoted himself to translating the Talmud into English.

Rogochover Gaon *see* ROZIN, JOSEPH.

***Rohling, August** (1839–1931). German scholar. He was born in the Rhineland. He became a professor at the University of Prague. He published a polemical work against the Talmud as well as anti-Semitic pamphlets. He was attacked by Joseph Bloch who accused him of deceit. Rohling sued Bloch, but later withdrew his suit, and resigned his teaching post.

Rojas, Fernando de (fl. 16th cent.). Spanish Marrano author. He was born in Puebla de Montalbán near Toledo. He was the author of one of the earliest Spanish tragedies, *La Celestina*. Members of his family suffered under the Inquisition.

Rokaḥ, Yisrael (1896–1959). Israeli communal leader and politican. He was born in Jaffa. He was a member of the

Tel Aviv city council from 1922, the city's deputy mayor from 1929, and mayor from 1937 to 1953. He was elected to the Knesset in 1949 as a General Zionist member, and later served as minister of the interior (1953–5) and deputy speaker of the Knesset (1957–9).

Rokeaḥ, Eleazar *see* ELEAZAR BEN JUDAH OF WORMS.

Rokeaḥ family *see* BELZ.

Rome. Capital of Italy. Its Jewish community is the oldest in Europe: the first record of Jewish settlement dates from the 2nd century BCE and in classical literature there are frequent references to Jews in Rome. In the Middle Ages the community dwindled, but it did not disappear; in the 13th century the city was a center from which Jewish loan bankers spread out into central and northern Italy. During the Renaissance Jews participated in new intellectual and cultural developments, but the Counter-Reformation brought about the renewal of anti-Jewish legislation, including the institution of the ghetto. It was not until 1870, when Rome became the capital of united Italy, that the Jewish population was granted full Emancipation.

Romm. Family of Lithuanian Hebrew printers. The first member of the family to be active as a printer was Baruch ben Joseph Romm (fl. 18th century), who established the first Hebrew printing press in Lithuania at Grodno; it was later transferred to Vilnius. His son Menaḥem (d. 1841) was responsible for the publication of the first "Vilna Talmud." Menaḥem's son Joseph Reuben (d. 1848) and grandson David (d. 1860) developed the firm. At the end of the 19th century the imprint of "the widow and brothers Romm" was to be found on many Hebrew works.

***Roosevelt, Franklin Delano** (1882–1945). American statesman, President of the US (1933–45). He was concerned about the plight of the Jews in Nazi Germany, and summoned a conference at Évian in 1938 to aid their emigration and resettlement. In 1944 he established a War Refugee Board to rescue victims of Nazism.

Rosales, Jacob [Jacob Hebraeus] (c. 1588–c. 1668). Marrano physician and author. He was born in Lisbon, and became a physician there. Later he settled in Rome, where he came under the influence of Galileo. During the 1630s he went to Hamburg. Emperor Ferdinand III bestowed the title of Count Palatine on him in recognition of his scientific achievements. Later he lived as a Jew in Livorno, assuming the name Jacob Hebraeus. He published works on medicine and astronomy.

Rosanes, Solomon Abraham (1862–1938). Bulgarian historian. He was born in Ruschuk. He was a businessman, but devoted himself to Jewish studies, and during World War I settled in Sofia, where he became librarian of the Jewish community. He published studies of Jewish history, including *A History of the Jews in Turkey and in the Orient*.

Rosen, Joseph (1877–1949). American agronomist. He was born in Moscow, and emigrated to the US in 1903. In 1921 he returned to Russia for the American Jewish Joint Distribution Committee on a relief mission to the Jews. In 1924 he initiated a land-settlement project in the Ukraine and Crimea for Jews who had been deprived of Soviet citizenship. In 1940 he directed Jewish colonization in the Dominican Republic.

Rosen [Rosenblüth]**, Pinḥas** (1887–1978). Israeli and Zionist leader, of German origin. He was born in Berlin. He served as chairman of the Zionist Organization of Germany (1920–23), and, after living in Palestine (1923–5), joined the Zionist Executive in London. In 1931 he returned to Palestine, where he practiced law. He was active in the Aliyah Ḥadashah party, and in 1948 he became president of the Progressive Party. From 1949 to 1968 he was a member of the Knesset, serving as minister of justice in successive coalition cabinets (1948–61).

Rosenbach, Abraham Simon Wolf (1876–1952). American bibliophile. He was born in Philadelphia, where later he founded the Rosenbach Company, a rare-book business. He wrote *An American Jewish Bibliography* and a historical study of Congregation Mikveh Israel in Philadelphia. He served as president of the American Jewish Historical Society, and was a benefactor of Graetz College.

Rosenbaum, Simon (1860–1934). Polish jurist and Zionist. He was born in Pinsk, and practiced law there and in Minsk. Active in the Ḥibbat Zion movement, he was a delegate to the Zionist Congresses until World War I; he was an opponent of the Uganda plan. During World War I, he worked for an independent Lithuania, and later became the country's deputy foreign minister; subsequently he served as minister of Jewish affairs. In 1924 he settled in Palestine, where he was chairman of the Supreme Jewish Peace Court.

***Rosenberg, Alfred** (1893–1946). German administrator. He was born in Reval, Estonia. He settled in Munich in 1918, and became involved in anti-Semitic circles; his book *The Myth of the Twentieth Century* had an important impact on Nazi ideology. In 1940 he became head of the Hohe Schule, which was planned to become the university of Nazism; his emissaries ransacked Jewish libraries throughout Europe and concentrated their holdings in Frankfurt am Main. In 1941 he became minister of occupied countries in eastern Europe and head of their civil administration. At the end of the war he was hanged after being tried for war crimes by the International Military Tribunal at Nuremberg.

Rosenberg, Isaac (1890–1918). English poet and painter. He was born in Bristol. Some of his poetry (such as *Chagrin*) expresses the rootless condition of the diaspora Jew.

Rosenblatt, Joseph (1882–1933). American cantor and composer. He was born in Belaya Tserkov' in the Ukraine, and in his youth toured eastern Europe as a child prodigy. He was initially cantor in Mukachevo, then moved to Bratislava in 1901, and to Hamburg five years later. In 1912 he emigrated to the US where he became ḥazzan of the Ohab Zedek Congregation in New York. He was the most popular cantor of his time. His collection of sacred songs, *Zemirot Yosef*, contains many of his best-known works.

Rosenblüth, Pinḥas *see* ROSEN, PINḤAS.

Rosenfeld, Isaac (1918–1956). American writer. He was born in Chicago. Some of his essays deal with Jews, Judaism, and Jewish life in America and Europe.

Rosenfeld, Morris (1862–1923). American Yiddish poet. He was born in Bolikshein in the Russian part of Poland, and grew up in Warsaw. After learning tailoring in London, he went to New York in 1886, where he worked in a sweatshop. Initially he published socialist poems. In 1894 he began editing a satirical weekly, and in 1905 the daily *New Yorker Morgenblat.* By this time he was recognized as a pioneer of Yiddish poetry and in 1908 he went on a tour of Galicia and western Europe. He wrote poems on proletarian, national, and romantic themes; he also published studies on Heinrich Heine and Yehuda Halevi.

Rosenheim, Jacob (1870–1965). Orthodox leader, of German origin. He was born in Frankfurt am Main. He first worked in a bank, and later founded the Hermon Publishing House. In 1906 he transferred publication of the weekly

Israelit from Mainz to Frankfurt where it became an influential organ of German Orthodoxy. He was a founder and leader of Agudat Israel, of which he was president from 1929. From 1940 he lived in the US and Israel; he helped to secure permission for Agudat Israel to participate in the Israeli government and Knesset. He wrote on various religious themes.

Rosenthal, Erwin Isak Jakob (b. 1904). British orientalist. He was born in Heilbronn, Germany, and settled in England in 1933, where he became a lecturer in Hebrew at University College, London. He taught Semitic languages and literature at Manchester University (1936–44) and later at Cambridge University. He wrote studies of Judaism, biblical exegesis, medieval philosophy, and Islam.

Rosenthal, Herman (1843–1917). American writer and pioneer of Jewish settlement in the US. He was born in Friedrichstadt, near Kiel, and initially worked as a printer in the Ukraine. During the Russo-Turkish War, he served with the Red Cross. After the pogroms of 1881, he organized a group of 70 people and set out for the US, where he attempted to establish an agricultural settlement for Russian Jews on Sicily Island, near New Orleans. In 1891 he participated in the establishment of an ICA colony in Woodbine, New Jersey. From 1898 he was the head of the Slavonic department of the New York Public Library.

Rosenthal, Leser (1794–1868). German bibliophile and bibliographer. He was born in Nasnelsk, Plock, Russia. He taught at Paderborn, Germany, and later was Klausrabbiner at Hanover. His library contained 32 manuscripts and 6000 printed volumes, including incunabula and rare books.

Rosenwald, Julius (1862–1932). American merchant and philanthropist. He was born in Springfield, Illinois. He first worked in his uncle's clothing store in New York, but later opened his own store. He began to manufacture summer clothing and in 1885 moved his business to Chicago. He became president of Sears, Roebuck, and Company, and subsequently chairman of the board. He was president of the Associated Jewish Charities of Chicago, and contributed to Jewish war relief during World War I and in the postwar period. He also supported the Hebrew Union College and the Jewish Theological Seminary.

Rosenwald, Lessing Julius (1891–1979). American merchant, bibliophile, and philanthropist, son of Julius Rosenwald. He was born in Chicago, where he later worked for Sears, Roebuck, and Company. In 1943 he helped to found the American Council for Judaism, and served as its president. Opposed to Zionism, he campaigned against the establishment of Israel.

Rosenwald, William (b. 1903). American philanthropist and financier, son of Julius Rosenwald. He was a director of Sears, Roebuck, and Company, but later concentrated on his own investments. He was chairman of the national United Jewish Appeal campaign and vice-chairman of the Joint Distribution Committee, and played an important role in the American Jewish Committee and United HIAS Service.

Rosenzweig, Franz (1886–1929). German theologian. He was born in Kassel. He studied at various universities, and eventually considered converting to Christianity. After attending an Orthodox high holy day service in Berlin, he embraced Judaism. Later he served in the German army, and he wrote *Star of Redemption* while confined to military hospitals in Leipzig and Belgrade. After returning home he established an institute for Jewish studies, the Freies Jüdisches Lehrhaus, in Frankfurt am Main. In 1921 he became partially paralyzed, but he continued to write. Together with Martin Buber he translated the Hebrew Scriptures into German.

Rosh *see* ASHER BEN JEHIEL.

Rosh bet din *see* AV BET DIN.

Rosheim, Josel(man) of *see* JOSELMAN OF ROSHEIM.

Rosh ha-Shanah ("Head of the year") **(i).** New Year. The Jewish New Year begins on the first day of Tishri, and marks the start of the Ten Days of Penitence, which end on the Day of Atonement. In the Bible Rosh ha-Shanah is referred to as falling on the first day of the seventh month (Leviticus 23.24). During the rabbinic period, it came to be regarded as a day of judgment for the entire world, on which each person's fate is inscribed in the Book of Life. During the festival service, which is traditionally celebrated in white vestments, the shophar is blown, and other rituals are introduced. In the diaspora Rosh ha-Shanah is observed for two days.

Rosh ha-Shanah ("Head of the year") **(ii).** Eighth tractate in the Mishnah order of Moed. It deals with the regulations regarding the sanctification of the new moon, the blowing of the ram's horn (or shophar) on Rosh ha-Shanah, and the special order of prayer for that occasion.

Rosh Ḥodesh ("Sanctification of the month"). The celebration of the appearance of the new moon, which marks the beginning of the month. A special sacrifice was offered in the Temple on this day, at which a musaph was recited (Numbers 28.11–15). The Bible mentions various observances that should take place on the day of the new moon; during the talmudic period these became more elaborate and included a proclamation of the new moon's appearance, communicated throughout and beyond Palestine by a system of beacons. In modern times the formal celebration is confined to the recital of the half Hallel and the addition of the musaph service to the Amidah on the first day of the month. It is announced in synagogues on the preceding Sabbath in a special ceremony (*see* NEW MOON, BLESSING OF THE).

Rosh yeshivah ("Head of the yeshivah"). Originally, the title accorded to one who directs an institution for the study of the Talmud. In modern times the title is used not only for the principals of yeshivot but also for the permanent members of the teaching staff.

Rosowsky, Shlomo (1878–1962). Israeli composer. In St. Petersburg he was an active member of the Society for Jewish Folk Music. In 1925 he emigrated to Palestine, where he composed music for the Hebrew theater. Besides composing, he studied Jewish music, and he published a work on the cantillation of the Bible. He later lived in the US and taught at the Jewish Theological Seminary.

Ross, Leonard Q. *see* ROSTEN, LEO CALVIN.

Rossi, Azariah ben Moses dei [Adummim; Azariah dei Rossi] (c. 1511–c. 1578). Italian scholar. He was born in Mantua, and lived in Bologna, Ferrara, and Mantua. His *Meor Enayim* shows how classical sources (such as the Letter of Aristeas) cast light on Jewish history and literature in the classical period. In the third part of this work ("Imrei Binah") he examined ancient Jewish history by comparing Hebrew texts with classical Jewish and non-Jewish sources. He also wrote poetry in Italian, Hebrew, and Aramaic. His writings provoked the hostility of a number of rabbis.

***Rossi, Giovanni Bernardo de'** (1742–1831). Italian priest and Hebraist. He made important contributions to the study of the text of the Bible and to Hebrew bibliography. His collection of

Hebrew books and manuscripts now form part of the Palatine Library in Parma.

Rossi, Salomone de' (fl. 17th cent.). Italian composer. He came from Mantua. He was the leading Jewish composer of the late Italian Renaissance, and a court musician of the Gonzaga rulers of Mantua. In 1587 he entered the service of Duke Vicenzo I as a singer and viola player. Later he became the leader of the duke's musical establishment and directed an instrumental ensemble. He published secular, instrumental, and vocal music, including a collection of Hebrew religious songs (*Ha-Shirim Asher li-Shelomoh*).

Rosten, Leo Calvin (b. 1908). American humorist. He was born in Łódź in Poland, and went to the US as a child. He later served in the US government. Under the pen name Leonard Q. Ross, he wrote *The Education of H*y*m*a*n K*a*p*l*a*n*, and *The Return of H*y*m*a*n K*a*p*l*a*n*. He also wrote the *Joys of Yiddish*.

Rostov-na-Donu. City in the southern USSR, on the River Don. Jews settled there in the 19th century. In 1905 the Jewish community was attacked and under the Soviet regime Jewish public life was suppressed.

Rotenstreich, Natan (b. 1914). Israeli philosopher. He was born in Sambor, Poland, and emigrated to Palestine in 1932. In 1955 he became professor of philosophy at the Hebrew University, and later dean of the faculty of humanities and rector. He wrote studies of Jewish thinkers and a survey of modern Jewish thought.

Roth, Cecil (1899–1970). English historian. He was born in London. He was a reader in Jewish studies at Oxford from 1939 to 1964, when he settled in Jerusalem and became visiting professor at Bar Ilan University. His publications include histories of the Jews of England and Italy, Jewish biographies, a history of the Marranos, a study of Jews in the Renaissance, and studies of Jewish art. He served as editor-in-chief of the *Encyclopaedia Judaica* from 1966.

Roth, Henry (b. 1906). American novelist. He was born in Austria, and went to the US as a child. He worked as a high-school teacher, precision metal grinder, and farmer. His *Call it Sleep* deals with Jewish immigrant life in New York's East Side.

Roth, Joseph (1894–1939). Austrian novelist. He was born near Brody in eastern Galicia. He worked from 1923 for the *Frankfurter Zeitung*. Later he lived in Paris. His novel *Job* describes eastern European Jewish life, and in *Juden auf Wanderschaft* he deals with the social position of Jews in eastern Europe.

Roth, Leon (1896–1963). English philosopher. He was a lecturer in philosophy at Manchester University from 1923 to 1927. He settled in Palestine and became (in turn) professor of philosophy at the Hebrew University, rector of the university (1940–43), and dean of the faculty of humanities. He returned to England in 1951. He wrote philosophical studies, translated philosophical classics into Hebrew, and published a study of the Jewish religion (*Judaism: a Portrait*).

Roth, Philip (b. 1933). American novelist. He was born in New Jersey. Many of his novels and short stories depict the struggle of American Jewish men, especially the conflict between their Jewish background and the attractions of American Christian culture. His writings include *Goodbye Columbus, Letting Go, Portnoy's Complaint, The Anatomy Lesson, The Breast, My Life as a Man, The Ghost Writer, Zukerman Unbound, The Counterlife, The Professor of Desire, The Great American Novel*, and *Reading Myself and Others*.

Rothenberg, Morris (1885–1950). American Zionist leader. He was born in Dorpat, Estonia, and was taken to the

US in 1893. During World War I he was a member of a federal commission charged with fixing the price of bread. In 1937 he became city magistrate of New York. He was a founder and executive committee member of the Jewish Welfare Board, a founder of the Joint Distribution Committee, and an executive committee member of the Council for German Jewry. He also served as president of the Zionist Organization of America.

Rothenburg. City in Bavaria, southern Germany. Its Jewish population dates from the 12th century. In the 13th century Meir ben Baruch settled there and attracted students to the city, but in 1298 the community was devastated during the Rindfleisch persecutions. The Jews were attacked again in 1349 in one of the series of massacres sparked off by the Black Death. Expulsions of the Jewish community from Rothenburg took place in the later 14th century and again in 1520.

Rothenstein, Albert Daniel *see* RUTHERSTON, ALBERT DANIEL.

Rothenstein, William, Sir (1872–1945). English artist. He was born in Bradford. He studied in London, Paris, and Oxford. During World War I he served as a war artist, and then became professor of civic art at the University of Sheffield. From 1920 to 1935 he was principal of the Royal College of Art. He painted portraits, still-lifes, and landscapes, as well as Jewish subjects and synagogue interiors.

Rothschild, Anthony, Sir (1810–1876). English communal leader, brother of Lionel Rothschild. He lived as a country gentleman and was active in the Jewish community. He served as the first president of the United Synagogue from 1870.

Rothschild, Edmond de, Baron (1845–1934). French philanthropist and art collector, son of James de Rothschild. He and his wife, Adelaide, were interested in Jewish affairs. When the first Zionist pioneers in Palestine appealed to Rothschild for assistance, he supported the colonization of Palestine. He sent agricultural experts and officials there to help in the settlement process, visited Palestine himself five times (1887, 1893, 1899, 1914, 1925), and purchased 125,000 acres of land in the country. In 1900 he transferred the management of the colonies to the ICA. Later he served as the honorary president of the Jewish Agency.

Rothschild, James de (1792–1868). French banker and communal leader. He settled in Paris in 1812, where he founded the firm Rothschild Frères. A financier to the Bourbon and Orléans kings of France, he later served Napoleon II. From 1840 the Rothschild family was active in the Jewish consistory of Paris, the Central Consistory of the Jews of France, and the Jewish Charity Committee of Paris. They also played a role in the Damascus Affair.

Rothschild, Karl (1788–1855). Italian banker. In 1821 he founded the Italian branch of the Rothschild family in Naples. He was instrumental in establishing a Jewish community there.

Rothschild, Lionel (1808–1879). English banker, brother of Anthony Rothschild. He was head of the family banking house at New Court in London. He was elected to parliament as a Liberal in 1847 but took his seat only in 1858, after the passing of the Jews' Disabilities Bill. The character Sidonia in *Coningsby* by Benjamin Disraeli is based on him.

Rothschild, Nathaniel, 1st Lord (1840–1915). English banker, son of Lionel Rothschild. He was head of the English branch of the Rothschild banking house, and became the first Jewish peer. He served as president of the United Synagogue.

Rov (Yiddish). Rabbi.

Rovina, Hanna (1892–1980). Israeli

actress, of Russian Origin. She was born in Berezino, Minsk, and first worked as head of an institute for refugee children at Saratov. In 1917 she joined a Hebrew theatrical studio in Moscow and became one of the founding members of the Ha-Bimah Theater Company. In 1928 she went to Palestine with the company and became the country's leading actress.

Rozin, Joseph [Rogochover Gaon] (1858–1936). Latvian talmudist. He was born in Rogochover, and became rabbi of the Ḥasidic community of Dvinsk in 1889. During World War I he fled to St. Petersburg, where he was the rabbi of a Ḥasidic community for ten years. He subsequently returned to Dvinsk. He wrote responsa and a commentary on Maimonides' *Mishneh Torah*. His collected works appeared under the title *Tzaphenat Paaneaḥ*.

Roziner, Felix (b. 1936). Israeli writer of Russian origin. He was born in Moscow, and lived there until his emigration to Israel in 1978. He worked initially as an engineer, but gave up his job in 1969 to write. His *A Certain Finkelmayer* deals with the Jew as a Russian intellectual. In *The Silver Cord* he depicts seven generations of a Jewish family who migrate from the shtetl to Israel.

Ruaḥ *see* Soul.

Ruaḥ ha-Kodesh *see* Holy spirit.

Rubens, Bernice (b. 1927). British novelist. She was born in Cardiff. She was first a schoolteacher, and later a writer and director of documentary films. Her early novels (*Set on Edge, Madame Sousatzka, Mate in Three*, and *The Elected Member*) deal with middle-class Jewish life.

Rubenstein, Richard L. (b. 1924). American theologian. He was born in New York. He served as chaplain to Jewish students at the University of Pittsburgh, and in 1970 became professor of religion at Florida State University. His writings include *After Auschwitz, The Religious Imagination*, and *The Cunning of History*.

Rubin, Solomon (1823–1910). Galician Hebrew writer. He was born in Dolnia. He became one of the most prolific writers of the Haskalah period, publishing studies of Jewish folklore, customs, and superstitions, and works about Spinoza.

Rubinstein, Isaac (1880–1945). Polish communal leader. He was born in Dotnuva, Lithuania. He was a rabbi in Genichesk, Ukraine, from 1906, and later became the government-appointed rabbi of Vilnius. In 1920 he was minister of Jewish affairs in Vilnius, and from 1922 to 1939 was a member of the Polish senate. He was also a leader of the Mizraḥi and active in the World Zionist Organization. In 1941 he emigrated to the US and taught at Yeshiva University.

Rufus Tinneius *see* procurator.

Rukeyser, Muriel (1914–1980). American poet, writer, and translator. She was born in New York, and taught at Sarah Lawrence College. Her poetry includes works about Rabbi Akiva.

Ruppin, Arthur (1876–1943). Palestinian Zionist, economist, and sociologist. He was born in Rawicz, in the Posen district, and initially worked in the grain trade. From 1903 to 1907 he directed the Bureau for Jewish Statistics and Demography in Berlin. In 1907 he went to Palestine as a representative of the Zionist Organization. Later he founded various settlement companies and helped to establish labor colonization in the country. He was deported by the Turks in 1916, but returned in 1920. Subsequently he became director of the Zionist Executive's colonization department in Jerusalem. From 1926 he taught sociology at the Hebrew University. His writings include sociological studies of Jewry.

Rutenberg, Pinḥas (1879–1942). Palestinian engineer and Zionist teacher, of

Ukrainian origin. He was born in Romny, in the Ukraine. He participated in the 1905 Russian Revolution, and after living for a time in Italy and the US, returned to Russia in 1917. He was again involved in revolutionary activities, but he left Russia in 1919 and settled in Palestine, where he founded the Palestine Electric Company. He was elected chairman of the Vaad Leumi in 1929.

Ruth (fl. 12th cent. BCE). Moabite woman. After her husband, Mahlon, died she went with Naomi (her mother-in-law) to Bethlehem, where she married Boaz. The Book of Ruth is one of the Five Scrolls, and is read during Shavuot.

Rutherston, Albert Daniel [Rothenstein, Albert Daniel](1881–1953). English artist and illustrator. He designed an important Haggadah (book of the Passover service).

Ruth Rabbah. Aggadic midrash, part of the Midrash Rabbah. It is exegetical in character. It utilizes earlier sources including the Palestinian Talmud, Genesis Rabbah, Leviticus Rabbah, and the Pesikta de-Rav Kahana.

Ruzhin, Israel of (1797–1851). Russian Ḥasidic rabbi. He established a Ḥasidic center at Ruzhin, where he lived in luxury. In 1838 he was accused of giving the order to put to death two Jewish informers. Imprisoned for 22 months, he was later released and settled in Sadagora in Bukovina, which also became a Ḥasidic center.

Ryback, Issachar (1879–1935). Russian artist. He was born in Yelizavetgradka in the Ukraine. He helped to establish an art section of the Jewish Cultural League in Kiev. From 1921 to 1925 he lived in Berlin, where he illustrated children's books in Yiddish, and published *The Shtetl* and *The Jewish Types of the Ukraine*; later he produced *On the Fields of the Ukraine.* In 1926 he moved to Paris.

Rybakov, Anatolii (b. 1911). Ukrainian writer. He was born in Chernigov, and moved to Moscow in 1919. He was arrested and sentenced to imprisonment in Siberia; after his release in 1935 he worked as a ballroom-dancing teacher, automobile mechanic, and driver. Later he served in the army, and began writing. His novel *Heavy Sand* deals with the Russian Jewish past and the Holocaust in the USSR.

S

Saad al-Daula (fl. 13th cent.). Persian physician and statesman. He served as a physician in government service in Baghdad, and later became Governor of Baghdad and Iraq. In 1289 he was appointed vizier by Arghun, the Mongolian ruler.

Saadyah Gaon [Saadyah ben Joseph] (882–942). Babylonian gaon. He was born in Pithom in the Faiym district of Egypt, and settled in Babylonia in 921. In 928 he became gaon of Sura, but two years later he was deposed by the exilarch David ben Zakkai; he was reinstated in 936. His earliest work was a polemic against the Karaite scholar Anan ben David. *Beliefs and Opinions* is his main philosophical treatise. His other scholarly works include a translation of the Bible into Arabic, Arabic commentaries on most biblical books, a Hebrew lexicon and grammar, and a list of biblical *hapax legomena*. He also produced a systematic compilation of the prayerbook, and wrote liturgical poetry. His *Sepher ha-Galui* is an account of his personal tribulations.

Sabbath (Hebrew "Shabbat"). Day of rest. It is observed weekly from before sunset on Friday until after nightfall on Saturday. According to tradition, the Sabbath is a memorial of the day of rest enjoyed by God after the Creation; its observance was enjoined by God, in one version of the Ten Commandments, to commemorate his bringing the Israelites out of Egypt. Work must cease on the Sabbath and rabbinic legislation stipulates 39 types of action which are forbidden; however, these regulations may be set aside if human life is in danger. The Sabbath day is an occasion for prayer, study, and refreshment of the spirit. Synagogue services include readings from the Torah and the Books of the Prophets, and the day concludes with the Havdalah service.

Sabbath, Great (Hebrew "Shabbat ha-Gadol"). The name given to the Sabbath before Passover. On that day a special haphtarah (Malachi 3.4–24) is read after the Torah portion, and a rabbinic discourse dealing with the laws of the approaching festival is delivered. The Ashkenazim read part of the Passover Haggadah during the afternoon service.

Sabbath lamp. Oil lamp kindled in the home on Friday night to symbolize the light of the Sabbath. Made of brass, copper, pewter, or silver, it was bowl-shaped and hung from the ceiling. In modern times candles have been substituted for oil.

Sabbath prayers. On Friday evenings the Maariv service is preceded by a special service in the synagogue known as "Kabbalat Shabbat" (Reception of the Sabbath). At home the kiddush prayer is recited before the meal, and Sabbath songs ("zemirot") are sung after it. The prayers recited on the Sabbath follow the same basic structure as on other days. However, the Amidah consists of only seven benedictions, and a fourth prayer service (musaph) is added to the three regular daily prayers. In addition many extra psalms and poetic compositions are included in the morning service. At the end of the Sabbath, Maariv is recited as on weekdays and is followed by the Havdalah service.

Sabbaths, special. Four Sabbaths are named after the special Torah readings that replace the ordinary maphtir (or concluding portion) of the weekly reading from the law: (1) 1 Adar or the preceding Sabbath is known as Shekalim from Exodus 30.11–16; (2) the Sabbath before Purim is known as Zakhor from Deuteronomy 25.17–19; (3) the Sabbath before Purim is known as Parah from Numbers 19.1–22; and (4) 1 Nisan or the preceding Sabbath is known as Ha-Ḥodesh from Exodus 12.1–20. In addition, three Sabbaths are named after the first word of the portion from the Books of the Prophets assigned to the day: (1) Sabbath Ḥazon (the Sabbath before the Ninth of Av) from Isaiah 1.1; (2) Sabbath Naḥamu (the Sabbath after the Ninth of Av) from Isaiah 40.1; and (3) Sabbath Shuvah (the Sabbath between New Year and the Day of Atonement) from Hosea 14.2. Similarly Sabbath Bereshit and Sabbath Shirah are named for the weekly biblical portions. Finally, the Sabbath during the intermediate days of Passover or Sukkot is known as Sabbath Ḥol ha-Moed, the Sabbath before Passover as Shabbat ha-Gadol.

Sabbatical year (Hebrew "Shemittah") [Year of Release]. Name given in Jewish law to every seventh year, when, according to Leviticus 25.3ff, no agricultural work should be done; all crops in this year are the property of the community. The Sabbatical year was also marked by the rescinding of debts, hence the alternative name "Year of Release." The year following seven Sabbatical years (that is, every 50th year) is a Jubilee (Leviticus 25.8), when cultivation is prohibited, slaves are freed, and land purchased since the preceding Jubilee reverts to its original owner. The laws relating to Sabbatical and Jubilee years are treated in the talmudic tractate Sheviit. They are now observed only by strict Orthodox Jews living in Israel.

Sabbetaians [Shabbetaians]. Name given to the followers of the Messianic leader Shabbetai Tzevi. After his death in 1676, they believed he would reappear as the savior of Israel. They eventually split into various sects, including the Dönmeh sect (followers of Shabbetai Tzevi's successor, Jacob Querido), the Cardoza sect (disciples of Abraham Miguel Cardoza), and the Mokiah sect (centered on Mordecai Mokiah).

Sabea [Sheba]. Ancient country in southern Arabia. Its language was Semitic, and numerous inscriptions that originated there cast light on biblical institutions and vocabulary. I Kings 10 mentions the Queen of Sheba, who visited Jerusalem to benefit from Solomon's wisdom. According to tradition, Judaism reached Sabea at the time of the destruction of the first Temple (586 BCE). During the 5th century CE several Jewish kings flourished there including Dhu Nuwas, an Arabian king of the Himyarite kingdom and a convert to Judaism.

Sabot, Elijah *see* ELIJAH BE'ER BEN SHABBETAI.

Sabra (Arabic). Native of Israel.

Sachar, Abram Leon (1899–?). American educator and historian. He was born in New York. He taught history at the University of Illinois, and later served as national director of the Hillel Foundation (1933–48). In 1948 he became the first president of Brandeis University, subsequently becoming its chancellor. His publications include *History of the Jews*, and a history of Jewish life between the two world wars.

Sachs, Michael Jehiel (1808–1864). German rabbi and preacher. He was born in Glogau, Silesia. He was a preacher in Prague, and later in Berlin, where he also served as dayyan of the bet din. He was an opponent of the reforming influence of Samuel Holdheim and his Berlin congregation. He translated the liturgy and parts of the Bible into German.

Sachs, Nelly (1891–1970). German poet. She was born in Berlin. She escaped to Sweden at the beginning of World War II. Some of her writing was inspired by the Holocaust. She received the Nobel Prize for literature in 1966.

Sackler, Harry (1883–?). American Hebrew and Yiddish author. He was born in Bohorodczany, Galicia, and went to the US in 1902. He worked as an attorney and served as an officer of various Jewish organizations. In his stories, novels, plays, and essays he recreated Jewry throughout the ages; his novel *Festival at Meron* depicts the period of the Bar Kokhba revolt (132–5 CE).

Sacks, Jonathan (b. 1948). English rabbi. He was born in London. He served as principal of Jews College, and in 1991 became chief rabbi of the United Hebrew Congregations of the British Commonwealth. His publications include *Traditional Alternatives*, *Tradition in an Untraditional Age*, and *The Persistence of Faith*.

Sacrifice. Ritual act involving an offering to a deity. In Judaism sacrifice was made to God to obtain his favor or atone for sin. The Canaanites sacrificed human beings (II Kings 3.27) but the story in Genesis of the binding of Isaac (22.1–19) teaches God's displeasure with this type of sacrificial act. In ancient Israel three types of sacrifice were offered in the Temple: animal sacrifice ("zeraḥ"), made as a burnt offering for sin, meal offerings ("minḥah"), and libations. The rituals and practices prescribed for the Temple sacrifice are set down in Leviticus 2 and 23, and Numbers 28–9.

Sacrifice of Isaac *see* AKEDAH.

Sacrilege (Hebrew "me'ilah"). The misuse or desecration of anything regarded as sacred or worthy of great respect. In biblical times it was regarded as sacrilege to appropriate Temple property for secular use, to put to secular use the formula for sacrificial incense, and to copy the design of the Temple candelabrum or other vessels for non-cultic purposes. Later it was decreed sacrilegious to use the synagogue improperly, to treat the Scroll of the Law with disrespect, to imitate Holy Writ for secular purposes, and to recite the Song of Songs as secular poetry. Concerning matters pertaining to death and burial, it is sacrilege to misuse a cemetery or to derive private gain from any activity involving a body or a shroud.

Sadagora. Town in Bukovina. Its Jewish community dates from the 19th century and most of the Jews who settled there were Ḥasidim. In the mid-century Israel of Ruzhin lived there and founded a dynasty of rabbis (known as the Sadagora rebbes); the family later moved to Vienna and eventually to Tel Aviv.

Sadan, Dov (b. 1902). Israeli Yiddish and Hebrew writer. He was born in Galicia, and emigrated to Israel in 1925. He first worked on the newspaper *Davar* and for the Am Oved publishing company. In 1952 he was appointed to teach Yiddish literature at the Hebrew University; he also taught Hebrew literature at Tel Aviv University. He was elected to the Knesset in 1965. He translated many works from Polish, German, and Yiddish, and published several collections of literary criticism.

Sadducees. One of the three main sects

of Judaism before the destruction of the Jewish state in 70 CE; the others were the Pharisees and the Essenes. The group comprised the priestly class, who officiated in the Temple. Unlike the Pharisees, the Sadducees did not subscribe to a belief in the resurrection of the dead. Encouraging adherence to the Written Law, they dispensed with an oral tradition. They were supporters of the Hasmonean kings, but lost influence under Salome Alexandra and suffered persecution at the hands of Herod the Great. After the destruction of the Temple in 70, the sect died out.

Sadeh, Pinḥas (b. 1929). Israeli writer. He was born in Tel Aviv. He has written in a wide variety of genres, including children's books, poetry, and literary articles; he has also published an autobiography and a novel, *Al Mazzavo Shel ha-Adam*.

Sadeh, Yitzḥak [Landsberg, Yitzḥak] (1890–1952). Israeli labor and military leader. He was born in Lublin, Poland. He served in the Russian army, then in 1920 left for Palestine, where he became the head of Joseph Trumpeldor's Labor Battalion. In 1941 he organized the Palmaḥ, which he commanded until 1945; later he served on the staff of the Haganah. After the creation of the State of Israel, he commanded the Eighth Armored Brigade. He published stories, plays, and memoirs.

Sadhe *see* TSADEH.

Safed. Town in Upper Galilee. It was of importance in crusading times. In 1140 Fulk of Anjou, King of Jerusalem, built a fortress there. In 1168 the town became the property of the Knights Templar, but it was destroyed by Baybars in 1266. In the 15th century Safed became a center of rabbinic and kabbalistic activity: Isaac Luria lived there as did Joseph Caro. In 1588 a Hebrew press was established in the town.

Sagerin *see* ZOGERIN.

Sahl ben Matzliah (fl. 11th cent.). Palestinian Karaite. He traveled extensively, spreading his teaching. His writings incorporate information on the Karaites and Palestinian Jewry; they include polemics against the rabbis and an Arabic commentary on the Torah.

Sahulah, Isaac ben Solomon *see* IBN SAHULAH, ISAAC BEN SOLOMON.

St. Petersburg [Leningrad; Petrograd]. Russian city and major port on the Baltic Sea; it was the capital of the Russian empire until 1918. Shortly after the foundation of St. Petersburg in 1703, some apostates or Marranos appeared there. In the 18th century Jewish physicians and financiers held various positions in the city. Catharine II attracted Jewish contractors, industrialists, and physicians to St. Petersburg, but under Nicholas I the position of the Jews deteriorated. Later, under Alexander II, the situation of the Jewish community improved, and the city played an important role in Russian Jewish life.

Salaman, Nina (1877–1925). English poet, wife of Redcliffe Salaman. She translated medieval Hebrew poetry. Her own writings included the collection *Apples and Honey*.

Salaman, Redcliffe (1874–1955). English pathologist and geneticist. He was the director of the Pathological Institute of the London Hospital from 1901 to 1904. In 1926 he became director of the potato virus research station in Cambridge. His writings include *Jewish Achievements in Medicine* and *Racial Origins of Jewish Types*. During World War I he served in Palestine, and published *Palestine Reclaimed*.

Salant, Samuel (1816–1909). Palestinian rabbi, of Polish origin. He was born near Białystok. He set out for Palestine in 1840, but was delayed in Constantinople, where he met Sir Moses Montefiore. In 1841 he reached Jerusalem, where he became rabbi of the Ashkenazi community. In 1878 he became Ashkenazi chief rabbi. He served various Jewish organizations and traveled widely in Europe to collect money for religious institutions in Jerusalem. A number of his novellae were published in talmudic journals.

Salanter, Israel [Lipkin, Israel] (1810–1883). Lithuanian scholar. He was born in Zhagory. He founded the Musar movement in Lithuania and Russia from around 1830, and set up "Musar houses" for the study of ethical literature. He also published a journal, *Tevunah,* to promote his views. His pupils helped to spread the Musar movement, particularly among the Torah students of Lithuania. Salanter also traveled to western Europe to propagate his ideas. Isaac Belzer collected his ethical writings in *Or Israel.*

Sale. According to the Talmud, a sale of any property is not legally binding until a "kinyan" (act of agreement or possession) has been drawn up; an oral agreement is not binding. In the case of movable property, the vendor may void the sale, even after money has been paid by the buyer, as long as a formal kinyan has not been exchanged. A sale is effected in cases of immovable property by payment of the full cost or by writing a kinyan.

Salem *see* JERUSALEM.

Saloman Yitzḥak ben Isaac *see* RASHI.

Salome (fl. 1st cent.). Palestinian princess, daughter of Herod's son Philip and Herodias. She is identified with the daughter of Herodias who was responsible for John the Baptist's death (Matthew 14.3–6; Mark 6.17–29). She married her uncle, the tetrarch Philip, and subsequently Aristobulus, King of Lesser Armenia.

Salome Alexandra [Shelom Tziyyon, Alexandra] (fl. 1st cent. BCE). Queen of Judea (76–67 BCE). She succeeded her husband Alexander Yannai. Reversing his policy toward the Pharisees, she gave them internal control of the country while retaining responsibility herself for the army and foreign policy. When she appointed her son Hyrcanus as high priest and heir, his younger brother Aristobulus denounced her action.

Salomon, Gotthold (1784–1862). German preacher and reformer. After an Orthodox education, he was sent to Dessau, where he was influenced by modern trends, such as new approaches to biblical criticism. He became a teacher and preacher in Dessau, and was later appointed rabbi of the Hamburg Reform temple. The publication of his new version of the liturgy in 1841 provoked considerable controversy.

Salomons, Sir **David** (1797–1873). English banker and communal leader. He was a founder of the joint stock banking system in England. An advocate of the admission of Jews into English public affairs, he was the first Jewish sheriff, alderman, and lord mayor of London. He was elected to parliament in 1851, and took his seat without taking the Christian oath; as a result he was ejected, which drew prominently to public attention the problem of Jewish parliamentary disabilities.

Salonica [Thessaloníki]. Port in northern Greece on the Aegean. Its Jewish community dates back to classical times. During the Middle Ages, the Jewish population was attacked by the crusaders, and the Jews of Salonica became the focus of messianic movements. Later the textile industry in Salonica attracted refugees from central Europe, and after the Jews were expelled from Spain in 1492 the town became a great center for exiles. In the 16th century Portuguese Marranos settled there; in 1568 the Jewish community was made autonomous. Salonica had a number of rabbinic academies and schools of poetry, and the printing of Hebrew works flourished there. In the 17th century Shabbetai Tzevi was active there, and later the town was the seat of the Judeo-Muslim sect of the Dönmeh.

Salt. In the Bible salt is used as a symbol of the eternal covenant between God and his people (Numbers 18.19; II Chronicles 13.5). According to ritual practice all sacrifices and meal offerings had to be salted before being placed on the altar in the Temple (Leviticus 2.13); salt for this purpose was stored in the Salt Chamber on the north side of the Temple court. After the Temple was destroyed, the meal table in the Jewish home became a symbol of the altar; salt is placed on it for all meals. Bread is to be dipped into salt after the Ha-Motzi blessing. Jewish law stipulates that all meat must be soaked in water and salted before it may be eaten.

Salten, Felix [Zalzmann, Felix] (1869–1945). Austrian novelist and critic. He was born in Budapest. He lived in Vienna, where he was a contributor to the *Neue Freie Presse*. He also wrote plays, essays, and stories, including the famous children's story *Bambi*. His Jewish interests are reflected in his novel *Simson*, and in essays about his visit to Palestine. In 1938 he settled in Hollywood, but after World War II returned to Europe to live in Zurich.

Salting *see* DIETARY LAWS; SALT.

***Salvador, Joseph** (1796–1873). French historian. He was born in Montpellier. He initially studied medicine, but after settling in Paris he began to work on the history of religions. In *Paris, Rome, Jérusalem, ou la question religieuse au 19e siècle* he propounded a universal creed of religion. He also wrote a history of Roman rule in Judea, a study of the institutions of Moses and the Jewish people, and a work about Jesus.

Salvation (Hebrew "yeshuah"). Divine deliverance. The term "yeshuah" (also "teshuah") occurs in biblical and liturgical texts, where it generally refers to deliverance from suffering, oppression, and exile. It is also linked with the concept of messianic redemption.

Samael. Prince of demons. He is identified with Satan and his wife Lilith is the queen of demons. He is mentioned in the Slavonik Book of Enoch and in midrashic and kabbalistic texts.

Samaria [Sebaste; Shomron]. Capital of the northern kingdom of Israel; the name is also sometimes used to refer to the northern kingdom as a political entity. The city Samaria was founded in the 9th century BCE by Omri, on a hill bought from one Shemer (I Kings 16.24). In 721 BCE it fell to Sargon II of Assyria. It served as an administrative center in the Persian period, and became a Macedonian colony in 331 BCE. It was taken by John Hyrcanus at the beginning of the 2nd century BCE, and was later rebuilt by Pompey. Herod the Great renamed the city Sebaste in honor of Augustus Caesar (Sebaste being the Greek form of his name); it was endowed with a new wall, a temple of Augustus, a forum, a basilica, and an acqueduct. During the Roman period it was an important center.

Samaritan. The language of the Samaritans is the Hebrew of the Torah, but it is pronounced differently from the Hebrew of the Ashkenazi and Sephardi rites. Modern Hebrew is a development of the Samaritan language. The old Defter liturgy is in Samaritan Aramaic as is the midrash Memar Marka. The Samaritans also possess a literature in Arabic.

Samaritans. Ancient people descended from the tribes of Ephraim and Manasseh (II Chronicles 34.9; Jeremiah 41.5) who intermarried with non-Israelite colonists (II Kings 17.24–41). Their capital was at Samaria. During the Persian period, Nehemiah foiled the Samaritan ruler

Sanballat, who attempted to obtain political and religious influence over Judah. When his son-in-law was driven from Jerusalem (Nehemiah 13.28), Sanballat built a rival Temple on Mount Gerizim; it was destroyed by John Hyrcanus in the 2nd century BCE. In modern times the Samaritans continue to live in Israel. Their synagogue, housing a Torah that is claimed to date from ancient times, is at Mount Gerizim, where they hold an annual Passover sacrifice.

Sambatyon. Mythical river which ceased to flow on the Sabbath. According to tradition, the Ten Lost Tribes of Israel were transported beyond the Sambatyon. It is referred to in the Targum by Pseudo-Jonathan to Exodus 34.10. The traveler Eldad ha-Dani (9th century) described it, Abraham Abulafia (11th century) wandered in search of it, and Shabbetai Tzevi (16th century) intended to journey there, marry the daughter of Moses, and restore the Ten Tribes to Palestine.

Samekh. 15th letter of the Hebrew alphabet. Its numerical value is 60.

Saminsky, Lazare (1882–1959). American composer, of Russian origin. He studied at the University of St. Petersburg and with Rimsky-Korsakov at the conservatory there. A founder of the Society for Jewish Folk Music, he went to the Caucasus in 1913 as a member of an ethnological expedition. In 1923 he settled in New York, where he became music director of Temple Emanu-El. He wrote symphonies, including *Jerusalem, City of Solomon and Christ*, liturgical choruses, and Hebrew services. His writings include *Music of our Day, Music of the Ghetto and the Bible,* and *Living Music of the Americas*.

Sampter, Jessie (1883–1938). American poet and Zionist writer. She grew up in the US, but later settled in Palestine, where she established evening classes for Yemenite working girls in Jerusalem. In 1920 she helped to organize the country's first camp for Jewish scouts. Subsequently she moved to Reḥovot, where she did social work. In *The Emek* she portrayed kibbutz life in a series of prose poems. She also wrote books, articles, and poems about Zionism and Jewish subjects.

Samson (fl. 12th–11th cent. BCE). Israelite judge, son of Manoah of the tribe of Dan (Judges 13–16). He was a Nazirite of enormous strength, but when his mistress, Delilah, revealed the secret of his strength as lying in his hair, he fell into the hands of the Philistines. His hair was cut, his eyes were put out, and he was forced to turn the prison mill. When he was taken to Gaza to be mocked for the entertainment of Philistines at a festival, his strength returned to him and he destroyed the palace, killing all those assembled there.

Samson ben Abraham of Sens (fl. 12th–13th cent.). French tosaphist. During the first Maimonidean controversy (1202), he spoke on behalf of the French rabbis. He opposed the teachings of Maimonides' *Mishneh Torah* and attacked his view of resurrection. The founder of the academy at Sens, he was one of the leaders of 300 rabbis who settled in Palestine at the beginning of the 13th century. He wrote talmudic commentaries (*Tosaphot Sens*) and liturgical poetry.

Samuel (i) (fl. 11th cent. BCE). Israelite prophet and judge. He was consecrated as a Nazirite by his mother before his birth, and served in the Sanctuary at Shiloh. There he foretold the destruction of the House of Eli. After the death of Eli and his sons, and the defeat of the Israelites by the Philistines, Samuel attempted to restore traditional religious worship. He lived at Ramah and judged the Israelites in Bethel, Gilgal, and Mizpah. Later he acceded to the Israelites' demand for a king and selected Saul. When Saul lost favor with God, Samuel was sent to Bethlehem, where at God's behest he annointed David as Saul's successor (I Samuel 1–16).

Samuel (ii). Biblical book (or, in the Christian tradition, books), part of the group known as the Former Prophets. It relates the history of the Israelites from the end of the period of the judges to the last days of David. It includes the biographies of Samuel (I Samuel 1–7), Saul (I 8–II 3), and David (I 16ff).

Samuel (iii) [Mar Samuel] (fl. 1st–2nd cent.). Babylonian amora. He was born at Nehardea, and became head of the academy there. He was acknowledged the outstanding authority on civil law; his debates with Rav about halakhic problems are recorded in the Talmud. He was also an expert astronomer, whose opinion on questions concerning the Hebrew calendar was often sought. He was on friendly terms with King Sapor I of Persia.

Samuel, Herbert Louis, Viscount (1870–1963). British statesman and philosopher. He was born in Liverpool. He entered parliament in 1902, becoming a privy councilor six years later. He served as postmaster-general and later home secretary. From 1920 to 1925 he was the first High Commissioner for Palestine. He was leader of the Liberal Party in both the House of Commons (1931–5) and the House of Lords (1944–55). He was also president of the Council for German Jewry from 1936, and in 1939 founded the Children's Movement to bring refugee children from Germany to Britain. He wrote various philosophical works.

Samuel, Maurice (1895–1972). American author and translator. He was born in Măcin, Romania, and was taken to England, where he grew up in Manchester. In 1914 he settled in the US. His writings include *You Gentiles, I, the Jew, Jews on Approval, The Great Hatred, The Gentleman and the Jew, Harvest in the Desert, The Second Crucifixion, On the Rim of the Wilderness, The World of Shalom Aleichem, Prince of the Ghetto, Certain People of the Book, Blood Accusation,* and *In Praise of Yiddish.* He translated Hebrew and Yiddish works.

Samuel, Midrash to. Midrash to the Book of Samuel. It was compiled in the 11th century from old midrashim.

Samuel ben Ali ha-Levi (fl. 12th cent.). Babylonian gaon. He was the head of the academy in Baghdad, and engaged in polemics with Maimonides about halakhic issues and about Maimonides' view of the resurrection of the dead.

Samuel ben Avigdor (1720–1793). Lithuanian rabbi. Between 1719 and 1746 he served (in succession) as rabbi of Pruzhany, Zelwa, Volkovysk, and Ruzhany. In 1750 he became rabbi of Vilnius, succeeding his father-in-law, Judah ben Eliezer. In 1777 the community decided to remove him from office because he was suspected of nepotism, but a compromise was reached. In 1782 the controversy broke out again, and the dispute was brought before Jewish and gentile courts. Samuel ben Avigdor was dismissed from his post and Vilnius was left without a rabbi. He was an ardent opponent of the Ḥasidim.

Samuel ben Hophni (fl. 10th–11th cent.). Babylonian gaon. He was appointed gaon of Sura in 997. One of the most prolific writers of the gaonic period, he wrote responsa, talmudic treatises, biblical exegesis, philosophy, theology, and polemics.

Samuel ben Meir [Rashbam] (c. 1085–1175). French biblical and talmudic commentator, grandson of Rashi. He was born in Ramerupt in northern France, and was a disciple of his grandfather. He engaged in sheep-farming and viticulture. His commentaries expound the simple and natural meaning of the Bible and Talmud texts. He completed Rashi's commentary on Bava Batra and Pesaḥim, and his works were quoted by the tosaphists.

Samuel ha-Katan (fl. 1st cent.). Palestinian tanna. His prayer Birkat ha-Minim expresses anathema against Judeo-Christians, sectarians, and informers. It was written at the request of Gamaliel II and was incorporated into the Amidah.

Samuel ha-Nagid *see* SAMUEL IBN NAGRELA.

Samuel ibn Adiya (fl. 6th cent.). Arabian poet. He lived in Tamya in Hejaz, northern Arabia. His poetry is similar to that of other pre-Islamic Arab poets.

Samuel ibn Nagrela [Ha-Nagid; Ibn Nagdela; Ibn Nagrela; Samuel ha-Nagid] (933–1055). Spanish statesman, scholar, and military commander. Born in Córdoba, he was forced to flee the city in 1013 and opened a spice shop in Málaga. He joined the staff of King Habbus, the Berber ruler of Granada, and was later appointed Vizier of Granada. In 1027 he became the nagid of Spanish Jewry. When Habbus died in 1037, Samuel ibn Nagrela supported his son Badis, taking on the administration of the kingdom and command of the armies. He composed poetry, wrote grammatical works, and completed an introduction to the Talmud. He was also a patron of numerous scholars.

Sanballat (fl. 5th cent. BCE). Satrap of Samaria. He held office during the reign of Artaxerxes I of Persia, when Israelite territory was under Persian rule. Sanballat attempted to halt Nehemiah's efforts to rebuild the walls of Jerusalem.

Sanctification *see* KIDDUSH.

Sanctification of the month *see* ROSH ḤODESH.

Sanctification of the name *see* KIDDUSH HA-SHEM; MARTYRS.

Sanctuary (Hebrew "bet ha-mikdash"). The most holy part of a place of worship. The term is applied to the Tabernacle at Shiloh, Jerusalem, and elsewhere. In Shiloh and Jerusalem, the sanctuary contained the Ark; in the Temple at Jerusalem the sanctuary was the Holy of Holies, where the Ark was kept, and the part of a modern synagogue where the Ark is positioned retains the name "sanctuary." The term also denotes a place of refuge for accidental killers. In ancient times, up to the period of the monarchy, this function was fulfilled by the altar (Exodus 21.14; I Kings 1.51; 2.28). Moses set aside six cities of refuge, where accidental killers could flee. The monarchy later took over the responsibility of dealing with such cases.

Sandak *see* CIRCUMCISION.

Sandalphon. Angel. In the kabbalah he plays an important role as the guardian of prayers and of Israel in exile. He is also depicted as the divine messenger at the time of the resurrection.

Sandmel, Samuel (1911–1979). American biblical scholar. He was born in Dayton, Ohio. He served as a Hillel rabbi (Jewish chaplain) at Yale University and was professor of Jewish literature and thought at Vanderbilt University (1949–52). In 1952 he became professor of Bible and Hellenistic literature at the Hebrew Union College. He published studies of Philo and the relationship between Judaism and Christianity.

Sanhedrin ("Assembly") **(i).** In the early rabbinic period an assembly of 71 scholars, which acted as a supreme court and legislature. It was headed by the nasi and an av bet din. Before the year 70 it convened in the Temple chamber called the Hall of Hewn Stone; later it met in various centers. Its duties consisted of proclaiming the new moon, declaring leap years, and reaching decisions on state offenses and questions of Jewish law. It was discontinued before the 4th century. During the 16th century Jacob Caro and Jacob Berab unsuccessfully attempted to revise ordination in Palestine and to establish a new Sanhedrin. Under Napoleon a modern form of the Sanhedrin was created (*see* SANHEDRIN, GREAT).

Sanhedrin ("Assembly") **(ii).** Fourth tractate in the Mishnah order of Nezikin. It deals with courts of justice and judicial procedure, particularly related to criminal law. It also includes a list of sins which exclude a person from entering into the after-life.

Sanhedrin, Great (French "Grand Sanhedrin"). Body of 71 members, convened by Napoleon to confirm the decisions of the Assembly of Jewish Notables. It comprised 45 rabbis and 26 lay members. Under the presidency of David Sintzheim, it met from 9 February to 9 March 1807.

Sannicandro. Town in southern Italy. 23 peasant families adopted Judaism there before migrating to Israel in 1949. Their conversion resulted from the vision of Donato Manduzio, in which he was told to return to the faith of Moses. With his disciples he became a Jew, but he died before the emigration to Israel. The group initially settled at Kephar Alma, but later dispersed.

San Remo Conference. Meeting convened by Great Britain, France, and Italy in San Remo, Italy, in April 1920 to consider problems arising from the Versailles Peace Treaty. The Zionist delegates proposed that the Jews return to Palestine and that Great Britain administer the country; the Palestine mandate was issued as a result of this gathering.

***Santa Maria, Paul de** [Paul of Burgos; Solomon ha-Levi of Burgos] (c. 1352–1435). Spanish churchman. As Solomon ha-Levi he served as a rabbi in Burgos. After converting to Christianity he became bishop of Cartagena, and then of Burgos. He was partly responsible for the anti-Jewish legislation enacted in Castile in 1412. His writings include biblical commentaries.

Santob de Carrion *see* CARRION, SANTOB DE.

Saphir, Yaakov *see* SAPIR, YAAKOV.

Sapir, Pinḥas (1907–1975). Israeli labor leader. He was born in Suwałki, Poland, and in 1924 went to Palestine, where he worked in the citrus groves. He later became head of the Negev settlements' Civil Defense. In 1953 he served as director-general of the ministry of finance, and from 1955 he was minister of commerce and industry. He became minister of finance in 1963, and general secretary of the Israel Labor Party and minister without portfolio in 1965; the following year he was again appointed minister of finance.

Sapir [Saphir], **Yaakov** (1822–1885). Palestinian writer and traveler. He was born in Oshmiany in the province of Vilnius; he was taken to Palestine in 1832 by his parents, who settled in Safed. In 1836 he moved to Jerusalem, where he became a teacher and scribe. In 1857 he traveled to oriental countries as an emissary of the Perushim community to raise funds for the construction of a synagogue. After returning to Jerusalem he recorded his travels in *Even Sappir,* which contains important information about Yemenite Jews.

Sapir, Yoseph (i) (1869–1935). Moldavian Zionist leader. He was born in Kishinev, and became a doctor. A supporter of Ḥibbat Zion, he founded a publishing house, Di Kopeke Bibliotek, to publish Zionist literature. In 1903 he wrote a popular study of Zionism; he also edited a Russian-language Zionist weekly. After the 1917 Revolution, he became chairman of the South Russia Zionist Organization. Following the Bolshevik Revolution he moved to Bessarabia, then to Palestine, where he served as director of a department of the Bikkur Ḥolim hospital in Jerusalem.

Sapir, Yoseph (ii) (1902–1972). Israeli communal worker. He was born in Jaffa. He was active in the Farmers' Federation of Israel and worked for the Pardes citrus fruit company. In 1940 he became mayor of Petaḥ-Tikvah, and later he served as a member of the Knesset; he was minister of transportation (1952–5), and minister of commerce and industry. In 1968 he was elected chairman of the Liberal Party.

Saragossa *see* ZARAGOZA.

Sarah [Sarai] (fl. 19th–16th cent. BCE). Israelite woman, wife of Abraham and mother of Isaac. After many years of barrenness, she gave Abraham her maidservant Hagar, who bore him a son, Ishmael. Later Sarah gave birth to Isaac. She is one of the four matriarchs of Judaism.

Sarajevo Haggadah. Illuminated codex (now in the public library at Sarajevo) of the Passover evening service. It was produced in northern Spain in the 13th century.

Sarasohn, Kasriel Hersch (1835–1905). American newspaper proprietor. He was born in Russia, and was active as a rabbi and merchant before settling in the US in 1871. He founded the weekly *Die New Yorker yiddishe zeitung* and *Die yiddishe gazetten*, which paved the way for the first Yiddish daily paper in the US, the *Yiddishes tageblatt*. He also published a Hebrew weekly (*Ha-Ivri*), and was a founder of HIAS.

Saratov. Town in the Russian SFSR, on the Volga. It was the scene of a ritual murder accusation in 1854. As a result of this affair, a government commission was appointed to investigate the blood libel charge in general. A pogrom took place in the town in 1905.

***Sargon** (fl. 8th cent. BCE). King of Assyria and Babylonia (722–705 BCE). He succeeded Shalmaneser V as King of Assyria and subsequently conquered Babylonia. He then proceeded to subjugate the Medes in the east and Samaria in the west. He was succeeded by Sennacherib.

Saruk, Israel (fl. 16th–17th cent.). Egyptian kabbalist. He created his own version of Isaac Luria's doctrines. From 1594 to 1600 he propounded his views in Italy and founded a school of kabbalists. Subsequently he lived in Ragusa and Salonica. He produced various kabbalistic works.

Sasportas, Jacob (1610–1698). North African rabbi. He was born in Oran, north Africa. He became rabbi of the Tlemcen community, and subsequently wandered throughout Europe. In 1664 he became Ḥakham in London, and later in Amsterdam. He was a critic of Shabbetai Tzevi, and in his *Tzitzat Novel Tzevi* reprinted certain Sabbetaian letters and pamphlets with his responses to their teaching.

Sassoon, David Solomon (i) (1792–1864). Indian businessman and philanthropist. He took over his family's business in Baghdad. In 1828 he went to Bushehr on the Persian Gulf, and later settled in Bombay. There he built a synagogue, contributed to various cultural and welfare organizations, helped to publish a Judeo-Arabic newspaper, and supported Jewish scholarship. In 1863 he built a synagogue in Poona, where he had his summer residence.

Sassoon, David Solomon (ii) (1880–1942). English Hebraist and bibliophile, son of Flora Sassoon. His collection included 1000 Hebrew and Samaritan manuscripts. His writings include *History of the Jews of Baghdad*.

Sassoon, Sir **Edward** (1856–1912).

English communal leader, grandson of David Solomon Sassoon (i). In 1899 he was elected to parliament as a member of the Conservative Party. He was involved in various aspects of English Jewish life.

Sassoon, Flora (1859–1936). English Hebrew scholar, daughter-in-law of David Solomon Sassoon (i). Initially she managed her husband's firm in Bombay; later she settled in England. In 1924 she gave a discourse on the Talmud at Jews College, and subsequently she published an essay on Rashi in the *Jewish Forum*.

Satan. The name of the devil. In the Bible he is referred to as a member of the divine household who functions as God's adversary (Job 1.6). Later he was conceived of as an evil spirit. In rabbinic literature, he is identified with the tempter, the accuser, the Angel of Death, and the arch-enemy of Israel. In kabbalistic texts other names are used for demonic rulers and princes of evil (*see* SAMAEL).

Satanov, Isaac (1732–1804). German Hebrew writer. He was born in Satanov, Podolia, and in 1771 settled in Berlin, where he was the director of a printing press of the Society for the Education of the Young. He wrote a Hebrew–German dictionary and thesaurus, studies of the liturgy, a collection of proverbs, an encyclopedia of arts and sciences, and commentaries on Maimonides' *Guide for the Perplexed* and Judah ha-Levi's *Kuzari*.

Satanower, Mendel *see* LEVIN, MENDEL.

Satire. The use of ridicule or irony to describe folly and wrongdoing in such a way as to expose them to contempt. Satire is found in the Bible, midrash, and Talmud. In medieval Spain it became a fashionable literary genre among Jewish writers, and in northern Europe it was a feature of compositions for Purim. In the modern period it has been used by such writers as Joseph Perl, Isaac Erter, Mordecai D. Brandstätter, J. L. Gordon, Peretz Smolenskin, and Mendele Mocher Sephorim.

Saul (fl. 11th cent. BCE). King of Israel. He was the first king of Israel, selected by Samuel in response to the request of the people for a king. He organized an army, and undertook expeditions against the Philistines, Moabites, Ammonites, and Arameans. Eventually a rift developed between Saul and Samuel (I Samuel 13); Saul persecuted David after his triumph over Goliath and drove him from the country. Saul fell in battle against the Philistines on Mount Gilboa together with three of his sons. (I Samuel 8–II Samuel 3).

Saul of Tarsus *see* PAUL.

Sayings of the Fathers *see* AVOT (i).

Scapegoat *see* AZAZEL.

Schaeffer, Susan Fromberg (b. 1941). American novelist and poet. She was born in Brooklyn, and taught at Brooklyn College. Her novel *Falling* deals with a young Jewish woman who attempts suicide. In *Anya* she tells the story of a victim of the Holocaust.

Schalit, Heinrich (1886–1976). American composer and organist. He was born in Vienna, and lived in Munich, where he was organist at the Munich Liberal synagogue. In 1932 he wrote *Freitagabend Liturgie*, a complete Sabbath Eve Service. He emigrated to the US and served various Jewish congregations. In 1948 he moved to Evergreen, Colorado. His works on Jewish themes include *Chassidic Dances, Builders of Zion, Sabbath Morning Liturgy*, and *Songs of Glory*.

Schapira, Hermann Tzevi (1840–1898). Lithuanian Zionist. He was born in Erswilken, and was initially rabbi and rosh yeshivah in a Lithuanian townlet. He later lived in Kovno, Berlin, and Heidelberg, where he taught mathematics at the university. After the pogroms in Russia in 1881 he joined the Ḥibbat Zion movement, and was a delegate to the

First Zionist Congress in 1897. At the Congress he proposed the foundation of the Jewish National Fund and the Hebrew University.

Schapiro, Israel (1882–1957). American bibliographer, orientalist, and librarian. He was born in Sejny, Poland. From 1907 to 1910 he taught at the Jerusalem Teachers Training College. He then emigrated to the US and in 1913 he was appointed head of the Semitic division of the Library of Congress in Washington; he also lectured on Semitics at George Washington University from 1916 to 1927. He left his post at the Library of Congress in 1944, and in 1950 he settled in Israel. He published studies of Jewish history and bibliography.

Scharfstein, Zevi (1884–1972). American Hebrew educator and publisher, of Ukrainian origin. He devoted himself to educational work and was the head of a Hebrew school in Tarnów, Galicia, from 1900 to 1914. After settling in the US, in 1916 he became an instructor at the Teachers Institute of the Jewish Theological Seminary in New York, where subsequently he became a professor of Jewish education. He published educational texts dealing with Hebrew language and literature, Jewish education, and the Bible.

Schatz, Boris (1867–1932). Palestinian painter and sculptor, of Lithuanian origin. He was born in Varna, in the province of Kovno. He studied sculpture in Paris, and in 1895 became court sculptor to Prince Ferdinand of Bulgaria. At the Zionist Congress of 1905 he proposed the idea of an art school in Palestine. In 1906 he went to Jerusalem, where he established the Bezalel School of Arts and Crafts. He produced sculptures dealing with Jewish religious practices, biblical subjects, and Jewish leaders.

Schechter, Solomon (1847–1915). British rabbinic scholar. He was born in Foscani, Romania. He became tutor in rabbinics to Claude Goldsmid Montefiore in London; in 1890 he became a lecturer in rabbinics at Cambridge University, and two years later reader. He was also professor of Hebrew at University College, London, from 1899. During this time he discovered the Cairo Genizah, the contents of which he took to Cambridge. In 1901 he was appointed president of the Jewish Theological Seminary of America. His writings include *Studies in Judaism* and *Some Aspects of Rabbinic Theology*.

Scheftelowitz, Isidor (1876–1934). British orientalist, of German origin. He was born in Sandersleben, in the Duchy of Anhalt. He worked at the British Museum in London and at the Bodleian Library in Oxford. In 1908 he returned to Germany and until 1926 was a rabbi and teacher of religion in Cologne; in 1923 he became professor of Sanskrit and Iranian philology at Cologne University. He later settled permanently in England and taught at Oxford University. He published studies of Sanskrit and Iranian philology and history, as well as comparative religion.

Scheiber, Alexander (1913–1985). Hungarian rabbi and scholar. He was born in Budapest, and became a professor and director of the Budapest Jewish Theological Seminary. He wrote studies of Jewish history, Jewish literature, comparative folklore, Jewish liturgy, bibliography, and Jewish art.

Schick, Baruch *see* BARUCH OF SHKLOV.

Schiff, David Tevele (fl. 18th cent.). German rabbi. He was born in Frankfurt am Main. He served as maggid in Vienna, head of the bet midrash in Worms, and dayyan in Frankfurt. In 1765 he became rabbi of the Great Synagogue in London. A volume of his responsa, *Leshon Zahav*, was published by his son.

Schiff, Jacob Henry (1847–1920). American financier and philanthropist. He was born in Germany, and went to the US in 1885, where he became head of the banking firm of Kuhn, Loeb, and Co. He was a founder of the American Jewish Committee, and contributed to a wide range of secular and Jewish organizations.

Schiff, Meir [Maharam] (1605–1641). German talmudist. He was born in Frankfurt am Main. He was rabbi of Fulda, where he also directed a yeshivah. His novellae on the Talmud are recorded in *Maharam Schiff.*

Schildkraut, Rudolph (1862–1930). German actor. He was born in Istanbul, and grew up in Romania. He was an actor in Vienna, Hamburg, and Berlin. In 1911 he settled in America, where he appeared in the Yiddish theater; later he acted in German and English productions in the US.

Schiller-Szinessy, Solomon Mayer (1820–1890). British scholar, of German origin. He was born in Altofen. He had a faculty appointment in Hebrew at Eperjes, where he also served the local community as its rabbi. In 1845 he attacked the Reform resolutions brought before the Frankfurt Rabbinical Conference. He was appointed rabbi of Manchester in 1851 and later taught talmudic and rabbinic literature at Cambridge University. His publications include the *Catalogue of Hebrew Manuscripts Preserved in the Cambridge University Library.*

Schindler, Alexander (b. 1925). American Reform leader. He was born in Munich, but left Germany in 1932, eventually settling in the US. He served in various congregations and became president of the Union of American Hebrew Congregations. In 1976 he became chairman of the Conference of Presidents of Major American Jewish Organizations.

***Schindler, Oskar** (1902–1975). German industrialist. During World War II he protected many hundreds of Jews from the Nazis in his factories in Kraków. After the war he settled for a time in South America, but finally returned to Germany. He was recognized and feted as a "righteous gentile" in the State of Israel. Thomas Keneally's novel *Schindler's Ark* tells the story of Schindler's war years.

Schipper, Ignacy (1884–1943). Polish historian and communal worker. He was born in Tarnów, Galicia. He was a member of the General Zionists from 1922. From 1922 to 1927 he served as a deputy in the Polish Sejm. Later he lectured on the history of Jewish economy at the Institute of Jewish Sciences in Warsaw. His writings include *The Economic Conditions of Medieval Polish Jewry, The History of Jewish Economy,* and *History of Jewish Theatrical Art and Drama.*

Schlettstadt, Samuel ben Aaron (fl. 14th century). Alsatian rabbi. He was born in Schlettstadt and became rabbi of Strasbourg. After sentencing an informer to death, he was forced to flee from Strasbourg because of a controversy surrounding the affair. He lived in a castle near Colmar, and later wandered to Babylonia and Jerusalem, before eventually returning to Strasbourg. He wrote an abridgement of *The Book of Mordecai* by Mordecai ben Hillel.

Schlossberg, Joseph (1875–1971). American journalist and trade union leader. He was born in Belorussia and emigrated to the US with his family when he was a child. He worked in the sweatshops of New York and was prominent in the Garment Workers' Union. In 1913 he was elected secretary of the Brotherhood of Tailors and in 1914 was a member of the group which seceded from the United Garment Workers of America to form the Amalgamated Clothing Workers of America. After his retirement in 1940 he devoted himself to community and Zionist affairs.

Schneersohn, Isaac (1879–1969). French communal leader. He was born in Kamenets-Podol'skiy in the Ukraine. He was a crown rabbi in Gorodnya from 1906. Later he settled in France, where he founded the Centre de Documentation Juive Contemporaine during World War II. He also encouraged the establishment of a memorial to the unknown Jewish martyr in Paris; this initiative came to fruition in 1956.

Schneiderman, Harry (1885–1975). American administrator. He was born in Saven, Poland, and went to the US in 1890. From 1909 he was a member of the staff of the American Jewish Committee and from 1914 to 1928 he served as its chief administrator. He was also editor of the *American Jewish Year Book* (1920–48).

Schnitzler, Arthur (1862–1931). Austrian playwright and author. Initially he practiced medicine in Vienna, only later devoting himself to writing. His views about the position of Jews in modern society are found in the play *Professor Bernhardi* and the novel *Der Weg ins Freie.*

Schocken, Gustav Gershom (1912–1990). Israeli publisher. He was the owner and chief editor of *Ha-Aretz* from 1939, and director of the family publishing house in Israel. He served in the Knesset from 1955 to 1959.

Schocken, Shelomoh Salman (1877–1959). German Zionist, publisher, and bibliophile. He was born in Margonin, in the province of Posen. A collector of rare books and manuscripts, he established the Research Institute for Medieval Hebrew Poetry in 1929 in Berlin, which was transferred to Jerusalem in 1936. He also founded a publishing house in Berlin, branches of which were later opened in Tel Aviv and New York. In 1934 he went to Jerusalem, but he eventually settled in the US.

Schoenberg, Arnold (1874–1951). Austrian composer. He was born in Vienna, and held teaching positions in Vienna, Berlin, and Amsterdam. In 1924 he settled in Berlin. He left Germany in 1933, and lived in the US. His compositions include the opera *Moses und Aron,* the Psalm *De profundis* to the original Hebrew words, and two works for chorus, speaker, and orchestra – *Kol Nidre* and *A Survivor from Warsaw.*

Schoffman, Gershon (1880–?). Israeli novelist. He was the editor of literary journals in Poland and Austria, before settling in Palestine in 1938. He published novels and short sketches.

Scholem, Gershom Gerhard (1897–1982). Israeli scholar. He was born in Berlin, and emigrated to Palestine in 1923, where he worked as a librarian in the Judaica collection at the Hebrew University. Subsequently he was appointed professor of Jewish mysticism at the university. His writings include *Major Trends in Jewish Mysticism, The Messianic Idea in Judaism and Other Essays in Jewish Spirituality,* and *From Berlin to Jerusalem.*

Schools *see* EDUCATION.

Schor, Ilya (1904–1961). American artist and silversmith, of Polish origin. He studied in Warsaw and Paris. In 1941 he settled in the US, where he worked as a silversmith, creating religious objects, and as a book illustrator. His art reflects eastern European Jewish life.

Schorr, Joshua Heshel (1818–1895). Galician scholar, editor, and leader of the Haskalah. He was born in Brody, and worked as a merchant there. In 1852 he established the periodical *He-Ḥalutz,* which he edited until 1887. In numerous articles he espoused religious and social reform. He engaged in satirical diatribes against Orthodox Judaism, and scholarly polemics against talmudic and rabbinic law. To the Jewish masses of eastern Europe he became a symbol of heresy.

Schorr, Moses (1874–1941). Polish rabbi and scholar. He was born in Przemyśl, Galicia. He was appointed a lecturer in Jewish religious studies at the Jewish Teachers Seminary in Lemberg in 1899. He eventually became professor of Semitic languages and ancient history at Lemberg University, and later taught at Warsaw University. In 1928 he was one of the founders of the Institute for Jewish Studies, which served as the rabbinical seminary of Poland; he taught there and became the institute's rector. In 1935–8 he was a member of the Polish Sejm. He wrote studies of Polish Jewish history, Semitic history and philology, and the history of Babylonian and Assyrian culture.

Schreiber, Abraham Samuel Benjamin [Ketav Sopher] (1815–1875). Hungarian rabbi, son of Moses Sopher. He succeeded his father as head of the Pressburg yeshivah, and became a leading critic of religious reform. He was known as "Ketav Sopher" after his collection of responsa, Bible commentaries, and talmudic glosses of that name.

Schreiber, Moses see SOPHER, MOSES.

Schreiner, Martin (1863–1926). Hungarian scholar. He was born in Nagyvárad. He was a rabbi in Csurgó (1887–92), and an instructor at the Jewish Teachers Training Institute in Budapest (1892–4). From 1894 to 1902 he was a professor at the Lehranstalt für die Wissenschaft des Judentums in Berlin. He spent the rest of his life in a sanatorium. He wrote studies of the Islamic influence on medieval Jewish thought, interfaith polemics, Jewish philosophy, and Karaism.

Schub, Kasriel *see* CHASANOWITSCH, LEON.

Schulman, Kalman (1819–1899). Polish Hebrew writer. He was born in Stari Bichov, Belorussia, and in 1843 settled in Vilnius, where he worked as a tutor. Later he taught Hebrew language and literature in the high school attached to the state rabbinical school. He eventually devoted himself to literary work. His writings, including translations, were intended to spread the Haskalah. He also published a history of Palestine and its environs.

Schulman, Samuel (1864–1955). US Reform rabbi. He was born in Russia, and went to the US as a child. He served as a rabbi in Helena (Montana), Kansas City, and at Temple Emanu-El in New York. He served as president of the Central Conference of American Rabbis and the Association of Reform Rabbis of New York.

Schulmann, Eleazar (1837–1904). Lithuanian Hebrew writer. He was born in Salantai, Lithuania, and lived in Odessa and Kiev. Financially independent, he devoted himself to research, publishing studies of Yiddish language and literature.

***Schürer, Emil** (1844–1910). German Protestant scholar. He wrote a history of the Jewish people from the Hellenistic period to 135.

Schutzjude (German: "protected Jew"). Term used in the 17th–18th centuries in Germany to refer to Jews who were given special privileges, such as being permitted to live outside the ghetto.

Schwab, Moise (1839–1918). French scholar. He was born in Paris. He served as secretary to Solomon Munk (1857–66), then from 1869 worked at the Bibliothèque nationale. He translated the Palestinian Talmud into French, and described the Hebrew manuscripts and incunabula in the library of the Alliance Israélite Universelle and other libraries. His writings include *Abravanel et son époque* and *Histoire des Israélites*.

Schwabe, Mosheh David (1889–1956). Israeli scholar, of German origin. He was born in Halle. After World War I he was head of the department of schools in the Lithuanian ministry of Jewish affairs. In 1925 he settled in Jerusalem, where he taught at the Hebrew University; he served there as dean of the faculty of humanities and rector. He was an authority on Greek and Greco-Jewish inscriptions.

Schwartz, Delmore (1913–1966). American poet, author, and critic. He was born in Brooklyn. He became a member of the literary-political group centered on the journals *Partisan Review* and *Commentary*. From 1940 to 1947 he taught at Harvard and Princeton universities. His writings include *Genesis*, which depicts the Jewish immigrant's experience of America.

Schwartz, Joseph J. (1899–1974). American communal leader and scholar. He was born in Russia, and went to the US in 1907. During World War II he negotiated the rescue of Jews from Germany and the occupied territories. After the war he directed the transfer of Jews to Israel from Europe, North Africa, and the Middle East; he also helped Jewish refugees emigrate to the US, Canada, and Latin America. He served as director-general of the American Jewish Joint Distribution Committee, vice-chairman of the United Jewish Appeal, and vice-president of the State of Israel Bond Organization. He published studies of Semitics and Jewish affairs.

Schwartz, Maurice (1890–1960). American Yiddish actor. He was born in the Ukraine, and went to the US in 1901. In 1918 he launched the Jewish Art Theater in New York. He subsequently acted throughout the Yiddish-speaking diaspora. In 1960 he went to Israel to establish a Yiddish art center.

Schwarz, Adolf (1846–1931). Hungarian rabbi and scholar. He served as a rabbi at Karlsruhe from 1875, then in 1893 he became head of the Israelitsch-Theologische Lehranstalt in Vienna. His writings include studies of talmudic hermeneutics.

Schwarz, Joseph (1804–1865). Palestinian rabbi and Palestinographer. He was born in Floss, Bavaria, and settled in Jerusalem in 1833. His publications include maps of Palestine and a descriptive geography of the country.

Schwarzbard, Shalom (1886–1938). Russian Yiddish poet. He was born in Izmail, Bessarabia. He was active in the revolutionary movement of 1905 and in 1906 fled from Russia to Paris, where he worked as a watchmaker. In World War I he served in the French Foreign Legion, but in 1917 he returned to Russia, where he joined the Red Guard. In 1920 he went on a mission to Paris to assassinate Simon Petlyura, who had carried out pogroms in the Ukraine. His autobiography *Inem loyf fun yoren* describes his experiences.

Schwarz-Bart, André (b. 1928). French author. He was born in Metz, and served in the Free French army before the Liberation. His novel *The Last of the Just* reinterprets the Jewish legend of the 36 righteous men ("lamed vav") in terms of the martyrdom of European Jewry.

Schwarzbart, Isaac Ignacy (1888–1961). Polish Zionist leader. He was born in Chrzanów, Galicia. He was the founder in 1929 of the World Union of General Zionists and served as its chairman. In 1938 he helped to establish a committee to coordinate the activities of the Zionists in western Galicia and Silesia. In the same year he was elected to the Polish Sejm. During World War II (1940–45) he was a member of the Polish government-in-exile in Paris and London. From 1946 he lived in the US, where he was active in the World Jewish Congress. His memoir *Between the Two World Wars* describes Jewish life in Kraków.

Schwarzman, Lev Isakavich *see* SHESTOV, LEV.

Schweid, Eleazar (b. 1929). Israeli scholar. He was born in Jerusalem, and became a professor at the Hebrew University. He published studies in the field of Jewish philosophy and Hebrew literature.

Sciaky, Leon (1893–1958). Greek-American writer. He was born in Salonica, and went to New York in 1915. His novel *Farewell to Salonika* deals with the Jewish community of his birthplace.

Science. Within certain Orthodox circles all non-fundamentalist biblical criticism, theories of evolution, and other scientific views are considered heretical. Non-Orthodox branches of Judaism, however, have generally accepted the authority of the sciences. There have been many eminent Jewish scientists.

Science of Judaism *see* WISSENSCHAFT DES JUDENTUMS.

Scopus, Mount *see* MOUNT OF OLIVES.

***Scott, Charles Prestwich** (1846–1932). English journalist. He was born in Bath. He was the editor of the *Manchester Guardian* and later a member of parliament (1895–1906). He helped Chaim Weizmann in his dealings with the British government over the implementation of the Balfour Declaration.

Scouts. International youth organization (properly the Scout Association) founded by Lord Baden-Powell in England in 1908. Jewish youth movements adopted the current organizational structures in their various countries. The Israeli scouting organization was based on the Baden-Powell scouting program but emphasized in addition the values of self-management and pioneering labor. There are Jewish members of scout troops throughout the world; but there are also exclusively Jewish scouting organizations, affiliated to the worldwide movement, in France (Éclaireurs Israélites), Switzerland, Italy, and Mexico, besides Israel.

Scribe (Hebrew "sopher"). Originally one who copies documents, but in Jewish usage a recognized scholar of the law. Under the Judean monarchy the king's scribe was the highest official of his household. Ezra is depicted as the "scribe" (that is, learned expert) of the law of the God of Heaven (Ezra 7.6). In the Book of Ecclesiasticus the scribe is described as a literate man, occupied with the study of the law. The New Testament links the scribes with the Pharisees. In the Mishnah the phrase "words of the scribe" refers to post-biblical legislation. Rabbinic sources reserve the term for those who write Torah scrolls and preserve textual traditions. The tractate Sopherim in the Talmud describes the rules for writing sacred documents.

Script. The ancient Israelites adopted alphabetic script from the Canaanites in the 12th or 11th century BCE; the Gezer Calendar from the late 10th century BCE is the earliest known Hebrew inscription. In the Talmud the early script is called "ketav ivri" (Hebrew script). After the Babylonian exile a square script, based on Aramaic, came into use; the Talmud refers to this as "ketav ashuri" (Assyrian script). Most talmudic scholars hold that Scripture was originally written in the ancient script, but was rewritten by Ezra. Detailed regulations are prescribed in the Talmud as to the ink and parchment to be used for writing sacred scrolls, as well as the writing to be employed. From the square script other cursive scripts later developed. *See also* ALPHABET; WRITING.

Scripture *see* BIBLE.

Scroll of the Law *see* LAW, SCROLL OF THE.

Scrolls, Five *see* FIVE SCROLLS.

Seal. A device impressed on wax or some other substance, fixed to a document as a mark of authentication. The Bible refers to the process of sealing, and numerous seals from the period of the monarchy have been discovered. They were used not only for documents but also to secure and attest the contents of jars. Seals continued to be used, often in the form of signet rings. During the Middle Ages they frequently bore the name of a person or his emblem. Jewish communities also had their own seals.

Sea of Galilee *see* GALILEE, SEA OF.

Sebaste *see* SAMARIA.

Second day of festivals. Before the days of scientific prediction of the moon's movements, the regulation of the calendar depended on the verbal testimony of witnesses, who came to the Sanhedrin in Jerusalem to report that they had seen the new moon. Messengers were then sent out every month to announce this; but, because it took some time to reach communities in the diaspora, there was some doubt as to which of two days was the first of the month, and thus which day marked the actual beginning of a festival. As a precaution, in the diaspora, two days were observed in celebrating the appearance of the new moon and in keeping holy days; this practice continues to the present day.

Second Passover *see* PASSOVER, SECOND.

Second Temple *see* TEMPLE (i).

Sects *see* CONTROVERSIES, RELIGIOUS. *See also* DÖNMEH; ESSENES; HEMEROBAPTISTS; PHARISEES; SADDUCEES; THERAPEUTAE.

Sedarot *see* SIDRAH.

Seder (*lit.* "order"). Ceremony that takes place on the first night of Passover in the home. The structure of the ritual is based on the Mishnah and its essential features are: the recitation of the Kiddush prayer, the reading of the Haggadah, the partaking of the special foods matzah and maror, the eating of the festival meal, the drinking of four cups of wine at specified intervals, the recitation of the Hallel, and the singing of songs.

Seder Eliyahu *see* TANNA DE-VE ELIYAHU.

Seder Olam Rabbah ("Major order"). The earliest post-biblical chronicle. It contains a chronological record from the Creation to the time of Alexander the Great (4th century BCE). It also includes an appendix that extends the account to Simeon Bar Kokhba (d. 135).

Seder Olam Zuta ("Minor order"). Chronology dating from the 8th century CE. It lists the names and dates of 50 generations from Adam to Jehoiakim, and those of 39 exilarchs in Babylonia from Jehoiakim to Zerubbabel.

Sedom *see* SODOM.

Seer *see* PROPHET.

Segal, George (b. 1924). American sculptor. He was born in New York. He began as a painter, then integrated free-standing plaster sculptures with his paintings, and eventually worked in sculptural forms alone. Some of his works refer to his Jewish background, and others to biblical subjects. He has also produced sculpture based on the Holocaust.

Segal, Lore (b. 1928). American novelist. She was born in Vienna. She taught creative writing at the University of Illinois at Chicago Circle. Her novel *My First American* explores the experiences of Jews and blacks. She has also written a collection of Bible stories, *The Book of Adam to Moses*.

Segal, Mosheh Tzevi Hirsch (1876–1968). Israeli Hebraist and Bible scholar. He was born in Myshad, Lithuania. He was a journalist in London, then in 1901 moved to Oxford, where he was minister to the Jewish congregation. In 1918 he went to Palestine as a member of the Zionist Commission. He settled there and became professor of Bible and Semitic Languages at the Hebrew University. His writings include *Grammar of Mishnaic Hebrew*, *Introduction to the Hebrew Bible*, and *The Pentateuch: its Composition and Authorship*.

Segall, Lasar (1891–1957). Brazilian

painter, of Lithuanian origin. He was born in Vilnius, and settled in Brazil in 1923. His works on Jewish themes include *Pogrom, Ship of Emigrants,* and *Concentration Camp.*

Segol. Sign indicating the short "e" vowel in Hebrew. It consists of three dots arranged in an inverted triangle, and is placed beneath the consonant preceding the vowel sound.

Segovia. Town in Castile, central Spain. Its Jewish community dates back to the 10th century. Segovia was an important Jewish center until the 14th century, but in 1391 a massacre of Jews there drove many into baptism. In 1410 a charge of desecration of the host led to the execution of the eminent physician Meir Alguades and the confiscation of the principal synagogue. During the expulsion of the Jews from the town in 1492 many took refuge in the surrounding hills.

Segrè, Joshua ben Zion (c. 1705–c. 1797). Italian dayyan and rabbi. He was born in Casale Monferrato. He was engaged as a children's tutor in Scandiano, but pretended to be a fully qualified rabbi, claiming to have graduated from the Mantua yeshivah; this led to a dispute with the rabbis under whose authority he worked. His *Asham Talui* is a polemic against Christianity.

Seixas, Gershom Mendes (1746–1816). American communal leader. He was the first Jewish minister to have been born in the US. In 1768 he became ḥazzan of Congregation Shearith Israel in New York. During the American Revolution, he moved to Connecticut, and then to Philadelphia, but in 1784 he returned to New York. He was one of the 13 clergy to participate in George Washington's inauguration.

Sekhirut *see* HIRING AND LETTING.

Selah. Word found in the Book of Psalms. Its meaning is unclear. It has been interpreted as meaning "forever"; as indicating a change in rhythm or tune when the psalm is chanted; as a eulogistic response to the words of the psalm; and as an acrostic of the Hebrew phrase meaning "return to the beginning."

***Selden, John** (1584–1654). English parliamentarian, lawyer, and antiquarian. He wrote studies of Jewish subjects, including an attempt to relate natural and international law to the Noachian laws. He also wrote a historical study of the Jews of England.

Seleucids. Hellenistic royal dynasty. It was founded by Seleucus Nicator, one of Alexander the Great's generals, and flourished from the 4th to the 1st centuries BCE. The Seleucids governed a vast empire comprising much of Asia Minor.

Self-defense. The law regarding the killing of a burglar in the act of breaking in (Exodus 22.1–2) is interpreted in the Talmud as the basis for its theory of justifiable homicide. Where a criminal act gives rise to a direct threat to life or reasonable certainty of such a threat, it is permitted to kill the criminal in self-defense or in defense of another. This course of action, however, should be adopted as a last resort. Moreover if the attacker is killed without an attempt's having been made to restrain him, his death is viewed as murder, though this is punishable only by an act of God.

Seligmann, Caesar (1860–1950). German leader of Liberal Judaism. He was born in Landau, and became the preacher of the Liberal synagogue in Hamburg in 1889. He then officiated as a rabbi in Frankfurt am Main (1902–39). In 1910 he published a two-volume prayerbook, and from 1910 to 1922 he edited the periodical *Liberales Judentum.* In 1929 he helped to publish the unified prayerbook, which included traditional and newly composed Liberal prayers. Among his other publications are a collection of lectures and a history of the

Reform movement. He moved to London in 1939.

Seligson, Esther (b. 1942). Mexican novelist. She was editor of the bi-monthly review of Jewish culture *Aqui estamos* in Oaxaca. Some of her writings deal with Jewish subjects.

Seliḥot ("penitential prayers"; *sing.* "seliḥah"). Prayers recited during the high holy day period and on fast days. Some date to the 1st century, but most were written by the Hebrew poets of Spain or by the liturgical poets of the 12th and 13th centuries. They deal with Jewish suffering, martyrdom, the destruction of the Temple, human weakness, confession, and God's forgiveness and mercy.

Semag *see* MOSES BEN JACOB OF COUCY.

Semaḥot *see* EVEL RABBATI.

Semaḥot of Rabbi Ḥiyya *see* EVEL ZUTRATI.

Semak *see* ISAAC BEN JOSEPH OF CORBEIL.

Semikhah see ORDINATION.

Séminaire Israélite de France. Rabbinical seminary, founded at Metz in 1829 as the École Rabbinique de France. It was transferred to Paris in 1859.

Semites. The name given to a group of ancient peoples originating in the Arabian peninsula. They settled in various areas from the Mediterranean coast to the mountains of Iran and Armenia. They included the Arabs, Hebrews, Phoenicians, Arameans, Babylonians, and Assyrians. The Bible attributes the origin of these peoples to Noah's son Shem.

Semitic languages. A branch or subfamily of the Afro-Asiatic family of languages, comprising various groupings. Eastern Semitic consists of Old Akkadian, Babylonian, and Assyrian; Northwestern Semitic of Amorite and Ugaritic; Canaanite of Hebrew, Phoenician, Punic, and Moabite; Aramaic of Old Aramaic, Imperial Aramaic, Biblical Aramaic, Nabatean, Palmyrenian, Palestinian Jewish Aramaic, Samaritan Aramaic, Christian Palestinian Aramaic, Jewish Babylonian Aramaic, Mandean, Modern Syriac, and Modern Aramaic of Malula; and Southern Semitic of Proto-Arabic, Arabic, ancient and modern southern Arabian languages, ancient Ethiopic, Amharic, Tigre, Tigrinya, Harari, Gafat Gurage, and Agobba. The word "Semitic" derives from the name of Noah's son Shem, mentioned in Genesis 10; it was first used by A. L. Schlözer in 1781.

Senator, Ronald (b. 1926). English composer. He was born in London. He became professor of music at London University, the University of Europe, and the Guildhall School of Music. His works on Jewish themes include *Kaddish for Terezin*.

***Senior, Abraham** (c. 1412–c. 1493). Spanish courtier. During the reign of Henry IV he was chief tax officer of Castile. From 1476 he was rabbi to the Jews of Castile and the assessor of Jewish taxes. He was appointed treasurer of the Hermandad, a military organization, in 1488. He eventually converted to Christianity.

***Sennacherib** (fl. 8th–7th cent. BCE). King of Assyria and Babylonia (705–681 BCE), son of Sargon II. He marched against the rebels of Syro-Palestine in 701 BCE, conquering various cities including Lachish. From there he sent a mission to Hezekiah to persuade him to surrender (II Kings 18.13–19.37; Isaiah 36–37); but although Sennacherib besieged Jerusalem, he failed to take the city and returned to Assyria.

Sepharad. Originally the name of a region of Asia, possibly north of Palestine, where exiles were deported after the destruction of the first Temple (Obadiah 1.20). In the medieval period, the name was used for Spain, and the term "Sephardim" was given to the Jews who resided there.

Sephardic Jewish Brotherhood of America. American welfare organization founded in New York in 1947. It acts as a coordinating body for Sephardi groups in the US, promoting the welfare and unification of its members.

Sephardim. One of the two main divisions of Jewry in the diaspora. The word comes from the Hebrew SEPHARAD, the name, originally, of an area to which the Jews were deported after the destruction of the first Temple. It was first used in the Middle Ages of the Jews of Spain; after the expulsion from Spain in 1492 the Sephardim settled in north Africa, Italy, Egypt, Palestine, Syria, the Balkans, and the Turkish Empire. Subsequently these communities were reinforced by refugees from Portugal. Sephardi congregations were established later in Amsterdam, London, Hamburg, Bordeaux, Bayonne, western Europe, the West Indies, and North America. In Mediterranean countries the Sephardim spoke Judeo-Spanish (Ladino). The Sephardim are distinguished from the Ashkenazim; aspects of liturgical practice and the pronunciation of Hebrew differ in the two groups.

Sepher *see* DEED.

Sepher Ḥasidim ("Book of the pious"). Devotional work of the medieval German religious movement known as Ḥaside Ashkenaz. It incorporates the teachings of Samuel ben Kalonymus he-Ḥasid, his son Judah ben Samuel he-Ḥasid of Regensburg, and Eleazar ben Judah of Worms. It consists of three sections dealing with piety, humility, and the fear of God. It was intended to serve as a guide to everyday religious conduct, stressing asceticism, humility, and strict ethical standards.

Sepher ha-Yashar *see* JASHAR, BOOK OF.

Sepher Mishlei *see* PROVERBS.

Sepher Mitzvot Gadol *see* MOSES BEN JACOB OF COUCY.

Sepher Mitzvot Katan see ISAAC BEN JOSEPH OF CORBEIL.

Sepher Torah *see* LAW, SCROLL OF THE.

Sepher Yetzirah ("Book of Creation"). Early Babylonian or Palestinian mystical work, dating from the 3rd-6th centuries. According to this treatise, the cosmos is derived from the Hebrew alphabet and the ten sephirot (manifestations of God). Knowledge of these mysteries, including significant letter combinations, allegedly conferred magical powers on the initiated. Thus the golem (an artificially created human being) was created by means of formulae from this volume. It greatly influenced later kabbalists, and from the gaonic period various commentaries were written on it.

Sephirat ha-Omer *see* OMER, COUNTING OF THE.

Sephirot. Kabbalistic term meaning the emanations or manifestations of God; ten sephirot are referred to. The concept, colored by Neoplatonism and Gnostic thought, was used to explain how a transcendent, inaccessible Godhead (En Soph) can relate to the world. In kabbalistic literature the nature of the sephirot is a matter of controversy. In the kabbalah a distinction is frequently made between the first three sephirot (regarded as the highest) and the remaining (lower) seven. The ten sephirot are: (1) the Supreme Crown; (2) Wisdom; (3) Intelligence; (4) Love; (5) Power; (6) Beauty; (7) Endurance; (8) Majesty; (9) Foundation; (10) Kingdom.

Sephorim, Mendele Mocher *see* ABRAMOWITSCH, SHALOM JACOB.

Sepphoris [Tzippori]. Ancient city in Galilee, the capital of Galilee during the second Temple period. Favoring peace with the Romans, its inhabitants surrendered in 67. It was the seat of the patriarchate from the time of Judah ha-Nasi until the 3rd century, when the patriarchs moved to Tiberias.

Septuagint (from Latin "septuaginta": 70). The principal Greek translation of the Bible (including the Apocrypha). According to tradition, the Pentateuch was translated into Greek at the command of Ptolemy II in the 3rd century BCE by 70 Jewish scholars, each of whom worked independently. The manuscripts of the Septuagint comprise the Great Codices (including the Alexandrinus, the Sinaiticus, and the Vaticanus) and the numerous Minor Codices.

Seraph. Supernatural being, depicted variously as a winged human or serpent-like figure. In Isaiah 6.12 the seraphim are members of the celestial court surrounding the divine throne in the Temple. In medieval literature they comprise one of the 10 hierarchical classes of angels.

Serekh. Word meaning "rule" or "order," used in the Dead Sea Scrolls.

Serene [Severus] (fl. 8th cent.). Syrian pseudo-messiah. He declared himself the Messiah in Syria in about 720, and attracted numerous followers. He was put to death by the Muslim authorities.

Sereni, Enzo (1905–1944). Italian pioneer of settlement in Palestine. He was born in Rome, and was one of the first in Italy to support settlement in Palestine. He went to Palestine in 1927, and worked on an orange grove. Initially a pacifist, he joined the British army during World War II; as a parachutist, he was dropped in occupied Italy, captured, and killed. His writings include *Arabs and Jews in Palestine* and *The Holy Spring*.

Serkes, Joel ben Samuel [Baḥ] (1561–1640). Polish codifier. He served as a rabbi in Polish and Lithuanian communities. His *Bayit Ḥadash* is a commentary on the *Arbaah Turim* of Jacob ben Asher. He also wrote responsa and talmudic glosses.

Serlin, Yoseph (b. 1906). Israeli politician, of Polish origin. He emigrated to Palestine in 1933 and was a founder of the General Zionist Party there. Elected to the Knesset in 1946, he served as deputy speaker (1951–2) and minister of health (1952–5).

Sermon. An address of religious instruction or exhortation, usually delivered in a service of worship. The institution of the sermon goes back to the time of the prophets. During the second Temple period, there was felt to be a need for a system of teaching and preaching, and this was provided by scholars, who read from the Torah and the prophetic books on Sabbaths and festivals. One method of teaching involved the translation of the biblical text into the Aramaic vernacular. After the destruction of the Temple, discourses in the form of midrashim were delivered in the synagogue. Eventually the sphere of the sermon was increased to include discourses for special events. During the medieval period preaching played an increasingly important role in Jewish life; in the 11th century professional preachers were known as "darshanin." The sermon became central to synagogue worship in western Europe, but in eastern Europe it was increasingly replaced by an ethical discourse preached by a "maggid" (official or itinerant preacher). In the modern world, the sermon has become a prominent feature of the synagogue service. *See also* HOMILETICS.

Serp *see* SEYMISTS.

Serpent. Literary or dialect word for "snake." In Genesis 3 the serpent persuaded Eve to eat from the Tree of Knowledge. As a consequence of its role in the fall of man, God condemned it to a state of enmity with humans. Moses made a brass serpent (Nehushtan), which cured people from snake bite; it was destroyed by Hezekiah because the Israelites worshipped it (II Kings 18.4). In Leviticus the serpent is forbidden as food (Leviticus 19.26).

Servant of the Lord. Title used in the Book of Isaiah, and variously interpreted. According to Isaiah 42.2–4, the Servant was chosen by God to convey divine truth to gentiles. In Isaiah 52.12–13 he is described as suffering vicariously. The Servant of the Lord has been variously identified as the Jewish people, the Messiah, the prophet Isaiah, and Jesus.

Seter, Mordekai (b. 1910). Israeli composer. He was born in Novorossisk, Russia. He went to Palestine in 1926, and taught at the Israel Academy of Music in Tel Aviv. His compositions include *Sabbath Cantata, Tikkun Hatzot,* and *The Legend of Judith.*

Seth. Third son of Adam. According to the Bible, he lived 912 years.

Setzer, Samuel Hirsch (1882–1962). American Yiddish and Hebrew journalist, of Polish origin. He was the literary editor of Naḥum Sokolov's Hebrew journal *Ha-Tzephirah* in Warsaw. Later he served as editor-in-chief of the Warsaw daily newspaper *Der Telegraph.* He lived in New York from 1912 to 1960, when he settled in Israel. He wrote studies of the German socialist writer Lassalle, Judah ha-Levi, the Baal Shem Tov, and Naḥman of Bratzlav.

Seudah shelishit. Third meal. During the Talmudic period it was customary for Jews to eat two meals a day. On the Sabbath, however, the rabbis stipulated that three meals should be eaten. Among the Polish Ḥasidim, the seudah shelishit was a major feature of religious life; at the table of the tzaddik the faithful would spend hours listening to his discourse and singing hymns.

Seudat havraah. Meal for mourners. It was traditionally provided by neighbors for the family and friends of one who had died on their return from the funeral.

Seudat maphseket. Last meal taken before the fasts of the Day of Atonement and the Ninth of Av.

Seudat mitzvah ("feast of the commandment"). Meal eaten after religious ceremonies and celebrations, such as weddings, circumcisions, and the redemption of the first-born, or to mark the completion of the study of a treatise of the Talmud.

Seven Benedictions (Hebrew "Sheva Berakhot"). The benedictions recited at the wedding ceremony after the bridegroom places the ring on the bride's finger. The first benediction is said over a cup of wine; the following three praise God; the fifth celebrates the restoration of Zion; the sixth refers to the joy of the first couple in Paradise; and the seventh thanks God for having created joy and gladness, and for the bride and bridegroom. During the seven days following the marriage, the Seven Benedictions are recited during grace after every meal.

Seventeenth of Tammuz *see* SHIVAH ASAR BE-TAMMUZ.

Severus *see* SERENE.

Seville. Port in south-west Spain. Jews lived there during the Roman period, and by the 11th century there was an important Jewish community in the town. In 1391 the preaching of Archdeacon Ferrand Martinez in Seville led to a wave of massacres. The Inquisition began its operations in Seville in 1480, and the town's Jews were expelled in 1483.

Sevoraim ("Reasoners"). Name given to Babylonian scholars of the period c. 500–700 (between the amoraim and the geonim).

Sexual intercourse. Jewish law stipulates that sexual relations must take place only within marriage. Homosexuality, prostitution, and various illicit sexual unions (*see* MAMZER) are forbidden. It is the duty of men to marry and procreate. Any form of physical contact between a man and his wife is forbidden during the menstrual period and for seven days afterward; the wife must take a ritual bath before sexual relations are resumed. Refusal of sexual relations by either partner is a ground for divorce in Jewish law.

Seymists. Name given to the members of the eastern European Jewish political party Serp. Derived from the Vozrozhdenia socialist party, the Seymists formed their own party in 1905, advocating a non-Zionist ideology of diaspora nationalism. In 1917 it merged with the Jewish Socialist Zionist Party, but later joined the communists.

Sforno, Obadiah ben Jacob (c. 1470–c. 1550). Italian biblical commentator. He was born at Cesena, Sforno. He taught Hebrew to Johannes Reuchlin in Rome (1498–1500). After living in various cities, he settled in Bologna, where he helped to reestablish a Hebrew printing house and organize the Jewish community. He founded and ran a bet midrash there. He wrote commentaries on the Pentateuch, Songs of Songs, Ecclesiastes, Psalms, Job, Jonah, Habbakuk, and Zechariah. He also wrote a commentary on Avot, a number of grammatical works, and a philosophical treatise.

Shaatnez. Fabric made of a mixture of wool and flax (the word is probably of Egyptian origin). The Bible prohibits the wearing of this material (Leviticus 19.19; Deuteronomy 22.11).

Shabbat (i) *see* SABBATH.

Shabbat ("Sabbath") **(ii).** First tractate in the Mishnah order of Moed. It sets out the general rules of the Sabbath and its observance, the 39 categories of work, and the regulations concerning the Sabbath Lamp.

Shabbat ha-Gadol *see* SABBATH, GREAT.

Shabbas goy (Yiddish). Non-Jew employed by Jews on the Sabbath to carry out tasks that they themselves are forbidden to perform.

Shabbazi, Shalom (fl. 17th cent.). Yemenite Jewish poet. He lived in a period of persecution and messianic expectations among the Yemenite Jews. According to legend he was a tzaddik and miracle worker. His poetry deals with exile and redemption, the Jewish people and God, wisdom and ethics, the Torah, and the after-life.

Shabbetaians *see* SABBETAIANS.

Shabbetai ben Meir ha-Cohen [Cohen, Shabbetai; Shak] (1621–1662). Lithuanian rabbi. He was born in Amstivov near Vilkaviškis, and became dayyan in the bet din of Moses Lima in Vilnius. He published *Siphte Kohen*, a commentary on *Yoreh Deah*. The alternative name, Shak, by which he was known, is derived from the initials of the title *Siphte Kohen*.

Shabbetai Tzevi (1626–1676). Turkish scholar and pseudo-messiah. He was born in Smyrna. He devoted himself to talmudic and kabbalistic studies. In 1665 he met Nathan of Gaza, who recognized him as the Messiah and became his prophet; in December of that year Shabbetai proclaimed himself the Messiah in the synagogue at Smyrna. The Jewish world was seized with enthusiasm. He went to Constantinople in 1666 to claim his kingdom from the sultan, but he was arrested and imprisoned at Abydos, which his followers regarded as the Migdal Oz ("Tower of strength") of the kabbalah. Eventually Shabbetai was summoned to appear before the sultan and adopted Islam to save his life. His apostasy caused great dismay, but a number of his followers (Sabbetaians) believed that his conversion was part of a divine plan.

Shabtai, Jacob (1934–1981). Israeli novelist and short story writer. His most famous work, *Zikron Devanim*, describes nine months in the protagonist's life, beginning and ending with a death;

despite its somber theme it is notable for its wit and penetrating insight.

Shadal *see* LUZZATTO, SAMUEL DAVID.

Shadar *see* MESHULLAḤ.

Shaddai ("Almighty"). One of the NAMES OF GOD, used in the Bible. It later appeared in kabbalistic formulae and on amulets. It is also frequently inscribed on the mezuzah.

Shadkhan ("negotiator"). Marriage broker. The shadkhan negotiated marriages, settlements, and dowries. The institution dates back to antiquity, and in the Middle Ages played an important role in Jewish life; it is still part of Jewish social custom in some communities.

Shaffer, Peter (b. 1925). English dramatist. He was born in Liverpool, and first worked as a coalminer. He spent some time in the US, where he worked at the New York Public Library. Later he was active as a literary and music critic in London. His play *The Salt Land* is set in a kibbutz in Israel. In *Yonadah* he adapted *The Rape of Tamar* by Dan Jacobson.

Shah (Yiddish). Exclamation, ordering someone to be quiet.

Shaham, Natan (b. 1925). Israeli author. He was born in Tel Aviv. He served with the Palmaḥ during the War of Independence, and later joined kibbutz Bet Alpha. He wrote fiction, plays, and stories for children.

Shahar, David (b. 1926). Israeli novelist. He was born in Jerusalem, and took part in the War of Independence. A number of his stories deal with the childhood recollections of a narrator who lived in Jerusalem under British Mandatory rule. Between 1969 and 1986 he published a series of five novels, *The Palace of Shattered Vessels*.

Shaharit [morning service]. The service of morning prayer. It consists of: the dawn benedictions, biblical verses related to the sacrificial system, and passages of rabbinicial writings for study; the Pesuke de-Zimrah with their benedictions; the Shema with its benedictions; the Amidah; the Taḥanun; and concluding prayers, including the Alenu. On Mondays, Thursdays, and occasions the Taḥanun is followed by the reading of the law, but on Sabbaths and festivals, when the Taḥanun is not recited, the reading of the law takes place after the Amidah.

Shahin (fl. 14th cent.). Persian poet. He lived in Shiraz. He based his work on the Bible; his *Sepher Sharḥ Shahin al ha-Torah* is a poetical paraphrase of the Pentateuch.

Shahn, Ben (1898–1969). American painter and graphic artist. He was born in Kovno, Lithuania. He settled in the US, but later traveled to Europe and North Africa. He made an early series of paintings based on the Dreyfus Affair. His later works include *Concentration Camp* and *This is Nazi Brutality*. He also produced works based on Hebrew letter forms and commissions for the decoration of synagogues.

Shaikevitch [Shomer]**, Nahum Meir** (1849–1905). Russian Yiddish novelist and dramatist. He was born in Nesvizh, Belorussia, and settled in Pinsk. He wrote Hebrew short stories and longer narratives, as well as about 200 Hebrew lyrics. Later he moved to Vilnius, where he wrote novels of suspense, and plays for the Yiddish stage. His plays were produced in the US, where he settled in 1889.

Shak *see* SHABBETAI BEN MEIR HA-COHEN.

Shaked, Gershon (b. 1929). Israeli scholar. He was born in Vienna, and settled in Palestine with his family at an early age. From 1959 he taught Hebrew literature at the Hebrew University, where he became professor in 1978. He has published various studies of Hebrew literature and drama.

Shaliaḥ. Emissary. The term (which is a synonym for MESHULLAH) applies particularly to an emissary sent from Israel to Jewish communities in the diaspora.

Shalkovitz, Leib *see* BEN AVIGDOR.

Shallum (i) (fl. 8th cent. BCE). King of Judah (747 BCE). He slew Zechariah, son of Jeroboam II and seized the throne (II Kings 23.29–34). He was subsequently killed and succeeded by Menaḥem.

Shallum (ii) *see* JEHOAHAZ (ii).

***Shalmaneser III** (fl. 9th cent. BCE). King of Assyria (860–825 BCE). He unsuccessfully fought against an alliance of Damascus, Hamath, and Israel. Later he devastated the territory of Hamath and received tribute from Jehu.

***Shalmaneser IV** (fl. 8th cent. BCE). King of Assyria (728–722 BCE). He fought against Sidon, Tyre, and Acre. Hoshea, the King of Israel, revolted against him, but was defeated. He died during the attack on Samaria.

Shalom. Word meaning well-being of various kinds: security, contentment, good health, prosperity, friendship, and peace of mind and heart. It is also used as in greetings and farewells when the meaning is "peace [be with you]."

Shalom [Sholem] **aleikhem** [aleichem]. Jewish greeting meaning "Peace be with you."

Shalom bayit ("domestic peace"). Term used specifically of harmonious relations between husband and wife. The rabbis formulated various regulations to bring about this situation.

Shalom Shabbazi *see* SHABBAZI, SHALOM.

Shamgar (fl. 13th cent. BCE). Israelite judge. He defeated the Philistines, killing 600 men with an ox-goad (Judges 3.31).

Shamir. According to legend, the name of a worm that could split stone and metal. It was used by Moses to engrave the names of the tribes on the high priest's breastplate. Later Solomon used it as an engraving tool in the construction of the Temple.

Shamir, Mosheh (b. 1921). Israeli author. He was born in Safed. He served in the Palmaḥ in 1944–5, and later was a member of the Knesset. He edited various Hebrew literary magazines. His works include novels describing Israel's struggle for independence and historical novels, which make indirect criticism of modern Israel.

Shamir, Yitzḥak (b. 1915). Israeli statesman. He was born in Ruzinoy, Poland. He emigrated to Palestine in 1935 and joined Irgun Tzevai Leumi. He later helped to reorganize the Central Committee of the Loḥame Ḥerut Yisrael. He was elected to the Knesset in 1973 and has served as foreign minister, vice-premier, and prime minister.

Shammai (fl. 1st cent. BCE). Palestinian rabbi. He was a contemporary of Hillel, and together they were the last of the zugot. He adopted a rigorous standpoint in moral and religious matters. The School of Shammai later disputed legal issues with the School of Hillel.

Shammash ("beadle"). Caretaker or sexton in the synagogue. The term also refers to the candle used in kindling the Hanukkah lights.

Shapero, Harold (b. 1920). American composer. He was born in Lynn, Massachusetts, and became professor of composition at Brandeis University in 1952. Some of his works deal with Jewish themes.

***Shapira, Constantin Abba** (1840–1900). Russian Hebrew poet. He lived in St. Petersburg, where he worked as a photographer. He converted to Christianity, but wrote Hebrew poetry and intended to settle in Palestine and return to Judaism. He died before he was able to carry out these plans.

***Shapira, Moses William** (c. 1830–1884). Polish dealer in antiquities. He was born a Jew but converted to Christianity. He dealt in antiquities in Jerusalem. In 1882 he offered what he claimed to be ancient manuscripts of parts of Deuteronomy to the British

Museum. When they were pronounced forgeries by C. S. Clermont-Ganneau, Shapira committed suicide.

Shapira, Mosheh Ḥayyim (1902–1970). Israeli politician. He was born in Grodno, Belorussia. He was a founder of the Mizraḥi youth movement. He settled in Palestine in 1925 and served on the executive of the Jewish Agency. After the founding of the State of Israel he represented the Ha-Poel ha-Mizraḥi in the Knesset, serving as minister of immigration, the interior, religious affairs, social welfare, and health.

Shapira, Shalom *see* SHIN SHALOM.

Shapiro, Harvey (b. 1924). American poet and editor. He was born in Chicago. He was editor of the *New York Times Book Review* from 1975 to 1983. His poetry is influenced by Jewish and, in particular, Ḥasidic themes.

Shapiro, Lamed (1878–1948). Polish Yiddish short-story writer. He was born in Rzhishchev, in the district of Kiev. He lived in Warsaw, where he came under the influence of Isaac Leib Peretz. In 1906 he went to the US, but he returned to Warsaw and worked for the Yiddish newspaper *Der fraynd.* Later he settled in Zurich, and finally in the US. He wrote stories about eastern European pogroms and Jewish life in New York; he also published a study of Yiddish literature and language.

Shapiro, Phinehas (fl. 18th cent.). Polish Ḥasidic writer. He lived in Koretz. A pupil of the Baal Shem Tov, he wrote *Midrash Pinḥas.*

Shaprut *see* IBN SHAPRUT.

Sharansky, Natan [Shcharansky, Anatoly] (b. 1948). Israeli human-rights activist, of Russian origin. He trained as a mathematician, but Israel's near defeat in the Yom Kippur War of 1973 provoked him into political activity. His ardent campaigns on behalf of Soviet *refuseniks* led to his imprisonment in 1978. After serving eight and a half years of a 13-year sentence he was released. He emigrated to Israel to join his wife, Avital, herself a constant campaigner for the rights of Soviet Jews. Sharansky continues to argue throughout the world on Zionist issues and for wider human rights. In 1987 he received the Simon Wiesenthal Centre's annual humanitarian award. His autobiography, *Fear No Evil*, was published in 1988.

Sharef, Ze'ev (1906–1984). Israeli politician. He was born in Izbor, Bukovina, and settled in Palestine in 1925. In 1948 he became secretary of the Emergency Committee and the National Administration, which laid plans for Israel's civil service. From 1948 to 1957 he was first secretary of the Government of Israel. Later he became director of the state revenues. As a member of the Knesset he served as minister of commerce and industry, minister of finance, and minister of housing.

Sharett [Shertok]**, Moshe** (1894–1965). Israeli statesman and Zionist leader, brother of Yehudah Sharett. He was born in Kherson, in the Ukraine, and settled in Palestine in 1906. Active in socialist circles, he became head of the Jewish Agency's political department in 1933. He was a leader of the campaign against the policy set out by the British in the White Paper of 1939. In 1946 he was interned at Latrun. Later he was appointed foreign minister of the provisional government of Israel, and led the Israeli delegation to the United Nations Assembly (1949–50). He subsequently served as foreign minister, and from 1953 to 1955 was prime minister. He was appointed chairman of the executive of the Jewish Agency in 1961.

Sharett [Shertok]**, Yehudah** (1901–1979). Israeli composer, brother of Moshe Sharett. He was born in Kherson, in the Ukraine, and went to Palestine as a child. He composed music, including children's songs, for his kibbutz, and published the *Yagur Passover Seder Service*.

Sharon. Part of the coastal plain of Israel, bounded in the north by Caesarea and in the south by the city of Joppa. In ancient times it was a fertile area, covered with oak forests, pastureland, and swamps. During the biblical period it formed part of the territory of the tribe of Ephraim. It was conquered in 732 BCE by the Assyrians. Greek and Roman cities, including Caesarea, later grew up there.

Sharon, Ariel (b. 1929). Israeli soldier and politician. He was born in Kephar Malal. He joined the Haganah, fought in the War of Independence, and later led a commando group. In the Six-Day War his brigade broke through the Egyptian positions. In 1969 he was appointed GOC Southern Command, and in the Yom Kippur War he commanded a division. He was elected to the Knesset in 1973 and served as minister of agriculture and minister of defense.

Shas. Abbreviation of the words "shishah sedarim" (six orders), referring to the six orders into which the Mishnah is divided and which form the basis of the Talmud. From the 16th century the term was used to refer to the Talmud.

Shaving. According to biblical law, it is forbidden to shave the "corners" of the head and the beard (Leviticus 19.27); the rabbis state that the corners are five in number, but they differ as to where on the head they are. The Talmud interprets shaving as removal of the hair with a knife or razor. Other methods are not forbidden in the Bible or according to rabbinic teaching. Thus the beard may be clipped with scissors and an electric razor may be used. It is forbidden to shave on holy days and during a period of mourning, as well as during the Counting of the Omer and the three weeks before the Ninth of Av.

Shavu ha-Ben *see* VAKHNAKHT.

Shavuot [Feast of Weeks; Pentecost]. One of the three pilgrim festivals, it is observed on 6 and 7 Sivan. According to tradition, it commemorates the giving of the law on Mount Sinai. It is also known as Pentecost because it begins on the 50th day after the completion of the seven-week period of the Counting of the Omer.

Shaygets (Yiddish). Gentile boy or man.

Shayner Yid (Yiddish: *lit.* "beautiful Jew"). Term used of a Jew whom other Jews esteem.

Shcharansky, Anatoly *see* SHARANSKY, NATAN.

Shear-Jeshub (fl. 8th cent. BCE). Israelite, son of Isaiah (Isaiah 7.3). The name means "the remnant shall return" and Shear-Jeshub symbolizes the remnant that would return to God after the suffering of the nation. On the Day of the Lord this remnant would be the perfect people of Israel cleansed of sin (Isaiah 10.21).

Sheba *see* SABEA.

***Sheba, Queen of** (fl. 10th cent. BCE). Ruler of a southern Arabian kingdom. She visited Solomon and returned to her country full of respect for him (I Kings 10).

Shechem. Ancient town in Cannan. The biblical patriarchs camped under Shechem's walls, and the town was pillaged by Simeon and Levi (Genesis 34). Later it was in the territory of Ephraim, and became the center of the House of Joseph. The northern tribes who broke away from Rehoboam encamped there when Jeroboam was made king (I Kings 12). Eventually it became secondary in importance to Samaria. In 72 Vespasian founded Neapolis nearby, which became an important city; during the period of the crusaders it was a royal seat. The site of Neapolis is now occupied by the town of Nablus.

She'elot u-teshuvot *see* RESPONSA.

Sheeny (Yiddish). Disparaging or contemptuous word for a Jew.

She-heḥeyanu. Opening words of a benediction, blessing God for preserving the speaker "until this season."

Sheḥita. Term used for the ritual slaughter of animals. It is carried out, using a special knife ("ḥallaph"), by a SHOḤET, who must be qualified to practice. The method is governed in detail by Jewish law.

Sheḥitat Ḥullin *see* ḤULLIN.

Sheitel (Yiddish). Wig worn by Orthodox women. Jewish law requires married women to cover their hair, and the sheitel is used in some very traditional circles for this purpose.

Shekalim ("Shekels"). Fourth tractate in the Mishnah order of Moed. It deals with the half-shekel tax, which was used to maintain Temple worship during the period of the second Temple.

Shekel. Unit of weight for measuring silver, later a coin; the shekel continues to be the unit of currency in modern Israel.

Shekinah. Divine presence. The Bible refers to God's dwelling in the midst of the children of Israel (Exodus 13.21–2; 40.34–8). Later the concept of the shekinah embodied God's presence in the world with the people as a whole and with individuals (*see also* INSPIRATION), sharing in Israel's suffering and exile. In kabbalistic sources the term "shekinah" refers to the tenth sephirah (or manifestation of God), representing God's feminine aspect.

Shekoaḥ *see* YISHAR KOAḤ.

Sheliaḥ tzibbur ("Emissary of the congregation"). The title given to the one who leads the public prayer in a synagogue. The term also refers to the ḥazzan.

Shelkowitz, Abraham Leib *see* BEN AVIGDOR.

Shelom Tziyyon, Alexandra *see* SALOME ALEXANDRA.

Shelom Zakhar *see* VAKHNAKHT.

Sheloshim ("30"). 30-day period of MOURNING that follows the death of a relative. Some of the customs of mourning observed during the shivah (seven-day) period continue in force for the duration of sheloshim. A public discourse was sometimes delivered at the end of the period.

Shem. Son of Noah. According to the Bible, the nations of Elam Asshur, Arpachshad, and Aram originated from him (Genesis 10.22). Arpachshad was the father of Eber and the ancestor of Abraham. Shem is thus regarded as the father of the Semitic peoples.

Shema ("Hear!"). Opening word (and hence the name) of a central prayer of the Jewish liturgy, incorporating a confession of faith. It is recited in the evening and morning. It consists of three passages from the Pentateuch (Deuteronomy 6.4–9; 11.12–21; Numbers 15.37–41), preceded by two blessings, and followed by a further benediction in the morning and two (sometimes three) benedictions in the evening. The Shema is also recited before going to sleep. Many martyrs met their death with the Shema on their lips.

Shemaiah (i) (fl. 5th cent. BCE). Israelite false prophet. During the rebuilding of the walls of Jerusalem, Shemaiah was hired by Tobiah and Sanballat to persuade Nehemiah to hide from his enemies in the Temple; their plan was to expose him as an irreligious coward (Nehemiah 6.10), but Nehemiah saw through Shemaiah and refused to follow his advice.

Shemaiah (ii) (fl. 1st cent. BCE). Palestinian rabbi. He was the head of the Sanhedrin in Palestine. He and Avtalyon were the fourth of the zugot.

Shema koli ("Hear my voice"). Opening words of a rhymed hymn ascribed to Hai Gaon. It is recited in the Sephardi ritual before the Kol Nidre prayer on the eve of the Day of Atonement.

Shem ha-Mephorash *see* GOD, NAMES OF.

Shemini Atzeret ("Eighth day of solemn assembly"). The final day of the festival of Sukkot. It takes its name from the regulations in Leviticus 23.36 on how it should be observed (that is, as a day of "solemn assembly"). In the diaspora it is celebrated for two days (22–3 Tishri); in Israel on a single day (22 Tishri), which is also SIMḤAT TORAH. A special prayer for rain is recited during the musaph service. Among the Ashkenazim, the yizkor memorial prayer is said on this day.

Shemittah *see* SABBATICAL YEAR.

Shemoneh Esreh *see* EIGHTEEN BENEDICTIONS.

Shemot *see* EXODUS (ii).

Shemot Rabbah *see* EXODUS RABBAH.

Shenhar [Shenberg]**, Yitzḥak** (1905–1957). Israeli author. He was born in Voltshisk, on the border of Galicia and the Ukraine, and settled in Palestine in 1921. From 1942 he was an editor for the publisher Schocken. His novels deal with Jewish life in eastern Europe and Israel. He also translated works from European literature into Hebrew.

Sheol. The dwelling-place of the dead, according to the Bible (Genesis 37.35; Isaiah 38.10). It is located below the earth (Isaiah 57.9).

Shepharam. Town in Lower Galilee. During the 2nd century it was the seat of the Sanhedrin under Judah ha-Nasi.

Shephatiah ben Amittai (fl. 9th cent.). Italian liturgical poet and religious leader. He lived in Oria in southern Italy. When Abu Aaron came to Italy, he passed on to Shephatiah kabbalistic secrets which Shephatiah used in performing deeds, as recorded in the *Chronicle of Ahimaaz*. In about 873 Shephatiah traveled to Constantinople to plead for the annulment of anti-Jewish decrees. His poem *Yisrael Nosha* is included in the Neilah service on the Day of Atonement in the Ashkenazi liturgy.

Shepher *see* RABINOWITZ, SAUL PHINEHAS.

Shepheya [Meir Shepheyah]. Israeli agricultural school. It was founded in the Carmel mountains by Baron Edmond de Rothschild in 1892. In 1904 Israel Belkind established nearby an agricultural school for orphans from the Kishinev pogroms. In 1923 a new school was opened, and in the 1930s it became an institution of Youth Aliyah and was adopted by Junior Hadassah of America.

Sherira Gaon (906–1006). Babylonian gaon. He was gaon of Pumbedita (968–98) in succession to his father, Ḥanina, and his grandfather, Judah. With his son Hai Gaon, Sherira maintained contact, by means of responsa, with Jews in north Africa, Spain, and elsewhere. In an important epistle in response to an inquiry from Kairouan, he described the origins of the Mishnah and the Talmud and the traditions of the sevoraim and the geonim. He also wrote commentaries on the Bible and talmudic tractates. During the last years of his life he was imprisoned by the caliph Kadir.

Shertok, Yehudah *see* SHARETT, YEHUDAH.

Sheshbazzar (fl. 6th cent. BCE). Israelite administrator. In 538 BCE he was appointed by Cyrus II, King of Persia, as governor over Judah. He was entrusted with the Temple vessels, which he took from Babylon to Jerusalem, and also laid the foundations for the construction of the second Temple (Ezra 1.8, 11; 5.14–16).

Sheshet (fl. 3rd–4th cent.). Babylonian amora. He lived at Shilhi on the Tigris. Although he became blind, he was still able to teach, since he could cite tannaitic sources from memory.

Shestov, Lev [Schwarzman, Lev Isakavich] (1866–1938). French philosopher, of Ukrainian origin. He was born in Kiev. He lived in France after the Russian Revolution of 1917. In 1922 he became professor of Russian philosophy at the University of Paris. His writings include *Speculation and Revelation* and *Athens and Jerusalem*.

Shetar *see* DEED.

Sheva. In Hebrew script, a sign resembling a colon, which indicates the absence of a vowel or the presence of a very short vowel.

Sheva Berakhot *see* SEVEN BENEDICTIONS.

Shevat. 11th month of the Jewish year.

Shevat, Fifteenth of *see* FIFTEENTH OF SHEVAT.

Sheviit ("Seventh year"). Fifth tractate in the Mishnah order of Zeraim. It deals with the laws of the Sabbatical year (Exodus 23.11; Leviticus 25.1–7). The release from debts (Deuteronomy 15.1–6) and the rabbinic institution of the prosbul are discussed in the last chapter.

Shevuot ("Oaths"). Sixth tractate in the Mishnah order of Nezikin. It deals with different types of oaths (Leviticus 5.4), and the laws applying to a person who becomes aware of being unclean (Leviticus 5.2–3).

Shewbread [showbread] (Hebrew "hapannim," "leḥem pannim"). The name given to the 12 loaves which were laid in two rows on the golden table in the inner shrine of the Temple. They remained there from one Sabbath to the next, and were then divided among the priests (Leviticus 24.1–9).

Shibboleth ("slogan," "test word"). Word used by Jephthah to test the nationality of wayfarers near the Jordan. In the Ephraimite dialect it was pronounced "sibboleth" and this enabled him to identify Ephraimites, with whom he was at enmity (Judges 12).

Shiddukh ("marital match"). In the Talmud the word is used to refer to the conversations between a prospective bridegroom or his parents and a possible bride or her parents, in preparation for betrothal. It has come to mean betrothal or marriage.

Shield of David *see* MAGEN DAVID.

Shikhḥah ("forgotten [ones]"). Term used specifically of sheaves which the landowner has overlooked during the time of reaping. According to Leviticus 19.9 they must be left for the poor.

Shikker (Yiddish). Drunk, or a drunkard.

Shikkun (from "shakken": to house). Term applied to a housing project, building development, or residence in Israel.

Shikseh (Yiddish). Non-Jewish woman.

Shiloaḥ *see* SILOAM.

Shiloh. Ancient place in the mountains of the territory of Ephraim, north of Jerusalem. It became the Israelite's first cultic center after the conquest of Palestine. The Ark of the Covenant and the Tabernacle were located there during the time of the Judges. The town and the Tabernacle were destroyed by the Philistines after the battle of Aphek in the 11th century BCE, and the Ark was captured.

Shimei (fl. 11th–10th cent. BCE). Israelite of the tribe of Benjamin, kinsman of Saul. He was a supporter of Saul, and uttered a curse against David when he fled from Absalom's revolt. David spared him on his return to Jerusalem, but Shimei was subsequently killed by Solomon (I Kings 2.35–46).

Shimoni [Shimonovitz]**, David** (1886–1956). Israeli poet, of Russian origin. He was born in Bobruisk, in the district of Minsk. He settled in Palestine in 1909, but later went to Germany to study, and returned to Russia at the outbreak of World War I. In 1921 he moved permanently to Palestine and taught at the Herzliyyah secondary school. He wrote poetry, parables, satires, meditations, and memoirs.

Shimshelevitz, Yitzḥak *see* BEN-ZVI, YITZḤAK.

Shin *see* SIN (i).

Shinar. Ancient country referred to in the

Bible. Its rulers included Nimrod (Genesis 10.10), and Amraphel (Genesis 14.1–9). After the destruction of the first Temple, exiles from Judah were banished there (Isaiah 11.11).

Shin Shalom [Shapira, Shalom] (b. 1904). Israeli poet, of Ukrainian origin. He was the son of the Ḥasidic rabbi of Drohobycz. From 1914 to 1922 he lived in Vienna, and then settled in Palestine. He wrote mystical religious poetry, an autobiographical novel, stories, and plays. He also translated the sonnets of Shakespeare into Hebrew.

Shir *see* RAPOPORT, SOLOMON JUDAH.

Shirayim ("leftovers"). Food left by the tzaddik. It is competed for by the Ḥasidim during the Sabbath and festival meals. According to Ḥasidism, these remains partake of the same holiness that traditionally resided in the part of a sacrifice which was not consumed upon the altar.

Shir ha-Kavod ("Song of glory") [Anim zemirot]. Hymn of praise. Among the Ashkenazim it is recited after the morning service and after the additional service on the Sabbath. The Ark is opened during its recitation. It takes the form of an alphabetic acrostic. Its opening words are "Anim zemirot" (I shall sing songs).

Shir ha-Maalot *see* SONG OF DEGREES.

Shir ha-Shirim Rabbah *see* SONG OF SONGS RABBAH.

Shir ha-Yiḥud ("Song of unity"). Ashkenazi hymn. It is a product of the 13th-century German religious movement of the Ḥaside Ashkenaz, and has been attributed to Samuel ben Kalonymus he-Ḥasid. It is divided into seven sections, one of which is read on each day of the week by the Ashkenazim. It glorifies the attributes of God.

***Shishak** (fl. 10th cent. BCE). Egyptian king (reigned c. 925 BCE). He offered refuge to Jeroboam on his flight from Solomon (I Kings 11.40). In the fifth year of Rehoboam's reign, he overran Judah and plundered the Temple (I Kings 14.25; II Chronicles 12).

Shitreet, Bekhor Shalom (1895–1967). Israeli politician. He was born in Tiberias. He was commander of the police in Lower Galilee and between 1935 and 1948 served as a magistrate in several towns. After the establishment of the State of Israel, he served as minister of police and minister of minorities, as a representative of Sephardi and Oriental communities. Subsequently he was a member of the Knesset for Mapai.

Shiur Komah ("The measure of the body"). Mystical work, concerning the nature of God; it dates from the gaonic period or earlier. It attributes colossal dimensions to God. It was denounced by various authorities as grossly anthropomorphic, but its defenders maintained that it should not be understood literally.

Shivah ("seven"). Seven-day period of mourning that follows the death of a relative. It is also known in the Talmud as "avelut" (mourning). During this period ordinary work is prohibited; sexual intercourse is also forbidden. The mourners sit without shoes on low stools or on the floor, a custom known as "sitting shivah." It is usual for friends to make visits to the mourners' home to offer prayers and condolences. The prohibitions of sheloshim also apply to this period. *See also* MOURNING.

Shivah Asar be-Tammuz (*lit.* "17th day of the month of Tammuz"). Fast day, originally commemorating the breach of the walls of Jerusalem three weeks before the fall of the city and the destruction of the Temple in 586 BCE; it is the "fast of the fourth month" mentioned in Zechariah 8.19. The Mishnah names four other events to be commemorated on this date, all associated with the destruction of the Temple in 70 CE: (1) the breaking of the two Tablets; (2) the cessation of the daily sacrifice; (3) the burning of the Scrolls of the Law by Apostomus; and (4) the erection of an idol in the sanctuary.

Shlemiel (Yiddish). A foolish or unfortunate person, or a simpleton.

Shlep (Yiddish). To drag, pull, or lag behind.

Schlimazel (Yiddish). An unlucky person.

Shlock (Yiddish). A shoddy, cheaply made, or fake article.

Shlonsky, Avraham (1900–1973). Israeli poet. He was born in Karyokov, in the Ukraine. He settled in Palestine in 1921, and in 1928 joined the staff of the newspaper *Ha-Aretz*. In 1943 he joined the editorial staff of the journal *Mishmar*, and subsequently edited the quarterly *Orlogin*. Associated with the Mapam party, he participated in the activities of the international world peace movement of the 1950s. From the 1950s he criticized the Soviet attitude to Israel and Jewish culture in the USSR. In addition to writing poetry, he translated classics from several languages into Hebrew.

Shlump (Yiddish). A tiresome person, or "wet blanket."

Shmaltz (Yiddish). Cooking fat. It is also used figuratively, particularly of music, to mean sugary and sentimental.

Shmatte (Yiddish). A rag or cheap junk; figuratively a person not worthy of respect.

Shmendrick (Yiddish). A person of no account.

Shmeruk, Chone (b. 1921). Israeli Yiddish scholar. He was born in Poland and emigrated to Palestine as a young man. From 1961 until his retirement he was professor of Yiddish literature at the Hebrew University. He is the chief editor with H. H. Paper of a complete edition of the works of Sholem Aleichem, and co-editor of *The Penguin Book of Modern Yiddish Verse*.

Shmo (Yiddish). A hapless fool, a "fall guy."

Schmuck (Yiddish). Penis; colloquially a foolish or stupid person.

Shmuss (Yiddish). To chat, or a chat.

Shnaps (Yiddish). Brandy.

Shneersohn, Dov Ber of Liubavich (1773–1827). Russian Ḥasidic leader. He was the successor of Shneour Zalman of Lyady. He founded the Ḥabad settlement at Hebron in Palestine, and advocated the establishment of Jewish agricultural settlements in Kherson province, in the Ukraine.

Shneersohn, Joseph Isaac (d. 1952). Russian Ḥasidic leader. He was imprisoned for his religious activities, and after his release in 1927 moved to Otwock in Poland. Later he emigrated to the US and settled in New York, where he founded yeshivot and schools in the Ḥabad tradition.

Shneersohn, Menaḥem Mendel (1789–1866). Russian Ḥasidic leader. He was the successor of Dov Ber Shneersohn of Liubavich (who was his father-in-law). He composed the halakhic work *Tzemaḥ Tzedek*.

Shneour Zalman (1887–1959). Russian Hebrew author. He was born in Belorussia, and lived in Vilnius, Berlin, Paris, the US, and Israel. In his poetic cycle *Luḥot Genuzim* he criticized the moral development of Judaism as found in biblical literature. His collections of stories *Peoples of Shklov* and *Noah Pandre* deal with Jewish life in the Pale of Settlement.

Shneour Zalman (ben Baruch) of Lyady (1747–1813). Russian Ḥasidic leader, founder of the Ḥabad movement. The pupil of Dov Ber of Mezhirich, he joined the Ḥasidim at the age of 20. In 1777 he succeeded Menaḥem Mendel of Vitebsk as the movement's leader, and became involved in controversy with the mitnaggedim. He was arrested by the Russian authorities and imprisoned in St.

Petersburg; although he was released, he was later rearrested. In 1804 he settled in Lyady. His teaching emphasized a rational approach and stressed the importance of study and contemplation. He wrote a liturgy, a code of laws, a mystic commentary on the Pentateuch, and a kabbalistic work, *Likkute Amarim* (also known as the *Tanya*).

Shnoder (Yiddish). To make an offering in the synagogue.

Shnook (Yiddish). An ineffectual person, a person to be pitied.

Shnorrer (Yiddish). Beggar.

Shnoz (Yiddish). Nose.

Shoham [Polakevich]**, Mattathias** (1893–1937). Polish author. He lived in Warsaw. He wrote plays based on the conflict between Judaism and idolatry, sensualism and spirituality, and war and peace.

Shoḥer Tov, Midrash. *See* PSALMS, MIDRASH ON.

Shoḥet. Ritual slaughterer. The Talmud decrees that any normal person who is not a minor may slaughter animals and poultry, as long as the act is performed in accordance with Jewish law (*see* SHEḤITA). Subsequently a shoḥet had to be correctly trained. In the modern period those who assume this role still have to be qualified and must in addition be learned in matters of halakhah.

Shoḥet u-vodek *see* BODEK.

Shokhen ad ("He who inhabits eternity"). First words of the final section of the Nishmat prayer. In the Ashkenazi rite the service of morning prayer on Sabbath and festivals begins at this point.

Sholem Aleichem [Rabinovitz, Solomon] (1859–1916). Ukrainian Yiddish author. He was born in Pereyaslav, and began writing novels, poems, and plays at an early age. In 1888–9 he published the literary annual *Die yidishe folksbiblyotek*. He subsequently created the character of Tevye the milkman, who exemplifies the experience of Jewish life in eastern Europe. He supported himself entirely by writing between 1900 and 1906, when he went to New York. He returned to Europe the following year. Many of his stories are set in an imaginary place called Kasrilevke, which was modeled on Voronkov, where he spent his childhood.

Sholem aleikhem [aleichem] *see* SHALOM ALEIKHEM.

Shomer, Nahum Meir *see* SHAIKEVITCH, NAHUM MEIR.

Shomer Yisrael ("Guardian of Israel"). Liturgical poem (piyyut), first found in a 13th-century manuscript among the penitential prayers (seliḥot) for 10 Tevet. Originally recited only on fast days, in the Ashkenazi and Ḥasidic rituals it was later incorporated into the Taḥanun; in other rites it is still reserved for fast days, and an additional stanza is used on the Ten Days of Penitence.

Shomron *see* SAMARIA.

Shool (Yiddish). Synagogue.

Shophar ("horn"). Ceremonial wind instrument, originally made of a ram's horn. The Bible stipulates that it should be sounded on the New Year and to proclaim the Year of Release (Leviticus 25.9). During certain periods it was also blown on fast days, in the ceremony of excommunication, before the start of the Sabbath, and at times of a famine or plague. The blowing of the shophar during the synagogue services in the month of Elul, on Hoshanah Rabbah, and at the conclusion of the Day of Atonement was introduced later.

Shopharot. The name of the last of the three central sections of the additional Amidah service on Rosh ha-Shanah (the others are Malkhuyyot and Zikhronot). It is composed of ten biblical verses that mention the shophar. It expresses hope for the messianic redemption, which will be heralded by the sound of the great shophar.

Shophetim *see* JUDGES.

Shorek, Brook of *see* NAHAL SOREK.

Shoshanat Yaakov ("The lily of Jacob"). Opening words of the final section of the piyyut "Who brought the counsel of the heathen to nought" by Asher Heni. It is recited on Purim after the reading of the Scroll of Esther at the evening and morning prayer services.

Showbread *see* SHEWBREAD.

Shroud *see* BURIAL.

Shtadlan (Hebrew from Aramaic: "persuader"). Title given to a representative of the Jewish community, skilled in negotiation and with access to dignitaries of state who worked at royal courts. In 18th-century Poland the position of shtadlan was a formal appointment and was sometimes salaried.

Shtetl (Yiddish). Small Jewish town in eastern Europe.

Shtif, Nochum [Baal Dimyon] (1879–1933). Ukrainian Yiddish critic and philologist. He was born in Rovno, Volhynia, and settled in Berlin in 1922. He was one of the founders of the Yiddish Scientific Institute (YIVO) in Vilnius in 1925. From 1926 he was in charge of the work of the linguistic section of the Institute for Yiddish Proletarian Culture in Kiev. Eventually he was appointed to the chair of Yiddish at the Kiev State Academy.

Shtik (Yiddish). A piece or part of a larger whole; figuratively a prank or trick, or misconduct.

Shtille (Yiddish) **khuppeh** (Hebrew). Secret wedding. Such a marriage is conducted in conformity with Jewish law, but does not follow civil regulations.

Shtreimel (Yiddish). A broad-brimmed black hat, trimmed with velvet or edged with fur; it is worn by religious Jewish men, particularly in Galicia and Poland.

Shtunk (Yiddish). An objectionable or offensive person, a fool, or an ungrateful individual; also a scandalous mess.

Shtup (Yiddish). To push, thus to fornicate; the act of copulation.

Shtuss (Yiddish). Foolishness or nonsense.

Shul (Yiddish). Synagogue.

Shulamite. Inhabitant of Shunem. The woman mentioned in the Song of Songs (6.13) is addressed by this name. From talmudic times the term referred to the Jewish people in relation to God owing to the allegorical interpretation of the Song of Songs.

Shulḥan Arukh *see* CARO, JOSEPH.

Shulklapper (Yiddish). The title of the official who knocked on the doors of Jewish houses to wake worshippers for early morning services in the synagogue. In eastern Europe he used a special hammer for this purpose.

Shum. Word derived from the initial letters of the German place names Speyer, Worms, and Mainz, and used to refer collectively to their Jewish communities, which were prominent in the Middle Ages. The regulations of their joint synod were called "takkanot Shum" and were binding on all German Jewry.

Shunem. Ancient town in the Valley of Jezreel in the territory of the tribe of Issachar. It was the home of the Shunammite woman whose dead son was revived by Elisha (II Kings 4).

Shuruk. The name given to the long vowel sound "u" in Hebrew.

Shushan. Ancient city about 150 miles north of the Persian Gulf; it was the capital of Elam, and later of Persia. The modern town of Susa stands on the same site.

Shvartzer (Yiddish). The colour black, or a black person.

Shvitzer (Yiddish). Literally one who sweats; figuratively a braggart.

Shylock. Jewish moneylender, the central character in William Shakespeare's *The Merchant of Venice.*

Siberia. Asiatic region of the USSR. Jews were probably sent into exile there as early as the 17th century; in 1827 they were prohibited from going there to join exiled relatives. In 1836 a government plan was proposed for the settlement of Jews in the regions of Tobolsk and Omsk, but this was later abandoned. The Jewish population in the region increased in the early 20th century as a result firstly of the establishment of the Jewish autonomous area of Birobidjan, and secondly of the Soviet policy of exiling Jews from the Baltic countries, Belorussia, and the Ukraine.

Sibylline Oracles. The name given to a series of prophecies in Greek hexameters, composed between the 5th century BCE and the 4th century CE. They are of pagan, Jewish, Christian, and mixed Jewish-Christian authorship. They sketch the history of the Mediterranean world in prophetic language, attack Israel's enemies, threaten disaster, and foretell messianic judgment and redemption.

Sicarii. Group of Jewish rebels active during the second Temple period. They were called after the dagger ("sica") they carried under their clothes. They killed their political enemies who advocated peace with Rome. Their numbers included Menaḥem ben Jair and Eleazar ben Jair.

Sick, prayers for the. The eighth benediction of the weekday Amidah is a petition for the healing of the sick. In addition any person may offer prayers for sick friends or relatives; these may be added to the eighth or the 16th benediction of the Amidah, or they may be offered anywhere at any time in the words of the worshipper. Prayers for the sick may also be offered in the synagogue after the reading of the law, and it is customary to read psalms on behalf of the sick. It also became usual for a special form of prayer (including psalms, petitions, and a brief confession of sin) to be recited by a sick person. A special prayer, including the CHANGE OF NAME, was composed for those very seriously ill.

Sick, visiting the (Hebrew "bikkur ḥolim"). Bringing comfort to those who are ill is an important duty in Judaism. According to the rabbis it derives its importance from God's visit to Abraham (Genesis 18.1) during his illness caused by circumcision.

Siddur ("order"). The term used by Ashkenazi Jews for the book containing daily prayers; Sephardim used the term "tephillah." The MAḤZOR contains the prayers for festivals.

Sidelocks *see* PAYESS.

Sidgwick, Cecily Ullman (1855–1934). British novelist, of German origin. She wrote short stories and novels dealing with Jewish characters.

Sidon. Ancient coastal city in Syria. It was the capital city of the Phoenicians, who are called "Sidonians" in the Bible. Jezebel was of Sidonian origin. Sidon was occupied by the Assyrians, was later subject to Persia, and eventually was captured by Alexander the Great. Under Roman domination it lost any form of autonomous government.

Sidrah ("order"). Portion of the Pentateuch read in the synagogue on the Sabbath. Each sidrah has a distinctive name, taken from the first important word in the text. The Pentateuch is divided into 54 sedarot so that the entire Pentateuch is read annually.

Sieff, Israel Moses, Baron (1889–1972). English industrialist and Zionist. He was born in Manchester. He was a collaborator of Chaim Weizmann and served as secretary of the Zionist Commission to Palestine in 1918. In 1934 he founded the Daniel Sieff Research Institute at Reḥovot. He contributed to various Zionist organizations.

Sieff, Rebecca (1890–1966). English Zionist, wife of Israel Moses Sieff. She was born in Leeds. She was a founder of the Woman's International Zionist Organization (WIZO) in London in 1920 and served as its president until 1963.

Sieff Institute *see* WEIZMANN INSTITUTE OF SCIENCE.

Siena. City in central Italy, formerly a city-republic. Jews lived there from the 13th century, and in time the city attracted a number of Jewish loan bankers. In the 16th century it became a center of Jewish scholarship. The Siena ghetto was established in 1571, when the city was annexed to the grand duchy of Tuscany. In 1799 the ghetto was attacked during the wave of Italian unrest occasioned by the French Revolution; an annual fast was instituted by the Jewish community to commemorate this event.

Sigilmessa. Town and oasis in Morocco. It was a center of Jewish scholarship during the early centuries of Muslim rule.

***Sihon** (fl. ?13th cent. BCE). Amorite king. He ruled in Transjordan, and his capital was Heshbon, north-east of the Dead Sea. He conquered much of this area from the Moabites (Numbers 27.21ff). When he refused to allow the Israelites passage across his territory, he was defeated and his land was partitioned between the tribes of Reuben and Gad.

Silbermann, Eliezer Lipmann (1819–1882). Prussian Hebrew journalist and editor. He lived in Lyck in East Prussia, where he worked as a shoḥet and cantor. He started the first Hebrew newspaper, the weekly *Ha-Maggid*, in 1856, and in 1862 helped to found the periodical *Mekitze Nirdamim.*

Silberschlag, Eisig (1903–1988). American Hebrew poet and critic. He grew up in Metri, Galicia. After emigrating to the US, he became professor in Hebrew literature at the Hebrew Teachers College in Boston. He published poetry, wrote critical studies in Hebrew and English, and translated Greek classics.

Silent prayer. No mention is made of silent prayer in the Bible. In the rabbinic period it became the custom for the members of the congregation silently to recite the Amidah before its repetition by the reader. Private prayers may be added to the 16th benediction of the silent Amidah.

Silkiner, Benjamin Nahum (1882–1933). American Hebrew poet. He was born in Vikija, Lithuania. He went to the US in 1904 and later taught at the Teachers Institute of the Jewish Theological Seminary in New York. He published texts for Hebrew schools, helped to produce an English–Hebrew dictionary, and wrote narrative poetry.

Siloam [Shiloaḥ]. Pool near Jerusalem fed by water from the Gihon spring. In c. 700 BCE Hezekiah cut a tunnel, through which the water of the Gihon spring could flow into the pool at Siloam (II Kings 20.20). The work on the tunnel began from both directions, and when the workmen met they commemorated the event by placing an inscription on the wall. This is one of the most ancient Hebrew inscriptions.

Silva, Antonio José da (1705–1739). Portuguese playwright. He was born in Rio de Janeiro, Brazil, and was of Converso origin. He moved to Lisbon, and studied at the University of Coimbra. While he was a student he wrote a satire, which led to his arrest; he was charged with Judaizing, but was later released. He became an important Portuguese dramatist. He was arrested by the Inquisition in 1737 and killed two years later.

Silva, Francisco Maldonado da [Nazareno, Eli] (c. 1592–1639). Chilean Marrano martyr. He worked as a physician in Chile, where he converted to Judaism, circumcised himself, and adopted the name Eli Nazareno. He was arrested by the Inquisition, but continued to practice Jewish rites even in prison. He was burned at an auto-da-fé in Lima.

Silva, Samuel da (fl. 16th–17th cent.). Portuguese Marrano physician. He was born in Oporto, but settled in Hamburg, where he lived as a Jew. He translated the section on repentance from the *Mishneh Torah* of Maimonides into Spanish. Later he wrote a reply to Uriel da Costa's criticism of the Jewish tradition entitled *Treatise on the Immortality of the Soul.*

Silver, Abba Hillel (1893–1963). American Reform rabbi. He was born in Sirvintos, Lithuania, and was taken to the US in 1902. He served as a rabbi in Wheeling, Virginia, and Cleveland, Ohio. In 1938 he became chairman of the United Palestine Appeal and joint chairman of the United Jewish Appeal. He led the meetings of the American Zionist Emergency Council in 1943, and later was appointed chairman of the American section of the Jewish Agency. His writings include *History of Messianic Speculation in Israel from the First Through the Seventeenth Centuries, The Democratic Impulse in Jewish History, Religion in a Changing World, Where Judaism Differed,* and *Therefore Choose Life.*

Silverman, Morris (1894–1972). American Conservative rabbi. He was born in Newburgh, New York. He served as rabbi of Mount Sinai Temple in Brooklyn (1917–20) and Emanuel Synagogue in Hartford, Connecticut (1923–61). He was active in various spheres of Jewish life and edited a series of prayerbooks.

Simeon (i) (fl. ?19th–16th cent. BCE). Israelite, second son of Jacob. To avenge the rape of his sister Dinah, he and Levi tricked the citizens of Shechem, captured the town, killed the male inhabitants, and took the women and children captive (Genesis 34).

Simeon (ii) (fl. 1st cent.). Palestinian Zealot leader, known as Simeon son of Judah the Galilean. He and his brother Jacob led the Zealots after their father's death. They were captured and crucified by the procurator Tiberius Julius Alexander.

Simeon bar Giora *see* BAR GIORA, SIMON.

Simeon ben Eleazar (fl. 2nd cent.). Palestinian tanna. A contemporary of Judah ha-Nasi, he lived in Tiberias. He is mentioned only infrequently in the Mishnah, but plays an important role in the Tosephta. He was a noted halakhist, aggadist, and polemicist.

Simeon ben Gamaliel I (fl. 1st cent.). Palestinian nasi. He was leader of the Sanhedrin at the time of the destruction of the second Temple in 70 CE. When the revolt against Rome began, in 66, he was among its leaders, but he later adopted a moderate policy. He is listed among the Ten Martyrs.

Simeon ben Gamaliel II (fl. 2nd cent.). Palestinian nasi, son of Rabban Gamaliel of Jabneh and father of Judah ha-Nasi. After the Romans destroyed the house of the nasi in revenge for the Bar Kokhba revolt (132–5), he was one of the few survivors. He was forced to go into hiding, but later became nasi of the Sanhedrin at Usha. Many of his decisions are quoted in the Mishnah and the Tosephta.

Simeon ben Isaac ben Abun [Simeon the Great] (d. c. 1015). German liturgical poet. He lived in Mainz. Many of his hymns are included in the Ashkenazi liturgy, notably that for the New Year. According to legend, he was the father of the pope Elhanan.

Simeon ben Lakish [Resh Lakish] (fl. 3rd cent.). Palestinian amora. In his youth he sold himself to men who hired participants in gladiatorial contests. According to legend, Johanan bar Nappaḥa persuaded him to study the Torah, and gave him his sister in marriage. Eventually Simeon became one of the most important sages in the Tiberias academy.

Simeon ben Mattathias *see* SIMON THE HASMONEAN.

Simeon ben Setaḥ (fl. 1st cent. BCE). Palestinian scholar. He was active during the reign of Alexander Yannai and Salome Alexandra (who was his sister). He and Judah ben Tabbai together formed one of the zugot. He was largely responsible for ensuring that the Pharisees were dominant in public and private life during the second Temple period; he managed to change the Sanhedrin into a Pharisaic body.

Simeon ben Tzemaḥ Duran *see* DURAN, SIMEON BEN TZEMAḤ.

Simeon ben Yoḥai (fl. 2nd cent.). Palestinian tanna. He was among the five pupils of Akiva who survived the failure of the Bar Kokhba revolt (132–5). When he expressed political opinions which were regarded by the Romans as seditious, he was forced to flee for his life; he is said to have hidden in a cave for 13 years. He was noted as a miracle worker, and was sent on a mission to Rome, where he succeeded in obtaining the withdrawal of a persecutory decree against the Jews. The authorship of the Zohar has been attributed to him, and he is frequently quoted in the Mishnah by his pupil Judah ha-Nasi. His tomb at Meron is a center of pilgrimage on Lag Ba-Omer (the traditional date of his death).

Simeon ha-Darshan *see* KAYYARA, SIMEON.

Simeon ha-Tzaddik (fl. ?4th–2nd cent. BCE). High priest. He played an important role in the Keneset Gedolah, which formulated the liturgy, established the canon of Scripture, and formed the Sanhedrin. Scholars have suggested that he belonged to the Hasideans and supported the Seleucids. He has also been credited with ensuring the central role of study in the Jewish tradition and stemming the influence of Hellenization.

Simeon Kahira *see* KAYYARA, SIMEON.

Simeon son of Judah the Galilean *see* SIMEON (ii).

Simḥah. Celebration.

Simḥah ben Samuel of Vitry (d. 1105). French scholar. He was a pupil of Rashi. He compiled the Maḥzor Vitry, which is regarded as an authoritative source for the prayerbook, synagogue customs, and the hymnology of medieval French Jewry.

Simḥat Bet ha-Shoevah ("Festival of the Water-Drawing"). Festival observed at the end of the first day of Sukkot (15 Tishri). Its ceremonies are described in the Mishnah (Sukkah 5): water was poured out in offering to God, huge bonfires were lit, and there was joyful dancing and singing. It ceased to be observed after the destruction of the second Temple.

Simḥat Torah ("Rejoicing in the law"). Holy day on which the annual completion of the reading of the Torah (*see* SIDRAH) is celebrated. It is observed on Shemini Atzeret (22 Tishri) in Israel (on the second day of Shemini Atzeret (23 Tishri) in the diaspora). It is customary to carry the Scrolls of the Law round the synagogue seven times or more. The last section of Deuteronomy is read by the Bridegroom of the Law (Ḥatan Torah), and the first section of Genesis is read by the Bridegroom of Genesis (Ḥatan Bereshit).

Simon, Ernest Akiva (1899–1973). Israeli educator and writer, of German origin. He was born in Berlin, where he co-edited the monthly journal *Der Jude* with Martin Buber. He settled in Palestine in 1928, and became a teacher and co-director of secondary schools and seminaries. He later was appointed professor of philosophy and history of education, and director of the school of education at the Hebrew University. He was an editor of the *Educational Encyclopaedia* and wrote books on education and philosophy.

Simon, James (1851–1932). German merchant and philanthropist. He helped to found the Hilfsverein der Deutschen Juden in 1901 and served as its chairman. He was an art collector and patron, and also financed archeological expeditions to Jericho and Tel el Amarna.

Simon, Sir **John** (1818–1897). British lawyer and politician. He was born in Jamaica, and went to England in 1833, where he studied law. He returned to Jamaica to practice as a lawyer, but eventually settled permanently in England, where he became a queen's counsel. From 1868 to 1888 he was a Liberal member of parliament and championed the cause of oppressed Jewry.

Simon, Julius (1875–1969). Zionist leader, of German origin. He was born in Mannheim, and engaged in banking in Switzerland and Alsace during World War I. Later he was invited by Chaim Weizmann to direct the economic activities of the Zionist Organization. In 1920 he was sent to Palestine to reorganize the Zionist Organization, but his report was not accepted by the Zionist Congress and he resigned from the organization. Between the wars Simon lived in Palestine and the US, and headed the Palestine Economic Corporation.

Simon, Sir **Leon** (1881–1965). English civil servant, brother of Maurice Simon. He was born in Southampton. He was director of telegraphs and telephones in the General Post Office and later director of the National Savings Bank. An ardent Zionist, he was active in the establishment of the Hebrew University. He lived in Jerusalem from 1946 to 1953 and worked in the Israel ministry of posts. He subsequently returned to England. His writings include *Studies in Jewish Nationalism*, *The Case of the Anti-Zionists: a Reply*, and *Zionism and the Jewish Problem*. He also translated Ahad ha-Am's writings into English.

Simon, Maurice (1874–1955). South African Hebraist and translator, brother of Leon Simon. He was born in Manchester. He moved to South Africa and later was associated with the Soncino Press. He was the co-translator into English of the Zohar and Midrash Rabbah, and helped with the Soncino translation of the Talmud.

Simon of Trent *see* TRENT.

Simonsen, David Jacob (1853–1932). Danish rabbi. He was born in Copenhagen, and served as a rabbi there. During World War I he assisted war victims and took an interest in the Palestine Jewish community. His library of books about Judaism contained about 40,000 volumes. He published various works of oriental studies.

Simon the Hasmonean [Simeon ben Mattathias] (fl. 2nd cent. BCE). Palestinian ruler and high priest, second son of Mattathias the Hasmonean. In 142 BCE he succeeded his brother Jonathan as head of the Jewish state. He captured Gezer, secured the evacuation of Greek troops from the Jerusalem area, and gained from Demetrius II exemption from the tribute previously paid to the Seleucids. Elected high priest (an office which then became hereditary), ethnarch, and general, he renewed the treaty with Rome and defeated Antiochus VII at Jabneh. He was killed by his son-in-law Ptolemy, and was succeeded by his son John Hyrcanus.

Simon the Just (fl. ?4th–2nd cent. BCE). High priest. According to Josephus, he is identifiable with Simeon I, the son of Onias I (4th–3rd cent. BCE). However, the Talmud identifies him as the father of Onias, who built a temple at Leontopolis in Egypt; according to this account he was Simeon II, the father of Onias III (c. 200 BCE). In rabbinic literature he is described as one of the last members of the Great Assembly.

Sin (i) [shin]. 21st letter of the Hebrew alphabet. Its numerical value is 300.

Sin (ii). Transgression of God's commandments. There are three main categories of sin: "ḥet" (sin committed in ignorance); "avon" (sin committed knowingly); and "pesha" (sin committed in a spirit of rebellion). No individual is without sin, but repentance leading to forgiveness by God cancels sin. For a sin against another person, restitution and placation are necessary.

Sin, Wilderness of. One of the four wildernesses on the Sinai peninsula, southwest of the Dead Sea. The Israelites crossed it during the Exodus on their journey from the Red Sea to Rephidim (Exodus 16.1; 17.1).

Sinai. Peninsula between the Gulf of Suez and the Gulf of Aqaba, the two northern gulfs of the Red Sea. Mount Sinai, roughly in the center of the peninsula, is the mountain where God revealed the Torah to Moses; the Israelites camped in the desert at the foot of the mountain and there received the divine law (Exodus 19.2).

Sinai Inscriptions. The name given to a series of inscriptions on stone tablets in a Semitic alphabetic script, dating from about the 15th century BCE. They were discovered by Flinders Petrie in 1906 in the southern Sinai Peninsula. The script used is a prototype of the ancient Hebrew script.

Sinai Operation. Military campaign prosecuted by Israel against Egypt from 29 October to 5 November 1956. Its aims were to break the encirclement created by the alliance of Egypt, Jordan, and Syria against Israel, to destroy Egyptian armaments, and to eliminate bases in the Gaza strip, in all of which it succeeded.

Sinclair, Clive (b. 1948). English author. He was born in London. His novel *Blood Libels* combines an account of the Israeli invasion of Lebanon and its repercussions in Israel with fantasies about the rise of anti-Semitism in England. His *Brothers Singer* is a biography of Isaac Bashevis Singer, Israel Joshua Singer, and Esther Kreitman.

Singer, Isaac Bashevis (1904–1991). American author, brother of Israel Joshua Singer and Esther Kreitman. He was born in Leoncin, Poland, and moved to Warsaw in 1923. In 1935 he settled in New York, where he worked for the Yiddish daily newspaper *Forverts*. In 1978 he won the Nobel Prize for Literature. He has written numerous novels about eastern European Jewish life.

Singer, Isidore (1859–1939). American writer and editor. He was born in Weisskirchen, Moravia. After working as an editor and as literary secretary to the French ambassador in Vienna, he settled in Paris in 1887, and took a post in the press bureau of the French foreign office. He was active in the defense of Alfred Dreyfus and founded and edited the short-lived periodical *La vraie parole* (1893–4). In 1895 he went to New York, where he became managing editor of the *Jewish Encyclopedia*.

Singer, Israel Joshua (1893–1944). Polish Yiddish novelist and playwright, brother of Isaac Bashevis Singer and Esther Kreitman. He was born in Biłgoraj, Poland, and lived in Warsaw and Kiev; he settled in the US in 1937. His writings include *Yoshe Kalb* and *The Brothers Ashkenazi*.

Singer, Simeon (1848–1906). English rabbi. He was headmaster of Jews College School, and later served as minister of the New East End Synagogue. He edited and translated the siddur as *The Authorised Daily Prayer Book*.

Sinkó, Ervin (1898–1967). Yugoslav

author. He initially wrote verse, fiction, and drama. After engaging in revolutionary activities, he fled to Paris, where he wrote *The Optimists*. He returned to Yugoslavia in 1939, and wrote novels, short stories, essays, and literary studies. His novel *The Love of Aaron* deals with a Jewish revolutionary who fought in the Spanish Civil War. In 1959 he became professor of Hungarian language and literature at the University of Novu Sacz.

Sin offering (Hebrew "ḥatta't"). Sacrifice for a sin committed unwittingly (Leviticus 4.1–3). A sin offering was also made after childbirth, the curing of leprosy, and the taking of the Nazarite vow. The offering consisted of either an animal or a bird.

Sintzheim, Joseph David (1745–1812). French rabbi. He was born in Trier. He was head of the yeshivot in Bischheim and Strasbourg. During the Reign of Terror he fled from France, but later returned to Strasbourg, where he served as rabbi. In 1806 he was appointed to the French Assembly of Jewish Notables, and formulated the replies to the 12 questions put by Napoleon to the Assembly. In 1807 he became president of the Great Sanhedrin and in 1808 chief rabbi of the Central French Consistory. His *Yad David* consists of responsa on sections of the Talmud.

Siphra (Aramaic: "Book") [Siphra de-ve Rav ("Book of the School of Rav"); Torat Kohanim ("Law of the Priests")]. Halakhic midrash on Leviticus. It is a product of the school of Akiva, and dates from the 2nd century.

Siphre to Deuteronomy. Exegetical midrash on Deuteronomy, dating from the 2nd century. It expounds the text chapter by chapter and verse by verse. Although primarily an halakhic midrash, its aggadic section is extensive. It contains a collection of various interpretations of the following passages of Deuteronomy: 1.1–30; 3.21–4.1; 6.4–9; 11.10–26; 15; 31.14; and 32.1ff.

Siphre to Numbers. Exegetical midrash on Numbers, dating from the 2nd century. It expounds the text chapter by chapter and verse by verse. It contains a collection of various interpretations of the following passages of Numbers: chapters 5–12; 15; 18–19; 25.1–13; 26.52–31.24; and 35.9–34.

Siphre Zuta (Aramaic: "Small books"). Halakhic midrash on Numbers, dating from the 2nd century. It is a product of the school of Akiva, and records differences of opinion between the schools of Shammai and Hillel.

Siphriyyat Poalim. Israeli publishing house. It was founded in 1940 at Merḥavyah by the organization of socialist kibbutzim Ha-Kibbutz ha-Artzi.

Sira, Jesus ben *see* BEN SIRA.

Sir Léon of Paris *see* JUDAH BEN ISAAC.

Sirota, Gershon (1874–1943). Lithuanian cantor. He was born in Podolia. He became ḥazzan in Odessa, and later served in Vilnius and Warsaw. He undertook concert tours in Europe and the US.

***Sisera** (fl. 12th cent. BCE). Canaanite general. He was in the service of Jabin, the Canaanite king, who lived at Hazor. He led the war against the Israelites under Barak and Deborah; he was defeated at the battle by the River Kishon, and was later killed by Jael the Kenite, in whose tent he had taken refuge (Judges 4–5).

Sivan. Third month of the Jewish year.

Six-Day War. War fought between Israel and Egypt, Jordan, Syria, and Iraq from 5 to 10 June 1967. During the course of the war Israel defeated the armies of its adversaries and occupied the Sinai Peninsula, the West Bank, and the Golan Heights.

613 commandments (Hebrew "Taryag mitzvot"). The laws as found in the Pentateuch. There are 248 positive commandments (traditionally relating to the number of bones in the body), and 365 negative commandments (equal to the number of days in the year). The first classification of the 613 commandments was made by Simeon Kayyara, and is set out in the Halakhot Gedolot. Maimonides later classified them in his *Sepher ha-Mitzvot,* and Moses of Coucy made a compilation of them in his *Sepher Mitzvot Gadol.*

Siyyum ("termination"). Term applied to the completion of the copying of a Torah scroll; it also refers to the completion of the study of a tractate of the Talmud. To celebrate either of these events a special meal is held ("seudat mitzvah"), where a concluding lecture ("hadran") is given.

Skoss, Solomon Leon (1884–1953). American Arabic and Hebrew scholar. He was born in Chusovoi, Siberia. He served in the Russian army, then in 1907 settled in the US. Later he taught at Dropsie College. His publications include a study of early Hebrew philology and an edition of the dictionary of the Karaite David Alfasi.

Slander (Hebrew "leshon ha-ra"). False report uttered maliciously to damage another person; the spreading of such a report. According to tradition, slander is a serious offence, and listening to slander is also forbidden. Rabbinic law empowered the courts to fine offenders, and to excommunicate them until they apologized to the satisfaction of the person injured. In certain instances fasting was also imposed as a punishment.

Slansky Trial. The name given to the trial in November–December 1952 of Rudolf Slansky, vice-premier of Czechoslovakia, and 13 of his associates, who were charged with Trotskyite-Titoist-Zionist activities. In December he and ten others were found guilty and executed.

Slaughter, ritual *see* SHEḤITA.

Slavery. The condition of a person who is the legal property of another and is bound to absolute obedience to his owner. Scripture stipulates that an Israelite can be made the slave of another Israelite for only a limited period; a manumission must take place in the seventh year of service, or in a Jubilee year. After the Babylonian exile, the institution of Israelite slavery disappeared, but non-Jewish slaves could be purchased from neighboring peoples. Male slaves had to undergo circumcision and all slaves were subject to Jewish law. A slave's marriage was arranged by the owner and the offspring of such a marriage became his property. During the Middle Ages some Jewish merchants engaged in the slave trade. Eventually Jews were prominent in the struggle that led to the abolition of slavery.

Sliosberg, Henry (1863–1937). Russian jurist and communal leader. He was born in Mir, Belorussia, and settled with his family in Poltava, in eastern Ukraine. In 1889 he became legal counsel on Jewish affairs to Baron Horace Günzburg. He intervened with the Russian government in Jewish affairs and was involved in several Jewish legal disputes. He also served as chairman of the Jewish community of St. Petersburg. In 1920 he moved to France, where he became head of the Russian Jewish community in Paris. His memoirs, *Bygone Days*, present an account of Jewish life in Russia before the Revolution.

Slobodka. Lithuanian town, suburb of Kovno. A yeshivah was founded there in 1882, which was associated with the Musar movement. Some of its students founded a yeshivah at Hebron in 1925; in 1929 they moved to Jerusalem. Former leaders of the yeshivah founded the Bene Berak yeshivah in 1947. A second yeshivah was opened in Slobodka in 1897;

during World War I it was moved to Kamenets.

Slonimski, Ḥayyim Selig (1810–1904). Polish Hebrew writer and editor. He was born in Białystok. During the Haskalah he wrote articles on popular science, and in 1834 he published the first part of a mathematics textbook; later he wrote a work on astronomy. He also invented a calculating machine and in 1862 founded a Hebrew newspaper, *Ha-tzephirah,* devoted to popular science.

Slouschz, Naḥum (1871–1966). Israeli scholar, archeologist, and historian, of Lithuanian origin. He was born in Smorgon, near Vilnius, and as a child went to Odessa, where he later became involved in political and cultural activities. In 1904 he was appointed to the chair of Hebrew language and literature at the Sorbonne in Paris; he also taught at the École Normale Orientale of the Alliance Israélite Universelle. He wrote various studies of Jewry in north Africa. In 1919 he settled in Palestine, where he participated in archeological explorations.

Slutzker Rav *see* RIDBAZ, YAAKOV.

Smilansky, Moshe (1874–1953). Israeli writer. He was born in the Ukraine and in 1890 emigrated to Palestine, where he started a farm near Reḥovot. He was a frequent contributor to the Zionist press. He also wrote a set of six autobiographical novels and several histories of the early days of agricultural settlement in Israel.

Smilansky, Yizhar [Yizhar, S.] (b. 1916). Israeli author. He was born in Reḥovot. He worked as a teacher and principal in various schools and served in the Knesset. His writings include the novel *The Days of Ziklag.*

Smolenskin, Peretz (1840–1885). Russian Hebrew novelist and editor. He was born in Monastyrshchina, in the province of Mohilev, Belorussia. He wandered for several years before settling in Odessa and later Vienna. In 1868 in Vienna he founded the Hebrew monthly journal *Ha-Shaḥar,* which served as a central organ of Hebrew literary activities and Jewish national thought. Ten years later he established the weekly *Ha-Mabbit.* He wrote numerous stories and romances about eastern European Jewish life. His articles promoted a Jewish national theory opposed to religious Orthodoxy and the Haskalah. After the pogroms in Russia in 1881, he supported the Ḥibbat Zion movement.

***Smuts, Jan Christian** (1870–1950). South African statesman. He served as a member of Britain's Imperial War Cabinet in World War I. A supporter of the Zionist movement, he helped to formulate the Balfour Declaration (1917) and the Palestine Mandate (1922).

Smyrna. Port in western Asia Minor; the modern port of Izmir in Turkey stands on the same site. The New Testament refers to Smyrna's Jewish community. Its numbers diminished in the Middle Ages, but increased with the settlement of refugees after the expulsion of the Jews from Spain in 1492. In the 17th and 18th centuries Jews played an important role in the economy of the city. Shabbetai Tzevi was born there, and the city became an important center of his movement.

Sneh, Mosheh [Kleinbaum, Mosheh] (1909–1972). Israeli politician. He was born in Radzyn, Poland. He joined the General Zionists in 1935. After the outbreak of World War II, he fled from Warsaw to Vilnius and then to Palestine. From 1941 he served as chief of the national command of the Haganah. He became a member of the executive of the Jewish Agency in 1945, but later resigned and joined the Mapam party. Eventually he established the Socialist Left Party (1953), which later joined the Israeli Communist Party (Maki). He was editor of the communist newspaper *Kol ha-Am* and wrote *Conclusions on the Jewish Problem in the Light of Marxism*.

Sobibor. Town in central Poland in the district of Lublin. A Nazi concentration camp, one of six extermination camps in Poland, was located in a wooded area near the town.

Sobol, Yehoshua (b. 1939). Israeli playwright. He was born in Tel Mond. He contributed to the leftist Israeli newspaper *Al Hamishmar*. From 1984 to 1988 he served as an art director at the Haifa Municipal Theater. His plays mostly explore life in modern Israel, but *Ghetto* depicts the existence of the Jewish community in the Vilnius Ghetto.

Socialism. Political and economic theory that advocates ownership and control by the community of the means of production, distribution, and exchange. Many Jews participated in the development of socialism in the 19th century. However, some socialists expressed a hostile attitude toward the Jewish community since they viewed Jews as an incarnation of social parasitism. Later in the century anti-Semitism came to the fore in certain socialist circles. Jewish socialists mostly espoused one of four approaches to the Jewish problem. According to the assimilationist view the Jews should be fully integrated with the communities in which they lived in the diaspora. The Territorialists were dedicated to the procuring of land where Jews could establish self-governing settlements. The Bundists believed that Jewish problems would be solved by the establishment of a socialist revolution, but that notwithstanding political circumstances Jewish cultural autonomy should be maintained. Zionist socialists aimed to establish a socialist territory in Palestine.

Social justice. The concept of equity for all members of society in matters of civil and social rights, access to social amenities, and so on. It is a central theme of biblical legislation and a primary concern of the prophetic books of the Bible. Rabbinic, medieval, and modern Jewish communal legislation continued to emphasize its importance.

Société des Études Juives. French society founded in 1880 by Isidore Loeb, Zadoc Kahn, and Israel Lévi. Its aims were to stimulate interest in the history of French Jewry and to spread a knowlege of Judaism. It published the *Revue des Études Juives*.

Society for the Advancement of Judaism. American Jewish congregation founded in 1922 by Mordecai M. Kaplan in pursuance of his views on the reconstruction of Judaism (*see* RECONSTRUCTIONISM). It aims to further the spread of Judaism, to which end it maintains a program of regular publications in association with the Reconstructionist Foundation.

Society for the Dissemination of the Enlightenment. Russian society founded in St. Petersburg in 1863 to promote secular education in the Russian language among Jews. It organized Jewish schools in which Russian was the language of instruction. In 1891 it established a scholarly society dedicated to the study of Jewish history and ethnography.

Sod ("secret"). Esoteric allegorical method of scriptural exegesis. It is based on the belief that the Torah has more than one level of meaning. It was used to interpret the Creation account in Genesis 1 (maaseh Bereshit) and Ezekiel's vision of the divine chariot in Ezekiel 1 (maaseh merkavah).

Sodom [Sedom]. Ancient Israelite city. Most important of the five cities (Sodom, Gomorrah, Admah, Zeboiim, and Zoar) of the Jordan plain. Lot settled there, but escaped when the city was destroyed because of the wickedness of its inhabitants (Genesis 19).

Sokolow, Naḥum (1859–1936). Polish Zionist leader. He was born in Wyszogrod, near Płock, Poland. He joined the editorial board of the journal *Ha-Tzephirah* in Warsaw in 1884, later becoming its manager. From 1905 to 1909 he served as secretary of the World Zionist Organization; during this period he edited the organization's journal *Die Welt* and also (in 1907) founded its Hebrew weekly *Ha-Olam.* At the outbreak of World War I he moved from Berlin to London, where he became involved in the negotiations concerning the Balfour Declaration. After the war he presided over the Comité des Délégations Juives during the Versailles peace conference in 1919. He was chairman of the executive of the Zionist Organization (1921–31), and president of the World Zionist Organization and the Jewish Agency. His writings include a study entitled *History of Zionism.*

Sola, David Aaron de (1796–1860). British rabbi. He was born in Amsterdam. He became ḥazzan of the London Sephardi community in 1818. His writings include *Forms of Prayer According to the Custom of the Spanish and Portuguese Jews* and *Eighteen Treatises of the Mishnah.*

Solis-Cohen, Solomon (1857–1948). American physician and poet. He was a professor of clinical medicine at Jefferson Medical College, Philadelphia (1904–27), and was also active in Jewish and Zionist organizations. He translated Hebrew poetry into English, including Ibn Ezra's *Selected Poems.*

Solomon (fl. 10th cent. BCE). King of Israel (965–931 BCE), son of David and Bathsheba. He became king before his father's death, through the influence of Bathsheba and Nathan, who promoted his accession to the throne in place of Adonijah, his elder brother. Solomon built the Temple in Jerusalem, constructed fortresses, store cities and chariot cities, and built a harbour at Elath; he also made administrative innovations, including the division of the country into 12 districts. The biblical books Song of Songs and Ecclesiastes are attributed to him, as is Psalm 72. According to the Bible, he was known for his wisdom.

Solomon, Norman (b. 1923). British rabbi. He was born in Cardiff. He served as minister of the Hampstead synagogue in London, and later became Director of the Centre for the Study of Judaism and Jewish Christian Relations at Selly Oak College in Birmingham. He served as the editor of the journal *Christian Jewish Relations.*

Solomon, Psalms of *see* PSALMS OF SOLOMON.

Solomon, Solomon Joseph (1860–1921). English painter. He painted portraits and figure compositions using Jewish motifs.

Solomon, Song of *see* SONG OF SONGS.

Solomon ben Adret [Solomon ben Abraham] *see* ADRET, SOLOMON BEN.

Solomon ben Isaac *see* RASHI.

Solomon ben Jeroham (fl. 10th cent.). Palestinian Karaite scholar. He lived in Egypt and Jerusalem. His writings include Arabic commentaries on the Bible and a Hebrew polemic against the Saadyah Gaon.

Solomon ha-Levi of Burgos *see* SANTA MARIA, PAUL DE.

Solomon Yitzḥak ben Isaac *see* RASHI.

Soloveichik, Ḥayyim (1853–1918). Lithuanian talmudist, son of Joseph Baer Soloveichik. He was born in Volozhin, and taught at the yeshivah there from 1880 to 1892. Later he lived in Brest-Litovsk, where he served as rabbi. He developed a new trend in talmudic study based on conceptual analysis. He also wrote novellae on talmudic tractates and on Maimonides' *Mishneh Torah.*

Soloveichik, Isaac Ze'ev (1886–1959). Lithuanian rabbi and halakhist, son of Ḥayyim Soloveichik. He was born in Volozhin, and became rabbi of Brest-

Litovsk in 1918 after the death of his father. During World War II he fled to Vilnius, and he later settled in Jerusalem, where he founded a kolel (academy for advanced study of the Talmud).

Soloveichik, Joseph (b. 1903). American talmudic scholar, son of Isaac Ze'ev Soloveichik. He was born in Pruzhany, Poland, and grew up in Hasloviz, Belorussia. In 1932 he emigrated to the US, where he served as a rabbi in Boston. He became professor of Talmud at the Isaac Elhanan Yeshiva in 1941. He was also professor of Jewish philosophy at the university's Bernard Revel Graduate School. His writings include *Ish ha-Halakhah*, an explanation of his theological position.

Soloveichik, Joseph Baer (1820–1892). Lithuanian talmudist. He lived in Volozhin, where he served as joint rosh yeshivah with Naphtali Tzevi Judah Berlin. Later he became rabbi of Slutsk, and, after a period spent in Warsaw (1875–8), of Brest-Litovsk. His *Bet ha-Levi* contains novellae on the Talmud, responsa, and sermons.

Sommerstein, Emil (1868–1946). Austrian soldier. He was born in Bukovina. He fought in Galicia during World War I, and later commanded the Austrian army that captured Burgenland. He served as head of the Austrian organization for Jewish war veterans. After the Anschluss he was put under house arrest, and in 1942 he was deported to Theresienstadt. He returned to Vienna at the end of the war; he later settled in the US.

Sommi, Leone de (1527–1592). Italian dramatist and poet. He was born in Mantua. He wrote and staged plays for the Gonzaga court theater, and eventually became renowned throughout Europe as a dramatist and director. In 1585 he bought property in Mantua on which he built a synagogue. His writings include plays, poems, canzones, and satires. His greatest works are the *Dialoghi*, an exposition on stagecraft, and his Hebrew comedy of betrothal, *Ẓaḥut Bediḥuta de-Kidushin.*

Soncino. Town in northern Italy. Israel Nathan Soncino set up a Hebrew printing press there in 1483; his work was continued by his son Joshua Solomon Soncino and his grandson Gershon ben Moses Soncino. The press, at Casalmaggiore for a time, which published books in Hebrew, Latin, and Italian, operated at Casalmaggiore for a time, returned to Soncino, and later moved to Naples, Brescia, Barco, Fano, Pesaro, Ortona, and Rimini. From 1526 it operated in Turkey.

Soncino Press. English Hebrew publishing company, founded in 1929. It was named after the Hebrew press set up at Soncino in Italy in the 15th century.

Song of Deborah *see* DEBORAH (i).

Song of Degrees (Hebrew "Shir ha-Maalot"). Title found at the head of each of the 15 psalms from 120 to 134. Various interpretations of the description have been advanced. It is thought that the word "degrees", having to do with ascent, may imply that the psalms were recited as the Jews returned from Babylon to Palestine, or that they are the songs of pilgrims on their way to Jerusalem. It has also been suggested that "degrees" should be interpreted more literally and that this group of psalms was recited in the Temple by the Levites on the 15 steps leading from the Court of the Israelites to the Women's Court at the Water-Drawing Festival.

Song of Moses *see* MOSES, SONG OF.

Song of Songs (Hebrew "Shir ha-Shirim") [Song of Solomon]. Biblical book, part of the Hagiographa. It is attributed to Solomon, and consists of a series of love poems. It was interpreted in the Talmud and by medieval Jewish commentators as an allegory depicting the love between God and Israel.

Song of Songs Rabbah (Hebrew "Shir ha-Shirim Rabbah") [Midrash Ḥazita]. Midrash to the Song of Songs, dating from about the 9th century. It is also known as Midrash Ḥazita after the opening word of its first verse (Proverbs 22.29).

Sonntag, Jacob (1905–1984). British scholar and editor. He was born in Wiznitz, northern Bukovina, and grew up in Vienna; he emigrated to England in 1938. In 1953 he founded the scholarly journal the *Jewish Quarterly*, which he edited.

Sons of God (Hebrew "Benei Elohim"). Term used variously in the Bible to designate demi-gods, angels, and mythological beings, as well as humans who have a special relationship with God. In the Apocrypha it also refers to the Messiah. Rabbinic literature applies the term to Israel or to man generally.

Sons of Man (Hebrew "Benei Adam"). Term used variously in the Bible to mean ordinary men or men of God. In Ezekiel 2.1 the prophet is called the Son of Man in the vision of the divine chariot. In the Book of Daniel the expression is first used in an apocalyptic context (Daniel 7.13), but is then applied to Daniel himself by the Angel Gabriel (Daniel 8.17). The name later passed into eschatological usage as a messianic title.

Sons of Light. Term found in the Dead Sea Scrolls, denoting the godly (in contrast to the Sons of Darkness – the ungodly). In the Qumran community, where the scrolls originated, the members of the community and their sympathizers were designated "Sons of Light."

Sopher *see* SCRIBE.

Sopher [Schreiber]**, Moses** [Ḥatam Sopher] (1762–1839). Slovakian rabbi. From 1903 he served as rabbi at Pressburg, where he founded a yeshivah. He was an influential preacher, halakhic authority, and opponent of Reform Judaism. His *Ḥatam Sopher* (after which he was known) contains responsa and novellae.

Sotah ("errant wife") **(i).** A married woman suspected of adultery (Numbers 5.11–31). The Bible prescribed a procedure to prove her innocence or guilt.

Sotah ("Errant wife") **(ii).** Sixth tractate in the Mishnah order of Nashim. It deals with the laws concerning a woman suspected of adultery (Numbers 5.11–31); the liturgical readings which may be recited in any language as opposed to those which must be recited in Hebrew; and the rite of breaking the neck of a heifer, performed when a murder by an unknown hand has been discovered. (Deuteronomy 21.1–9). It also contains a discussion of declining standards after the destruction of the Temple, and depicts the chaos that will precede messianic redemption.

Soul. The spiritual, immaterial part of man, held to survive death. There are three biblical words translated as "soul": "nephesh," "ruaḥ," and "neshamah"; all derive from words meaning "breath" or "wind." The Bible makes an intimate connection between the soul and life itself, and speaks of the soul as the means by which the body is animated. After death the soul has only a shadow existence in Sheol. During the Hellenistic period the concept of the soul's existing independently of the body became current; it was understood as originating in Heaven and was believed to join the body at the moment of birth. In kabbalistic Judaism metempsychosis ("gilgul") was an important doctrine.

Souls, transmigration of *see* METEMPSYCHOSIS.

Spalato *see* SPLIT.

Spector, Mordecai (1858–1925). Ukrainian Yiddish novelist and editor. He was born in Uman. Initially he wrote sketches and novels, including *Der yidisher muzhik*, which advocated the return of the Jews to productive labor in Palestine. In 1857 he settled in Warsaw, where he wrote travel sketches, short stories, and novels, and also edited a series of anthologies; in 1894 he helped to set up the important anthology *Yontev bletlekh*. He moved to New York in 1921, and shortly before the end of his life wrote a volume of memoirs, *Mayn lebn*.

Spektor, Isaac Elhanan [Isaac Elhanan] (1817–1896). Lithuanian rabbi. He was born in the province of Grodno, Russia. He served as a rabbi in various towns, eventually settling in Kovno, where he officiated until his death. He established a yeshivah in Kovno, and organized aid for stricken communities; he was the only rabbi invited to attend the conference of Jewish leaders held in St. Petersburg in 1881–2 to discuss the plight of Jewry. Subsequently he supported the Ḥibbat Zion movement. The Isaac Elhanan Yeshiva in New York (later incorporated into Yeshiva University) was named for him.

Sperber, Manes (1905–1984). Austrian author. He was born in Zabolotov, Galicia, and moved to Vienna in 1916. He taught in Berlin from 1927 to 1933 and then settled in Paris. His novels about shtetl life include *Like Tears in the Ocean* and *All our Yesterdays*.

Speyer [Spires]. Town in western Germany on the River Speyer, close to its confluence with the Rhine. Jews settled there in the 11th century, and in 1096 the bishop of Speyer protected the Jewish community from the crusaders. At this time the town was a center of Jewish scholarship, one of a group with Worms and Mainz which held joint rabbinical synods. However, the Jews of Speyer suffered massacre during the Black Death (1348–9), and discrimination and expulsion in the following century.

Spicehandler, Ezra (b. 1921). American Hebrew scholar. He was born in Brooklyn. He became professor of modern Hebrew literature at the Hebrew Union College in 1952. In 1966 he was appointed director and then dean of the Hebrew Union College in Jerusalem. He published works dealing with modern and medieval Hebrew literature, Zionism, Judeo-Persian studies, and talmudic history.

Spices. Aromatic woods were used in producing incense for the Temple. At the close of the Sabbath it is the custom to smell fragrant spices, and the spice boxes used for this practice have become a form of Jewish ritual art. Specific benedictions are prescribed to be recited on smelling aromatic woods or cloves. In the Middle Ages Jews were involved in the spice trade between Asia and Europe.

Spiegel, Shalom (1899–1984). American scholar and educator. He was born in Romania, and educated in Vienna. From 1923 to 1929 he taught in Palestine, but then settled in New York, where he was professor of medieval Hebrew literature at the Jewish Theological Seminary. His publications include studies of the biblical prophets, and an edition of the liturgical compositions of Eleazar Kallir.

Spiegelman, Art (b. 1948). American cartoonist, of Swedish origin. His cartoon strip *Maus* is a depiction of the Holocaust based on the metaphor of the Nazis as cats and the Jews as mice.

***Spiel, Hilde** (1911–1990). Austrian author. She was born in Vienna. She went to Britain in 1936 and later lived in both Vienna and London. Although she was a Roman Catholic, she was interested in Jewish life. Her novel *Fanny von Arnstein* is a description of the Jewish contribution to the Enlightenment.

Spielman, Sir **Isidore** (1854–1925).

English communal leader. He was the founder and director of the art exhibits branch of the Board of Trade. In 1887 he organized an exhibit on British Jewry under the title the Anglo-Jewish Historical Exhibition; he also served as president of the Jewish Historical Society (1902–4).

Spielvogel, Nathan (1874–1956). Australian author. He was born in Ballarat, in the state of Victoria. He was a country schoolteacher and traveled frequently in the eastern Australian outback. In his writing he portrayed Jewish immigrants who arrived in Australia from England and Europe.

***Spina, Alfonso de** (d. 1468). Spanish priest. He was General of the Franciscan order, rector of the University of Salamanca, and confessor to Henry IV of Castile. He helped to introduce the Inquisition into Spain. His *Fortalitium fidei* contains anti-Jewish polemics.

Spinoza [De Spinoza; Espinoza]**, Benedict** (1632–1677). Dutch philosopher. He was born in Amsterdam. He had a traditional education, but his heretical views led to his excommunication in 1656. From 1660 he lived away from Amsterdam, earning his living as a lens polisher. His *Theologico-Political Treatise* initiated modern biblical criticism. In his *Ethics* he applied Euclidean methods to demonstrate a metaphysical concept of the universe with ethical implications.

Spire, André (1868–1966). French poet and Zionist leader. He was born in Nancy. He became a member of the Conseil d'État in 1894, specialized in employment problems at the French Ministry of Labor (1898–1902), and served as inspector-general in the Ministry of Agriculture (1902–26). He played an active part in the Dreyfus Affair. He became an advocate of Zionism, and in 1919 represented the French Zionists at the Paris Peace Conference. During World War II he lived in the US. His writings include *Poèmes juifs* and *Quelque Juifs et demi-Juifs*.

Spires *see* SPEYER.

Split [Spalato]. Port in Yugoslavia on the Dalmatian coast. Its development as a free port in the 16th century was due to the former Marrano, Daniel Rodriguez. Its Jewish community was confined to the ghetto in 1738 but was emancipated by the French in 1797.

Sport. The Bible records the use of lances, swords, and slings for sport or training. In the 2nd century BCE a gymnasium was established in Jerusalem to train Jewish youths. Herod the Great constructed stadia and organized Palestinian teams to take part in the Olympic Games. In talmudic and post-talmudic times physical training was not regarded as a priority. In the modern period, however, Jews have been involved in a wide variety of sports activities. Since 1932 international gatherings of Jewish athletes have been held under the auspices of the MACCABIAH.

Sprinzak, Yoseph (1885–1959). Israeli politician. He was born in Russia, where he was one of the founders of the socialist youth movement Tzeire Zion. He settled in Palestine in 1908, where he became active in labor politics. A founder of the Histadrut and Mapai, he represented Mapai in the Knesset, and later became speaker of the Knesset.

***Stahl, Friedrich Julius** (1802–1861). German statesman. He was born in Würzburg, Bavaria, and converted to Lutheranism in 1819. In 1840 he was appointed professor of law at the University of Berlin. He became a member of the Upper House of the Prussian parliament in 1848, and led his party's opposition to the Emancipation of the Jews.

Stamps. The first postage stamps issued by the State of Israel appeared on 16 May 1948. Special stamps have been issued for anniversaries, congresses, and memorial days, and for each Jewish New Year and Independence Day.

Starer, Robert (b. 1924). American composer. He was born in Vienna. He fled the Nazis in 1938 and settled in Palestine, where he became staff pianist for the BBC Palestine. Later he taught at the Juilliard School in New York and became professor of composition at Brooklyn College. His compositions include settings of the Psalms, and liturgical cantatas such as *Kohelet*, *Ariel*, and *Joseph and his Brothers*.

Star of David *see* MAGEN DAVID.

Starr, Joshua (1907–1949). American historian and communal worker. He was born in New York. He was secretary of the Commission for European Jewish Cultural Reconstruction in 1947–9. He published studies of Byzantine and post-Byzantine Jewish history.

State of Israel *see* ISRAEL, STATE OF.

Statistics. The Bible records several instances of a census (as in the Book of Numbers). Subsequently attempts were made from time to time to number Jewry. In the 12th century Benjamin of Tudela estimated the Jewish population in each place he visited. The scientific gathering of statistical information about Jewish communities took place from the 18th century onward; for example, the German Büro für Statistik der Juden (Institute for Jewish Demography) in Berlin published a journal giving such information until the mid-1920s. Statistics on the population of the State of Israel are maintained by the Statistical Bureau.

***Stein, Edith** (1891–1942). German philosopher. She was born in Breslau. She converted to Catholicism in 1922; she was appointed lecturer at the Institute for Pedagogy at Münster in 1932, but in 1933 abandoned her post and entered the Carmelite convent in Cologne as Sister Theresa Benedicta of the Cross. In 1938 she moved to the Netherlands. Under the Nazis she was deported to Auschwitz, where she died. Her collected works were published in five volumes.

Steinberg, Ben (b. 1930). Canadian composer, conductor, organist, and educator. He was born in Winnipeg. He taught music in public schools in Toronto, and from 1988 he served as director of music at the city's Temple Sinai. He has written Jewish liturgical music, and *Echoes of Children* commemorating the children who died during the Holocaust.

Steinberg, Isaac Nachman (1888–1957). Russian revolutionary and writer. He was born in Dvinsk, worked as a lawyer in Moscow before World War I. He was arrested and exiled because of his revolutionary activities, but returned to Russia in 1910. In 1917–18 he was commissar for law. Later he lived in Berlin, London, and New York. He was prominent in the Yiddish and Territorialist movements, and published studies of the Russian Revolution and Jewish issues.

Steinberg, Judah (1863–1908). Bessarabian writer and educator. He was born in Lipkany. His early works include a writing manual, a book of proverbs, and a children's storybook. In 1897 he became a teacher in Leovo, Moldavia, and later settled in Odessa, where he was the correspondent of the New York daily *Di warheit*. He published textbooks, children's stories, feuilletons, and fables. A number of his stories deal with Ḥasidic life.

Steinberg, Milton (1930–1950). American rabbi and novelist. He was born in Rochester, New York, and became rabbi at New York's Park Avenue Synagogue. His publications include *As a Driven Leaf*, *The Making of the Modern Jew*, *Basic Judaism*, *A Partisan Guide to the Jewish Problem*, and *A Believing Jew*.

Steinberg, Yaakov (1887–1947). Hebrew author. He lived in Warsaw, Switzerland,

and Palestine. His stories, set in the Ukraine, illustrate the difficulties of life in the diaspora.

Steiner, George (b. 1929). British scholar. He was born in Paris. He became professor of comparative literature at Geneva University and a fellow of Churchill College, Cambridge. Many of his writings deal with Jewish themes; they include *The Death of Tragedy*, *After Babel*, *In Bluebeard's Castle*, and *The Portage to San Cristobal of A.H.*

Steinhardt, Jakob (1887–1968). Israeli artist. He was born in Zerków, Poland, and in 1933 settled in Palestine, where he became director of the Bezalel School of Arts and Crafts in Jerusalem. He produced woodcuts dealing with Jewish and biblical themes, as well as Palestinian landscapes.

Steinheim, Solomon Ludwig (1789–1866). German philosopher. He was born in Bruchhausen, Westphalia, and practiced as a physician in Altona from 1813 to 1845. Later he settled in Rome. His writings include *Revelation According to the Doctrine of the Synagogue* and *The Doctrine of the Synagogue as Exact Science*.

Steinman, Eliezer (1892–1970). Israeli writer. He was born in Obodovka, in the Ukraine, and became a part-time Hebrew teacher in Odessa. In 1920 he left Russia, and settled in Warsaw, where he wrote stories, essays, articles, and a novel; he also published collections of Yiddish essays and stories about the pogroms against Ukrainian Jews. In 1924 he settled in Tel Aviv, where he wrote for *Ha-Aretz* and *Ha-Olam* and published stories and novels. He later became a columnist for *Davar*.

Steinschneider, Moritz (1816–1907). German bibliographer and orientalist. He was born in Prossnitz, Moravia. He taught in Prague and Berlin, where he also preached, officiated at weddings, worked as a translator, and wrote Hebrew textbooks. He was appointed lecturer at the Veitel-Heine-Ephraimsche Lehranstalt in 1859, and taught there for 48 years. From 1869 he was also assistant librarian at the Berlin State Library. He produced catalogs of the Hebrew books at the Bodleian Library, Oxford, and of the Hebrew manuscripts at Leyden, Munich, Hamburg, and Berlin. His other publications include studies of the history of Jewish literature and Hebrew typography. From 1858 to 1882 he edited the *Hebräische Bibliographie*.

Steinthal, Heymann (1823–1899). German philologist and philosopher. He studied in Berlin and was appointed lecturer in philology and mythology at Berlin University in 1850. In 1872 he became professor of biblical studies and philosophy of religion at the Hochschule für die Wissenschaft des Judentums. He and Moritz Lazarus were the originators of the science of racial psychology.

Stencl, Avrom-Nokhem (1897–1983). Polish Yiddish poet. He was born in Czeładzy, Poland. He went to the Netherlands in 1919, then moved to Germany, and eventually settled in England. His publications include *Londoner sonetn* and *Vaytshepl shtetl d'Britn*.

Sterilization. The Bible contains prohibitions against castration and against the marriage of a man "crushed or maimed in his privy parts" (Deuteronomy 23.2). On the basis of these laws, the rabbis concluded that it is forbidden to impair the reproductive organs in humans, beasts, or birds. In males this includes the mutilation of the penis, testicles, or seminal ducts (even after any previous impairment). The use of oral contraceptives and of sterilizing agents is also forbidden, as is the sterilization of females. The marriage ban applies only to those injured by human means rather than through an act of God or through illness.

Stern, Abraham Jacob 1762–1842). Polish maskil and mathematician. He was born in Hrubieszów, and lived in Warsaw. He invented a calculating machine and a threshing machine, and acted as government censor for Hebrew books.

Stern, Avraham [Yair] (1907–1942). Palestinian underground fighter. He was born in Suwałki, Poland. He went to Palestine in 1925 and became active in the Irgun Tzevai Leumi. In 1940 he formed an underground organization, Loḥame Ḥerut Yisrael (known as the Stern Gang). He was killed by the British police while he was being arrested.

Stern, Gladys Bronwyn [Holdsworth, Mrs.] (1890–1973). English novelist. She was born in London, and worked as a writer and journalist. Many of her novels deal with Jewish themes; they include *Matriarch Chronicles, Children of No Man's Land, Tents of Israel,* and *Mosaic.*

Sternberg, Erich Walter (1891–1974). Israeli composer. He was born in Berlin, and settled in Palestine in 1932. His early compositions incorporated material from eastern European Jewish folklore. Many of his works are based on biblical themes and Jewish liturgical traditions.

Sternberg, Sigmund (b. 1921). British communal leader and philanthropist. He was born in Hungary, and settled in Britain. He has been active in various Jewish organizations, supporting Jewish education and interfaith activities.

Stern Gang *see* LOḤAME ḤERUT YISRAEL.

Stern-Täubler, Selma (1890–1989). American historian, wife of Eugen Täubler. She was archivist of the American Jewish Archives in Cincinnati from 1947 to 1956. She wrote about the history of German Jewry and about court Jews.

Stiebel (Yiddish: "small room"). Side room in a synagogue, used for public prayer. The term is also applied to the meeting place of Ḥasidic Jews.

***Stiles, Ezra** (1727–1795). American Hebraist. He was born in North Haven, Connecticut, and served as minister of the Congregational church in Newport, Rhode Island. He was a friend of Raphael Ḥayyim Isaac Carigal. When he became president of Yale University in 1778, he made the study of Hebrew compulsory.

Stobi. Ancient Greco-Roman town in Macedonia. The remains of a synagogue have been found there.

Stockade and tower *see* ḤOMAH U-MIGDAL.

***Stöcker, Adolph** (1835–1909). German politician. He was imperial court chaplain in Berlin from 1874. In 1878 he founded the Christian Social Workers' Party, and from 1879 to 1898 he was a member of the Prussian Diet. He also served in the Reichstag (1881–1908), where he advocated anti-Semitic attitudes.

Stoicism. Philosophical doctrine founded in c. 300 BCE in Athens. The stoics made virtue the highest good, advocated control of the passions, and inculcated indifference to pleasure and pain. Stoicism flourished during the Greco-Roman period; it exercised an influence on Hellenistic Jewish thought, as well as on medieval Jewish theology.

Stone, Elihu D. (1888–1952). American Zionist. From 1922 to 1934 he was assistant attorney for Massachusetts. He founded a Zionist organization for the New England region.

Stone, Mickey *see* MARCUS, DAVID.

Stone worship. The use of stones in religious worship was current from ancient times, but is forbidden in the Bible: the Israelites were commanded not to erect a pillar or bow down to figured stone (Leviticus 26.1). Stones however were used as memorials of historic events (Joshua 4.9; 8.32; I Samuel 7.12) and as markers (Genesis 31.48–52).

***Strack, Hermann Leberecht** (1848–

1922). German orientalist. He was born in Berlin, and became founder and director and professor of oriental languages of the university's Institutum Judaicum. He was the leading non-Jewish scholar in the fields of Bible, Talmud, Hebrew and Aramaic linguistics, and Masorah. He also engaged in missionary work. His writings include *Introduction to the Talmud and Midrash.*

Stranger (Hebrew "nokhrim," "zarim"). According to the Bible, strangers must be shown consideration and should be treated like native-born Israelites (Leviticus 19.33–4). The rabbis asserted that in order to qualify for the protection offered by Jewish law, the stranger must adhere to the Noachian Laws.

Strashun [Zaskovitzer]**, Samuel** (1794–1872). Lithuanian talmudic scholar. He was born in Zaskovitzer; he was initially named after his birthplace, but later adopted the name of his father-in-law, David Strashun. He lived in Vilnius, where he devoted himself to scholarship. He wrote annotations and glosses on almost all the tractates of the Mishnah and the Talmud.

Straus, Nathan (1848–1931). American merchant and philanthropist, brother of Oscar Solomon Straus. He was commissioner first for parks then for health in New York, and a member of the New York Forest Preserve Board. He established a milk pasteurization laboratory and milk distribution stations in New York, an emergency relief system to distribute coal and food to the poor, and a chain of boarding houses for the destitute. He also established the Pasteur Institute in Palestine and endowed child welfare stations and health centers there.

Straus, Oscar Solomon (1850–1926). American diplomat and jurist, brother of Nathan Straus. He served as American minister in Turkey, and later was appointed to the International Court of Arbitration at The Hague. He was secretary of commerce and labor in the US (1906–9) and then ambassador to Turkey. He helped to found the American Jewish Committee, served as an officer of the Baron de Hirsch Fund, and was president of the American Jewish Historical society. In his writings he illustrated the impact of Hebrew concepts on American culture.

Strauss, Leo (1899–1973). American philosopher and political scientist, of German origin. After emigrating to the US, he taught at the New School for Social Research in New York (1938–49) and was appointed professor of political science at the University of Chicago. He wrote studies of political philosophy and the relation between philosophy and theology.

***Streicher, Julius** (1885–1946). German journalist. He was involved in Hitler's Munich putsch, and edited the newspaper *Der Stürmer* from 1923 to 1945.

Streisand, Barbra (b. 1942). American singer and actress. She was born in Brooklyn. She appeared in Broadway musicals and in films, some of which have Jewish subjects.

Stricker, Robert (1879–1944). Austrian Zionist leader and journalist. He was born in Brünn, and became an engineer for Austrian state railways. Before World War I he edited the Vienna *Jüdische Zeitung*, and in 1915 he founded the Jewish War Archives. He became president of the Jewish People's Party, and in 1919 was elected to the Constituent National Assembly of the Federal Austrian Republic. From 1919 to 1928 he edited the *Wiener Morgenzeitung* and later *Die Neue Welt.* In 1931 he joined the Union of Zionist Revisionists, then in 1933 was one of the founders of the Jewish State Party.

Stroock, Alan Maxwells (1907–1985). American lawyer, son of Solomon

Marcuse Stroock. He started his career as a law clerk to Supreme Court Justice Benjamin Cardozo (1934–6), then joined the Stroock family legal firm Stroock and Stroock, where he became a partner. He served as chairman of the board and later president of the corporation of the Jewish Theological Seminary in New York, and was also active in various other Jewish organizations.

Stroock, Solomon Marcuse (1874–1945). American communal leader. A specialist in constitutional law, he was the chairman of various legal committees. He served as president of the New York branch of the Young Men's Hebrew Association, the Federation for the support of Jewish Philanthropic Societies in New York, and the American Jewish Committee.

Struma. Name of an immigrant ship, which left Romania for Palestine in 1941. It reached Istanbul, but turned back when it was learned that the British Mandatory government would refuse its refugees entry into Palestine. The ship foundered in the Black Sea with the loss of all those on board.

Student Zionist Organization [SZO]. American student organization. Zionist activities on American college campuses were initially sponsored by Avukah, founded in the mid-1920s. In 1945 Avukah was superseded by the Intercollegiate Zionist Federation of America (IZFA), which was replaced in its turn by the Student Zionist Organization.

Stutschewsky, Joachim (1891–1981). Israeli cellist, composer, and historian, of Ukrainian origin. He worked as a cellist in Switzerland and in Vienna, where he contributed essays on Jewish music to the periodical *Die Stimme*. In 1938 he settled in Palestine. He organized concerts of Jewish music in Tel Aviv. He composed works for cello, numerous songs, and arrangements of folk songs. He also engaged in historical research on Ḥasidic musicians.

Suarès, André (1866–1948). French author, of Portuguese Jewish descent. He was born near Marseilles. Although he adopted a negative attitude to Judaism, he rallied to the defense of the Jews after the advent of Nazism.

Subbotniki. Name of a group of Russian Sabbatarians, which emerged at the end of the 18th century. Most of the Subbotniki practiced Jewish customs but acknowledged the New Testament in addition to the Hebrew Scriptures; others accepted the Hebrew Scriptures but not the Talmud. Under Nicholas I they were banished to Siberia and conscripted into the army, but from 1905 they enjoyed religious freedom. Some of their descendants reverted to traditional Judaism and settled in Palestine.

Suffering. The problem of human suffering occupies a central place in the Bible and the Talmud. A theme of the Book of Job is that the righteous person may be forced to endure suffering in order to prove that he is capable of piety. Other books of the Bible assume a direct relationship between suffering and sin. The rabbis also adopted this view, but conceded that suffering can come upon an innocent person without explanation or apparent justification. Central to Jewish theology is the belief that the righteous will be rewarded in the world to come.

Suicide. Taking one's own life is regarded, in the Jewish faith, as a crime equivalent to murder. A person who had committed suicide was denied normal burial and mourning. Suicide is clearly differentiated from martyrdom which is extolled in Judaism.

Sukenik, Eliezer Lipa (1889–1953). Israeli archeologist. He was born in Białystok, and settled in Palestine in 1912. He became professor of archeology at the Hebrew University. He excavated the Third Wall of Jerusalem, the city of Samaria, and the synagogues in the town of Beth Alpha.

Sukkah ("tabernacle") **(i).** Booth erected during the festival of Sukkot. According to Leviticus, Jews are obliged to dwell or at least eat in it for the seven days of Sukkot (Leviticus 23.42). It symbolizes God's protection of the Israelites during their 40 years of wandering in the desert. According to custom it is decorated with curtains, fruits, and symbols of the holy day. In modern times it is usually constructed near the synagogue, and a token meal is eaten there after the service on each day of the festival.

Sukkah ("Tabernacle") **(ii).** Sixth tractate in the Mishnah order of Moed. It deals with the laws concerning the festival of Sukkot and it also contains a description of the Festival of the Water-Drawing, which in the first and second Temple periods was celebrated at the same time.

Sukkot ("Tabernacles") [Ḥag ha-Asiph; Ingathering Festival]. One of the three pilgrim festivals. It begins on 15 Tishri and lasts for seven days (eight days in the diaspora). The eighth day (22 Tishri) is a separate holy day, Shemini Atzeret. Work is prohibited on the first day of Sukkot (or two days in the diaspora), and on Shemini Atzeret. The festival is also known as "Ḥag ha-Asiph" (Festival of the Harvest) or simply "Ḥag," and marks the end of the agricultural year (hence the English name Ingathering Festival, derived from Exodus 23.16). During the Temple period the first day of Sukkot was also celebrated as a water libation festival (*see* SIMḤAT BET HA-SHOEVAH). Sukkot is celebrated by taking four species of plant – palm (lulav), citron (etrog), myrtle, and willow – and carrying them in procession in the synagogue (*see* HOSHANAH RABBAH); according to Leviticus (23.42), it is also required to dwell or at least eat all meals in the sukkah.

Sulzbach. Town in Baden-Württemberg, western Germany. A Hebrew press was set up there in 1669 and continued in operation until 1851. It printed the Bible, the Talmud, and the Zohar, as well as works in Yiddish.

Sulzberger, Mayer (1843–1923). American jurist and communal leader. He was born in Heidelsheim, Germany, and emigrated to the US in 1849. He became a lawyer in Philadelphia, and in 1895 was elected a judge of the Court of Common Pleas. He lectured on Hebrew jurisprudence and government at Dropsie College and the Jewish Theological Seminary. He served as president of the American Jewish Committee and the Young Men's Hebrew Association of Philadelphia. His writings include *The Am ha-Aretz – the Ancient Hebrew Parliament: a Chapter in the Constitutional History of Ancient Israel*, *The Policy of the Ancient Hebrews*, *The Ancient Hebrew Law of Homicide*, and *The Status of Labor in Ancient Israel.*

Sulzer, Solomon (1804–1890). Austrian cantor. He was born in Hohenems, in the Tyrol, and served as a cantor in Vienna from 1826. He sought to revive traditional cantorial music by incorporating modern musical innovations. His *Shir Tziyyon* purified many melodies from their later embellishments and included recitatives in the original Polish tradition.

Sumeria. Region of southern Mesopotamia, later part of ancient Babylonia. It was inhabited by a non-Semitic people (the Sumerians) who migrated there in prehistoric times and founded a series of city-states. Its culture was the basis of Babylonian civilization.

Summerfield, Woolfe (1901–1976). English lawyer and author. He was born in Manchester. Under the pseudonym Ben Mowshay he published two novels set in Kidston (Manchester) about the life of a Jewish hero, Abraham Bear Davis.

Sumptuary laws. Regulations limiting private expenditure. In Jewish communities laws that restricted extravagance in dress and festivities were known in talmudic times, and became common in the Middle Ages. They governed matters such as the number of guests that could be invited to private festivities, the dishes that could be served, the jewelry and dress that could be worn, and the nature and number of wedding gifts.

Sun, Blessing of the (Hebrew "Birkat ha-Ḥammah"). Blessing recited once in every 28 years on the first Wednesday of Nisan, when the sun is believed to be in the same place in the heavens as at the time of Creation.

Superstition. Credulity about the supernatural or mysterious. The Bible forbids divination and magic. In the Talmud superstitious practices and beliefs are frequently referred to, including the belief in demons, amulets, and sorcery, and the significance of dreams and chance occurrences. In the Middle Ages a number of Jewish authorities declared all forms of superstition to be nonsense. Nonetheless, such beliefs, enhanced by kabbalistic influences, have persisted in the form of folk customs.

Supplication *see* BAKKASHAH.

Sura. Ancient city in southern Babylonia. An academy was founded there by Rav in the early 3rd century and flourished for eight centuries. Here the Babylonian Talmud was largely compiled by Ashi and Ravina during the 4th–5th centuries. From the time of Mar bar Huna (591) the heads of the academy were called "gaon." The Sura academy eventually merged with the academy at Pumbedita, around the 11th century.

***Surenhuys, William** (1698–1763). Dutch orientalist. He was a professor of Greek and Hebrew at the University of Amsterdam. He published a Latin translation of the Mishnah together with the commentaries of Maimonides and Obadiah of Bertinoro.

Susa *see* SHUSHAN.

Susannah, History of [Susannah and the Elders]. Apocryphal book. It describes a plot by two elders against the virtue of Susannah and how Daniel exposed their guilt by uncovering contradictions in their account of the event.

Sushan-Dukht (fl. 5th cent.). Persian queen. The daughter of the exilarch, she married King Yezdegerd I of Persia (399–420), and became the mother of Bahram V (420–38). According to tradition, she founded the Jewish settlement in Isfahan.

Susita. Ancient Palestinian town on the eastern shore of the Sea of Galilee. During the 2nd century BCE it was renamed Hippos. It was captured from the Syrians by Alexander Yannai early in the 1st century BCE, and subsequently established as a city of the Decapolis by Pompey. Augustus gave the city to Herod the Great, but it eventually reverted to Syria. It was attacked by the Jews during the war against Rome (66–70 CE).

Sussmann, Heinrich (1904–1986). Austrian painter. He was born in Tarnopol, Galicia, and went to Vienna in 1914. He later lived in Berlin and (from 1933) Paris. His later work deals with themes of the Jewish diaspora, including memories of his childhood in Galicia.

Sutro, Adolph (1830–1898). American engineer. He was born in Aachen, Prussia. He went to the US in 1848 and first worked as a miner. After moving to San Francisco he dealt in real estate; he later served as the city's mayor. He amassed a large library, including numerous Hebrew manuscripts.

Sutskever [Sutzkever]**, Avraham** (b. 1913). Polish Yiddish poet. He was born in Smorgon, Belorussia. His family moved to Siberia then to Vilnius. He belonged to the "Yung Vilne" school of Yiddish poets. In 1941–3 he was incarcerated in the Vilnius ghetto, but escaped and joined the partisans. He settled in Paris in 1949. Many of his poems deal with European ghetto life and the Holocaust.

Swaythling, Baron *see* MONTAGU, SAMUEL.

Swine. Pig (or, collectively, pigs). According to the Bible, the meat of the pig is forbidden as food for Jews (Leviticus 11.7; Deuteronomy 14.8).

Swope, Gerard (1872–1957). American electrical engineer and philanthropist. He was born in St. Louis. He became president of the International General Electric Company. He made substantial contributions to the Haifa Technion.

Sykes–Picot Treaty. The name by which a series of secret agreements made between Britain, France, and Russia in 1914–16 are known. The agreements provided for the partition of the Turkish Empire after World War I, including the dismemberment of Palestine: Upper Galilee was to come under French control and the Haifa Bay area under British control; the Hauran was to become a French-protected Arab state, and the Transjordan and the Negev a British-protected Arab state; the remainder of central Palestine was to form an Anglo-French-Russian condominium. When Zionist leaders discovered the terms of the treaty in 1917, they protested against its provisions, but with little success.

Symmachus (fl. 2nd cent.). According to various traditions, he was an Ebionite, a Samaritan proselyte to Judaism, or a pupil of Meir. He translated the Bible into Greek.

Synagogue. Meeting place of a Jewish congregation, where services of public prayer are held. The synagogue originated in the 6th century BCE among the Babylonian exiles as a substitute for the Temple; it served as a place of prayer, study, and public assembly. By the 1st century it had become an established institution in Jewish life. From the 3rd century synagogues were decorated with figured carvings, mosaics, and frescoes. In the Middle Ages they became centers of study and most had a rabbinical school ("bet midrash") attached. Although synagogues are built to different plans they have certain common features: the Ark containing the Scrolls of the Law is built into the wall facing Jerusalem and the reading desk is placed on the bimah, or platform, before the Ark; in the past men and women sat separately, and they still do so in Orthodox Judaism. The officers of the synagogue include the gabbai, ḥazzan, and shammash. In the 19th century the Reform movement introduced the organ into the synagogue, abolished the women's area, and moved the reader's platform from the center of the building to the east wall; Reform Judaism also altered the synagogue liturgy and changed the name of the institution to "temple."

Synagogue Council of America. Body founded in 1926 to represent the voice of the religious Jewish community in the US; it thus acts on behalf of Orthodox, Conservative, and Reform Judaism.

Syncretism. Attempt to unify or reconcile differing schools of thought, beliefs, or principles. The term is applied specifically to the mixing of Greek and oriental religions during the Hellenistic period.

Synod. Religious council responsible for the government of organized religion. The most important Jewish synod in ancient times was that held in 138 at Usha in Lower Galilee to reorganize Jewish life after the Hadrianic persecutions. Local and regional rabbinical synods were held during the Middle Ages. In the 15th century a series of synods was held in Italy to combat anti-Jewish legislation by the Church. The Council of Four Lands served as the central governing body for Jewry in Poland and Lithuania from the 16th to the 18th centuries, though Lithuania had its own independent council from 1623. During the 19th century Reform rabbinical conferences were held in Europe. In the US, conferences of the Reform, Conservative, and Orthodox rabbinates take place annually.

Synthetic Zionism *see* ZIONISM.

Syria. Eastern Mediterranean country to the north of Israel. Modern Syria is cognate with the land called Aram in the Bible. There was constant friction between Syria and the kingdoms of Israel and Judah until the 8th century BCE, when Syria was overrun by the Assyrians. During the period of the Seleucids (late 4th–late 2nd centuries BCE) a large Jewish population was located at Antioch, one of the principal Syrian cities. Few Jews lived in Syria during the talmudic period, but the population increased with the Arab conquest in the 7th century. During the Middle Ages, Jews settled in Aleppo, Damascus, and Palmyra; their numbers increased after 1492 when an influx of refugees arrived in the Middle East after the expulsion of the Jews from Spain and Sicily. In 1840 the Damascus Affair in which a murder charge was brought against members of the Jewish community provoked a worldwide reaction. In modern times Syria has been constant in its opposition to the State of Israel, and since World War II there has been considerable emigration from Syria to Israel.

Syrkin, Marie (1899–1988). American author and educator. She was born in Berne, Switzerland, and was taken to the US as a child. She became the editor of the Labor Zionist monthly *Jewish Frontier*, and taught English at Brandeis University. Her writings include *Woman with a Cause* and *Blessed is the Match.*

Syrkin, Nachman (1868–1924). American leader of Socialist Zionism. He was born in Mohilev, Belorussia, and moved with his family to Minsk in 1884. Later he lived in Berlin, where he helped to found the Russian-Jewish Scientific Society, and participated in the first Zionist congresses. In 1907 he settled in New York and became active in Zionist work; he also contributed to Yiddish journals. During World War I he helped to establish the American Jewish Congress. He was a member of the Comité des Délégations Juives at the Paris Peace Conference in 1919. He published studies of Socialist Zionism.

Szenes, Hannah (1921–44). Palestinian poet and resistance fighter. She was born in Budapest, and moved to Palestine in 1939. She joined Kibbutz Sedot Yam, and began to write poetry. In 1942 she became one of a group of parachutists organized by the Haganah to rescue prisoners of war and organize Jewish resistance in Europe; she was dropped in Yugoslavia, and crossed the border into Hungary, where she was arrested and executed by the Nazis.

Szichman, Mario (b. 1945). Argentine novelist. In 1967 he went to Columbia, and later settled in Venezuela. He served as a foreign reporter for Jacobo Timerman's *La opinión* and as a correspondent for the Italian news agency. In 1980 he moved to the US, where he has continued to work as a correspondent. His novels trace the history of an eastern European family's attempt to adapt to life in Argentina.

Szigetti, Imre (1879–1975). Australian graphic artist and illustrator, of Hungarian origin. He was born in Budapest, and emigrated to Australia in 1939. A number of his drawings depict Hungarian Jewish life.

Szold, Benjamin (1829–1902). American rabbi. He was born in Nemiskert,

Hungary. He emigrated to the US and served as a rabbi at Congregation Oheb Shalom in Baltimore. With his daughter Henrietta Szold he organized study groups and a library for immigrants. He published studies and commentaries on the Bible.

Szold, Henrietta (1860–1945). American Zionist and philanthropist, daughter of Benjamin Szold. She ws born in Baltimore. She was secretary of the Jewish Publication Society (1892–1916), in which capacity she edited and translated many books and edited the *American Jewish Year Book.* In 1912 she organized Hadassah, the Women's Zionist Organization of America. She was the first woman to become a member of the executive of the Zionist Organization, in which she took responsibility for education and health. After the rise to power of the Nazis, she worked as a leader of Youth Aliyah.

Szomory, Dezső (1869–1944). Hungarian writer. He trained as a musician, studying at the Academy of Music in Budapest, before turning to writing. He later settled in Paris. Some of his works explore the problem of Jewish assimilation.

Szyk, Arthur (1894–1951). American artist. He was born in Łódź. After studying in Kraków and Paris, he specialized in book illumination. He produced illuminated versions of the Passover Haggadah and the Israeli Declaration of Independence. He lived in France and England, before settling in the US, where he produced book illustrations, and anti-Nazi caricatures.

T

Taanit ("Fast"). Ninth tractate in the Mishnah order of Moed. It deals with the designation of fast days during times of drought, as well as with the timing and form of prayers for rain. Other communal fasts are also discussed.

Tabatznik, Mendel (1894–1975). South African Yiddish essayist and poet. He was born in Kletsk, in Belorussia, and became the director of a Yiddish elementary school in Mir. In 1927 he settled in Johannesburg, South Africa, where he taught Yiddish and published articles about pedagogical issues. He also wrote poetry and an autobiographical novel.

Tabernacle [booth] (Hebrew "sukkah"). Portable habitation used as the sanctuary during the Israelites' years of wandering. Set up by Moses in the wilderness (Exodus 26–7), its chief architects were Bezalel and Oholiab. It was constructed of acacia wood overlaid with gold, and contained layers of curtains and animal skins, which gave it a tent-like appearance. Inside the tabernacle was the Holy of Holies, containing the Ark of the Covenant, the seven-branched menorah, the table where the shewbread was laid, and the golden altar for incense. The term "tabernacle" is also used of the booth constructed for the festival of Sukkot (*see* SUKKAH (i)).

Tabernacles *see* SUKKOT.

Tablets of the Law *see* TEN COMMANDMENTS; LAW, TABLETS OF THE.

Tabor, Mount. Mountain in Lower Galilee. Deborah and Barak concentrated their forces there before the battle with the Canaanites under Sisera (Judges 4). During Hellenistic times Mount Tabor was a royal fortress; it was refortified by Josephus, and stormed by the Romans under Titus. According to Christian tradition, Jesus was transfigured there in the presence of his disciples.

Tachlis (Yiddish). Achievement, or the substance of the matter.

Tadmor. Ancient city in Syria between the Euphrates and Orontes rivers. It was known as Palmyra to the Romans. During the Jewish rebellion against the Romans (66–70) citizens of Palmyra served in the Roman army. In the 3rd century Jews served in Roman military units raised from the city. Benjamin of Tudela found 2000 Jews living in Tadmor in the 12th century.

Tadshe. Opening word (and hence title) of a midrash dating from the late 2nd century and attributed to Phinehas ben Jair (it is also known as the "Baraita of Phineas ben Jair"). It deals with the symbolism of numbers.

Tag ("crown"). The name given to a short vertical stroke added to the top of various Hebrew letters when they are used in the Torah and other parts of Scripture. According to the Masorah, the letters shin, ayin, tet, nun, zayin, gimel, and tsadeh require three crown strokes. Other letters require one or none. The kabbalah stresses the mystical meanings of the tagin.

Taḥanun ("Supplication"). The name of a prayer for grace and forgiveness. It is recited daily (except on Sabbaths, festivals, and days of celebration) after the morning and afternoon Amidah. Its wording was established after the gaonic period.

Taharah *see* TOHORAH.

Taḥkemoni *see* AL-ḤARIZI, JUDAH.

Takhrikhim. Shroud.

Takkanah ("directive"). The name given to any of the regulations which supplement the law as laid down in the Torah. The Talmud attributes to Moses the takkanah of reading the Pentateuch on Sabbaths, festivals, the New Moon, and the intermediate days of festivals. The Amidah is traditionally regarded as a takkanah issued by men of the Great Synagogue. Tannaitic takkanot include the provision that a wife's marriage settlement is to be a general mortgage on the whole of the husband's property, that communities must appoint elementary school teachers, that a father must support his minor children, and that compulsory education is to be provided for children from the age of six. In the Middle Ages Gershom ben Judah issued 25 ordinances which were accepted as binding in Ashkenazi custom. Takkanot prescribed by a bet din remain valid even if the reason for their enactment no longer exists; only another bet din of greater authority can annul them. Notwithstanding the status of the takkanot, many lapsed with the passage of time.

Tal [Grünthal]**, Yoseph** (b. 1910). Israeli composer and teacher. He was born in Pinne, in the Poznań district. He moved to Palestine and in 1937 joined the faculty of the Academy of Music in Jerusalem. Later he became head of the department of musicology at the Hebrew University. Many of his compositions are based on biblical motifs and liturgical poetry.

Tallit. Prayer shawl. It is worn by adult males during morning prayer, at the afternoon service on the Ninth of Av, and at all services on the Day of Atonement. The shawl is a four-cornered garment, usually made of wool. Fringes are knotted on the corners in accordance with biblical law (Numbers 15.37–41). Often the area that is draped over the head is adorned with a strip of silver or gold referred to as the "atarah" (crown). A smaller garment, the "tallit katan" (small tallit), also referred to as "arba kanphot" (four corners), is worn at all times under the outer clothes.

Talmid Ḥakham. Person who is expert in Jewish study.

Talmon, Jacob Leib (1916–1980). Israeli scholar. He was born in Rypin, Poland. In 1934 he went to Palestine, where he became professor of modern history at the Hebrew University. His writings include *The Origins of Totalitarian Democracy*, *The Nature of Jewish History: its Universal Significance*, *The Unique and the Universal*, *Romanticism and Revolt*, and *Political Messianism: the Romantic Phase*.

Talmud ("Study"). Name given to each of two collections of records of the discussion and administration of Jewish law by scholars and jurists in various academies in the period c. 200–500. The two Talmuds are the Babylonian and Palestinian (also known as the Jerusalem Talmud) and although they are distinguished from each other their contents overlap to a considerable extent. Both Talmuds contain the Mishnah together with Gemara (a commentary and supplement to the Mishnah text); both also contain aggadic digressions. The authorities referred to in the Palestinian Talmud lived before c. 400; those mentioned in the Babylonian Talmud lived before c. 500. The Babylonian Talmud contains more material than the Palestinian, and is regarded as more significant.

Talmud, burning of the. From the Middle Ages the attempted suppression of Judaism led at intervals to the wholesale destruction of copies of the Talmud and other Jewish texts. The first official burning of the Talmud took place in Paris on 17 June 1242, in response to the Disputation of Paris of 1240. From that time on, similar destruction of rabbinic texts was carried out intermittently. On 9 September 1533 vast numbers of rabbinic texts were destroyed in Rome; this was followed by similar attacks throughout northern Italy. In the 18th century thousands of copies of the Talmud were burned in Poland after a disputation in 1757.

Talmud commentaries. The first commentaries on the Talmud consist of textual comments found in the writings of the later geonim. The earliest full commentaries are those of Sherira Gaon, Hai Gaon, and Samuel ben Hophni, from the 10th to 11th centuries. In the 11th century Nissim ben Jacob of Kairouan and Hananel ben Hushiel produced important commentaries. The focus of talmudic study then moved to Germany and France. The early 11th-century commentary by Gershom ben Judah laid the foundation for the work of Rashi, who was followed by the Tosaphists. Later important commentaries were written by Naḥmanides and Solomon ben Adret, and in the 16th century Solomon Luria, Samuel Edels, and Meir Lublin produced significant works. In the modern period scientific studies of the Talmud have been produced by various Jewish scholars.

Talmud Torah ("study [of the] law"). Term which refers to religious study. The term was adopted as a name (Ḥevra Talmud Torah) by voluntary associations that fostered religious education; it was also applied to their schools, and ultimately to Jewish religious schools in general. The institution of the Talmud Torah flourished in Europe and among immigrant communities in western countries. It should be distinguished from the elementary school (ḥeder) and advanced academies for talmudic study.

Tam, Jacob ben Meir *see* JACOB BEN MEIR TAM.

Tamar (i) (fl. ?19th–16th cent. BCE). Israelite woman, wife of Er, the eldest son of Judah, and later wife of Er's brother, Onan. After Onan's death, Judah refused to allow Tamar to marry his third son, Shelah. In protest she disguised herself as a prostitute and bore twins by Judah (Genesis 38).

Tamar (ii) (fl. 10th cent. BCE). Israelite woman, daughter of David. She was raped by Amnon, her stepbrother (II Samuel 13), who was killed in revenge by her brother Absalom.

Tamid ("perpetual offering") **(i).** The name given to the whole offering or sacrifice made twice daily (in the morning and the evening) in the Temple (Numbers 28.1–8).

Tamid ("Perpetual offering") **(ii).** Ninth tractate in the Mishnah order of Kodashim. It deals with the regulations for the daily burnt offerings in the Temple (Exodus 29.38; Numbers 28.1–8) and with the organization of the Temple in general.

Tammuz (i). Babylonian and Sumerian deity. The annual cycle of winter and spring was accounted for by his captivity in the underworld and his resurrection by Ishtar. A cult of Tammuz existed in ancient Palestine (Ezekiel 8.14).

Tammuz (ii). Fourth month of the Jewish year. On 17 Tammuz a fast is observed which commemorates the destruction of the Temple walls by Nebuchadnezzar (586 BCE) and Titus (70 CE).

Tammuz, Benjamin (b. 1919). Israeli

writer and journalist. He was born in Khar'kov, in the Ukraine, and went to Palestine in 1924. From 1965 he was the editor of the weekend literary supplement of *Ha-Aretz*, for which he wrote art criticism. In 1971 he became cultural attaché at the Israeli embassy in London. He wrote short stories, novels, and children's books, and translated several books into Hebrew.

Tanakh. The Hebrew Bible. The name derives from the initial letters of the words "Torah," "Neviim," and "Ketuvim" (Pentateuch, Prophets, Hagiographa).

Tanḥum ben Joseph of Jerusalem (c. 1220–1291). Palestinian philologist and biblical exegete. He lived in Palestine and Egypt. He wrote a lexicon to Maimonides' *Mishneh Torah*.

Tanḥuma [Midrash Tanḥuma; Yelammedenu]. Palestinian Midrashic collection attributed to Tanḥuma bar Abba. It covers the entire Pentateuch and contains discourses usually based on the opening verse of the portion of the week according to the triennial Palestine cycle. It is also known as "Yelammedenu" from the opening phrase of each sermon: "Yelammedenu Rabbenu" (Let our teacher pronounce).

Tanḥuma bar Abba (fl. 4th cent.). Palestinian amora. He developed the art of homiletics and, according to tradition, was the author of many midrashim which begin "Yelammedenu Rabbenu" (Let our teacher pronounce), including those that make up the Midrash Tanḥuma.

Tanna (Aramaic, from "teni": to teach). Term used of a teacher in the mishnah or baraita, during the 1st–2nd centuries CE. The tannaitic period begins with the death of Hillel and Shammai, and ends with the generation after Judah ha-Nasi. The term was also applied during the talmudic period to a reader of tannaitic texts in the academies.

Tanna de-ve Eliyahu [Seder Eliyahu]. Ethical religious text consisting of Eliyahu Rabba and Eliyahu Zuta. The work is comprised of a series of moral homilies emphasizing the love and study of the Torah, love of Israel, and social justice. Although it is assigned to the talmudic period, it was probably copied in the 10th century.

Tanya (i). Opening word and hence the title of a code of laws extracted from Zedekiah ben Abraham Anau's *Shibbole-ha-Leket*. It was prepared in Italy, probably in the 14th century.

Tanya (ii) [Likkute Amarim]. Ḥasidic kabbalistic work written by Shneour Zalman of Lyady. It guides the believer to the attainment of devekut. Based on the kabbalah, it is also deeply influenced by talmudic literature and medieval Jewish philosophy.

Tappuḥim ("apples"). The fruit-shaped ornaments used to decorate the staves of the Torah scroll, particularly in Spain; *see* TORAH ORNAMENTS.

Tarbut. Hebrew educational and cultural organization. It was started in Poland in 1919 but soon had branches in Lithuania, Russia, and Romania. It maintained schools in eastern European countries between the two world wars. Instruction was given in Hebrew and in biblical and modern Hebrew literature. Zionist in orientation, it promoted pioneer settlement in Palestine.

Tareph *see* TEREPHAH.

Targum (Aramaic, from Assyrian "targumanu": interpreter). The name given to any Aramaic translation of the Bible or book of the Bible, oral or written. According to the Talmud, the custom of adding an Aramaic translation to the public reading of Scripture goes back to Ezra and became established in the second Temple period. This oral targum was both a translation and an interpretation of the text. The three written targums to the Pentateuch are: Targum

Onkelos; Targum Jonathan; and Targum Yerushalmi. The targum to the Former and Latter Prophets is called after Jonathan ben Uzziel. The targums to the books of the Hagiographa are midrashic in character, especially that to the Five Scrolls.

Targum Sheni ("Second targum"). Aramaic paraphrase of the Book of Esther, dating from c. 500–1000. Additional to the ordinary targum (hence its name), it is more midrashic in character.

Tarnopol. Town in Galicia. Jews settled there in the 16th century. In 1648 the community participated in the defense of the town against the Cossacks. When it was annexed to Russia in 1809, Joseph Perl founded a Jewish school there, which influenced the cultural development of Jews who were later active in the Haskalah and Zionist movements.

Tarphon (fl. 1st cent.). Palestinian tanna. He served with his priestly family in the Temple, and studied with Johanan ben Zakkai and Gamaliel I. He was active in discussions at the academy at Jabneh. The Mishnah refers to differences of opinion between him and Akiva regarding the halakhah.

Tarshish. Distant port from which silver, iron, tin, ivory, monkeys, and peacocks were brought to Palestine (I Kings 10.22). Its location is uncertain. According to the Book of Jonah, Jonah took a boat going to Tarshish rather than to Nineveh (Jonah 1.3).

Tartakower, Aryeh (1897–1982). Israeli sociologist and communal leader. He was born in Brody, in eastern Galicia, and taught at the Institute of Jewish Sciences in Warsaw. In 1939 he went to the US, where he was director of relief and rehabilitation for the World Zionist Action Committee. He settled in Palestine in 1946 and taught at the Hebrew University. From 1948 to 1971 he was chairman of the Israeli section of the World Jewish Congress. He wrote studies of the Jewish labor movement, migration problems, the history of Polish Jewry, anti-Semitism, and the Jewish communities of the diaspora.

Taryag mitzvot *see* 613 COMMANDMENTS.

Tas ("plaque"). A silver plaque placed on the Torah scroll to indicate the festival for which the scroll had been made ready; *see* TORAH ORNAMENTS.

Tashlikh ("Thou shalt cast"). Custom practiced on the first day of the New Year (or the second when the first takes place on the Sabbath). Prayers are recited near a stream or a body of water, preferably where there are fish. The term derives from Michah 7.19 ("Thou shalt cast all their sins into the depths of the sea.").

Tashmishei kedushah ("appurtenances of holiness"). Religious articles and objects pertaining to the practice of the liturgy in the synagogue; they include the tallit, shophar, and Torah ornaments.

Tata (Yiddish). Papa.

Täubler, Eugen (1879–1953). American historian and biblical scholar. He was born in Gostyn, in the district of Poznań. He taught at the universities of Berlin, Zurich, and Heidelberg, where he was a professor from 1925 to 1935. He emigrated to the US, where he taught at Hebrew Union College in Cincinnati. He wrote various studies of Jewish history.

Tav. 22nd letter of the Hebrew alphabet. Its numerical value is 400.

Taxation. According to the Book of Exodus, a poll tax was imposed on the Israelites during their years in the wilderness (Exodus 30.11–16). Later a system of tithes was used to maintain the Temple and the priesthood, and additional levies were used to help the poor. After the destruction of the Temple, the Romans imposed the FISCUS JUDAICUS on the Jewish community, and this was revived during the Middle Ages as the

OPFERPFENNIG. In the 17th–18th centuries in Italy Jewish communal dues were exacted by a tax on capital ("capella"). In modern times such special Jewish taxes have disappeared, except in some countries where the Jewish community has the right to impose taxes on all its members to maintain communal institutions. *See also* TEMPLE TAX.

Tcherikover, Avigdor (1894–1958). Israeli historian, of Russian origin. He settled in Palestine in 1925 and became professor of ancient history at the Hebrew University. He published studies of the Jews in Palestine and Egypt during the Hellenistic and Roman periods.

Tcherniakov [Tchernikhovski]**, Adam** *see* CHERNIAKOV, ADAM.

Tchernikhovski, Shaul *see* TSCHERNIKHOVSKI, SHAUL.

Tchernowitz, Chaim (1871–1949). American talmudic scholar. He was born in Sebesh, Russia. He founded a yeshivah in Odessa and adopted the pseudonym "Rav Tzair." In 1923 he settled in the US and taught Talmud at the Jewish Institute of Religion in New York. He published studies of rabbinic literature, an abridgement of the Talmud, and histories of Jewish law.

Teacher of Righteousness. In the Dead Sea Scrolls, the title given to the organizer of the sect of the Qumran community. The name appears in the Zadokite Fragments and from Qumran commentaries on books or sections of the Bible.

Tebah *see* ALMEMAR.

Technion, Haifa *see* HAIFA TECHNION.

Tehillim *see* PSALMS.

Teḥinnah ("supplication"). Any prayer of private devotion, or a prayer composed for private use. During the talmudic period private prayers were said after the Amidah; they were later replaced by the recital of the Taḥanun. Teḥinnot from the talmudic period include prayers for the forgiveness of sin, for divine blessing and protection, and for blessing in the study of the Torah. Many were subsequently incorporated into the prayerbook. From the gaonic period many teḥinnot were composed in the vernacular. Collections of such private devotions include prayers to be said when visiting the sick or at a cemetery, supplications for the blessing of scholarly and pious children, and prayers for use when baking Sabbath cakes or lighting Sabbath candles. Devotional books in Yiddish for women were also known as teḥinnot.

Teitel, Jacob (1851–1939). Russian jurist and communal worker. He was born in Cherny Ostrov, Podolia. He was one of the first Jews in Russia to be employed in the judicial service during the czarist regime. Devoted to communal work, he helped Jews who were oppressed by the authorities, and was a founder of a relief enterprise which supported Jewish youth. In 1921 he left the USSR and became president of the Union of Russian Jews in Germany. When the Nazis came to power, he moved to France, where his memoirs were published.

Teitelbaum, Moses (1759–1841). Galician Ḥasidic leader. He was born in Przemyśl and served as a rabbi at Sieniawa and Ujhely. He was among the first to spread Ḥasidism in the northern and central districts of Hungary, and became known as a wonder-working tzaddik. He wrote a homiletic work (*Yismaḥ moshe*) and responsa.

Teixeira, Abraham Senior (1581–1666). Portuguese Marrano financier and diplomat. He was born in Lisbon, the son of Dom Francisco de Melo and Donna Antonia de Silva Teixeira, lady-in-waiting to the queen. In 1643 he moved to Antwerp, where he became consul and paymaster for the government of Spain. After moving to Hamburg, he and his sons were circumcised; this caused a scandal, and led to an (unsuccessful) attempt by the imperial Viennese court to confiscate his property. Teixeira established an international banking house in Hamburg and took a leading role in Jewish affairs there, serving as the head of the city's Sephardi congregation. From 1655 he was resident diplomatic and financial minister for the Swedish crown in Hamburg.

Teixeira, Isaac Ḥayyim Senior (1625–1705). Dutch communal leader, son of Abraham Senior Teixeira. He became head of the Portuguese community in Amsterdam. He was unsuccessful in his attempt to intercede on the behalf of the Jews of Austria when they were threatened with expulsion in 1670.

Tekoa (i). Ancient town in Palestine, south of Bethlehem. Amos was born there.

Tekoa (ii). Ancient town in Upper Galilee. In biblical times it was noted for its olives and oils.

Tel Aviv. Israeli city. It was founded in 1909 as a garden suburb of Jaffa, and named after the Hebrew translation of Theodor Herzl's novel *Altneuland*. It developed rapidly under the British Mandate, and became a separate town in 1921. Jaffa and Tel Aviv were amalgamated in 1949 under the official name Tel Aviv–Jaffa. Tel Aviv is now a major city in Israel.

Tel Aviv University. Israeli university established in 1956. It has faculties of humanities, social sciences, and natural sciences, a medical school, more than 30 research institutes, and various specialized departments.

Tel el Amarna. Site of the capital of Pharaoh Amenhotep IV in Middle Egypt; it is near the modern town of Beni Hasan. In 1887 many cuneiform tablets were discovered there; these include letters from Canaanite kings complaining about disorder in the country caused by the incursion of the Habiru.

Tels. Small town in Lithuania. Its yeshivah flourished from its foundation in 1881 until after World War II. Later the surviving teachers of the yeshivah founded the Telse Rabbinical College in Cleveland, Ohio.

Temple (i) (Hebrew "bet ha-mikdash," "hakhal"). In Jewish usage the name given to the principal place of worship of the Jews in Jerusalem until 70 CE. The first Temple was built by Solomon c. 950 BCE. It served as a shrine for the Ark of the Covenant and the sacred vessels, and as a place for the offering of sacrifice and prayer. It consisted of an outer court opening into a hall, behind which was the shrine; beyond the shrine was the inner sanctum (the Holy of Holies). These areas were surrounded by cells and rooms used for storing vessels and treasure. Worship was performed in the shrine, which was entered from the hall through two cedar doors. The Holy of Holies, where the Ark was kept, had a raised floor and was windowless. A small altar made of cedar overlaid with gold stood in the shrine at the entrance to the Holy of Holies. The main bronze altar was in the court before the hall and was surrounded by a ditch. On the south-east side of the court stood a huge cauldron resting on figures of bulls; close by were bronze bases for the lavers. At the entrance from the court to the hall were two columns, Boaz and Jachin. Solomon's Temple was destroyed in 586 BCE by the Babylonian troops of Nebuchadnezzar. The Temple was rebuilt in the Persian period, and completed and dedicated in 515 BCE. Herod the Great completely reconstructed the building, beginning in 55 BCE and (according to St. John's Gospel) continuing for 46 years. This Temple was destroyed by the

Romans in 70 CE. The only part surviving is the Western Wall.

Temple (ii) *see* SYNAGOGUE.

Temple of Onias *see* ONIAS IV.

Temple Scroll. One of the DEAD SEA SCROLLS. It originated in the community at Qumran around the 2nd century BCE. It contains quotations from the Bible, rewritten so that God speaks throughout in the first person. The text describes the Temple, various festivals, and the king's army; it also contains halakhot on a number of topics.

Temple tax. According to Exodus 30.13, each Israelite paid half a shekel for the maintenance of the sanctuary. During the second Temple period the half-shekel was levied as an annual tax in Palestine and the diaspora; the tractate Shekalim in the Mishnah deals with its collection. After the destruction of the Temple in 70, the Romans replaced this tax by a compulsory levy paid into the "fiscus judaicus." The Zionist Organization revived the tax by a decree passed at the First Zionist Conference in 1897.

Templo, Judah *see* LEON TEMPLO, JACOB JUDAH ARYEH.

Temurah ("Exchange"). Sixth tractate in the Mishnah order of Kodashim. It deals with the regulations concerning the exchange of an animal consecrated for sacrifice and associated problems (Leviticus 27.9–10).

Tenant. One who occupies land or property under a landlord. According to talmudic law, a distinction is made between agricultural and urban tenancy. In the former case, two types of tenant are recognized: the "aris" and the "ḥokher." The aris gives the landlord a percentage of the produce from the land; the ḥokher pays a fixed amount in rent. In both kinds of agricultural tenancy local custom serves as the prime factor determining the law regarding landlord and tenant relationship. In the Mishnah urban tenancy is treated separately: the tenant is called a "sokher" (hirer) and the provisions of the lease grant him possession of the property for the duration of the lease. Acceptance of advance payment has the binding character of a lease. If a term is not specified for the duration of the lease it is presumed that the rental is for the winter season or for the summer period. However, in large towns tenancies were assumed to be of 12 months' duration.

Ten Commandments [Decalogue]. Ten laws proclaimed by God to Moses on Mount Sinai (Exodus 20.2–14; Deuteronomy 5.6–18). Moses wrote them on two stone tablets, which he later broke in anger when he found the Israelites worshipping the Golden Calf. He reascended Mount Sinai and brought down a second set of tablets inscribed with the Ten Commandments, which were placed in the Ark of the Covenant.

Ten Days of Penitence (Hebrew "Aseret Yeme Teshuvah"). The name given to the first ten days of Tishri, from the beginning of the New Year to the close of the Day of Atonement. According to tradition, individuals are judged at the New Year and the judgment is proclaimed on the Day of Atonement; clemency may be obtained through sincere repentance during the Ten Days of Penitence. Penitential prayers ("seliḥot") are said daily, fasts take place, and there are alterations to the liturgy emphasizing God's kingship.

Ten Lost Tribes of Israel. The ten tribes constituted the population of the northern kingdom of Israel from the time of Jacob until they were taken into captivity by the Assyrians in the period 721–715 BCE. They never reemerged from this captivity and are assumed to have intermarried with the Assyrians; those who remained in Israel intermarried with the Canaanites and became Samaritans. It was hoped that the lost tribes would be rediscovered intact; Ezekiel associated such a rediscovery with the final redemption of the Jews, involving the reunion of the whole house of Israel (Ezekiel 37.16). Various travelers reported their discovery: Eldad ha-Dani claimed that they were in the mountains of Africa; Benjamin of Tudela heard of them in central Asia; David Reuveni stated that he was the brother of one of their rulers in a region of Arabia; and Antonio de Montezinos reported that he had found them in South America. Shabbetai Tzevi appointed rulers over the various tribes.

Ten Martyrs. The name given to ten rabbis, who according to tradition were executed by the Roman government after the Bar Kokhba revolt. They were killed for defying the prohibition against Jewish observances and Jewish religious teaching. Their identity is uncertain and not all of those usually named among the ten lived at the time of the Bar Kokhba revolt. The following names are those most commonly found in the various sources that list the Ten Martyrs: Akiva ben Joseph, Ishmael ben Elisha, Eleazar ben Dama, Ḥanina ben Teradyon, Judah ben Bava, Ḥutzpit the Interpreter, Yeshevav the Scribe, Eleazar ben Shammua, Ḥanina ben Ḥakhinai, Simeon ben Gamaliel I, and Ishmael the high priest.

Ten Plagues *see* PLAGUES, TEN.

Ten Tribes *see* TEN LOST TRIBES OF ISRAEL.

Tenuat ha-Moshavim ("Moshav movement"). Israeli organization of cooperative smallholders' settlements. It was founded in 1928 and its membership comprises all the MOSHAV OVEDIM.

Tephillah. A prayer, or, specifically, the Amidah or EIGHTEEN BENEDICTIONS. The term is also used by the Sephardim to mean a prayerbook.

Tephillat ha-Derekh ("Prayer for the journey"). Prayer recited before setting off on a journey. Its original text ran: "May it be Thy will that Thou leadest me in peace and settest my steps. Blessed be Thou who hearest prayer." Under kabbalistic influence, additional verses were interspersed with the phrases of the prayer.

Tephillin ("phylacteries") **(i).** Name given to two small leather boxes each containing four passages from the Torah written on parchment (Exodus 13.1–10; Exodus 11–16; Deuteronomy 6.4–9; Deuteronomy 13–21). In accordance with Deuteronomy 6.8, they are worn by adult male Jews, bound by leather straps to the arm and the head. Their purpose is to remind the wearer to keep the law. Tephillin are worn on weekdays, but not on Sabbaths and festivals; custom differs regarding their use on the intermediate days of festivals. Originally they were worn all day, but they are now worn only during morning prayer (only during afternoon prayer on the Ninth of Av).

Tephillin ("Phylacteries") **(ii).** Minor pseudo-talmudic tractate. It discusses regulations regarding the wearing of tephillin and their preparation.

Terah. Father of Abraham. He left Ur of the Chaldees with his son and nephew Lot. Intending to journey to the land of Canaan, they stopped at Haran, where Terah died at the age of 205 (Genesis 11.31–2).

Teraphim. Household gods. According to Genesis, images of the household gods were stolen by Rachel from her father's house (Genesis 31.19). Teraphim were denounced by the Israelite religion, but were nevertheless frequently used, perhaps for divination.

Tere Asar (Aramaic: "12"). Traditional name for the books of the 12 Minor Prophets.

Terephah ("unfit"). Term applied to food that is not kosher; the Sephardi word is "tareph." *See* KASHRUT.

Territorialism *see* JEWISH TERRITORIAL ORGANIZATION.

Terumot ("Heave-offerings"). Sixth tractate in the Mishnah order of Zeraim. It deals with the HEAVE-OFFERING due to the priest from the Israelite (Numbers 18.8; Deuteronomy 18.4) and the Levite (Numbers 18.25ff).

Teshuah *see* SALVATION.

Teshuvah *see* REPENTANCE.

Testaments of the 12 Patriarchs. Pseudepigraphic work. Dating from the second Temple period, it purports to give the testaments of the sons of Jacob to their descendents. The testaments are modeled on the blessing of Jacob to his sons (Genesis 49); each of the patriarchs describes the merits and sins of his own life and instructs his children to live righteously. Most of the testaments contain an apocalyptic ending.

Tet. Ninth letter of the Hebrew alphabet. Its numerical value is 9.

Tetragrammaton (Greek: "four letters"). A word of four letters, especially the Hebrew name of God written YHVH. Because the Jews would not pronounce the divine name itself, God was referred to by various other names descriptive of his attributes (*see* GOD, NAMES OF).

Tetrarch. Subordinate ruler. The title was given to minor rulers in the provinces of Judea and Syria during the Roman period. They were appointed by the Roman emperor and were subject to him. Important tetrarchs of Jewish history include Phasael, Herod Antipas, and Herod Philippus.

Tetuan. Town and port in northern Morocco. Jews settled there after they were expelled from Spain in 1492. In 1578 a local Purim festival was introduced to commemorate the thwarting of a Portuguese invasion. The Jewish community later became the largest in Morocco. In the 18th century the Jews of Tetuan were persecuted, and anti-Jewish riots took place during the war between Morocco and Spain in 1860.

Tevel. Agricultural produce which has not been tithed and which therefore may not be put to profane use. On the basis of Deuteronomy 26.13 the rabbis ruled that liability for tithes begins only when the crop is gathered in; thus tevel could be eaten by the agricultural worker in the field.

Tevet. Tenth month of the Jewish year. Tevet (the Fast of Tevet) commemorates the besieging of Jerusalem by Nebuchadnezzar (II Kings 25.1).

Tevul Yom ("One who has bathed that day"). Tenth tractate in the Mishnah order of Tohorot. It deals with the minor degree of ritual uncleanness which remains after ritual bathing until sunset (Leviticus 15.7–18).

Textual criticism *see* BIBLICAL CRITICISM.

Thank offering. Sacrifice offered in the Temple as a token of thanks to God. The regulations for such an offering are contained in Leviticus 7.12–15.

Thanksgiving (Hebrew "berakhah"). Biblical expressions of thanksgiving frequently begin with the word "Barukh" (Blessed be). Thus the statutory opening formula of benedictions said in thanksgiving to God before enjoying anything in the world is "Blessed art thou, o Lord our God, king of the universe." Other prayers of thanksgiving are recited on special occasions, on hearing good news, on the occurrence of joyful events, and on deliverance from evil. Thanksgiving is the theme of many of the psalms included in the liturgy.

Thanksgiving Psalms. One of the DEAD SEA SCROLLS. It contains many prayers, beginning with the words "I thank thee, o Lord."

Theater. Jewish playwrights are known to have been active in Alexandria as early as the 2nd century BCE, but during the Roman period Jewish sages denounced the theater. From the medieval period Purim farces were performed in central and western Europe. In the 16th century Marrano poets wrote plays in Spanish and Portuguese, and Jews in Italy took an active role in the theater. An attempt was made in Venice in the 17th century to establish a ghetto theater. From the 18th century there were outstanding Jewish actors in western Europe, and German Jewry produced famous theater critics and dramatists. In eastern Europe and later the US, Yiddish theater played an important role in Jewish life. In the modern period Jews have been involved in drama, film, and television.

Theft (Hebrew "genevah"). In Jewish law, theft is distinguished from robbery: a thief is one who appropriates another person's property secretly, while a robber steals without attempting to hide the deed. The convicted thief must pay double the value of the stolen property (Exodus 22.3). It is not permissible to buy stolen property, or property which the prospective buyer has reason to believe may have been stolen (for example, from an employer).

Theism (from Greek "theos": god). Belief in the existence of gods, or (specifically) a God having an existence independent of the world which he has created, and sustaining a personal relationship with his creatures.

Theocracy (from Greek "theos": god). Form of government directly by God or through a priestly order; the term is used specifically of the Jewish commonwealth from Moses to the time of the monarchy. Josephus used the term to describe the government of the Jewish people under Moses. Samuel was reluctant to create a monarchy because he feared it might undermine the recognition of God as ruler and his commandments as law. According to tradition, Jewish kings ruled by God's appointment and were pledged to heed the voice of the prophet who spoke in God's name. Persian and Hellenistic kings recognized the high priest as the supreme Jewish authority and the Torah as the basis of law. This belief was supported by the Maccabees, but ended by Herod.

Theodicy (from Greek "theos": god; and "dikē": justice). Vindication of God's justice in the face of human suffering. The problem of the suffering of the righteous exercised biblical writers, the rabbis, medieval philosophers and kabbalists, and modern Jewish thinkers.

***Theodora** (fl. 14th cent.). Bulgarian czarina. She came from a Byzantine Jewish family, but was baptized and married Czar Ivan Alexander. Her son, Czar Ivan Shishman III of Bulgaria, allowed Jews from Hungary to settle in Nicopolis, Plevna, and Murad.

Theodotion (fl. 2nd cent.). Ephesian scholar. According to Christian tradition, he was a proselyte originating from Ephesus (or possibly Pontus). He translated the Bible into Greek. His version is based on the Septuagint and is less literal than Aquila's.

Theology. The study of the existence and nature of the divine. Although Jews have traditionally been more concerned with religious practice than orthodox beliefs, theological speculation has been current among Jewish thinkers from early times. Particularly in the Middle Ages Jewish scholars produced systematic expositions of theology. Prominent among them were Saadyah Gaon's *Beliefs and Opinions*, Judah ha-Levi's *Kuzari*, and Moses Mendelssohn's *Guide for the Perplexed*. The theological tradition was continued in modern times by such thinkers as Moses Mendelssohn, Leo Baeck, and Franz Rosenzweig. *See also* GOD, ATTRIBUTES OF; JUDAISM.

Therapeutae (Latin: "Healers"). Jewish religious sect in Egypt in the 1st century. It was described by Philo. Its members (both male and female) lived in solitude, poverty, and (so far as possible) celibacy, spending their time in meditation on sacred writings. Every 50th day they gathered for a meal, and spent the night in religious singing and dancing.

Theresienstadt. Garrison town in Bohemia (now Terezín, Czechoslovakia). It was transformed into a ghetto by the Nazis in November 1941. The Jews who were incarcerated there maintained a form of autonomous Jewish life, presided over by a council of elders. The Nazis regarded it as a model ghetto, to which they sent prominent Jews.

Thessaloníki *see* SALONICA.

Theudas (fl. 1st cent.). Palestinian religious leader and pseudo-messiah. He persuaded the people to gather up their possessions and follow him to the Jordan, where at his command he claimed the river would part. The Roman procurator Cuspius Fadus sent cavalry after them. Theudas was caught and decapitated, and his head was taken to Jerusalem.

13 attributes of mercy. The attributes of God, according to Exodus 34.6–7. Before the Tablets of the Law were given to Moses a second time, God proclaimed himself the Lord (1), the Lord (2) God (3), merciful (4), gracious (5), long-suffering (6), and abundant in loving-kindness (7) and truth (8), keeping mercy unto the thousandth generation (9), forgiving iniquity (10), transgression (11), and sin (12), and able to clear the guilty (13). Alternative enumerations of the attributes have been formulated. The 13 attributes are of importance in the liturgy, especially in the penitential prayers recited on fasts, in the seliḥot days before and after the New Year, and in the service of the Day of Atonement. *See also* GOD, ATTRIBUTES OF; SEPHIROT.

13 principles of faith. Principles of the Jewish faith enumerated by Maimonides. They state that: (1) God the Creator exists; (2) that God is one; (3) that God is incorporeal; (4) that God is eternal; (5) that prayer is for God alone; (6) that the prophets are true; (7) that Moses is supreme above all other prophets; (8) that the Pentateuch was given to Moses; (9) that the Torah is immutable; (10) that God is omniscient; (11) that divine retribution will be carried out; (12) that the Messiah will come; and (13) that the dead will be raised. These principles are reproduced in the prayerbook.

32 paths of wisdom. Mystical concept, originating in the Sepher Yetzirah. The "32 Paths of Hidden Wisdom" used there refers to a system based on the 22 letters of the Hebrew alphabet and the ten elementary and primordial numbers that constitute the elements of creation. In kabbalistic sources the notion of the 32 paths was reinterpreted in terms of the doctrine of the SEPHIROT: the highest sephirah emanates or descends into the lower sephirot by way of 32 paths or channels.

Thomashefsky, Boris (1866–1939). American Yiddish actor, of Ukrainian origin. He went to the US in 1881. He produced, wrote, adapted, and acted in many plays performed at New York's Yiddish theaters. He also initiated the visit of a Yiddish theater company from London.

Thon, Osias (1870–1936). Polish rabbi and Zionist, brother of Yaakov Thon. He was born in Lemberg. He became an associate of Theodor Herzl, whom he assisted in preparing the First Zionist Congress. From 1897 he was a rabbi in Kraków. In 1919 he was appointed vice-president of the Comité des Délégations Juives at the Paris Peace Conference; in the same year he was elected to the Sejm, where he served until 1935 and was head of the Jewish members' organization. He wrote a biography of Herzl and essays on Zionism.

Thon, Yaakov (1880–1950). Palestinian communal leader, brother of Onias Thon. He was born in Lemberg, and in 1907 went to Palestine, where he became Arthur Ruppin's deputy in the management of the Palestine Office of the Zionist Organization; he took Ruppin's place during his exile in Turkey (1916–20). In 1917 Thon organized the Jewish community council in Jerusalem, which he served as its chairman. Later he prepared a report on conditions in Palestine during World War I. In 1921 he became managing director of the Palestine Land Development Corporation.

Three Weeks (Hebrew "Bein ha-Mezarim": *lit.* between the straits). Period of mourning observed from 17 Tammuz (when the walls of Jerusalem were breached by Nebuchadnezzar) to 9 Av (the anniversary of the destruction of the Temple). The celebration of marriages, other festive occasions, and cutting of the hair are forbidden during this time; during the latter part of it the eating of meat and the drinking of wine are proscribed except on the Sabbath. On the three Sabbaths the prophetical readings in the synagogue consist of prophecies of doom (Jeremiah 1, 2, and Isaiah 1).

Throne of God. Visions of the throne of God are recorded in various books of the Bible (I Kings 22.19; Isaiah 6.1; Ezekiel 1). Ezekiel's vision gave rise to the tradition of chariot mysticism (maaseh merkavah); this evoked ecstatic states, in which the mystic's soul left the body, ascended to heaven, and there beheld the vision of the Throne of God.

Thursday *see* MONDAYS AND THURSDAYS.

Tibbon *see* IBN TIBBON.

Tiberias. Israeli town on the western shore of the Sea of Galilee. Founded in the 1st century by Herod Antipas, it was named after the emperor Tiberius. Its inhabitants participated in the war against Rome (66–70) and surrendered to Vespasian. In the 3rd century the patriarchate was transferred there, and an academy was founded. The town became the capital of Jewish Palestine until the academy moved to Jerusalem in the 7th century. It later became a center of masoretic study.

***Tiberius** (fl. 1st cent.). Roman emperor (14–37). In 19 he expelled the Jews from Rome, and 4000 young Jews were sent to Sardinia to fight brigands. Under his rule, Palestine was harshly administered. The crucifixion of Jesus took place during this period.

Ticho, Anna (1894–1980). Israeli artist. She was born in Brünn, Moravia, and went to Jerusalem in 1912. She made numerous drawings of the Judean landscape.

***Tiglath-Pileser III.** King of Assyria (745–726 BCE). In 743 BCE he invaded Syria and levied tribute on Menaḥem of Israel. In 734 BCE he invaded Philistia, conquered Damascus, seized a large part of the kingdom of Israel, and banished the population of Galilee to Transjordan. He exacted tribute from Ahaz of Judah as well as from Ammon, Moab, and Edom. Later he also ruled over Babylon.

Tigris (Hebrew "Hiddekel"). River flowing from Turkey, through Iraq, to the Persian Gulf. According to Genesis, it was one of the four rivers emerging from the Garden of Eden (Genesis 2.14). The Babylonian talmudic academy Maḥoza was located on its banks.

Tik. Sephardi term for the wood or metal case in which the Scroll of the Law is kept.

Tikkun ("passage") **(i).** Name given to any of several collections of biblical, mishnaic, and kabbalistic passages instituted by kabbalists for reading on special occasions. The Tikkun Ḥatzot ("Midnight service") consists of selections of psalms, lamentations, and petitions recited at midnight in memory of the destruction of the Temple. The Tikkun lel Shavuot is read on the night of Shavuot. The Tikkun Hoshana Rabbah includes readings from Deuteronomy, Psalms, and the Zohar, and special kabbalistic prayers recited on the night of Hoshanah Rabbah. A similar tikkun is observed on the night of 7 Adar (the anniversary of the birth and death of Moses) and 5 Av (the anniversary of the death of Isaac Luria).

Tikkun (ii) *see* KABBALAH.

Tikkun sopherim ("scribal emendation"). Term used specifically of any of the 18 emendations of the Bible attributed to the scribes; they deal mostly with pronominal suffixes. The term is also applied to an unpointed copy of the printed Pentateuch, which is used for practice in reading the Scroll of the Law.

Tiktin, Gedaliah (c. 1810–1886). German rabbi, son of Solomon Tiktin. He became Landrabbiner in Breslau in 1854. He joined his father in a feud with Abraham Geiger.

Tiktin, Solomon (1791–1843). German rabbi. He became a rabbi in Breslau. In 1838 he opposed the appointment of the reformer Abraham Geiger as assistant rabbi, preacher, and dayyan in Breslau. He and his son, Gedaliah Tiktin, engaged in a campaign against Geiger, which divided the community.

Time *see* DAY.

Timerman, Jacobo (b. 1923). Argentine journalist. He was born in Russia, and went to Argentina in 1942. He became a political journalist and founded *La opinión* in Buenos Aires. His *Prisoner without a Name, Cell without a Number* explores anti-Semitism in Argentina.

Timişoara. City in the Banat region of Transylvania, western Romania. Spanish Jews settled there from the 16th century. After 1716, when the Turks lost the city to Hungary, the Jewish community was subjected to various restrictions which were not lifted until the late 18th century.

Timna. Wadi descending to the Arabah valley, north of Elath. One of Solomon's copper mines was known by this name.

***Tinneius Rufus, Quintus** (fl. 2nd cent.). Roman administrator, Governor of Judea (130–33). From 130 he was the commander of the Tenth Legion. Unprepared for the Bar Kokhba revolt, he evacuated Jerusalem and appealed to the legate of Syria for aid. He failed to overcome the rebels, and was replaced by Julius Severus.

Tiomkin, Vladimir (1860–1927). Russian Zionist leader. He was born in Yelizavetgrad in the Ukraine. He was a founder of the Ahavat Zion Society in St. Petersburg, and later became head of the executive committee of the Russian Ḥovevei Zion in Jaffa. He returned to Russia and joined the Zionist movement, participating in Zionist congresses. During World War I he directed relief projects in southern Russia; after the 1917 Revolution he resumed his Zionist activities. In 1920 he settled in Paris and joined Vladimir Jabotinsky's Revisionist Zionist movement.

Tirado, Jacob (c. 1560–1625). Portuguese religious leader. He was born in Portugal into a family of Conversos. He settled in Amsterdam, where he returned to Judaism. In c. 1608 he helped to found the first Sephardi community in the city. Before 1616 he went to Palestine and settled in Jerusalem.

Tirzah. Ancient Samarian city, capital of Samaria before the time of Omri (I Kings 15.21). It served as Menaḥem's base of operations in his uprising against Shallum.

Tish (Yiddish: *lit.* "table"). In Ḥasidic tradition, a meal taken by the tzaddik with his followers. Three such meals are held on Sabbaths, holidays, and the anniversaries of the deaths of tzaddikim. During the tish the tzaddik gives a discourse, sings hymns with his followers, and distributes shirayim; on the Sabbath the proceedings conclude with dancing.

Tisha b'Av *see* NINTH OF AV.

Tishbite *see* ELIJAH.

Tishby, Isaiah (b. 1908). Israeli scholar. He was born at Sándor Schwartz in Sanislo, Hungary. In 1933 he settled in Palestine, where he became a professor at the Hebrew University. His publications include studies of the kabbalah.

Tishri. Seventh month in the Jewish calendar. The following festivals take place during Tishri: 1 Tishri (1 and 2 Tishri in the diaspora), Rosh ha-Shanah (New Year); 10 Tishri, Yom Kippur (Day of Atonement); 15–21 Tishri, Sukkot (Tabernacles); 22 Tishri, Shemini Atzeret (Eighth Day of Solemn Assembly) (in the diaspora it is observed also on the 23rd as Simḥat Torah (Rejoicing in the Law)). The Fast of Gedaliah takes place on 3 Tishri.

Tiszaeszlar. Town in Hungary. It was the scene in 1882 of a ritual murder accusation, which gave rise to an outburst of anti-Jewish hostility in Hungary. After the prisoners were acquitted, outbreaks against the Jewish population occurred throughout the country.

Tithe (Hebrew "maaser"). Tenth part of one's produce, set aside as a religious offering. According to Jewish law, there are various types. The "first tithe" (Numbers 18.24) was given to the Levites after the heave offering ("terumah") for the priests had been separated from it. During the second Temple period the first tithe was given as a whole to the priests. This subject is dealt with in the tractate Maaserot in the Mishnah. The "second tithe" (Leviticus 27.30–31; Deuteronomy 14.22–6) was a tenth part of the first tithe, and was consumed by the owner himself in Jerusalem; it applied in the 1st, 2nd, 4th, and 5th years in the Sabbatical cycle, and is dealt with in the tractate Maaser Sheni in the Mishnah. The "poor tithe" (Deuteronomy 14.28–9; 26.12) was calculated in the same way as the second tithe and was paid in the 3rd and 6th years of the Sabbatical cycle; it was given to the poor. The "tithe of the animal" (Leviticus 17.32) took place three times a year when the animals were counted; the selected animal was sacrificed. The animal tithe is dealt with in the tractate Bekhorot in the Mishnah. The Levites also paid a tithe from what they received (Numbers 18.26), in the form of an offering to God.

***Titus** (fl. 1st cent.). Roman emperor (79–81), son of Vespasian. He took over control of the Roman army in Judea from his father in 70, and destroyed the Temple in Jerusalem.

Titus, Arch of. Arch in Rome erected by the senate in honor of Vespasian and Titus. It commemorates the victory over the Jews in the war of 66–70.

Tobiads. Name given to the descendants of Tobiah (fl. 3rd cent. BCE), a landowner who married the sister of the high priest Onias III. In the struggle over Palestine between Egypt and Syria, Hyrcanus, the younger son of Tobiah's son Joseph, supported the Ptolemies, whereas Joseph's other sons supported the Seleucid Antiochus III. When Antiochus IV Epiphanes came to power, Hyrcanus committed suicide. The other Tobiads encouraged the Hellenizing movement that supported Antiochus IV, who replaced the high priest Onias III with Jason. Later Antiochus deposed Jason in favor of Menelaus. Jason endeavored to regain power, but Menelaus and his followers reported that an anti-Seleucid revolt was taking place in Jerusalem; this led to Antiochus' persecution of the Jews. The Hasmonean uprising (c. 160 BCE) put an end to the Tobiads as an important influence in Jewish life.

Tobiah ben Eliezer (fl. 11th cent.). Bulgarian talmudist and poet. He wrote *Lekaḥ Tov* (or *Pesikta Zutarta*), a midrashic commentary on the Pentateuch and the Five Scrolls.

Tobiah ben Moses (fl. 11th cent.). Turkish Karaite scholar, biblical exegete, and liturgical poet. After studying in Jerusalem under Yeshuah ben Judah, he lived in Constantinople. He translated the Arabic works of his sect into Hebrew. His writings include *Yehi Meorot* on the biblical commandments, *Otzar Neḥmad* on Leviticus, and *Zot ha-Torah* on the Pentateuch.

Tobias, Lilly (1887–1984). Welsh novelist. She was born in Swansea. Her works deal with various modern Jewish themes. Her publications include *The Nationalists and other Goluth Studies*, *My Mother's House*, and *The Samaritan*.

Tobias the Doctor *see* COHEN, TOBIAS.

Tobit. Apocryphal book. It describes how Tobit, a blind exile at Nineveh, sent his son Tobias to Persia to collect a debt. On his journey, Tobias visited a relative, whose daughter Sarah had been married seven times, but each of whose bridegrooms had been killed on the wedding night by the demon Ashmedai out of jealousy. With the assistance of the archangel Raphael, the demon was exorcised. Tobias then married Sarah and Tobit's blindness was cured.

Tochis (Yiddish). Rear end, buttocks.

Tog, Der. American Yiddish daily newspaper, published in New York. Founded in 1914, it endorsed Zionism and cultural pluralism. In 1919 it absorbed the daily *Wahrheit*. Later it merged with the *Morgen-Journal* to become the *Day-Jewish-Journal*.

Tohorah [taharah] ("purification"). Ceremonial washing of the dead before burial. The ceremony is performed by the Ḥevra Kaddisha. The body is laid on a board and thoroughly rubbed and cleansed with lukewarm water. The head and the front part of the body are scrubbed with a beaten egg, and nine measures of water are poured over the body while it is held upright. The body is then dried and dressed in a shroud.

Tohorot ("purifications") **(i).** The rules of ritual cleanliness. The term is also applied to foods that may be eaten only by those who are in a state of cleanliness.

Tohorot ("Purifications") **(ii).** Sixth order of the Mishnah. It deals with the laws concerning purity and impurity.

Tohorot ("Purifications") **(iii).** Fifth tractate in the Mishnah order of Tohorot. It deals with minor degrees of ritual uncleanliness, the effects of which last only until sunset.

Tokheḥah ("reproof"). The name given to two sections of the Pentateuch (Leviticus 26 and Deuteronomy 28), which prophesy a series of punishments to be visited upon the Israelites if they forsake the Torah.

Toledano, Yaakov Mosheh (1880–1960). Israeli rabbi. He was born in Tiberias. He served as a rabbi in Alexandria, and in 1941 was appointed chief Sephardi rabbi of Tel Aviv. He served as minister for religious affairs in the Israeli government.

Toledo. City in Castile, central Spain. Jews settled there in Roman times. Under the Visigoths the Jewish community of Toledo was the most important in Spain. In the 7th century a series of Councils of Toledo formulated legislation designed to extirpate Judaism from Spain, but under Arab rule from the 8th century the community flourished. After the Christian reconquest in 1085 Jewish rights were secured. When the Almohades persecuted Jews in Muslim Spain, the city became the most important center of Jewry in the peninsula. During the next centuries Jews prospered there and established a tradition of scholarship. In 1391 massacres claimed many Jewish victims in the city, and left behind a large number of converts to Christianity; Toledo thus became one of the great centers of the Marranos. Later it was the seat of an Inquisitional tribunal.

Toledot Yeshu ("Histories of Jesus"). Medieval Hebrew work on the life of Jesus. It describes Jesus as the illegitimate son of Joseph Pandera. It records that he performed miracles but was conquered by an emissary of the rabbis and condemned to death.

Toleranzpatent (German: "edict of toleration"). Law issued by Emperor Joseph II on 2 January 1782. It relieved the Jews in the Austrian dominions from various disabilities, and encouraged them to engage in agriculture and handicrafts.

Tombs. Jewish tombs in Palestine initially consisted of rock-cut chambers. In the Hellenistic and Roman periods, the tomb was commonly one of a series of such chambers linked by doors or passages, in which bodies were placed in cists or sarcophagi on ledges, or in galleries; arched niches containing cists began to be used in the 3rd century. Large structures of this type are known as catacombs. Tombs or mausolea above ground also originated during the Hellenistic period. Later individual tombs became common; they were marked by upright or recumbent tombstones bearing inscriptions (often in Hebrew).

Tombs of the Kings. Large burial complex near Jerusalem, dating from the second Temple period. It originally consisted of a staircase, a rock-cut court, a porch, and six chambers in two stories with dozens of sepultures; it was once surmounted by three pyramids. The tomb was closed by rolling a stone against the opening. According to Josephus, the tomb was the mausoleum of the royal family of Abiadene.

Tombstone *see* EPITAPH.

Topheth. High place in the Valley of Hinnom, south-west of Jerusalem. Children were sacrificed there to Moloch (Jeremiah 7.31).

Topol, Ḥayyim (b. 1935). Israeli actor. He was born in Tel Aviv. He appeared at the Haifa Municipal Theater, and later in *Fiddler on the Roof* in Tel Aviv. Subsequently he starred in the film production of the play.

Torah ("Law") **(i)** [Pentateuch]. In the narrow sense the term is synonymous with Pentateuch. The Pentateuch (also known as the Five Books of Moses) is the Written Law. The five books are Genesis, Exodus, Leviticus, Numbers, and Deuteronomy, and according to tradition, they were given by God to Moses on Mount Sinai; along with the Written Law, God gave Moses a detailed explanation of its commandments (known as the Oral Law or Oral Torah). Thus, in its broad sense the term Torah refers to both the Written and Oral Law.

Torah (ii) *see* LAW, SCROLL OF THE.

Torah, reading of the *see* LAW, READING OF THE.

Torah, study of the (Hebrew "talmud Torah"). The study of the Torah is a religious duty; the blessing preceding the reading of the Shema in the morning and evening services asks for grace to carry out this duty. Rabbinic Judaism stresses that when groups (or individuals) engage in such study, the divine presence dwells among them.

Torah ornaments. General term for the covering and decorations of the Scroll of the Law. Special coverings for the scroll are mentioned in the Talmud; they assumed their present form in the Middle Ages. The binder ("mappah") is used to fasten the scroll and a mantle ("me'il") is placed over it. The mantle is surmounted with a silver crown ("keter," "atarah"). In medieval Spain it was common to decorate the ends of the staves on which the scroll was rolled with fruit-shaped ornaments known initially as "tappuḥim" (apples), and later as "rimmonim" (pomegranates). In Italy, the crown and rimmonim were used together. In Ashkenazi communities a silver plaque ("tas") was placed on the scroll, and a pointer ("yad"), made of precious metal and used in the reading of the law, was hung over it. In oriental and Sephardi communities the Torah scroll was kept in a wooden or metal case ("tik").

Torah Umesorah. American organization of Jewish day schools. Founded in 1944 by Feivel Mendlowitz, it is the largest national body serving Orthodox day schools in the US and Canada. It sponsors teacher training, publishes magazines for children, parents, and teachers, and administers US federal educational aid.

Torah va-Avodah ("Torah and labor"). Slogan of the Zionist religious pioneering movement, and hence the name given to its ideology. The phrase was also adopted as its name by the world confederation of pioneer and youth groups of the Mizraḥi movement.

Torat ha-Kohanim *see* LEVITICUS.

Torczyner, Harry *see* TUR-SINAI, NAPHTALI HERZ.

***Torquemada, Tomas de** (1420–1498). Spanish Dominican monk. He was born in Valladolid, and became prior of the monastery of Segovia. He was confessor to Queen Isabella and King Ferdinand, and was appointed inquisitor-general in 1483. He was influential in obtaining the decree of expulsion of the Jews from Spain in 1492.

***Torres, Luis de** (fl. 15th–16th cent.). Spanish explorer. He was interpreter to Christopher Columbus on the expedition of 1492 which led to the discovery of the New World. Born a Jew, Torres was baptized before the expedition set sail.

***Torrey, Charles Cutler** (1863–1956). American biblical scholar. He was born in East Hardwick, Vermont. He taught at Bowdoin College, Andover Theological Seminary, and Yale University. He published studies of the Bible, the Apocrypha, and Jewish influences on Mohammed. He argued that the Gospels were translations of Aramaic originals.

Tort. In legal usage, an act that damages a person, his property, or his reputation, and which demands compensation; default on a contract is also a tort. The talmudic tractate Nezikin deals with legislation regarding tort in Jewish law.

Tortosa. City in northern Spain. Its Jewish community dates from the Roman period. The Disputation of Tortosa in 1413–14 was forced on representatives of Spanish Jewry by the anti-pope Benedict XIII, who presided over it. They debated with the Christian convert Geronimo de Santa Fé (Joshua Lorki), who attempted to prove the truth of Christianity from the Talmud and Hebrew literature.

Tosaphot ("addenda"). Critical and explanatory notes on the Talmud, composed by French and German scholars from the 12th century to the 14th. These scholars, known as tosaphists, initially produced supplements to Rashi's commentary on the Talmud, but eventually they evolved their own method of talmudic study. The first tosaphists were Rashi's two sons-in-law, Meir ben Samuel and Judah ben Nathan; the greatest was his grandson Jacob ben Meir, known as Rabbenu Tam. Other important tosaphists were Samuel ben Meir, Samson ben Abraham of Sens, Judah ben Isaac of Paris, and Samuel of Falaise.

Tosephta ("Addition"). Tannaitic work that parallels and supplements the Mishnah. It dates from around the 2nd century. It has six orders with the same names as those of the Mishnah. Some of its paragraphs (known as "baraitot") are alternative versions of mishnaic paragraphs; others supplement the Mishnah or provide elucidation; and still others are independent of mishnaic law. Many of the baraitot in the Tosephta are identical with or are versions of baraitot quoted in the Talmud.

Tötbrief. In Germany a royal edict issued to cancel debts due to Jews or the interest on them.

Toulouse. City in southern France. Jews lived there from the 8th century. A custom of smiting an elder of the community on the cheek on Good Friday was abolished in the 12th century. Jews were expelled from the city in 1306. In the 16th century Toulouse became a Marrano center.

Touro, Abraham (1774–1822). American philanthropist, brother of Judah Touro. He was born in Newport, Rhode Island, and with his brother helped to support Newport's synagogue. His will made possible the building of residential units in what later became the new city of Jerusalem.

Touro, Judah (1775–1854). American philanthropist, brother of Abraham Touro. He was born in Newport, Rhode Island. He worked as a merchant and supported Christian and Jewish charities.

Touroff, Nissan (1877–1953). American educator. He served as director of the Bureau of Hebrew Education in Palestine from 1914 to 1919. He was dean of the Boston Hebrew Teachers' College (1921–26), and taught at the Jewish Institute of Religion.

Tov Elem *see* BONFILS, JOSEPH BEN SAMUEL.

Tovele shaḥarit *see* HEMEROBAPTISTS.

Tower of Babel *see* BABEL, TOWER OF.

Tower of David. Name of the main tower of the Jerusalem citadel, south of the Jaffa Gate. Its base contains the foundation of Phasael's Tower constructed by Herod the Great.

Trade unions. The first Jewish trade union was a tailors' union founded in London in 1874. In contrast to gentile labor associations, Jewish trade unions developed from political organizations; in Poland between the wars trade unions had Social Democratic (Bund), Poale Zion, or Communist affiliations. From eastern Europe Jewish trade unions spread to France, the Netherlands, the US, Argentina, Uruguay, and Palestine.

Tradition. Teachings and laws passed on from one generation to another. This oral tradition was collected and recorded in the Mishnah and Gemora and in later rabbinic responsa. Orthodox Judaism regards itself as the upholder of the Jewish tradition.

***Trajan** (c. 53–117). Roman Emperor (98–117). In 105–6 he annexed the Nabatean kingdom, which included the Negev and the Transjordan. During his reign Jewish uprisings took place in Crenaica, Egypt, Cyprus, and Alexandria, where the Greek population took retaliatory action. As a consequence, in 116 Trajan ordered a preventative massacre of Jews in Mesopotamia, and Judea was kept under control by his general Lucius Quietus.

Trani. Port in southern Italy on the Adriatic. Its Jewish population dates from the Middle Ages, when it became a center of Jewish scholarship. At the end of the 13th century the Jews of Trani were forced to convert to Christianity, and the city developed a strong community of Neofiti (new Christians), who remained loyal to the Jewish tradition.

Trani, Isaiah (ben Mali [Elijah]**) di** (fl. 12th cent.). Italian talmudist. He was born in southern Italy but lived in the north. His commentaries on the Talmud carried the conception of contemporary French tosaphists to Italy.

Trani, Joseph di (1568–1639). Palestinian rabbi and scholar, son of Moses ben Joseph di Trani. He was born in Safed, and founded a yeshivah there. Later he settled in Jerusalem, where he did research on the design and plan of the Temple. He returned to Safed and became head of the Sephardi community. Eventually he moved to Constantinople, where he directed a yeshivah, and became chief rabbi of Turkey.

Trani, Moses ben Joseph di (1505–1585). Palestinian rabbi. He was born in Salonica. He was one of the four scholars ordained by Jacob Berab in his attempt to reintroduce ordination and establish an authoritative Jewish leadership. Trani served as a rabbi and dayyan for 54 years, eventually becoming spiritual head of the Safed community.

Transjordan. Area of Palestine east of the Jordan. It consists of Golan, Gilead, Ammon, Moab, and the mountains of Edom.

Translations. The rise of communities of Aramaic- and Greek-speaking Jews during the second Temple period created the need for translations of the Bible, the Apocrypha and the Pseudepigrapha from Hebrew into those languages (*see* TARGUM, SEPTUAGINT). Until 1200 the bulk of translations from other languages into Hebrew was of Arabic works, and in the 13th century translators turned their attention to Arabic philosophical and scientific texts; after 1250 a number of Latin texts were translated. During the Renaissance and the Reformation period the process was reversed and Hebrew works, such as mystical writings, grammars, and rabbinic texts were translated into Latin. Scientific translations from many languages into Hebrew flourished from the 18th century. The creation of a Jewish state stimulated the translation into modern Hebrew of a variety of works of all kinds, from fiction to scholarship.

Translations of the Bible *see* BIBLE, TRANSLATIONS OF THE.

Transmigration of souls *see* METEMPSYCHOSIS.

Travelers. From the earliest period of the diaspora Jews have, sometimes perforce, sometimes voluntarily, traveled widely. The memoirs of some Jewish travelers are valuable sources of information about the traditions of the various communities they visited. In the 8th century a deputation sent by Charlemagne to the caliph Haroun al-Raschid included a Jew named Isaac. Jewish merchants known as Radanites undertook journeys from Europe to the Orient in the 9th century, and at about that time Eldad ha-Dani made numerous journeys in Spain and north Africa. In c. 970 the Caliph of Córdoba sent a deputation to Germany including one Ibrahim ibn Jakub. Perhaps the best-known Jewish traveler was Benjamin of Tudela, who in the 12th century journeyed widely in Europe and the Middle East. A later notable Jewish traveler was Pethahiah of Regensburg, and others of the medieval period include Abraham ibn Ezra, Judah al-Harizi, and Estori ha-Parḥi. In the 15th–17th centuries some Jews went on English and Portuguese expeditions of exploration. Like many of his predecessors, the late 18th-century traveler Samuel Romanelli of Mantua left a written account of his experiences. In the 19th century a number of Jewish explorers were active in Africa and Asia: Joseph Wolff traveled to Bokhara, Nathaniel Isaacs explored Zululand and Natal, Arminius Vámbéry went to central Asia, and Emin Pasha traveled to central Africa.

Trayf (Yiddish). Any food which is not kosher; an animal which is not slain according to ritual law.

Treason. The Bible recounts a number of

instances of rebellion and regicide (as in II Samuel 18.14; II Kings 11.1). The imposition of the death penalty for disobedience to the king is based upon the declaration made by the people to Joshua that whoever rebelled against his word should be put to death (Joshua 1.18). Rabbinic law has transferred rights previously enjoyed by the king to the state.

Treblinka. Village in central Poland on the Bug River, north-east of Warsaw. It was the site of a Nazi concentration camp, known principally as the place where the Jews of the Warsaw Ghetto were put to death.

Tree of Life. One of the two trees mentioned in the biblical account of the Creation as growing in the Garden of Eden (Genesis 2.9). Whoever ate from it lived forever. After Adam and Eve broke God's commandment and ate fruit from the second of the trees, the Tree of Knowledge of Good and Evil, they were expelled from the garden.

Treinin, Avner (b. 1928). Israeli poet. He was born in Tel Aviv and taught chemistry at the Hebrew University. His poems are concerned with the Holocaust and recent events in Jewish history.

***Treitschke, Heinrich von** (1834–1896). German historian. In 1876 he wrote an article, "Unsere Aussichten" (published in the *Preussische Jahrbücher*), in which he justified anti-Semitism. He was also the author of a popular German history, *Deutsche Geschichte im 19. Jahrhundert*, published in five volumes between 1879 and 1894.

***Tremellius, John Immanuel** (1510–1580). Italian Hebraist. He was born in Ferrara. He became a Catholic, then a year later converted to Protestantism. In 1542 he was appointed professor of Hebrew at the University of Strasbourg. He moved to England, where he was King's Reader in Hebrew at the University of Cambridge, and then to Germany to take the position of professor of Old Testament at the University of Heidelberg. He published a Latin translation of the Bible from Hebrew and Syriac.

Trendel *see* DREIDEL.

Trent. Town in northern Italy. A Jewish community existed there from the 14th century, but in 1475 it was eliminated on the charge of having put to death a Christian child named Simon for ritual purposes on Passover; this allegation was instigated by Bernardino da Feltre. Simon was beatified in 1582 and venerated until 1965, when the Catholic Church proclaimed that the accusation against the Jews was false.

Trespass. Legal term applied in Jewish usage to a variety of acts, including offenses against another person's rights or property, transgressions against divine law, and certain specific offenses that require a particular form of sacrifice (*see* TRESPASS OFFERING).

Trespass offering. Sacrifice required of a person guilty of certain offenses or trespasses. The acts for which such an offering was laid down were: perjury committed in denying a robbery; profane use of sacred objects; and violation of a betrothed handmaid. In cases of doubt concerning the commission of a trespass the offering might be suspended. A trespass offering was also brought by a Nazirite after being cleansed from ritual defilement and by a leper after his purification. The sacrifice consisted of a two-year-old ram, which was consumed by the priests.

Treves, Johanan (d. 1429). French rabbi, son of Mattathias ben Joseph Treves. When his father died he became chief rabbi of Paris. Later Isaiah ben Abba Mari claimed the sole right of appointing rabbis in France and of conducting a yeshivah. With the help of Meir ben Baruch of Vienna, he attempted to remove Johanan from his post. The expulsion of Jews from France in 1394 ended the dispute, and Johanan went to Italy.

Treves, Mattathias ben Joseph (c. 1325–c. 1385). French rabbi. He was born in Provence, and lived in Spain. He returned to France when the edict of expulsion of the Jews was repealed in 1361. He founded a yeshivah in Paris, and in 1363 became the city's chief rabbi.

Tribes of Israel. The 12 tribes into which the ancient Israelites were divided. They derived from the sons of Jacob: Reuben, Simeon, Levi, Judah, Issachar, Zebulun, Joseph, Benjamin, Dan, Naphtali, Gad, and Asher (Genesis 49). Moses conferred the priestly office on the tribe of Levi, and divided the tribe of Joseph into Ephraim and Manasseh. After Solomon's death the country split into two kingdoms: the tribes of Judah and Simeon, and most of the tribe of Benjamin peopled the southern kingdom of Judah, and the remaining tribes the northern kingdom of Israel. After the invasion of the Assyrians under Tiglath-Pileser III and Sargon in the 8th century BCE, the northern tribes were exiled (*see* TEN LOST TRIBES OF ISRAEL). A large part of the population of the southern kingdom was exiled by Nebuchadnezzar to Babylon in 586 BCE.

Tribunal. Court of justice, or a judicial body. During the biblical period, the tribunals of the Israelites were constituted by rulers of groups of 10, 50, 100, and 1,000 families (Exodus 18.21–6). After the institution of the monarchy, elders sitting at the city gateway served as a tribunal subject to the authority of the judges. Eventually by the second Temple period the bet din of three persons (or 23 in the cases of a regional tribunal acting in major cases) constituted the tribunal. The Sanhedrin of 71, also established in the second Temple period, had overriding authority. Throughout the Middle Ages a bet din of three scholars served as the normal Jewish tribunal. During the ghetto period, lay leaders of the community occasionally constituted a tribunal to arbitrate civil cases.

Triennial cycle *see* LAW, READING OF THE.

Trietsch, Davis (1870–1935). German Zionist writer. He was born in Dresden. During a period spent in the US (1893–9) he wrote several works on Jewish migration. He participated in the First Zionist Congress (1897), advocating Jewish settlement in Cyprus and the Sinai peninsula. Later he published schemes for Jewish settlement in Palestine. He himself moved to Palestine in 1932. He was a founder of the journals *Ost und West*, *Palästina*, and *Jüdischer Verlag*.

Tripoli. North African port, capital of Libya. Jews lived there from the 3rd century BCE. The Jewish population increased in Roman times and under Muslim rule.

Troki. Small town in Lithuania, near Vilnius. In the 14th century Grand Duke Witold of Lithuania settled 330 Karaite families from Crimea in Troki. The Jewish community was granted considerable autonomy in the next century and from that time continued to flourish.

Troki, Isaac ben Abraham (c. 1533–c. 1594). Lithuanian Karaite scholar. He was born in Troki. He wrote an apologia for Judaism, *Ḥizzuk ha-Emunah* ("Strengthening of the faith").

Trope. Traditional formula to which the Torah is intoned.

Troyes. Town in north-eastern France. Jews first settled there in the 10th century. The home of Rashi, it became a major center of Jewish learning. In the 13th century 13 Jews were put to death in the town on a ritual murder charge, and in 1306 the Jewish community was expelled.

Trumpeldor, Joseph (1880–1920). Palestinian soldier. He was born in Pyatigorsk in the northern Caucasus. He volunteered for the Russian army and became an officer. In 1912 he moved to Palestine, where he attempted to found a cooperative agricultural settlement. In Egypt during World War I he and Vladimir Jabotinsky tried to establish a Jewish unit to fight against the Turks in Palestine. In 1917 Trumpeldor went to Russia to organize Jewish groups who would settle in Palestine. Two years later he returned to Palestine as leader of a pioneer group and organized volunteers to protect Jewish settlements in Upper Galilee.

Truth *see* EMET.

Tsadeh. 18th letter of the Hebrew alphabet. Its numerical value is 90.

Tschernikhovski [Tchernikhovski]**, Shaul** (1875–1943). Palestinian Hebrew poet, of Russian origin. He was born in Mikhailovka, and during World War I served in the Russian medical corps. From 1922 to 1931 he lived in Germany, and later he moved to Palestine. He wrote poetry, stories, essays, and philological studies, and translated ancient and modern verse. His poetry had an important impact on Jewish youth.

Tschlenow, Jehiel (1863–1918). Russian Zionist leader. He was born in Kremenchug in the Ukraine, and became a physician. Active in the Ḥibbat Zion movement, he was one of the leaders of the Tziyyone Zion group founded in opposition to the plan for a Jewish homeland in Uganda. In 1906 Tschlenow convened the Helsingfors Conference. He later lived in Copenhagen and London, where he was an active Zionist. After the 1917 Revolution, he returned to Russia and convened a Russian Zionist Conference. His writings include *The Second Zionist Congress*, *Five Years of Work in Palestine*, and *The World and our Prospects*.

Tsederboym, Aleksander *see* ZEDERBAUM, ALEXANDER.

Tsimmes (Yiddish). Side dish of mixed cooked vegetables and fruits, or a dessert of stewed fruits.

Tsinberg, Yisrael (1873–1939). Russian literary historian. He was born in a village near Lanovits, Volhynia, and lived in St. Petersburg, where he became head of a chemical laboratory. He published a popular science book in Yiddish, critical and literary-historical studies, and a history of Jewish literature.

Tsuris (Yiddish). Troubles, suffering, or problems.

Tubal-Cain. Son of Lamech. According to Genesis, he was the first craftsman in iron and copper (Genesis 4.22).

Tu b'Av *see* FIFTEENTH OF AV.

Tu bi-Shevat *see* FIFTEENTH OF SHEVAT.

Tucker, Richard (1916–1975). American tenor. He was a successful synagogue cantor. From 1945 he made a career as an opera singer at the Metropolitan Opera in New York.

Tucker, Sophie (1889–1966). American entertainer. She was born in Russia, and went to the US as a child. The songs for which she was known included *My Yidishe Momma*.

Tudela. Town in northern Spain, formerly the chief city of Navarre. The establishment of a Jewish population there antedated the reconquest of Spain from the Arabs in 1114. Attacked during unrest in 1235, the community suffered again in a wave of massacres in 1321. In 1492 refugees from elsewhere in Spain increased the size of the population, but in 1498 the Jews were expelled from the town.

Tudesco (Ladino: "German"). Sephardi expression applied to the Ashkenazim.

Tugendhold, Jacob (1794–1871). Polish author. He was born near Kraków. He founded a modern Jewish school in Warsaw, which alienated Orthodox Jews. He served as vice-censor of Hebrew books, and from 1856 to 1863 was head of the government rabbinical seminary in Warsaw.

Tumarkin, Yigal (b. 1933). Israeli painter and sculptor. He was born in Dresden, and went to Palestine as a child in 1935. Later he lived in Germany, the Netherlands, and Paris. He constructed a number of sculptural monuments in Israel.

Tunkel, Joseph (1881–1949). Russian Yiddish humorist and cartoonist. He was born in Bobruisk, Belorussia. In 1906 he went to the US, where he edited the comic magazines *Der kibitzer* and *Der groyse kundes*. He returned to Warsaw in 1910 and became editor of *Der moment*. In 1939 he fled to France and in 1941 to the US. He wrote under the pseudonym "Der Tunkeler."

Turim, Baal ha- *see* JACOB BEN ASHER.

Turin. City in northern Italy. Jews settled there in the 15th century. A ghetto was established in the city in 1679. In the 19th–20th centuries Turin's Jewish community was one of the most important in Italy.

Tur Malka. Aramaic appelation of Har ha-Melekh ("Kings mountain"), the administrative district of Jerusalem during the period of the second Temple.

Tur-Sinai, Naphtali Herz [Torczyner, Harry] (1886–1973). Israeli philologist and Bible scholar. He was born in Lemberg. In 1933 he went to Palestine, where he taught at the Hebrew University. He wrote commentaries to the Book of Job, a study of Proverbs, essays on Biblical texts, rabbinic Hebrew, and problems in the history of the Hebrew language, and a work on the Lachish Letters.

Tuv Elem *see* BONFILS, JOSEPH BEN SAMUEL.

12 Minor Prophets *see* PROPHET.

12 tribes of Israel *see* TRIBES OF ISRAEL.

Twersky. Dynasty of Ḥasidic tzaddikim, active in Chernobyl from around 1750. It was founded by Menaḥem Nahum, the maggid of Chernobyl. Its influence declined after the Russian Revolution.

Twersky, Menaḥem Nahum (1730–1783). Lithuanian Ḥasidic leader. He was a pupil of Israel ben Eliezer Baal Shem Tov and Dov Ber of Mezhirich. He practiced as an itinerant preacher, stressing the importance of purifying moral attributes. He was the founder of a dynasty of tzaddikim. His son, Mordecai of Chernobyl (1770–1837), lived in some splendour and was greatly revered.

Twersky, Yoḥanan (1900–1967). Israeli novelist. He was born in Shpikov in the Ukraine. He went to the US in 1926 and taught at the Hebrew College in Boston. In 1947 he settled in Israel, where he served on the editorial staff of the Dvir Publishing House in Tel Aviv. His novels include *Uriel Acosta*, *Aḥad ha-Am*, *Alfred Dreyfus*, *Rashi*, and *Rom u-Tehom*.

Twilight (Hebrew "bein ha-arbayim," "bein ha-shemashot"). The soft light occurring when the sun is just below the horizon, especially after sunset; the period of evening when this light occurs. For halakhic purposes, it is deemed that as long as only two stars of medium size are visible, it is still twilight; the appearance of the third star marks the onset of night.

Tyre. City on an island off the shore of Phoenicia. Hiram of Tyre sent cedarwood and artisans to Solomon to help in constructing the Temple. Owing to the marriage of Jezebel with King Ahab, the worship of Baal and Ashtoreth spread from Tyre to Israel. Herod built a temple for the city and during the Roman period it became a center of commerce and the craft of purple dyeing. After 1071 the Palestinian gaonate was transferred there.

Tzaddik ("righteous man"). Word used to describe a person of faith and piety. Such figures are praised in the Bible (Habakkuk 2.4; Proverbs 20.7), and the Talmud states that the world depends for its continued existence on the presence in every generation of 36 tzaddikim. In the Ḥasidic movement the concept of the tzaddik was developed by Dov Ber of Mezhirich and Jacob Joseph of Polonnoye into one of a spiritual leader. Regarded as the intermediary between God and man, he brought down divine blessings. Individuals frequently visited the tzaddik for advice, and on Sabbath and festivals multitudes of Ḥasidim gathered at his festival table for a meal known as a "tish."

Tzarfati [Zarfatti]**, Joseph** (fl. 15th–16th cent.). Italian poet and physician. He was active in Jewish affairs in Rome. He wrote poetry about a wide range of topics and his translation of the Spanish comedy *Celestina* initiated Hebrew drama.

Tzarfati [Zarfatti]**, Samuel** (fl. 15th–16th cent.). Italian physician. He was in the service of the Medici family in Florence, and of several popes in Rome. He was active in Jewish affairs.

Tzedakah. Charity, philanthropy.

Tzedakah box. Box in the synagogue for gifts of money for charity. Located near the door, the contributions left there are used for local and Jewish charities. A box is also passed among the congregation for collections during week-day services and at funerals.

Tzeire Zion ("Young men of Zion"). Zionist socialist youth movement. Formed in Russia and Galicia from 1903, it spread throughout eastern Europe. After World War I it merged with Ha-Poel Ha-Tzair to form Hitaḥdut.

Tzemaḥ, Nahum David (1890–1939). Theater producer. He formed a Hebrew dramatic group in Vienna, which became the Ha-Bimah company. From 1930 to 1937 he directed the Tel Aviv Bet Am.

Tzemaḥ, Shelomoh (b. 1886). Israeli author, of Polish origin. He lived in Palestine in 1903–9, and again from 1921. His stories describe life in Israel.

Tz'enah u-Re'enah *see* ASHKENAZI, JACOB.

Tzere. Long "e" vowel sound in Hebrew.

Tzeva Haganah le-Israel ("Israel defense army"). Full name of the Israeli army. It developed from underground organizations in Palestine under British Mandatory rule. Established in 1948, it developed into a regular army by the end of the War of Independence the following year. It is composed of a standing army as well as reserves.

Tzidduk ha-din ("justification of the judgment"). Term used to acknowledge the justice of any evil occurrence that can be accounted for, including death. By extension it has come to refer to the burial service.

Tzimtzum ("divine contraction"). Kabbalistic doctrine which teaches that God makes a space in which the process of creation can take place.

Tzippori *see* SEPPHORIS.

Tzitzit ("fringes"). The Bible commands the wearing of fringes on the corners of garments (Numbers 15.37–41). Initially all garments had fringes, but later an undergarment with fringes on the corners ("tallit katan") was devised for daily use. *See also* TALLIT.

Tziyyone Zion ("Zionists of Zion"). Zionist political group. Founded in 1904 as a result of the controversy over the establishment of a Jewish homeland in Uganda, it was opposed to Theodor Herzl's tendency to accept territory outside Palestine. At the Seventh Zionist Congress it vigorously opposed the case of the Territorialists. Subsequently its members were instrumental in the drive for practical colonization work in Palestine. When the Territorialists left the Zionist Organization in 1905, its activities ceased.

Tzom ("fast"). Term used as a component

in the titles of particular fast days, such as "Tzom Gedaliah" (Fast of Gedaliah).

Tzoraat *see* LEPROSY.

Tzur mi-Shello ("Rock from whose store we have eaten"). Song sung at the Sabbath table. Its four stanzas correspond to the four benedictions of the Grace after Meals.

Tzur, Yaakov (b. 1906). Israeli diplomat and public figure. He was born in Vilnius, and emigrated to Palestine in 1921. He worked in the head office of the Jewish National Fund from 1929 to 1948. After the establishment of the State of Israel, he represented Israel in Argentina and other South American countries, as well as in France. He later returned to Israel, where he became director of the Jewish National Fund.

U

Uganda proposal. Plan set out in 1903 by Joseph Chamberlain, the British colonial secretary, to establish a Jewish homeland in Africa. The Seventh Zionist Congress rejected the proposal in 1905.

Ugarit. Ancient Canaanite city on the north Syrian coast; the modern town of Ras Shamra occupies the same site. Archaeological discoveries made there have cast light on Canaanite culture and religion in biblical times.

Uktzin ("Stalks"). 12th tractate in the Mishnah order of Tohorot. It deals with the transference of ritual impurity to a harvested plant when its roots, stalks, or pods come into contact with an unclean person or thing.

Ullendorff, Edward (b. 1920). British scholar. He was born in Zurich. He lectured in Semitics at the University of St. Andrews and was later professor at the universities of Manchester and London. He published numerous works on aspects of Semitics, notably in the field of Ethiopian studies.

Ullstein. German publishing house. It was founded in Berlin in 1877 by Leopold Ullstein, and was carried on by his descendants. It published four daily newspapers and 13 weeklies and monthlies, as well as books.

Ulpan ("study"). Institute for advanced study. The term is also used to refer to intensive courses in Hebrew for new immigrants to Israel.

Unbeshrieen (Yiddish: *lit.* "without evil omen"). Exclamation made after praising someone, in order to ward off the evil that is thought to result from good fortune.

U-Netannah Tokeph *see* AMNON OF MAINZ.

Union of American Hebrew Congregations. Association of Reform congregations in the US. It was founded in Cincinnati in 1873 by Isaac Mayer Wise; the Hebrew Union College was founded under its auspices in 1875. The Union runs departments dedicated to education, synagogue administration, public information, synagogue services, and interfaith activities. Its headquarters are now located in New York.

Union of Orthodox Jewish Congregations of America. Association of Orthodox synagogues and related institutions in the US. Founded in 1898, its members are chiefly synagogues, yeshivot, and day schools. The "U" symbol of the organization is widely used to designate approved kosher products.

Union of Orthodox Rabbis of the United States and Canada [UOR]. Organization dedicated to the encouragement of Orthodox Judaism in North America. It assists yeshivot and promotes Orthodox observance.

Union of Sephardic Congregations. American organization founded in New York in 1929. It promotes the interests of Sephardi Jews and supports rabbinic students.

Unions *see* TRADE UNIONS.

United Hebrew Trades. American labor organization representing Jewish workers in New York. Established in 1888, it works to eliminate discrimination in employment and housing.

United HIAS Service *see* HIAS.

United Jewish Appeal. American organization which coordinates fund raising for Israel. Established in 1939, it originally coordinated the campaigns of the United Palestine Appeal, the American Jewish Joint Distribution Committee, and the National Refugee Service.

United Nations. International organization of independent states formed in 1945 to promote peace and international cooperation. The United Nations' concern with the Jewish people has centered on its role in the establishment of the State of Israel, its attempt to resolve differences between Israel and the Arab world, and its influence on the concerns of Jewish communities outside Israel.

United Palestine Appeal. American Zionist fund-raising body, founded in 1927. In 1939 the United Jewish Appeal was founded to coordinate the fund-raising efforts of the United Palestine Appeal and the American Jewish Joint Distribution Committee.

United Service for New Americans. Organization formed in 1946 as the result of a merger between the National Refugee Service and the National Office of the Service to the Foreign-Born. It helped Jewish displaced persons and immigrants to the US. In 1954 it merged with HIAS and the Overseas Emigration Service of the American Jewish Joint Distribution Committee to form the United HIAS Service.

United Synagogue. British association of Ashkenazi congregations. It was established in London in 1870 and authorized by an Act of Parliament. It supports the office of the chief rabbi and the London bet din. After World War II its activities were expanded to include congregations outside the capital.

United Synagogue of America. Association of Conservative congregations in the US. It was formed by Solomon Schechter in 1913. It is associated with the Rabbinical Assembly, the Cantors' Assembly, the Educators' Assembly, the National Association of Synagogue Administrators, the National Women's League, the National Federation of Jewish Men's Clubs, and the United Synagogue Youth. It runs departments of Jewish education, youth activities, and music, maintains the Commission on Social Action, the Kashrut Commission, the Commission on Congregational Standards, and the Ramah Commission, and supports the National Academy of Adult Jewish Studies.

Universalism. The claim of a religion that it is true for all humankind; it is contrasted with particularism. Judaism combines aspects of both universalism and particularism, since, although it advocates the vision of a united humanity, it perpetuates the survival of the Jewish people as a distinct entity. Jewish universalism is based on the recognition of the absolute sovereignty of God and the doctrine of the messianic redemption of humankind. The theme of the liturgy on high holy days is God's rule over all people, and the second section of the Alenu prayer intercedes for the perfection of humanity in the Kingdom of God. Some Jewish thinkers have attempted to reconcile universalism and particularism in the Jewish faith by emphasizing Israel's mission as a herald of the divine promise for all people.

Universities. As in other areas of life, Jews have been excluded from university education for much of the history of the Jewish community in the diaspora. Not until Emancipation in the 18th century did Jews begin to be admitted on equal terms with other students to universities in Europe. According to legend, Jews attended the medical school at Salerno during the Middle Ages. In the 14th century a few Jews studied medicine in universities such as that at Montpellier. In 1466 Sicilian Jews obtained royal authorization to set up their own university, but this does not appear to have occurred. The University of Padua admitted Jews from Italy and elsewhere, again to study medicine, from the 16th century. Dutch universities accepted Jews in the 17th century, German universities in the 18th, and British universities in the 19th. In the US Jewish graduates were not known until the American Revolution. In modern times Jews attend university throughout the world, and several universities have been founded in Israel.

Unleavened bread *see* PASSOVER.

Unterfirer (Yiddish). Person (usually a close relative) who, during the marriage ceremony, conducts the bride or groom under the wedding canopy.

Unterman, Issar Yehudah (1886–1976). Israeli rabbi and scholar. He was born in Brest-Litovsk, Belorussia. He served as rosh yeshivah in Vishova, Lithuania, and later as a rabbi in various Lithuanian communities. After moving to England, he became rabbi of Liverpool in 1924. In 1946 he was appointed chief rabbi to the Ashkenazi community in Tel Aviv–Jaffa, and in 1964 Ashkenazi chief rabbi of Israel. His writings include *Shevet mi-Yehudah* on problems of Jewish law.

UOR *see* UNION OF ORTHODOX RABBIS OF THE UNITED STATES AND CANADA.

Ur. Ancient city of southern Mesopotamia or Chaldea (later in Sumeria and then Babylonia). Abraham lived there before his family left for Haran (Genesis 11.29–31).

Urbach, Ephraim Elimelech (1912–1991). Israeli scholar. He studied at the Breslau Rabbinical Seminary and at the universities of Breslau and Rome; he later taught at the Breslau seminary (1935–8). In 1938 he settled in Palestine, where he became a schoolteacher and headmaster of grammar schools in Jerusalem. In 1958 he became professor of Talmud at the Hebrew University. His publications include a study of the tosaphists and their methods.

Uri, Phoebus ben Aaron Levi [Witzenhausen, Joseph] (1623–1715). Dutch printer. In 1658 he established a press in Amsterdam, which published rabbinical and religious works in Hebrew and Yiddish. He also published the first Yiddish newspaper, *Dienstagishe und Freytagishe Kurant*, from 1680. In 1692 he moved to Zholkva, Poland, where he is supposed to have been invited by the king, John Sobieski, to print Hebrew books.

Uriah ben Shemaiah (fl. 7th cent. BCE). Israelite prophet. A contemporary of Jeremiah, he foretold the destruction of Jerusalem and Judah. He was persecuted by Jehoiakim and fled to Egypt. Later he was brought back and put to death (Jeremiah 26.20ff).

Uriah the Hittite (fl. 10th cent. BCE). Israelite soldier. He was in the service of David, who, when he had taken Bathsheba, Uriah's wife, for his mistress, sent Uriah to the front line where he was killed in battle. David's sin was denounced by the prophet Nathan (II Samuel 11–12).

Uriel. According to mystical literature, one of the four Angels of the Presence.

Urim and Thummim. Instruments of divination attached to the breastplate of the high priest; their form is uncertain. The process of divination involved the use of two stones or tablets by means of which an answer of "yes" or "no" could be obtained to important questions (I Samuel 23.10–12; 30.8).

Uris, Leon (b. 1924). American novelist.

He was born in Baltimore. His novels include *Exodus*, which tells the story of the birth of the State of Israel, and *Mila 18*, about the uprising in the Warsaw Ghetto.

Ury, Lesser (1861–1931). German artist. He was born in Birnbaum, Prussia, and went to Berlin at the age of 12. He studied art in Düsseldorf, Brussels, Paris, and Italy, later returning to Berlin. Some of his paintings deal with Jewish themes.

Usha. Town in Lower Galilee. It was an important center of learning during mishnaic and talmudic times. Around 140, at the end of the period of persecution following the Bar Kokhba revolt, the surviving scholars reestablished the Sanhedrin there; among those who served as nasi in Usha was Simeon ben Gamaliel II. While the Sanhedrin was centered there Usha also had an academy.

Ushpizin ("visitors"). According to the Zohar, the term refers to seven guests (Abraham, Isaac, Jacob, Joseph, Moses, Aaron, and David) who in succession visit the sukkah or booth of every pious Jew during the festival of Sukkot to partake of a meal with him.

Usque, Abraham [Pinhel, Duarte] (fl. 16th cent.). Portuguese printer. He fled from the Inquisition around 1543 to Ferrara, where he became associated with the Hebrew and Italian press established by Yom-Tov ben Levi Athias. His name appears in connection with the 1553 translation of the Bible into Italian (*The Ferrara Bible*).

Usque, Samuel (fl. 16th cent.). Portuguese poet and historian. He was born in Spain, but his family emigrated to Portugal in 1492. His *Consolation for the Tribulations of Israel* was designed to persuade Marranos to return to Judaism.

Usque, Solomon [Lusitano, Salusque] (c. 1530–1595). Portuguese poet. He lived in Italy and Turkey. In collaboration with Lazzaro di Graziano Levi, he wrote the earliest known Jewish drama in the vernacular, a Purim play in Spanish. He also published a Spanish translation of the final part of Petrarch's sonnets. In Constantinople he engaged in Hebrew printing.

Ussishkin, Menaḥem Mendel (1863–1941). Russian Zionist leader. He was born in Dubrovno in the district of Mohilev in Belorussia; he moved to Moscow in 1871. He was a founder of the Zionist youth group Bilu in 1882, and of the Bene Zion society in 1884; in 1897 he attended the First Zionist Congress as a delegate. He published a pamphlet, *Our Program*, in 1903, advocating a policy of political activity and practical work in Palestine. In the same year he convened an assembly of Palestinian Jews at Zikhron Yaakov and a teachers' conference. After returning to Russia, he organized the Tziyyone Zion (1904) in opposition to the proposal for a Jewish homeland in Uganda. In 1906 he went to Odessa, where he became leader of the Ḥovevei Zion. He later settled in Palestine, where he was appointed chairman of the Jewish National Fund.

Usury *see* MONEYLENDING.

Utz (Yiddish). To nag, to goad.

U-va le-Zion ("And a redeemer shall come unto Zion"). Opening words of a prayer used in various services. It is one of the concluding prayers in the morning service; on Sabbaths and festivals it is recited in the afternoon service; on the Day of Atonement it occurs in the concluding service; and, except for the first section, it is incorporated in the Saturday evening service. The prayer consists of Isaiah 59.20–21; Isaiah 6.3; a prayer based on verses from I Chronicles, the Book of Psalms, and Micah; and a prayer for enlightenment in understanding the law (made up of verses from Psalms, Jeremiah, and Isaiah).

Uziel, Ben Zion Meir Hai (1880–1954).

Israeli rabbi. He was born in Jerusalem. He became Ḥakham Bashi at Jaffa in 1912, and Rishon le-Zion in 1939. His writings include studies of Jewish law.

Uziel, Isaac ben Abraham (fl. 17th cent.). Dutch rabbi. He was born in Fez, and in 1610 was appointed rabbi of the Neveh Shalom synagogue in Amsterdam. He wrote poetry, a Hebrew grammar, and a translation of legends and fables.

Uzziah [Azariah] (fl. 8th cent. BCE). King of Judah (c. 780–c. 740 BCE). He conquered Philistia and led a league of kings opposed to Tiglath-Pileser of Assyria; he also rebuilt the port of Elath. He eventually fell victim to leprosy and ceded power to his son Jotham.

V

Vaad Arba Aratzot *see* COUNCIL OF FOUR LANDS.

Vaad ha-Lashon ha-Ivrit [Hebrew Language Council]. Israeli institution concerned with the development of the Hebrew language. It was founded in 1890 in Jerusalem by Eliezer Ben-Yehudah, David Yellin, and others as a branch of the Saphah Berurah Hebrew-speaking society. It was reorganized in 1904, and in 1953 its functions were transferred to the Academy of Hebrew Language.

Vaad Hatzala Rehabilitation Committee. American welfare organization. It was established in 1939 to rescue Jewish victims of Nazism. It succeeded in helping thousands of Jewish families, especially those of religious leaders, to escape Nazi persecution.

Va-ani tephillati ("And as for me, may my prayer"). Opening words of verse 14 of Psalm 69, which is recited at the opening of the afternoon service on the Sabbath. The verse is also included in the Mah Tovu prayer recited when entering the synagogue at the beginning of morning prayer.

Vajda, George (1908–1981). French Arabist and Hebraist. He was born in Budapest. In 1928 he settled in Paris, where he became professor of Bible and theology at the Séminaire Israélite. He also lectured at the École Pratique de Hautes Études, and was active in the oriental department of the Institut de Recherches et d'Histoire des Textes. From 1950 he edited the scholarly journal *Revue des Études Juives*. In 1970 he became a professor at the University of Paris. His writings include studies of Arabic and Jewish philosophy, the kabbalah, and Arab manuscripts.

Vakhnakht (Yiddish: "Watchnight"). Feast celebrated on the night preceding the circumcision ceremony, or (later) on the Sabbath eve before. Formerly called "Shavua ha-Ben," it is spent in feasting and reciting special prayers. The feast is also called "Zakhar" (or "Shelom Zakhar") after the first word of a hymn recited on the occasion.

Valladolid. City in central Spain. It had an important Jewish community in the Middle Ages. During the Civil War between Pedro I and Henry of Trastamara (1367), the Jewish quarter was attacked. In 1473 many Marranos were killed in the city. Later Valladolid became the seat of an Inquisitional tribunal.

Valley of Hinnom *see* GEHINNOM.

Valley of the Kings. Central area of the Kidron Valley to the north-east of Jerusalem, facing the city. By the reign of David it had become a royal domain. The King's Pool, which irrigated the royal gardens, was situated there (Nehemiah 2.13–14).

***Vámbéry, Arminius** (1832–1913). Hungarian orientalist and traveler. He was born in Dunajska, Streda, on the island of Schütt, and lived in Constantinople, where he worked as a tutor in European languages. After becoming a Muslim, he became secretary to Mehmet Fuad Pasha. In 1863–4 he traveled through Armenia, Persia, and Turkestan, disguised as a Sunnite dervish; he published an account of his experiences as *Travels and Adventures in Central Asia.* He later became a Protestant and taught oriental languages at the University of Budapest. His writings include studies of oriental languages and ethnology.

Varnhagen von Ense, Rachel *see* LEVIN, RACHEL.

***Varus, Publius Quintilius** (fl. 1st cent. BCE). Roman governor of Syria (6–4 BCE). In 4 he suppressed a revolt against Roman rule.

Vashti (fl. 5th cent. BCE). Persian queen, wife of King Ahasuerus. According to the Book of Esther, she was divorced after refusing to answer the king's summons to appear before him at a banquet. Her place in the royal household was taken by Esther.

Vav. Sixth letter of the Hebrew alphabet. Its numerical value is 6.

Va-yekhullu ("And they were completed"). Opening word (and thus the name) of the concluding paragraph of the Creation account in Genesis (Genesis 2.1–3). The paragraph is recited on Friday evening during and after the Amidah and in the Kiddush at home.

Va-Yikra *see* LEVITICUS.

Vazsonyi, Vilmos (1868–1926). Hungarian politician and lawyer. He founded the club of Junior Democrats in Budapest around 1890. In 1894 he was elected to the Budapest municipal council, and in 1901 to the lower house of the Hungarian parliament; during World War I he served as minister of justice. He advocated assimilation of the Jews in the diaspora and was an opponent of Zionism.

***Vecinho, Joseph** (fl. 15th cent.). Portuguese scientist and physician. A pupil of Abraham Zacuto, he translated his teacher's astronomical tables (*Almanach perpetuum*) into Spanish. Together with Martin Behaim and the court physician Rodrigo, he participated in a commission investigating navigation. He was forcibly converted in 1497, adopting the name Diego Mendes Vecinho.

Vegetarianism. According to the rabbis, the permission to eat animal food was not part of the original dispensation given by God to Adam at the time of the Creation; humankind was given dominion over the animals, but was allowed to eat only fruit and vegetables. However, the covenant made with Noah after the Flood permitted human beings to eat "every moving thing that liveth ... even as the green herb" (Genesis 9.3). Jewish law dictates that only those animals that have been specifically permitted may be eaten, and that they must be killed according to established ritual practice (*see* SHEḤITA).

Ve-hu raḥum ("And he, being merciful"). Opening words of verse 38 of Psalm 78. The verse occurs in the prayerbook as the introduction to the weekday evening service; and the opening of a seliḥah recited before the Taḥanun prayer on Mondays and Thursdays.

Venetianer, Lajos (1867–1922). Hungarian rabbi and historian. He was born in Kecskemét. He served as rabbi in Csurgó (1893) and Lugos (1896), and from 1897 as chief rabbi in Ujpest. He was also professor at the Budapest Rabbinical Seminary. His publications include studies of Christian liturgy and Judaism, the history of Hungarian Jewry, and the organization of Jewish communities.

Vengeance (Hebrew "nekamah"). Different attitudes to vengeance are expressed in biblical, rabbinic, moral, and legal texts. In the Bible it is regarded as a divine prerogative and part of the system of divine retribution, and is thus restricted as a human act. The Bible and the

Talmud contain numerous instances of forebearance and abstention from vengeance.

Venice. City and port in north-east Italy, formerly an independent republic. Jews lived there from the 12th century. In 1509 the German invasion of the Veneto drove many Jewish refugees there, and in 1516 they were segregated in the so-called New Foundry (Ghetto Nuovo); Jewish traders from the Levant were segregated in the Old Foundry (Ghetto Vecchio) in 1541, and at the end of the century they were joined by the "Ponentines" (Marranos who had been allowed to settle in Venice after 1589). During the next century the ghetto became a center of Jewish life in Italy. When French Revolutionary forces entered the city in 1797, the ghetto gates were destroyed and the Venetian Jews were emancipated.

Veprik, Alexander (1899–1952). Russian composer. He was born in Balta. He taught orchestration at the Moscow conservatory from 1923 to 1942. His works include *Songs and Dances of the Ghetto*, *Jewish Songs*, and *Kaddish*.

Verband der Vereine für Jüdische Geschichte und Literatur ("Association of Societies for Jewish History and Literature"). German organization dedicated to maintaining the aims of the traditional bet midrash. It was founded in Berlin in 1893 and was directed by Gustav Karpeles.

Verbitsky, Bernardo (1902–1979). Argentine novelist and academic. He was born in Buenos Aires. He wrote prose fiction and essays; some of his work deals with the problem of Jewish identity.

Verga, Ibn *see* IBN VERGA.

Vermes, Geza (b. 1924). British scholar, of Hungarian origin. He taught at the University of Newcastle, and later became professor of Jewish studies at the University of Oxford. He has published studies of the Dead Sea Scrolls, early Jewish biblical exegesis, and the Jewish background to the New Testament.

Versailles, Treaty of. Treaty imposed on Germany in 1919 after World War I; the most important of the five treaties that concluded the war. At the preceding Paris Peace Conference, Jewry was represented by the Zionist Organization and the Comité des Délégations Juives, as well as other minor organizations.

Ve-shameru ("And they shall keep"). Opening word of the passage from Exodus 31 (verses 16–17) recited before the Amidah in the Friday evening service, and on the Sabbath during the Amidah in the morning service and the Kiddush after the service.

Vespasian (fl. 1st cent.). Roman military commander and emperor (69–79). He was sent by Nero in 67 to subdue the Judean rebellion. By 68 he had conquered Galilee, Transjordan, and the Judean coast. In 69 he became emperor and the campaign was concluded by Titus.

Vessels, sacred (Hebrew "kelei kodesh"). Term applied originally to vessels and other implements and furnishings used in the tabernacle during the wilderness years and in the Temple. They included the Ark, seven-branched menorah, veil, table, laver, altar, coal shovels, and large shovel. The vessel chambers, which surrounded the temple, contained vessels of silver and gold which were taken to Babylon when the Jews were exiled there (II Kings 25.13–17); according to Cyrus' edict, the vessels were returned to Jerusalem with the homecoming exiles. Later they were looted from the second Temple by Titus and taken to Rome. The term "sacred vessels" is used in modern times to refer to synagogue appurtenances.

Vichy Government. Name by which the collaborationist government led by Marshal Pétain during the German occupation of France (1940–44) is commonly known; the government had its seat at Vichy in central France. Among its departments was a commissariat for Jewish affairs, directed by Xavier Vallat and then Darquier de Pellepoix; its policies were implemented through the Union Générale des Israélites de France, founded in 1941.

Vidal-Naquet, Pierre (b. 1930). French historian. He was born into an assimilated Jewish family, but his attitude to Judaism was changed by the Holocaust, in which his parents were killed. He has led a campaign against Revisionist historians, who claim that the Holocaust did not take place.

Viddui *see* CONFESSION OF SIN.

Vienna. Capital of Austria. Jews resided there from the 10th century and in the Middle Ages the community was a major center of Jewish scholarship. A ghetto was introduced in the 13th century, and in the 14th the Jewish population was devastated in anti-Jewish unrest resulting from a ritual murder accusation. The community was re-formed at the beginning of the 17th century, but expelled in 1670. The Jews of Vienna participated in the Revolution of 1848, and in 1867 were granted equal rights. In the 19th–20th centuries Jews attained a prominent position in the political, economic, cultural, and scholastic life of the city.

Vienna, Congress of *see* CONGRESS OF VIENNA.

Vienna Rabbinical Seminary [Israelitisch-Theologische Lehranstalt]. Founded in 1893, it served the Austro-Hungarian Empire and later its successor states as a training school for rabbis and teachers of Judaism. It was closed after the Nazis annexed Austria in 1938.

Vigée, Claude (b. 1921). French poet and essayist. He was born in Bischwiller. He was active in the Jewish Resistance in France during World War II, but in 1942 escaped to Spain and the following year emigrated to the US. He taught at various American universities, before becoming a professor at the Hebrew University in 1963. He wrote poems, stories and recollections, many of which deal with Jewish themes.

Villages, children's *see* YOUTH VILLAGES.

Vilna *see* VILNIUS.

Vilna Gaon *see* ELIJAH BEN SOLOMON ZALMAN.

Vilnius [Vilna]. City now in the western USSR, capital of Lithuania. Jews lived there from the 15th century but were banished in 1527. They were permitted to return later in the 16th century, and in the 17th they were allowed to engage in various trades. In 1655 the Jews of Vilnius were massacred by the Cossacks. From the 18th century the city became a center of rabbinical study and of the Haskalah movement. It was also a center of Zionism, the birthplace of the Jewish socialist party the Bund, and an important focus for Yiddish culture.

Vimpel [wimpel] (Yiddish). Fabric strip used as a binder round a Scroll of the Law (*see* MAPPAH). A vimpel was frequently presented to a synagogue to commemorate the birth of a male child.

Virtues (Hebrew "middot tovot"). In the Jewish tradition virtue is regarded as consisting of practices, actions, and states of mind that conform to God's will. Certain types of virtue, as well as the virtuous life, are extolled in the Bible. In rabbinic and medieval literature, the moral virtues, such as humility, patience, and contentment, are discussed according to various principles of classification. They are treated in the context of halakhic law or as mental and temperamental qualities conducive to the good life.

Vision. A mystical or religious experience in which a supernatural event or person is seen, or knowledge beyond normal human understanding is gained. A vision may be sought by mystical practices or may occur spontaneously. It may reveal terrestrial events removed in space and time, or spiritual realities and symbols. On the highest level in the Jewish tradition visions are the means by which God's will and purpose are made known to prophets. Visionary accounts occur frequently in apocalyptic literature, and are discussed in talmudic texts, though the Talmud does not itself generally record visions. Visionary experiences were cultivated in mystical circles among the ancient rabbis and medieval kabbalists.

Visiting the sick *see* SICK, VISITING THE.

Vital, Ḥayyim (1543–1620). Palestinian kabbalist. He was a student of Moses Cordovero and Moses Alshekh, and was associated with Isaac Luria during his last years in Safed. After Luria's death, Vital claimed that he alone had an accurate account of Luria's teaching. He boasted that his soul was that of the Messiah, son of Joseph, and he became known in oriental countries as miracle worker. His notes on Lurianic kabbalah were transcribed and published as *Etz Ḥayyim*. From 1590 he lived in Damascus, where he wrote kabbalistic works and preached the coming of the Messiah.

Vital, Samuel (fl. 17th cent.). Syrian rabbi and kabbalist, son of Ḥayyim Vital. He lived in Damascus and later went to Cairo. He edited his father's works on Lurianic kabbalah.

Viterbo, Carlo Alberto (1889–1974). Italian Zionist. He was born in Florence. He became president of the Italian Zionist Organization in 1931. He was imprisoned in the Sforzacosta concentration camp during World War II and released by the Allies in 1944. After the war he relaunched the periodical *Israel*, which continued until his death.

Vitkin, Yoseph (1876–1912). Palestinian Zionist pioneer. He was born in Mogilev, Belorussia. In 1897 he went to Palestine, where he worked as a laborer, and later as a schoolteacher and headmaster. His writings include a number of pamphlets on pioneering, such as *A Call to the Youth of Israel whose Hearts are with their People and with Zion* and *A Group of Young People from Eretz Israel*.

Vitry. Small town in north-eastern France. Vitry was the home of Rashi's disciple, Simḥah ben Samuel of Vitry, who gave his name to the Maḥzor Vitry (11th century). In 1317 the Jewish population was massacred on suspicion of having poisoned the town well.

Vocalization [vowelization]. The indication of vowel sounds in Hebrew script by means of marks or points placed above or below consonants. Originally Hebrew was written only with consonants, which were "vocalized" to show where vowel sounds occurred and what vowels should be sounded. Eventually the letter yod came to represent the long i and e sounds, and the letter vav the long u and o sounds. At the end of the talmudic period a system of distinctive signs to indicate vowels began to develop, and eventually three so-called "punctuation" systems evolved: Babylonian, Palestinian, and Tiberian. The Tiberian system became fixed in two different forms associated with the masoretic schools of Ben Asher and Ben Naphtali. The Ben Asher system passed into common use and is found in printed Bibles.

Vogel, David (1891–1944). Russian Hebrew poet and writer. He was born in Satanov, Russia, and settled in Vienna in 1912. He suffered periods of imprisonment during World War I (to 1916) and World War II (in French detention camps, to 1941), before being arrested by the Nazis in 1944. He wrote novels as well as poetry and is regarded as an important forerunner of Hebrew modernism.

Volcani [Volkani], **Yitzḥak Avigdor** *see* ELAZARI-VOLCANI, YITZḤAK AVIGDOR.

Volhynia. Province in north-west Ukraine. The Jewish community dates from at least the 15th century. In the 17th century it was brought under centralized organization as part of the Council of Four Lands. At this time Volhynia was a center of Jewish scholarship, but in 1648–9 the community was devastated during the Cossack onslaught. In the 18th century Ḥasidism flourished strongly in the province.

Volkisten *see* FOLKISTEN.

Volozhin. Small town in Lithuania. It was known for its yeshivah, which attracted students from various countries. The principals of the yeshivah were Ḥayyim of Volozhin (1802–21), his son Isaac of Volozhin (1821–49), Eliezer Isaac Fried (1849–53), and Naphtali Tzevi Judah Berlin (1853–92). The yeshivah was closed after 1892 but reopened in 1899.

Volterra, Meshullam [Meshullam ben Menaḥem of Volterra] (fl. 15th cent.). Italian financier. He inherited his father's loan bank in Florence. In 1481 he traveled to Palestine; after a month's stay he returned to Florence via Venice. His *Massa Meshullam mi-Volterra be-Eretz Yisrael* is an account of his voyage.

Voskhod. Russian Jewish monthly journal. It appeared in St. Petersburg from 1881 to 1906 under the editorship of Adolph Landau and later S. Gruzenberg. Until 1904 it was the only Russian-language Jewish periodical.

Vow. A solemn pledge binding on the person making it. In Jewish tradition it was common to make religious vows undertaking voluntarily to perform a specific act or behave in a certain way. In talmudic law there are two types of vow: a promise to provide Temple sacrifices or to make gifts of property to the Temple or to charity; and the commitment to abstain from eating specified food or from the financial exploitation of specified property. Vows are binding even if no special formula or invocation of the divine name is used in making them.

Vowels *see* VOCALIZATION.

Vozrozhdenie. Russian Jewish socialist party. It was the precursor of the SEYMISTS.

Vulgate. The principal Latin translation of the Bible. It was made in Palestine at the end of the 4th century by Jerome.

W

Wadi Kumran *see* QUMRAN.

***Wagenseil, Johann Christoph** (1633–1705). German Hebraist. From 1667 he was a professor at Altdorf. His *Tela ignea satanae* is a collection of Jewish polemical writings critical of Christianity.

Wages. According to the Bible, the employer is enjoined to pay wages without delay (Leviticus 19.13). The Talmud explains that a person hired for the day is to be paid not later than the next morning; one hired for the night by the following evening. Whoever withholds such payment violates several biblical prohibitions.

Wahl, Meir (fl. 17th cent.). Lithuanian talmudist, son of Saul Wahl. He was rabbi of Brest and a founder in 1623 of the Council of Lithuania, an autonomous governing body for Lithuanian Jewry.

Wahl, Saul (1541–1617). Lithuanian financier. He was the son of Samuel Judah ben Abraham, who was rabbi at Venice and Padua. Wahl became court agent to Sigismund III, and used his influence on behalf of Jews in Poland and Lithuania. According to legend, he was chosen to be King of Poland for a day.

Wailing Wall *see* WESTERN WALL.

Wald, Herman (1906–1970). South African sculptor. He was born in Cluj, Hungary. He went to Paris in 1933 and later to London; in 1937 he settled in South Africa. Some of his art is influenced by Jewish subjects.

Waldman, Morris David (1879–1963). American communal worker. He was born in Bartfa, Hungary, and was taken to the US as a child. From 1908 to 1917 he was managing director of the United Hebrew Charities of New York. In 1921–2 he organized relief for central European Jewish communities, and from 1928 he served as executive secretary of the American Jewish Joint Distribution Committee. His writings include an autobiography, *Not by Power*, and *Sieg Heil*, a study of Hitler's treatment of the Jews.

Waley, Jacob (1818–1873). English lawyer and communal leader. He served as professor of political economy at University College, London (1953–60). He was a founder of the United Synagogue, president of the Anglo-Jewish Association, and president of the Jews Hospital and Orphan Asylum.

Waley Cohen *see* COHEN, ROBERT WALEY.

Walk, Joshua *see* FALK, JOSHUA BEN ALEXANDER HA-COHEN.

Walkowitz, Abraham (1878–1965). American painter. He was born in Siberia, and went to the US in 1889. His works include *Faces from the Ghetto*.

Wallant, Edward (1926–1962). American novelist. He was born in New Haven, Connecticut, and worked in a New York advertising agency. His novels deal with Jewish characters.

***Wallenberg, Raoul** (1912–c. 1947). Swedish diplomat. He was stationed in Hungary during World War II and helped to save thousands of Jews from the Nazis.

Wallenstein, Meir (b. 1903). British orientalist. He was born in Jerusalem. He taught in Palestine (1925–9), and Manchester (1932–8), then from 1946 was reader in medieval and modern Hebrew at Manchester University. He settled in Jerusalem in 1970. His publications include studies of Moses Judah Abbas and his contemporaries, hymns from the Judean scrolls, and piyyutim from the Cairo Genizah.

Wandering Jew [Ahasuerus]. Figure from a medieval Christian legend. The story concerns a Jerusalem cobbler called Ahasuerus, condemned to wander eternally for taunting Jesus on his way to the crucifixion. Among many literary treatments of the legend are David Pinski's Yiddish play *The Eternal Jew*, Rudyard Kipling's short story *The Wandering Jew*, and a novel by Stefan Heym, also called *The Wandering Jew*.

Warburg, Edward (b. 1908). American communal leader, son of Felix Warburg. He was involved in a variety of cultural, communal, and philanthropic activities. He served as chairman of the American Jewish Joint Distribution Committee (1941–66) and of the United Jewish Appeal. In 1967 he became president of the United Jewish Appeal of Greater New York.

Warburg, Felix (1871–1937). American banker and communal leader, brother of Max Warburg. He was born in Hamburg, and in 1894 went to the US, where he became a partner in the banking firm of Kuhn, Loeb and Co. in New York. He served as chairman of the American Jewish Joint Distribution Committee (1914–32) and supported Jewish educational institutions, including the Hebrew Union College, the Jewish Theological Seminary, and the Graduate School for Jewish Social Work.

Warburg, Max (1867–1946). German banker, brother of Felix Warburg. He served as a German delegate to the Paris Peace Conference at the end of World War I and was active in Jewish affairs. He settled in the US in 1939.

Warburg, Otto (1859–1938). German botanist, cousin of Max and Felix Warburg. He was born in Hamburg. He became professor at the University of Berlin in 1892. An active Zionist, he was instrumental in founding the Palestine Office at Jaffa in 1908, and served as president of the World Zionist Organization from 1911 to 1920. From 1921 he was head of the Jewish Agency's experimental station at Tel Aviv, and he also taught at the Hebrew University.

War criminal. One who commits a crime in wartime in violation of accepted rules of war. During World War II, the Allied Powers declared that Germans responsible for crimes against humanity would be tried and judged. For this purpose, after the surrender of Germany, an International Military Tribunal was created. Heads of the Nazi government and armed forces were charged and tried for crimes against the Jews and others. In addition to the International Military Tribunal, national courts to deal with war criminals were established in occupied zones.

War of Independence. War for Israeli independence fought in Palestine in 1947–9. After the UN resolution passed on 29 November 1947 to partition Palestine into Jewish and Arab states, Palestinian Arabs initiated hostilities against the Jewish population; they were soon joined by volunteers from Arab states. Jewish forces were largely organized in the Haganah. In May 1948 the forces of the Arab League invaded the country. Eventually, between February and July 1949, armistice agreements were signed between Israel and Egypt, Jordan,

Lebanon, and Syria; these permitted Israel to maintain a defensive force in the Negev desert.

Warsaw. Capital of Poland. It had a Jewish community from at least the 15th century, but the Jews were expelled from the city in 1483. A number were living there again by the 18th century, and rights were granted to the Jewish community in 1862. From the early 20th century the city was a center of Hebrew and Yiddish culture. In October 1940 the forces of German occupation established a ghetto in which were incarcerated the Jews of Warsaw and deportees from other parts of Poland. In April and May 1943 the Jews of Warsaw unsuccessfully attempted to rise against the Germans, the ghetto was demolished, and its surviving inhabitants sent to concentration camps.

War Scroll. One of the DEAD SEA SCROLLS. It describes the war at the end of time between the Sons of Light and the Sons of Darkness.

Wassermann, Jakob (1873–1934). German novelist. He was born in Fürth, and from 1898 lived in Vienna. His works include *My Life as a German and Jew*, *The Jews of Zirndorf*, *Caspar Hauser*, *The Goose Man*, and *The Maurizius Case*.

Wassermann, Oscar (1869–1934). German banker and communal leader. He was born in Bamberg. He became a director of the Berlin branch of his family bank, and in 1912 joined the board of directors of the Deutsche Bank, which later merged with the Disconto-Gesellschaft. Later he was appointed a member of the Council of the Reichsbank. In 1933 he was dismissed from these posts. An active Zionist, he held various positions in the Jewish community including the presidency of the Keren ha-Yesod in Germany.

Waten, Judah (1911–1985). Australian novelist, critic, and essayist. He was born in Odessa. In 1914 he emigrated with his family to Perth, where later he worked as a literary critic. In the 1940s he served as a member of the Jewish Council to Combat Fascism and Anti-Semitism. Some of his work deals with Jewish themes.

Water (Hebrew "mayim"). Biblical and rabbinic law prescribe ablutions and immersions in water for various occasions (*see* ABLUTION; IMMERSION; MIKVEH; PURIFICATION AFTER CHILDBIRTH; PURITY, RITUAL). In the aggadah water is regarded as a symbol of the Torah.

Water-Drawing, Festival of the *see* SIMḤAT BET HA-SHOEVAH.

Waters of Merom *see* MEROM, WATERS OF.

Waxman, Meyer (1887–1969). American scholar. He was born in Slutsk in Belorussia. In 1905 he emigrated to the US, where he became principal of the Mizraḥi Teachers Seminary, and later director of the Mizraḥi Zionist organization. In 1924 he joined the faculty of the Hebrew Theological College in Chicago; he was later appointed professor of Hebrew literature and philosophy there. His writings include *A Handbook of Judaism*, *Judaism: Religion and Ethics*, and *A History of Jewish Literature*.

Wedding *see* MARRIAGE.

Weeks, Feast of *see* SHAVUOT.

Weidman, Jerome (b. 1913). American writer. He has written 200 short stories, as well as plays and novels. In much of his work he draws on the conflict between Jewish and American culture. Among his better-known works are the novels *The Center of the Action* and *Fourth Street East*.

Weights and measures. In biblical times the unit of weight for silver was the shekel; there were various standard weights based on this unit. Hollow measures included the ephah, the seah, the hin, the ḥomer, the omer, the kav, and the log. For ritual purposes the measures "olive-sized" and "egg-sized" were used. There were two systems of measuring length, the ordinary ammah ("cubit"), about 46 cm, and the large ammah, 52 cm. The cubit was divided into two units of a zeret ("span"), six units of a tephaḥ ("hand's breadth"), or 24 units of an etzba ("finger").

Weil, Gotthold (1882–1960). Israeli orientalist and librarian, of German origin. He was born in Berlin. He became director of the oriental department at the Berlin State Library in 1906, and in 1920 professor at Berlin University. He was appointed professor of Semitic languages at the University of Frankfurt in 1934. After moving to Palestine he served as head of the National and University Library in Jerusalem (1935–46) and was professor of Turkish studies at the Hebrew University. He published works on Arabic and Turkish subjects.

Weil, Gustav (1808–1889). German orientalist. He was born in Salzburg, Baden. He worked as a French instructor at a medical school in Cairo, then, after returning to Germany, as a librarian and teacher in Heidelberg. He wrote studies of Jewish influences on the Koran, Muslim history, and Arabic literature. He also translated the *Arabian Nights* into German.

Weil, Simone (1909–1943). French religious writer. She was born in Paris. She gave up teaching philosophy to become a factory worker. In 1936 she joined the Republicans in the Spanish Civil War. After the Nazi invasion of France she worked as a farm laborer in the south. She spent a period in the US, but returned to France to join the Resistance. She was fiercely critical of Judaism.

Weiler, Moses Cyrus (b. 1907). South African rabbi. He was born in Riga, Latvia, and was educated in Palestine and later in the US. In 1933 he settled in South Africa where he founded the non-Orthodox Progressive movement and served as a rabbi. He moved to Israel in 1958 to teach at the Hebrew Union College in Jerusalem.

Weill, Alexandre (1811–1899). French philosopher. After a talmudic education he abandoned traditional Judaism. A friend of Hugo, Balzac, and Baudelaire, he was prominent in the literary world. In later life he returned to a study of the Bible.

Weinberg, Elbert (b. 1928). American sculptor. He was born in Hartford, Connecticut. Some of his works deal with biblical subjects and others with the Holocaust.

Weinberger, Jacob (1879–1956). American composer. He was born in Odessa, and taught there from 1915 to 1921. He emigrated to Palestine in 1922, and later settled in the US. His works include the opera *The Pioneers*, and a number of choral works, among them *Prayers for the Sabbath*, *Isaiah*, and *The Life of Moses*.

Weinberger, Jaromir (1896–1967). American composer. He was born in Prague, and taught there and in various other cities. In 1937 he emigrated to the US, settling in St. Petersburg, Florida. His compositions include works based on biblical themes.

Weiner, Lazar (1897–1982). American composer, of Russian origin. He settled in the US in 1914. His compositions include a setting of the Friday evening service and other liturgical works.

Weingreen, Jacob (b. 1908). English Hebrew grammarian and biblical scholar. He was born in Manchester. He became professor of Hebrew at the University of Dublin. His works include *A Practical Grammar for Classical Hebrew*, *Themes of Old Testament Stories*, *English Versions of the Old Testament*, and *The Concepts of Retaliation and Compensation in Biblical Law*.

***Weininger, Otto** (1880–1903). Austrian philosopher. He was born in Vienna into a Jewish family, but later converted to Protestantism. His *Sex and Character* deals with the nature of anti-Semitism.

Weinreich, Max (1894–1969). American scholar. He was born in Kuldiga, Latvia. He served as research director of YIVO in Vilnius from 1925, and later at the institute's new center in New York. From 1947 he was professor at City College, New York. He published studies of Yiddish linguistics, folklore, literary history, psychology, pedagogy, and sociology.

Weinreich, Uriel (1925–1967). American scholar of linguistics, editor, and educator, son of Max Weinreich. He was born in Vilnius, and emigrated to the US in 1940. He became professor of Yiddish language, literature, and culture at Columbia University in 1959. His writings include *College Yiddish: an Introduction to the Yiddish Language and to Jewish Life and Culture*, *Language and Culture Atlas of Ashkenazic Jewry*, and *Modern English–Yiddish, Yiddish–English Dictionary.*

Weinryb, Bernard Dov (1900–?). American economic and social historian. He was born in Turobin, Poland. He worked as the librarian of the Breslau Rabbinical Seminary, before emigrating in 1934 to Palestine, where he lectured at the School of Social Work and School of Economics. Later he settled in New York and held a succession of teaching posts – at the Herzliah Teachers' Seminary, the Jewish Teachers' Seminary, Brooklyn College, Columbia University, and Yeshiva University. From 1949 he was professor of Jewish history and economics at Dropsie College. He wrote studies of Jewish life and history.

Weisgal, Meyer Wolf (1894–1977). Israeli Zionist. He was born in Kikol, Poland, and moved to the US in 1905. He served as national secretary of the Zionist Organization of America, and as Chaim Weizmann's political representative in the US. Later he became secretary-general of the Jewish Agency for Palestine. He subsequently settled in Israel and became president and chancellor of the Weizmann Institute of Science at Reḥovot.

Weisgall, Hugo (b. 1912). American composer and educator. He was born in Ivančice (now in Czechoslovakia), and settled in the US in 1920. He taught at Queens College, New York, and served as chairman of faculty at the Cantors Institute of the Jewish Theological Seminary. He has lectured extensively on the subject of Jewish music.

Weiss, Isaac Hirsch (1815–1905). Moravian talmudic scholar. He lectured at the Vienna bet midrash from 1861. His *Dor Dor ve-Doreshav* is a history of the development of the Oral Law down to the Middle Ages.

***Weiss, Peter** (1916–1982). German playwright. He was born in Berlin. In 1939 he settled in Sweden, where he was active as a painter, film producer, and writer. In his play *The Investigation* he made use of documentation produced at the Frankfurt trial of Nazi war criminals.

Weizel, Naphtali Herz *see* WESSELY, NAPHTALI HERZ.

Weizmann, Chaim (1874–1952). Israeli Zionist leader and statesman. He was born at Motel near Pinsk, in Belorussia. He settled in England and in 1904 became a lecturer in biological chemistry at Manchester University. In 1916 he was appointed director of the British Admirality Chemical Laboratories. His Zionist activities began when he became associated with the Democratic Fraction in 1901; the following year he and Berthold Feiwel proposed the creation of the Hebrew University (the foundation stone of which Weizmann, as chairman of the Zionist Commission finally laid in 1918). In 1903 Weizmann opposed the plan for the establishment of a Jewish homeland in Uganda and became a supporter of synthetic Zionism. He was the prime mover behind the Balfour Declaration of British support for Zionism in 1917. At the Paris Peace Conference of 1919 Weizmann (together with Menaḥem Mendel Ussishkin and Naḥum Sokolow) represented the Zionist movement, and in the same year he became president of the World Zionist Organization. He later retired to Reḥovot to work at the Weizmann Institute, which he had helped to found. In 1948 he became the first president of the State of Israel.

Weizmann, Ezer (b. 1924). Israeli military commander, nephew of Chaim Weizmann. He served as a pilot in the British Air Force (the RAF) during World War II, then in 1958 became commander of the Israeli air force. He was appointed chief of operations of the Israeli general staff in 1966, and played an important role in the Six-Day War in 1967.

Weizmann Institute of Science. Israeli research institute. It was founded in 1949 in Reḥovot as an extension of the Daniel Sieff Research Institute, set up in 1934 by Israel Moses Sieff under the direction of Chaim Weizmann. The Weizmann Institute engages in research into the exact sciences. In 1952 the Yad Chaim Weizmann was established as a foundation to develop cultural and scientific projects; it administers the institute and cares for Weizmann's residence and for his grave.

***Wellesz, Egon** (1885–1974). British musicologist and composer. He was born in Vienna. After moving to England in 1938 he was baptized and took up a teaching post at Oxford University. His work as a scholar demonstrated the affinity of early church music with ancient Jewish cantillation.

***Wellhausen, Julius** (1844–1918). German biblical scholar. He was born in Hameln. He was professor of theology in Greifswald (1872–82), and of oriental studies in Halle (1882–5), Marburg (1885–92), and Göttingen (from 1892). His publications include *Prolegomena to the History of Ancient Israel.*

Welt, Die. Journal of the World Zionist Organization, published from 1897 to 1914. It was founded and first edited by Theodor Herzl in Vienna. Later its offices moved to Cologne (1906–11) and then Berlin (1911–14).

Wengeroff, Pauline W. (1833–1916). Russian writer. She was born in Bobruisk, Belorussia, and became the wife of Ḥanan Wengeroff, a banker and communal worker in Minsk. Her memoirs depict the life of a rich Jewish family in the period before and after the Haskalah.

Werblowsky, Raphael Juda Zwi (b. 1924). Israeli scholar. He was born in Frankfurt am Main. He taught first in England (at the universities of Leeds and Manchester), and then at the Hebrew University. He has written extensively on areas of Jewish studies and served as co-editor of the *Encyclopedia of the Jewish Religion*, published in the US in 1966.

Werfel, Franz (1890–1945). Austrian novelist, playwright, and poet. He was born in Prague, and served in the Austrian army. From 1940 he lived in the US. Some of his writing deals with Jewish themes.

Werner, Eric (1901–1988). American musicologist. He was born in Vienna. He lectured at the rabbinical seminary in Breslau before moving to the US in 1938. He became professor of liturgical music at the Hebrew Union College in Cincinnati, and in 1948 founded the college's School of Sacred Music. From 1967 to 1971 he served as head of the department of musicology at Tel Aviv University. He wrote studies of early Christian, medieval, and Renaissance music, and of the relationship between ancient Greek and Hebrew hymnology and musical theories.

Wertheimer, Joseph von (1800–1887). Austrian educator and author. He was born in Vienna, where he later was active as a merchant. He founded the city's first kindergarten in 1830, and in 1843 set up a Jewish kindergarten. His other acts of philanthropy included the establishing of a society to assist released criminals and provide guidance for juvenile delinquents, and (in 1860) the founding of the Society for the Care of Needy Orphans of the Israelite Community. He also played a leading role in the struggle to achieve equal social and political status for Jews.

Wertheimer, Leopold *see* BRUNNER, CONSTANTIN.

Wertheimer, Samson (1658–1724). German court Jew. He was born in Worms. In 1684 he went to Vienna to join the bank of Samuel Oppenheimer, and he eventually became a court banker. In 1719 Carl VI appointed him chief rabbi of Hungary. Wertheimer was active on behalf of Jewish communities, and in 1700 obtained an order from the Emperor Leopold which resulted in the withdrawal from circulation of Johann Eisenmenger's anti-Jewish book, *Entdecktes Judentum.* He also created a fund to help paupers in Palestine.

Wesker, Arnold (b. 1932). English playwright. He was born in London. He held various jobs, including kitchen porter and pastry cook, before becoming a full-time writer. His plays include *Chicken Soup and Barley*, *Roots*, *I'm Talking about Jerusalem*, and *Chips with Everything*.

Wessely [Weizel]**, Naphtali Herz** (1725–1805). German Hebrew writer and leader of the early Haskalah movement. He was born in Hamburg, and lived in Copenhagen; his business affairs also took him to Amsterdam and Berlin. His first work was a study of the origins of Hebrew words, and synonyms in the Hebrew language. Later he published a commentary on Avot and an annotated Hebrew translation (from the original Greek) of the Wisdom of Solomon. He also participated in the writing of Moses Mendelssohn's commentary on the Pentateuch. Wessely's *Words of Peace and Truth*, written under the influence of Joseph II's Edict of Toleration, advocated an educational program for Jewish youth in the spirit of the Haskalah. Subsequently he published the epic story *Shire Tipheret*, which relates biblical events from the Exodus to the revelation on Mount Sinai.

Western Wall (Hebrew "Kotel Maaravi") [Wailing Wall]. Name given to the surviving part of the outer wall of the Temple, dating from c. 35 BCE. Owing to its proximity to the Holy of Holies at the west end of the Temple, the wall is regarded as sacred. Regular services have been held there since the 10th century.

Whitehall Conference. Conference of lawyers, clergy, and merchants convened in London by Oliver Cromwell in 1655. Its purpose was to consider Manasseh ben Israel's petition for the readmission of Jews to England. It was dissolved by Cromwell to prevent it from producing a negative report.

White Paper, Churchill. Document issued by the British government in June 1922, following a statement by Winston Churchill. It claimed that the McMahon Letters (1915) did not refer to Palestine, and that the intention of the Balfour Declaration (1917) was to create a Jewish national home but not necessarily a state under Jewish sovereignty; further, it made Jewish immigration into Palestine dependant on absorptive capacity. As a result of this document, the Transjordan was excluded from the area to which the Balfour Declaration applied.

White Paper, Passfield. British statement

of policy on Palestine. It was issued in October 1930 by Lord Passfield. Based on the Hope-Simpson report, it argued that Jewish land acquisition and settlement were creating a landless peasantry and unemployment among the Palestinian Arabs. To combat this, it ruled that Jewish immigration and land purchase should be restricted. In protest against the provisions of the White Paper Chaim Weizmann resigned as president of the World Zionist Organization.

White Paper of 1939 [Macdonald White Paper]. British statement of policy on Palestine. Prepared under the aegis of the British Colonial secretary, Malcolm Macdonald, it was issued in May 1939. It declared the British intention of establishing after ten years an independent Palestinian state in which both Jews and Arabs would participate in the government. 75,000 Jews would be allowed to enter Palestine over 5 years to 1944, after which Jewish immigration would be subject to Arab agreement, and land sales to Jews would also be restricted. The document evoked a hostile response from the Zionist movement. The plans it set out were overtaken by events and were never implemented.

Whitman, Ruth (b. 1922). American translator and poet. She was born in New York. She lectured on poetry at Harvard University and Radcliffe College. She edited and translated *An Anthology of Modern Yiddish Poetry* and has published several volumes of her own poetry.

Whole offering (Hebrew "kalil"). Term used in the context of the Temple sacrifice to denote any offering that was consumed entirely when it was burnt. Specifically it is used of the meal offering consumed in this way (Leviticus 6.15–16). In this more limited sense "whole offering" is parallel to "burnt-offering" (olah), the one referring to a sacrifice of meal and the other to an animal sacrifice.

Wicked Priest. In the Dead Sea Scrolls, the figure portrayed as the opponent of the Teacher of Righteousness. Initially he was on the side of truth, but later betrayed the law for gain and persecuted the Teacher of Righteousness.

Widow. According to the Bible, a widow is a privileged person, who is to be protected and maintained (Exodus 22.21; Deuteronomy 27.19). She is entitled to payment of the sum stipulated by her husband in the marriage contract, or alternatively to support by her husband's descendants.

***Wiener, Leo** (1862–1939). American philologist. He was born in Białystok, Poland. In 1882 he settled in the US, where he became a professor at Harvard University. His publications include *History of Yiddish Literature in the Nineteenth Century*. He became a Unitarian.

Wiener Neustadt. Austrian town, about 30 miles south of Vienna. Jews settled there in the 12th century but were expelled in 1496. After a long interval the community was re-established in the 18th and 19th centuries.

Wiernik, Peter (1865–1936). American Yiddish writer, of Lithuanian origin. He went to the US in 1885. He served as editor of the Yiddish daily *Morgen-Journal* from its foundation in 1901, and also of the weekly *Der Amerikaner*. His writings include *History of the Jews of America*.

Wiesel, Elie (b. 1928). American author. He was born in Sighet, Romania. A survivor of the concentration camps, he later lived in Paris and New York. He became a foreign correspondent for an Israeli daily newspaper, and from 1957 worked for the *Jewish Daily Forward*; in 1976 he was appointed professor of humanities at Boston University. His works include *Night*, *The Gates of the Forest*, *Legends of our Time*, *The Jews of Silence*, *A Beggar in Jerusalem*, and *The Trial of God*. In 1986 he was awarded the Nobel Peace Prize.

Wig. From talmudic times it was common practice for women to wear wigs. According to Jewish law, married women must cover their hair, and from the 15th century it became customary to fulfil this prescription by wearing a wig (known as a "sheitel").

Wilderness *see* SIN, WILDERNESS OF.

Wilensky, Mosheh (b. 1910). Israeli composer. He was born in Warsaw, and settled in Palestine in 1932. He wrote many popular Israeli songs.

Wilkansky [Wilkanski], **Yitzḥak Avigdor** *see* ELAZARI-VOLCANI, YITZḤAK AVIGIDOR.

Will. The declaration (usually written) of a person's wishes regarding the disposal of his property after his death. According to Jewish law, the property owned by a person at the time of death passes (after all debts have been paid) to the next of kin (Numbers 27.8–11). Nevertheless it is possible for an estate to be distributed differently. This may be ensured by the making of a will (embodying the correct legal formulae) while a person is sound in body and mind. If no will exists an individual may, during his final illness, dispose of all or any part of his property by issuing verbal instructions before witnesses; if he recovers, however, these instructions are regarded as void.

***William of Norwich** (d. 1144). English apprentice boy. It was alleged that he was the victim of a ritual murder by members of the Jewish community of Norwich. He was venerated locally as a saint.

Willow. One of the four species of plant, branches of which are used ceremonially on the feast of Sukkot. Willows growing near Jerusalem supplied adornment for the altar during the festival and branches were carried during the hakkaphot circuits. The shaking of willow twigs and leaves on Hoshanah Rabbah symbolically expresses the desire for rain.

Willstätter, Richard (1872–1942). German organic chemist. He was born in Karlsruhe. From 1902 he taught at the University of Munich, but in 1924 he resigned his chair in protest against the university's anti-Semitic policy. He received the Nobel Prize for chemistry in 1915.

***Wilson, Woodrow** (1856–1924). American statesman, president of the US (1912–20). In 1918 he endorsed the Balfour Declaration. At the Paris Peace Conference after World War I, he fought for the inclusion in the treaties of clauses to protect the rights of minorities.

Wimpel *see* VIMPEL.

Winchevsky, Morris (1856–1933). Lithuanian Yiddish poet and essayist. His activities as a socialist agitator led to his being imprisoned and banished from Germany and Denmark. He moved to London in 1879, and later lived in New York. He wrote poetry for Yiddish periodicals; he is regarded as the founder of Yiddish socialist literature.

Winder, Ludwig (1889–1946). Moravian novelist. He was born in Schaffa. He worked as a journalist on the *Deutsche Zeitung Bohemia* in Prague until 1938. A number of his works deal with Jewish topics.

Wine. In ancient Israel wine was drunk at meals (though ascetics such as the Nazirites and Rechabites abstained from it). In the Temple it was poured on the altar with the sacrifices. Wine has also played an important role in later rituals, such as Kiddush, Havdalah, and the Passover seder; a special benediction is recited before and after drinking it. At the festival of Purim and on Simḥat Torah overindulgence in wine is encouraged as part of the celebration. Vine leaves and grapes were used on Jewish coins during the second Temple period, and in synagogue art during the talmudic period. The wine of the gentiles is forbidden according to Jewish law (*see* NESEKH).

***Wingate, Charles Orde** (1903–1944). British soldier. During the Arab riots of 1936–9 in Palestine, he organized formations of Jewish volunteers (Special Night Squads) to counter Arab terrorism.

Wischnitzer, Mark (1882–1955). Russian historian, sociologist, and communal worker. He lived in Galicia, Vienna, and Berlin. After returning to Russia, he lectured at the institute of Baron David Günzburg in St. Petersburg (1909–12). From 1914 to 1916 he was the editor of the periodical *History of the Jewish People* in Moscow. He lived in London for a time, then moved to Germany and served as secretary to the Hilfsverein der Deutschen Juden; in the period 1933–7 he helped to organize the emigration of Jews from Germany. Subsequently he became professor of Jewish history at Yeshiva University in New York. His writings include studies of eastern European Jewish history.

Wischnitzer, Rachel (1882–?). Polish art historian. She was born in Minsk in Belorussia. A pioneer of the study of Jewish art, she edited some of the first periodicals on this subject. From 1934 to 1938 she served as director of the Jewish museum in Berlin. In 1940 she went with her husband to New York, where she published studies of synagogue art.

Wisdom (Hebrew "ḥokhmah"). According to the Bible wisdom results from education and experience, and is conferred by God. It is not spoken of as existing only in Israel, but is found among other nations as well. The Book of Proverbs emphasizes its significance. In the post-exilic period wisdom was identified with knowledge of the Torah and the law.

Wisdom literature. Term used of a body of biblical and apocryphal literature in which wisdom is portrayed as being based on fear of God and knowledge of the commandments. The works concerned are the books of Proverbs, Job, and Ecclesiastes, and Psalms 37, 49 and 73, and the apocryphal books Ecclesiasticus, Wisdom of Solomon, and IV Maccabees.

Wisdom of Ben Sira *see* ECCLESIASTICUS.

Wisdom of Solomon. Apocryphal book. It is devoted to the promise of wisdom: chapters 1–5 praise wisdom in human life and emphasize the superiority of the wise over the wicked; chapters 6–9 describe Solomon's wisdom; and chapters 10–19 glorify wisdom and its role in history.

Wise, George S. (1906–1987). Israeli administrator. He was born in Pinsk, Belorussia, and emigrated to the US in 1926. He was associate director of the Bureau of Applied Social Research from 1949 to 1952. After moving to Israel he served as chairman of the Hebrew University's board of governors (1953–62). From 1963 he was president of Tel Aviv University.

Wise, Isaac Mayer (1819–1900). American Reform leader. He was born in Steingrub, Bohemia, and emigrated to the US in 1846. He served as rabbi of Congregation Beth El in Albany, then in 1854 became minister of a congregation in Cincinnati, where his most important work was carried out. He founded an English-language weekly, *The Israelite*, and a German-language weekly, *Die Deborah*; he also published an American Reform prayerbook, *Minhag America.* In 1855 he attempted to found a rabbinical seminary, Zion College; though he was unsuccessful at that time he was later a prime mover in the establishing of the Hebrew Union College in 1875. He summoned rabbinic conferences in 1869 and 1871, helped to form the Union of American Hebrew Congregations in 1873, and in 1889 organized the Central Conference of American Rabbis.

Wise, James Waterman (1901–1983). American editor and author, son of

Stephen S. Wise. He served as director of the Stuyvesant Neighborhood House in New York, and national secretary of Avukah, the American students' Zionist Federation. He also was editor of *Opinion*. His writings include *Liberalizing Liberal Judaism*, *Jews are like that*, *Legend of Louise*, and *A Jew Revisits Germany*.

Wise, Louise Waterman (d. 1947). American communal worker, artist, and translator, wife of Stephen S. Wise. She established the Free Synagogue's Child Adoption Committee in 1914, and in 1933 became president of the Women's Division of the American Jewish Congress. She translated various works, and painted works on the theme of persecuted Jewry.

Wise, Stephen Samuel (1874–1949). American rabbi and Zionist leader. He was born in Budapest, and emigrated to the US as a child. He served as rabbi of Congregation B'nai Jeshurun in New York, and later in Portland, Oregon. In 1907 he established the Free Synagogue of New York, and in 1922 founded the Jewish Institute of Religion. He was secretary to the Federation of American Zionists, which subsequently became the Zionist Organization of America, and chairman of the Provisional Committee for Zionist Affairs (1916–19). For many years he was president of the American Jewish Congress (1925–9, 1935–49).

Wiseman, Adele (b. 1928). Canadian novelist. She was born in Winnipeg. Some of her works, including *The Sacrifice*, and *Crackpot*, deal with Jewish life.

Wissenschaft des Judentums [Jüdische Wissenschaft] (German: "Science of Judaism"). Term applied to the scientific study of Jewish history, literature, and religion. The methodology developed in Europe in the 19th century as a result of the Haskalah and the rise of Reform Judaism; its first exponents are generally considered to be Leopold Zunz and Abraham Geiger. Despite its connection with the Jewish Enlightenment and liberal religious views, Orthodox scholars also adopted this approach.

Wissotzky, Kalonymos Ze'ev (1824–1904). Russian merchant, philanthropist, and Zionist. He was born in Zhagare. In 1858 he moved to Moscow and established a tea firm. An active supporter of Ḥibbat Zion, he visited Palestine, where he supported religious settlers, and contributed to the foundation of the Haifa Technion. He founded the Hebrew monthly *Ha-Shiloaḥ* in 1896.

Witchcraft *see* MAGIC.

Witness (Hebrew "'eid"). According to Jewish law, a person who is in possession of evidence concerning an event is obliged to testify before a court. In civil cases the testimony of a single witness obligates the accused to take an oath that he is not liable for the claim made against him. Similarly, in matters of religious law regarding things permitted or prohibited, the testimony of one witness is valid. In all other cases the evidence of two witnesses is needed to prove a charge.

Wittels, Fritz (1880–1950). Austrian psychoanalyst. He was born in Vienna. He was the first biographer of Sigmund Freud. In 1904 he wrote *Der Taufjude* (The convert Jew), which argued that Jews should resist the temptation to join the majority culture and should stand up for their own interests.

Witzenhausen, Joseph *see* URI, PHOEBUS BEN AARON LEVI.

WIZO [Women's International Zionist Organization]. International body founded in London in 1920. Its original aims were to train Jewish girls and women for labor in Palestine and to promote care for mothers and children there. The organization was initially headed by executives in London and Palestine, but after 1948 the direction was centered in Israel. WIZO's activities include child care, and agricultural and vocational training, instruction in home sciences, and job guidance for Israeli women.

Wolf, Johann Christoph (1683–1739). German Hebraist. He was born in Wernigerode, Prussia, and became professor of oriental languages and literature at the Hamburg gymnasium. His *Bibliotheca hebraea* is a list of Hebrew books based on the collection of David Oppenheimer.

Wolf, Lucien (1857–1930). English historian, journalist, and communal worker. He was born in London. He was foreign editor of the *Daily Graphic* (from 1890) and editor of the *Jewish World* (1906–8), and also edited the periodical *Darkest Russia*. In 1917 he became Secretary of the Joint Foreign Committee of the Board of Deputies of British Jews and the Anglo-Jewish Association. After World War I he attended the Paris Peace Conference in 1919. He published articles and works dealing with the period between the expulsion and resettlement of English Jewry (c. 1290–1650) and with the mission of Manasseh ben Israel to Oliver Cromwell.

Wolf, Simon (1836–1923). American communal leader. He was born in Hinzweiler, Germany, and emigrated to the US in 1848. Living in Washington, he intervened with presidents and other government officials to obtain equity for Jews in America and abroad. From 1878 to 1911 he was chairman of the standing committee of the Board of Delegates of Civil and Religious Rights. He also served as consul-general to Egypt (1881–2), and as president of B'nai B'rith (1904–5).

***Wolff, Joseph** (1795–1862). German missionary. He was born in Weilersbach, Bavaria. He converted to Catholicism in 1812, but later he joined the Anglican Church, serving as a vicar in England. He traveled as a missionary to the Jews in Palestine, Kurdistan, Mesopotamia, Turkey, Persia, Khurasan, Bukhara, India, Yemen, Abyssinia, and various European countries.

Wolffsohn, David (1856–1914). German Zionist leader. He was born in Dorbiany, Lithuania, and lived in Cologne, where he was a timber merchant. An active Zionist, he was a co-founder of a society to promote Jewish agricultural work and handicrafts in Palestine. Later he became an assistant to Theodor Herzl, who entrusted him with the preparations for the founding of the Jewish Colonial Trust. In 1898 he went with Herzl to Palestine to meet Kaiser William II. Wolffsohn was elected to succeed Herzl as president of the World Zionist Organization in 1905.

Wolfskehl, Karl (1869–1948). German poet. He was born in Darmstadt. In 1934 he left Germany and lived successively in Italy, Switzerland, and New Zealand. He was influenced by the poet Stefan George; his series of poems, *Die Stimme spricht*, gives expression to the German Jewish tragedy.

Wolfson, Harry Austryn (1887–1974). American historian of philosophy. He was born in Belorussia, and emigrated to the US in 1903. In 1925 he became professor of Hebrew literature and philosophy at Harvard University. His publications include studies of Ḥasdai ben Abraham Crescas, Spinoza, and Philo.

Wolfson, Sir **Isaac** (1897–1991). Scottish businessman and philanthropist. He was born in Glasgow. He became chairman of Great Universal Stores in 1946. After World War II he devoted himself to philanthropic activities. The Edith and Isaac Wolfson Trust provided funds for building the Supreme Rabbinical Center in Jerusalem, 50 synagogues throughout Israel, and the Kiryat Wolfson housing project for new immigrants. Wolfson also served as chairman of the Joint Palestinian Appeal of Great Britain and Ireland, and president of the United Synagogue.

Wolpe, David (b. 1912). South African Yiddish writer. He was born in Keidan, Lithuania. He went to Palestine in 1930, but in 1936 returned to Lithuania, where he joined the army. In 1942 he was confined in the Kovno Ghetto, and later he was sent to the concentration camp at Dachau. In 1951 he settled in South Africa, where he became editor of the journal *Dorem Afrike*. One of the central topics of his writing is the Holocaust.

Woman. According to the Bible woman was created as a helpmate for man (Genesis 2.23–4). Under rabbinic law, women are granted various rights, such as the right to own property, but they are restricted in certain spheres: they may not, for example, give evidence in a court of law. Rabbinic Judaism focuses on the woman's role in the home; women are exempt from observing the numerous religious obligations enjoined on men by the positive commandments. The position of women in Jewish society changed significantly with the effective abolition among Ashkenazi Jews of polygamy around 1000. Nevertheless women continued to occupy an inferior position in terms of education, especially in eastern Europe. In the modern period women have played a central role in Jewish life, in the Zionist movement, and in religious education; among non-Orthodox congregations girls receive the same religious instruction as boys and celebrate an equivalent to the bar mitzvah (*see* BAT MITZVAH). Recently women have been trained as rabbis and cantors in non-Orthodox movements, though in Orthodox Jewry they continue to take no active part in the worship of the synagogue. *See also* MARRIAGE; MOTHER; WIDOW.

Women's International Zionist Organization *see* WIZO.

Women's League for Israel. American charitable organization. It was founded in New York in 1928 to aid women immigrants to Palestine. It established hostels in Haifa, Jerusalem, Tel Aviv, and Netanyah, and built the Women's Student Residence Center at the Hebrew University.

Women's Zionist Organization of America *see* HADASSAH (ii).

Woodbine. Town in the US, in southern New Jersey. It was founded by the Baron de Hirsch Fund as a Jewish agricultural colony with an industrial annexe. In 1892 60 families from southern Russia arrived there and an agricultural school was later established. In 1903 Woodbine became the first all-Jewish municipality in the US.

Woodhead Commission. Body appointed by the British government in November 1937 to formulate practical proposals for the partition of Palestine. The commission submitted three proposals in 1938, none of which was accepted. The idea of partition was superseded by that of a Palestinian state ruled jointly by Jews and Arabs, as set out in the White Paper of 1939.

Work *see* LABOR; OCCUPATIONS.

Workmen's Circle. Fraternal insurance society, active in US and Canada. Formed by Jewish immigrant workers in 1900, it helped to establish unions in the needle and other trades. In 1933 it was involved in the creation of the Jewish Labor Committee, which was formally established the following year.

World Hebrew Union *see* BERIT IVRIT OLAMIT.

World Jewish Congress. International representative body of Jews. Founded in 1936 in Geneva, it succeeded the Comité des Délégations Juives. It protects Jewish rights and interests, fosters unity of action, supports Jewish cultural activities, and serves as a representative body.

It has American, European, and Israeli sections. In 1940 it set up the Institute of Jewish Affairs to deal with Jewish issues.

World Union for Progressive Judaism. International organization of Liberal and Reform Judaism. Founded in London in 1926, it coordinates the activities of Liberal and Reform Jewish groups throughout the world; it holds a conference every two years.

World Union of General Zionists *see* GENERAL ZIONISTS.

World Union of Pioneer Women's Organizations *see* PIONEER WOMEN.

World Union of Zionist Revisionists *see* REVISIONISM.

World Zionist Organization *see* ZIONIST ORGANIZATION.

Worms. German town, 30 miles south of Frankfurt am Main. Jews first settled there in the 10th century. In 1074 and 1090 Emperor Henry IV passed decrees granting them considerable privileges. The community was massacred during the first crusade, but was reestablished shortly afterward. In the Middle Ages, Worms became a center of Jewish scholarship and was closely associated with Speyer and Mainz. The community was again attacked in the outbreaks of anti-Jewish violence following the spread of the Black Death in 1349. The Jews were expelled from Worms in 1615, and in 1689 another massacre took place, perpetrated by the soldiers of Louis XIV. The Jewish community of Worms was emancipated at the end of the 18th century.

Wouk, Herman (b. 1915). American novelist and playwright. He was born in New York. Initially he worked as a radio scriptwriter, but later served in the US Navy as a line officer. His writing includes *The Caine Munity*, *Marjorie Morningstar*, and *This is my God*.

Writing. In ancient times writing was done with a pen and ink on potsherds or on leather scrolls. It was common in the upper classes to dictate to a scribe. During the tannaitic period (c. 100 BCE–200 CE) there were elaborate rules for writing holy books: the parchment was ruled with a stylus and the letters were written suspended from the line; there was also a fixed orthography. Until the modern period Jews used Hebrew script for writing both Hebrew and other languages. Although Hebrew presses have existed for centuries, Jewish law dictates that certain books and documents must be handwritten: the Scrolls of the Law and the Scrolls of Esther for use in the synagogue, the parchments enclosed in phylacteries and mezuzot, and divorce documents; marriage certificates are also often written by hand. *See also* ALPHABET; SCRIPT.

Writing on the Wall *see* MENE MENE TEKEL U-PHARSIN.

Writings *see* HAGIOGRAPHA.

Written Law. The law given by God to Moses on Mount Sinai; according to tradition, the Written Law is the Pentateuch. By extension the term is also used for the prophetic books and the Hagiographa. The Written Law is complemented by the Oral Law, which is traditionally believed to originate in God's revelation to Moses of the interpretation of the law.

***Wünsche, August** (1839–1913). German scholar of Hebrew literature. He was born in Haimwalde. He wrote commentaries on Joshua and Joel and studies of rabbinic literature, and translated the aggadot of the Jerusalem and Babylonian Talmuds into German. He also published an anthology of post-biblical Jewish literature.

Würzburg. German town, about 60 miles south-east of Frankfurt am Main. The Jewish community there dates from the 12th century. In 1147 crusaders and townspeople killed a number of Jews, and forcibly baptized others. Eliezer ben Joel ha-Levi and Isaac ben Moses of Vienna were rabbis in Würzburg, and students at the yeshivah included Meir of Rothenburg and Mordecai ben Hillel. In 1298 and again in 1349 the community was destroyed. In 1567 the reestablished settlement was expelled, but it was again restored in the 18th century. The Jews were attacked once more during the Hep Hep riots of 1819, and many were killed or driven out.

Wyner, Yehudi (b. 1929). American composer and educator. He was born in Calgary, Canada, and went to the US at an early age. He taught at Yale University, and at SUNY at Purchase. He wrote a number of compositions for the synagogue.

Y

Yaaleh ("May it arise"). Opening word (and hence title) of a hymn sung in the synagogue during the evening service on the Day of Atonement; it occurs in the Italian, Ashkenazi, and (in an altered form) Polish rites, and introduces the seliḥot. It is based on the prayer *Yaaleh ve-yavo.*

Yaaleh ve-yavo ("May it arise and come"). Opening words of a paragraph added to the Amidah and Grace after Meals on New Year and festivals. In the Spanish and Yemenite rites it is also added to the Amidah in the additional service for the New Year and the Day of Atonement.

Yaari, Avraham (1899–1966). Israeli scholar, of Galician origin, brother of Yehudah Yaari. He settled in Palestine in 1920; after teaching at a school in Tel Aviv, he worked in the Hebrew National Library and Tel Aviv University Library. He published studies dealing with Hebrew bibliography and the history of Jewish settlement in Palestine.

Yaari, Yehudah (1900–1982). Israeli writer and diplomat, of Galician origin, brother of Avraham Yaari. He emigrated to Palestine in 1920 and served in the head office of Keren ha-Yesod. He held a number of diplomatic posts – as cultural attaché to the Israeli legation in Scandinavia (1955–7), director of the department for cultural relations of the Israeli foreign ministry, and as consul-general in Amsterdam. He wrote stories and romances dealing with eastern European life during the 20th century and with pioneer youth in Israel.

Yad ("hand"). Pointer used to indicate the place during the reading of the Torah scroll.

Yadayim ("Hands"). 11th tractate in the Mishnah order of Tohorot. It sets down rabbinic decrees concerning ritual impurity of hands, and the means of their ablution. It also deals with the canonicity of the Song of Songs and Ecclesiastes, the Aramaic language in Ezra and Daniel, the ancient Hebrew script, and disagreements between the Pharisees and Sadducees.

Yad Chaim Weizmann *see* WEIZMANN INSTITUTE OF SCIENCE.

Yad Ḥazakah *see* MAIMONIDES.

Yadin, Yigael (1917–1984). Israeli archeologist and soldier. He was born in Jerusalem. He became a member of the Haganah and served in various official positions: he was chief of operations during the Israeli War of Independence, and chief of staff of the Israeli army from 1949 to 1952. He then taught archeology at the Hebrew University, where he became professor. He published studies of the Dead Sea Scrolls and directed excavations at Hazor and Masada.

Yad va-Shem ("Monument and Name"). Israeli official body, whose charge it is to commemorate the Holocaust and its victims. It was instituted by a bill passed in the Knesset in 1953, by which it was authorized to carry out commemorative projects, and collect and publish documents dealing with the Nazi period. Its headquarters are in Jerusalem on Memorial Hill, adjoining Mount Herzl; they include a shrine, archives, and a library.

Yaḥad ("unity"). Term used in the Dead Sea Scrolls to describe the unifying spirit of the sect that produced the scrolls.

Yaḥia *see* IBN YAḤIA, DAVID BEN JOSEPH.

Yah Ribbon Olam ("God, master of the universe"). Opening words (and hence title) of an Aramaic hymn. Composed by Israel ben Moses Najara, it is generally sung at the table during the Sabbath meal.

Yahrzeit (Yiddish). Term used by Ashkenazi Jews for the anniversary of the death of a relative. It is observed by kindling a light and reciting the kaddish. In some communities it is also marked by fasting.

Yahuda, Abraham Shalom (1877–1951). Palestinian orientalist. He was born in Jerusalem. He taught at the Hochschule für die Wissenschaft des Judentums, in Berlin and at the University of Madrid. In 1942 he became professor at the New School for Social Research in New York. He published biblical and philological studies, attempted to establish correspondences between Egyptian texts and the Pentateuch, and edited the Arabic text of Baḥya ibn Pakuda's *Duties of the Heart*.

Yahweh *see* GOD, NAMES OF.

Yair *see* STERN, AVRAHAM.

Yaknehaz (i). Mnemonic for the order of the blessings in the Kiddush recited on a festival that begins on Saturday night. The letters stand for "yayin" (wine), "kiddush" (sanctification), "ner" (light), "havdalah" (blessing for the end of the Sabbath), and "zeman" (the benediction She-heḥeyanu). The term has been associated with the German phrase "jag den Has" (chase the hare); for this reason manuscripts of the Passover Haggadah were often illustrated with hunting scenes.

Yaknehaz (ii). Pseudonym of Isaiah N. Goldberg (1858–1927), Lithuanian and Yiddish author. He was a teacher in Lithuania from 1880, and served as permanent assistant on the Hebrew newspaper *Ha-Melitz*. He wrote stories and sketches for the Hebrew and Yiddish press.

Yalkut ("compilation"). Title of several midrashic compilations including the *Yalkut Shimoni*, *Yalkut ha-Meiri*, and *Yalkut Reuveni*.

Yalkut Reuveni ("Compilation of Reuben"). Anthology of homiletic and mystical writings on the Pentateuch. Composed in the 17th century by Reuben Kahana of Prague, it is arranged in order of the weekly portions assigned to be read in the synagogue.

Yalkut Shimoni (Compilation of Simeon"). Anthology of midrashic writings on all the books of the Bible. It was compiled by Simeon Kayyara.

Yamin Noraim ("Days of Awe"). Term used of the New Year (Rosh ha-Shanah) and Day of Atonement (Yom Kippur), and also of the period between them – the Ten Days of Penitence. According to Jewish tradition all people stand before the divine throne of judgment at the New Year, and judgment is pronounced upon them on the Day of Atonement.

Yanait, Rachel *see* BEN-ZVI, YITZḤAK.

Yannai (i) (fl. 3rd cent.). Palestinian amora. He was a pupil of Judah ha-Nasi and Ḥiyya. He established an academy at Akhbara in Upper Galilee, the teachings of which are cited in the Palestinian and Babylonian Talmuds as "de-ve Rabbi Yannai" (school of Rabbi Yannai).

Yannai (ii) (fl. ?6th cent.). Hebrew liturgical poet. He probably lived in Palestine. He introduced rhyme into religious poetry, wrote piyyutim related to the weekly portion of the Torah, and determined the final form of the Kerovah. His piyyutim (with the exception of *Az rov nissim* in the Ashkenazi rite for the Passover Haggadah) were forgotten until the 19th century, when scholars discovered others of his poems. Further examples were found in the Cairo Genizah.

Yannai, Alexander *see* ALEXANDER YANNAI.

Yaoz-Kest, Itamar (b. 1934). Israeli poet and fiction writer. He was born in Szarvas, Hungary. He survived incarceration at the concentration camp at Bergen-Belsen in 1944–5. In 1951 he went to Israel where he became an editor in the publishing house Eked. Some of his work deals with modern Jewish history.

Yarmulke. Skull cap, worn by male Jews. It is worn by observant Jews at all times, and for prayer even by the less Orthodox (*see also* COVERING OF THE HEAD). The derivation of the word is unknown.

Yashar *see* REGGIO, ISAAC SAMUEL.

Yashar, Sepher ha- *see* JASHAR, BOOK OF.

Yavetz *see* EMDEN, JACOB ISRAEL.

Yavneh *see* JABNEH.

Year, Jewish *see* CALENDAR; MONTHS.

Year of Release *see* SABBATICAL YEAR.

Yeb *see* ELEPHANTINE.

Yehalel *see* LEVIN, JUDAH LEIB.

Yehoash *see* BLOOMGARDEN, SOLOMON.

Yehoshua, Avraham (b. 1936). Israeli writer. He was born in Jerusalem. He served in the Israeli army. After living in Paris for a time, he settled in Haifa. He published stories about heroes haunted by indecision.

Yehudai (fl. 8th cent.). Babylonian gaon. He was born in Pumbedita. He succeeded Solomon bar Ḥasdai as head of the Sura academy in 757 and served until 761. He entered into relations with Jewish communities in north Africa, and attempted to enforce Babylonian usages in Palestine. His code of the law, *Halakhot Pesukot*, was written down for him by his pupils, since he was blind.

Yehudi ben Sheset (fl. 10th cent.). Spanish grammarian. A pupil of Dunash ben Labrat, he wrote a reply (consisting of 150 verses of introduction and a prose section) to the polemic directed against Dunash by the pupils of Menaḥem ben Saruk. This was in response to a criticism leveled by Dunash against Saruk.

Yekke (Yiddish). A German.

Yekopo. Russian aid organization (the name is an acronym based on the Russian for "committee for Jewish assistance"). Founded in 1915, it aided Jews who were expelled by the Russian military command from Baltic provinces.

Yekum purkan (Aramaic: "May redemption come"). Opening words of two Aramaic prayers. The first is for the welfare of the communal and scholastic heads of Palestine and Babylonia; the other is for the general community. Composed during the gaonic period, they are recited in Ashkenazi communities after the reading of the law on the Sabbath.

Yelammedenu *see* TANḤUMA.

Yellin, David (1864–1941). Palestinian scholar. He was one of the organizers of the founding conference of the Teachers' Association at Zikhron Ya'akov in 1903; later he was the association's president. He served as deputy director (from 1912) of the teachers' seminary founded by the Hilfsverein der Deutschen Juden in Jerusalem, and also lectured on Hebrew poetry of the Spanish period at the Hebrew University. He published studies of medieval Jewish poetry and Hebrew philology, a Hebrew dictionary and grammar, and an edition of the poems of Todros Abulafia. Besides his scholarly work, he was deputy mayor of Jerusalem (1920–25) and head of the Vaad Leumi (1920–28).

Yenta (Yiddish). A shrew, a gossipy woman, or a woman of vulgar manners.

Yeshivah ("academy"). Jewish school devoted to the study of the Talmud and rabbinic literature. The institution of the yeshivah is a continuation of the academies in Babylonia and Palestine during the talmudic and gaonic periods. Many modern yeshivot teach a program of secular studies to complement the traditional talmudic studies.

Yeshivah bucher (Yiddish). A young man who studies at a yeshivah, or a scholarly person; by extension an inexperienced individual.

Yeshivath Torah Vodaath and Mesivta. American Orthodox educational institution, founded in 1918 in Brooklyn. It comprises elementary and high schools, a teachers' college, and a rabbinical seminary.

Yeshiva University. American university in New York. It originated from the Etz Chaim yeshivah founded in 1886 and the Isaac Elhanan Yeshiva founded in 1896. In 1915 these institutions merged, Yeshiva College was opened in association with them in 1928, and Yeshiva University was founded in 1945. It includes a theological seminary, separate colleges for men and women, graduate schools of education, social work, mathematics, and medicine, and a cantorial institute.

Yeshuah *see* SALVATION.

Yeshuot *see* NEZIKIN.

Yetzer ha-ra. Evil inclination; *see* GOOD.

Yetzer ha-tov. Good inclination; *see* GOOD.

Yetzirah, Sepher *see* SEPHER YETZIRAH.

Yevamot ("Levirates"). First tractate in the Mishnah order of Nashim. It deals with the status of the widow of a man who has died childless. His brother must contract a levirate marriage with her or carry out the ceremony known as Ḥalitzah.

Yevin, Shemuel (1896–?). Israeli archeologist, of Russian origin. He went to Palestine before World War I, participating in various archeological explorations. He was secretary of the Vaad ha-Lashon, and from 1948 to 1959 was director of the Israeli government's Department of Antiquities. His publications include studies of the Bar Kokhba revolt.

Yevsektzia. Jewish branch of the Russian Communist Party, formed in 1918 and active until 1930. It was responsible for the elimination of Jewish communal organizations and institutions, the boycotting of synagogues, and activities against Judaism and the Hebrew language. It initiated plans for Jewish territories in the Crimea in 1926, and later in Birobidjan. It published the daily paper *Emes*.

Yezierska, Anzia (1885–1970). American novelist, of Russian origin. She went to New York at the age of 16 and worked in a tailor's shop; later she found better-paid work and ran away from home. Her short stories and novels deal with the adjustment of the Jewish immigrant to American life. Her publications include *Hungry Hearts*, *Salome of the Tenements*, *Children of Loneliness*, *Bread Givers*, *Arrogant Beggar*, and *All I could never be*.

YHVH *see* GOD, NAMES OF; TETRAGRAMMATON.

Yiches (Yiddish). Family status.

Yid. A disparaging and offensive term for a Jew.

Yiddish. Language spoken by Ashkenazi Jews from the Middle Ages. It derives from Hebrew, Loez, German, and Slavic. Since its formation in c. 1000–1250, Yiddish has undergone constant development. It can be classified chronologically into Old Yiddish (1250–1500); Middle Yiddish (1500–1750); and modern Yiddish (1750–20th century). Different Yiddish dialects were spoken in Lithuania (the northern dialect) and in the area extending from Romania and Poland across the Ukraine (the southern dialect). The standard pronunciation of modern Yiddish is based on the northern dialect. The language is written in Hebrew letters; its spelling was standardized in 1937 by YIVO.

Yiddishe Gesellshaften Komitet (Yiddish: "Jewish public committee") [Yidgazkom]. Jewish public committee. Founded in 1920 by the Jewish Commissariat and the American Jewish Joint Distribution Committee, it coordinated Jewish relief and social activities in Soviet Russia. It ceased its activities in 1924.

Yiddishkeit (Yiddish). Jewish culture.

Yiddish literature. The first important works of Yiddish literature date from the 16th century. The most popular romance was the *Bovo-buch* (or *Bovo-maase*). The *Shmuel-buch* is a heroic epic of Old Yiddish, and the *Maase-buch* a prose collection of talmudic legends and folktales. The *Tz'enah u-re'enah* is a combination of stories and teachings based on the Bible; other sacred works in Yiddish include devotional prayers ("tekhines") composed for women. During the 19th century Yiddish was used as a medium of enlightenment by writers of the Haskalah. They were followed by a group of classic Yiddish writers: Mendele Mocher Sephorim, Isaac Leib Peretz, and Sholem Aleichem; in fiction contemporaries of the classicists were Jacob Dinesohn, Mordecai Spector, and S. An-Ski, and Shomer. Abraham Goldfaden is traditionally regarded as the father of the Yiddish theater. In the 20th century playwrights wrote for the Yiddish theater in the US, and in both Europe and the US Yiddish writers continue to produce lyrics, short stories, and novels. Prominent among modern Yiddish writers are Sholem Asch and Isaac Bashevis Singer. YIVO, founded in Vilnius in 1925 and later transferred to New York, is the principal institution for the study of Yiddish literature.

Yideneh (Yiddish). Derogatory term for an older Jewish woman; also a gossipy shallow person.

Yidgazkom *see* YIDDISHE GESELLSHAFTEN KOMITET.

Yigdal ("May he be magnified"). Opening word (and hence title) of a liturgical hymn. Based on Maimonides' 13 principles of faith, it originated in Italy in c. 1300; its author may have been Daniel bar Judah, who was a dayyan in Rome at that time. It is recited on the Sabbath eve in the Sephardi and Italian rites; among the Ashkenazim it is used as an opening hymn for the daily morning service. On high holy days it is chanted to a special melody.

Yiḥus. Distinguished ancestral descent.

Yimaḥ shemo ("May his name be blotted out"). Phrase uttered when mentioning the name of an enemy of the Jewish people.

Yishar koaḥ ("May your strength increase"). Phrase of congratulation spoken to a person who has read or spoken in public. It has been shortened to "Shekoaḥ."

Yishtabbaḥ ("May his name be praised"). Opening word (and hence title) of the concluding blessing of the Pesuke de-Zimrah. It contains 15 terms of praise and adoration and in some rites is recited standing.

Yishuv. Settlement or population group. In the modern period it refers specifically to the Jewish community of Israel.

YIVO Institute for Jewish Research. The Yiddisher Visnshaftlekher Institut (known in English as the Yiddish Scientific Institute) was founded in Vilnius in 1925 to promote the scientific study of Jewish life, with particular reference to eastern European Jewry and its Yiddish-speaking descendants throughout the world. At the outbreak of World War II, its center was transferred to New York and in 1956 its name was changed to YIVO Institute for Jewish Research.

Yizhar, S. *see* SMILANSKY, YIZHAR.

Yizkor ("He shall remember"). Opening word (and hence title) of the prayer in commemoration of the dead, recited in Ashkenazi communities on the last days of Passover, Shavuot, and Sukkot and on the Day of Atonement. The term is also applied to the memorial service held on each of those days, at which the members of the congregation remember their relatives who have died.

Yod. Tenth letter of the Hebrew alphabet. Its numerical value is 10.

Yoma ("The Day"). Fifth tractate in the Mishnah order of Moed. It describes the Temple service of the high priest on the Day of Atonement. It also contains discussions of the regulations regarding the fast, and the significance of atonement and repentance.

Yom Atzmaut [Independence Day]. Anniversary of Israel's Declaration of Independence made on 14 May 1948 (5 Iyyar 5708). It is observed as a public holiday in Israel.

Yom Kippur *see* DAY OF ATONEMENT.

Yom Kippur Katan ("Minor Day of Atonement"). Fast observed on the day before the New Moon. The practice of fasting on this day existed in Palestine in the 16th century. It was brought from there to Italy by Moses Cordovero, and it eventually spread to Germany. The day is marked by a special order of prayer, consisting of psalms and seliḥot, added to the usual afternoon prayer service.

Yom Tov ("A good day"). A term, applied to all festivals, which connotes joy and festivity.

Yomtov ben Abraham Ishbili [Ritba] (c. 1250–1330). Spanish talmudist. A student of Aaron ha-Levi of Barcelona and Solomon ben Adret, he became a ḥakham and dayyan in Zaragoza. His talmudic commentaries contain summaries of the views of previous authorities. He also wrote a defense of Maimonides and a commentary on the Passover Haggadah.

Yomtov ben Isaac of Joigny (d. 1190). Liturgical poet, of Spanish origin. He settled in York in c. 1180. He wrote commentaries on the Bible and engaged in anti-Christian polemics. He composed an elegy on the Blois martyrs of 1171 and the hymn *Omnam Ken* for the eve of the Day of Atonement. According to tradition, he inspired the heroic mass suicide of the Jews of York in 1190 (*see* YORK).

Yomtov Lipmann *see* MÜHLHAUSEN, YOMTOV LIPMANN.

Yontif (Yiddish). Holiday or celebration.

Yoreh Deah *see* JACOB BEN ASHER.

York. City in north-east England. In 1190 on the Sabbath before Passover (16 March) the Jewish community of York, led by Josce and Yomtov ben Isaac of Joigny, was besieged in the keep of the castle. Rather than be slaughtered by the mob, they killed one another.

Yose ben Halaphta (fl. 2nd cent.). Palestinian tanna. A pupil of Akiva, he became the head of the academy in Sephoris, and one of the leaders of the assemblies at Usha and Jabneh after the abolition of the Hadrianic decrees against the practice of Judaism. According to tradition, he was the author of the chronological work *Seder Olam Rabbah*. In the Talmud he is referred to as "Rabbi Yose".

Yose ben Joezer (fl. 2nd cent.). Palestinian rabbi and nasi. He and Yose ben Johanan of Jerusalem were the first of the scholars known as the "zugot." A disciple of Antigonus of Sokho, he served as nasi (head of the Sanhedrin).

Yose ben Yose (fl. ?5th cent.). Palestinian liturgical poet (the first paytan known by name). He lived in Palestine. His poems were highly regarded by the Babylonian geonim, and some were incorporated into the high holy day liturgy (notably the Avodah of the Sephardi rite for the Day of Atonement).

Yose ha-Gelili (fl. 2nd cent.). Palestinian tanna. At an early age he went to Jabneh, where he engaged in discussions with Tarphon and Akiva. His halakhot are found throughout the Mishnah, especially in the order Kodashim. He was known for the efficacy of his prayers for rain.

Yoseph, Dov (1889–?). Israeli public figure. He was born in Canada, and settled in Palestine in 1921. From 1945 to 1948 he was a member of the executive of the Jewish Agency, and later (1957–61) he served as its treasurer. During the War of Independence he served as military governor of Jerusalem. He was elected to the Knesset in 1949 as a member for Mapai, and held several cabinet positions, as minister of commerce and industry (1951–3), of development (1953–5), and of justice (1961–6).

Yotzer ("He createth"). Name derived from the opening word of the first of the blessings that frame the Shema and applied to various elements of the liturgy. In some rites it is used of the service of morning prayer (Shaḥarit). It also applied to a hymn preceding the Shema. More generally it denotes all the special hymns added to the blessings of the Shema on Sabbaths and festivals. The term is misleadingly used in the plural ("yotzerot") to mean the entire group of liturgical hymns added at various points in the morning service.

Young Israel. American organization dedicated to fostering Orthodoxy and the study of the Torah. Founded in 1912 in New York, it has branches throughout the US, and affiliates in Canada, the Netherlands, and Israel. The National Council of Young Israel was formed in 1922 and establishes the policies of the organization. Most branches maintain a synagogue with its own rabbi, a Hebrew school, an adult study group, and youth activities.

Young Judea. American Zionist youth movement. It was founded in 1909 by Emanuel Neumann. It supports summer camps and weekend institutes.

Young Men's [Women's] **Hebrew Association** *see* JEWISH COMMUNITY CENTER.

Youth Aliyah. Organization for settling and educating youth in Israel. The movement was founded by Recha Freyer in Berlin in 1932, and from 1933 to 1945 was led by Henrietta Szold in Baltimore in the US. The first group went to Palestine from Germany in 1934. By May 1948 nearly 30,000 children and young people had been transferred to Palestine and educated in labor villages, agricultural institutions, and special centers. A further 44,000 arrived by the end of 1956 from Asia, north Africa, the Balkans, and Europe.

Youth villages. Israeli educational and agricultural settlements for young people. Of the approximately 50 such villages in Israel, the majority are associated with Youth Aliyah. The education system they employ is based on study in an elementary school context, but many also have agricultural secondary schools. The first settlement was the agricultural school of Mikveh Israel, founded in 1870; Shepheyah (1892) and Ben Shemen (1927) are the oldest youth villages.

Yudghan (fl. 8th cent.). Persian religious leader. A disciple of Abu Issa al-Isfahani, he lived in Hamadan. He was influenced by the doctrines of Islamic Sufism: he maintained that he was a prophet, advocated a mystical interpretation of the Torah, and argued that all religious symbols are allegories; he also supported the prohibition on wine and animal food introduced by the Issavites. A group of disciples grew up around him, which became known as the Yudghanites.

Yushkevich, Semyon (1868–1927). Russian novelist and playwright. He was a physician in Odessa. In his plays and narrative works he contrasted poor and virtuous Jews with their vulgar, rich co-religionists. After the 1917 Bolshevik Revolution he settled in the US.

Z

Zabara, Joseph *see* IBN ZABARA, JOSEPH.

Zach, Nathan (b. 1930). Israeli poet. He was born in Berlin, and went to Palestine in 1935. He has published poetry, translated Arabic folk songs, and edited the selected works of Ya'akov Steinberg.

Zacuto, Abraham [Abraham ben Samuel Zacut] (1452–c. 1515). Spanish astronomer and historian. His ancestors were French Jewish exiles who went to Castile in 1306. He studied and taught in Salamanca. His *Ha-Ḥibbur ha-Gadol*, a Hebrew work on astronomy, was translated into Spanish and Latin. He was the first to make a metal astrolabe, and he also drew up astronomical tables, which were used by Christopher Columbus. When Jews were expelled from Spain in 1492, he became astronomer and astrologer at the court of John II of Portugal; he was consulted by Vasco da Gama before his journey to India. Eventually he settled in Tunis, where he completed his *Sepher Yuḥasin* on the history of rabbinic scholarship.

Zacuto, Moses ben Mordecai (c. 1620–1697). Italian kabbalist and poet. He was born in Amsterdam. During a pilgrimage to Palestine he was persuaded to go to Italy, where he served as a rabbi in Venice and Mantua. He composed mystical and devotional poetry, some of which was used in the Italian liturgy. He wrote responsa, a poetical vision of the after-life (*Topheth Arukh*), and a drama about Abraham (*Yesod Olam*).

Zadok (fl. 11th cent. BCE). Israelite priest. He was a descendant of Aaron. He went to David at Hebron after Saul's death, and, with Abiathar, became David's chief priest. He was loyal to David during Absalom's rebellion, and at David's behest he annointed Solomon as the next king. Solomon subsequently appointed Zadok's son high priest in the Temple. From that time onward the high priesthood remained in the Zadokite family until the beginning of the Hasmonean dynasty (2nd cent. BCE).

Zadokite Fragments. Name given to two manuscripts found in the Cairo Genizah and first published in 1910 by Solomon Schechter. In 1952 fragments of other copies of the same documents were found in a cave near Khirbet Qumran. All the manuscripts form part of the literature to which the Dead Sea Scrolls belong. They preserve parts of two works: a sermon on the history of humanity and of the Qumran sect, and a collection of sectarian laws and rules.

Zadon *see* INTENT.

Zaftig (Yiddish). Plump, buxom, by extension provocative; used figuratively it means juicy.

Zakhar *see* VAKHNAKHT.

Zakhur la-tov ("May he be remembered for good"). Expression of respect and blessing uttered in connection with the name of a person who has died. It has now largely been replaced by the expression "Zikhrono li-verakhah" (May his memory be for a blessing).

Zalzmann, Felix *see* SALTEN, FELIX.

Zamenhof, Ludwig Lazarus (1859–1917). Polish philologist. He was born in Białystok, and lived in Warsaw. In 1887 he published a pamphlet that set out the fundamentals of Esperanto. In 1905 he convened the first international Congress of Esperantists. He translated the Bible as well as German, Russian, and English literature into this new language.

Zangwill, Israel (1864–1926). English author. He was born in London, where he later taught at the Jewish Free School. His writings include *Children of the Ghetto*, *Ghetto Tragedies*, *Ghetto Comedies*, and *The King of the Shnorrers*. He also produced essays on Jewish themes, and translations of Jewish liturgical poetry and the poems of Solomon ibn Gabirol. Initially an enthusiastic Zionist, he helped to found the Jewish Territorial Organization in 1905.

Zaragoza [Saragossa]. Spanish city, formerly capital of the state of Aragon. Jews lived there from the Moorish period (10th–15th centuries), and in the 11th century Jekuthiel ibn Ḥasan was vizier. Under Christian rule Zaragoza's Jewish community prospered.

Zaragoza, Purim of. Festival celebrated by oriental Jews to commemorate the deliverance in 1380 (or 1420) of the community in Zaragoza from a false accusation of plotting against the king. It is celebrated on 17–18 Shevat with the reading of a special megillah.

Zarfatti *see* TZARFATI.

Zarim *see* STRANGER.

Zaritsky, Yosef [Zarfutti, Yossef] (1891–1985). Israeli painter. He was born in the Ukraine, and went to Palestine in 1923. He painted watercolours of Safed, Tiberias, and Jerusalem, and his later works chiefly depict the Israeli landscape.

Zaskovitzer, Samuel *see* STRASHUN, SAMUEL.

Zavim ("Sufferers from flux"). Ninth tractate in the Mishnah order of Tohorot. It deals with ritual uncleanliness caused by a flux in both men and women (Leviticus 15). It also describes how a person or thing can become unclean through contact with a person suffering from a discharge.

Zayde (Yiddish). Old man, grandfather.

Zayin. Seventh letter of the Hebrew alphabet. Its numerical value is 7.

Zbahrz, Velvel of *see* EHRENKRANZ, BENJAMIN WOLF.

Zealots. Jewish political party active during the second Temple period. Founded by Judah the Galilean and Zadok the priest, the Zealots' first purpose was to oppose the Roman demand for a census under Quirinius, the governor of Judea. They developed their own religious outlook and proclaimed God the sovereign ruler of the nation. Suppressed by the procurators, they continued to struggle against Roman rule. After the conflict with Rome began (66 CE), Menaḥem (the son of Judah the Galilean) claimed messianic status, and was slain by Eleazar ben Hananiah, the captain of the Temple; Menaḥem's comrades (the Sicarii), led by Eleazar ben Jair, fled to Masada. After a Zealot uprising in Jerusalem, the Zealots under Eleazar ben Simeon were driven into the inner court of the Temple, but they eventually regained control of the city. At the time of the destruction of Jerusalem in 70, many of the Zealots were killed, others committed suicide or fled the country.

Zebulun (fl. ?19th–16th cent. BCE). Israelite, sixth son of Jacob and Leah. His descendants, the tribe of Zebulun, received territory in central Palestine.

Zechariah (i) (fl. 8th cent. BCE). King of Israel (743 BCE), son of Jeroboam II. He was assassinated by Shallum of Jabesh, who seized the throne (II Kings 15.8–13).

Zechariah (ii). Biblical book, one of the books of the 12 Minor Prophets. It records the prophecies of the Israelite prophet Zechariah (fl. 6th century BCE), who predicted material prosperity, the ingathering of the exiles, liberation from foreign domination, and the expansion of Jerusalem; he also encouraged the people to rebuild the Temple.

Zedekah *see* RETRIBUTION.

Zedekiah (i) [Mattaniah] (fl. 6th cent. BCE). King of Judah (597–586 BCE), son of Josiah. He was originally called Mattaniah, but took the name Zedekiah when he was appointed king by Nebuchadnezzar in succession to Jehoiachin. Initially he refused to join an anti-Babylonian coalition, but later conspired with Egypt against Babylonia; as a result, the Babylonians invaded Judah and captured Jerusalem. Zedekiah was subsequently imprisoned in Babylon (II Kings 25; Jeremiah 52).

Zedekiah (ii) (fl. 9th cent. BCE). Israelite false prophet. He incorrectly predicted that Ahab would be successful in his invasion of Ramoth Gilead. He made iron horns to symbolize Ahab's victory. (I Kings 22).

Zederbaum, Alexander [Tsederboym, Aleksander] (1816–1893). Polish editor and author. He was born in Zamość, and lived in Lubin and Odessa. He founded the Hebrew newspaper *Ha-Melitz* in 1860, and in 1862 began to issue *Kol mevaser* in Yiddish. Later he settled in St. Petersburg where he established the city's first Russian Jewish periodical (*Vyestnik russkikh yevreyev*) and first modern Yiddish periodical (*Yidishes folks-blat*).

Zeira (fl. 4th cent.). Babylonian amora. He was a pupil of Huna and after moving to Palestine became an important teacher himself.

Zeira, Mordechai (1905–1968). Israeli composer. He was born in Kiev in the Ukraine, and went to Palestine after having been arrested as a member of a Zionist youth organization. He initially found employment as a construction worker and fisherman, but in 1927 he moved to Tel Aviv and joined the Ohel Theater. Later he worked for the Palestine Electric Corporation. He wrote numerous songs, which were in part influenced by eastern European cantorial and Ḥasidic idioms.

Zeit, Die (i). American Yiddish monthly journal, published in New York in 1897–8.

Zeit, Die (ii). English Yiddish daily newspaper. It was founded in London in 1913 by Morris Meyer. It initially served as the organ of the working-class Jewish movement, but later advocated Zionism. It continued to publish until 1950.

Zeit, Die (iii). American Yiddish daily newspaper. It was published in New York from 1920 to 1922.

Zeitlin, Hillel [Cejtlin, Hillel] (1871–1942). Russian philosopher. He was born in Korma, Belorussia, and in the 1890s lived in Homel. Initially he was a Zionist, but in reaction to the Kishinev pogrom he became a supporter of Territorialism. After settling in Vilnius, he published works in Yiddish opposing assimilation and secularism. In the 1920s he returned to Zionism. He is an important representative of Ḥasidic thought in modern Yiddish literature.

Zeitlin, Solomon (1892–1977). American scholar, of Russian origin. He emigrated to the US in 1915 and taught at Yeshiva College. In 1921 he became professor of rabbinics at Dropsie College. He wrote studies on rabbinics, Josephus, the Apocrypha, Christianity, and the Dead Sea Scrolls. He also served as editor of the *Jewish Quarterly Review*.

Zekhor Berit ("Remember the Covenant"). Penitential hymn composed by Gershom ben Judah. It is recited on the eve of Rosh ha-Shanah in the Ashkenazi rite; the day before New Year is therefore called Zekhor Berit. The hymn is also recited during the concluding service on the Day of Atonement.

Zekhut Avot ("Merit of the Fathers"). In Jewish tradition, the idea that the pious deeds of the fathers help to protect and gain salvation for their descendants. The concept is applied particularly to the patriarchs, Abraham, Isaac, and Jacob.

Zelda *see* MISHKOVSKY, ZELDA.

Zelophehad, daughters of (fl. ?13th cent. BCE). Name given to the five daughters of the Manassite Zelophehad (Numbers 26.33). When Zelophehad died, they asked Moses for a ruling upon their title to their father's prospective property in the Promised Land. They received an affirmative reply, and their claim was put into effect when Joshua conquered Canaan (Joshua 17.3–6). The case served as a precedent for later generations and led to the decree that, in the absence of sons, a man's property might pass to a daughter, provided she were married to a member of her father's tribe (Numbers 27.1–11; 36.6–8).

Zemirot ("songs," "hymns"). Among the Ashkenazim the term refers to hymns and songs sung during Sabbath meals and at the end of the Sabbath. Although the zemirot were composed largely during the 16th and 17th centuries, some are the works of earlier poets. Printed prayer-books include zemirot for the Sabbath eve, the Sabbath day, and the end of the Sabbath. In the Sephardi and Yemenite rites the term designates the part of the morning prayer service known as the Pesuke de-Zimrah.

Zeno Papyri. Name given to a group of papyrus documents discovered during World War I at Rabbath Ammon. They are named after Zeno, a treasury official under Ptolemy II, who visited Palestine in 259 BCE. The documents cast light on the economy, administration, law, and mode of life in Ptolemaic Egypt.

Zephaniah (i) (fl. 7th cent. BCE). Judean prophet. He was a member of a noble Judean family, and his prophecies were uttered during the early part of Josiah's reign. He described the Day of the Lord, when the wicked will be punished, the poor will inherit the land, and the Lord will be universally acknowledged.

Zephaniah (ii). Biblical book, one of the books of the 12 Minor Prophets. It contains the account of Zephaniah's prophecies.

Zeraḥ *see* SACRIFICE.

Zerahiah Levi [Ferrer Saldin] (fl. 15th cent.). Spanish scholar and poet. A disciple of Ḥasdai Crescas, he served as rabbi of Zaragoza and all the communities of Aragon. He was a talmudist, preacher, physician, and translator, and also participated in the Disputation of Tortosa.

Zeraim ("Seeds"). First order of the Mishnah. It deals with agricultural laws, and also with the laws of prayer.

Zerubbabel (fl. 6th cent. BCE). Israelite leader, grandson of Jehoiachin. With the consent of Cyrus II of Persia, he returned to Judah from Babylon to help rebuild Jerusalem. Together with Joshua the priest, he set up an altar, reestablished the festivals, and began the rebuilding of the Temple.

Zevaḥim ("Animal sacrifices"). First tractate in the Mishnah order of Kodashim. It deals with the laws governing the offering of sacrificial animals and birds.

Zhirkhova, Yelizaveta *see* ELISHEVA.

Zhitlovski, Chaim (1865–1943). Russian philosopher and essayist. He was born in a small town near Vitebsk, Belorussia. He initially was involved in the revolutionary activities of the Narodniki. Later he founded the Jewish section of the Socialist Revolutionary Party, which advocated Jewish national emancipation and Yiddish as the language of national rebirth. In 1888 he left Russia and settled in Switzerland, where he edited the *Russian Worker.* He returned to Russia after the revolution of 1905 and helped to found the Seymist party. In 1908 he went to New York, where he edited *Dos neie leben.*

Zhitomin. Town in the Ukraine, 80 miles west of Kiev. Jews settled there from the 18th century. In 1845 Zhitomir and Vilnius had the only Hebrew printing presses in Russia. Zhitomir was the seat of a Russian rabbinical college (1848–73), a state college for Jewish teachers (1813–85), and a state Jewish crafts school (1862–84). The town suffered a pogrom in 1905.

Zidfeld, Simeon *see* NORDAU, MAX.

Zikhrono li-verakhah ("May his memory be for a blessing"). Expression of respect and blessing, uttered when mentioning someone who has died.

Zikhronot ("Remembrances"). The name of the second of the three sections in the additional Amidah service on Rosh ha-Shanah (the others are Malkhuyyot and Shopharot). It contains ten biblical verses with an introductory paragraph and a concluding blessing. The shophar is sounded after its recital.

Ziklag. Ancient Palestinian city, in the territory of the tribe of Simeon. During the time of Saul it was held by the Philistines, who handed it over to David. It subsequently remained in the territory of Judah (I Samuel 27.6).

Zilpah (fl. ?19th–16th cent.). Israelite woman, handmaid of Leah. Leah gave Zilpah to Jacob as a wife. She bore Gad and Asher (Genesis 30.9–13).

Zimra, David ben Solomon ibn Avi [David ben Solomon ibn Zimra; Radbaz] (fl. 16th cent.). Spanish talmudist and kabbalist. He was born in Spain, and studied in Safed, Fez, and Cairo, where he became chief rabbi. He later returned to Spain and served as a dayyan. He composed responsa, a commentary on Maimonides' *Mishneh Torah,* kabbalistic works, and talmudic novellae.

Zimri (i) (fl. ?13th cent. BCE). Israelite, head of a clan of the tribe of Simeon. He consorted with a Midianite woman, and with her was stabbed by Phinehas, the grandson of Aaron. This act ended a plague which had been visited on the Israelites for commiting harlotry with Midianite women and worshipping Baal Peor (Numbers 25).

Zimri (ii) (fl. 9th cent. BCE). King of Israel (855 BCE). As captain of half the chariots of the Israelites, he killed Elah, son of Baasha, when he had reigned for only a short time. After Zimri assumed power he executed all the male relatives and admirers of Baasha (I Kings 16.11). However, he reigned for only seven days. Omri was proclaimed king by his own men and besieged Tirzah the capital city. Zimri set his own palace on fire and died in the blaze, thus evading capture.

Zinberg, Israel (1873–1939). Ukrainian historian of Hebrew and Yiddish literature. He was born near Kremenets, Volhynia, and worked as a chemical engineer. He wrote eight volumes of a history of Jewish literature from the Spanish period (c. 10th century) to the end of the Russian Haskalah.

Zion (i). Jebusite stronghold in Jerusalem. It was captured by David and became part of the City of David (II Samuel 5.6–7). Its location is uncertain. During the Maccabean period, Mount Zion was identified with the Temple Mount and the City of David to the south-east, but Josephus identified Zion with the Upper City on the western ridge. The name is used in poetic and prophetic language to refer to Jerusalem as a whole. In religious terms Zion symbolizes the spiritual capital of the world, the messianic city of God. In this sense it also became a symbol of Jewish restoration.

Zion (ii). Hebrew quarterly, founded in 1936. Devoted to Jewish history, it was published by the Israel Historical Society, and its editors included Yitzḥak Baer, Ben Zion Dinur, and Israel Heilprin.

Zionides *see* JUDAH HA-LEVI.

Zionism. International political and ideological movement devoted to securing the return of the Jewish people to the Land of Israel. Modern political Zionism was conceived by Theodor Herzl and launched at the First Zionist Congress in 1897. His vision drew on a long religious tradition of messianic hope in the restoration of Zion, and at the same time aimed to solve the problem of the Jewish community in the diaspora by meeting the need and desire for a Jewish homeland. As an ideology Zionism was opposed by large numbers of Orthodox Jews, who claimed that divine intervention in history should not be usurped by human action. In addition many reform Jews were opposed to Zionism as a political policy. After the death of Herzl in 1904, Russian Zionists demanded the immediate beginning of practical colonization work ("practical Zionism") in Palestine. Other Zionists advocated diplomatic activity ("diplomatic Zionism"), pursuing Herzl's attempt to win support from Turkey and the European powers for a Jewish homeland. In 1911 a compromise between practical and diplomatic Zionism ("synthetic Zionism") was adopted as a general policy following Herzl's death. After the establishment of a Jewish state in 1948 the Zionist movement continued its activities, raising money to support settlement in Israel and encouraging immigration.

Zionist Commission. Commission appointed by the British government and sent to Palestine in 1918. Its purpose was to advise the British military authorities on the implementation of the Balfour Declaration. Led by Chaim Weizmann, it included prominent members of the Jewish communities of several countries. The commission organized an administrative center at Jaffa to replace the Palestine Office and another in Jerusalem to handle food supplies, immigration, and education. After the 12th Zionist Congress in 1921, its functions were given over to the executive of the Zionist Organization in Palestine.

Zionist Congresses. Series of conferences attended by representatives of the Zionist movement. Instituted by Theodor Herzl in 1897, they served as the supreme legislative forum of the Zionist Organization. Their main functions were to receive reports from the administrative institutions of the Zionist Organization, supervise the organization's work, determine the policy of the executive institutions, fix the budget, and elect the organization's principal officers.

Zionist Organization. International body, founded at the First Zionist Congress in Basle in 1897. It has served as the structural framework for the international Zionist movement. In 1960 it changed its name to the World Zionist Organization.

Zionist Organization of America [ZOA]. American Zionist body. Founded in 1897, it is affiliated to the World Confederation of General Zionists. Its activities include public relations, education, the promotion of investment in Israel, Israel tourism, community relations, and fund raising.

Zionists-Revisionists *see* REVISIONISM.

Zion Mule Corps. Company of ammunition carriers in the British army. It was enrolled in World War I in Egypt on the initiative of Vladimir Jabotinsky and Joseph Trumpeldor, and consisted of

Jews expelled from Palestine by the Turks. The British rejected the proposal to form these men into a Jewish military unit, but agreed to organize them as companies of mule-drivers to carry ammunition in Gallipoli. The corps was commanded by John Henry Patterson, with Trumpeldor as his second in command. It was disbanded in 1916. *See also* JEWISH LEGION.

Zipporah (fl. ?13th cent. BCE). Israelite woman, wife of Moses. She was the daughter of Jethro, priest of Midian. She travelled to Egypt with Moses to plead with Pharoah for the release of the Israelites; on the journey she saved the life of her son Gershom by circumcising him (Exodus 4.24–6). She returned alone to her father, with her sons Gershom and Eliezer; Jethro later took them to rejoin Moses on Mount Sinai (Exodus 18.1).

Zirelsohn, Judah Löb (1860–1941). Romanian rabbi and communal leader. He was born in Kozelets in the Ukraine, and served as rabbi of Priluki and Kishinev. He initially was a supporter of Zionism, but later dissociated himself from the movement. In 1912 he was one of the founders of Agudat Israel. When Bessarabia was incorporated into Romania in 1920, he became chief rabbi of Bessarabia and the leader of Orthodox Jewry there. In 1922 he was elected a deputy in the Romanian parliament, and in 1926 a senator. His writings include responsa, homilies, eulogies, essays, and poems.

Zitron, Samuel Löb (1860–1930). Russian writer. He was born in Minsk, Belorussia. He studied at Lithuanian yeshivot and became interested in the ideas of the Haskalah. In 1876 he went to Vienna, and later studied in Germany. He contributed to the Yiddish press and to Hebrew periodicals in the diaspora. His writings include studies of the Zionist movement and its precursors, and Hebrew literature.

Zodiac. Imaginary zone in the sky divided into 12 equal areas, called "signs of the zodiac," each named after the constellation in which it once lay; the paths of the planets and the sun appear to move across the zodiac. The signs of the zodiac are discussed in midrashic literature where the 12 constellations are correlated with the 12 tribes of Israel. They also play a role in Jewish art.

Zogerin [sagerin] (Yiddish: "sayer"). Title given to the woman who recites in the synagogue the prayers in the vernacular for those women unable to read Hebrew. This was a common practice in Russia and Poland.

Zohar. Mystical commentary on the Pentateuch and parts of the Hagiographa. According to tradition, it was composed in the 2nd century by Simeon ben Yoḥai, his colleagues, and disciples. It was first published in Spain by Moses de Leon in the 13th century. The work is written partly in Hebrew and partly in Aramaic; lengthy homiletic passages alternate with short discourses and parables. The Zohar is one of the principal kabbalistic works, and all subsequent mystical writing is based on it. The most important commentaries on the Zohar are *Ketem Paz* by Simeon ben Lavi, *Or ha-Ḥammah* by Abraham Azulai, and *Mikdash Melekh* by Shalom Buzaglo.

***Zola, Emil** (1840–1902). French novelist. He was active in the Dreyfus Affair as a supporter of Dreyfus. His article "J'accuse," published in *L'aurore* in 1898, condemned the conviction of Dreyfus and had an important influence. Sentenced to imprisonment for libel as a result of the article, he fled to England, where he continued the struggle to clear Dreyfus.

Zorach, William (1887–1966). American sculptor. He was born in Eurburg, Lithuania, and emigrated to the US in 1891.

He studied art in Cleveland, New York, and Paris. In his later works he utilized Jewish subject matter.

Zoroastrianism [Parsiism]. Ancient religion of Persian origin, taught by Zarathustra (c. 660–583 BCE). It is based on the belief that the task of human beings is to struggle for light and good against an evil power. It embraces belief in individual judgment after death, a final era of redemption, and the appearance of saviors. In talmudic times and subsequently Jews were persecuted by certain followers of this religious sect referred to as "Magi" (fire-worshippers). In the 7th and 8th centuries Muslim persecution almost extinguished Zoroastrianism, but some of its adherents fled to India; their descendants, the Parsis, still practice the religion there.

Zuckermandel, Moses Samuel (1836–1917). Moravian talmudist. He served as a rabbi in Moravia and Germany. He compiled what became the standard edition of the Tosephta, published in 1880.

***Zuckmayer, Carl** (1896–1977). German playwright. He was born in Nackenheim. Although he had a Jewish mother, he was raised as a Catholic. From 1919 he worked in the theater and as a freelance writer. In 1924 he joined Bertholt Brecht at Berlin's Deutsches Theater. He moved to Switzerland in 1938, and later settled in the US. Jewish characters play a role in a number of his dramas.

Zugot ("pairs"). Term designating the pairs of Palestinian sages who for five generations led the rabbinic tradition of Judaism (2nd century BCE to 1st century CE). They are listed in Avot. According to tradition, one was the president of the Sanhedrin (nasi) and the other head judge (av bet din) of the court (bet din). The zugot were: Yose ben Joezer and Yose ben Johanan; Joshua ben Peraḥyah and Nittai the Arbelite; Judah ben Tabbai and Simeon ben Shetaḥ; Shemaiah and Avtalyon; and Hillel and Shammai.

Zukunft. American Yiddish monthly, founded in 1892. It paralleled the approach of the socialist Yiddish daily *Forverts*. Its publication was suspended in 1940, but the journal was revived the following year by the Central Yiddish Culture Organization.

Zulay Menaḥem (1901–1954). Israeli scholar. He was born in Oschcianci, Galicia, and settled in Palestine in 1920. He worked at the Schocken Institute for the Study of Hebrew Poetry. He was an expert on early Palestinian piyyutim and edited the collection of such poems discovered in the Cairo Genizah, among which the most notable were those of Alexander Yannai.

Zunser, Eliakum (1836–1913). Lithuanian Yiddish poet. He was born in Vilnius. He was conscripted into the military, and later worked in Kovno as a braider of gold lace for uniforms. He became Russia's foremost wedding bard. In 1889 he moved to New York. Many booklets of his poems were published.

Zunz, Leopold (1794–1886). German historian. He was born in Detmold. He helped found the Verein für Kultur und Wissenschaft der Juden in Berlin in 1819, and his work is regarded as having laid the foundations for the scientific study of Jewish history (Wissenschaft des Judentums). From 1840 to 1850 he served as principal of the Berlin Teachers' Seminary. His early writings include a biography of Rashi, a history of Jewish homiletics, and a survey of Jewish names from biblical times. Among his later publications are a history of Jewish geographical literature, a history of Jewish liturgy, studies of medieval piyyutim and their authors, and Bible studies. He also edited the works of Naḥman Krochmal.

Zutra, Mar, I (d. c. 414). Babylonian

exilarch (401–9). He was the successor of Mar Kahana and a contemporary of Ashi.

Zutra, Mar, II (c. 496–520). Babylonian exilarch (512–20), son of Huna. He defeated the Persians and set up a Jewish state, which lasted for seven years; during this time he made Maḥoza his residence.

Zutra, Mar, III (fl. 6th cent.). Babylonian exilarch. Although he served as exilarch he left Babylonia and settled in Palestine.

Zweifel, Eliezer Tzevi (1815–1888). Russian Hebrew author and essayist. He was born in Mohilev, Belorussia. He wandered through Russia stopping in various towns, and worked as a preacher and teacher. In 1853 he was appointed lecturer in Mishnah and Talmud at the government rabbinical seminary in Zhitomir. Later he lived in Russia and Poland and finally settled in Glukhov in the Ukraine. In his *Shalom al-Yisrael*, he defended Ḥasidism, and demonstrated the movement's kabbalistic roots.

Zweig, Arnold (1887–1968). German novelist and playwright. He was born in Gross-Glogau, Silesia. He worked as a freelance writer in Bavaria and Berlin, where he edited the Zionist journal *Jüdische Rundschau*. After moving to Haifa, he coedited the weekly *Orient* in 1942–3. In 1948 he settled in East Berlin. A number of his works deal with Jewish themes.

Zweig, Stefan (1881–1942). Austrian author. He was born in Vienna and became a member of the Young Vienna group of Jewish intellectuals. In 1918 he wrote the pacifist play *Jeremiah*. His works include a number of biographies, *The Buried Candelabrum*, and *Beware of Pity*.